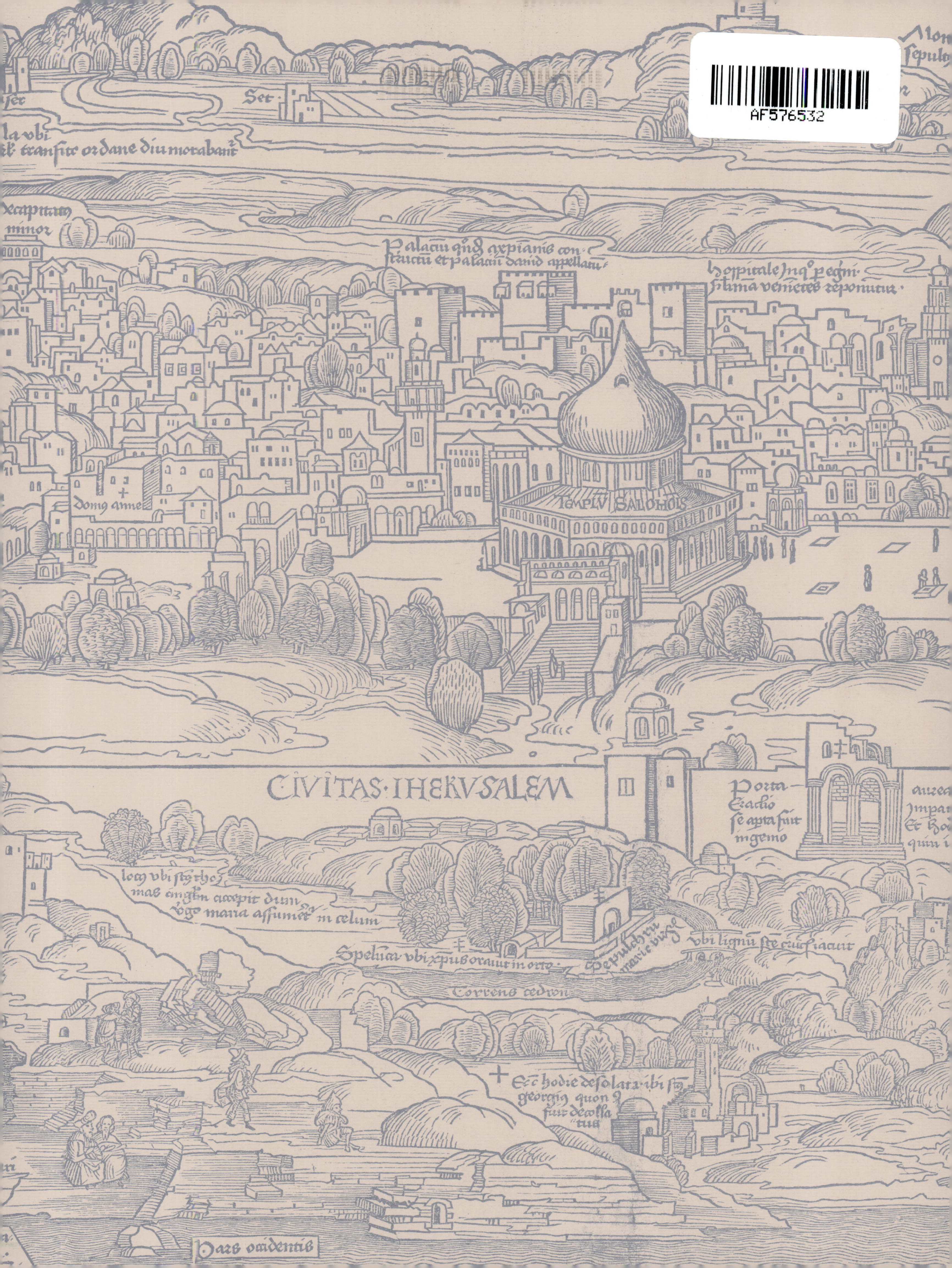
AF576532
Set
CIVITAS·IHERVSALEM
TEMPLV SALOMOIS
Torrens cedron
Pars occidentis

JERUSALEM • 1000–1400
EVERY PEOPLE UNDER HEAVEN

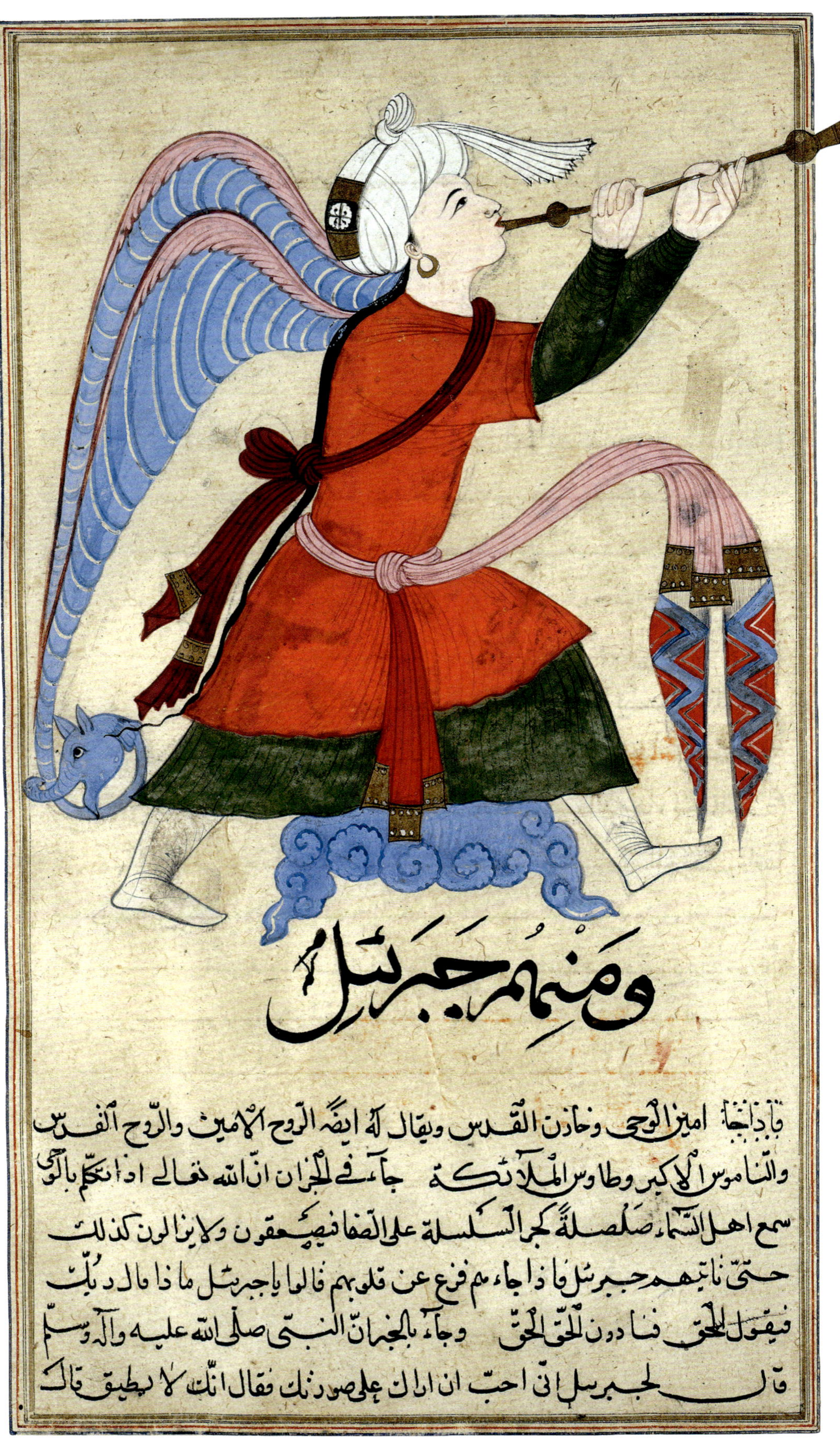
ومنهم جبرئيل
امين الوحي وخازن القدس ويقال له ايضا الروح الامين والروح القدس
والناموس الاكبر وطاوس الملائكة جاء في الخبر ان الله تعالى اذا تكلم بالوحي
سمع اهل السماء صلصلة كجر السلسلة على الصفا فيصعقون ولا يزالون كذلك
حتى ياتيهم جبرئيل فاذا جاء فزع عن قلوبهم قالوا يا جبرئيل ماذا قال ربك
فيقول الحق فينادون الحق الحق وجاء في الخبر ان النبي صلى الله عليه وآله وسلم
قال لجبرئيل اني احب ان اراك على صورتك فقال انك لا تطيق ذلك

JERUSALEM • 1000–1400
EVERY PEOPLE UNDER HEAVEN

EDITED BY BARBARA DRAKE BOEHM AND MELANIE HOLCOMB

THE MET The Metropolitan Museum of Art, New York
Distributed by Yale University Press, New Haven and London

CONTENTS

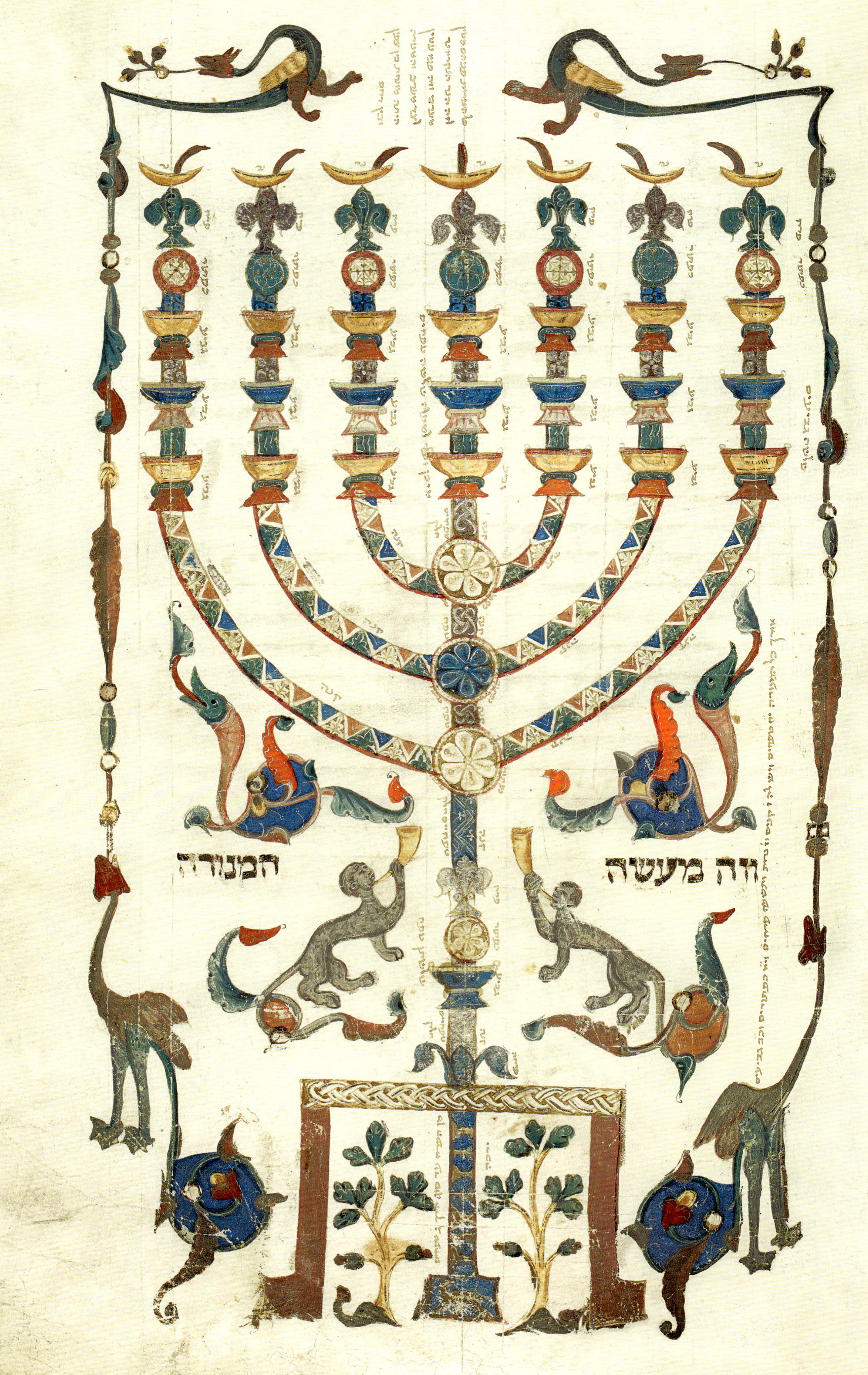

זה מעשה
המנורה

DIRECTOR'S FOREWORD

From today's vantage point, Jerusalem seems destined to host unending, unrelenting conflict among the three Abrahamic religions that deem it holy: Judaism, Christianity, and Islam. Sectarian conflict is sadly the easiest tale to spin, but Jerusalem's history is in fact much more nuanced. From the years 1000 to 1400, when the city was home to more cultures, faiths, and languages than at any other period, Jerusalem was both a site of productive coexistence and the backdrop for strife. Through times of peace and of war, it inspired art of great beauty and fascinating complexity. *Jerusalem, 1000–1400: Every People Under Heaven* explores – for the first time – the ways in which multiple competitive and complementary religious traditions, fueled by an almost universal preoccupation with that singular, sacred place, gave rise to one of the most creative periods in the city's history. This publication and the exhibition it accompanies demonstrate the key role that the Holy City played in shaping medieval art, whether in works that were created in situ or from afar. It in turn shows how this critical period left an indelible mark on the Holy City.

Given Jerusalem's unique place in history and in the hearts of people across the world, it is not surprising that works of art from the Holy Land can be found in major collections across the globe. For this exhibition, nearly two hundred works have been gathered from sixty lenders in over a dozen countries, representing an extraordinary level of international cooperation (all are listed on page xiv). Some of these treasures reside in major museums in the Middle East, Europe, and the United States; others are in unexpected or difficult-to-access places, above all private collections and the closed treasuries of religious communities.

Our greatest debt is to the lenders in Jerusalem, from which a quarter of the objects come. We are deeply grateful for their vision and promotion of culture as a bridge to the past and a witness to the present. Jerusalem's diverse religious communities are fittingly among our most significant lenders. They have served for centuries as the custodians of Jerusalem's sacred art, and it was a leap of faith for them to entrust us with their treasures, many of which have never left the Holy City. The Custodia Terrae Sanctae opened its storerooms, archives, and museums to us, while the Greek Orthodox Patriarchate endured the disruption of hand trucks and hoists as we packed up heavy sculpture from the garden and storage areas for a trip to New York. The Armenian Patriarchate graciously tracked down rare objects in its possession, as did the kind clergy at the Church of Saint Peter in Gallicantu. We were repeatedly welcomed into the Islamic Museum, which houses many of the riches of the Haram al-Sharif. Public collections in Israel of course feature prominently: the Israel Museum, the Israel Antiquities Authority, and the National Library of Israel were among the earliest advocates of the exhibition and are among our most generous lenders.

The list of lenders outside Jerusalem is long, and we also thank them for their willingness to support this project. A special debt of gratitude is owed to a number of institutions, including the staffs of the British Library, London; the Morgan Library and Museum, New York; and the Museum of Islamic Art, Doha, who expressed particular enthusiasm for the topic and parted with an exceptional number of prized works for the duration of the show.

The exhibition is made possible by a diverse group of individuals and organizations whose commitment to this project springs from deeply held links to the Holy Land and to The Metropolitan Museum of Art. We extend our thanks to The David Berg Foundation, which gave two grants at crucial stages; The al-Sabah Collection, Kuwait; the Sherman Fairchild Foundation; the William S. Lieberman Fund; The Polonsky Foundation; Diane Carol Brandt; The Andrew W. Mellon Foundation; the Ruddock Foundation for the Arts; and Mary and Michael Jaharis. Additional support is provided by the National Endowment for the Arts, The Chapman Family Charitable Trust, the Doris Duke Foundation for Islamic Art, the Alice Lawrence Foundation, Michael H. and Judy Steinhardt, and the Florence S. Daniels Fund. The catalogue is made possible by The Andrew W. Mellon Foundation, the Michel David-Weill Fund, Tauck Ritzau Innovative Philanthropy, the Ruddock Foundation for the Arts, Christopher C. Grisanti and Suzanne P. Fawbush, and Helen E. Lindsay.

At The Met, Paul and Jill Ruddock Senior Curator Barbara Drake Boehm and Curator Melanie Holcomb proposed this project to me some six years ago, and the extraordinary range, rarity, and high quality of objects attest to the curators' great love of the Holy City, their deep engagement with the subject, and the bonds they have established with colleagues near and far. Conservator Jack Soultanian, Jr., proved a great ally in the endeavor, demonstrating special expertise that made possible many of the most important loans. Former Associate Director for Exhibitions Jennifer Russell provided critical guidance and enthusiasm for this project since its inception. Its presentation coincides with her retirement, and this exhibition offers a fitting tribute to the breadth of her commitment to The Met. Thanks go as well to the heads of numerous Museum departments, who made works from their collections available for the exhibition. *Jerusalem, 1000–1400* benefits from the extraordinary depth of The Met's collection and includes works from the departments of Arms and Armor, Asian Art, Drawings and Prints, Islamic Art, and Medieval Art and The Cloisters.

There was more to medieval Jerusalem than East meets West. History records the harmonious and dissonant voices of people from many lands, passing in the narrow streets of a city not much larger than midtown Manhattan. The exhibition cannot fail to find resonance in today's New York, with its similarly rich mosaic of heritages living side by side. Ultimately, *Jerusalem, 1000–1400: Every People Under Heaven* bears witness to the crucial role that the city has played in shaping world culture, a lesson vital to our common history.

Thomas P. Campbell
Director
The Metropolitan Museum of Art

ACKNOWLEDGMENTS

WHILE WORKING on this exhibition, we have been privileged to collaborate with professionals around the world whom we now treasure as colleagues and friends. An undertaking of this nature would not have been possible without the support and assistance of many individuals and institutions near and far. These few words of gratitude can scarcely express the extent of our indebtedness to them all.

Many of our most generous lenders have come from Jerusalem itself, and we thank all the members and staff of the religious communities, museums, and libraries there who have graciously, and repeatedly, opened their doors and welcomed us. Among the friars of the Custodia Terrae Sanctae, we are forever grateful for the trust extended to us by Father Pierbattista Pizzaballa, former Custos of the Holy Land, and by Father Francesco Patton, the current Custos; Fr. Stéphane Milovich; Fr. Eugenio Alliata; Fr. Sergey Loktionov; and Harout Simonian. Fr. Xavier John Seubert in New York and Fr. Garret Edmunds in Washington, D.C., provided us with crucial introductions to those fine men. We also thank Diana Kattan and Sarah Zabel for their efforts on our behalf. Thanks to the introductions of Archbishop Demetrios of America and Mary and Michael Jaharis, we were graciously welcomed by His Beatitude Theophilos III, Greek Patriarch of Jerusalem. We were also assisted in our many visits to the Greek Orthodox Patriarchate by Archbishop Aristarchos of Constantina, Theodosios Mitropoulos, and Anna Koulouris. Père Jean-Daniel Gullung at the Church of Saint Peter in Gallicantu is owed special thanks for his persistent search for their missing Crusader capital, appropriately found one Christmas Eve. We will never forget the fine meal we enjoyed at the Christmas Hotel with His Beatitude Archbishop Nourhan Manougian, the Armenian Patriarch of Jerusalem, on an early visit to Jerusalem. We owe a deep debt of gratitude to him and to Archbishop Aris Shirvanian and Archbishop Sevan Gharibian, Fr. Tiran Hakobyan, and Fr. Samuel Aghoyan for their hospitality and helpfulness. Archbishop Khajag Barsamian and Aso Tavitian, both in New York, played key roles in forging links between us and the Brotherhood of Saint James, which has never before sent any of its treasures across the ocean. Nor has the Islamic Museum on the Haram al-Sharif. We are indebted to H.R.H. Prince Ghazi bin Muhammad, Sheikh Abdel al-Azeem Salhab, and Sheikh Azzam al-Khatib, and to our dear friends Yusuf Natsheh, Mustafa Abu Sway, and Khader Salameh for welcoming us at the Aqsa Mosque, for teaching us about their research and collections, and for making these loans possible.

Each visit to Jerusalem has confirmed our profound appreciation for our colleagues at the Israel Museum, which has been unsparing in its generosity. Our utmost gratitude extends to James S. Snyder, Tania Coen-Uzzieli, Na'ama Brosh, Daisy Raccah-Djivre, Anna Nizza Caplan, Michal Dayagi-Mendels, Rachel Sarfati, Ariel Tishby, Daniel Kobrinski, and Henk van Doornik. We have enjoyed an exceptionally warm relationship with the Israel Antiquities Authority, facilitated by Jacob Fisch. The staff there opened their vast storerooms for us, while Gideon Avni led us on our first tour of the Church of Holy Sepulchre. We much appreciate the efforts of Miki Saban, Uzi Dahari, Ayala Lester, Robert Kool, and Helena Sokolov on behalf of this project. At the National Library of Israel, we benefitted from the guidance and support of Aviad Stollman, Raquel Ukeles, and Haggai Ben-Shammai. Our thanks too to Oren Weinberg, Rachel Misrati, and Michal Moav. Rachel Hasson welcomed us at the L. A. Mayer Museum for Islamic Art. We also acknowledge the assistance there of Nadim Sheiban, Idit Sharoni, and Deena Lawi.

At the generous invitation of our trustee Sheikha Hussah Sabah al-Salem al-Sabah, Barbara was honored to lecture about our forthcoming exhibition for the Dar al-Athar al-Islamiyyah in Kuwait City. We are deeply grateful to all the staff there, especially Salam Kaoukji and Fahad al-Najadah. At the Museum of Islamic Art in Doha, we thank Sheikha Nasser Al-Nassr, William Greenwood, Jonathan Wilson, Leslee Katrina Michelsen, Nancy Konstantinou, and Mounia Chekhab-Abudaya.

Absolutely vital to the exhibition are the extraordinary works of art on loan to us from the United Kingdom. We are indebted to our colleagues at the British Library, which has lent treasures in many languages from many cultures that hold Jerusalem dear. Roly Keating, Scot McKendrick, Ilana Tahan, Colin F. Baker, Andrea Clarke, Leslie Thomas, and Barbara O'Connor greeted this project from the start with enthusiasm and generosity. At the British Museum, thanks are due to Neil MacGregor, Jill Maggs, and Dean Baylis, as well as to James Robinson and Mahmoud Hawari for early advice. John Lewis, Heather Rowland, and, most especially, Anooshka Rawden have proven enormously helpful with our loans from the Society of Antiquaries of London. At the Victoria and Albert Museum, we benefitted from the guidance of Martin Roth, Tim Stanley, Mariam Rosser-Owen, Moya Carey, Olivia Horsfall Turner, Paul Williamson, Marian Campbell, Bill Sherman, and Katherine Elliott, especially during the enjoyable time that Barbara spent there as an exchange curator. Kent Rawlinson of the Royal Institute of British Architects, James Allan of Oxford University, and Rachel Ward, formerly of the British Museum, likewise shared their expertise. Christopher de Hamel from the Parker Library at Corpus Christi College, University of Cambridge, remains an invaluable colleague, and we thank him as well as Steven Archer and Elizabeth Dumas. At the Bodleian Libraries, University of Oxford, we received a warm welcome from Gillian Evison, Alasdair Watson, and Bruce Barker-Benfield. Our thanks as well to César Merchán-Hamann and Richard Ovenden, the Head Librarian. Without the blessing of Robert and Carole Hillenbrand we might never have been able to borrow from the University Library, Edinburgh. Our thanks as well to Joseph Marshall and Jill Forrest for their support of our request.

We greatly appreciate the kindness of numerous private collectors in the United Kingdom. We thank our trustee Sir Paul Ruddock for introducing us to the Sarikhani family and to Nasser D. Khalili. We express our gratitude to Ina Sandmann, Ali Sarikhani, Sabine Sarikhani, and Susan Richardson, and to Professor Nasser D. Khalili, Nahla Nasser, and Suzanne Tuck. The family of Jasim Y. Homaizi has graciously allowed a work from their collection to be on long-term loan to the Metropolitan Museum, and we are pleased to be able to include it in the exhibition.

The exhibition would be far less rich if it did not include the extraordinary works on loan to us from Germany. We are indebted to Peter van den Brink, the late Georg Minkenberg, Gertraut Sofia Mockel, and Monica Paredis-Vroon at the Domkapitel Aachen. At the Bayerisches Nationalmuseum in Munich, we received kind assistance from Renate Eikelmann and Raphael Beuing. At the Thüringisches Landesamt für Denkmalpflege und Archäologie in Weimar, our appreciation is due to Karin Sczech and Sven Ostritz; at the Alte Synagogue in Erfurt, we thank Ines Beese and Anselm Hartinger. In Bremen, we owe our gratitude to Bernd and Eva Hockemeyer for their longstanding generosity to our institution.

In Italy, we extend our appreciation to our new colleagues Pier Francesco Fumagalli, Franco Buzzi, and Elena Fontana at the Veneranda Biblioteca Ambrosiana in Milan. Thanks are due to Evelyn Cohen for her introduction. At the Museo di Capodimonte in Naples, our thanks go to Sylvain Bellenger, Linda Martino, Patrizia Piscitello, and Brigitte Daprà. We benefitted from the assistance given to us by many individuals at the Biblioteca Apostolica Vaticana in Vatican City, especially Cesare Pasini, Amalia D'Alascio, Maria Adalgisa Ottaviani, and Paolo Vian.

At the Furusiyya Art Foundation, we received the welcome support of Bashir Mohamed, Shahnaz Mohamed, Debra Noël Adams, and Charles-André Junod. It has been a pleasure to collaborate with our colleagues at the Koninklijke Bibliotheek in The Hague, and we extend our appreciation to Lily Knibbeler, Ed van der Vlist, and Madeleine van den Berg. At the David Collection in Copenhagen, we would like to thank Kjeld von Folsach and Anne-Marie Keblow Bernsted.

We depended again on the abiding friendship and unfailing generosity of colleagues in Paris. We owe thanks beyond measure to Jean-Luc Martinez, Jannic Durand, Pierre-Yves Le Pogam, Florian Meunier, Yannick Lintz, and Laurent Creuzet at the Musée du Louvre, and, as always, to our devoted friend Élisabeth Taburet-Delahaye at the Musée de Cluny, Musée National du Moyen Âge, as well as to Rachel Beaujean-Deschamps. At the Bibliothèque Nationale de France, we relied upon the support of Bruno Racine, Delphine Mercuzot, Laurent Héricher, Julien Spinner, and Chiara Pagliettini. Among the priests and staff of Saint-Sulpice, we acknowledge the kind assistance of Fr. Ronald D. Witherup and Agnès Jauréguibéhère. For his help, we extend our gratitude as well to Pierre-Jean Riamond. At the Musée des Beaux-Arts in Chartres, Séverine Berger, Irène Jourd'heuil, and Philippe Bihouée generously lent their support. In Lyon, Jérôme Sirdey welcomed Austin B. Chinn of our department's Visiting Committee, who graciously offered to represent our interest in their collection during his stay in the city. Thanks too to Marianne Besseyre and Gilles Eboli. In the Limousin and at Toulouse, notwithstanding a gap of several decades since our last engagement with them, our colleagues have reaffirmed their friendship with New York. Olivier Poisson provided critical initial support, and we were guided at every step by secular and ecclesiastical authorities. We express our appreciation to Adeline Rabaté, Judith Kagan, Nicolas Vedelago, and Josette Libert, as well as to Fr. Vincent Gallois, Fr. Michel Lateras, Évelyne Ugaglia, Catherine Gaich, and Claudine Jacquet. In Angers, Ariane James-Sarazin, Delphine Galloy, Sylvia Niveau, and Nathalie Besson-Amiot of the Musée des Beaux-Arts kindly saw to their important loans.

In Namur, Belgium, our heartfelt gratitude to Baroness Françoise Tulkens of Fondation Roi Baudouin; Fadila Laanan at the Ministry of Culture, Fédération Wallonie-Bruxelles; and Marie-Françoise Degembe, Anne De Breuck, Anna Trobec, and Fiona Lebecque at the Musée des Arts Anciens du Namurois for their able assistance. We especially recognize our long-standing colleague Jacques Toussaint.

We cannot overlook the kindness of the many institutions in the United States that have sent their invaluable objects to our Museum and have graciously allowed us to study their collections. At the Walters Art Museum in Baltimore, we are grateful to Julia Marciari-Alexander, Amy Landau, Lynley Anne Herbert, Martina Bagnoli, Robert Mintz, and Jenn Harr for their help. We thank Brian Henderson, Bret Bostock, and Ed Gyllenhaal at the Glencairn Museum in Bryn Athyn, Pennsylvania, and James Rondeau, Douglas Druick, and Natasha Derrickson at the Art Institute of Chicago for their generous assistance. We would like to thank our colleagues at the Cleveland Museum of Art, namely William M. Griswold, Stephen Fliegel, Fred Bidwell, and Colleen Snyder for their involvement and support. In Columbus, we extend our appreciation to Jay and Jeannie Schottenstein, and Ari Kinsberg. We recognize the efforts of Maxwell Anderson, Sabiha Al Khemir, and Tricia Dixon at the Dallas Museum of Art and thank them for their involvement. At the Library of Congress, we would like to thank Levon Avdoyan, Maricia Battle, Rachel Waldron, and Jonathan Eaker. Anjuli Lebowitz, a fellow at the Metropolitan Museum, was particularly helpful in research for this loan. In nearby New Haven, we extend our thanks to Edwin C. Schroeder at the Beinecke Library of Yale University, and to Beinecke Trustee Stephen K. Scher, while in neighboring Princeton, we thank Don Skemer, Paul Needham, and John Walako at the Princeton University Library.

Sister institutions in New York City have generously allowed us to display some of their rarest works. At the Library of The Jewish Theological Seminary, David Kraemer, Sharon Liberman Mintz, Menahem Schmelzer, Jerry Schwarzbard, Sarah Diamant, Jay Rovner, and Akiko Yamazaki-Kleps merit our deepest gratitude. We are grateful for the encouragement and generosity of Colin Bailey, Peggy Fogelman, William Voelkle, Roger Wieck, John Marciari, Jennifer Tonkovich, Margaret Holben Ellis, and Sophie Worley at the Morgan Library and Museum. Our thanks as well are conveyed to our counterparts at the New York Public Library, Anthony Marx, Stephen D. Corrsin, Deborah Straussman, and Adrianne Rubin. We also express gratitude for the generosity of numerous private lenders who have chosen to remain anonymous.

Our Exhibition Advisory Council offered important advice and broadened our perspective as we developed the exhibition. Helen C. Evans, Jaroslav Folda, Abby Kornfeld, Yusuf Natsheh, Avinoam Shalem, and Elizabeth Dospěl Williams were all open in spirit and generous with their time. We could not have anticipated the impact on our exhibition that came from dialogue with our students both in a seminar at the Graduate Center, City University of New York, and in the Curatorial Studies class jointly administered by The Metropolitan Museum of Art and the Institute of Fine Arts, New York University. Those conversations echo throughout the pages of this catalogue.

This project has also benefitted from discussions with Adnan Abdelrazek, Ghiora Aharoni, Neshan Balian, Ben Balint, Jennifer Ball, Lisa Bessette, Keith Christiansen, Kathleen Fleck, Rula Jebreal, Marilyn Jenkins-Madina, Abu Khalaf, Rashid Khalidi, Rebecca Kohn, Bianca Kühnel, Howard Lay, Joseph and Karen Levine, Milka Levy-Rubin, Merav Mack, Vivian Mann, Laura Morreale, Suleiman Ali Mourad, Hashim Natsheh, Lawrence Nees, Christina Nielsen, Jonathan

Phillips, Barbara Porter, Elchanan Reiner, Nina Rowe, Rehav Rubin, George Saliba, Robert Schick, Priscilla Soucek, David Stern, Anne Strauss, Sasha Suda, Thelma K. Thomas, David Wachtel, Jacob Weiss, and Hani Zalatimo. The advice of Jiří Fajt, Sam Fogg, Francesca Galloway, William and Lisa Gross, Theo Jülich, Abby Kaufthal, Tara Kelly, Natia Khuluzauri, Gerhard Lutz, Christoph Mackert, Aneta Samkoff, Jane Suda, David Sulzberger, Michele Tocci, and Hiltrud Westermann-Angerhausen has also been much appreciated. Last but not least, Sylvia Auld, Jennifer Ball, James Carroll, Helen C. Evans, Jaroslav Folda, Carole Hillenbrand, Robert Hillenbrand, Martin Jacobs, Abby Kornfeld, David Kraemer, Nabil Matar, Yusef Natsheh, Meira Polliack, Avinoam Shalem, Xavier John Seubert, and Elisabeth Dospěl Williams wrote highly informative essays for this publication. In addition, nearly fifty scholars, listed on page xv, shared their research and innovative ideas in the catalogue sections throughout the book.

No person ever works in isolation, and this exhibition would not have been possible without the support of our friends and colleagues at the Metropolitan Museum. We are grateful to our director, Thomas P. Campbell, for his unstinting support of this endeavor from its inception. We owe an enormous debt to Jennifer Russell for her early and ongoing encouragement of the project. Linda Sylling, as well as Patricia Gilkison, expertly oversaw the installation and planning of this exhibition. Martha Deese and Chris Coulson deserve special thanks for their frequent and always astute counsel. This exhibition involved skilled navigation and negotiation of the many details of shipping, insurance, and customs, for which we extend our thanks to Aileen Chuk and Meryl Cohen in the Office of the Registrar. Legal intricacies are part and parcel of every exhibition, but we needed to look no farther than the legal expertise of our colleagues in the Counsel's Office, specifically Sharon H. Cott and Amy Desmond Lamberti, with assistance provided by Maria E. Fillas and Nicole Sussmane, to whom we are very grateful. In our Office of Institutional Advancement, Clyde B. Jones III, Nina McN. Diefenbach, Stephen A. Manzi, Christine S. Begley, Sarah Higby, Elizabeth Burke, Lindsey Schneider, and most especially Jason Herrick have brought their skills to this project.

As the exhibition designer, Michael Langley creatively turned our vision into a physical reality. We are grateful to Mortimer Lebigre, Ria Roberts, Emile Molin, and Susan Sellers for their patience and attention to our curatorial concept. We would like to thank wholeheartedly the staff in the Digital Department for their involvement in this project, particularly Christopher A. Noey. In a world where online accessibility translates into raised interest, viewership, and attendance, Annie Dunleavy worked creatively to give our exhibition a presence on the Museum's website. We are indebted to Staci Hou and Nina Diamond for their work in shaping an audio guide that translates our words into an educational experience for the visitor.

Our deep appreciation goes out to our colleagues in Education who help disseminate the message of our exhibition through their educational programming, namely Jennifer Mock, Jessica S. Bell, Joseph Loh, and Sandra Jackson-Dumont, Frederick P. and Sandra P. Rose Chairman of Education. Erin Flannery and Limor Tomer in Concerts and Lectures helped us plan nuanced programming that built upon the complexity and beauty replete in the exhibition.

Every exhibition involves a strong research component and we owe much to our colleagues at the Thomas J. Watson Library who have been instrumental from start to finish of this project. In particular, we would especially like to thank the ever-helpful Kenneth Soehner, Arthur K. Watson Chief Librarian; Robyn Fleming; Guinevere C. Mayhew; Michael K. Carter; Jessica Ranne; Ronald Fein; Fredy Rivera; and Patrick J. Raftery.

We acknowledge the important contributions of our colleagues in conservation for their outstanding efforts on behalf of this project. In particular, we thank Drew Anderson, Mechthild Baumeister, George Bisacca, Kathrin Colburn, Pete Dandridge, Yana van Dyke, Ellen Howe, Edward A. Hunter, Lucretia Kargère, Nora Kennedy, Hermes Knauer, Jean-François de Lapérouse, Michael Alan Miller, Janina Poskrobko, Karen Stamm, Wendy Walker, and Florica Zaharia. Jack Soultanian, Jr., who traveled with us to Jerusalem, deserves special recognition for his contributions as both a conservator and a diplomat.

This catalogue would never have come to fruition without the endeavors of the Museum's Publications and Editorial Department. Our thanks go to Mark Polizzotti, Gwen Roginsky, Peter Antony, and Michael Sittenfeld for their refined perspective and support. As our co-captains on the journey toward this catalogue's completion, Cynthia Clark and Kamilah Foreman earn our continued thanks and gratitude for their insight and passion as editors; they were assisted by Anne Blood, Amelia Kutschbach, and Briana Parker, among others. Penny Jones and Ellen Hurst brought their acumen to the notes and the bibliography. The catalogue was beautifully designed by Christopher Kuntze, while its production was overseen by the unflappable Christopher Zichello, with image-acquisition support provided by Crystal A. Dombrow. New photography for the catalogue was produced by Anna-Marie Kellen, Peter Zeray, and Hyla Skopitz of the Museum's Imaging Department. In the Office of the Senior Vice President for Marketing and External Relations, we would like to thank Cynthia L. Round, Elyse Topalian, Ann M. Bailis, Christopher P. Gorman, Rachel Ferrante, Egle Žygas, and Harold Holzer.

We are in the privileged position of being able to draw upon the richness of the Metropolitan Museum's own collection, and this exhibition draws together some of the finest pieces within our own holdings. As the inclusion of these treasures are the result of continued cooperation among various curatorial departments, we would like to thank our colleagues for their support and involvement in our exhibition. In Arms and Armor, we thank Donald J. LaRocca; Pierre Terjanian, Arthur Ochs Sulzberger Curator in Charge; and Stuart W. Pyhrr for their involvement. In Arts of Africa, Oceania, and the Americas, we thank Alisa LaGamma, Ceil and Michael E. Pulitzer Curator in Charge. We are grateful to Maxwell K. Hearn, Douglas Dillon Chairman, and Denise Patry Leidy in Asian Art for their steadfast support. We benefitted as well from Nadine M. Orenstein, Drue Heinz Chairman; Femke Speelberg; and Elizabeth Zanis in Drawings and Prints. Jeff L. Rosenheim was a great partner in thinking about nineteenth-century photography of the Holy Land. Finally, we relied heavily upon the counsel and collection of the Department of Islamic Art, and we extend particular thanks to Sheila Canby, Patti Cadby Birch Curator in Charge; Deniz Beyazit; Maryam Ekhtiar; Navina Najat Haidar; Matthew Saba; Annick des Roches; and Douglas C. Geiger for their generosity.

The continued support of the staff within the Department of Medieval Art and The Cloisters deserves our deepest gratitude. Particularly, we would like to thank our colleagues C. Griffith Mann, Michel David-Weill Curator in Charge; Timothy B. Husband; Charles T. Little; Helen C. Evans, Mary and Michael Jaharis Curator of Byzantine Art; Peter Barnet; and Nancy Wu. The administrative, logistical, and technical support provided by Christine E. Brennan, Thomas C. Vinton, Andrew Winslow, and Hannah Korn was crucial. We owe thanks as well to an accomplished group of interns: Yitzchak Schwartz, Dina Akhmadeeva, Oriane Beaufils, and Emma Kate Lindsay.

Throughout the past several years, we have been blessed by the eager and steadfast assistance of a remarkable team. Elizabeth Eisenberg, Francesca Dorwart, Tanushree Naimpally, and Christine D. McDermott have set an unmatched example of professionalism, academic rigor, diplomacy, patience, and tenacity. Such a combination of talents is seldom found in a single person; it is abundant in each of them. Their achievements are far beyond their compensation or their recognition. They have our unending gratitude. We can only hope that the experience has proven worth the commitment and investment they have made in *Jerusalem*.

Finally, we express our personal thanks to Judy Baldwin; Allison Barlow; Elaine Buice; Karin Genis; Rachel and Wendell Green; Melissa Hall; Roy and Michele Holcomb; Laura Kates; Marcia Lerner; Thanassis and Helen Mazarakis; David Ochshorn; Michelle O'Malley; Anne and Michael Wilson; Amelia and Ida Holcomb; Douglas and Sophie Shapiro; Michael, Alexander, David, and Ben Porcelli; and Linda Zrida. Each of them knows how much we have depended upon them.

Barbara Drake Boehm & Melanie Holcomb

LENDERS TO THE EXHIBITION

Armenian Patriarchate, Jerusalem

Art Institute of Chicago

Basilique Saint-Sernin, Toulouse

Bayerisches Nationalmuseum, Munich

Beinecke Rare Book and Manuscript Library, Yale University, New Haven

Biblioteca Apostolica Vaticana, Vatican City

Bibliothèque Municipale, Lyon

Bibliothèque Nationale de France, Paris

Bodleian Libraries, University of Oxford

British Library, London

British Museum, London

Church of Saint Peter in Gallicantu, Jerusalem

Cleveland Museum of Art

Compagnie des Prêtres de Saint-Sulpice, Service des Archives, Paris

Corpus Christi College, University of Cambridge

David Collection, Copenhagen

Dallas Museum of Art

Domkapitel and Domschatzkammer, Aachen

Furusiyya Art Foundation, Vaduz

Glencairn Museum, Bryn Athyn, Pennsylvania

Greek Orthodox Patriarchate, Jerusalem

Bernd and Eva Hockemeyer, Germany

Islamic Museum and Al-Aqsa Library, Jerusalem

The Israel Antiquities Authority, Jerusalem

The Israel Museum, Jerusalem

Keir Collection on long-term loan by Ranros Universal S.A. to the Dallas Museum of Art

Koninklijke Bibliotheek, The Hague

Nasser D. Khalili Collection of Islamic Art, London

L. A. Mayer Museum for Islamic Art, Jerusalem

Library of Congress, Washington, D.C.

The Library of The Jewish Theological Seminary, New York

Mairie d'Ambazac

Morgan Library and Museum, New York

Musée de Cluny, Musée National du Moyen Âge, Paris

Musée des Beaux-Arts, Chartres

Musée du Louvre, Paris

Musées d'Angers

Musée Provincial des Arts Anciens du Namurois, Namur

Museo Nazionale di Capodimonte, Naples

Museum of Islamic Art, Doha

The National Library of Israel, Jerusalem

New York Public Library

Princeton University Library

Private collection, in honor of Jasim Y. Homaizi

Private collection, United Kingdom

Private collections

The al-Sabah Collection, Dar al-Athar al-Islamiyyah, Kuwait

Sarikhani Collection, Oxfordshire

Jay and Jeannie Schottenstein, Columbus

The Society of Antiquaries of London

Terra Sancta Museum, Basilica of the Annunciation, Nazareth

Terra Sancta Museum, Jerusalem

Thüringisches Landesamt für Denkmalpflege und Archäologie, Weimar

University of Edinburgh

Veneranda Biblioteca Ambrosiana, Milan

Victoria and Albert Museum, London

Walters Art Museum, Baltimore

CONTRIBUTORS TO THE CATALOGUE

DA Dina Akhmadeeva
Rijksmuseum, Amsterdam

MA Mabi Angar
University of Cologne

MAS Mustafa Abu Sway
Al-Quds University, Jerusalem

BDB Barbara Drake Boehm
The Metropolitan Museum of Art, New York

CB Colin Baker
British Library, London

DB Deniz Beyazit
The Metropolitan Museum of Art, New York

HB Heather Badamo
University of California, Santa Barbara

JB Jennifer Ball
Brooklyn College, City University of New York Graduate Center

NB Na'ama Brosh
The Israel Museum, Jerusalem

OB Oriane Beaufils
Château de Fontainebleau

PB Peter Barnet
The Metropolitan Museum of Art, New York

EMC Evelyn M. Cohen
Independent scholar, New York

SRC Sheila R. Canby
The Metropolitan Museum of Art, New York

MCA Mounia Chekhab-Abudaya
Museum of Islamic Art, Doha

MD Marek Dospěl
Institut für Papyrologie, Ruprecht-Karls-Universität, Heidelberg

EE Elizabeth Eisenberg
The Metropolitan Museum of Art, New York

HCE Helen C. Evans
The Metropolitan Museum of Art, New York

ME Maryam Ekhtiar
The Metropolitan Museum of Art, New York

JF Jaroslav Folda
University of North Carolina, Chapel Hill

CG Christiane Gruber
University of Michigan, Ann Arbor

MH Melanie Holcomb
The Metropolitan Museum of Art, New York

MHA Melanie Hanan
Stern College, Yeshiva University, New York

RH Robert Hillenbrand
Edinburgh University

AK Abby Kornfeld
City College, New York

LK Lev Kapitaikin
Tel Aviv University

RK Robert Kool
The Israel Antiquities Authority, Jerusalem

SK Salam Kaoukji
The al-Sabah Collection, Dar al-Athar al-Islamiyyah, Kuwait

SAK Sabiha Al Khemir
Dallas Museum of Art

AL Ayala Lester
The Israel Antiquities Authority, Jerusalem

DLR Donald LaRocca
The Metropolitan Museum of Art, New York

PYLP Pierre-Yves Le Pogam
Musée du Louvre, Paris

AEM Alaa El-Din Mahmoud
The Egyptian Museum, Cairo

CGM C. Griffith Mann
The Metropolitan Museum of Art, New York

VBM Vivian B. Mann
The Jewish Theological Seminary, New York

YN Yusuf Natsheh
Islamic Museum and Al-Aqsa Library, Jerusalem

AS Avinoam Shalem
Columbia University, New York

EJS Edna J. Stern
The Israel Antiquities Authority, Jerusalem

HS Harout Simonian
Franciscan community, Jerusalem

YT Yasser Tabbaa
Independent scholar

EVDV Ed van der Vlist
Koninklijke Bibliotheek, The Hague

AW Alasdair Watson
Bodleian Libraries, Oxford University

EDW Elizabeth Dospěl Williams
Dumbarton Oaks, Washington, D.C.

NOTE TO THE READER

A cross-cultural approach to the Holy City necessarily involves a challenging array of languages and names. To add to the complexity, almost every spot in Jerusalem has multiple appellations attached to it. Our aim is to make our text approachable to the general reader. We have therefore elected to use the names most accessible and familiar to an English-speaking audience, and, sometimes, multiple spellings of the same name (such as Sion and Zion; while we opted for Sion, used in many early translations of pilgrims' accounts, quotations from some sources use Zion). With places that have several preferred designations, we rely on context to determine which to use. When discussing a Jewish perspective on the sacred esplanade where the Ancient Temple once stood, for example, we refer to the area as the Temple Mount. When discussing Muslim sites on that same space, we refer to it as the Haram al-Sharif or the Noble Sanctuary.

The region in which Jerusalem sits also has many names (and many borders), depending on the culture, religion, politics, and era of the person describing it. We have largely chosen to call it the Holy Land, because that speaks to the feature that everyone can agree upon. Some of our authors have departed from that model, deeming it appropriate to use a name that speaks to the context they describe.

Our work relies upon the voices of many visitors and residents of the city. We supply references to the English translation of those primary sources whenever possible so that the broadest number of our readers may discover these voices for themselves. Multiple editions of these sources are grouped in the bibliography under the name of the original writer.

We looked to context to decide which translation of the Hebrew Scriptures we would use. When discussing Jewish art, we cite both Jerusalem and Babylonian Talmud passages, followed by reference to an English translation. Medieval scholars are likewise cited first, with the location of the Hebrew passage followed by an English translation. For Christian art, we rely upon the Douay-Rheims translation of the Bible. With a few exceptions requested by our authors, quotations from the Qur'an are taken from *The Holy Qur'an: English Translation of the Meanings and Commentary* (Medina, 1992–93); all sources are listed in the bibliography.

Except where an object bears a specific date, we make use of the dating system of the Gregorian calendar, while recognizing that many calendars were and are still current. It is the style of the Museum to use B.C. and A.D. We have used these abbreviations minimally and, we hope, with sensitivity.

At every stage this exhibition and catalogue have developed from an extraordinary collaborative partnership. Our jointly written catalogue entries simply give our initials in alphabetical order. To underscore the joint authorship of our essays, we have elected to alternate the sequence in which our names appear. The reader will appreciate that our approach to all of these points mirrors the subject of our book, the multifarious experience of Jerusalem in the Middle Ages.

JERUSALEM • 1000–1400
EVERY PEOPLE UNDER HEAVEN

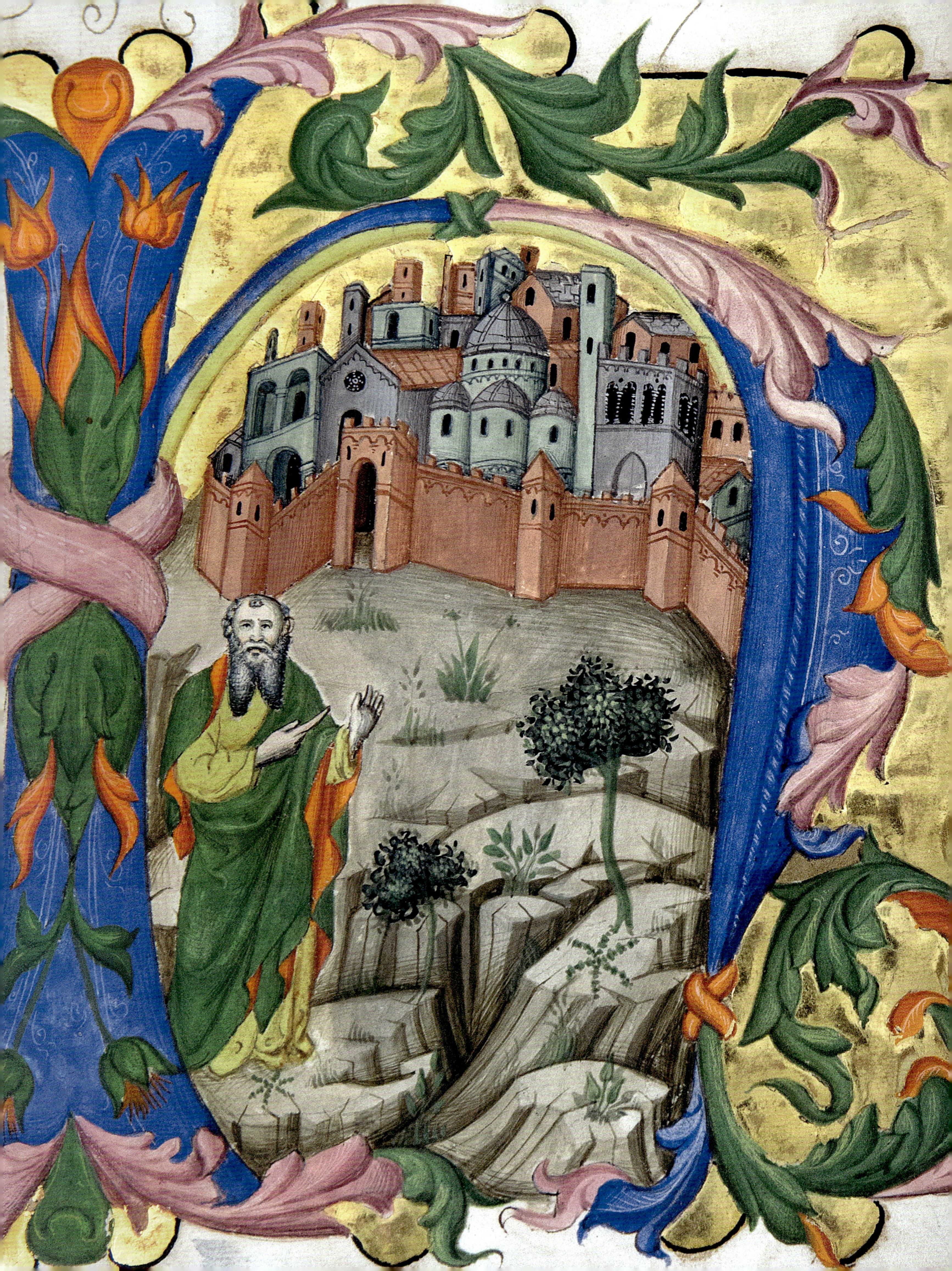

INTRODUCTION

Art and Medieval Jerusalem

The city which you see is the cause of all our labor

— Baldric of Dol, Abbot of Bourgueil, historian of the First Crusade (ca. 1050–1130)

BARBARA DRAKE BOEHM AND MELANIE HOLCOMB

The British Journal of Psychiatry reported in the year 2000 that, over the course of a decade, some twelve hundred international tourists had been admitted to hospital with "severe, Jerusalem-generated mental problems," occasioned by a visit to the Holy Land in which fixation on Jerusalem became "pathological."[1] Categorizing the syndrome into three types, the authors noted one that developed in people with no previous history of mental illness and who recovered on returning home. Caught up in the spectacle of the place, those stricken would don a hotel bedsheet, recite scripture, process to Jerusalem's holy places, and deliver sermons.[2]

Whatever the credibility of the modern syndrome, there is no question that from roughly the eleventh through the fourteenth centuries much of the world was indeed in the grip of a kind of Jerusalem fever — a profound obsession rather than a temporary mental lapse. Across three continents — from Islamic, Christian, and Jewish traditions alike — thousands made their way to the Holy City. Generals and their armies fought over it. Merchants profited from it. Patrons, artists, pilgrims, poets, and scholars drew inspiration from it. Focusing their attention on this singular spot, they praised its magic, endowed its sacred buildings, and created luxury goods for those who passed through its streets. Medieval Jerusalem attracted the devotion of people from as far north as Scandinavia, as far west as Spain, as far south as Ethiopia, and as far east as present-day China. As a result, the Holy City played a key role in shaping the art of this period.

In about the year 1000 an extraordinary convergence of circumstances brought new attention to the medieval city, which continued unabated for the next four centuries. These included natural disasters, political turmoil, intense religious fervor, and a notable uptick in world travel. In the 1020s the Fatimid caliph al-Zahir in Egypt made agreements with Italian merchants and then with the Byzantine emperor to join him in rebuilding the city after a series of earthquakes and a campaign of destruction waged by the caliph's mad predecessor. Meanwhile, with Messianic fervor, the Karaites, a distinctive community of Babylonian Jews, had proclaimed with renewed vigor the need to move to Jerusalem. In 1099 European Christians achieved their improbable dream of conquering and claiming faraway Jerusalem as theirs, and they celebrated their victory in glorious buildings and works of art. By 1187 Saladin, founder

FACING PAGE
Fig. 1. The initial "H" showing the prophet Isaiah at the walls of Jerusalem, from an antiphonary. Detail of cat. 1[illegible]4a, fol. 45v

of the Ayyubid dynasty, retook the city for Islam, reasserting his claim by rededicating and endowing its sanctuaries, hospitals, and centers of learning. In the thirteenth and fourteenth centuries, Jerusalem was nurtured by those Mamluk sultans blessed with stable reigns who, although based in Cairo, promoted the city as a spiritual and scholarly center, accessed by passing under handsome gates and into domed houses of prayer and study.

This publication and the exhibition that it accompanies are the first to define these four centuries as a singularly creative moment in a singularly complex city. Indeed, this period as a whole has barely received a nod, even within presentations that have attempted to trace the city's millennia-long history.[3] A number of previous exhibitions have focused exclusively on the Crusades, reinforcing the problematic assertion that the arrival of Western warriors was the single driving force in the region, historically and aesthetically.[4] Meanwhile, exhibitions devoted to Islamic art of the Fatimid or Mamluk periods have overlooked Jerusalem's artistic heritage because the city, which was not a political capital, has been dismissed as provincial.[5] Moreover, Jerusalem's contentious history over much of the last century has not been conducive to an international celebration of the city's artistic legacy.[6] Approaches that are beholden to political history or the academic compartmentalization that separates works of art by religious tradition suppress the overlapping histories, points of contact, and complexity that the city engendered and that find their brilliant reflections in works of art.

From 1000 to 1400 the city's power and wealth rested either with Christians from Europe or Muslims from the region. Not surprisingly, the art reflects their dominance. By contrast, written testimonial indicates that the Jews of Jerusalem were among her poorer citizens. While we have evidence of Jewish scholarly creativity and activity as traders and in some cases makers of goods, we have to look to the wealthier communities of the Diaspora, and particularly to Europe, for spectacular works of art inspired by the city.

Longing for Jerusalem is a recurring theme here. If the city's devotees could not come to the city, they yearned to. If they could not lay their eyes on the city, they imagined it. In terms of artistic production, the envisioned Jerusalem was sometimes more magnificent than the city itself. Exile and attendant longing for Jerusalem was, and still is, deeply embedded into Jewish ritual and prayer. Evocations of the Temple that once overlooked the city thus figured in Hebrew Bibles, service books, and even wedding rings (cats. 62a–c). Matthew Paris (ca. 1200–1259), a monk in Saint Albans who never traveled out of his native England, produced maps — page after page detailing the journey from England to Jerusalem via the port of Acre — that make clear his intense desire to go there in his imagination (cat. 1). Contemporary chroniclers tell us that the Zangid military leader Nur al-Din commissioned a great minbar in Aleppo for the Aqsa Mosque. It symbolized his aspiration to one day take back Jerusalem from the Crusaders and embellish it with a great work of art (cats. 93a, b).

WALKING ABOUT SION (PSALMS 48:13)

Pilgrims who come to Jerusalem today almost invariably focus on the city's biblical past. Tour guides point out archaeological remnants from the ancient Temple. Scale models reconstruct the city as it appeared under Roman rule. Groups of pilgrims trace the steps of Jesus. Seeing the city through that lens certainly makes for a powerful experience, but it obscures the rich layering of history that is everywhere evident. No archaeological dig is required to uncover the historic, artistic, and spiritual significance of this extraordinary place. So much of what we see today is medieval — and beautiful — and often hiding in plain sight.

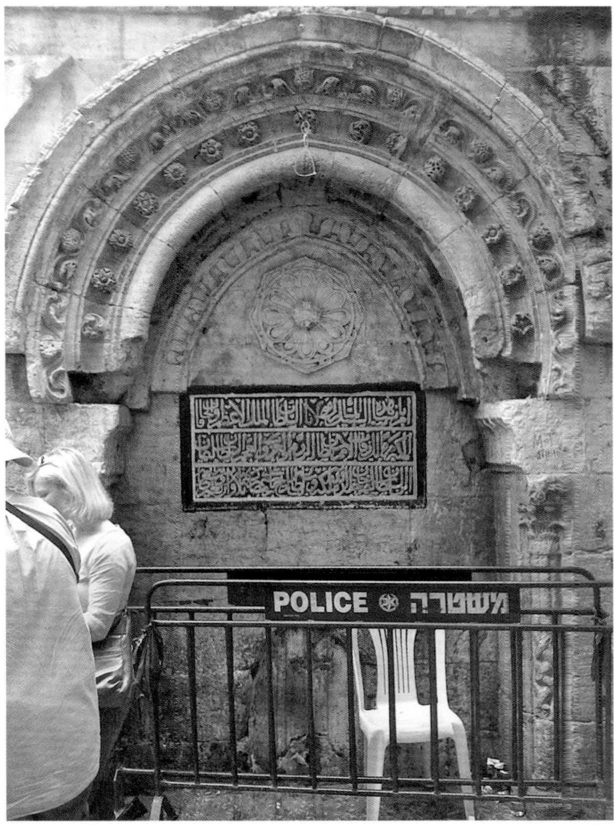

Fig. 2. The Fountain of the Inspector, Jerusalem

At a jog in Al-Wad Street in Jerusalem stands the Fountain of the Inspector (Sabil al-Nazir) (fig. 2). One of several fountains around the Old City completed during the Ottoman period, it presents a particularly handsome assemblage of parts.[7] While its engineering and elaborate inscription date from the sixteenth century, most of its decorative elements — the impressive arch, the grand medallion beneath the arch, and the elegant braided columns to each side — were carved by master sculptors in the twelfth.[8] No sign draws attention to it. It is not part of any standard tourist itinerary today, and pilgrims and shoppers alike pass it by without notice. Blue police barricades steer the throngs intent on following the Stations of the Cross on the Via Dolorosa, but the faithful miss this spot, a source of life-sustaining water with its own inherent tranquility and spiritual impact. Such works of art testify as powerfully to Jerusalem's history as do the prominent, officially designated spots. Throughout the city, whole worlds exist behind doors, realms within realms. We aim to bring them into the light.

To focus on the eleventh through the fourteenth centuries is to be reminded that, though Jerusalem can seem eternal, it has undergone enormous change. Seemingly immutable elements of its sacred topography were understood differently in this period. The Old City today is famously divided into four quarters: Armenian, Christian, Jewish, and Muslim, but it has not always been so. Some of those designations find their roots in the medieval period. The Byzantine emperor likely negotiated a small Christian quarter within the Muslim-controlled city from Caliph al-Zahir as part of his agreement to help rebuild the walls of the city after the earthquakes of the early eleventh century.[9] Scholars debate the location of the Jewish Quarter at this time, though evidence suggests there were Jewish neighborhoods on either side of the city walls in the vicinity of the Sion Gate.[10] The centuries-old Armenian community lived, then as now, around its Cathedral of Saint James and grew during our period.[11] Hard borders, however, were not a feature of medieval Jerusalem.[12] Neighborhoods evolved with the needs of the city and its inhabitants. The Crusaders designated quarters for the patriarch, Armenians, Syrians, the Hospitallers, and the Templars.[13] Under Saladin, North African Muslims endowed a Maghrebi Quarter.[14] By the late fifteenth century, the Muslim judge and historian Mujir al-Din enumerated not four but nine zones, including one dubbed the "quarter of the Feather."[15]

With this exhibition and publication we hope to unravel the various cultural traditions and aesthetic strands that made medieval Jerusalem a magnet for so many. The project has been something of an experiment, inspired in part by the forgotten Fountain of the Inspector. What would happen if we eschewed the division of works of art by religious belief and cultural heritage? Suppose we set aside political history as a means to define cultural history so that we could better explore the variety, richness, continuities, and interconnectivity of the city, its people, and its art? We do not offer a time line. In lieu of a chronological framework, we provide a thematic approach.

In the following discussions, we examine six specific factors that made medieval Jerusalem an exceptional source of artistic inspiration:

The Pulse of Trade and Tourism. Often understood as the crossroads of the known world, Jerusalem in the medieval period was a thriving urban center catering to both residents and pilgrims. Indeed, it was the special mix of locals and religiously motivated tourists that fueled the economy. Commerce, then as now, had a way of cutting across cultural and religious divides and even working around armed conflict.

The Diversity of Peoples. During this time the city was home to more cultures, faiths, and languages than ever before. Even calendars varied. Dozens of denominations and communities – sometimes competitive and other times complementary – contributed to the artistic and spiritual richness of the city.

The Air of Holiness. Sanctity is the most salient feature of Jerusalem. We have attempted to evoke the city's sacred iconic monuments, with their layered history and shared spaces. In discussing those monuments we have given pride of place to the voices of medieval visitors, what features struck them, how their own expectations informed what they saw, and what sorts of cultural exchange occurred when they inevitably encountered the art of the other.

The Drumbeat of Holy War. Intimately bound with the belief in Jerusalem's sanctity and the sense of exclusive ownership it instilled is the ideology of Holy War. This period witnessed the intensification of both crusade in Christianity and jihad in Islam. We have an important opportunity to present these concepts, so charged in our own day, and consider the ways in which art was placed in their service. We recognize that conflict can result in wanton destruction, but we find, sadly and paradoxically, that it can also spark creativity.

The Generosity of Patrons. War notwithstanding, the medieval city was blessed with generous patrons who built and reshaped its sanctuaries and public spaces. We explore the motivations and projects of the men and women who altered the aesthetic landscape of Jerusalem.

The Promise of Eternity. We juxtapose works of art that spring from a belief – commonly held by the three Abrahamic faiths – that Jerusalem stands at the gates of heaven. This is art of dreamlike beauty, born of hope and sometimes mixed with a sense of foreboding.

SPEAK TENDERLY TO JERUSALEM (ISAIAH 37:10)

Our conception of this project was shaped by an early conversation with an extraordinary man. Theophilus, the Greek Orthodox patriarch of Jerusalem, graciously agreed to receive us in his imposing office. In keeping with social convention, we were offered a hot beverage, and the distinguished churchman listened attentively as we pitched our ideas and the necessity of his community's involvement in realizing them. A pregnant pause ensued. In a quiet voice the patriarch inquired: "Whose story do you intend to tell?"

With his question, we were reminded of the depth of feeling and history that pervades almost every aspect of life in Jerusalem. Our reply was, "we hope to tell everyone's story, and no one's." Yet even with the best of intentions, everyone tells his or her own story. In presenting ours we have relied as much as possible on the voices of our medieval predecessors who, like us, have fallen in love with the city. As historians of Jerusalem, we are blessed with an abundance of written sources from the medieval period. Coming from different lands and traditions, representing "every people under heaven," they form a veritable chorus.[16] Though not always singing the same lyrics in the same language in harmony, they enrich our understanding of the city called Jerusalem, Sion, al-Quds, Bayt al-Maqdis. . . .

Our many medieval accounts have revealed that visitors to Jerusalem used the stories from their own traditions to set their courses through the city. We expect that readers of this publication and visitors to the exhibition will, to some extent, do the same. Our hope, however, is that people, whatever their background or expectations, will also turn their attention to the unexpected beauty waiting just at the jog in the road, off their prescribed itinerary. The British artist Selina Bracebridge, in a watercolor she painted in the early twentieth century (fig. 3), seems to advocate exactly this approach to the Old City. With great subtlety, her image captures the spiritual cool and quiet of the Fountain of the Inspector. Bracebridge does not place it at the center of her composition, but just a little bit to the side, waiting to be fully discovered. The morning sun leaves the wide and familiar road in darkness; it illuminates only the art.

NOTES FOR THIS ESSAY APPEAR ON PAGE 300

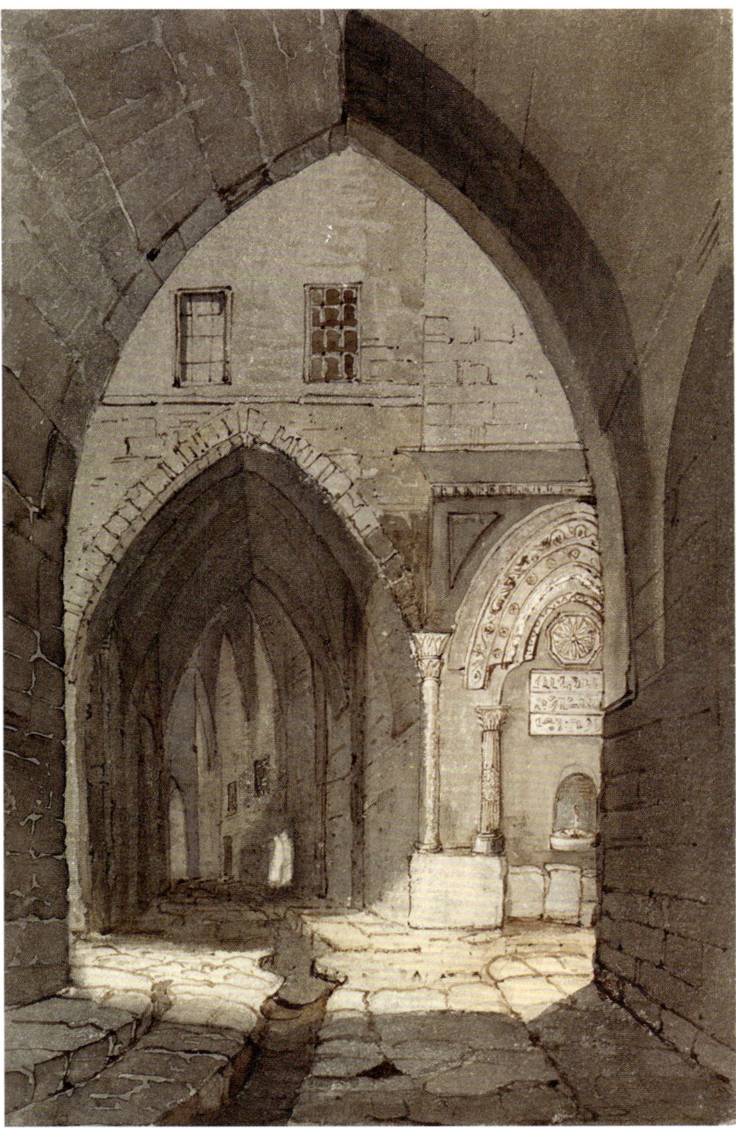

Fig. 3. The Fountain of the Inspector. Watercolor by Selina Bracebridge, 19th century. Victoria and Albert Museum, London (SD.158:1)

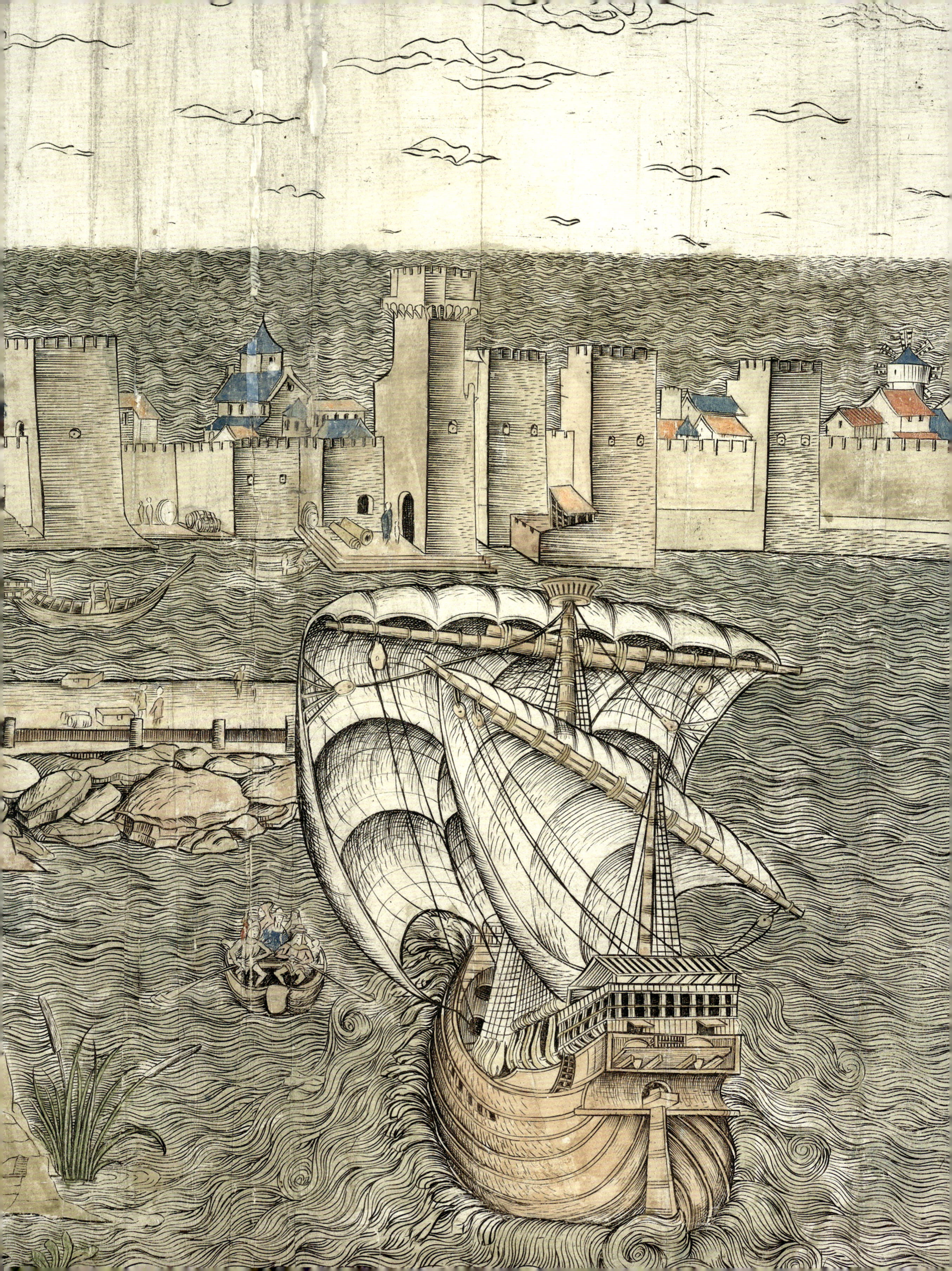

Trade and Tourism in Medieval Jerusalem

Travelers will come and go – Ibn Jubayr

MELANIE HOLCOMB AND BARBARA DRAKE BOEHM

FACING PAGE
Fig. 4. Ship bound for the Holy Land, at port in Methoni, Greece, from *Journey to the Holy Land* (*La peregrination en Terre Sainte*). Detail of cat. 47

SAILING FROM GENOA to the Holy Land in 1216, Jacques de Vitry (ca. 1160/70–1240), newly appointed bishop of Acre, and his fellow travelers encountered a terrible storm: "The fore part of our ship was now lifted up towards the stars, the next moment it was sunk into the depths. The storm lasted continuously for two days and nights; so that some of our people could hardly bear the violence of the winds, which laid low the forecastle of our ship, and broke down [in panic], while others did not eat nor drink for the fear of death."[1] Deadly storms en route to the Holy Land had been described in equally dramatic terms a century earlier by an Anglo-Saxon monk known as Saewulf and the Spanish poet Judah ha-Levi.[2] Yet for many sea travelers, storms were the least of their concerns. When Felix Fabri set sail in the company of 329 others in the fifteenth century, he endured over the six-week journey not only high winds and waves but also pirates, disagreeable fellow voyagers, and regular encounters with "fleas and lice, flies, mice and rats."[3] Given the life-threatening dangers and discomfort encountered by seafarers on the Mediterranean, one wonders why anyone would have traveled to Jerusalem, by sea or by land.

But travel they did. In 1248, four years after the Europeans' final loss of Jerusalem, the Genoese vessel *Oliva* expected to carry 1,100 passengers to Acre; the numbers leaving from Marseille in the 1250s were comparable.[4] In the fourteenth century, two to three ships, full of Europeans bound for Jerusalem, sailed to Jaffa from Venice each year (fig. 4).[5]

Many visitors were inspired by religious belief. Felix Fabri was a Dominican cleric from Ulm, setting out on a pilgrimage in order to deepen his faith, but he reported that only a third of the group on board had kindred motivations.[6] What drew the rest? Felix Fabri did not say, but it had already been apparent to Jacques de Vitry two centuries earlier that religious conviction was not the only reason for travel: "Some light-minded persons went . . . to the holy places, not so much out of devotion as out of curiosity and love of novelty, that they might travel to unknown lands, and with great toil might prove the truth of the strange and, to the ignorant, miraculous stories which they had heard about the East."[7] The bishop of Acre's testimony speaks of a taste for the unknown, a yearning for adventure, and a sense – at least for Europeans – that an exotic and magical world awaited, if only they survived the trip. More practical matters drew the many merchants from Italy, India, and lands in between, who saw the Holy Land as a lucrative market and source for salable goods. Merchants might even combine business with religious duties as they sought economic advantage from well-timed ventures.

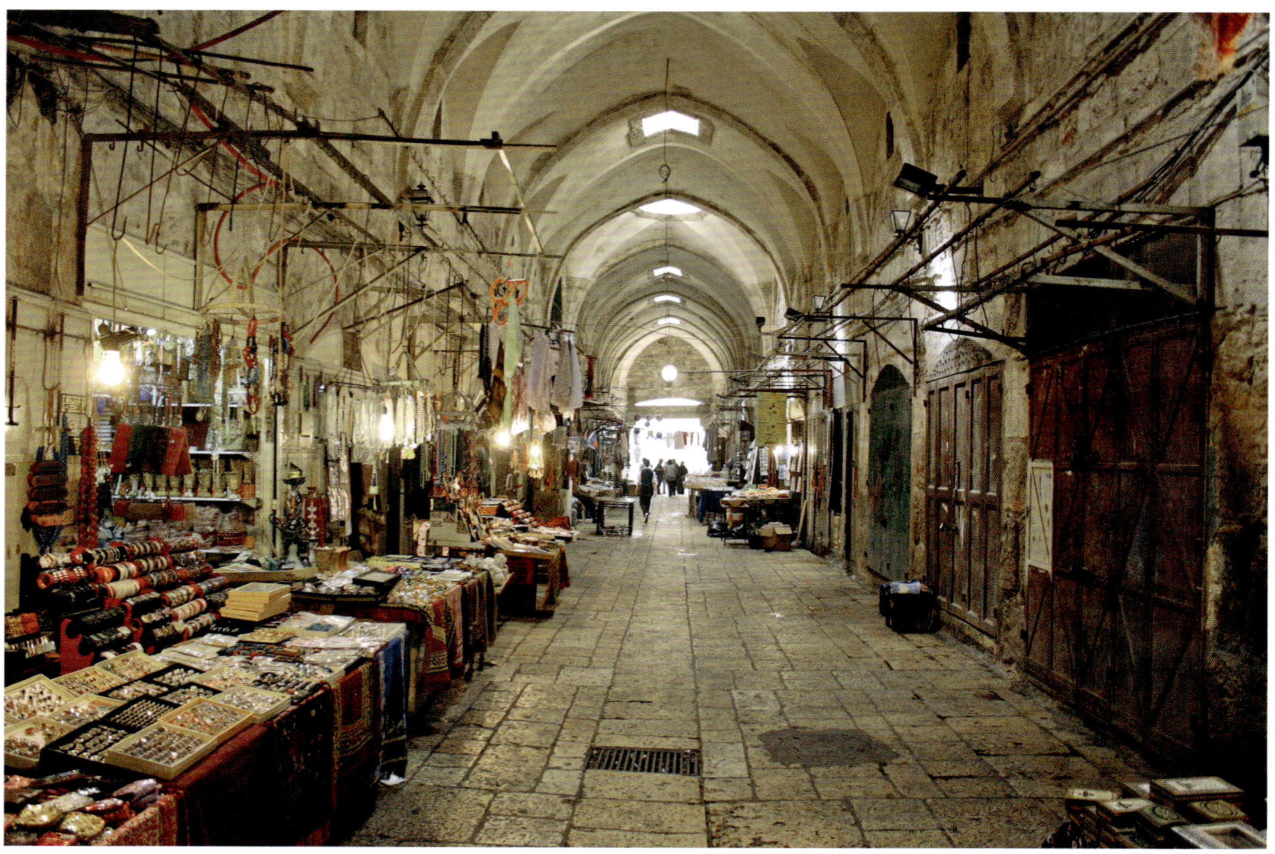

Fig. 5. The Cotton Market, Jerusalem

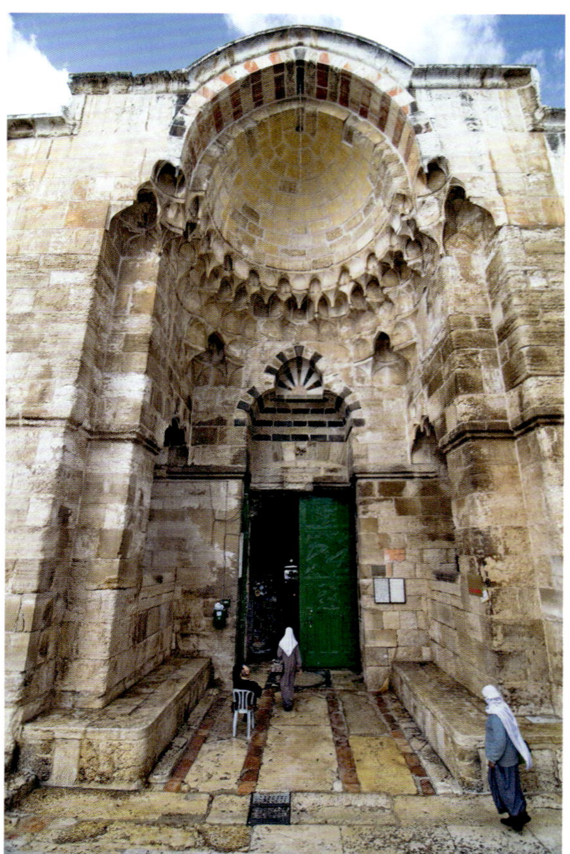

Fig. 6. Gate of the Cotton Market, Jerusalem

Jerusalem's streets were "never . . . empty of strangers," remarked al-Muqaddasi, a native of the city in the late tenth century, an observation that highlights one of its most distinguishing features.[8] The Holy City offered a special mix that drew thousands every year. Neither a capital like Cairo nor a booming commercial center like Damascus, it nevertheless enjoyed a peculiar position as a tourist destination and economic hub, but, unlike any other place, one that was fed by the influx of religious pilgrims, adventurers, and merchants of many faiths and from around the world.

On arrival in Jerusalem, visitors, whether from Europe or elsewhere, were as astounded by the city's markets as by its holy sites. Nasir-i Khusraw, who visited from Persia in 1047, noted the bazaars as well as the numerous specialized artisans who worked in them.[9] Later travelers were more expansive in their observations. Pietro Casola, a fifteenth-century Milanese cleric who was surely no stranger to the beauty of the urban landscape, was effusive in his praise: "What delighted me most was the sight of their bazaars — long, vaulted streets extending as far as the eye can reach."[10] For Simone Sigoli, a late fourteenth-century Florentine Franciscan, not only were the streets beautiful and the shops exceptionally clean, but also "the streets are all, or the greater part of them, covered with roofs or vaulted, and they have windows which give light so that when it rains the streets remain dry."[11] Today the triple suq, the beautiful allée created by three long, vaulted markets set side by side, still astounds, as does the Cotton Market with its skylights (fig. 5). Built in the fourteenth century, the Cotton Market's "height and solidity" impressed those who saw it.[12] "There are many cities where one cannot find its equal," remarked Mujir al-Din (1456–1522), another Jerusalem native.[13] Al-Umari, a fourteenth-century visiting scholar from Damascus, declared the carved and gilded stone gate at the market's end, leading up to the Haram al-Sharif, to be nothing short of "perfect" (fig. 6).[14]

In the city, tradesmen offering similar goods congregated in proximity to one another and according to shoppers' needs. This business strategy is still used today, whether in New York's lighting stores on the Bowery or the Forty-Seventh Street diamond district. In Jerusalem's triple suq, one section of the market was dedicated to the spice merchants, another to the vegetable vendors, and a third to the traders in silk or cotton, with each named according to its trade.[15] Although focused almost entirely on holy sites, a Jewish pilgrim's scroll in the exhibition identifies the same set of markets in Jerusalem (cat. 21). Still today, a cluster of incense shops is only steps away from the Church of the Holy Sepulchre. In this compact city, food and precious goods were sold in shops set cheek by jowl, and a cacophonous, odiferous atmosphere must have surrounded the Holy Sepulchre, where the goldsmiths worked in curious proximity to the vendors of chickens and birds. The goldsmiths themselves conversed in different languages: Syrian gold workers were on the right; European goldsmiths on the left.[16]

Not far from the goldsmiths' shops sat the currency exchange. Writing in the tenth century, al-Muqaddasi asserted that Jews largely handled the quality control of coin and the money exchange in Jerusalem.[17] In addition to banking, tenth-century Jews were involved in trade, manuscript copying, and the production and marketing of Jerusalem's textiles.[18] While the welfare of the Jewish community fluctuated in the centuries that followed, reaching its nadir when European Christians controlled the city,[19] Jews had returned to Jerusalem when the city was once more governed by Muslims and by the fifteenth century were employed as goldsmiths, shoemakers, carpenters, weavers, silk producers, and silk merchants.[20]

While many eyewitness accounts provide a sense of the hubbub of Jerusalem's streets and the remarkable variety of its wares, specific details about the kind and quality of goods are much harder to retrieve. Goldsmiths' work from the century of European Christian domination of Jerusalem, for instance, rarely survives in situ (cat. 97), as much of it was carried off when Saladin (1137/38–1193), founder of the Ayyubid dynasty, captured Jerusalem in 1187.[21] The few extant examples, created almost uniquely for religious use, owe their survival to having been sent back to Europe or buried (fig. 7, cat. 25c). In terms of textiles, however, fourteenth-century documents preserved at the Haram suggest the range found in Jerusalem: colorful pillows, carpets, and prayer rugs from Syria and Anatolia (cat. 9c), along with shirts of linen and wool brought from Upper Egypt.[22] Nompar de Caumont, an early fifteenth-century pilgrim from Aquitaine, purchased in Jerusalem silks, woolens, and textiles from India (cat. 9a, b).[23] Considering the diversity of peoples and goods flowing through this cultural

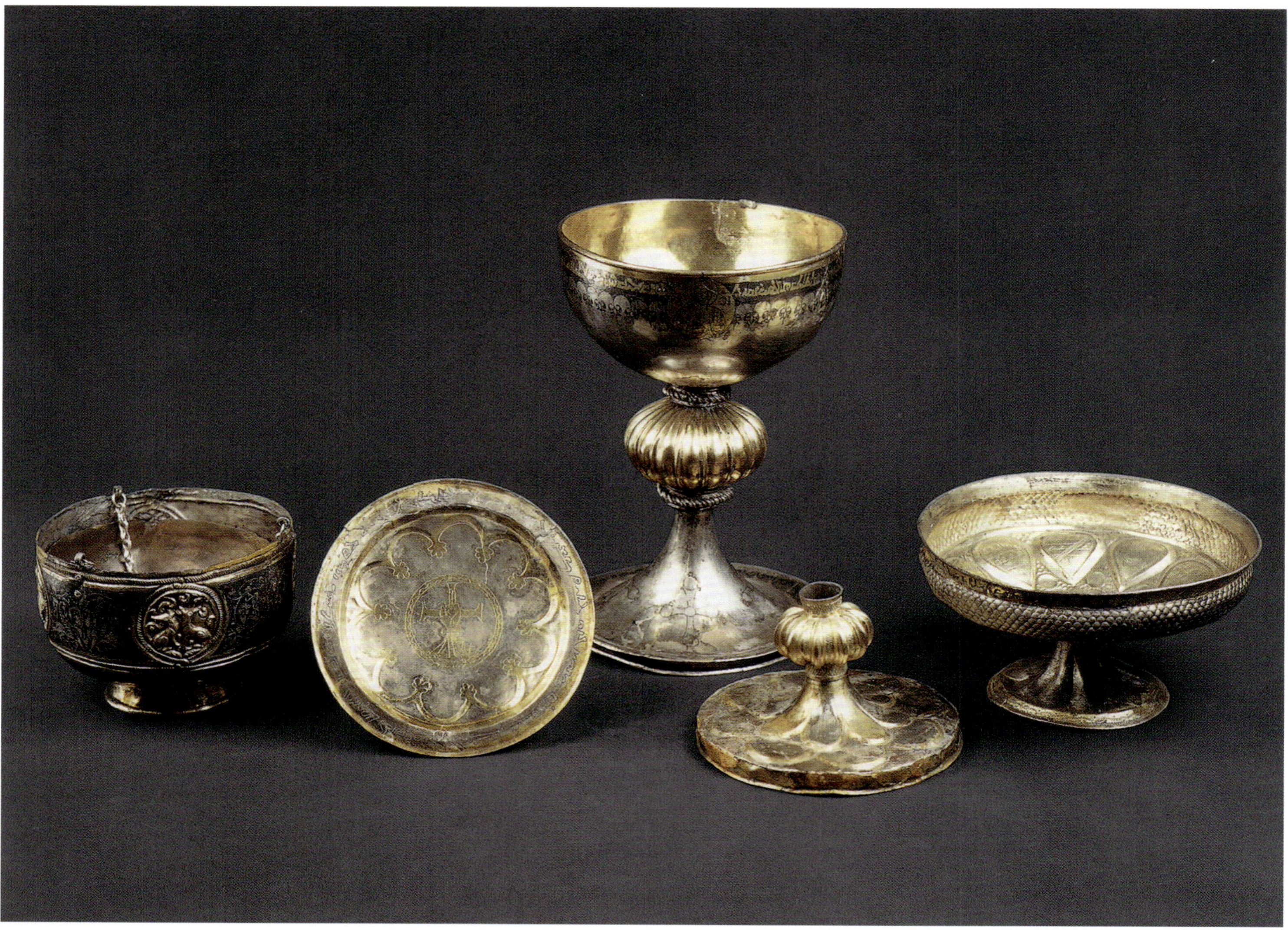

Fig. 7. The Resafa hoard (discovered in Resafa — known in Roman times as Sergiopolis — in present-day Syria, in the courtyard of the Basilica of the Holy Cross), ca. 1243–59. Silver. National Museum of Damascus, Syria (29313/15, AN 30; 29134, AN 32; 29311, AN 29; 29316, AN 31; 29312, AN 29)

crossroad, it is unsurprising that enameled glass vessels reflect the vibrant, colorful, and international world in which they were created (cats. 24a–c).

No visitor to Jerusalem failed to mention the food. Even Pietro Casola, who reminisced about the chestnuts sold on the streets back home, marveled at the variety of comestibles in Jerusalem's suq, while his fellow countryman Simone Sigoli remarked that the markets had many more kinds of meat than Italian markets had.[24] The always observant Felix Fabri noted the city's many kitchens, commenting that "no woman is ever seen near the fire."[25] One can imagine that, as in Cairo, simple ceramic vessels were used for carryout orders.[26]

The abundance and assortment of foods were remarkable. Al-Muqaddasi held the conviction that God himself had provided the wide array of delicacies in his native land, including "the citron, the almond, the date, the nut, the fig, and the banana, besides milk in plenty, and honey and sugar."[27] The German Dominican Burchard of Mount Sion who traveled in the Holy Land from 1274 to 1284 not only listed the many marvelous foods of the region but also described how the more exotic, like bananas and sugar, were grown and prepared.[28] Local abundance notwithstanding, foods were transported to Jerusalem to meet the demand of visitors, including grapes from Cairo brought in for the pilgrimage.[29]

One wonders if the grapes did well, for some said that the greatest pleasure was to eat bananas in the shadow of the Dome of the Rock.[30]

Such chroniclers richly portrayed the ways in which agriculture and industry sustained the pilgrim trade. Nasir-i Khusraw observed oxen and mules grinding flour all day long in the many mills of Hebron, as well as the slave girls charged with baking bread. He also described the special tradition of feeding visitors lentils cooked with olive oil, bread, and raisins.[31] Both he and al-Muqaddasi recognized "the custom of Abraham" in the hospitality offered at Hebron, considering it the best example of charity "in all of Islam."[32]

Reports of travelers spanning several hundred years attest to this custom in Muslim Hebron. An inscription in marble preserved over the gate of a portico leading to the city's kitchens and bakeries celebrates the charitable distribution of food through the generosity of the late thirteenth- to early fourteenth-century sultan al-Nasir Muhammad ibn Qala'un.[33] According to Yitgaddal, an Egyptian Jewish scribe writing in the early fourteenth century, "4,000 pieces of bread and cooked lentils" were publicly distributed during the Islamic afternoon prayer and "whoever wishes may partake."[34] Rabbi Obadiah of Bertinoro, renowned as the revitalizer of Jerusalem's Jewish community in the fifteenth century, also remarked that the offering in Hebron was extended to non-Muslims: "Every day, they distribute bread, a stew of lentils or some other dish of legumes to the poor — be they Ishmaelite [Muslim] or Jewish or uncircumcised [Christian]."[35] Impressed by both the volume and the variety of offerings, Meshullam of Volterra, a late fifteenth-century Jewish banker, merchant, and sometime correspondent of Lorenzo de Medici, was impressed by both the volume and variety of offerings. He cited numbers of biblical proportions, "at least 13,000 loaves of bread a day in honor of Abraham, Isaac and Jacob," and described a sumptuous feast befitting his aristocratic tastes: "In honor of Abraham, they distribute bread, tongues in mustard, and tender and delicious veal, such as Abraham gave to the angels, and in honor of Isaac, venison and delicacies such as he loved and in honor of Jacob, bread and lentil stew, such as he gave to Esau and this is held constantly every day and without fail."[36]

If serving food was linked to Abraham, the cooking vessels were linked in contemporary thought to King Solomon. According to al-Qalqashandi, a fourteenth-century scribe in Cairo, cooking pots were the proud possessions of royalty, symbols of their prosperity and generosity. Genies, or djinns, he explained, produced the pots of Solomon.[37] Surviving vessels from a Fatimid merchant's and metalsmith's hoards, found nearby in Caesarea and Tiberias (cats. 10, 11), as well as their more ostentatious Mamluk counterparts connote hospitality embraced as a sacred calling.

Whether in Hebron or Jerusalem, food and religion were intertwined, mixed with commerce, and necessitated by the sheer volume of visitors. The number of mouths to be fed was exponentially greater in the Holy City: "Jerusalem, which the people of Syria and that region call 'Quds,' is visited during the season by the people of the area who are unable to make the Pilgrimage to Mecca. They perform the requisite rituals and offer a sacrifice on the customary holiday. Some years more than twenty thousand people come during the first days of Dhu I-hejja bringing their children to celebrate their circumcision."[38] For Christians, food was available in the central market on a street whose name carried its own implicit warning: Malquisinat Street. On this Street of Bad Cooking, pilgrims could find prepared food and have their heads washed before they entered the Holy Sepulchre.[39]

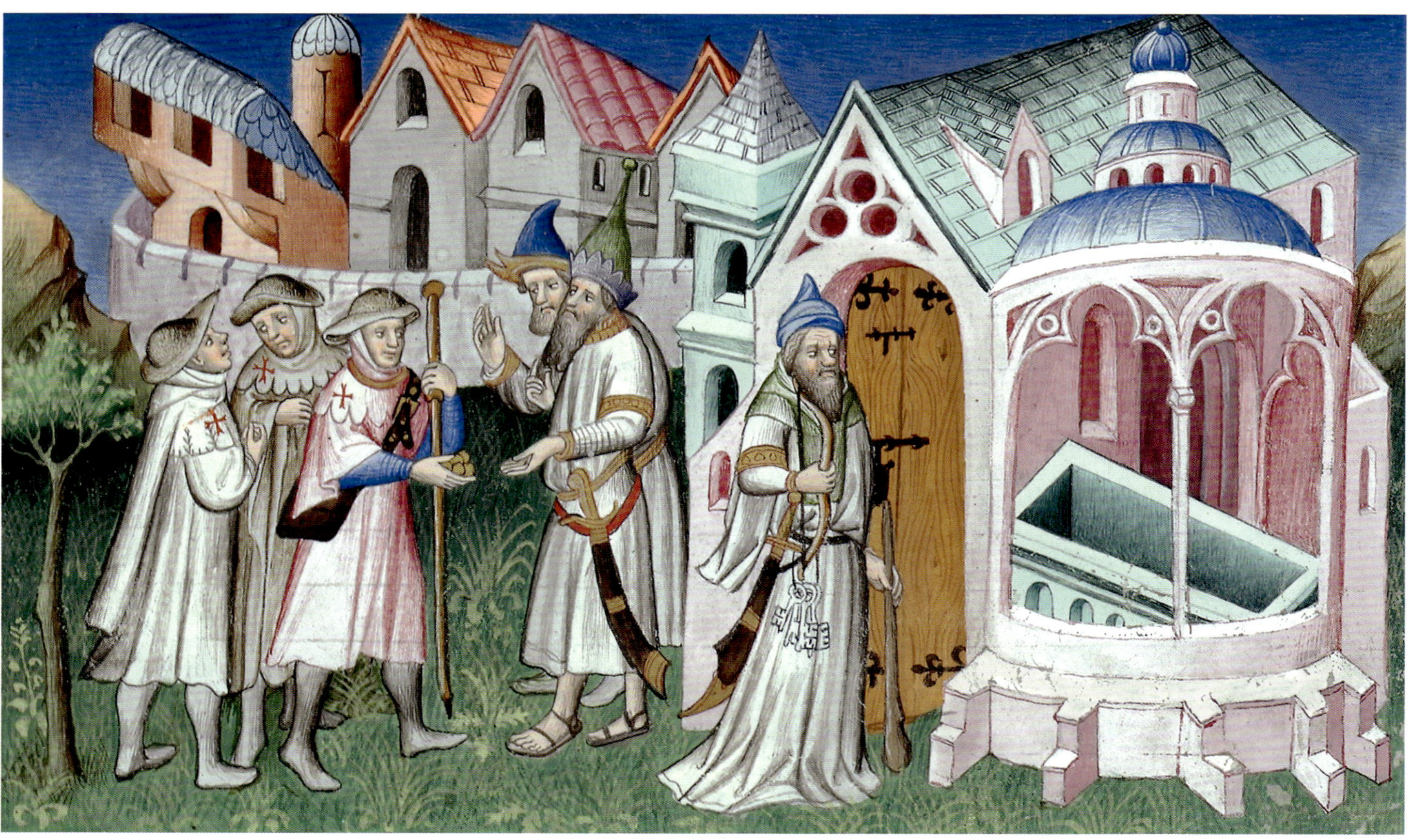

Fig. 8. Pilgrims at the Holy Sepulchre, from the *Pilgrimage Book* (*Liber peregrinationis*) by Riccoldo da Monte Croce. Paris, 1410–12. Tempera, gold leaf, and ink on parchment. Bibliothèque Nationale de France, Paris (MS Fr. 2810, fol. 274r)

It is significant that Nasir-i Khusraw realized that religious tourism applied not only to his own tradition but also to that of Christians and Jews: "From the Byzantine realms and other places too come Christians and Jews to visit the churches and synagogues located there."[40] Those seeking refuge from the hurly-burly of Jerusalem's marketplaces would not have found it in that church, whose interior could be every bit as boisterous as the crowded streets outside (fig. 8). Felix Fabri described with dismay a lively suq flourishing inside the church itself:

> Whenever the pilgrims enter the Church of the Holy Sepulchre, those traders come in together with them, carrying their wares. They . . . establish themselves straight in front of the door of the church, spread out a cloth on the pavement and set out their wares upon it for sale. Some of the pilgrims . . . stayed awake all that night bargaining, and bought all kinds of things, for the traders there had for sale not only Pater Noster beads and precious stones, but also cloths of damask, of camlet, and of silk, and round about these merchants there was much disturbance and noise, even as in a marketplace.[41]

This mania for commerce was obviously not a new phenomenon. In 1350 Ludolph von Suchem related a similar scene taking place twice a year: "From Good Friday to Monday after Easter, and from the Eve of the Invention of the Holy Cross till the morrow of the feast – the Christians . . . are let into the church for nothing, and locked in, and then one finds shops in the church where sundry things and victuals are sold, even as in this country they do in markets and fairs, and then one hears talk and songs in divers tongues."[42]

For Christians, the visit to Jerusalem was commemorated by the souvenir, a memento sometimes procured from the city's merchants and sometimes not. Felix Fabri described pilgrims in acts of "vicious curiosity," chipping off bits of stone from the Holy Sepulchre to take home, despite having been warned on more than one occasion not to.[43] He also lamented the pilgrims' habit of leaving their mark by attaching their heraldic arms to holy sites, thus "spoil[ing] works artistically wrought with great labor and expense."[44] A noble fourteenth-century visitor from Florence took bits of stone from Bethlehem for friends back home, stone from the Golden Gate for himself and a travel companion, and a piece of Lazarus's tomb from the village of Bethany, just east of Jerusalem, for himself. He also obtained from the Tomb of Abraham at Hebron holy oil that, as Frescobaldi observed, was eagerly sought by Jews, Muslims, and Christians alike.[45] The English mystic Margery Kempe (ca. 1373–after 1438) chose "a staff like Moses' rod."[46] In the twelfth century, Guy of Blond carried a host of relics back to the Limousin in central France, including two pieces of the Cross along with a list detailing the source of each.[47]

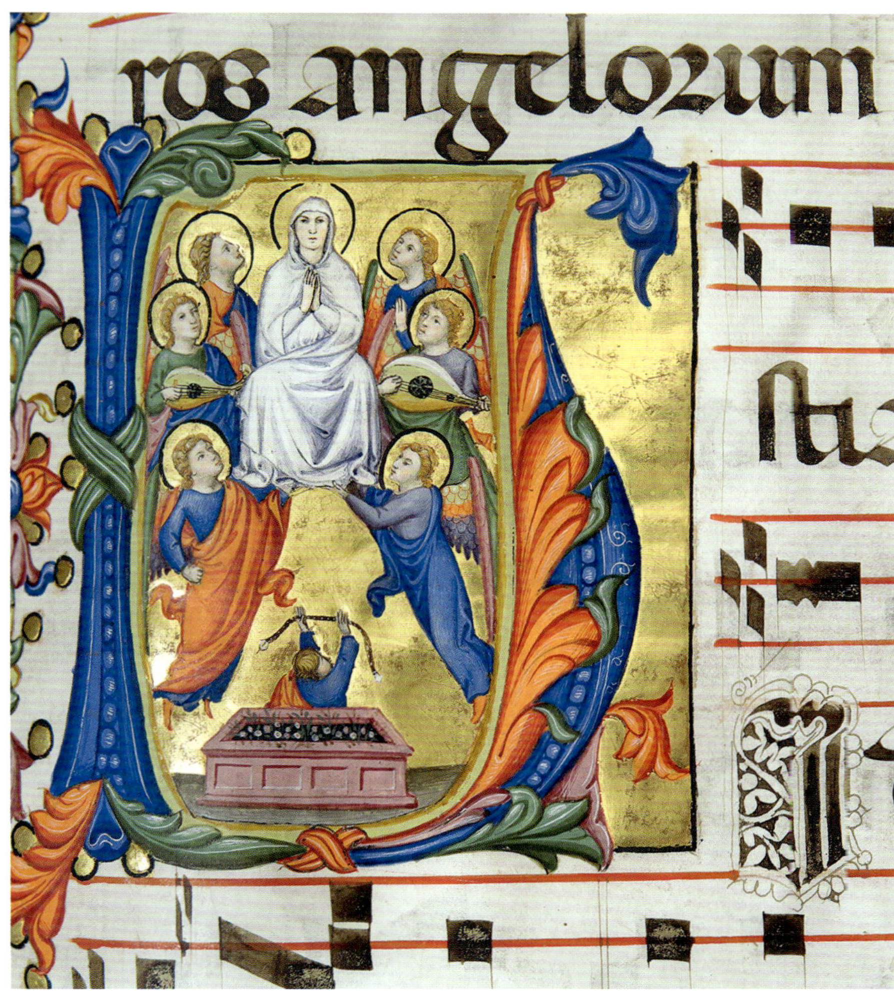

Fig. 9. Initial "V" with the Assumption of the Virgin Mary and Saint Thomas receiving her belt, from an antiphonary made for the Franciscan community of Bethlehem. Detail of cat. 134c

When an Italian merchant from Prato married a woman from Jerusalem in 1141, he received as dowry the belt of the Virgin Mary that, according to legend, she had dropped from heaven to Saint Thomas as evidence of her Assumption. The miracle is illustrated in the antiphonary presented to the Franciscans of the Holy Land (fig. 9, cat. 134c); the Virgin's belt is shown with the gleaming silver medallions, buckle, and tab that characterize Italian luxury belts (cat. 18). When the merchant returned to Prato with his bride, he carried the relic with him on board ship. A fresco by Agnolo Gaddi (active by 1369; d. 1396) preserved in Prato attests to the veracity of the story, with the merchant and his bride in white clutching a box containing the relic as the ship sails through stormy waters (fig. 10), a presentation that echoes a reliquary made to authenticate the tale of the transport of the Cross to Toulouse (cat. 25e). Today the relic of the Virgin's belt (*la sacra cintola*) is the great treasure of the cathedral in Prato.

Icons painted in the Holy Land, especially at Acre, are venerated today at the Monastery of Saint Catherine on Mount Sinai.[48] By legend, the famous image of the Virgin and Child preserved at Saidnaya in Syria, revered by both Muslims and Christians to this day, was purchased by a monk from Constantinople in Jerusalem, on behalf of a lady in Damascus. It was barely out of the shop before it performed its first miracles, protecting its bearer from lions and thieves.[49] One gains a sense of how such a shop might have looked in an illumination from the *Canticles of Saint Mary* (*Cantigas de Santa Maria*) manuscript of Alphonso the Wise (1221–1284), in which the monk in his hooded cloak selects the icon from among several choices presented by a helpful merchant and his son (fig. 11).[50]

Some souvenirs were purely devotional, but those more worldly in material or manufacture were equally available in Jerusalem. In 1420 Nompar carried home a treasure chest made of cypress wood, filled with a remarkable array of precious objects, some religious, some made sacred by contact with religious sites, and some worldly, acquired in Jerusalem for his wife and neighbors. In addition to other textiles, he purchased gold cloth, an embroidered purse, leather gloves, silk belts, more than a dozen Turkish knives, and rosaries of gold, of ivory, of precious stones, of crystal, and of cypress. Water from the Jordan River was transported in a flask along with a palm frond. Crosses had been imbued with sacredness by contact with the Holy Sepulchre, as had a pair of gilded spurs, four *roses d'outre-mer*, and scores of finger rings.[51]

Merchants of different religious persuasions stood ready to accommodate the likes of Nompar, and ease of movement was essential to the economy. Indeed, many accounts of the eleventh to fourteenth centuries reveal that, then as now, business is business. The traveler and poet Ibn Jubayr (1145–1217), writing in the late twelfth century, was astonished to see that "Muslim and Christian travelers will come and go without impediment."[52] Less than a year after Saladin's reconquest of Jerusalem in 1187, trade with the Franks was reestablished.[53] European visitors spoke favorably of the lodging that was provided in Muslim mercantile centers.[54] Traveling merchants lodged in well-appointed hotels (*funduqs*).[55] Jacques de Vitry, observing trade from his seat at the port of Acre, the last European stronghold in the Holy Land, realized that cooperation among the diverse Christian communities was essential to the marketplace, agriculture, and industry.[56] Meanwhile, in 1434, Elijah of Ferrara wrote, "The Jews ply

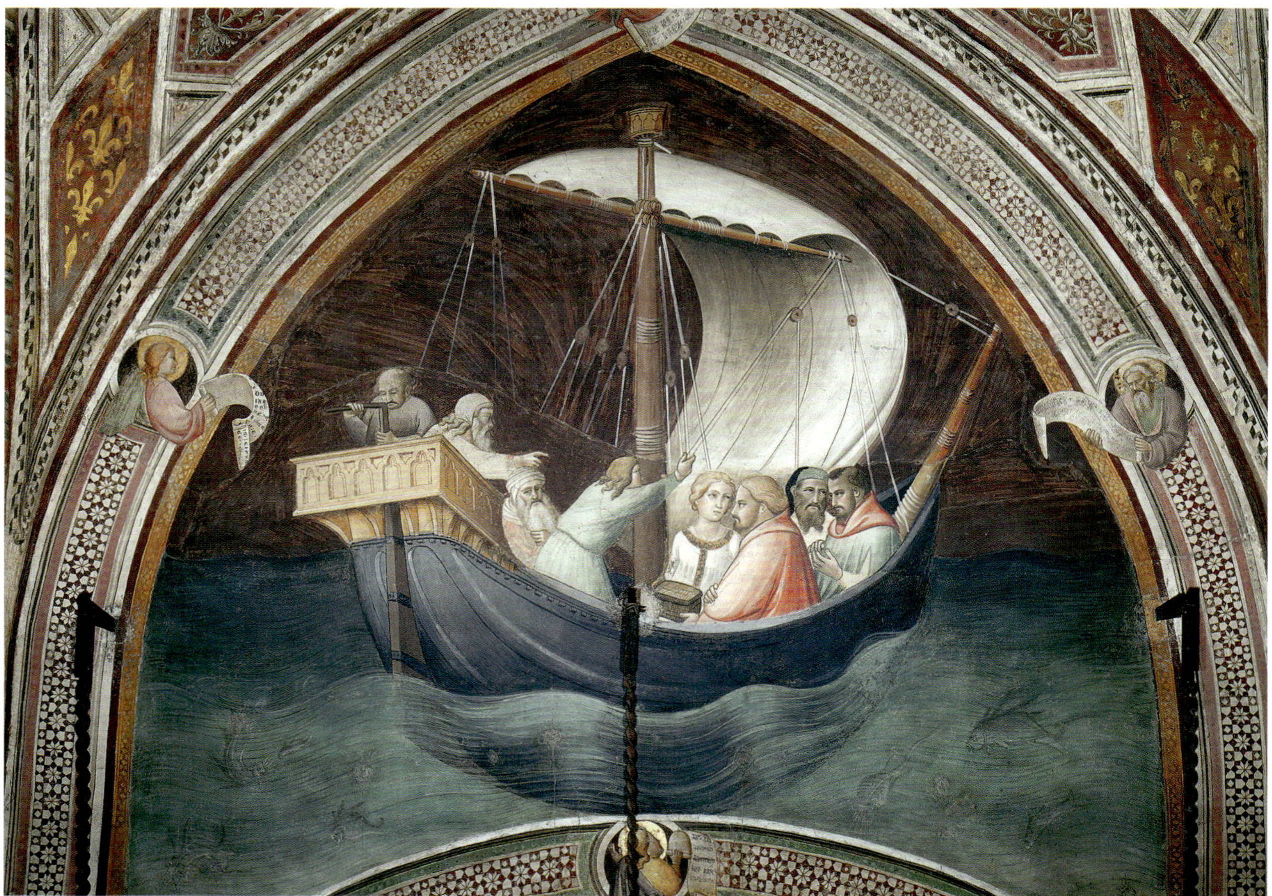

Fig. 10. Fresco showing the voyage from the Holy Land to Tuscany. Agnolo Gaddi, 1392–95. Chapel of the Holy Belt, Cathedral of Saint Stephen, Prato, Italy

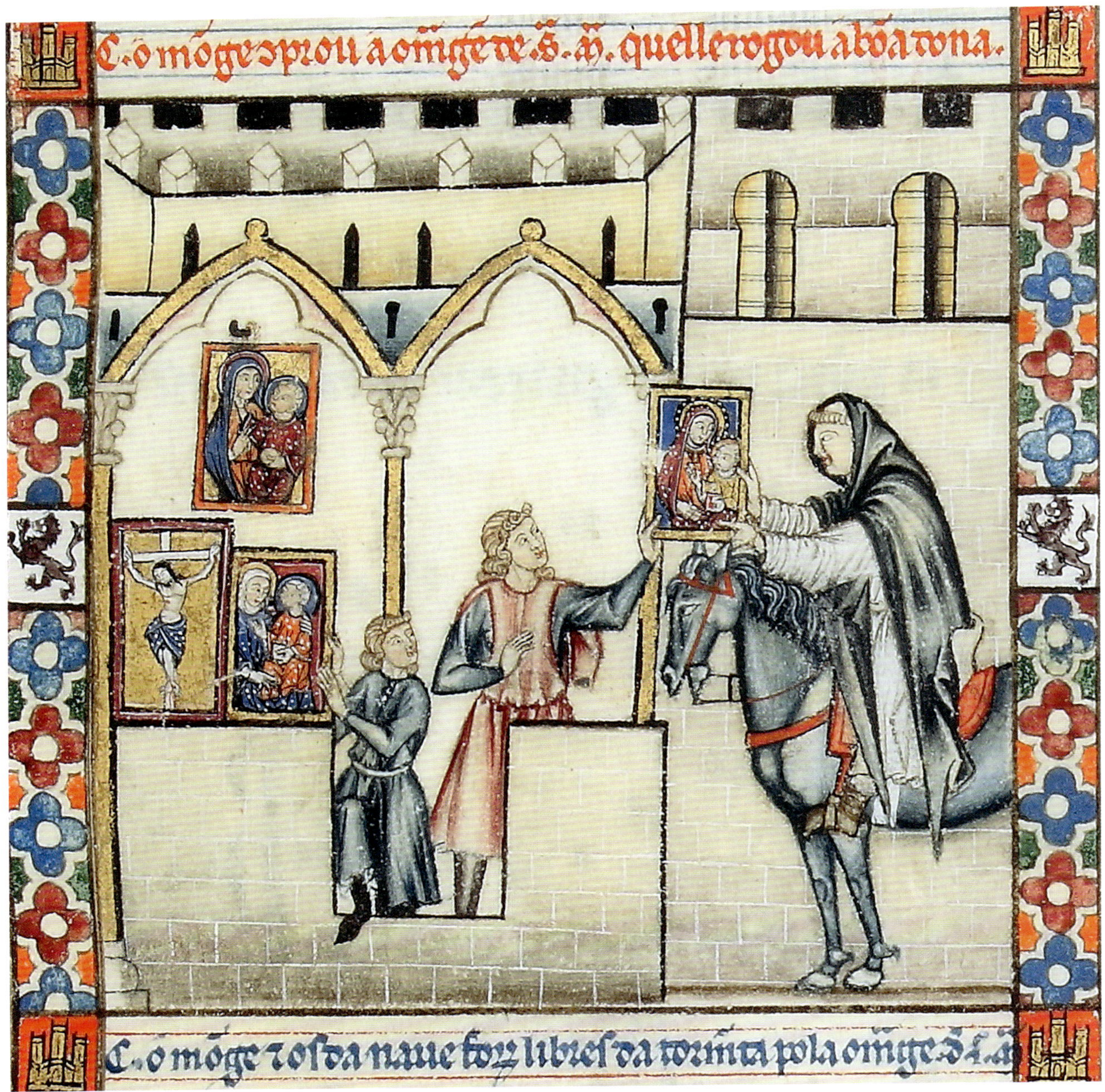

Fig. 11. Detail from canticle 9, "How the Monk Bought the Image of the Virgin which the Good Lady Had Asked of Him," from the *Canticles of Saint Mary* (*Cantigas de Santa Maria*) of Alphonso the Wise. Spain, ca. 1280–84. Tempera, gold, and ink on parchment. Real Biblioteca de El Escorial, Madrid (MS B.I.2, fols. 38v–39v)

their trades side by side with the Ishmaelites, and no jealousy between them results such as I remarked in other places."[57] Paid Arab guides escorted Christian pilgrims, protecting them from bandits along the road.[58] Even when Muslim and Christian armies were at war, "still the caravans passed successively from Egypt to Damascus, going through the lands of the Franks without impediment from them."[59] Trade and travel between Europe and the Holy Land provided common cause, even in times of war, and afforded peoples from different worlds opportunities to meet through the shared language of commerce.

NOTES FOR THIS ESSAY APPEAR ON PAGE 300

SEE CATS. 1–26

DOMESTIC GOODS FROM THE SUQ TO THE HOME: IMAGINING JERUSALEM'S INTERIORS

Elizabeth Dospěl Williams

The sensual pleasures of the sights, sounds, tastes, textures, and smells of Jerusalem's suqs make these marketplaces among the city's most memorable sites. Perhaps even more significantly, the suqs impress visitors as areas where the city's social distinctions collapse. The marketplace is a meeting place of goods (both locally made and imported), people (from all regions and confessions), and public and private space. There the public realm of commerce meets the private domain of goods, many acquired for domestic interiors.

In the Middle Ages, Jerusalem's suqs extended across the city, largely along the same contours as they do today.[1] Its marketplaces were certainly smaller than those of the medieval metropolitan emporia of Cairo, Constantinople, and Damascus, yet they operated along similar lines. Medieval marketplaces were organized by the types of products sold, rather than by the religious identities of shopkeepers or customers. In Jerusalem, among the plethora of items available were not only tourist or pilgrim souvenirs but also goods for local consumers.

Arabic sources known as *hisba* manuals illuminate the craft and sale of such goods in medieval marketplaces, which were regulated by a local official known as a *muhtasib*.[2] Reflecting fabric's enormous economic significance, the *hisba* manuals contain more than a dozen terms for cloth producers and merchants, with words specifically related to textile production, use, and material. The *qattan*, for example, processed or traded cotton; the *hariri* made and sold silk; the *khayyat*, or tailor, fashioned items of dress; the *mutarriz* created embroidered designs; and the *bazzaz* dealt in bedding and drapery.[3] Likewise, the physical organization of the suq reflected the narrow specialization of merchants and craftsmen. Persian poet and traveler Nasir-i Khusraw's eleventh-century account of his visit to Jerusalem described a place with "many artisans in the city, each group having its own separate streets."[4] Western travelers to the city similarly observed the organization of intensely specialized stalls in different sections of the suqs, including a dedicated street where one could buy icon paintings (fig. 11).[5]

Medieval archaeological and textual sources, especially legal documents, make it possible to follow purchases from the marketplace to the city's interior spaces. Accounts of property drawn up for marriages, divorces, deaths, and estate disputes provide exacting descriptions of consumer goods along with their monetary values, giving an immediate impression of the belongings of individuals from a range of social and religious backgrounds. The most informative and widely studied documents come from a trove known as the Cairo Geniza (fig. 12). Discovered in the nineteenth century in the attic space of the Ben Ezra synagogue in Fustat (Old Cairo), the texts paint an evocative picture of the lives of medieval Jewish merchants and their families around the eastern Mediterranean and beyond.[6] Among the finds are numerous trousseau lists that shed light on the entire spectrum of social classes. The marriage contract of a Karaite Jewish bride named Sarwa composed in 1028 in Jerusalem lists the general categories of gold (jewelry), clothing (personal dress), copper (including eating and cooking vessels), and bedding (pillows, sofas, and bedcovers). Each subcategory in turn details the appearance, function, and value of Sarwa's possessions, which together reached the relatively modest sum of 61½ dinars.[7] In contrast, the trousseau of a particularly wealthy bride from about 1140 tallied up to 2,100 dinars, approximately the amount found in a gold hoard uncovered off the shore of Caesarea (cat. 4). Among the bride's gifts were several pairs of earrings, bracelets, rings, and necklaces; clothing made of various kinds of silk, including Byzantine (*rumiyya*) style clothing; brocaded bedcovers, silk sofas, and a couch made of reeds (*saman*); and several metal lamps, copper bowls, and candlesticks (cat. 10). In addition to jewelry,

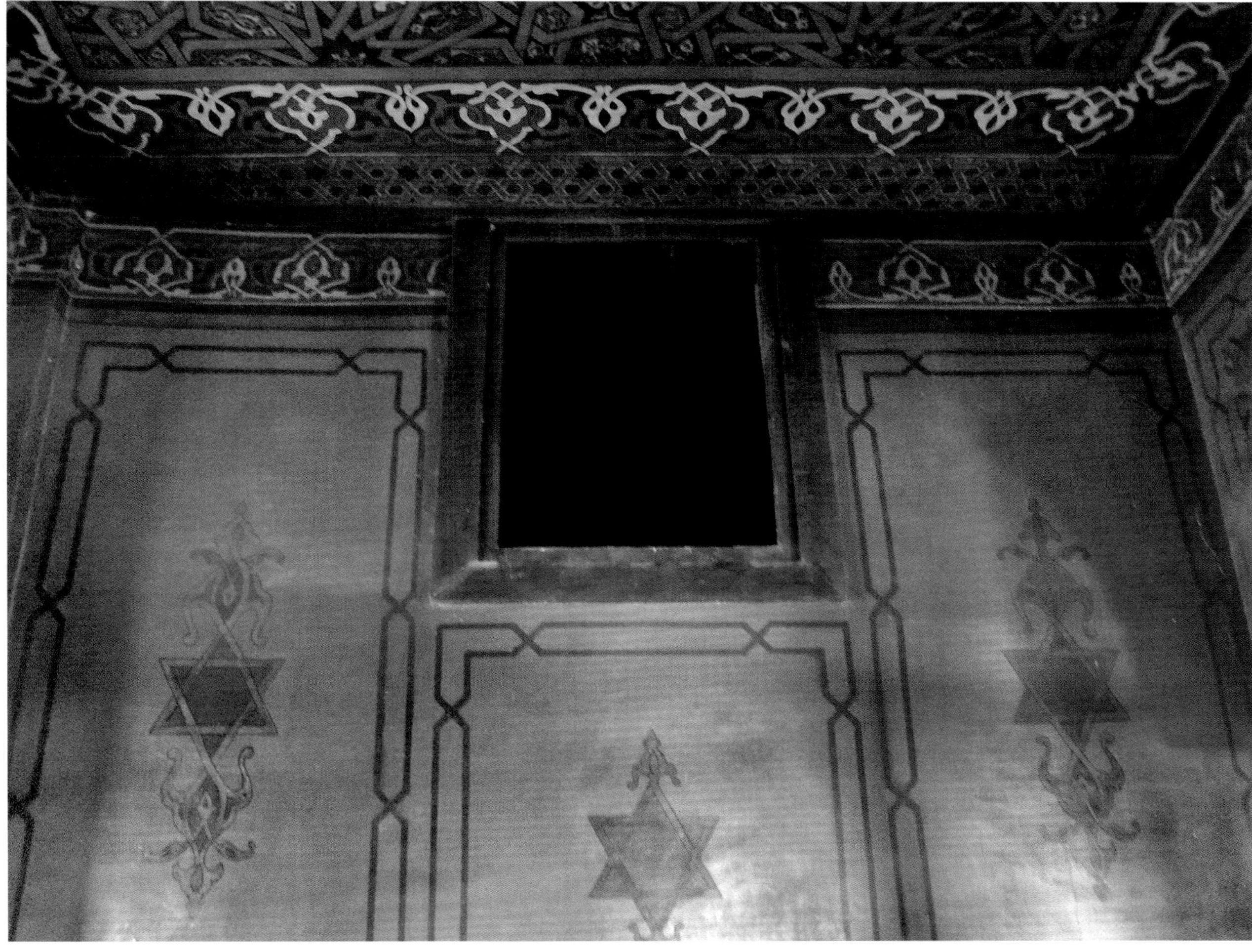

Fig. 12. The opening to the geniza, or storage area, in the attic of the women's section of the sanctuary of the Ben Ezra Synagogue, Fustat (Old Cairo)

clothing, and housewares, her possessions included servants (recorded with colorful Arabic names translating to Glory, Coquetry, Rainbow, and Fidelity) and 250 dinars' worth of books.[8] The names of the goods, many of which were derived from other languages, including Greek, Arabic, and Persian, reflect the interconnected, multilingual world of the medieval Middle East.

The estate inventory of Eudes (1231–1266), count of Nevers in Burgundy, provides an exceptional opportunity to learn about the possessions of an upper-class Crusader living about the same time as the Jewish brides listed in the Cairo Geniza documents.[9] Eudes died in Acre in 1266, just one year after arriving in the Holy Land on crusade. His list of possessions, written in old French, documents the kinds of items that wealthy Crusaders might hold in their homes. They included objects both brought from Europe and acquired in the Holy Land: for example, the list mentions fabric purchased in Troyes or Burgundy, while other items are noted as recent purchases.[10] Among Eudes's extensive property were jewelry; elaborate clothing; basins, cups, and other vessels; furnishing textiles for couches, tables, and bedrooms; and, unsurprisingly, armaments and weaponry. Eudes's records also enumerate items he stored in his personal chapel, which contained fragments of the Cross, prayer books, and liturgical garments for the celebrating priest.

The approximately nine hundred Islamic legal documents discovered at the Haram al-Sharif in Jerusalem in 1974–76 are equally important for understanding the possessions of the city's Muslim inhabitants.[11] Among these is a series of late fourteenth-century texts related to the estate of a Levantine merchant named Shams al-Din Muhammad al-Ba'labakki, known as Ibn Jamal, and his wife Almalik, residents in the Maghrebi Quarter.[12] The highly legalistic language

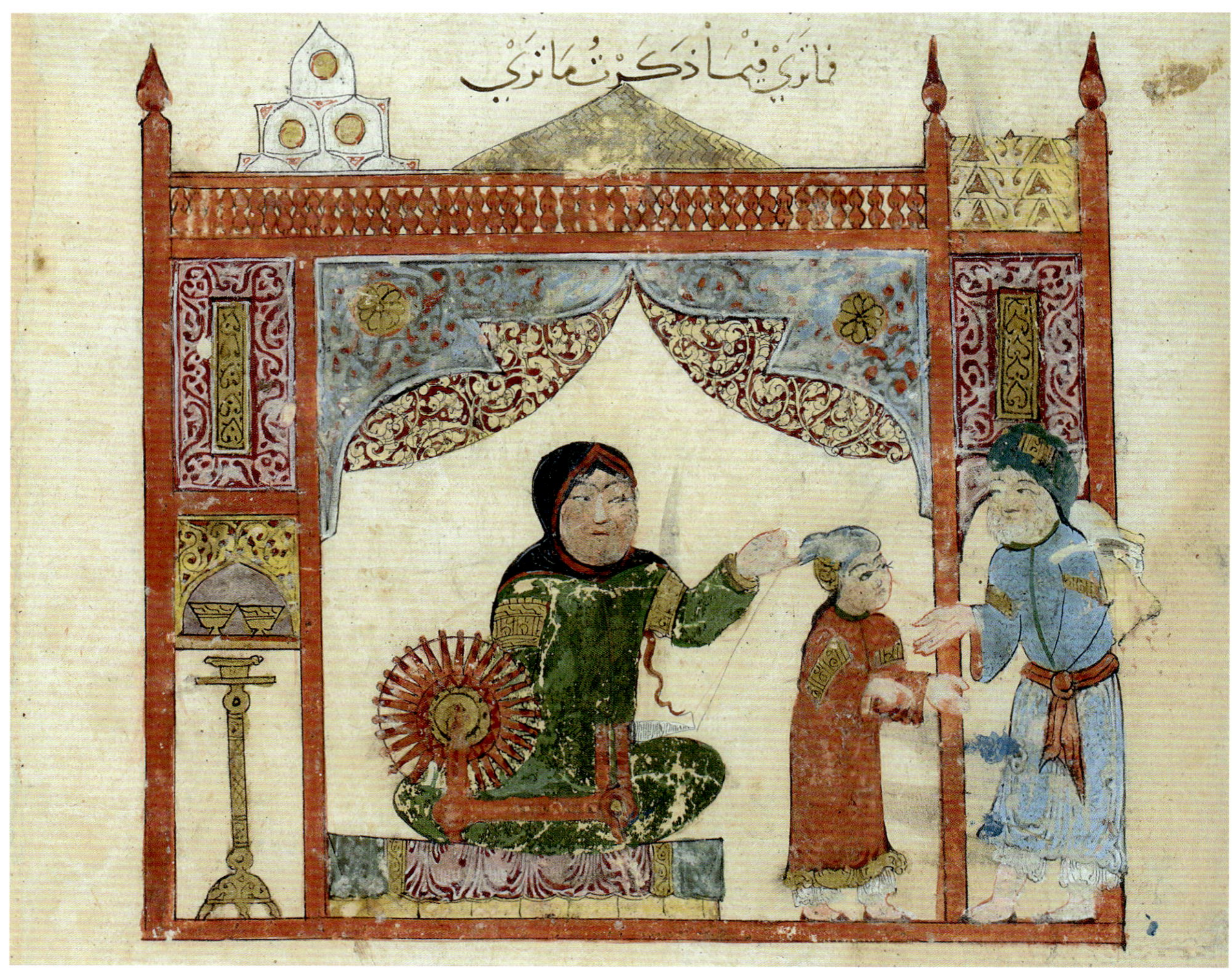

Fig. 13. "Woman Spinning in a Room Hung with Textiles," from the *Assemblies* (*Maqamat*) of al-Hariri. Copied by al-Wasiti. Baghdad, 1237. Paper. Bibliothèque Nationale de France, Paris (MS Arabe 5847, fol. 13v)

of the documents conveys Ibn Jamal and Almalik's relatively impoverished living situation. Interestingly, the texts take pains to describe the family's textiles, including an "old carpet," suggesting that the fabrics were the most, or perhaps the only, valuable items in the house (cat. 9c). Merchants like Ibn Jamal are similarly mentioned in the Cairo Geniza documents, showing the networks of traders throughout the Levant, North Africa, and beyond. Another Geniza document relayed the advice of a Jewish merchant on importing silk to Jerusalem; while black and sky blue were among the most popular colors, one should bring crimson as well, in case "Persians should happen to arrive."[13]

The accuracy of textual descriptions, whether from the Geniza or the Haram, is confirmed by archaeological finds from several sites in the Holy Land.[14] By comparing extant written sources and objects, it is possible to envision the kinds of goods acquired in Jerusalem's suqs and open the doors of the city's homes in our imagination (fig. 13).

NOTES FOR THIS ESSAY APPEAR ON PAGE 300
SEE CATS. 9–20

JEWISH-MUSLIM ENCOUNTERS IN THE HOLY LAND

Martin Jacobs

MOST EXTANT descriptions of Jewish-Muslim encounters in the Holy Land during the Middle Ages were penned by European Jewish travelers, as opposed to Middle Easterners.[1] During much of the period covered in this volume, the Jewish population of the Holy Land, in particular, was relatively small. That said, Jewish communities flourished in Sidon, Tyre, Tiberias, Ramle, and Jerusalem under Fatimid rule. Except for the reign of Caliph al-Hakim (996–1021), Jewish-Muslim relations seem to have been largely peaceful. Sacred space was clearly divided between Muslims, who controlled the Haram al-Sharif, and Jews, who held prayer services on the Mount of Olives facing the former Temple's site. But the Crusader conquest of Jerusalem in 1099 ended this arrangement, and the Jewish community was uprooted. In the thirteenth century the port city of Acre, then the capital and commercial hub of the second Crusader kingdom, hosted again a growing number of Jews, largely of European origin. The Crusader period was also the time when Hebrew travel accounts emerged as a literary genre, creating a corpus that sheds much light on Jewish-Muslim encounters in the region. However, not all Jews who recorded a Holy Land pilgrimage hailed from Christian-ruled countries. Some pilgrims and merchants came from other parts of the Middle East or from Muslim Iberia (al-Andalus), such as Judah ha-Levi, the famous twelfth-century poet and philosopher, whose travels to the Levant are echoed in both correspondence and poetry.[2]

Following Saladin's victory over the Crusaders in 1187, the major sacred sites, such as Jerusalem's Haram and Hebron's Tomb of the Patriarchs (Cave of Machpelah to Jews, Haram al-Khalil to Muslims) were off limits to non-Muslims. (Non-Christians had been largely excluded from the same places under the previous Frankish rule.) Even so, Jews from then on were allowed to pray at a window in the outer walls of the sacred compound at Hebron. Surprisingly to modern readers, Jewish pilgrims voiced little disappointment about this unequal access. In fact, they praised Muslim charity in honor of Abraham that included the public distribution of bread and lentils, known as "Abraham's hospitality" (Arabic, *diyafat al-khalil*), of which all visitors partook.

While the major holy places in Jerusalem and Hebron, hallowed by all three Abrahamic religions, saw only limited encounters between the different communities (the one in power usually claimed exclusive control), Jewish and Muslim worshippers frequently intermingled at less renowned sites, including the traditional tombs of biblical figures and rabbinic sages outside Jerusalem or in the Galilee. Arguably, interfaith relations were more relaxed at these local shrines since they were less significant to each community's self-definition than the highly contested sanctuaries of Jerusalem and Hebron.

Time and again, the sources mention that the burial sites of Jewish holy men and women (such as the biblical Rachel) also attracted Muslim devotees who revered them for their alleged powers of healing and intercession (fig. 14).[3] In fact, local Muslims frequently served as guides for Jewish pilgrims, showing them less familiar grave sites. During the late Mamluk era, the Italian Jewish merchant Meshullam of Volterra, for instance, mentioned in the diary of his 1481 journey that "the Ishmaelites [Muslims] honor all these places . . . and they say to the Jews: Why don't you go to the tomb of such a righteous man or to the tomb of the prophet whose name is such?"[4]

Local pilgrimages (Arabic, *ziyara*) by Jews and Muslims were differentiated from the central or canonical pilgrimage to Jerusalem (Hebrew, *'aliyyah le-regel*) or Mecca (Arabic, hajj). They came with few social restrictions and thus were frequently criticized by religious authorities on both sides. These local holy places seem to have functioned as liminal spaces in which the boundaries of religion, social status, and gender were

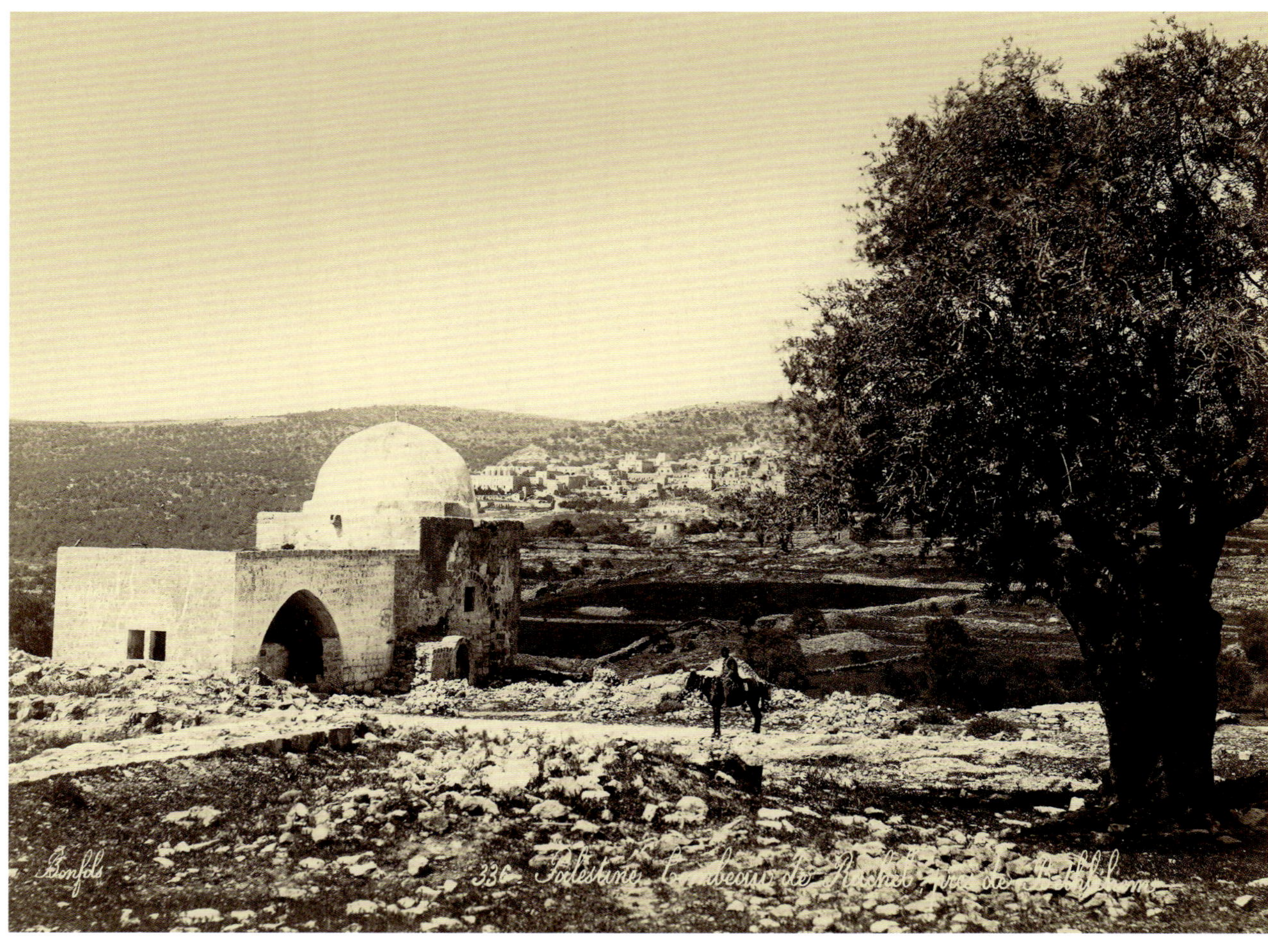

Fig. 14. Rachel's Tomb, Bethlehem. Photograph by Félix Bonfils, 1870–79. Albumen silver print. J. Paul Getty Museum, Los Angeles (84.XM.1021.8)

relaxed.[5] Together with the universal customs of prayer, processions, and prostrations, Jewish and Muslim devotees kindled lights, made votive offerings, and engaged in the common pleasures of eating and drinking.

In other localities, Jews and Muslims rubbed shoulders but disagreed over the identity of the person buried at a shared shrine. Since the thirteenth century, for example, Jews believed that a certain tomb in Yavneh (Yibna for Muslims, Ibelin for the Franks), south of Jaffa, belonged to Gamliel of Yavneh, a late first-century founding figure of rabbinic Judaism. According to Muslim tradition, however, the domed Mamluk shrine erected on the site shielded the grave of Abu Hurayra, a seventh-century companion of the Prophet Muhammad (cat. 92).

At some mutually venerated places, such as the putative tomb of the prophet Samuel (Nabi Samwil), northwest of Jerusalem, members of the dominant religion (Islam) tried to assert their ownership rights and limit Jewish access over the course of centuries. Nonetheless, the competition over holy space between Muslims and Jews seems to have been less fierce than that between Muslims and Christians, probably because Jews did not potentially threaten Muslim sovereignty. Similarly, many Jewish pilgrims highlight in their accounts that during their travels they experienced no hostility on the part of local Muslims.

NOTES FOR THIS ESSAY APPEAR ON PAGES 300–301

SEE CATS. 21–23

TERRA MIRACULA: BLESSED SOUVENIRS FROM THE HOLY LAND

Avinoam Shalem

IN TERMS of time and memory, souvenirs present tangible challenges to a sequential order of events. Usually framed by nostalgia, they activate memories, bring the past into the present, and at the same time continually alter the present by resurfacing varied links between the remembered past and the cognizant present. More than just aide-mémoire, they not only help one access past memories that are guarded by the screen of oblivion, but they also reshape the past and present again and again. In short, souvenirs become relevant in different ways at each moment we ponder them.

From an artistic point of view, souvenirs usually display the most expected image, turning the iconic into banal kitsch, as they helplessly try to replace the original with its copy. Moreover, in some cases, they even "caricature the self-image that local and national agencies want to promote."[1] In medieval times, with the growth of tourism, mass productivity, and miniaturization, the drive to fulfill both necessities of the souvenir – that it represents the site and is portable – downgraded artistic creativity through mass-manufacturing processes. On the one hand, mass-production dictates deemphasized the substance's quality, diminished excellence in terms of fabrication, and most of all, ended such artistic values as singularity and uniqueness. On the other hand, miniaturization can impart an air of the ridiculous or mockery and, as is the case with small things, suggests less importance or even triviality.[2]

The Holy Land had a long tradition of producing a great variety of souvenirs and blessings. With the emergence of pilgrimages as early as the fourth century, the production of memorabilia flourished, a tradition that has continued almost without interruption until the present day (fig. 15). In fact, moments of ruptures such as the Muslim conquest of the Holy Land in 641, the fall of Jerusalem to the Franks in 1099, and the Crusade era did not affect production.[3] On the contrary, the manufacture of keepsakes was quickly adapted to meet changing circumstances and clientele.

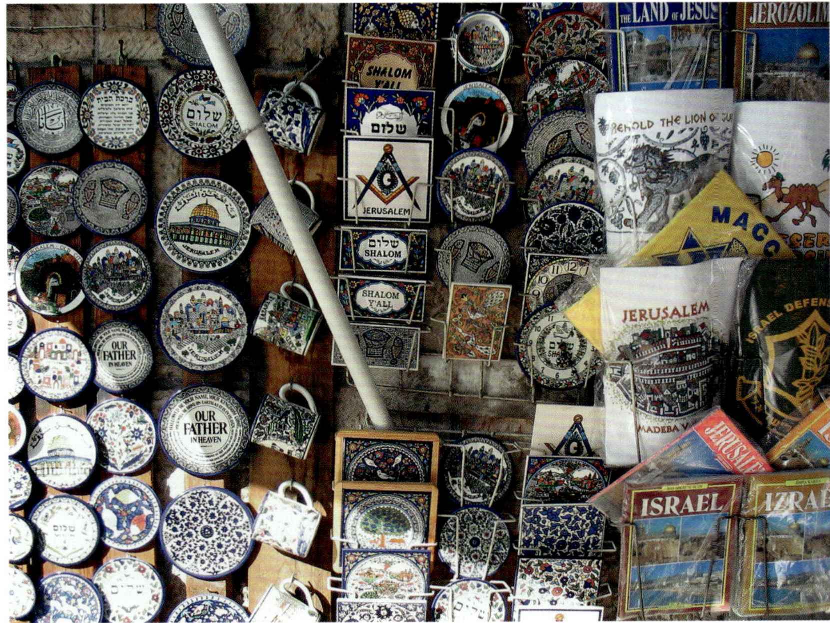

Fig. 15. Souvenirs in present-day Jerusalem

Moving beyond commercial production, however, since by tradition the whole earth was sanctified by the steps of Christ, some pilgrims regarded any item collected while traveling as a souvenir.[4] The majority of keepsakes were probably perishable and might have included plants, fruits, oil, and aromatic substances such as balsam. As a plethora of the Terra Sancta souvenirs were procured to convey blessings, or eulogia, these sanctified mementos ranged from minute holy particles detached from original relics to substances sanctified by their sheer proximity to the sacred and finally to blessings that materialized the sacred but did not have physical form.[5] Of course, a legitimate relic, or at least a small particle of it, was the most desired object, and some pilgrims bit off tiny pieces of the Holy Cross in the Church of the Holy Sepulchre while kissing it or stole small pieces from the slab that covered the Tomb of Christ or the sacred rock in the Dome of the Rock.[6] Not only were sacred, tangible objects collected but also light, as in that of the Holy Fire on Easter (fig. 48) or of any lamp in a sacred shrine, which was procured by capturing some of its burning oil in a portable container.[7] Sanctified substances were usually carried in containers such as boxes, like the famous one in the Sancta Sanctorum in the Vatican; phials and ampoules made of cheap glass, clay, lead, and metal; vessels made of costly, fragile materials like cut glass, rock crystal, and enameled glass; and possibly cases of expensive woven textiles.[8]

Beyond their uses as mementoes of the past and physical confirmations of a visit to the Holy Land, the souvenirs have a benedictory character, turning the entire object into a vessel of miraculous nature. The pilgrimage was, and still is, designed as a walk in Christ's steps with the pilgrim's experience gradually amplifying, as in a crescendo, along the journey through visits to the stations of Christ's Passion and culminating in an encounter with the empty tomb in the Holy Sepulchre, where the chief miraculous episode of his apotheosis was made visible. The void imparted validity. The ultimate goal was to witness, as the angels and Holy Women did, the miracle of Christ's Resurrection. Moreover, the ongoing public visibility of the Holy Fire on Easter Eve asserted that divine phenomena still occur. These miracles authenticated holy spaces, validated the biblical story of the "living and risen Christ," and, by continuing to appear in holy shrines, transformed Terra Sancta into Terra Miracula.[9]

Perhaps the best account of Terra Miracula was written by the anonymous pilgrim from Piacenza, who traveled to the Holy Land about 570 and related that "at the moment when the cross is brought out of this small room for veneration, . . . a star appears in the sky and comes over the place where they lay the cross, and they offer oil to be blessed in little flasks, when the mouth of one of the little flasks touches the wood of the cross, the oil instantly bubbles over, and unless it is closed very quickly it all spills out."[10] The bubbling oil probably marked a change of matter, from liquid into vapor, as if symbolically proposing that in this sacred space form becomes spirit. Moreover, the appearance of the star exactly above the cross suggests a cosmic intervention, similar to the appearance of the Star of Bethlehem announcing the birth of Christ. Numerous pilgrims reported that miracles occurred in these holy sites. The Piacenza pilgrim described manna falling from the sky in the Horeb Valley, near the Monastery of Saint Catherine. This manna, he continued, was collected by monks and placed in little flasks for sale as blessings.[11] Niccolo of Poggibonsi, whose trip to the Holy Land was between 1346 and 1350, wrote about the healing power of the pool in Jerusalem where Christ once healed the paralytic and added that "the first person to enter (this pool) after the motion of the water was healed of whatsoever infirmity he lay under."[12] He also testified that holy manna flowed like oil out of the mouth of the venerated body of Saint Catherine in the eponymous monastery in Sinai.[13] Finally, Father Simon Fitzsimonis, whose voyage was between 1322 and 1324, claimed that protection from illness was granted to the sick, who bathed in the Fountain of the Virgin in Matariyya, near Cairo.[14] The most spectacular miracle, however, performed in Jerusalem for pilgrims' public view continues to be the descent of the Holy Fire at the Holy Sepulchre, which, according to Orthodox belief, took place each year on the Great Saturday of Easter.[15] Envisioning this miracle in the Holy Sepulchre, at the spot where the Resurrection took place, likely filled the pilgrims' hearts with joy, allowing them to feel transformed and, perhaps like Christ, reborn.

These accounts stress that pilgrims were more than just visitors to miraculous spaces. Rather, the visits created a new bond between devotee and site that on the one hand sealed the pilgrim's experience and on the other hand personalized the holy space through the pilgrim's actual experience of the site.[16] Past and present collided in this moment of spectacle. Like the Resurrection, the past reappeared in the present and in the pilgrim's presence, imbuing the moment with the full reappearance of holiness.[17]

Apart from the obvious role that decorative motifs — that is, the usual depictions of Christ's crucifixion on Calvary, the famous aediculae on his grave in the Holy Sepulchre (fig. 46), and other scenes relating to his suffering on the Via Dolorosa in Jerusalem — play on eulogia as authenticating markers of sacred topography, these images also distinguish the pilgrim experience in these sites. In addition, several images include specific details concerning the state of these sites, and certain motifs, mainly hanging lamps, relate to the acquiring of blessings from lamp oil. This visual evidence suggests

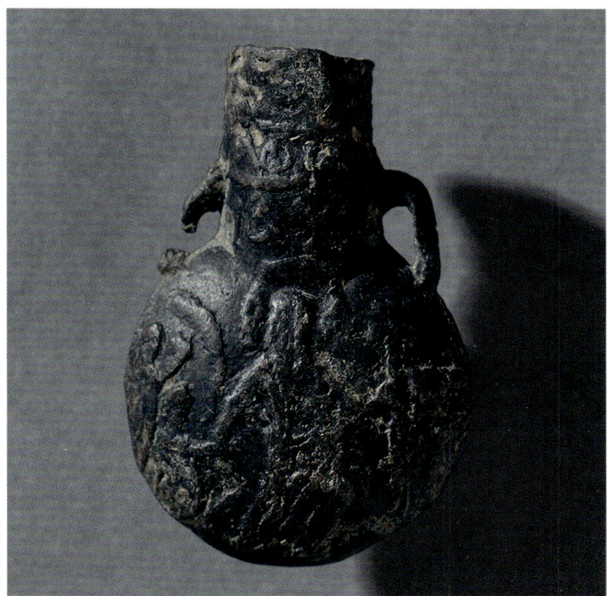

Fig. 16. Pilgrim's flask. Latin Kingdom of Jerusalem, ca. 1099–1200. Lead. Cleveland Museum of Art (1999.234)

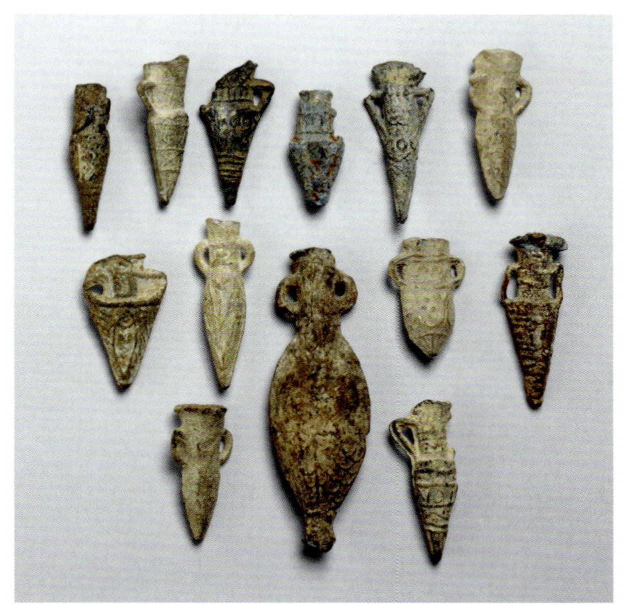

Fig. 17. Miniature lead amphora-shaped phials. Byzantine period. Musée Sainte-Anne, Collection of C. Schmidt, Collection of the Wolff Family, Jerusalem

that souvenirs were meant not only to bring back evidence of past biblical stories but also to integrate the contemporaneous experiences of pilgrims into the biblical past, achieving synchrony between then and now.

It was mainly during the twelfth and thirteenth centuries that images of the present were incorporated into this iconography. Depictions of the newly erected bell tower next to the main Crusade facade of the Holy Sepulchre, of specific warrior saints associated with the Crusade conquest and protection of Jerusalem, and of minarets start to appear on ampoules and other souvenirs of the Frankish kingdom of the Holy Land.[18] The new eulogia commemorating visits to Jerusalem incorporate narrative and anecdotal elements into the traditional iconic images of Terra Sancta. Several lead ampoules of the Crusade era and numerous small flat, amphora-like phials excavated in Bet She'an might be regarded as souvenirs, specifically containers for storing the sanctified oil of the Holy Fire (figs. 16, 17).[19] The usual stamped decoration on small ampoules and tiny pendant containers again reveals the mass production of items authenticating the pilgrim experience.[20] On a practical level, however, the stamped image suggests its being cast from a singular, allegedly genuine mold, as if the potency of stamped blessings was ensured through the long history of recurring contact with the sacred.[21] Symbolically, perhaps, the significant quantity of this type of blessing can be understood as part of the miraculous act of multiplication. In any case, sealed, sometimes in front of the pilgrim's eyes, and carried as a personal private object during the return home, the eulogium of the Terra Miracula entered its next phase as an object of the future. It conveyed spiritual power that could secure the pilgrim's long and dangerous travel back home and ensured that the miraculous could happen again. The souvenir blessing was anything but just a memorial to an authentic past. It merged into the pilgrim's present, revitalized his experience in front of the holy, and augmented the future with the full incarnational impact of the miraculous sanctity contained within.

NOTES FOR THIS ESSAY APPEAR ON PAGE 301
SEE CATS. 24–26

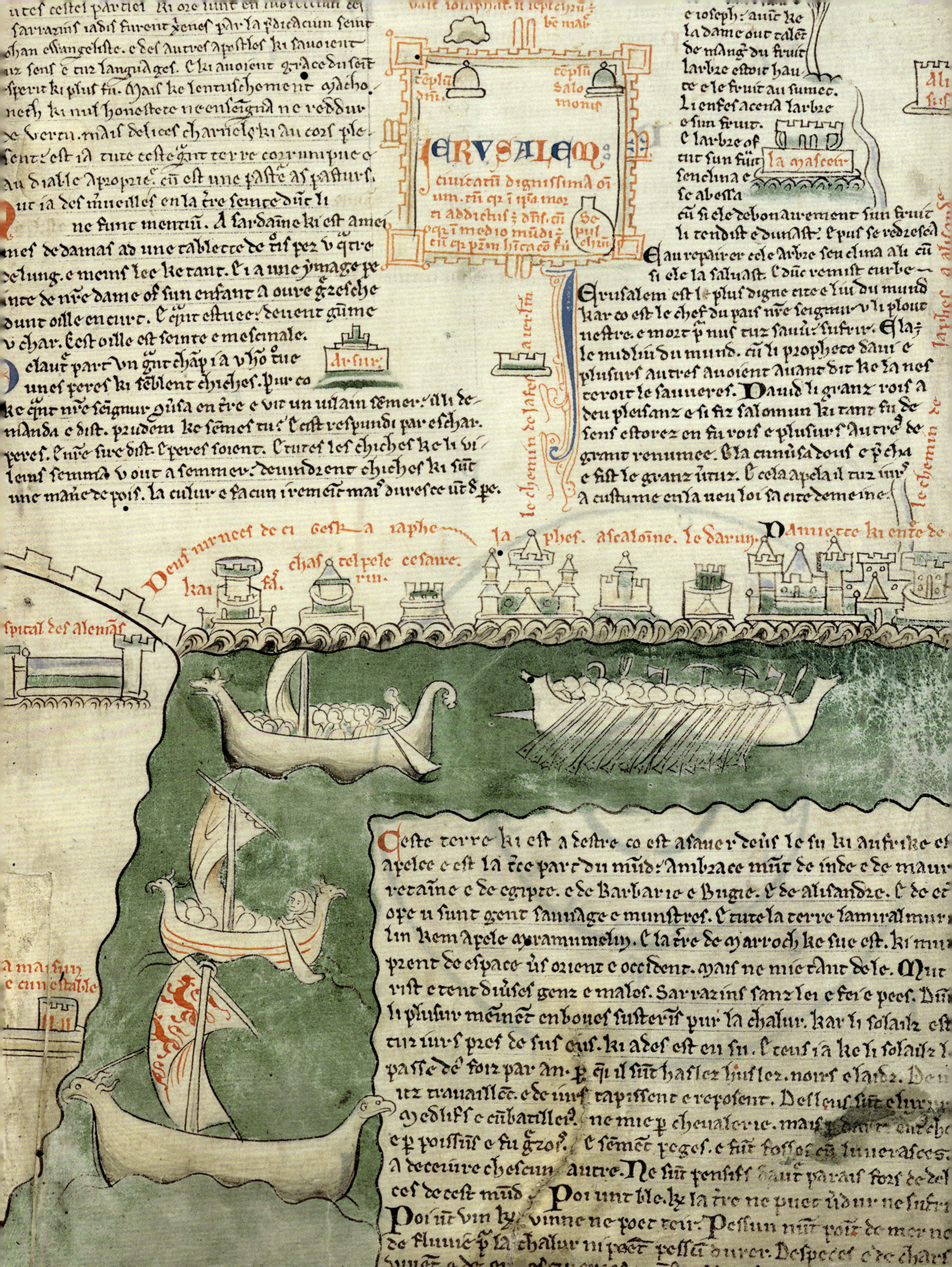
Jerusalem
Arsur
la maseun
la phes
ascaloine
le darun

1

Map of the Holy Land

From *Chronica majora*, vol. I
Saint Albans, England, ca. 1240–53
Written and illustrated by Matthew Paris
(ca. 1200–1259)
Opaque watercolor and ink on parchment; 151 fols.
14¼ × 9¾ in. (36.2 × 24.8 cm)
Corpus Christi College, University of Cambridge
(MS 26)

Western Europe's fascination with the Holy Land during the thirteenth century finds perhaps no better expression than the itinerary map created by the Benedictine monk Matthew Paris. Inserted in Matthew's multivolume chronicle of world history, this seven-page set of maps marvelously evokes the route from London to Dover and across France, Italy, and finally the Adriatic Sea.[1] The reader or pilgrim moves along from city to city, page by page, until arriving at last at the resplendent terminus. There, at the port of Acre and the city of Jerusalem, space, time, and even the book itself seem to expand through foldout flaps. The linear format of the strip maps on the preceding pages (fig. 18) gives way to a dense vista of cities, significant sites, and explanatory texts. The places include Mount Ararat in Armenia, the site of Noah's ark shown at the top of the left page; Saidnaya in Syria, mentioned in the text on the right page, home of a miraculous icon of the Virgin Mary that exudes sacred oil; and, on the attached extension to the left, the legendary headquarters of the Old Man of the Mountain, founder of an Islamic sect known in the West as the Assassins and greatly feared by the Crusaders.[2] The entire map offers the armchair traveler an opportunity for exploration, contemplation, and education. Curiously, it was a journey of the imagination for Matthew, who never traveled beyond England; yet it remarkably captures the emotional crescendo one discovers in the accounts of medieval travelers who did make the journey.

Given the singular spiritual importance of Jerusalem, it seems odd that the city occupies only a small portion of the map, an unremarkable square dotted with a few key

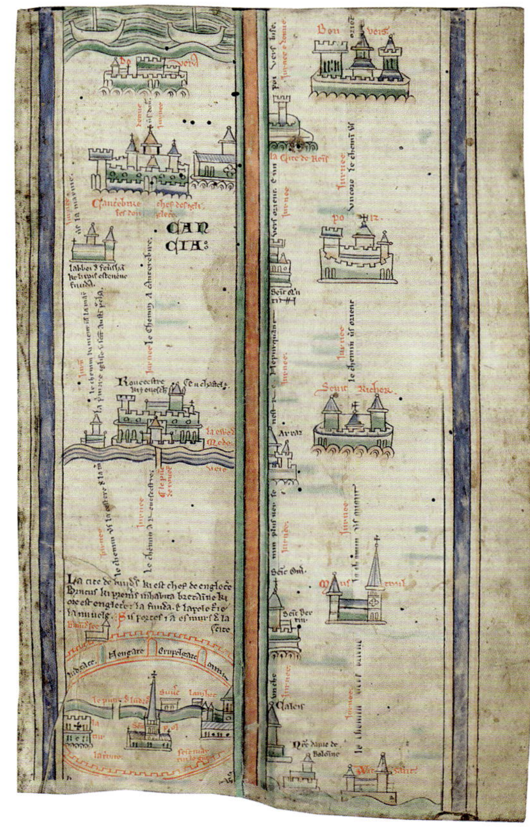

Fig. 18. The route from London to Beauvais, France Detail of cat. 1

1, fols. iiiv–ivr

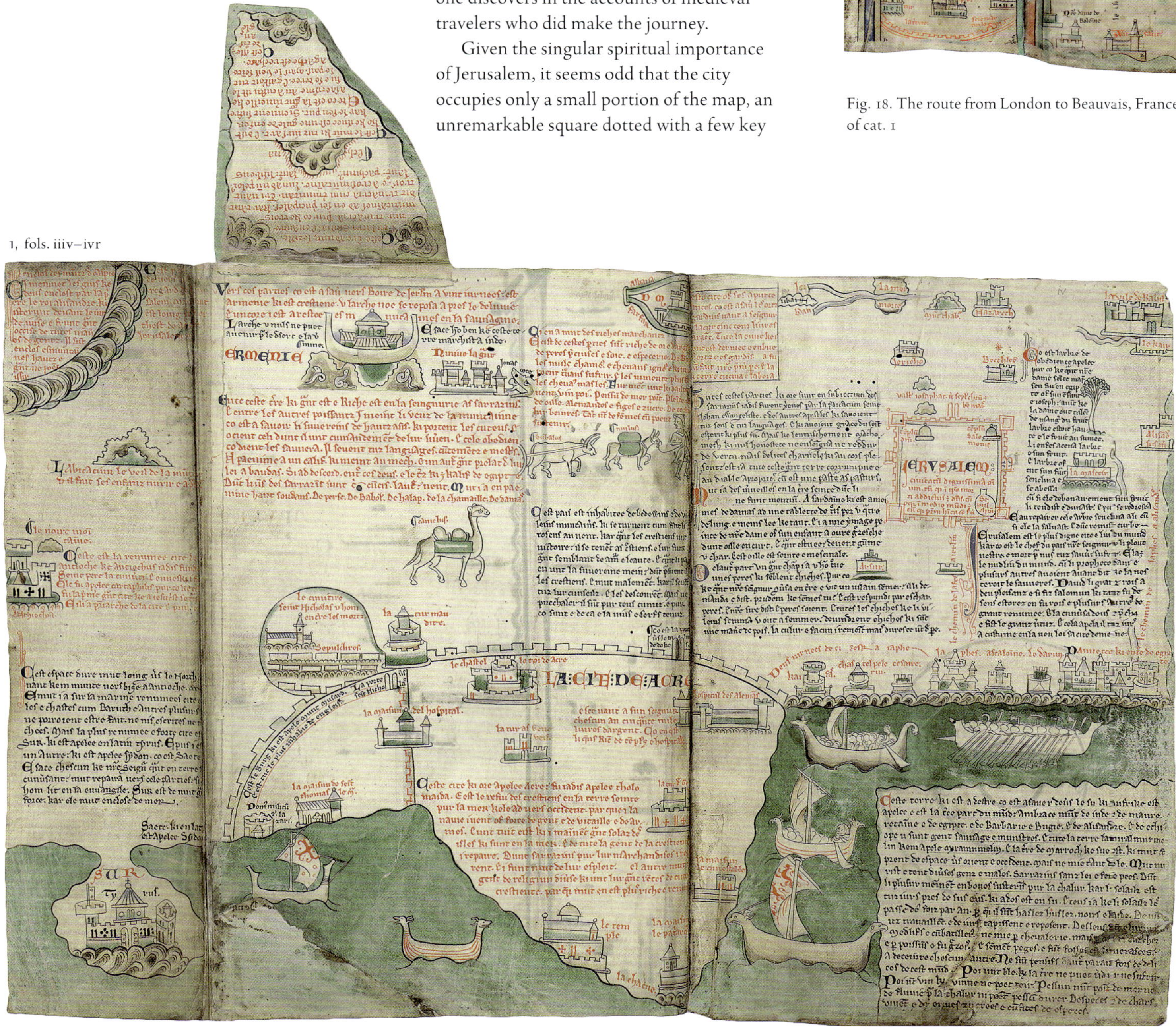

domed monuments. It is Acre, rather, that receives pride of place. Thus the map reflects then-current political reality. Nestled into its harbor and protected by crenelated walls, Acre stretches across both pages, and Matthew has labeled the various quarters of the city and designated its important sites. At the time the map was created, Acre was both the port city and the administrative and commercial center of the Crusader Kingdom of Jerusalem; Jerusalem itself had been under Muslim rule for decades. The map's many lengthy inscriptions, almost all written in Anglo-French, often underscore the intertwined nature of crusade and commerce.[3] Matthew pays homage to Jerusalem's spiritual significance with a few descriptive lines in Latin, but his scribal and artistic energies announce that it is clearly Acre, the most important city in the Holy Land still in Western hands, that excites him.

MH

Selected References: Connolly 2009; Harvey, P., 2012, pp. 74–93; Whatley 2014.

1. Matthew created several versions of this map. See Harvey, P., 2012, pp. 74–93.
2. Lewis, B., 1955. On Matthew's understanding of this secret sect, see Lewis, S., 1987, pp. 349, 352.
3. Whatley 2014.

2a–c

Planispheric Astrolabes

a. Arabic Astrolabe

Andalusia, A.H. 466 (1073)
Designed by Muhammad ibn Sa'id al Sabban
Gilded brass
Diam. 5 in. (12.6 cm)
Bayerisches Nationalmuseum, Munich (33/243)

b. Judeo-Arabic Astrolabe

Probably Spain, ca. 1300
Designed by Abraham
Brass with silver
Diam. 7⅜ in. (18.5 cm)
Nasser D. Khalili Collection of Islamic Art, London (SCI 58)

c. Latin Astrolabe

Catalonia, ca. 1300
Brass
Diam. 4 in. (10 cm)
The Society of Antiquaries of London

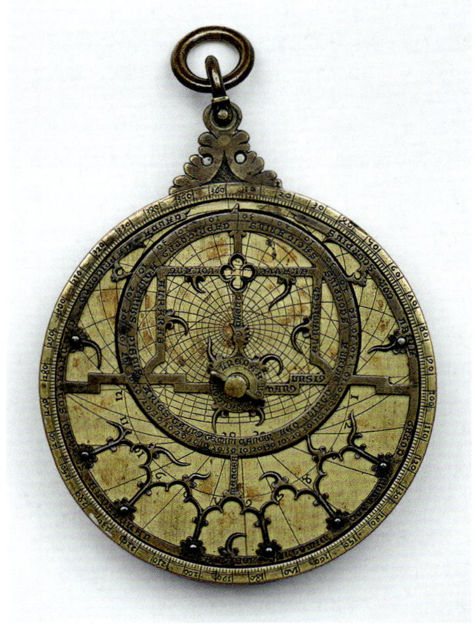

2c

The planispheric astrolabe is an analogue computing device widely used from the ninth to the seventeenth centuries to tell time, cast horoscopes, and make simple observations regarding the movement of the sun and stars. The back often features a variety of tables and scales for reference, but the instrument's distinct utility lies in the time and location-specific information yielded by its interactive format. The front displays an openwork rete (Arabic, *'ankabut*), or a rotatable star map, a single spin of which approximates the daily movement of the celestial sphere. The rete sits atop a fixed circular plate engraved with coordinate lines for a specific geographic latitude.

2a

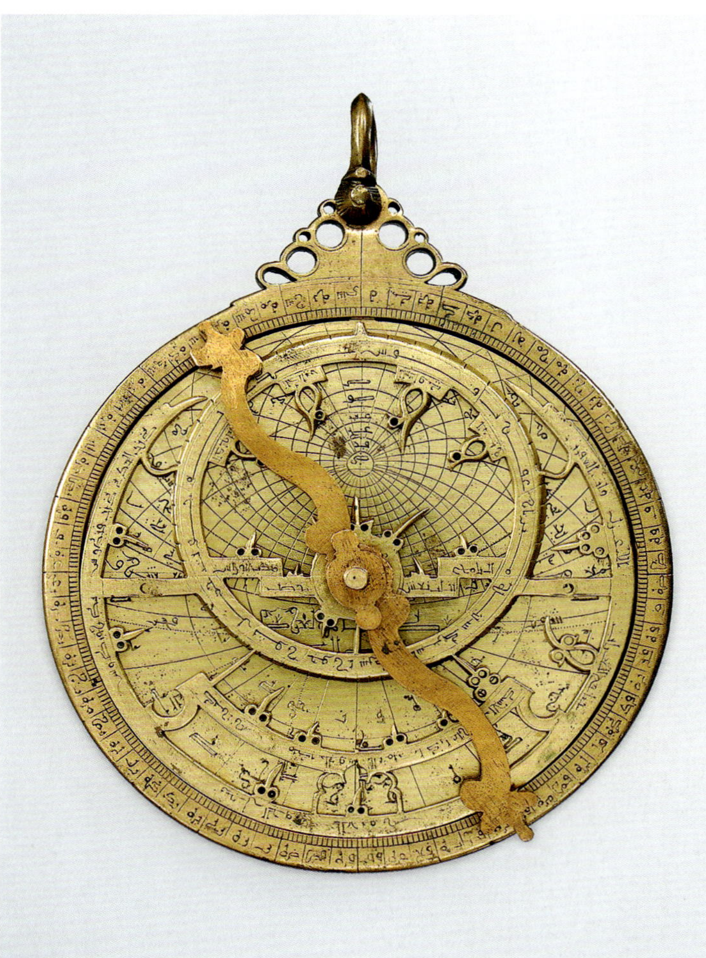

2b

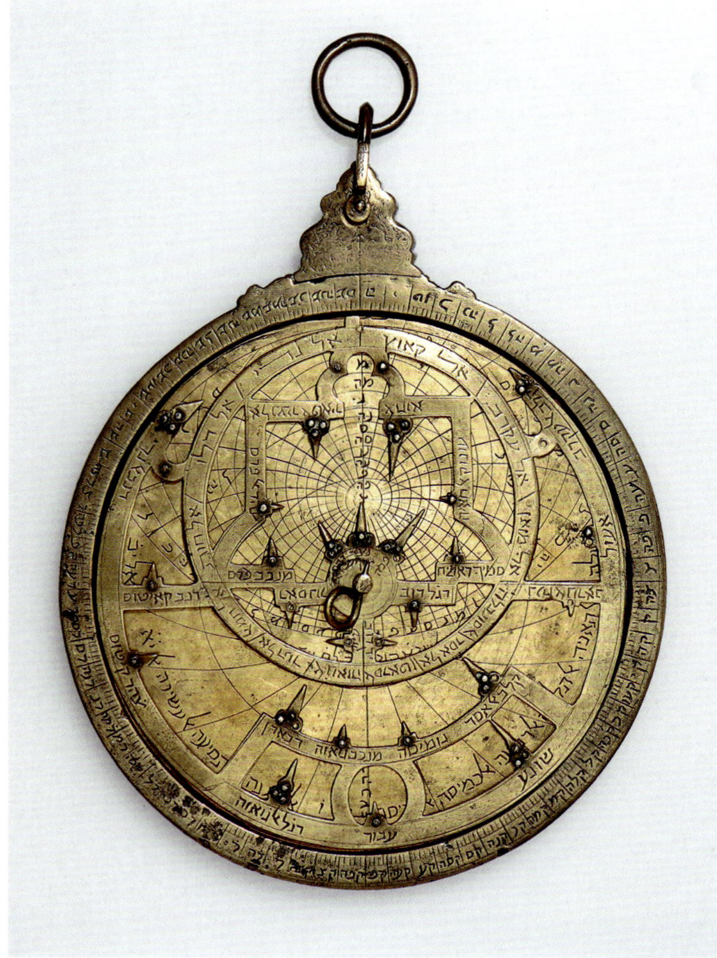

The circular plate could easily be removed, and most astrolabes were equipped with a set of several, all fitted for the same rete, to allow the instrument to be used in more than one location.[1]

To examine the latitudes featured on the plates of these three early astrolabes is to gain a glimpse of the possible travel patterns of their owners. Not surprisingly, given their place of manufacture, all emphasize cities on the Iberian Peninsula, with Córdoba appearing on all three. Inscribed on the plates and inside the casing, the locations featured on the Arabic astrolabe (cat. 2a), likely intended for a Muslim owner, include many major Middle Eastern cities: Mecca, Cairo, Mosul, Baghdad, and Tiberias.[2] The plates on the Judeo-Arabic astrolabe (cat. 2b), which seem to designate Tunis, Marrakech, Cairo, and Sijilmasa, indicate that its Jewish owner might have traveled regularly to North Africa.[3] Though the Latin astrolabe (cat. 2c), probably made for a Western Christian, is missing two plates, those that survive prioritize more important European cities such as Genoa and perhaps Rome.[4]

A seemingly exceptional feature, Jerusalem appears on all three astrolabes.[5] Given the emphasis on Maghrebi and European cities in the Judeo-Arabic and Latin astrolabes, faraway Jerusalem seems an unusual inclusion. One wonders whether our travelers ever made it there, and all three raise questions about the owners' relationship to the Holy City: was it a focus of business travel, pilgrimage, or religious devotion from afar? MH

Selected References: Cat. 2a: Stautz 1999, pp. 145–59, no. 1. Cat. 2b: Maddison and Savage-Smith 1997, pp. 214–17, no. 124. Cat. 2c: King and Maier 1996.

1. For an introduction to the use of these instruments, see Maddison and Savage-Smith 1997, pp. 186–99; Savage-Smith 1992, pp. 18–28. See also Schechner 2008.
2. Stautz 1999, p. 151.
3. One of only four surviving astrolabes inscribed in Hebrew, the object is unique in its use of Judeo-Arabic, a form of Middle Arabic using Hebrew letters, used by Jewish communities in Arabic-speaking lands. However, the rarity of such astrolabes says little about Jewish ownership as Jews were important figures in the astronomical sciences. One of the most influential treatises in the Latin West had a Jewish author, Abraham ibn Ezra (1089–1167), who also oversaw its translation into Latin and French. See Rodríguez Arribas 2014. One presumes that in most cases Jews used astrolabes inscribed in the primary language of the regions they lived and worked in.
4. See King and Maier 1996, pp. 690–94, on the difficulties concerning the localities intended for this astrolabe.
5. Though the city is regularly included in Islamic geographic tables, the Munich device (cat. 2a) is one of just three Islamic astrolabes made before 1100 to present it explicitly. See King 1999, p. 9.

3

Map of Greater Syria

Possibly Syria, 13th–15th century
Ink and opaque watercolor on paper
12½ × 8¼ in. (31.5 × 20.7 cm)
Private collection, Riyadh

Jerusalem sits at the halfway point on the inland route between Damascus and the port of Ascalon in this early regional map of Greater Syria, which conforms to a type associated with the Balkhi school of mapmaking, named for the tenth-century geographer Abu Zayd Ahmad ibn Sahl al-Balkhi (d. 934). Though his geographical treatise no longer survives, the commentaries and maps produced by several of his followers are thought to be derived from his.[1] This map was likely once part of a regional atlas, composed of approximately twenty-one maps that presented caravan itineraries across the Islamic world. Each map lays stages along well-traveled routes, and precise distances are neglected in favor of a clear sequence of dependable stops. Only the most significant geographical landmarks — major mountain ranges, rivers, and other bodies of water — are included.

The map is oriented with south at the top and is divided diagonally by a chain of mountains, their silhouette reminiscent of a flattened crown. Known to medieval Arabic geographers as the Lukkam Mountains, they formed the frontier between northern Syria and Byzantium. All that remains to suggest the Mediterranean Sea, at one time a band of color along the right edge of the page, is a series of small huts that indicate its ports. The large double-banded circle in red and blue just to the left of the mountains marks the great Syrian city of Damascus. To find Jerusalem one must look at the simply rendered huts along the thin line that stretches from the right corner down to the Lukkam Mountains. The line traces a path from Gaza to Ramle, from Ramle to Jerusalem, labeled al-Quds. One continues from there to Tiberias, then through the mountains before reaching Damascus. In this dispassionate rendering of the Holy Land's sites, the needs of trade and travel trump spiritual significance, making clear Jerusalem's long-standing role along the established commercial routes of the Levant.

MH

Selected References: Riyadh 1985, p. 67, no. 49; Hillenbrand, C., 1999, p. 270, pl. 5.

1. His followers included the tenth-century geographers al-Istakhri, Ibn Hawqal, and the Jerusalemite al-Muqaddasi. For a discussion of the complex relationship of texts to their maps, see Tibbetts 1992. On the map of Greater Syria specifically, see Savage-Smith 2003.

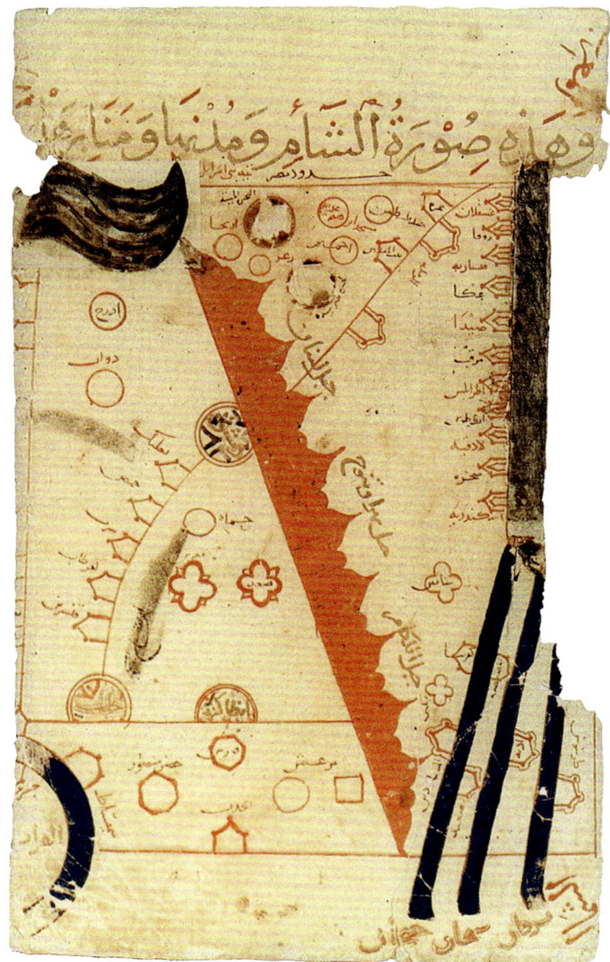

3

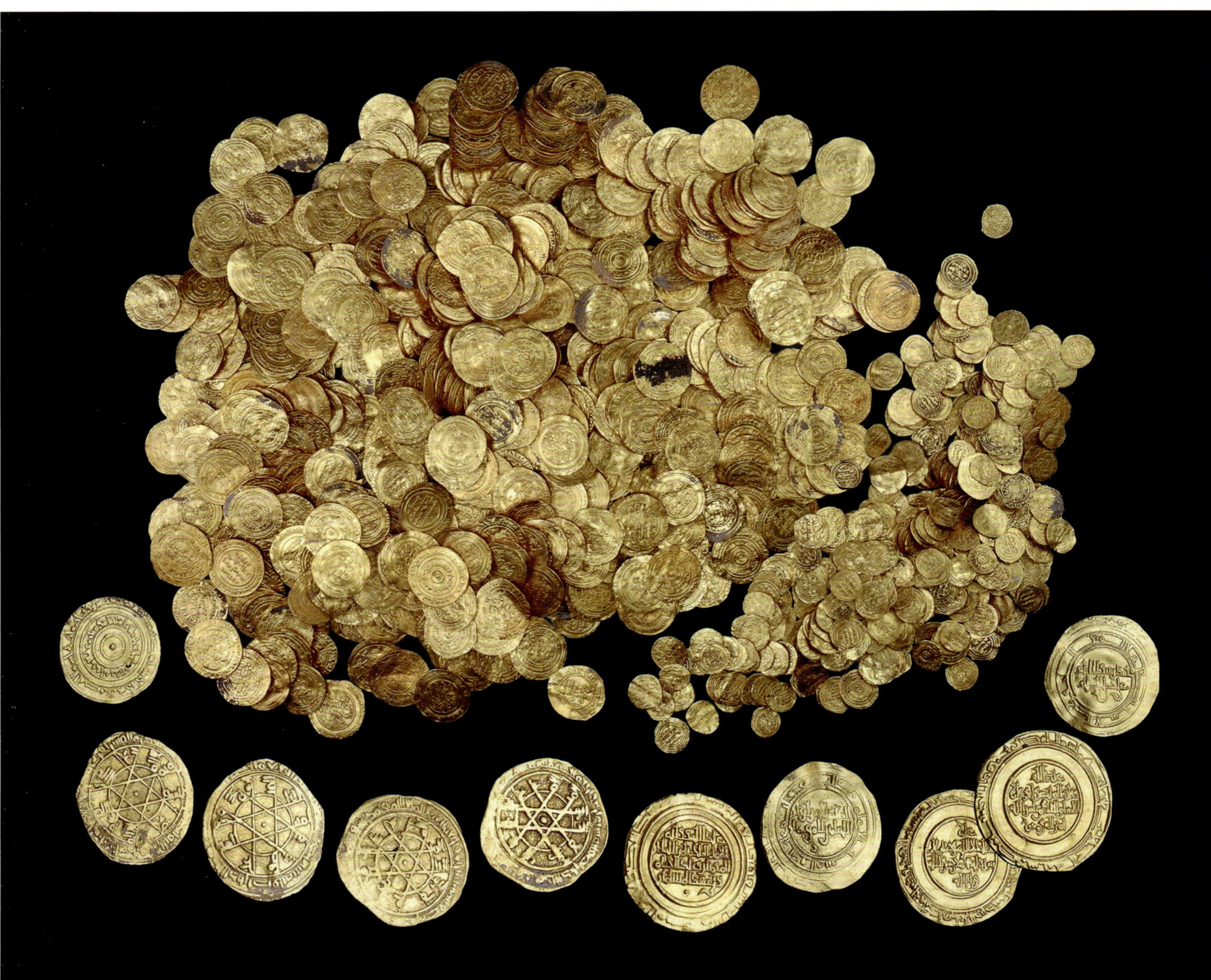

4

4

Selections from a Large Fatimid Coin Treasure

Caesarea, early 11th century
Gold
Dimensions variable
Courtesy of the Israel Antiquities Authority, Jerusalem (IAA 150254-152117)

This large gold treasure, dated to the early eleventh century, was discovered in the port of Caesarea in early February 2015. The treasure consists of more than 2,600 gold coins, totaling some 16.5 pounds (7.5 kg) of pure 24 karat gold. It contains two types of coins: gold dinars weighing around 0.14 ounces (4 g) each and gold quarter dinars weighing 0.03 ounces (1 g). These were the most common coins of the period, as silver coins were rare and bronze coins were not used at all.

The treasure dates to the time of the Fatimid caliphs of Egypt, who ruled an empire stretching from North Africa to northern Syria and Yemen during the tenth and eleventh centuries. A Shi'ite dynasty, the Fatimids were renowned for their enormous wealth and splendid gold coinage. The gold for these elaborate coins came from mines in the Soninke Kingdom of Ghana, situated between the Niger and Senegal rivers. Sold to North African merchants in the form of nuggets and gold dust, it traveled through the Sahara to the trade entrepôt of Sijilmasa in southern Morocco, where it was transported eastward to the Fatimid heartland.[1] Struck into coins in the empire's mints, the gold fueled a global trading network that reached as far east as China and India to the Byzantine Empire, Amalfi on the Italian coast, and as far west as the Iberian caliphate of Córdoba.

On visiting Fatimid Cairo in 1047, around the time that the treasure was lost, the Persian poet and traveler Nasir-i Khusraw wrote, "I could discover no end or limit to their wealth, and I never saw such ease and comfort anywhere."[2] The amount of coins produced in Fatimid mints was huge, even by contemporary standards. The Cairo treasury alone contained 24 million gold dinars in the second half of the tenth century.[3] Merchants, officials, and soldiers traveled with money, often sealed in purses of 50, 100, or 300 coins, throughout the empire and beyond. Archaeological excavations in urban centers such as Arsuf (present-day Israel), Jerusalem, Ramle, and Tiberias have yielded a large number of gold dinars, in both singular finds and hoards, sometimes accompanied by exquisitely crafted jewelry.[4]

The earliest coins in the treasure are quarter dinars minted in Sicily in the second half of the ninth century, when the island was ruled by the Aghlabids, an Islamic North African dynasty. The hoard also contains dinars minted in the Tunisian city of Kairouan by the Fatimid caliphate's founder 'Ubayd Allah al-Mahdi Billah (873–934). Most of the coins, however, belong to the era of the

Fatimid caliphs al-Hakim (985–1021) and his son al-Zahir (1005–1036) and were minted in Egypt and North Africa.

Hundreds of thousands of documents preserved in the Cairo Geniza record in detail prices of wages and goods of the Fatimid period. Prices were noted in gold dinars or silver dirhams, with one dinar the equivalent of approximately forty silver dirhams. For example, the dowry of a Karaite bride in Jerusalem in 1028, during the same period in which the Caesarea treasure was lost, amounted to 61½ gold dinars, a substantial sum at the time.[5] To purchase a shop in eleventh- to twelfth-century Jerusalem, one paid the sum of 70 gold dinars, while a large house could cost 150 gold dinars or more.[6]

In adherence with the Islamic religious prohibition against graven images, only inscriptions appear on the coins, and they mention the ruler's name, his honorific titles, the oneness of God, and the acceptance of Muhammad as God's prophet. Particularly important for the Fatimids is a reference to ʿAli, the Prophet's cousin and son-in-law whom the Shiʿa consider the first imam after Muhammad as "God's intimate." These inscriptions also include the name of the mint and the exact date when the coin was issued, making them extremely important historical documents.

Salvage excavations conducted near the treasure trove by the Israel Antiquities Authority in 2015 uncovered five iron anchors used on ships of this period, suggesting that the coins may have belonged to a lost ship. Further underwater research will, one hopes, reveal more about the context and circumstances under which this large gold treasure was lost. RK

1. Al-Bakri 1913 ed., pp. 300–335.
2. Nasir-i Khusraw 2001 ed., p. 55.
3. Lev 2007.
4. For a listing of these hoards, see Tal, Kool, and Baidoun 2013, p. 269.
5. Goitein 1967–93, vol. 4, pp. 314–15.
6. Ashtor 1969, p. 257; Goitein 1967–93, vol. 4, pp. 282–88.

5

Selections from the Jewelry Hoard from Caesarea

Caesarea, 11th century
Gold, silver, rock crystal, glass, and semiprecious stones
Dimensions variable
Courtesy of the Israel Antiquities Authority, Jerusalem, exhibited at the Israel Museum, Jerusalem (IAA 1960-.834–1960.859)

Discovered during excavations at Caesarea in 1960, this jewelry hoard — containing gold beads, silver jewelry, and a variety of beads made from rock crystal, glass, and semiprecious stones — was hidden in an eleventh-century glazed clay juglet.[1] The most prominent pieces are the three large openwork gold beads made of filigree wire decorated with granulation into symmetrical patterns of convoluted, unequal S-shapes with figure-6 shapes filling the intervals and creating tendril patterns. Such pieces were the most valued jewelry in the dowry lists of the Cairo Geniza, in which they were described as *mushabbak* (lattice work).[2] For example, in an agreement written in Ascalon and dated 1100, a string of beads with a central interlaced gold bead was assessed at thirty-five dinars, a huge sum considering that two dinars was a typical monthly income for a lower-middle-class family.[3]

Other gold beads include a group of elliptical ones made of gold sheet and decorated with granulation, along with spherical spacer units, each fabricated from nine small beads soldered together. Another biconical spacer bead mirrors the largest openwork bead mentioned above. The silver pieces consist of a pair of earrings, two amulet cases with benedictory inscriptions, a silver-mounted agate pendant, another silver pendant with an animal's tooth, and a small bell. The materials used to form the beads range from rock crystal inlaid with carnelian to marvered glass beads to tiny barrel-shaped glass, the latter of which was employed to make a necklace. Lastly, a rectangular silver amulet inlaid with niello is inscribed with *Surat al-Ikhlas* (Purity [of Faith]), chapter 112 of the Qur'an.[4] The epigraphical character of the inscription dates the object to between the end of the eleventh century and the beginning of the twelfth century, in line with the history of Caesarea. On May 17, 1101, the city was subdued by Crusader armies, a terrifying event for local inhabitants, who probably concealed their valuables.[5] Gold and silver pieces from the cache are typologically and stylistically similar to items found in the Kairouan hoard, dated A.H. 436 (1044/45).[6] The Caesarea hoard extends the chronological scope of this group of jewelry to the end of the eleventh and the beginning of the twelfth centuries. Moreover, due to the large number of pieces made of gold wire and granulation, an active workshop probably existed in the region.[7] AL / NB

Selected References: Rosen-Ayalon 1977, pp. 195–201, pl. 14.3; Brosh 1987, p. 10; Vienna 1998–99, p. 123, no. 88; Dayagi-Mendeles and Rozenberg 2010, pp. 195–97, fig. 3

1. Brosh 1987, p. 10.
2. Goitein 1967–93, vol. 4, pp. 211–12, 219.
3. For the agreement, Friedman 1981, pp. 388–93; Goitein 1967–93, vol. 4, pp. 211–12, 218. For the income of a lower-middle-class family, see Goitein 1967–93, vol. 1, p. 359.
4. Rosen-Ayalon 1977, pp. 200–201, pl. 14.3.
5. Petersen 2005, pp. 86–87.
6. Marçais and Poinssot 1948–52, vol. 2; Jenkins 1988a, p. 39.
7. Rosen-Ayalon 1991; Lester 1991, p. 23, fig. 7; Amitai-Preiss 1992.

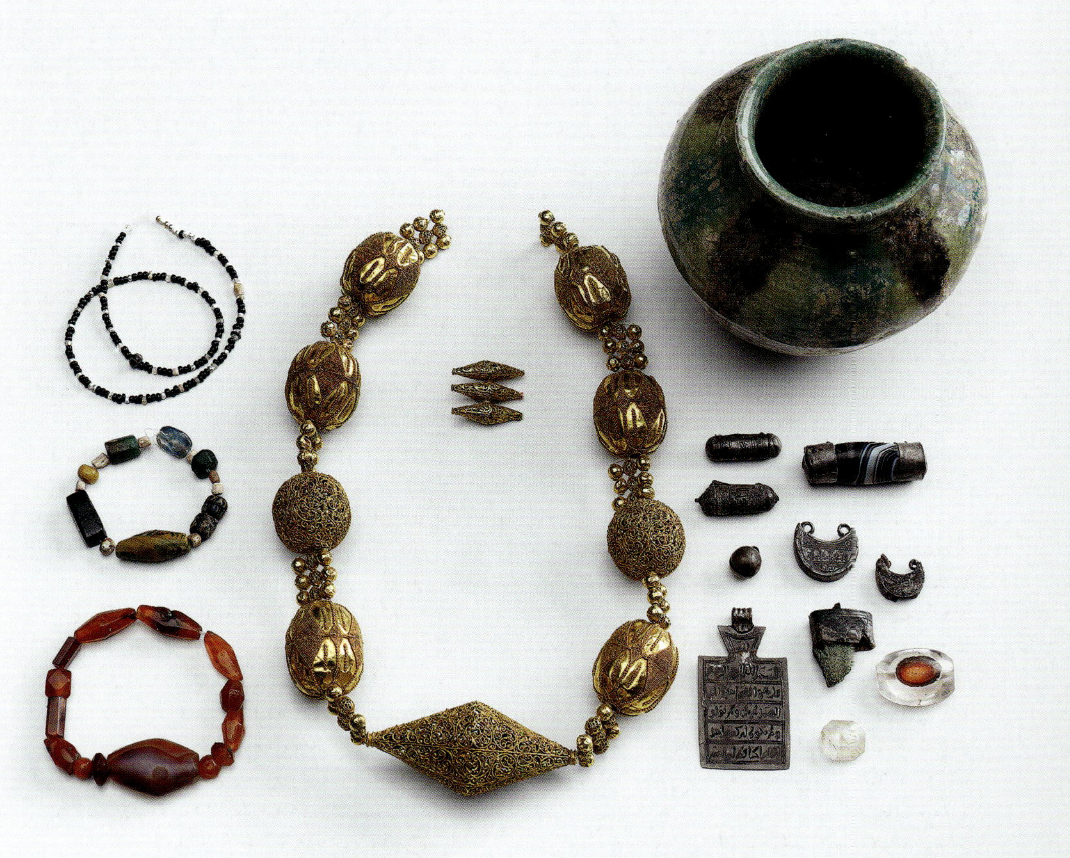

5

6

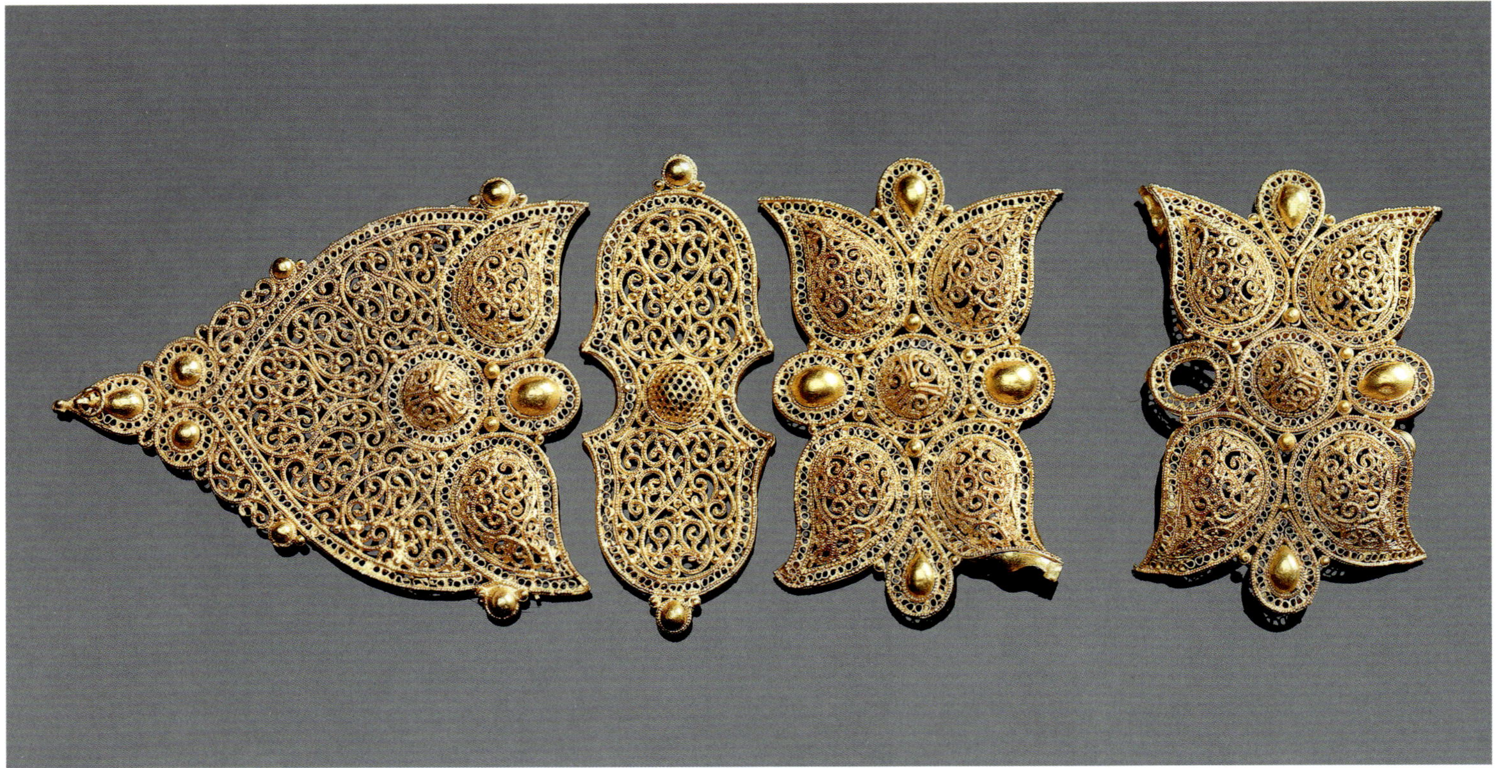

6

Gold Ensemble for the Head or Neck

Ascalon, 11th–12th century
Gold filigree, wire, granulation, strips, beads, and sheet
H. 2–2⅝ in. (5.1–6.7 cm), W. 1–2 in. (2.5–5.1 cm)
Courtesy of the Israel Antiquities Authority, Jerusalem, exhibited at the Israel Museum, Jerusalem
(IAA 1986.672, 1986.673, 1987.939, 1987.940)

These four components that make up a larger item of gold jewelry were found on the Tell at Ascalon, two in 1986 and the others in 1987. All pieces were fabricated from filigree wire covered with granulation, decorated with gold beads, and hammered from gold sheet. The back sides were reinforced by small strips of flat wire. Composed of asymmetrical S-shape wires with figure-6 units and small round pieces of filigree filling the spaces, the decorative patterns are based on a central palmette or half-palmettes flanked by tendrils and framed by a flat band of figure 8s. The largest element is arch-shaped while two others resemble a flower composed of four teardrop-shaped units with a central round boss and beads in the intervals. The fourth could be likened to a violin. Together the four pieces create a harmonious stylistic balance further enhanced by the use of a vertical axis in each piece and a horizontal axis that extends through all the elements of the jewel.

The original ensemble probably included at least one element of each type, with violin and flower shapes alternating and arch shapes at the terminals. Thus the total would have been at least seven pieces. All four parts shown here have a circumscribing flat strip on the back for attaching it to the brocade or velvet fabric.[1]

The piece could have been a head ornament (*'isaba*), similar in concept to that in the drawings of Andromeda, Cassiopea, and Herakles in manuscripts by the tenth-century Persian astronomer al-Sufi.[2] A head ornament, made of gold adorned with pearls, is mentioned in the Cairo Geniza and could have been a tiara or a diadem. Valued from fifty to eighty dinars, such pieces were very expensive.[3] Other kinds of jewelry such as the *khanaqa*, or *hanak* choker, and the *mihbas*, a jeweled collar, would also have been composed of several pieces.[4]

The ensemble under discussion dates to the eleventh to twelfth century, slightly later than the dating of the Caesarea hoard, which includes beads made in the same technique (cat. 5).[5] AL

Selected References: Rosen-Ayalon 1991; Rosen-Ayalon 2008.

1. Rosen-Ayalon 1991, p. 16.
2. For the image of Cassiopea, see Wellesz 1959, figs. 5, 6. For Andromeda, see ibid., p. 21, fig. 55; Rachel Hasson in Jerusalem 1987, p. 25, pl. 2b.
3. Goitein 1967–93, vol. 4, pp. 213–14.
4. Ibid., pp. 216–17.
5. Rosen-Ayalon 1991, p. 8.

7

Ta'widh Pendant

Greater Syria or Egypt, 11th century
Gold, worked in granulated filigree
a: H. 1⅞ in. (4.6 cm), W. 2⅝ in. (6.5 cm), D. ⅝ in. (1.5 cm); b: H. ⅝ in. (1.5 cm), W. 2⅜ in. (6 cm), D. ½ in. (1.2 cm)
The al-Sabah Collection, Dar al-Athar al-Islamiyyah, Kuwait (LNS 1216 J a,b)

An object of great rarity, this exquisite filigree *ta'widh* pendant (amulet or talisman) constitutes part of a hoard of jewelry fragments most likely buried or hidden for safekeeping during an imminent crisis; as the quality of the remaining hoard fragments is superb, it is unlikely that this pendant was part of a jeweler's workshop that was broken up and destined for recycling.

Filigree is a process that involves the creation of intricate motifs in fine gold, silver, or copper wire, often twisted into a plait augmented with gold granules and set on a substrate or backed with strips of gold sheet. Among the finest known, the filigree work of Fatimid Syria is characterized by being worked with no sheet or other support on the back.

Box-constructed in granulated filigree and fitted with a cylindrical sliding cover, probably to enclose a talismanic scroll, the pendant is fitted with rings for suspension. Compartments filled with palmette scrolls on the front and back are bordered by bands of scrolling vines, which incorporate an inscription on the front.[1] *Ta'widh*s were generally inscribed with

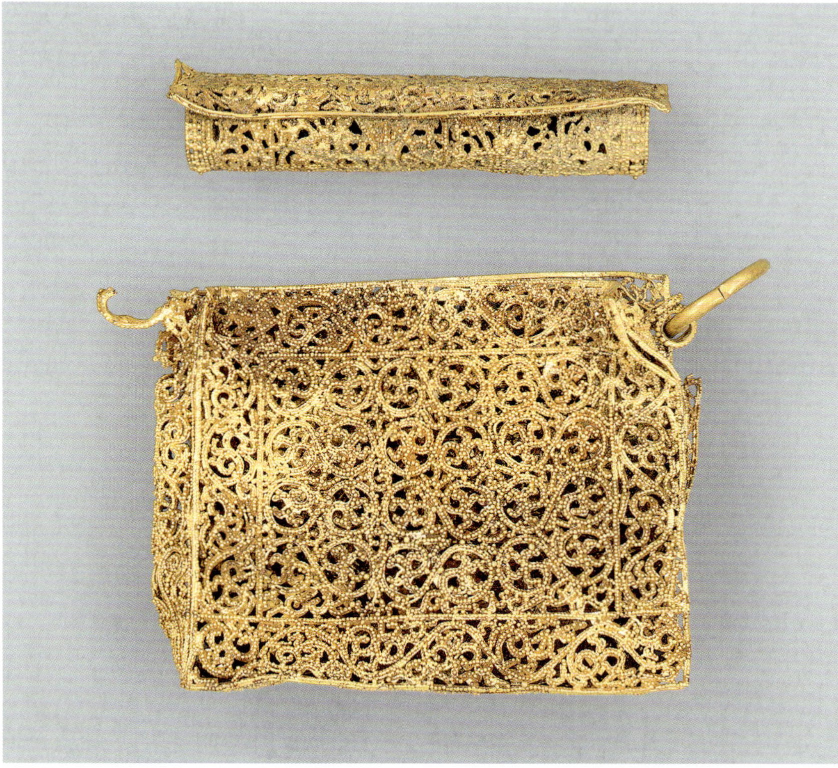

7

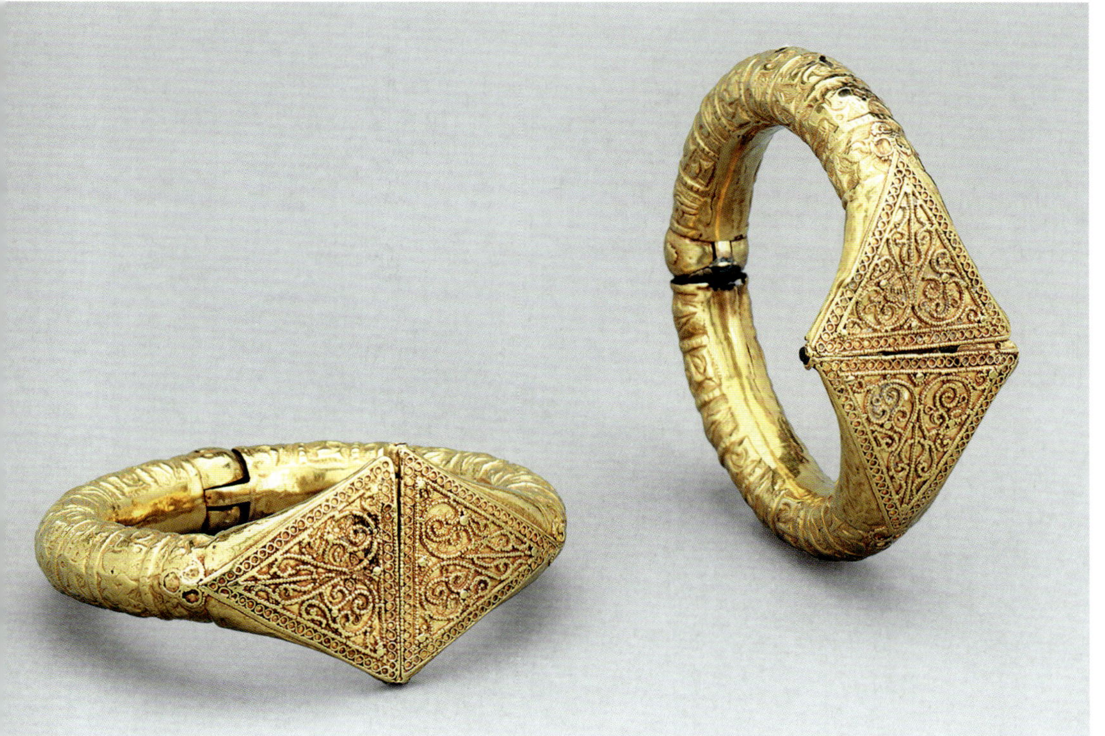

8

invocations seeking God's protection or magic formulas to protect the owner. Although scarcely discernible, the text includes a few words of benedictory nature such as "prosperity" (*'izz*), "furtherance" (*iqbal*), and "happiness" (*yumn*), dedicated "to the owner" (*li-sahibihi*).[2] The remaining surfaces are filled with scrolling palmette vines, and the hollow cylindrical cover is fitted on a flat sheet of gold to allow it to slide across the opening.[3] SK

1. For a Fatimid filigree finger ring incorporating an inscription, see Houston 2015–17, no. 60.

2. Benedictory inscriptions on early medieval objects, even ones from the Iranian world, are always in Arabic.

3. For different types of *ta'widh* pendants in the al-Sabah Collection, see, for example, a gold pendant from tenth-century Iran in Jenkins et al. 1983, p. 33; and a jeweled pendant from seventeenth-century India in London and other cities 2001, no. 1.5.

8

Pair of Bracelets

Egypt or Greater Syria, 11th century
Repoussé gold sheet, wire, and granulation
a: W. 1¼ in. (3.2 cm), Diam. 2¾ in. (7 cm);
b: W. 1¼ in. (3.2 cm), Diam. 2⅝ in. (6.5 cm)
The al-Sabah Collection, Dar al-Athar al-Islamiyyah, Kuwait (LNS 7 J ab)

From a region steeped in the arts of late antiquity, especially those of the Greco-Roman and Byzantine periods when bracelets were most often depicted worn in pairs, this set of gold bracelets perpetuates the practice of using broad, decorated shank terminals, which here serve as a clasp. The bracelets are of a type that appears to have been the fashion during the eleventh century, as evident from other near identical examples in museums, and particularly pieces in a hoard of jewelry in the al-Sabah Collection that includes catalogue 7.[1]

The tubular shanks are fitted in the center with a ball-and-socket joint and worked in repoussé with transverse bands alternately featuring the word "blessing" (*baraka*) in Kufic script and birds flanking trefoils. The wide triangular clasps are elaborately decorated with granulation set in between pairs of twisted wire that form vegetal motifs.[2] SK

Selected References: Jenkins et al. 1983, p. 65; Geneva 1985, p. 342; Baltimore and other cities 1990, p. 143; Ermete, Gleba, and Endlich 2006, p. 97; Schallaburg 2007, p. 61; Los Angeles and Houston 2011–12, p. 27; Provo 2012, p. 34.

1. Museum of Islamic Art, Cairo, no. 1/16326: 6326/2; Musée du Louvre, Paris, no. MAO 495; Museum of Islamic Art, Doha, no. JE.118.

2. For ancient examples of filigree work, see Tait, ed. 1986 for the ca. 2500 B.C. gold roundels from the Sumerian city of Ur (no. 28); ca. 1600 B.C. pendants from Tell al-'Ajjul, Palestine (nos. 52–55); seventh-century B.C. Etruscan bracelets and ear stud from Tarquinia (nos. 130–31); fourth-century B.C. Greek gold necklace from Tarentum, Greece (no. 136); ca. fourth- to third-century B.C. Hellenistic jewelry found on the east coast of Turkey (nos. 189–90); first- to third-century A.D. Roman jewelry (nos. 191–93); ca. seventh-century A.D. Byzantine necklace and earrings from Egypt (no. 222); and the pair of eleventh- to twelfth-century earrings and rings from Egypt or Syria (nos. 336–38).

9a–d

Selection of Furnishing and Clothing Textiles

a. Textile with Foliated Scrolls

Probably India, 13th–14th century
Cotton, block-printed and resist-dyed
8½ × 6 in. (21.6 × 15.2 cm)
The Metropolitan Museum of Art, New York, Purchase, V. Everit Macy Gift, 1930 (30.112.25)

b. Textile with Blue and White Pattern

Probably India, 13th–14th century
Cotton, block-printed and resist-dyed
6⅝ × 10 in. (16.8 × 25.4 cm)
The Metropolitan Museum of Art, New York, Purchase, V. Everit Macy Gift, 1930 (30.112.41)

c. Piece of a Carpet with Geometric Design

Anatolia, 14th century
Wool (warp, weft, and pile), symmetrically knotted pile
12 × 9½ in. (30.5 × 24.1 cm)
The Metropolitan Museum of Art, New York, Rogers Fund, 1927 (27.170.91)

d. Textile with Stripes

Egypt, 12th century
Linen and silk, plain weave and tapestry weave
19¼ × 11 in. (48.9 × 27.9 cm)
The Metropolitan Museum of Art, New York, Gift of George D. Pratt, 1931 (31.19.4)

Although today many textiles are considered inexpensive, disposable objects, fabrics counted among the most valuable goods available for sale in the medieval marketplace. Current knowledge of textiles from this period is largely filtered through finds from cemeteries and rubbish piles in Egypt, where dry conditions helped to preserve these otherwise fragile items. Textual sources, too, aid in understanding textile production and trade, particularly when compared to objects from museum collections or excavation. Pieces like catalogues 9a–d suggest the range of textiles available in Jerusalem in the twelfth through fifteenth centuries.

Most scholarship on medieval textiles has focused on clothing, which can usually be identified through details like the cut of the cloth, fineness of weave, inclusion of seams, or overall quality of the cloth itself.[1]

One fragment, catalogue 9d, is similarly woven in a combination of linen and silk, and its small size and fine details also suggest it was once part of an article of dress. Weaving precious silk with more quotidian linen was an economical choice for garments and other items intended for popular consumption. While pure silk was largely unobtainable for the average consumer, objects made partly of silk offered a similar effect at a much more accessible price. The survival of significant pieces of silk garments points to the material's popularity in the eastern Mediterranean. Interestingly, Islamic trade manuals regulating marketplace practices (*hisba*) are concerned only with the relative purities of silk and are largely silent on the legitimacy of wearing it, a topic that normally arises in Islamic jurisprudence.[2] In addition, lists of Jewish women's trousseaux and men's estates from the Cairo Geniza include silk garments, highlighting sartorial use by both genders.[3]

Furnishing textiles, in contrast, have received much less attention in scholarly literature, despite overwhelming evidence of their central importance in day-to-day life. Although fragmentary, catalogue 9c can be identified as part of a rug, thanks to its knotted-pile technique and geometric design. Geniza documents employ a multitude of terms to describe carpets, which stresses their omnipresence and multiple uses in homes and places of worship, including the dwellings of the poor, palaces of the elite, and interiors of holy places, at times serving as wall coverings, bedding, or prayer rugs.[4] Curtains receive special attention in the textual sources and are indeed the most frequently cited object in the Geniza's accounts and in Byzantine wills.[5] Curtains, too, served a variety of functions in interior spaces, acting as room dividers, doorways, bed curtains, and sanctuary screens, among other possibilities.

In many cases it is difficult to tell the exact purpose of a surviving fabric because it lacks clearly identifiable traits. Such uncertainty complicates efforts to identify its original function as clothing or household decoration. At the same time, however, overlaps between furnishing and dress fabrics are compelling because they signal continuities in the appearance of the clothed body and the decoration of the home, thus revealing clues about the broader visual culture of the medieval eastern Mediterranean. Catalogues 9a and b illustrate this point. Large numbers of textiles created in a block-print technique on cotton were found in rubbish heaps in Fustat, just outside modern-day Cairo. Still more were found in port cities on the Red Sea, pointing to their trade through these places.[6] Technical details on these sorts of fabrics point to usages both as furnishings and dress. Carbon dating of several fragments in the Ashmolean Museum, Oxford, shows a date range from the eleventh to the seventeenth century, a testament to the

9a

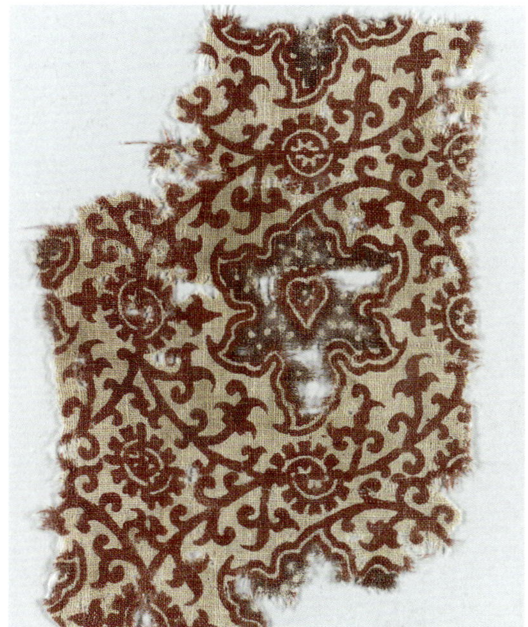

9b

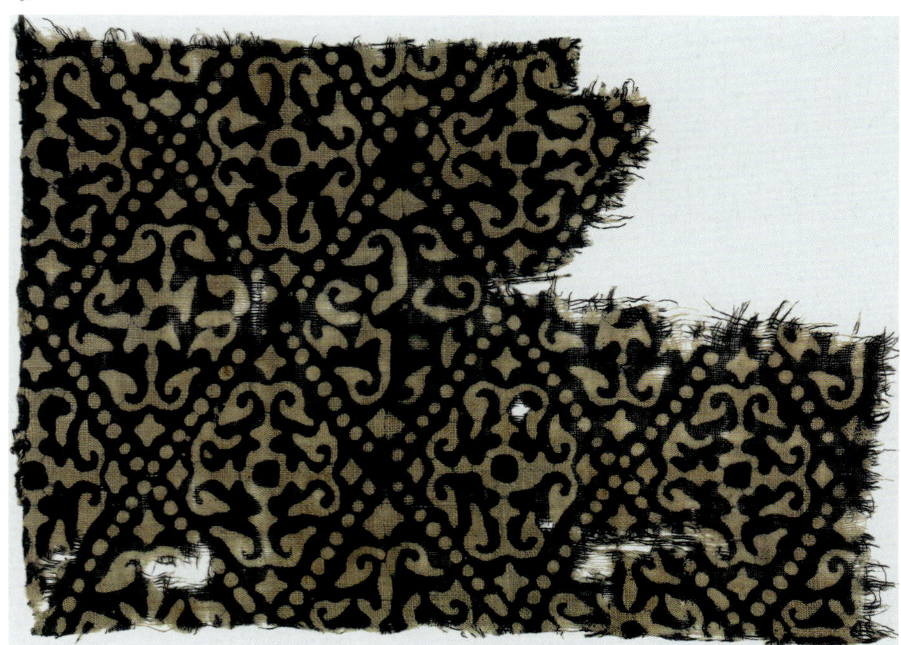

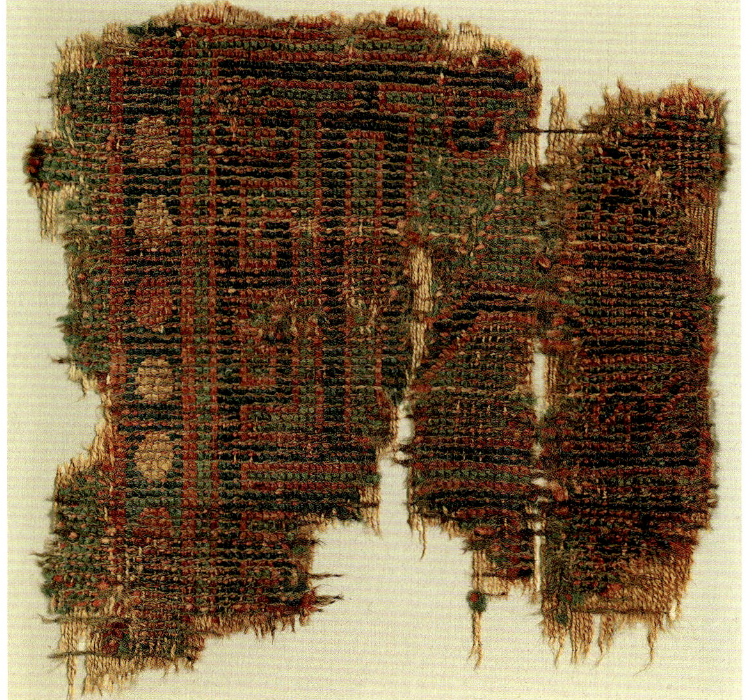

9c

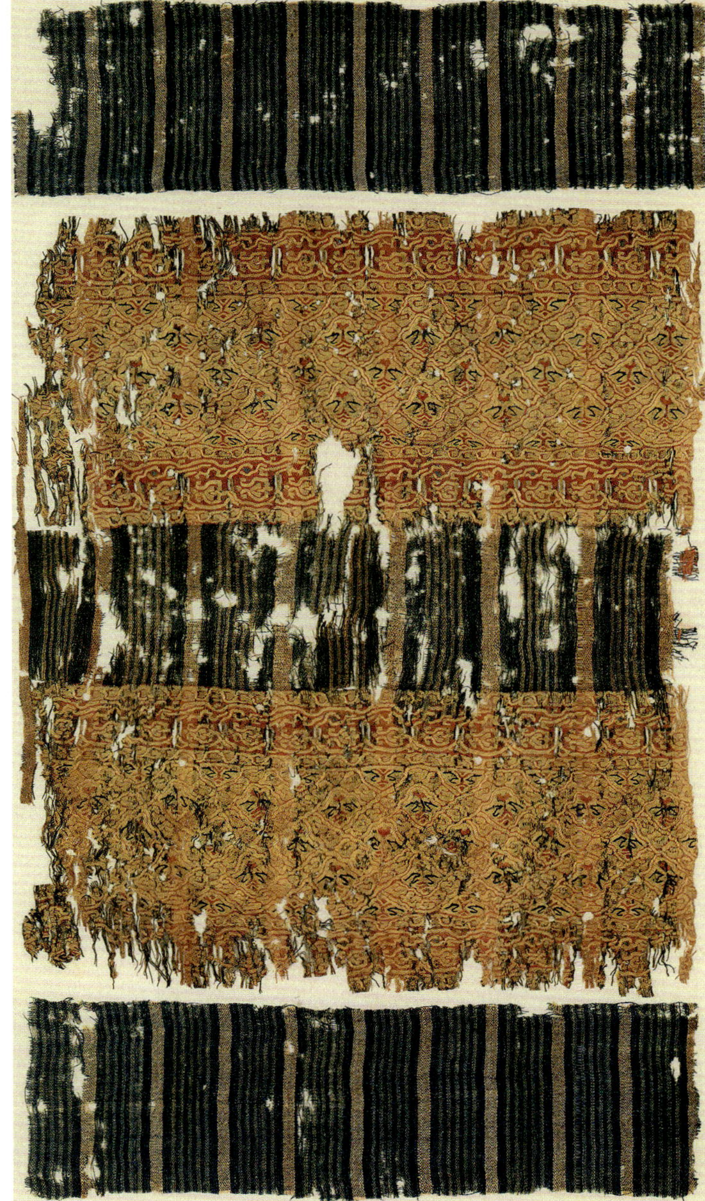

9d

enduring taste for block-print textiles in the Egyptian market. Yet the material, method of decoration, and designs indicate production in India's Gujarat region, suggesting they were imported in large numbers to Egypt due to popular demand.[7] However, at the same time, the survival of block-printed pieces with Arabic inscriptions, including one made of linen possibly naming the Mamluk sultan al-Nasir Muhammad ibn Qala'un, allude to the development of a local industry in Egypt.[8] Taken together, the range of textiles presented here provides an important contribution to our conception of the colorful clothing of Jerusalem's citizens and the richly patterned interiors of their homes. EDW

1. For background on medieval dress in the Middle East, see Ball 2005 and Stillman 2000.

2. Ghabin 2009, pp. 221–23. For a scholarly evaluation, see Steensgaard et al. 1971; Al-Bukhari's chapter "Kitab al-Libas" (The Book on Clothing) in the *Sahih al-Bukhari* is typical of the traditions prohibiting the wearing of silk; Al-Bukhari 2011– ed.

3. Goitein 1967–93, vol. 4, pp. 310–44, appendix D, docs. I–VI describe women's trousseaux; docs. VII–IX are from men's inventories. See especially docs. IX, VII, the inventory of the physician Abu 'l-Rida, dated to 1172.

4. Goitein 1967–93, vol. 4, pp. 123–27.

5. A concise discussion of written sources is in Helmecke 2009. See also Goitein 1967–93, vol. 4, pp. 117–22.

6. Barnes 1997. For recent work, see Wild and Wild 2005.

7. Machado 2009.

8. Museum of Islamic Art, Cairo, no. 8204; see O'Kane et al. 2012, p. 297.

10

Selections from the Metal Hoard from Tiberias

Tiberias, 11th century
Various metals
Dimensions variable
Courtesy of the Israel Antiquities Authority, Jerusalem, exhibited at the Israel Museum, Jerusalem (IAA 1999-3638; 1999-3639; 1999-3645; 1999-3661–1999-3633; 1999-3699; 1999-3704/1-2; 1999-3706; 1999-3720/1,2; 1999-3722; 1999-3727; 1999-3739; 1999-3855; 1999-3856; 1999-3858; 1999-3860–1999-3862; 1999-3864; 1999-3890; 1999-3891; 1999-3971)

During salvage excavations at the foot of Mount Berenice in Tiberias in 1998, a cache was discovered in three large storage jars (Greek, *pithoi*) in a two-room building with a courtyard. The cache comprised lampstands, ewers, bowls, boxes, trays, ladles, buckets, cooking vessels, mortars and pestles, a great variety of supporting feet and handles, parts of boxes (such as hinges and clasps), small pieces of sculpture to adorn vessels, two bracelets, two molds for the preparation of beads, metal bells for domestic animals, two molds for sand casting, and a few pieces of lacework. Altogether the cache included 646 artifacts as well as 551 pounds (250 kg) of metal manufacturing waste and 85 coins dated to between 978 and 1078.

Containing 350 artifacts, the largest *pithos* (h. 43⅜ in. [110 cm], diam. 33½ in. [85 cm]) was found in the western corner of the rear room, standing on the beaten-earth floor and supported by a low curved wall that was probably built to hide it. In the front room, another storage jar (h. 27⅝ in. [70 cm], diam. 19¾ in. [50 cm]) was buried under the floor covered by a basalt slab. It held 20 bronze vessels and 250 kilograms of manufacturing waste and coins. In the courtyard, below the beaten floor, a third storage jar, filled with hundreds of small bronze artifacts, was found.

The location was identified as a workshop based on the huge amount of production

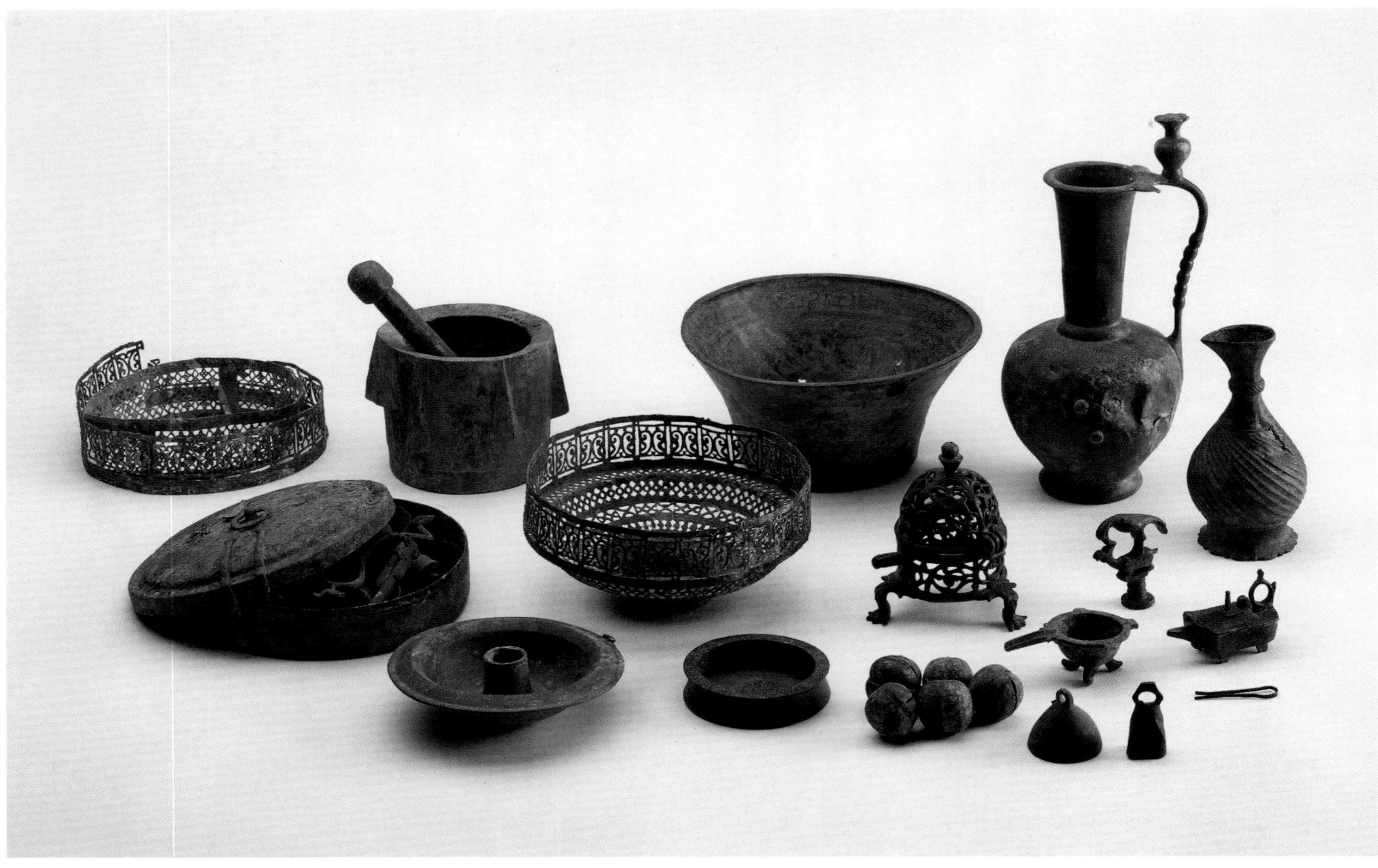

10

waste and base metal found in the *pithoi*. Base metal had been dispersed all over the floor and stuck to the walls, while the courtyard was covered with metal flakes and bronze scrap.[1] An examination of the production waste sheds light on the techniques used and points to the extensive hammering of brass sheets and trimming using scissors. These practices resulted in a wide array of spirally twisted strips among the scrap. Following hammering, the vessels were polished on a lathe, which was the source of the accumulated base metal. Two sets of sand-cast molds along with the huge number of solid handles and feet indicate the extensive use of this technique in the workshop.

One tripod lampstand base features the inscription *ʿamal ʿAbbas* (work of ʿAbbas), similar to one found at Caesarea though lacking the words "in Damascus," probably due to a lack of space (cat. 11). This near-identical text confirms that the lost-wax vessels — mainly the bases and shafts of lampstands — were imported from Damascus. The workshop at Tiberias may have specialized in hammering and sand casting to produce items of high-quality workmanship. Furthermore, the numerous vessel parts, such as bases, bodies, and necks, argue for local production.

The typology of the vessels largely adheres to Roman-Byzantine prototypes. Their decoration follows the repertoire of the Fatimid decorative arts, with inscriptions as well as vegetal and geometric decor. The inscriptions invoke well-being, good fortune, blessings, and felicity for their owners. The vegetal patterns are generally heart-shaped palmette leaves with involuted scrolls, while the geometric ones usually fill secondary and marginal bands, continuing a Roman-Byzantine tradition of zigzag and lozenge patterns filled with dots or other embellishment. The most prevalent pattern on the metalware involves pairs of circles, produced on a lathe, on the outer walls and bases — a format whose Roman heritage dates to the first and second centuries.[2]

The considerable similarity between the Tiberias and Caesarea assemblages is to such a degree that solid feet with identical flaws were found in both sites. By contrast, some more richly decorated vessels found at Caesarea suggest that they may have been especially ordered for particular clients, while at Tiberias the vessels were produced serially and with modest decoration.

Another assemblage of vessels was found in Denia on the western coast of Spain at the beginning of the twentieth century. The vessels, most of them broken, were found packed in one large *pithos*.[3] Identical to the Tiberias and Caesarea hoards, the cache may have been shipped from Tiberias for melting and reuse. Both cities took part in the dynamic trading activities of the eleventh century; Geniza documents describe merchandise being traded throughout the Mediterranean basin and beyond. The Caesarea hoard has facilitated greater understanding of the previously unknown subject of Fatimid metal vessels, and the Tiberias hoard has enabled a deeper insight into production techniques and the physical extent of their distribution.

In terms of dating, the latest coin is dated to the reign of the Byzantine emperor Michael VII Doukas (1071–78). The dating of the workshop is connected with political events in Palestine during the second half of the eleventh century and the raids of Turkish tribesmen originating in central Asia. They first appeared as nomadic tribes with their families and herds and also served as mercenaries. Within a few years they became a military force that opposed the Fatimid regime, with a base near Tiberias. In 1074 they plundered the city, and, as a result, the population fled and the workshop ended. AL

Selected References: Bijovsky and Berman 2008; Hirschfeld et al. 2008; Khamis 2013; Lester 2013; Lester 2014.

1. Hirschfeld et al. 2008, pp. 20–30; Lester 2014, pp. 437–44.
2. Strong and Brown 1976, pp. 34–35.
3. Ruíz 2012, pp. 21–134.

11

Selections from the Metal Hoard from Caesarea

Caesarea, 11th century
Various metals
Dimensions variable
Courtesy of the Israel Antiquities Authority, Jerusalem, exhibited at the Israel Museum, Jerusalem (IAA 1996-390/1,2,3; 1997-3267; 1997-3271; 1997-3272; 1997-3421; 1997-3428; 1995-3496–1995-3502; 1995-3507/1,2,3,4,5; 1995-3509; 1995-3510; 1995-3520; 1996-402; 1996-407)

In 1995, during an excavation in southeastern Caesarea, a hoard of 136 brass vessels, 23 clay objects, and 13 glass articles was found in a cavity beside a staircase and a retaining wall on the platform of the temple to Roma and Augustus. Prior to this discovery, only a few metal vessels from museums and private collections had been identified as Fatimid.[1] The clay and glass groups include unique vessels such as glazed bowls, jars, juglets, and a cooking pot that until then were known through shards only.

Among the brass vessels are lampstands, ladles, ewers, basins, boxes, braziers of different sizes, trays, buckets, and a large group of solid handles and feet. Prominent are the lampstands composed of three parts — a tripod base, shaft, and tray — and made in sizes ranging from 6⅛ to 32¾ inches (15.5–83.2 cm) in height. The bases and shafts were produced using the lost-wax technique, with inner cores made of mud, remnants of which can be seen on the insides of these parts. Probably fabricated using a stone mold, the heavy round trays of these lampstands are decorated with pairs of circles worked on a lathe and clusters of circles produced by punches of various diameters.[2]

A major characteristic of the group is the stylistic association of the base and shaft. A round base had a cylindrical shaft and a polygonal base had a ribbed shaft, creating a harmonized set. The parts of one striking lampstand are uniquely decorated, its round base featuring tendrils and half-palmettes that recur on the tray where they are integrated into a six-pointed star in a pattern that appears on the shaft together with a benedictory inscription.

Another significant group consists of nine buckets, five of which are similar in size and were probably used in the bathhouse, continuing a Roman-Byzantine tradition. Such buckets were mentioned in trousseau lists in the Geniza of the Ben-Ezra synagogue at Fustat.[3] One bucket is luxuriously decorated with alternating compositions of tendrils and palmettes over the entire surface. It has a splendid benedictory inscription below the rim, and a heavy sand-cast handle terminating in a carved vegetal pattern and a loop for suspension.

The hoard includes several ladles very similar to globular Roman ones but trapezoid in shape. One ladle, decorated with a band of half-palmettes, is inscribed *Barakah li-ṣahibihi* (blessing to its owner) on its base. When not in use, the ladle was suspended on the wall with the inscription facing out, emphasizing the power of the written word for believers.

Two trays typify the hoard. The first is made of thick brass sheet engraved with a central scene of an eagle attacking a gazelle, a common theme in Fatimid decorative arts.[4] The scene, popular since the Hellenistic and Roman periods, may have been interpreted as a conquering force overcoming a weaker rival and had a religious significance. The theme appears again on a sculptural adornment on the upper part of a vessel found at Tiberias. This tray, with its convex walls, was influenced by a group of trays from the middle Byzantine period.[5] The shape was later adopted in the Eastern Islamic world during the twelfth and thirteenth centuries, and such trays were used to serve fruits and sweets.[6] The second tray, on the other hand, produced from a thin sheet, has straight walls and a central rosette with punched circles. The straight walls enabled the soldering of small feet to the tray so that it could be raised above the floor and used to serve food.

Inscribed on the bottom of the most important lampstand base is *ʿamal ʿAbbas bi-Dimashk* (the work of ʿAbbas in Damascus), a notation that sheds light on the Syrian origin

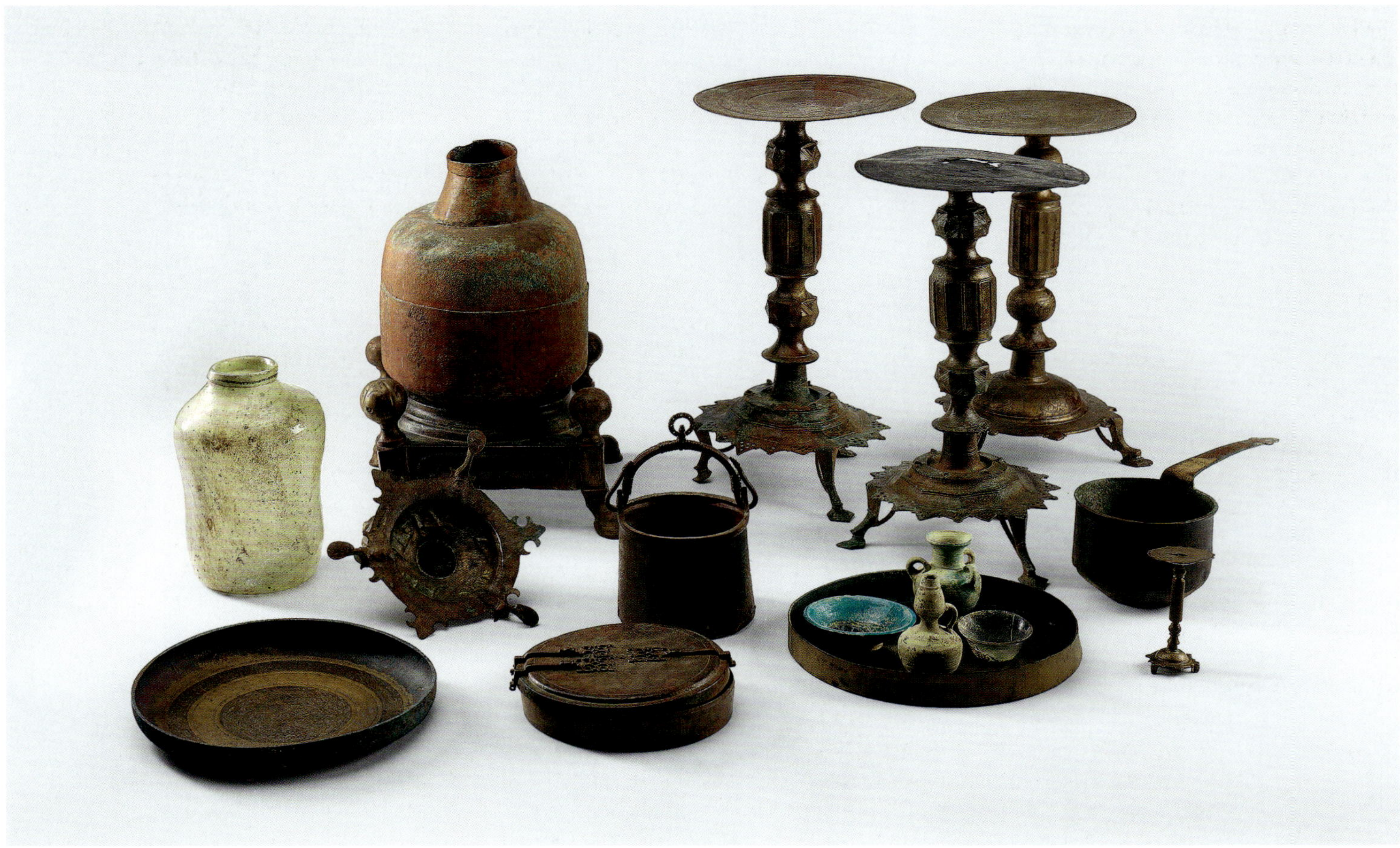

11

of this group of lampstands. Of the variety of fabrication types and styles, thick brass and figures of animals, inscriptions, palmettes, and tendrils as adornment were used on the most splendid and valued items. Articles of inferior quality were hammered from a thinner brass sheet and decorated on the lathe with pairs of circles. Thus the owner of the assemblage, probably a merchant, was familiar with his clients and knew their financial capacities. The reference to Damascus also helps to identify Syria as the origin of the clay vessels.

A bowl, coated with alkali glaze, is made of red-pinkish clay typical of eleventh-century clay vessels in Syria.[7] A juglet with a swollen neck produced from greenish buff clay seems to be the forerunner of this group with swollen necks of the Ayyubid period as no other comparisons for the vessel have been found.[8] The merchant may have purchased the clay vessels during his travels in Syria.

The intact storage jar made of thick free-blown glass was produced locally and can be compared with shards found in several sites in the region.[9] It was probably used to store chunks of sugar, a new regional product that was exported to Europe less than a decade after the Crusader occupation of the Holy Land at the turn of the twelfth century.[10] Except for lampstands that were probably produced in Damascus, the vessels originated in a workshop either in Tiberias or Caesarea. Tiberias was abandoned in 1072, following the settlement of Turkman tribes around the city, and a Caesarean metal workshop with large quantities of production waste, under which the jewelry hoard (cat. 5) was hidden, was excavated in 1960.[11] This finding may indicate the establishment of a metal workshop in Caesarea, after the desertion of Tiberias, which would have existed for about twenty-five years, prior to the conquest of Caesarea in 1101. AL

Selected References: Haifa 1999; Lester 2011; Lester 2014.

1. Grube 1965; Fehérvári 1976, pp. 39–54; Lester 2004.
2. Strong and Brown 1976, pp. 33–34.
3. Goitein 1967–93, vol. 4, pp. 317–21.
4. Ettinghausen, Grabar, and Jenkins-Madina 2001, pp. 202, 206, figs. 317, 329; Paris 1998, pp. 118, 128, 219, figs. 45, 81, 200; Hoffman, E., 1999, p. 406, figs. 5, 6, 7.
5. Ballian and Drandaki 2003, pp. 52, 56, figs. 4a–b, 7.
6. Welch 1976, pls. 52, 76.
7. I wish to thank Robert Maison from the Royal Ontario Museum, Toronto, for this information.
8. Avissar and Stern 2005, pp. 109, 167, fig. 45.4, .5, .6, pl. 30.2.
9. Gorin-Rosen 2004, p. 60, fig. 1.10.
10. Peled 1999.
11. For the abandonment of Tiberias, see Gil 1983, p. 338. For the 1960 excavation, see the archive of the Israel Antiquities Authority, Jerusalem, file no. C-24/1962.

12

Perfume Sprinkler (*Qumqum*)

Probably Syria, Ayyubid period (1169–1260)
Glass; blown, with applied decoration and blown foot
H. 10¼ in. (26 cm), W. 5⅜ in. (13.4 cm), D. 3¼ in. (8.3 cm)
The Metropolitan Museum of Art, New York, Purchase, Richard S. Perkins Gift, 1977 (1977.164)

This sprinkler consists of a flattened, ring-shaped body with a long tapering neck decorated with applied trails on its lower third and set on a cushion-topped foot with a splayed base. The ring form had a useful function; one could hook a thumb or finger into the central hole and shake the bottle vigorously without losing one's grip. Although aromatics were

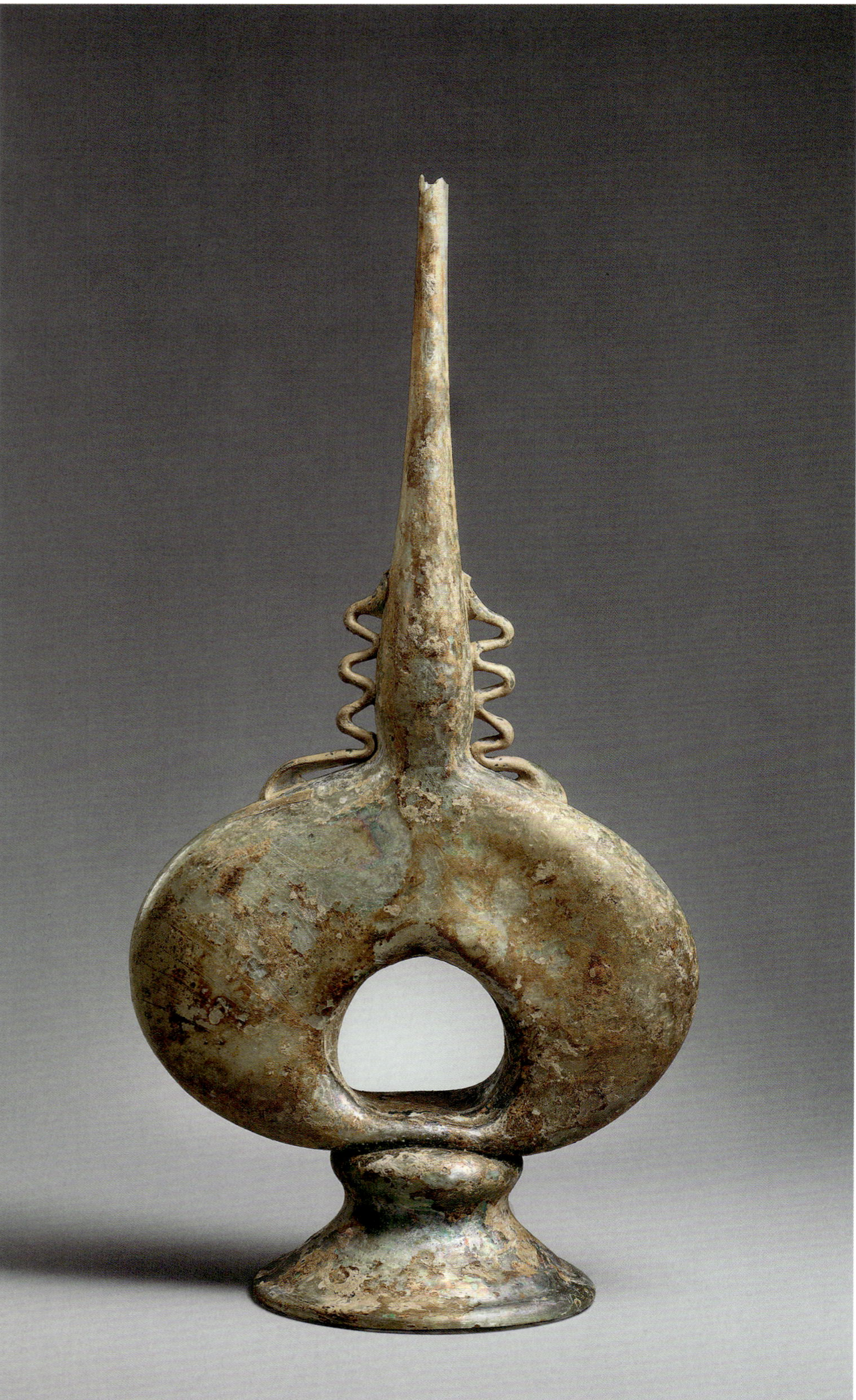

12

used in the Middle East from Roman times on, sprinklers of this and related shapes first appear in Syria and Egypt in the eleventh and twelfth centuries.[1] They would have been traded throughout the Levant, including in Jerusalem, where an example has reportedly been excavated.[2]

While such sprinklers most often contained rosewater, dilutions of other fragrant substances such as musk and ambergris could be used alone or in combination with a range of ingredients. Following a meal, people not only rinsed their mouths with rosewater but also sprinkled their clothes and faces with it. Other practices included sprinkling rosewater on the shrouds of the dead. For such purposes long-necked sprinklers would have been employed, whereas differently shaped containers held the precious attar of rose. In the medieval period an important source of rosewater was Fars province in Iran. References to the alembic, used to distill rosewater, appear as early as the tenth century in an Arabic translation of the first-century Greek physician Pedanius Dioscorides's *De Materia Medica*, suggesting that rosewater was also produced in the Arab regions of the Middle East.[3] Substantial quantities of rosewater must have been required for the perfuming of the Dome of the Rock carried out by Saladin's nephew after the reconquest of Jerusalem.[4] SRC

Selected References: Jenkins 1986, p. 35, fig. 42; Welch et al. 1987, pp. 44–45, fig. 31; Canby 2012, pp. 126–27, fig. 15; New York 2016, p. 106, no. 35.

1. Tait et al. 1991, pp. 128–29.
2. See the example in the Israel Museum, Jerusalem, no. 380; museum website catalogue record.
3. Wiedemann and Plessner 1960.
4. Imad al-Din, as cited in Gabrieli, ed. 1969, pp. 171–72.

13a–e

Selection of Ceramics

a. Vase

Egypt, 9th–11th century
Stonepaste, white slip, and glaze
H. 5⅝ in. (14.3 cm), Diam. 5 in. (12.7 cm)
Victoria and Albert Museum, London, Given by Major W. J. Myers (746-1897)

b. Bowl

Damascus, late 12th–13th century
Stonepaste, paint, and transparent glaze
H. 4⅛ in. (10.5 cm), Diam. 8⅞ in. (22.5 cm)
The Metropolitan Museum of Art, New York, H. O. Havemeyer Collection, Gift of Horace Havemeyer, 1941 (41.165.2)

c. Plate

China, Yuan dynasty, 14th century
Stoneware and celadon glaze
H. 2½ in. (6.4 cm), Diam. 13 in. (33 cm)
The Metropolitan Museum of Art, New York, Gift of Mr. and Mrs. Stanley Herzman, 1980 (1980.471.2)

d. Vase

Probably Egypt or Syria, 14th century
Stonepaste, paint, and transparent glaze
H. 15⅜ in. (39 cm), Diam. 10½ in. (26.5 cm)
Victoria and Albert Museum, London (618-1864)

e. Stem Cup

Jerusalem(?), 14th century
Stonepaste, molded decoration, and glaze
H. 3⅛ in. (7.8 cm), Diam. 5¼ in. (13.3 cm)
By kind permission of the Keir Collection on long-term loan by Ranros Universal S.A. to the Dallas Museum of Art

The wide variety of ceramic finds in Jerusalem suggests that its residents enjoyed access to the lively trade routes crisscrossing the region. The vast majority of surviving ceramics are remnants of vessels, simply glazed if at all, which were used for cooking, eating, lighting, and storage. These works are useful records of daily life but aesthetically unremarkable. The many extant shards of brightly colored pots, however, attest to an appreciation for the sophisticated glazing practiced by potters in the region as well as for the distinctive wares produced in more distant lands.[1]

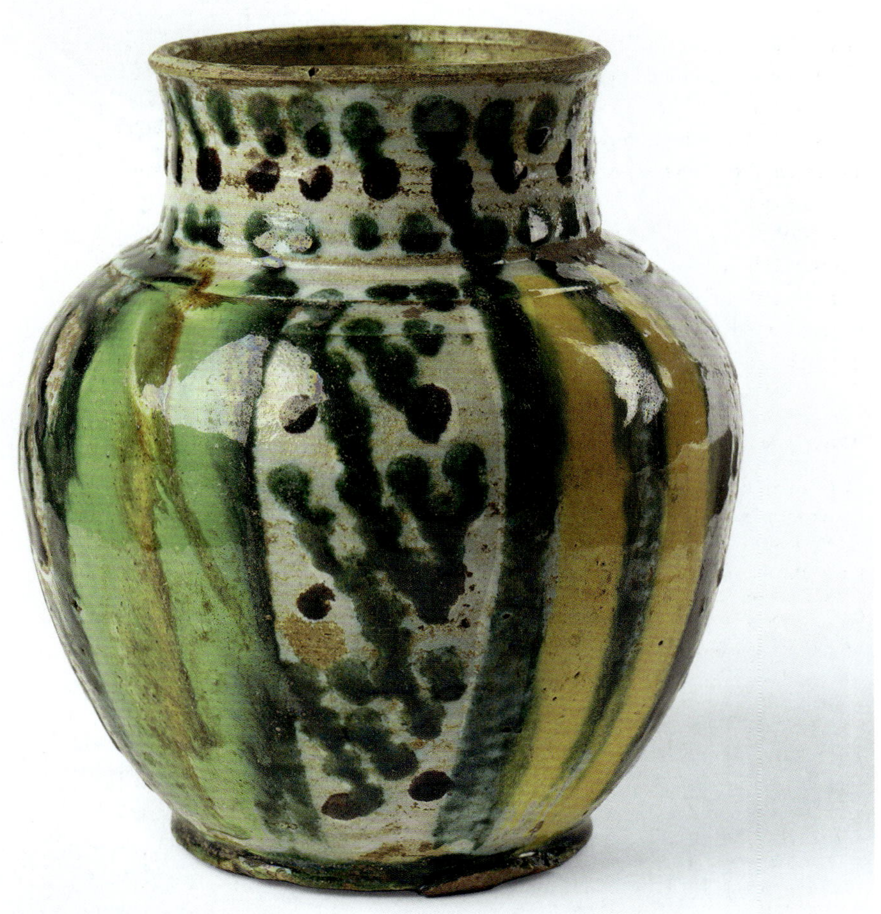

13a

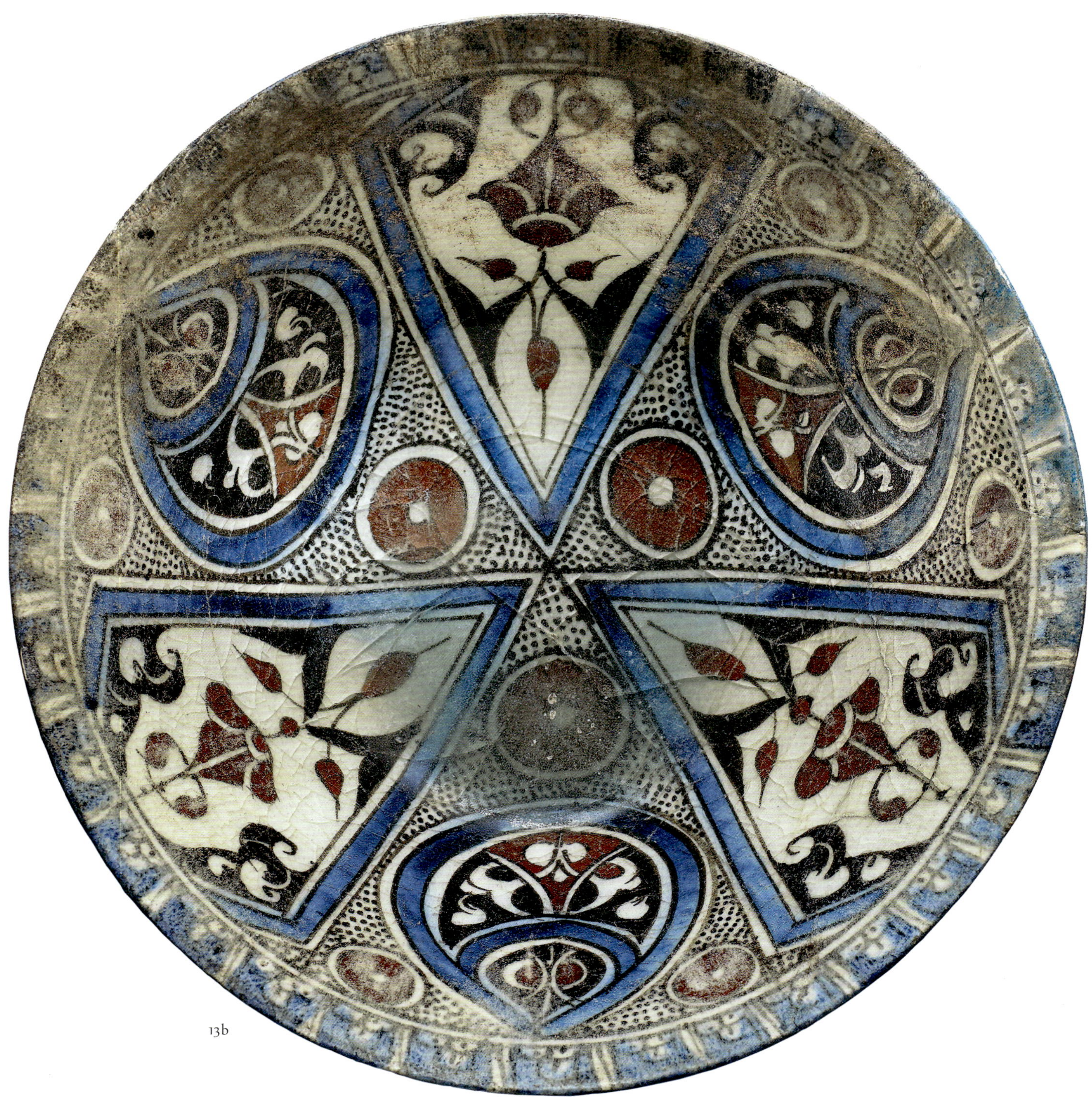

13b

Documents from the Cairo Geniza make clear that the ceramic trade and industry in the region was highly developed, with vessels of various shapes and functions produced by their own specialist makers. Though pottery rarely appears in trousseau lists, it figures prominently in the inventories of pharmacists, doctors, and merchants. Ceramics were also an integral feature of private households, and families might place an order for whole sets of painted platters, bowls, and cups, with specifications given as to color and design.[2]

Some of the finest pottery did not travel far to reach Jerusalem and neighboring cities, and the extensive assortment of ceramics from Egypt that were found in the coastal city of Caesarea, some sixty miles northwest of Jerusalem, offers a cross section of Fatimid glazing techniques.[3] These include monochrome vessels dipped in vivid blue, green, or ochre glazes, often with incised decoration (cat. 11) as well as splash-and-striped wares, similar to the charming vase from the Victoria and Albert Museum (cat. 13a), appealing for their improvisatory design. (Shards of splash-and-striped ware were also found in various parts of the Old City in Jerusalem.)[4] In addition, the Caesarean hoard yielded numerous examples of the iridescent lusterware for which Fatimid potters were famous and in which lively designs were painted with metallic oxides onto an opaque white surface (cat. 33).[5]

Among the finds in a garden of the Armenian patriarchate in Jerusalem are fragments of several bowls, similar in shape, design, and palette to one in the Metropolitan Museum's collection (cat. 13b).[6] All are typical of the stonepaste wares associated with Syrian kilns of the twelfth to thirteenth century, and analysis of the clay suggests they may have been produced in Damascus.[7] Pigments of black, blue, and red are applied on ceramic

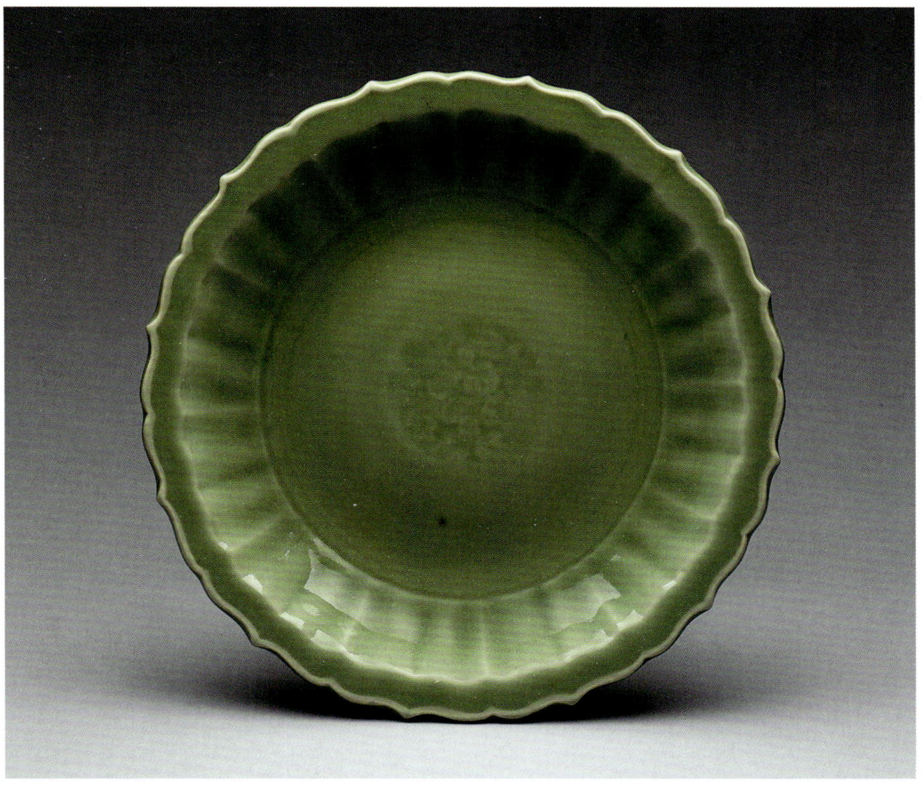

13c

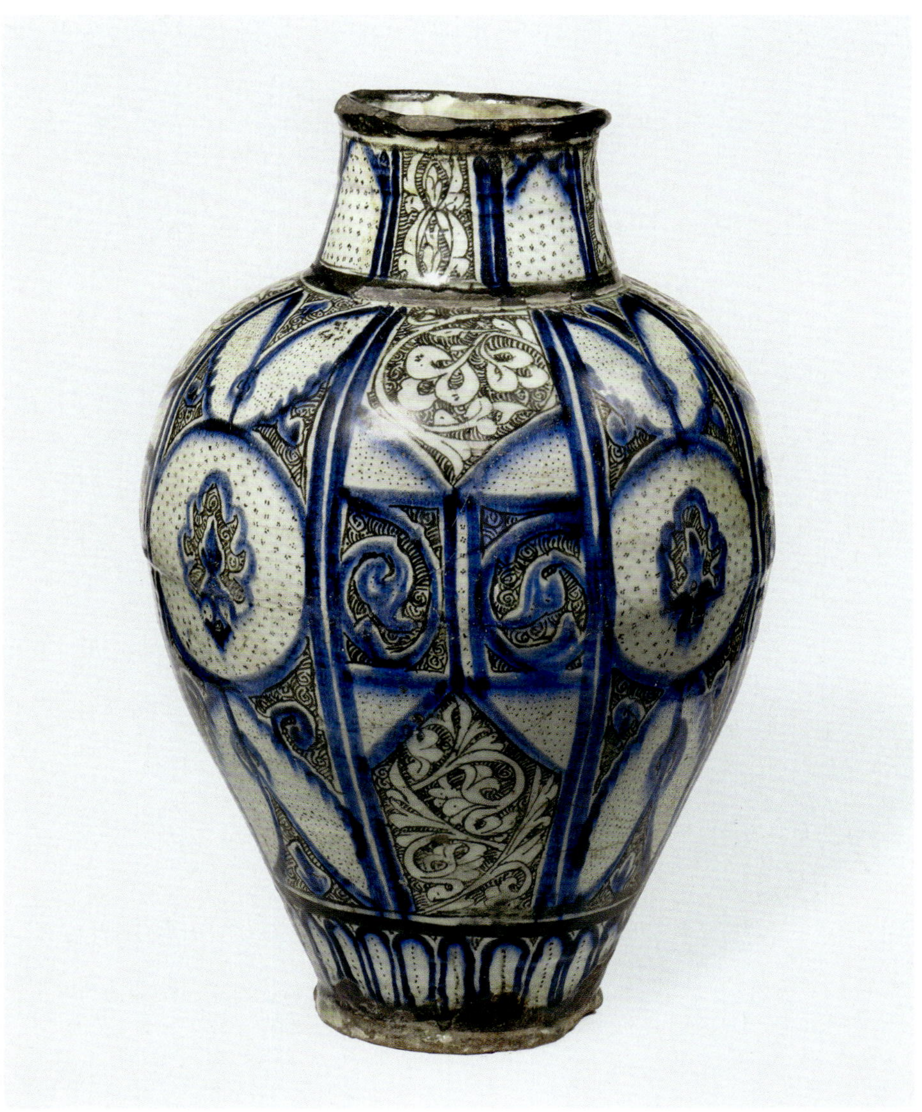

13d

bodies before coating with a transparent glaze. Often painted with a radial design inside, they all display a simple border of a repeating caliper shape on the exterior.

The high quality of ceramics from Egypt and Syria did not eliminate the demand for imports from other, sometimes more distant producers. When Europeans occupied the Kingdom of Jerusalem, they looked perhaps unsurprisingly to Italy and Sicily for painted vessels with motifs keyed to their tastes (cat. 14). These wares seemed to have been particular favorites of the Italian merchants who settled in cities on the Mediterranean coast. Enormously popular in the Crusader era were pots with incised design (sgraffito) known as Port Saint Symeon ware, after the Antioch port where a large quantity of this type was found (fig. 19).[8] Archaeological excavations indicate that they were made in Saint Symeon and other sites throughout the eastern Mediterranean, likely for clients of all sectarian stripes. The wide-ranging imagery includes mounted warriors, courtly cupbearers, astrological symbols, and heraldic motifs.[9]

Then as now, China was synonymous with fine ceramics: the records of local merchants refer to porcelain or imitations of porcelain as "sini."[10] Celadon produced in the area around Longquan was an important Chinese export (cat. 13c). Though shards bearing the characteristic green-gray glaze are rare, they have been found in Alexandria, Antioch, Acre, Safed, and perhaps Jerusalem and seem to have traveled to the Holy Land via Egypt.[11] Chinese pottery had an impact on local taste with blue-and-white Ming ware serving as models for some of the elegant Mamluk ceramics created in Cairo and Damascus (cat. 13d).[12]

Little evidence of significant ceramic production is found in Palestine itself, though Jerusalem potentially offers a notable exception. Mamluk potters working on the Haram al-Sharif during the fourteenth century may have been responsible for the distinctive green-glazed stem-fitted cups inscribed with benedictions (cat. 13e).[13] As products of the Holy City, these vessels and the wishes they offered for the prosperity and honor of the person who drinks from them may have had special resonance. MH

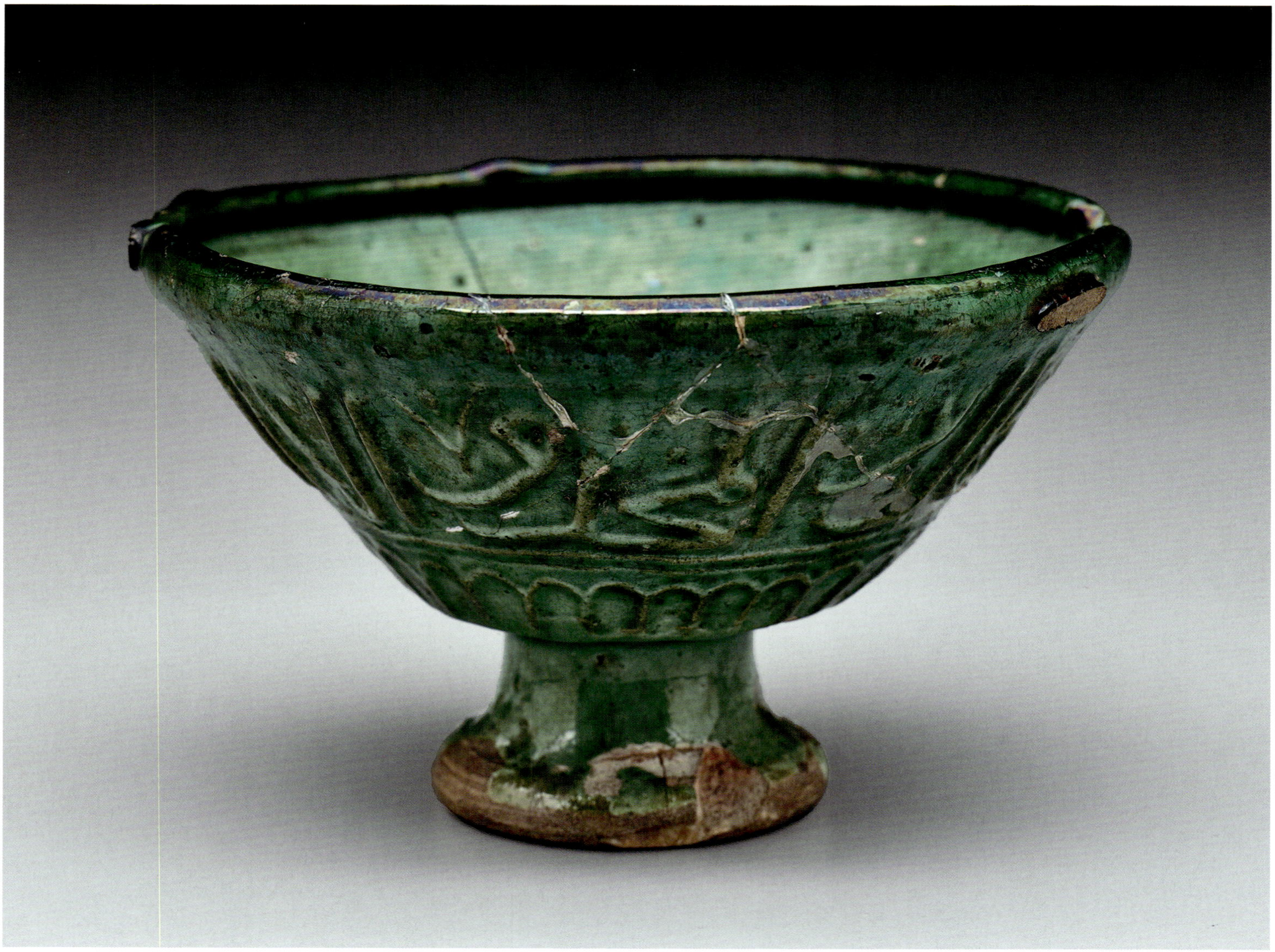

13e

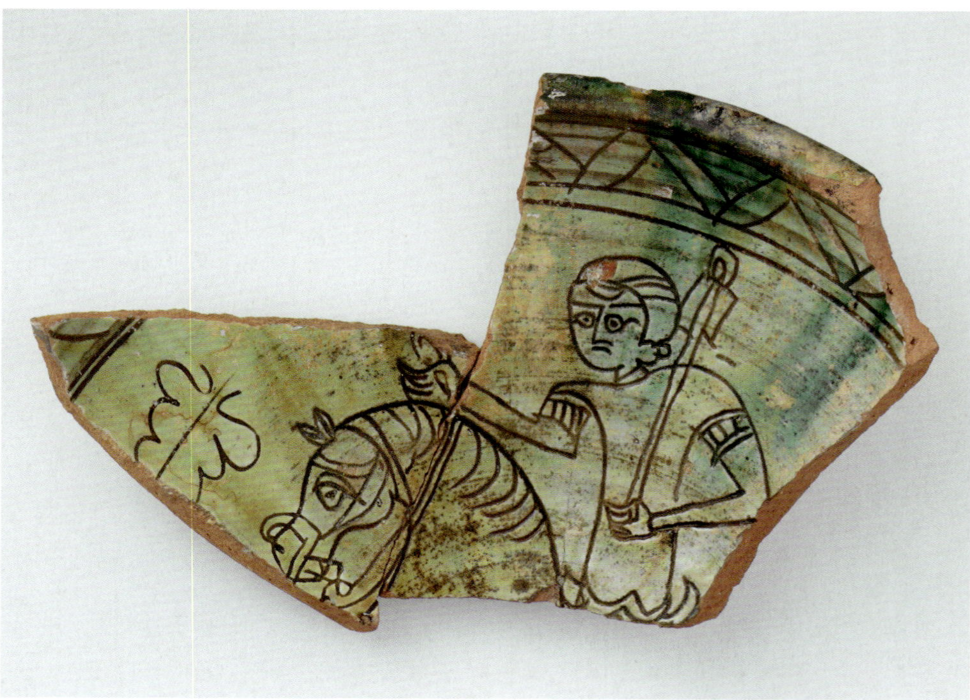

Fig. 19. Fragment of a bowl with a horse and rider. Port Saint Symeon (present-day Al-Mina/Samandağ, Turkey), 1200–1268. Terracotta with green glaze over slip, decorated in sgraffito. The Metropolitan Museum of Art, New York, Purchase, Anonymous Gift, 1984 (1984.181)

Selected References: Cat. 13b: New York 2011, pp. 5, 138, 149–50, no. 97. Cat. 13d: Gayraud 2012, p. 89, fig. 14. Cat. 13e: Grube 1976b, pp. 154–57, no. 102 (as Egyptian?).

1. For an overview of ceramic finds in the region during this period, see Avissar and Stern 2005; Stern, E., 1999; Milwright 2009.

2. Goitein 1967–93, vol. 1, pp. 110–11; vol. 4, pp. 106, 145–48.

3. Generally speaking, port cities seem to have had access to a wider variety of imported ceramics than those inland, including Jerusalem.

4. Avissar 2003, p. 433; see also Williams, G., 2013, pp. 83–84.

5. Brosh 1986.

6. Tushingham et al. 1985, figs. 34.34, 40.8, 40.17, 44.4.

7. Mason 2004, pp. 98–99.

8. Avissar and Stern 2005, pp. 52–56; Blackman and Redford 2005.

9. Redford 2004.

10. Goitein 1967–93, vol. 4, pp. 145–46.

11. Avissar and Stern 2005, pp. 78–79.

12. On the Chinese export market and the impact of Chinese ceramics on Mamluk production, see Gayraud 2012, pp. 88–91; and Haddon 2012, pp. 100–101.

13. Ben-Dov 1985, p. 364; Avissar and Stern 2005, pp. 22–24; Haddon 2012, p. 109.

14

Bowl with a Woman Spinning

Brindisi, 13th century
Tin-glazed earthenware
H. 2⅜ in. (6 cm), Diam. 10⅝ in. (27 cm)
Courtesy of the Israel Antiquities Authority, Jerusalem, exhibited at the Israel Museum, Jerusalem
(IAA 1985.49)

This vessel of a type known as proto-maiolica is made of pale brown fabric. The interior is covered with white tin glaze on which the designs were painted in dark brown, dark yellow, and blue. A woman engaged in hand spinning is the main motif. Her dress and head cover are identical to that of a woman depicted in a contemporary church mural in the Salento region of southern Italy, and the facial features are similarly illustrated.[1] Spinning was a common daily task for medieval women and an emblem of female virtue. In imagery of the time, the Virgin Mary is often depicted spinning.[2]

Found in Acre in the early 1980s, the bowl is dated to the thirteenth century and seems to have been produced in the workshops of Brindisi in southern Italy.[3] Proto-maiolica was transported to the Latin Kingdom of Jerusalem, the Principality of Antioch, as well as to Frankish Greece by Genoese, Pisan, and Venetian merchant ships that sailed to the eastern Mediterranean via the port of Brindisi. These ceramic bowls apparently served as a secondary cargo, or less profitable freight, and ballast in these ships that carried more lucrative goods. The bowls were later sold in the markets to both the Franks and locals.[4]

EJS

Selected References: Jerusalem 1999, p. 60; Sheffer and Druks 2000.

1. Compare with the woman in a dark dress standing in the middle of the bottom register of the left nave vault of the Church of Santa Maria della Croce in Casaranello. See Safran 2014, pp. 73, 268, no. 33sc.2.
2. Schaus, ed. 2006, pp. 150, 152.
3. Patitucci-Uggeri 1979.
4. Stern, E., 2012, vol. 1, pp. 76–80, 139–58.

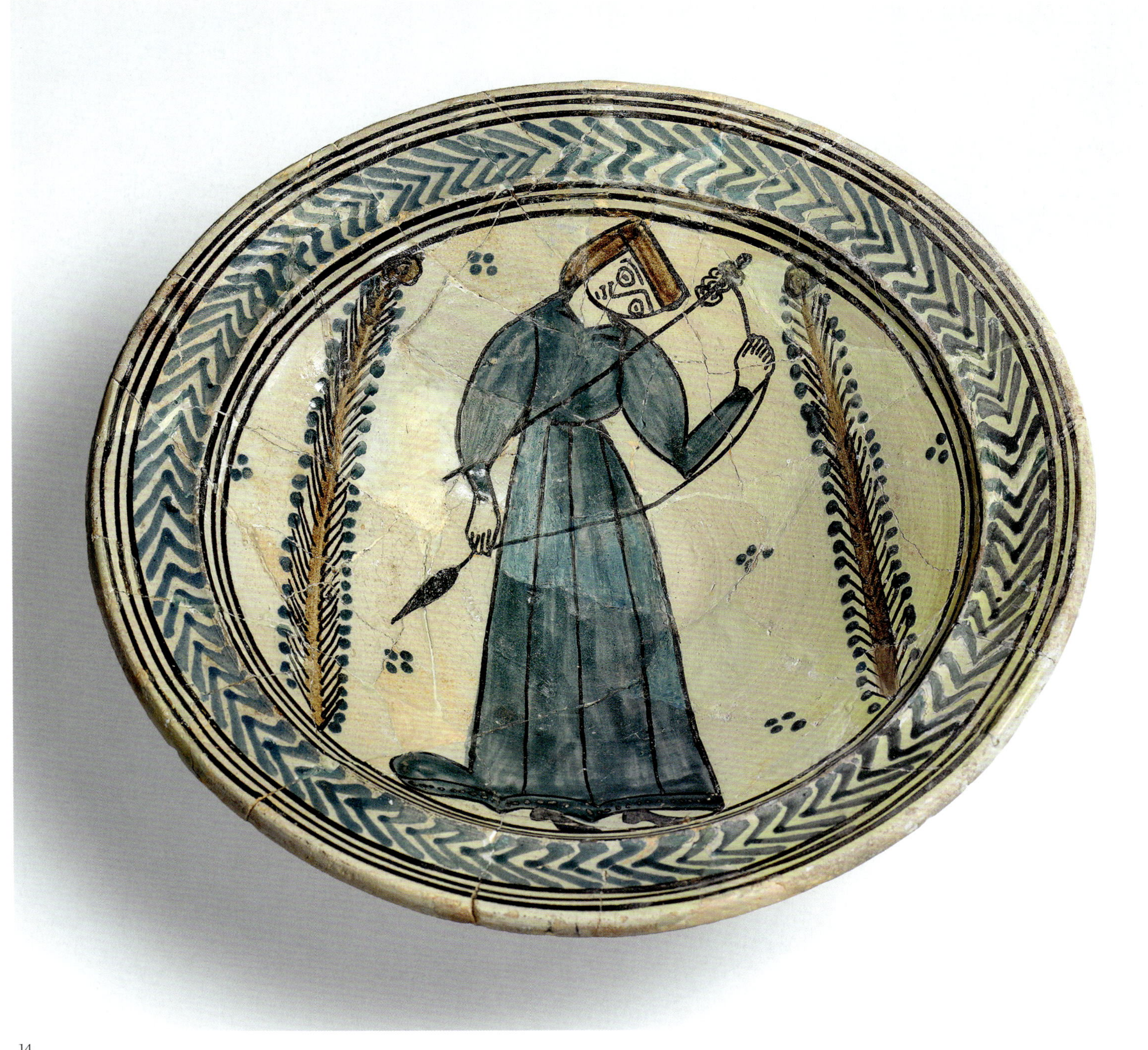

14

15

The Asseburg-Hedwig Beaker

Possibly Sicily, ca. 1175–1225
Free-blown glass, cut, polished, and engraved
H. 4 in. (10.2 cm), Diam. 3¾ in. (9.5 cm)
Lent by Bernd and Eva Hockemeyer, Germany

The presence of sophisticated glassmakers in the Latin Kingdom is well documented in contemporary texts.[1] The chronicler William of Tyre, writing before 1167, mentioned that the "glass [of Tyre] is exported to distant provinces, and it provides material suitable for vessels that are remarkable and of outstanding clarity."[2] Jacques de Vitry, bishop of Acre between 1216 and 1226, wrote of the "purest glass . . . made with cunning workmanship out of the sands of the sea."[3] Linking Tyre's shipping business with its renowned glassmaking, the intrepid traveler Benjamin of Tudela, while visiting the Holy Land in the twelfth century, related that "the Jews own sea-going vessels, and there are glassmakers among them who make fine Tyrian glassware, which is prized in all countries."[4]

It is tempting to tie the glass that these writers describe in such admiring terms to the distinctive, somewhat puzzling group known as the Hedwig Beakers. Scholars have yet to agree on the origins of these vessels, named after the saint who, tradition held, owned such a glass and for whom the water poured into it would miraculously turn to wine. Approximately thirteen such vessels survive intact.[5] Though varying in size and motif, they share a number of features: a squat shape, thick walls, faceted lip, and deeply cut ornament. Their color ranges from smoky gray to honey and looks like quartz. All have been found in European contexts and seem to date from the twelfth to thirteenth century.[6] Their presence in church treasuries and noble collections suggests that they were prized from an early date.

Their appreciation by Europeans cannot be doubted, but their decoration and overall aesthetic have little in common with European precious objects of the same date. They strongly resemble Fatimid rock-crystal carvings, even as they differ in detail. Chemical analysis is not entirely conclusive, but the soda-lime composition with low traces of magnesium in the nearly half-dozen examples that have been tested aligns them more closely with Islamic glass of the Levant than to European wares.[7]

How then to resolve this cross-cultural conundrum? Is this European glass that seeks to emulate Islamic glass in style and chemical composition or Islamic glass made exclusively for the European export market? Prompted by the chroniclers' accounts, an intriguing theory that marries both points of view has emerged. The glassmakers of Tyre might have supplied glass as a raw material to workshops in Sicily, where the vessels were fashioned and from which they then traveled on to European treasuries.[8] MH

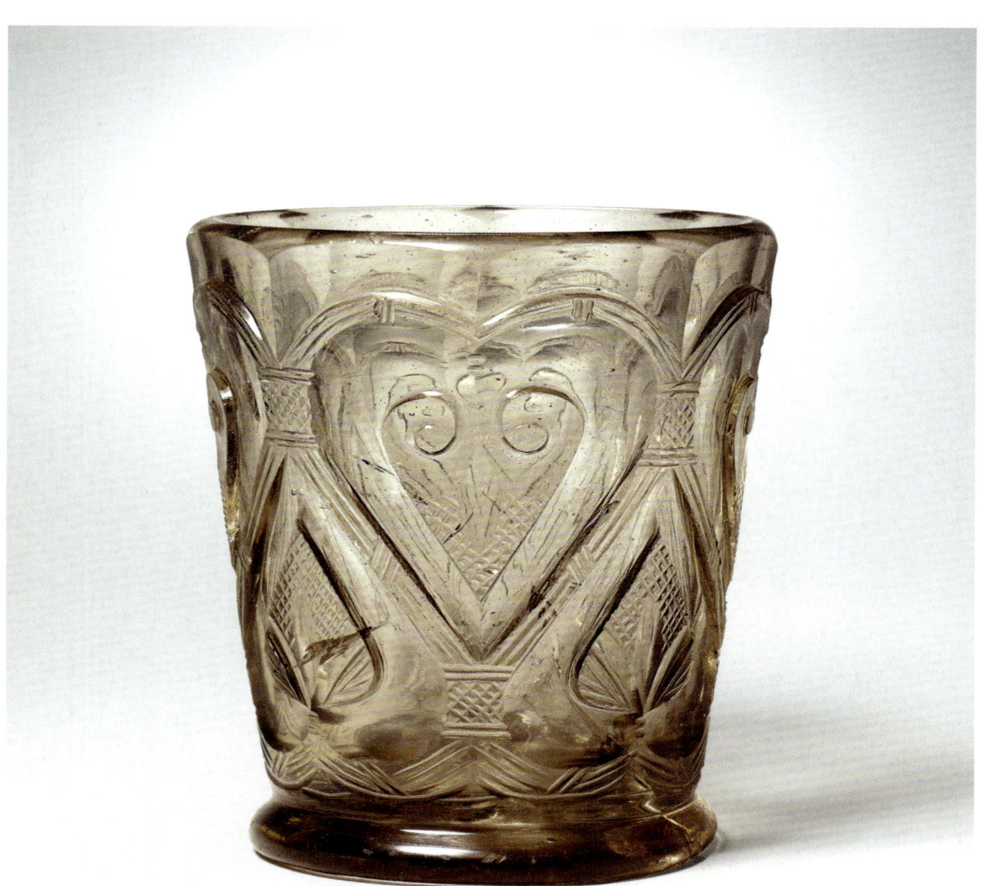

15

Selected Reference: Husband 2009.

1. Carboni, Lacerenza, and Whitehouse 2003; archaeological evidence also attests to a medieval glass factory in Tyre. See Aldsworth et al. 2002.
2. William of Tyre 1943 ed., vol. 2, p. 6.
3. Jacques de Vitry 1896 ed., pp. 92–93.
4. Benjamin of Tudela 1983 ed., p. 79.
5. See Husband 2009, pp. 60–62, for a helpful list of all extant beakers. Remnants of approximately eleven others survive.
6. Two Hedwig glasses, said to be gifts from Jacques de Vitry to the Treasury of Oignies, are in the Musée Provincial des Arts Anciens du Namurois, Namur, Belgium.
7. Wedepohl 2005.
8. See Whitehouse 2010, pp. 333–37, which includes a summary of the various scholarly stances toward their manufacture.

16

Chalice and Paten

Levant, 14th or 15th century
Glass
Chalice: H. 5¾ in. (14.6 cm), Diam. 3⅝ in. (9 cm); paten: Diam. 4⅛ in. (10.5 cm)
Lent in honor of Jasim Y. Homaizi

In the Levant from the ninth century onward, glassmaking underwent a series of profound technological changes, including modifications to the chemical composition of glass, which updated methods inherited from the Roman period and drastically changed the appearance and technical effects of the medium.[1] Scientific analysis of surviving examples is crucial in understanding the chemical makeup of the glass, which in turn can suggest the objects' date and place of production. This chalice and paten are made of sodium carbonate, calcium carbonate, and silicon dioxide, a soda-lime-silica composition, and contain significant amounts of alumina, magnesia, and potash. This chemical combination was typical of Levantine glass of the later medieval period, pointing to the pieces' manufacture in the Middle East.[2]

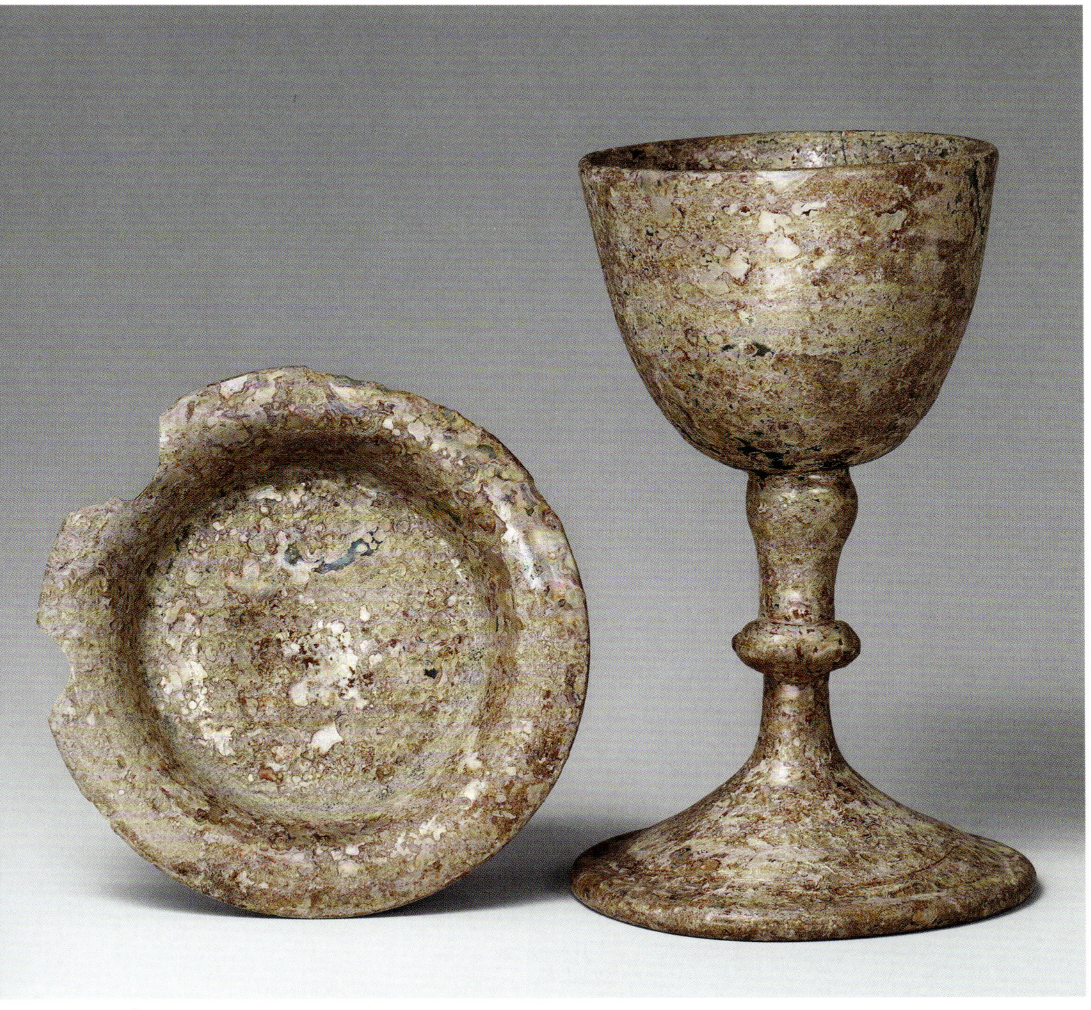

16

Glass weights, vessels for domestic uses, and equipment for mosques (such as sprinklers or lamps, as in cats. 12, 91) count among the most common surviving glassworks from the medieval Levant. By contrast, this chalice and paten are rare survivals of Christian liturgical glass vessels, a category of objects known mostly from textual sources.[3] Because they are lightweight and small, it seems likely that the chalice and paten were made for individual use rather than for church services, though it is difficult to tell precisely for whom. In addition, the shape of the chalice and paten points to Western prototypes rather than to local Christian ones, and the fact that so many glass vessels were brought back from the Holy Land to European church treasuries certainly strengthens the argument that the pieces were made for a Western patron. Their portability suggests they were intended for performing the liturgy during travel and possibly carried back from the Levant to Europe by a returning pilgrim or Crusader. EDW

1. Henderson 2002.

2. Recent chemical analyses of the glass, carried out by Mark Wypyski, Research Scientist, Department of Scientific Research, The Metropolitan Museum of Art, showed that the glass also contains alumina, magnesia, and potash, which point to production with sand and plant ash. For a useful technical glossary, see Corning Museum of Glass 2002– . I thank Christine Brennan for this information.

3. Thurston 1908.

17

The Book of Secrets of the Faithful of the Cross (Liber secretorum fidelium Crucis)

Venice, 1319–21
Written by Marino Sanudo Torsello the Elder (ca. 1270–1343)
Tempera, gold, and ink on parchment; 115 fols.
11⅞ × 9⅜ in. (30.2 × 23.7 cm)
Biblioteca Apostolica Vaticana, Vatican City (MS Vat. Lat. 2972)

In the early fourteenth century Marino Sanudo Torsello the Elder, a wealthy merchant from a prominent Venetian family, set about persuading church leaders and nobles of the feasibility of his scheme to retake the Holy Land.[1] Though many such proposals circulated at the time, his stood out for its detailed strategy derived from his knowledge of Venetian maritime prowess.[2] Sanudo's plan, written from 1300 to 1321, hinged on a complete embargo of the Mamluk sultan's lands, specifically Egypt, a lucrative international entrepôt through whose ports precious and base metals, gemstones, silks, wools, fancy foodstuffs, and slaves regularly passed. For Sanudo the most crucial commodities to restrict from the West were those required for shipbuilding: wood, iron, and pitch.

Sanudo's text reveals deep awareness of the intricacies of Levantine politics. He saw Armenia as a crucial stronghold and hoped to forge alliances with Nubian Christians and the "Tartars" (Mongols) of Persia and Chaldea. No less important than the ideas was their presentation. Sanudo specially commissioned a series of illustrated copies to distribute to influential parties. As he had established his plans within a broader discussion of history and geography, regional and world maps were frequently incorporated along with marine charts.[3]

This manuscript, presented to Pope John XXII in September 1321, is among the most elaborate of the twenty or so surviving copies. Colorfully painted and highlighted with gold leaf, it concludes with a small atlas of six maps. As meticulously conceived as the text they accompany, the illuminations use an allegorical system devised by Sanudo. The Mamluk sultan regularly appears as or with a panther, while a lion represents the "Emperor of the Tartars." Particular headgear, flags, and equipment help to differentiate among the various players. Skin color, too, sometimes serves as a marker of difference.[4]

This page illustrates two specific sections of the text.[5] The left-hand scene portrays the enmity between Mongols and Mamluks as the light-skinned Tartars, clad in helmets and armor, drive out the dark-skinned and turbaned Mamluks from a destroyed town.

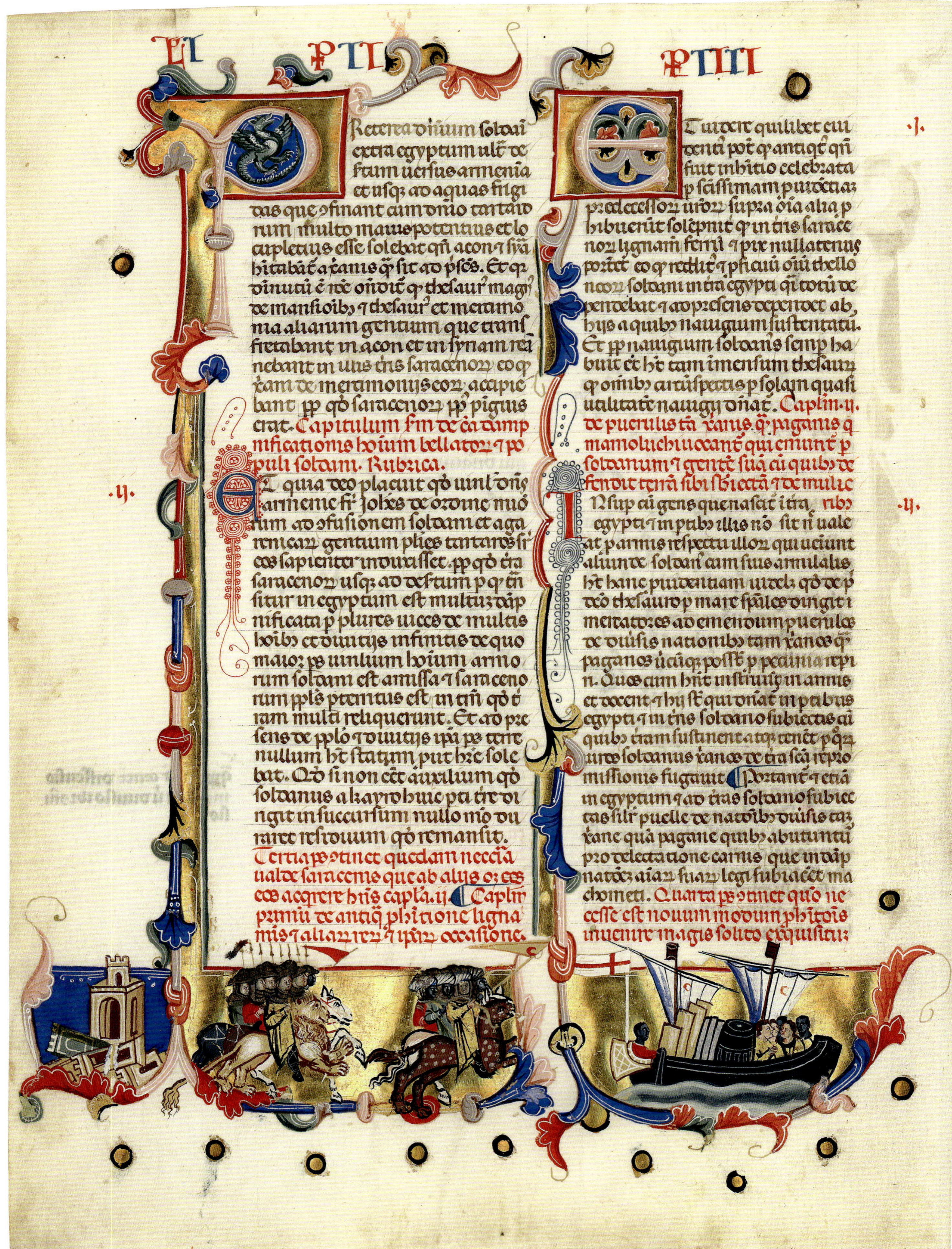

17, fol. 11v

The scene on the right captures the details of commercial exchange between European Christians and the Mamluks. A Latin cross stands behind a ship, its sails marked by Islamic crescents. The dark-skinned Mamluks pilot the boat, loaded with planks of wood, plates of iron, and a barrel of pitch, while the light-skinned passengers are human cargo intended as slaves.

As a whole, the book is emblematic of Sanudo's ambitious and comprehensive program of persuasion, which ultimately failed. The pope responded to the gift by setting up a commission to study the proposal and depositing the book safely in the papal library. MH

Selected Reference: Degenhard and Schmitt 1973, p. 22, no. 2.

1. For an English translation, see Sanudo 2011 ed.
2. Among the many works that discuss Sanudo and efforts to muster a new Crusade in this period, see Tyerman 1982; Leopold 2000; Stantchev 2014.
3. Edson 2004.
4. Not all Sanudo manuscripts depict dark-skinned figures. Even in the papal copy, skin color is not a stable indicator of identity. On other folios, Mamluks are portrayed with light skin in order to differentiate them from the "black Christians" that Sanudo mentions in the text. For a medieval depiction of Muslims from North Africa, see Blackmore 2009, pp. 2–32. For later representations, see Baltimore and Princeton 2012–13.
5. Sanudo 2011 ed., bk. 1, pt. 2, chaps. 1–2, pp. 54–55, and bk. 1, pts. 3–4, pp. 55–63, respectively.

18
Belt

Possibly Genoa, mid-14th century
Silver, with traces of enamel and gilding
L. 65⅜ in. (166 cm), W. 1⅜ in. (3.3 cm), D. ⅝ in. (1.4 cm)
The Metropolitan Museum of Art, New York, The Cloisters Collection, 2015 (2015.705)

In tales of the Holy Land, precious belts play an unexpectedly large role. Legend claims that the belt of the Virgin Mary was miraculously given to Saint Thomas at the moment of her assumption into heaven and that it was eventually passed as dowry to an Italian merchant who had wed a Jerusalem bride (figs. 9, 10). In a purely secular context, the celebrated Renaissance poet Giovanni Boccaccio (1313–1375) tells of a silver belt stolen from a virtuous Genoese woman offered for sale in the market at Acre, a scenario that seems to echo an illumination of a Genoese merchant's shop that also features carpets and vessels associated with the eastern Mediterranean (fig. 20).[1]

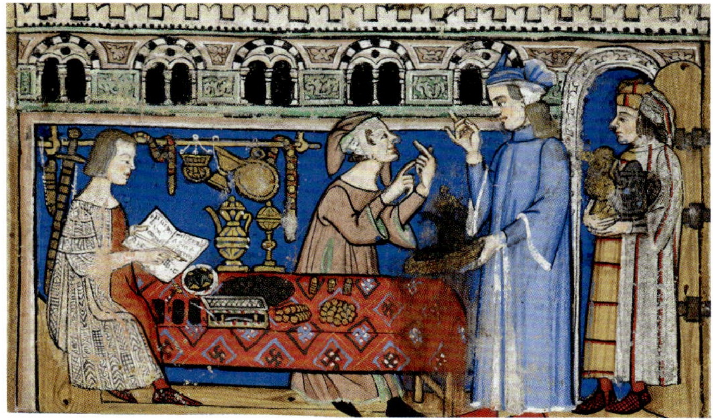

Fig. 20. Detail of a Genoa merchant's shop from a Latin prose treatise on the Seven Vices. Master of the Cocharelli Codex. Genoa, ca. 1330–ca. 1340. Tempera, gold, and ink on parchment. British Library, London (Add. MS 27695, fol. 7v)

The early history of The Cloisters belt is not known; examples of similar date and form have been found from Italy to the Crimea. Reflecting international taste animated by commerce in the Mediterranean, this one combines typically European images like that of a woman spinning with others of men with exotic costumes and bearing, inspired by the clothing of contemporary Persians, trading partners envied and admired for their luxuriant dress.

Like charms on a lady's bracelet today, these silver medallions boast of the wide world in which the owner lived, the world to which Marco Polo belonged and of which others were equally proud. Some medallions on this belt compare closely to belt elements thought to be Italian found in 1967 at Simferopol in the Crimea. That treasure includes dinars of Indian sultans struck at Delhi in the late thirteenth and first half of the fourteenth centuries, as well as objects of Mamluk manufacture.[2] BDB

1. It is told in the ninth story of the second day in Boccaccio's *Decameron*.
2. I am grateful to Nikolas Kontogiannis for bringing this treasure to my attention. See Fedorov-Davydov, ed. 2001, pp. 58–59, nos. 20–38. For the Mamluk pieces, see Jenkins 1988a; Watt 2002–3, p. 67.

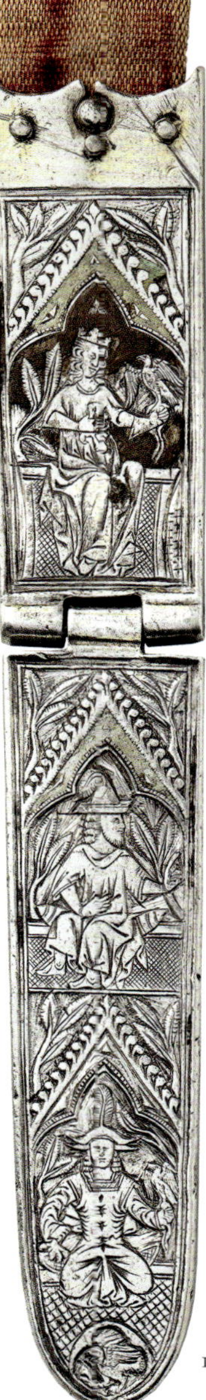

18 detail

18

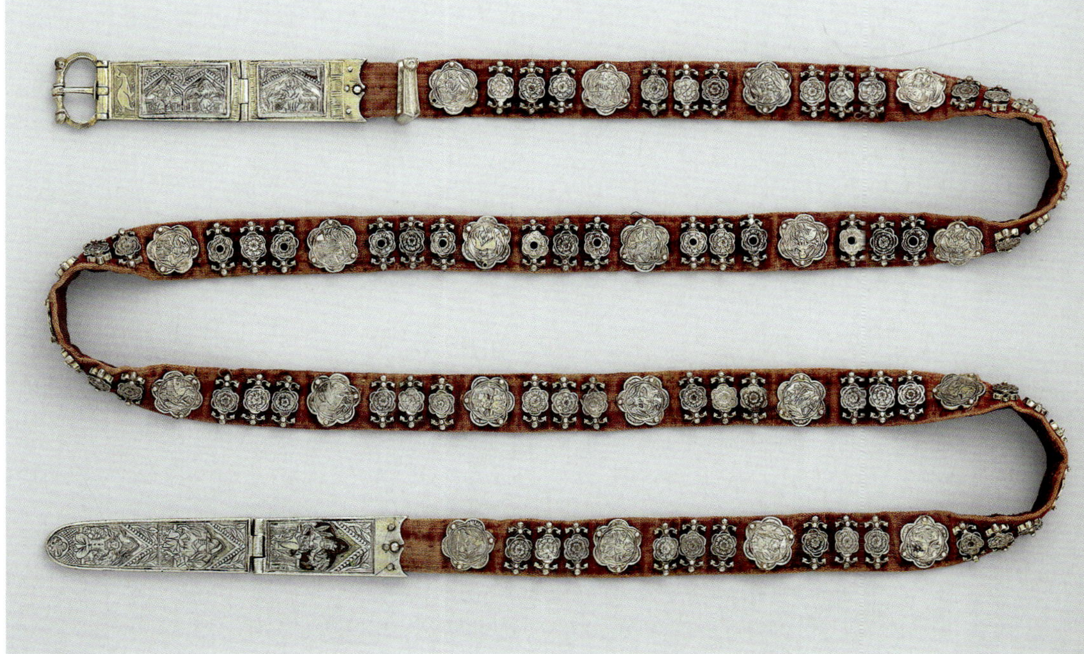

19a

Platter with Lusignan Arms

Egypt or Syria, ca. 1324–1330
Copper alloy and traces of silver, gold, and black-paste inlay
H. 3¾ in. (9.5 cm), Diam. 16⅜ in. (41.5 cm)
Musée du Louvre, Département des Arts de l'Islam, Paris (MAO 1227)

19b

Bowl with the Arms of Hugh IV of Lusignan

Egypt or Syria, 14th century
Copper alloy with silver inlay and engraving
H. 4⅜ in. (11 cm), Diam. 8⅞ in. (22.5 cm)
Courtesy of the L. A. Mayer Museum for Islamic Art, Jerusalem (M 6-68)

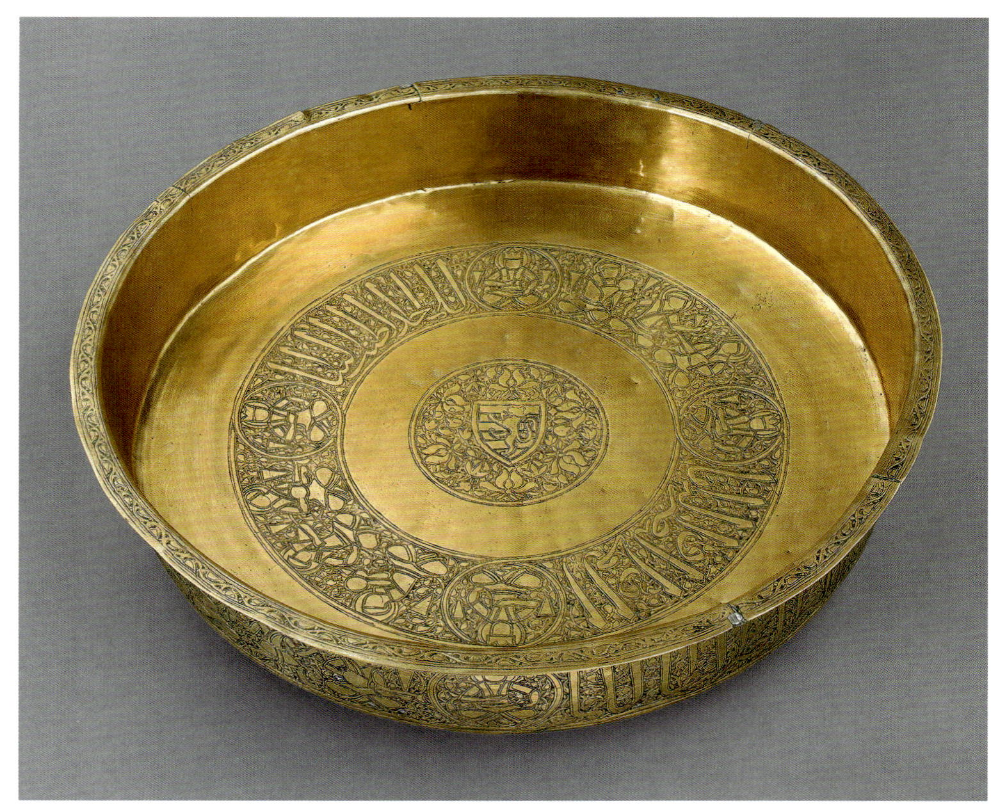

19a

19b

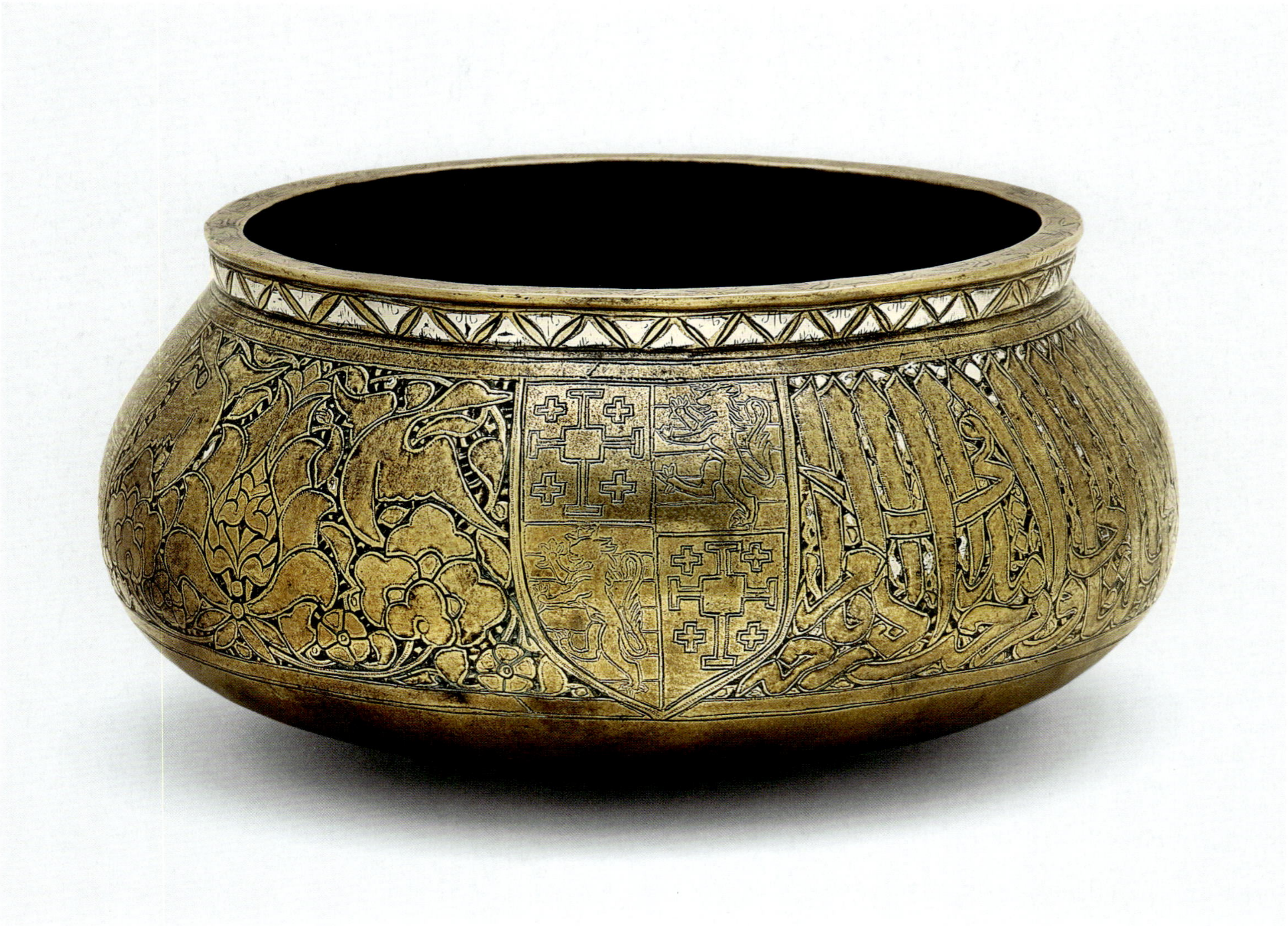

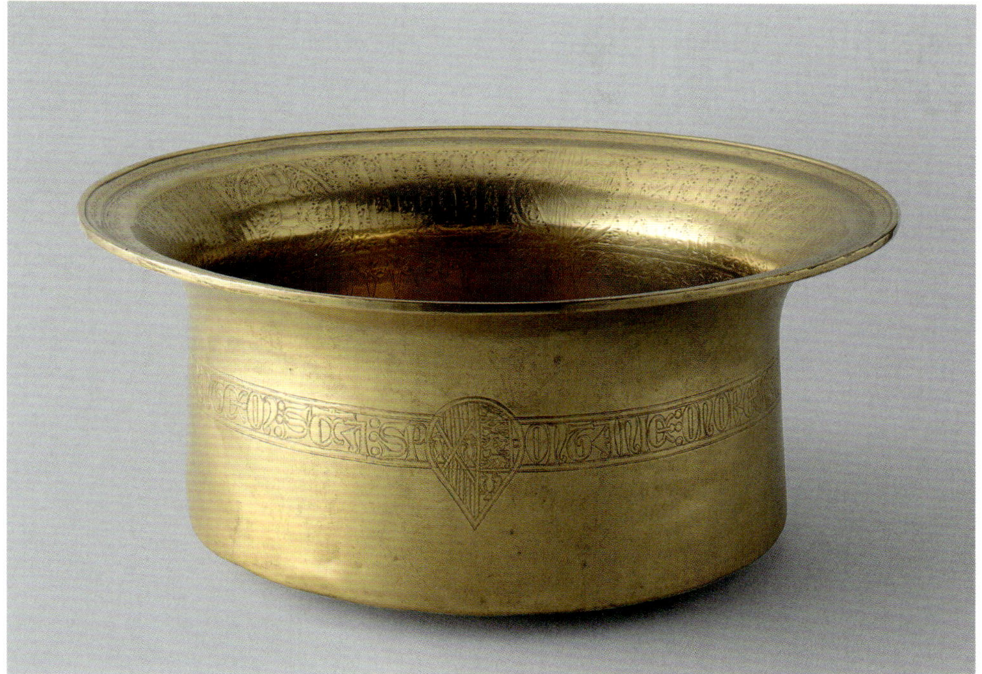

Fig. 21. Basin of Elizabeth of Carinthia. Possibly Egypt or Syria, ca. 1323–50. Brass. Rijksmuseum, Amsterdam (BK-NM-7474)

The numerous surviving pieces of Islamic metalwork in European collections open up fascinating questions of historical exchange between East and West in the Middle Ages. Most Ayyubid and Mamluk pieces name elite Muslim patrons and were made in Egypt or the Levant. However, a sizable subgroup includes vessels created for Western markets. Technical and stylistic similarities to those made for Muslims suggest that they were fabricated in the same workshops, yet European blazons, inscriptions in Latin and French, and explicit mention of Western patrons all point to a Christian clientele.[1]

Metal vessels featuring the coat of arms of the Lusignans, a powerful Crusader dynasty based in Cyprus, present a particularly enigmatic subgroup. For example, a platter housed in the Musée du Louvre (cat. 19a) bears the family's heraldic device surrounded by an Arabic inscription wishing the owner blessings and a long life.[2] A bowl in the collections of the L. A. Mayer Museum for Islamic Art (cat. 19b) also features an Arabic inscription and Lusignan arms, intersected with symbols associated with the Kingdom of Jerusalem.[3] These details suggest it was made for Hugh IV of Lusignan, who bore the title King of Cyprus from 1324 to 1358 and was the nominal King of Jerusalem until his death in 1359. At least two other surviving vessels are associated with the family, suggesting that the dynasty's rulers specifically sought luxury Mamluk metalwork. A large basin at the Louvre includes the arms of the Kingdom of Jerusalem and Arabic and French inscriptions explicitly naming Hugh IV.[4] A shallow, unfinished basin lacking silver inlay, now in private hands, features a design of seated figures and an Arabic inscription surrounding Lusignan emblems.[5]

A basin at the Rijksmuseum similarly attests to these cross-cultural exchanges. The exterior of the vessel features the coat of arms of Elizabeth of Hapsburg-Carinthia (ca. 1300–ca. 1350), wife of Peter II of Sicily, embedded in a grammatically incorrect Latin text derived from a prayer associated with Saint Agatha (fig. 21).[6] The interior contains generic Arabic blessings and epithets organized in an unusual style, interspersed with depictions of courtly figures typical of Ayyubid and early Mamluk metalwork. The Arabic formulations, the vessel's shape, and the details of manufacture make them comparable to the Lusignan pieces, raising the possibility that the objects were all manufactured in the same workshop. The prayer to Agatha, patron saint of Catania in Sicily, on an object dedicated to the island's queen, indicates the piece was a special commission.

The technical, stylistic, and epigraphic evidence on these three objects raises questions about their production and eventual arrival in Europe. It is noteworthy that several examples with European arms or inscriptions lack precious-metal inlay, a technical detail indicating that they were left unfinished. The incomplete manufacture and the atypical, at times incorrect inscriptions exclude the possibility that the objects were intended as high-level diplomatic gifts between courts. Instead, they were probably special orders, souvenirs, or curiosities commissioned in the Middle East by Europeans eager to acquire the kinds of objects owned and exchanged among Mamluk elites in the region. EDW

Selected References: Cat. 19a: d'Allemagne 1899, pp. 754–55, fig. 2; d'Allemagne and Janneau 1948, vol. 2, pls. 153, 154; Makariou et al. 2002, pp. 41–44; Makariou et al. 2012, pp. 268–70, fig. 175. Cat. 19b: Rüdt de Collenberg 1977, p. 143, pl. 41.

1. Despite the extensive discussion of Islamic metalwork in European collections and objects for trade, few articles deal specifically with objects bearing European coats of arms, Western patrons' names, or Latin or French inscriptions. For a discussion of the market, see Ward 1989, and a more recent evaluation in Ward 2007.

2. The Arabic inscription, published in Makariou et al. 2012, p. 270 n. 7, reads "power, victory, and long life to the noble, the good; praise and greatness, glory and excellence."

3. The Arabic inscription is unpublished. For an image of the interior of the piece, see Rüdt de Collenberg 1977, p. 143, pl. 41.

4. The basin in the Louvre (MAO 101) has recently been published in Makariou et al. 2012, pp. 268–70. The Louvre's platter and basin were both once part of the Henri-Réne d'Allemagne collection.

5. This piece was sold at Christie's London, on April 20, 1999, pp. 232–33, lot 516. It was also once part of the d'Allemagne collection.

6. Mols 2012. The inscription along the exterior reads "MENTEM SCA SPONTANIE ONOREM DEI PATREM LIBERACIONIS," which Jan De Hond and Luitgard Mols argue is a derivation of "Mentem sanctam spontaneam honorem Deo et patriae liberationem," an epithet associated with Saint Agatha. They translate the phrase as "she had a holy and generous soul, gave honour to God, and accomplished the liberation of her country." See De Hond and Mols 2011, pp. 25–27.

20

View of Jerusalem

From *Journey to the Holy Land (Peregrinatio in terram sanctam)*
Mainz, 1486
Written by Bernhard von Breydenbach (1440?–1497?), designed by Erhard Reuwich (ca. 1455–ca. 1490), and published by Peter Schöffer the Elder (1425–1503)
Woodcuts on paper
H. 12⅝ in. (32 cm), W. 9⅛ in. (23 cm), D. 1⅜ in. (3.5 cm)
The Metropolitan Museum of Art, New York, Rogers Fund, 1919 (19.49.3)

Commanding the center of a seven-page foldout, this bird's-eye view of Jerusalem set within the great expanse of the Holy Land provides a majestic climax to the earliest illustrated printed book that recounts a Christian pilgrimage to the region. When the German cleric and nobleman Bernhard von Breydenbach set out from Europe in 1483, he seemed already to have envisaged a book project. Wanting to take full advantage of the new technology of printing, he made the unusual decision, as noted in the preface, to take with him what he called "a skillful artist," one Erhard Reuwich of Utrecht who would illustrate Breydenbach's text. An enormous success, the book was published in six languages by 1500 (cat. 47), and Reuwich's image

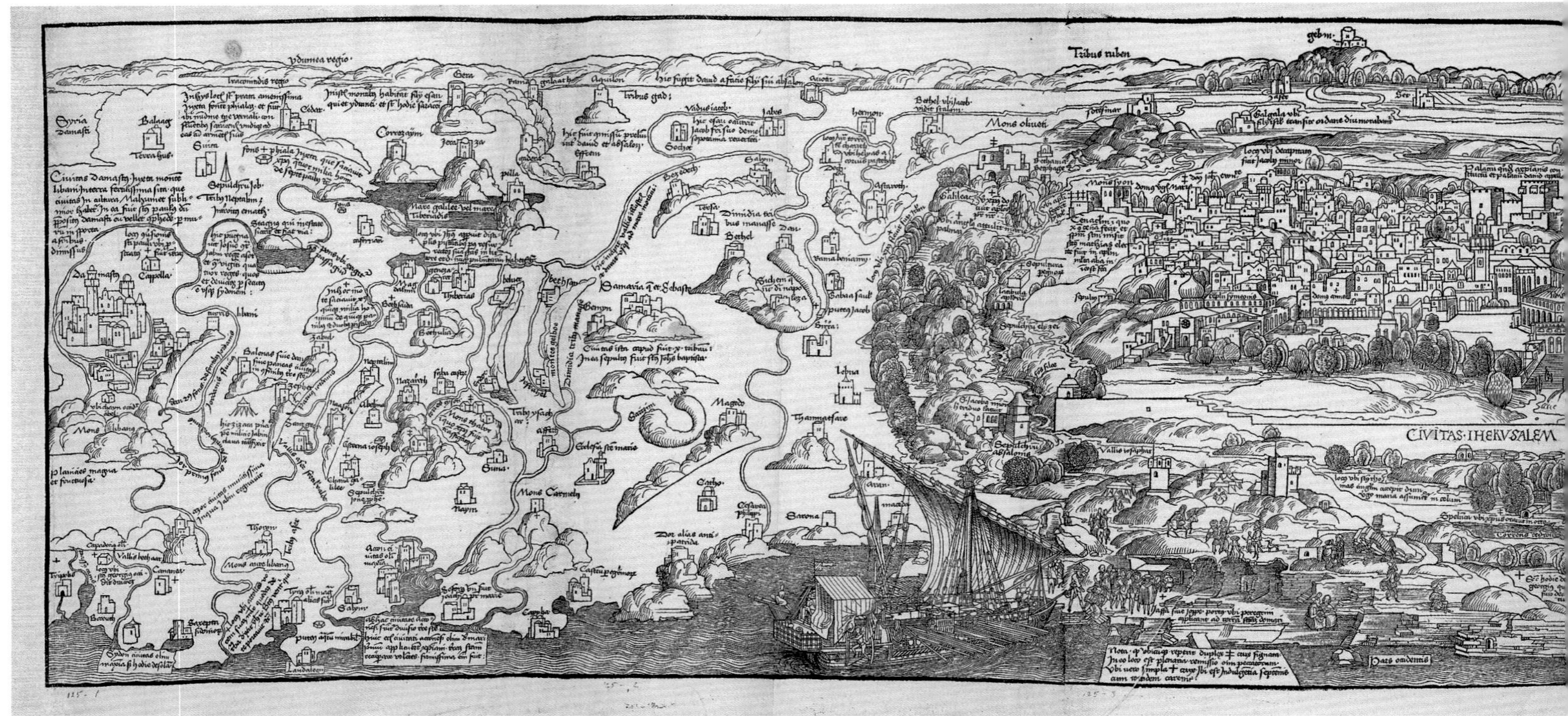

20, fol. 119r with foldout

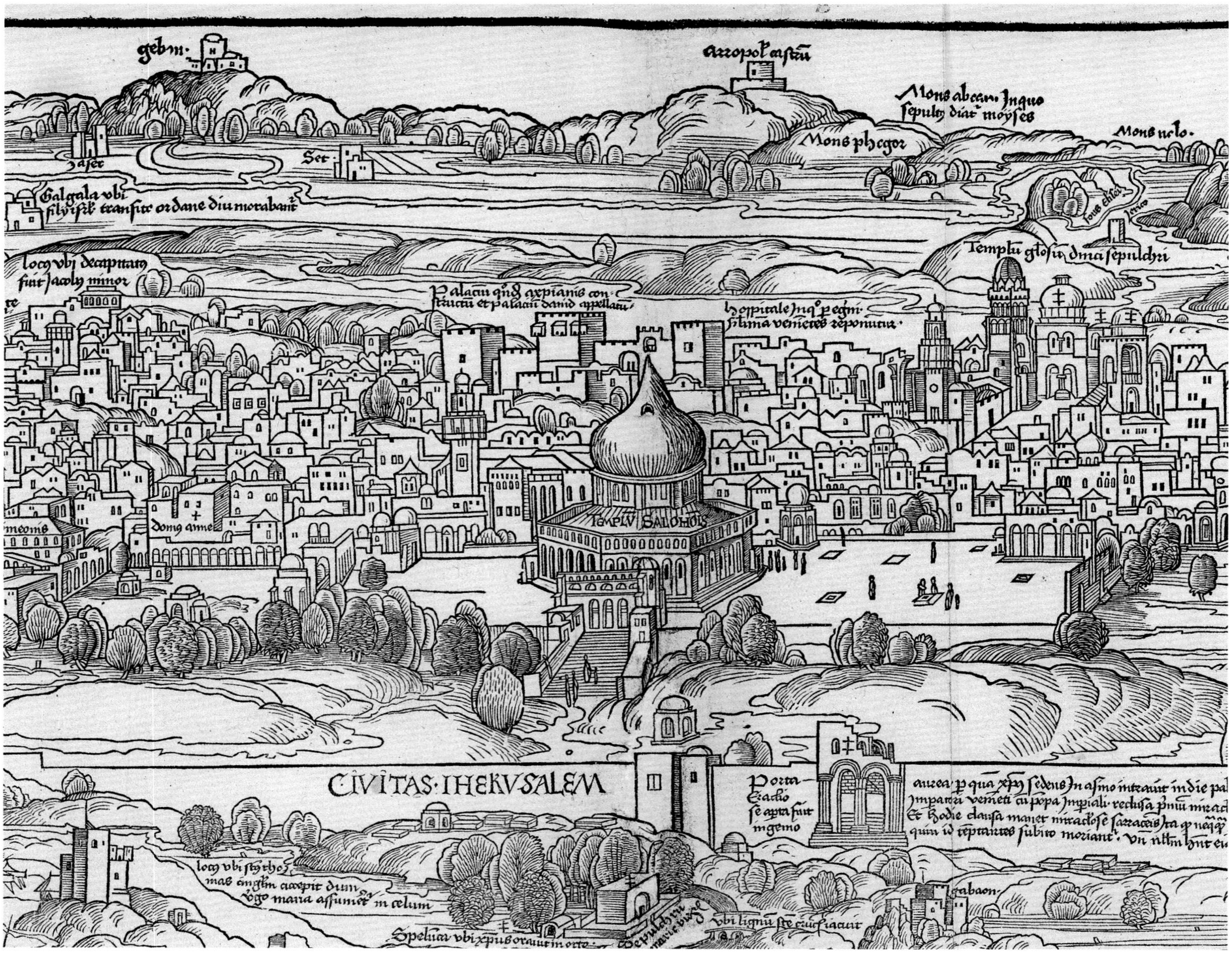

20 detail, fol. 119r

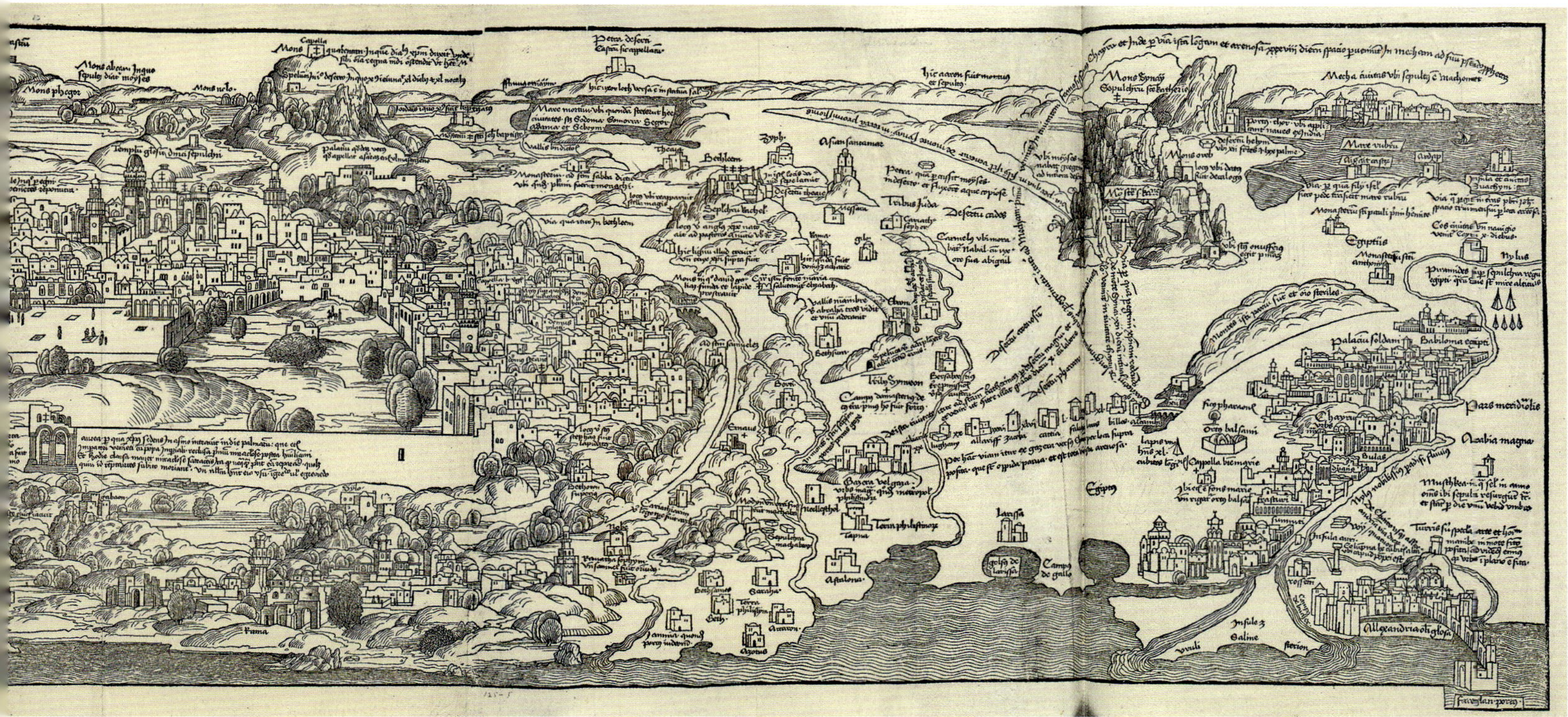

of Jerusalem established a standard for subsequent European artists who sought to capture its distinctive topography.

Jerusalem is one of five cities included to evoke the extended voyage. The book begins with Venice, its sprawling harbor spread over nine folded pages, and continues with several smaller ports along the way. Jerusalem is second to Venice in the number of illustrations but unique among the set in detail and extensive annotations. At a single glance Breydenbach's readers could take in the region's major sites, grasping their appearance, relative location, and religious significance.

Though the level of detail convinces one of its verisimilitude, the image of Jerusalem is carefully composed to provide the most advantageous Christian view of the city and its surrounds.[1] It might seem surprising to set the Dome of the Rock at the center of the composition, but it is clearly labeled "Temple of the Lord" in accordance with the long-standing view of Western Christians, thereby justifying its prominence. Other Muslim monuments are largely absent.

Like a Cubist painting, the Jerusalem image incorporates multiple perspectives into a pleasing whole. The Mediterranean Sea at the bottom positions the viewer in the east looking westward, while the city itself appears from the west facing the east. The Church of the Holy Sepulchre, the multidomed structure right of center, has been tipped up and turned around so as to give visual access to the courtyard entrance.

Text and additional pictures take the reader deeper into the Holy City, with anecdotal images of "Saracens" (Muslims), Jews, and Eastern Christians, whom the text describes in terms of their errant theology, along with two views of the Holy Sepulchre and animals thought to be native to the region. Seven alphabetic charts for the languages of each community in the city round out the account, a compelling mix of practical advice, anthropological observation, and religious polemic.

MH

Selected References: Timm 2006; Ross 2014.

1. See Ross 2014, esp. pp. 141–84.

21

Genealogy of the Patriarchs (Yihus ha-Avot)

Probably Jerusalem, 16th century
Tempera and ink on parchment
55⅛ × 4⅞ in. (140 × 12.2 cm)
The National Library of Israel, Jerusalem
(MS Heb. 8° 1187)

While the Temple stood, Jews fulfilled the commandment to travel to Jerusalem thrice yearly for the pilgrimage festivals, bringing offerings and participating in Temple services.[1] Pilgrimage continued even after the Temple's destruction in the year 70, albeit with a shift from joyous celebration to mournful longing. For centuries the locations of the holy sites were transmitted orally, until lists and travel accounts such as that of Benjamin of Tudela emerged in the twelfth century, greatly shaping Diasporic perceptions of Jerusalem.[2] An influx of European pilgrims in the thirteenth century necessitated the transcription of detailed itineraries, which later evolved into decorative commemorative scrolls like the one depicted here.[3]

Hung on a wall, the manuscript with its almost talismanic illustrations served as both a virtual pilgrimage to the Holy Land and a constant reminder of its sanctity and its Jewish communities.[4] The introductory images of Temple vessels, Zechariah's prophetic menorah, and the walled city of Jericho signify hope for the divine deliverance of both Temple and land, illustrating the sentiments with which physical pilgrimage was undertaken.[5] Depicting the Temple as the Dome of the Rock was common in European Christian art and attests to the strength with which the spiritual significance of the land permeated its contemporary monuments. Here the Aqsa Mosque, which Crusaders had dubbed the Palace of Solomon (*Mikdash Shlomo*) is labeled the "(House of) Study of Solomon" (*Midrash Shlomo*).[6] The larger dome spanning the site of the Temple is depicted to the right of the smaller one, indicating an eastern approach to the city. This is in accordance with medieval pilgrimage itineraries, which stressed the importance of the Gates of Mercy, sealed until Redemption, and the Mount of Olives, upon which the Divine Presence awaited Israel's repentance before the Temple's destruction.[7]

The Gates of Mercy are here identified with the gateway that King Solomon, builder of the First Temple, designed to promote acts of kindness (*gemilut chasadim*).[8] One wicket is labeled "Mourners," the other, "Bridegrooms." On Sabbath, Jerusalemites sat between the two in order to console the mourners entering on one side and congratulate the bridegrooms entering on the other. Medieval features of the city are highlighted as well, such as its three markets and the synagogue established by the renowned thirteenth-century Spanish scholar Nachmanides (Rabbi Moshe ben Nachman) on his immigration to the Holy Land in 1267. The holy cities of Hebron, Tiberias, and Safed are included among other stops along the illustrated pilgrimage route. EE

Selected References: Reiner 2002, p. 17; Sarfati 2002, p. 22; Sarfati, ed. 2002, no. and pls. 12 I–II.

1. The festivals are Passover, Shavuot, and Sukkot; the biblical commandment is given in Exodus 34:23.

2. For the account of Benjamin of Tudela (and those of other Jewish pilgrims throughout the centuries), see Adler, ed. 1930, pp. 38–63. For a fuller explanation of this evolution of Jewish pilgrimage documents, see Sarfati 2002.

3. Earlier Jewish pilgrimages to Jerusalem had mostly originated from within the Holy Land or from elsewhere in the Middle East. The Crusades opened up Western sea travel to the region, eventually enabling European Jews passage to the Holy Land. The right to visit Jerusalem had to be negotiated, however, and the Crusaders did not allow Jews to remain in the city overnight. Reiner 1999, p. 211. For a detailed evolution of scrolls to souvenirs, see Reiner 2002.

4. Sarfati 2002, p. 21; Reiner 2002, p. 17, proposes that when hung on the wall, these scrolls assumed the role of the *zecher l'churban*, the visual reminder of the Temple's destruction traditionally manifested in one's home.

5. Zechariah 4:1–14. The divine deliverance of Jericho is outlined in Joshua 6.

6. There seems to be no deliberate motive for the shift, which perhaps originated when a scribe or pilgrim mistook one similar-sounding and similar-looking Hebrew word for another.

7. Beside the image of the Gates of Mercy, the scroll cites Lamentations 2:9: "Her gates are sunk in the earth." For the import of the Mount of Olives, see cat. 67.

8. Tractate Soferim 19:11 in Cohen, A., ed. 1965, vol. 1, pp. 308–9; Friedlander, ed. 1916, p. 122. The Italian merchant Meshullam of Volterra also noted the same connection when he visited Jerusalem in the fifteenth century (Rabbi Meshullam ben R. Menahem of Volterra in Adler, ed. 1930, p. 191).

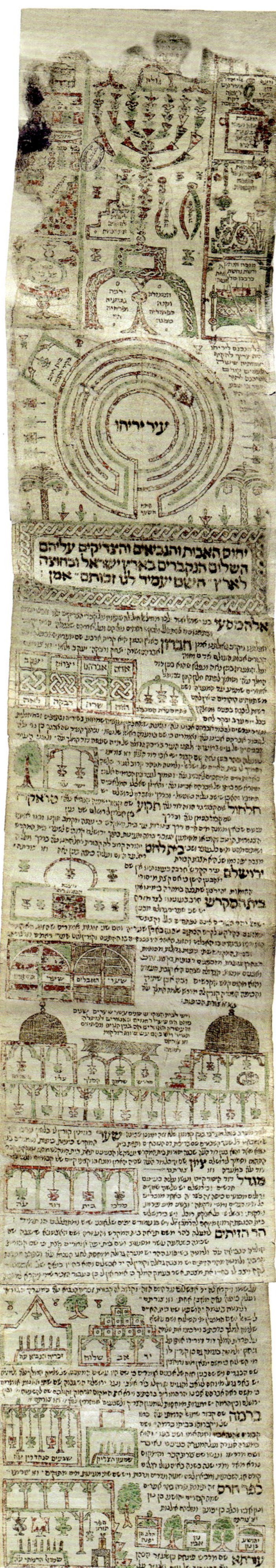

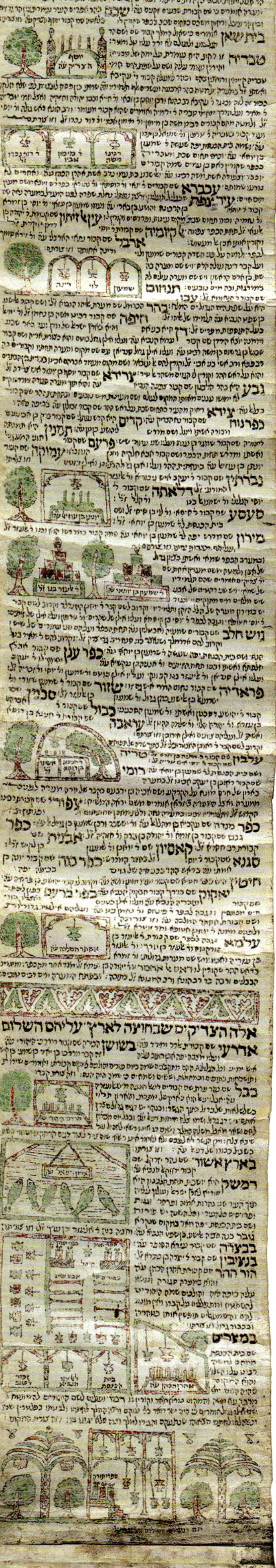

21

22

Letter from Judah ha-Levi in Toledo to Halfon ben Nathanel al-Dimyati in Spain

Toledo, 1125
Ink on paper
8⅝ × 7⅜ in. (21.9 × 18.7 cm)
The Library of The Jewish Theological Seminary, New York (ENA NS 1.5 L 41)

Judah ha-Levi rose to prominence in Toledo as an esteemed physician, community leader, scholar, and author of both secular and religious poetry.[1] The defining theme of his writing is his love for the Land of Israel and his longing for God's presence to return there. In his most heartrending poem, one of many integrated into official liturgy, the narrator cries out, "Sion! Will you not ask after the wellbeing of your captives, those who seek your peace, the remnants of your flocks?!"[2] Ha-Levi's burning desire to immigrate to the Holy Land is eloquently expressed in his famous elegy, "My heart is in the East, and I am in the uttermost West."[3]

The sentiment is reiterated in this letter, in which ha-Levi tells his friend, "I have no other wish than to go East as soon as I can," a wish he made reality in 1140.[4] The letter also refers to an early draft of his *Kuzari*, a philosophical defense of Judaism phrased as a dialogue between a rabbi and the king of the Khazars, a Turkic dynasty residing in the Caucasus. The king ultimately recognizes the religion's truth but questions risking one's life to journey to

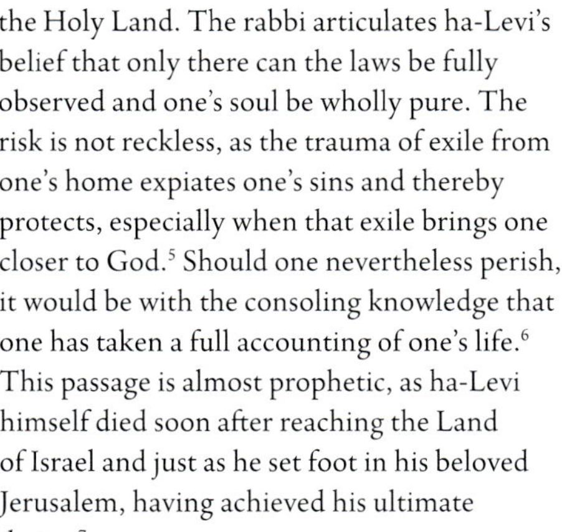

the Holy Land. The rabbi articulates ha-Levi's belief that only there can the laws be fully observed and one's soul be wholly pure. The risk is not reckless, as the trauma of exile from one's home expiates one's sins and thereby protects, especially when that exile brings one closer to God.[5] Should one nevertheless perish, it would be with the consoling knowledge that one has taken a full accounting of one's life.[6] This passage is almost prophetic, as ha-Levi himself died soon after reaching the Land of Israel and just as he set foot in his beloved Jerusalem, having achieved his ultimate desire.[7] EE

Selected References: Goitein 1967–93, vol. 5, pp. 456, 464–65; New York 2000–2001, p. 85, no. 36.

1. Ha-Levi was held in such high regard by the Muslim aristocrats of Toledo that he could only see his other patients on Fridays, when the Muslims were otherwise engaged in their day of public worship (Goitein 1967–93, vol. 5, p. 456). As a community leader, he was involved in fund-raising for the ransoming of Jews taken captive by Crusaders (ibid., vol. 5, pp. 453, 462).
2. Scheindlin 2008, pp. 172–73, poem 16, with slight revisions to the translation by the author. The poem was integrated into the official liturgy of Tisha b'Av, the day of mourning for the destruction of the Holy Temple, as early as the writing of the 1272 Worms Mahzor (cat. 58). Brodt 2011a, p. 755.
3. Scheindlin 2008, pp. 168–69, poem 15, with slight revisions to the translation by the author.
4. He continued, "if I am so enabled by [divine] decision." Goitein 1967–93, vol. 5, p. 465.
5. On exile atoning for one's sins, see Babylonian Talmud, Tractate Sanhedrin 37b; for English, Schottenstein Talmud 1990–2005, Tractate Sanhedrin (1993), p. 37b.
6. Ha-Levi 1964 ed., p. 293.
7. On ha-Levi's arrival in the Holy Land and the circumstances of his death, see Brodt 2011a; for English, Brodt 2011b.

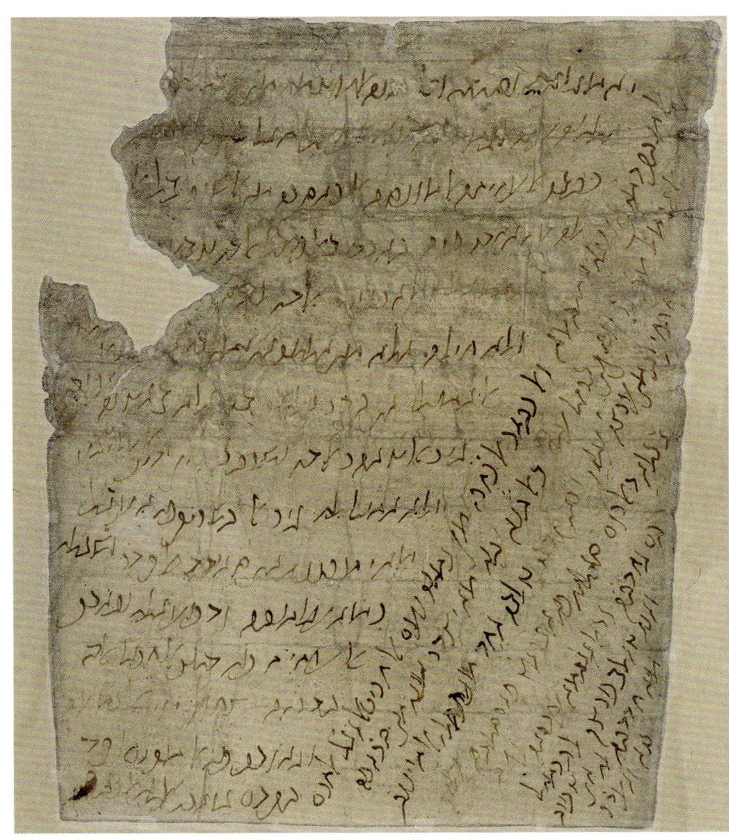

22

23

'Umra Certificate

Iraq, probably Najaf, A.H. 21 Muharram 837 (September 6, 1433)
Ink, opaque watercolors, and gilded paint on paper
262¼ × 13⅜ in. (666 × 34 cm)
Museum of Islamic Art, Doha (MS 267.1998)

Acquired in Mecca at the end of the voyage or elsewhere along the way, a pilgrimage certificate served as the personal and official record that a person had fulfilled the journey. Usually presented on scrolls, the easiest format for transport, these legal documents are arranged vertically, and the illustrations within generally follow traditional depictions of sacred geography, with representations of the sites visited, starting with Mecca and different holy places of the hajj (undertaken during the final month of the Islamic calendar) or *'umra* (undertaken at any other time of year), followed by Medina, Jerusalem, and sometimes the shrines of Iraq. They would often include at the bottom the type of pilgrimage (hajj or *'umra*) along with the names of the person who had performed it and of witnesses.

Gradually over time, the representations and calligraphic texts became standardized, as evinced by surviving examples. According to the limited research conducted thus far, *'umra* certificates were more often created than ones for the hajj.[1] While the final use of these documents is uncertain, it is possible that they were hung in such places as a mosque or the pilgrim's house to demonstrate his newly elevated social status.[2]

This certificate was made in Iraq, probably in Najaf, on A.H. 21 Muharram 837 (September 6, 1433) for a pilgrim named Sayyid Yusuf bin Sayyid Shihab al-Din Mawara al-Nahri, who undertook the *'umra*. The document features the most important Islamic sites including the Ka'ba, Masjid al-Haram, and the *mas'a* path that pilgrims run between the Safa and Marwa hills, all in Mecca; the Prophet's mosque with its minbar (pulpit) along with the mihrab and the tombs of Abu Bakr and 'Umar in Medina; the Dome of the Rock with the Aqsa Mosque in Jerusalem; the Cave of the Patriarchs in Hebron; the shrine to 'Ali in Najaf; and the Tomb of Husayn in Karbala. Also included is an image of the Prophet's sandal.

Combining Persian inscriptions and iconography found throughout tradition and scripture — and in some places in quite curious ways — the representation of Jerusalem contains two green domed arches in the center, one symbolizing the Aqsa Mosque and the other, the Dome of the Rock.[3] The two arches are composed of a rectangle decorated with suspended lamps and a minaret at each corner.[4]

The Aqsa Mosque includes a minbar and a domed structure designated as the Station of Abraham (*maqam Ibrahim*), which, according to tradition, is located in Mecca. Two doors lead to the mosque and bear similar names to those of the Meccan sanctuary: Ali's Gate (Bab 'Ali) and Peace Gate (Bab al-Salam). To the right of the image of the Dome of the Rock, the name of the site is inscribed in Persian, and its minarets are noted as well.[5] Beneath is a red circle with an inscription that could be read as *Separ-e Hamza*, a reference to the shield of the Prophet Muhammad's uncle.[6] Farther to the right of the circle are a green structure, a black knife that recalls the story of Abraham's sacrifice, and a colored staff that evokes Moses by inscription.[7] Moses's staff never seems to have been identified with Jerusalem, but several biblical episodes associate it with a sacred stone, one as sacred as the Dome of the Rock. An inscription underneath commemorates the footprint of the Prophet Muhammad during his heavenly ascent, the *mi'raj*.[8] To the left of the inscription is a structure that symbolizes the Church of the Holy Sepulchre, and a circular shape to the right of the Dome of the Rock is named Adam's cave; biblical tradition locates his grave in Jerusalem.[9] Probably referring to the Jahanam Valley west of the city, a door, Jahanam Gate (Bab Jahanam), provides access to the Dome of the Rock. MCA

1. Roxburgh 2008, p. 769.
2. Certificates were still issued into the mid-twentieth century, by which time they had become simple printed documents in which pilgrims could fill in their names and the date they had performed the pilgrimage.
3. This mixed iconography is not a curious conflation of tradition but rather a reflection of religious diversity. For example, one tradition locates the footprint of Abraham on the Dome of the Rock, while others locate it in Mecca.
4. The minarets are marked *manar masjid aqsa* (minaret of the Aqsa Mosque).
5. The Dome of the Rock is marked *gonbad sakhra* and the minarets *manar qubba sakhra* (minaret of the Dome of the Rock).
6. The shield was supposedly part of the relics of the Dome of the Rock but is no longer part of the sanctuary.
7. Inscribed in Persian are the knife *kard-e Isma'il* (Isma'il's knife) and the staff *'asa-ye Musa* (staff of Moses).
8. The inscription reads . . . *sakhra va . . . qadam hazret Mustafa 'alayhi al-salam* (. . . rock . . . foot of his holiness Mustafa, peace be upon him).
9. The Holy Sepulchre is marked . . . *'Îsâ 'alayhi al-salâm* (Jesus peace be upon him), while the red circle contains the text *taghâr-e Adam* (Adam's cave).

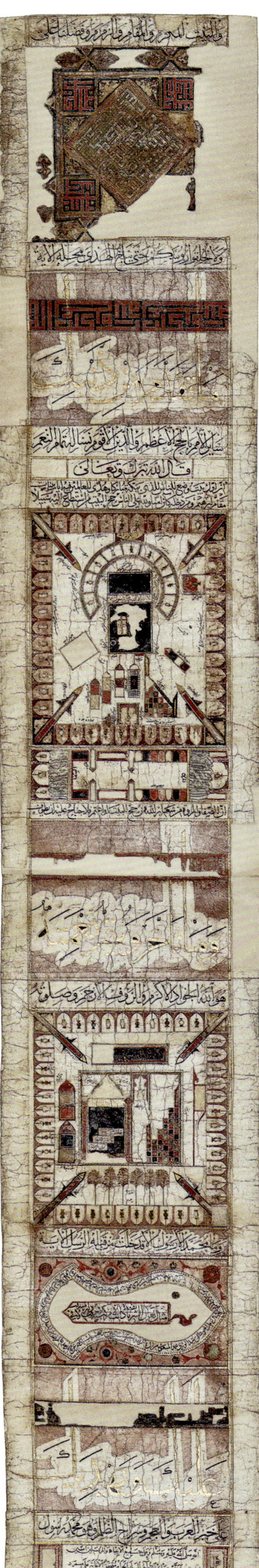

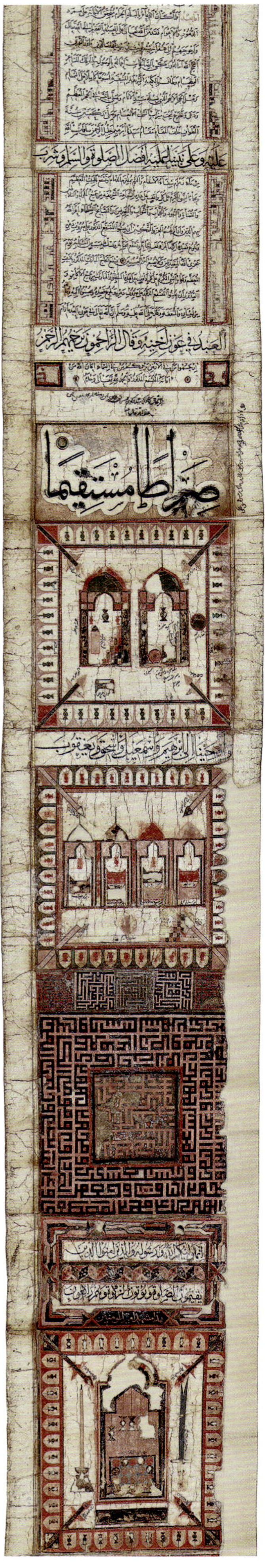

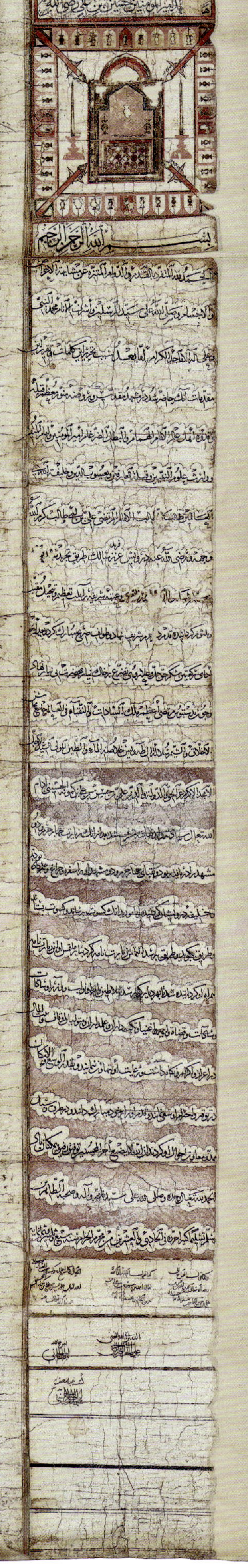

23

24a–c

Enameled Glass from the Holy Land

a. Beaker

Syria, ca. 1260
Glass, gold, and enamel
H. 7⅜ in. (18.5 cm), Diam. 4¾ in. (12.1 cm)
Walters Art Museum, Baltimore (47.17)

b. Beaker

Syria, ca. 1260
Glass, gold, and enamel
H. 6¾ in. (17 cm), Diam. 4⅜ in. (11.1 cm)
Walters Art Museum, Baltimore (47.18)

c. Bottle with Christian Scenes

Syria, Ayyubid period, mid-13th century
Glass, gold, and enamel
H. 11⅛ in. (28.2 cm), Diam. 7 in. (17.8 cm)
Furusiyya Art Foundation (R-3012)

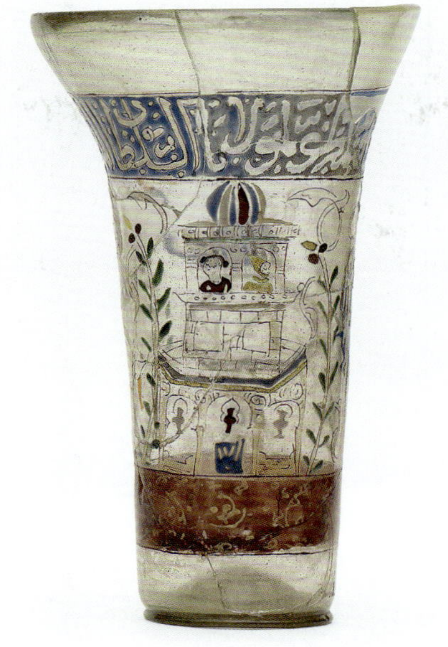

24a

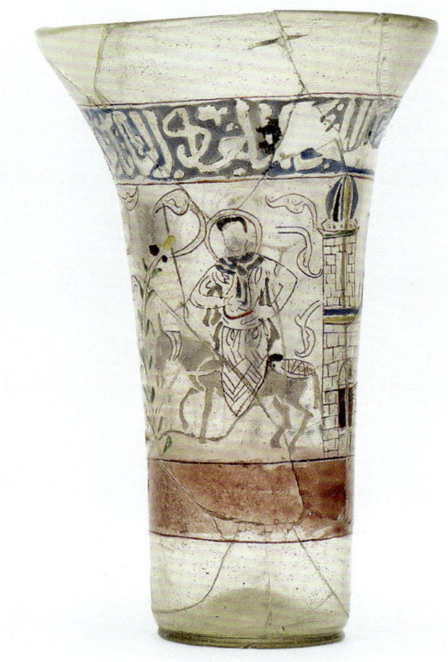

24b

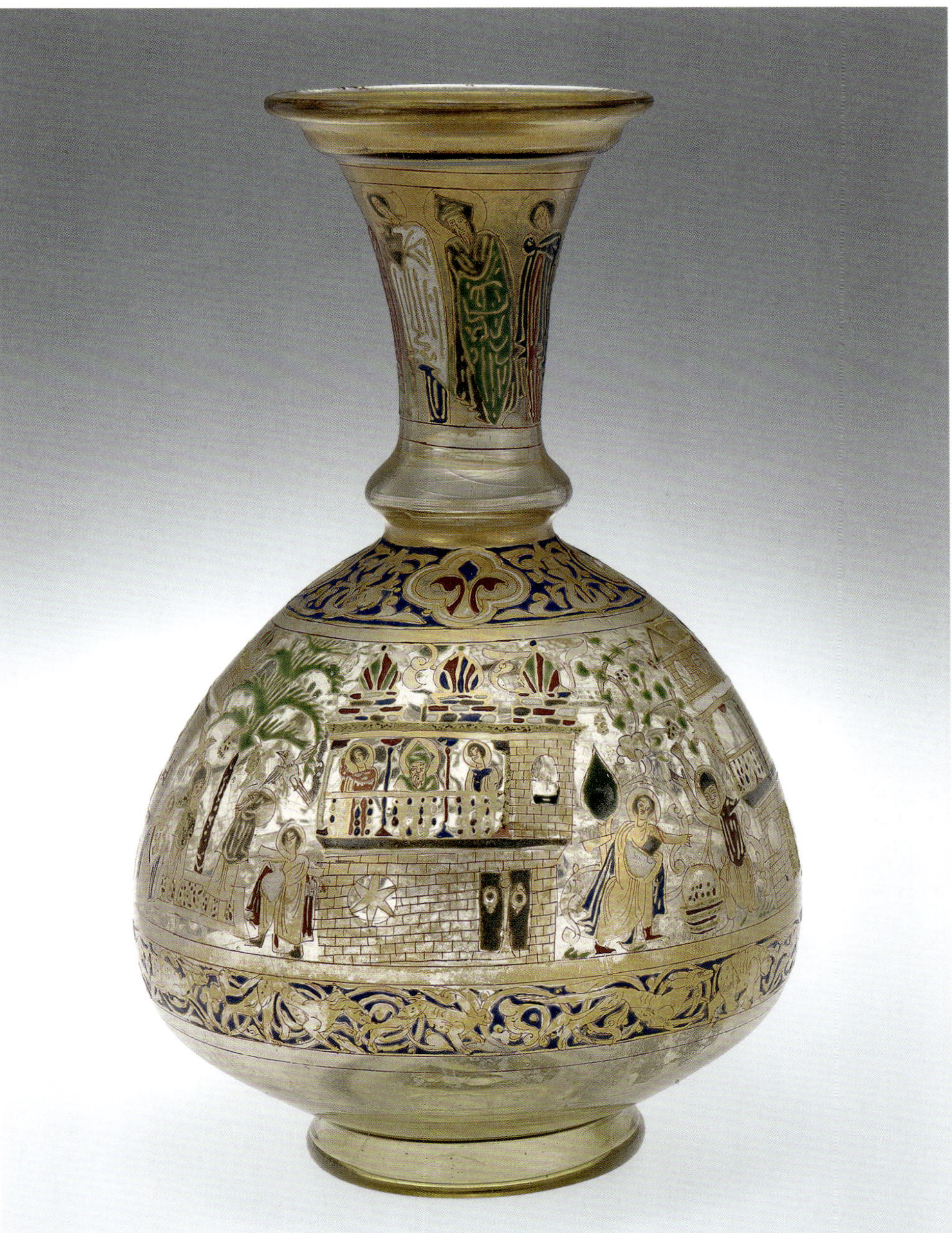

24c

Despite the abundance of surviving medieval enameled-glass objects, many of which were exported to the West around the time of their production, mainly between the thirteenth and the fifteenth centuries, very few medieval records on trade goods from the East list this type of luxury artifact. This silence is quite remarkable, yet the collection inventories of European royal families and noblemen do include them.[1] The terms recorded — *l'ouvrage de damas*, *à la façon de damas*, *vetro domaschino*, and *vetro da Domascho* — all associate this type of glass, sometimes defined as *smalto* (enameled), with Damascus.[2]

The richness of these items — conical beakers, bottles with long necks, bowls, basins, flat dishes, mosque lamps with globular bodies and flaring necks, and goblets, all decorated with floral and geometric patterns, figural scenes and, in many cases, Arabic inscriptions and blazons — in shape, decor, and especially bright and lucid colors made them desirable objects of extravagance. They were usually made of a fine, transparent free-blown glass and decorated with translucent glazed colors of fresh green, citrus yellow, subtle brick-red, indigo blue, and gold. The overall decoration is outlined by thin, red contours and then painted with accurate brushstrokes of intense color, a combination of both precision and aesthetic freedom that indicates a professional artistic hand.

Several figures on these objects suggest that the major decorative themes were mainly focused on royal leisure activities, like banquets and hunting (cat. 24b). However, a relatively large group has engaged the attention of scholars because its decor displays pilgrims' activities at holy sites.[3] The two beakers from Baltimore (cats. 24a, b), a globular bottle from the Furusiyya Art Foundation (cat. 24c), the small bottle from Paris (fig. 22), and

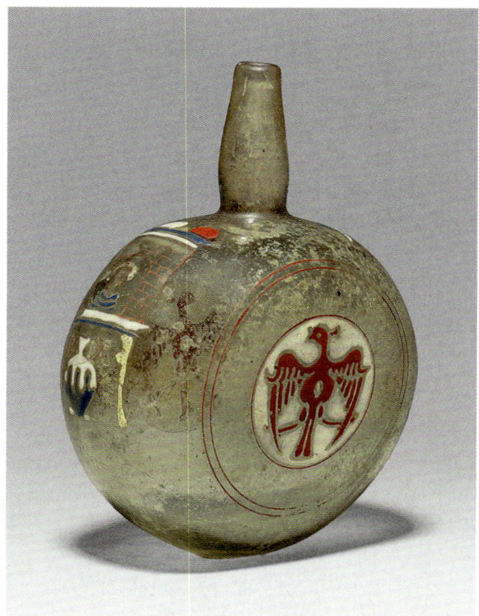

Fig. 22. Vial with an eagle crest. Egypt or Syria(?), ca. 1250. Blown glass, enamel, and gold. Musée du Louvre, Paris (OA7244)

several fragments of enameled glass objects demonstrate the new tendency of illustrating narrative scenes that usually include monks (Franciscan?) and other travelers shown within local architecture. This trend most probably started with the emergence of illustrated manuscripts of rhymed prose around 1200 in Syria – for example, the popular illustrated *Assemblies* (*Maqamat*) of al-Hariri.[4] In addition, the motif of a hanging lamp or a vessel such as a large amphora is seen within these architectural composites: these vessels frequently appear as if they were dripping their sacred contents (fig. 22).[5] This detail might relate to the specific accounts of the miraculous overflowing oil in holy shrines that visitors collected as blessings, especially that gathered at the Church of the Holy Sepulchre during the Miracle of the Holy Fire.[6] Other depictions, meanwhile, of horsemen, banquet scenes, and wild fantastic animals on the surfaces strongly recall the delicate twelfth- and thirteenth-century Mina'i decoration and luster painting on Central Asian ceramics of the same period. Despite the dissimilar technique – Mina'i and luster painting both involve the application of enamel and gold paint usually on the white ground of a ceramic – their commonalities might allude to a parallel artistic desire for a dazzling decorative effect.[7] The accuracy of the floral and geometric patterns and especially the prodigious use of gold also suggest a powerful aesthetic link to silver-inlaid Mamluk metalwork.[8] In terms of function, small enameled containers, similar in size and shape to the so-called pilgrims' bottles, were likely used to transport sanctified substances or holy relics; the enameled pilgrims' bottles from the Cathedral of Saint Stephen in Vienna, which are said to contain soil from Bethlehem stained with the blood of the Holy Innocents, are famous examples (fig. 23).

Who were the individuals who took the trouble of bringing these fragile objects to the West and what did they contain? According to pilgrims' accounts, high-ranking clergy and aristocrats acquired and owned these objects. Unlike other travelers' mementoes, which were usually made from sturdy, inexpensive materials designed for travel, these objects were expensive and fragile. For example, as early as the eighth century, Saint Willibald of Bavaria, who traveled to the Holy Land between 724 and 730, secured a flagon of balsam by using a hollow cane cut to the size of the object.[9] Other materials, such as woven cases of wicker, cane, and raffia and even pieces of cotton, were likely used for packing glass vessels.[10] In addition, several extant leather cases (fig. 24), all datable to the High Middle Ages and classified as European based on their manufacturing technique, were apparently used to protect the artifacts.

In any case, the fragility and preciousness of these enameled artifacts, whether made to contain blessings or simply exported as luxury glassware, probably contributed to their amulet-like virtues, thought to ensure health and long life as long as they remained intact.

AS

Selected References: Cats. 24a, b: Carswell 1998. Cat. 24c: Corning, New York, and Athens 2001–2, pp. 242–45, no. 121; Seville and Dallas 2013–14, p. 130, fig. 86.

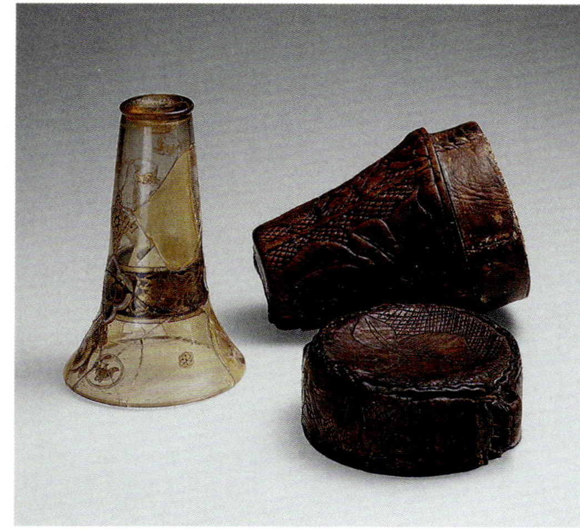

Fig. 24. Glass beaker from the Aleppo Group (Syria, mid-13th century), with a leather case (Germany, 14th–15th century). Museum für Angewandte Kunst, Cologne

1. Rogers 1998; Spallanzani 2012. See also the sources on glass listed in Lamm 1929–30, vol. 2, pp. 483–521.
2. For more about their possible manufacturing centers, see Carboni 2001–2. See also Lamm 1929–30, vol. 2, pp. 483–521; Kenesson 1998; Gibson 2005.
3. For the Paris bottle, see Munich 1910, pl. 168; Lamm 1929–30, vol. 1, p. 327, vol. 2, pl. 126, no. 16. For the enameled-glass fragments, see Lamm 1929–30, vol. 2, pl. 122. For the new narrative scenes, see Carswell 1998, pp. 61–63; Moore 2010; see also Avinoam Shalem, "Terra Miracula," pp. 23–25, in this volume.
4. See mainly, Hoffman, E., 2000; see also Hoffman, E., 1982; Grabar, O., 1970; Grabar, O., 1984; Guthrie 1994; O'Kane 2012; George 2012; Roxburgh 2013.
5. Lamm 1929–30, vol. 2, pl. 122, esp. nos. 21–28.
6. Lidov 2014, pp. 241–49.
7. Watson 1998.
8. Ward 1998.
9. Cited in Wilkinson 1977, p. 132.
10. Shalem 1998.

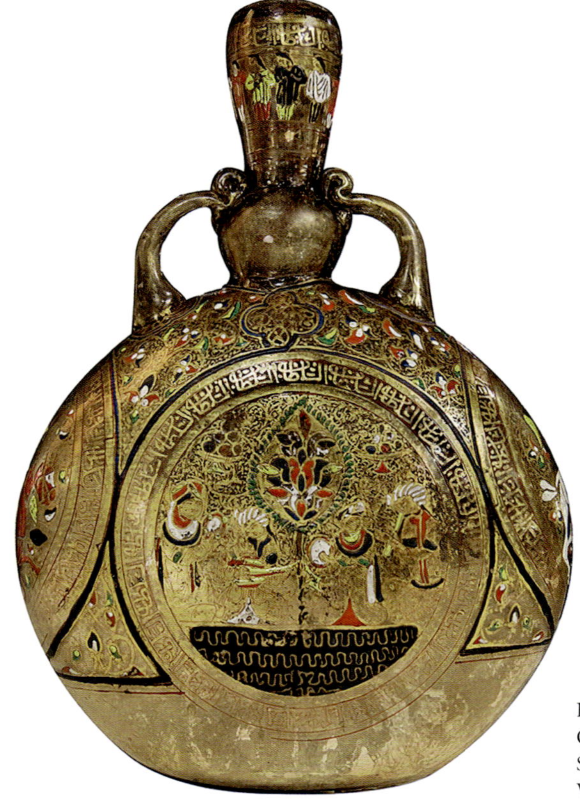

Fig. 23. Pilgrim's flask with Arabic inscription and Christian relics from the Holy Land. Probably Syria, 1275. Glass, enamel, and gold. Dom Museum, Vienna (L-6)

25a–f

The Cross of Jerusalem

a. Phylactery with the Finding of the Cross

Meuse Valley (present-day Belgium), 1160
Gilded copper, émail brun, champlevé enamel, gems, rock crystal, and wood
H. 8⅞ in. (22.5 cm), W. 8¾ in. (22 cm), D. 1¼ in. (3 cm)
Private collection, United Kingdom

b. Reliquary Cross of La Roche Foulques

Western France, ca. 1000/ca. 1180
Gold, semiprecious stones, antique intaglios, and wood
H. 11¼ in. (28.4 cm), W. 6⅞ in. (17.2 cm), D. 1¼ in. (3 cm)
Musées d'Angers (MAGF 1816)

c. Reliquary Cross

Latin Kingdom of Jerusalem, 12th century
Gold and wood
H. 4⅛ in. (10.5 cm), W. 2⅛ in. (5.3 cm), D. ⅝ in. (1.5 cm)
Cleveland Museum of Art, Purchase from the J.H. Wade Fund (1983.208)

d. Reliquary Cross

Limoges, probably Abbey of Grandmont, France, ca. 1180
Gilded silver, rock crystal, glass, and wood
H. 11¾ in. (29.8 cm), W. 5 in. (12.5 cm), D. 1 in. (2.5 cm)
The Metropolitan Museum of Art, New York, Purchase, Michel David-Weill Gift, The Cloisters Collection, and Mme. Robert Gras Gift, in memory of Dr. Robert Gras, 2002 (2002.18)

e. Reliquary of the Cross

Limoges, France, 1178–98
Gilded copper and champlevé enamel
H. 5⅛ in. (12.9 cm), W. 11½ in. (29.2 cm), D. 5½ in. (14 cm)
Basilique Saint-Sernin, Toulouse

f. Reliquary of the Cross

Rhine or Meuse Valleys, ca. 1214
Silver, gilded silver, niello, semiprecious stones, and walnut
H. 17⅜ in. (44 cm), W. 12¼ in. (31 cm), D. 1⅞ in. (4.7 cm)
Cleveland Museum of Art, Purchase from the J.H. Wade Fund (1952.89)

You who ask about the Cross: Read!
— Inscription, cat. 25f

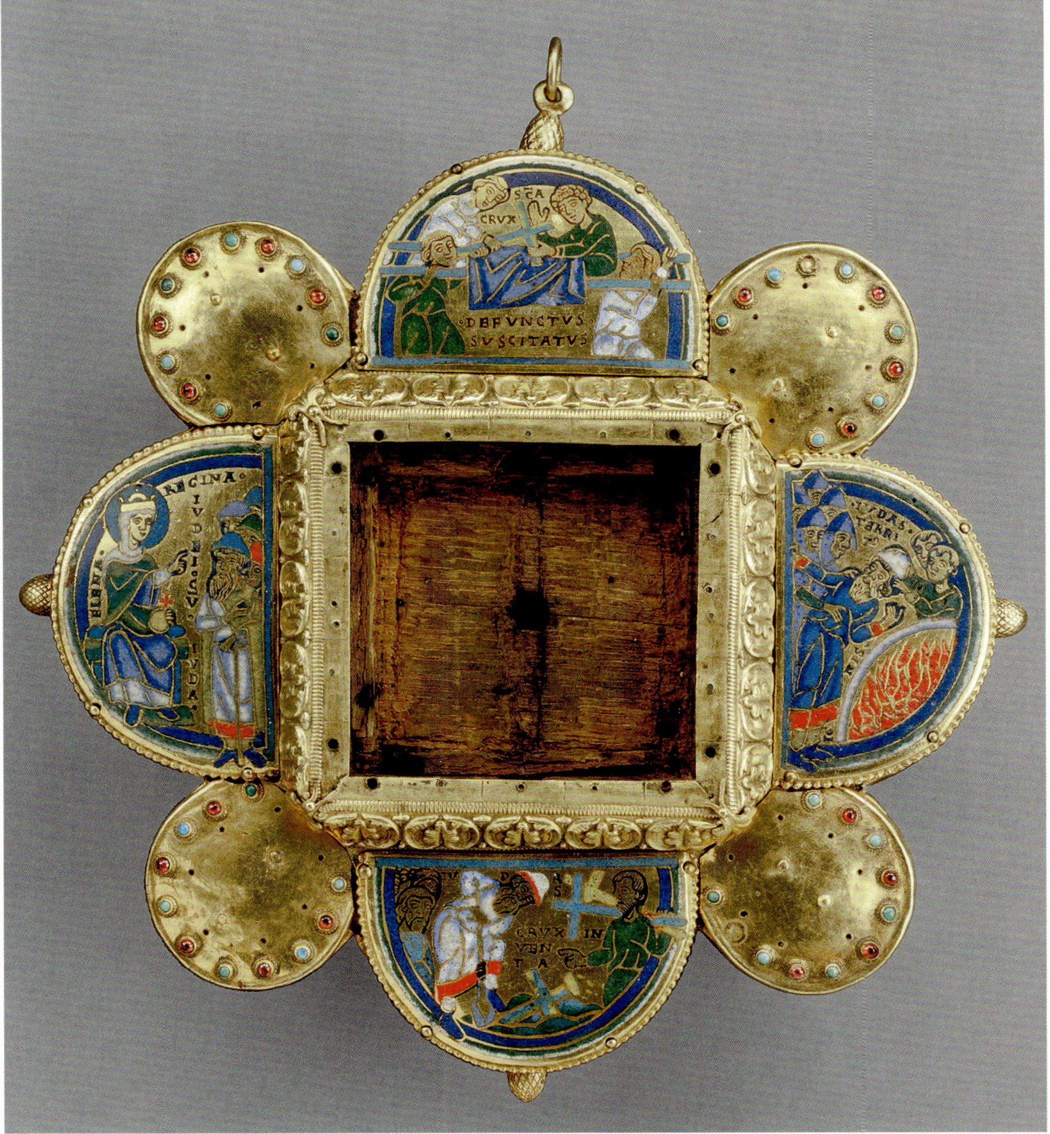

25a

Numerous chronicles tell how reliquaries of the Cross from Jerusalem were prized, featured in the liturgy, and deployed in battle in the Holy Land, but not a single example from the eleventh to fourteenth century can be seen by visitors to Jerusalem today. Instead, they are found in European churches and museums.[1] The works of art gathered here offer compelling stories of devotion and even intrigue.

The phylactery (cat. 25a), intended to be suspended over an altar or worn around a priest's neck, seems to anticipate nagging questions of the authenticity of the relic by offering a step-by-step account of the discovery of the Cross. At left, Empress Helena, mother of Constantine the Great (ca. 273–337), who legendarily took on the search as a personal mission, confers with Judas Cyriacus and other Jewish authorities in Jerusalem. Opposite, Helena's soldiers threaten the Jews with fire for withholding information about the location of the Cross. At the bottom, Judas, coerced, digs up three crosses, one hoped to be that of Jesus, the others of the two thieves who died at his side. At the top, Jesus's Cross is positively identified, as it is used to resurrect a dead man. The authenticity of the relics (principally bits of wood still present in the nineteenth century) is the vitally important theme here, one that appears on other religious objects as well: the artist of the Stavelot Triptych presents the same account of the Cross's discovery (cat. 110).

From its first publication in 1878, the phylactery has been linked to Saint-Pierre de Lobbes, an abbey of Benedictine monks in present-day Belgium. Since the tenth century, the church at Lobbes had a Chapel of the Cross,

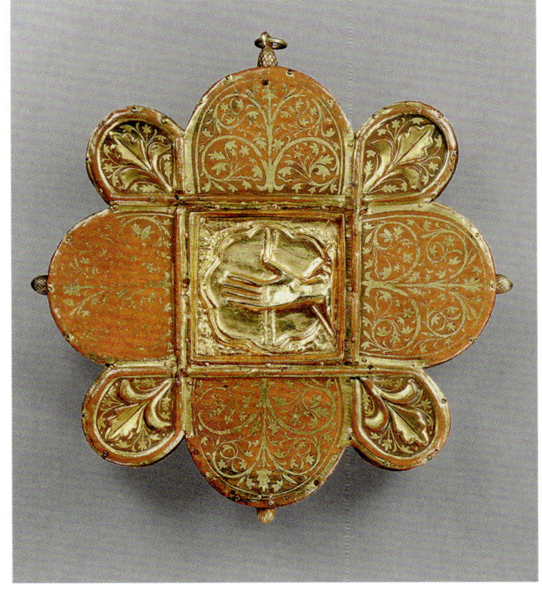
25a back view

and thus likely a relic. The abbey's connection to Jerusalem solidified when its leadership was inspired by the charismatic preaching of Bernard of Clairvaux (1090–1153) to join the Second Crusade: thus Léonius, the abbot from 1131 to 1137, embarked for the Holy Land with

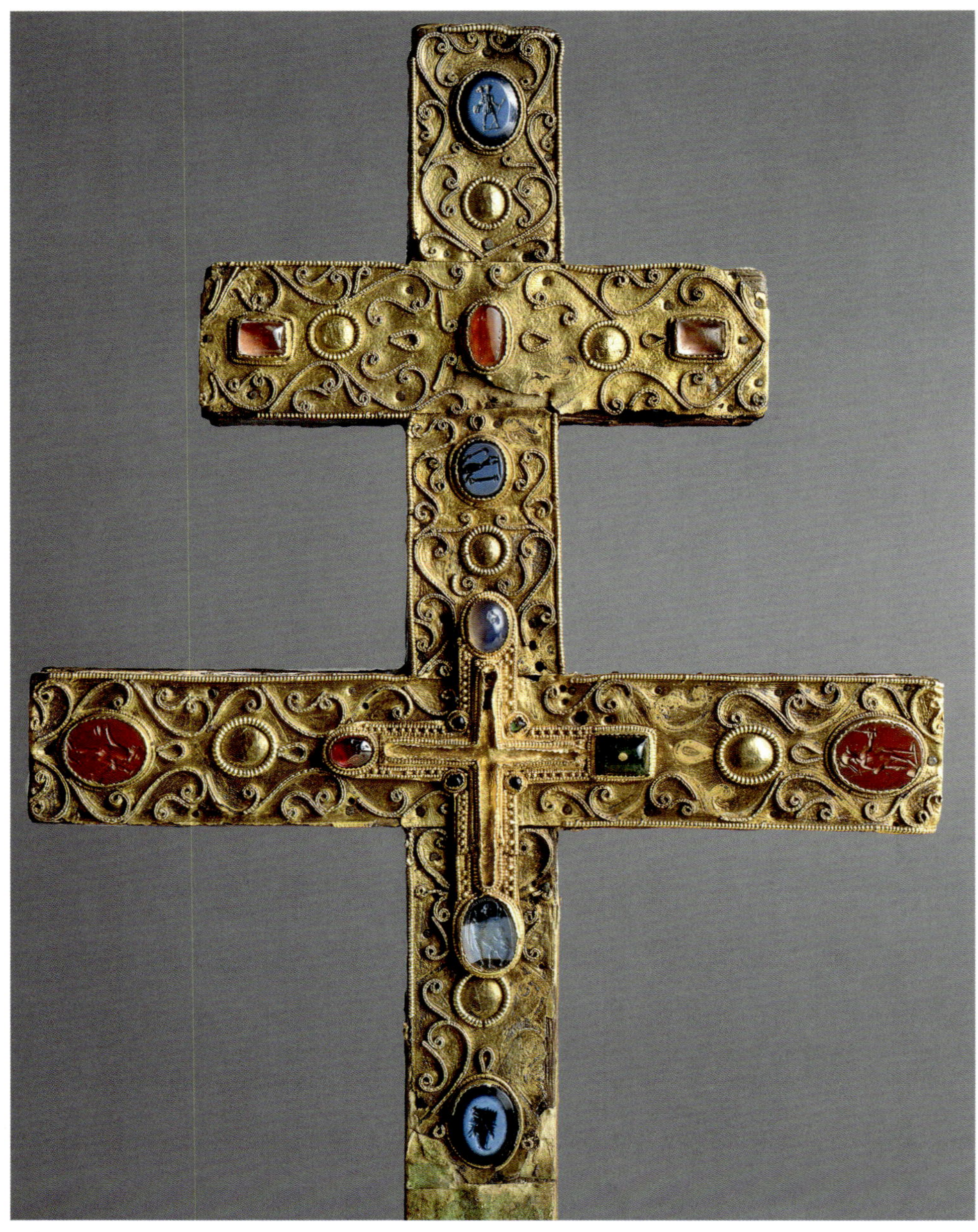

25b

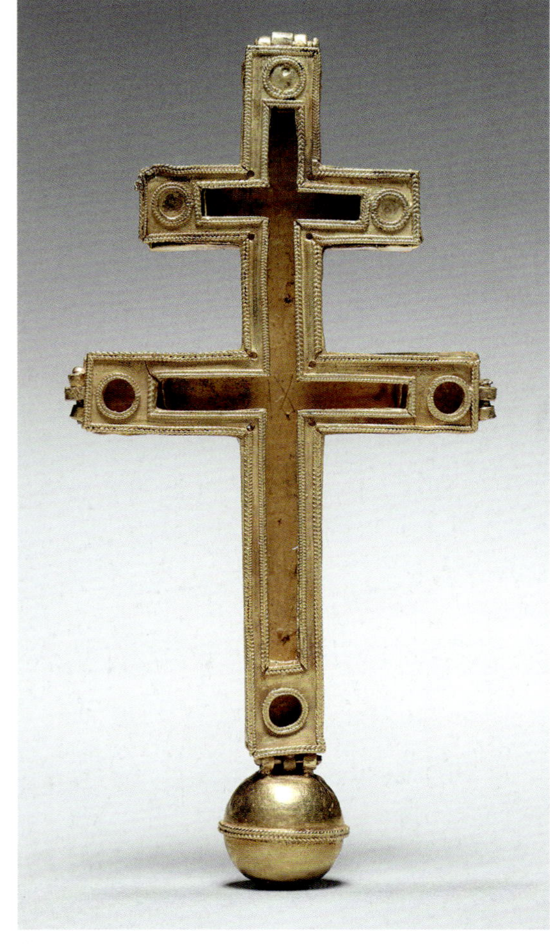

25c

Thierry of Alsace, count of Flanders. No record of a Cross relic for Lobbes is recorded from that journey; however, a vial said to contain the blood of Christ was brought back to be worn around the abbot's neck.

Nobles were as involved as churchmen in the acquisition and transport of relics of the Cross. Foulques de Cleers and his son Geoffroi founded a Chapel of the Holy Cross near their chateau in Soucelles in 1158, from which the Reliquary Cross of la Roche Foulques comes (cat. 25b). Its double-arm form was specifically associated with the Holy Land and therefore proclaims its genuineness at first glance.

More explicitly, a rare gold double-arm reliquary cross (cat. 25c) bears inscriptions on one side enumerating the relics it once contained, the largest of which was of the Cross. Irregularly placed and variously sized, the texts surely correspond to the original setting of the relics within. Such an erratic disposition would have been anathema to the ordered sensibilities of medieval goldsmiths; its use here unequivocally identifies the relics and evinces their direct connection to the Cross.

On a Cross from The Cloisters (cat. 25d), inscriptions atypically set along the sides of the shaft and arms likewise validate the relics once perceptible behind the glass cabochons; special prominence is accorded the relic of the Cross, superimposed on the front. The ensemble constitutes a virtual tour of key sites of the Holy Land, including the Church of the Holy Sepulchre, the Church of the Virgin in the Valley of Jehoshaphat, and the Church of the Nativity in Bethlehem. The curiously placed inscriptions were a feature of reliquary crosses at the abbey of Grandmont, outside Limoges, but details of the goldsmith's work of the reverse — notably the embossed rosettes — compare with the Cross of Jacques de Vitry in Namur, Belgium, raising the question of whether both were fabricated in the Holy Land (cat. 126).

The Toulouse reliquary (cat. 25e) is exceptional among Cross reliquaries in form. Did this elongated rectangular box with pitched roof contain the silver double-arm crosses mentioned in the local church inventory in 1246? Unlike the phylactery, the Toulouse reliquary depicts Helen's finding of the Cross on a plaque relegated to the short side only. Instead, the prominent long sides focus on recent chapters in the relic's history, detailing its gift and transport from Jerusalem to France. First, Jean, abbot of the Church of the Virgin in the Valley of Jehoshaphat from 1178 to

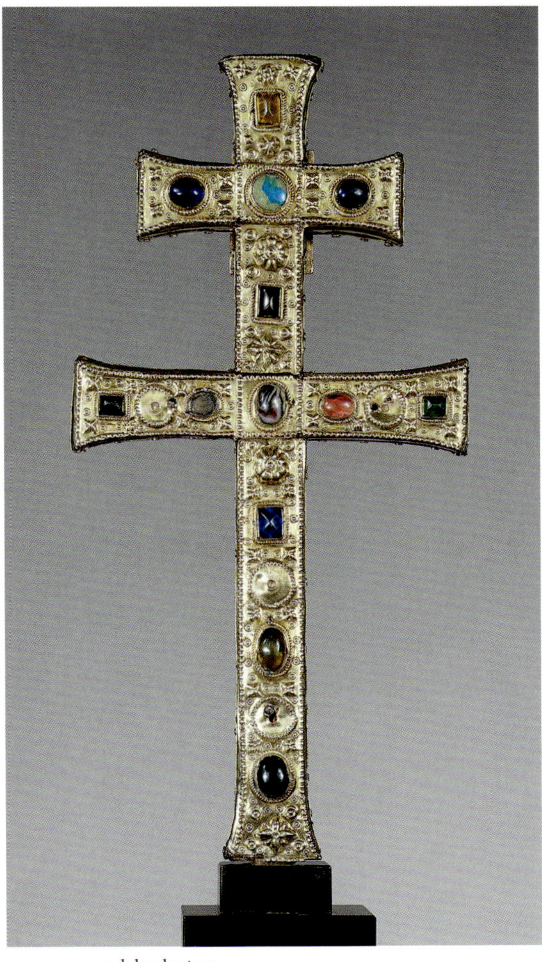

25d back view

1186, standing next to the walls of Jerusalem, hands the double-arm Cross to Raymond Botardelli, a scribe from Toulouse. "Oremus," written on his scroll, indicates that they are linked by prayer. Botardelli then steps into a boat to transport it across the sea; on arrival, he presents it to the abbot of Saint-Sernin, Toulouse. On the other long side Botardelli kneels with the Cross before the abbot, and the doors of the church of Toulouse are flung wide to receive it.

The rectangular reliquary from the Cleveland Museum of Art (cat. 25f), the latest of the group assembled here, is the only one of the ensemble definitely created after Saladin's reconquest of Jerusalem in 1187. Its lengthy inscription begins with an exhortation to "You who ask about the Cross" and then tells an extraordinary tale of malfeasance on the

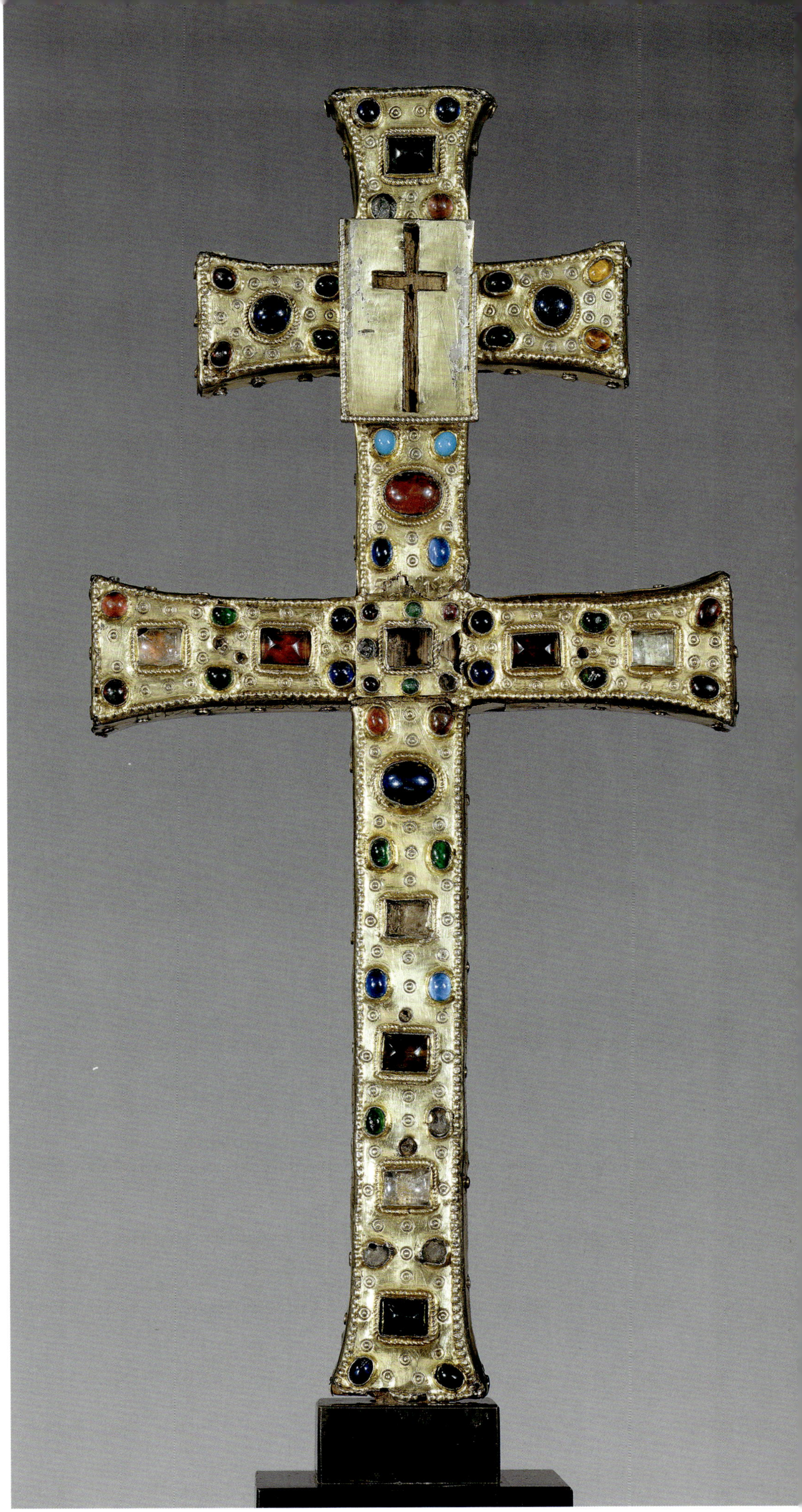

25d

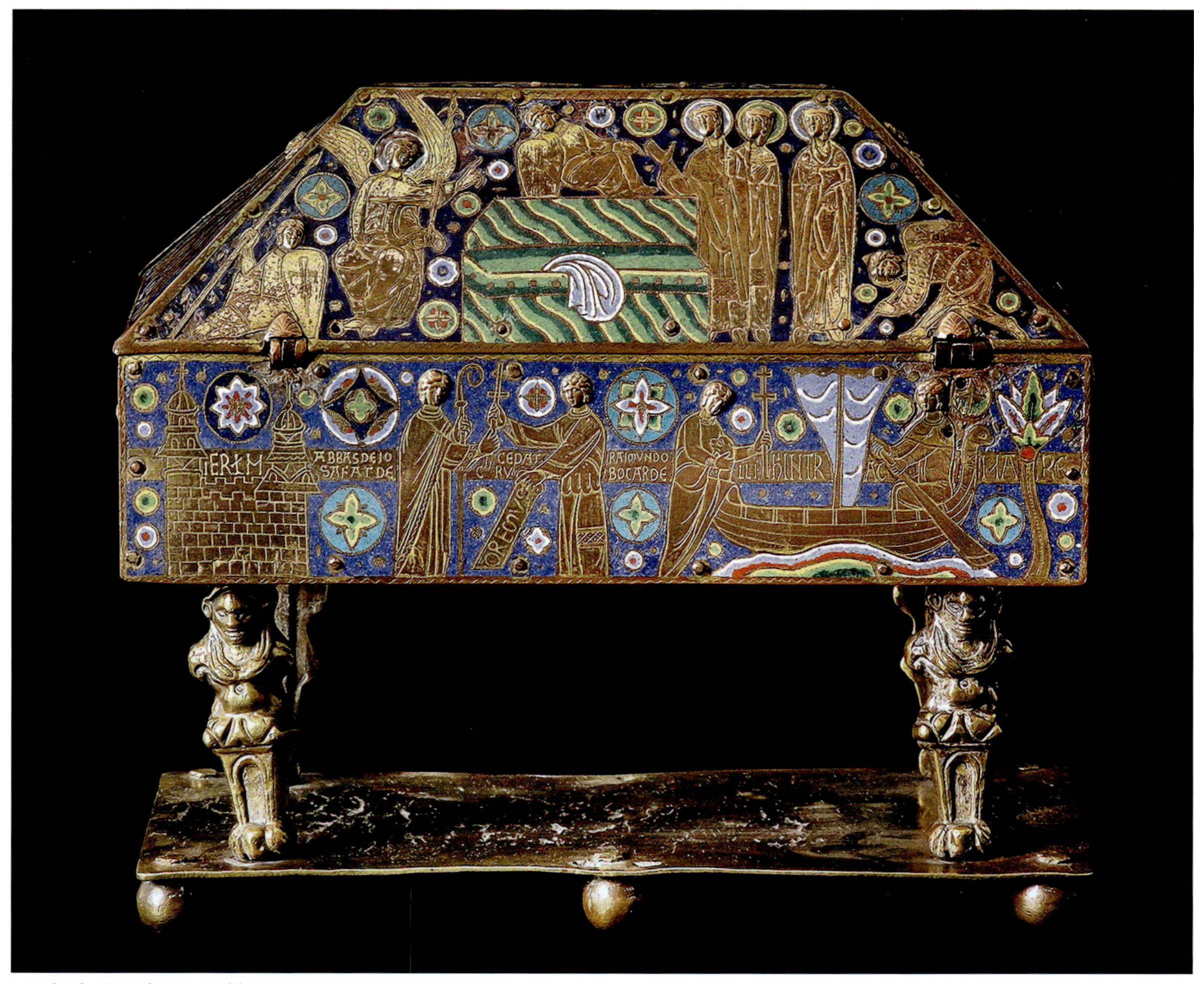

25e back view, showing Abbot Jean in Jerusalem

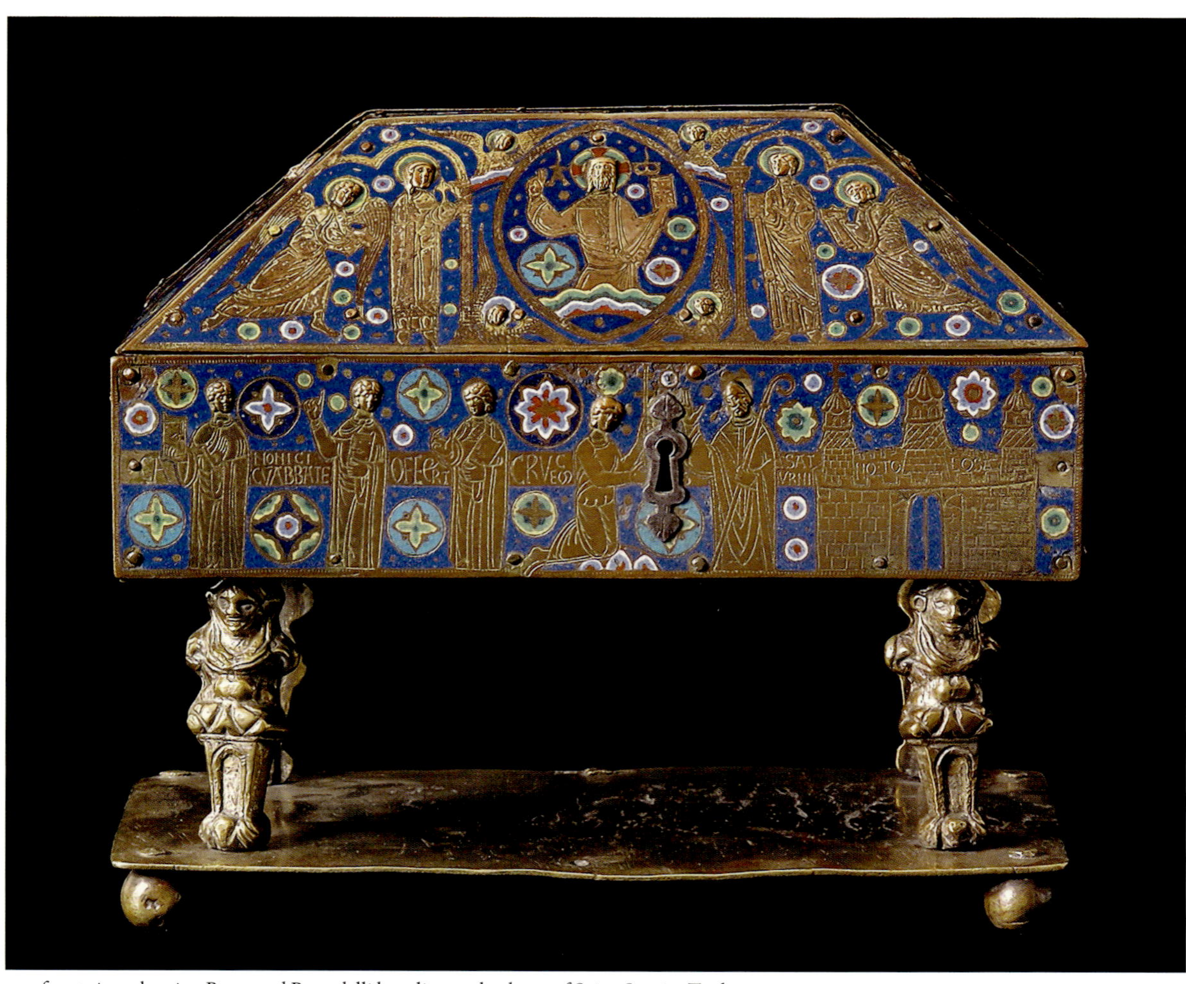

25e front view, showing Raymond Botardelli kneeling at the doors of Saint-Sernin, Toulouse

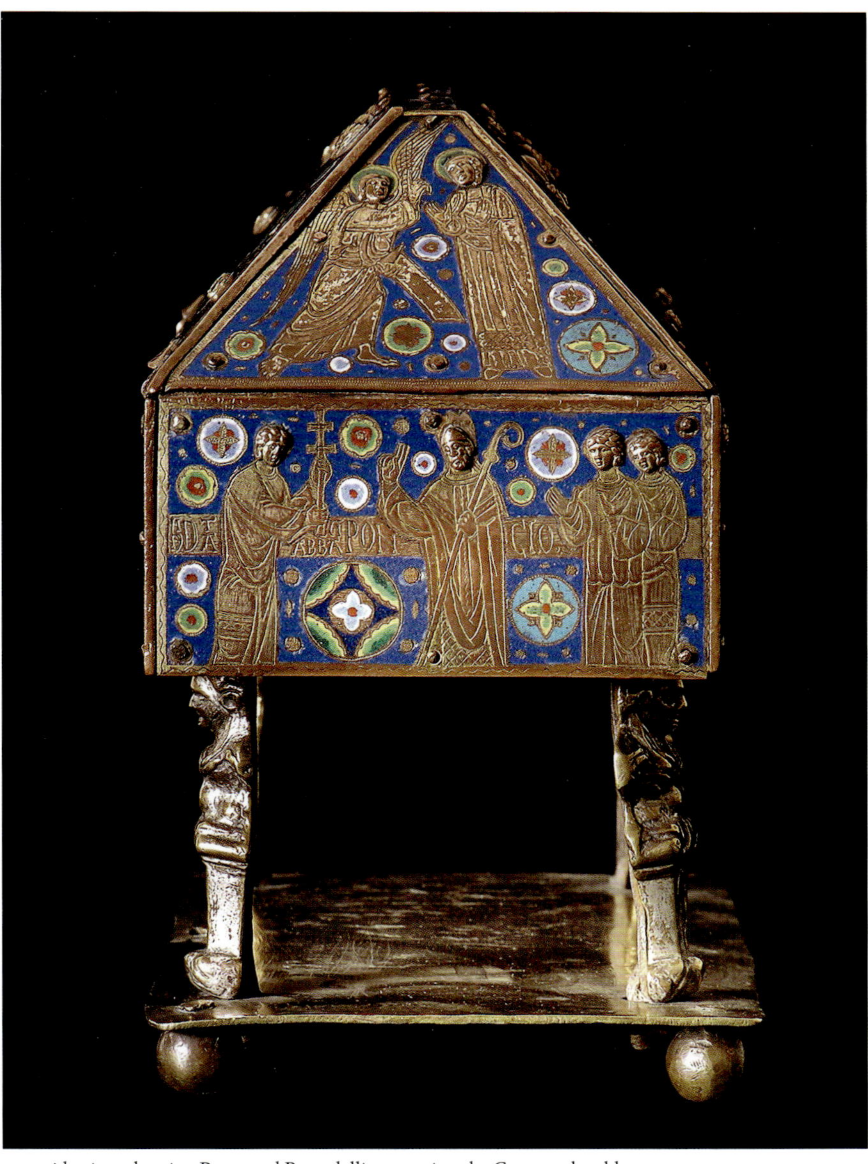

25e side view, showing Raymond Botardelli presenting the Cross to the abbot

part of a Christian priest, who stole the relic, presumably from the Syrian community or the Cathedral of the Holy Cross at Acre, and then sailed for Europe. His crime provoked a raging storm on the Mediterranean. Through the intercession of the Virgin Mary, the priest relinquished the relic, gifting it to the Knights Templar. On the point of death he asked to be thrown overboard to calm the seas. The pilgrims then "happily disembarked at Brindisi and returned peacefully to their country with the relic of the Cross, which you see beautifully set in its container."[2] Set at the southern tip of Italy on the Adriatic, Brindisi was a major port for travel to and from the Holy Land and where the Knights Templar, the beneficiaries of the Cross relic contained here, maintained a prominent presence. BDB

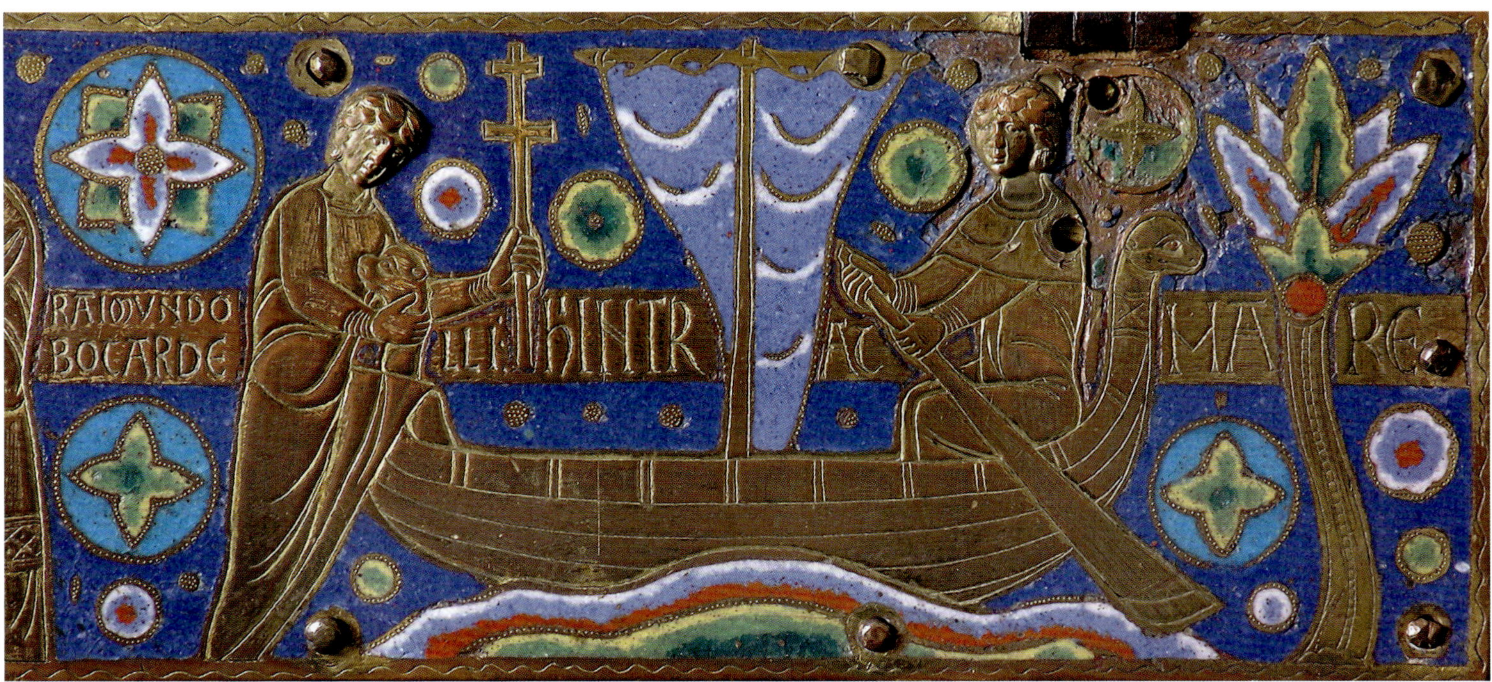

25e detail, showing Raymond Botardelli embarking for France

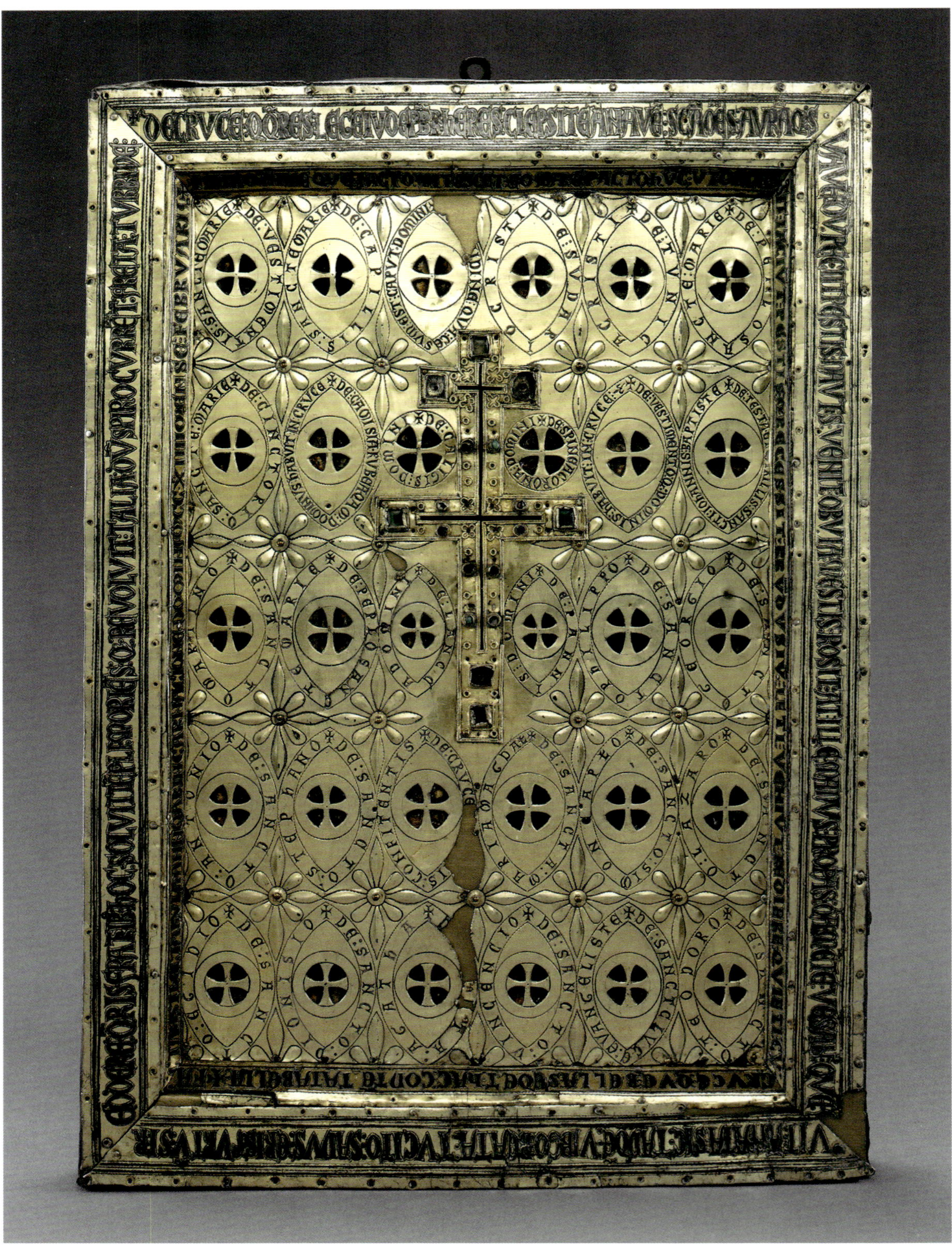

25f

Selected References: Cat 25a: Van Bastelaer 1880, pp. 2–52; van den Bossche et al. 2007, p. 152, fig. 1; Cleveland, Baltimore, and London 2010–11, p. 180, no. 88; Frojmovic 2012, pp. 173–79, fig. 9. Cat. 25b: Frolow 1961, p. 337, no. 350; Gaborit-Chopin 1992. Cat. 25c: Cleveland, Baltimore, and London 2010–11, pp. 88–89, no. 46. Cat. 25d: Boehm 2006; Cleveland, Baltimore, and London 2010–11, pp. 89–90, no. 48. Cat. 25e: Paris and New York 1995–96, pp. 165–67, no. 40; Watin-Grandchamp, Cabau, and Cazes 2007; Cleveland, Baltimore, and London 2010–11, pp. 122–23, no. 62. Cat. 25f: Frolow 1961, pp. 407–8, no. 494; Gauthier 1983, pp. 96–97, no. 53 (as Levantine and South Italian); Cologne 1985, vol. 3, pp. 130, 133, no. H.43 (as South Italian?); Cleveland, Baltimore, and London 2010–11, pp. 90–91, no. 49 (as Kingdom of Jerusalem and Rhenish-Mosan); Lupis 2012, pp. 188–89, fig. 8.

1. For more on Crosses, see Frolow 1961, p. 310; Frolow 1965; Bresc-Bautier 1971; Meurer 1985; Murray 1998; Jaspert 2014.

2. As translated in the Cleveland Museum of Art website catalogue record.

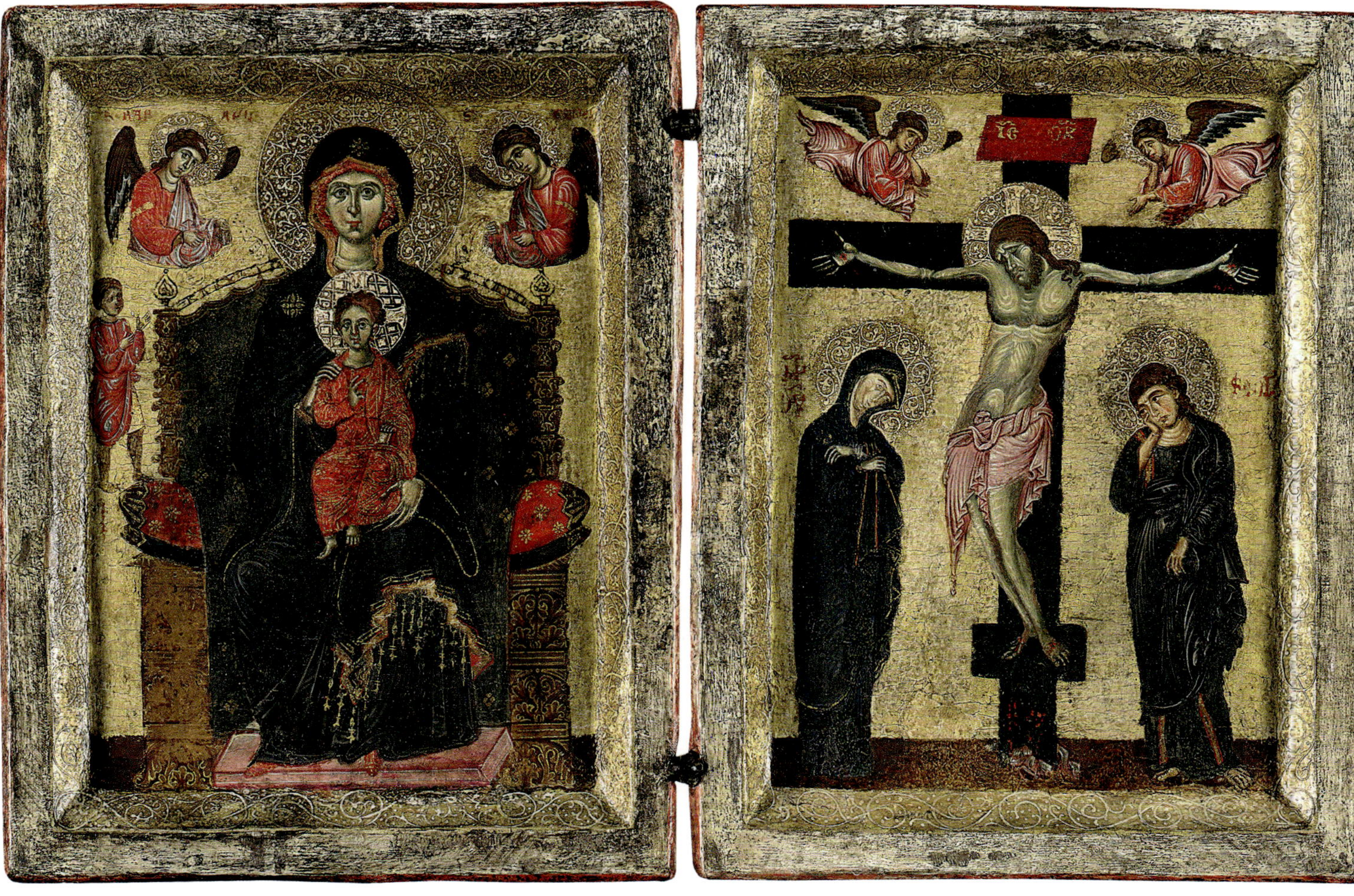

26

26

The Ryerson Diptych: Virgin and Child Enthroned with Angels and Donor; The Crucifixion with the Virgin Mary, Saint John the Evangelist, and Two Angels

Acre, ca. 1275–85
Tempera and gold on wood panels with gilded plaster pastiglia
Each wing: 15 × 11⅝ in. (38 × 29.5 cm)
Art Institute of Chicago, Mr. and Mrs. Martin A. Ryerson Collection (1933.1035)

This diptych depicts on the left wing the icon of the Virgin and Child *Nikopoios* (victory maker) on a round-backed throne with a cloth of honor, flanked above by two bust-length angels and with a diminutive donor standing to the left. On the right wing is an icon of the Crucifixion of Christ accompanied by the grieving Virgin, Saint John the Evangelist, and two sorrowful angels above the cross arm. The imagery combines for devotional purposes a cult image found in early Byzantine ivories, textiles, and apse mosaics and frescoes with the crucified Christ and its Eucharistic connotations.[1]

No doubt commissioned for individual devotional use, the diptych appears to have been created for a pilgrim — possibly Venetian — to the Holy Land, as were some of the encaustic icons on the columns in the Church of the Nativity in Bethlehem, which also depict pilgrims with the holy figures. The small image of the pilgrim suspended against the gold ground to the left of the throne compares to other depictions of pilgrims who appear next to an enthroned nursing Virgin and Child, or *Galaktotrophousa* (milk giver), and to the standing figure of Saint James the Greater in Bethlehem.[2]

The diminutive icon of the Virgin and Child enthroned with angels was one of the most popular cult images of the last third of the thirteenth century in the Crusader East, Constantinople, and Tuscany and Umbria in Italy. Echoing Byzantine models, this type is the well-known *Nikopoios* without chrysography, or writing in gold — rather than the greatly venerated Virgin and Child *Hodegetria* (she who shows the way) with chrysography — and enjoyed widespread popularity after the 1250s on Crusader and Italian icons, panel paintings, and altarpieces.[3] The work appears to have been made in the Crusader East at Acre, judging by the red Greek and Latin titles, pastiglia relief in the gold background, and stylistic similarities with contemporary Crusader paintings from Acre.[4] JF

Selected References: Garrison, Ed., 1949, p. 57, no. 241; Buchthal and Wormald 1957, pp. 49–51, pl. 145; Kermer 1967, pp. 70–71, pl. 88; New York 2004, p. 471, no. 288; Folda 2005, pp. 296, 298, 302, 566–68, figs. 412, 413.

1. For the ivories, see Olenka Pevny in New York 1997, pp. 140–41, no. 87 (tenth/eleventh centuries). For the textiles, see Rutschowscaya 2000, p. 224 (sixth century). For the apse mosaics and frescoes, see Cormack 2000.
2. Kühnel, G., 1988, pp. 22–26, pls. 2–6 (dated 1130), and pp. 40–43, pl. 13.
3. Folda 2015.
4. Rebecca W. Corrie in New York 2004, p. 479.

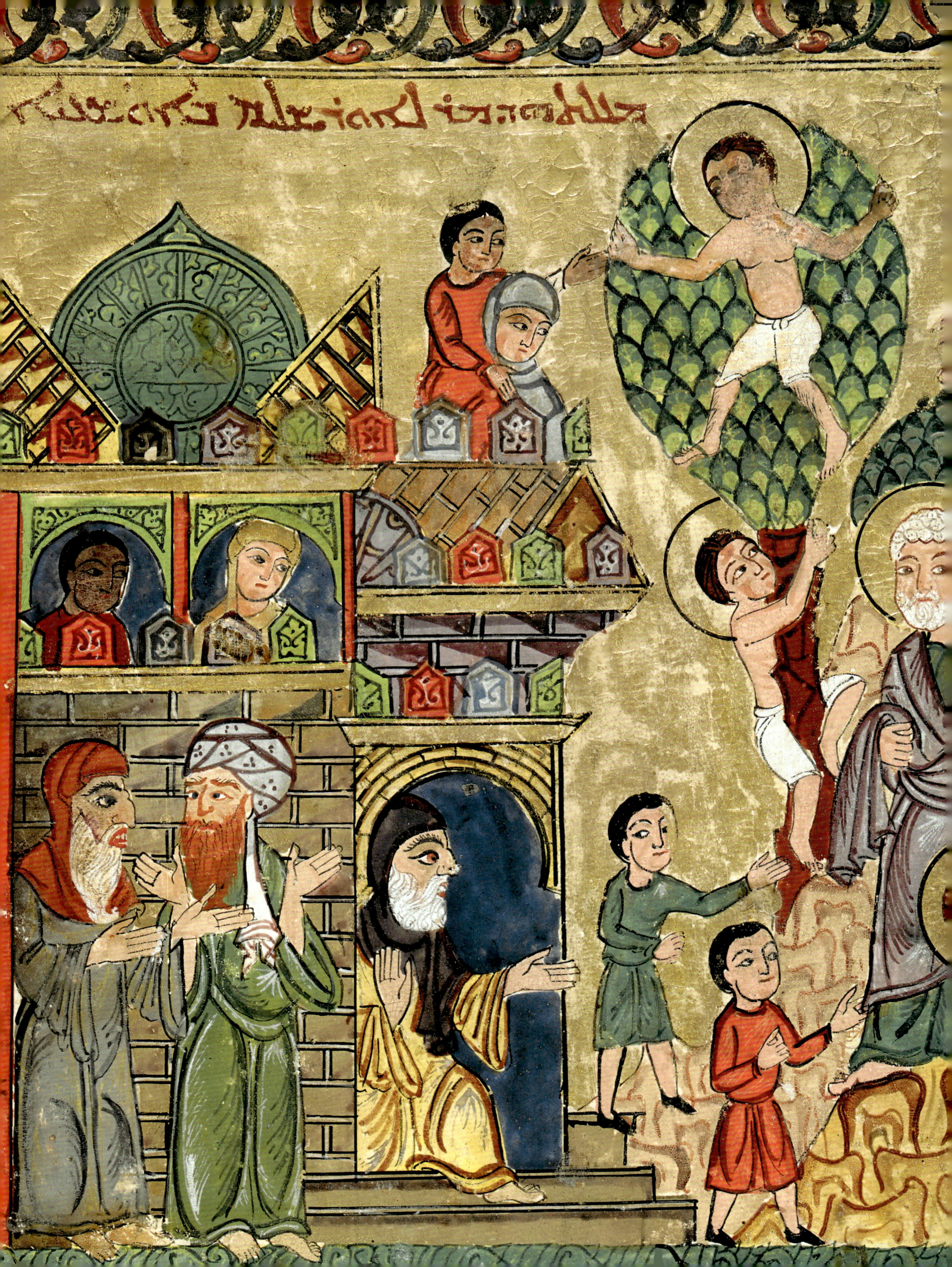

Pluralism in the Holy City

People of all tongues — Benjamin of Tudela

BARBARA DRAKE BOEHM AND MELANIE HOLCOMB

FACING PAGE
Fig. 25. *Syriac Lectionary*. Detail of cat. 27

In a scene set against a field of gold, a crowd gathers at the gates of a city (fig. 25).[1] Two men standing at left converse; one, with a red beard, sports a turban of purple-gray fabric. His companion is clearly old and perhaps venerable, as is his white-bearded counterpart seated under a golden stone arch. In the windows above, we see a man and a woman, side by side. He has black skin; hers is white. Another light-skinned woman, also with her head covered, holds a child with black hair, whose tawny hand reaches out to a lighter-skinned boy in a nearby tree. Young and old, men and women, people of many races, all cluster in the colorful context of a vibrant urban landscape. This is not just any city: "This is Jerusalem . . . set in the midst of the nations and countries that are around about her."[2]

For the thirteenth-century Syriac artist who illustrated the lectionary (a collection of readings from Christian Gospels; cat. 27) in which this scene appears, it was a point of pride that the population of Jerusalem was so diverse.[3] And he was not alone in his sentiments. Bishop Sulëyman al-Ghazzi, writing in the early eleventh century, had described the Christian communities he knew from his experience of Jerusalem and Gaza:

> God has favored a Church
> Whose stones are gathered from all corners and climes . . .
> All bodily creatures are pleased to see it
> When it appears in races and colors . . .
> White, blond, and brown in their churches
> Praise God with the yellow and the black.[4]

The rich mix of people on the streets of Jerusalem was a feature of the city no visitor failed to notice. Its astounding variety occurred across multiple dimensions: religious, linguistic, ethnic, and cultural. Locals, both longtime residents and recent immigrants, claimed a heritage of extraordinary diversity, while visitors, whether pilgrim or merchant, soldier or diplomat, traveled there from every part of the known world. Political leadership changed throughout the years 1000 to 1400, as did the demographic balance. Minorities of various kinds fared better or worse depending on the moment.[5] What remained constant was the city's insistent heterogeneity. Even in the aftermath of extreme ethnic and religious cleansing, as when victorious Crusaders mercilessly slaughtered most of the city's inhabitants, demographic homogeneity simply could not take hold. Within a generation of the Crusaders' conquest in

1099, Syrian Christians from Transjordan were invited back to repopulate the city.[6] Pilgrims, diplomats, and merchants of multiple faiths from around the world continued to visit.

Though many cities — by virtue of their political, religious, or mercantile importance — could claim a vibrant combination of inhabitants and visitors, Jerusalem stood out for its spectacularly international character. Neither Cairo nor Damascus, Mecca nor Constantinople held the same appeal for Western travelers.[7] Venice, Rome, Paris — none of these cites tolerated the same degree of religious diversity. Laws, living arrangements, linguistic affinities, and sartorial codes were among the many mechanisms that encouraged or even forced individuals and groups to retain and display their distinct identities. Yet the city's small size, its many shared sacred sites, its religious rituals, and the practical aspects of living ensured that few could exist in splendid isolation. Much of its visual, aural, and textual richness drew from its mixed, often hybrid character. Among the most interesting art and texts to survive are those that reveal how visitors and inhabitants navigated Jerusalem's extreme multiculturalism. They show how identities frequently overlapped, and barriers intended to divide were regularly traversed.

The color of the city owed much to the varied appearance of its visitors and inhabitants. Robes, belts, headgear, and facial hair all served as indices of cultural difference. Westerners, in particular, marveled at the array of people they saw, and authors of many chronicles and travel accounts made a point of cataloguing, to the best of their abilities, the region's multiple religions and ethnicities, with an emphasis on appearance. Jacques de Vitry, a European bishop stationed in Acre in the early thirteenth century, considered beards to be a distinguishing characteristic, noting, for instance, that "[the Syrians] do not shave their beards as do the Saracens, Greeks, and almost all Easterns, but cherish them in great care and especially glory in them, holding the beard to be a sign of manhood."[8] Perhaps unsurprisingly for a cloth merchant, Jean of Tournai, who visited Jerusalem in 1488, focused on headdress and fabric selection. He noted that "Moors wear white, with head wraps of fine cotton or 'toile de Hollande.'" The hat of the Mamluk, he further stated, was red, secured by a white cloth with a striped border. Jews wore yellow, Christians blue and white linen.[9] Bernhard von Breydenbach's pilgrimage chronicle of the late fifteenth century offers a visual catalogue of Jerusalem's sartorial diversity (cat. 20). The illustrations by Erhard Reuwich show Syrians wearing turbans (cat. 47). Of two Saracen women, one has a completely veiled face, the other, an elegant and elaborate headdress. In another image, a Greek monk is hooded and carries prayer beads (fig. 26).

Levantine variations in costume could inspire both curiosity and anxiety. Laws established by Western Christian authorities in Nablus during the Frankish occupation of the Holy Land forbade Muslims from adopting Frankish modes of dress.[10] In contrast, when a Melkite physician from Jerusalem moved to Damascus, he was advised to discard his Frankish uniform — a head shawl, turban, and collared coat — if he hoped to advance his career within the Ayyubid court.[11] Some high-ranking Franks embraced local costume to the dismay, it would seem, of folks back home. When Heraclius (ca. 1128–1190/91), the Latin patriarch of Jerusalem, made a trip to Europe, he was mocked for his excessive use of perfume and the extravagant Eastern fabrics of his robes.[12]

To walk in medieval Jerusalem was to experience a polyglot world. Numerous distinct alphabets could be seen and different languages of prayer and commerce heard: Arabic, Persian, Greek, Armenian, Syriac, Coptic, Geez, Latin, and Hebrew were among the many that filled Jerusalem's streets, markets, and places of worship. Breydenbach's illustrated pilgrim's guide paid tribute to that

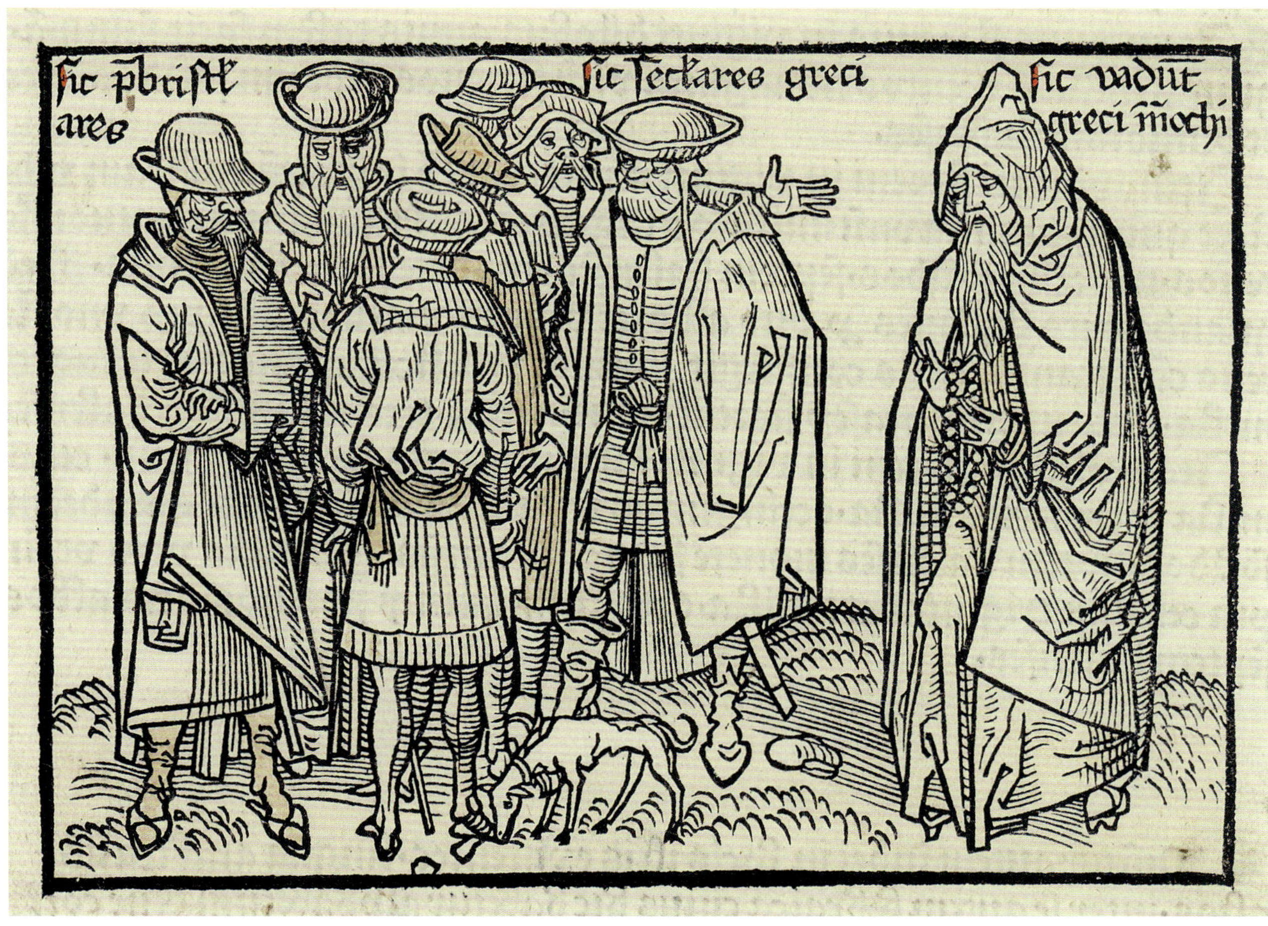

Fig. 26. A Greek monk hooded and carrying prayer beads, from *Journey to the Holy Land* (*Peregrinatio in terram sanctam*). Detail of cat. 20, fol. 66v

linguistic diversity, even as it critiqued the religious beliefs of the varied speakers. Alongside images of Jerusalem's inhabitants, he included alphabetic charts of seven different languages spoken there (fig. 27). And though Western Europeans shared a common faith and hence a common liturgical language, they were often divided by the vernacular, as Felix Fabri (ca. 1437/38–1502) noted several times in his travel account. Fluent in German and Italian, Felix Fabri was particularly attuned to misunderstandings that arose among speakers of those languages.[13] Commenting on the linguistic diversity of the clergy aboard the ship sailing to the Holy Land, he remarked that "there were many Latin priests — Slavonians, Italians, Lombards, Gauls, Franks, Germans, Englishmen, Irishmen, Hungarians, Scots, Dacians, Bohemians, and Spaniards" and marveled at how song united them all.[14]

The linguistic variety of Jews in Jerusalem reflected the wide geographic range of the Jewish diaspora. Although the language of prayer among Jews coming to Jerusalem from Italy, Spain, Germany, France, Persia, Yemen, and northern Africa was Hebrew, they conversed in the languages of their native lands. Indeed, Hebrew could not always be counted on to bridge national or regional divides even in a religious setting: prayer shifts at the city gates bewailing the "desolation" of the Holy City were conducted by Karaite Jews in Hebrew, Persian, and Arabic, presumably to accommodate the many linguistic needs of the participants.[15]

In such an environment, nimble code-switching was an asset. Translations were a necessary enterprise in Jerusalem, and the Georgians were among those who excelled in this area. The Menologion — a collection of saints' and martyrs' lives read on their commemoration days — copied by George

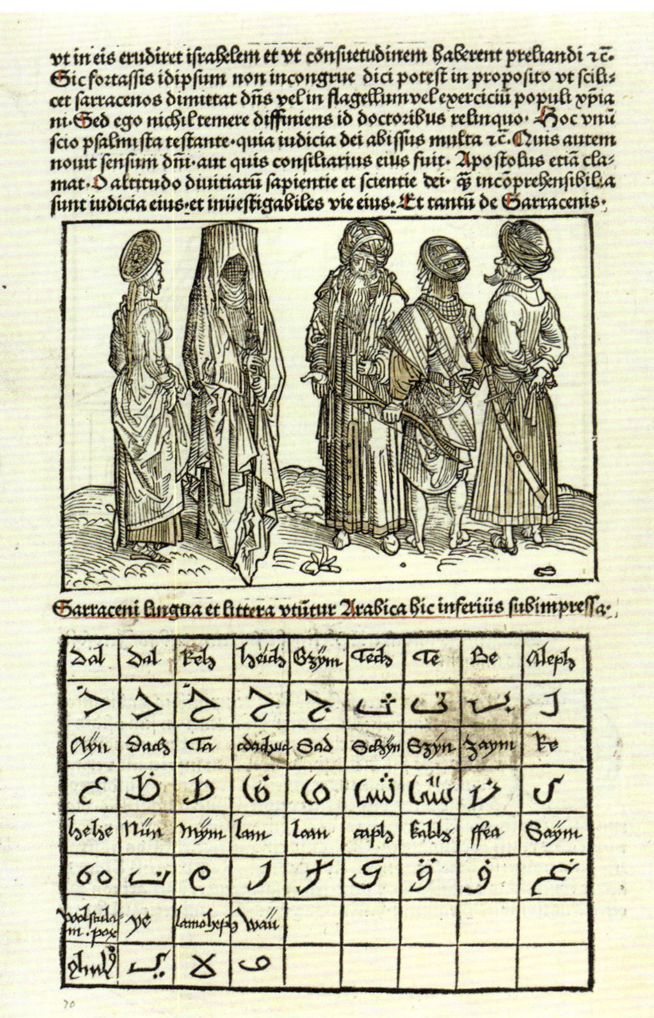

vt in eis erudiret israhelem et vt consuetudinem haberent preliandi rc. Sic fortassis idipsum non incongrue dici potest in proposito vt scilicet sarracenos dimittat dñs vel in flagellum vel exerciciũ populi xpiani. Sed ego nichil temere diffiniens id doctoribus relinquo. Hoc vnũ scio psalmista testante. quia iudicia dei abissus multa rc. Quis autem nouit sensum dñi. aut quis consiliarius eius fuit. Apostolus etiã clamat. O altitudo diuitiarũ sapientie et scientie dei. q̃ incõprehensibilia sunt iudicia eius. et inuẽstigabiles vie eius. Et tantũ de Sarracenis.

Sarraceni lingua et littera vtũtur Arabica hic inferiũs subimpressa.

Dal	Dal	Keh	Heich	Gzym	Tech	Te	Be	Aleph
ذ	د	خ	ح	ج	ث	ت	ب	ا
Ayn	Dadh	Ta	[illegible]	Sad	Schym	Szyn	Zaym	Re
ع	ظ	ط	ض	ص	ش	س	ز	ر
helhe	Nun	Mym	lam	lam	caph	kabh	ffea	Gaym
[illegible]	ن	م	ل	[illegible]	ك	ق	ف	غ
[illegible]	ye	lamalepfh	Wau					
[illegible]	ي	[illegible]	[illegible]					

Fig. 27. Saracens and the Arabic Alphabet, from *Journey to the Holy Land* (*Peregrinatio in terram sanctam*). Detail of cat. 20, fol. 64r

Prokhorus (cat. 29), the founder of the Monastery of the Holy Cross outside Jerusalem's then-borders (fig. 28), included a Georgian translation of what was likely an Arabic translation of a now-lost Greek account of the Sassanian conquest of Jerusalem.[16] The Georgian community at the Holy Cross Monastery not only preserved documents in Arabic attesting to their property rights but also presented them at hearings in the Islamic courts.[17]

We learn of more informal modes of translation from Arnold von Harff, who traveled to Jerusalem in the late fifteenth century. While in the Holy Land, he developed an Arabic-German lexicon that included an Arabic alphabet and transliterations of many useful phrases. An encounter with two Christian converts to Judaism and a number of German Jews in Jerusalem allowed him to augment the lexicon with Hebrew. We gain a sense of Arnold's priorities from his repertory of phrases: "God give us good wind"; "How much does it cost"; and "Woman, let me sleep with you tonight."[18]

Two copies of a Frankish-Arabic lexicon, both from about 1300, present Frankish words transcribed into Coptic letters and followed by an Arabic translation.[19] The appearance of words such as "spice merchant," "parfumer," "fabric merchant," "goldsmith," and "copper workers" suggests that this word-book would have catered specifically to the needs of merchants and pilgrims. It noted the names of many animals as well as fruits and stars and included helpful phrases as well: "Do you want to go to the baths? To the garden?" Demonstrating that Arnold was not alone in certain interests, the manuscript also provided the word for "prostitute."[20]

One imagines that much of the communication in Jerusalem took place through pidgin languages – a feature that clearly enchanted Fulcher of Chartres: "People use the eloquence and idioms of diverse languages in conversing back and forth. Words of different languages have become common property known to each nationality."[21] French was spoken among the nobility of the Crusader states until the fifteenth century,[22] but if any language could claim to be Jerusalem's (and the region's) true lingua franca, it would surely be Arabic. A liturgical manuscript from the ninth century bears numerous marginal notes in Arabic explaining the Greek rubrics, suggesting that at least by then the vernacular among local Christians was Arabic.[23] A twelfth-century liturgical manuscript for the Church of the Holy Sepulchre recommended translating the homily into Arabic "so that those who do not know how to read Greek may be comforted and that all the people may have joy, exultation, and merriment, both the small and the great."[24] Within a decade or two of their occupation of Jerusalem, Latin Christians had begun to learn the local language,[25] and numerous Christian manuscripts and objects from the region incorporate Arabic (cats. 54, 56).

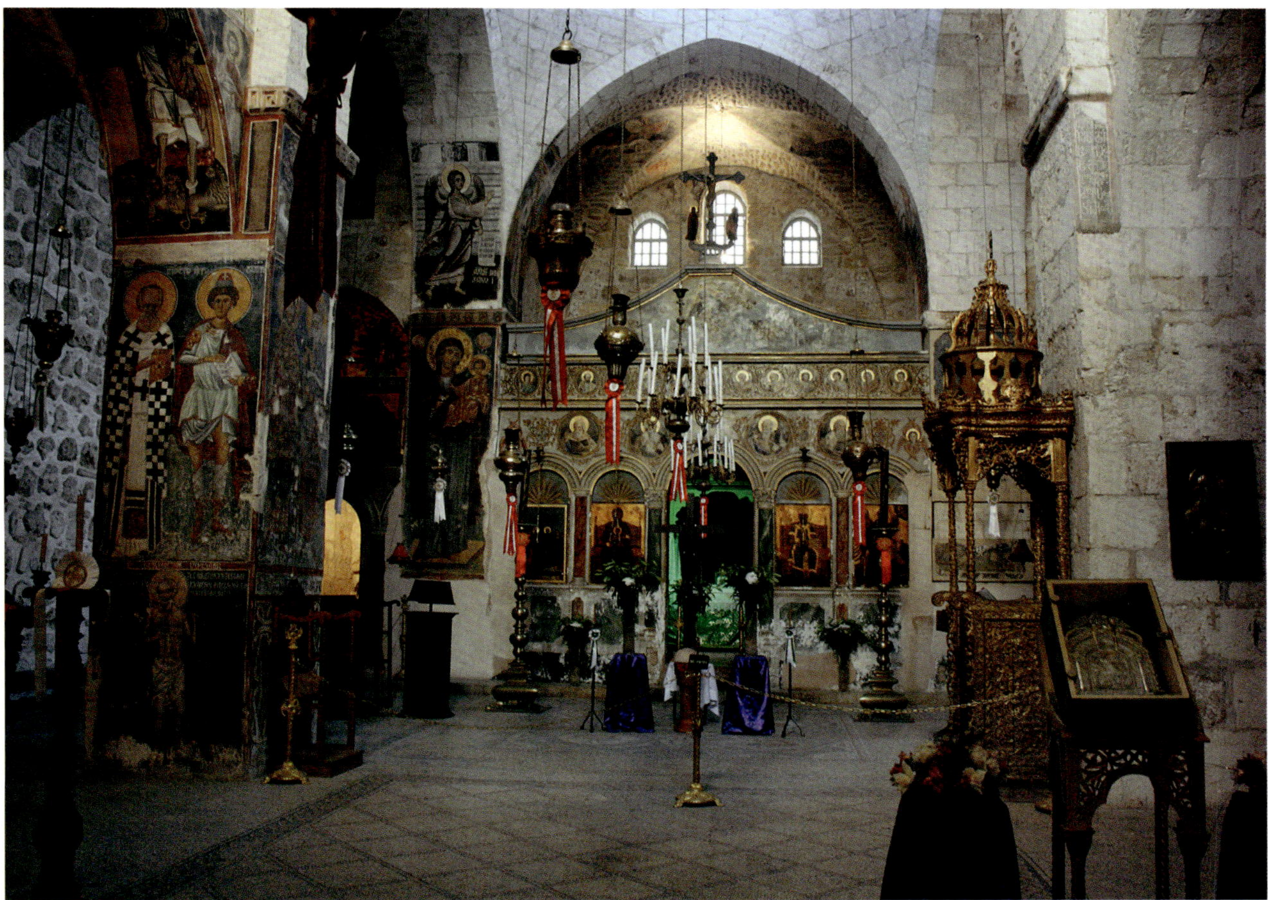

Fig. 28. Interior of the church at the Monastery of the Holy Cross, Jerusalem

In this respect, local Christians played a key role. The Jerusalem native al-Muqaddasi, writing in the tenth century, indicated that all scribes in the region were Christians.[26] Ibn Jubayr, a famous twelfth-century traveler, reported that clerks of the Acre customhouse were Arabic-speaking and Arabic-writing Christians (with ebony inkstands ornamented with gold).[27] The amirs of Saladin (1137/38–1193) and his successors had Coptic administrators, possibly explaining the Coptic-Frankish-Arabic lexicon mentioned above.[28] The Franks, perhaps surprisingly, preserved the Arabic language for some administrative matters and seem to have relied largely on indigenous Christians as scribes: seventeen such scribes are mentioned in Frankish charters, nine with Christian names, one with a typically Muslim name, and others that could be either.[29]

The ability to inhabit two worlds made local Christians useful for both Western Christians and local Muslims. Syrian Christians helped to guide invading Crusaders to Jerusalem,[30] yet the Latins were wary of them precisely because they spoke the language of the area. Jacques de Vitry, who did not hold a high opinion of the local population, alleged that the Syrians "become spies and tell the secrets of the Christians to the Saracens, among whom they are brought up, whose language they speak."[31] Eastern Christians may well have been the interpreters Saladin relied on in his negotiations with Richard the Lion-Hearted. Or perhaps they were key to his strategy of having his ships masquerade as Christian vessels in order to get supplies to his troops. Affixing crosses on his ship, he then required his sailors to "imitate Christian speech."[32]

The use of Arabic bound local Jews together as well. The vast majority of documents from the Cairo Geniza were also written in Judeo-Arabic, a form of Arabic written in Hebrew script, as Arabic was the spoken language of commerce among Jewish merchants working in the region.[33] This practice could have posed problems for Jewish immigrants to the area. In a thirteenth-century Geniza document, for example, community elders in Alexandria invoked a statute requiring judges to be Arabic speakers, excluding those Byzantine or Western Europeans who could only "[deliver] judgment by means of a translator."[34] The great twelfth-century philosopher Maimonides (Rabbi Moshe ben Maimon), leader of the Jewish community in nearby Fustat (Old Cairo), spoke Arabic, and many of his treatises and letters were written in Judeo-Arabic.

Jerusalem has often been described as a city of three faiths, a truism that underestimates its religious complexity. No religion was in fact monolithic, and the city's artistic and intellectual culture benefitted from the distinct perspectives and rivalries that often emerged from various sects. Among Jews, for example, Karaites and Rabbanites often clashed over matters of religious law, as the Karaites did not recognize the authority of the Midrash or the Talmud. Each community therefore produced its own school of scholarship, often pointedly in opposition to the other. The Samaritans, though claiming ancestry from the Ancient Israelites, did not consider themselves Jewish. They used a form of Hebrew (cat. 37c) and upheld the sanctity of Mount Gerizim near Nablus as opposed to the Temple Mount in Jerusalem.[35] The attention bestowed on Jerusalem by the Fatimids may have derived in part from their eagerness to link the form of Shi'a Islam they practiced to the city and the Prophet. Similarly, the Turkish military leader Nur al-Din's focus on Jerusalem in the mid-twelfth century was a means to unite the region's many Sunni communities against the Franks. Nuances of doctrine and questions of allegiance split Christians into a dizzying number of distinct sects, and Jerusalem boasted churches for many of them, including (according to contemporaneous sources) Armenian (fig. 29), Coptic, Ethiopian, Georgian, Latin, Maronite, Nestorian, Orthodox, and Syriac Christians.[36]

In a land seemingly fixated on religious distinctions, overlap among them was more common than we might imagine. The celebrated mystic Ibn al-'Arabi (1165–1240) held that a follower of God could find solace in sites sacred to different faiths: "A cloister for the monk, a fane for idols, the tables of the Torah, the Qur'an. Love is the faith I hold."[37] Conversions happened across all religious divides. Maimonides, writing from Fustat to the sages in Tyre, affirmed the acceptability of preparing Muslims and Christians for conversion to Judaism.[38] Obadiah the Proselyte (cat. 37b) was likely a Christian priest before converting to Judaism in 1102; one of his letters included a medieval Jewish chant in Gregorian notation.[39] Numerous Latin chroniclers recount anecdotes about Crusader rulers effecting conversions to Christianity.[40] We learn from Fulcher of Chartres, for instance, that the Latin king of Jerusalem Baldwin I (r. 1100–1118) marched to the Dead Sea in the company of "local inhabitants who were previously Saracens, but have recently become Christians."[41] The first Mamluk madrasa founded at the edge of the Haram al-Sharif was endowed in 1318 by a high court official, Karim al-Din 'Abd al-Karim, a Copt who had converted to Islam.[42] When his personal physician became a Muslim, Saladin hosted an elaborate ceremony.[43] Evangelism was not welcome, however. The wryly observant diplomat Usama ibn Munqidh (1095–1188) complained of the Templars' efforts to bring about conversion by showing icons of the Virgin and Child to Muslims and declaring, "This is God as a baby" (cat. 26).[44]

Exposure to other cultures could affect not only religious practice, but also professional training — in this case, in the arts. Usama told the story of a Frank named Raoul, who, after he was taken captive in Syria, converted to Islam and learned to be a sculptor of marble. (Small wonder that art

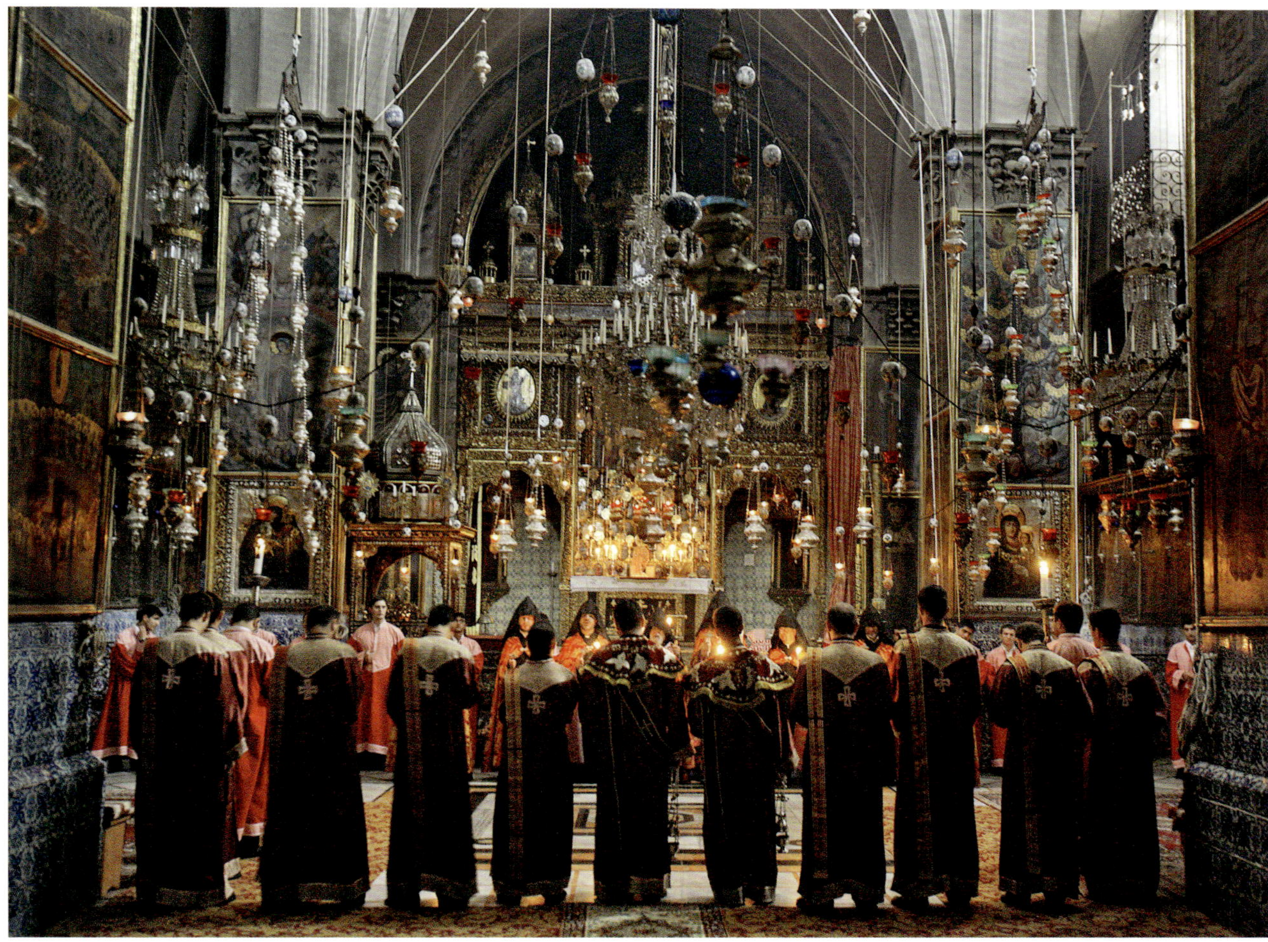

Fig. 29. Interior of the Cathedral of Saint James, Jerusalem

historians struggle to identify the artistic sources of sculpture from the Holy Land.) He went on to marry a woman "of a pious family," who bore him two sons. One day, to everyone's surprise, he became Christian again, together with his children, "after having practiced Islam with its prayers and faith." Usama could not contain his disdain for Raoul's fickleness: "May Allah . . . purify the world from such people!"[45] Marriage occasioned conversion not just between Muslims and Christians, but among different Christian communities as well – and not simply for political expediency, as with the marriage of Frankish kings and Armenian princesses.[46]

Fluid religious identity was not limited to the laity. Felix Fabri described with unease a cleric who served both the Greek Orthodox and Latin churches: "In all respects he conformed himself to the rite of each, for on Sundays he first celebrated Mass in the Latin church and consummated it in the Western fashion with unleavened bread and when this office was finished he crossed over to the Greek church, and consummated in the Eastern fashion with leavened bread."[47] This ecumenical priest was surely an anomaly. We find many more stories of wariness among Jerusalem's various Christian communities, in spite of – or perhaps because of – the many holy spaces they shared. Such circumstances make the letter of Theorianus, an Orthodox priest in service of the Byzantine emperor Manuel Comnenus (1118–1180), all the more touching. The priest, an envoy to the Catholicos (or head) of the Armenian church, had been informed of disputes between Orthodox and Latin Christians on issues such as the Sabbath fast, Communion, priestly marriage, beards, and so on. His advice to his fellow clergy: "Love the Latins as brothers, for they are orthodox and the sons of the Catholic Church, just as you are."[48]

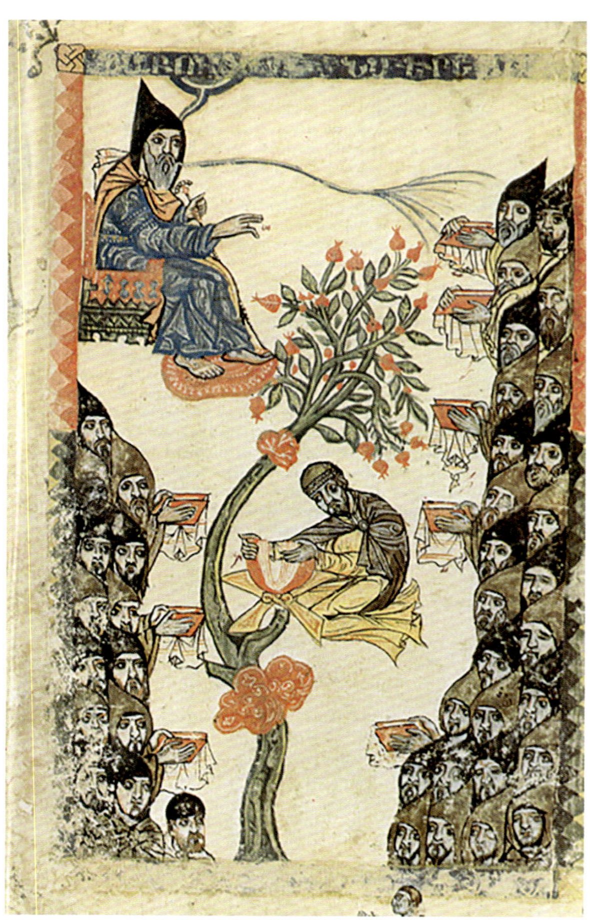

Fig. 30. "Archbishop Esayi of Netch Teaching His Pupils in Glatsor," from *Isaiah Commentary of 1299*. Jerusalem, early 14th century. Paint and ink on paper. Armenian Patriarchate, Jerusalem (MS 365, fol. 2)

If anything could be said to connect the many religious communities that held Jerusalem dear, it was a shared reverence for the written word. All fundamentally understood themselves as "people of the book," having a faith and practice rooted in a rich body of foundational texts. The study and interpretation of those texts were among the holiest of pursuits (fig. 30). For all of these communities, books served as tools to instill social cohesion by preserving the language, liturgy, traditions, and beliefs that gave each one its distinctive character. Books written in, brought to, or sent from the Holy City thus exhibit an astonishing diversity of language and style.

Few Hebrew codices from the city survive, but contemporary sources attest to local book production (fig. 31). With ambitions to copy the entire Talmud and numerous tractates for anyone willing to pay for the service, a certain Israel ben Nathan set up business as a scribe in Jerusalem, importing the necessary supplies from Fustat in 1060.[49] In contrast, manuscript production by Christians is evidenced by surviving codices rather than by documentation. The Library of Congress preserves a manuscript penned by the abbot for the Armenian community at Jerusalem (cat. 49); Georgians wrote books at the Holy Cross Monastery and at Mar Saba (cats. 29, 31); and the Greeks copied sacred texts as well as books of grammar at Mar Saba (fig. 34). During the reign of the Latin kings of Jerusalem, the Holy Sepulchre housed a scriptorium. A missal (the service book of the Mass), one of many deluxe manuscripts made there (cat. 77), was clearly produced in collaboration with Armenian Christians, for its individual gatherings or sections are numbered in Armenian.[50]

A reverence for books and the cultivation of scholarship went hand in hand. Jerusalem's role as a center of learning is often undeservedly ignored, in spite of the fact that scholarship was intertwined with religious vocation. The city's many madrasas, its centers for Jewish learning, and its Christian monasteries contributed to Jerusalem's diversity, attracting students and scholars from afar.

Karaite Jews flocked to the city in the ninth and tenth centuries. From an extensive list compiled by one Ibn al-Hiti in the fifteenth century we know the names of many Karaite scholars who contributed to this flourishing academic scene.[51] Study groups formed around prominent scholars, including Yusuf ben Bakhtawayh, known as the "teacher to the diaspora," who apparently gathered students in a courtyard. In addition to such notable scholars as Daniel ben Moses al-Qumisi (d. 946) (cat. 36a), al-Hiti mentions Shaykh Abu Yakub ben Noah, who "had a college in Jerusalem" with some seventy "learned men."[52] Almost the entire corpus of Karaite scholarly literature, which included biblical commentaries, Hebrew grammars, and works of religious poetry and philosophy, was composed in Jerusalem during these years.[53]

The number of madrasas, *zawiya*s, and *khanqa*s mentioned by Mujir al-Din (1456–1522), a judge and historian from Jerusalem, in his description of the city from the end of the fifteenth century exceded seventy-five, most of them clustered around the Haram and a not insignificant number of them

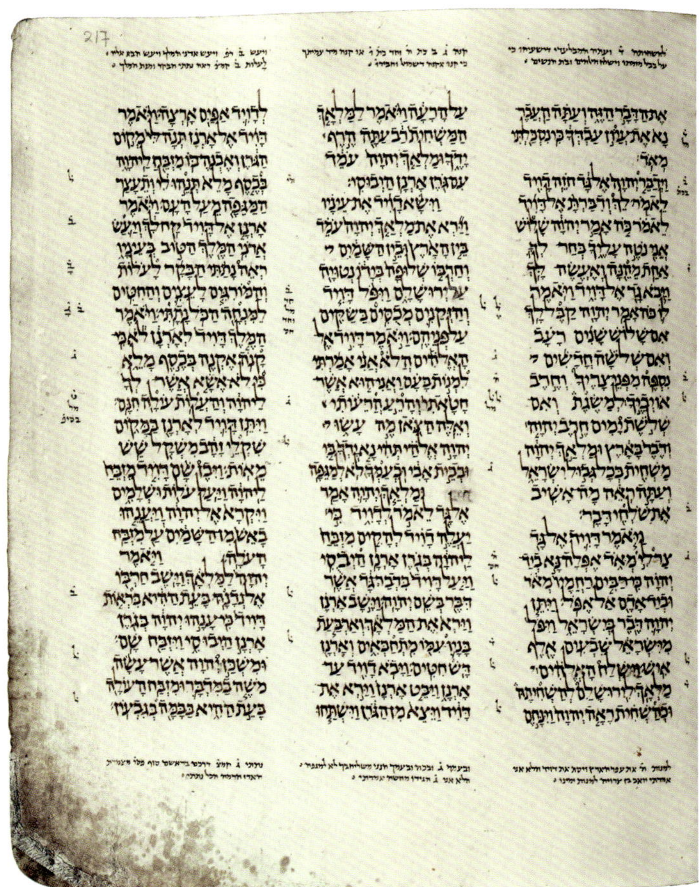

Fig. 31. Folio showing 1 Chronicles 21:8–29, from the Aleppo Codex. Written by Shlomo ben Buya'a; vocalized and edited by Aaron ben Asher. Tiberias, ca. 920. Parchment. Ben-Zvi Institute, Hebrew University, Jerusalem

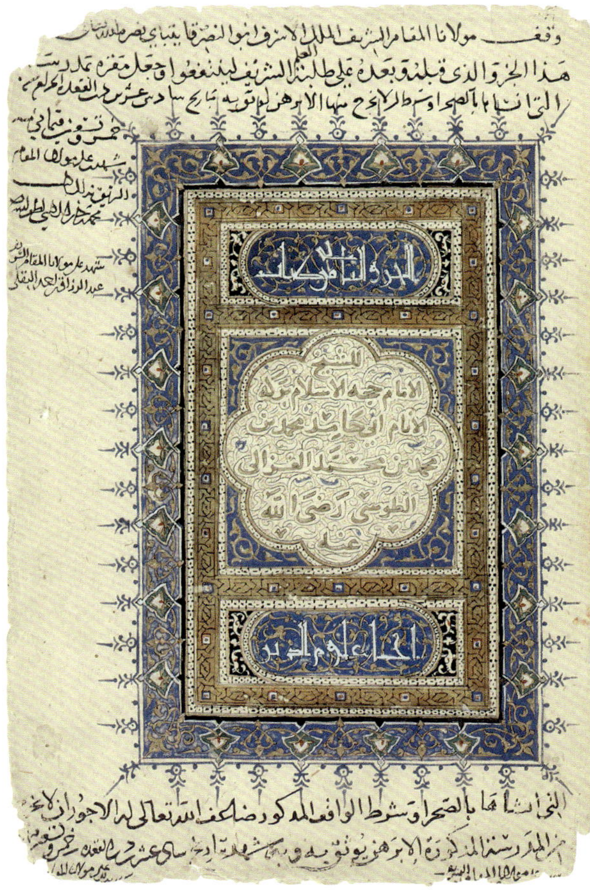

Fig. 32. Eighth section of *Revival of the Islamic Sciences* (*Ihya' 'ulum al-din*) by al-Ghazali. Endowed by Sultan Qa'it Bay (r. 1468–96) to his madrasa. Egypt, 1468–96. Ink, opaque watercolor, and gold on paper. Los Angeles County Museum of Art, The Nasli M. Heeramaneck Collection, gift of Joan Palevsky (M.73.5.516)

founded by women (cat. 136).[54] In the madrasa the fundamental Islamic sciences, in particular the study of Islamic law, formed the curriculum. After Saladin's conquest of Jerusalem, centers for the study of all four schools of Sunni Islam could be found on the Haram.[55] *Khanqa*s and *zawiya*s were lodges of sorts, fostering community among the devout. Housing madrasa staff as well as students or novices, they also provided accommodation for short-term visitors, among them wandering scholars or mystics.[56] While wealthy patrons sometimes paired their endowment of an institution with the gift of a sacred or scholarly manuscript (fig. 32), small-scale Qur'an manuscripts from Jerusalem, such as the example in the British Library (cat. 45), were made in Jerusalem for individual study rather than collective or congregational use. In addition, Mujir al-Din proudly enumerated the many distinguished personages affiliated with Jerusalem, concluding with the great Muslim theologian and philosopher al-Ghazali (ca. 1058–1111), and called particular attention to those scholars who made outstanding contributions in the field of Merits of Jerusalem (Fada'il al-Quds), an Arabic genre of praises for the city (cats. 41, 43).[57]

Part of Jerusalem's vibrancy derived from the steady stream of scholars, Sufis, and students constantly coming and going.[58] For a madrasa he founded in Cairo in the fourteenth century, the Mamluk sultan Barquq (d. 1399) designated special funds for professors to travel to Jerusalem on paid leave whenever they chose.[59] As early as the eleventh century, when the Muslim scholar Abu Bakr ibn al-'Arabi (as distinct from the twelfth-century mystic) reached Jerusalem with his father en route from Spain to Mecca, the many circles of study and disputation in Jerusalem were so impressive that he ended up staying there. "If you intend to go on pilgrimage to Mecca, go as is your wish," al-'Arabi told his father. "As for me, however, I will not leave this city [al-Quds] until I have plumbed the knowledge of those in it, and set it as an example of knowledge and a ladder to its virtues."[60] Reminiscing about his time in Jerusalem and the intellectual openness there, which he found far superior to Cairo, he eloquently stated that "the full moon of knowledge shone for me and I was illuminated by it for more than three years."[61] The "full moon" that so entranced Ibn al-'Arabi, however, did not have the same effect on all who came to study there. A Shafi'i (one of the four schools of Sunni Islamic law) teacher told a story about himself as a young man coming to Jerusalem to study at the Khanthaniyya *zawiya*. Once, before dawn, his shaykh found him napping when he was supposed to be engaged in more elevated matters. Prodding him with his foot, the shaykh said, "My son, your family sent you here for religious study, not for sleep."[62]

The end of Crusader control of Jerusalem permitted a fresh wave of Jewish immigration to the city after 1187. One source indicates that "more than 300 rabbis" came from France and England in the year 1211 alone.[63] While that number is undoubtedly an exaggeration, there was unquestionably a large migration of Jews from northern France, Provence, Languedoc, and Germany during the thirteenth century, many of them notable scholars. Among these immigrants were Rabbi Yehiel of Paris, the head of the Parisian Academy, who came to Jerusalem about 1249, and the exceptionally learned rabbi Nachmanides (Rabbi Moshe ben Nachman), who came in 1267 and established a school and synagogue there, harkening back to when Jerusalem was the seat of the great yeshiva. Abraham, the son of Maimonides, admired some of the French rabbis who passed through Egypt on their way to Palestine: "We saw that they were great sages, possessing wisdom, understanding, piety and sense. We rejoiced in them and they were happy with us and we did them honor as was our obligation."[64]

A native of Jerusalem, William of Tyre (d. 1186) brought a unique scholarly perspective.[65] Educated in Jerusalem[66] and then in Paris and Bologna, he remained enamored of his homeland, eager to return "to the embrace of my pious mother . . . in holy Jerusalem beloved by God."[67] He dedicated himself to writing its history. To do so, he scoured archives, consulted existing histories, and interviewed his contemporaries.[68]

In his chronicle of the kingdom of Jerusalem, William described the complicated relationships between the Eastern Latin clergy, the Pope and papal legatees, the Byzantine patriarchies, the military orders (such as the Knights Templar), and others. In addition to this history, William wrote a history of Islam, from the time of Muhammad until 1184. He deemed Saladin to be "a man of keen and vigorous mind, valiant in war, and of an extremely generous disposition."[69] Of Nur al-Din (d. 1174), he wrote that this "greatest persecutor of the Christian name and faith" was nonetheless "a just prince, valiant and wise, and . . . a religious man."[70] William died in 1186, on the eve of the fall of the kingdom to Saladin.

As the tutor to the future king of Jerusalem Baldwin IV (1161–1185), William of Tyre touchingly described how he first noticed the prince's leprosy. The historian was skeptical of the talents of the physicians in royal service, specifically those of local doctors.[71] Predictably, most chroniclers expressed confidence in physicians from their own communities. Usama ibn Munqidh, for example, recounted the tragic tale of a Frankish doctor who sneered at the cures proposed by one of his eastern Mediterranean colleagues; insisting on a surgical intervention, the Frankish doctor provoked his patient's untimely death.[72]

Religious affiliation was less important in medicine than in other professions. There were doctors of all faiths at the court of Saladin and his successors.[73] When the Frankish king of Jerusalem Amalric (d. 1174) asked his Fatimid allies in Egypt for a good doctor, they initially suggested Maimonides (who later became the physician of Saladin).[74] Ultimately, Abu Sulëyman Dawud, an Eastern Christian physician from Jerusalem, was chosen.[75] The Greek Orthodox physician Ya'qub b. Siqlab, a native of Jerusalem, practiced medicine for the Muslim court in Damascus. Sectarian indifference could extend to patients as well. A hospital in Frankish Jerusalem admitted not only Christians but Jews and Muslims as well, even accommodating dietary restrictions by making chicken available for those who did not eat pork.[76]

Such "doctors without borders" exemplified how scholarship could help bridge the divides between cultures. A few religious scholars were also remarkable for their focus on points of intersection between faiths. Al-Ghazali wrote extensively about Jesus; it appears that Maimonides was aware of the work of a number of Islamic scholars, including al-Ghazali. The title of Maimonides's *Guide for the Perplexed* may have been inspired by al-Ghazali's designation of that attribute to God.[77] Ibn al-'Arabi admired the spirited intellectual jousting he witnessed between learned Jews and Muslims during his sojourn in Jerusalem.[78] William of Tripoli, a thirteenth-century Dominican resident in Acre, combed the Qur'an for passages relating to the "Story of Mary and Jesus" and, though eager to encourage conversion, saw Islam in a newly positive light.[79] Learning, too, could serve as the currency of diplomatic entente. The historian Ibn Wasil recounted that, in negotiations with al-Malik al-Kamil (d. 1238) over the status of Jerusalem, Holy Roman Emperor Frederick II (1194–1250) posed queries on "difficult philosophic, geometric and mathematical points to test the men of learning at his [the sultan's] court."[80] Scholarly exchange formed the basis for mutual respect, and, as a result, the emperor and the sultan managed within a matter of months and without bloodshed to forge a temporary truce. The Treaty of Jaffa of 1229 was an imperfect agreement, but it opened the Holy City to the subjects of both rulers for a decade.

The multiethnic, multireligious, multilinguistic stew that was medieval Jerusalem yielded an environment of perpetual instability. Who was foreign? Who was native? Who was culturally dominant? Who was marginal? While questions of power never disappeared, the city's inhabitants and visitors found ways to manage. Life in Jerusalem entailed a ceaseless bumping up against difference. Even as these intercultural interactions could produce misunderstandings, hostility, dishonesty, and distrust, the diversity of the city's population was also sometimes celebrated, as is clear from the comments of Niccolo of Poggibonsi, a Franciscan from Tuscany who visited Jerusalem in the fourteenth century. His description of Palm Sunday rituals recalls the image from the Syriac lectionary with which this essay opened. Noting men in olive trees shouting in "shrill voices," Poggibonsi asked an interpreter what they were saying. "And he [the interpreter] replied that he understood not, as those on one tree shouted in Arabic, and those on the other in Ethiopic; 'and I am an interpreter for the Hebrew and Saracenic languages.' And yet the truth is that they spoke very good words and the multitude around them all sang in a loud voice, each one in his own tongue."[81]

NOTES FOR THIS ESSAY APPEAR ON PAGES 301–2
SEE CATS. 27–57

SAINT SABAS AND THE MONKS OF THE HOLY LAND

Jennifer Ball

Just as Jerusalem is the queen of all cities, so is the lavra of Sabas the prince of all deserts, and so far as Jerusalem is the norm of other cities, so too is St. Sabas the exemplar for other monasteries. — PASSION OF SAINT MICHAEL THE SABAITE

ONE OF the most influential monks of the Eastern Orthodox Church, Saint Sabas (439–532) was revered for leading a great monastic movement and for writing a set of liturgical rules for his monks.[1] Born in 439 and raised from boyhood in a monastery near his childhood home in Asia Minor, he left Cappadocia at about the age of eighteen for the Holy Land, where he later founded the Great Lavra, a monastic complex in the Valley of Jehoshaphat between Jerusalem and the Dead Sea.[2] Known in Arabic as Mar Saba, the Great Lavra still exists today (fig. 33).

Sabas is best known for his development of a distinct "Sabaite" form of monasticism and its accompanying liturgical practice, written in a book known as the Sabaite typikon.[3] Sabaite monasticism blended elements of cenobitic (or communal) monastic living with the practices of hermit monks, especially those of the Egyptian desert.[4] Sabas spent his first years in the Holy Land living in various cenobitic monasteries. In 469 he went to live as a solitary monk in a cave outside the walls of the monastery of Abba Theoktistos. During the week he lived an ascetic life, depriving himself of food while praying and weaving baskets (at a rate of fifty baskets a week).[5] On Saturdays and Sundays he returned to Theoktistos to attend services and replenish supplies, a practice he maintained for five years and later used as the model for the Great Lavra monastery that he established.

Desiring to live completely on his own, Sabas soon began to wander in the desert. No longer reliant on supplies from Theoktistos, he lived off of wild plants and the occasional sundries offered by nomads. Although Sabas had some interactions with other wandering monks during these years, for the most part he struggled to survive in the wilderness in a Christlike, athletic battle against Satan, as portrayed in the story of his life (*vita*), written by Cyril of Scythopolis in 556.

Choosing in 483 a cave in the Valley of Jehoshaphat purportedly pointed out to him by an angel, Sabas decided to take on disciples in adjacent rock-hewn caves described by Daniel the Abbot (1106–1178) as "cells fixed to the rocks like stars in the sky."[6] The dramatic setting for his lavra, on the sides of a steep cliff almost three hundred yards from the valley floor at its highest point, distinguished it from lavriote settings in other parts of the late antique world.[7] Living in solitude during the week, the monks came together for services and provisions at the week's end. Sabas and his community of monks, whose ranks grew to 150, enlarged a cave to build a church, now dedicated to Saint Nicholas.[8] Over time Sabas expanded the monastery — with support from the patriarch of Jerusalem and his own inheritance — to include a second church dedicated to the Virgin, cisterns, a hostel, an oven, and a hospital. A number of pilgrims briefly described the church, which reportedly had a blue-green dome.[9] According to the Greek pilgrim John Phocas, the church was "full of delightful things, being very large, long, full of light, with its pavement adorned with marbles, which though of small cost and brought from the wilderness are nevertheless colourfully worked."[10] The buildings of Mar Saba as they exist today had to be rebuilt after a devastating earthquake on May 13, 1834.[11]

Sabas eventually founded a total of ten monasteries, with his disciples starting four others.[12] In 493 he rose to the position of archimandrite, leading all anchorites (hermits) in the Judean Desert as well as some cenobitic houses, or about five hundred monks in total. Because of the substantial number of monks under his leadership and the dissemination of his typikon, one can speak of a Sabaite form of monasticism.

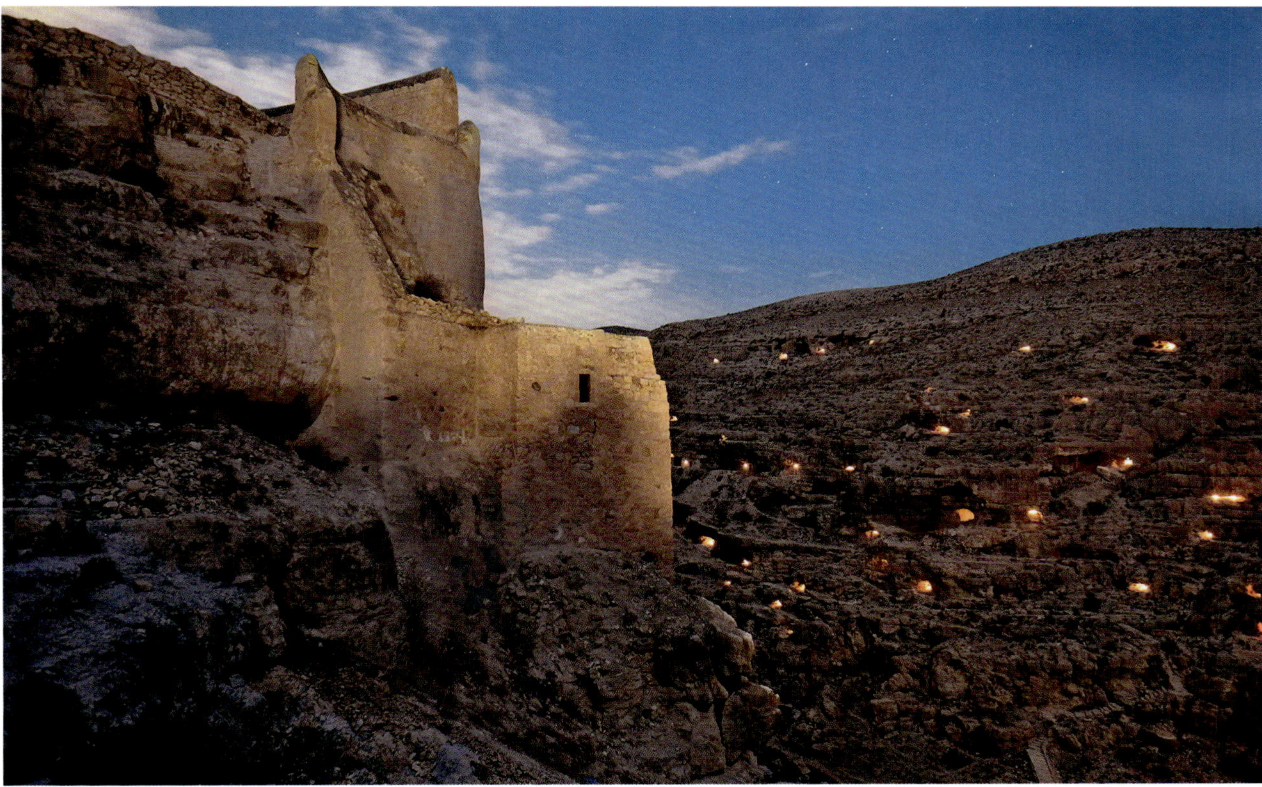

Fig. 33. Candles illuminating the caves in the Judean Desert near the Monastery of Mar Saba on the Feast of Mar Saba, December 17, 2015

Sabas's innovations were adopted by the influential Stoudios Monastery in the Byzantine capital of Constantinople. These included the use of hymns, previously known only in lay churches,[13] and all-night vigils on Saturdays between the observation of Divine Offices and the Divine Liturgy.[14] The Sabas monastery produced several famous hymnographers, including Kosmas the Hagiopolite and Stephanos the Melodist, as well as the most famous Sabaite monk, John of Damascus (ca. 675–749), who perfected the Canon of the Orthodox Church, which was incorporated into a liturgical typikon at Sinai in 1214.[15] Although John's famous defense of images was taken up by iconophiles during the Byzantine controversy over images (723–842), it was likely written to counter Muslim accusations of idolatry while he lived under the policies of the Umayyad caliph Yazid II (687–724).[16]

The longevity of Mar Saba can be attributed to its dramatic setting and the prolific writers and theologians who spread not only Sabas's own teachings but also those of the great intellectual community that flourished there. At the behest of the patriarch of Jerusalem, in 511 and again in 532 Sabas traveled to Constantinople for imperial audiences, beginning a long tradition of the monastery's involvement in doctrinal disputes. In 614 the monastery was sacked by the Persians. Scores of monks were martyred then, and again at the time of Arab attacks in 638 and 797. Their stories cemented the reputation of Sabaites as defenders of Orthodoxy as well as hero-martyrs.[17] The Graptoi brothers, Theodore and Theophanes, martyrs of the Iconoclast controversy, were also Sabaites.

Long after Sabas's death in 532, the Great Lavra continued to be known as a major intellectual center, housing a number of renowned theologians. Because the Great Lavra housed Greek, Georgian, and Syrian monks in a single community, it served a vital role in translating works into many languages, including Arabic (cat. 35). The first redaction of the Georgian bible, made after 980, is known as that of "Saint Sabas."[18] A twelfth-century Greek Grammar from the library at Mar Saba (fig. 34), for example, attests to the monastery as a center of learning, even long after Greek was no longer its primary spoken language. In addition,

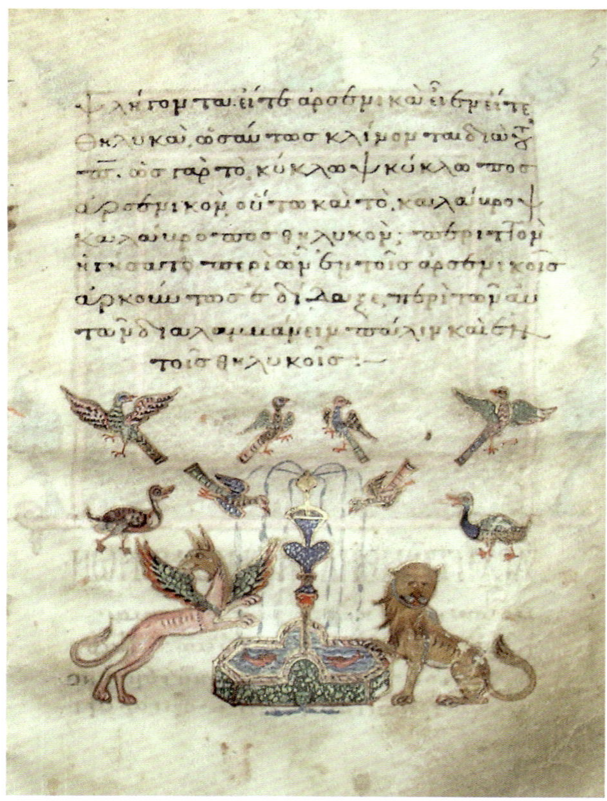

Fig. 34. "On Feminine Rules," from *Greek Grammar.* Monastery of Mar Saba, 12th century. Tempera and gold on parchment. Greek Orthodox Patriarchate, Jerusalem (Taphou 52, fol. 50r)

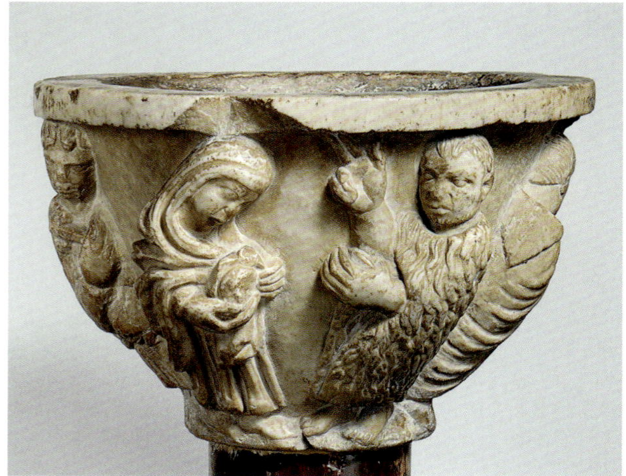

Fig. 35. Capital of Saint Rainer of Pisa, monk of the Holy Land (reused as a font). Follower of Guglielmus. Probably Pisa, ca. 1160–65. Carrara marble. The Metropolitan Museum of Art, New York, The Cloisters Collection, 1964 (64.96)

the library of the Great Lavra included thirteenth-century copies of works by Aristotle and other classical authors.[19]

Along with biblical sites, the Great Lavra and other monastic communities were a focus of Orthodox pilgrimage.[20] Latin Christians knew little of Mar Saba until the Crusader period, when Western pilgrimage grew, as did interest in the life of Saint Sabas himself. The Englishman Saewulf, traveling to the Holy Land about 1102, included in his account a discussion of Sabas.[21] Melisende, queen of Jerusalem (r. 1131–53), gave three properties to the monks of Saint Sabas, the income from which was to be donated to the poor.[22] Orthodox monks had parochial responsibilities in the Latin Kingdom of Jerusalem, and their ascetic lifestyle influenced not only the faithful of their own sect but also European monks such as Rainer of Pisa (fig. 35). Though the relics of Sabas were taken from the monastery during the Crusades and brought to Venice, they were returned in 1965.[23]

Like the Monastery of Saint Catherine at the foot of Mount Sinai in Egypt, Mar Saba is one of the few continuously operated Orthodox monasteries in the world, which is especially remarkable given the tumultuous history of the region and the Great Lavra's proximity to Jerusalem. Today Mar Saba continues to maintain Byzantine time, in which midnight begins at sunset. Once a week, a monk climbs to the top of the monastery and sets the time to midnight just as the last rays of the sun touch the cave of Saint Sabas.

NOTES FOR THIS ESSAY APPEAR ON PAGE 302
SEE CATS. 30–34

THE KARAITES

Meira Polliack

KARAISM, a branch of Judaism, is one of many manifestations of medieval Jewish culture and identity. This distinctive form of Judaism focuses on the Hebrew Bible, as reflected in the names given to its followers – *kara'im*, *benei-miqra*, *ba'alei miqra* – all of which are derived from the word *miqra*, the Hebrew root for "Bible." The Karaite movement crystallized in the second half of the ninth century among the Jewish communities of Iran and Iraq. In the early tenth century the Karaites founded an intellectual center in Jerusalem, which remained active until the late eleventh century (fig. 36). During this two-hundred-year-long golden age in Jerusalem, they produced major works of Hebrew grammar, Bible translation, exegesis, law, and philosophy. These texts had an enduring effect on medieval Judeo-Arabic culture and influenced medieval Jewish thought and literature as a whole.

The major geographical centers of the Karaites eventually shifted from Jerusalem to Turkey, the Crimea, Lithuania, and Egypt. Today they have come full circle, as the majority of Karaite Jews, estimated at several thousand, live in Israel (their major community centers and synagogues are in Ashdod and Ramle). Smaller offshoot communities can be found in the United States. In Eastern Europe there are still some small communities of "Karaim," a group whose ethnic connection to the Middle Eastern Karaites has been debated among scholars and who from the late nineteenth century ceased to define themselves as Jews.[1]

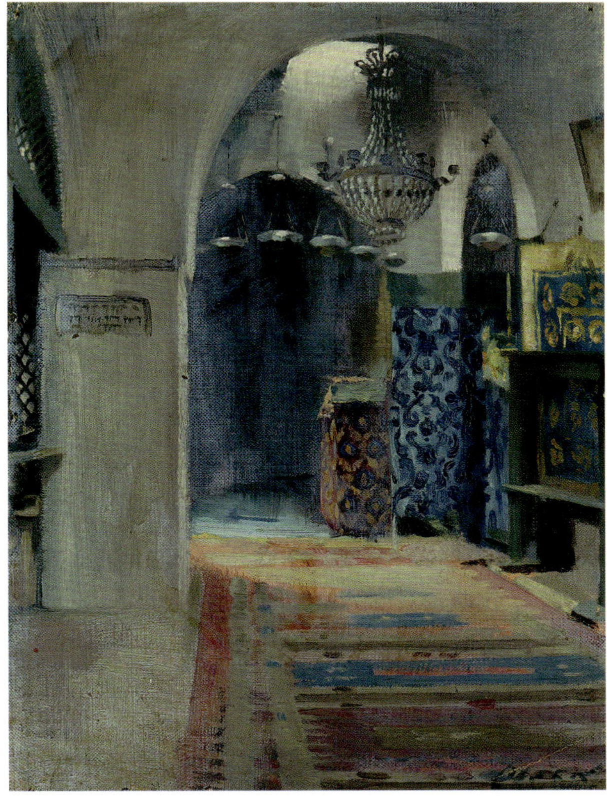

Fig. 36. *Old Karaite Synagogue, Jerusalem* (built on the site of the original medieval synagogue). James Clark. 19th century. Oil on canvas. Palestine Exploration Fund, London

HISTORICAL BACKGROUND

Beginning in the seventh century, the region of Palestine, in which various Jewish communities had existed since ancient times, was ruled by several successive Muslim dynasties. The first Muslim conquerors in 634 permitted the rebuilding in Jerusalem of a Jewish community that thrived until its expulsion by the Crusaders in 1099. According to sources found in the Cairo Geniza, the Jewish center of learning known as the Palestine Academy (Yeshivat Eretz Yisrael) relocated from Tiberias to Jerusalem about 922–25 and was active in the city until 1076. This yeshiva led Palestine's Rabbanite (non-Karaite) community and strove to retain its status in the face of frequent challenges from the two leading Babylonian yeshivas near Baghdad. In Jewish historiography this era is known as the Geonic period, after "Gaon," the title by which the yeshiva heads were commonly called. It was marked by immense creativity as well as by intellectual and political tensions between the two main centers, in Palestine and Babylonia, each of which adhered to its distinctive literary and religious traditions.

Into this communal diversity entered the Karaite Jews, who began immigrating to Palestine from Iraq about 880, led by the exegete and activist Daniel

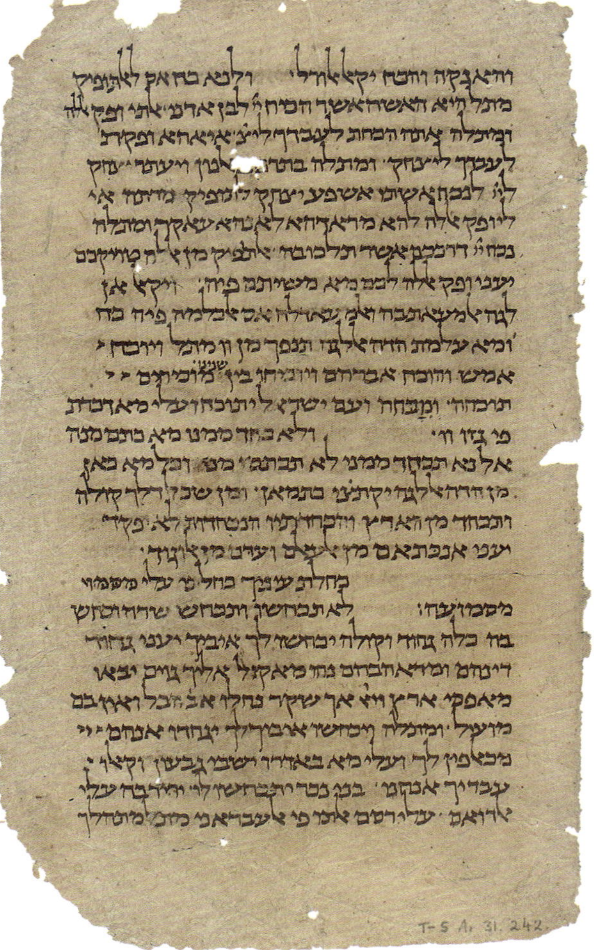

Fig. 37. Hebrew-Arabic lexicon. Written by David ben Abraham Alfasi. Second half of the 10th century. Ink on paper. Cambridge University Library, Taylor-Schecter Genizah Collection (T-S Ar.31.242, fol. 1r)

al-Qumisi (cat. 36a). They founded a thriving community in Jerusalem, which they named with the biblical epithets Mourners of Sion (*aveley tziyon*) and Lilies (*shoshanim*). They also established a learning precinct in the city, known in Arabic as *dar lil-'ilm* (house of study), associated with the figure of the leading Karaite grammarian Yusuf ibn Nuh. Several generations of Karaite scholars regularly met there. During this formative period, the Jerusalem community became the most important Karaite group of its day and remained so until its destruction by the Crusaders.

Tensions between the Rabbanite and Karaite communities of Jerusalem persisted throughout this time and are reflected in various historical sources. The groups lived in different neighborhoods in the city and sometimes clashed over their interpretations of Jewish religious observance (cat. 68). Yet both groups considered each other as belonging to the Jewish people, and both were treated by the Muslim authorities as Jews, albeit of different denominations.

In the wake of the Crusader conquest, many Jews were expelled and their communities destroyed, including those of Jerusalem. The Karaite Jews, whose entire ethos was based on a return to the Bible and the Promised Land, harbored Messianic hopes and received the severest blow. From Jerusalem they fled to Byzantium, Egypt, and Spain. Eventually they succeeded in reorganizing their community life and ideology around a diasporic model. In Byzantium they translated many classical works into Hebrew and created new anthologies, adapting their religion and literature to their new situation.[2] In Egypt the Karaites joined forces with Rabbanite brethren in ransoming Jewish books and prisoners (cat. 39). While some would claim that the intellectual challenge they represented within medieval Judaism, particularly in their Jerusalem golden age, was unmatched by their later achievements, others would see Jerusalem as just one episode in a rich historical and literary Karaite tradition. The continued yearning for Jerusalem was reflected in many medieval sources, both Karaite and Rabbanite, and furnished many themes of Jewish poetry and thought (cat. 22), as well as sporadic waves of pilgrims and immigrants to the Holy Land, up to the modern era.

LITERATURE

The Karaites' rejection of the Rabbinic Oral Law, and their desire to return to the Hebrew Bible as the sole basis for Jewish religious practice, led them to focus afresh on the biblical text; the language, syntax, and discourse of the Hebrew Bible were their building blocks of biblical exegesis (cat. 36a). They produced manuscripts of interpretation that closely followed the text, usually quoting the full verse in Hebrew, translating it into Arabic, and commenting on it in Arabic (cats. 37a). Like most Jews of the region up to modern times, Karaites wrote their manuscripts mainly in Judeo-Arabic, a medieval form of classical Arabic transcribed into Hebrew script, with some unique ethnic and religious features (fig. 37). Some manuscripts, however, were written in Arabic script (fig. 38). The Karaites produced books on Jewish religious law (*sifrei mitzvot*), Hebrew grammar, and traditions of reading the Bible (Masora), as well as biblical dictionaries. They also created theological compositions influenced by the rationalist philosophy of the Mu'tazilite school of Islamic *kalam*, a form of rationalist philosophy and theology (cat. 36b).

The Karaite conflict with the Rabbanites resulted in polemical works, especially against the Rabbanite scholar who most strongly opposed the Karaite movement, Rabbi Sa'adia Gaon (882–942).[3] The important Karaite exegetes and scholars who lived in Jerusalem during the tenth and eleventh centuries included al-Qumisi, David ben Abraham Alfasi, Salmon ben Jeruham, Yefet ben 'Eli, Yusuf ibn Nuh, 'Abu al-Faraj Harun, and Yeshu'ah ben Yehudah. As a center of so many forms of creativity, Jerusalem was a magnet for Karaites from all corners of the Diaspora. The eleventh-century Byzantine Karaite Tobias ben Moses, who sojourned in Jerusalem, disseminated Karaite doctrine when he returned to his birthplace by translating some of the works of the Jerusalem Karaites from Arabic into Hebrew. According to Rabbi Abraham ben David (the Rabad), a twelfth-century Talmudic authority in southern France, Ibn al-Taras, who spread Karaism in Spain, studied with Yeshu'ah ben Yehudah in the city during the eleventh century.

Throughout its long history, Karaism experienced transformations and resurgent cycles of creativity: its ethos and creed were adapted and redefined; its language and literature diversified and grew. These variations in self-definition and religious practice have suggested to some the notion of "Karaisms" (similar to the notion of "Judaisms"). Nevertheless, the past

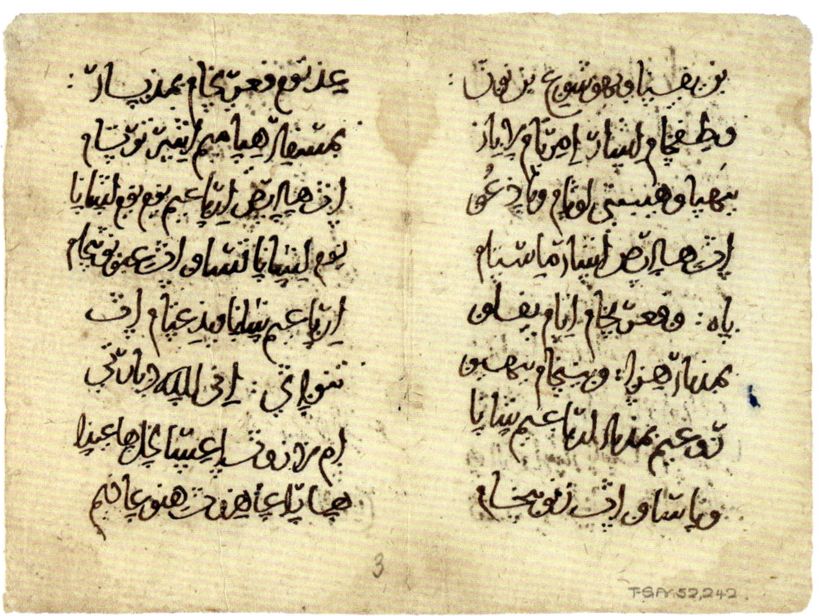

Fig. 38. Karaite-Arabic transcription of the book of Numbers (14:33–35). Ink on paper. Cambridge University Library, Taylor-Schecter Genizah Collection (T-S Ar.52.242, fol. 3r)

millennium has witnessed a striking consistency, with Karaites maintaining their scripturalist ethos and their Jewish identity. Focus on the Hebrew Bible made the movement an unrivaled "alternative voice" within premodern Judaism. Recently — within the past decade — there has been an increase in the number of publications on medieval and modern Karaism, including the preparation of long-awaited critical editions of major medieval Karaite works, updated historical monographs, and important bibliographical tools.[4]

NOTES FOR THIS ESSAY APPEAR ON PAGE 302
SEE CATS. 30–34

MAIMONIDES AND JERUSALEM

David Kraemer

PHILOSOPHER, scholar, and physician, Maimonides – Rabbi Moshe ben Maimon (1135–1204) – was recognized as the rabbinic authority of his generation as well as one of the most brilliant and influential Jews of all time. Of great interest to scholars and historians, the details of his life and work have been scrutinized time and again. One of the many areas of dispute among those who study his legacy is his relationship to Jerusalem.

When speaking of Maimonides's relationship to Jerusalem, we must consider two matters: first, the nature of Maimonides's own visit to the Holy Land and Jerusalem, and second, his attitudes toward Jerusalem as expressed in his legal writings. Given the fact that Maimonides's reported conduct in Jerusalem and the Holy Land contradicted his legal rulings in significant respects, we must also ask how and whether these apparently conflicting realities can be reconciled.

Maimonides visited the Holy Land for nearly a year, immediately after leaving behind years of difficulty in North Africa. Forced to flee a new, oppressive Muslim regime in his native Spain, in 1159 Maimonides and his family had found their way to Morocco, the very center of the restrictive Almohad caliphate. How or whether they managed to maintain their Jewish practice in North Africa is a matter of dispute; some scholars believe that Maimonides converted to Islam, at least outwardly.[1] But it is clear that life for Jews in Morocco must have been very challenging, and in 1165 Maimonides and his family fled by ship, arriving in Acre on May 16. Did Maimonides intend to stay in the Holy Land or was his visit devised as an atoning pilgrimage? While we cannot answer that question, we do know that his sojourn there lasted less than a year and that in 1166 he relocated to Fustat.

Our knowledge of Maimonides's visit to the Holy Land comes primarily from a letter that he wrote.[2] According to Maimonides's account, he spent but a few days in Jerusalem – Thursday, October 16, to Sunday, October 19 – after which he traveled to Hebron to visit the Tomb of the Patriarchs. On the first of those days, Maimonides recorded, he "entered the great and Holy House and . . . prayed in it."[3] The meaning of this statement has been the subject of considerable discussion. The Jewish Temple in Jerusalem (fig. 39) had been destroyed by the Romans many centuries before Maimonides visited the city, and it is unlikely that Maimonides would describe the Dome of the Rock (not the Aqsa Mosque, which is not on the site of the Temple) using this kind of language. In addition, in his compendium of Jewish religious law, the *Mishneh Torah*, Maimonides forbade treading on the sacred space of the Temple. Consequently, some scholars believe that Maimonides must have been speaking of the Western Wall. Others take him at his word and understand him to mean that he prayed in the space of the destroyed Temple. In this scenario, Maimonides did not follow the law as he himself understood it.

This is all we know about Maimonides's experience in Jerusalem. Of his attitudes, however, we know something more – if his legal rulings may be taken as expressions of such. Maimonides wrote more about the Holy Land in general than of Jerusalem in particular. Surprisingly, he does not list the obligation for a Jew to settle in Eretz Yisrael (the Land of Israel) in his accounting of the 613 commandments of the Torah, a fact that through the ages has generated great consternation among scholars, among them Nachmanides (1194–1270).

Instead, Maimonides wrote at length about the superiority of the land and the obligation to live and remain there once one had entered it. Drawing on the teachings of the Talmud, he declared that one who lives in the land is forgiven all his sins and that one who walks a distance of merely four cubits in the land merits a place in the World to Come.[4] He also confirmed the superiority of Jerusalem in particular over the land in general.[5] Maimonides most eloquently expressed the sacredness of Jerusalem thus: "Why do I say that the original sacredness of the Temple and Jerusalem are eternal? . . . Because the sacredness of the Temple and Jerusalem is on account of the Divine Presence, and the Divine Presence is never annulled. Behold, the Torah says, 'I will lay waste your holy places' (Leviticus 26:31), and our sages said, 'even though they are wasted, they remain holy.'"[6] Even long after the destruction, the Temple Mount must be treated as though the Temple were still standing.[7]

For Maimonides, Jerusalem was the eternal home of the Divine Presence, regardless of whatever mundane power rules its precincts and whatever its state of repair or ruin. Does this mean that Maimonides broke his own law when he prayed in the "great and Holy House"? If he did, we may imagine that his personal conduct was inspired by his very sense of the holiness of the place where he found himself. To be sure, he would not be the only righteous person who was inspired to break the law for what he saw as a holier purpose. Less than a year after arriving in the Holy Land, Maimonides abandoned his own directives and left for Egypt, where he lived until the end of his life. What do his actions tell us about his relationship with Jerusalem and the Holy Land? Perhaps nothing more than that ideals are ideals, but life must be lived in the real world.

NOTES FOR THIS ESSAY APPEAR ON PAGE 302
SEE CATS. 38, 39

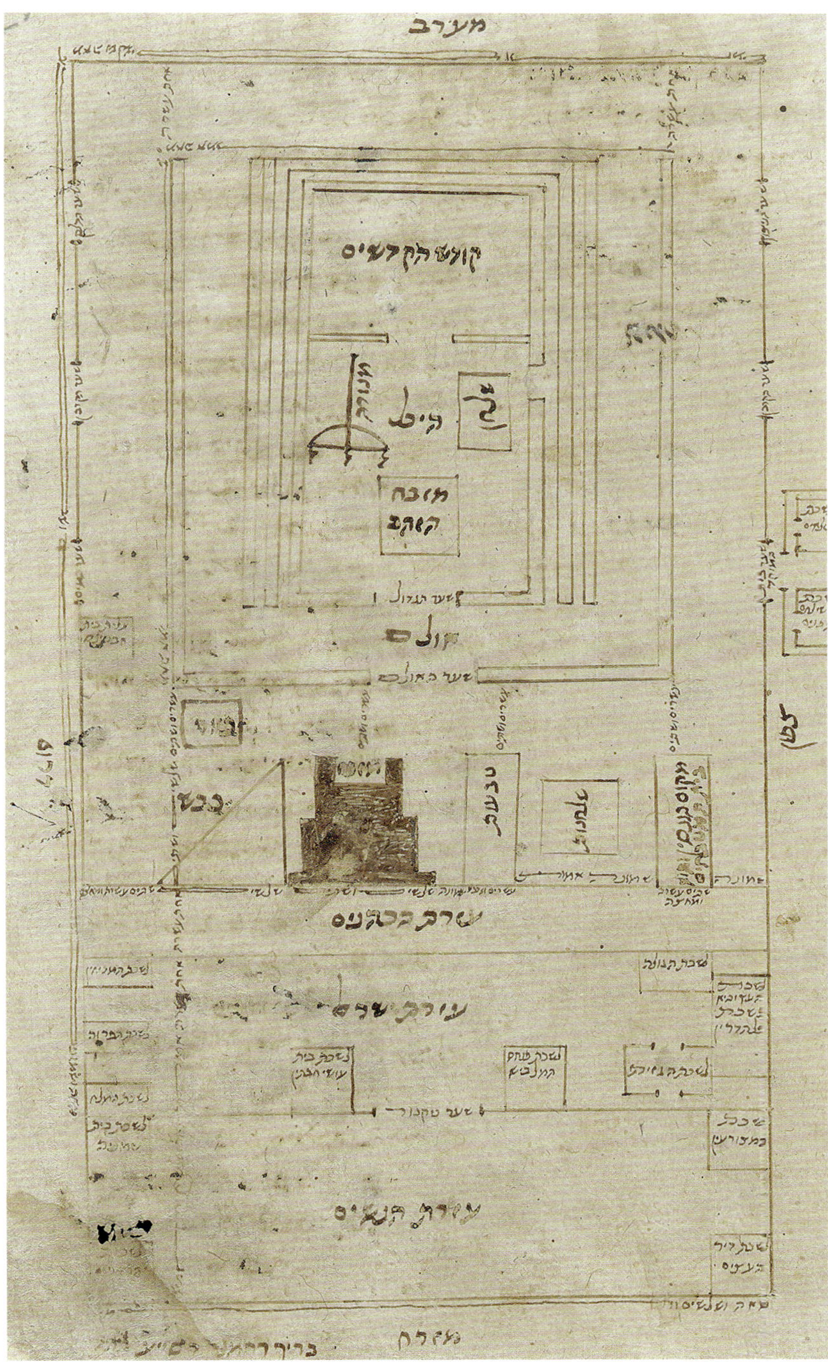

Fig. 39. Temple diagram from Maimonides's *Commentary on the Mishnah*. Detail of cat. 38, fols. 294v–295

MERITS OF JERUSALEM (FADA'IL AL-QUDS)

Carole Hillenbrand

THE FIRST Muslim dynasty, the Umayyads, with their capital in Damascus, beautified Jerusalem by building the Aqsa Mosque and the Dome of the Rock. Their successors, the Sunni Abbasid caliphs in distant Baghdad, paid little attention to Jerusalem, but their rivals, the Shi'ite Fatimid caliphs in Egypt, generally venerated the city. By 1099, when the Crusaders captured Jerusalem, it had acquired the status of the third most sacred city in Islam, after Mecca and Medina (fig. 40). From 1099 to 1187 Jerusalem was in the hands of the Christians, and as the twelfth century progressed, its loss became increasingly painful to the Muslims of Syria and Egypt. Their military leaders, and above all Nur al-Din and Saladin, used a variety of methods to induce a spirit of jihad among the Muslim inhabitants of Syria and Egypt in order to recapture Jerusalem and especially the sacred sites of the Dome of the Rock and the Aqsa Mosque. Saladin took back the city in October 1187.

MERITS OF JERUSALEM (FADA'IL AL-QUDS) LITERATURE

The sacred status of Jerusalem in Islam received special attention in writings called the Merits of Jerusalem (Fada'il al-Quds).[1] The first known work of this kind, titled the *Merits of the Holy House* (*Fada'il al-bayt al-maqdis*), was compiled by the Muslim scholar al-Ramli (d. 912). Although no longer extant, his book can be reconstructed almost completely by quotations that appeared in later works, particularly those of two eleventh-century scholars, al-Wasiti (d. after 1019) and Ibn al-Murajja'.[2] Al-Ramli was fully aware that the sacred heritage of Jerusalem was shared by all three Abrahamic religions. Gradually, however, a new, specifically Islamic view of the sanctity of Jerusalem was adopted by later scholars, a view especially emphasized in the twelfth century. The Crusader appropriation of the Aqsa Mosque and the Dome of the Rock must have deeply shocked Muslims in the Holy Land and Syria, and with Jerusalem in Crusader hands, the Merits of Jerusalem genre gradually gathered momentum. In the 1160s in Syria, the public reading of these works in the mosques both encouraged the Muslim faithful and helped to increase their desire to repossess the Holy City.

FORMAT AND THEMES OF THE MERITS OF JERUSALEM BOOKS

Muslim traditions emphasizing the sanctity of Jerusalem can be traced to seventh- and eighth-century collections of hadith (canonical sayings of the Prophet Muhammad). Familiar elements of the Merits of Jerusalem literature had already appeared in the famous Qur'an commentary of Muqatil (d. 767) and in Muslim travel and geographical writings dating to before the twelfth century.[3] The Persian traveler Nasir-i Khusraw (d. 1088), for example, noted that a prayer said in Jerusalem was worth twenty-five thousand ordinary ones. A single silver coin given in Jerusalem as alms rescued the donor from the fires of hell, as did a day of fasting there.[4]

Almost all the compilers of the Merits of Jerusalem books came from the Holy Land and Syria. Nevertheless, the most famous preacher of his time, Ibn al-Jawzi (1126–1200), who lived in Baghdad, also wrote such a work, although it is very unlikely that he ever visited Jerusalem.[5] The content of these books is highly predictable, for their "authors" derive themes, and indeed very often even exact wording, from earlier works of this kind. Rarely do they comment personally on the material. It is, on occasion, hard to tell from the content and phrasing whether such a book was composed in the twelfth or the fifteenth century.

The earliest Merits of Jerusalem works spoke of the biblical heritage that made Jerusalem sacred to Jews and Christians while also developing the concept of the sanctity of Jerusalem within the Islamic tradition. They emphasized that the city was the first Muslim direction of prayer (qibla) and that Muhammad made his Night Journey into the heavens from there. They described the many sacred sites in Jerusalem; stressed the extra value of prayer, pilgrimage, and other religious exercises carried out there; and pointed out that it is especially meritorious to die or be buried in the city. After the Crusaders had been removed from Jerusalem, the scholars who compiled books of this genre focused much more exclusively on the city's Muslim heritage.

Eschatological themes connected with Jerusalem also figured prominently in these works. On the Day of Judgment, every soul will have to tread the Narrow Path (Sirat al-Mustaqim) mentioned in the Qur'an. Stretching from the Aqsa Mosque to the Mount of Olives and no wider than a human hair, the path leads to paradise for those blessed souls who can cross it. For those who fall, the fire of hell awaits.

That the Merits of Jerusalem literature played a key role in efforts to revive jihad in Syria and Egypt and recapture Jerusalem is clearly demonstrated in the famous sermon of the preacher Ibn al-Zaki (d. 1192) given in the Aqsa Mosque in October 1187 to celebrate Saladin's victorious entry into the city. The words of al-Zaki, recorded by Saladin's biographers, echo the themes found in the Merits that highlight the sacred nature of the Holy City: its status as Abraham's dwelling place, the site of the Prophet Muhammad's Night Journey, the first direction of prayer in Islam, and the home of the saints. At some future time, all mankind would assemble outside Jerusalem to receive God's judgment on the Last Day.

Not surprisingly, the Merits of Jerusalem books remained popular for several centuries and served as an encouragement for Muslims to make visitations to Jerusalem and to perform prayer, pilgrimage, and other acts of piety there.

NOTES FOR THIS ESSAY APPEAR ON PAGE 302
SEE CATS. 40–57

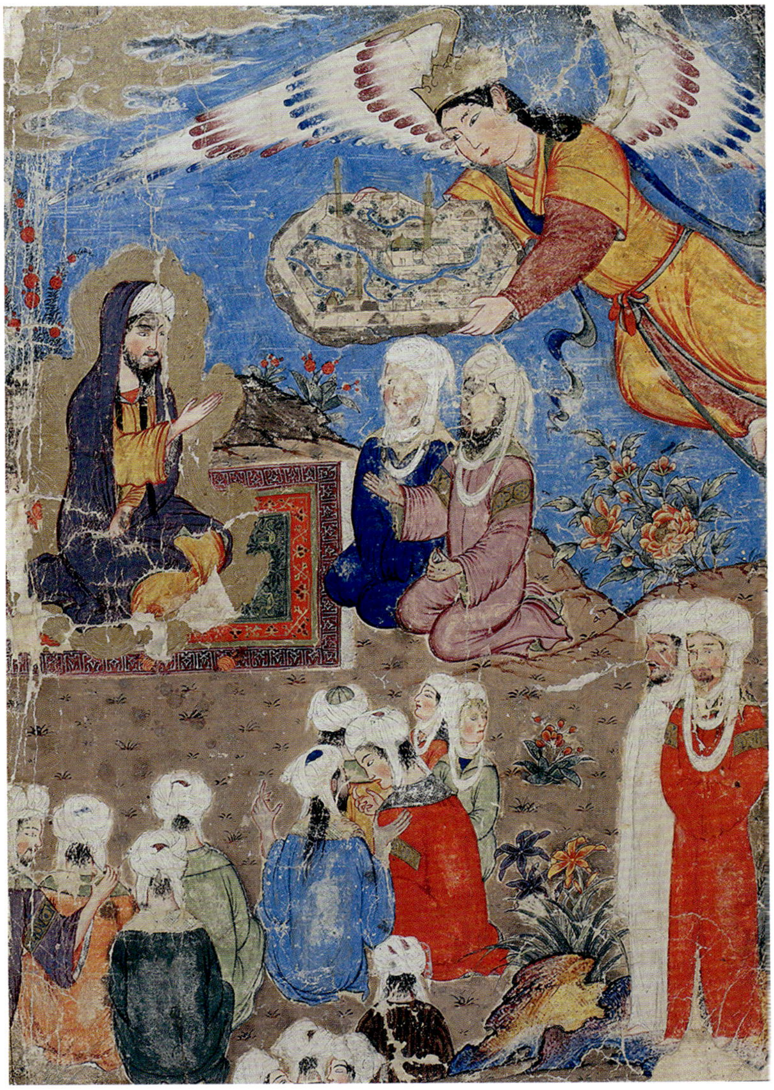

Fig. 40. "The Prophet Describes Jerusalem after His Night Journey," from a *Book of Ascension* (*Mi'rajnama*). Probably Tabriz, Iran, ca. 1317–35. Paint and gold on paper. Topkapı Sarayı Museum Library, Istanbul (Hazine 2154, fol. 107r)

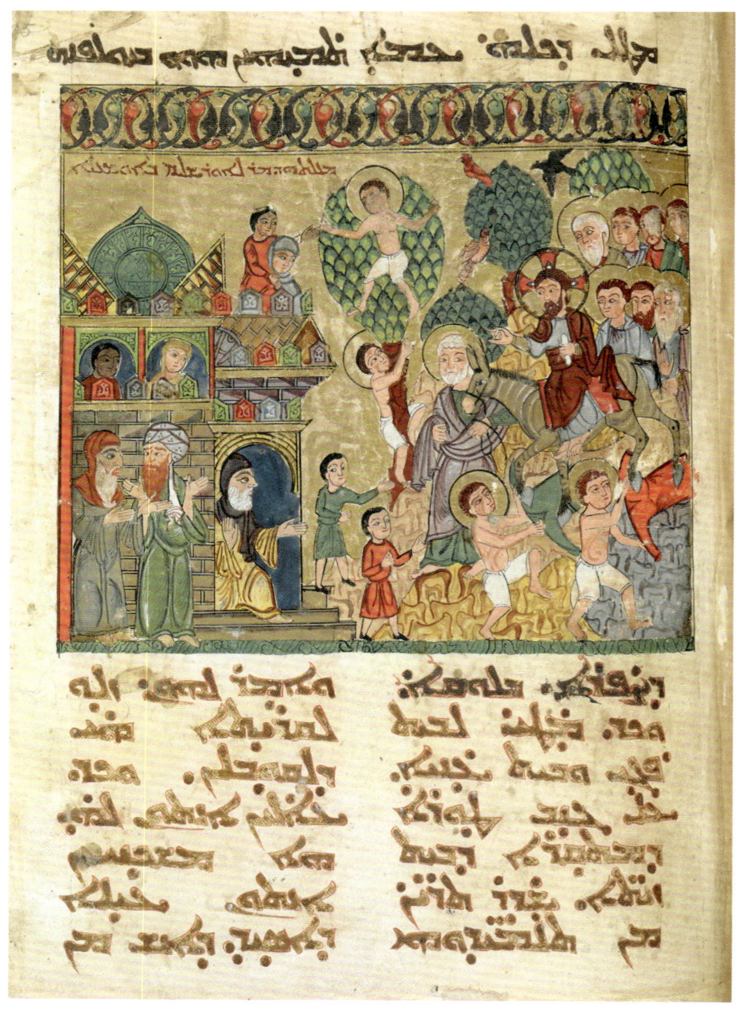

27, fol. 115

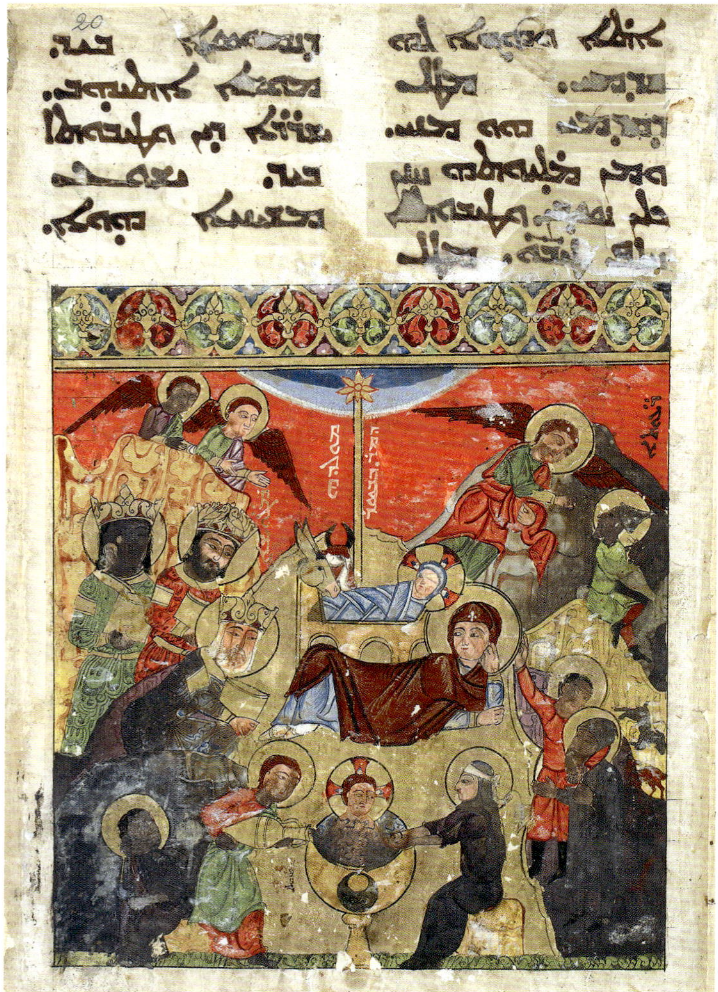

27, fol. 21r

27

Syriac Lectionary

Iraq, possibly Monastery of Mar Mattei, 1216–20
Tempera, ink, and gold on paper; 264 folios
17½ × 13¾ in. (44.5 × 35 cm)
British Library, London (Add. MS 7170)

A lectionary contains the Gospel readings appointed for services throughout the church year. The text of this lectionary, written in a Syriac script known as Estrangela and reading from right to left, is richly decorated with some forty-eight miniatures, including scenes from the Life of Christ as well as images of the Virgin and Constantine and Helen with the Cross of Jerusalem. A note in gold letters on blue at the end of the readings for Easter indicates that the manuscript was created in the time of the abbot Mar Ioannes (1208–1220), "patriarch of all the earth," and the *maphrian*, or prelate, Mar Ignatius (1216–1222).

A sister manuscript is in the Vatican Library (Syr. 559); it was completed at the Monastery of Mar Mattei, near Mosul, in present-day Iraq, from which it may be inferred that this book comes as well (this manuscript was purchased in Mosul in 1820). There is a noteworthy distinction between

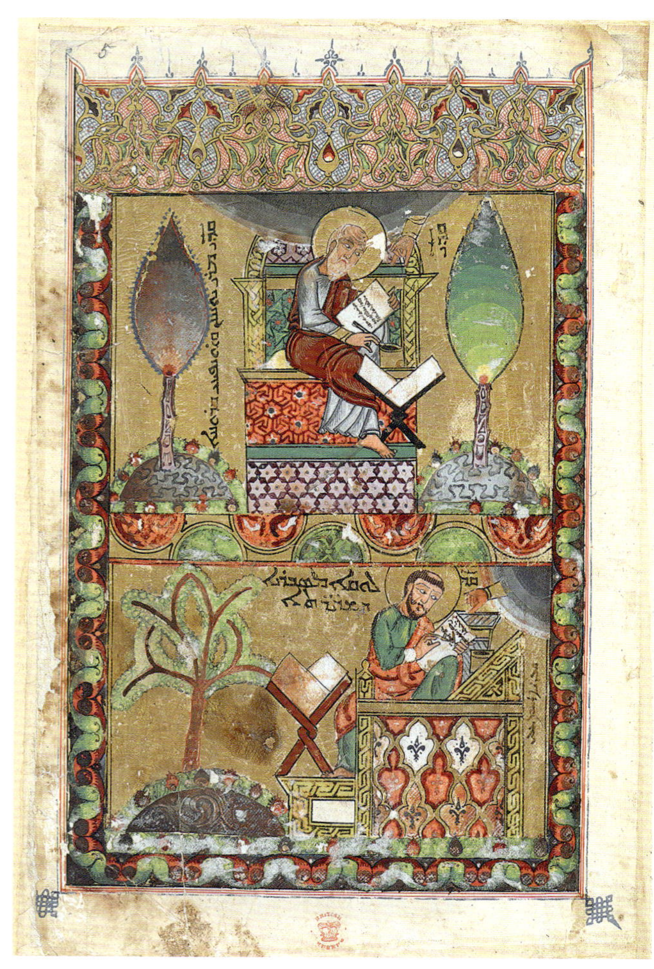

27, fol. 6r

the two, however. In the scene depicting the Entry to Jerusalem (folio 115) in the present lectionary, people from distinct backgrounds have gathered to witness the procession; in the Vatican Library's manuscript, a much more homogeneous group has assembled.[1] The artist responsible for this manuscript has clearly made a deliberate effort not only to portray various people in this image but also to represent the Magi in the illustration of the Nativity (folio 21 recto) as "from the East," giving them features associated with the Mongols.

An inscription written by a certain "Basel Maphrianus" in 1408 indicates that this manuscript was restored and rebound; the image of the Anastasis on folio 157 verso, considered to be particularly dependent on Byzantine example, was added at that time. Aspects of the decoration dependent on Islamic example are equally remarkable, whether the minbar (pulpit) behind the Evangelist on folio 6 recto, or the ornate green dome of the Entry to Jerusalem. BDB / MH

Selected References: Leroy 1964, pp. 302–13; Hunt 1985, pp. 131–35; New York 1997, pp. 384–85, no. 254; Paris 2001–2, pp. 110–11, no. 90.

1. Paris 2001–2, pp. 110–11, no. 90.

28

Embroidered Textile with Four Saints

Possibly Egypt, possibly 13th century
Cotton, embroidered in gold thread and silk
Overall: 13½ × 9½ in. (34.3 × 24.1 cm)
The Metropolitan Museum of Art, New York, Gift of Mrs. Edward S. Harkness, 1929 (29.106a, b)

Densely embroidered, these textile fragments probably came from an ecclesiastical vestment or liturgical cloth. By the thirteenth century in Eastern Orthodox churches, such embroidered vestments and altar cloths with haloed figures under arcades were common, and the fashion of covering the entire surface of the fabric in embroidery was seen frequently, beginning in the fourteenth century. Here the specific technique is a distinct variation on couching and is not identifiable with a particular culture. The dress of the figures, however, suggests that this textile was made in the Coptic Church in the thirteenth century.

The figure on the far right in the triad, carrying a processional cross, is a Coptic deacon or priest, identified by his wearing of an orarion, a stole of crosses that wraps the shoulders and hangs down one side of the body, over a sticharion, a type of tunic or long robe.[1] His belt and lack of beard indicate that he might also be a monk. Two of the figures carry Gospel Books, appropriate to apostles or theologians of some sort.

Yet the figures' attire includes leggings, typical of secular figures in the Islamic sphere.[2] The wearing of leggings beneath greatcoats originated in ancient Persia and was known in early Islam. In the Mamluk period men wore belted coats (*aqbiya*) over leggings (*ran*), with variations in sleeves, fabric, and other ornament to illustrate their status. All the men, except for the beardless man on the right of the group of three, display this type of dress, seen in many illuminations of the *Assemblies* (*Maqamat*), an Arabic compendium of tales, which date to the twelfth and thirteenth centuries.[3] Due to losses, it is unclear if the beardless man on the left carried anything. JB

1. Innemée 1992, pp. 13–61.
2. Stillman 2003, pp. 62–72.
3. Grabar, O., 1984.

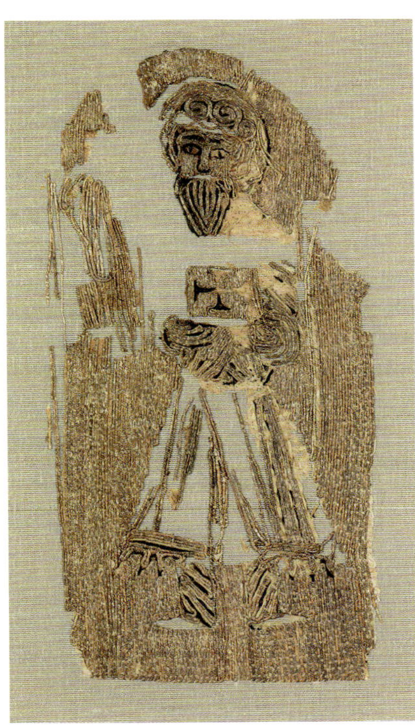

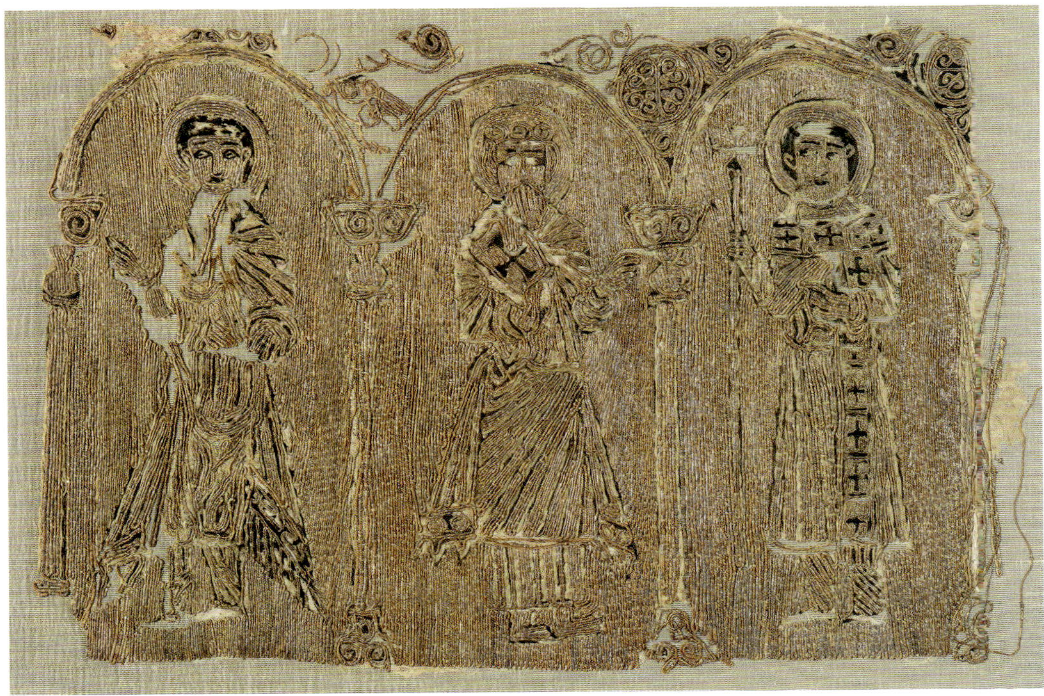

28

29

Menologion for March to August and Biographies of Saintly Women

Monastery of the Holy Cross, Jerusalem, ca. 1038–40
Written by the monk George Prokhorus
Ink on parchment; 509 folios
15⅜ × 9⅞ in. (39 × 25 cm)
Bodleian Libraries, University of Oxford
(MS Georg.b.1)

This Georgian-language menologion, a collection of saints' and martyrs' lives, was penned by George Prokhorus, the founder of the Monastery of the Holy Cross, located just outside Jerusalem.[1] Beginning in 1038, Prokhorus established the monastery on the remains of a sixth- or seventh-century Christian church built on the site where, legendarily, Lot had planted the tree that was to become the Holy Cross.[2]

Sections of the menologion specific to saints' commemoration days were, most likely, read aloud at the monastery's services on those days,[3] structuring the prayer life of the community around the temporal rhythm of an early Christian past. The language of the menologion attests to the Monastery of the Holy Cross as a center of scholarly endeavor and part of a larger network for translation activity.[4] The May 20 prayer for the seventh-century Sabaite monk Antiochus Strategos offers a Georgian version of his Greek-language witness account of the Sassanian conquest of Jerusalem in 614. The "feeling" of Arabic syntax within the Georgian version of the text offers evidence that the account was translated not directly from Greek but via Arabic and demonstrates that the monastery's preservation of an unbroken lineage — that of Jerusalem's history and of a deeper Christian past — was filtered through the lens of linguistic pluralism.[5] DA

Selected References: Antiochus Strategos 1909 ed.; Peeters 1912.

1. For a Latin summary of the work's contents, see Peeters 1912.
2. Seawulf 1892 ed., p. 21.
3. Ševčenko 1991.
4. For the role of Judean desert monasteries in translating Greek into Arabic and Georgian, see Griffith 1992 and Griffith 1998.
5. Nicholas Marr's philological study of the Georgian text offered this insight into the translation; see Antiochus Strategos 1909 ed. Tamar Pataridze gives a holistic account of the scholarship on Greek and Syriac works passed down through Arabic translation; see Pataridze 2013, pp. 47–66.

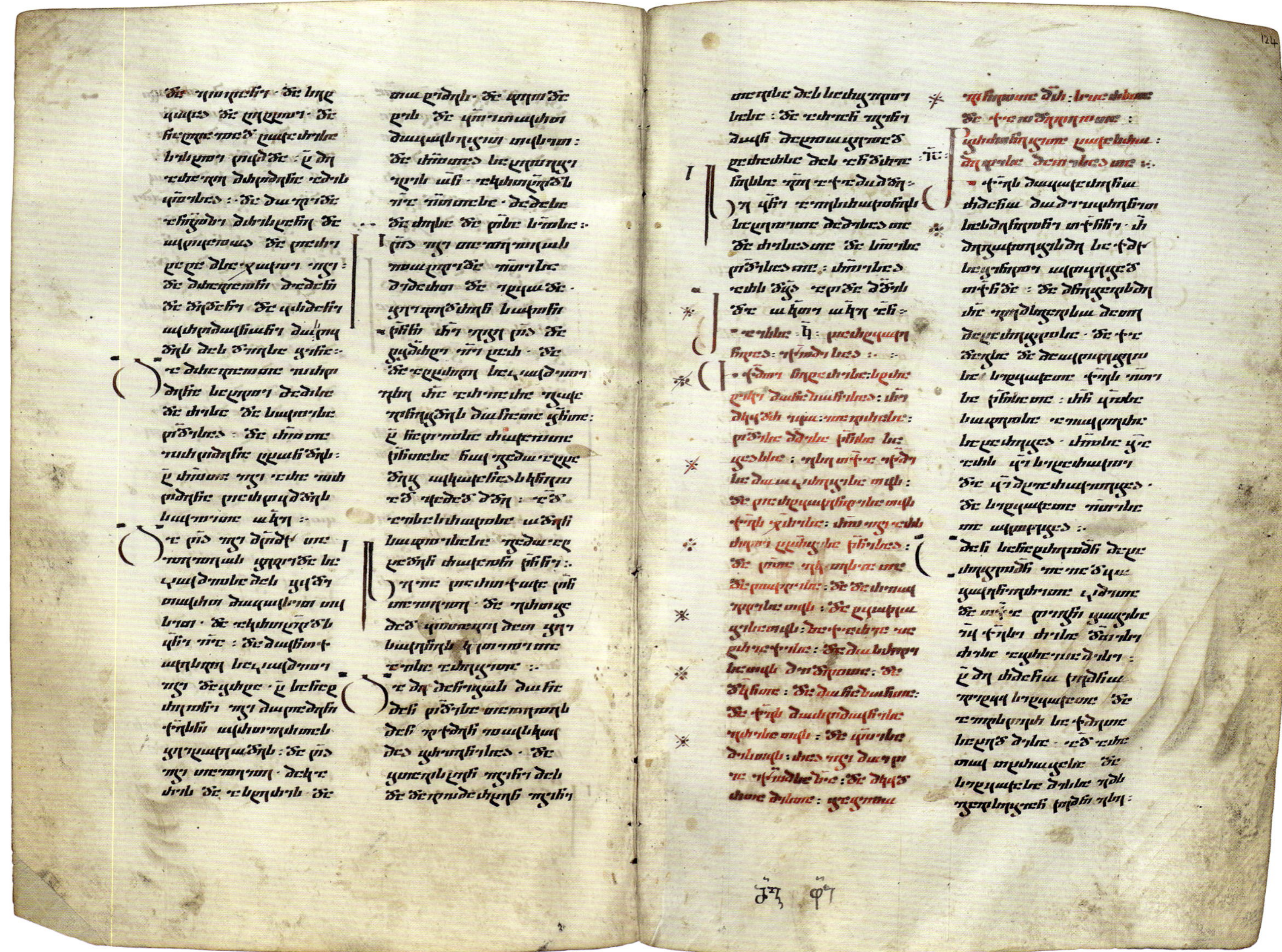

29, fols. 123v–124

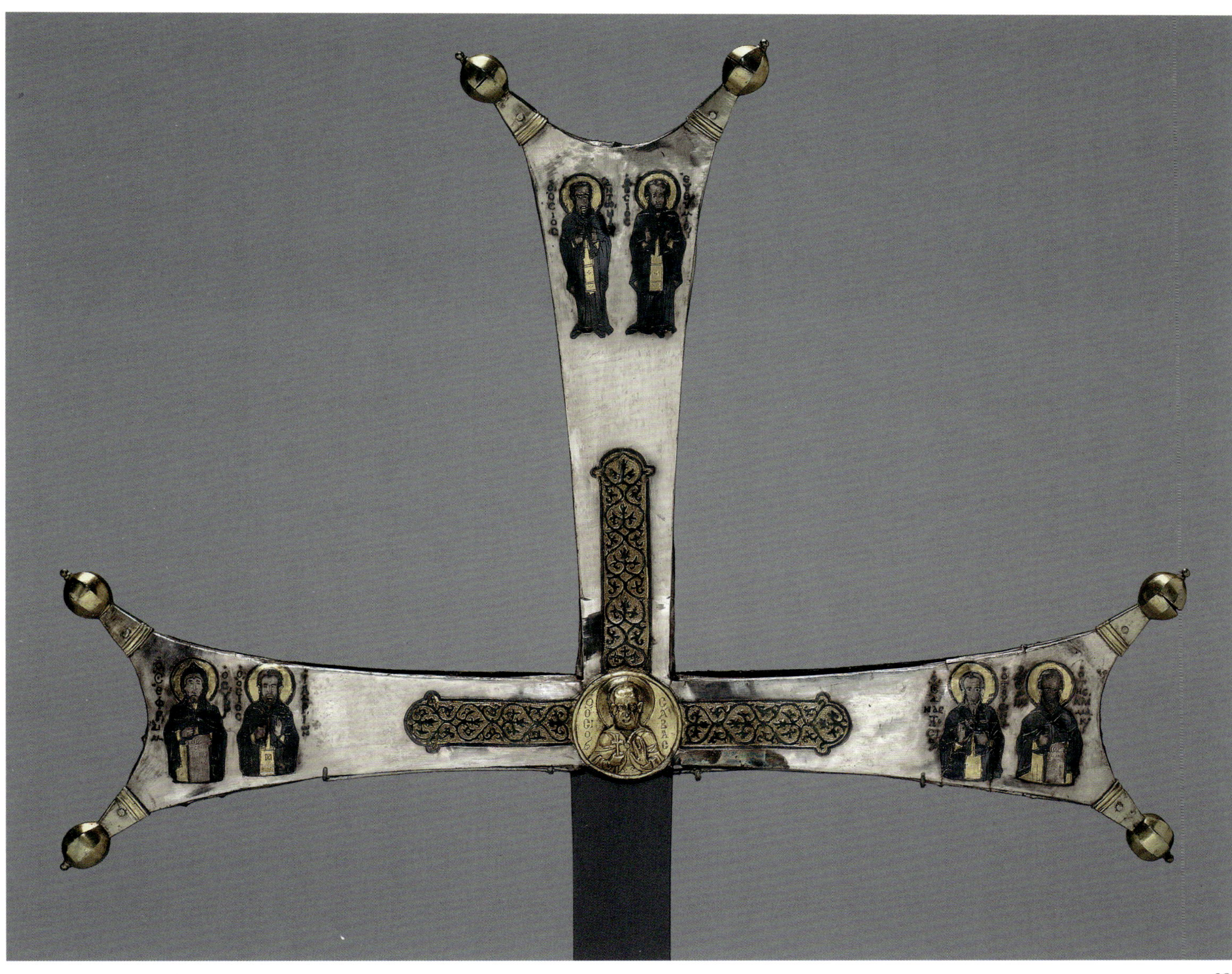

30

30

Processional Cross

Byzantium, ca. 1050
Gilded silver and niello
H. 12¾ in. (32.3 cm), W. 17⅝ in. (44.8 cm), D. 2¼ in. (5.7 cm)
Cleveland Museum of Art, Leonard C. Hanna, Jr. Fund (1970.36)

Part of a group of stunning silver repoussé crosses, this fragmentary processional cross displays on the front an image of Christ Pantocrator in the center medallion, flanked on the side arms by the Virgin and John the Baptist (Prodromos, or precursor of Christ), the three figures together forming a scene of intercession known as the Deesis.[1] The Archangel Michael inhabits the medallion on the top arm. Crosses like these were carried in imperial and military ceremonies, processions for feast days related to the Cross, as well as during the Divine Liturgy.[2]

This cross is unique because the back is decorated in niello with a group of monastic saints: Saint Sabas in the center, Anthony the Great and Euthymius the Great on the upper arm, Ephraim the Syrian and Hilarion on the left arm, and Anastasios of Sinai and John Climacus on the right arm. It was surely made in a monastic setting and was likely a votive offering from its monastic patron, as a now-lost inscription tells us: "This precious cross was beautifully worked in the name of our blessed father Sabas by Nicholas the monk and presbyter and founder of the Monastery of Glastine [?]."[3]

The fine quality of the metalwork, with handworked, as opposed to stamped, ornament across the front, suggests that Nicholas paid a considerable amount for this object. The dedicatory inscription to Saint Sabas, whose portrait is the central focus of the reverse, might mean that this cross was made for a monastery in the circle of the Great Lavra that Sabas founded or at least for a Palestinian monastery, though the "Glastine Monastery" of the inscription is unknown in any sources. Each saint depicted on the cross represents a varying form of monastic practice from a different region, the result being a devotional object that lauds the institution of monasticism itself. JB

Selected References: Cotsonis 1994, pp. 68–75, no. 2; New York 1997, pp. 60–62, no. 24.

1. Two examples in the group of silver processional crosses include one from the Musée de Cluny, Musée National du Moyen Âge, Paris (no. Cl.23295) and another from the George Ortiz Collection, Geneva (no. 260), both published in New York 1997, pp. 64–66, nos. 26 and 27, respectively.
2. Cotsonis 1994, pp. 8–29.
3. Ibid., p. 70.

31

Menologion with the Life of Saint Sabas

Monastery of the Holy Cross, Jerusalem, 11th century
Copied by the monk Black John
Ink on parchment; 369 folios
13⅞ × 9⅞ in. (35 × 25 cm)
British Library, London (Add. MS 11281)

This eleventh-century menologion from the Monastery of the Holy Cross on the outskirts of Jerusalem records the lives of fifteen saints local to Palestine, Syria, and Egypt, to be read on their commemoration days. Included is Saint Sabas, whose cult flourished among the Georgian communities in the Holy Land as well as in Georgia and whose distinct form of monasticism had a great impact on the Holy Cross Monastery.[1]

Written in the Georgian language by a monk who, on folio 1 recto, gave himself the name Black John, the life of Saint Sabas, in addition to five of the other lives contained in the menologion, are translations from Cyril of Scythopolis's sixth-century Greek-language *Peri tou Megalou Euthymiou Syngraphē* (Writing on Euthymius the Great), known in English as *The Lives of the Monks of Palestine*, written at the Great Lavra founded by Saint Sabas. The commemoration of the saint within the Monastery of the Holy Cross's services using a Greek-language hagiographic model from Saint Sabas's own monastery demonstrates not only the long-standing connection between these two communities, but also the role of both monasteries within an intellectual network that translated between Greek, Arabic, Georgian, and Syriac.

The fortunes of the Georgian community at the Monastery of the Holy Cross rose and fell with the changing political landscape. It was under royal protection at the end of the eleventh century and again at the end of the twelfth.[2] In the late thirteenth century the property was confiscated by Sultan Baybars, but at the beginning of the fourteenth it was returned by Sultan al-Nasir Muhammad ibn Qala'un.[3] Over time, fewer monks arrived from Georgia,[4] and their circumstances had significantly declined by the late fifteenth-century visit of the Dominican theologian Felix Fabri. DA

Selected Reference: Peradze 1935, pp. 82–83.

1. For possible reasons for Sabas's popularity among the Georgians, see Gagoshidze 2001, p. 363.
2. Ehrhard 1892, p. 161.
3. Pringle 1993–2009, vol. 2, p. 34.
4. Janin, R., 1913, p. 35.

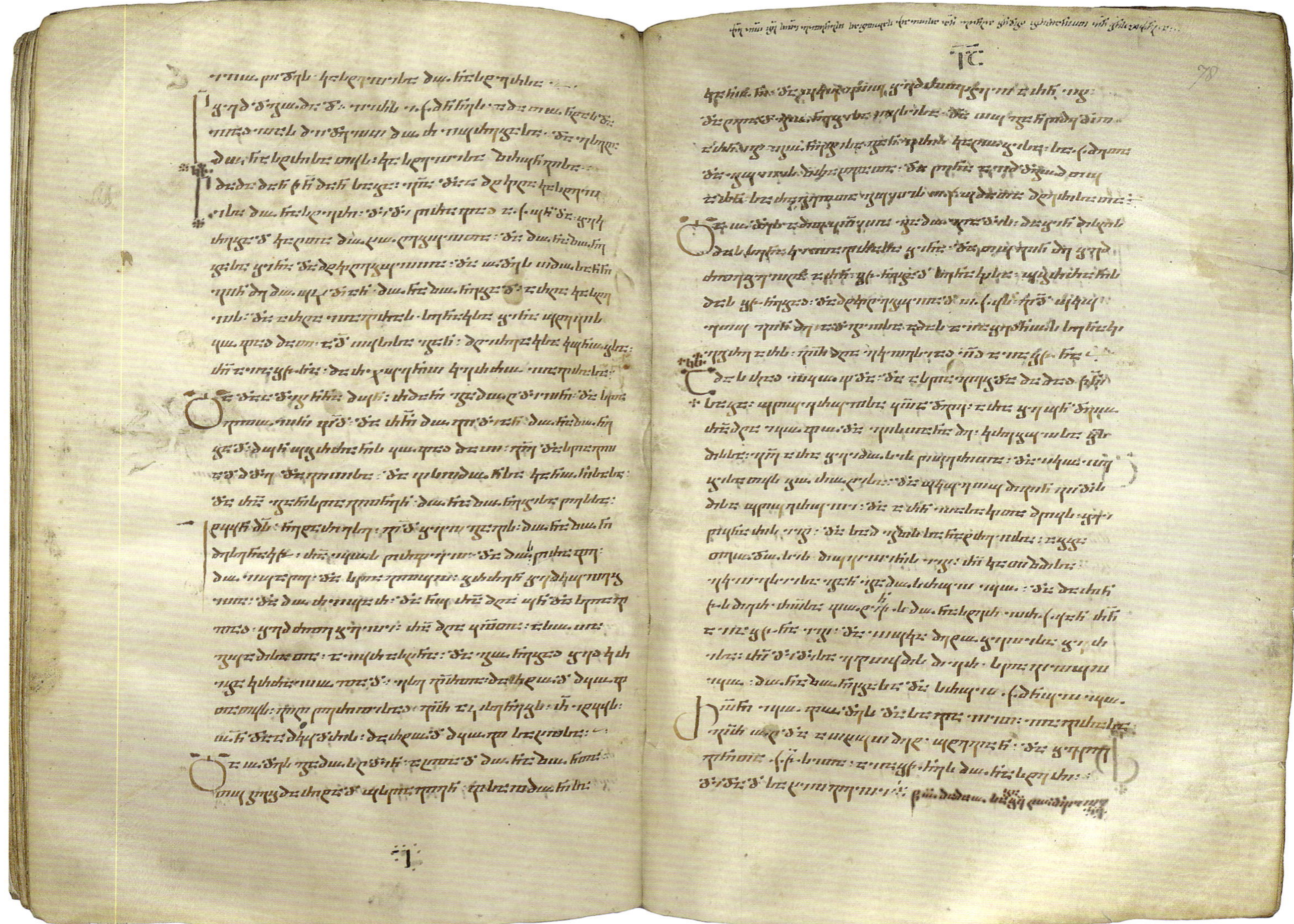

31, fols. 77v–78

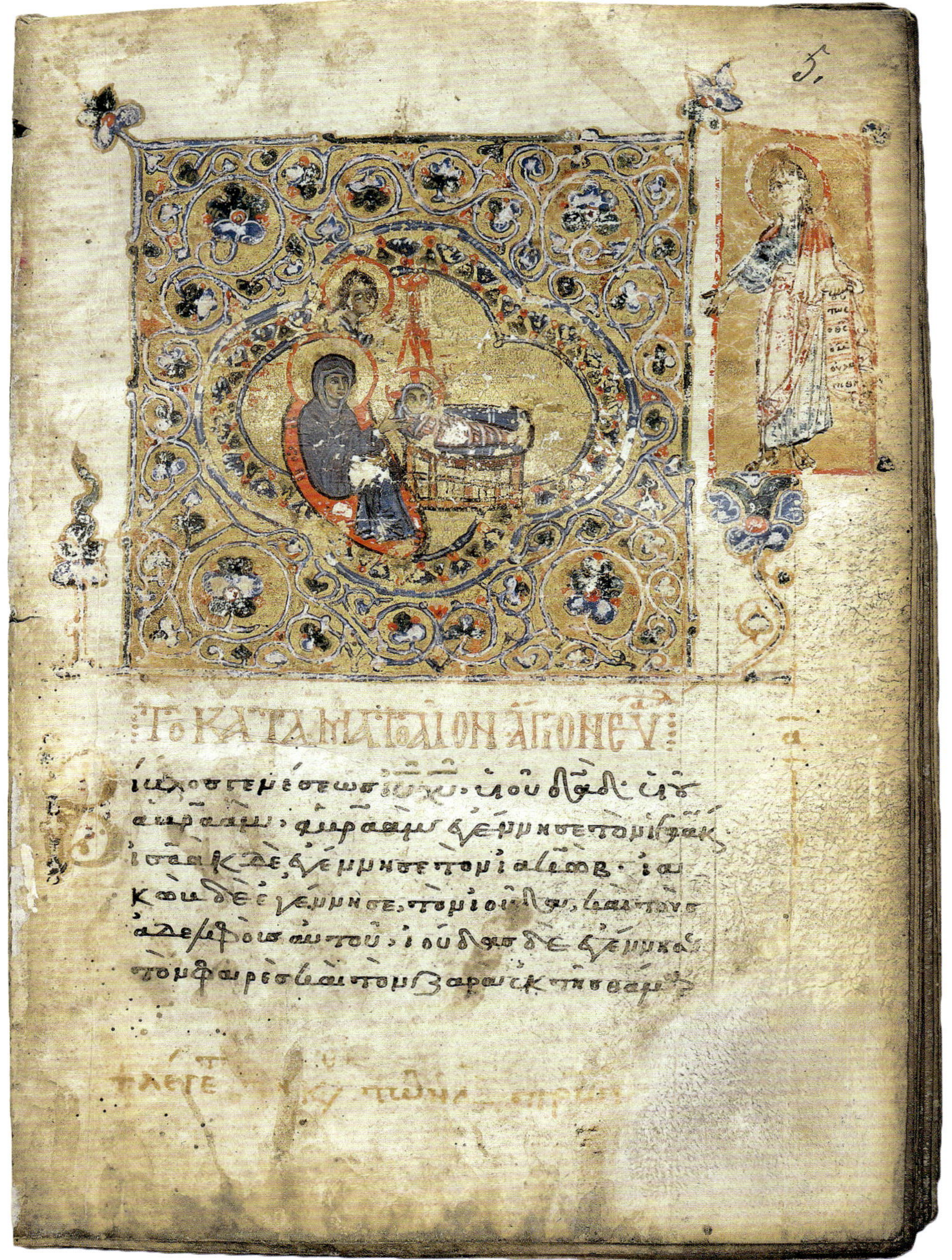

32, fol. 5

conceived in the Virgin's womb through the Holy Spirit. In a red-framed gold rectangle in the margin, Isaiah stands holding a scroll that recalls what Christians consider to be his prophecy of the Incarnation (Isaiah 9:6), which is quoted in the Gospel of Matthew (Matthew 1:23) that follows this opening image.[2] Isaiah's scroll, however, depicts the words from Jeremiah, "This is our God; no other can be compared to him" (Baruch 3:35), which is a passage typically read on the Eve of the Nativity, Christmas.[3] The complicated pictorial and textual relationships among Matthew, Isaiah, and Jeremiah, each pointing to the Incarnation highlighted in red, reflects the erudition of the community at the Great Lavra of Saint Sabas where the patron lived. JB

Selected References: Spatharakis 1981, vol. 1, p. 42; Kotzabassi, Ševčenko, and Skemer 2010, pp. 19–25.

1. Natalia Teteriatnikov in Princeton 1986, p. 178, no. 154.
2. Anne Van Buren in Princeton 1973, p. 140, no. 37.
3. Kotzabassi, Ševčenko, and Skemer 2010, p. 22. Baruch is an apocryphal book that was included in the Septuagint, the Greek translation of the Hebrew Bible, and the Vulgate, the Latin translation of the Bible, but is not canonic in Judaism or Protestantism.

32

The Four Gospels

Great Lavra of Saint Sabas, 1136
Tempera and gold on parchment; 278 folios
7 × 5⅛ in. (17.8 × 13 cm)
Manuscripts Division, Department of Rare Books and Special Collections, Princeton University Library (MS Garrett 3)

According to the colophon on folio 260 verso, this copy of the Four Gospels was made at the Great Lavra of Saint Sabas in the Judean desert at the behest of a monk there named John. John held two monastic offices: *oikonomos* (steward) and *xenodochos* (in charge of guests). He likely commissioned the book for his personal use, befitting his high status in the monastery.[1]

In addition to decorated canon tables — a type of concordance of the events in Christ's life as they appear among the Gospels of Matthew, Mark, Luke, and John — there were originally four evangelist portraits, of which only the portraits of Mark and John remain. Each portrait faced a festal image, of which only the Nativity (folio 5), originally paired with Matthew, survives. Enclosed in a quatrefoil frame with an allover floriated vine motif, this Nativity scene shows the Virgin resting on a red cushion, while the Child Jesus, swaddled, lies in a crib beside her. Above, a bust-length angel bursts through the frame, pointing to the rays of the Holy Spirit shining down on the infant.

The focus here is the Incarnation, that is, the Christian belief that Christ is God

33

Bowl with a Coptic Monk-Priest

Egypt, probably Cairo, 1050–1100
Stonepaste with luster overglaze
H. 4⅛ in. (10.4 cm), Diam. 9¼ in. (23.5 cm)
Victoria and Albert Museum, London, Purchased with the assistance of The Art Fund and the Bryan Bequest (C.49-1952)

This bowl depicts a figure in the garb of a monk-priest, swinging a censer. He wears a monastic hooded mantle, decorated with armbands and an allover pattern of swirls, over another tunic, which is visible at the wrists. His identity as a priest derives from the censer he carries and from his stole, known as an orarion in the Coptic Church, which encircles his neck and drapes down his front.[1] He also wears a belt, which may have been part of the priestly vestments that served to distinguish him from clergy of other denominations.[2]

Beside him stands an ankh, which in Ancient Egypt signified "life" and later was used by Coptic Christians to symbolize Christ. The form has also been interpreted as a cypress tree, conjuring a monastic garden scene common in Arabic poetry.[3] Surely here it is meant to convey both references at once.

On the bowl's exterior the word *Sa'd*, or "good luck," is written twice. While it could be a man's name, it is more likely a blessing used as the mark of a pottery workshop.[4] There are forty-six known pieces associated with this atelier, whose potters worked in Egypt and Syria beginning in the eleventh century.

The pottery techniques used in Egypt demonstrate extensive networks of influence. This bowl is made of fritware, or stonepaste, a compound of white clay and quartz created to mimic smooth, white Chinese porcelain, and to eliminate the need for a glaze layer.[5] First developed in Egypt, fritware spread eastward to Iran, via Syria, by the eleventh century. Conversely, the luster glaze used to create this piece's metallic sheen moved westward from Iraq and proliferated in Egypt in the tenth century, probably because the potters themselves migrated. JB

Selected References: London 2003–4, p. 152, no. 81; Washington, D.C., and other cities 2004–6, p. 118, fig. 137.

1. "Coptic" is the term used to refer to Egyptian Christians and is derived from the Greek word for Egyptian, *Agyptos*.
2. For a full discussion of the Coptic priestly vestments, see Innemée 1992, pp. 44–60.
3. Information on the object from the Victoria and Albert Museum refers to the cypress tree theory. Tim Stanley, in Washington, D.C., and other cities 2004–6, p. 118, favored the idea that it is an ankh. As it is very common for symbols to be multivalent, both references seem apt.
4. Jenkins 1988b, pp. 67–73.
5. Bernsted 2003, pp. 23–27.

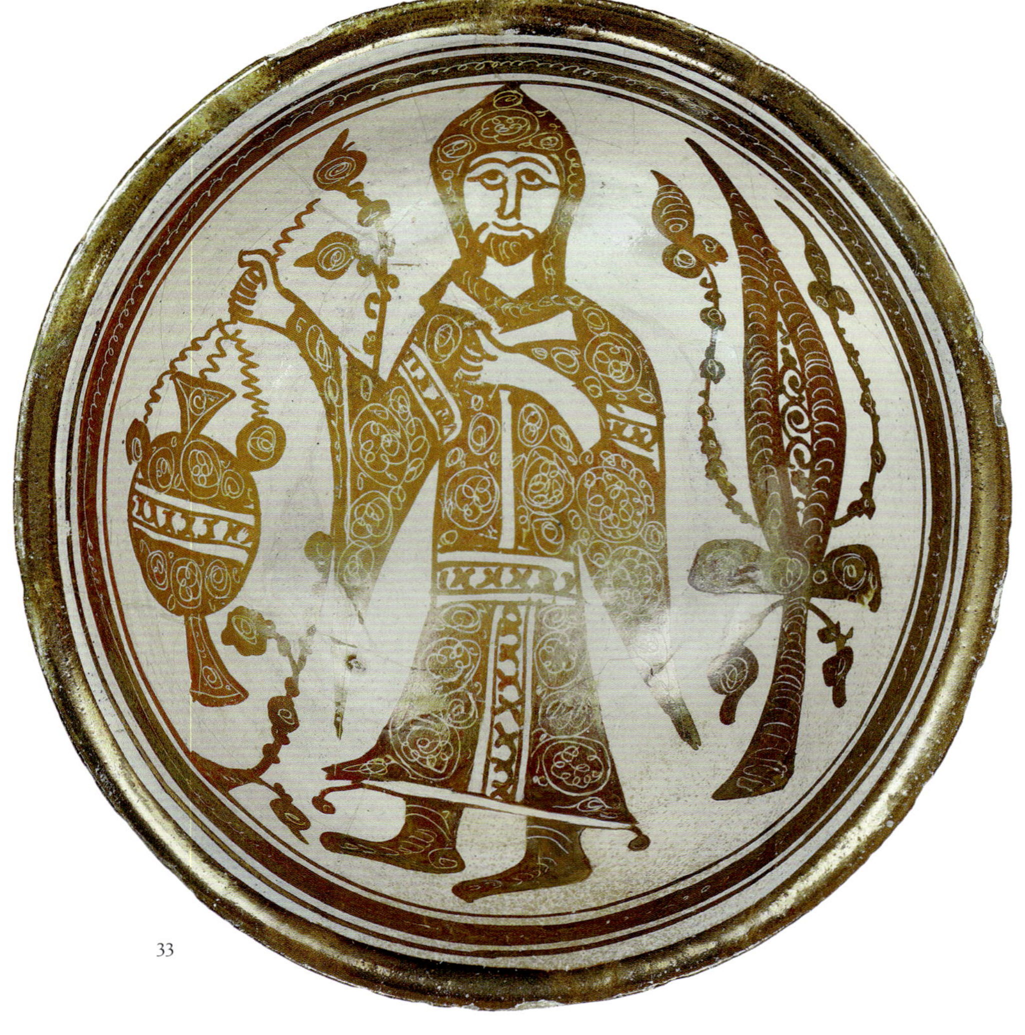
33

34
The New Testament ("Peshitta")

Mar Aziza, Zerini (Jilu), Turkey, 1212/13
Scribe and illuminator: Bôkhtiso
Opaque watercolor, pen, and ink on parchment; 322 folios
10½ × 7⅜ in. (26.7 × 18.8 cm)
Morgan Library and Museum, New York (MS M.235)

This manuscript, written in Syriac, comes from the church of the Monastery of Saint Aziza (Mar Aziza) in the southeast of present-day Turkey. The brief surviving account of the saint's life attests that he founded this eponymous monastery in his native village of Zerini in the fourth or early fifth century, after returning from a trip to Jerusalem and Mount Sinai.[1] Pilgrimage to the Holy City was of central importance to Syriac Christians, whether monks, priests, or layfolk, and is a common theme in their saints' stories.[2]

The earliest Syriac Christian manuscript to survive from the area,[3] this version of the New Testament is known as "Peshitta."[4] The scribe and illuminator, Bôkhtiso, penned his name on folio 319 verso; he is perhaps the man of the same name given on folio 124 verso of the Peshitta Gospels, dated about 1241, now in the Staatsbibliothek in Berlin.[5] Like Hebrew and Arabic, Syriac reads from right to left.

Bôkhtiso has decorated the manuscript in classic Syriac fashion, with simple geometric shapes that frame — almost enshrine — the text. The manuscript includes two full-page ornamental crosses and twelve decorative introductory pages. The opening shown here features side-by-side crosses of green set within almond-shaped frames.

Pertaining to the family tree of Jesus as given in the Gospels of Luke (at right) and Matthew (at left), the text addresses the complicated issue, first tackled by Eusebius of Caesarea,[6] of the variously given fathers of Joseph (Heli, in Luke 3:23; Jacob, in Matthew 1:16)[7] and traces the ancestry through different sons of David (Nathan, in Luke 3:31; Solomon, in Matthew 1:6). The juxtaposition of these pages forcefully demonstrates that, whether traced through Mary's or Joseph's lineage, Jesus was a descendant of David, as the Messiah was foretold to be. HS

Selected Reference: Casey 1951, p. 67.

1. See Fiey 1966, pp. 429–33.
2. See Bitton-Ashkelony 2010.
3. Notwithstanding its mountainous terrain, the region has been subject to periodic attack. For more information, see *World Heritage Encyclopedia* n.d.
4. It is called "Peshitta" (Syriac, simple version) in contrast to other versions that have more critical apparatus.
5. Staatsbibliothek, Berlin, MS 14, Sachau 304 (information from the Morgan Library and Museum, New York, museum website catalogue record).
6. For more detail, see Eusebius 1993– ed.
7. Joseph was called the "son [in law] of Heli" by marriage to Mary.

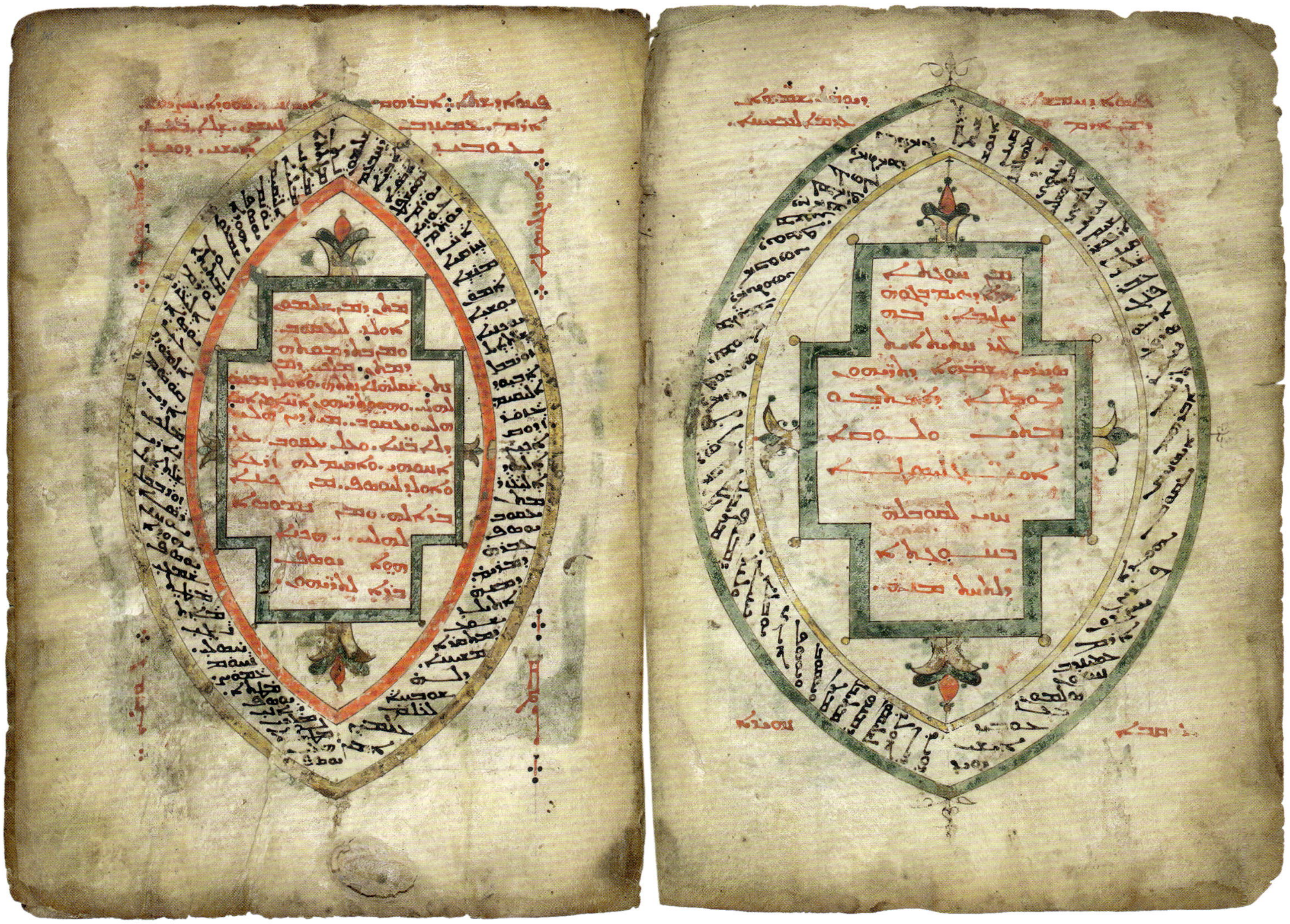

34, fols. 9v–10r

35

Seal of Tsemach, Son of Asah, the Prince

Fustat, Egypt, 1000–1050
Carnelian
H. ⅞ in. (2.2 cm), Diam. 1 in. (2.4 cm)
Private collection, Alon Shvut

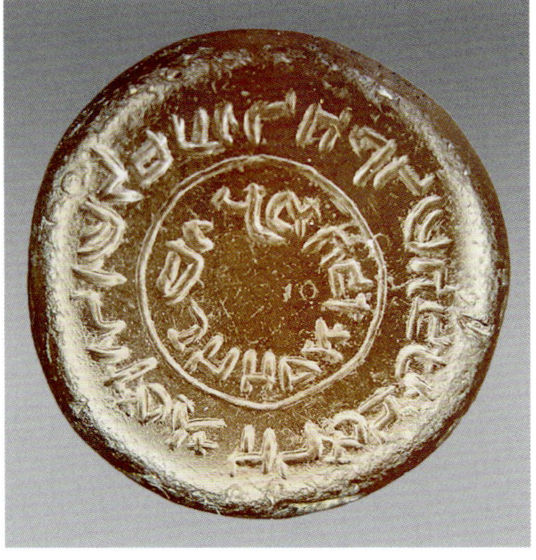

35

Although the seventh-century caliph ʿUmar forbade non-Muslims the wearing of seal rings, which were a sign of distinction, he made an exception for the exilarch, the leader of the Jewish Diaspora in Babylon.[1] The position was hereditary, stemming from the line of King David.[2] When the Karaites split from the mainline (Rabbanite) Jewish community, they established their own imperially recognized exilarchs,[3] who continued to stress their royal lineage from the Davidic line.[4]

This dome-shaped carnelian seal, which would have been threaded on a necklace, features two concentric lines of text inscribed in reverse, so that when pressed into wax, the resulting relief reads correctly. The inner circle proclaims the owner's name, "Tsemach, son of Asah, the Prince," leader of the Karaite community in Fustat in the early eleventh century. The outer circle exclaims, "Jerusalem, the Holy City, may it be built soon, Amen!"

Scholars justify the Fustat prince's claimed connection to Jerusalem through his familial ties to the Davidic dynasty or through a hypothetical regency during a break between leaders in the Holy City.[5] However, it should perhaps be understood as a prayer or motto — the literary equivalent of a seal's emblem — rather than as an address.[6] The rebuilding of Jerusalem was, after all, the rallying cry of the Karaites. EE

Selected References: Ben-Shammai n.d.; Glatzer, M., n.d.

1. Avigad 2007, esp. p. 226.
2. Olszowy-Schlanger 1998.
3. The Abbasid caliph al-Maʾmun (786–833) acknowledged the Karaite leader as *nasi*, or prince, of his community. Neusner and Bashan 2007, esp. p. 603.
4. Their honorifics in Karaite documents include the "Descendant of the Man of Peace," a reference to King Solomon taken from I Chronicles 22:9, and "His virtuous fathers the kings, in the Garden of Eden, Garden of God." Olszowy-Schlanger 1998, p. 152, nos. 52 and 56.
5. Ben Shammai n.d., p. 3, proposes that the seal may have been produced during the period after the death of the Jerusalem prince Shlomo ben David ben Boaz in the early eleventh century but before the ascension of his sons Hezekiah and Josaiah as leaders.
6. Other examples of such mottos on seals are "May God have Mercy" or "The Work of God." Jacobs, J., and Wolf 1906.

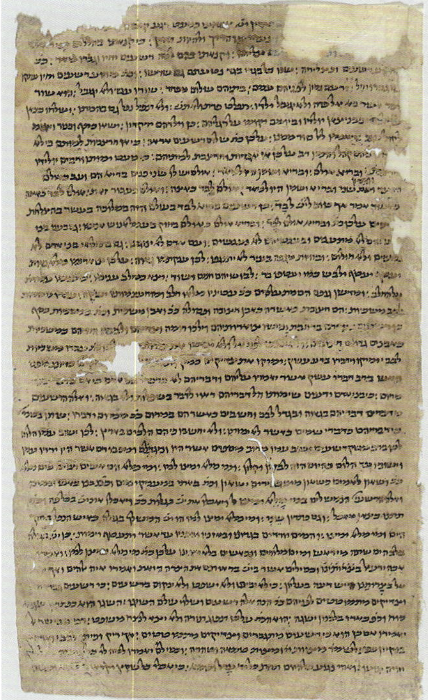

36a

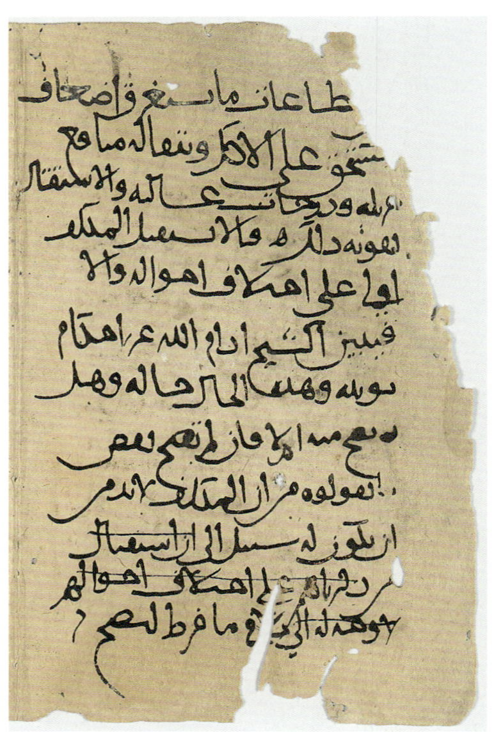
36b

36a

Commentary on Psalms (73–82)

Jerusalem(?), late 9th–early 10th century
Written by Daniel ben Moses al-Qumisi (d. 946)
Ink on paper
14¾ × 8¾ in. (37.2 × 22 cm)
The Library of The Jewish Theological Seminary, New York (ENA 2778.1)

36b

Responsa (Questions and Answers)

Jerusalem(?), second quarter of the 11th century
Written by Joseph ben Abraham al-Basir (960/80–1037/39)
Ink on paper
5½ × 3⅝ in. (14 × 9.2 cm)
The Library of The Jewish Theological Seminary, New York (MS 3448)

The golden age of the Jerusalem Karaite community can be divided into two flourishing periods, each exemplified by a leading Karaite scholar, Daniel al-Qumisi and Joseph ben Abraham al-Basir.[1]

It was al-Qumisi who, after immigrating to Jerusalem from Iran, first exhorted the Karaites to gather in Jerusalem and mourn the destroyed Temple, thereby speeding the coming of the Redemption, and it was he who first named them the "Mourners of Zion."[2] His commentary on the Psalms (cat. 36a) embodies two fundamental Karaite principles: adherence to the Biblical text and yearning for Redemption. He stated, "Every word in the Bible has but one [true] interpretation, not two. But since people do not know [scripture's true] meanings, they will [continue to] interpret it in various ways until the advent of the Teacher of Righteousness," by which he meant the return of the prophet Elijah at the time of Redemption.[3]

Al-Basir, who immigrated to Jerusalem from Iraq, was one of the greatest authorities of the Karaite academy and a key member of the city's scholarly community. He wrote theological and legal treatises, polemics, and works on the Mu'tazilite *kalam* doctrines of divinity. There is some debate as to whether his epithet the Seer (*ha-Basir*) referred euphemistically to blindness, as previously thought, or, more likely, honored either his great wisdom or his magnum opus, *Book of Insight* (*Kitab al-Istibsar*, a compendium of religious law).[4] Al-Basir's authority is verified by the fact that he was one of the few contemporary Karaites who wrote Responsa (cat. 36b), answering legal and theological questions addressed to him by followers near and far.[5]

EE

Selected Reference: Cat. 36a: Marmorstein 1916.

1. Sklare 1995, pp. 249–50.
2. Gil 1996, pp. 617–19.
3. On Psalms 74:6, see Marmorstein 1916, p. 196; translation from Frank 2004, p. 61 n. 10.
4. Schwarb 2010.
5. Sklare 1995, pp. 251, 259 and n. 31. It appears that this manuscript and another in The Library of The Jewish Theological Seminary, New York (MS 3443), originally formed one manuscript.

37a

Arabic Transliteration of the Hebrew Text of Jeremiah 20:3–5

Egypt–Palestine, 10th–11th century
With Arabic translation and commentary by Yefet ben 'Eli
Ink on paper
7⅞ × 7⅛ in. (19.9 × 17.9 cm)
The Library of The Jewish Theological Seminary of America, New York (ENA 3913.3)

37b

Page from the Chronicle of Obadiah the Proselyte

Egypt, ca. 1121
Written by Obadiah the Proselyte
Ink on paper
8⅜ × 5¾ in. (21.1 × 14.5 cm)
The Library of The Jewish Theological Seminary of America, New York (ENA 3098:7)

37c

Samaritan Bible

Yavneh (Yibna), 1232
Ink on parchment; 522 folios
12¼ × 10 in. (31 × 25.5 cm)
Dorot Jewish Division, New York Public Library, Astor, Lenox, and Tilden Foundations (MS Heb. 228)

A multitude of distinct languages and scripts were employed in Jerusalem during this period even among those who shared the common linguistic heritage of Hebrew.

Although translation of biblical texts into vernacular Arabic was not uncommon for educational purposes, transliteration of those Hebrew texts into Arabic characters was a uniquely Karaite phenomenon. It seems to have stemmed from their desire to create a single authorized reading tradition of the Bible independent of the multiple Rabbanite interpretations gleaned from the nonvocalized Hebrew text.[1]

The transliterated biblical text seen in catalogue 37a is layered with Arabic translation and commentary by the Karaite exegete Yefet ben 'Eli, who left Basra (present-day Iraq) for Jerusalem in the tenth century and was considered the foremost Karaite commentator of his time.[2] The passage from Jeremiah (20:3–5) foretells the fall of Jerusalem to Babylon, resulting in the destruction of Solomon's Temple in 586 B.C.

Born into Italian nobility and ordained a priest, Obadiah the Proselyte converted to Judaism after the First Crusade.[3] He chronicled his journeys in both verse and prose and conferred with leading religious authorities,[4] all in a fluent and elegant Hebrew script learned alongside the schoolchildren of Baghdad.[5] Obadiah here (cat. 37b) recounted a humorous exchange with a Karaite Messianic

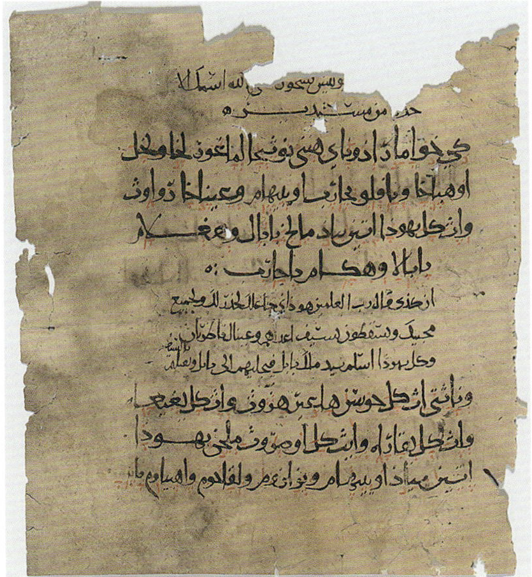

37a

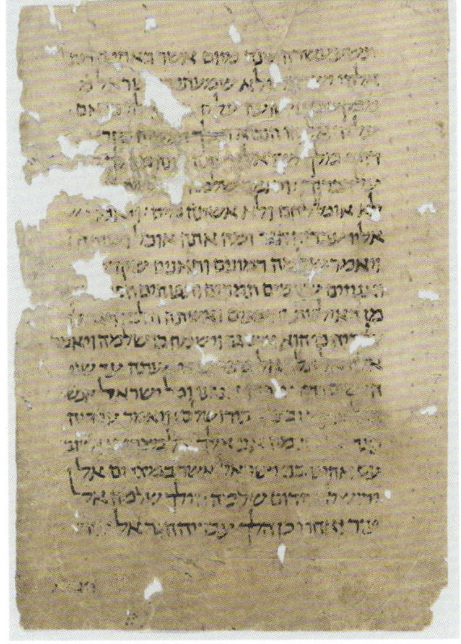

37b, fol. 7

pretender in Banias, a site near Caesarea, an encounter that highlights the eschatological fervor concentrated on the Holy City at this time. When the pretender asks why Obadiah is not headed toward Jerusalem in anticipation of his arrival, Obadiah reassures him that should what he says be true, Obadiah will be in-gathered with the rest of the exiles.[6]

This Samaritan Bible (cat. 37c) is inscribed in the Samaritan alphabet, a direct descendant of the ancient Paleo-Hebrew once used by all Jews. While the Jews banished in the Babylonian Exile adopted a derivative of the Aramaic alphabet that eventually evolved into Hebrew square script, the Samaritans remained in the Land of Israel and retained their script unchanged.

The chapters displayed (Numbers 34:16–35:14) discuss preparations for entering the Holy Land, including defining its borders, appointing leaders from each tribe, and designating the inheritance of the Levites. The circular composition of this folio relates to this last point, for rather than receiving a single fixed territory, the Levites were apportioned the land surrounding each of the other tribes' domains.[7] EE

Selected References: Cat. 37a: New York 2000–2001, p. 73, no. 28. Cat. 37b: New York 2000–2001, pp. 82–83, no. 35; Golb 2004, pp. 11–13. Cat. 37c: New York 2010–11, http://exhibitions.nypl.org/threefaiths/node/83?nref=36&key=8.

1. Khan 1992, esp. p. 175; note that both Rabbanites and Karaites venerated the original Hebrew text. The Karaites would therefore never have made changes to that text and only did so in Arabic (ibid., pp. 175–76). Using Arabic also allowed the Karaites to concretize the vocalization of the text without recognizing any one Rabbanite tradition (New York 2000–2001, p. 73).
2. Ben-Shammai 2007.
3. New York 2000–2001, p. 82, no. 35.
4. See "Letter to Obadiah the Proselyte," in Twersky, ed. 1972, pp. 475–76; letter of recommendation by Rabbi Baruch ben Isaac (Bodleian Libraries, University of Oxford, MS Heb. 2873; English translation in Golb 2004, pp. 13–19).
5. The head of the academy in Adina (Baghdad) invited him to learn "the Torah of Moses and the words of the prophets in the script of the Lord and the language of the Hebrews." Kauffman Genizah Collection, Budapest, MS 134, fol. 2r; for English, Golb 2004, p. 6.
6. Golb 2004, pp. 11–13. As proof of his divinity, the pretender tells Obadiah that he requires neither bread nor water to survive. When Obadiah presses him to discover what he does eat, he admits, "Pomegranates, figs, almonds, nuts, sycamore-fruit, dates and apples . . . and I drink milk."
7. The composition includes Numbers 35:5–8 and starts with verse 5: "You shall measure from outside the city, two thousand cubits on the eastern side, two thousand cubits on the southern side, two thousand cubits on the western side, and two thousand cubits on the northern side, with the city in the middle; this shall be your cities' open spaces."

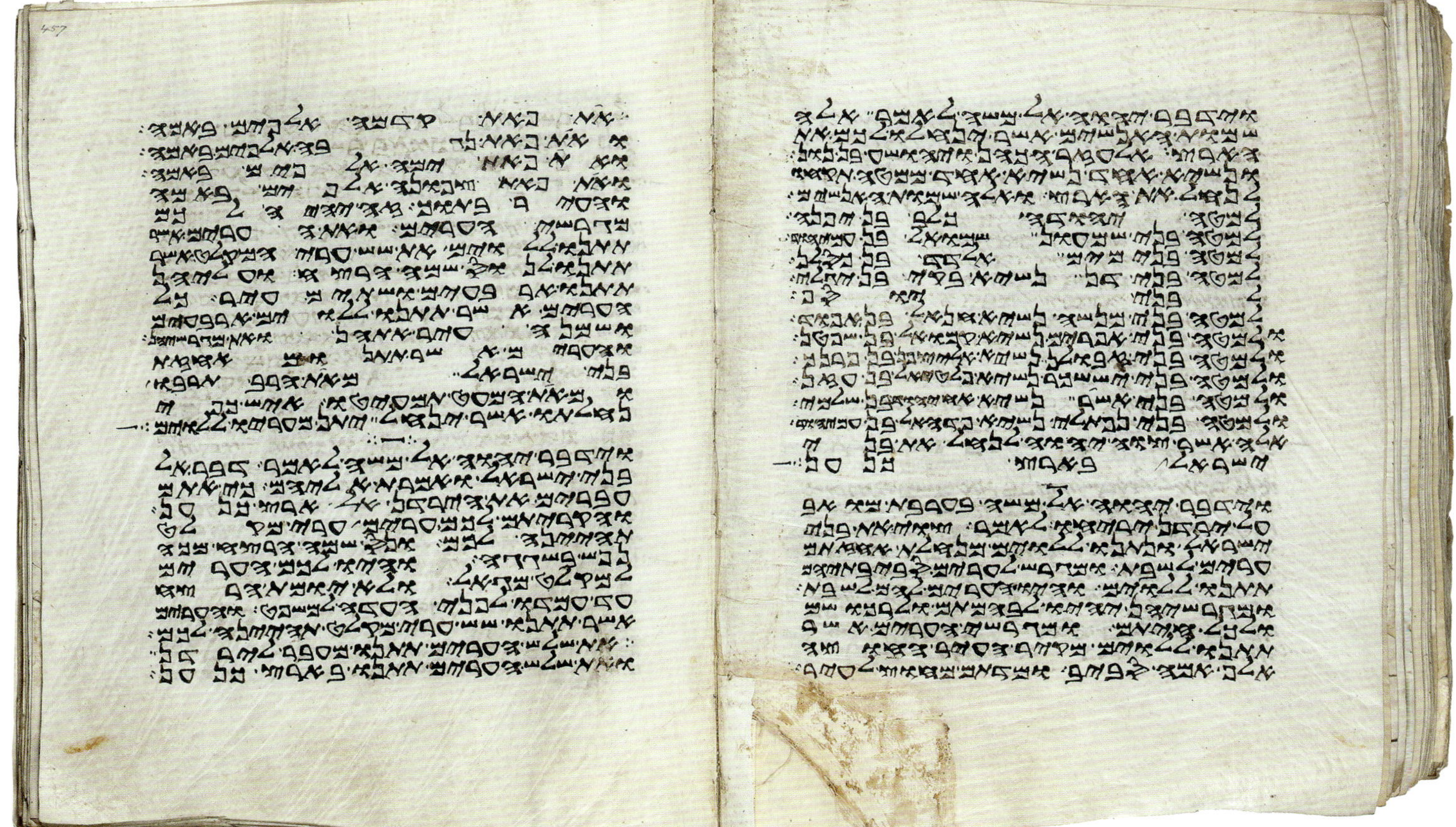

37c, fols. 457v–458r

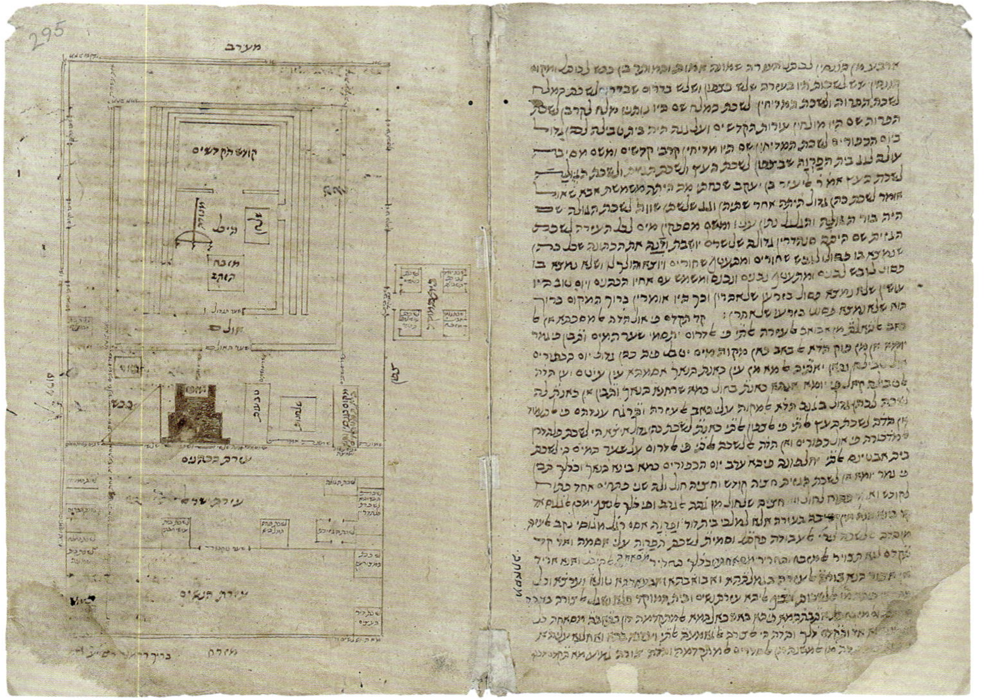

38, fol. 295r

38

Plan of the Temple

Fustat, Egypt, after 1167/68
From *Commentary on the Mishnah*
Written by Maimonides (1135–1204)
Ink on paper; 310 folios
11 × 7½ in. (28 × 19 cm)
Bodleian Libraries, University of Oxford (MS Poc. 295)

The Temple in Jerusalem that was twice destroyed prompted Jewish scholars, artists, and patrons to ponder its past form and furnishings. Among them was the great twelfth-century philosopher Maimonides, who traveled to Jerusalem in 1165 and seems to have visited the Temple Mount. He remarked in a letter that he "was privileged to pray [there], when it was ruined."[1] It is impossible to know the impact of that experience on his studies, but within a few years he developed his *Commentary on the Mishnah*, an important collection of Jewish oral law. One of its tractates, Middoth, described the architectural layout and function of the Temple complex in depth, and the commentary on this tractate, thought to be written in Maimonides's own hand,[2] is remarkable for its many diagrams illustrating features of that lost structure.[3]

This page (folio 295 recto) presents a floor plan of the Temple. The top half shows a series of walled enclosures that surround the Holy of Holies, the innermost sanctuary at the Temple's western end. The single line projecting from a semicircular stand represents the menorah, the great candelabrum. The dark, stepped structure near the center of the page refers to its sacrificial altar. The images are drawn from and work in tandem with his text.[4] None of the diagrams look to visual precedents for inspiration nor aim for abstract geometric elegance; rather we see here Maimonides's attempts to explore and explicate his own ideas about the intricate, often confusing, layout of the Temple through drawing. MH

Selected References: Wischnitzer 1974; Goldman 2005.

1. Prawer 1988, pp. 141–43.
2. Beit-Arié et al. 1994, p. 62. Some have argued that it may have been written by a scribe under Maimonides's direction; Stern, S., 1955.
3. The manuscript includes ten drawings illustrating the Temple's layout and implements. Later copies of the commentary as well as his *Mishneh Torah* make use of these same images. They often pay greater attention to aesthetic concerns but lose the original's exactitude. See, for example, The Library of The Jewish Theological Seminary, New York (MS R350), illustrated in Goldman 2005, p. 97, fig. 5.
4. The text, written in Arabic with Hebrew characters, occasionally directs the reader to the accompanying picture; see Wischnitzer 1974, p. 24.

39

Letter Requesting Funds to Ransom Captives

Egypt, 1170
Written by Maimonides (1135–1204)
Ink on paper
7½ × 5⅝ in. (19.1 × 14.2 cm)
The Library of The Jewish Theological Seminary, New York (MS 8254)

One of the preeminent philosophers, Torah scholars, and physicians of the Middle Ages, Maimonides actively participated in the welfare of the community.[1] In addition to definitive philosophical and legal treatises, he composed circular letters soliciting donations to ransom captive Jews — in this case, those taken by the Crusader king Amalric of Jerusalem during the 1169 siege of Bilbays, Egypt.[2] Penned by his secretary and signed by Maimonides himself, the letter accompanied emissaries who were charged with publicly reading the message and returning with the collected funds. Ransoms had been set so exorbitantly high that the fundraising campaign spanned Egypt, as no one community could absorb the cost.[3] The wider Jewish population was forced to pool anything of value to meet the demand.[4]

In his monumental *Mishneh Torah*, Maimonides outlined the levels of charity. He declared ransoming captives to be the highest religious duty, for one is not only aiding the destitute but also saving a life.[5] He therefore strongly urged his letter's audience to contribute to the cause, declaring that he had personally collected and donated "as much as we ourselves are able to."[6] Maimonides's leadership role in ransoming the captives attests to the esteemed reputation his erudition had earned him so soon after his arrival in Egypt, where he was already known as *ha-Rav ha-Gadol be-Yisrael* (the Great Rabbi in Israel).[7] His scholarly authority was such that Jews from near and far, including the Holy Land, sought his rulings on religious and legal queries.[8] EE

Selected References: Goitein 1980; New York 2001, p. 15, no. 3; Cohen, M., 2005a, pp. 114–18; Cohen, M., 2005b, pp. 69–71, no. 33; Kraemer 2008, pp. 272–73.

1. Maimonides wrote his six-volume *Commentary on the Mishnah* between the ages of twenty-three and thirty. In a famous letter of 1199 to Samuel ibn Tibbon, the translator of his *Guide for the Perplexed*, the sage related how his role as court physician in Cairo and his medical practice in Fustat were so time-consuming that it was only on the Sabbath that he could grant audiences to the members of Fustat's Jewish community. Löwy, ed. 1872–77, vol. 1, pp. 223–25.

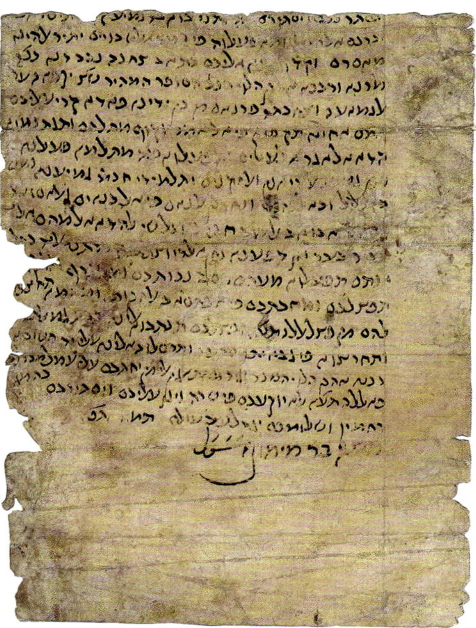

39

2. This is one of possibly five surviving such letters circulated by Maimonides. See Cohen, M., 2005a, pp. 115–17. On the date of this letter, see Cohen, M., 2005b, pp. 70–71 and n. 7.

3. "The sum required to ransom even one person, 33⅓ dinars, or gold pieces, was enormous, more than many craftsmen or shopkeepers could save during a lifetime." Goitein 1980, p. 157.

4. An early eleventh-century letter illustrates just how exorbitant the ransoms were and the degree to which the Jewish communities rallied: "The gentiles were astonished in the face of such sacrifices for entirely strange persons and said: 'Blessed is the people that is of such a condition. Yea, blessed is the people, whose God is the Lord.'" Goitein 1967–93, vol. 2, p. 137.

5. Maimonides 2005 ed., pp. 172–73, The Book of Gifts to the Poor, 8:10.

6. For a translation of the letter, see Goitein 1980, pp. 156–57; Cohen, M., 2005b, pp. 70–71.

7. The title *ha-Rav ha-Gadol* designated one "whose legal opinions carried religious authority" (Goitein 1980, p. 161). Scholarly consensus is that Maimonides was appointed Ra'is al-Yahud – political head of Egyptian and Syrian Jewry – by the Fatimids shortly after his arrival in Egypt. His role in ransoming the captives would have helped propel him to such prominence in so short a time (Goitein 1980, pp. 160–62; Kraemer 2008, pp. 216–27). For the argument that Maimonides never held this position, see Davidson 2004, pp. 54–64. Maimonides was uniquely honored in receiving the additional designation *be-Yisrael* (Kraemer 2008, p. 223).

8. Maimonides 1910 ed., nos. 72 and 105, cited in Prawer 1988, pp. 118–19.

40

Pen Box

Probably Egypt, ca. 1345–46
Brass with silver and gold
H. 3⅛ in. (8 cm), W. 12 in. (30.5 cm), D. 3½ in. (8.8 cm)
Bibliothèque Nationale de France, Cabinet des Médailles, Paris (55.539)

Lavishly inlaid oblong pen boxes (*dawat* or *qalamdan*) appeared in the Islamic world along with the development of inlaid metalwork during the twelfth century in the Khorasan (present-day Iran), and, beginning in the early thirteenth century, in Mosul (present-day Iraq), whence they spread to Syro-Palestine, Anatolia, and Egypt.[1] Inlaid pen boxes such as this one probably served as esteemed gifts for a highly literate and cultivated elite society and may have been used not only by viziers but also by rulers or their scribes and personal advisers to write missives or chronicles. Emblematic of the high regard in which scholarship was held, these objects served as status symbols for high-ranking officers as well as the wealthy and elite classes.[2] Representations of oblong boxes similar to this one being held by attendants standing next to enthroned rulers, and depictions in manuscripts of figures presenting such boxes to rulers, suggest that this shape was preferred for royal or state inkwells under the Seljuq successors in Syro-Palestine and the Jazira (encompassing present-day Syria, Lebanon, Jordan, Israel, Palestinian territories, northern Iraq, and southeastern Turkey) and was also adopted by the Mamluks and Ilkhanids.[3]

Characteristics of Mamluk art, and specifically inlaid metalwork, seen here are the epigraphic blazons and the lotus flower, a symbol that also reflects the Mamluk preference for Ilkhanid chinoiserie after 1320. The figural motifs on this pen box are limited to simple pairs of ducklike birds that are almost hidden within the vegetal decoration.[4]

The inlaid inscriptions, most of which are written in elegant cursive script with elongated shafts typical of the Mamluk period, are arranged in circular radiant medallions or monumental friezelike cartouches against dense floral scrolls. Several of them give the honorific titles and names of the royal owner of this pen box, the Mamluk sultan al-Kamil Sha'ban (r. 1345–46).[5]

Typical of the time is the interior division of the pen box into several compartments, a longer one (*miqlama*) to hold *qalam*s and other writing tools and two smaller circular cavities, one to contain sand to dry the ink on the paper and the other to hold glue to seal secret messages in the presence of the sultan.[6] A larger semicircular cavity served as the holder of the ink cloth and the inkwell (*mihbara*), which preferably was circular in form to retard the thickening or deterioration of the ink in the corners of an angular well.[7] DB

Selected References: Kalus and Naffah 1983; New York 2016, pp. 273–74, no. 174b.

1. One of the earliest datable inlaid brass objects in the characteristic "glittery" style is a pen box with a comparable shape, now in the collection of the State Hermitage Museum, Saint Petersburg; see Giuzalian 1968, pp. 95–119. Earlier oblong pen boxes with rectangular edges are known in carved steatite, a common medium from early medieval Nishapur, Iran, one example of which is in the Metropolitan Museum, acc. no. 39.40.34. On the Khorasani inlaid metalwork school, see Ward 1993, pp. 71–79; Blair 2014, pp. 57–111; Deniz Beyazit in New York 2016, pp. 155–56, no. 85. For references on the renowned inlaid metalwork known as "al-Mawsili" (from Mosul), see cat. 56.

2. Melikian-Chirvani 1986, pp. 70–94; Taragan 2005, pp. 39–40.

3. See Beyazit in New York 2016, pp. 142, 273–74, nos. 72, 174a, b. In the famous Mamluk-period Saint Louis basin in the Musée du Louvre, Paris, a standing attendant holds a rectangular box inscribed with a *dawat*, an attribute of the amir *dawadar* (Melikian-Chirvani 1986, p. 83, fig. 18). In an Ilkhanid manuscript painting of Rashid al-Din's *World History* (*Jami' al-tawarikh*), such an oblong pen box is presented to the ruler (Melikian-Chirvani 1986, p. 72, fig. 1). According to the Mamluk historian al-Qalqashandi, writing about 1400, it was common in his time for chancellery and treasury scribes to use brass or steel pen boxes, whereas judges and their clerks, as well as some government notaries, used pen boxes of ebony or red sandalwood; as an additional distinction, government scribes used long pen boxes with rounded ends, while treasury scribes used long square-cornered ones; see Kalus and Naffah 1983, pp. 113–14.

4. Meinecke 1972, pp. 213–87; Rogers 1973, p. 387; Kalus and Naffah 1983, pp. 106–7; Ward 1993, pp. 106–20.

5. All inscriptions except the benedictory ones are transcribed in Arabic and translated into French in Kalus and Naffah 1983, pp. 108–13.

6. Some pen boxes have a lattice (to filter out larger grains of sand) or other cover on top of the smaller circular cavities; for one such example in the British Museum, London, no. OA 1884.7-4.85, see Ward 1993, p. 83, fig. 62.

7. Al-Qalqashandi gave the full description and function of such pen boxes with their medieval terms; see Kalus and Naffah 1983, pp. 114–16.

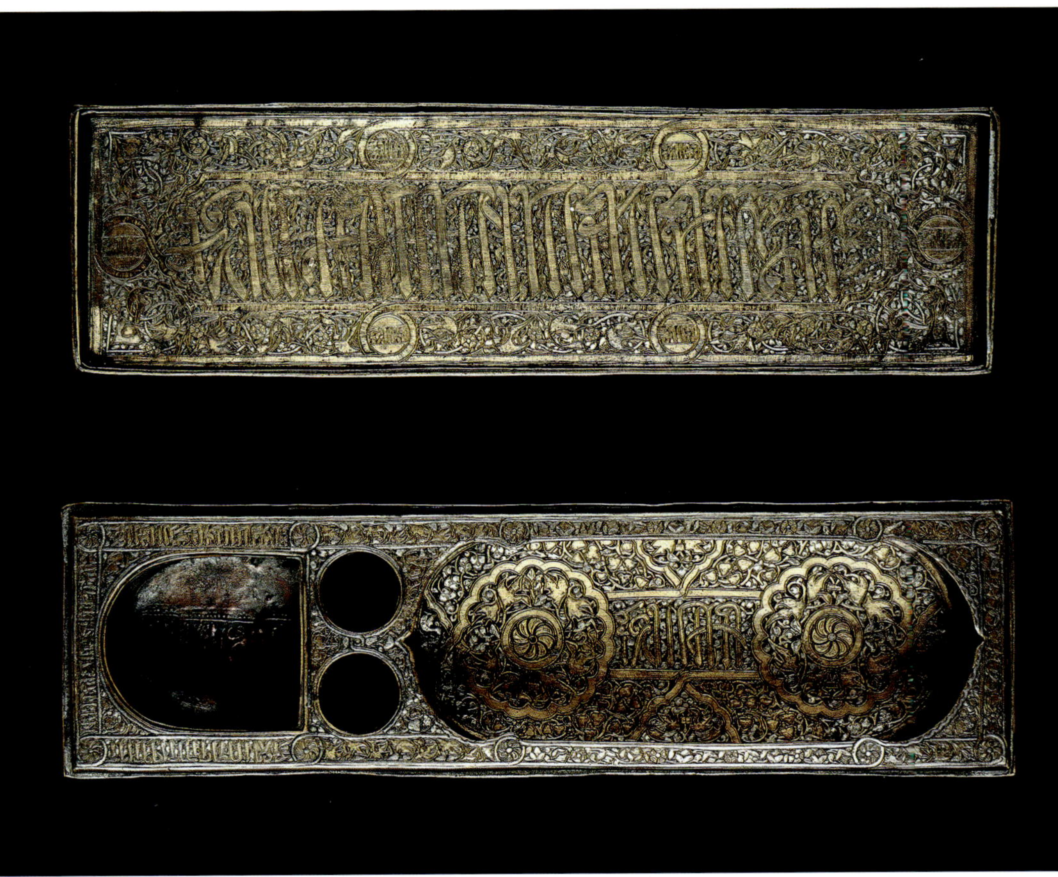

40

41

The Book of Arousing Souls to Visit the Divinely Guarded Jerusalem (*Kitab ba'ith an-nufus ila ziyarat al-Quds al-mahrus*)

Possibly Damascus, dated 1477
Written by Ibrahim ibn 'Abd al-Rahman ibn Ibrahim al-Fazari, also known as Ibn al-Firkah (d. 1328)
Ink on paper; 72 folios
6¾ × 5 in. (17.1 × 12.7 cm)
Beinecke Rare Book and Manuscript Library, Yale University, New Haven (Landberg MS 117)

Ibrahim ibn 'Abd al-Rahman ibn Ibrahim al-Fazari, also known as Ibn al-Firkah, was a Shafi'i scholar who came from a rural Egyptian family but was born and raised in Damascus. His *Book of Arousing Souls to Visit the Divinely Guarded Jerusalem* is a classic of the *fada'il* (merits of) genre, which reflects on the spiritual merits of places such as the Aqsa Mosque in Jerusalem and the Tomb of Abraham in Hebron or of broader regions such as al-Sham (Greater Syria). The purpose was to encourage the general public to embark on religious pilgrimages.

Ibn al-Firkah mentions in the introduction that he has relied on two sources for his book: primarily, *The Comprehensive Compilation of the Merits of the Aqsa Mosque* (*Al-Jami' al-mustaqsa fi fada'il al-masjid al-aqsa*) by Abu Muhammad al-Qasim ibn Hibat-Allah ibn 'Asakir (d. 1293), and, to a lesser extent, *The Merits of Jerusalem* (*Fada'il bayt al-maqdis*) by Abu al-Ma'ali al-Mushrif ibn al-Marjihi ibn Ibrahim al-Maqdisi (d. 1098). (He gives the name of the latter whenever it is quoted to differentiate the two sources.) To simplify the text, Ibn al-Firkah omitted the chains of narrators whenever he reported prophetic traditions.

The book is divided into thirteen chapters that cover the merits of visiting and performing acts of devotion at the Aqsa Mosque and the tomb of the prophet Abraham. Chapter two mentions visiting and praying in Bethlehem, while chapter thirteen culminates with the Prophet endowing land in Hebron to his companion, Tamim al-Dari. MAS

Selected References: Al-Jubeh 1991, pp. 161, 168, 170; Mitchell 2004, pp. 105, 249, 288; Sezgin, Ehrig-Eggert, and Neubauer 2007, vol. 3, pp. 233, 285; el-Awaisi 2008, pp. 27, 48, 49.

41

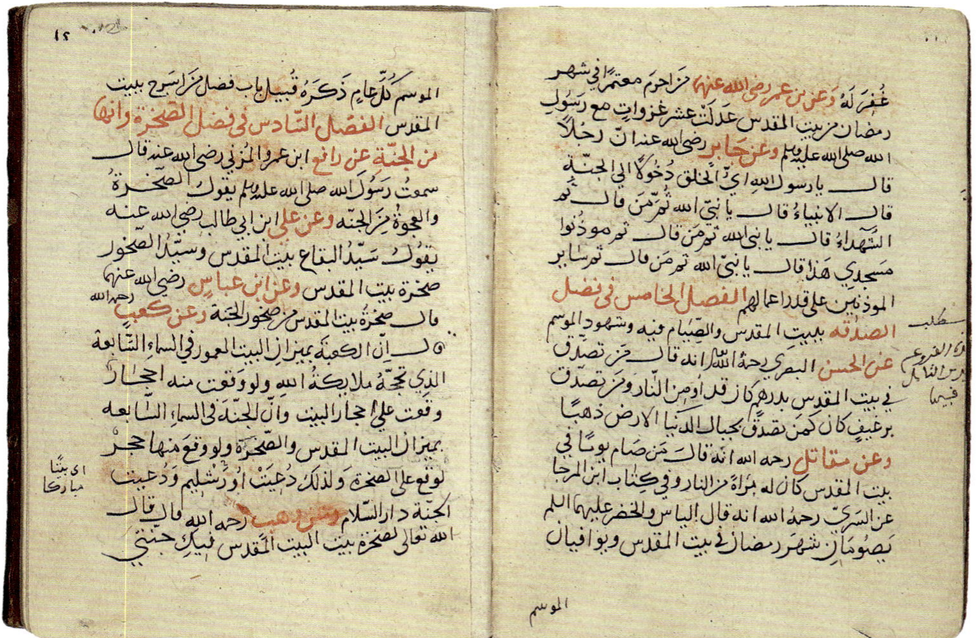

42

Celestial Globe

Syria or Egypt, A.H. 622 (1225/26)
'Alam al-Din Qaysar (1178/79–1251)
Copper alloy inlaid with silver and copper
Diam. 8⅝ in. (22 cm)
Museo Nazionale di Capodimonte, Naples

Covered with forty-eight constellation figures and 1,025 stars graduated in size to convey relative magnitude, this splendid celestial globe bears witness to the high regard in which both fine metalwork and astronomical erudition were held by Ayyubid rulers. A celestial globe is an object of utility and of conspicuous display, and this one excels on both counts. Its most basic function is to illustrate the relative positions and sizes of major stars and constellations. With supplementary instruments and calendrical tables, it could perform many of the same functions as an astrolabe.[1] This example incorporates such tools in its design: two gnomons and graduated arcs for determining the elevation of the sun are hidden in the base. The surface dazzles: stars are indicated by inlaid silver dots, while figures are expertly and elegantly engraved in copper. The globe presents the constellations not as seen from the earth but as if one is looking down upon the night sky, a position that allows its owner to track the movement of the stars from a realm beyond the celestial sphere. Its pleasure lay in the indulgence of a majestic, breathtaking conceit: that one could, literally and figuratively, grasp the entire universe.[2]

That Sultan al-Malik al-Kamil, named in one of the two inscriptions on the object, would own a well-crafted celestial globe should hardly surprise. The Ayyubid leader found such enjoyment in academic inquiry that he was known to discourse with invited scholars through the night.[3] The globe reflects precisely the sort of up-to-date technology that he might have commissioned to outshine his rival brothers, who also appreciated luxurious astronomical devices,[4] or to impress a foreign leader, such as the Holy Roman Emperor Frederick II, to whom he sent a mechanical tree with singing birds in the course of their negotiations over the shared status of Jerusalem.[5]

Mathematics and the related fields of astronomy, astrology, geometry, engineering, and music were among the most highly regarded disciplines, and the maker of this globe, 'Alam al-Din Qaysar, mentioned in a second inscription, enjoyed a considerable reputation as a master.[6] He studied with the renowned teacher Kamal al-Din Musa bin Yunis in Mosul and found ready patronage within the Ayyubid courts. Under Muzaffa Mahmud, amir of Hama, Syria, he built observation towers and a watermill. Al-Ashraf Musa (d. 1237), brother of al-Kamil, had him construct an octagonal palace in Ra's al-'Ayn, also in Syria. When Frederick II sent a series of learned questions to al-Kamil as part of his diplomatic wooing, the sultan directed the mathematical questions to none other than 'Alam al-Din Qaysar.[7] A reference to Ptolemy's *Almagest* in one of the inscriptions serves the practical function of indicating the standard against which this globe is calibrated, while also conveying in a public manner the maker's mastery of and reverence for this classic Greek source.[8] MH

Selected References: Savage-Smith 1985, pp. 25–26, 72, 218–19; Dekker 2013, p. 328, no. IG4.

1. On the many uses of celestial globes, see Savage-Smith 1985, pp. 74–80.
2. A pleasure also clearly enjoyed by a later user, as indicated by a scale subsequently added that showed the size used for the first five magnitudes and Latin zodiacal names.
3. Al-Maqrizi, in his obituary for al-Kamil, describes the sultan's laudable and noteworthy patronage of "men of learning." Al-Maqrizi 1980 ed., pp. 229–30.
4. Still extant are the exquisite astrolabes created for al-Mu'azzam Isa (1176–1227) and al-Ashraf Musa, now in the Naval Museum, Istanbul, no. 264, and the Museum of the History of Science, University of Oxford, no. 37148, respectively.

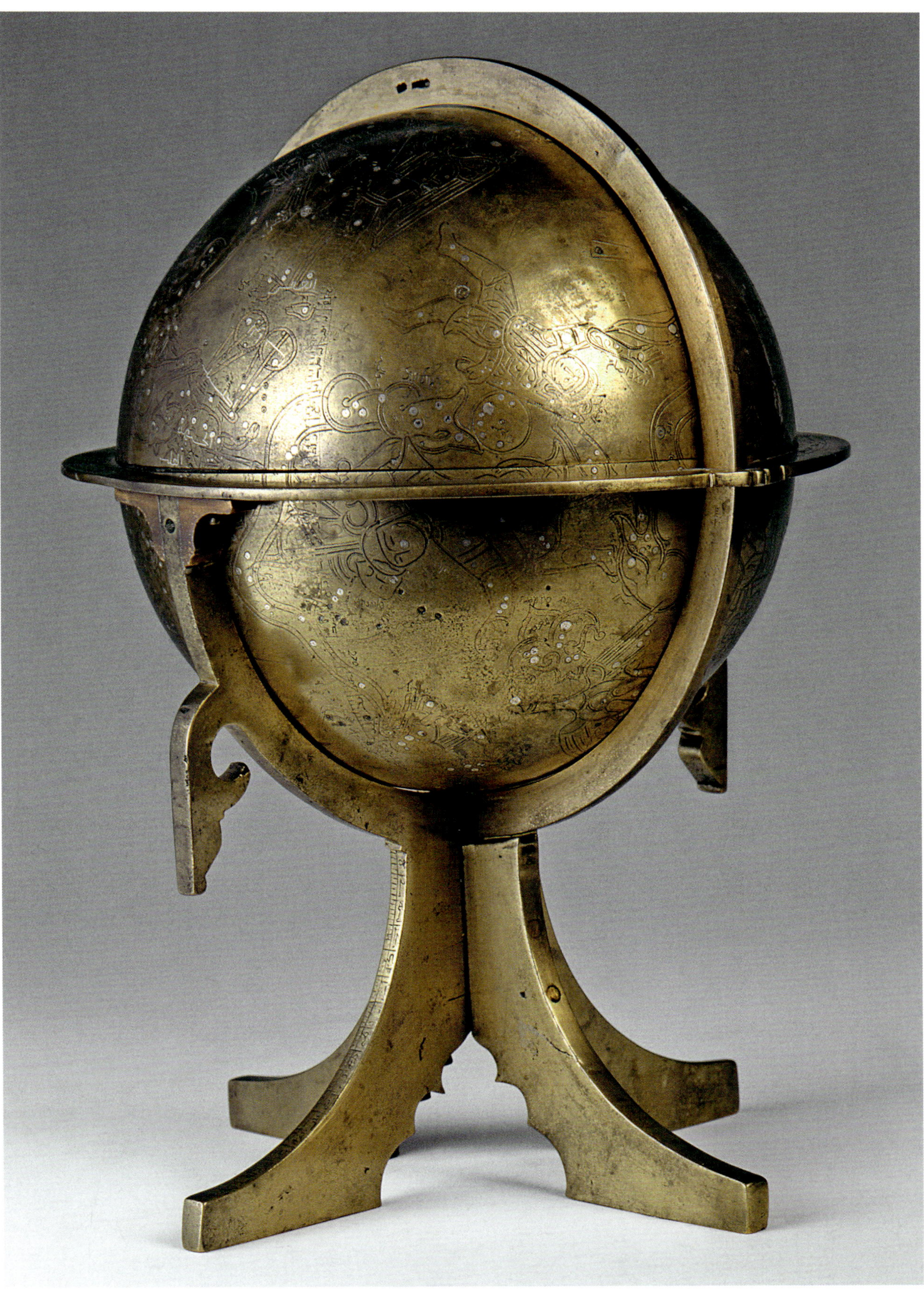

42

5. Here, too, al-Ashraf competed with his brother, sending Frederick an astronomical clock. Müller-Wiener 2009, p. 420.

6. Brentjes 2011. See especially her remarks on pp. 342–44. For a brief biography of Qaysar, see Mayer, L., 1956, p. 80.

7. Ibn Wasil in Gabrieli, ed. 1969, p. 270.

8. One of the most important sources on ancient astronomy in the Islamic world, the *Almagest* was written in Greek in the second century A.D. and included discussions on the construction of celestial globes.

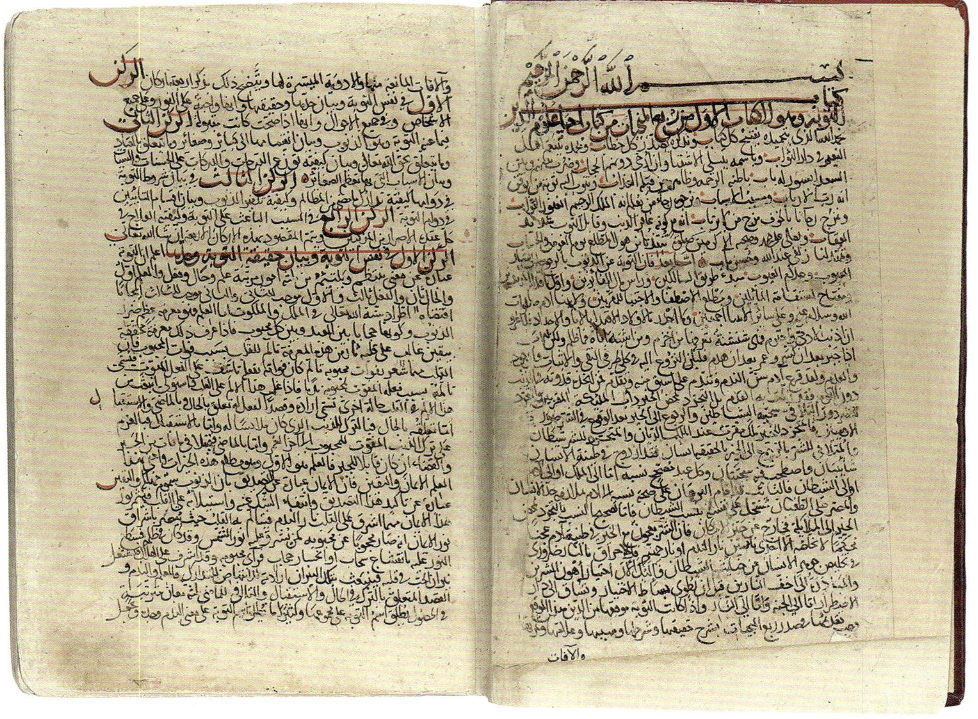

43

43
Revival of the Islamic Sciences (Ihya' 'ulum al-din)

Jerusalem, A.H. 631 (1233/34)
Written by al-Ghazali (ca. 1058–1111)
Ink on paper; 131 folios
10⅞ × 7⅝ in. (27.7 × 19.5 cm)
Museum of Islamic Art, Doha (MS 788-03)

Imam al-Ghazali, one the most influential Muslim scholars of all time, achieved fame and fortune before he underwent a profound spiritual crisis that led him to renounce worldly affairs. He gave up his teaching position at the Nizamiyyah College of Baghdad, distributed his wealth, and went on an eleven-year earthly and spiritual trip to cleanse his heart and attain sincerity. The trip took him to Damascus, Jerusalem, Hebron, Medina, and Mecca for pilgrimage.

Al-Ghazali's magnum opus, *The Revival of the Islamic Sciences* (*Ihya' 'ulum al-din*), is an unparalleled work of spirituality in which Muslim law was used as a vehicle for the religious message. At least part of the work — the second chapter of the first section, titled "The Jerusalem Treatise of the Creed" — was written in Jerusalem, where al-Ghazali resided in rooms above the Golden Gate. During that period, education flourished in the city, as entire schools were endowed inside and outside the Aqsa Mosque.

The Revival of the Islamic Sciences is a voluminous work divided into four major "quarters," each containing ten chapters: the Quarter of the Acts of Worship (*Rub' al-'ibadat*); the Quarter of the Norms of Daily Life (*Rub' al-'adat*); the Quarter of the Ways to Perdition (*Rub' al-muhlikat*); and the Quarter of the Ways to Salvation (*Rub' al-munjiyat*). The manuscript pages seen here contain the beginning of the Book of Repentance (*Kitab al-tawbah*), the first chapter of the fourth quarter. MAS

Selected References: Abu-Sway 1996, pp. 101–23; al-Ghazali 2010 ed.

44
Ode to the Mantle (Qasidat al-Burda)

Egypt, late 1361
Written by al-Busiri (ca. 1212–ca. 1295)
Copied by Muhammad al-Firuzabadi al-Shirazi
Ink, opaque watercolor, and gold on paper
Overall: 13⅝ × 17⅝ in. (34.6 × 44.8 cm)
The National Library of Israel, Jerusalem (Yah. Ar. 784)

The thirteenth-century Sufi imam al-Busiri's *Ode to the Mantle* (*Qasidat al-Burda*), also known as *The Glittering Stars in Praise of the Best of Creation* (*al-Kawakib al-durriya fi khayr al-bariyya*), is among the most frequently recited poems in the Islamic world. Written in elegant Arabic, it is a mystical ode in praise of the Prophet Muhammad. The *Burda* is associated with miracles (*mu'jizat*s) and is believed to embody curative and talismanic properties and have the power to procure intercession and salvation. Its verses are worn as charms, written on the walls of mosques and houses, and chanted at funerals.[1] The introduction to the present manuscript recounts the story of al-Busiri's miraculous recovery from a state of semiparalysis after he composed the poem and dreamed that the Prophet had placed his sacred mantle, or cloak, over him.[2]

Over time the original *Burda* has generated countless commentaries, expansions, and imitations. The present verse is an expansion (*takhmis*) by 'Izz al-Din Muhammad 'Abd al-'Aziz ibn Ahmad ibn Sa'id al-Dirini al-Dumairi (d. 1297), who is also credited with writing the introduction.[3] The manuscript contains seventeen illuminated folios in *muhaqqaq* and *naskhi* scripts. Copied by a Persian calligrapher, Muhammad Firuzabadi al-Shirazi, toward the end of 1361, it was reportedly produced in Jerusalem. Its connection to the city is based on evidence that the renowned scholar and calligrapher Muhammad Firuzabadi, author of the great lexicon *Comprehensive Dictionary* (*Qamus al-Muhit*), taught in the holy city between 1358 and 1368. A Persian annotation in nastaliq script added to the very end of the manuscript in 1911 is signed by the owner, Muhammad Kazim, who mentions that he compiled these folios over a period of twenty years and had them restored and the borders repainted.

Al-Busiri composed the *Qasidat al-Burda* in Mamluk Egypt during the thirteenth century at a time of heightened religious fervor and a growing popularity and influence of Sufism. As the Mamluk military elite were of Turkic origin, on conversion to Islam many were educated in Arabic language, literature, and Islamic science as well as in Sufi poetic texts. Religious prose, poetry, and biographies of the prophets, particularly Muhammad, flourished under Mamluk patronage. Rulers and

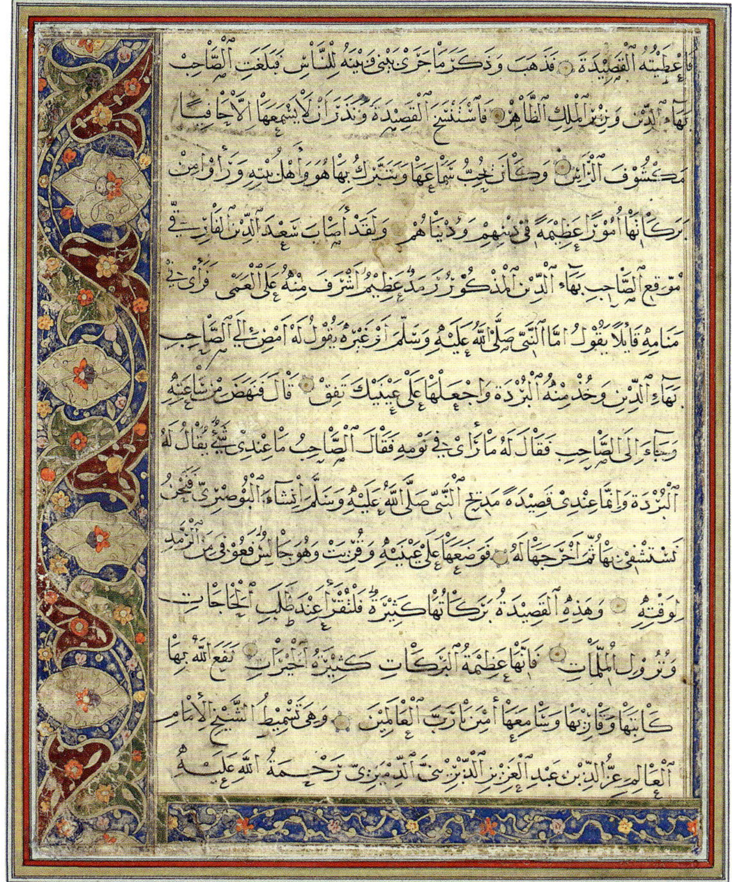
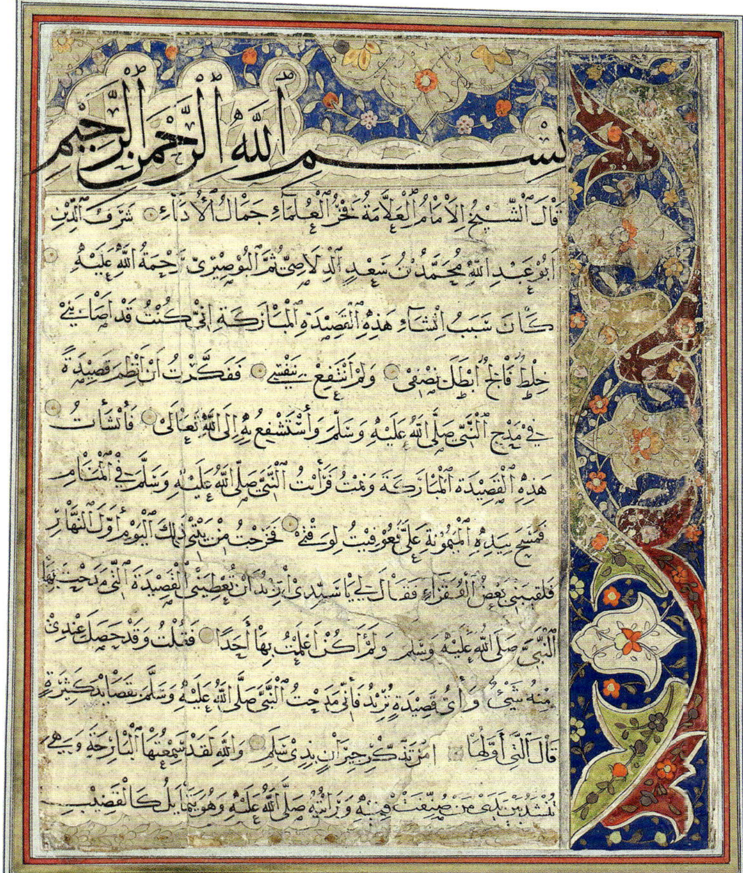

44, fols. 2v–3

elites copied them as a pious exercise and had ample resources to hire talented calligraphers and illuminators to embellish their work.[4] An illuminated copy of the *Burda* produced about 1470, dedicated to the Mamluk sultan Qa'it Bay (r. 1468–96), and a second copy commissioned by the Mamluk amir Yashbak ibn Mahdi (d. 1480) and dated 1472/73 are currently preserved in the Chester Beatty Library in Dublin.[5] ME

1. Newman 2008. See also Stetkevych 2006 and Stetkevych 2010. Verses from al-Busiri's *Qasidat al-Burda* are inscribed on the painted-and-gilded wood panels of the winter reception room from Ottoman Damascus dated A.H. 1119 (1707) in the Metropolitan Museum's collection, acc. no. 1970.170.

2. Basset 1960.

3. It became common practice with religious poems to interweave one's own lines with the original verses. A *takhmis* (the making of five) is a derivative poem in which a second poet takes a base text and adds three hemistiches to two of the original, for a total of five hemistiches per verse.

4. Flemming 1977, p. 259.

5. Chester Beatty Library, Dublin, MS 4168 and MS 4169. See Washington, D.C., and other cities 1981–83, p. 47 and note; Irwin 2003.

45

Qur'an Manuscript

Jerusalem, 1390
Copied by Muhammad ibn Ahmad ibn Isa, known as Ibn al-Bulaybil al-Hijazi
Opaque watercolor, gold, and ink on paper
7⅛ × 4¾ in. (18 × 12 cm)
British Library, London (Or. 12809)

Produced in Jerusalem, this Qur'an manuscript is representative of the ornately illuminated examples made in Egypt, Syria, and the Holy Land under Mamluk rule between 1250 and 1517. The relative richness of its decoration and its convenient size for study and prayer suggest that it was commissioned for personal use. A conventional feature of these Qur'ans is the tripartite division of the decorative page,

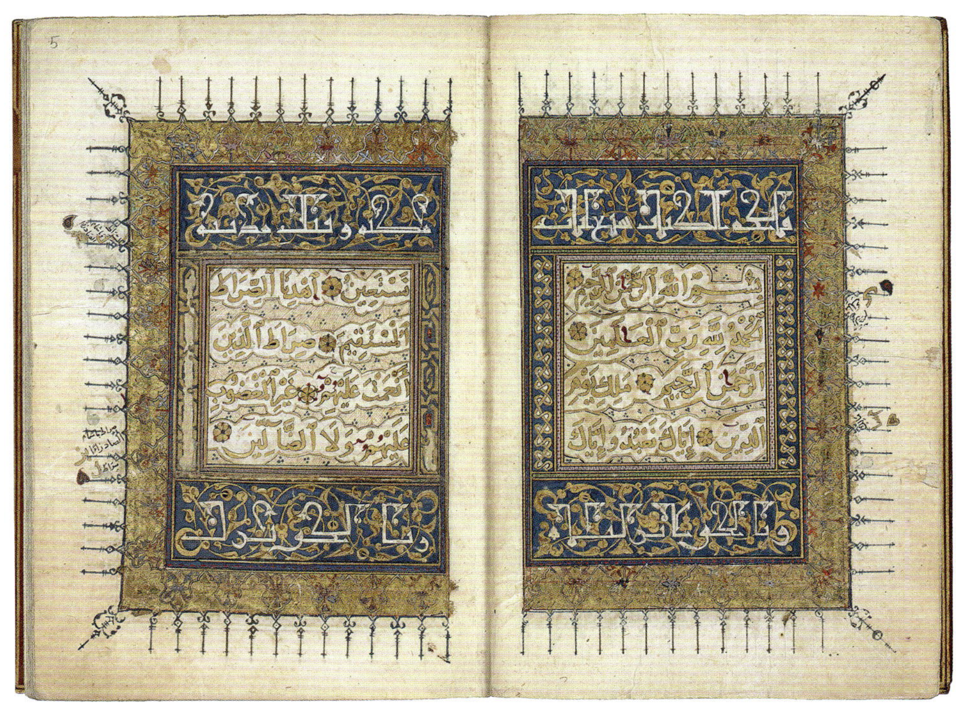

45, fols. 4v–5r

with a central panel to carry the text and upper and lower panels to carry inscriptions. The central panels here encase the whole of chapter one of the Qur'an, that is, the seven verses of *Surat al-Fatihah*, spread over both pages of the opening. The text itself is in gold *naskhi* script, finely outlined in black ink within a flowing, cloudlike motif, between which is a delicately hatched pattern, also in gold. Gold rosettes speckled with red, green, and blue dots mark the end of each verse. The upper and lower horizontal panels of both pages contain inscriptions written in a white Eastern Kufic script against a blue-based gold-foliate background. In the upper panels, the inscription states the name of the chapter, the number of its verses, and the fact that they were revealed in Mecca. The inscription in the lower panels quotes from *Surat al-Isra'* (17:105), "With the truth we have sent it down, and with the truth it has come down."[1] The central, lower, and upper panels are encased on three sides within a gold border decorated with red, blue, and pink floral designs and edged with blue finials into the margin. CB

1. Arberry 1955, p. 286.

46

Godefroy de Bouillon and His Men Embark on the First Crusade

From *History of Outremer* (*Livre d'eracles*) by William of Tyre (d. 1186)
Northern France, Paris(?), ca. 1295–1300
Tempera, ink, and gold on parchment; 362 folios
13⅜ × 9⅝ in. (34 × 24.5 cm)
Walters Art Museum, Baltimore (MS W.137)

The *History of Outremer*, also known as the *Livre d'eracles* from the first line of the text, is an old French translation of the Latin *Historia*.[1] William I, archbishop of Tyre, wrote this history of the Crusader Kingdom in the twelfth century and carried the story up to 1184. The second highest ecclesiastical official in the Latin Kingdom, William composed the work there, presenting it from the point of view of Jerusalem. He was also adviser to King Amalric and then, from 1177, chancellor under the youthful King Baldwin IV. The translation into Old French was carried out in France in the early 1220s,[2] and various Old French continuations were added by anonymous authors during the thirteenth century.[3] In this manuscript, executed in northern France, the continuation goes up to 1232. This manuscript (MS W.137) and another in the Walters Art Museum (MS W.142) are the only two codices with this text in the United States.[4]

All illustrations in this manuscript are historiated initials, one placed at the start of each book of William's translated text. No system had yet developed for how to illustrate the texts of the continuations. The rubrics seen here, above the initial "V," identify the scene as "la muete Godefroi et ces compaignons," a reference to the departure of Godefroy de Bouillon and his men on the First Crusade in August 1096. It is the classic image of Western Crusaders starting their journey eastward to liberate the holy sites of Jerusalem, Bethlehem, and Nazareth. The lead knight holds a spear with a cross on its banner, but none of the soldiers wears the cross insignia on his shoulder that would signify he had "taken the cross," that is, made the vow to go on Crusade. The two knights wearing thirteenth-century-type French barrel-helmets (*heaumes*) reveal the artist's contemporary interest in a simplified naturalism, applied here to a scene from the late eleventh century. Although clearly French, this artist chose scenes for his cycle of historiated initials from manuscripts originating in the Crusader Holy Land. Nonetheless, the closest comparison manuscript for the present work is now in the Bibliothèque Municipale, Epinal, France (MS 45), a contemporary codex with a similar text and comparable illustrations, also possibly done in Paris by a different scribe and a different artist.[5] JF

Selected References: Folda 1976, pp. 148–51, 168, 208–11; Randall 1989, pp. 123–27, no. 50; Edbury 2007, pp. 75ff.; Handyside 2015, pt. 2, pp. 123ff.

1. The title of the Latin text is often given as *Historia rerum in partibus transmarinis gestarum*, but we do not know what title William of Tyre himself used; Handyside 2015, pp. 1–2. Edbury and Rowe 1988, p. 1, suggest *Historia Ierosolymitana*, but Philip Handyside uses *Historia*, as here.
2. Handyside 2015, pp. 114ff.; Edbury 2007, p. 69.
3. Edbury 1997, pp. 139–53; Morgan 1982; Morgan 1973.
4. They were used as the two base manuscripts for the edition of the *History of Outremer* published by A. Firmin-Didot in 1879–80. See William of Tyre 1879–80 ed.
5. Folda 1976, pp. 146–50, 205–6.

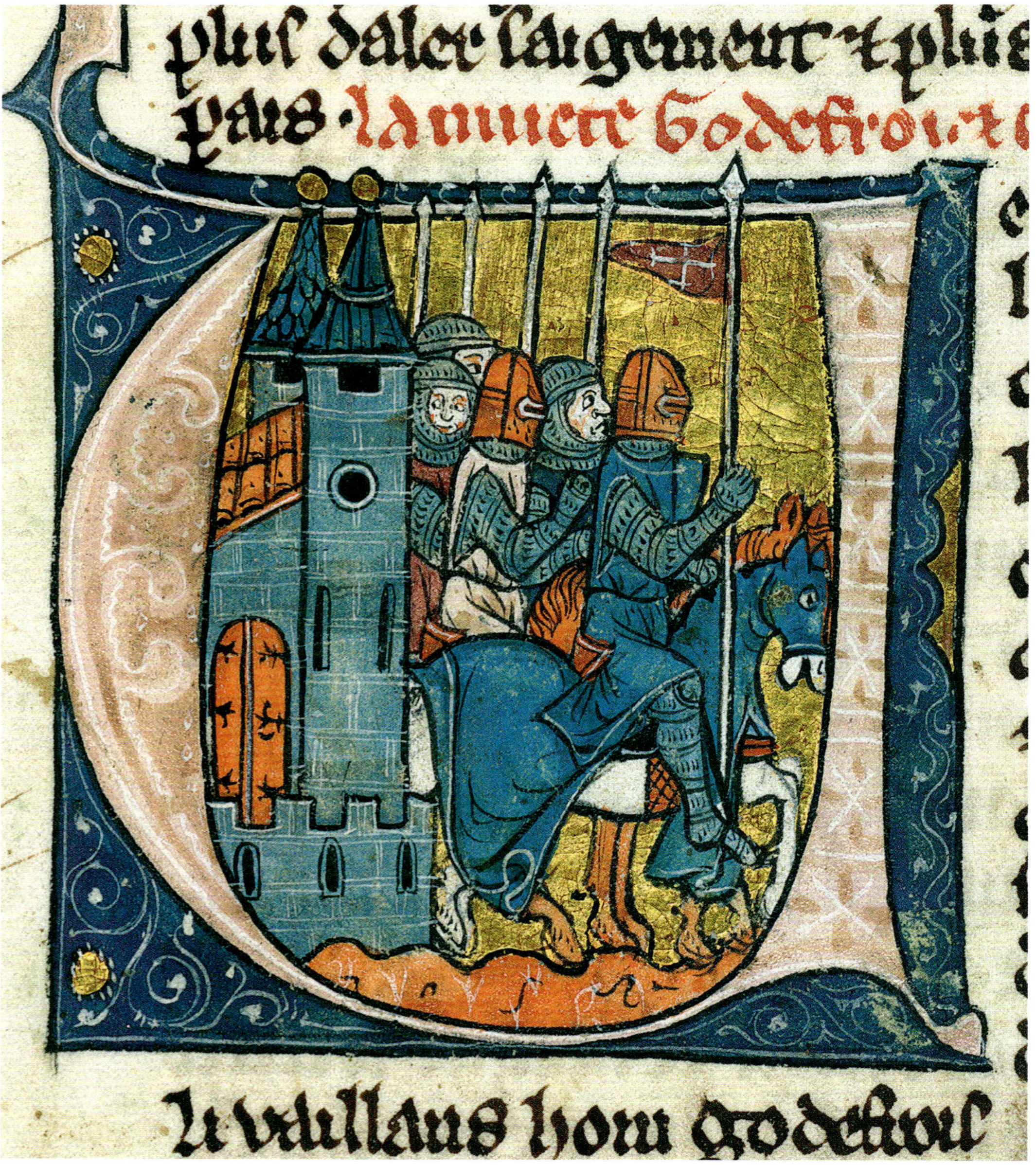

46, fol. 15r

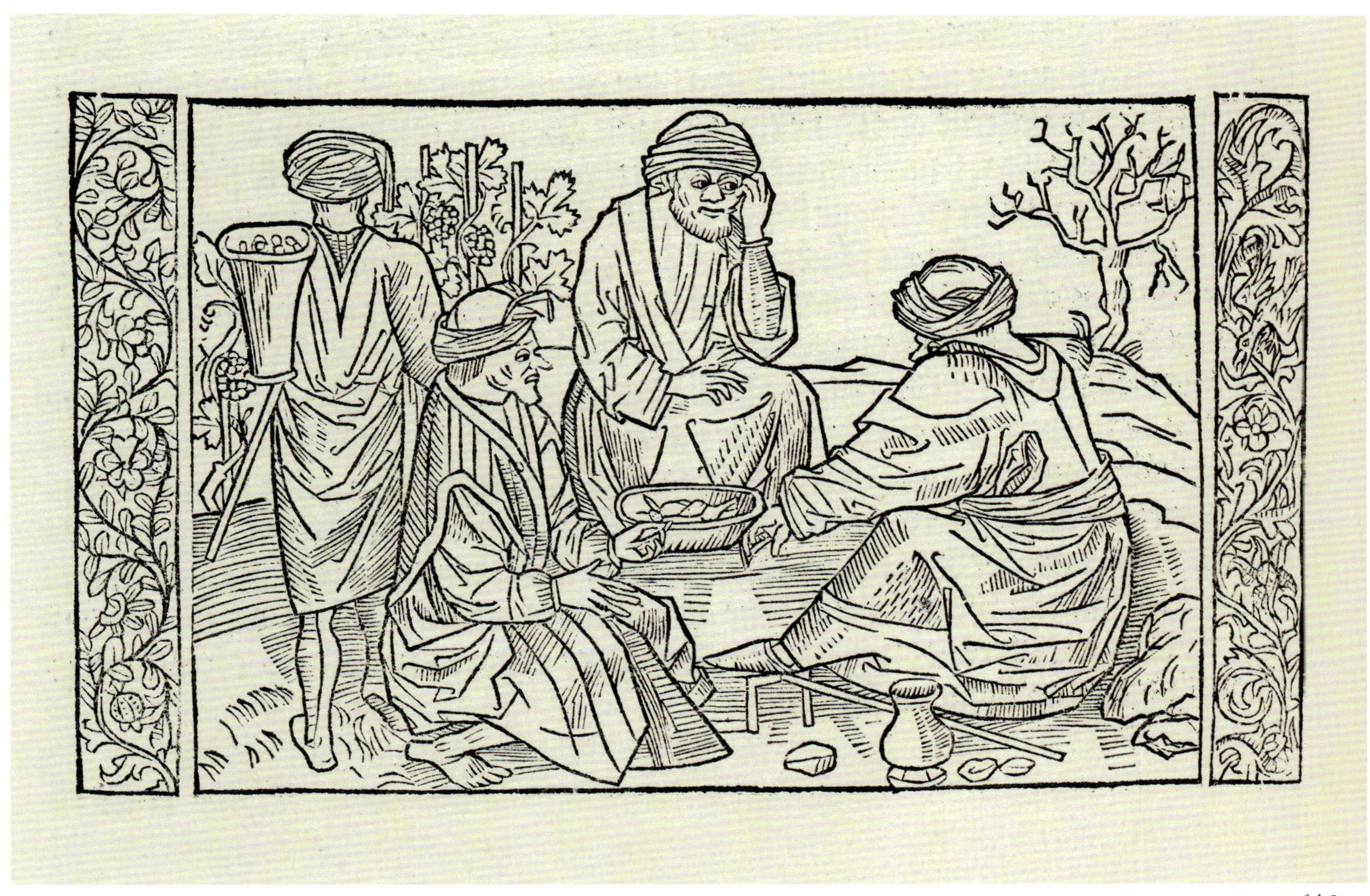

47, fol. L.3v

47

The Syrian Christians of the Holy Land

Lyon, 1488
From *Journey to the Holy Land* (*La peregrination en Terre Sainte*)
Written by Bernhard von Breydenbach (1440?–1497?); translated by Nicolas Le Huen (active 15th century); illustrated by Erhard Reuwich (ca. 1455–ca. 1490); published by Topie, Lyon
Hand-colored engraving; 131 folios
11½ × 8¾ in. (29.2 × 22.3 cm)
The Metropolitan Museum of Art, New York, Harris Brisbane Dick Fund, 1928 (28.86.2)

Long before the publication of Bernhard von Breydenbach's account of his trip to the Holy Land, European pilgrims' guides had advised travelers in search of wine in the region to seek out the fine vineyards of local Christians.[1] Perhaps then it is not surprising that the illustration of Syrian Christians, one of six images of local peoples included in the book, depicts them as vineyard workers, taking a break from their labors. While the accompanying text concedes that they are hard workers, it perpetuates a long-standing perjorative — that these Arabic-speaking Christians cannot be trusted for they are likely to transmit the secrets of their co-religionists to their Muslim neighbors.[2] MH

Selected References: Timm 2006; Ross 2014.

1. See, for instance, the comments of the Seigneur d'Anglure, writing in the fourteenth century: "We laid in a supply of wine, which was delivered by the consul at Jerusalem. Because the Saracens themselves drink no wine, the pilgrims can get it only at very great danger and at a high price. . . . Beit Jala is populated more by Christians than by Saracens. The Christians work the vineyards where these good wines grow and you may be sure that one can properly call them good wines." Browne 1975, pp. 41–42.
2. Jacques de Vitry 1896 ed., p. 67.

48

Copto-Arabic Book of Prayers

Egypt, Dal al-Suriyan(?), Wadi al-Natrun, 17th century(?)
Ink on paper; 44 folios
8⅞ × 6⅝ in. (22.5 × 16.8 cm)
The Metropolitan Museum of Art, New York, Rogers Fund, 1919 (19.196.3)

This collection of Christian exhortative texts for morning and evening communal devotions focuses on the Cross and the mysteries of salvation. Bilingual by design, it contains versions in Arabic and in the Bohairic dialect of Coptic Egyptian written in two adjacent columns. The original scope of the manuscript remains unknown, as the last extant page ends in the middle of a sentence and the covers are missing; the preserved canons (of prayers) are numbered 1 to 22, followed by five pages of a similar text in Coptic only. Although it is not illustrated, several pages exhibit elaborately drawn capital letters. The dating of the book depends entirely on external features, which can be very deceptive; while the Coptic scribal hand suggests the fifteenth century, the extant three-crescent watermarks indicate a later, Ottoman period.[1] The text itself, however, is likely a copy of an older composition.

The acquisition of the manuscript is linked to the Metropolitan Museum's excavations at the Monastery of the Syrians (Dayr al-Suriyan) in Wadi al-Natrun (ancient Scetis), where it was either found in the excavations or acquired from the library.[2] Alternatively, it may come from the Monastery of Saint Macarius the Great (Dayr Abu Maqar), whose library was investigated by the same mission.[3] Both monasteries belong to ancient foundations in Scetis that have remained active to the present day. After the first monastic communities were established in Scetis, in the fourth century the area developed into the premier Christian site of medieval Egypt. Monastery libraries grew accordingly to reflect the various Christian traditions represented in the area, including the Coptic, Syrian, Armenian, and Ethiopian.

The present manuscript testifies to the gradual linguistic change following the transformation of the country after the Arab conquest in the 640s. By the time it was penned, even the Egyptian clergymen were native speakers of Arabic, and their command of Coptic was rather poor. MD

I had the opportunity to study and discuss this manuscript with Alzahraa K. Ahmed, Matthew Saba, and Thomas Vinton.

1. The watermarks were first noticed by Metropolitan Museum conservator Yana van Dyke, Department of Paper Conservation.
2. The findings of the excavations were published between 1926 and 1933 by Hugh G. Evelyn-White in three volumes titled *The Monasteries of the Wadi 'n Natrûn*. Headed by Stephen J. Davis, a project is currently under way to catalogue Coptic, Arabic, and Ethiopic manuscripts at the library of Dayr al-Suriyan.
3. Evelyn-White 1926–33, pt. 1. The present manuscript is not part of the selection introduced in the book, but Evelyn-White recounts his visits to the library on pp. xli–xlii.

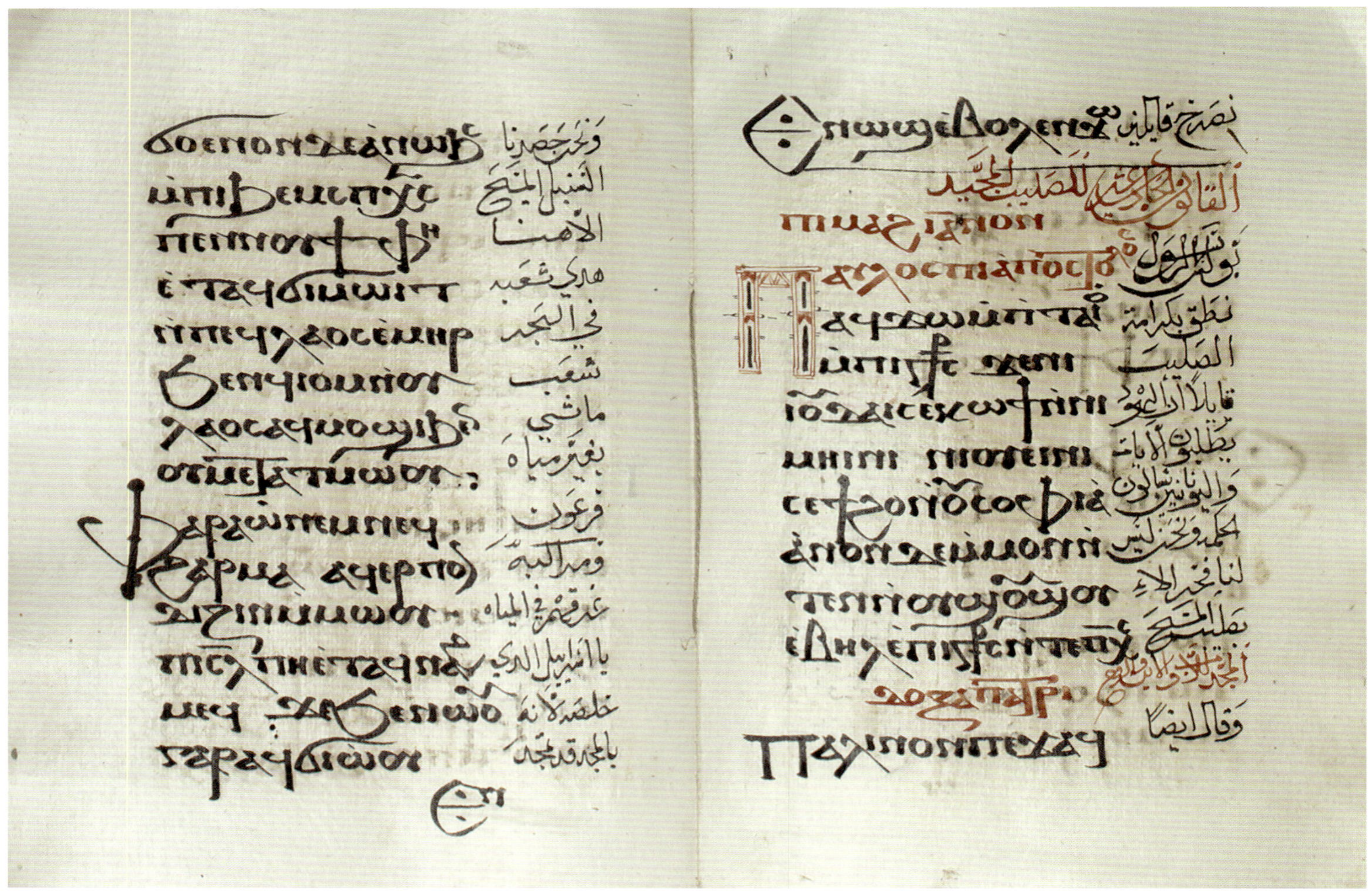

48

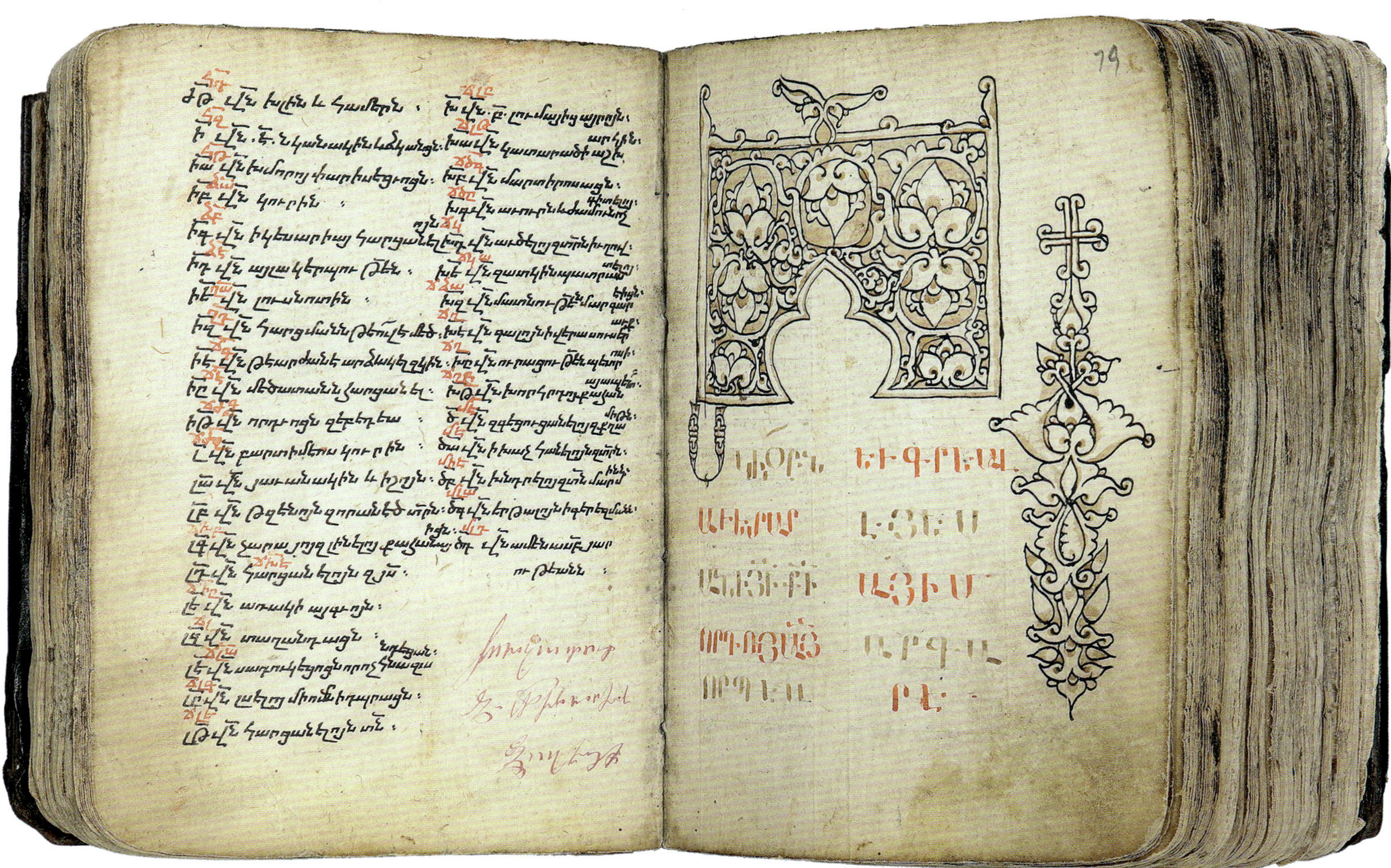

49, fols. 78v–79r

49

Gospel Book

Jerusalem, 1321
Written by Nerses the Abbot
Wash and ink on paper; 284 folios
6¾ × 5 in. (17 × 12.5 cm)
Library of Congress, Washington, D.C. (MS Orien Nr. East: 6003)

Nerses the Abbot copied the text of this Gospel Book while Jerusalem was under the rule of the Mamluk sultan al-Nasir Muhammad, whose patronage is represented elsewhere in this volume (cat. 129). Rather than recognizing the ruler of the city, the dedication places the manuscript and its donor within the Armenian world by dating the work to the reign of the Armenian king of Cilicia and the Armenian patriarch.[1] The first (incipit) page of the Gospel of Mark, on the right, is written in *erkatagir*, the original, vertical form of the Armenian alphabet. On the previous page, the text is in *bolorgir*, the cursive form of that alphabet that became popular by the thirteenth century. With its trilobed arch drawn gracefully in shades of brown ink, the headpiece continues the floral patterns and form of the first letter developed centuries earlier in Byzantine manuscript illumination (cat. 72). The manuscript retains much of its original leather binding, which is decorated with an embossed cross, a reference to the Cross on which Jesus was crucified originally preserved in Jerusalem (cat. 25a–f). This work reflects both the importance given to the word in the Armenian faith and the significance of the Armenian monasteries in Jerusalem in producing and protecting manuscripts. HCE

Selected References: Sanjian 1976, pp. 767–71; Washington, D.C. 2012, n.p.

1. Sanjian 1976, p. 767.

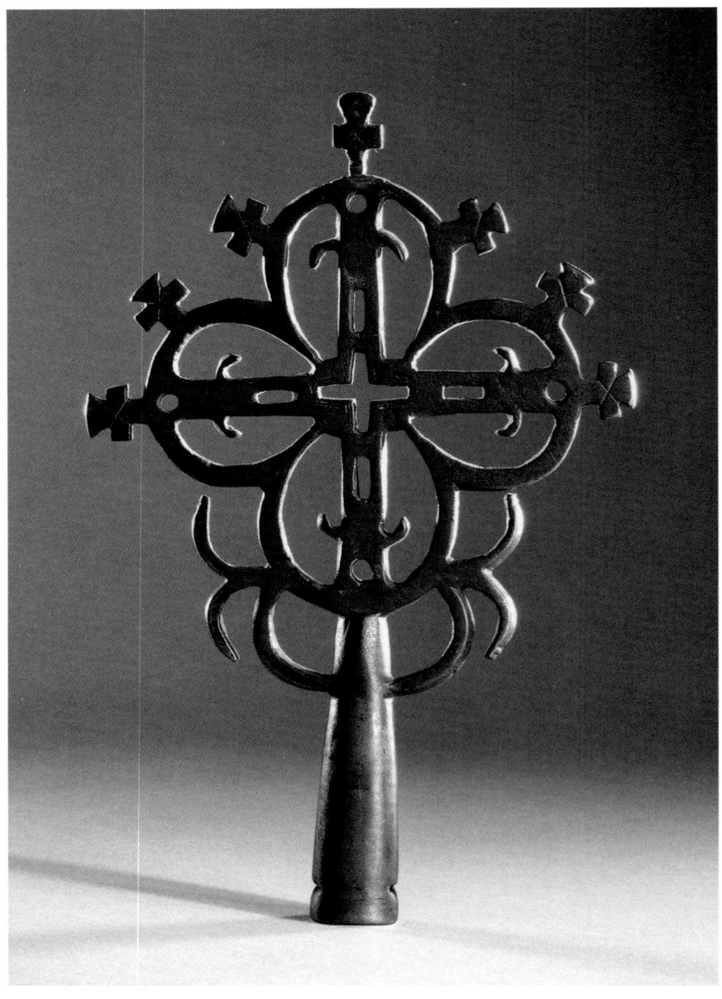

50

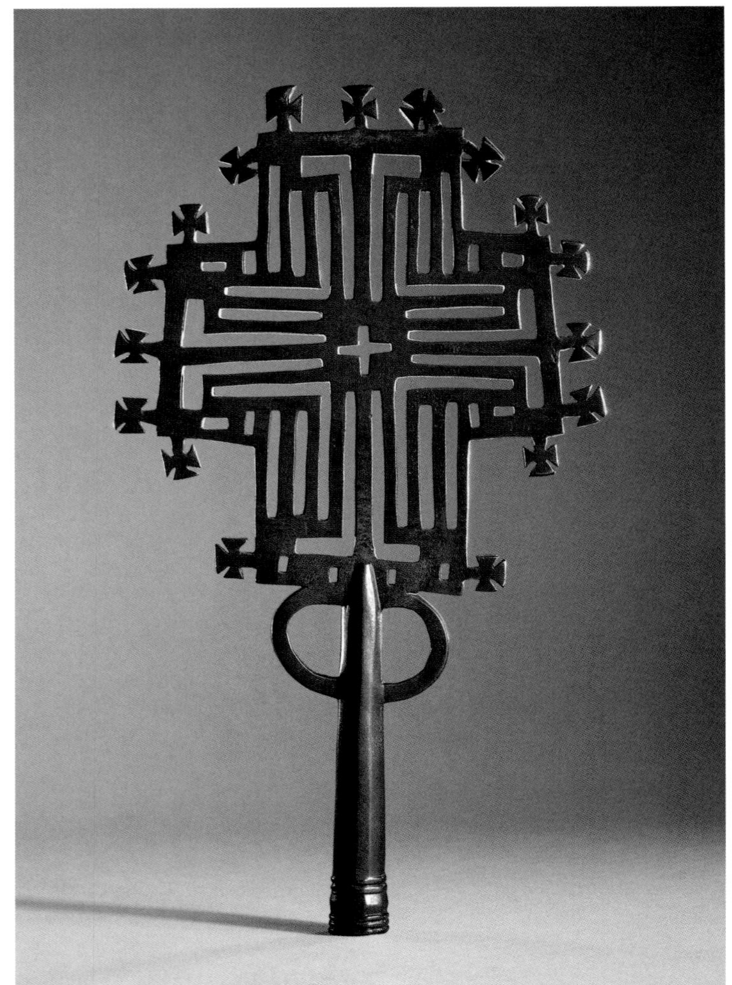

51

50

Cross

Ethiopia, 14th century
Copper
8¼ × 5⅜ in. (20.8 × 13.8 cm)
Private collection, United Kingdom

Openwork metal crosses are emblematic of Ethiopian Christians. The solidity and weight of the copper are offset by openwork patterning and fanciful ornamentation that create an overall lacelike delicacy. When used in procession, this cross would have been affixed to a wood pole and embellished by colorful cloth bands attached to the loops at the bottom.

Ethiopians trace their links to Jerusalem to the time of Solomon. The Acts of the Apostles tells of Saint Philip's baptism of an Ethiopian (8:26–40), and disciples of Saint Jerome (d. 420) mention Christian monks from Ethiopia among those streaming to the Holy Land.[1] Ethiopian pilgrimage grew significantly in the twelfth century.[2] Niccolo of Poggibonsi, a fourteenth-century Franciscan visitor to Jerusalem, noted that Ethiopians carrying full-size olive trees processed with Armenians on Palm Sunday.[3]

In 1290, around the time this cross was made, Emperor Yagbe'u Seyon dispatched letters and gifts to the Ethiopian community in Jerusalem, along with one hundred candles to be lighted in the churches of the city.[4] BDB

Selected References: Jerusalem 2000–2001, p. 38; Di Salvo 2006, p. 137, fig. 2.

1. O'Mahony 1996, p. 143.
2. Isaac 1984–86, p. 53.
3. Cerulli 1943–47, vol. 1, pp. 123–24.
4. O'Mahony 1996, p. 146.

51

Cross

Ethiopia, 15th century
Copper
15½ × 9⅛ in. (39.5 × 23.1 cm)
Private collection, United Kingdom

Ethiopian crosses typically create pattern from the interplay of solids and voids. The form of this example, with its openwork crosses framed within a square cross, seems to echo the shape of the thirteenth-century Church of Saint George (Bete Giyorgis) near the town of Lalibela in Ethiopia, one of the eleven rock-cut churches built after the loss of Jerusalem to Saladin and intended as a surrogate means for religious pilgrims to visit Jerusalem without leaving their own land.[1]

Meskel, meaning "cross," is the name given to the great feast commemorating the discovery of the Cross by Saint Helena (Eleni), which is celebrated annually by Ethiopian Christians, beginning with a celebratory bonfire on the evening of September 26. It is believed that part of the Cross was sent to Ethiopia from Jerusalem. BDB

Selected Reference: O'Mahony 1996, p. 144.

1. O'Mahony 1996, p. 144.

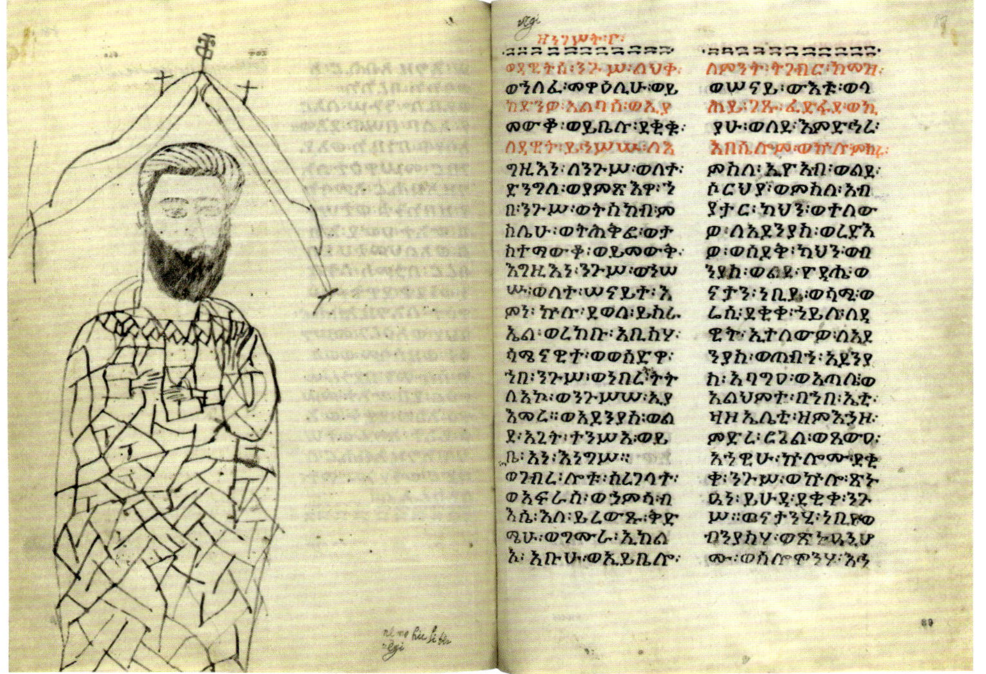

52, fols. 88v–89r

52

The Book of Kings

Aksum(?), Ethiopia, 1344
Ink on parchment; 187 folios
14⅜ × 10⅝ in. (36.5 × 27.1 cm)
Biblioteca Apostolica Vaticana, Vatican City (Borg. Et. 3)

An inscription dated 1637 in this book reveals that the manuscript was sent from Jerusalem to Rome — temporarily — to serve as an exemplar for study. A second note, penned some sixty years later, states that the Ethiopian king ʿAmda Seyon I (Pillar of Zion, r. 1314–44) gave it to the Church of the Virgin in Jerusalem, either the Chapel of Mary at Golgotha or an altar of the Virgin of Jehoshaphat, over which the Ethiopians presided from at least the mid-fourteenth to the seventeenth century.

It is not clear whether the figural drawings in the manuscript are contemporary with the text, although their placement at the beginning of significant sections indicates that illustrations were intended. There are images of Hannah and her son, Samuel; a king; and the bearded man seen here, said to be likely Saul or David. The complicated patterning and decorative neckline of the man's robe connote luxury and authority. Holding a small book in his tiny hands, he stands under a stylized canopy topped with small crosses, the center one resembling a typical decorative Ethiopian example (cats. 50, 51).

There are only passing references to the Ethiopian presence in Jerusalem before the thirteenth century. Tantalizing evidence of their devotions there can be gleaned from this manuscript; its rubrics (the instructions in red) mark the readings for particular holy days, such as the highly celebratory Feast of the Cross, known as Meskel. Where the text mentions the carrying of the Ark into the Temple in Jerusalem and Solomon's prayer, the rubric reads *bazeja ʿeten* (incense administered). BDB

Selected References: Roupp 1902, pp. 299–304; Cerulli 1943–47, vol. 1, pp. 130–31; Tamrat 1972, p. 251.

53

Textile with Musicians

Spain, 13th century
Silk and gilded animal substrate around silk core; lampas
4 × 4¼ in. (10.3 × 10.8 cm)
The Metropolitan Museum of Art, New York, Rogers Fund, 1928 (28.194)

Surviving examples of cloth from medieval Spain showcase the remarkable achievements of textile workshops in the Western Islamic world. Silks and fabrics with gold or gilded threads were especially esteemed, thanks to the sheer financial investment in the cloth. This piece was once part of a larger textile that featured a repeating design of medallions with musicians playing tambourines beneath a hanging lamp.[1] Other fabrics of the same period and place of production are woven with representations of drinkers, seated figures making a toast, and entwined animal designs.[2] The large size of at least one fabric with such festive patterns suggests that this small example was originally part of a furnishing textile, probably a curtain. Indeed, "Maghrebi" silk curtains appear numerous times in documents from the Cairo Geniza, where the term suggests their provenance in the western Mediterranean.[3] After Saladin's conquest of Jerusalem, significant numbers of both Muslims and Jews from the Maghreb settled in the city.

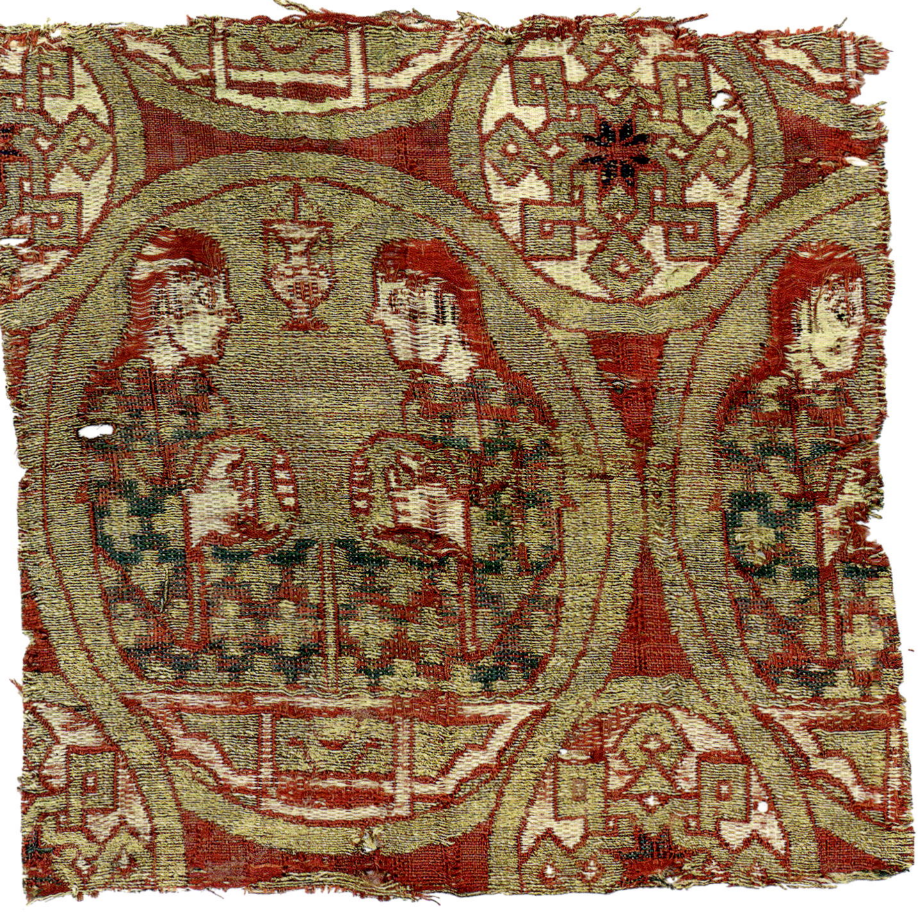

53

Such depictions of dancers, musicians, and partygoers are associated with Islamic court culture throughout the Mediterranean, particularly during the Fatimid period of the tenth to twelfth century. The iconography is common in ceramics, stone sculpture, ivory, and woodwork intended for domestic settings. However, these images were also deemed appropriate for Christian churches. A wood altar screen at the eleventh-century Church of Sitt Barbara in Cairo and the ceiling of the twelfth-century Cappella Palatina in Palermo, for example, both prominently feature courtly figures in their decor.[4] Luxury textiles with secular themes also served elite audiences of diverse religious confession. Despite the secular nature of their iconography and their production in workshops controlled by Spain's Muslim rulers, there is good evidence that these textiles were used in Christian sacred contexts: more than a dozen fragments of the same design with tambourine players were once integrated into a thirteenth-century manuscript held in the treasury at the Cathedral of Vich in Spain.[5] EDW

Selected References: Dimand 1944, p. 275, fig. 183; New York 2011, p. 80, no. 47.

1. The present piece is almost certainly from the same fabric as those in the Abegg-Stiftung, Riggisberg; the Museum of Fine Arts, Boston; and the Wadsworth Atheneum, Hartford. These are listed in Otavsky and Salim 1995, pp. 194–95, no. 107.
2. A textile of similar inspiration but different technique at the Cooper-Hewitt, Smithsonian Design Museum, New York, shows figures holding chalices (no. 1902-1-82; museum website catalogue record).
3. Related textiles from different fabrics include a large example at the Hispanic Society of America, New York, measuring 56¼ × 42½ inches (143 × 108 cm), which is the most complete version of a textile with courtly scenes. See May 1957, pp. 134–41, frontispiece, figs. 89, 90. For Maghrebi curtains, the second most frequently cited type of curtain in the Geniza documents, see Goitein 1967–93, vol. 4, pp. 120–21.
4. Photographs of the wood screen at Sitt Barbara appear in Pauty 1930, pls. 1–15. A recent publication on the Cappella Palatina, with full color photographs, is Brenk et al. 2010.
5. Noted by Olga Bush in New York 2011, p. 80, no. 47.

54

The Four Gospels in Arabic

Palestine, A.H. 20 Jumada I 737
(December 25, 1336)
Opaque watercolor, gold, and ink on paper; 205 folios
10⅝ × 7⅞ in. (27 × 20 cm)
British Library, London (Add. MS 11856)

The various languages in which the Gospels were written included Arabic, as in this 1336 version from Palestine, which speaks to the plural Christian populations in the region during Mamluk rule of the thirteenth to the sixteenth century.[1] Arabic became the primary language of government in Syria and Palestine by the mid-eighth century. By the ninth century Arab Christians had acculturated into Islamic society, although Greek (as well as Syriac, Aramaic, and Armenian) continued to be used by Christians, especially in Jerusalem, for Gospel and liturgical books and for theological treatises.[2]

The earliest known copy of any biblical text translated into Arabic is found in a Gospel Lectionary of 859.[3] The British Library Gospel discussed here is a copy of what has become known as the Arabic Vulgate version, a translation developed by the thirteenth century that utilized Greek, Syriac, and Coptic versions of the texts.[4] This became the standard Arabic Gospel version into modern times.

The present manuscript demonstrates that the illuminators also looked to various pictorial traditions. The decorative headpieces at the beginning of the Gospel of Luke borrow from Qur'anic illumination. Five star patterns in white enclose blue and red quatrefoil and rosette designs; the title, reading right to left, is framed above and below. Two

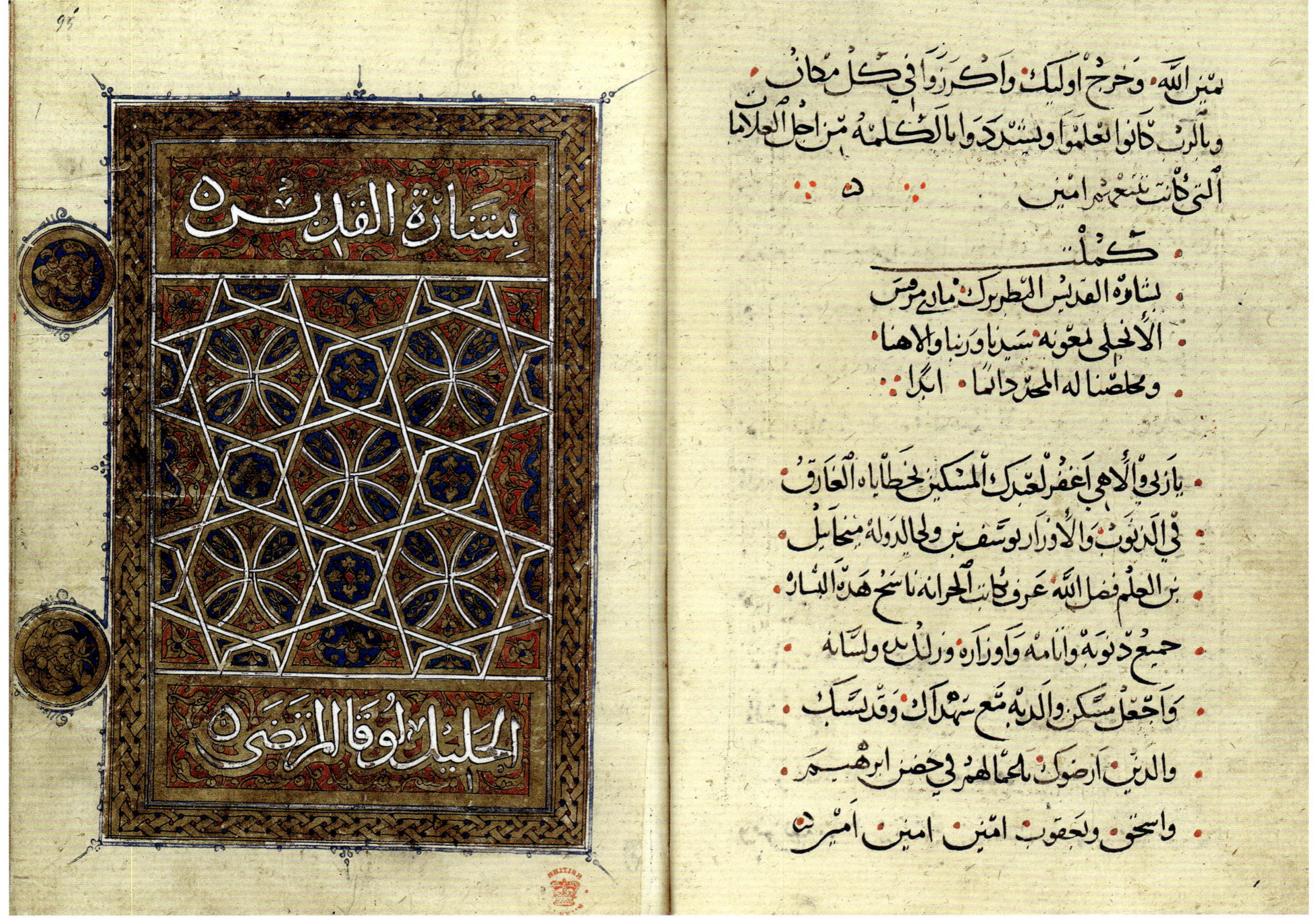

54, fols. 94v–95r

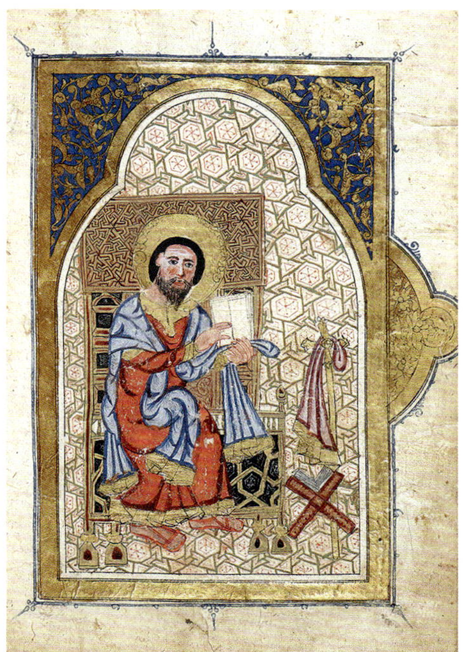

Fig. 41. Gospel of Luke, from *The Four Gospels in Arabic* (cat. 54, fol. 95v)

medallions are to the left of the central abstract design. On the following page, however, the artist has used a model from Byzantine manuscript illumination to picture the evangelist-author Luke, who is seated beneath an archway, showing us his text (fig. 41). JB

Selected References: Guidi 1888, p. 31; Wardrop et al. 2003, pp. 13–23; Kashouh 2011, p. 55.

1. This manuscript has been published as being made in 1337; using an Islamic date converter for A.H. 20 Jumada I 737, however, one gets December 25, 1336, which concurs with the date given in the British Library publication Wardrop et al. 2003, p. 19.
2. Griffith 2012, p. 60.
3. The Monastery of Saint Catherine, Sinai, Egypt, Arabic New Finds Manuscript 14 and 16. Published in New York 2012, pp. 61–62, no. 34.
4. The term "Vulgate" refers to the standard Latin translation of the Bible made by Saint Jerome in the fourth century. The standard Arabic version then was given the nickname "Arabic Vulgate" by scholars. It used to be known as the Alexandrian, or Egyptian, Vulgate, so named by Georg Graf and those who followed him (Graf 1944–53, vol. 1, p. 161), because it was thought to have taken into account only Egyptian Coptic sources. See Kashouh 2011, pp. 205–6.

55

Pyxis

Jazira or Syro-Palestine region, early to mid-13th century
Brass inlaid with silver and copper
H. 3⅜ in. (8.5 cm); Diam. 3¼ in. (8.3 cm)
Victoria and Albert Museum, London (320-1866)

During the course of the thirteenth century, a distinctive group of exquisitely inlaid metalwork was created in the regions of Syro-Palestine and the Jazira, among them this example.[1] Characteristic of these works is the use of imagery that relates to Christian iconography, such as figures of saints and ecclesiastics as well as scenes from the life of Jesus, including the Annunciation, the Nativity, the Presentation in the Temple, and the Entry to Jerusalem.[2] Alterations to the standard iconography of these scenes confirm that the "borrowing" was deliberate, and scholars have discussed whether the craftsmen either did not fully understand the imagery or were not concerned with the established canon. The juxtaposition of Christian themes alongside motifs typical of medieval Islamic art known as the "courtly cycle"[3] and images from astrology highlights the diverse and complex multicultural milieu in which these brasses originated.[4] Some may have been ordered by local Christian patrons, others as souvenirs for Crusader knights. Suitable for Muslim and Christian courts, as prestigious diplomatic gifts or as luxurious export works, they reached rulers and elite individuals both within and beyond the Middle East, as far away as Europe.[5]

This pyxis is one of three small cylindrical boxes with lids that belong to this particular group of inlaid metalwork.[6] Typical in style and motif are the bands of scrolling arabesque and chasing animals — evocative of the hunt, one of the courtly pastimes of medieval Islamic rulers — that border the box, as well as the interlacing star pattern on the lid. More significant are the two inscriptions on the lid: one, along the side, is a benedictory pseudo- or abbreviated inscription in Kufic script;[7] the other, encircling the geometric composition and in *naskhi* script, gives a corrupt rendering of two verses by al-Nabigha al-Dhubyani, a pre-Islamic Arab poet who lived about half a century before the Prophet Muhammad.[8] In the central register on the side of the box is a frieze of twenty-four figures wearing Christian apparel and carrying crosses and censers or holding staves, plus two seated men receiving the blessings. This scene has been interpreted as the ordination of a priest, a liturgical theme common in contemporary Latin, Syriac, and Armenian manuscripts.[9] However, here the artist has deliberately adapted the scene, emphasizing the procession rather than the liturgical act. The ecclesiastic figures are stereotyped, and the principal personage is hardly differentiated from the rest

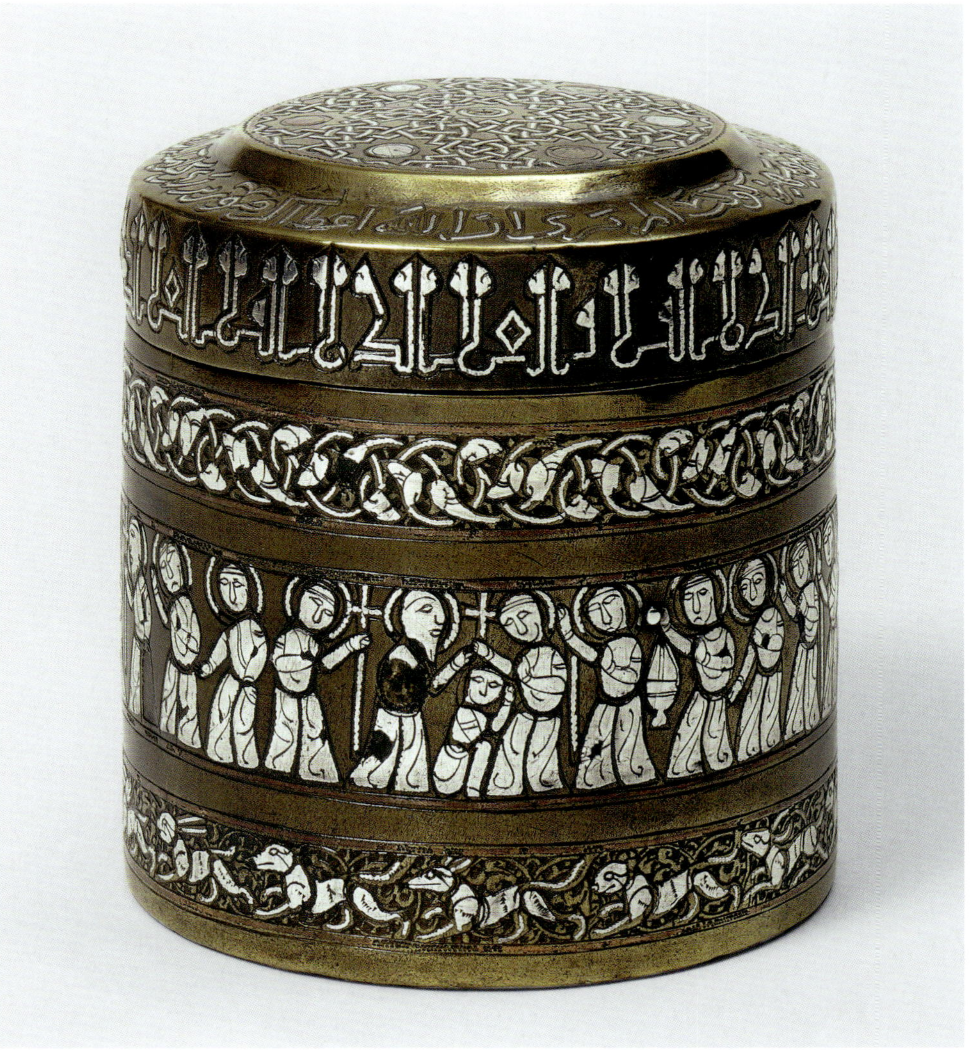

55

of the clergy, while the kneeling or inclining novices appear simply as figures crouching on the floor. DB

Selected Reference: New York 2016, pp. 265–67, no. 168a–c.

1. These brasses, of which there are at least nineteen, are often signed by the renowned "al-Mawsili" (from Mosul) artists or are comparable in style with their remarkable craftsmanship. Several generations of scholars have researched al-Mawsili inlaid metalwork. For the most recent contribution, with extensive bibliography, see Raby 2012; Raby 2014. For more references and discussion, see also Deniz Beyazit in New York 2016, pp. 62–65, 74–75, 120, 138–39, 142, 151, 160–61, 209, 232–33, 265–67, nos. 12a,b, 13a,b, 15, 49, 68, 69, 72, 79, 90, 125, 145, 155, 168a–c, 174b.

2. The foundational study remains Baer 1989, which discusses eighteen metal objects with Christian imagery. See also Katzenstein and Lowry 1983; Washington, D.C. 1985–86, pp. 124–46; Hoffman, E., 2004; Ward 2005; Auld 2009a; Beyazit in New York 2016, pp. 265–67, nos. 168a–c, adding the casket with combination clock lid from the Khalili Collection, London, to the group of eighteen objects.

3. "Courtly cycle" imagery presents an idealized view of the ruler and life at court and includes enthronement scenes and hunting or musical parties.

4. Scholars have associated these brasses with Ayyubid Syria; however, recent research confirms that the Jazira and, specifically, Mosul were likewise relevant production centers. See, for example, the discussion of the Homberg ewer by Beyazit in New York 2016, pp. 265–67, nos. 168a–c, or the discussion of the Freer canteen in Ecker and Fitzherbert 2012. Ward 2005, p. 321, emphasizes that conclusions of attribution, patronage, and meaning should be reassessed individually. For a broader perspective regarding Christian imagery and iconography and their interaction with the Muslim world, see Snelders 2010.

5. These sophisticated objects belonged to the households of the ruling elite and members of the court of medieval society. They were luxury objects used on festive and ceremonial occasions and, as prestige gifts, played a role in diplomatic exchanges and negotiations. See Raby 2012, pp. 28–29. To celebrate the circumcision of his brother Muhammad in Cairo in 1293, for instance, the Mamluk sultan Khalil distributed one hundred brass candlesticks inscribed with the sultan's titles, as well as other metalwork; see Ward 1993, p. 26. For an example from the Byzantine world, see Ballian 2009, p. 114.

6. Of the other two, one is in the Museum of Islamic Art, Cairo (no. 225; see Baer 1989, pp. 13–15), and the other is in the Metropolitan Museum (acc. no. 1971.39a, b; see Beyazit in New York 2016, pp. 265–67, nos. 168a–c). Pyxes were intended for use as liturgical receptacles to carry the Eucharist to those unable to receive the consecrated host in church. In the medieval Islamic world such boxes may have held *ushnan*, a vegetal-ash soda used to launder clothing (Stefano Carboni in Paris 2001–2, p. 114, no. 97). Sophisticated inlaid-brass examples such as this one might also have held aromatics, jewelry, or other more precious items.

7. Such inscriptions evocative of protection and blessings addressed to the owner are very common in medieval Islamic art, especially on metalwork.

8. The lines are taken from an apology and panegyric composed for Nu'man ibn Mundhir, the king of Hira, and should read according to al-Nabigha al-Dhubyani's *Diwan*: "Don't you see that God has granted you a degree of power which makes all the kings (grovel at your feet)? For you are a sun; the kings, stars. When the sun rises no star will be seen." Rice, D. S., 1950, pp. 631–32. According to the Victoria and Albert Museum, London, the lid may be a later addition.

9. Baer 1989, p. 33, pl. 89.

56
Chalice

Egypt or Syria, 1250–1350
Brass with silver inlay
H. 6¾ in. (17 cm); Diam. 4⅛ in. (10.6 cm)
Victoria and Albert Museum, London (761-1900)

This brass drinking vessel combines a Christian shape with silver-inlaid Arabic inscriptions encircling the bowl. The shape follows that of a traditional chalice, a sacred object in Christian liturgical worship that is used in the Eucharist to serve the sacramental wine. Its Christian patron chose to have the chalice inscribed in Arabic, reflecting the common linguistic traditions of Eastern Christian and Muslim believers during this period. The result demonstrates the plurality and inclusiveness of Mamluk society in the mid-thirteenth and early fourteenth century. The inscription reads "Made at the order of the reverend father at a certain Dayr al-Madfan (Monastery of the Tomb)." It has been suggested that this is perhaps a reference to the Church of the Holy Sepulchre in Jerusalem.[1]

The decoration and imagery on this vessel are akin to those seen on inlaid metal objects produced in northeastern Iran and diffused throughout the Jazira, possibly through the city of Mosul. The style of the *naskhi* calligraphy and the pair of facing ducks in roundels closely resemble the same elements found on an inlaid circular box with a domed lid made for the Mamluk sultan al-Nasir Muhammad in the Museum of Islamic Art in Doha, Qatar (cat. 129a). ME

Selected Reference: Washington, D.C., and other cities 2004–6, pp. 28–29.

1. Tim Stanley in Washington, D.C., and other cities 2004–6, pp. 28–29; Victoria and Albert Museum, London, museum website catalogue record.

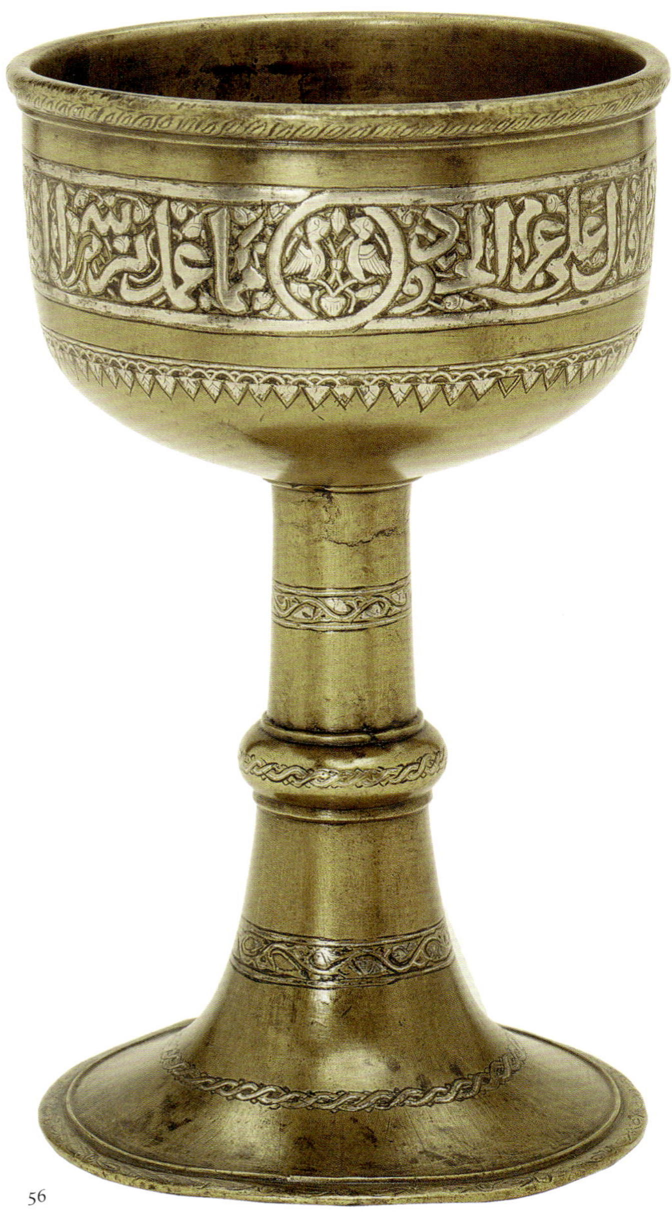

56

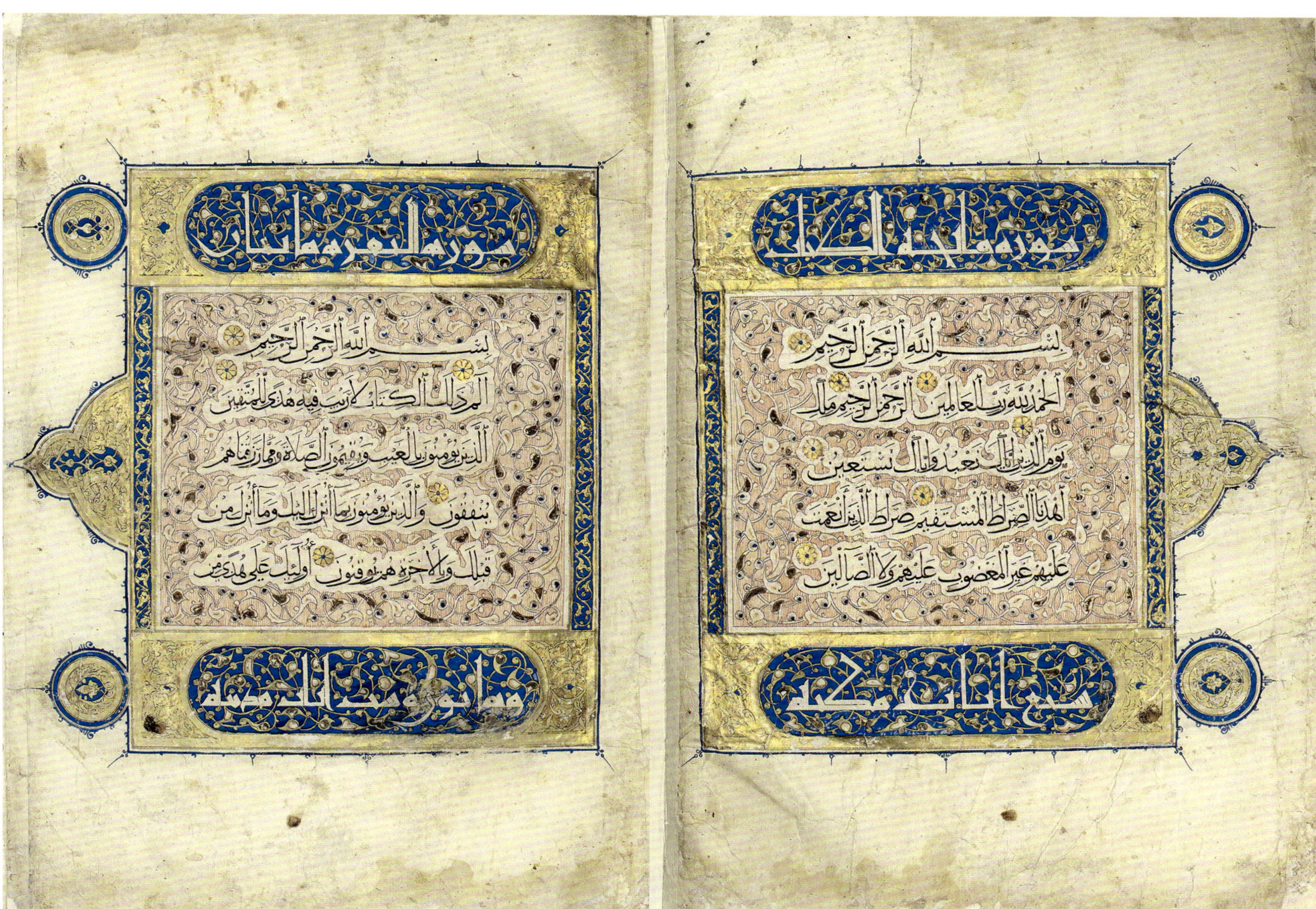

57

57
Qur'an Manuscript

Egypt or Syria, A.H. 25 Ramadan 746
(January 19, 1346)
Ink, colors, and gold on paper; 302 folios
21 × 16⅞ in. (51.5 × 38 cm)
The al-Sabah Collection, Dar al-Athar al-Islamiyyah, Kuwait (LNS 47 MS)

A sumptuous example of the arts of the book produced in Mamluk territories, this Qur'an manuscript was completed during the reign of Sultan al-Kamil Sha'ban, who ruled briefly between August 1345 and September 1346.[1] Dated A.H. 25 Ramadan 746 (January 19, 1346), it is signed by Asanbugha ibn Taray [of] al-Sayfi Arghun Shah al-Ustadar al-Maliki al-Nasiri, majordomo of the official household, whose name or *nisbah*, al-Nasiri, associates him with his royal patron.[2]

The manuscript opens with a beautifully illuminated double-page frontispiece of geometric patterns incorporating octagons, stars, and six-sided polygons augmented with vegetal arabesques, which, atypically, are not identical. The folio that should have faced folio 1 verso has been replaced by folio 301 verso, which was brought forward from the back of the manuscript and inverted. The fact that folio 301 verso would also have originally faced a matching page clearly indicates that the manuscript once had illuminated double-spread end-pages. Framing the geometric patterns are wide outer borders with medallions set against scrolling palmette vines, rendered in the style of Sandal, the renowned illuminator of the Baybars al-Jashnagir Qur'an manuscript copied in Cairo during the first decade of the fourteenth century (British Library, London, MS 22406).[3]

The illuminated opening text pages are written in five lines of contoured *muhaqqaq* script on a ground of scrolling palmette vines against fine pink hatching. The chapter headings are inscribed in gold Kufic script on a ground of scrolling vines. Rounded palmettes and lobed medallions extend into the margins. Gold rosettes mark the verse endings.

The remaining text is written with eleven lines to a page, with chapter headings in thuluth script and illuminated cartouches in Kufic. The verse count is indicated in the margins by circular and drop-shaped medallions.

SK

Selected References: Jenkins et al. 1983, p. 78; James 1988, no. 22; Lisbon 1997–98, p. 50; Provo 2012, pp. 68–69 Houston 2015–17, pp. 28–29.

1. Behrens-Abouseif 2007, p. 317.
2. See James 1988, p. 138 and p. 255 n. 8, in which the author states that Asanbugha ibn Taray must have been a *mamluk* (military slave) of Sayf al-Din Arghun Shah al-Maliki al-Nasiri, who was appointed governor of Safad in Palestine in 1346–47, thus concluding that the manuscript must have been produced while Arghun Shah was still in Egypt.
3. Ibid., pp. 34–38, no. 1.

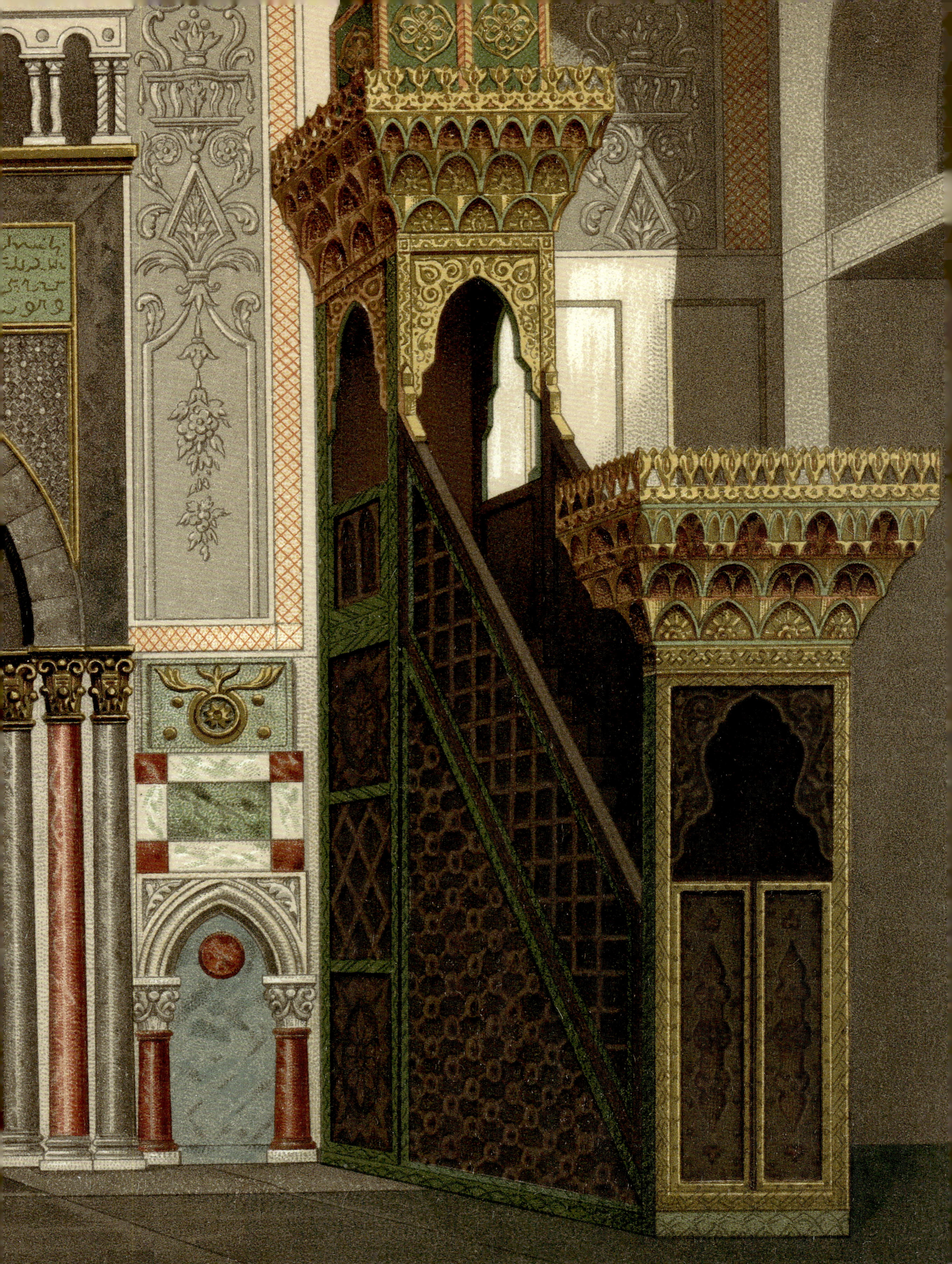

Experiencing Sacred Art in Jerusalem

Where saints . . . and angels . . . visit – Saladin

MELANIE HOLCOMB AND BARBARA DRAKE BOEHM

FACING PAGE
Fig. 42. The minbar in the Aqsa Mosque, Jerusalem. Lithograph published in 1884 after a photograph and watercolor by Gustave Le Bon

No fewer than three contemporary chroniclers felt compelled to remark upon the beauty of the majestic pulpit, or minbar (fig. 42), installed by Saladin in the Aqsa Mosque after his retaking of Jerusalem from the Crusaders in 1187.[1] According to the historian Ibn Jubayr (1160–1233), "The art of ornamental carving has exhausted its resources in this minbar, for I have not seen in any other country a minbar which resembles its shape and the uniqueness of its manufacture. . . . It rises like an enormous crown above the mihrab until it reaches the ceiling. Its top part is arched and opened with balconies. It is all inlaid with ivory and ebony, and this inlay work continues to the mihrab and beyond to the qibla wall without any apparent division, so that the eyes enjoy one of the most beautiful sights in the world."[2] Towering above the heads of all, the pulpit was deeply and intricately carved, its surface a mesmerizing pattern of overlapped scrolling vines contained within a complex lattice of interlocking geometric shapes. Paired doors opened to reveal a steep and private staircase that led to a covered platform, from which the imam would address the faithful. Both entryway and preacher's platform were graced by elaborate cornices. The costliness of the wood, in a region whose many blessings do not include forests, and the virtuosity of its carving made plain the reverence in which the spoken word was held.

One account even attests to the effect this work of art had on a visitor from a different faith. After Sultan al-Malik al-Kamil and Holy Roman Emperor Frederick II negotiated the Treaty of Jaffa in 1229, Frederick paid an official visit to Jerusalem. With the permission of the sultan, he was escorted to the Haram al-Sharif by the qadi, a Muslim judge. Frederick expressed his admiration for the construction of both the Aqsa Mosque and the Dome of the Rock (the site from which the Prophet Muhammad is believed to have ascended into paradise). On seeing the minbar in the mosque, Frederick climbed its stairs to the very top. His exuberant response to this sacred work of art was no doubt a violation of protocol, but that did not concern Ibn Wasil, our chronicler. Rather, he touchingly noted that, when Frederick descended, he took the qadi by the hand and the two went out together.[3]

This remarkable story reminds us of the capacity of sacred works of art to move their viewers. In this instance, a shared aesthetic experience prompted the joining of hands, mediating an encounter between adversaries that extended beyond mere tolerance. These are moments when the mystery inherent in a work of art transforms its viewers. Saladin's minbar (cat. 93) was one of these objects, but Jerusalem between the years 1000 and 1400 was blessed with many such monuments and works of art.

Many still survive; those that do not were often described by contemporaries who saw them. As the story of Frederick suggests, a viewer need not be of the same culture or religious tradition for which a work of art was intended to feel its power.

BEHOLDING THE CITY

It could be argued that the experience of a great work of art like the minbar was intensified by its location in a city where visitors were primed for the miraculous. Sources tell us the very sight of Jerusalem could provoke an ecstatic response. The Dominican Felix Fabri (ca. 1437/38–1502) compared the impact to being struck by lightning: "Casting our eyes to the right, lo! Like a flash of lightning the oft-mentioned and oft-to-be-mentioned holy city of Jerusalem shone forth. When we beheld with our eyes the long-desired holy city, we straightaway dismounted from our asses and greeted the holy city, bowing our faces to the earth."[4]

Companions traveling with the Christian mystic Margery Kempe (ca. 1373–after 1438) had to hold her up when she collapsed in ecstasy upon seeing the city of Jerusalem.[5] This was not a new phenomenon; during his decade-long sojourn in the Holy Land (1274–84), the German Dominican Burchard of Mount Sion described the delirious response of monks and nuns from around the world: "Who could tell how many . . . from Georgia, Greater and Lesser Armenia, Chaldae, Syria, Media, Persia, India, Ethiopia, Nubia, Nabatenia, of the Maronite, Jacobite, Nestorian, Greek, Syrian and other sects, at this day roam over [the Holy Land] in groups of one or two hundred each, visit each holy place, and with burning zeal . . . worship the spots on which they have heard that sweet Jesus ate, stood, or wrought any work?" As Burchard reported, the experience of this international assemblage was contagious, affecting Muslims who witnessed it as well: "Beating their breasts, weeping, groaning and sighing by turns, the outward bodily show of the religious which they . . . possess inwardly, moves many even of the Saracens to tears."[6]

Jewish visitors approached the city with a unique sense of expectancy — for they came prepared to mourn. A guidebook found in a treasure trove of documents known as the Cairo Geniza offered instructions on the proper approach, incorporating ancient rituals for mourning the dead. "If you are worthy to go up to Jerusalem, when you look at the city from Mount Scopus [you should observe the following procedure]. If you are riding on a donkey, step down; if you are on foot, take off your sandals, then rending your garment say: 'This [our] sanctuary was destroyed.'"[7] Rabbi Samuel ben Samson, a traveler to Jerusalem in 1210, called the first glimpse of the city "a moment of tenderest emotion" that caused him and his companion to "weep bitterly."[8] Whatever the expectations of its visitors, Jerusalem's monuments and works of art contributed to and reinforced the idea of its sanctity.

A CITY OF GATES AND DOMES

The city's gates had been a means of defining the sacred landscape of Jerusalem since biblical times: "The Lord loveth the gates of Sion above all the tabernacles of Jacob" (Psalms 87:2). The Geniza guidebook mentioned above invoked Psalm 48 in advising pilgrims to "circle all the gates of the city and go round all its corners, make a circuit and count its towers." The very names of the gates signaled their spiritual significance. In the time of the Jerusalem geographer al-Muqaddasi (ca. 946–991), a visitor would encounter either the Sion gate, the Gate of Jeremiah's Pit, or the Gate of the Prayer Niche of David. Later visitors describe Saint Stephen's Gate, the Mercy Gate, the Gate of Jehoshaphat, the Gate of the Friend of God (Abraham), and the Gate of Judgment. In an illuminated choir book made for the Franciscans of the Holy Land (fig. 1), the Hebrew prophet Isaiah stands, sentinel-like, at the walls of Jerusalem to mark the hymn "Jerusalem." Staring out at the choristers who would have gathered around this grand book to sing the hymn, Isaiah points to one of the city's open gates.

The great domes within Jerusalem (fig. 43) were perceptible from afar and thus also became emblematic of the city. Any visitor understood them as according honor and prestige to Jerusalem's holy sites.[9] The sense one has even now that the city's domes compete with one another is affirmed by writers from an earlier period. Al-Muqaddasi claimed that the caliph ʿAbd al-Malik oversaw the building of the glorious Dome of the Rock in the seventh century in response to the Church of the Holy Sepulchre: "Noting the greatness of the Dome [of the Holy Sepulchre] and its splendour, fearing lest it should beguile the hearts of Muslims, [ʿAbd al-Malik] erected, above the Rock, the dome you now see there."[10] It could be argued that the Western Christians who took over the city in the late eleventh century perpetuated that rivalry. Not only did they renovate the dome of the Holy Sepulchre, but they also provided the church with a second one over the spot in the church complex that was designated the navel of the world. Amid Jerusalem's massive domes were smaller ones, such as those found over a number of the tombs visited by Jews on pilgrimage (cat. 21).[11] Some, such as the aedicule (fig. 46) within the Holy Sepulchre, were nested within larger domed structures to create a space of concentrated holiness.

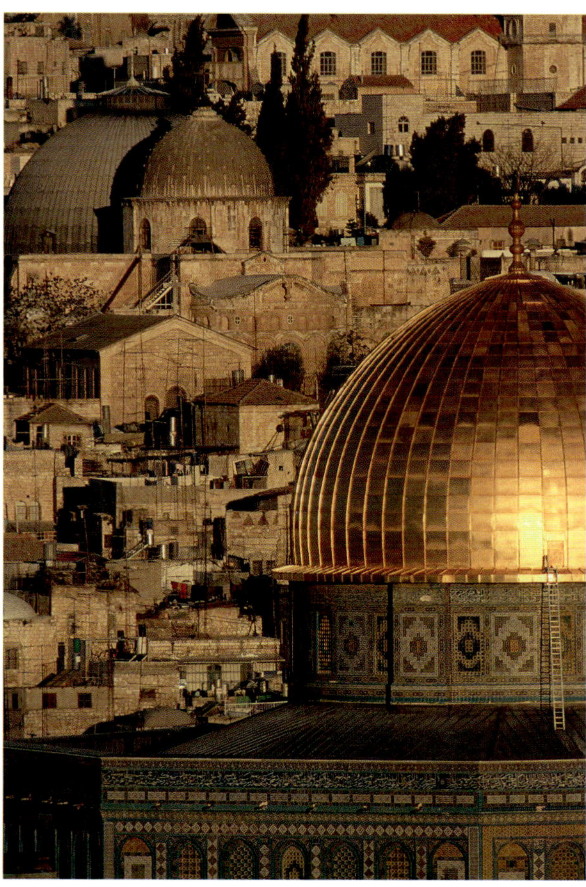

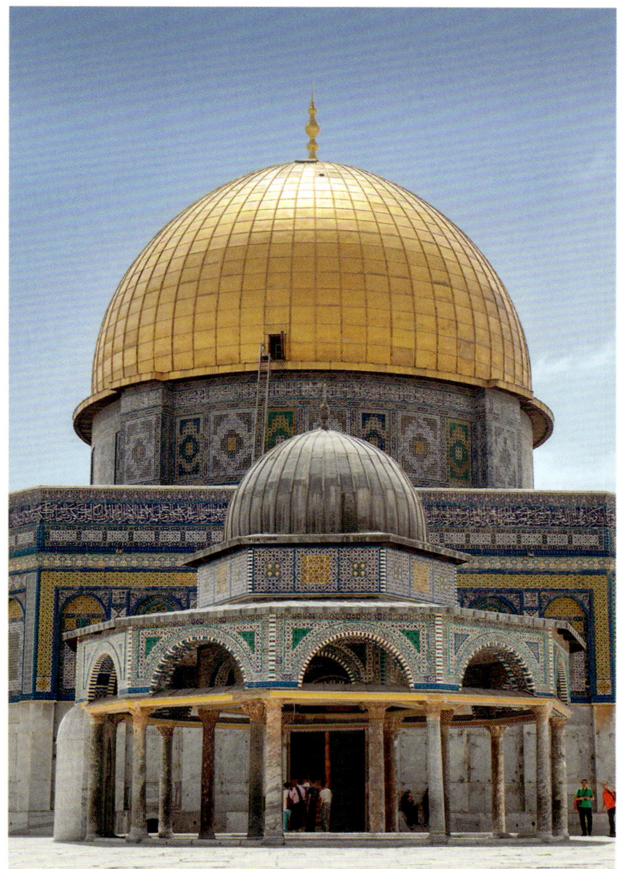

Fig. 43. *Left:* The domes of Jerusalem, including the Dome of the Rock in the foreground and the Church of the Holy Sepulchre. *Right:* The Dome of the Chain in the foreground and the Dome of the Rock

Others, such as the many domed structures on the Haram al-Sharif, stand like respectful offspring, near and around more impressive religious monuments (fig. 43).

Once inside the gates, as visitors entered the magical realm of Jerusalem's crowded streets and majestic holy buildings, the impact of the city was no less affecting. The holiest spaces in Jerusalem were noteworthy for their layers of decoration created from a dizzying array of materials. Writers repeatedly noted the gleaming marbles and colorful mosaics that adorned churches, mosques, and shrines. The perfumed air was intoxicating. One visitor remarked that so much incense emanated from the Dome of the Rock "that its fragrance could be detected in the markets of the city below."[12] Jerusalem was a noisy city, filled with the music of prayer that respected no barriers. In the days of al-Muqaddasi, there was a common saying: "There is no place in Jerusalem where you cannot get water or hear the call to prayer."[13]

THE HOLIEST SITES

Church of the Holy Sepulchre

Among Christians, Fulcher of Chartres (1059–after 1128) spoke of a "symphony" of singing by Greeks, along with prayers in Latin and the sound of trumpets at the Easter Vigil in the Holy Sepulchre, the culmination of any Christian's trip to Jerusalem.[14] Within the walls of this church, known to Eastern Christians as the Church of the Resurrection (or Anastasis), are the sites where Christians believe that Jesus was crucified, taken down from the Cross, and buried.

In the twelfth century, as today, the faithful entered through one of two large doorways that offered almost immediate access to two of the holiest spots. These were framed and laden with sculpture that reinforced the experience of pilgrimage (fig. 44). The arrangement of scenes on the lintel over the entrance, although carved by sculptors familiar with European conventions, had no equivalent in contemporary European churches. The narratives traced key moments of Jesus's life and ministry in an

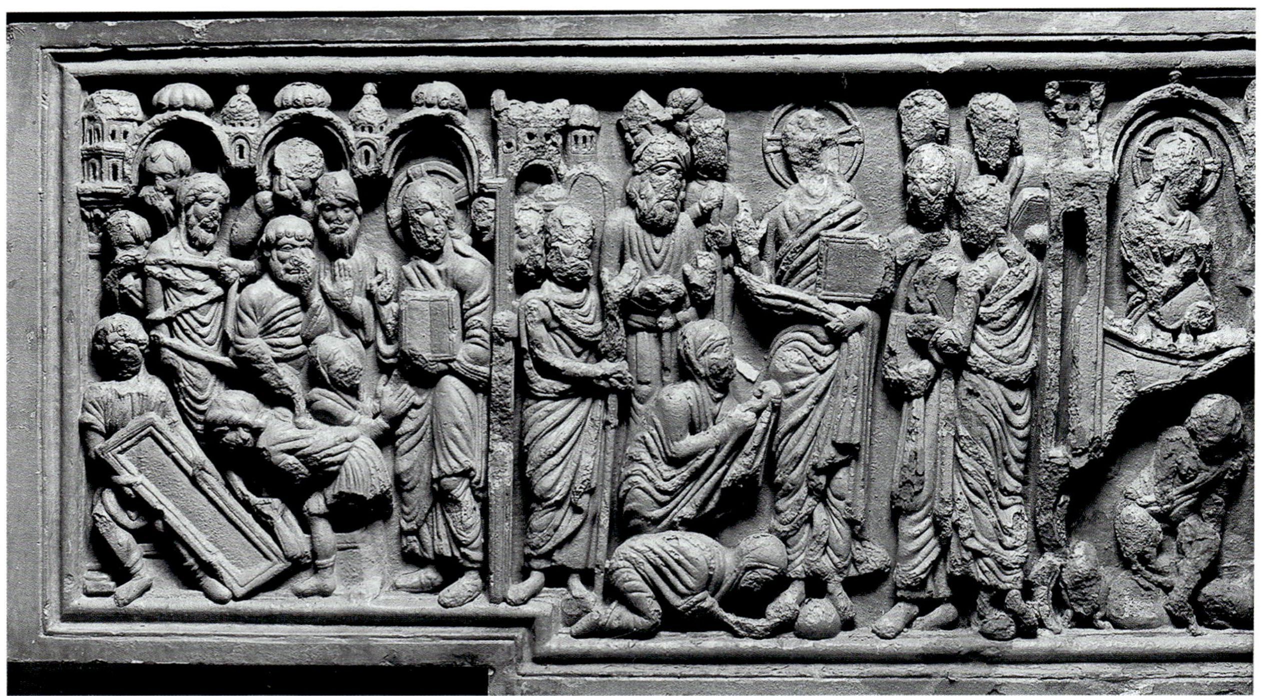

abbreviated sequence that follows the geographical order of a pilgrimage. They begin with the Raising of Lazarus, in Bethany, and end with the Entry into Jerusalem and the Last Supper, mimicking a pilgrim's progress from Bethany through Jerusalem's gates to the cenacle of Mount Sion, site of the Last Supper (fig. 45).[15]

The building incorporates the natural rock outcroppings on which it sits and invests them with meaning. Nearly destroyed in the early eleventh century by earthquakes and at the hands of the mad caliph al-Hakim (985–1021), the church's reconstruction was completed in 1048 by the Byzantine

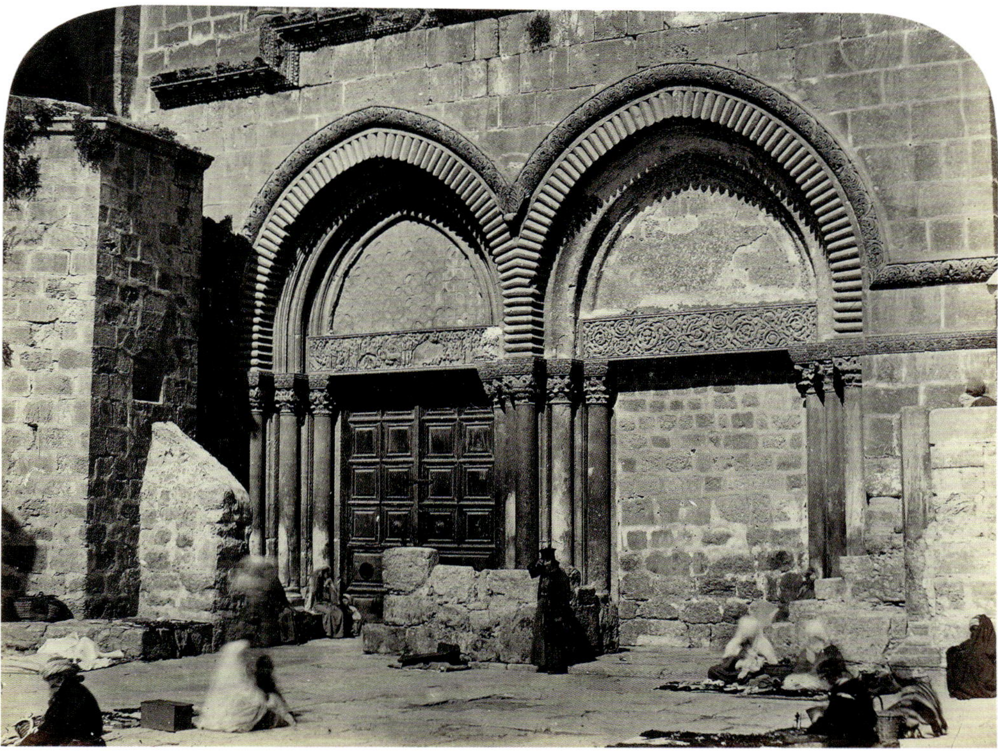

Fig. 44. The entrance to the Church of the Holy Sepulchre, Jerusalem

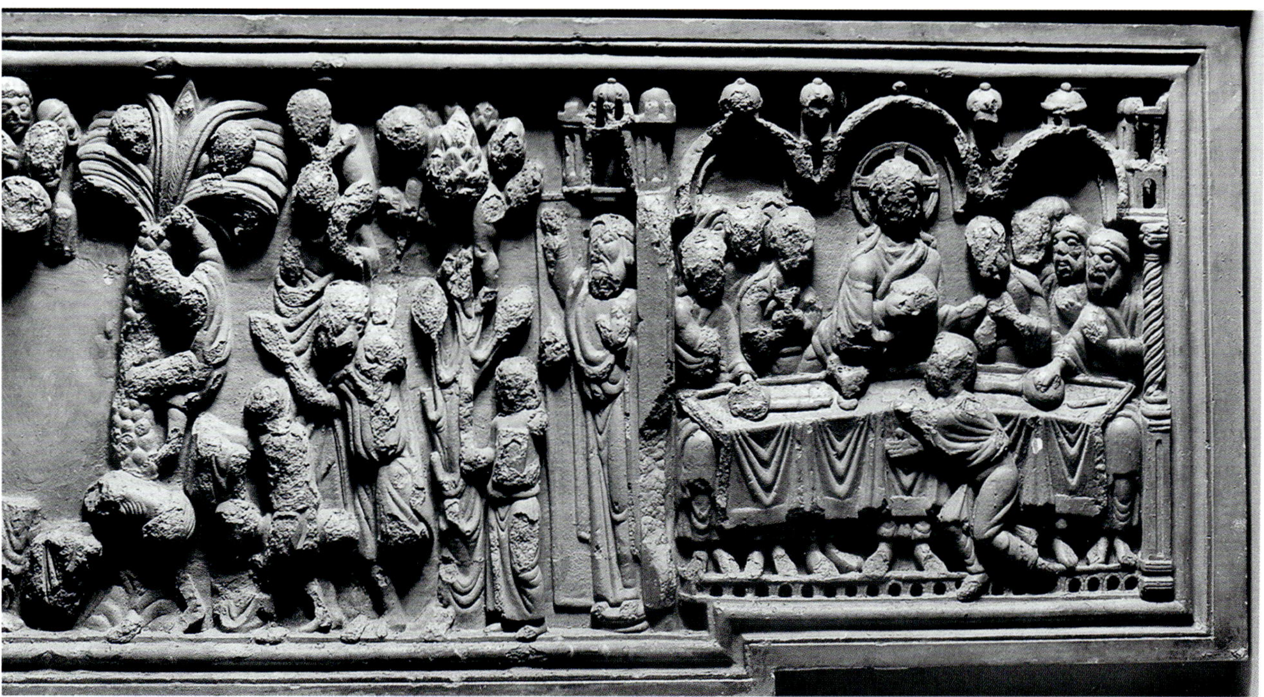

Fig. 45. The figural lintel above the entrance to the Church of the Holy Sepulchre, Jerusalem

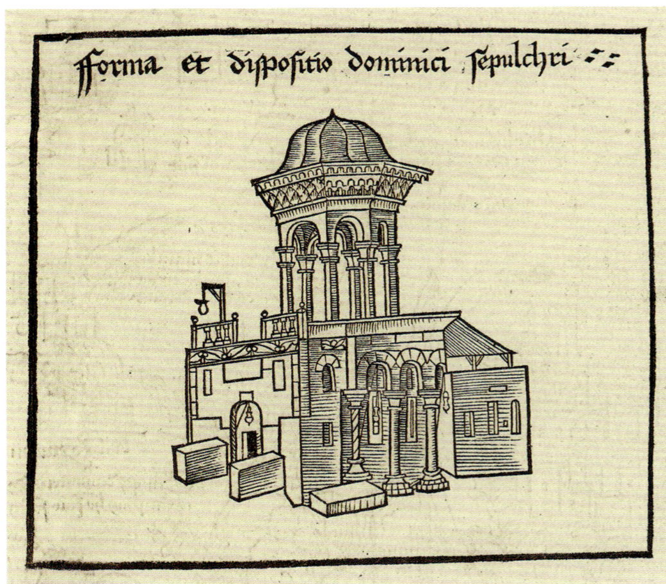

Fig. 46. The aedicule of the Church of the Holy Sepulchre, Jerusalem, from *Journey to the Holy Land* (*Peregrinatio in terram sanctam*). Insert from cat. 20

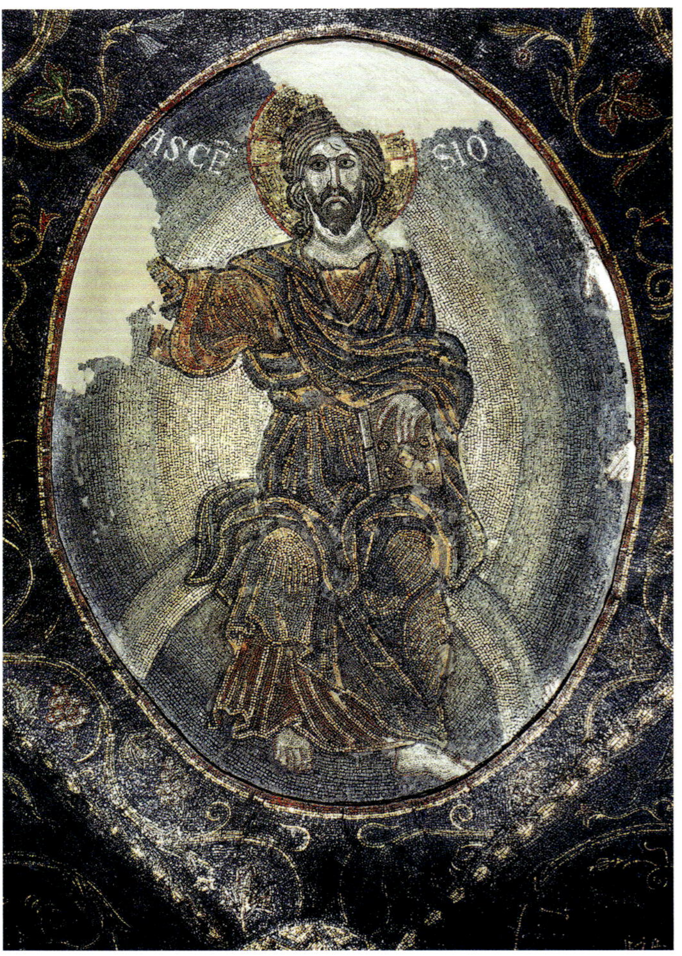

Fig. 47. Mosaic of the Ascension set in the vault of the Calvary Chapel, Church of the Holy Sepulchre. Jerusalem, 12th century

emperor Constantine IX Monomachus (r. 1042–55), who concentrated the remains of the original architecture of the church into two points of focus: a rotunda and a courtyard comprising numerous shrines.[16] Likely overseen by a master mason from Constantinople, both Constantinopolitan and local construction techniques were used in the rebuilding of the church. Western Christians then dramatically rebuilt and refurbished the Byzantine church in the twelfth century.[17] The bipolar plan of Constantine IX Monomachus's church was transformed into a single grand edifice that made some effort at re-creating the basilica plan found at Europe's pilgrimage churches. Even so, the layout of the Crusader church would have been surprising to a visitor of the time. The scale and variety of the columns and capitals of the interior create a forestlike canopy of Constantinian and Crusader workmanship. With each successive building campaign, the public spaces of the interior became increasingly idiosyncratic, yet visitors admired the new Crusader structure. The German monk Theoderich, who visited the Holy Land in the 1170s, predictably asserted that the Frankish workmanship was "marvelous,"[18] but even Muhammad al-Idrisi (1100–1165), a Muslim geographer from Sicily with no parochial agenda, referred to the new building as a "great and venerable church."[19]

Far from passive tourists, Christians responded to the building in a variety of ways. Taking the measure of the church – literally – was an act of devotion that proved remarkably enduring.[20] Hundreds of small crosses carved into the stone wall of the Holy Sepulchre (fig. 92) offer quiet testimony to the path taken by centuries of devout pilgrims. Words were everywhere – on entryways, cornices, arches, and walls. Inscriptions in Latin and Greek, drawn from scripture and sacred song, guided the visitor's experience, clarifying the meaning of pictures and places for the literate visitor and reinforcing the rituals that took place in the church. We know that at least some studied the texts carefully. Both Theoderich and fellow German monk John of Würzburg made a point of recording them, and Theoderich, ever thorough, even expressed his disappointment that he and his companions could not read half the verses on the aedicule because "of the fading colours."[21]

The church encompassed a circuit of holy sites, from the prison where Jesus was kept by Pontius Pilate to the place where Empress Helena found the Cross on which he was crucified. Among the most poignant was the site of the entombment of Jesus. Set within the great rotunda of the church, the tomb itself was a small cave that contained two significant features: a carved shelf on which the body had been laid and the stone from the doorway that was removed when Jesus is believed to have risen from the dead. The cave was illuminated by lanterns; the great dome marking it overhead was "open to the sky above."[22] A chapel-like structure, "a large sort of round ciborium," known as the aedicule (fig. 46) mediated the two.[23] The site encouraged a ritualized approach, as Theoderich conveyed: "The mouth of the cave cannot be entered by anyone without bending his knees. But arriving there, he finds the treasure for which he has longed, the Sepulchre in which our most benevolent Lord Jesus Christ rested for three days. It is wonderfully decorated with Parian marble, gold and precious stones. In the side it has three round holes through which travelers give the kisses they have for so long desired to give to the stones on which the Lord lay. . . . The floor . . . has enough space for five people with their faces towards the sepulcher to kneel down."[24]

Pilgrims regularly commented on the contrast between the rustic bare rock of the cave and the luxurious marble framing it outside and in.[25] In addition, about 1106, Daniel the Abbot, who traveled to the Holy Land from his monastery in Kievan Rus, wrote of a statue of "Christ made in silver and larger than a man" that stood atop the structure above the tomb.[26] A few decades later, Theoderich mentioned a gilded Cross with a dove above, which crowned what was likely a new and imposing aedicule built by the Crusaders.[27] By 1177 the shrine was more glittering still. A Greek visitor, John Phocas, noted that the shelf had received a sheath of "pure gold" as a gift from the Byzantine emperor.[28]

Images blanketing the interior intensified the majesty and message of the church. Theoderich mentioned a mosaic showing Jesus's entombment over the entry to the tomb as well as images of prophets, apostles, and saints. Daniel the Abbot gave us the sense that the sanctuary was peopled with holy figures greeting the faithful, describing "holy prophets, represented as if they are alive," and "marvelous mosaics" on the eastern wall of Calvary Chapel, the site of the Crucifixion, with the crucified Christ "skillfully and marvelously done just as if alive and even more so, just as it was then."[29]

Anyone visiting after the Crusader renovation would have found a mix of mosaics of Frankish and earlier Byzantine manufacture; Theoderich discerned the difference, noting that the mosaics he saw near the choir were worked in the same style as a recent Crusader mosaic, "but old." Though he described the workmanship of the mosaics as "delicate," "graceful," and "very fine," he was sometimes disappointed in the viewing conditions. Coming upon a ceiling mosaic in the Calvary Chapel (fig. 47), he declared: "No work on earth would equal that if only it were possible to see it clearly."[30] A painting of the Crucifixion at the entry to the cloister of the canons he deemed particularly moving, as it "excites all who see it to penitence."[31]

While one can admire Theoderich's art-historical acumen in distinguishing between Byzantine and Frankish workmanship, it is stunning to realize that the eleventh-century Persian poet Nasir-i Khusraw (d. 1088) not only described Byzantine workmanship, but also recognized the image of Jesus, proclaiming, "They have portrayed Jesus – peace be upon him!"[32]

Indeed, the visitor who best captured the spiritual import and impact of the decoration of the Holy Sepulchre was not a Christian but rather another Persian, the historian Imad al-Din (1125–1201):

> The Franks said: . . . This is our Church of the Resurrection. . . . We love this place, we are bound to it. . . . Here is the place of the crucifixion and our goal, the altar and the place of sacrifice . . . the place

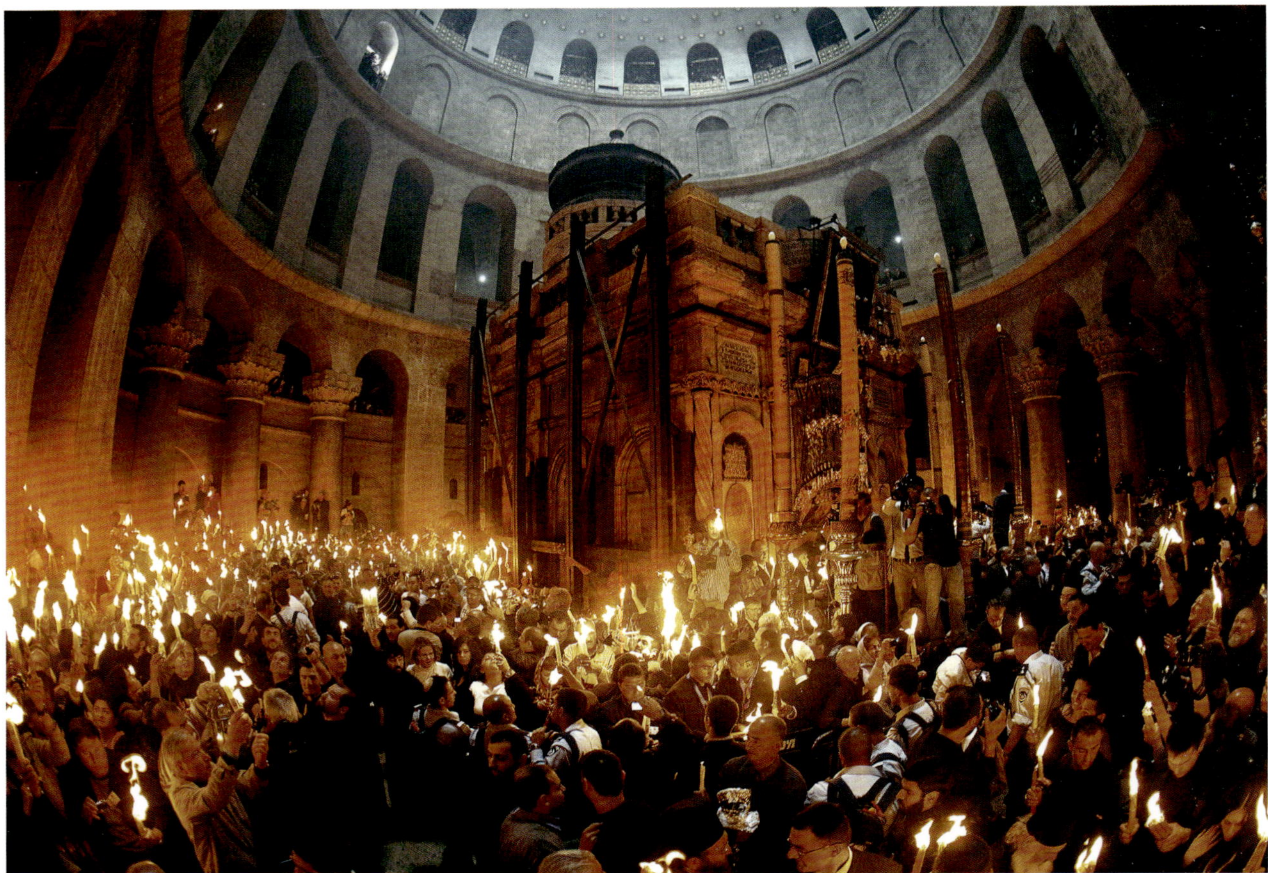

Fig. 48. The Miracle of the Holy Fire in the Church of the Holy Sepulchre, Jerusalem

> for ornament and decoration, the prologue and epilogue, the food and the nourishment, the works of marble and intaglio, the permitted and the forbidden places, the pictures and the sculptures, the views and configurations, the lions and the lion-cubs (cat. 80a), the portraits and likenesses, the columns and slabs of marble, the bodies and souls. Here are pictures of the Apostles conversing, Popes with their histories, monks in their cells, priests in their councils, the Magi with their ropes, priests and their imaginings; here the effigies of the Madonna and the Lord, of the Temple and the Birthplace, of the Table and the fishes, and what is described and sculpted of the Disciples and the Master, of the cradle and the Infant speaking. Here are the effigies of the ox and the ass, of Paradise and Hell, the clappers and the divine laws. Here, they say, the Messiah was crucified.[33]

The very things that Imad al-Din found most curious were those that contributed most to the impact of the space and the works of art on the Christian visitor. He understood the church's role as the culmination of the pilgrim's journey, and he perceived that part of its magic depended on its division into public and private spaces. These were not the open spaces of a mosque interior but a juxtaposition of zones "permitted" and "forbidden." With his lengthy catalogue of image types, Imad al-Din effectively conveyed the sheer accumulation of pictures. He no doubt meant to affirm for his image-averse audience their sense of the idolatrous nature of Christian art,[34] yet he also revealed his impressive knowledge of the Christian story, with details like the "Infant speaking" and the Magi's ropes that reflected his own Muslim belief.[35]

The Holy Sepulchre was and is more than a series of stopping points for the pilgrim. It served as a setting for communal ceremony and ritual.[36] At different moments in the structure's long history, various denominations have celebrated their faith there; today its use on a single day follows a uniquely orchestrated rhythm and ceremony. Theoderich attested to the shared use of the church in the twelfth century, noting in particular the sound of trumpets, which he attributed to the Syriac Christians.[37]

Of the many services held there, the most dramatic was the Miracle of the Holy Fire, which to this day takes place on the eve of Orthodox Easter (or Pascha) (fig. 48). The miracle, in which fire appears in the lamp above the tomb, is described in numerous medieval accounts — some purely descriptive, some analytical, some even critical — but none better conveys the simultaneous fear and thrill experienced by a participant than that of Daniel the Abbot, who provided a moment-to-moment account of his experience, beginning with the purchase of a very large glass lamp, which he filled with pure oil.[38] Daniel described the frighteningly chaotic conditions as crowds "from every corner of the earth" gathered at the church to await the miracle:

> And there is a great crush and terrible suffering for the people, and many are suffocated from the pressure of the vast number of people. All these people stand with unlit candles and wait for the church doors to open. . . . Then the church doors are opened and the people enter into the church and there is a great crush and pushing and the church is filled and all the galleries are full, for the church cannot contain all the people. . . . And all the people . . . say nothing but "Lord have mercy." They cry out ceaselessly and shout so loudly that the whole place resounds and echoes with the shouts of the people. And the faithful weep torrents of tears: if a man had a heart of stone he would weep then.[39]

Haram al-Sharif

The pulsating fervor that informs the Holy Fire ceremony at the Holy Sepulchre seems perfectly to suit its setting, embedded as it is in the dense fabric of the bustling city. By contrast, the Dome of the Rock and the Aqsa Mosque are poised on a great esplanade in a parklike setting that opens up as one moves uphill from the city and passes through deep, towering gates. According to the account of his visit, Nasir entered by what would have been a newly built gate, part of the mid-eleventh-century refurbishment of the Haram al-Sharif.[40] "Thirty ells high and twenty wide," this "splendid" new gate, which Nasir referred to as the Gate of David, was "adorned with designs and patterned with colored tiles set in plaster. The whole produces an effect dazzling to the eye." The doors were faced with Damascene brass, which looked like gold, while the enameled inscription above was positioned so that "when the sun strikes this, the rays play so that the mind of the beholder is absolutely stunned."[41]

Once inside the gate, a visitor encountered a holy, peaceful landscape (fig. 49). Whereas the Crusaders sought to contain a host of shrines within the confines of the Holy Sepulchre, the many patrons of the Haram took advantage of the expanse of real estate at their disposal. Structures of varied sizes and types — colonnades, domed buildings, prayer niches, monuments, minor mosques, ablution places, madrasas, residences for holy men (*zawiyas*), and other places of assembly — were liberally disposed over the space. Al-Muqaddasi described Muslim shrines "scattered over the sacred area," including not only the Dome of the Rock and the Aqsa Mosque but also the Oratories of Mary, Zachariah, and Jacob, prayer stations of the Prophet and of Gabriel, as well as the curiously named Place of the Ant, the Place of the Light, Place of the Ka'ba, and the Bridge al-Sirat, which divides Heaven and Hell.[42]

Instead of presenting a specified circuit, the space encouraged visitors to move fluidly between indoors and out. Al-Idrisi was impressed by "a beautiful garden, planted with all sorts of trees."[43]

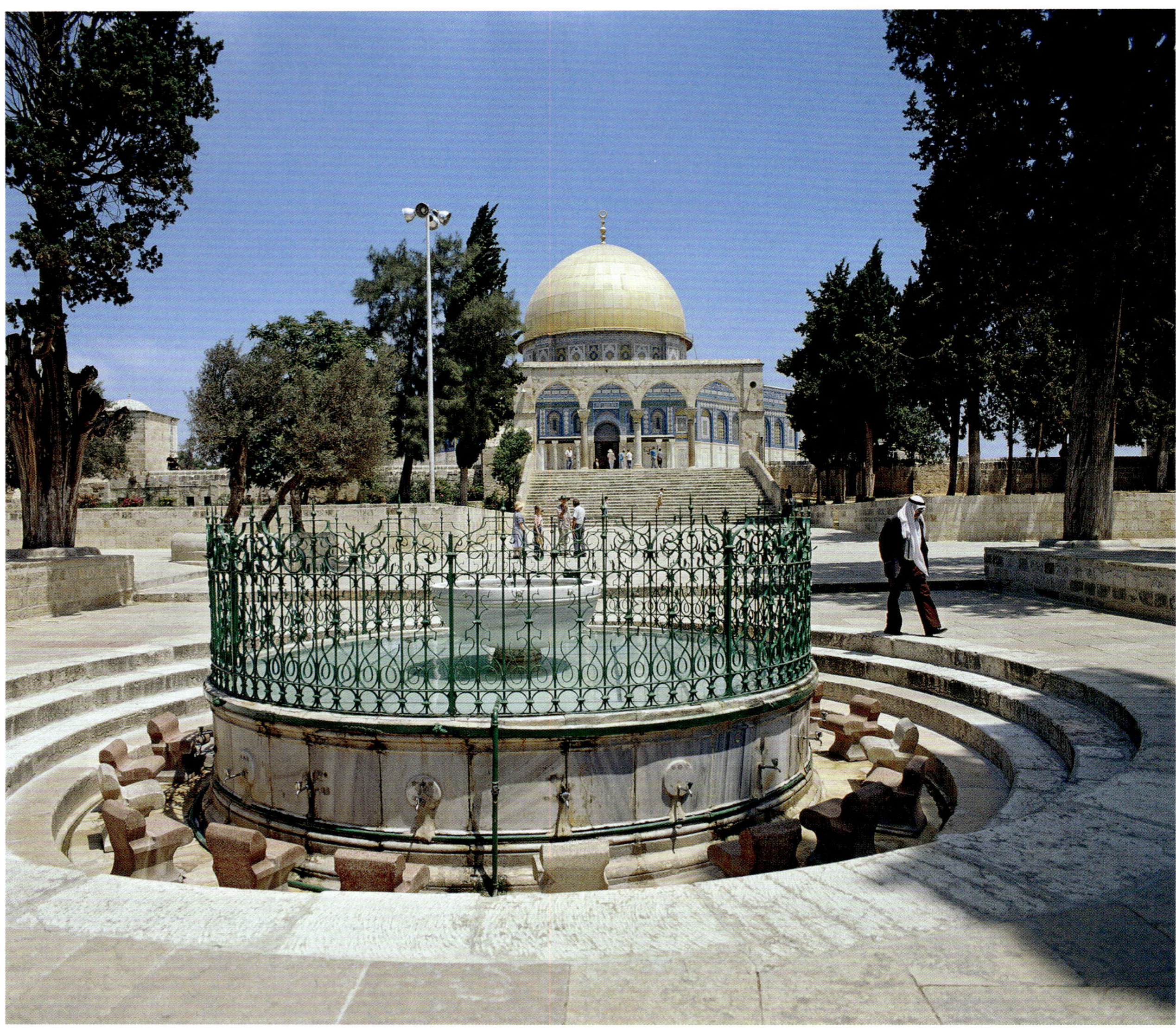

Fig. 49. The Al-Kas Fountain, Jerusalem

Nasir specifically mentioned olive groves, which remain much in evidence to this day. Here above the city, a pilgrim could stroll and admire, convene, learn, and pray without the pressing obligation that Christians had to retrace episodes of a sacred story.[44]

An abundance of water, necessary for ritual ablutions, contributed to the atmosphere. Nasir, a government bureaucrat who had abandoned his post to go on pilgrimage, took particular interest in the water infrastructure of Jerusalem, noting the solid construction and efficiency of its cisterns and conduits, some of which he was prepared to attribute to King Solomon himself.[45] Even within a city where water was as well managed as Jerusalem's, the supply on the Haram al-Sharif stood out: "Of all the city, the greatest abundance of water is found in the Friday mosque."[46] He described the means by which the water was kept from going to waste and its purity maintained, and he noted that the water from the tank under the Dome of the Rock was "the cleanest and best water in the entire sanctuary complex."[47] He marveled at the tank that supplied the water used for ablutions within the precinct's walls,[48] "for the mosque is so large, that if you had to leave it, you would certainly miss your prayer."[49] Nasir's comments aptly distill the reactions of many others. Water, space, light, and greenery — features at a premium in a crowded city at the edge of a desert — were as critical to the sense of sacred resplendence as the marble and mosaics that adorned the Haram's many structures.

The Dome of the Rock and the Aqsa Mosque

"In the center of the court rises the mighty dome known as the Dome of the Rock. In its midst is the Rock (fig. 50), which is said to have fallen down [from heaven]," reported al-Idrisi.[50] Like the Holy Sepulchre, the Dome of the Rock crowns and enshrines a natural rock outcropping of significant size, believed to be the site of both Abraham's sacrifice and Muhammad's Ascent to paradise. Octagonal in plan, it is a building of encircling, gemlike richness, theatrically disposed "in the middle of the court… in the middle of the platform."[51]

Caliph Abd al-Malik had the shrine constructed in the late seventh century, with, it would seem, a vast audience in mind. From its elevated stage at the apparent center of a hilltop esplanade, it commands the attention of the city and its surrounds below. With its prominent siting, majestic dome, highly legible exterior decoration, and the fourfold symmetry of its overall shape, the structure was legendary. According to Nasir, "The great dome . . . is so shaped that from one good parasang away it appears like a mountain."[52] Nasir specified its height at thirty cubits from the base of the dome to the top.[53] The Spanish geographer and poet Ibn Jubayr (1145–1217), who never visited Jerusalem, nonetheless indicated that its dome was the standard against which other buildings, even the great mosque in Damascus, could not compare.[54] And al-Muqaddasi, attuned to the light of his native city, observed of the dome, "rising high into the air, . . . as soon as the beams of the sun strike the cupola and the drum radiates the light then indeed is this marvelous to behold" (fig. 43).[55]

As impressive as the Dome's elegantly simple structure was, its most remarked upon feature was the delicate mosaic work that adorned the building both inside and out (fig. 54, cat. 82).[56] The fourteenth-century Moroccan traveler and scholar Ibn Battuta used the word "indescribable" and then proceeded to try to articulate its effect: "Both on its exterior and inside it is adorned with such a variety of decoration and such brilliance of execution to defy description. The greater part of this decoration is surfaced with gold, so that it glows like a mass of light and flashes with the gleam of lightning; the eyes of him who would gaze on its splendor are dazzled and the tongue of the beholder finds no words to represent them."[57]

In Jerusalem, mosaics and marble were both markers of opulence on important public buildings. The Dome of the Rock made use of both, but its "excellent mosaics," flowering and leafy as a garden in full bloom, seemed in the eyes of medieval visitors to surpass all other examples.[58] The interior was no less impressive than the exterior, with successive tiers of mosaics set in counterpoint to a clear rhythm of columns. So straightforward was its floor plan that one could understand the layout of the entire building at a glance and yet get lost in the dizzying richness of the mosaic work. Nasir also described doors of teak, columns of marble, pillars and arches covered with gold and enamel designs, balustrades of flecked green marble, carpets of silk, candles of ambergris, and lamps of silver.[59]

Everyone proclaimed its beauty, even non-Muslims. Giorgio Gucci, a fourteenth-century Tuscan pilgrim, realized that the building was for Islamic worship, "but to see it from the outside it appears a great building and a work of art."[60] Felix Fabri, who looked at it from the windows of the Ashrafiyya Madrasa at the western edge of the Haram, declared it "a noble and exceedingly costly building, great and round."[61] Pietro Casola, a fifteenth-century Milanese canon, deemed it Jerusalem's one beautiful building.[62]

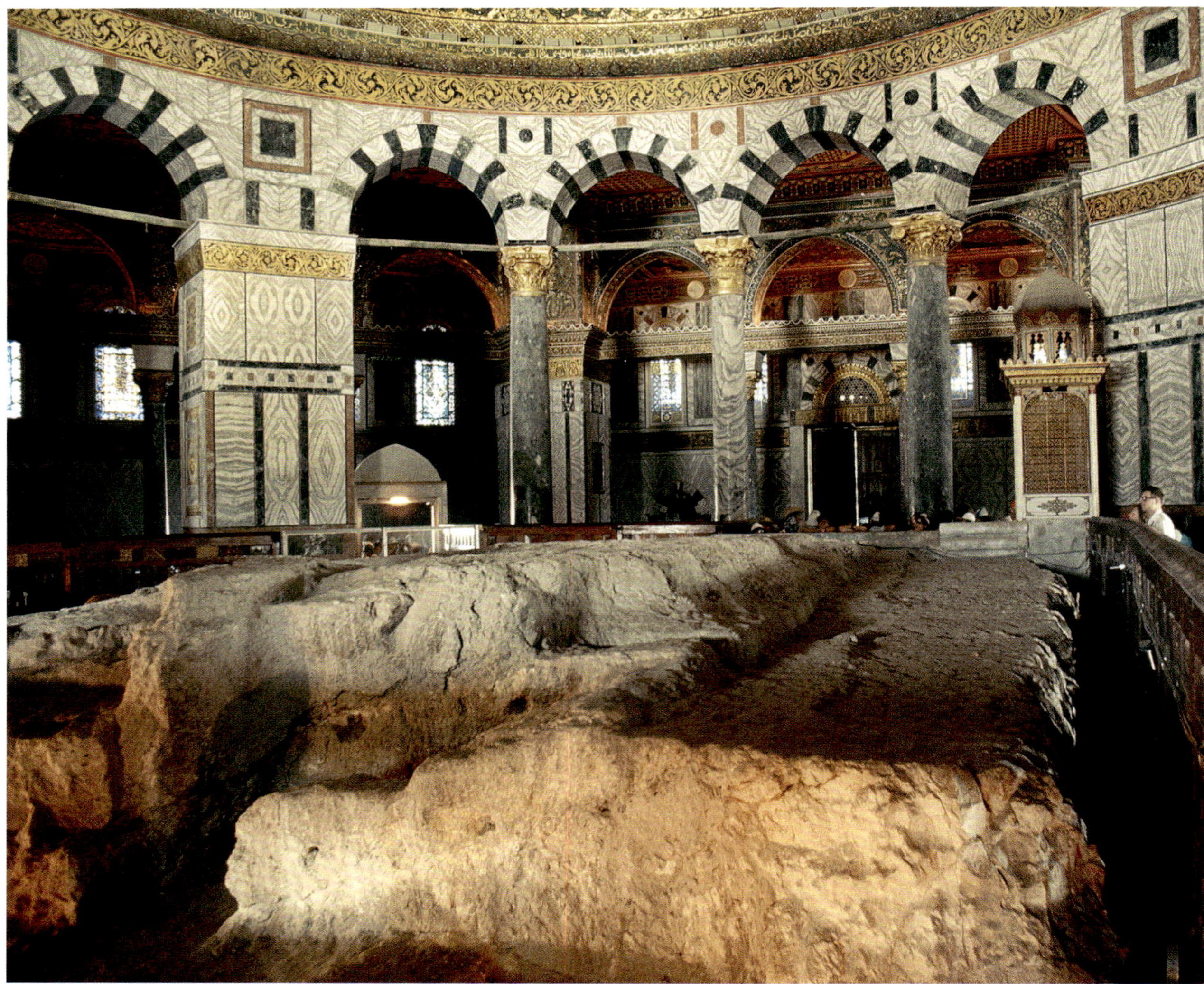

Fig. 50. The Foundation Stone, inside the Dome of the Rock, Jerusalem

Nasir's chronicle provides a sense of the vast open spaces of the nearby Aqsa Mosque, just after the renovations undertaken by the early eleventh-century Fatimid caliph al-Zahir. Like many others before and after, he marveled at the scale of the building.[63] Inside he found a parade of marble columns with great sculpted capitals, 280 by his own count.[64] He made note of a dome "ornamented with enamel work" above the *maksurah*, a separate space designated for officials. There too he found "Maghribi matting" and "lamps and lanterns, each suspended by its separate chain." He described several mihrabs, one "inlaid with tile" and flanked by marble columns "the colour of red carnelian," and the roof constructed of "beautifully sculpted" wood. He mentioned some fifteen gateways, one of which was so marvelously wrought it looked like gold burnished with silver niello: "When all these gates of the mosque are set open the interior of the building is light, as though it were a court open to the sky."[65]

Candles and lamps were signature features of both the Dome of the Rock and the Aqsa Mosque. Mujir al-Din (1456–1522), qadi of Jerusalem, proudly proclaimed that "there is no other mosque in this world, in our empire, where one lights so many lamps," citing 750 at Aqsa and 550 at the Dome of the Rock.[66] The late fifteenth-century traveler Arnold von Harff from Cologne, who resorted to disguise and bribery to gain access to the building, gave similar numbers, 800 in Aqsa and at least 500 in the Dome of the Rock burning continuously.[67]

Claiming the Sacred Esplanade

When Crusaders assumed control of the city in 1099, they altered the buildings on the Haram al-Sharif to suit their needs and assert their dominance. The biblical Temple loomed large in the Christian imagination, particularly for the role it had played in the life and teaching of Jesus. The Dome of the Rock became the Temple of the Lord (*Templum Domini*) and the Aqsa Mosque, the Temple or Palace of Solomon (*Templum Salomonis*). The names, which were to endure for European Christians well after the end of Crusader rule, represented a linguistic sleight of hand. Christians understood that the original Temple of Solomon had been sacked in the sixth century before the birth of Jesus and the rebuilt Temple of Herod destroyed in the first century, about four decades after his death. According to the Gospels, Jesus had predicted its ruin; Christians claimed the extant buildings anachronistically, making them part of their sacred landscape.[68] As in the Holy Sepulchre, they incorporated images and inscriptions at the Dome of the Rock to spell out the significance of the site.[69] Given that no surviving account has commented on the elegance or beauty of these additions, even among those visitors with a demonstrated interest in art, one might surmise that their emphasis was more educational than aesthetic. The great rock at the center of the building, which had been protected by a marble balustrade, was sheathed with marble and an altar erected over it.[70] Imad al-Din further asserted that improper images and statues had been set inside, including "flocks of animals, among which I saw species of pig . . . carved in marble."[71] (This claim, emphasizing the forbidden pig, was surely intended for shock value.) Perhaps most galling of all for Muslims of the time was the placement of a cross at the top of the dome.[72]

The Aqsa Mosque underwent even greater change under Crusader rule. In 1099 the Knights Templar, whose original charge was the protection of pilgrims to the Holy Land, seized the mosque, transforming it and the adjacent area into a sprawling complex replete with "houses, dwellings and outbuildings for every kind of purpose," including stables for their thousands of horses. They added an enormous new multistoried building with cellars and refectories. This ambitious campaign completely reconfigured the space. Some of the finest sculpture surviving from the Crusader occupation is a product of the prolific masons' workshop associated with the Templar endeavors (cat. 80a–c).[73]

When Saladin conquered Jerusalem in 1187, he immediately reclaimed the Haram, intent on restoring the sacred places to their earlier state. The cross on the Dome of the Rock was the first to go. Then, in a gesture of tremendous symbolic import, Saladin had the "sumptuous building" over the great rock inside removed. As Imad al-Din recorded, "The Rock was . . . brought to light again for visitors and revealed to observers, stripped of its covering and brought forward like a young bride. . . . Now it appeared in all its beauty, revealed in the loveliest revelations. Candelabra gleamed upon it, light on light and over it was placed an iron grille."[74] He quickly razed the walls and structures that had divided the spaces of the Aqsa Mosque and its courtyards. He had the interior purified with rose water and refurnished it with deep carpets, candelabra, and prayer mats. The twelfth-century historian Ibn al-Athir indicated that Saladin "gave every encouragement to its embellishment"; no expense was spared. Marble "of unrivalled quality" was imported, as were "golden tesserae from Constantinople," in order to face the walls with mosaics.[75] Beautiful Qur'an manuscripts were brought to the mosque and set up on stands to be admired by visitors — not to mention protected by responsible "curators" — as was the extraordinary minbar that would one day enchant Frederick II.

Embellishment of the Haram al-Sharif continued under Saladin's successors. Augmenting its water features, al-Malik al-Adil, Saladin's brother, built a drinking fountain between the Dome of the Rock and the Aqsa Mosque.[76] Using salvaged material from Crusader structures, his nephew al-Mu'azzam repaired the entrance porch of the mosque and added a dome and new facade.[77] Al-Mu'azzam, like many of the Mamluk rulers subsequently, took a keen interest in reinforcing the sense that the Haram was a space of learning, building numerous pious institutions at its edges.[78]

Medieval accounts leave no doubt as to the impressive scale and beauty of the structures and spaces within the Haram al-Sharif, but what was it like for a Muslim of the period to worship there, amid the splendor? Imad al-Din again served as an eloquent spokesman for the visitor's experience. After detailing the changes Saladin ordered, Imad al-Din described the prayerful activity that followed. Writing about a single emotion-filled moment, he nonetheless captured the essential character of the space when filled with the faithful. He emphasized, with his own fulsome prose, the critical way in which words — in the form of prayers, sermons, lessons, and disputations — activated the mosque's interior. In so doing, he celebrated a tradition in which he himself clearly excelled. Yet equally important is that he assigned an active role to the work of art — the minbar — as a participating witness.

> They [Muslim worshippers] joined in groups to pray and prostrate themselves, humbling themselves and beating their breasts . . . standing and sitting, keeping vigil and committed to prayer by night. . . . The pulpit raised its voice, the preacher expounded his truths; the crowd met and surged in. . . . The traditionalists recited, the holy orators comforted men's souls, the scholars disputed, the lawyers discussed, the narrators narrated, the tradition[al]ists transmitted canonic traditions. The spiritual guides performed pious exercises, the pious ascetics acted as guides, the worshippers adored God with devotion, the sincere devotees lifted their prayers to heaven.[79]

The Absent Temple

In stark contrast to the richly appointed Christian and Muslim shrines of medieval Jerusalem is the poignant absence of the biblical Temple, once Jerusalem's most magnificent structure. Medieval Jews who lived in or visited the city invariably framed their experience of its sanctity in terms of desolation and destruction, giving less attention to sites where great events from Jewish biblical history took place.[80] The "Prayer at the Ruin of Jerusalem," in which the great rabbi Nachmanides (1194–1270) called for a Jewish return to Jerusalem, epitomized this line of thinking: "I weep, because in the city there is nothing but desolation and destruction. Our house of Holiness and Glory in which our forefathers praised God was burned down and all our delights were destroyed."[81] In the early thirteenth century, the Spanish poet Judah al-Harizi (1165–1225) sounded a bittersweet note when he described his days in Jerusalem "as if they had been carved from rubies, cut from the trees of life, or stolen from the stars of heaven. And each day we would walk about on its graves and its monuments to weep over Sion . . . and to lament over the destruction of her palaces and the remnant of her buildings."[82]

It was customary to speak of the city's desolation even in the face of relative prosperity, a contrast seemingly difficult to reconcile. The eminent Italian scholar Rabbi Obadiah of Bertinoro (ca. 1450–before 1516), who became a leading figure in Jerusalem's Jewish community, marveled that the city possessed beautiful and bountiful marketplaces "notwithstanding the city's destruction."[83] Similarly, the international merchant Meshullam of Volterra (before 1443–after 1507), conceded that the population was sizable, the buildings fine, and the fruits choice even though "through our sins [Jerusalem] is all in ruins." He summed up the contradiction nicely: "The land flows with milk and honey although it is hilly and ruined and desolate."[84] In the eyes of the Jewish pilgrims, a land bereft of her children was desolate land, regardless of her fruitfulness. Nachmanides likened the bountiful land to a nursing mother whose own infant died, forcing her to nourish others with her milk.[85] Al-Harizi mourned Sion, while Sion "mourned for her children until the streams of tears dug pits in her face."[86] Pilgrims lamented the land's desolation in penitential tones, hoping to atone for the collective sins that had brought about their exile and the earlier destruction of Jerusalem.

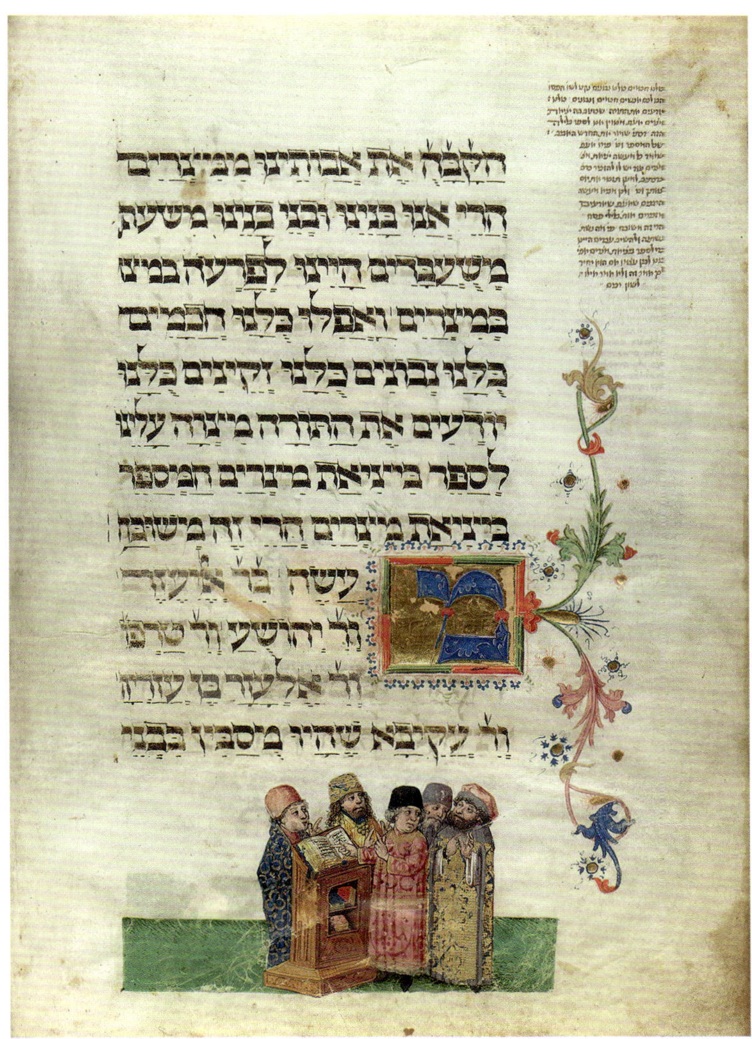

Fig. 51. Rabbis Eliezer, Yehoshua, Elazar Ben Azaryah, Akiva, and Tarfon, whose tombs were among those visited by Jewish pilgrims to the Holy Land. From a Haggadah. Germany, ca. 1460. Tempera, gold, and ink on parchment. British Library, London (MS Add. 14762, fol. 7v)

If nothing remains, why make a pilgrimage at all? If the function of pilgrimage is an experiential validation of religious history, what was there for a medieval Jewish pilgrim to see, to touch, to experience? Today Jews travel to the Western Wall, an exposed portion of the ancient retaining wall of the destroyed Temple complex built by Herod that is the closest point accessible by Jews to the Holy of Holies. There they can place written prayers in the cracks between the blocks of stone. Medieval pilgrims, however, organized itineraries in the Holy Land around the tombs of esteemed ancestors, reinforcing their sense of historic connection to the place (fig. 51).[87] In the Holy City itself, they focused their prayers at the Gates of Mercy – beneath which lay the gateway to the Temple – scratching their names and prayers for peace into the stone.[88] In both cases, Jewish pilgrims strove to tie their practices to the physical historical record, but in the face of exile and destruction, they organized their rituals around the notion of absence. "There [in Jerusalem] they weep upon its stones, roll in its dust, and circle its walls, and pray."[89]

Visitors to the city followed the expected protocol of prayer. As Nachmanides attested, "I recited over [Jerusalem] as it is proper: 'Sion is become a wilderness; Jerusalem a desolation.'"[90] In the mid-thirteenth century, when Rabbi Jacob the Emissary visited Jerusalem on behalf of the prominent Rabbi Yehiel of Paris, he went so far as to stand outside the city and map out the individual buildings of the complex he could not see. "When we reach Jerusalem, we go on one of the ruins and look at the Temple Mount and the wall of the Court of Women and the Court of Israel, the site of the Altar, and the site of the Temple and the Sanctuary."[91]

Such prayers largely took place not within the city walls but at the periphery, at the city's gates or on the Mount of Olives,[92] the historic site where the priest of the Temple slew the red heifer for ritual purification.[93] It was also believed to be the place where the Divine Spirit, having departed from the Temple before its destruction, rested before ascending to the heavens. Medieval Jews paid for the right to pray on this holy site, the spot to which, it was prophesied, the Divine Spirit would one day return.[94] This significant prospect just east of the city also afforded the best view of the closed gate and the Temple platform. Pilgrims therefore concluded their circuit around the city's gates at the Mount of Olives, praying that the "King of Glory" will come back through the gate.[95] The site figured heavily in holiday celebrations, and an eleventh-century letter from the Cairo Geniza described the Jews' "ascent to the Mount of Olives in song, and their stance facing the Temple of God on the holidays, the place of the Divine Presence, his strength and footstool."[96] On Tisha b'Av, the day on the Jewish calendar set aside each year to mark the destruction of the Temple, Jews chose that same spot to lament the Divine Spirit's departure and the loss of what they could no longer see. Under these conditions, even the miraculous took the form of conspicuous absence. Meshullam told how each year, on that same holiday, "all the lamps in the Temple Court go out of their own accord, and cannot be kindled again."[97]

But of course the Temple Mount the medieval Jews saw was neither a desert nor a desolation — far from it. Great domed buildings crowned it, with hundreds of lights. Even as pilgrims standing on the Mount of Olives focused their prayers in the direction of buildings long gone, they perceived the very present structures before them. And, like their Muslim contemporaries viewing the Holy Sepulchre or their Christian counterparts visiting the Dome of the Rock, they were impressed by the great works of art that stood before them. Rabbi Jacob reported that "the Ishmailite [Muslim] Kings have built a very beautiful building for a house of prayer and erected on the top a very fine cupola."[98] Rabbi Petachia of Regensburg, writing in the 1170s, described "a beautiful palace which the Ishmaelites [Muslims] built in ancient times," and recalled a king, "a friend of the Jews," who, having ascertained the location of the destroyed Jewish Temple, built over it a "temple of marble stone, a beautiful structure of red, green and variegated marble."[99] Chroniclers also told of a Jewish woman called Stella, who had seen the Aqsa Mosque and declared that it was "made of extremely beautiful stones," "radiant and pure as the very heavens."[100]

FOR ALL VISITORS, the beauty of Jerusalem was to be expected. It had biblical authority: Isaiah had called it "a crown of beauty in the hand of the Lord" (Isaiah 62:3); the Psalmist called it "beautiful in elevation" (Psalms 48:2). At prayer in Jerusalem, even as the faithful held in their mind's eye the city of their own religious convictions, they could not help beholding the city that stood before their open eyes nor could they avoid others' realities. That was when art worked its special magic, and visitors realized it. They tell us that domes were "beguiling," stones were "heavenly," prophets were "alive," and a minbar "raised its voice" in prayer. Together, then as now, works of art create an exceptional atmosphere of holiness, a transcendent realm where heaven and earth touch, nowhere more than in Jerusalem.

NOTES FOR THIS ESSAY APPEAR ON PAGES 302–3

THE CLOSED GATE

Melanie Holcomb

A GATE IS by definition an opening. It presupposes a barrier that separates two discrete zones and makes possible passage between them. What then are we to make of Jerusalem's double-arched Golden Gate, also known as the Beautiful Gate or the Gates of Mercy and Repentance, an entrance known for being intriguingly, reliably closed (fig. 52)? There is scarcely a medieval account by visitors to the city that fails to mention it, as either an historic site, a place of miracles, or an indicator of the End of Time. Whatever else was said about the gate, its sealed doorways were its defining feature.

Architecturally undistinguished, the gate visible today is a sixteenth-century reconstruction of a gate likely built in the late seventh century on the ruins of an ancient gate.[1] Were its portals open, it would serve as the closest point of passage between the Mount of Olives and the Temple Mount, or Haram al-Sharif, the elevated platform that is the pinnacle of the walled city of Jerusalem. The current gate structure bears some resemblance to that depicted in a fifteenth-century print (cat. 20). A tall edifice, rectangular in plan, it presents to the outside two doorways articulated by a double-arched molding. Medieval accounts speak of an imposing pair of closed doors covered with bronze or iron, with a column or wall between them. The column and doors are now gone, replaced by post-medieval masonry that spans the height and width of the earlier opening. The gated structure, then as now, served as an imposing facade to a vaulted and columned vestibule. So much did the gate and its vestibule, or court, impress medieval viewers that they often attributed it to King Solomon himself.

Nasir-i Khusraw, a Persian poet who visited the city from Mosul in the tenth century, asserted that Solomon constructed the gate to please his father, David.[2] An anonymous Christian pilgrim writing in the twelfth century claimed it was indeed the only structure in the entire precinct that could be traced back to Solomon's time.[3] Jews knew it as the gate through which the red heifer was led to the Mount of Olives for a purification ceremony when the ancient Temple still stood.[4] Christians traditionally understood it to be the location of multiple events related to the life and mission of Jesus: the gate where his grandparents, Joachim and Anna, met and rejoiced over the conception of their daughter Mary, his mother; the gate through which Jesus entered on Palm Sunday; and the place where the apostle Peter cured the paralytic. Muslims claimed it to be the place where King David repented.

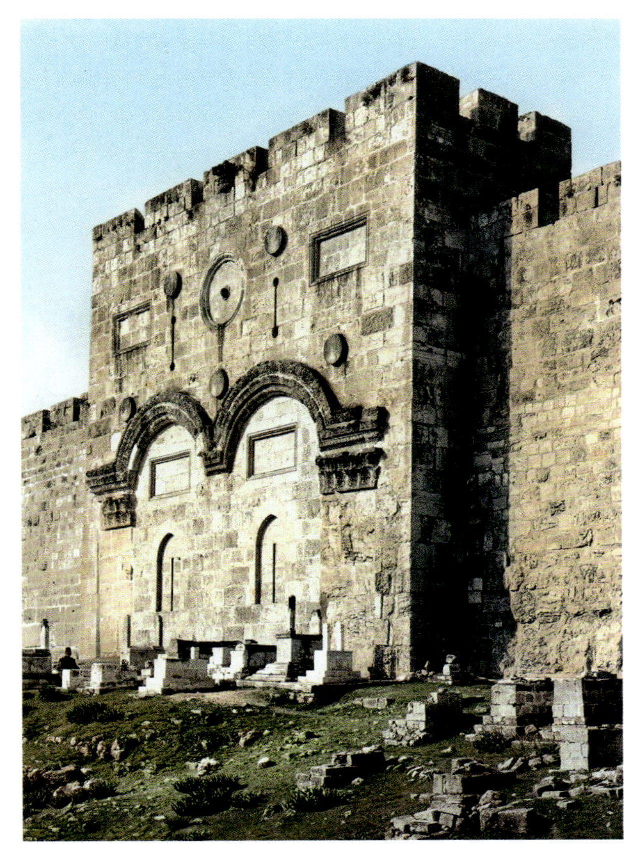

Fig. 52. The Gates of Mercy, Jerusalem

The gate's link to sacred history was but one component of its attraction. Medieval visitors assigned special properties to it. Christian and Jewish visitors presented similar tales of its indestructibility, imagining its stones as a bulwark against the destructive impulses of enemies. The eleventh-century French rabbi and biblical scholar Rashi, who never visited Jerusalem, nonetheless knew the gate and explained in his commentary on Lamentations 2:9 that "enemies had no power over it." Both Friar Niccolo of Poggibonsi in the mid-fourteenth century and Rabbi Obadiah of Bertinoro more than a century later told of foes — Mongols for Niccolo, Arabs for Obadiah — who, in their admiration for the gate, attempted to dig it up and take it away, only to be foiled because its foundation was so deep in the ground.[5] The Dominican Felix Fabri was one of a number of visitors who remarked on both the many Christians who took away nails and other pieces of the door (because such architectural relics were believed to cure illnesses) and the guards who were theoretically there to prevent it.[6]

Yet the gate's most salient aspect, the evidence of its connection to the divine, involved its opening and closing. Often considered a threshold of supernatural power, it was thought capable of reading and responding to the character and intention of those who wished to pass through it. When King Solomon brought the Ark of the Covenant to the Temple Mount, according to the Talmud, the gates rose up, elongating their aperture to allow the ark to pass.[7] Christians recounted the tale of the triumphant arrival of the Byzantine emperor Heraclius (ca. 1128–1190/91), carrying a relic of the Cross of Jesus back into the city. When he attempted to ride through the gate on horseback, the gate closed into a solid wall. Not until he dismounted and prepared to walk through the gate in a proper state of humility did the stones retract and permit him entry.[8]

These accounts presuppose an open gate, but medieval pilgrims invariably encountered a closed one. When did it close and when would it open? It is not clear. Medieval Jews, citing a passage from Ezekiel (44:1-3), declared it had not opened since before the days of exile. Nor could it be opened: they told of gentiles who had wanted to clean and open it, but an earthquake — clearly an intervention from above — signaled the imprudence of that endeavor. Niccolo of Poggibonsi was certain that the gate was sealed permanently after Jesus's fateful entry through it on a donkey. The scholar Mujir al-Din attributed its closing to Caliph 'Abd al-Malik, the very man who probably had the gate built at the same time as the Dome of the Rock. Mujir al-Din explained that the caliph apparently saw it as a vulnerability and, in closing it, sought to protect the Haram al-Sharif from an unspecified heretic enemy.[9]

If the reasons for its closing validated particular religious histories, predictions of its opening invoked the end of an age. For Jews the gate would only become unsealed at the moment of redemption. Hence medieval pilgrims stood on the Mount of Olives facing the Gate of Mercy, praying that it would open. Saladin himself affirmed the significance of the gate at the End of Time: those passing through would gain the right to dwell in paradise.[10] The Qur'an (*Surat al-Hadid* 57:13) put it more starkly: inside is mercy, outside is torment. Though Mujir al-Din asserted that Christians had told him it would not be reopened until the descent of the Lord Jesus, no surviving Christian account makes such a claim. Perhaps that is why Latin Christians, in the one hundred or so years when they ruled over the city, felt emboldened to open the gate from time to time.[11] They sensed, after all, that they were key players in Christian history. In that intoxicating environment of divinely sanctioned privilege, why not reopen the Golden Gate on Palm Sunday to reenact Jesus's ride into the city, or on the day marking Heraclius's return of the relic of the Cross, or at the coronations of their kings?[12] The sixteenth-century Ottoman sultan Süleyman the Magnificent, no less certain of his place in history than the Crusaders, saw fit simply to remove the doors and block up the openings with masonry during his restoration of the city walls between 1537 and 1541. Gone were the source of relics, the need for guards, and the tantalizing sense that the gates could be opened by human hands.

Pilgrims came to medieval Jerusalem with the expectation that the very dust and stones of the place would confer authenticity to the narratives said to have taken place there. What fascinated people about the great closed gate on the eastern wall was that it provided tangible evidence of sacred history — for visitors of many faiths — and at the same time it harbored mystery. Its paradoxical state begged for explanation. As such, it not only validated sacred stories, but also gave rise to them.

NOTES FOR THIS ESSAY APPEAR ON PAGE 303
SEE CATS. 58–69

SHARING THE CHURCH OF THE HOLY SEPULCHRE DURING THE CRUSADER PERIOD

Jaroslav Folda

JERUSALEM WAS already a multicultural center when Christianity was born and long before Islam came into existence. Over the centuries the residents and visitors changed repeatedly as the Holy City served as "the strategic battlefield of clashing civilizations."[1] From the time that the Church of the Holy Sepulchre – first built by Constantine the Great (ca. 273–337) – was rebuilt by the Byzantines and the Crusaders, the history of the church provides a focal point of great importance for understanding the conflicts and compromises of the three great faiths, Judaism, Christianity, and Islam, that shared space in the Holy City.

When Jerusalem was conquered in 1099 during the First Crusade, the Holy Sepulchre, the holiest site in Christendom, became its premier pilgrimage site. Also that year, the Crusaders retook two other major dominical sites: the Church of the Nativity in Bethlehem, where Jesus was born, and the Church of the Annunciation in Nazareth, where the angel Gabriel announced to the Virgin Mary that she was to be the mother of God and where the Incarnation of Jesus took place in her womb. Crusader possession of these sites, along with the increased popularity of places in Western Europe – Rome and Santiago de Compostela – generated fresh enthusiasm for pilgrimage to Jerusalem and the Holy Sepulchre.

As Crusader control of the Holy Land was gradually reestablished, Christian pilgrims gained greater access, focusing on the places where Jesus had been crucified on Calvary hill, buried in the Holy Sepulchre, and risen from the dead – all defining events of Christ's death and resurrection as recorded in the Four Gospels. These sites were all contained in the Holy Sepulchre, also known as the Church of the Anastasis or the Church of the Resurrection, which the mad caliph al-Hakim partially destroyed in 1009 and which was further damaged by an earthquake in 1033. It was heroically rebuilt by the Byzantine Greeks in the 1040s with the support of the Byzantine emperor and Greek Orthodox patriarch of Jerusalem. Pilgrims came to pray, be inspired by firsthand experience of these holy sites, do penance for their sins, and receive the grace of a new life marked by an increased intimacy with Christ and a fuller understanding of the meaning of his life and teachings.[2] They came from all over Christendom to join the faithful who already lived in Jerusalem and were present at the church.

The First Crusaders, who were members of the Western Latin Catholic Church of Rome, experienced a major culture shock when they discovered a multiplicity of other Christian peoples and confessions, most of which they were unfamiliar with.[3] Those other devotees, who worshipped there at their own altars, included the Greek Orthodox, who had rebuilt the church and whose liturgical language was Greek; the Armenian Orthodox, who had their own patriarch and retained their ancient Armenian language (fig. 53); the Syrian Orthodox, or Syrian Jacobites, whose official tongue was Syriac; the Copts, whose altar was in a chapel at the western side of the aedicule and who worshipped in Coptic; and finally the Ethiopians, who had resided there since early Christian times and prayed in Geez.[4]

Even more than local worshippers, the pilgrims who came to Jerusalem were numerous and diverse. Later travelers, such as Theoderich and John of Würzburg who came in the 1160s and 1170s, cite some of these peoples, as for example John's impressive list: "for there are Greeks, Bulgars, Latins, Germans, Hungarians, Scots, people of Navarre, Britons, Angles, Franks, Ruthenians, Bohemians, Georgians, Armenians, Jacobites, Syrians, Nestorians, Indians, Egyptians, Copts, Capheturici, Maronites and many others."[5] Moreover, impressive numbers of Scandinavians such as the Norwegians, Swedes, and Danes, as well as the Russians, were among the others who visited in the twelfth century.[6]

Remarkably, even during times of hostility and conflict, visitors of diverse faiths still visited Jerusalem. By 1110 both Jews and Muslims returned to the Holy

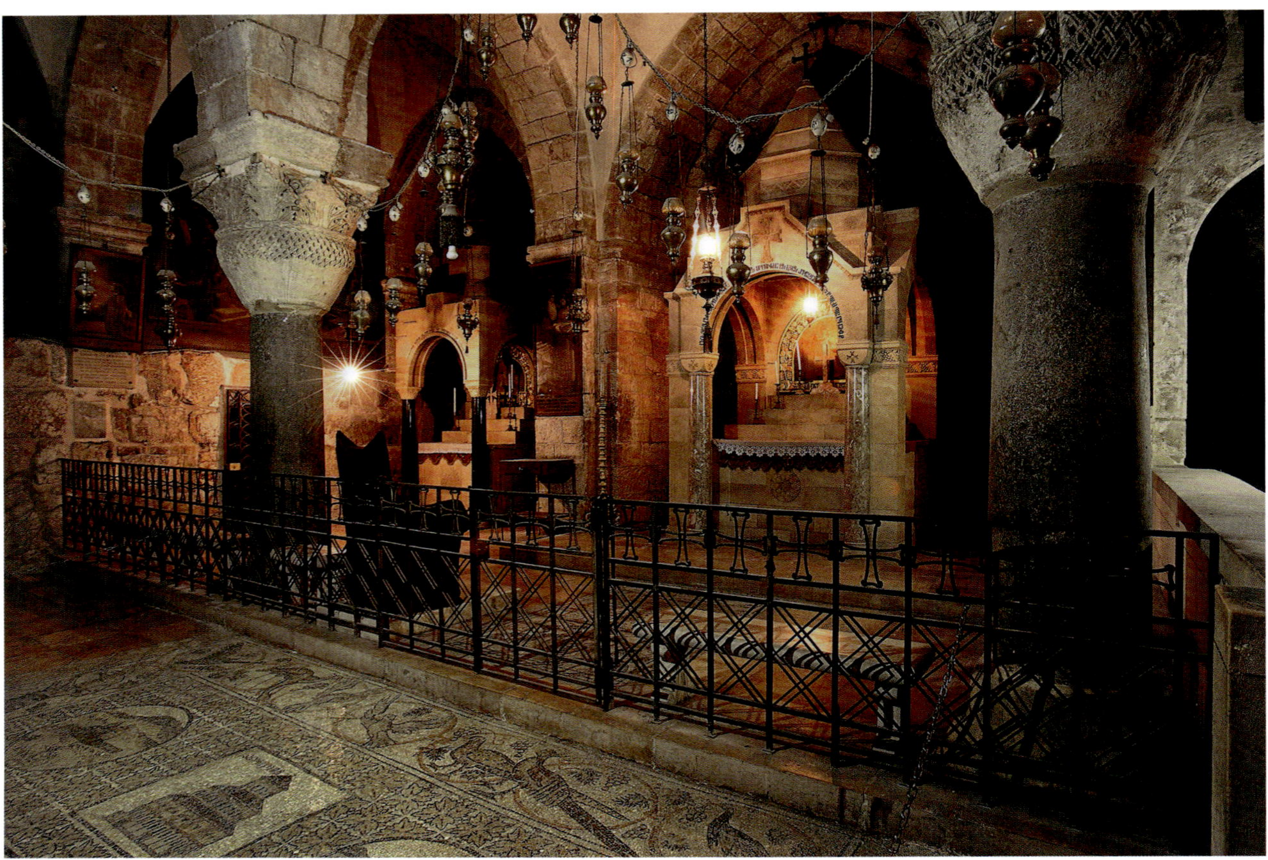

Fig. 53. The Chapel of Saint Helena in the Church of the Holy Sepulchre, Jerusalem

City, but the Crusaders did not allow them to live there, save for a small Jewish community near the citadel.[7] Yet Jewish pilgrimage became frequent during this time, with travelers arriving in part to contemplate the Temple area from the Mount of Olives, a custom for centuries. Jews began to emigrate in great numbers to other parts of the Latin Kingdom, especially Acre, Ascalon, and Tyre, but it was not until Saladin conquered the city in 1187 that Jewish immigrants were welcomed, as the Spanish-Jewish poet Judah al-Harizi recorded of an 1189–90 declaration: "And Saladin ordered to proclaim in every city, to let it be known to old and young: 'Speak ye to the heart of Jerusalem, let anybody who wants from the seed of Ephraim come to her.'"[8]

While there is no particular record of Jews sharing the Holy Sepulchre as visitors, the situation differs for Muslims. In Islam, Jesus is a prophet worthy of reverence, though Muslims do not recognize him as the son of God. Nonetheless, on his Night Journey the prophet Muhammad came to Jerusalem and was said to have prayed at the birthplace of Jesus in Bethlehem.[9] Mary, who appears as a central figure in two suras of the Qur'an, was also highly revered (cat. 95).[10] Along with Christian pilgrims, many Muslims visited the Tomb of the Virgin in the vale of Jehoshaphat, one of a number of holy sites venerated by both faiths.[11] Of course, Muslims visited the Holy Sepulchre for private devotion and directly shared this supreme Christian site in certain important ways.[12] For one thing, despite the anomaly of Caliph al-Hakim's destruction in 1009, Muslim conquerors – twice – protected the church for Christian worship. Relating the first instance, Imad al-Din, secretary to Saladin, noted that "when 'Umar [ca. 581–644], prince of the believers, conquered Jerusalem in the early days of Islam [638], he confirmed to the Christians the possession of the place, and did not order them to demolish [the Holy Sepulchre] on it."[13] Imad al-Din recounted this event shortly after recording contemporary arguments for saving the church again in 1187, with the majority advocating that "demolishing it and destroying it would serve no purpose, nor would it

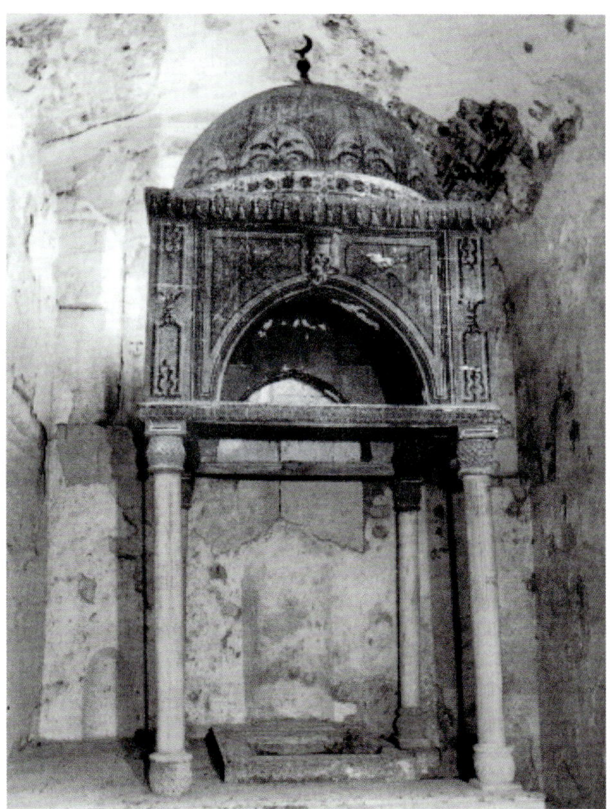

Fig. 56. The Cradle of Jesus on the Haram al-Sharif, Jerusalem

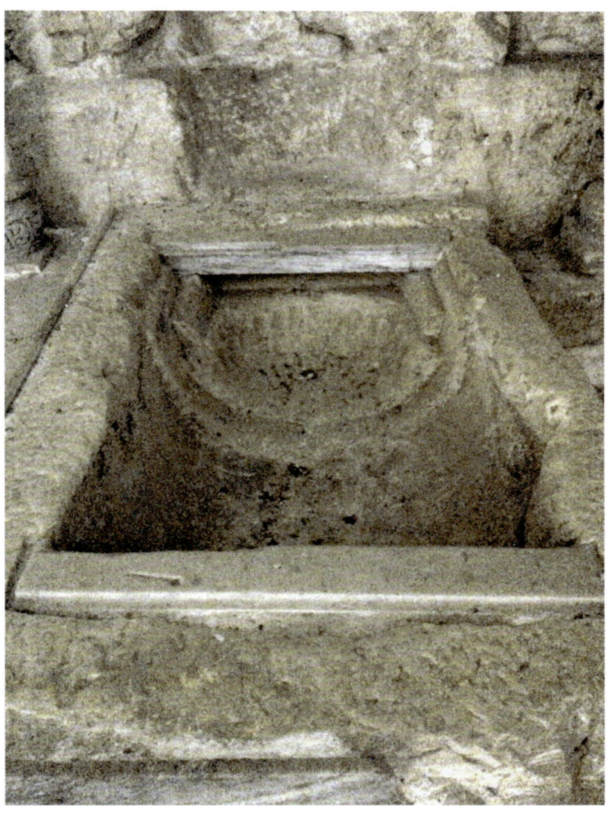

Fig. 57. Detail of the Cradle of Jesus on the Haram al-Sharif, Jerusalem

place of our master Gabriel, peace be upon him, and there is another place which, it is said, is where the disciples of Jesus, peace be upon him, worshipped. It is said that prayers there are accepted by God. So we prayed two prostrations.[12]

Of all the sanctuaries built for prophets near the Prophet Muhammad's locus of divine encounter, the Haram became the only place in the Islamic world that contained the history of God in all his prophetic revelations, from Abraham and Solomon to Jesus and Muhammad. It was therefore not surprising that Muslims began to view Jerusalem and the Haram as a piece of heaven on earth, the center of the world — the omphalos (*surra*) in the words of the scholar Ibn al-Firkah (1262–1329).[13] With the Haram at its center, Jerusalem became the city of the Qur'anic prophets of God.

NOTES FOR THIS ESSAY APPEAR ON PAGE 304
SEE CAT. 95

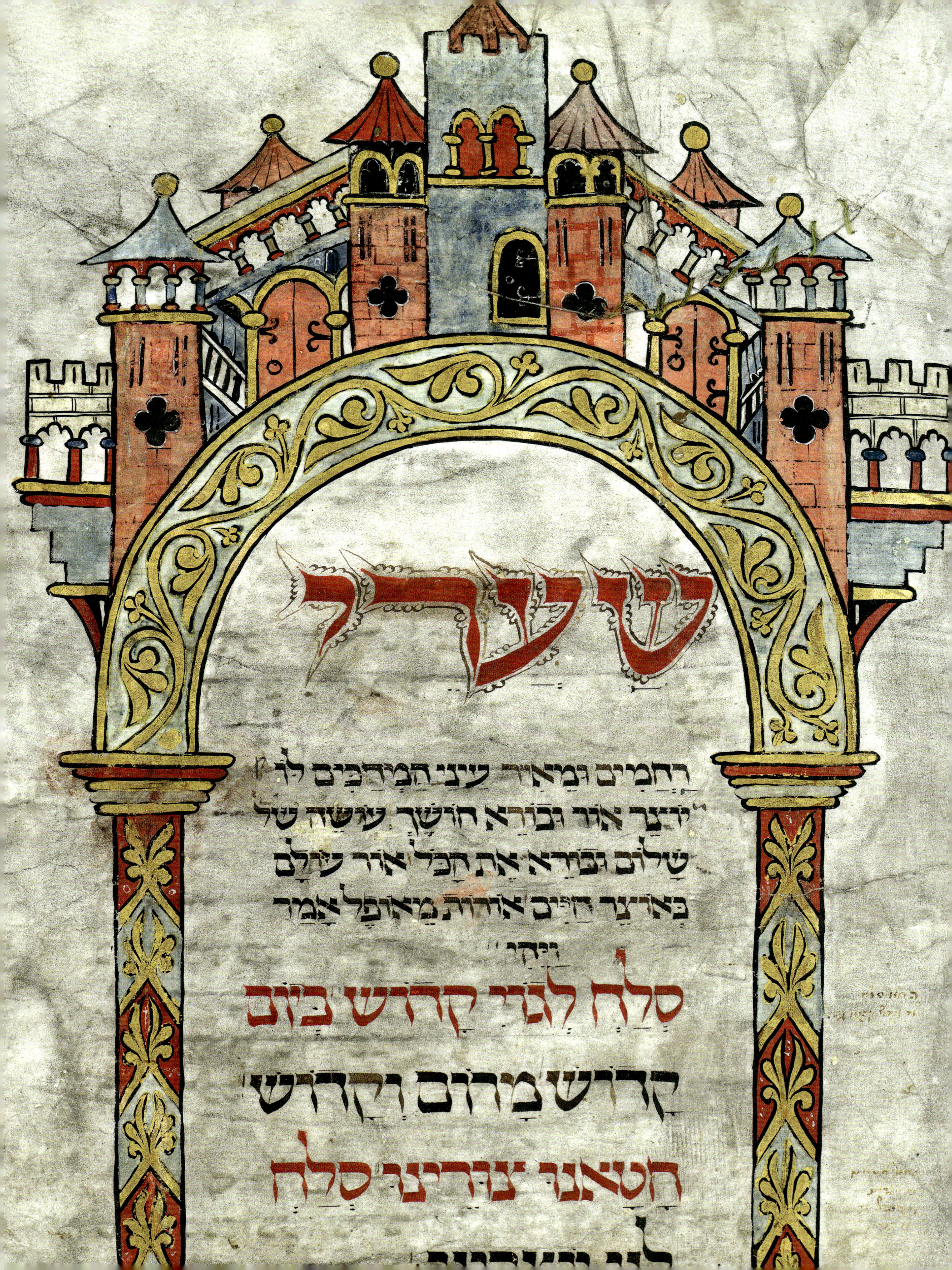

רחמים ומאיר עיני המרכבים לו
יוצר אור ובורא חושך עושה של
שלום ובורא את הכל אור עולם
באוצר חיים אורות מאופל אמר
ויהי
סלח לגוי קדוש ביום
קדוש מרום וקדוש
חטאנו צורינו סלח

58

The Gates of Mercy

From the Worms Mahzor, vol. II
Southern Germany, ca. 1280
Gold, ink, and tempera on parchment; 219 folios
17¾ × 12¼ in. (45 × 31 cm)
The National Library of Israel, Jerusalem
(MS. Heb. 4°781/2)

On the annual Day of Atonement, worshippers invoke God, who "opens for us the Gates of Mercy and enlightens the eyes of those who yearn for Your pardon." In thirteenth- and fourteenth-century German mahzors — the prayer books used during holidays — this prayer is often framed in a gateway, illustrating the heavenly Gates of Mercy open to receive supplicants' prayers. Here, a majestic blue and red archway decorated with golden palmettes and acanthus vines dominates the page (folio 73 recto). Otherworldly blue lions stalk the entrance, their knotted tails barring entry, symbolizing the ordinarily closed status of the gate. Glimpsed over the crown of the arch are the towers and balustrades of a glittering city — the heavenly Jerusalem? — painted in the same regal palette as the gate.

Correspondence between these heavenly Gates of Mercy and their earthly counterparts in Jerusalem can be assumed via the firm correlations established between the physical and heavenly Temples, each of which is situated within a physical or heavenly Jerusalem. Upon waking from his dream of angels traversing the ladder, the patriarch Jacob declared, "How full of awe is this place! This is none other than the House of God, and this is the Gate of Heaven" (Genesis 28:17). The preeminent medieval biblical and Talmudic scholar Rashi (Rabbi Solomon ben Isaac of Troyes, 1040–1105) taught that Jacob was speaking of Jerusalem, a place where Israel's prayers ascend instantly to heaven[1] because the heavenly Temple is directly over the earthly one.[2] From Psalms 122:3 — "Jerusalem that is built like a city joined within itself" — Rashi learned that the earthly and heavenly Jerusalems are tied to each other.

These concepts were well known to medieval Jews, imparted by both their scholars and their liturgical poets. From the commandment to build the Sanctuary, Exodus Rabbah[3] deduced that "all that God created above, He created below," bringing as examples biblical passages that draw direct parallels between specific elements of the physical and heavenly Temples.[4] These connections were celebrated in liturgical poems by the famous seventh-century poets Yannai and his pupil Eleazar ben Kalir, both of whom likely lived in the Holy Land.[5] Thus medieval Jews correlated the heavenly and earthly Jerusalems, the heavenly and earthly Temples, and — one can infer — the heavenly and earthly Gates of Mercy.

This second volume of the Worms Mahzor was not originally related to the first (cat. 65). Being of similar style and almost contemporaneous in date, it was adjoined to the first volume sometime in the sixteenth century to replace its lost second half, thereby re-forming a complete cycle of yearly prayers.[6] EE

Selected References: Landsberger 1961, pp. 294–95; Sed-Rajna 1983, pp. 16, 20, pl. 5; Cohen-Mushlin 1985, vol. [2], pp. 94–96 and fig. 30, and reproduced in facsimile vol. [1]; Jerusalem 1985, pp. 22, 43, no. 33; Jerusalem 2000, pp. 55–58, no. 18.

1. Pirkei de-Rabbi Eliezer in Friedlander, ed. 1916, chap. 35, pp. 265–66: "All who pray in Jerusalem, it is as if he is praying before the Heavenly Throne, for the Gate of Heaven is there, and it is open to hear the prayers of Israel, as it is said, 'And this is the gate of heaven.'"
2. Genesis Rabbah 69:7. Nachmanides expresses a similar opinion. Among further biblical passages ascertaining that the heavenly Temple is directly above the earthly Temple are Exodus 15:17 and 38:21. For more on the heavenly and earthly Temples and Jerusalem, see Aptowitzer 1931, abridged English translation in Aptowitzer 1989, and Idal 1991.
3. A tenth-century collection of writings on the Book of Exodus.
4. Exodus Rabbah 33:4 quotes Rabbi Berachia, who connects Exodus 25:2 with I Chronicles 29:11: "Yours, Oh Lord, are the greatness, and the strength, and the glory, and the victory, and the majesty, for all that is in the heavens and on the earth [is Yours]."
5. Yannai's poem for Shabbat Chanukah was rediscovered amongst Geniza fragments by Menachem Zulay. The poem can be found in Rabinowitz 1985, pp. 241–43; Eleazar ben Kalir's poem is included in the opening liturgy for Shabbat Parah. It is in Mirsky 1985, pp. 26–27.
6. Beit-Arié 1985, p. 14.

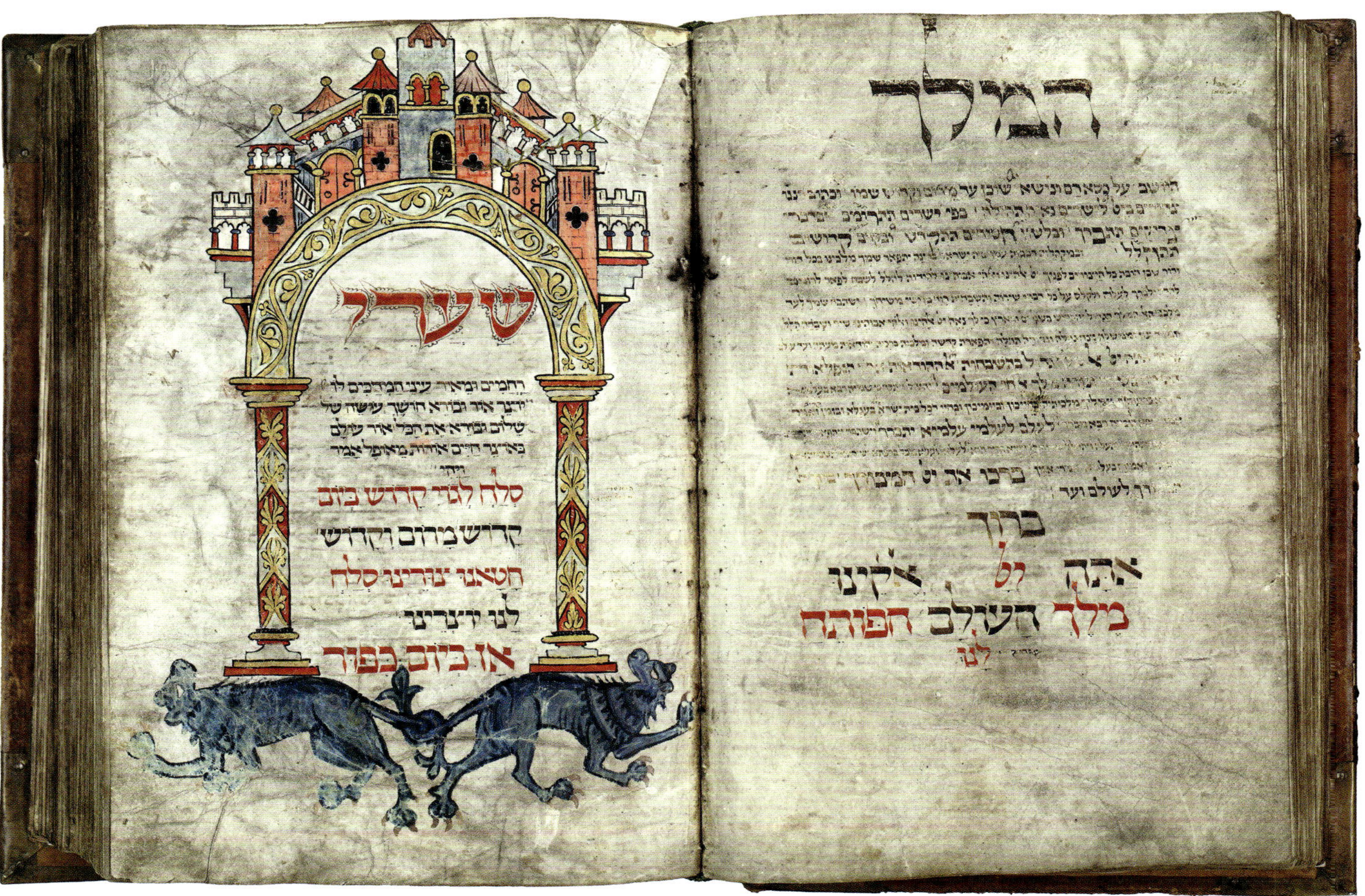

58, fols. 72v–73r

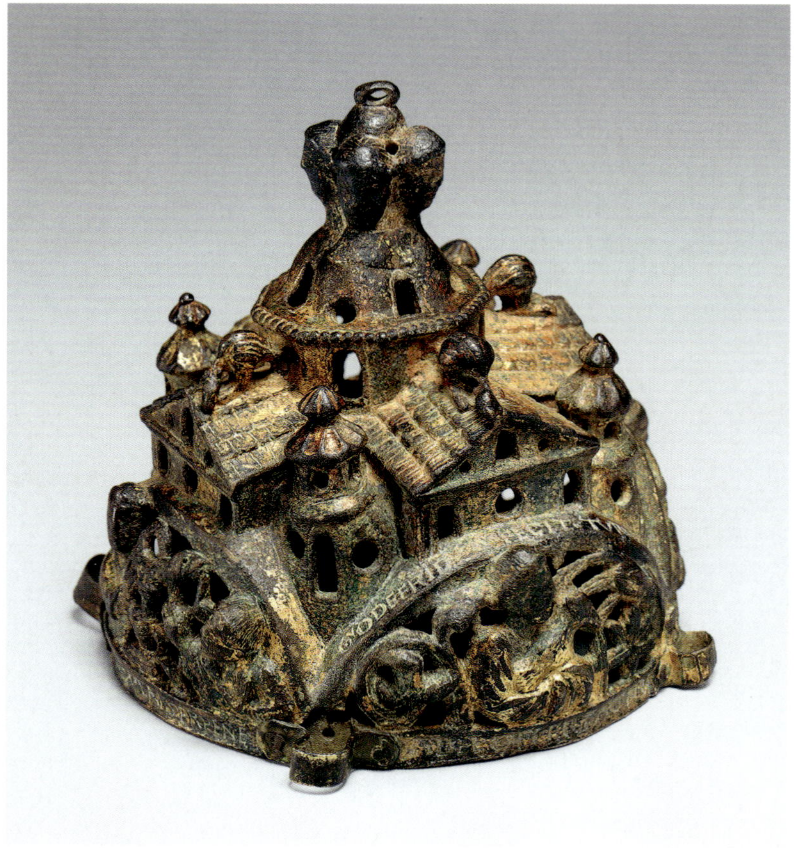

59

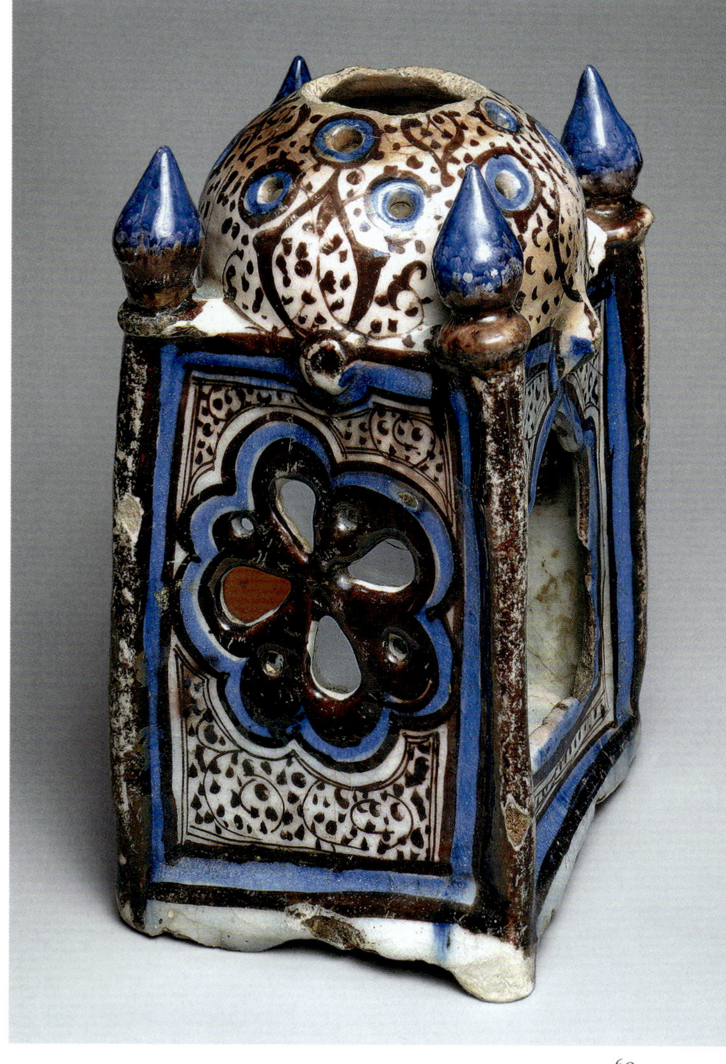

60

59

Cover of a Censer

Meuse Valley (present-day Belgium), mid-12th century
Made by Godefridus
Gilded copper alloy
4⅛ × 4⅛ in. (10.5 × 10.5 cm)
The Metropolitan Museum of Art, New York,
The Cloisters Collection, 1979 (1979.285)

The decoration and structure of this cover for an incense burner draw from two strands of medieval thought. The first is the exegetical tradition that compared a censer to the body of Christ, a metaphor extended in each of the scenes depicted in the lunettes.[1] There, we see four episodes from the Old Testament that were thought to prefigure aspects of Christ described in the New. Whether the lamb sacrificed by Abel or the snake exalted by Moses, whether the grapes brought to the Israelites by Joshua and Caleb or the bread offered to Abram by the priest Melchizedek,[2] each was understood as a prophetic symbol for the sacrifice on the Cross of Jesus incarnate and therefore a demonstration of the divinely crafted coherence of history.

The second strand pertains to Christian ideas about the glorious conclusion of history called the Apocalypse (book of Revelation). In this book, the final chapter of the Christian Bible, Saint John described the descent from heaven of a glittering new Jerusalem, its gates harmoniously disposed to face each of the cardinal directions. The practical requirements of a censer neatly aligned with this geometrically balanced conception of the Holy City. Indeed, an artist's handbook from the twelfth century describes how a metalsmith can, with extra effort, specially craft a censer to resemble the city seen by John in his vision.[3]

It would seem that the artist who made this object did expend the effort. In so doing, he transformed a seemingly simple object into an elegant and evocative cityscape, one that serves as a framework to convey the significance of history and the imminence of its end. MH

Selected References: New York 1999, pp. 63–64, no. 76; New York 2006, p. 184, no. 44.

1. Gousset 1982, p. 104 n. 63.
2. The inscriptions on the cover are as follows: Above, on the arch: GODEFRIDVS FECIT TVRIBVLVM: ABEL OFFERT AGNV[M] (Genesis 4:4); IOSVE ET CALEP FER[VN]T BONTR[VM] (Numbers 13:23); [MO]YSES EXALTAT SERPENTE[M] (Numbers 21:9); MELCHISEDEC PANEM (Genesis 14:18).
3. Theophilus 1961 ed., pp. 132–38.

60

Lantern

Syria, probably Raqqa, early 13th century
Stonepaste, underglazed luster paint
H. 9⅜ in. (23.8 cm), Diam. 6 in. (15.2 cm)
The Metropolitan Museum of Art, New York,
Edward C. Moore Collection, Bequest of
Edward C. Moore, 1891 (91.1.138)

The Holy City was a luminous one. Visitors of all creeds remarked upon the abundance of lamps that illuminated its sacred spaces. This charming domed lamp, associated with the famous kilns at Raqqa, speaks to the ecumenical appreciation of light. It pairs a rose window with an ogive arch, emblematic of Christian and Islamic architecture, respectively. The same combination appears in the Aqsa Mosque, where the Knights Templar, who used the structure for their headquarters, installed a chapel replete with a rose window on the east wall. In reclaiming the mosque, Saladin retained the window, and the space is now known as the mihrab of Zachariah. MH

Selected References: Paris 2001–2, p. 217, no. 234; Jenkins-Madina 2006, p. 116.

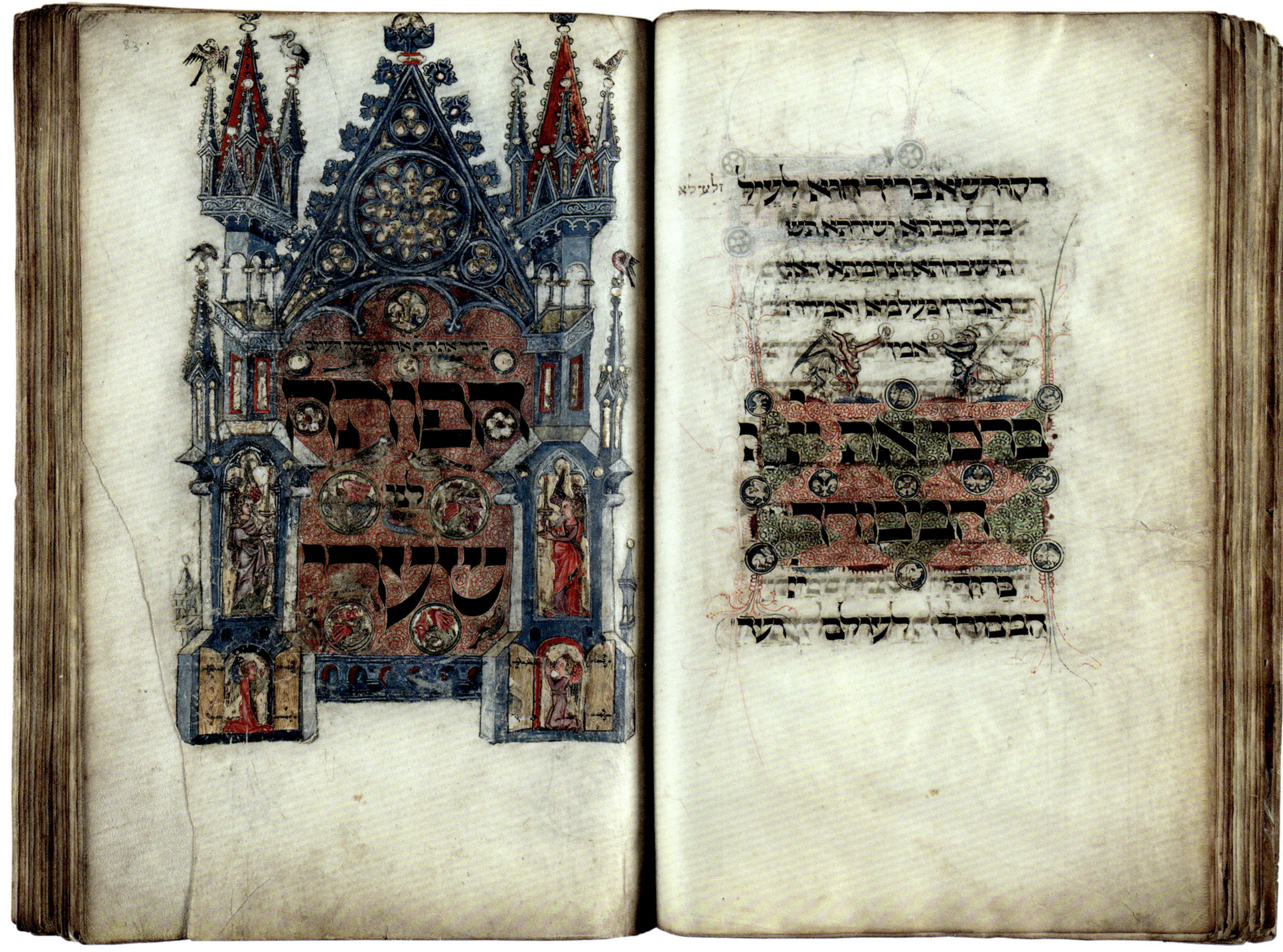

61a, fols. 82v–83r

61a

The Gates of Mercy

From the Moskowitz Rhine Mahzor
Northern Rhineland, 1340s
Tempera, gold, and ink on parchment; 179 folios
9⅛ × 6 6⅛ in. (23.3 × 15.4 cm)
The National Library of Israel, Jerusalem
(MS. Heb. 4° 5214/1)

61b

The Gates of Mercy

From the David bar Pesah Mahzor
Rhine Valley, 1348
Scribe: David bar Pesah
Tempera, gold, and ink on parchment; 577 folios
15 × 10⅝ in. (38.2 × 27 cm)
Dorot Jewish Division, New York Public Library, Astor, Lenox, and Tilden Foundation (**P, MS. Hebr. 248, vol. 2)

On Yom Kippur, the Day of Atonement, worshippers pray for the opening of the heavenly Gates of Mercy, illustrated here as contemporary Gothic edifices.

A celestial glow emanates from within the Moskowitz Rhine Mahzor's gateway on folio 83 recto, hinting at what lies beyond. Its dazzling architecture — soaring spires, hanging arches, and ethereal tracery — is described in an elaborate three-dimensional perspective, the wood grain on its shutters captured in intricate detail. Angels direct worshippers' pleas with guiding candles and clasped hands. Dragons are contained in roundels, while birds perch on every surface, adding their song to the prayer. Small spires in the lower corners suggest the city beyond.

Although compact and sturdy, the structure on folio 353 verso of the David bar Pesah Mahzor seems to strive heavenward through its rising pinnacles, the straining upward arc of its crockets, and the birds poised for flight. The undulating tonal patterns on the red columns suggest a semiprecious stone such as agate or jasper — a truly heavenly portal. Although guarded by teeth-baring lions, the open tracery of the upper register gives the gateway a sense of accessibility.

While the heavenly Gates of Mercy are invoked in this prayer, the physical Gates of Mercy were also central to Yom Kippur. During the Temple eras, the high priest would stand at the gate before the holiday, familiarizing himself with the animals to be sacrificed so that all would proceed smoothly the next day.[1] It was through this gate that the scapegoat was led into the wilderness, where its sacrifice symbolized both the futility and the banishment of the nation's collective sins.[2]

The concluding service of Yom Kippur is Ne'ilah, from Ne'ilat ha-She'arim — the Closing of the Gates. The Jerusalem Talmud relates a debate between two third-century sages as to whether this refers to the closing of the gates of heaven or the gates of the Temple.[3] The discussion continued into the Middle Ages, when both Rashi and Maimonides (Rabbi Moshe ben Maimon) addressed the question.[4] While the liturgy has come to stress the heavenly aspect, the Talmudic reasoning seems to resolve in favor of the Temple gates.[5]

The prayer "Who Opens for us the Gates of Mercy" is inserted in the first of the blessings preceding the morning Shema, the twice-daily declaration of faith in God's oneness.[6] In the Temple, priests readied the morning offering but would not perform the sacrifice until the Gates of Mercy had been opened.[7]

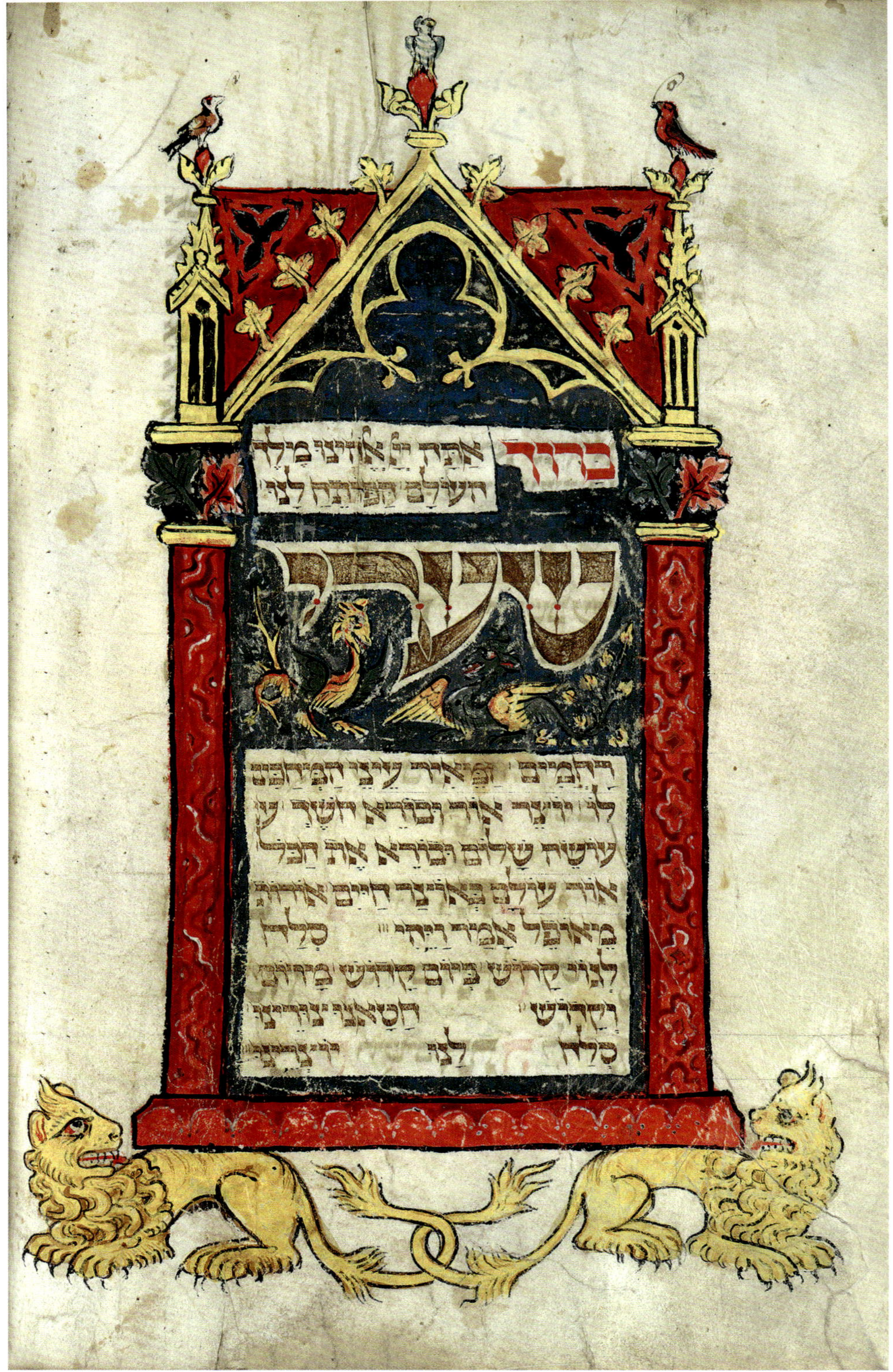

61b, fol. 353b

They next recited the blessing preceding the Shema, the Ten Commandments, and the Shema itself.[8] Structured to recall Temple services, Jewish liturgy follows this sequence.[9] A correlation thereby appears between the timing of the blessing "Who Opens for us the Gates of Mercy" in the liturgy and the opening of the physical Gates of Mercy in the Temple. In both prayer and practice, the day of Yom Kippur is bookended by the opening and closing of the Gates of Mercy. EE

Selected References: Cat. 61a: Sed-Rajna 1975, pp. 181, 187, ill. p. 186; Sed-Rajna 1986–87, pp. 47–50; Lachter 2015, pp. 193–95, fig. 227. Cat. 61b: New York 1988–89, p. 202, no. 59, cover ill.

1. Mishnah Yoma 1:3; for English, *Mishnah* 1933 ed., p. 162.
2. Mishnah Yoma 4:2; *Mishnah* 1933 ed., p. 166.
3. Rav (Rabbi Aba bar Aibo; Abba Aricha) takes the first position, Rabbi Yochanan (Rabbi Yochanan bar Nafchah) the second. Jerusalem Talmud, Tractate Berachot 4:1 (31a); for English, Jerusalem Talmud 2000 ed., pp. 345–46.
4. For Rashi, Babylonian Talmud, Tractate Taanit 26a; for English, Schottenstein Talmud 1990–2005, Tractate Taanit (1991), p. 26a: "When is Neilah? There are those who say the closing of the gates of the Temple, and there are those who say the closing of the gates of Heaven, that close at the time of evening when Tefillah is finished. And our custom has been to pray the Tefillah of Neilah at all fasts in the way that we pray on Yom Kippur." For Maimonides, *Mishneh Torah*, Hilchot Tefillah and Birkat Kohanim 1:7; for English, Maimonides 1989a ed., pp. 106–9: "This is called the Ne'ilah prayer, as if to say that the Gates of Heaven are closed behind the sun, which becomes hidden, since it is recited only close to sunset."
5. Jerusalem Talmud, Tractate Berachot 4:1 (31a); for English, Jerusalem Talmud 2000 ed., pp. 345–46 (with some revisions to the translation by the author): "A Mishnah supports Rabbi Yochanan (Mishna Taanit 4:1): 'At three periods of the year the priests shall raise their hands [to bless the people] four times in one day, in the morning service, additional service, afternoon service, and at the locking of the gates. [The three mentioned periods are on] the fast-days, at support services [*ma'amadot*], and on the Day of Atonement.' [The priestly blessing can only be recited during daytime, therefore] can one say that the gates of heaven are locked while it is still daytime?" Rav later refers to *Ne'ilah* as the Closing of the Gates of the Temple, but because "he needed a lot of time to pray, he reached the Locking of the Gates of Heaven."
6. *Yotzer Ohr* – Fashioner of Light.
7. The "Great Gate." Mishnah Tamid 3:7; for English, *Mishnah* 1933 ed., p. 584.
8. Mishnah Tamid 5:1; *Mishnah* 1933 ed., p. 586. For the debate as to which of the blessings preceding the Shema this was, see Babylonian Talmud, Tractate Berachot 11b; for English, Schottenstein Talmud 1990–2005, Tractate Berachot (1997), p. 11b; and Jerusalem Talmud, Tractate Berachot 1.8 (9b); Jerusalem Talmud 2000 ed., p. 122, and Maimonides on Mishnah Tamid 5:1.
9. Minus the Ten Commandments, which were removed from the liturgy in the Mishnaic period (70–200). The Shema serves as the opportunity to commemorate the Ten Commandments. On the deliberate structuring of liturgy to mirror Temple service, see Babylonian Talmud, Seder Zeraim, Tractate Berachot 26b; Schottenstein Talmud 1990–2005, Tractate Berachot (1997), p. 26b.

62a–c

Medieval Jewish Marriage Rings

a. Jewish Wedding Ring

Germany, first half of the 14th century
Gold with enamel
H. 1⅝ in. (4 cm), W. 1 in. (2.6 cm), D. ⅝ in. (1.7 cm)
Private collection, New York

b. Jewish Wedding Ring

Germany, first half of the 14th century
Gold with enamel
H. 1⅜ in. (3.5 cm)
Musée de Cluny, Musée National du Moyen Âge, Paris (Cl. 20658)

c. Jewish Wedding Ring

Germany, first half of the 14th century
Gold
H. 1⅞ in. (4.8 cm), W. 1 in. (2.5 cm), D. 1 in. (2.5 cm)
Thüringisches Landesamt für Denkmalpflege und Archäologie, Weimar (5067/98)

In 1826 the first discovery of a coin and object hoard dating before 1348, the era of the Black Death, was unearthed in Weissenfels, near Speyer, Germany.[1] Among the jewelry was a gold ring with a house-shaped bezel engraved with the Hebrew words *mazal tov* (good luck), a traditional wish at weddings (fig. 58). The

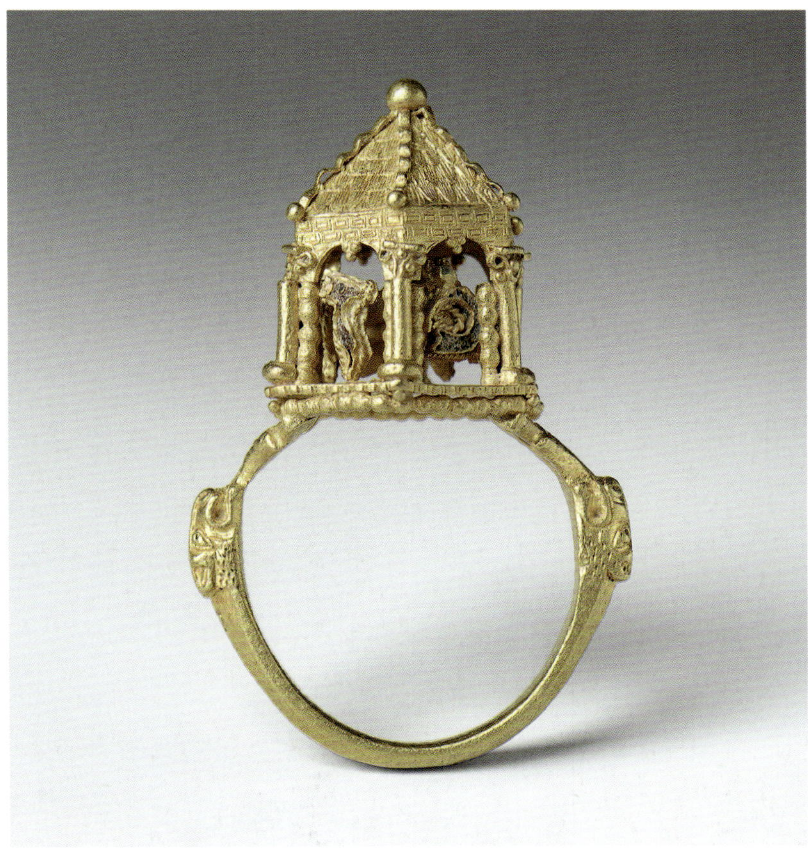

62a

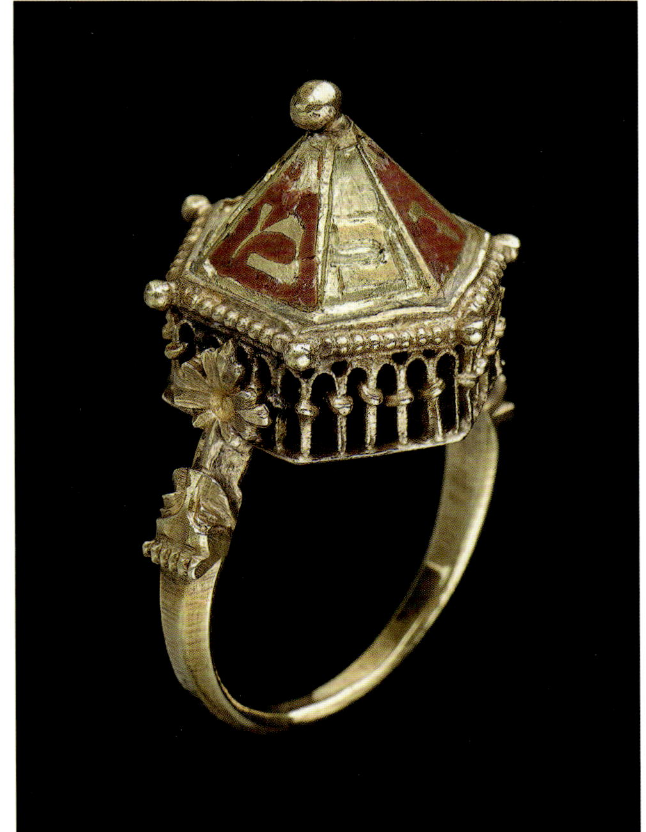

62b

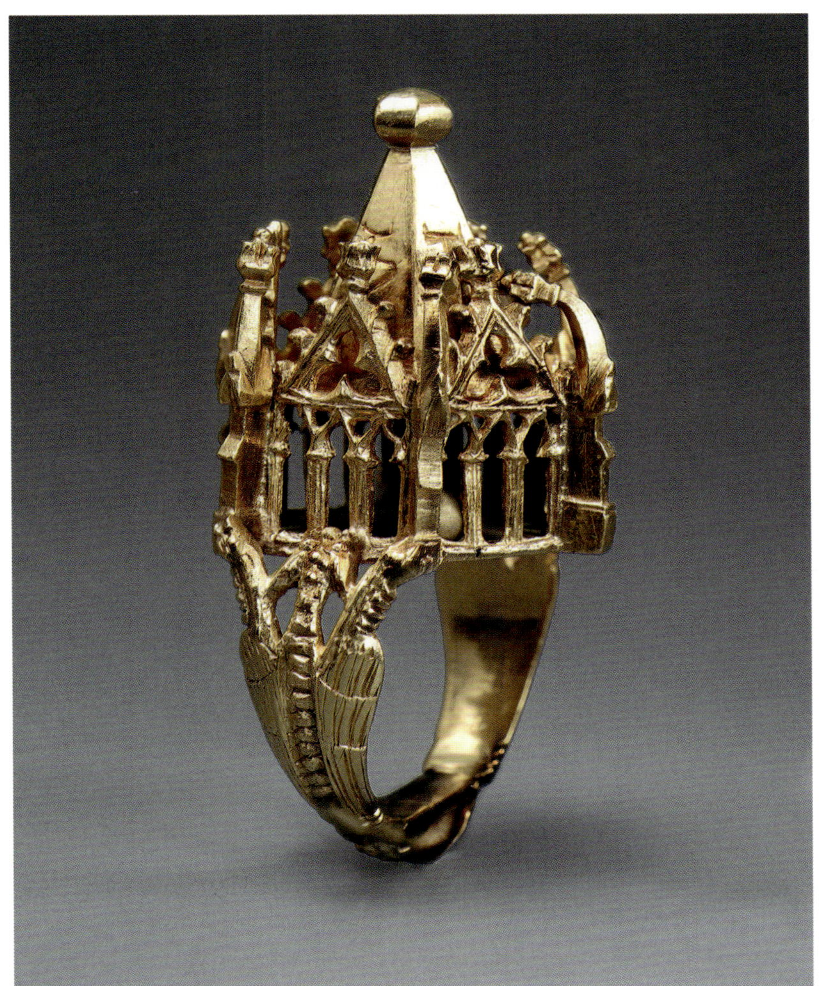

62c

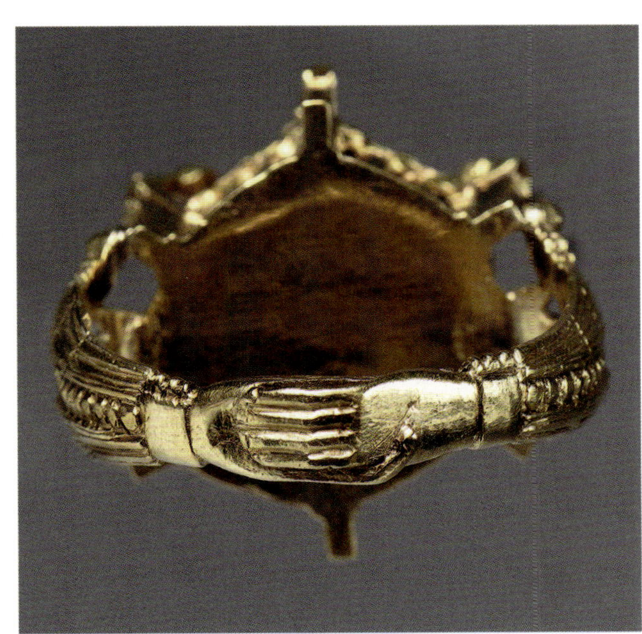

62c back view

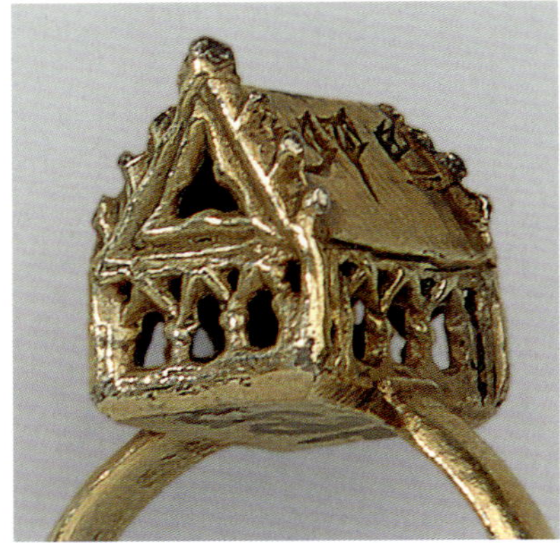

Fig. 58. Jewish wedding ring, from the Weissenfels treasure. Early 14th century. Silver. Staatliche Galerie Moritzburg, Halle, Germany (Mo. LMK. E.162)

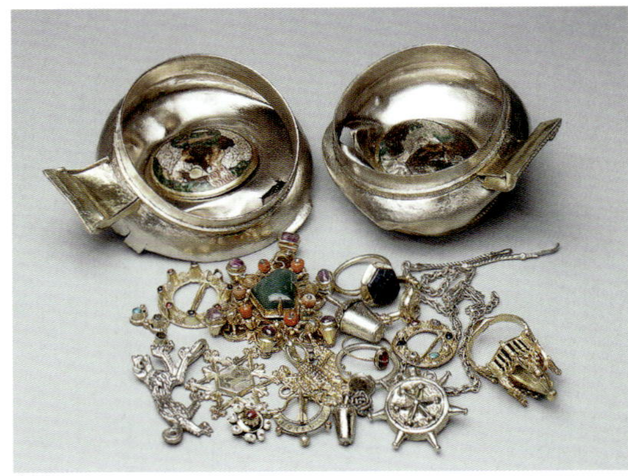

Fig. 59. The Erfurt hoard. Erfurt, Germany, 14th century. Gold, silver, bronze, iron, and organic material. Thüringisches Landesamt für Denkmalpflege und Archäologie, Erfurt

next hoard appeared in Colmar, in present-day France, in 1863. It consisted of a wider range of objects of art and jewelry, including another gold ring surmounted by a hexagonal bezel supported by columns whose facets are inlaid with red enamel, each with a Hebrew letter that together spell *mazal tov* (cat. 62b). The discovery of these two hoards in the nineteenth century was followed by several others in the twentieth century and by the finding of precious objects presumably immured in the same period, such as the nested silver beakers uncovered from the wall of a Gothic house in Kutná Hora (formerly Kuttenberg, a center for silver mining in medieval Bohemia).[2] The most recently found hoard, that from Erfurt, is also the largest: 3,141 coins, the latest a *tournois* of Adolph VIII of Berg last minted in 1348; 600 works fashioned by goldsmiths – jewelry, clothing ornaments, and drinking vessels; and fourteen rare, hallmarked silver ingots (fig. 59).[3] Among the jewelry is a large marriage ring with an architectural bezel whose hexagonal roof is inscribed *mazal tov* (cat. 62c). Only two other Jewish marriage rings with architectural bezels were published prior to the discovery of the Erfurt hoard; one in the Munich Schatzkammer, dating to before 1598, in the form of a Gothic tower,[4] and another found in Pest featuring a gabled house.[5] The sixth extant medieval ring, in a private collection (cat. 62a), also has an architectural bezel with a hexagonal roof.[6]

Although the Black Death probably came to Europe aboard ships sailing from the East, the Jews in German lands were blamed and persecuted. By March 1349 the plague had reached Erfurt; in the same month, over one hundred Jews were killed and more died of the plague, with the result that the Jewish community there disbanded for ten years.[7] The same scenario repeated in numerous German cities, so that many of the owners who had hidden coins and objects did not return to retrieve them. The significance of the hoards for a history of Gothic silver is reflected in the estimate that less than one percent of the silver works fashioned in the Gothic period survive, and that 90 percent of those works belonged to the Church.[8] The discovery of the hoards has greatly enlarged the corpus of secular silver dated to the late thirteenth and fourteenth centuries.

Some of the drinking vessels may have been used in Jewish ceremonies, yet their forms are indistinguishable from those made for Christians.[9] The rings, however, are singular in having architectural bezels inscribed *mazal tov*, which indicates their use in connection with Jewish weddings and may represent the oft-cited Talmudic trope that the groom's "wife is his house."[10] But the hexagonal shape of four of the six architectural bezels suggests these rings incorporate the image of a particular building, the Dome of the Rock, built between 687 and 691, which represented the Temple to the Crusaders, who named it the Templum Domini.[11]

While the placing of the ring on a bride's finger signifies her consecration to the groom and is an integral part of a Jewish wedding, the ceremony also incorporates customs expressing the obligation to remember the destruction of the Temple even at moments of intense joy. Crushing a glass at the conclusion is one example of the customs still practiced.[12] By contrast, the rings with architectural bezels that reference the Temple were used only in the first half of the fourteenth century and became known after the publication of the Weissenfels hoard in 1826. Subsequently, the possession of an elaborate Jewish marriage ring, with or without architectural bezels, became highly desired by collectors and led to the predictable consequence: the production of fakes and copies.

The exact use of the genuine fourteenth-century rings within a Jewish marriage is still unknown. Jewish law (Halakah) requires that the ring given to a bride at her wedding be worth a specific monetary value; therefore, it should be without stones and easily evaluated.[13] What can be said with certainty is that travel and pilgrimages to Jerusalem and other holy sites in the Land of Israel increased under the influence of the Crusaders and, at the same time, disseminated an image of the Temple as the hexagonal Dome of the Rock. VBM

Selected References: Fritz 1982, pp. 231, 238, 275; Mann, V., 1988, pp. 13–14; Stürzebecher 2010, pp. 167, 170, 220, 278.

1. For a recent discussion of all the hoards, see Stürzebecher 2010, pp. 158–89, and catalogue, nos. 214–302. On the 1998 Erfurt finds, see Ostritz, ed. 2010a, pp. 65–133. For technical analyses of these objects, see Ostritz, ed. 2010b.
2. Stürzebecher 2010, pp. 174–76. The beakers were one of three Jewish works published in Fritz 1982: p. 231, no. 318, the Weissenfels wedding ring; p. 238, no. 376, the five nested beakers from Kutná Hora; and p. 275, no. 641, the Double Cup from Erbach (with mistranslated Hebrew inscription).
3. Stürzebecher 2010, pp. 185–89, and catalogue, nos. 1–77.
4. Cologne 1963–64, no. E162, fig. 50.
5. Scheiber 1983, pp. 385–87.
6. A seventh medieval ring, now lost, is described in the 1853 catalogue of Lady Londesborough's collection as acquired from the Debruge-Dumenil sale. As on the Colmar and Erfurt rings, lions' or dragons' heads support a faceted bezel inscribed "two" and a variant of "good." Croker et al. 1853, p. 5, no. 2.1.
7. Stürzebecher 2010, p. 156; Lämmerhirt 2010, pp. 347–49.
8. Fritz 1982, pp. 33–35.
9. Mann, V., 1988, pp. 16–22.
10. Mishna Yoma 1.1.
11. The earliest representation of the Temple as the Dome of the Rock in Jewish art appears in a fifteenth-century manuscript of Maimonides's *Mishneh Torah* (cat. 64), for which earlier pilgrimage guides may have served as a source. On the association of the Dome of the Rock with the Temple, see Berger 2012 and Weiss 1997–98.
12. Daniel Sperber has suggested that the bride's wearing of a ring with a house-shaped bezel signified her marking of the destruction of the Temple amid the joy of marrying (Sperber 1989, pp. 143–48). He erred, however, in accepting the authenticity of Jewish marriage rings modeled on the fourteenth-century examples, rather than seeing them as fakes created for collectors in the nineteenth century. In actuality, the rings with architectural bezels have a short history, whereas the customs associated with the groom have been ongoing, which suggests that the medieval rings with house-shaped bezels were not considered essential to the marriage ceremony.
13. Sperling n.d., par. 974.

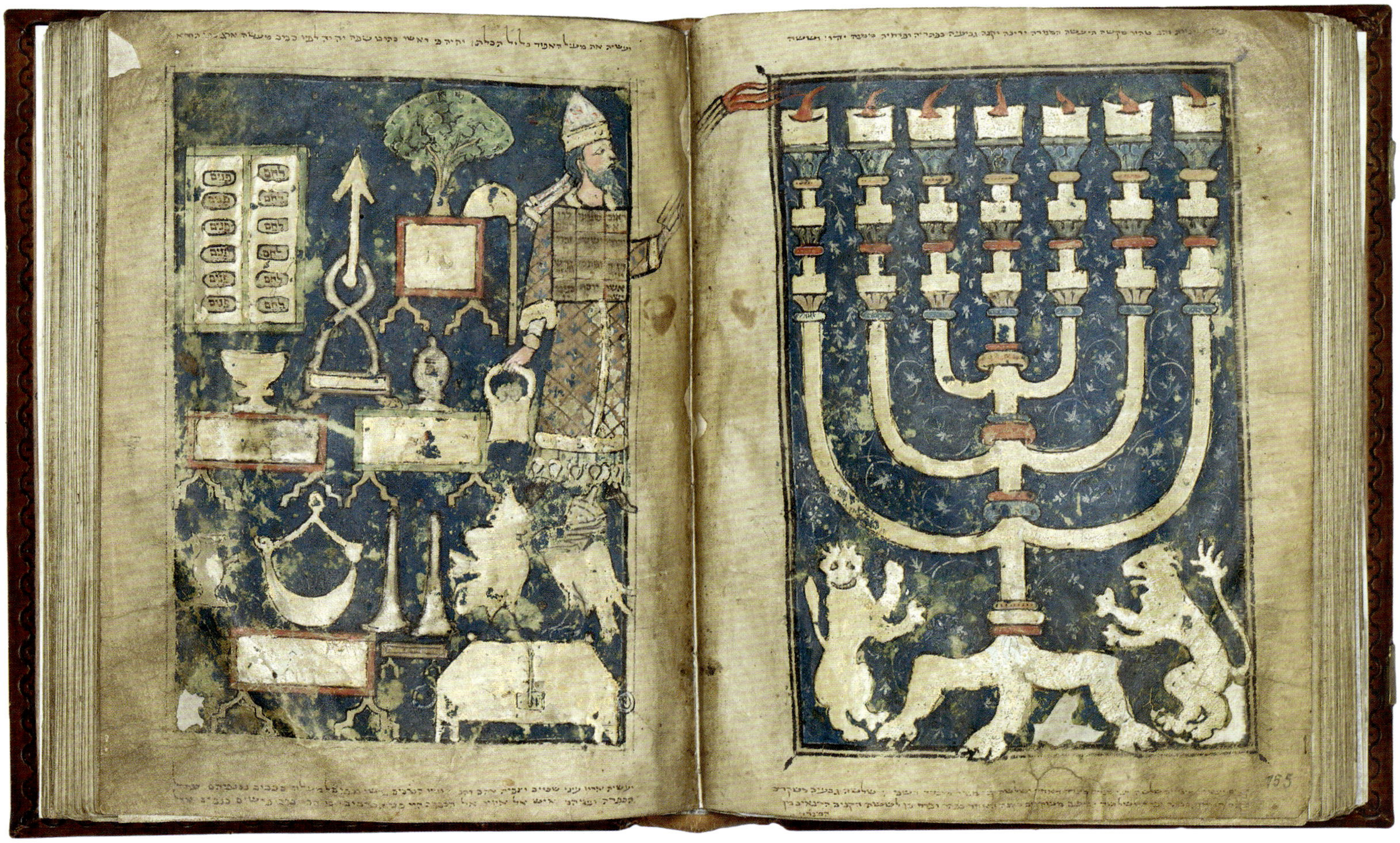

63, fols. 155v–156r

63

Aaron Lighting the Temple Menorah

From the Regensburg Pentateuch
Regensburg, Germany, ca. 1300
Scribes: David ben Shabetai and Baruch
Masorete: Jacob ben Meir and three anonymous collaborators
Tempera, gold, and ink on parchment; 246 folios
9⅝ × 7¼ in. (24.5 × 18.5 cm)
The Israel Museum, Jerusalem (BOS.0009)

Created for Gad ben Peter ha-Levi, head of the Jewish community of Regensburg, this manuscript contains the text of the Five Books of Moses, or the Torah, as well as special liturgical readings from Prophets (Nevi'im) and Writings (Ketuvim). Three full-page images mark the transition from the book of Deuteronomy to the book of Esther: first, Moses receives the Ten Commandments from God and transmits the law to the Israelites (folio 154v); then, the high priest Aaron tends to God's sanctuary on earth by lighting the menorah (folios 155 verso–156 recto); finally, Esther and Mordecai triumph over Haman, saving the Jewish people from an impending massacre (folio 157). Together, this series of images forms a bridge joining two disparate texts and emphasizes the relationship among law, ritual, and redemption. In addition, it reminds the modern viewer that figural imagery was occasionally used to illuminate Hebrew manuscripts.

Only the image of the sanctuary vessels is accorded two full folios. In it, Aaron reaches across the margin in order to light the enormous seven-branch menorah. He wears all the trappings of the high priest: the miter, breastplate, and long robe fringed with bells. He is surrounded by the accoutrements for God's dwelling place on earth – whether the portable sanctuary erected in the desert or, later, the Temple in Jerusalem. These ritual implements, which were once completely gilded, would have shimmered brilliantly against the blue background. They provide visual representations of the artifacts of the holy sanctuary – drawn from descriptive biblical texts and reimagined in rabbinic commentaries – that would spur imagination and contemplation. They also highlight the inextricable link between the Bible and the Temple and God and the Jewish people. AK

Selected References: Narkiss 1969, pp. 98–99, pl. 29; Frojmovic 2007, pp. 11–22, pl. 2.1; Kogman-Appel 2009, pp. 245–77.

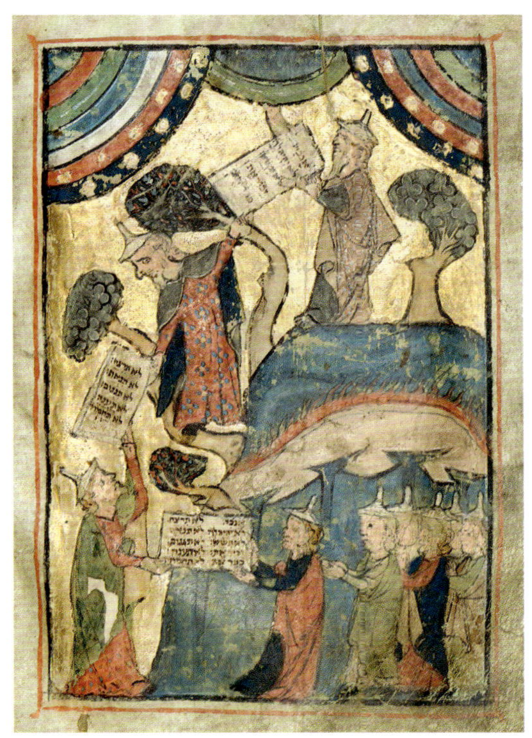

63, fol. 154v

64

The Book of Divine Service

From the *Mishneh Torah* of Maimonides (1135–1204)
Illumination attributed to the Master of the Barbo Missal
Scribe: Nehemiah for Moshe Anauv be Yitzchak
Northern Italy, ca. 1457
Tempera, gold leaf, and ink on parchment; 346 folios
Folio: 9 × 7¼ in. (22.7 × 18.4 cm)
Jointly owned by the Israel Museum, Jerusalem, and The Metropolitan Museum of Art, New York, 2013. Purchased for the Israel Museum through the generosity of an anonymous donor; René and Susanne Braginsky, Zurich; Renée and Lester Crown, Chicago; Schusterman Foundation, Israel; and Judy and Michael Steinhardt, New York. Purchased for The Metropolitan Museum of Art with Director's Funds and Judy and Michael Steinhardt Gift (2013.495)

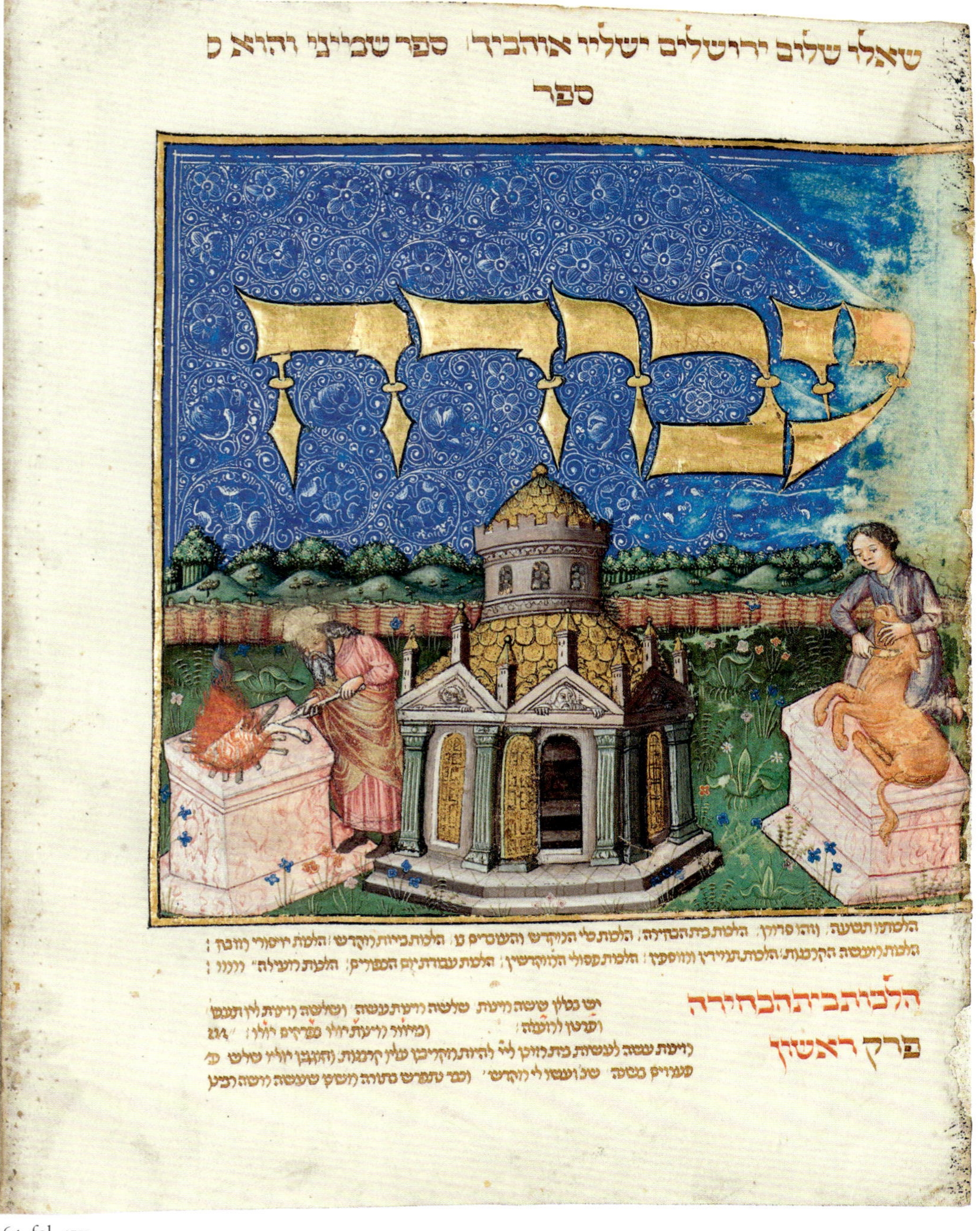

64, fol. 41v

In the courtyard of the Temple, two priests perform ancient sacrificial rites. Between them, the Temple glitters brilliantly while, beyond, the Judean hills roll softly into the distance. Overhead, emblazoned on an intricately patterned azure sky is the word *Avodah*, meaning "divine service." This illumination illustrates a manuscript copy of the eighth book of Maimonides's magnum opus, the *Mishneh Torah*, originally written between 1170 and 1180.[1] In this monumental work, Maimonides codified and clarified all of Jewish law, distilling biblical, Talmudic, and rabbinic sources into a lucid and systematic guide. He wrote its fourteen volumes in Hebrew rather than Talmudic Aramaic so that the contents would be accessible to all, no matter the reader's level of scholarship.[2]

This section of the *Mishneh Torah* is devoted to the construction and worship of the Holy Temple, including detailed descriptions of its services and vessels. The Temple had been destroyed for over a millennium before Maimonides's writing, yet it is described in the present tense. This sense of immediacy and the desire to understand the Temple's blueprint on a technical level were crucial to a community that was not only studying the historic Temple but also forever readying itself for the Messianic one.[3] Maimonides prefaced this section with a passage from Psalms: "Pray for the peace of Jerusalem, may those who love [it] enjoy tranquility" (Psalms 122:6). He numbered among those, recalling with reverence his own time spent on the Temple Mount,[4] a day he vowed to commemorate in perpetuity as "a festival, a day of prayer and rejoicing in God, for festivities and eating and drinking."[5]

Such sumptuous illuminations are rare for a book of law, and their commission from an artist employed by the highest echelons of Italian society attests to the high esteem in which Maimonides's work was held, as well as to the taste of the patron.[6] The artist modeled the illustrations after his known world, visible in the contemporary dress and architectural details, as well as in the textually inaccurate—albeit magnificent—pink-veined marble altars.

EE

Selected References: Wischnitzer 1935, pp. 51–52, figs. 3–5; Narkiss 1969, pp. 160–61, pl. 60; Boehm and Holcomb 2014.

1. Maimonides himself calls it his *hibbur hagadol*, or "great treatise." Maimonides 1987 ed., vol. 1, p. 236, ll. 9–10.

2. See Maimonides's preface to the *Mishneh Torah*. For English, see Maimonides 1989b ed., pp. 30–33. Hebrew was the single common language of Jewish communities around the globe, and, by 1191, Maimonides spoke of his great work having gained renown in every corner of the Jewish world, from Asia and Africa to Europe.

3. Maimonides 2007 ed., p. 106, Hilchot Beit ha-Bechira 7:7: "Even though the Temple is now in ruin, . . . a person must hold it[s site] in awe, as one would regard it when it was standing."

4. Maimonides did not prohibit entering the Temple complex but only standing within the footprint of the Temple building itself; so great a scholar of the Temple would have known where the permissible areas such as the courtyard would have once been. Maimonides 2007 ed., p. 108, Hilchot Beit ha-Bechira 7:7: "One should not enter except where one is permitted. One should not sit in the Temple courtyard or act frivolously while standing at the Eastern Gate." Maimonides is outlining proper conduct, not prohibiting access. The Hebrew terms used by Maimonides sometimes refer to the complex as a whole, not merely the building itself.

5. Azkari 1981 ed., pp. 253–54. He also recalled the visit in his Epistle to Yemen: "When we departed from the West to gaze upon the graciousness of the Lord, to visit his Temple" (Twersky, ed. 1972, pp. 437–62, sec. 1), as well as in a letter to Japheth ben Eli of Acre: "All four of us [Maimonides's father, brother, Japheth, and himself] walked together in God's house in fear and trepidation. . . . I shall not forget our wandering together in wastelands and forests after the Lord" (Maimonides, letter to Japheth ben Eli, in Maimonides 1987 ed., vol. 1, p. 230; for English, Kraemer 2008, p. 137).

6. The artist decorated manuscripts for the aristocracy and for high-ranking religious officials, patrons who were "known for their discerning taste and lavish expenditures" (Holcomb and Boehm 2014, p. 23).

65

Opening Prayer for Shabbat Shekalim

From the Worms Mahzor, vol. I
Probably Würzburg, Germany, 28 Tevet 5032 (1272)
Scribe: Simcha ben Yehudah, for his uncle, R. Baruch ben Yitzchak
Tempera, gold, and ink on parchment; 242 folios
15⅜ × 12¼ in. (39 × 31 cm)
The National Library of Israel, Jerusalem (MS 4° 781/1)

Opening this mahzor is a liturgical poem for Shabbat Shekalim, one of the four Sabbaths of the year with an additional Torah portion (folio 1 verso).[1] The reading describes a yearly census of the Israelites conducted by collecting a half-shekel coin from every adult male.[2] The tax subsidized communal sacrifices and maintenance of the Tabernacle — and later the Temple in Jerusalem. After the Temple's destruction, the funds were allocated for worthy causes, with some medieval communities in the Rhineland reserving their donations for those traveling to the Holy Land, in commemoration of the collection's original destination.[3]

The figure under the arch could be a money changer exchanging foreign currency for the prescribed half-shekel coin outside the Temple gates.[4] The scales bear the words *shekel* and *Israel*, perhaps illustrating the tallying of the census by the counting of coins, but the imbalance suggests that the fate of the nation is being weighed against a sum of money. Shabbat Shekalim coincides with the start of the month of Adar (alluded to by the calendrical imagery of the heavenly luminaries), and the holiday of Purim falls shortly thereafter.[5] The Talmud explains that the shekel collection was instituted preemptively to counteract the money paid by Haman, the antagonist of Purim, for the right to annihilate the Jews.[6] This figure could alternatively represent Haman himself, noticeably lacking the hat identifying all Jewish figures in the Mahzor and depicted further on in similar red garb.[7] The expiatory significance of the tax is inherent in both the poem and the Bible, which calls it "silver of atonement,"[8] and is reinforced by imagery of savage beasts threatening the balance while the Hebrew word *El* (God) hovers protectively above.[9]

Inscribed in red within the black initial letter, perhaps by the owner himself, is the message "Mine, Baruch son of Yitzchak, may his memory be a blessing." EE

Selected References: Narkiss 1969, pp. 92–93, pl. 26; Metzger, T., and Metzger 1982, p. 257; Beit-Arié 1985; Jerusalem 1985, p. 22, no. 33, pl. 6.

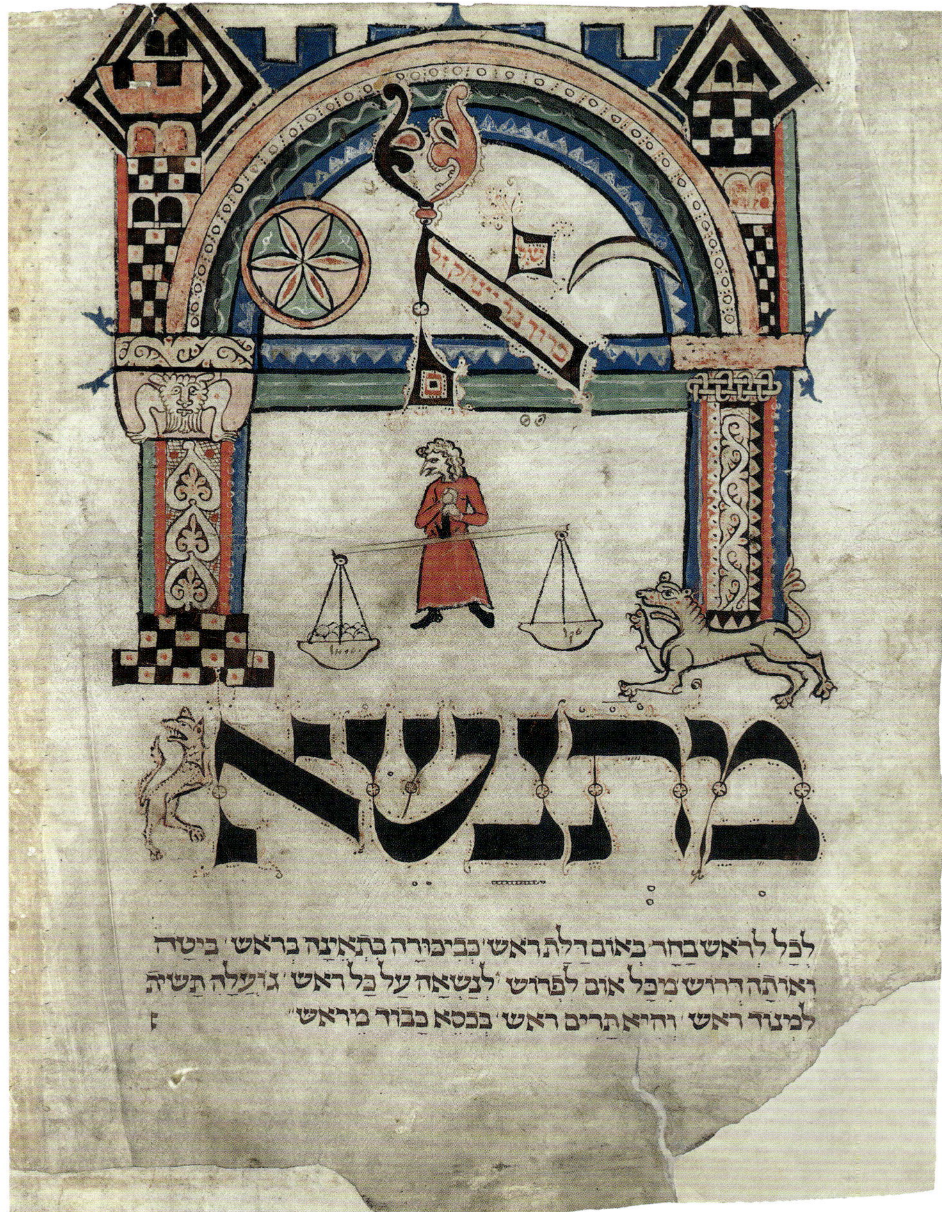

65, fol. 1v

1. Attributed to R. Eleazar ben Kalir (c. 570–c. 640).
2. Exodus 30:11–16.
3. As decreed by the great German rabbinic authority, Rabbi Jacob ben Moshe ha-Levi Moelin (called the Maharil, ca. 1365–1427), "The half-shekel is given to support those who go to the Holy Land for the sake of Heaven." Moelin 1960 ed., p. 596.
4. Wischnitzer 1960, p. 24.
5. The imagery is repeated on Shabbat HaChodesh, fol. 26v, which commemorates the commandment to sanctify the start of each month.
6. Babylonian Talmud, Tractate Megillah 13b, quoted in Offenberg 2014, p. 5. This ancient idea is reiterated in the Holy Land in the ninth century in Tractate Soferim 21:4 (Cohen, A., ed. 1965, vol. 1, p. 318).
7. Only Haman's family, illustrated on fol. 19r, and the personifications of both the zodiac and the months are depicted without the Jewish hats.
8. Exodus 30:16.
9. Wischnitzer 1960, p. 25.

66

Menorah

From a Hebrew Bible
Rome or Bologna, Italy, last quarter of the 13th century
Tempera, gold, and ink on parchment; 262 folios
15⅜ × 10¼ in. (39 × 26 cm)
British Library, London (MS Harley 5710)

Yoav Fosco bar Binyamin was a member of the Italian banking company that lent vital funds to the cities of Perugia and Todi at the end of the thirteenth century on the heels of the declaration of the expulsion of the Jews from Perugia in 1279.[1] The company granted the loan on the condition that the cities acknowledge and protect the religious and civil liberties of their Jewish citizens.[2] Yoav owned a number of the most beautiful Italian Hebrew illuminated manuscripts, including this two-volume Hebrew Bible.[3]

Richly painted initial word panels elaborated with delicate pen work introduce each book of the Bible, and the monumental menorah of the Temple marks the end of the Pentateuch (folio 136 recto). The large text just below its arms quotes Numbers 8:4: “And this is the work of the Menorah.” Its structure and details conform to the biblical text and the scholarship of Maimonides; each section of the menorah — its flames, flowers, knops, cups, stem, and base — is annotated with labels, measurements, and exegetical elaborations drawn from both sources.[4] The flowers — whose petals curve outward, as specified by Maimonides — are here charmingly interpreted as fleurs-de-lis.[5] While the Temple menorah was made of pure gold, the artist has utilized an array of rich colors that highlight the textural patterns of its surface.[6]

Beneath the menorah’s base, two trees sprout from small mounds, calling to mind illustrations of the Mount of Olives in Jerusalem (cat. 69). They flank the central leg, which encases a fleeing hare — sometimes seen as a symbol of persecution.[7] This configuration could be the visual manifestation of a hope for the Messianic deliverance of an oppressed people (see cat. 68). The inclusion of this folio at the completion of the Pentateuch and the presence of the shofar-blowing hybrid creatures suggest the menorah’s larger significance as a sign of the Temple as a whole. The menorah and other Temple implements were popular and powerful images in Jewish art throughout the centuries and across geographic borders.[8]

EE

Selected References: Narkiss 1969, pp. 36–37; Narkiss 1998, pp. 84–85; Tahan 2007, p. 30, fig. 17.

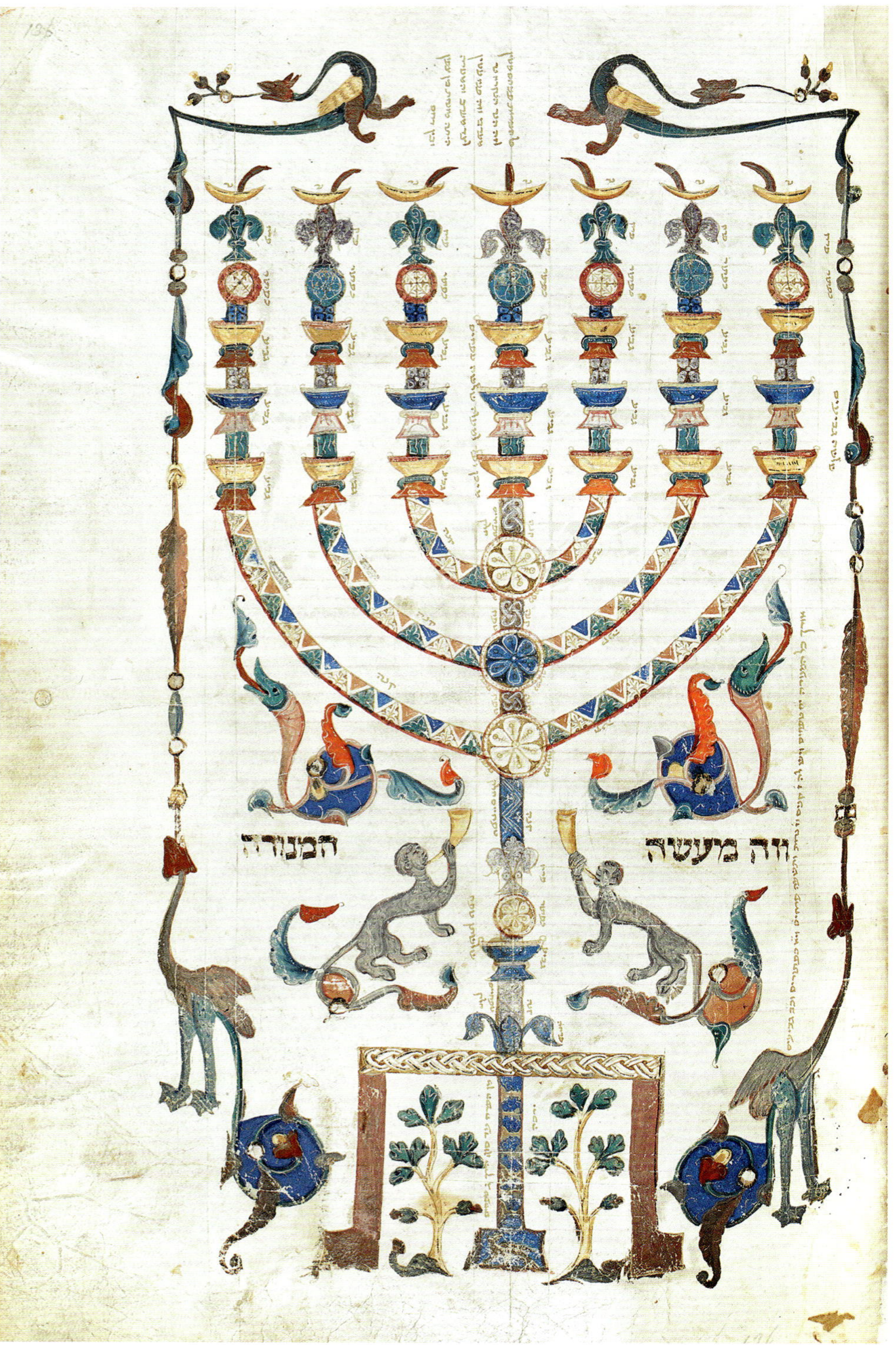

66, fol. 136r

1. “Fosco di Beniamino” in the charters. Mortara Ottolenghi 1993–94, pp. 87–88.

2. For the respective charters, see Toaff 1993, p. 19, doc. 25; p. 29, doc. 28 (which refers to p. 22, doc. 27, for its conditions).

3. Mortara Ottolenghi 1993–94, pp. 87–88.

4. Exodus 25:31–37 and Maimonides, *Mishneh Torah, Sefer Avodah*, Hilchot Beit ha-Bechira, chap. 3; for English, Maimonides 2007 ed., pp. 42–55. Knops are ornamental knobs or bulbs.

5. Maimonides, *Mishneh Torah, Sefer Avodah*, Hilchot Beit ha-Bechira 3:9; Maimonides 2007 ed., pp. 48–49: “The flowers resemble the flowers of a column. They are shaped like bowls, with the edges bent over outward.”

6. Exodus 25:31: “And you shall make a menorah of pure gold”; Maimonides, *Mishneh Torah, Sefer Avodah*, Hilchot Beit ha-Bechira 3:2; Maimonides 2007 ed., pp. 42–45. Maimonides understood the words to mean embossed or hammered all over, so that the surface pattern resembled little almonds. Rashi on Exodus 25:33 interpreted the word as *niello*. For English, Rashi 1995–2008 ed., vol. 2, p. 338, 25:33.

7. “In medieval Jewish art the hunting of a deer or a hare allegorized the persecutions of Jews.” Offenberg 2011, p. 12, and see his n. 9 for earlier literature.

8. Early depictions of the menorah are found in the Magdala Stone, 100–50 B.C., Israel Antiquities Authority, Jerusalem; the Beit Alpha Synagogue floor mosaic, near Beit She’an, Israel, 6th century; the First Saint Petersburg Pentateuch, 929, National Library of Russia, Saint Petersburg, Firkovich Collection, MS II B17. For Catalan and Castilian examples of depictions of menorahs, see cat. 137a–d; for Ashkenazic and Italian examples, see Stern, D., 2012, pp. 46–47 n. 109.

67

Opening Prayer for Shabbat Parah

From the Michael Mahzor
Germany, 1257–58
Scribe: Judah bar Samuel (Zaltman)
Tempera and ink on parchment; 136 folios
16¼ × 11 in. (41.3 × 27.9 cm)
Bodleian Libraries, University of Oxford (MS Mich. 617)

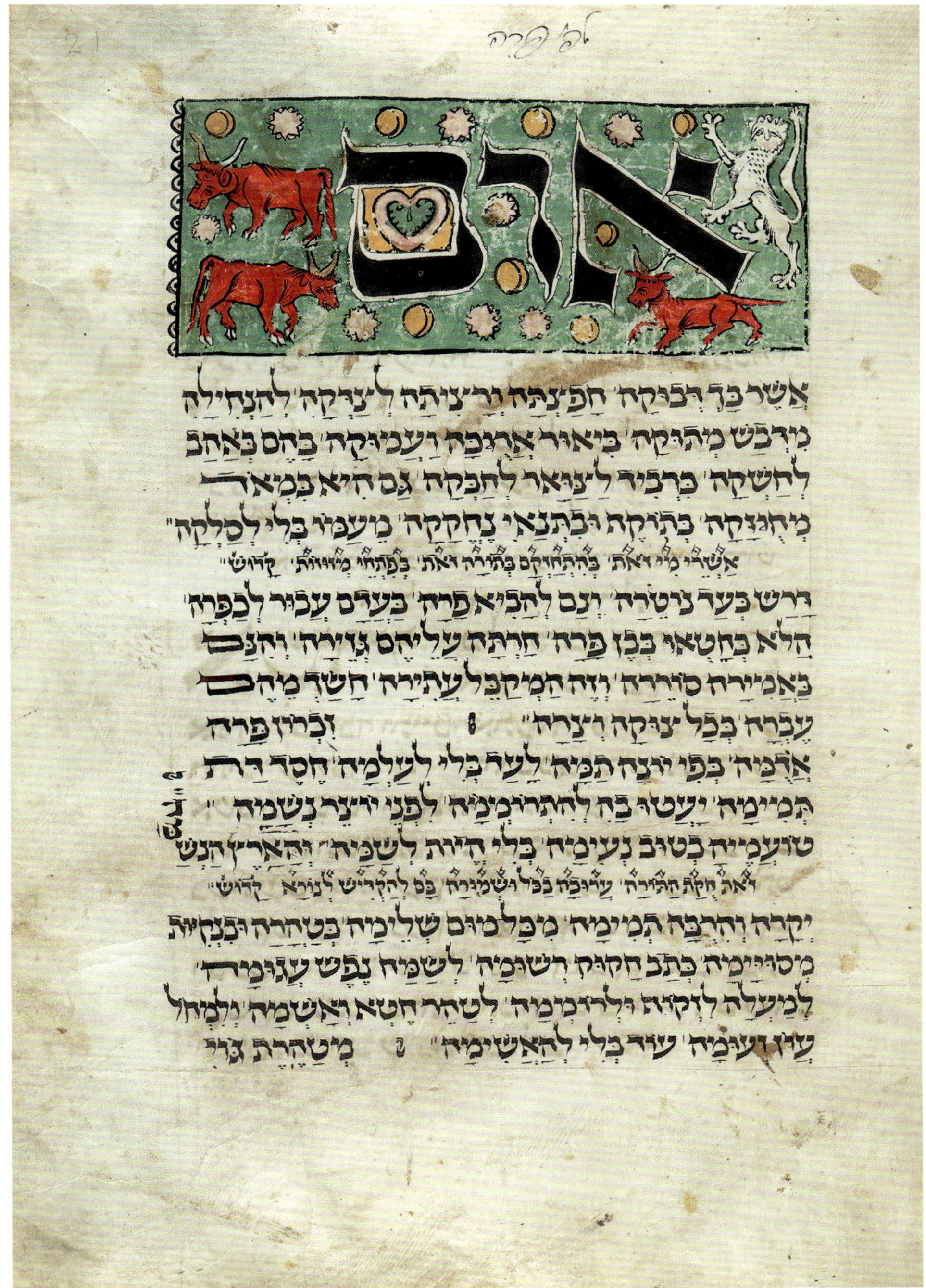

67, fol. 21r

In this earliest of dated mahzors, a herd of red heifers ambles across a green field dotted with suns, moons, and a rampant lion, marking the introductory prayers of Shabbat Parah (folio 21 recto). During the Temple periods, Jews celebrated the holidays of Passover, Shavuot, and Sukkot by traveling to Jerusalem to offer sacrifices and participate in Temple services. Before presenting the Passover offering, pilgrims underwent a ritual purification that involved the sprinkling of the ashes of a red heifer.[1] The High Priest would pass through the Eastern Gate, ascend the Mount of Olives, and there conduct the ceremony while directing his gaze back over the eastern wall toward the Temple itself.[2]

The process is outlined in Parshat Parah, an excerpt from the Book of Numbers read on one of four special Sabbaths of the year to receive an extra Torah portion.[3] Recited three weeks before Passover on the Sabbath following the holiday of Purim, the selection served as a timely reminder to ready oneself for pilgrimage to Jerusalem, as it was a two-week journey from the farthest border of the Land of Israel and the purification process itself spanned one week.[4] This duration is perhaps made reference to in the depiction of eight suns and eight moons alongside the heifer, indicating the seven days one remained impure, emerging cleansed on the eighth day.[5]

Accompanying this reading, the Haftarah (the corresponding selection from Prophets that is read aloud after the Torah on Sabbaths and festivals) discusses ultimate purification at the time of Redemption, revealing the Messianic import of Parshat Parah itself.[6] The continued yearly recitation of this call to the Temple epitomizes the immediacy with which Medieval Jews longed for the Redemption, always looking toward Jerusalem. EE

Selected References: Sed-Rajna 1983, pp. 13–14, 63–64; Frojmovic 2009, p. 48.

1. Although ritual purification was required before the bringing of any sacrifice, Parshat Parah was recited before Passover because, unlike other sacrifices required only of specific segments of the population, the Passover offering involved the entire nation, and therefore everyone was included in the reminder (Babylonian Talmud, Tractate Pesahim 91b, on those required to bring the sacrifice; for English, Schottenstein Talmud 1990–2005, Tractate Pesahim [1997], p. 91b).

2. On the Eastern Gate, see Mishnah Middot 1:3; for English, *Mishnah* 1933 ed., p. 590. On the Mount of Olives, see Rashi on Numbers 19:4 (Rashi 1995–2008 ed., vol. 4, p. 227), Mishnah Middot 1:3 (*Mishnah* 1933 ed., p. 590), and Mishnah Parah 3:6 (*Mishnah* 1933 ed., p. 670). Mishnah Middot 2:4 relays that the Eastern wall was built low specifically for this reason (*Mishnah* 1933 ed., p. 592).

3. Numbers 19:1–22.

4. Rashi on Babylonian Talmud, Tractate Megillah 29b; for English, Schottenstein Talmud 1990–2005, Tractate Megillah (1991), p. 29b.

5. Leviticus (14:10 and 14:23) states that after the skin of one who has been afflicted with leprosy has been inspected and deemed unblemished, he retains an impure status for seven full days, bringing his expiating offering "on the eighth day of his cleansing" (Leviticus 14:23).

6. Ezekiel 36:16–38, specifically: "And I will sprinkle clean water upon you, and you will be clean; from all your impurities and from all your abominations will I cleanse you" (Ezekiel 36:25); upon redemption, "I will multiply [the Israelites] like . . . the flocks appointed for the holy offerings, like the flocks of Jerusalem on its festivals" (Ezekiel 36:37–38). Rashi on Ezekiel 36:38 explains, "Like the flocks appointed for the holy offerings: which come to Jerusalem at the times of the Passover sacrifices" (Rosenberg, trans. 2000, vol. 2, p. 317).

68

Letter from Eli ben Ezekiel in Jerusalem to Ephraim ben Shemariah in Fustat

Jerusalem, ca. 1030
Ink on paper
6½ × 4 in. (16.5 × 10 cm)
Courtesy of The Library of The Jewish Theological Seminary, New York (ENA 4010:32)

This letter from one Jerusalem yeshiva member to another, written in Judeo-Arabic, tells of a ban of excommunication declared upon the Karaites by a few contentious Rabbanites during the festival of Hoshana Rabba.[1] The controversial decree was included among the yearly bans and blessings proclaimed on the Mount of Olives on this holiday, the seventh day of Sukkot, perhaps the most important pilgrimage of the three yearly pilgrimage festivals.[2]

The Mount of Olives is unparalleled for both its commemorative and Messianic significance. Together with the recitations of prayers on the city's gates, a visit to the mount was considered the essence of pilgrimage to Jerusalem.[3] On Sukkot, pilgrims poured into Jerusalem from near and far,[4] and on Hoshana Rabba, they encircled the Mount of Olives seven times while bearing willow branches, led by priests and accompanied by the blowing of the shofar, praying, singing, and dancing.[5] The community leader issued rulings, announced appointments to the yeshiva, and bestowed honorary titles.[6] Public mention at this ceremony was considered the highest of honors not only because of the large audience gathered[7] but also because these proclamations were issued from a most sacred site.

According to Talmudic tradition, the Divine Presence reluctantly withdrew from the First Temple in ten stages.[8] Its last post was the Mount of Olives, where it awaited the nation's repentance for three and a half years before resignedly ascending heavenward, making way for the Temple's destruction.[9] It is from this spot – called "the Footstool of God"[10] – that the Hoshana Rabba announcements were made, and it was prophesied that it is from this spot on the Mount of Olives that the Divine Spirit will return to Jerusalem at the time of Redemption.[11]

The spiritual power of the Mount of Olives was foremost in the minds of medieval Jews. Letters from Jerusalem to Fustat are filled with variations on the refrain, "We pray for you regularly on the Mount of Olives."[12] The community acquired land there after the Arab conquest and dedicated a synagogue.[13] It was only when Crusader control limited access to the site that it lost its centrality as the lifeblood of Jewish pilgrimage.[14]

EE

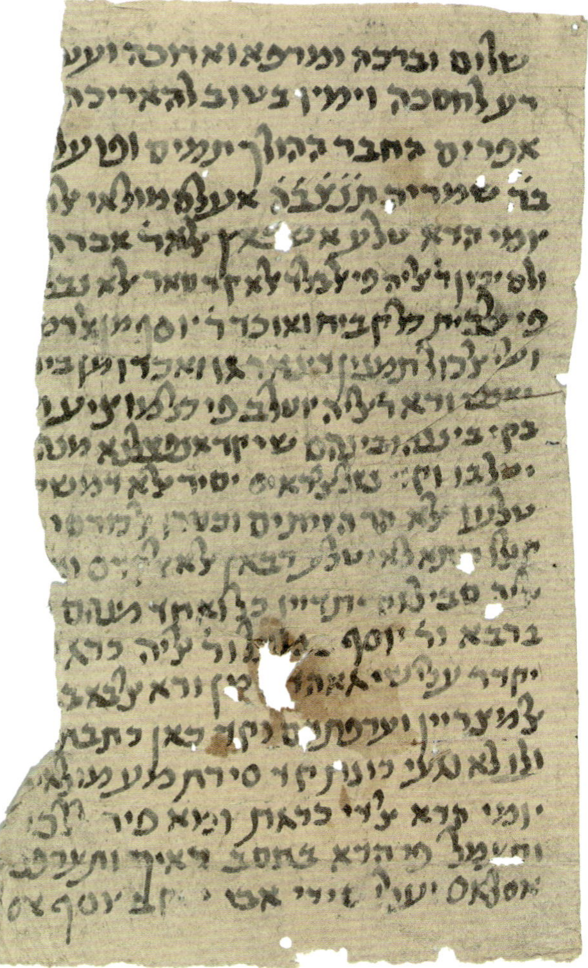

68

Selected Reference: New York 2000–2001, p. 78, no. 31.

1. The ban faced major opposition within the Rabbanite community itself and was resolved by the intervention of the Muslim authorities, who jailed the instigators in Damascus. See Gil 1992, pp. 560–61, 630, 812–13.

2. Reiner 2004, p. 41; Gil 1992, p. 628.

3. Reiner 2004, p. 38. For the prayers on the gates of Jerusalem, see Fleisher 1998.

4. Rabbi Eliyahu ben Menachem discusses the ceremony in eleventh-century France; Reiner 2004, p. 43.

5. The Jews paid an expensive tax to the Muslim authorities in return for access to the city and the holy sites and for permission to hold ceremonies and pray aloud; Gil 1996, pp. 106, 178; Gil 1992, p. 627.

6. Such rulings included the setting of the calendar.

7. Gil 1996, p. 195.

8. Buber, ed. 1899, pp. 29–30, Petichta (Opening) 25. The Babylonian Talmud, Tractate Rosh Hashana 31a relates the same concept of ten stages of removal, but the Mount of Olives is listed as the penultimate station. For English, Schottenstein Talmud 1990–2005, Tractate Rosh Hashana (1999), p. 31a.

9. Derived from Ezekiel 11:23: "And the glory of the Lord went up from the midst of the city, and stood over the mount that is on the east side of the city." The concept of the Divine Spirit resting on the Mount of Olives "was already familiar to Eusebius, the fourth-century Church historian" (Goldhill 2008, p. 75).

10. "Hadom Raglei Hashem" (Reiner 2004, p. 41); the term is found in letters of the period (Gil 1992, p. 627). The spot was also referred to in medieval times as the "Chair of the Cantors" (Gil 1996, pp. 180–81).

11. Zechariah 14:4: "And on that day His feet shall stand on the Mount of Olives, which is before Jerusalem from the east. And the Mount of Olives shall split in the midst thereof – toward the east and toward the west – a very great valley. And half the mountain shall move to the north, and half of it to the south."

12. For specific examples see Gil 1996, pp. 172, 177, and Gil 1992, pp. 626–28.

13. A letter from the Jerusalem yeshiva written in 1057 relates that after the Arab conquest of Jerusalem in 637, the Jews "bought the Mount of Olives, where the Divine Spirit had stood" (Gil 1992, p. 627). There is some disagreement as to whether this means that they purchased the land (Prawer 1988, p. 133) or rights to hold ceremonies there (Gil 1992, p. 627).

14. The Mount of Olives, Gates of Mercy, and Kidron Valley were all part of one eschatological narrative (Reiner 2004, p. 59). During Crusader rule, with Jewish pilgrims' access restricted, more "modest" modes of worship were required. The ceremonies and prayers of encircling the gates and ascending the Mount of Olives were only recalled faintly, and all the eschatological import associated with God's departure and Messianic return was transferred to the Gates of Mercy (Reiner 2004, pp. 137–38).

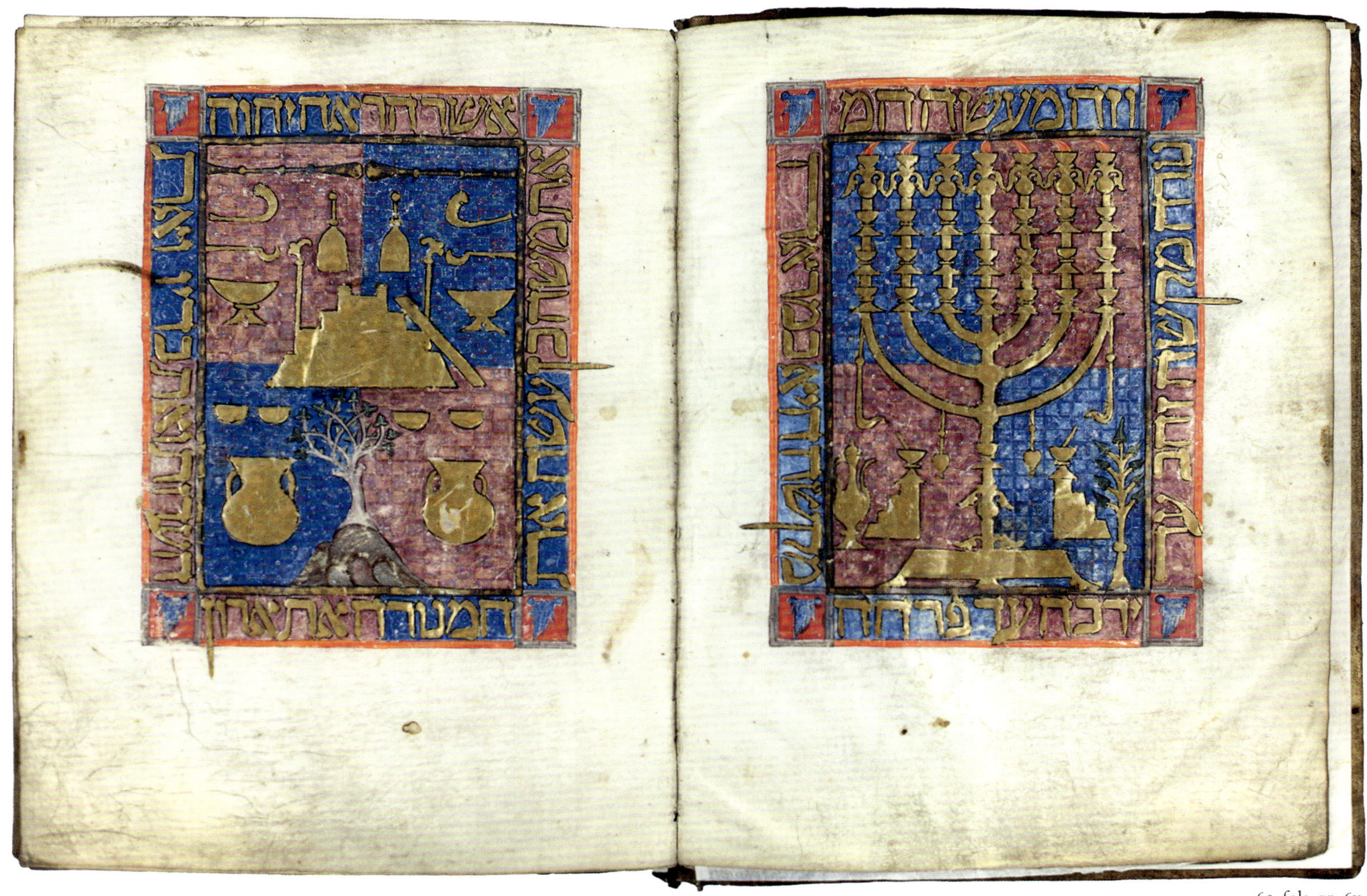

69, fols. 5r–6v

69

Temple Implements

From the Foa Bible
Catalonia, possibly Barcelona, ca. 1370–90
Tempera, gold, and ink on parchment; 344 folios
14⅛ × 10⅝ in. (36 × 27 cm)
Compagnie des Prêtres de Saint-Sulpice, Service des Archives, Paris (MS 1933)

Medieval illuminated Catalan Bibles often open with a brilliant array of the implements of the Temple, symbolizing the ascendancy of Bible study as the ultimate devotional practice after the destruction of the Temple and the cessation of sacrifice.[1] Here, the golden menorah illuminates folio 5 verso. Its tongs and scoops hang from its branches, and the steps used by the priest to light its wicks are stationed below. To its right is the flowering rod of Aaron, while the vessel of manna is on the left. The facing page illustrates the sacrificial altar with its ramp and service implements. Strikingly, the Mount of Olives – at first glance, seemingly unrelated imagery – swells below, signifying hope for the Redemption and the building of the Messianic Temple. Various vessels and musical instruments complete the display. Framing the assemblages are shining biblical passages that dictate the creation of the very implements they surround.[2] Illustrated on the following folios are the Ark of the Covenant, the incense altar, laver, shewbread table, a labeled ewer of oil, and – an unusual inclusion in Catalan Bibles – the breastplate of the High Priest.[3]

French Gothic, Italian, and Islamic artistic influences are visible within the typically Catalan style and can be found in the delicate diaper pattern and quartered red and blue background exhibited here as well as in the carpet pages and rich foliation decorating the following pages. The forms of the implements signal a knowledge of biblical scholarship, especially apparent in the inclusion of the menorah steps, which are not mentioned in the Bible and on which, Maimonides relayed, the priests would rest the oil vessels while lighting the menorah.[4] This desire on the part of the patron to capture the form of the vessels with scrupulous accuracy demonstrates the dedication of medieval Jews to both the commemoration of and preparation for the Temple in Jerusalem. EE

Selected References: Garel 1979, pp. 78–85; Sed-Rajna 1994, pp. 59–64, no. 22; Kogman-Appel 2004, pp. 150–51.

1. Wieder 1957, p. 171.
2. Fol. 5v: Numbers 8:4; fol. 6r: Numbers 8:4 and Exodus 39:35; continued on the succeeding implement pages are Exodus 39:35–37 and Exodus 28:30.
3. Fols. 7v and 8r. The intervening pages are decorative carpet pages. The High Priest's breastplate is also included in cat. 137.
4. Maimonides, *Mishneh Torah, Sefer Avoda*, Hilchot Beit ha-Bechira 3:11; for English, Maimonides 2007 ed., pp. 48–49.

70

Reliquary of Saint Anastasios the Persian

Holy Land, 969–70
Silver repoussé, gilding, and niello
H. 7¾ in. (19.6 cm), W. 7⅞ in. (20 cm), D. 15⅜ in. (39 cm)
Domkapitel and Domschatzkammer, Aachen

A fascinating gold work in the shape of a centralized church surmounted by a ribbed dome set on a drum, the Reliquary of Saint Anastasios the Persian (d. January 628) has often been linked to the Church of the Holy Sepulchre, also known as the Church of Anastasis (Resurrection), especially since the object's inscribed psalms mention "Sion" and the "City of God," thereby evoking Jerusalem as well as the concept of Heavenly Jerusalem from the Apocalypse (book of Revelations). The reliquary's design, reminiscent of Byzantine and Armenian churches; decorative elements such as horseshoe-shaped doors and niello; and Greek inscriptions of the donor's name and Psalm verses (86:3, 131:8, 131:13) constitute its overall Byzantine, or, more broadly, Middle Eastern appearance.[1] The donor Eustathios Maleïnos, a Cappadocian magnate, served as *strategos*, or military leader, of Antioch around 969–70, when the multiethnic city at the eastern border of the Byzantine Empire was reconquered from the Muslims.

Though its original function is unknown, the object is commonly understood as an *artophorion*, a container for consecrated bread, which, due to different liturgical practices, was transformed into a reliquary for the cranium of Saint Anastasios the Persian in its new religious context in Europe. Anastasios the Persian was not significantly venerated in Aachen, whereas he was a popular saint in Byzantium; therefore, it cannot be excluded that the object from the very beginning served as a reliquary for the saint's relics, especially since, according to legend, the Persian convert was baptized in the Holy Sepulchre. Thus, any allusions of the microarchitecture to Jerusalem could also be interpreted in a specific hagiographic context. MA

Selected References: Kaentzeler 1858; Aachen 1972, pp. 46–47; Saunders 1982, pp. 211–19; New York 1997, pp. 460–61, no. 300; Angar 2016.

1. For the inscriptions, see Robert Ousterhout in New York 1997, pp. 460–61, no. 300.

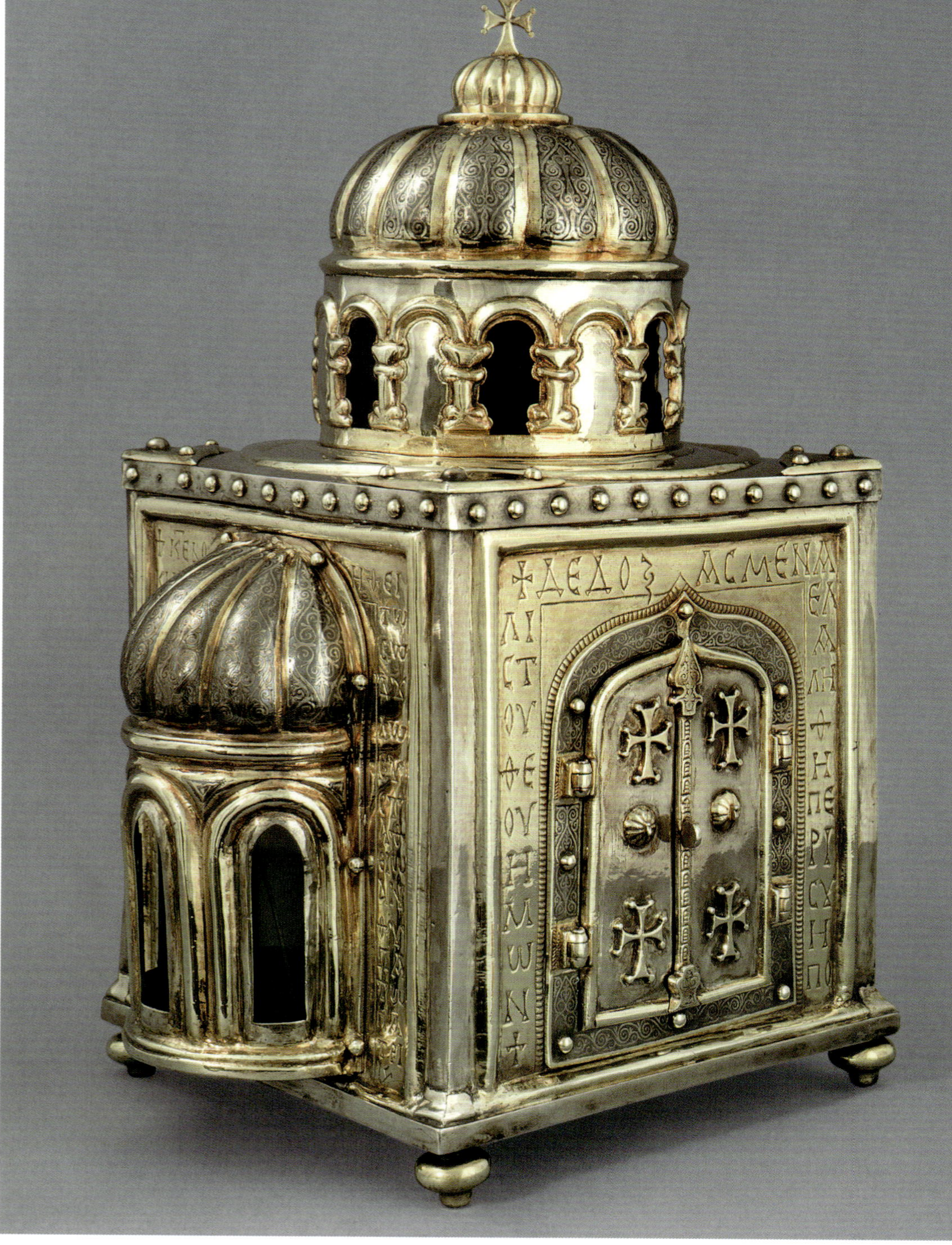

70

71

Portion of a *Transenna* Panel

Jerusalem, 10th–11th century
Marble
H. 26¾ in. (68 cm), W. 22 in. (56 cm), D. 1⅝ in. (4 cm)
Terra Sancta Museum, Studium Biblicum Franciscanum, Jerusalem (CTS-SB-09460)

This panel is from a tomb in the Church of the Holy Sepulchre that the eighteenth-century Franciscan friar Elzear Horn illustrated and described in his *Ichnographiae Monumentorum Terrae Sanctae (1722–1744)*. His drawing (fig. 60) labeled it "Tomb of Baldwin II or Tomb of Fulk" and showed the fragment as part of a panel extending from the left of a simple rectangular tomb to cover two-thirds of its face: Baldwin II, count of Edessa, ruled Jerusalem from 1118 to 1131, his successor Fulk, count of Anjou, from 1131 to 1143.[1] Unlike the drawing, however, Horn's text suggests that the tomb might have been assembled as late as 1560.[2] While the Crusader rulers from the twelfth century and beyond buried nearby had elaborate Western-style tombs with inscriptions, the simpler, non-Western style of the fragment lends support to Horn's proposed later date for its reuse in the construction of a tomb.[3] A remnant of a *transenna*, or low screen that defines the altar area, the panel, especially in its size and design, is typical of Middle Byzantine examples of the type. It may have been created during the restoration of the Holy Sepulchre by the Byzantine emperor Constantine IX Monomachus in 1042–48(?) after its infamous desecration in 1009 by the mad Fatimid caliph al-Hakim.[4] HCE

Selected References: Bagatti 1930, p. 131, no. 224; Horn 1962 ed., pp. 1–3, 72 n. 2, 72–73; Buschhausen 1978, pp. 160–61, figs. 68, 87.

1. The text is in the Vatican Library, Vat. MS 9233. Horn 1962 ed., pp. 1 n. 1, 73, fig. 9; Buschhausen 1978, p. 161, fig. 87.
2. See Horn 1962 ed., p. 72, where he associates the tomb with Alphonso the Wise (1221–84), king of Spain, or "the two Counts Holland and the Dukes of Burgundy, whose hearts . . . in 1467 and 1560 were buried in Jerusalem." Bagatti 1930, p. 131, no. 22; and Buschhausen 1978, pp. 19, 161, figs. 68, 87, accept the attribution on the drawing's label.
3. See Horn 1962 ed., figs. 7, 8, 10, for the Crusader tombs of rulers of Jerusalem Godfrey de Bouillon (r. 1099–1100), Baldwin I, count of Edessa (r. 1100–1118), and Baldwin V (r. 1183–86); Buschhausen 1978, figs. 73, 86, 88.
4. Bagatti 1930, p. 131, no. 224; see Ousterhout 1989, pp. 68, 77, on the restoration where he questions if marble was imported for rebuilding the site.

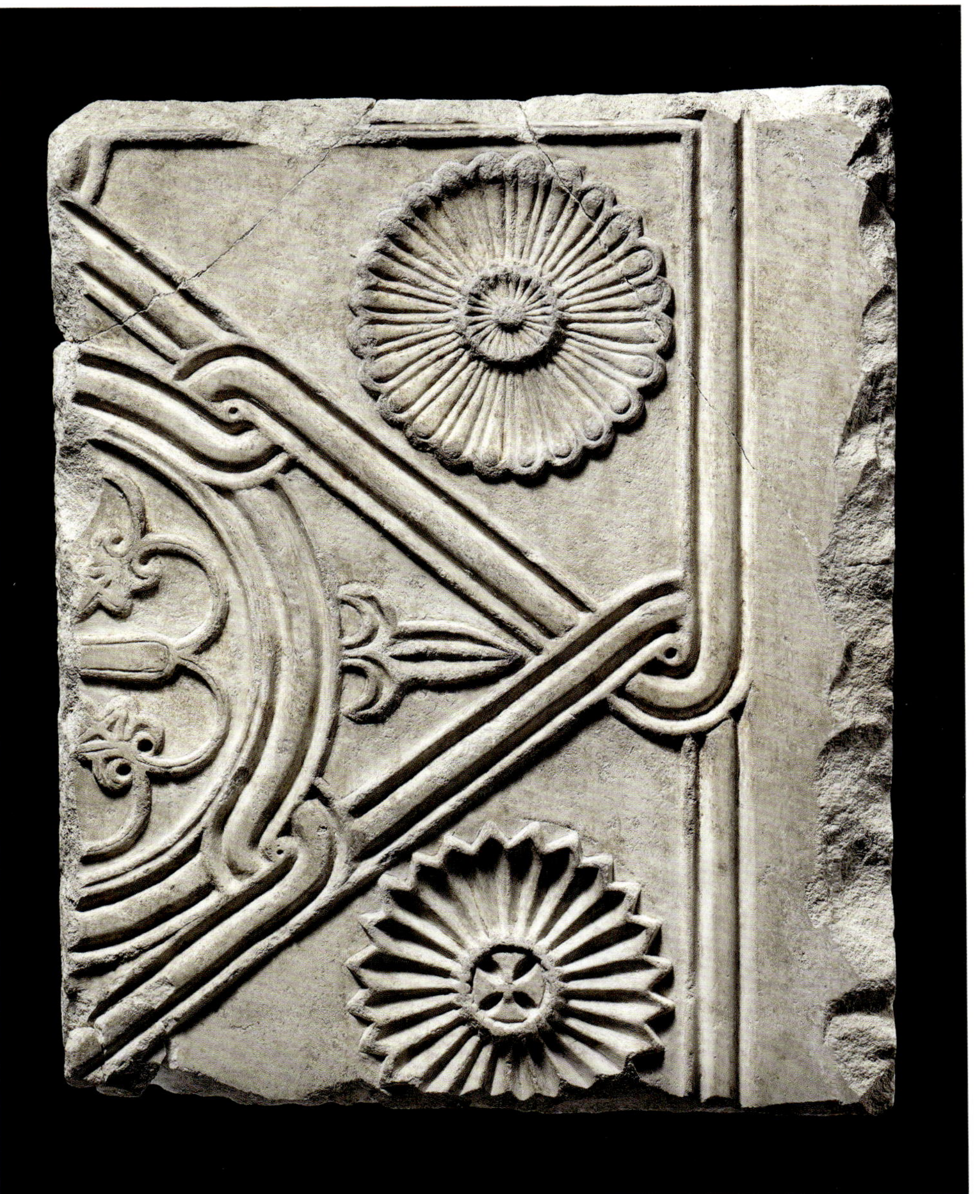

71

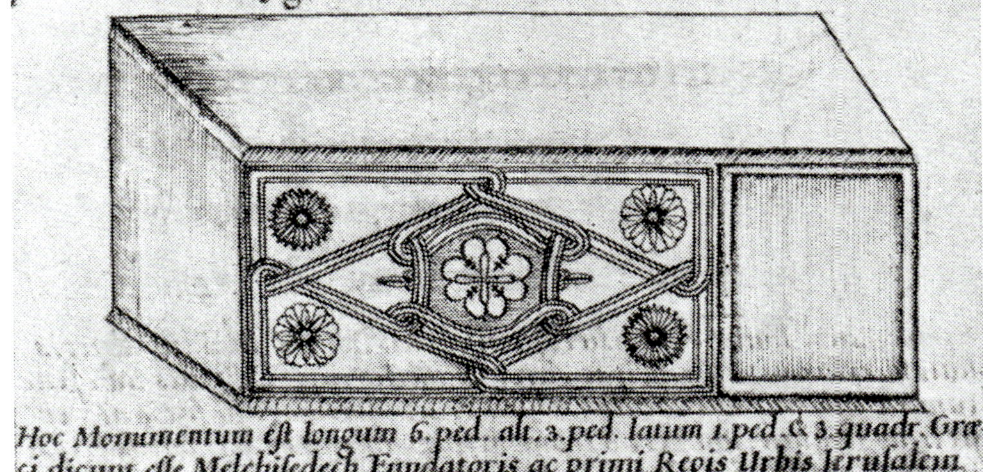

altitud. 1. ped. & 3. quadr; stat erectum i regione prioris ad dexteram in meridionali parte, cui Sepulchrum aliud interposita solum palistida est proximum in hac figura: (61).

Hoc Monumentum est longum 6. ped. alt. 3. ped. latum 1. ped. & 3. quadr. Graeci dicunt esse Melchisedech Fundatoris ac primi Regis Urbis Jerusalem.

Fig. 60. Tomb of Baldwin II or Fulk of Anjou. Drawing by Elzear Horn, 1724–44. Biblioteca Apostolica Vaticana, Vatican City (MS 9233)

72

Canon Table

From a Gospel Book
Constantinople(?), late 11th century
Tempera, gold, and ink on parchment; 192 fols.
8¾ × 6⅞ in. (2.2 × 17.5 cm)
Scheide Library, Princeton University Library
(Scheide MS 70)

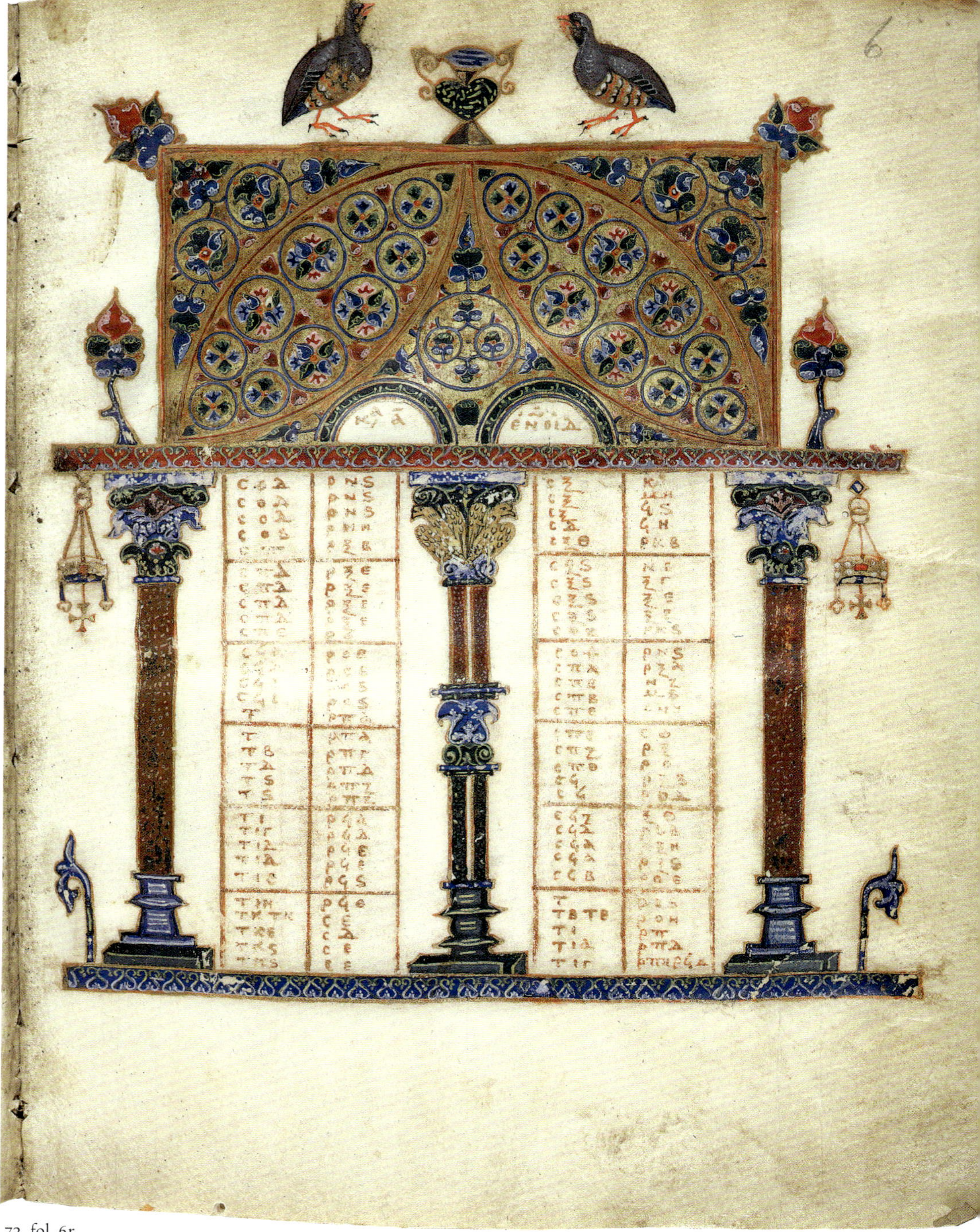

72, fol. 6r

This handsomely decorated page is from the canon tables, a concordance to the Gospels developed in the first half of the fourth century by Eusebius of Caesarea. In a letter to his pupil Karpianus, Eusebius described how to use his tables that coordinate the events in the life of Christ with the Gospels in which they appear, and the tables became so popular that they were bound to the front of Gospels in all translations throughout the medieval world.[1] In this Greek manuscript, the leaves date to the late eleventh century by their resemblance to the canon tables in two Gospel Books, attributed to Constantinople and now housed on Mount Athos in northern Greece. All these manuscripts include canon tables decorated with gold votive crowns hanging from each end of the base of their headpieces.[2] The format of columns supporting elaborate headpieces topped by pairs of opposing creatures, here partridges, is typical of the period. The saturated jewel-like colors and graceful flower petal–style embellishment on the richly gilded ground of the headpieces is reminiscent of the contemporary Byzantine taste for cloisonné enamels. The intricate design, at times the only richly adorned element of a manuscript, encouraged symbolic interpretations of the illuminations, including allusions to their representing Heavenly Jerusalem.[3] This manuscript was in the library of the Church of the Anastasis (Holy Sepulchre) by 1897. HCE

Selected References: Princeton 1973, pp. 130–31, no. 33; Princeton 1986, pp. 148–49, no. 174; New York 1997, p. 93, no. 46; Kotzabassi, Ševčenko, and Skemer 2010, pp. 210–17, figs. 226–38.

1. Jeffrey C. Anderson in New York 1997, p. 93, no. 46.
2. Natalia Teteriatnikov in Princeton 1986, p. 149; Kotzabassi, Ševčenko, and Skemer 2010, p. 213.
3. Mathews et al. 1991, pp. 207–11.

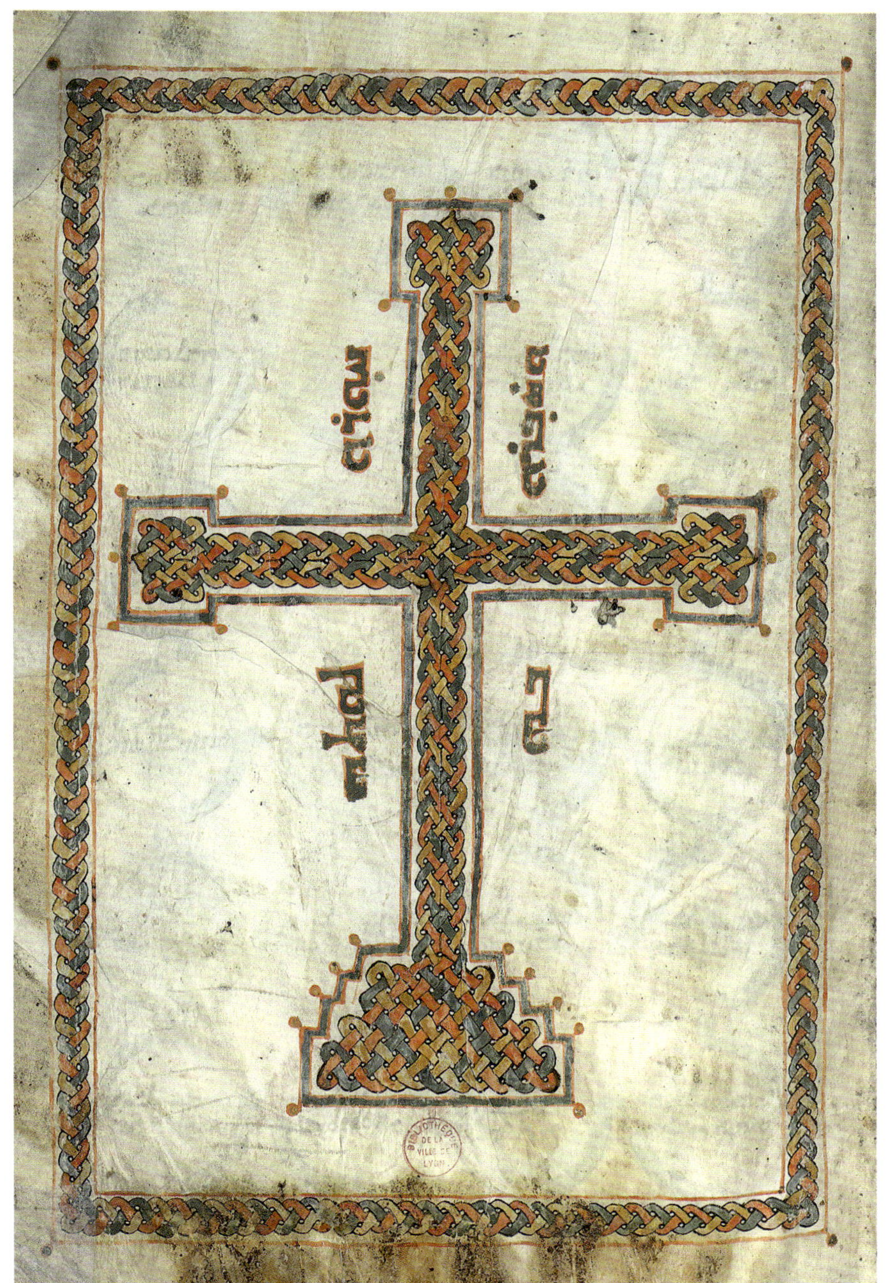

73, fol. 2r

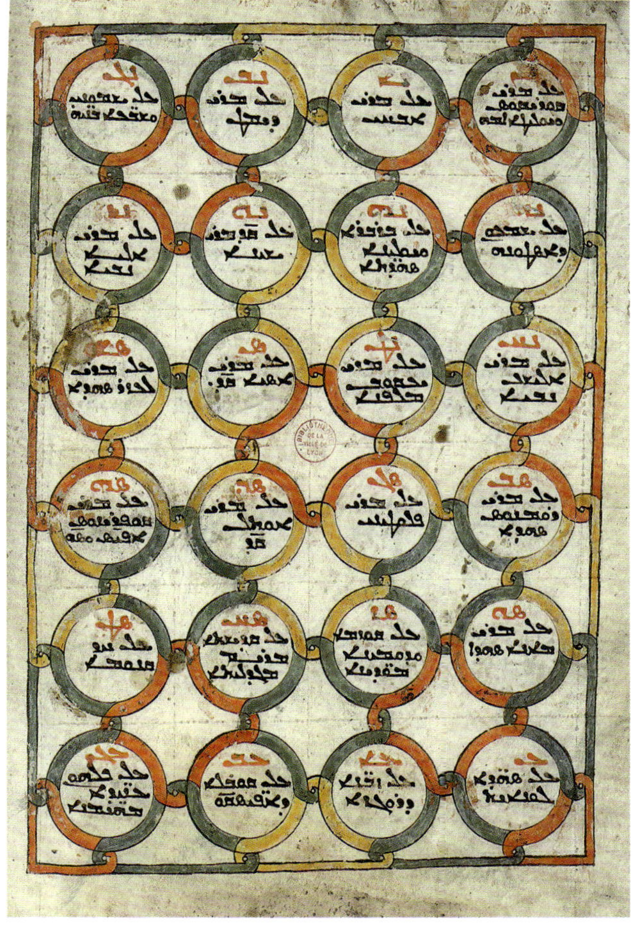

73, fol. 3v

73

Syriac Breviary

Jerusalem, 1138
Copied by Michael de Mar'ach
Tempera and ink on parchment
H. 14⅝ in. (37 cm), W. 10¼ in. (26 cm), D. 6⅜ in. (16 cm)
Bibliothèque Municipale, Lyon (Ms Syr 001)

Created in the Monastery of Mary Magdalene and Saint Simon the Pharisee in Jerusalem and dated February 10, 1138, this manuscript bears witness to the Syriac community's presence during the time when Fulk and Melisende were the Latin king and queen of Jerusalem. The large cross dominating the opening page is typical of Syriac manuscripts. The inscriptions set vertically that border the Cross (folio 2 recto) read "Look at him [Jesus] and your hope be in him," indicating that the image served as a focus of contemplation.[1] The pages immediately following have interlaced circles, each featuring the name and feast day of a given saint, ranging from the apostles to George and Barbara to Syriac theologians like James of Saroug.

This breviary, or *Fenqito*, contains the texts for services, beginning with the Dedication of a Church and continuing to the feasts through the end of the summer. The book reads from right to left and uses Estrangela, the Syriac alphabet, which has twenty-two letters, all consonants. Parts of the manuscript are in verse, with texts by known Syriac hymnists. Notes in the book state that it was copied by a monk named Michael de Mar'ach and checked for accuracy by Ignatius II, the Syriac bishop of Jerusalem from 1125 to 1138. In addition to the sacred writings, the manuscript includes important information about the growth of the Syriac community under Ignatius. He expanded the monastery in Jerusalem, adding three rooms with vaulted ceilings and a square loggia, all intended to serve as lodging for pilgrims and foreigners.

In 1684, the Syriac patriarch and a Syriac archbishop presented this manuscript, by that time in Aleppo, to the French consul, who gave it to the city of Lyon, where it was housed in the Jesuit college of the Trinity. At an unknown point in its history, the manuscript was mislabeled as a Qur'an. HS / BDB

Selected References: Martin, J., 1888–89, pp. 33–80; Kenaan 1973; Briquel-Chatonnet 1997, pp. 195–96, no. 1; *E-Corpus* 2011–12.

1. We thank Laila Daliappo for translating the inscription.

74

Gospel Book

Tegray, Ethiopia, early 14th century
Tempera and ink on parchment; 248 folios
H. 10½ in. (26.7 cm), W. 6¾ in. (17 cm), D. 4½ in. (11.4 cm)
Walters Art Museum, Baltimore, Museum purchase with funds provided by W. Alton Jones Foundation Acquisition Fund, 1996 (W.836)

The facing pages of this Gospel Book belong to a short prefatory cycle depicting key episodes in the life of Christ. At left, the Lamb of God perches above a jeweled cross flanked by the crucified bodies of the two thieves. The gemmed Cross, absent the body of Christ, rises between two soldiers. Their discarded shields hovering nearby, the soldiers stand at the base of the picture field in adoration of the central object in the composition. The Cross has been interpreted as a reference to the great triumphal cross that Theodosius II (r. 408–50) erected in the Chapel of Golgotha, the site of Christ's crucifixion.[1] The opposite page features the Holy Women arriving at the tomb, where an angel greets them, and the women swing incense burners beside red-veined columns. An angel, hand outstretched in speech, sits on a yellow tomb pierced by a black opening. On learning that the tomb is empty, the women raise their left hands in surprise. The domed cupola and lamps succinctly evoke the domed rotunda erected over the Holy Sepulchre, again blending the Gospel narrative with recognizable references to holy sites in the region.

In northern Ethiopia, where this manuscript was illustrated, images like these called Jerusalem powerfully to mind, drawing on pilgrimage imagery developed as early as the sixth century.[2] This Gospel Book has been associated with Tegray based on inscriptions that indicate that it belonged to the Church of Saint George in Däbrä Mä'ar. The Gospel text that follows was written by the scribe Mätre Krestos in Geez, the liturgical language of the Ethiopian Church.[3] CGM

Selected Reference: Baltimore 2001, pp. 96–97.

1. Baltimore 2001, pp. 96–97.
2. M. Heldman in Baltimore and other cities 1993–96, p. 119, nos. 54–56; and Paris and Girona 2000–2001, pp. 44–45.
3. Getatchew 2008–14.

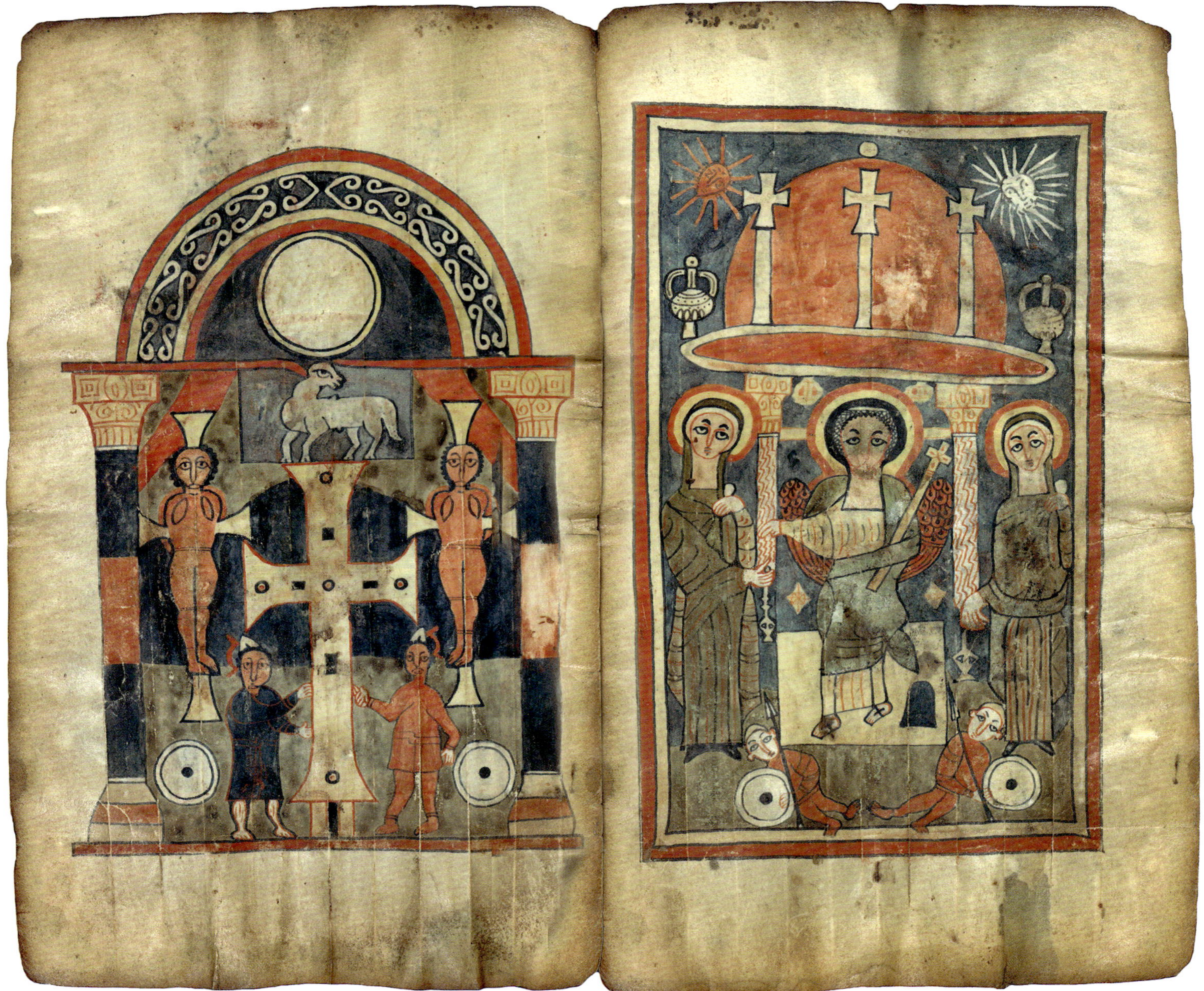

74, fols. 6v–7r

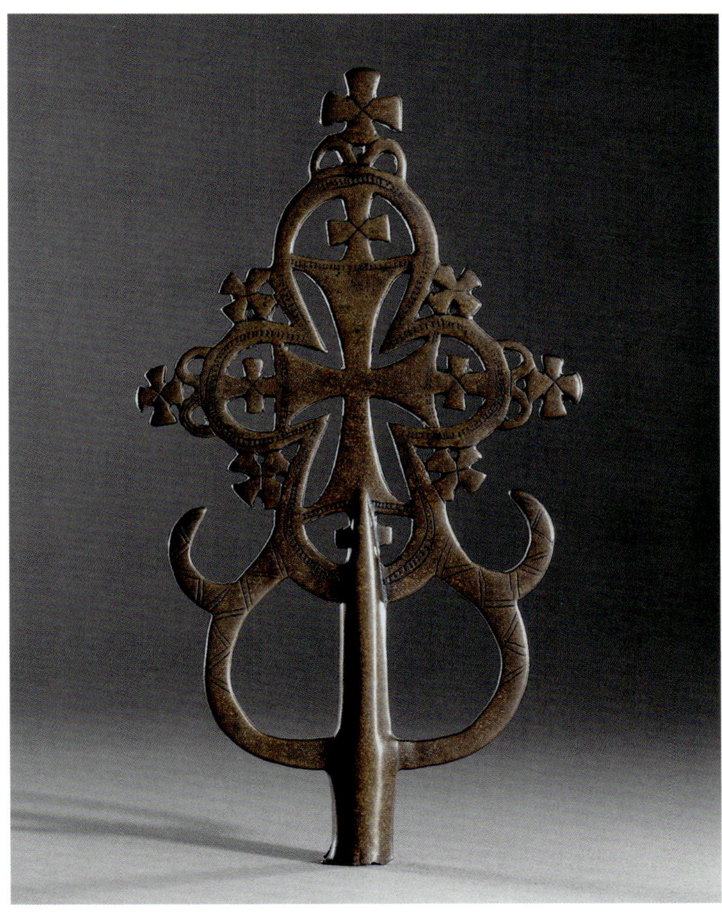

75a

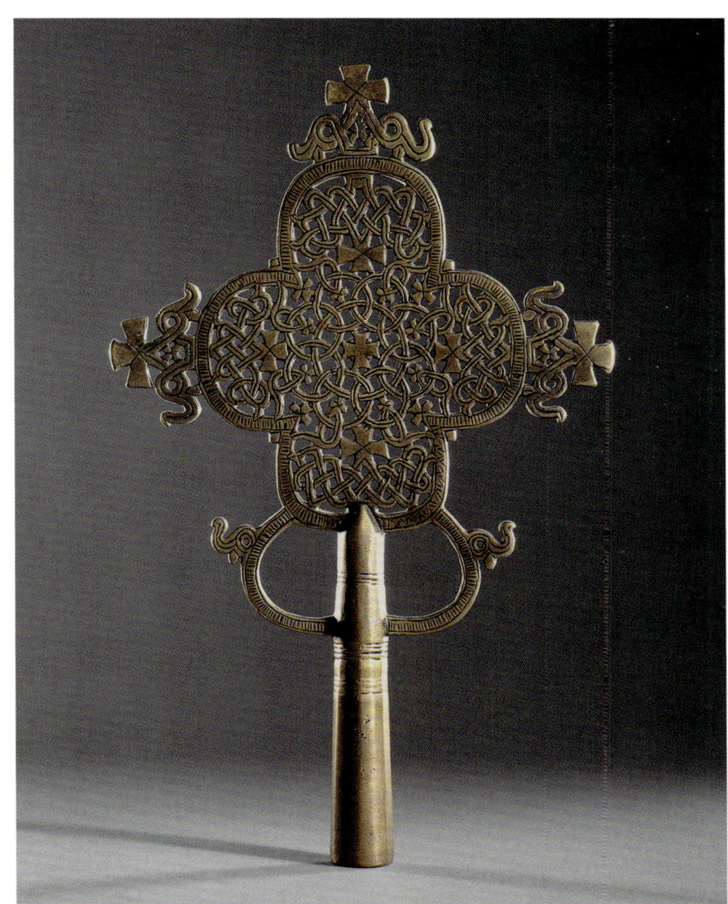

75b

75a, b

a. Cross

Ethiopia, 14th century
Copper
H. 7⅞ in (20 cm), W. 4⅜ in. (11 cm)
Private collection, United Kingdom

b. Cross

Ethiopia, 14th–15th centuries
Copper
H. 11½ in. (29 cm), W. 7⅜ in. (18.5 cm)
Private collection, United Kingdom

Visitors to Jerusalem over the centuries mention an Ethiopian presence at a number of holy sites, including Bethlehem, the Grotto of King David on Mount Sion, a Chapel of the Virgin on Golgotha, the Chapel of the Disgrace (where Jesus was crowned with thorns), and the Church of the Holy Sepulchre, where the community worships today in a second-story chapel above the Chapel of Saint Helena. It is reached either by a door to the right of the main entrance or from the roof, on which the Ethiopian monks' spare residence is found.[1]

There is no early written record of Ethiopian metalwork in Jerusalem, but a cross appears to crown a canopy drawn over the head of a figure in the Book of Kings that was a royal gift from the Ethiopian sovereign to the Ethiopian community in Jerusalem (cat. 52). An inventory of the possessions of the Ethiopians in Jerusalem transcribed and translated in 1900 lists sixteen crosses, including six of brass.[2] Whether portrayed in manuscripts (cat. 74) or carried in procession, such crosses often appear in multiples. These two examples attest to the variety achieved by metalsmiths working with the same material and to the same end. On the first, the repeating cross form is clearly discernible; on the second, tiny crosses merge into a maze of pattern. BDB

1. Ethiopian possessions acquired since the Middle Ages include the Monastery of Dabra Gannat on Ethiopian Street in West Jerusalem. See Isaac 1984–85, p. 54.
2. Littmann 1902, p. 123.

76

Canon Tables

From a Gospel Book
Monastery of Poghoskan (P'awloskan, Pawoskan), near Hromkla, Turkey, 1193
Tempera, gold, and ink on parchment; 316 folios
H. 10¼ in. (26 cm), W. 7¹⁄₁₆ in. (18 cm), D. 3 in. (7.6 cm)
Walters Art Museum, Baltimore, Acquired by Henry Walters (Ms. W.538)

The pair of elaborate canon tables are the last tables of Eusebius of Caesarea correlating the events in the Gospels (see cat. 72). The tabernacle atop the final table on the right represents the new Heavenly Jerusalem as envisioned by the Armenian theologian Nerses Shnorhali, catholicos of the Armenians from 1166 to 1173, in the introduction to his *Commentary on the Gospel of Saint Matthew*. Viewing canon-table illuminations as making "invisible things . . . visible," he described the last table as the "mystery of the highest tabernacle . . . the new Jerusalem," which is associated with the Second Coming of Christ in Christian tradition.[1] The extended colophon (folios 311 recto–313 verso) in the text narrates such contemporary events in Jerusalem as Saladin's advance and capture of the city in 1187, his arrest of men in the military order the Frères, his advance on Antioch, and his threatened invasion of Cilicia, which was averted. The colophon also records the sadness of Armenian Catholicos Grigor IV (r. 1173–93) at the conquest of Jerusalem, his prayers for its liberation, his writing to the Byzantine and Latin rulers urging them to assist the Christians there as well as the arrival of the Holy Roman Emperor Frederick I Barbarossa (r. 1155–90), his death by drowning that led to the dispersion of his army, and other events of the Third Crusade (1189–92).[2] The dedicatory inscription on folio 12 verso indicates the Gospel was made in 1193 at the Monastery of Poghoskan for Bishop Karapet, who is known to have resided at the Armenian catholicate at Hromkla, originally in the Crusader Kingdom of Edessa. The style of the manuscript's canon tables are closely linked to other works from Hromkla, making it probable that the monastery was in the same area.[3] HCE

Selected References: New York 1970, p. 295, no. 288 (mislabeled no. 528); Der Nersessian 1973, pp. 6–9; Sanjian 1976, pp. 173–93; Der Nersessian 1993, vol. 1, pp. 4, 6–7, 15, 17–18, 32–33, 37, 39, vol. 2, figs. 7, 8; New York and Baltimore 1994, p. 149, no. 7; Der Nersessian et al. 2013.

1. Mathews et al. 1991, pp. 171, source of the text, and 207–11, esp. 211 for a translation of the text.
2. Der Nersessian 1973, p. 6; Der Nersessian et al. 2013, introductory text.
3. Helen C. Evans in New York and Baltimore 1994, p. 149, no. 7; Der Nersessian 1973, p. 7; Der Nersessian 1993, vol. 1, pp. 3–4.

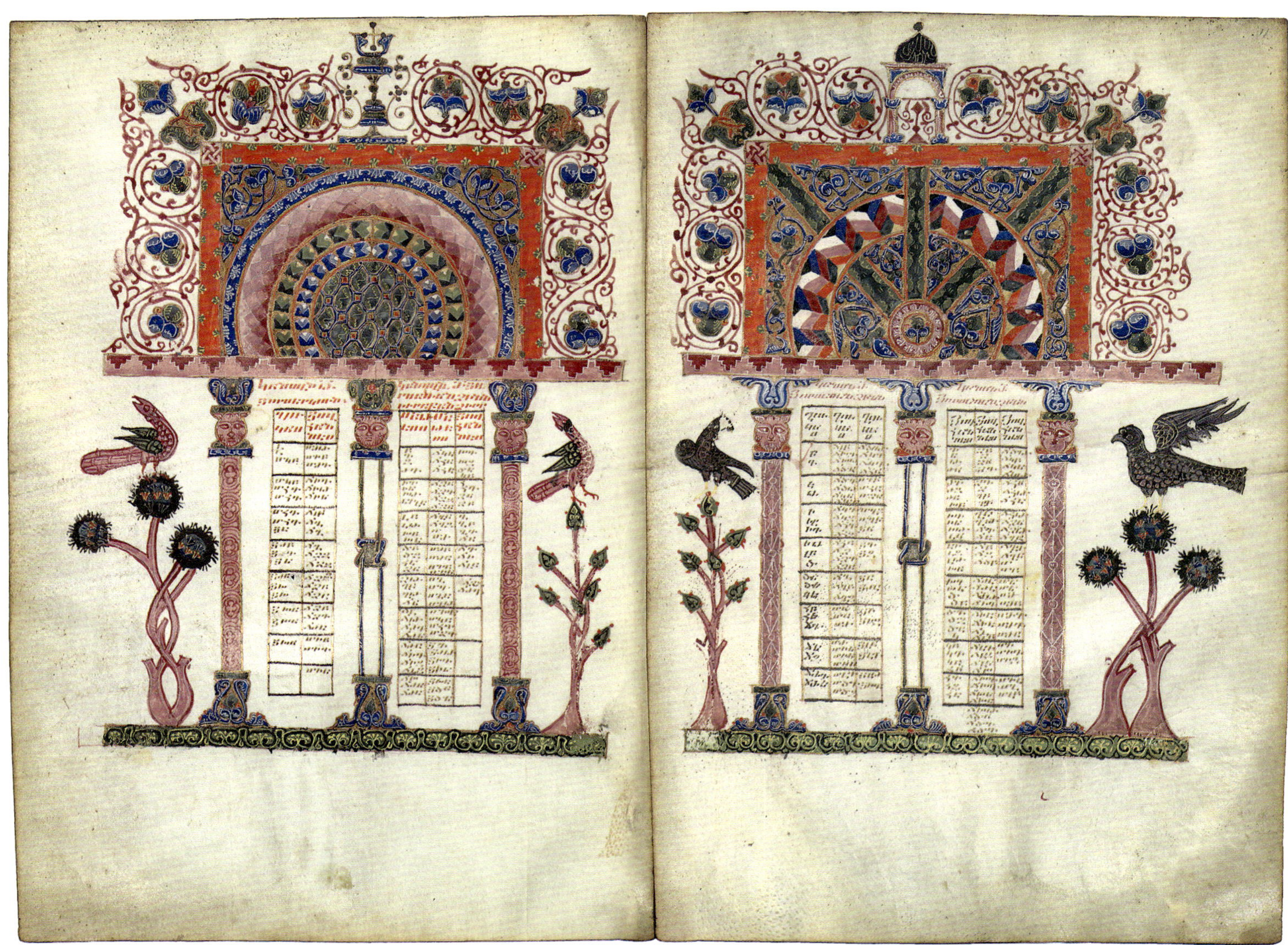

76, fols. 10v–11r

77

Missal of the Holy Sepulchre

Jerusalem, ca. 1135–40
Tempera, gold, silver, and ink on parchment
H. 11⅞ in. (30 cm), W. 7⅞ in. (20 cm), D. 2⅞ in. (7.5 cm)
Bibliothèque Nationale de France, Paris (Latin 12056)

The calendar and certain prayers of this manuscript indicate that it was used to celebrate Mass at the Church of the Holy Sepulchre. The names of sainted bishops of Jerusalem appear regularly, as do those of Saint Sabas, and the patriarchs Abraham, Isaac, and Jacob, venerated in Hebron. Even more compellingly, a prayer on folio 301 verso refers to God as the builder of Jerusalem and the *custos* (guardian) of the city and its people, day and night.[1] The calendar includes the Franks' capture of Jerusalem on July 15, which occurred in 1099, but not the dedication of Holy Sepulchre in 1149; a date before that year can therefore be inferred.[2]

The missal once had full-page illuminations of the Crucifixion and of Christ in Majesty; it retains four large, thirty-five medium, and many small initials. A number of letters have framing devices that seem to mimic enamel work, perhaps echoing lost work of goldsmiths from the area.[3] Notably, silver is used on two letter *O*s found on folios 101 verso and 102.

The gatherings are, exceptionally, numbered in both Latin and Armenian characters. Therefore, at the very least, the book represents a cooperative venture between Europeans and Armenians and possibly the work of a bilingual scribe. The palette is unusually rich in pinks and purples used in startling combinations.[4] An Armenian influence may be also discerned in the vibrant palette of Christ flanked by angels and in the facial features. Both the palette and the images have been compared to the Melisende Psalter (cat. 121); accordingly, it has been suggested that that Latin queen of Jerusalem, whose mother was an Armenian princess, commissioned the book.[5] BDB

Selected Reference: Folda 1995, pp. 159–63.

1. Perhaps surprising for its date, the Missal includes prayers for heretics and schismatics (fol. 103r), and for the Jews (fol. 103v), asking God not to remove his mercy from them.
2. The calendar references to both Jerusalem and the Augustinians at the Holy Sepulchre have been discussed in the literature; the prayer *ante portas* with God as the *custos* of Jerusalem has not previously been remarked.
3. The letters are, for example, a "D" with Christ Blessing on fol. 69v, the upright of the letter on fol. 168r, and a "D" with Saint George on fol. 188v.
4. On the image of Holy Women at the Tomb (fol. 121v), the stone of the tomb is ochre like Jerusalem stone. Note also the unusual combination of olive green and burgundy in the calendar.
5. In this context, the prayers "for my mother and father" found on fol. 289r merit further attention.

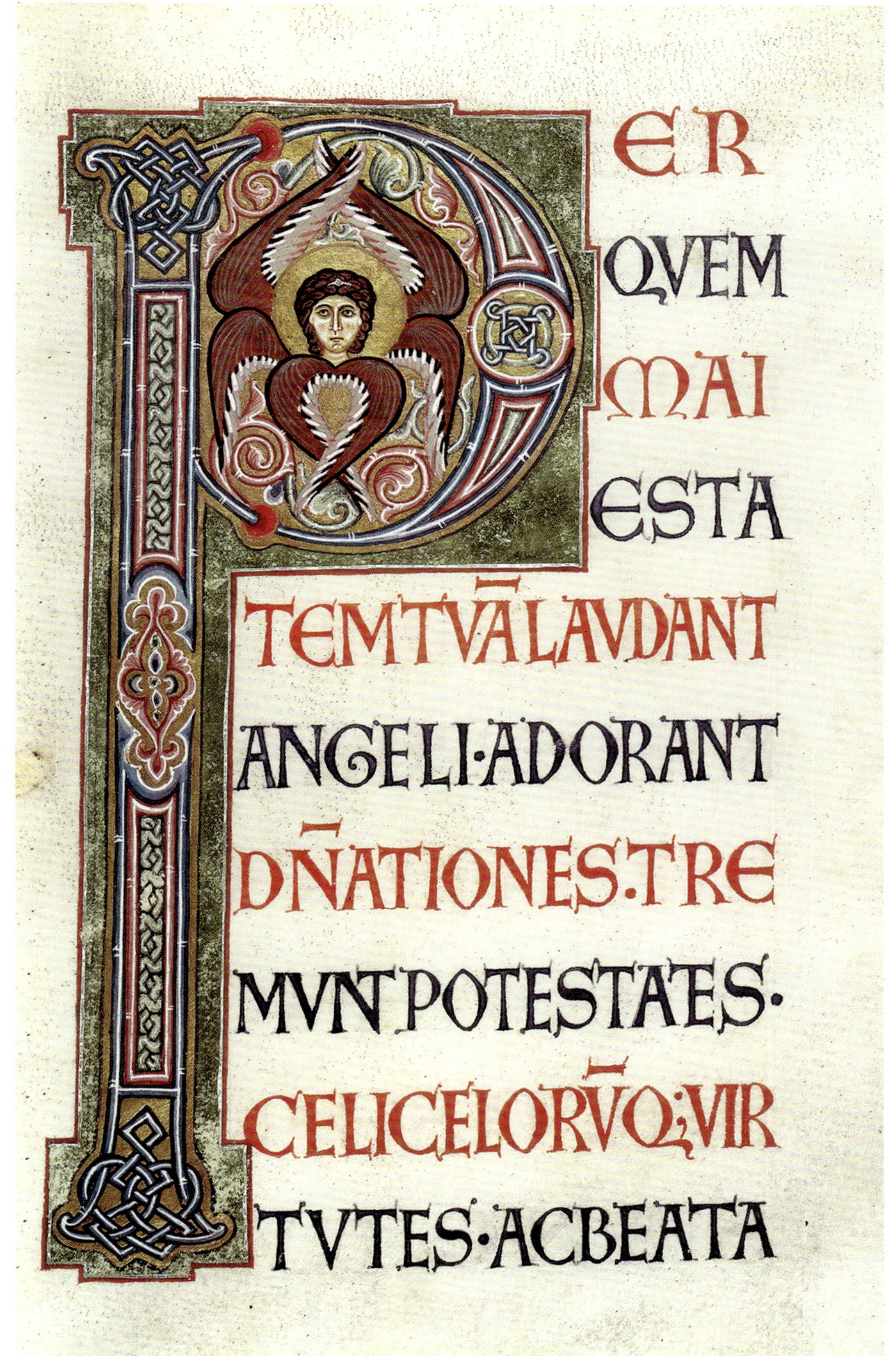

77, fol. 169r

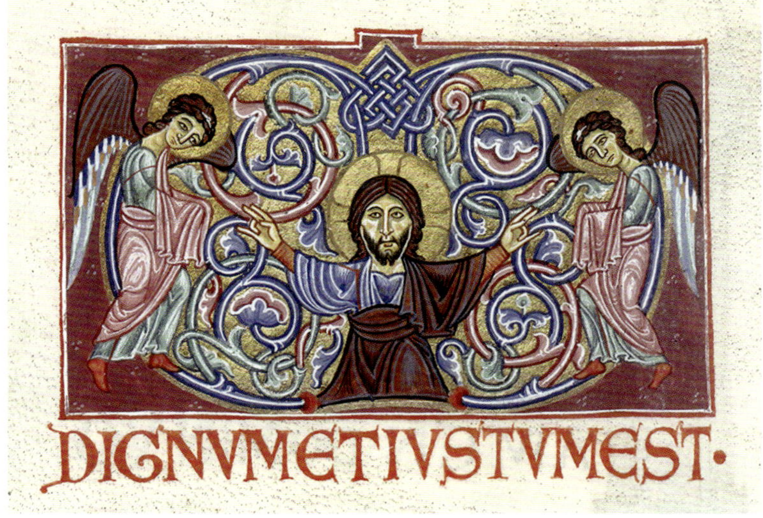

77 detail, fol. 168v

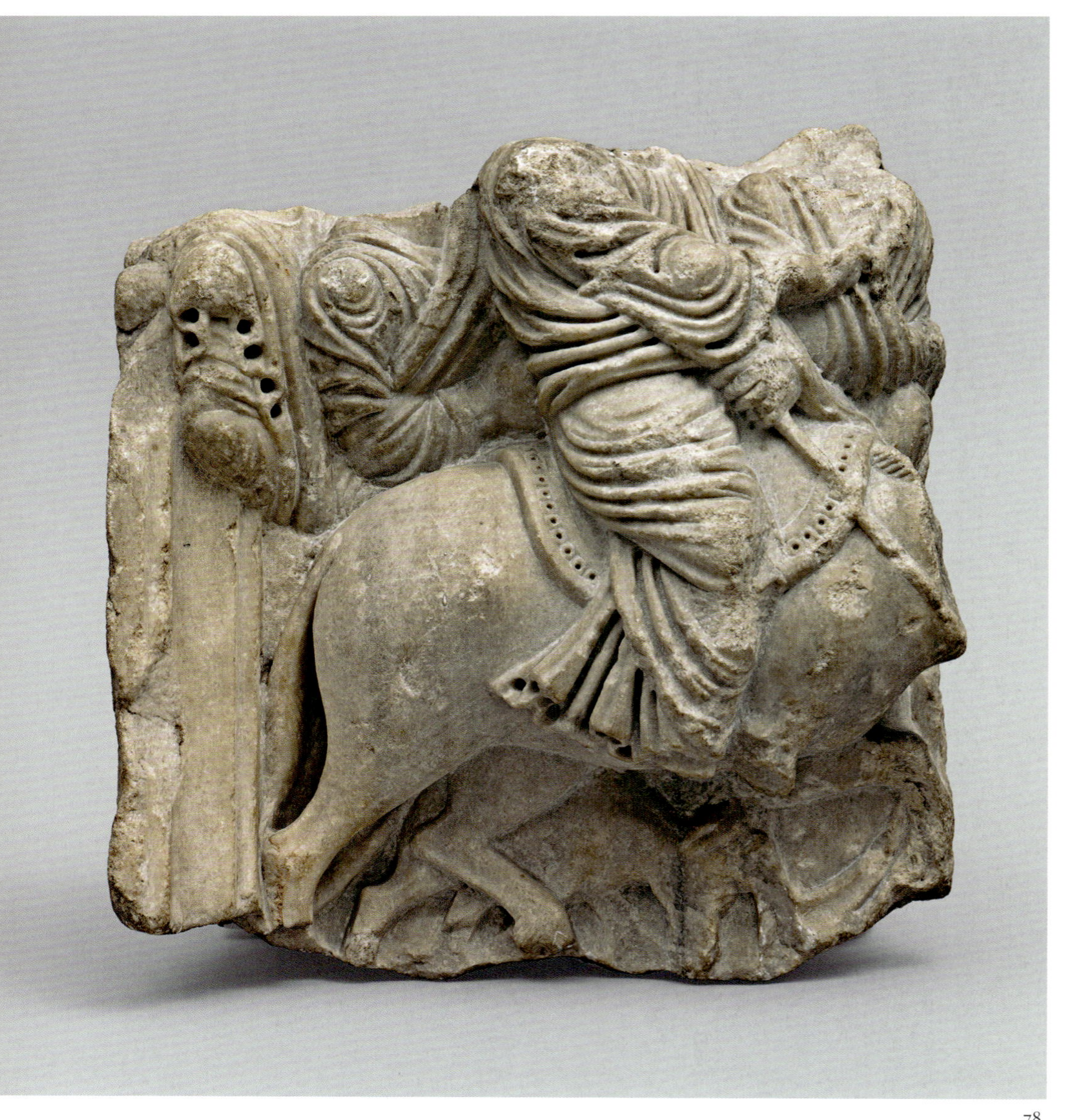

78

78
Entry to Jerusalem

Probably Jerusalem, second half of the 12th century and before 1187
Marble
H. 9⅞ in. (25 cm), W. 10⅝ in. (27 cm), D. 5¾ in. (14.5 cm)
Musée du Louvre, Département des Sculptures, Paris (RF 855)

While only parts of the relief have been preserved, it is possible to identify the primary animal visible, a donkey, on the basis of its feet, as well as the lower part of a colt in the background. This last detail allows one to name the scene with certainty: it is the entry of Jesus into Jerusalem on the back of a donkey accompanied by her foal. The proximity of three other extremely damaged figures to Christ (and the fact that they are not palm bearers) indicate that they are apostles or disciples.

The work was discovered in 1881 in a working-class neighborhood of Jerusalem near the Damascus Gate. The relief had been attributed to the lintel of the left door of the Church of the Holy Sepulchre because of its shape, which seemed to match a missing section perfectly. But experiments using a mold demonstrated early on that the Louvre fragment could not be inserted into the lintel in situ.[1] In any case, the work probably comes from a church in Jerusalem, where the theme of the entry of Jesus into the city was particularly appropriate, not only for topographical reasons but also because it could be interpreted as the model for the triumphal entry of European knights into the Holy City during the First Crusade. The extent of the drill work links the relief to Provençal sculpture, that of the Rhone Valley in France, and, more loosely, the art of the late twelfth-century Master of Cabestany. It was produced before 1187, and the comparisons mentioned by different researchers date it to a time shortly before Saladin's reconquest of Jerusalem in that year.

PYLP

Selected References: Clermont-Ganneau 1885, p. 171, no. 20, pl. 9A; Vincent and Abel 1912–26, vol. 2, p. 152, pl. 29; Henschel-Simon 1946; Baron et al. 1996, p. 56; Gaborit et al. 2005, p. 82.

1. Archaelogist Father Louis H. Vincent abandoned that identification in a letter to Paul Deschamps in 1930, though the idea was published in 1946 by another researcher.

79
Corinthian Capital

Jerusalem, ca. 1160–80
Marble
H. 24⅝ in. (62.5 cm), D. 29½ in. (74.9 cm), Diam. 20¼ in. (51.4 cm)
Greek Orthodox Patriarchate, Jerusalem

This substantial marble capital harks back to the classical Corinthian type that spread through the Roman world, including Jerusalem, where Hadrian rebuilt the city as a Roman colony in the second century. For medieval sculptors, remnants from this period served as both sources of inspiration and reusable materials.[1] The capital also shows some knowledge of Byzantine workmanship, notably the crisp carving that defines the foliate forms with sharp little valleys, whereas the sense of energy in the leaves that appear to grow up the corbel is closer to the naturalistic creations of the Abbasid period.[2]

The capital bears many resemblances to an ensemble said to come from the Church of Saint Mary the Great in the Hospitallers district, directly south of the Church of the Holy Sepulchre.[3] They share the unusual bulbous bottom part and the general composition with a double row of acanthus leaves and large lotus-like flowers on the upper part.[4] The carving style is also comparable: the use of the drill and a sharp-edged chisel created a dramatic interplay of light and shadow between protruding scallop-shaped leaves and the low-relief smaller leaves. Similar features can be seen on a set of capitals that are now rearranged on the prayer platform, or *dikka*, at the Aqsa Mosque. According to several pilgrim sources, the Knights Templars had undertaken a monumental building campaign at the south end of the Haram district.[5] Though this site was later destroyed by Saladin, many elements, especially architectural marble sculpture with rich foliate decoration, were reused in the Aqsa Mosque. The artists responsible for this ensemble, to which the present capital could belong, have been described as the Templar workshop.[6]

The origin of these artists is a long-debated question: they could have come from Provence or southern Italy, places where Romanesque interpretation of the Corinthian capital were to be found. They could also be local artists influenced by the various traditions

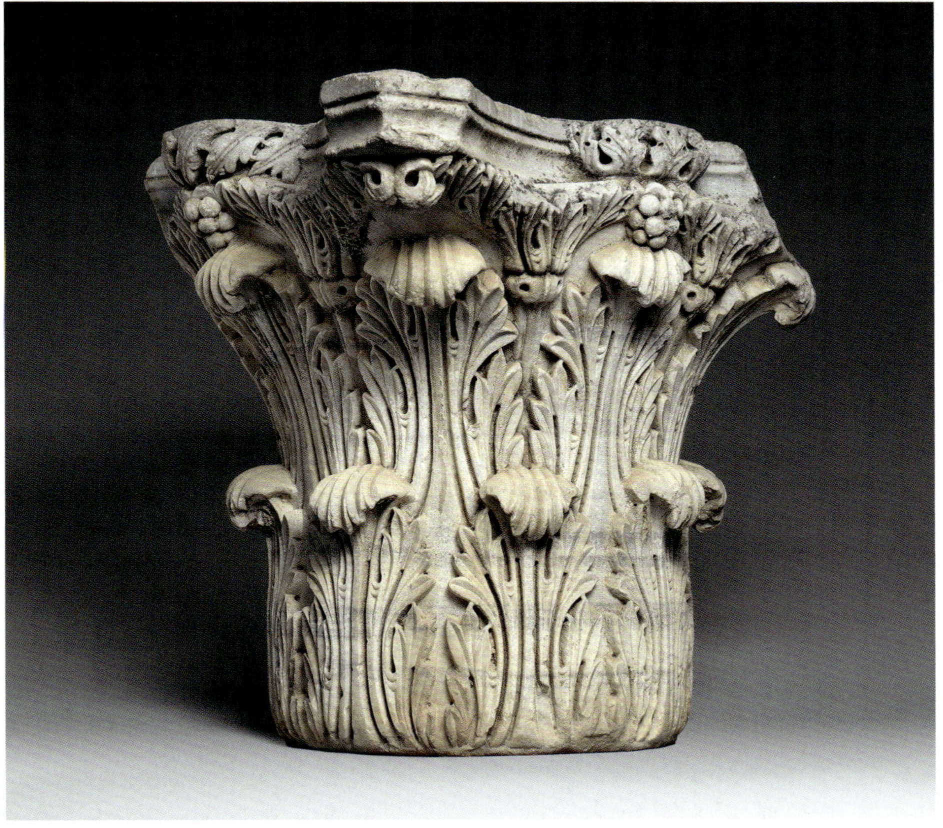

79

in twelfth-century Jerusalem under Latin rule that gave birth to what has been called Crusader Art. OB

1. Buschhausen 1978, pp. 245–46.
2. See the Theodosian-style pilaster capital in the Byzantine and Christian Museum, Athens, BXM 00330, or Wilkinson 1987, pp. 58–62, nos. 21–26.
3. Excavated in the Muristan around 1900–1901, the ensemble is cited in Buschhausen 1978, pp. 245–46, pls. 213–24, where he described them as antique pieces from Hadrian's period reused later on. See also Folda 1995, p. 278.
4. See for example in Pringle 1993–2009, vol. 3, p. 259, pl. 133g.
5. See the accounts of John of Würzburg and Theoderich in Folda 1995, p. 441.
6. A highly comparable object in terms of the plasticity of the leaves and the carving in shallow relief is illustrated in ibid., p. 448, pl. 10.14c–d. Folda stated that despite the vicinity of these capitals to the Hospitallers' quarter, the plasticity is closer to the Templar workshop output. For an extensive description of the development and production of the Templar workshop, see Jacoby, Z., 1982.

80a–c

Sculpture from the Templar Workshop

a. Frieze with Animals Fighting

Probably from the Templar complex, Jerusalem, ca. 1160–80
Marble, with traces of paint
H. 13⅝ in. (34.5 cm), W. 15¾ in. (40 cm), D. 4¾ in. (12 cm)
Terra Sancta Museum, Studium Biblicum Franciscanum, Jerusalem

b. Arcade

Templar complex, Jerusalem, ca. 1160–80
Marble
H. 10 in. (25.4 cm), W. 42 in. (106.7 cm), D. 8½ in. (21.6 cm)
Greek Orthodox Patriarchate, Jerusalem

c. Abacus

Probably Templar complex, Jerusalem, ca. 1160–80
Proconnesian marble
H. 15½ in. (39.4 cm), W. 15½ in. (39.4 cm), D. 6⅜ in. (16.2 cm)
Greek Orthodox Patriarchate, Jerusalem

Pilgrims' accounts from the 1170s describe the enormous building projects undertaken by the Knights Templars, a military order organized to protect pilgrims. Lauded by the Cistercian leader Bernard of Clairvaux as a monastic knighthood, they established a powerful military presence in Jerusalem with their headquarters at the Aqsa Mosque.[1] Though Saladin dismantled much of the Templar complex when he conquered the city in 1187, many of the sculptural elements found a new home in both the Aqsa Mosque and the Dome of the Rock, where, the sophistication of their carving evidently appreciated, they were reused in new structures. Other remnants from the destroyed buildings and the masons' yard likely established there are scattered throughout Jerusalem and beyond.[2] An attentive eye can spot pieces not only in local museums but also set into buildings, walls, and fountains (fig. 3).

Among the most elegant carvings produced during the Crusaders' ninety-year rule in Jerusalem, sculpture from the Templar workshop typically displays rolling acanthus vines.

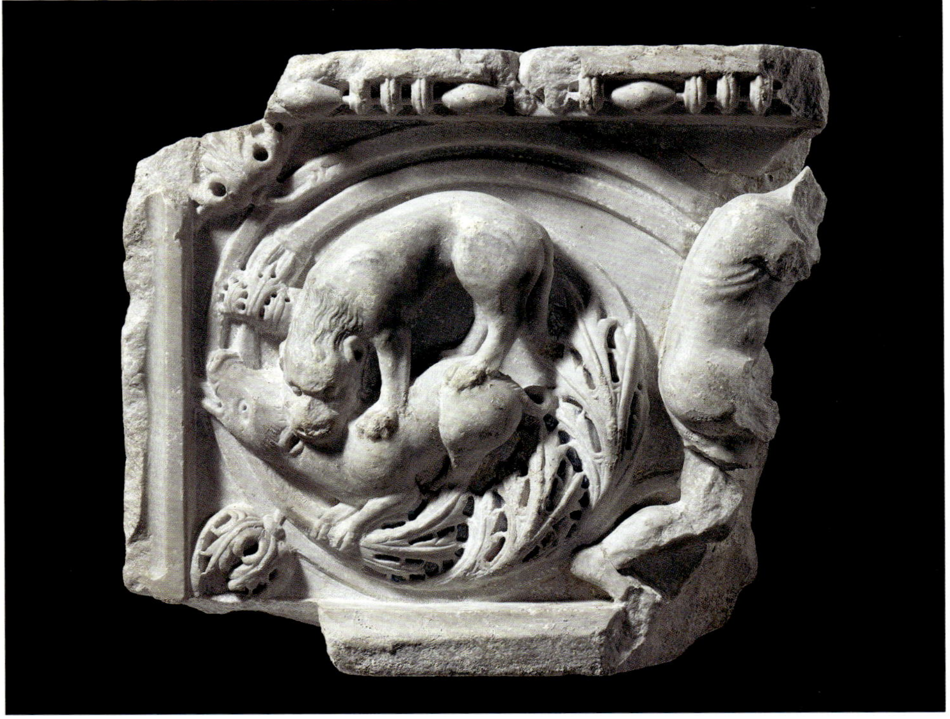

80a

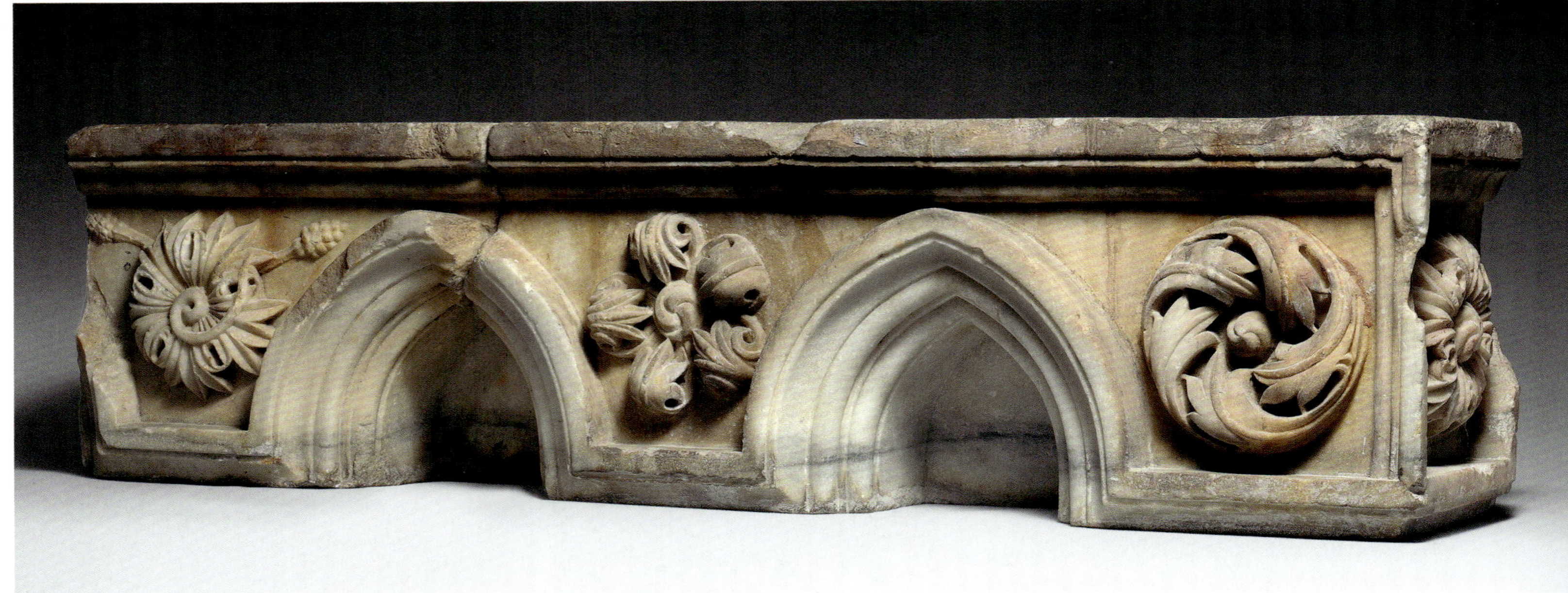

80b

Their slender leaves and spiky tips curve in an emphatically convex form. The vines provide a unifying framework, inhabited by sirens, animals, hunting birds, and naked figures.[3] Other distinguishing motifs include leafy medallions and pine cones. Even the smallest fragments display a characteristically gracious composition, which allows ample space for each foliate element. The same style appears in Puglia in the late twelfth century, suggesting that some sculptors responsible later found work in southern Italy after Saladin's arrival deprived them of further employ in Jerusalem.[4]

BDB / MH

Selected References: Cat. 80a: Milan 2000, p. 109. Cat. 80c: Jacoby, Z., 1982, p. 330 n. 11, fig. 9.

1. Bernard of Clairvaux 1977 ed.
2. On the Templar workshop, see Buschhausen 1978; Jacoby, Z., 1982; Folda 1995, pp. 441–56.
3. The traces of paint on cat. 80a were recently observed by Jack Soultanian Jr., Conservator, Department of Objects Conservation, The Metropolitan Museum of Art.
4. See for example Jacoby, Z., 1982, pp. 389–94. She pointed notably to the churches of Santa Maria Maggiore at Barletta (four abaci and one capital of the ciborium), Santa Trinità at Brindisi (two abaci in the crypt of the church), and San Clemente at Casauria. These elements share with those from Jerusalem the spiky carving of the leaves, the bulbous shape of capitals, and the contrast between flattened and fleshy areas.

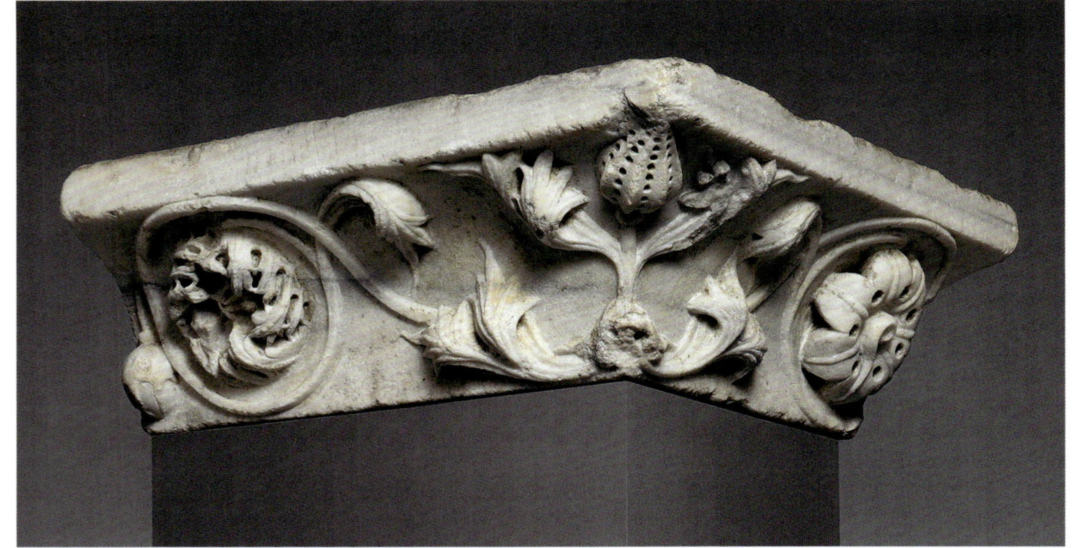

80c

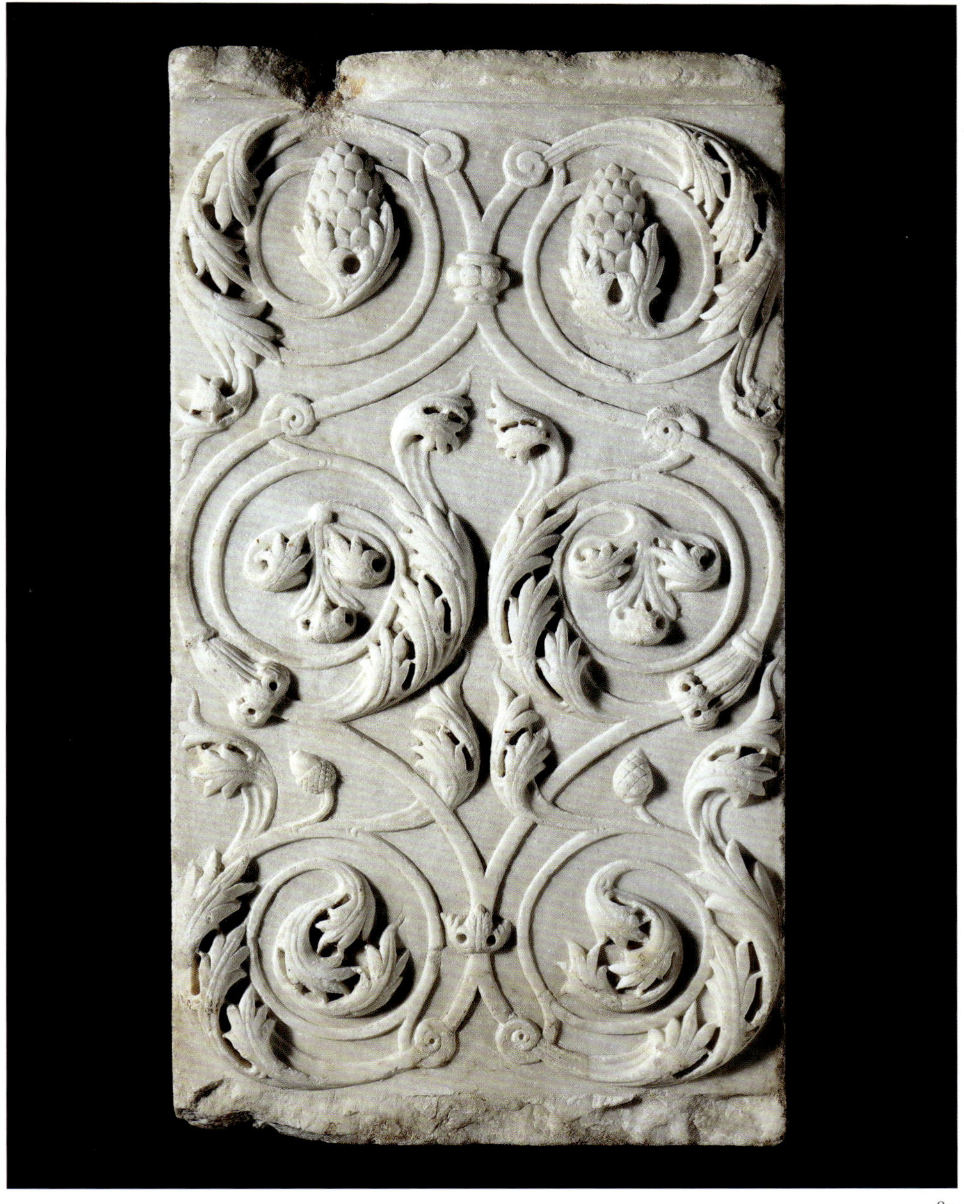

81

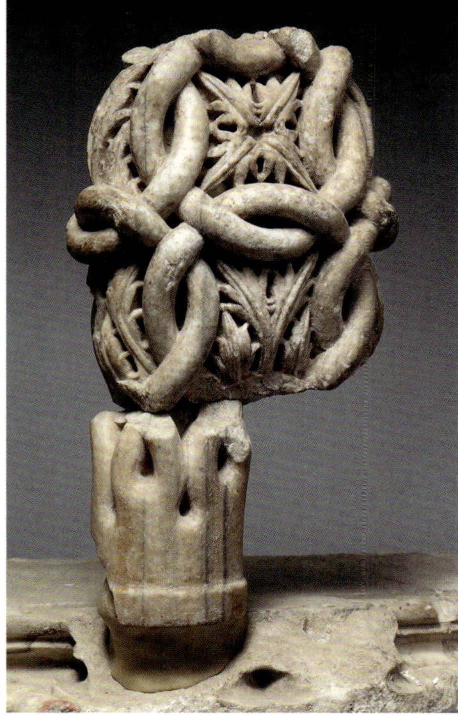

81

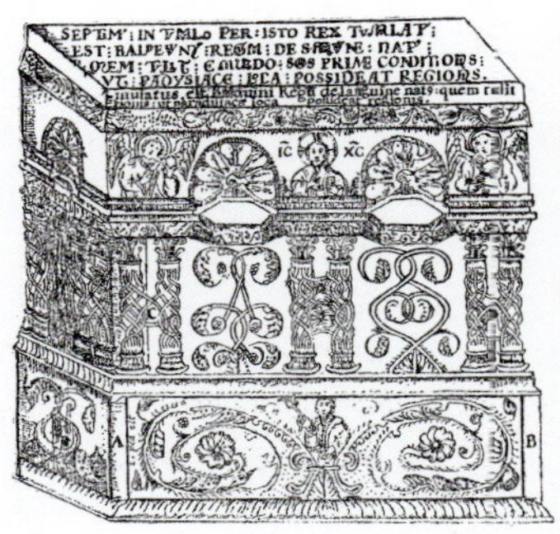

Fig. 61. Tomb of Baldwin V. Drawing by Elzear Horn, 1724–44. Biblioteca Apostolica Vaticana, Vatican City (MS 9233)

81

Elements from a Tomb in the Holy Sepulchre

Latin Kingdom of Jerusalem, 1180s
Marble
Plaque: H. 28 in. (71.1 cm), W. 15¾ in. (40 cm), D. 2⅜ in. (6 cm); braided element: H. 11 in. (27.9 cm), W. 6⅜ in. (16.2 cm), D. 3⅜ in. (8.6 cm)
Greek Orthodox Patriarchate, Jerusalem

In 1186, a year before Saladin's capture of Jerusalem, the Latin Kingdom of Jerusalem saw the death of Baldwin V, the seventh Crusader king. He was laid to rest alongside his predecessors in a spectacular tomb not far from the main entrance of the Church of the Holy Sepulchre. A sickly child crowned at age five, Baldwin had been a mere pawn in a factionalized, threatened state, and the extravagance of his tomb was inversely proportional to his political significance.[1]

Though the tomb was destroyed in the early nineteenth century, a drawing by Elzear Horn, who saw it in the first half of the eighteenth, provides a sense of its splendor (fig. 61). With its elaborate three-tiered design, it showcased the remarkable workmanship of the Templar atelier, a prolific and highly skilled group of sculptors likely located near the Aqsa Mosque, where the Templars were headquartered. The tombs of the earlier kings were notably austere; Baldwin V's by contrast was graced with sizable marble panels displaying elegant foliate designs. Conch-shaped niches and half-length portraits of Christ and angels adorned the upper register, which rested on interlaced pairs of the distinctive knotted columns in which the workshop specialized.

These two fragments might have come from Baldwin V's tomb, as the elegant marble plaque remarkably resembles those shown in Horn's drawing. Alternatively they may be from another tomb, perhaps that of the leper king Baldwin IV, Baldwin V's uncle, who died only eighteen months before him.[2] History has left few details concerning the design of the older Baldwin's tomb, but it would likely have benefitted from the talents of the Templar sculptors.[3] If neither tomb was the source, they surely came from liturgical furniture within the Holy Sepulchre. Whatever their original location, the two marble fragments partake of the same aesthetic as the tomb depicted by Horn and attest to the ambitious commissions and high level of sculptural production taking place in Jerusalem, even in the waning days of Crusader rule. BDB / MH

Selected References: Jacoby, Z., 1979; Folda 1995, pp. 467–69.

1. Jaroslav Folda views the tomb as a statement of political alliances on the part of the Templars; Folda 1995, p. 469.
2. Their location in the Greek Patriarchate also suggests they might have come from tombs. As Zehava Jacoby has discussed, the tombs were removed by the Greeks during renovations after an 1808 fire. See Jacoby, Z., 1979, pp. 8–9.
3. See Folda 1995, p. 461.

82

Drawing of the Cross-Section of the Dome of the Rock

Jerusalem, 1909
William Harvey (1883–1962)
Pen, ink, watercolor, Indian ink, and gold on paper
35¾ × 47¾ in. (90.8 × 121.3 cm)
Victoria and Albert Museum, London (E.1266-1963)

Created by an English engineer during his stay in Jerusalem, this meticulous watercolor presents the medieval interior of the iconic Dome of the Rock. The focus of the drawing, the section plan shows three levels: the dome, the drum of the dome, and the arcade level that supports the dome and the drum.

The dome is in reality two domes made of wood, separated by a space of 8¼ feet (2.5 m). The exterior was coated in lead, then covered with gold when Caliph ʿAbd al-Malik oversaw its construction in 691, and the interior one is probably the oldest Islamic structure still in use, decorated with vibrant ornamentation in plaster as well as calligraphic inscriptions from the Qur'an in various styles.[1] The embellishment and the inscriptions chronicle the history of the Dome's continued restorations by Muslim sultans, including Saladin and al-Nasir Muhammad ibn Qala'un (1285–1341). The drum is divided into two sections: the upper is pierced with sixteen windows, only seven of which are visible in the drawing, while the lower is of hollow concrete. The interior volume covered by the dome and the octagonal arcades reaches approximately 12,900 square feet (1,200 sq m). Considered the largest in the Mediterranean, it was favorably compared to the Great Mosque of Damascus.[2] Adorned with beautiful Umayyad-style mosaics dating to 691, the drum is remarkable for its state of preservation, brilliant decoration, ornate inscriptions, and geometric design. In accordance with prevailing Islamic doctrine, it is devoid of animal and human imagery. The third part of the section shows columns, piers, and arches of the arcade, constructed with a remarkable array of colored marbles.

To the left of the section plan is the ground plan of the arcade level and to the right, a section and plan of the cave containing the Rock. At the center of the octagonal arcade is the irregularly shaped Rock, surrounded by two rings of passageways. The external passage is bordered by the eight-sided external walls on one side and a ring of arches resting on eight columns and sixteen piers on the other, while the internal passage is articulated with four columns and twelve piers. Situated on the southeast side of the Old City, the Dome of the Rock is redolent with spiritual, religious, ornamental, architectural, historical, and aesthetic value. YN

Selected Reference: Harvey, W., 1922, p. 490, fig. 3.

1. The present dome is sheathed in copper, further embellished with a ¾ in. (2 mm) thick layer of gold leaf, thanks to the late Jordanian king Hussain bin Talal (1935–1999).

2. Grabar, O., 2006, p. 80. See "Experiencing Sacred Art in Jerusalem," p. 123, in this volume.

82

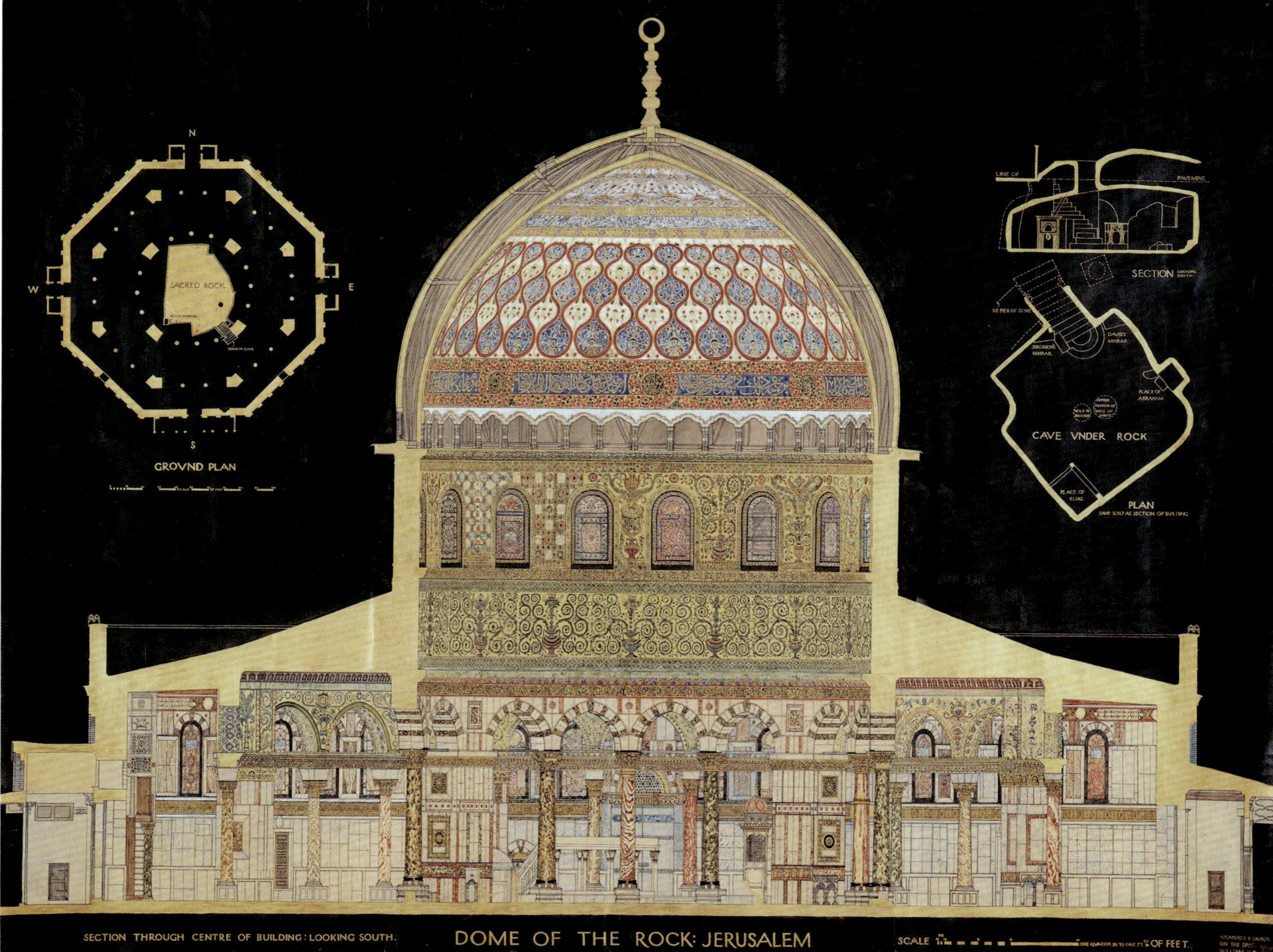

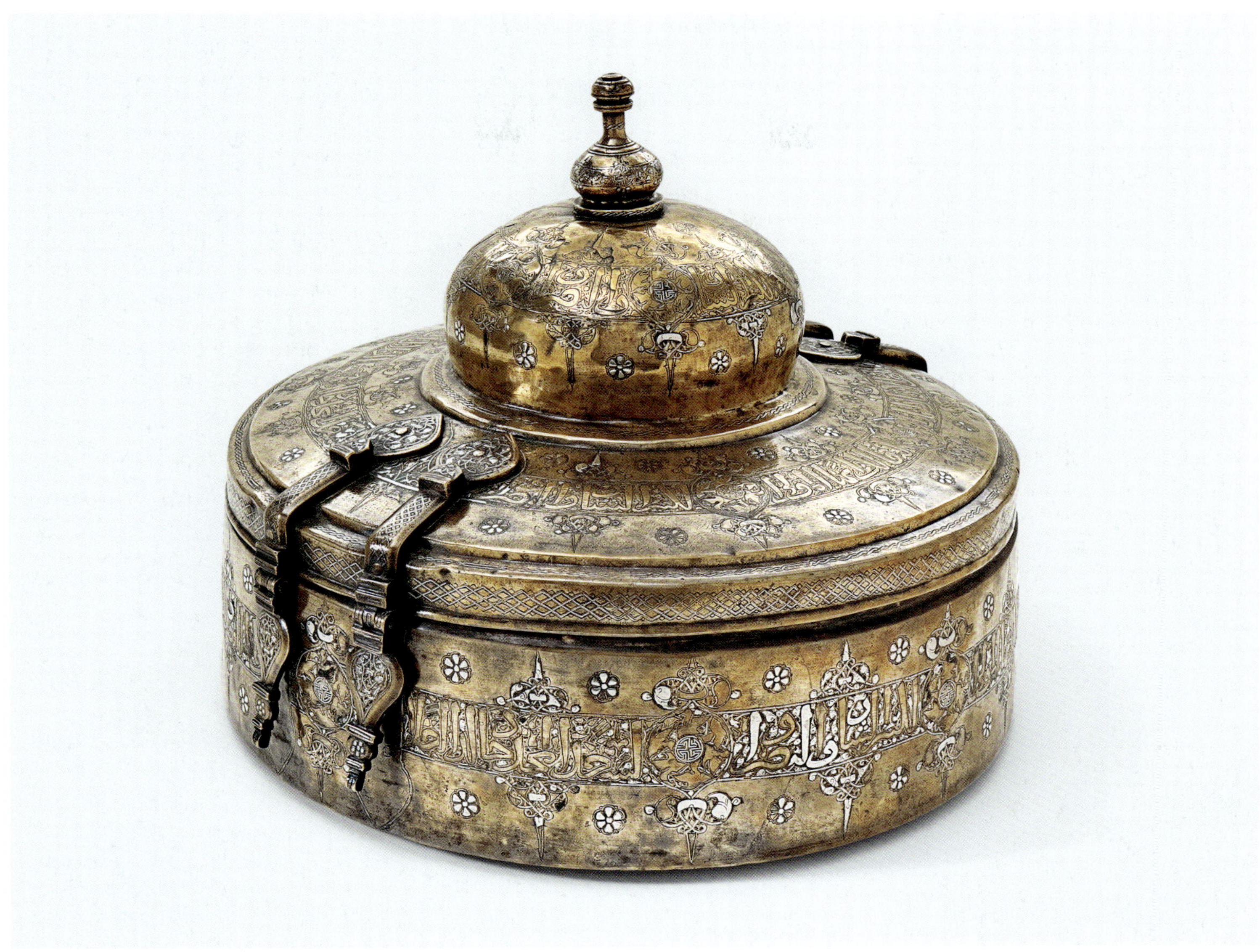

83

83

Box

Syria, late 13th–early 14th century
Brass with silver inlay
H. 5 in. (12.6 cm), Diam. 14¾ in. (37.5 cm)
Couresty of the L. A. Mayer Museum for Islamic Art, Jerusalem (M 144–71)

Architecture likely served as the inspiration for this storage container with a dome centered on a wide cylindrical base. Domed structures have a long history in Islamic architecture, especially on palaces, religious buildings, and funerary monuments. Loosely linked to abstract notions of honor and prestige, domes designated the most significant spaces of a building, whether seen from outside or experienced from within.[1] In post-Crusader Jerusalem, they seem to develop a particular association with the madrasa as a symbol for the transmission of knowledge.[2]

Domes feature on an array of Persian and Syrian containers — inkwells, incense burners, and storage containers of various sizes — from the twelfth to fourteenth century.[3] The makers of these buildings-in-miniature may well have looked to established architectural forms to convey structural solidity, aesthetic distinction, or prestige. Though this box, one of the largest of this shape to survive, bears a lengthy inscription praising its original unidentified owner and his potential for glory, we know neither its function, which may have varied, nor its owner.[4] MH

Selected References: Baer 1983, pp. 77–78, fig. 58; Jerusalem 1995, n.p., no. 40.

1. Grabar, O., 1963.
2. Jarrar 1998.
3. For examples, see Baer 1983, pp. 66–68, 77–79.
4. The Arabic inscription with a Hebrew translation is published by Rachel Hasson in Jerusalem 1995, n.p., no. 40.

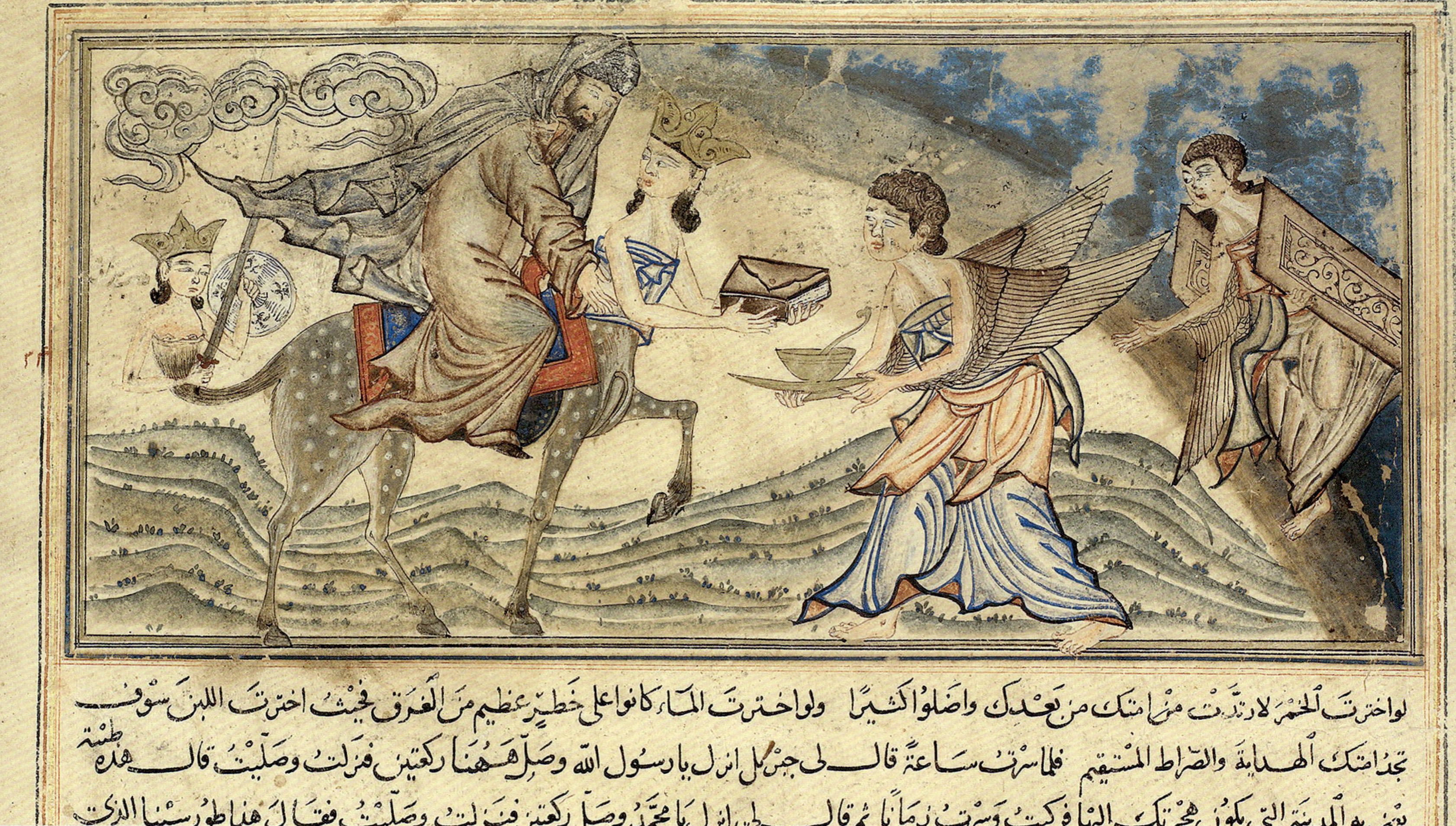

84, fol. 55

84

Night Journey of the Prophet Muhammad

From the *World History* or *Compendium of Chronicles* (*Jami' al-tawarikh*)
Tabriz, Iran, Ilkhanid period, 1314
Written by Rashid al-Din (1247–1318)
Opaque watercolor, gold, and ink on paper; 151 fols.
17½ × 26⅜ in. (44.5 × 67 cm)
Courtesy of the University of Edinburgh (Or. Ms. 20)

One of the supreme masterpieces of Persian book painting, the *Jami' al-tawarikh* (commonly known as the *World History*) is datable to 1314 and was produced in Tabriz in northwest Iran. Its extreme rarity, huge size, lavish illustration, and very early date propel it to the forefront of noteworthy illustrated Islamic manuscripts. It was produced at the command of Rashid al-Din, the Persian vizier to the Mongol ruler of Iran. An intellectual enterprise of the first order and one unique in medieval world history, its original four volumes cover Mongolia, China, India, Russia, and Europe as far west as Ireland.[1] Native informants provided the raw material for the 2,000 elephant folio text, by far the largest illustrated volume of Mongol times, with probably some 800 illustrations in all.

The largest surviving portion of this pioneering text produced in the lifetime of its compiler is the Edinburgh fragment, which is interesting for several reasons. First, it contains much material from Hebrew and Christian scriptures, the Apocrypha and the Midrash, all seen through Muslim eyes; second, it features the first coherent cycle of images of the Prophet Muhammad, images that had hitherto been taboo in the Islamic world; and third, its historical coverage is particularly rich for the tenth and eleventh centuries, adding great detail to the few extant chronicles of this period.

Moreover, its seventy associated paintings document a crucial period of transition in Persian and indeed Islamic painting, when Arab, Persian, and Byzantine traditions encountered those of China, resulting in an unprecedented fusion of east and west. Historically and culturally, this is a very important document, since it is the first true world history to survive, spanning all of Eurasia from Far West to Far East. By contrast, the numerous world histories produced at the same time or slightly earlier in the West have no pretensions to encompass the world of Asia or Africa. Similarly, while the *Jami' al-tawarikh* can be slotted into the tradition of medieval Islamic historical and annalistic writing — owing a certain debt to Tabari (ninth century), al-Bundari (twelfth century), and Ibn al-Athir (thirteenth century) — its scope extends far wider than these texts.

The manuscript stands at a crossroads of history and art history, as the principal surviving illustrated document of the largest continuous land empire that the world has ever seen, stretching from Korea to Eastern Germany and from the Sea of Japan to the Baltic. The multiconfessional flavor of text and images alike reflects these expansive horizons, when most of Asia was briefly united under the Pax Mongolica. A pronounced tolerance of other faiths and remarkably ecumenical character inform the text and reflect the unprecedented favor that the Mongol rulers showed to Jews and Christians.

This folio, which depicts the Prophet's Night Journey from Mecca to Jerusalem to the heavens on his hybrid half-human steed Buraq, is the earliest known attempt by a Muslim painter to illuminate this otherworldly experience. The doors of heaven open as Muhammad is welcomed by angels who offer him a copy of the Qur'an and beverages: water, milk, wine, and honey. He chooses milk, thereby saving his community from drowning, drunkenness, and unbelief. Buraq's tail ends in a zoomorphic figure brandishing sword and shield, a zodiacal reference to Sagittarius that underlines the syncretic nature of the image.

RH

Selected References: Rice, D. T., 1976; Rashid al-Din 2015 ed.

1. No complete manuscript has survived.

85

Reed Mat

Tiberias, first half of the 10th century
Hemp (warp), straw (weft); weft-faced plain weave, brocaded
63⅜ × 33⅞ in. (161 × 86 cm)
The Metropolitan Museum of Art, New York, Purchase, Joseph Pulitzer Bequest, 1939 (39.113)

Medieval Arabic manuals of market regulation (*hisba*) refer to floor coverings made of reed, papyrus, or other plant-derived fibers such as *hasir*, *hasira*, or *husur*.[1] In many sources, *hasir* are associated with shrines and places of prayer.[2] The eleventh-century traveler Nasir-i Khusraw used the term when describing floor coverings in the Aqsa Mosque and the Tomb of the Patriarchs at Hebron.[3] Reed mats were also used in domestic settings: an eleventh-century letter from a Jewish merchant in Fustat includes an order with precise measurements for reed mats, which he requested to arrive before Passover.[4]

Various texts make clear that *hasir* were made in a number of centers around the Mediterranean. Khusraw describes the mats he saw in Jerusalem as "Maghrebi" (from the Maghreb, or perhaps meaning "Western" more generally) and claims that the ones in Hebron had been sent from Egypt. Palestine, too, was a center of production: the Metropolitan's prayer mat is almost identical to one in the Benaki Museum, Athens, which bears an inscription saying that it was made in the workshop (*tiraz*) of Tabariya (Tiberias).[5]

EDW

Selected References: Dimand 1942; New York 2011, pp. 50–51, no. 28.

1. Ghabin 2009, pp. 242–43.
2. Numerous hadiths mention reed mats, as cited in ibid., p. 242 n. 346. A typical ritual can be found in the book "Establishing the Prayer and the Sunnah Regarding Them" in the *Sunan Ibn Majah*: "It was narrated that 'Aishah said, 'The Messenger of Allah had a reed mat [*hasir*] that he would spread out during the day, and make into a compartment at night, towards which he would perform prayer.'" Ibn Majah 2011– ed.
3. Nasir-i Khusraw 2001 ed., pp. 33–34, 44–45.
4. Goitein 1967–93, vol. 4, pp. 127–29.
5. The Metropolitan's piece provides generic wishes, reading "Complete blessing and universal prosperity and continued happiness and joy to its owner." The example in the Benaki is similar, yet specifies it was made in Tiberias. Mina Moraitou in New York 2012, pp. 263–64, no. 185.

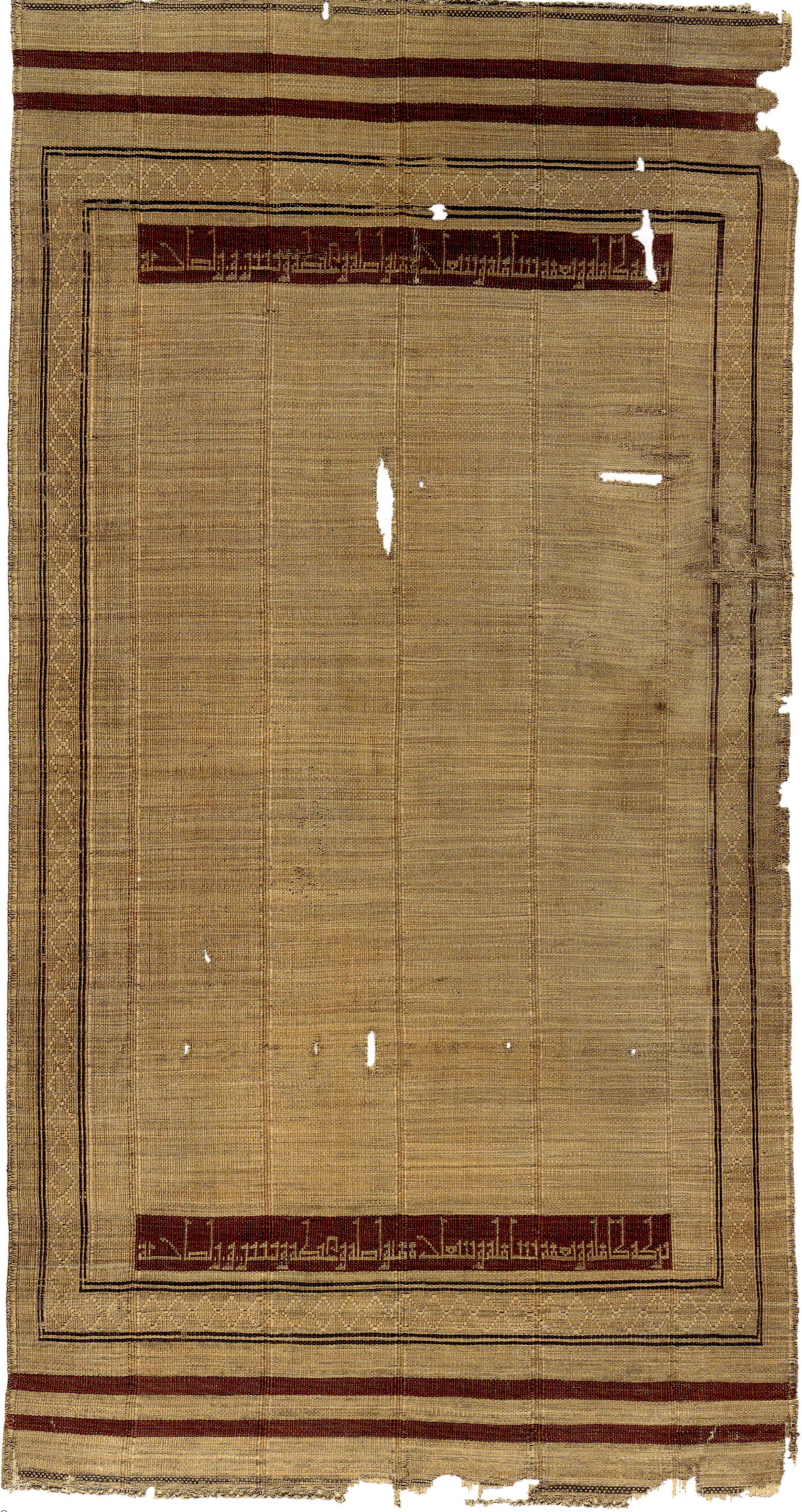

85

86

Portion of a Garment with Geometric Patterns

Egypt, 12th century
Linen, silk, and metal-wrapped thread, plain weave and tapestry weave
16 × 19¼ in. (40.6 × 48.9 cm)
The Metropolitan Museum of Art, New York, Rogers Fund, 1929 (29.136.4)

This finely woven textile was likely once part of a garment, possibly a cloak. The large medallion features patterns woven in gemlike reds, greens, blues, and yellows, as well as the word "Allah" repeating around its outer edge. The piece includes silk and gold metallic threads, signs that it was once an exceptionally valuable cloth. EDW

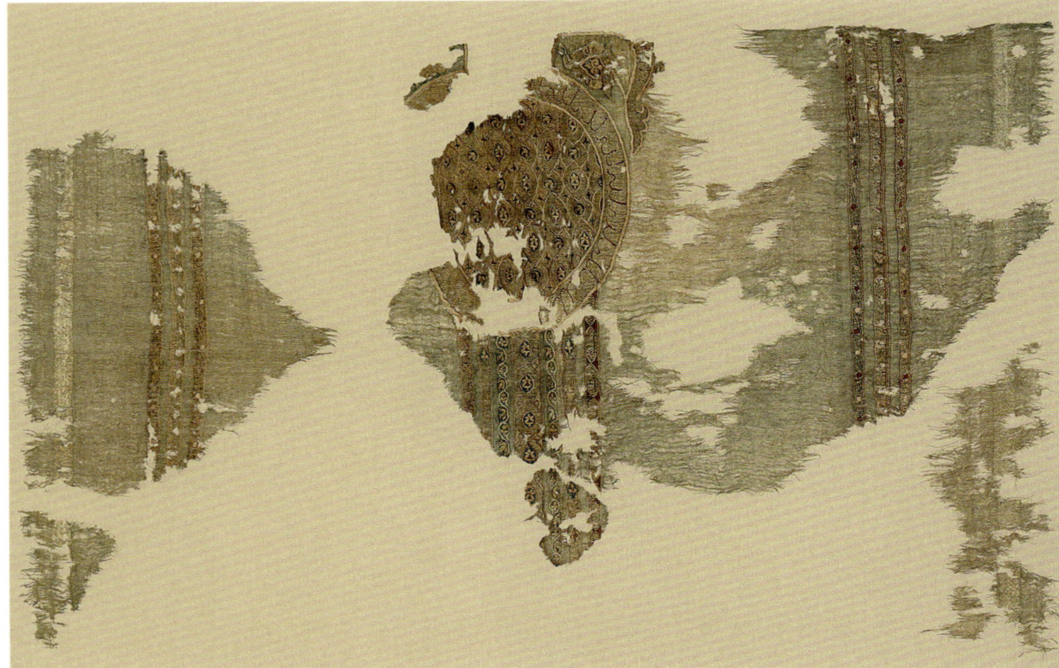

86

87

Textile Featuring Arabic Inscriptions

Egypt, 12th century
Linen and silk; tapestry weave
10¾ × 7½ in. (27.3 × 19.1 cm)
The Metropolitan Museum of Art, New York, Rogers Fund, 1929 (29.136.2)

The practice of embroidering, weaving, or painting textiles with inscriptions expanded greatly in the early Islamic period. Textiles with such inscriptions in Arabic are known as *tiraz* and were especially popular during the Abbasid and particularly the Fatimid periods for clothing, furnishings, and other fabrics. The Metropolitan's pieces can be dated to the Fatimid era thanks to the bright colors and decorative motifs, most notably the braided design.[1] The fragmentary inscription includes the *shahada*, the foundational pronouncement of Islamic belief. The prayer starts with the *bismallah* ("In the name of Allah, the Merciful and Compassionate") and continues with a statement of the uniqueness of God ("There is no God but God"). The lower registers use a shorthand catchphrase derived from the Qur'an, "Victory is from Allah."

Inherently valuable objects, textiles were admired across a wide social spectrum in the Middle Ages. Many inscribed pieces include the word "Allah" as part of their generic prayers or blessings, yet such textiles could be admired by people of different religious backgrounds, as Arabic-speaking Christians share the same word for God. The explicit statement of faith and victory on this fragment, however, reminds us that luxury goods could at times serve specific communal identities and needs. Far from blurring the boundaries between groups, textiles like this one emphatically proclaim sectarian difference. EDW

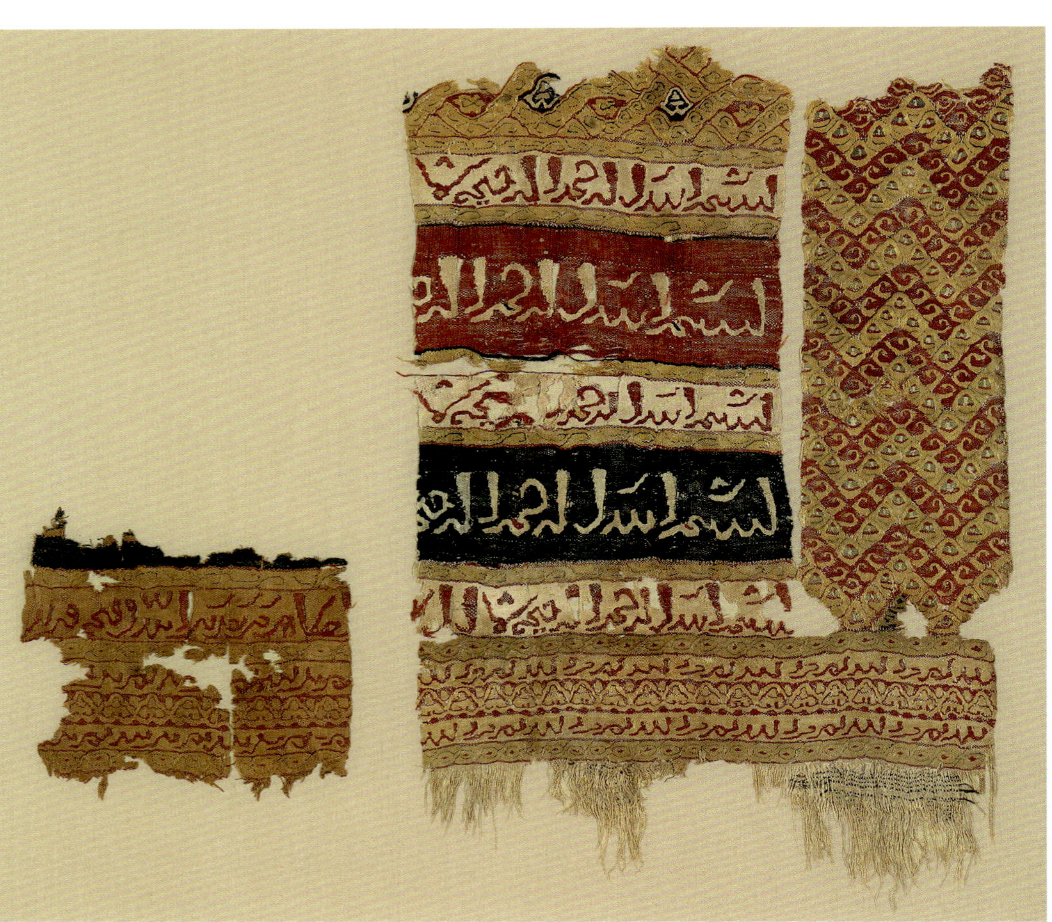

87

Selected Reference: Schimmel 1992, p. 13, fig. 15b.

1. Textiles with similar color schemes and decorative motifs include two fragments at the Brooklyn Museum of Art (39.90, 86.227.102) and one at the Art Institute of Chicago (1976.60).

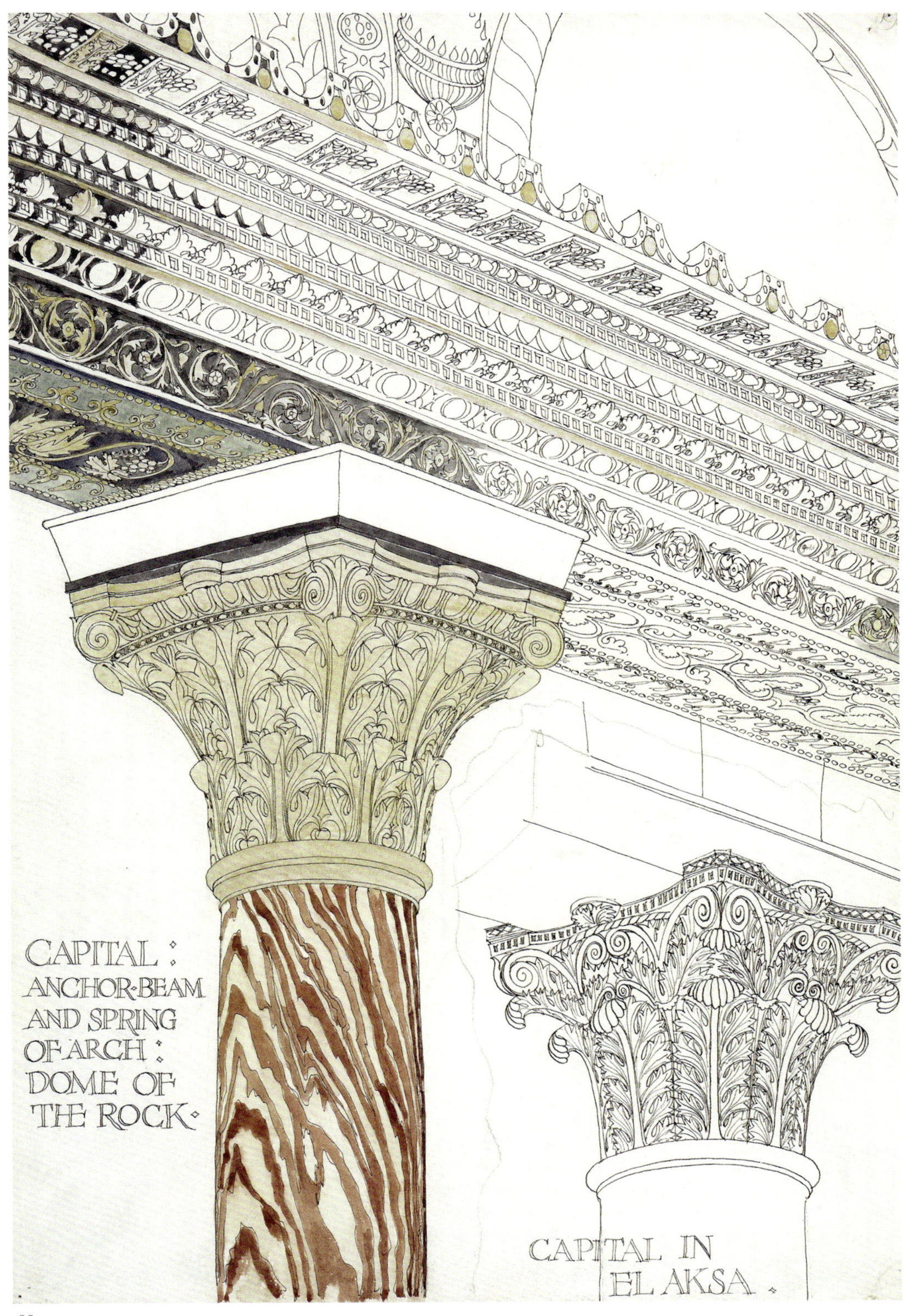

88

88

Drawing of Corinthian Capitals in the Dome of the Rock and the Aqsa Mosque

Jerusalem, 1909
William Harvey (1883–1962)
Pen, ink, watercolor, Indian ink, and gold
20 × 14 in. (50.8 × 35.6 cm)
Victoria and Albert Museum, London (E.1266-1963)

This carefully rendered drawing displays side-by-side architectural sculpture from the two greatest monuments on the Haram al-Sharif: a part of the variegated marble column and capital of one arch along the external octagon of the Dome of the Rock, and a capital from the Aqsa Mosque, located in the sanctuary to the south of the building.

Both Corinthian, these capitals were created in the Byzantine period and reused in the Dome of the Rock and in the mosque. Such recycling was common, due to the scarcity of white marble after the closure of quarries that had exported to the region around 550. Visitors to the Holy Land, whatever their ethnic or religious background, often remarked on the finely carved marble, still seen in abundance across the city today. As long as its ornamentation and artistry did not interfere with Islamic doctrine, Muslim artists widely adapted marble sculpture, particularly in subsequent restorations in the Aqsa Mosque. YN

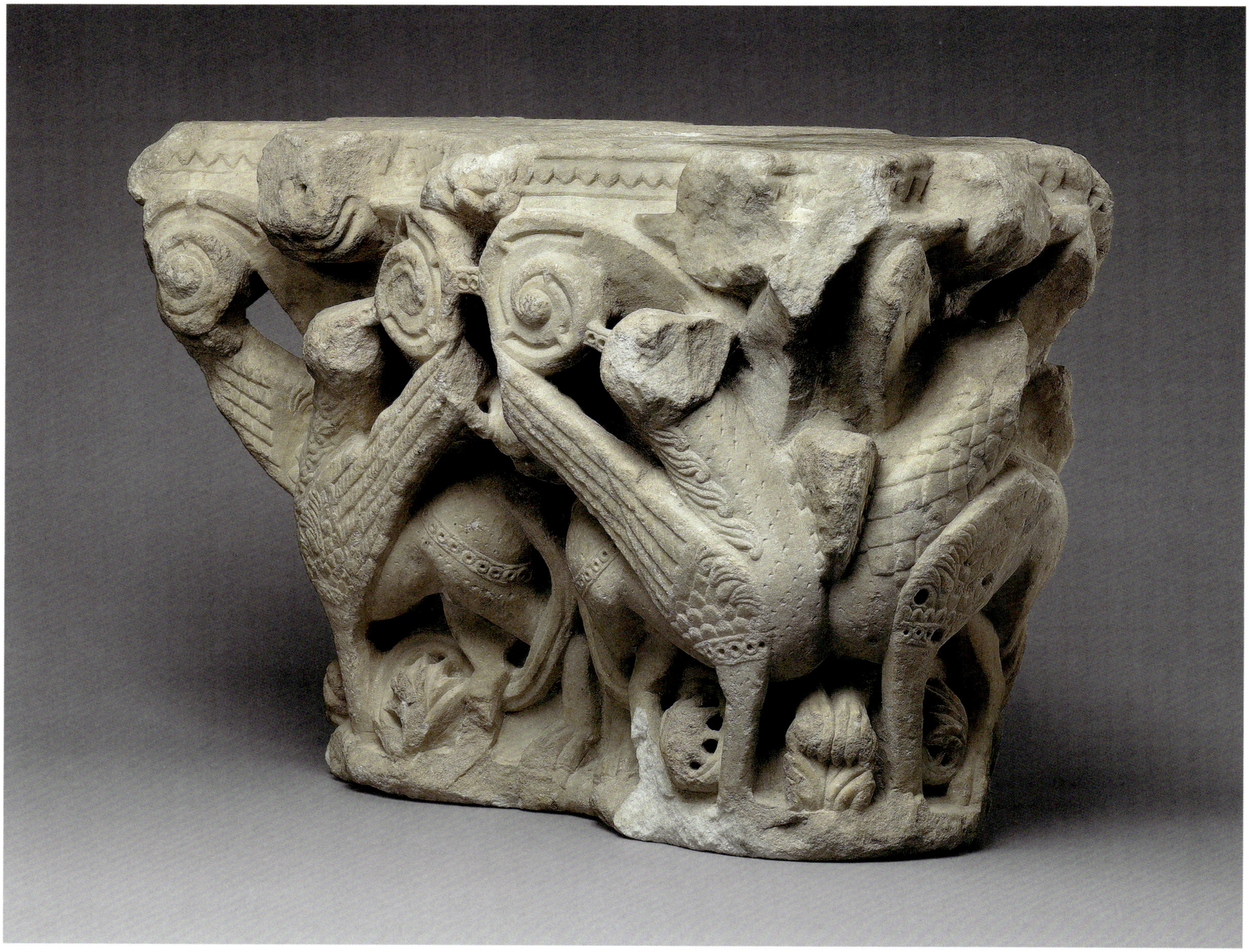

89

89

Double Capital with Griffins

Latin Kingdom of Jerusalem, ca. 1140–50
Marble, H. 14⅝ in. (37 cm), W. 19 in. (48 cm), D. 10⅝ in. (27 cm)
Church of Saint Peter in Gallicantu, Jerusalem

This imposing double capital attests to the ambitions of patrons and the capabilities of sculptors in the Latin Kingdom of Jerusalem. Though unavailable locally, white marble was used extensively on Crusader buildings like the Church of the Ascension and the Qubbat al-Mi'raj, the latter of which is thought to have served as the baptistery for the Crusaders. Details of the griffins — the feet poised on the lower ledge of the capital, the animals' nicely rounded haunches, the articulation of the wings — echo similar details on the birds found on single capitals at the Church of the Ascension, and the lion and lioness on the capital from the Islamic Museum (cat. 99). The proposed date for this double capital, first recorded by the French archaeologist Charles Simon Clermont-Ganneau, who had purchased it from a merchant near Jerusalem in the nineteenth century, is extrapolated from the Crusader dedication of the Dome of the Rock as the "Temple of the Lord" (*Templum Domini*) in 1141, a date that seems to be reinforced by comparison to a similar double capital of Crusader manufacture incorporated into the Aqsa Mosque and preserved there today (fig. 62). BDB

Selected References: Kühnel, B., 1977; Folda 1995, p. 272.

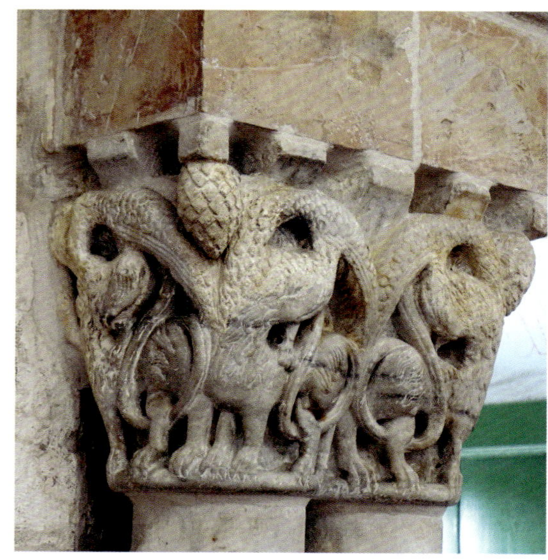

Fig. 62. A double capital in the Aqsa Mosque, Jerusalem

90

Sections 13 and 53 of the Qur'an of Nur al-Din

Damascus, A.H. Dhu'l-Hijja 562 (September 1167)
Calligraphy by 'Ali bin Ja'far bin Asad
Opaque watercolor, gold, and ink on paper and parchment
7⅝ × 6⅜ in. (19.5 × 16 cm)
By kind permission of the Keir Collection on long-term loan by Ranros Universal S.A. to the Dallas Museum of Art (ex. Keir Coll. VII 3 and 4)

These two Qur'an sections (13 and 53) come from a manuscript that once numbered sixty sections (*juz*'s), of which other parts are in the Damascus Museum and the Museum of Turkish and Islamic Art, Istanbul.[1] Each section begins with a decorated double frontispiece that appears on the right page under the number of the section, instead of the usual title of the chapter, and on the left under the repeated phrase "out of sixty sections." The chapter headings are contained within a golden guilloche frame and written in a rather plain Kufic script in white ink outlined with gold over an arabesque background in blue and gold. Below the section headings are just two lines written in cursive *naskhi* script, separated by an amorphously outlined cartouche that is either left plain or divided into rhomboids filled with simple repetitive ornament. Decorative palmettes in gold, red, and blue emerge out of the frame surrounding the text, level with the first line. The two volumes still retain their original leather binding, which is stamped and molded in the form of a lobed square, a design also found in contemporary carved stone ornament.

The body of each section contains four lines, also in *naskhi*, but somewhat smaller and more cursive than the frontispiece script. Unframed and minimally decorated, each page presents a perfectly balanced and easily legible text, conforming to a trend toward readability in Qur'anic scripts that had started in the early eleventh century and was actively pursued by the patron of this Qur'an, the Zangid ruler Nur al-Din, particularly in public inscriptions. The verses are separated by golden rosettes, while each fifth and tenth verse is marked in the margin by roundels in red framed by gold. The last page of each section reverts to two lines per page, which are bound by a golden border.

Section 53 ends with a colophon that gives the name of the calligrapher 'Ali bin Ja'far bin Asad, who may have been a scribe in the chancery of Nur al-Din and whose name also appears in a section in the Damascus Museum. The endowment deed (*waqfiyya*), inscribed in the last folio of section 53 and also in the portion at the Damascus Museum, states that the Qur'an was dedicated by Nur al-Din for his Hanafi madrasa in Damascus in A.H. Dhu'l-Hijja 562 (September 1167).[2] This is no doubt the Madrasa al-Nuriyya al-Kubra in Damascus, which he founded in A.H. 567 (1172) and named after himself.

One of the most striking features of this manuscript is that it is, at least partly, written on parchment, rather than on paper exclusively, making it one of the latest Qur'ans to use this material. Paper had begun replacing parchment in Qur'ans as early as the last quarter of the tenth century, and the first written in *naskhi* on paper is that of Ibn al-Bawwab, created in A.H. 390 (1000–1001). The more expensive material may have been chosen, about one and a half centuries after it was no longer widely used, for its durability, an important factor in a manuscript that is frequently handled by Qur'anic reciters. The division of the manuscript into sixty sections without regard to chapter divisions also conforms to Qur'ans that were intended to be read in specific measures, here as part of the endowment requirement.

By 1167, Nur al-Din was at the peak of his powers, having unified Aleppo and Damascus, asserted symbolic control over Mosul, and sent two expeditions to conquer

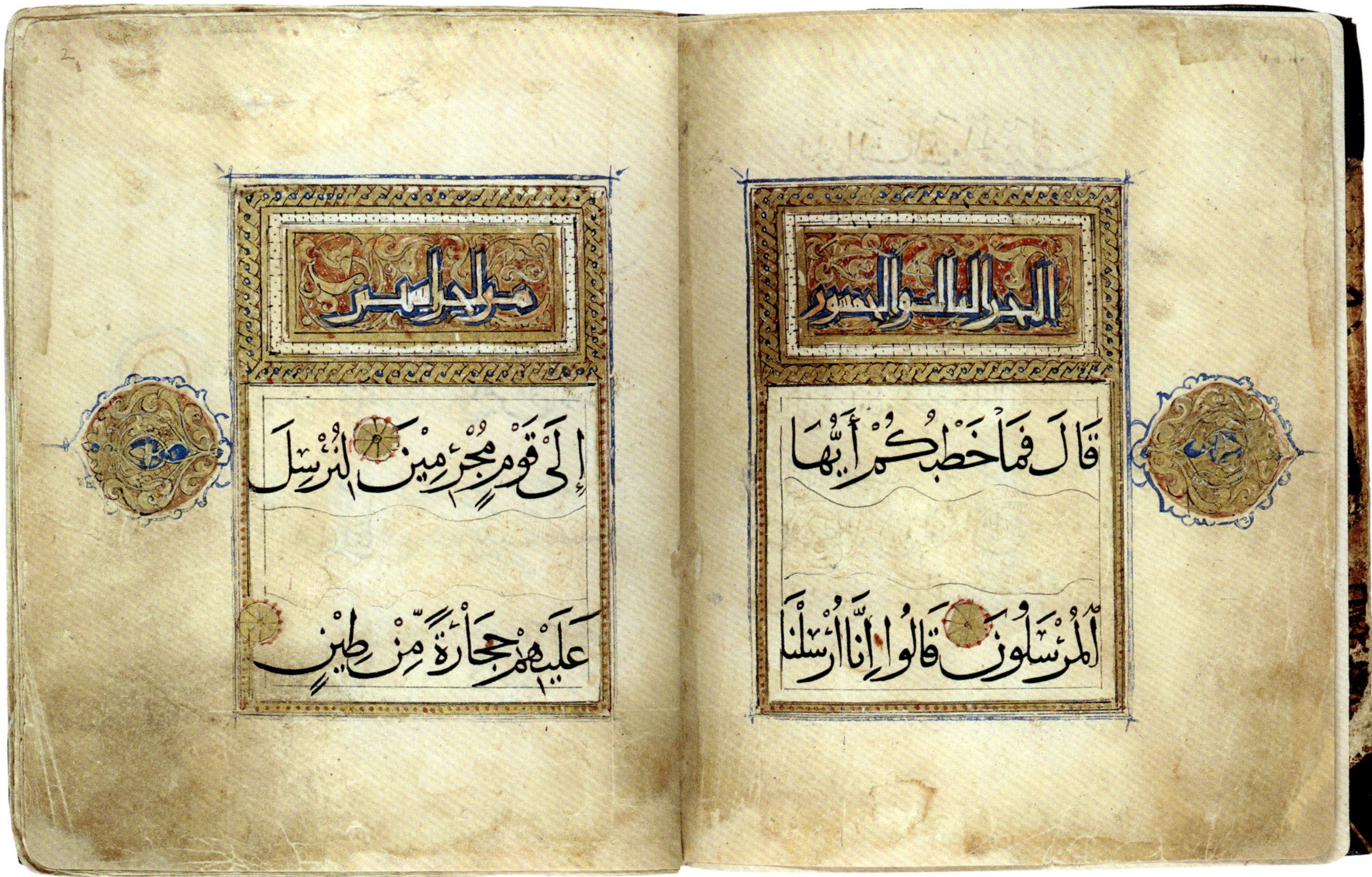

90 section 13, fols. 1v–2r

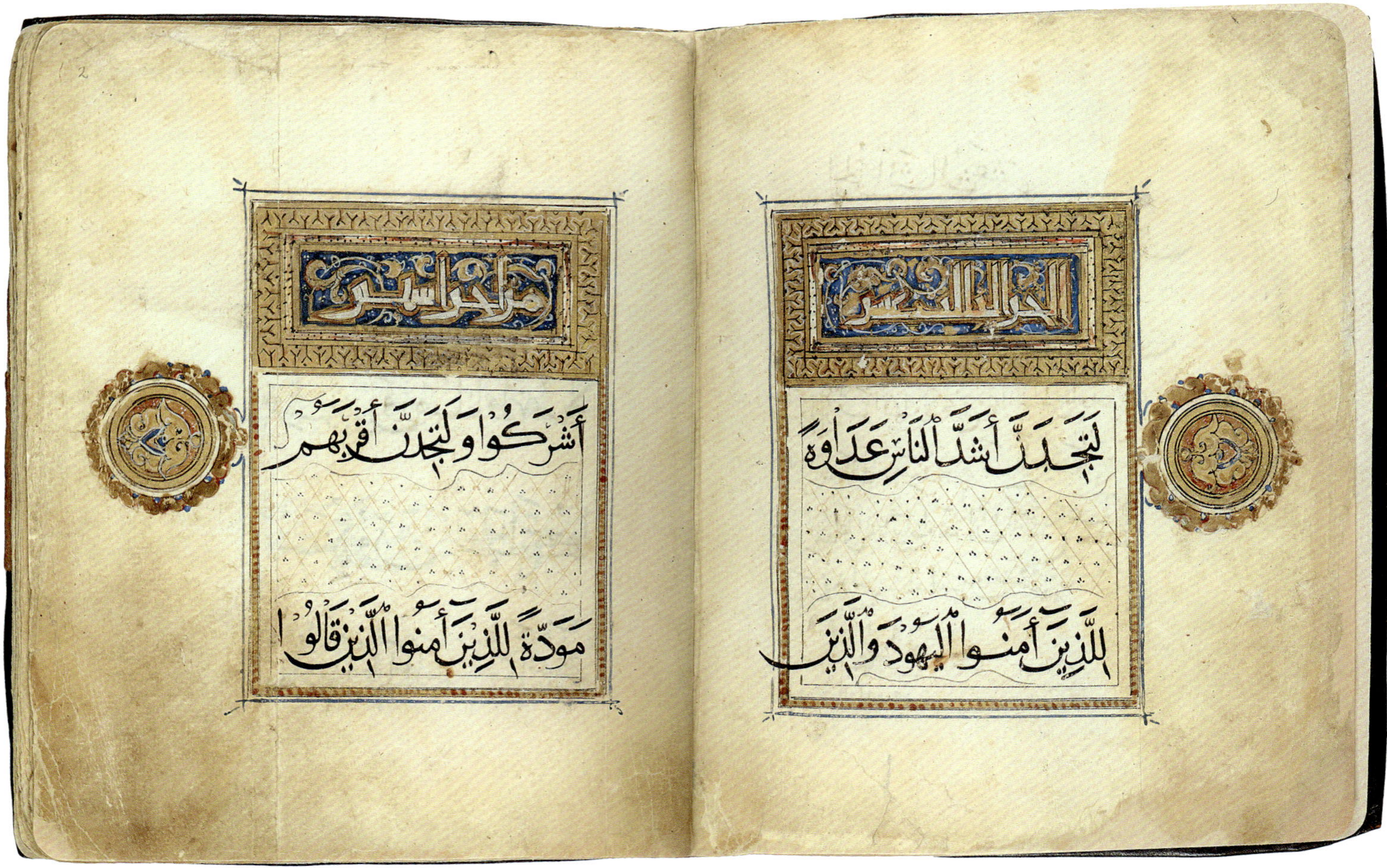

90 section 53, fols. 1v–2r

Fatimid Egypt, first in 1163 and next in 1167, led by his commander Saladin. Nur al-Din's determination to defeat the Ismai'li Fatimids, which he would finally achieve in 1171, signals a decisive shift from his earlier jihad against the Crusaders to advancing the Sunni revival by ending the state that was seen to represent the excesses of Shi'ism. In fact, his program of madrasa building represents a concerted policy to educate jurists in the Sunni traditions in order to further the aims of the Sunni revival. One could therefore infer that, for Nur al-Din, the suppression of an alleged heresy within Islam took precedence over the conquest of Jerusalem, which was not achieved until 1187 by Saladin.

Interestingly, the Madrasa al-Nuriyya is the first preserved college to include the mausoleum of its founder, here Nur al-Din, who acquired sainthood shortly after his death. It survives today as a courtyard-based structure with the attached mausoleum facing the Suq al-Khayyatin (tailors' market) through a double-grilled window. His arched cenotaph, covered in arabesque ornament and surmounted by an elaborate *muqarnas* (stalactite vaulting) dome, was quite likely the place where this Qur'an was intended to be read. The *waqfiyya* inscribed in the lintel above the main portal lists various income-generating structures (baths, shops, and agricultural lands) to support the college's educational and charitable functions but does not specify the normal dispensation of these funds, such as for the regular Qur'anic recitations upon the soul of the deceased founder. But judging from slightly later Ayyubid *waqfiyya*s, one can be fairly certain that this manuscript was read aloud daily by reciters whose voice would float through the window grilles and mingle with the hubbub of the street. YT

Selected References: Safadi 1978, p. 62; James 1988, p. 20; Tabbaa 1991; Tabbaa 2001; Paris 2001–2; New York 2016, p. 282, no. 182.

1. Section 13 begins with verse 82 of chapter 5, *Surat al-Ma'ida* (The Table Spread) and section 53 with verses 31–33 of chapter 57, *Surat al-Dhariyat* (The Winnowing Wind).
2. Hanafism is one of the four schools (*madhhab*) of Sunni jurisprudence. Most Turks, including the Zangids, followed this *madhhab*, which is considered to be the most permissive in legal matters.

91

Mosque Lamp of Sultan al-Zahir Baybars

Damascus, probably A.H. 676 (1277)
Brass, inlaid with silver and black compound
H. 11½ in. (29 cm), Diam. 11⅝ in. (29.3 cm)
Museum of Islamic Art, Doha (MW.117.1999)

Created for the Tomb of Sultan Baybars, this oil lamp of brass inlaid with silver was most likely crafted in Damascus in 1277, the year the sultan died. Currently in two parts, it lacks its original base. The decoration of the upper part (the neck) consists of a Mamluk inscription: "This is what was made for the blessed mausoleum of (al-Malik) al-Zahir (Baybars), may God sanctify his spirit and illumine his tomb." The middle of the body has large medallions, detailed with the supplication: "Oh God, in your mercy and Your grace, incline towards the tomb of our master the Sultan al-Malik al-Zahir Rukn al-Din."[1]

Among the most prominent early Mamluk leaders, Baybars ruled for seventeen years (1260–77) and played a significant role in resisting and expelling the Franks, exploits that eventually became the subject of popular tales, culminating in the *Life of Baybars* (*Sirat al-malik az-zahir Baybars*). He was unquestionably attentive to his administrative duties, maintaining strong links to Jerusalem and Palestine and patronizing architectural projects in the region.

Most extant lamps of the period are made from transparent glass overlaid with enamel and gold; few of pierced metal survive. Such lamps derive their status from the *Surat al-Noor* (The Light), chapter 24 of the Qur'an, in which Allah is called the light of the heavens and the earth, the Light being one of the ninety-nine names of God in Islam. The example of God's light is compared to a glowing lamp, lit from a "blessed Tree, An Olive, neither of the East, Nor of the West."[2] YN

Selected Reference: Paris, Brooklyn, and Doha 2006–7, pp. 132–35.

1. Doha 2002, p. 70.
2. Qur'an 24:35.

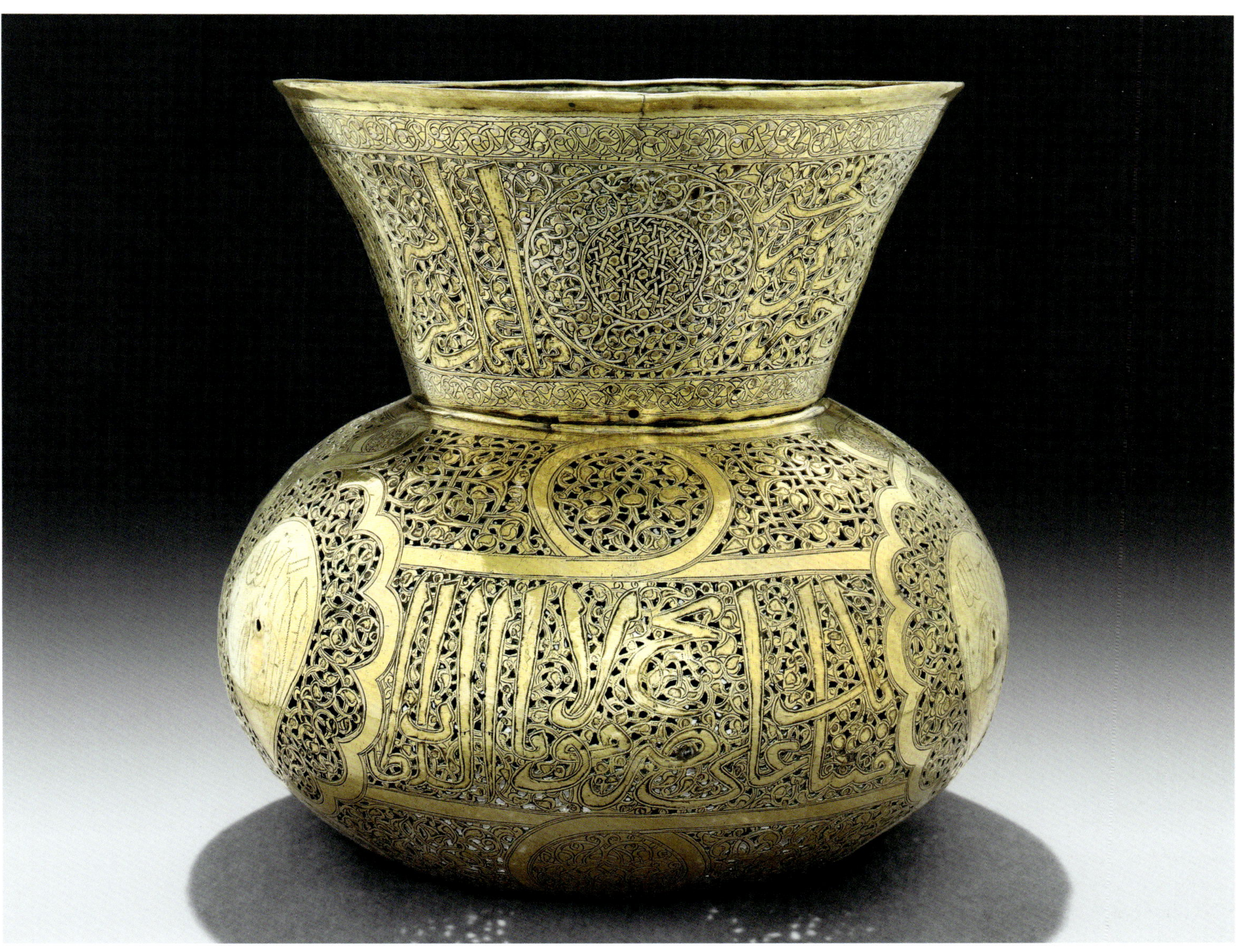

91

92

Commemorative Inscription from the Mausoleum of Abu Hurayra

Yavneh (Yibna), A.H. 673 (1274)
Marble
H. 28 in. (71 cm), W. 43 in. (109 cm), D. 1⅝ in. (4 cm)
Courtesy of the Israel Antiquities Authority, Jerusalem, exhibited at the Israel Museum, Jerusalem (2005-1891, 2008-1453)

This early Mamluk inscription, written in *naskhi* script and carved in relief, contains five lines in a rectangular frame with diacritical marks, many of which served as decorations, together with other embellishments such as foliated scrolls with palmettes and half-palmettes. The inscription commemorates the renovations of the tomb that were carried out by Khalil, governor of Ramle, under the order of Sultan Baybars, in A.H. 673 (1274).[1] Khalil built the portico leading to the tomb chamber that existed at the site prior to Baybars's arrival.

The tomb has dual attribution. It is believed to be that of Abu Hurayra, a companion of the Prophet Muhammad, who is best known for having transmitted 3,500 hadiths authored by Muhammad.[2] Although Abu Hurayra died in Medina and was buried there, tombs bearing his name are found in Yavneh and elsewhere. Since the thirteenth century, Jewish pilgrims have referred to the mausoleum as that of Rabbi Gamliel, president of the Sanhedrin, the Jewish high court, who lived at the end of the first and beginning of the second centuries.[3] NB

Selected References: Clermont-Ganneau 1896, p. 177; Taragan 2000.

1. The inscription is translated in Clermont-Ganneau 1896, p. 177.
2. The Persian traveler Ali al-Harawi (d. 1215) wrote, "Yavneh is a town between Jaffa and Ashkelon [Ascalon] where the tomb of Abu Hurayra is found." Taragan 2000, p. 122.
3. Written between 1266 and 1291, the *Ele Masa'ot* states, "And there is the tomb of Rabbi Gamliel, surmounted by a very beautiful dome, and it serves as a house of prayer for Ishmaelites, an imposing building known as Abu Hurayra." Taragan 2000, pp. 122, 139.

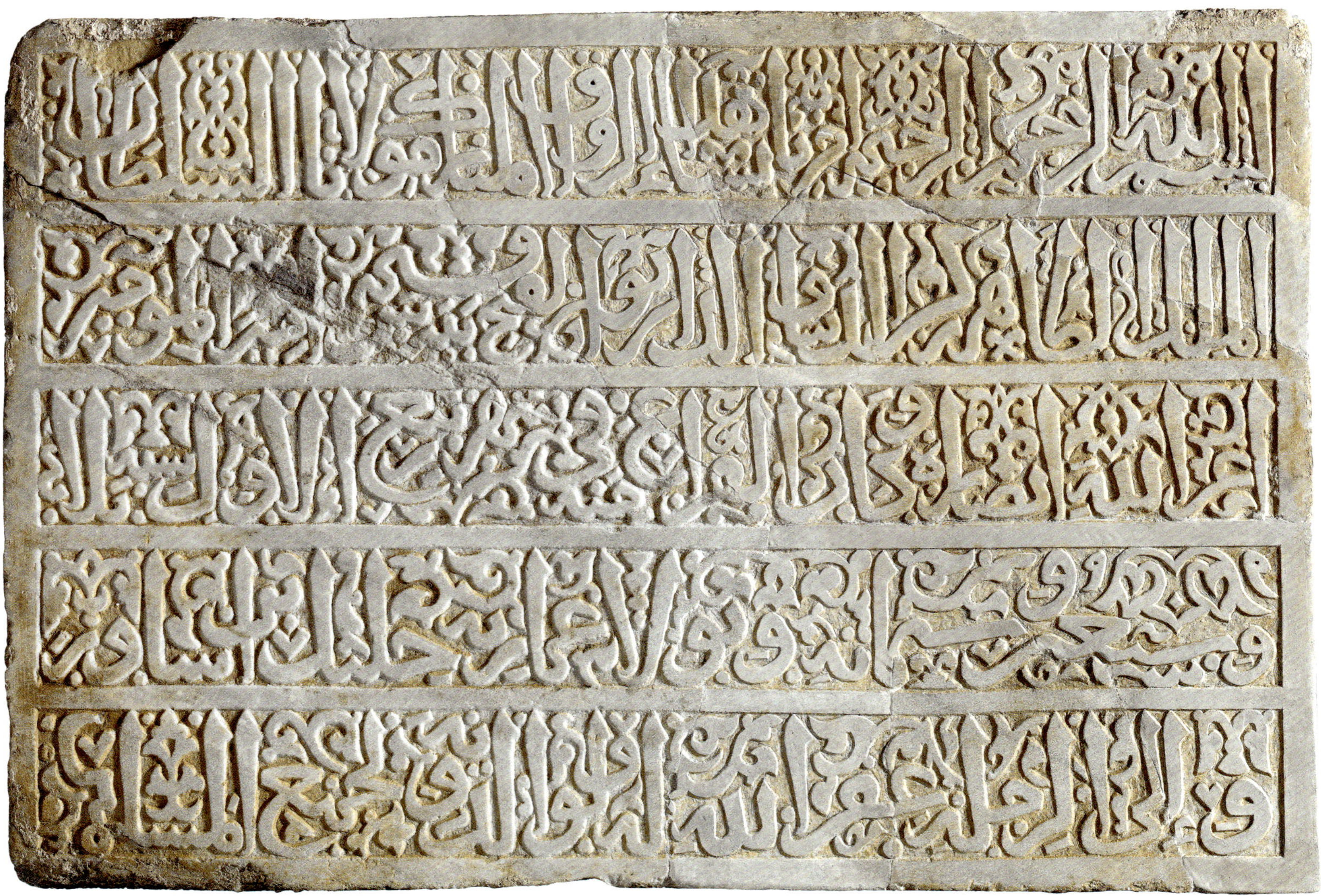

92

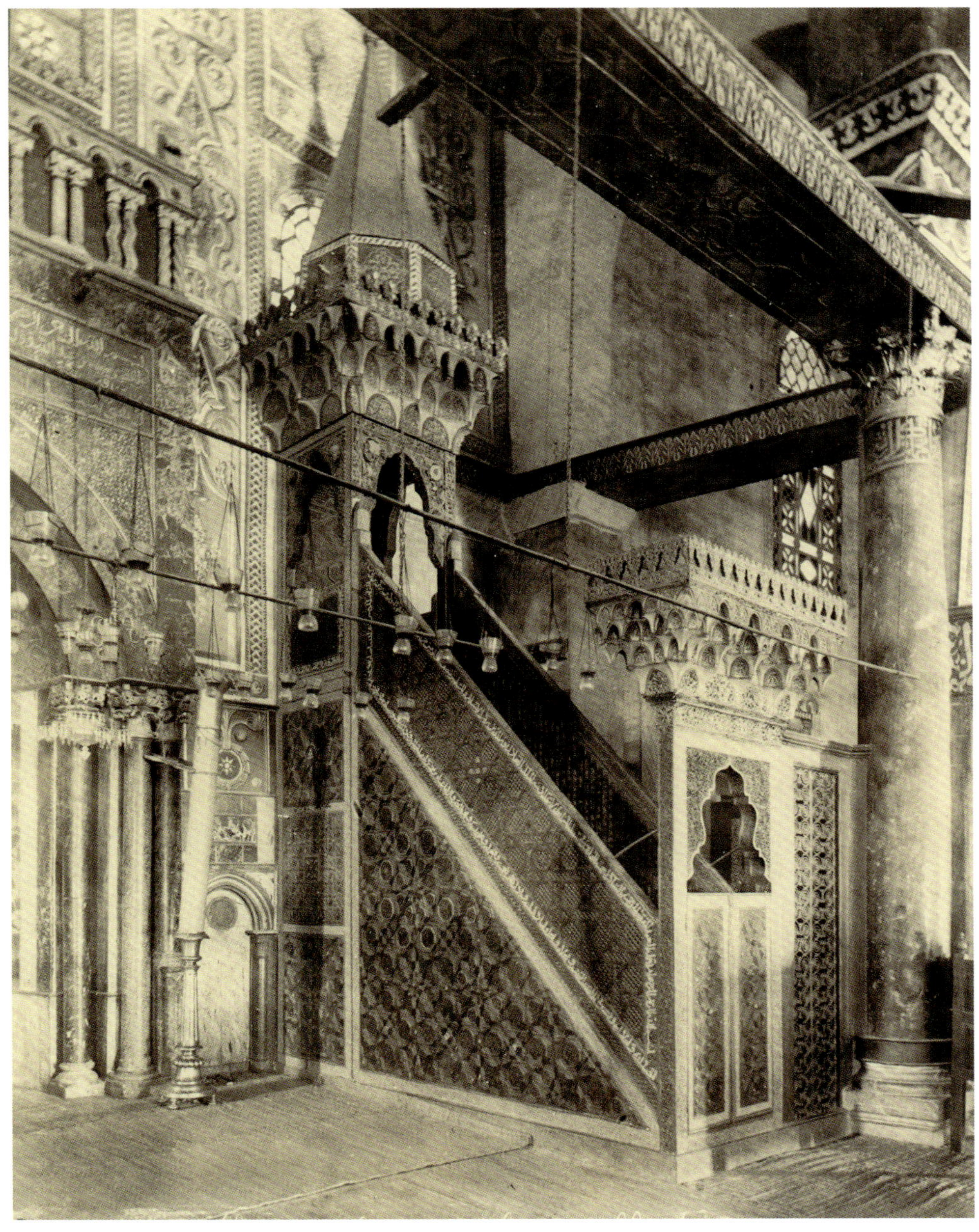

93a

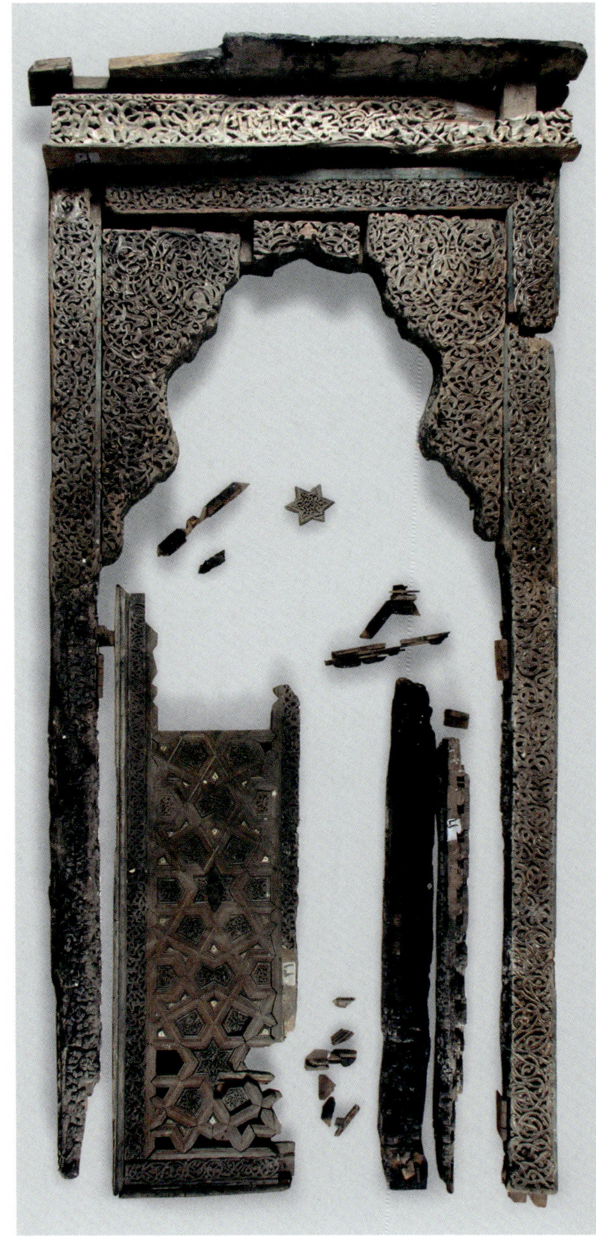

93b

93 a, b

a. The Minbar of Nur al-Din in the Aqsa Mosque

Jerusalem, ca. 1867–99
Félix Bonfils (1831–1885)
Albumen print
Image: 10⅞ × 8½ in. (27.5 × 21.5 cm), mat: 14 × 11⅛ in. (35.5 × 28 cm)
Library of Congress, Prints and Photographs Division, Washington, D.C. (LOT 13550, no. 216)

b. Remains of the Minbar of Nur al-Din

Aleppo, 1169–74
Carved pine, mother of pearl, pearls, and ivory or bone
Dimensions variable
Islamic Museum, Jerusalem (142/40)

The photograph by Félix Bonfils is one of the few images that document the monumental minbar, or pulpit, that graced the Aqsa Mosque from 1188 until August 1969, when, tragically, it was set on fire by Michael Dennis Rohan, a radical Evangelical Christian, leaving only fragmentary remains. Among the most beautiful minbars of the Levant, it was commissioned in 1168–69 by Nur al-Din, who aimed to liberate the city and the mosque from the Franks. The work was completed in 1174–75 during the reign of his son al-Saleh Ismail, but as the twelfth-century historian Ibn al-Athir has explained, it was Saladin who, after his conquest of Jerusalem, triumphantly transferred the minbar from Aleppo to Jerusalem in 1187.[1]

The word *al-Minbar* derives from the trilateral verb *na-ba-ra*, which means to tower and rise. Height and elevation, which traditionally characterize the pulpit, are emblematic of the stature of the orator who preaches on Fridays and other religious occasions. Socially, the minbar functioned much as the media and centers of learning do today. At the same time, it is inextricably linked to prayer, which, along with the personal declaration of faith (*shahada*), is central to Islamic observance. Indeed, Friday prayer is not considered valid without a sermon. The artistic value of this minbar, still discernible from the few treasured pieces that survive, arises in part from its prized materials and the sophisticated interlocking (*ta'sheeq*) that joins them mechanically, without the use of glue or nails. The inscriptions, largely religious in nature, include the names of not only Nur al-Din and his son but also the artists. YN

Selected References: Singer, ed. 2008; Abweini et al. 2013; al-Jubeh 2016.

1. Ibn al-Athir in Gabrieli, ed. 1969, p. 145.

94

Section of a Qur'an

Syria, the Jazira, or Egypt, 13th century
Opaque watercolor, gold, and ink on paper; 274 folios
20 × 13¼ in. (50.8 × 33.7 cm)
The Metropolitan Museum of Art, New York, Fletcher Fund, 1924 (24.146.1)

This section of a Qur'an is lavishly illuminated with text written entirely in gold letters outlined in black. The preserved suras (Qur'an chapters) represent the second half of a once large Qur'an.[1] Many of the sura headings, as well as the three fully illuminated pages that survive, are set against a background of vegetal scrolls on a deep blue ground. Verse endings are marked with illuminated disks inscribed with the word *aya* (verses), while the fifth and tenth verses and prostration points are noted by marginal disks or teardrop-shaped medallions. The text, generally eleven lines per page, is written in a cursive script comparable to what medieval sources referred to as *ash'ar* or *thuluth ash'ar* (that is, thuluth outlined in hairline strokes).[2]

The sophistication and luxuriousness of this Qur'an suggest that it was intended for a wealthy if not courtly owner, while its monumental size indicates that it might have been intended to be used in a mosque or madrasa (school offering higher education in Islamic law and theology), public buildings that were often furnished with precious and colorful artworks, including Qur'ans and other books. Such manuscripts emphasized the importance given at that time to the color and beauty of the written word or calligraphy. Usama ibn Munqidh, a courtier and diplomat under Saladin, wrote about a Qur'an copied by his father: "One of the copies was a huge one which he wrote in gold in which he included all the sciences of the Koran — its different readings, its obscure terms, its Arabic style and grammar, . . . its commentary, reasons for its revelation, and its jurisprudence. This copy, which he styles *al-Tafsir al-Kabir* [the great commentary], was written in black ink alternating with red and blue. Another copy he transcribed with letters of gold, but this had no commentary. The rest of the copies were written in black ink with the following in gold: the first words of the tenth and fifth parts of the book, the number of verses, the first word of the surahs [chapters], the titles of the surahs and the headings of the sections."[3] DB

Selected Reference: New York 2011, pp. 141–42, no. 90.

1. For a recent discussion and more references on this Qur'an manuscript, see Ellen Kenney in New York 2011, pp. 141–42, no. 90.

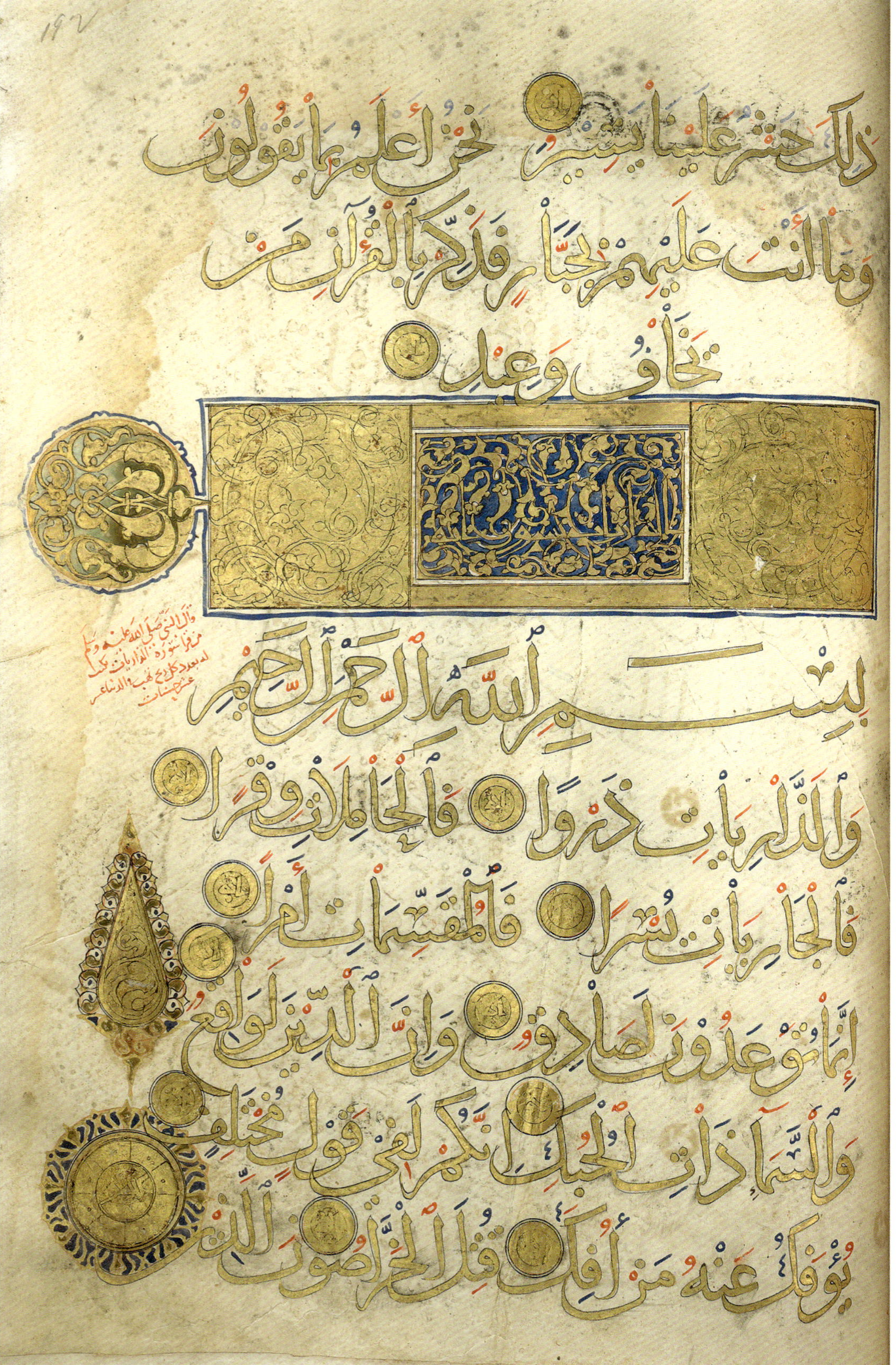

94, fol. 192

2. James 1999, p. 19. As pointed out by Kenney (in New York 2011, p. 142 n. 4), some aspects of the script rather compare with *tawqi'* and *tumar*, especially the way the final letter of *Allah* is open or how the letter *mim*'s relative short tail hooks upward.

3. Quoted in Usama ibn Munqidh 2000 ed., p. 81.

95

Folio from a Qur'an Manuscript with Verses from *Surat Maryam*

Egypt or Syria, 14th century
Opaque watercolor, gold, and ink on paper
13 × 10⅝ in. (33 × 27 cm)
The Metropolitan Museum of Art, New York, Purchase, Ehsan Yarshater Gift, 1975 (1975.29.1)

This illuminated folio in *naskhi* script contains verses from *Surat Maryam* (Qur'an 19), the only chapter of the holy book dedicated to the Virgin Mary, mother of Jesus. The elaborate heading at the top of the folio encloses the name of the sura ("of Maryam"), the number of verses (89), and the place of revelation (Mecca). The text focuses on Mary's motherhood and describes her childbirth in detail. Her exalted place in Islam is also discussed in Sura 3 (*al-'Imran*, The Family of 'Imran), where it is stated that she was revered and chosen above all women.[1]

There are many powerful associations between the birth of Jesus and the Holy City of Jerusalem. The Cradle of Jesus is located on the Haram al-Sharif at the northern corner of the court at the entrance to Solomon's stables. It is a small rectangular room believed to be where Jesus was laid down by Mary after he was presented at the Temple when he was only forty days old.[2] For centuries the Cradle of Jesus was an important place of worship and pilgrimage for both Christians and Muslims. According to the Florentine Giorgio Gucci, who traveled to Jerusalem in the late fourteenth century and visited the Church of the Tomb of the Virgin Mary, "Every morning early, many Saracen women and men enter the said church to worship, and more women than men: and this is the reason, because the said women have great reverence for Our Lady and have great faith in her. And every morning, while making the visits, we met Saracen women doing the visits, which, it is said, Our Lady made every morning for XIV years, which she lived after Our Lord; and in these devout and notable places they kneel and make reverence as we Christians."[3] The Presentation of Jesus at the Temple is thus a momentous event ingrained in the collective memory of believers of both faiths. ME

1. Qur'an 3:42, "Behold! the angels said: 'O Mary! Allah hath chosen thee and purified thee — chosen thee above the women of all nations.'"

2. See "The Cradle of Jesus and the Oratory of Mary on Jerusalem's Haram al-Sharif," pp. 138–39, in this volume.

3. Quoted in Frescobaldi, Gucci, and Sigoli 1948 ed., p. 129.

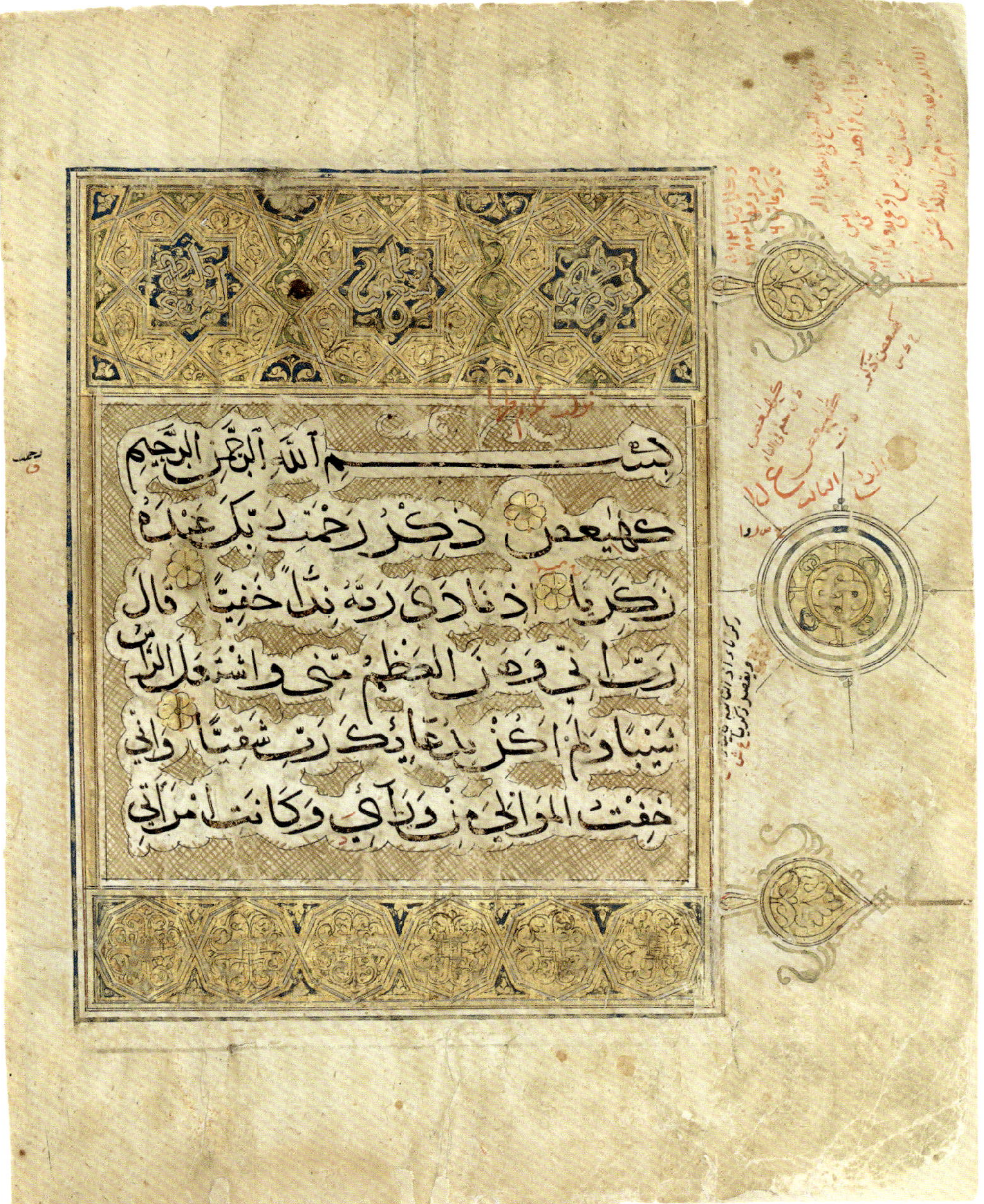

95

Roads to Jerusalem

Some wishing to visit the Holy Places of the chosen Land of Promise should begin from Nazareth where our salvation had its beginning.[1]

With Jerusalem as the goal, pilgrimage meant visits to a number of sites in the Holy Land. For Christians like Marino Sanudo the Elder (1260–1338) — who never actually made the trip — it meant stops at places described in the Gospels, beginning in Nazareth, where Jesus's birth was first heralded. For Jews, it included visits to the Tomb of the Patriarchs and ancestors who stood in silent witness to their history in the Holy Land.[2] An overlapping itinerary informed Muslim pilgrimage, whether undertaken in addition to, or in lieu of, pilgrimage to Mecca.

Where sites became sacred, artistry followed. As in Jerusalem itself, sanctuaries were built, ornamented, embellished, endowed by patrons, and recorded in pilgrims' writings. The works of art gathered here hail from three of the most important holy sites beyond the city of Jerusalem: Bethlehem, honored by both Christians and Muslims as the birthplace of Jesus; Hebron, sacred to all three faiths; and Nazareth, in Galilee, where Jesus's family lived and from which his ministry was launched.

BDB / MH

1. Sanudo 2011 ed., p. 403.
2. Prawer 1988, p. 174.

96

Watercolors of the Mosaics in the Nave and Transepts of the Church of the Nativity, Bethlehem

Bethlehem, 1909
William Harvey (1883–1962)
Graphite and watercolor on paper
Each: 32¼ × 46⅝ in. (81.9 × 118.4 cm)
The Society of Antiquaries of London
(Scharf 95 and 96)

In 1909 the British-trained architect William Harvey (1883–1962), a graduate of the Regent Street Polytechnic and Royal Academy Schools, rendered his first important service in the preservation of the Church of the Nativity in Bethlehem.[1] Under extraordinarily difficult circumstances, he prepared watercolor drawings of the surviving wall mosaics in the nave and transepts of this venerable church, the first renderings of the mosaics in color.[2]

Among the mosaics reproduced by Harvey, there are, on the north wall of the nave, symbols (summary texts) of the provincial councils at Sardis and Antioch in Greek, and above, in the clerestory, striding angels with a Latin inscription at the feet of the central angel.[3] On the east wall of the north transept are scenes of Doubting Thomas and a fragment of the Ascension. On the east wall of the south transept is the Entry into Jerusalem. On the south wall of the nave are, to the left, the summary texts, in Greek, of the ecumenical councils at Nicaea, in 325 (line endings only, at left), and Constantinople, in 381 (with letters *B* and *C*); to the right, Ephesus, in 431 (half survives), and Chalcedon, in 451 (right); below are seven bust-length portraits of ancestors of Christ — Iac[o]b, Math[an], Eleazar, [Ab]iud, Achi[m], Sadoch, Azor — from Matthew 1:1–16.[4]

Harvey's watercolors are clearly important; nonetheless, one must use some imagination. For example, what Harvey represented as a yellow ground is actually a brilliant metallic gold that has its own distinctive coloristic and reflective properties. Given the magnificence of the designs, the lavishness of the materials (gold, silver, mother of pearl, and rich colors), and how difficult it was for Harvey to see the details in dim light and under layers of dust, soot, and water leakage from the roof and windows, the watercolors are a signal achievement and a valuable resource.[5]

The origins of these surviving mosaics are still debated. Some scholars favor the idea that they were originally done in the seventh to eighth centuries, then were repaired, renovated, and added to in the twelfth century. Others think that the mosaics were entirely set in the twelfth century.[6] These Bethlehem mosaics are the only extant examples of large-scale figural mosaic programs in a major dominical holy site. In the Church of the Holy Sepulchre in Jerusalem, by contrast, only one small fragment — an image of Christ on a rainbow — in the Chapel of Calvary survives

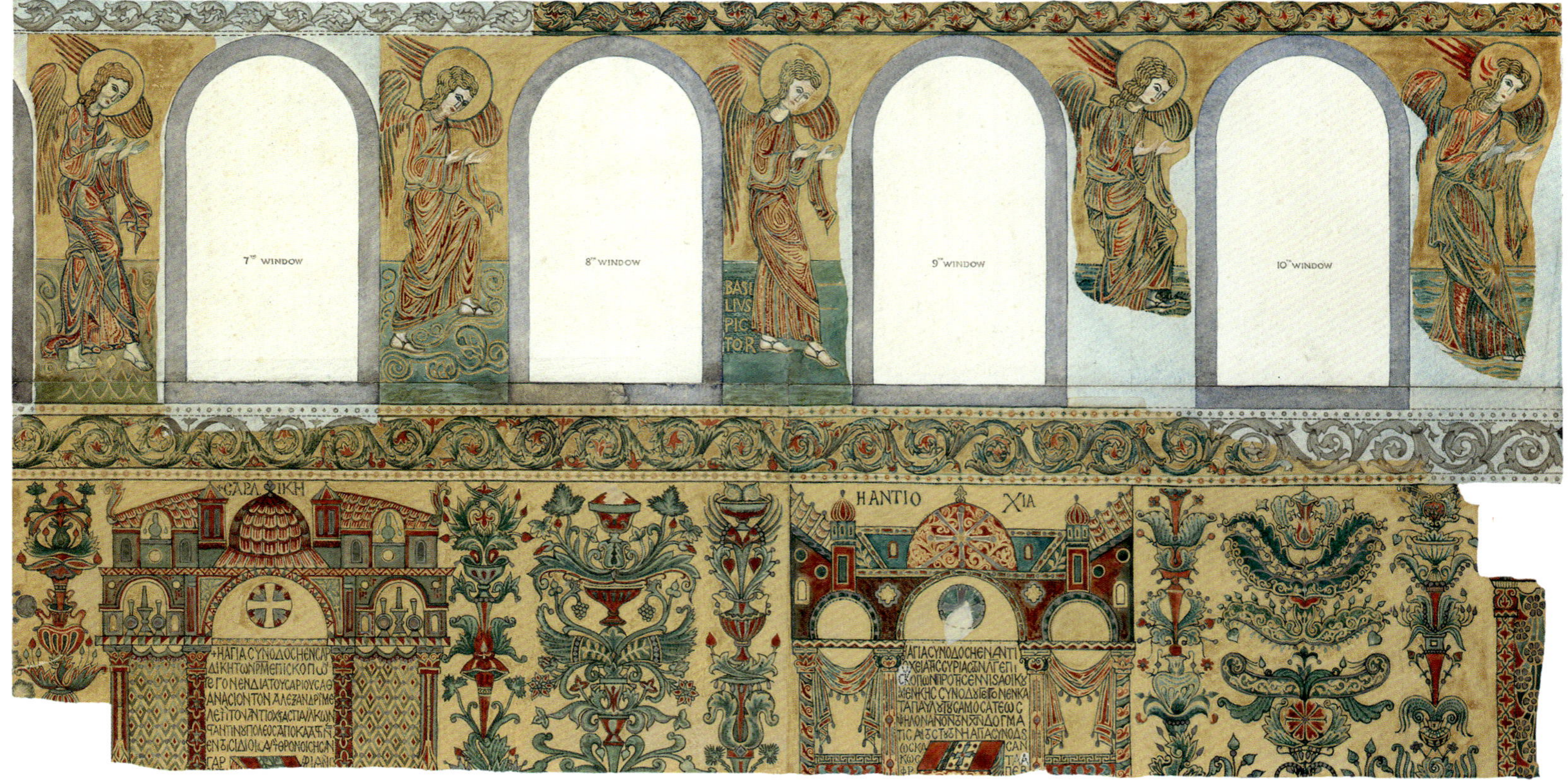

96 North wall of nave

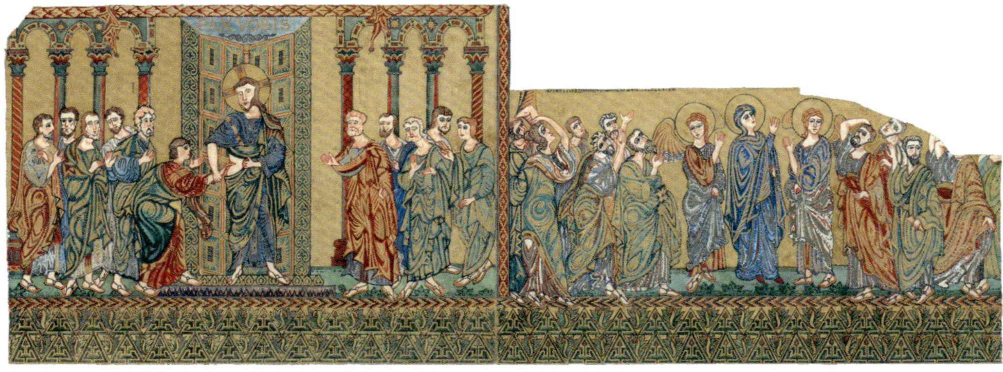

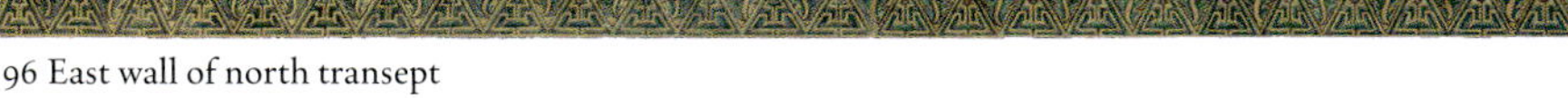

96 East wall of north transept

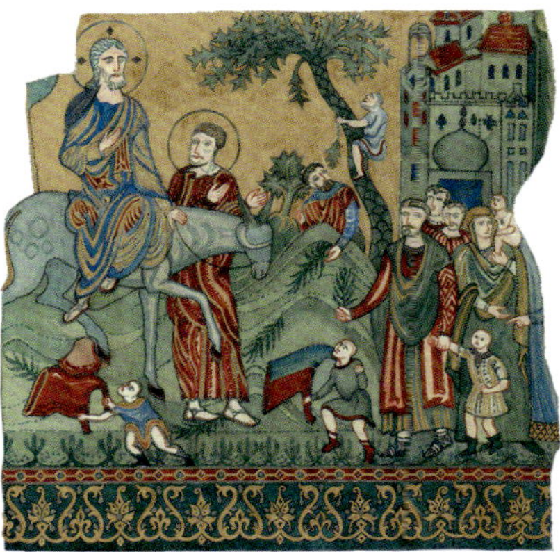

96 East wall of south transept

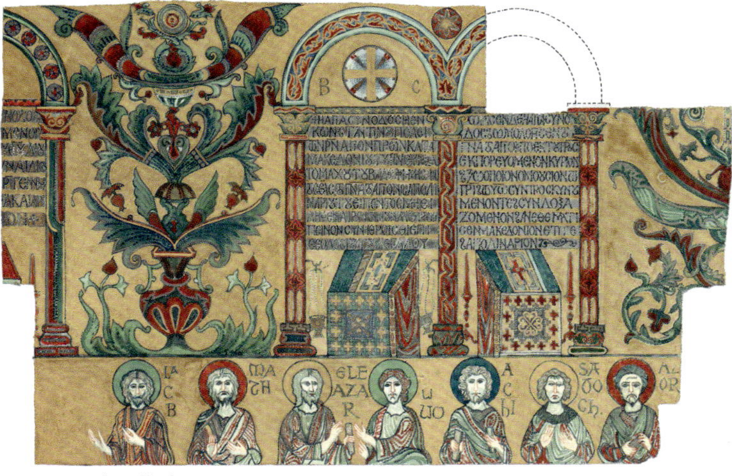

96 South wall of nave

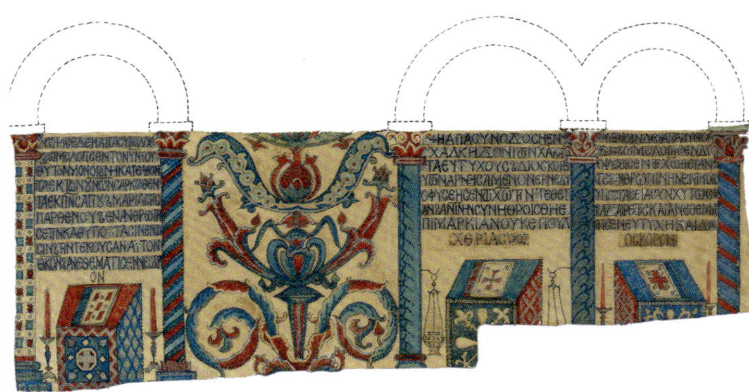

from a sizable program in that church complex (fig. 47). Harvey's watercolors still enable us to imagine what the surviving mosaics in Bethlehem looked like in their colorful glory.[7]

JF

Selected References: Schultz, ed. 1910, pp. 1–12, pls. 10, 11; Vincent and Abel 1914, pp. 143–83; Stern, H., 1936, 1938, 1948, and 1957; Hamilton, R., 1947, pp. 51–69; Bagatti 1952; Tzaferis 1981; Kühnel, G., 1988, 1993–94, 1999; Hunt 1991; Pringle 1993–2009, vol. 1, pp. 137–56; Folda 1995, pp. 347–64; Hunt 2005–6; Keshman 2013.

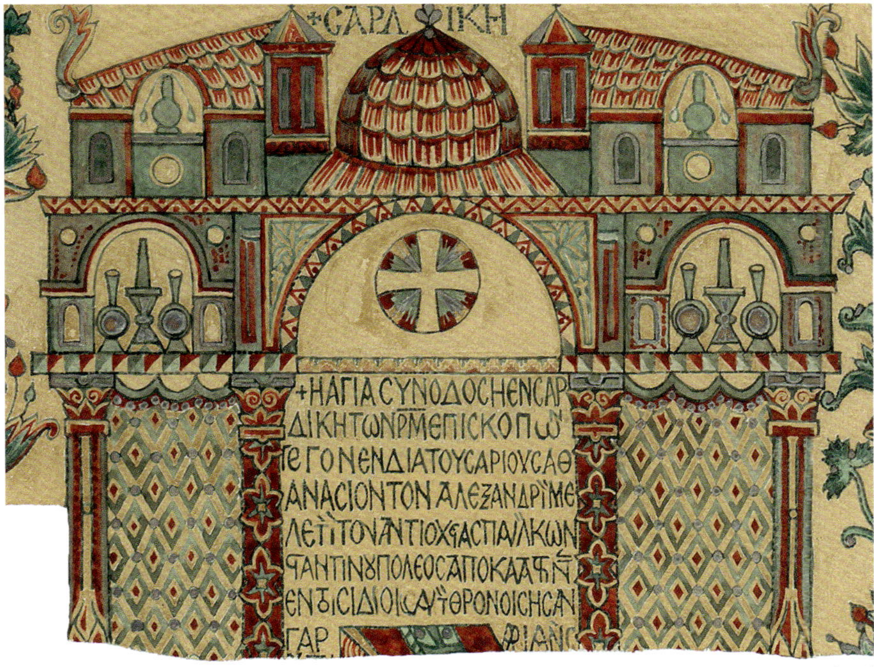

96 detail

1. *RIBA* 1962. Additional details on William Harvey are found in the finding aid for his collection of papers in the Surrey History Centre, Woking, England, item no. 623.

2. Earlier representations included the detailed written description of Quaresmius in 1626 (Quaresmius 1639, vol. 2, pp. 469–510), followed by Ciampini in 1693 (Ciampini 1693, pl. 33, between pp. 150 and 151).

3. The north wall mosaics are published in Schultz, ed. 1910, as pl. 10.

4. Published in ibid., as pl. 11.

5. Harvey's striking account of his labors demonstrates that he spared no pains in attempting to capture an accurate record of their appearance under difficult circumstances: "The drawings of the mosaics were made entirely on the spot in the church. . . . Extreme care was taken. . . . Every letter recorded in the inscriptions having been checked by means of powerful opera-glasses from many different standpoints on the church floor, and upon a high step-ladder in the middle of the nave. . . . The colours had to be determined by reference to those in the comparatively small portions accessible for adequate cleansing and thorough investigation; and having been put on paper in the gloom of a church interior in wintry weather, fail to do justice to the beauty of the original tints" (William Harvey in ibid., p. 32). While Harvey's attempt at accuracy is impressive, in at least one instance the problem of seeing inscriptions covered with grime could not be overcome: in the watercolor, the angel in the clerestory on the north wall of the nave was given the Latin inscription "Basilius pictor" (Basil the deacon depicted [this]; Folda 1995, pp. 351–52) at the lower left of the figure; Harvey could not see the Syriac inscription at the lower right of this figure, which only became visible after Gustav Kühnel cleaned it in the early 1990s.

6. A book-length study on the subject, begun by Gustav and now being completed by Bianca Kühnel, is in progress. See Keshman 2013, pp. 257–69.

7. The Ma'an News Agency, based in Bethlehem, reported (February 20, 2016) news of the cleaning and conservation of these mosaics currently in progress. The find of an ancient icon embedded in the wall of the church was also mentioned.

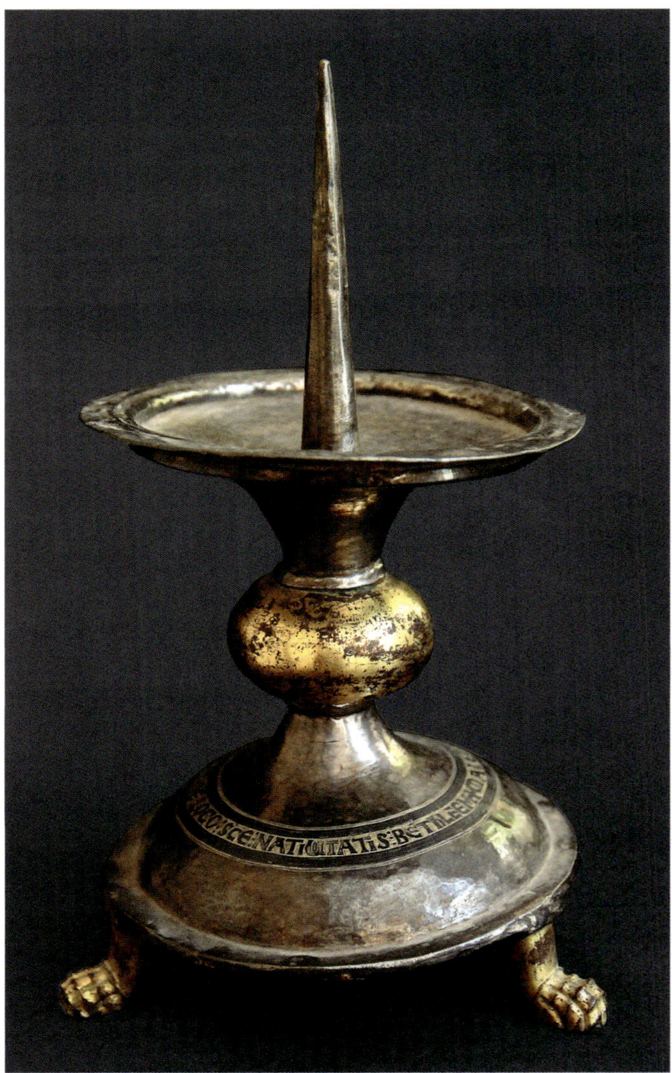

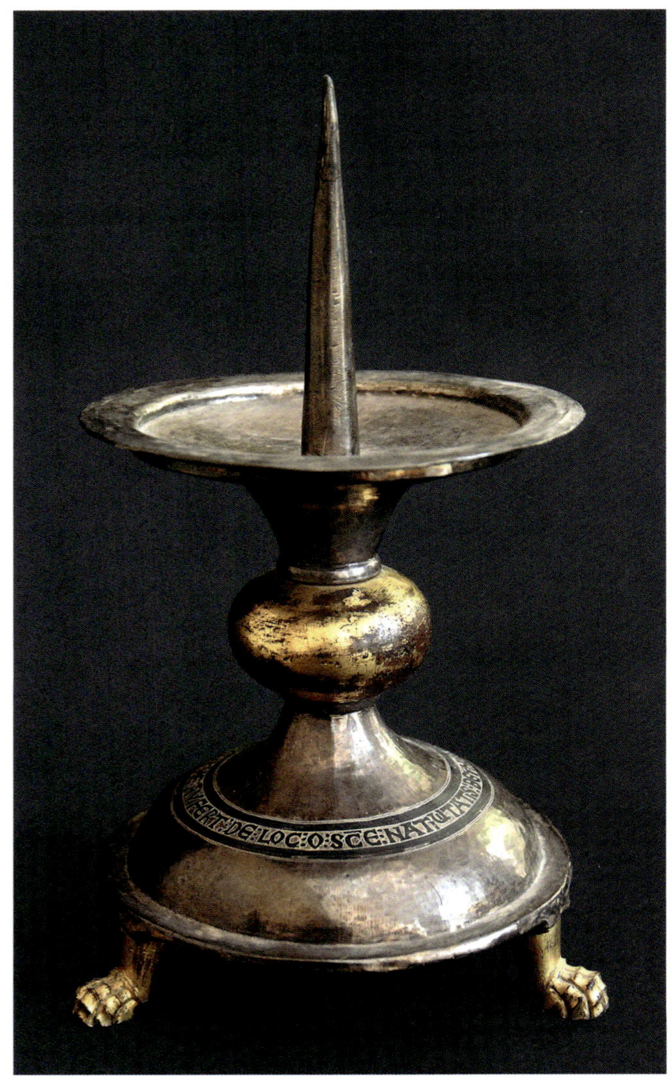

97

97

Pair of Candlesticks

England(?) or Latin Kingdom(?), first half of the 13th century
Silver with niello and some gilding
H. including pricket 10⅝ in. (27 cm), W. 6¼ in. (16 cm), D. 6¼ in. (16 cm)
Terra Sancta Museum, Studium Biblicum Franciscanum, Jerusalem (CTS-SB-01326/7)

These silver candlesticks would have been used on the altar of the Church of the Nativity in Bethlehem for a variety of services, among which the liturgy, known in the Western church as the Mass, was the most frequent and important. Candles were used widely in the church to symbolize the divine presence for those gathered in God's name and the Christian passage from darkness into the light of the Word of Jesus.

The history, rarity, and particular inscriptions of these Bethlehem candlesticks make them especially remarkable. In the Middle Ages liturgical vessels made of precious metals were highly susceptible to theft and were frequently melted down for the value of their metal content. These examples from Bethlehem are prized survivals, as nothing comparable remains from the Church of the Holy Sepulchre in Jerusalem or the Church of the Annunciation in Nazareth. Both candlesticks have special inscriptions on their bases to protect them from theft. Done in niello on silver, they read: "Maledictur qui me aufert de loco sce nativitatis bethleem" (Anathema to him who would take me away from the site of the holy Nativity in Bethlehem).[1]

The candlesticks were apparently part of a celebrated ecclesiastical affair in which Giovanni Romano, former bishop of Bethlehem, improperly sold off liturgical property of the See of Bethlehem following the loss of Jerusalem and Bethlehem to the Khwarezmian Turks in 1244. When the new bishop, Gottifredo de' Prefetti de Vico, was named in 1245, he immediately petitioned Pope Innocent IV to recover the lost property. With the pope's support, in 1247 the items, which included certain specific relics and very likely these two candlesticks, were reclaimed.[2]

JF

Selected References: Enlart 1925–28, vol. 1, pp. 193–94; Bagatti 1952, pp. 72–73, 113; Boas 1999, pp. 157–58; Milan 2000, p. 252; Folda 2005, pp. 208–9.

1. Folda 2005, p. 209.
2. Ibid., pp. 208–9.

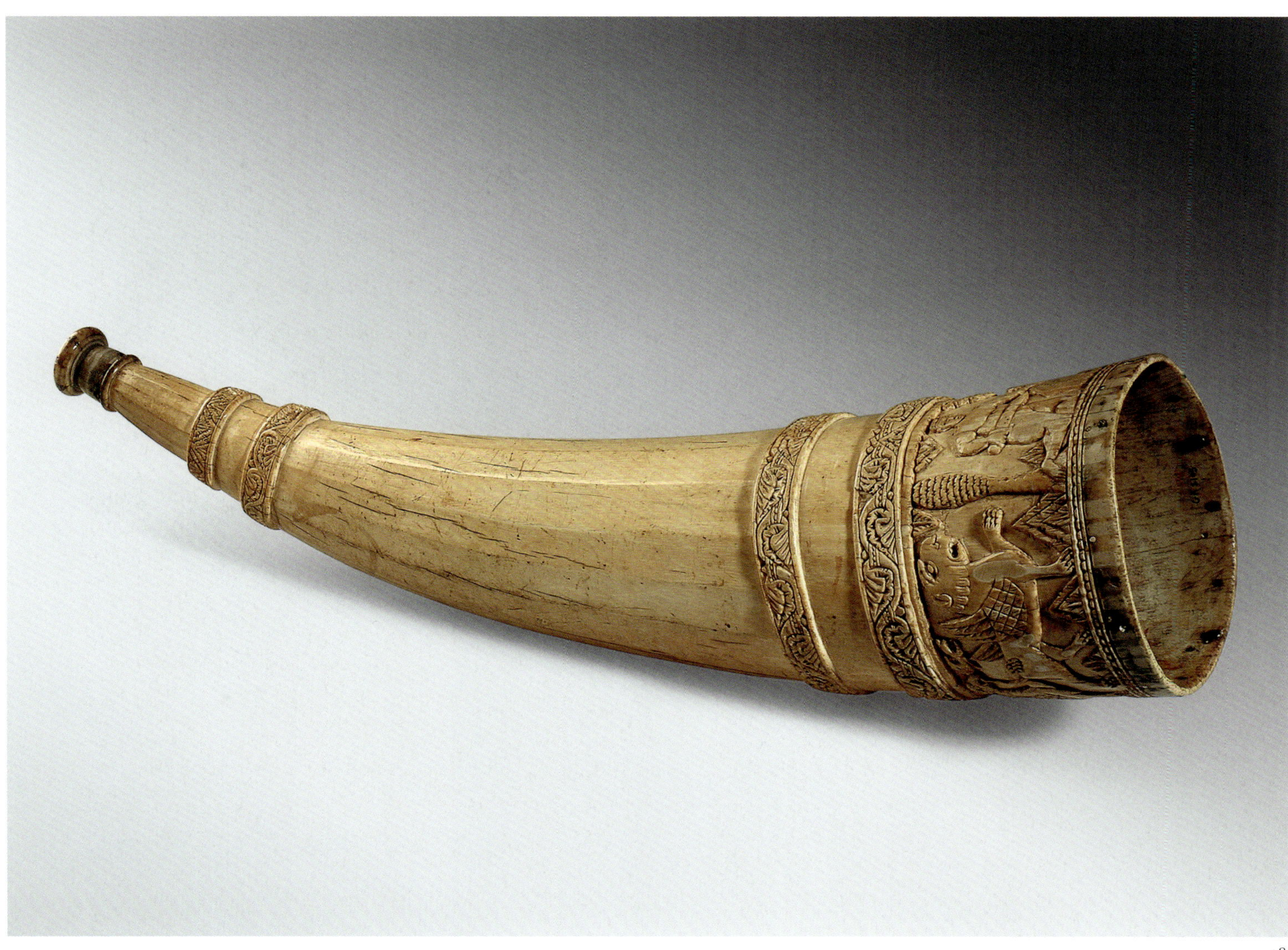

98

98

Ivory Horn (Oliphant)

Eastern Mediterranean or Sicily, 12th century
Elephant ivory
23⅝ × 5⅜ in. (60 × 13.5 cm)
Musées d'Angers (MA 1 R 99-69)

Horns of elephant ivory are among the most ubiquitous treasures preserved from the Middle Ages, yet their individual histories are often lost. This example, evocative of far-away lands both by virtue of its material and its representation of a lion hunt—complete with a camel ridden by a small naked man sounding a horn—also has documentary evidence that links it to the Holy Land. In 1255 an oliphant was listed in the inventory of the cathedral of Saint Maurice in Angers, with the precise information that it contained the relics of the "four patriarchs, Abraham, Isaac, Jacob and Sarah," along with remnants of the Last Supper and other relics, mentioned secondarily, and a document attesting to their authenticity.[1]

The bodies of the patriarchs at Hebron were, according to both Christian and Muslim accounts, discovered beneath their cenotaphs in June 1119. Henceforth, they ranked among the most celebrated in the Holy Land. Accordingly, the church of Saint Abraham at Hebron was made a cathedral in 1168. Churchmen and nobles visiting the Holy Land acquired pieces of the prized relics over the course of the twelfth century.[2] The ivory horn was mentioned in a later listing of the gifts to the cathedral from its bishop, Guillaume de Beaumont (r. 1202–40).[3] By that time, Hebron had been conquered by Saladin and was no longer under Christian control. Did the bishop of Angers obtain the relics in Acre, to which he had traveled in 1217 as a participant in the Fifth Crusade,[4] or are the relics the same ones described in Angers in 1211?[5]

BDB / MH

Selected Reference: Shalem 2014, pp. 311–14, no. B15.

1. The bodies of the patriarchs were discovered alongside those of their wives. The Angers inventory, in what may be a slip of the pen, mentions Sarah as one of the four patriarchs, rather than as the wife of Abraham.
2. See Pringle 1993–2009, vol. 1, p. 228, which also discusses the Muslim accounts. For the importance of the discovery and an English translation of the European medieval accounts, see Whalen 2001.
3. See Farcy 1898, p. 468.
4. See Pletteau 1876, p. 157. The bishopric of Hebron was vacant between 1189/91 and 1252, when the bishop became resident in Acre. See Pringle 1993–2009, vol. 1, p. 228.
5. Noted in Shalem 2014, p. 314.

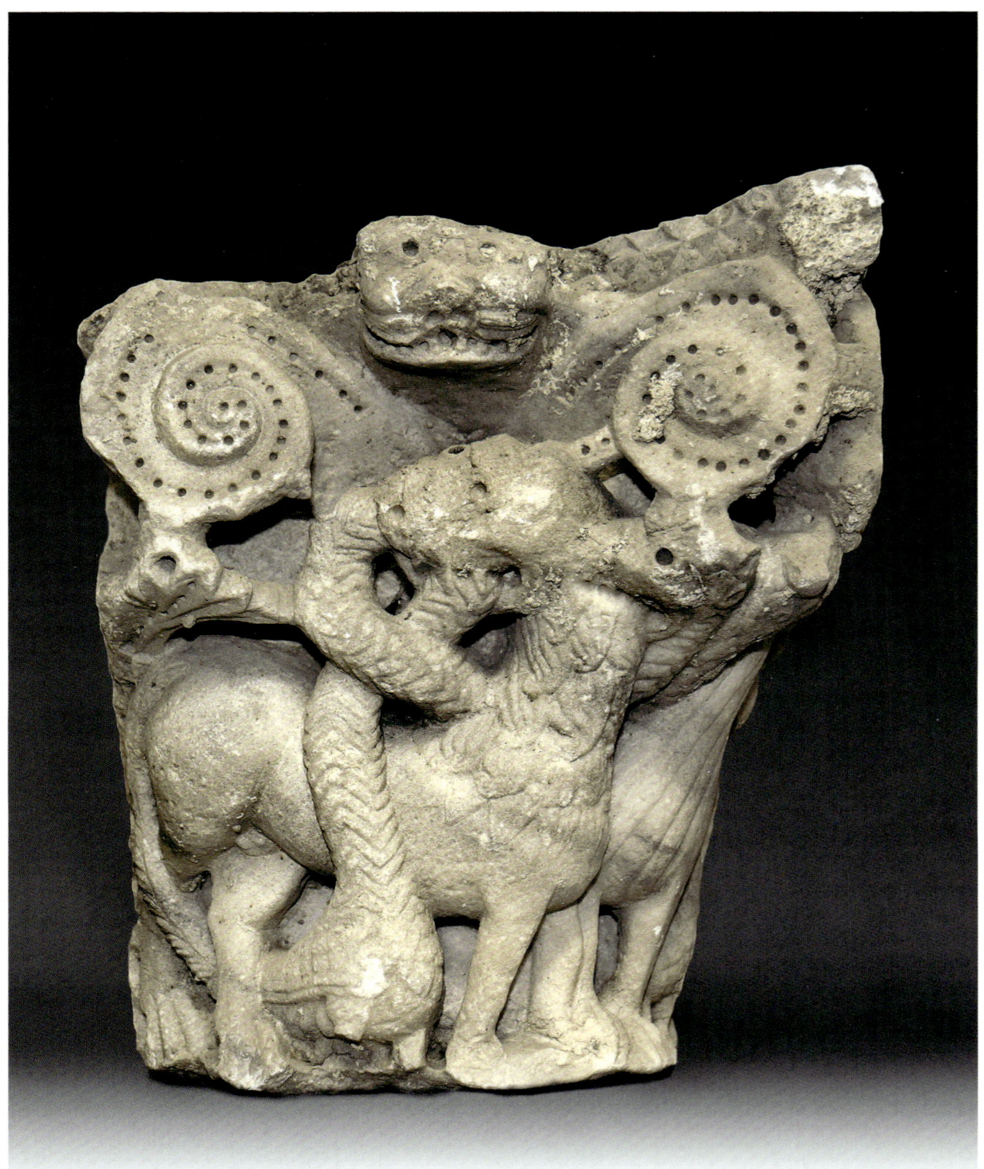

99

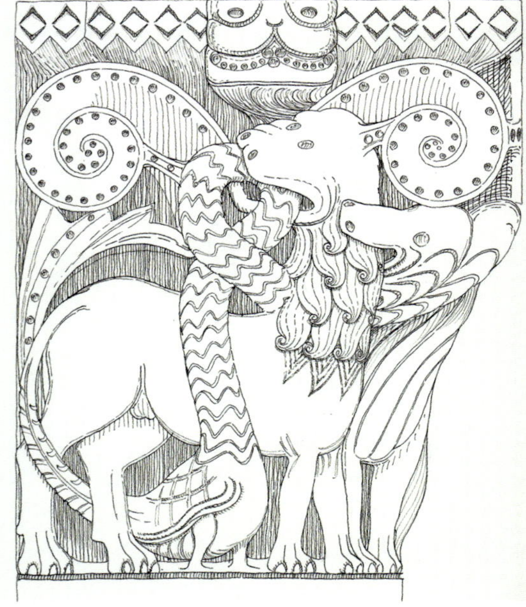

Fig. 63. Drawing of a capital with lions and serpents in the Mosque of ʿAli al-Bakka in Hebron. William Harvey, ca. 1909. Pen and ink. Victoria and Albert Museum, London (E.1247-1963)

99

Capital with Lions and Serpents

Latin Kingdom of Jerusalem, ca. 1140–50
Marble
H. 12⅝ in. (32 cm), W. 7⅞ in. (20 cm), D. 7⅞ in. (20 cm)
Islamic Museum, Jerusalem (inv. no. 45)

As the historian Ibn al-Athir recounted, when Saladin reconquered Jerusalem in 1187, the Franks left unwieldy artistic treasures behind — "even superb columns of marble and slabs of marble and mosaics in large quantities."[1] This deftly carved capital, with its intertwined, battling lions and serpents, is among the most charming examples of this phenomenon.

Its general layout recalls the capitals with birds (created before 1150) on the exterior of the Church of the Ascension and a double capital with lions in the Aqsa Mosque from the Crusader era (fig. 62). While the original destination of this sculpture is unknown, its aesthetic appeal was apparently such that it was adapted to use in a prominent window of the Shaykh ʿAli al-Bakka Sufi Mosque in Hebron, which was built by Sultan Baybars in 1269. The capital could still be seen in 1909, when it caught the eye of William Harvey, who made several drawings of it (fig. 63).[2] BDB

Selected References: Boehm 2014; al-Jubeh 2015.

1. Cited in Gabrieli, ed. 1969, p. 146.
2. The mosque was in damaged condition when it was photographed for the archives of K. A. C. Creswell, inspector of monuments in Mandate Palestine beginning in 1919. The capital is perceptible in photo J454 at the École Biblique in Jerusalem, which, to judge from the other images adjacent to it in a bound volume of photographs, was probably taken after the earthquake of 1927. The mosque was rebuilt in 1978; however, the capital likely entered the collection of the Islamic Museum in Jerusalem after the earthquake in 1927, along with textiles and metalwork from Hebron.

100

The Annunciation

From the Four Gospels
Cyprus or Palestine(?), late 12th–13th century
Tempera, gold, and ink on parchment; 270 fols.
8⅞ × 6½ in. (22.5 × 16.5 cm)
British Library, London (MS Harley 1810)

Integrated into the body of the text written in Greek, the illuminations for this Gospel focus on narratives of the life of Christ that are among the Great Feasts, the religious holidays of the Orthodox Church.[1] In the Gospel of Luke, the Annunciation to the Virgin shows the Archangel Gabriel advancing toward the Virgin against a luminous gold ground. Seated on a throne, she spins thread, an activity associated since antiquity with virtuous women.[2] Above the archangel, rays from the heavens indicate the descent of the Holy Spirit. The manuscript's small size suggests it was used for personal devotion, possibly by a Christian resident in the Holy Land or by an Orthodox pilgrim there.[3] Stylistically inspired by earlier works of the Byzantine capital, Constantinople, the work's relatively unsophisticated execution is now associated with Cyprus or Palestine.[4] Possible evidence of links with Jerusalem include the association of the image's background buildings with Nazareth, long a site of Christian pilgrimage;[5] the similarities of the work to manuscripts at the Monastery of Saint Sabas outside Jerusalem;[6] and a later inscription in the text mentioning a Monastery of Elijah, which might be Mar Elias, on the road between Jerusalem and Bethlehem, restored by the Byzantine emperor Manuel I Comnenus in the twelfth century following an earthquake.[7] HCE

Selected References: London 1978, p. 19, no. 10; Carr 1987, pp. 251–81, with microfiche, no. 70; London 1994, pp. 179–80, no. 194; Yota 2001, pp. 114–19.

1. Carr 1987, pp. 3, 58–59; Yota 2001, p. 241.
2. Mathews 1982, p. 204.
3. Carr 1987, pp. 1, 145; Yota 2001, p. 254.
4. Carr 1987, pp. 1, 66, 151, 153; John Lowden in London 1994, p. 179, no. 194; Yota 2001, p. 45.
5. Yota 2001, p. 119.
6. Carr 1987, pp. 67, 78; Yota 2001, pp. 24–25.
7. Carr 1987, p. 68; Yota 2001, pp. 42, 70.

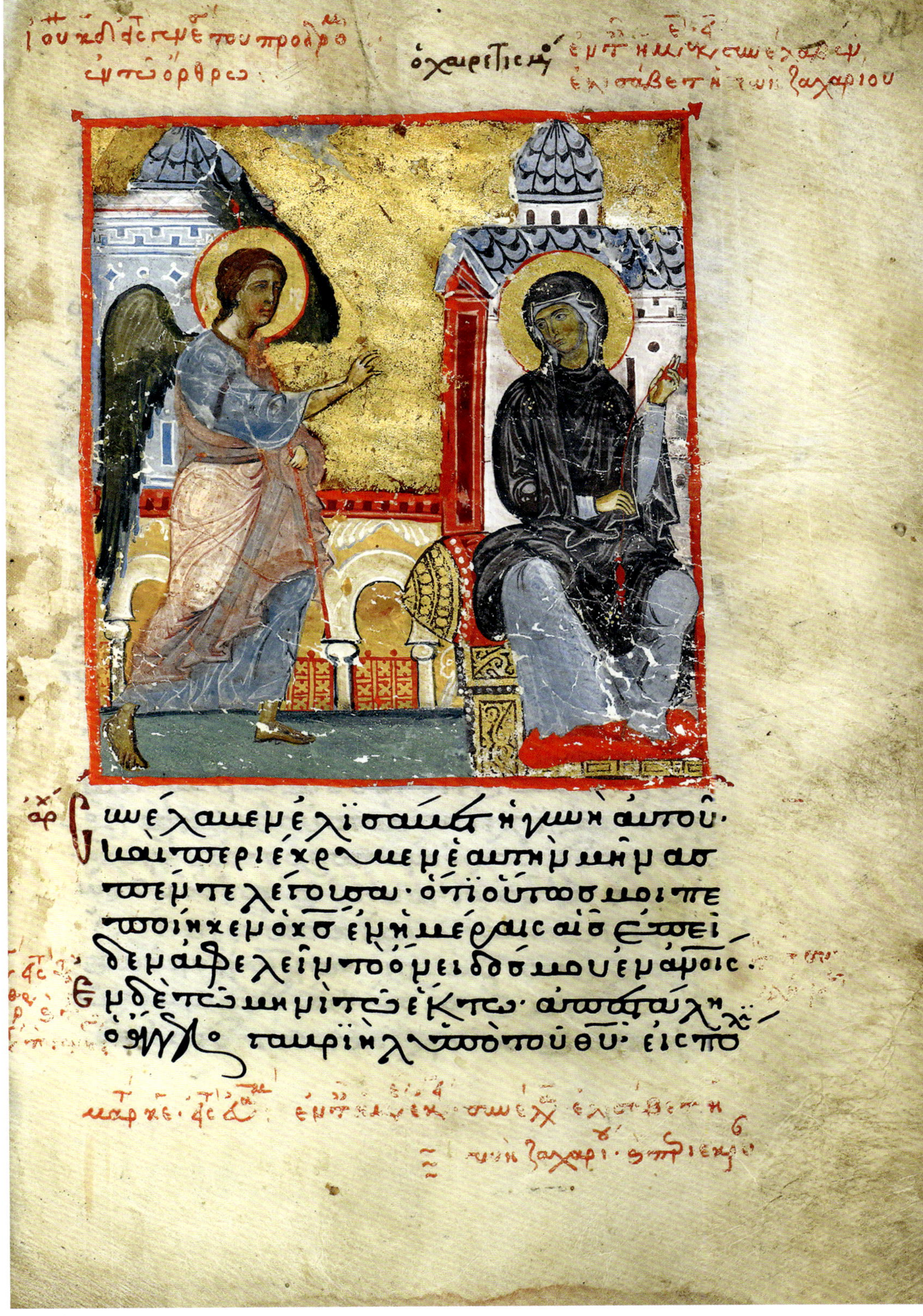

100, fol. 142r

101 a–e

Crusader Sculpture at the Church of the Annunciation in Nazareth

Beginning in the 1140s, Jerusalem became the center for Crusader architectural sculpture, with major works at the Church of the Holy Sepulchre and various other sites, among them the Hospitaller Quarter adjacent to the church, the so-called Baptistry of the Templum Domini, the Church of the Ascension, and the Tomb of the Virgin.[1] Nonetheless, the most remarkable figural sculpture commissioned for a holy site in the Latin Kingdom of Jerusalem in the late twelfth century is found at Nazareth, at the site of the Annunciation to the Virgin Mary and the Incarnation of Jesus. At least one artist active there probably came from the mason's yard of the Holy Sepulchre. This sculptor may have trained the artists who executed both the large statues carved to adorn the entrance portal of the new Crusader cathedral at Nazareth in the early 1170s and the "five famous figural capitals" (cats. 101a–e) for the Shrine of the Annunciation inside the church.

Archbishop Lietard II built the cathedral at Nazareth after the great earthquake of 1170.[2] The large and ambitious plan for sculptural decoration abruptly ended, however, with some work apparently unfinished, when Saladin took Nazareth, shortly after the fall of Jerusalem on October 1, 1187. Even though the holy places had been profaned, the Church of the Annunciation remained standing, and the cave grotto inside the church, where the Incarnation was believed to have taken place, was intact for those pilgrims who managed to visit. The treaty of 1229 negotiated by Emperor Frederick II enabled greater pilgrim access, but no further work appears to have been done on the program of decoration.[3] Between 1244 and 1263 Nazareth remained the only major Christian holy site in Crusader hands after the Khwarezmian Turks captured Jerusalem and Bethlehem. When the Mamluks largely destroyed the cathedral in Nazareth in 1263, the figural sculpture from the church portals was left broken on the ground with other ruins. Only some sculpture – the five capitals apparently prepared for the Shrine of the Annunciation, which had not yet been put in place by 1187 – was saved intact, because it had been buried in the workshop just outside the church.

The first Crusader figural sculpture remains from Nazareth were discovered in 1867 during early excavations at the cathedral site.[4] Other, more extensive excavations were done in 1907–9 and again in 1955–70, at the time of the construction of the modern Church of the Annunciation, dedicated in 1969. These digs have yielded large amounts of high-quality sculpture, including the so-called "five famous capitals" in 1908, and a torso of Saint Peter in 1966. One other comparable torso in the same distinctive Franco-Crusader style from Nazareth, thought to be that of a prophet, has also been identified in the collection of the Dukes of Devonshire at Chatsworth (fig. 64).

As if they had just been removed from the sculptor's workshop, the five capitals emerged from the ground unweathered, only lightly damaged by the excavators' shovels and exhibiting a remarkably dynamic style.[5] Extraordinary in design and execution and exceptionally well preserved, they appeared at first glance to be closely related to French Romanesque sculpture in Burgundy and the Rhone Valley, especially sculpture at Plaimpied and Vienne.[6] This led some scholars to believe that they must have been carved in France and shipped to Nazareth. However, further study has revealed that the stone is local to Nazareth, and the design, style, and imagery, while related to French Romanesque work, are in fact a unique blend of Crusader style and imagery from Jerusalem, including French and possibly Muslim elements (discussed below).

As an ensemble, four of the five capitals – all polygonal in shape – shown here were probably prepared for a two-storied shrine monument in honor of the Annunciation, in the north aisle of the church at Nazareth. Although the Shrine of the Tomb of Christ in the Holy Sepulchre may have provided some inspiration,[7] the Shrine of the Annunciation at Nazareth is unique in its design and its own program of brilliantly carved figural capitals. The proposed reconstructed program incorporating the four polygonal capitals differs from the programs at sites such as the Holy Sepulchre in Jerusalem and the Nativity of Christ in Bethlehem and is also distinctly configured, unlike other holy sites claiming apostolic foundation in honor of the Virgin, such as the Church of Saint Mary on Mount Sion in Jerusalem and the Church of Our Lady in Tartus.[8]

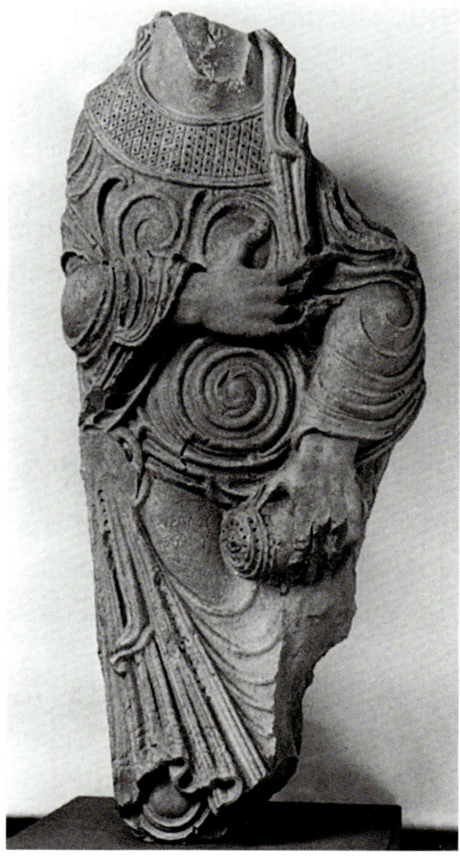

Fig. 64. Torso of a prophet(?), from the Church of the Annunciation, Nazareth. Latin Kingdom of Jerusalem, 1170s. Stone. Chatsworth, Devonshire Collection, United Kingdom

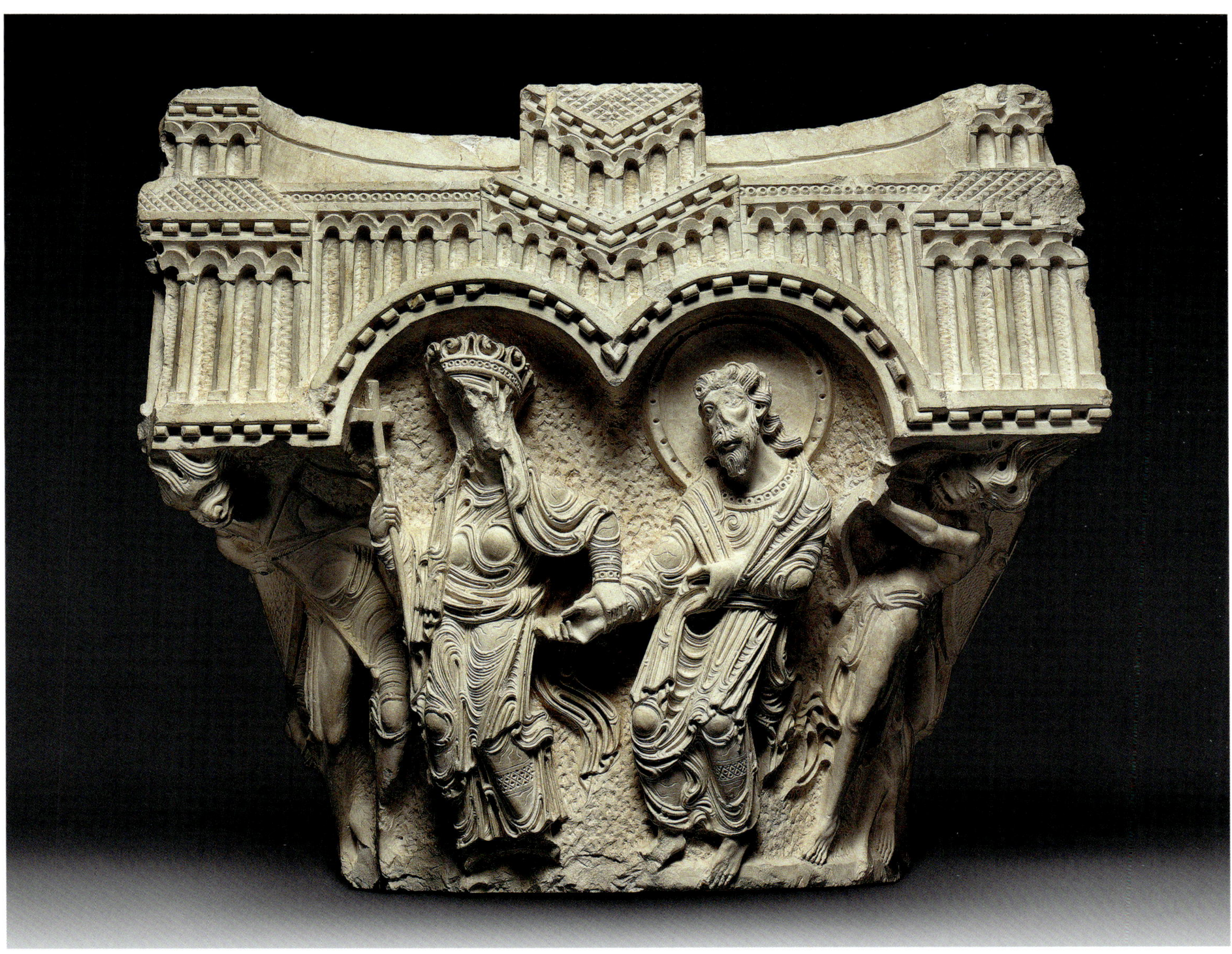

101a

101a

The Virgin and Apostle Capital

Nazareth, early 1170s
Limestone
H. 24½ in. (62 cm), W. 28⅜ in. (72 cm), D. 13⅜ in. (34 cm)
Terra Sancta Museum, Basilica of the Annunciation, Nazareth

On the front face of this capital — the largest of the five in this group and the only one with a rectangular rather than a polygonal superstructure — under the double arch, the Virgin, represented as a crowned figure without a halo and carrying a cross staff, leads an unspecified apostle, represented as a bearded male with a halo and wearing a tunic and cloak. On the two side faces, four armed demons threaten Mary and the apostle as they make their way through hell. All the figures actively "dance" on the rounded molding, which forms the ground line below.

The content of this scene is derived from the Greek tradition of Mary leading the apostles into hell, where they witness terrible things.[9] Later, Mary pleads with her son, Jesus, to have mercy on the condemned souls. It is a unique iconography in which the Virgin Mary, depicted as the Church personified, leads an apostle through hell in the manner of Jesus Christ at the Anastasis (the Resurrection).[10] While the Nazareth artist would have seen Anastasis images in local Byzantine churches, the most celebrated example was in the mosaic of the main apse of the Holy Sepulchre in Jerusalem, an image that was later destroyed but is directly reflected in the miniature now found in the Melisende Psalter (cat. 121).[11] The imagery of Christ in Jerusalem at his Resurrection is linked to that of Mary here in Nazareth.

One special feature of this capital is the presence of the four demonic figures with spears, bows, and arrows who threaten the Virgin. The appearance of demons on Romanesque capitals in France was widespread, but here the diversity of the demons is remarkable. Demons are also major figures on the Saint James and Saint Matthew capitals (cats. 101d, e). Some of the Nazareth demons have human bodies and grotesque heads, while others have furry bodies or what might be interpreted as slimy or scaly bodies, as on the Saint James capital, where one demon has huge talons for feet and another, a fierce animal head. Almost all the demons are full size. Clearly the figures personify the wickedness that Christ and the apostles encounter and discuss in the New Testament, and which stands in contrast to the apostles' good actions.

Although the intended location of this capital inside the cathedral would not have been as part of the Shrine of the Annunciation, it was probably meant to be placed near the shrine on the interior of the church.[12] However, given the fact that these five well-preserved

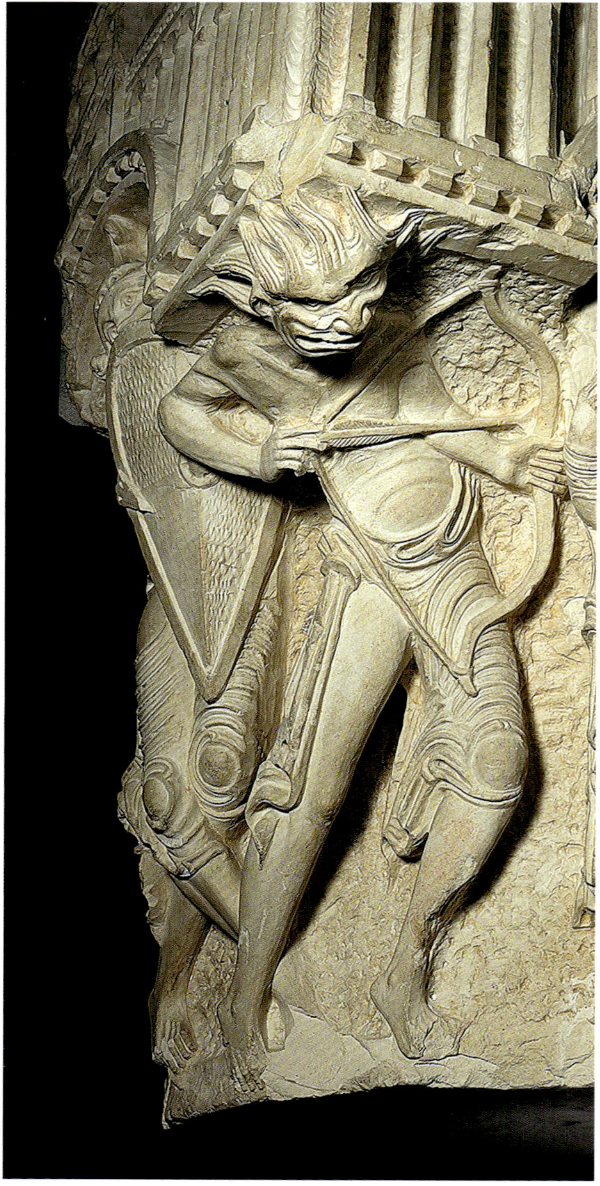

101a Demon, detail

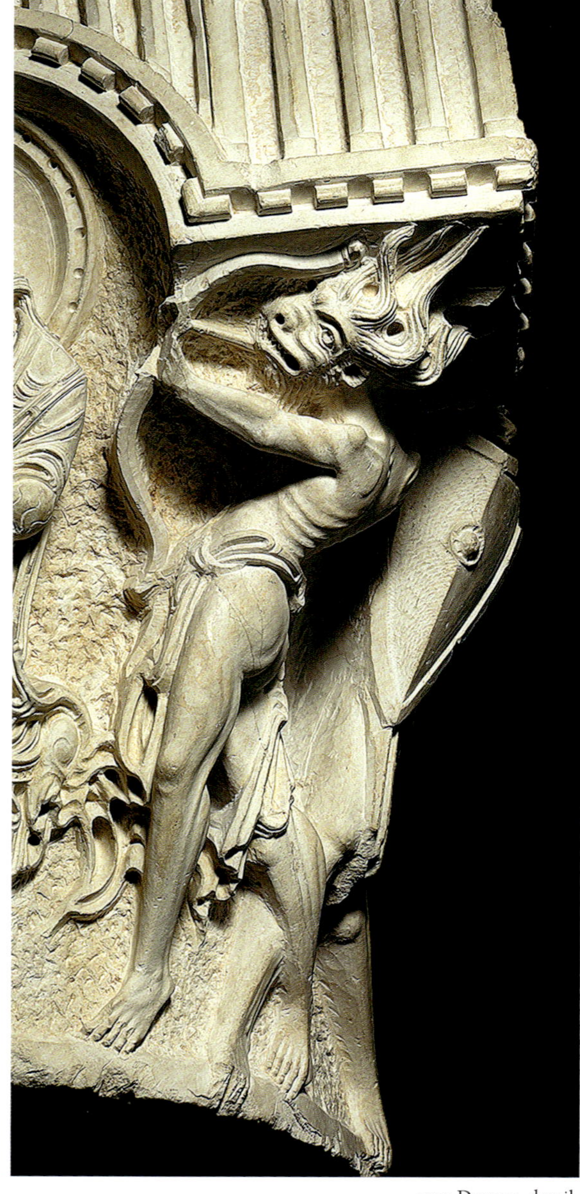

101a Demon, detail

capitals represent only about 10 percent of the intended program of figural sculpture for the Cathedral of the Annunciation and its associated shrine, attempts to reconstruct their locations, function, and meaning remain speculative. JF

Selected References: Viaud 1910, pp. 156–57, figs. 76–78; Enlart 1925–28, vol. 1, pp. 129–33, vol. 2, pp. 302, 304–5, atlas, pl. 131, figs. 412, 413; Bagatti and Alliata 1984, p. 99, fig. 37, pl. 38; Folda 1995, pp. 414–38; Stratford 2015, pp. 320–24.

101b

The Saint Peter Capital

Nazareth, early 1170s
Limestone
H. 16⅝ in. (42 cm), W. 21¼ in. (54 cm), D, 21⅝ in. (55 cm)
Terra Sancta Museum, Basilica of the Annunciation, Nazareth

Saint Peter appears twice on this capital, in two important roles drawn directly from the New Testament: as a newly named apostle at the Sea of Galilee (John 21:1–17) and as a miracle worker who raises the wealthy, charitable woman Tabitha from her deathbed in Jaffa (Acts 9:36–43). By showing Jesus – from the onlooker's perspective – between two significant images of Saint Peter and considering the importance of Peter among the apostles, we can surmise that this capital was most likely located in a very prominent location on the canopied arcade of the shrine over the holy site.

On this capital, as with the others, the architectural canopy is meant to be read as a generic framework relating to the shrine, and not as a specific setting for the scenes below. This use of architectural elements, characteristic of Romanesque capitals in Europe, is also found in examples in the Holy Sepulchre in Jerusalem. The Nazareth capitals, however, are unusual because of their scooped-out faces and the roughened surfaces below the arches. In the absence of comparable Romanesque examples for this configuration, it seems likely that the Nazareth sculptor took advantage of his Middle Eastern context and perhaps found inspiration in the *muqarnas* – a form of Islamic honeycomb-like ornamental vaulting – he could have seen in the region. The scalloped bases, hollowed faces, and blossoming rising profiles of these Nazareth capitals find interesting parallels in twelfth-century examples of *muqarnas* on buildings in Cairo, Damascus, and Aleppo.[13]

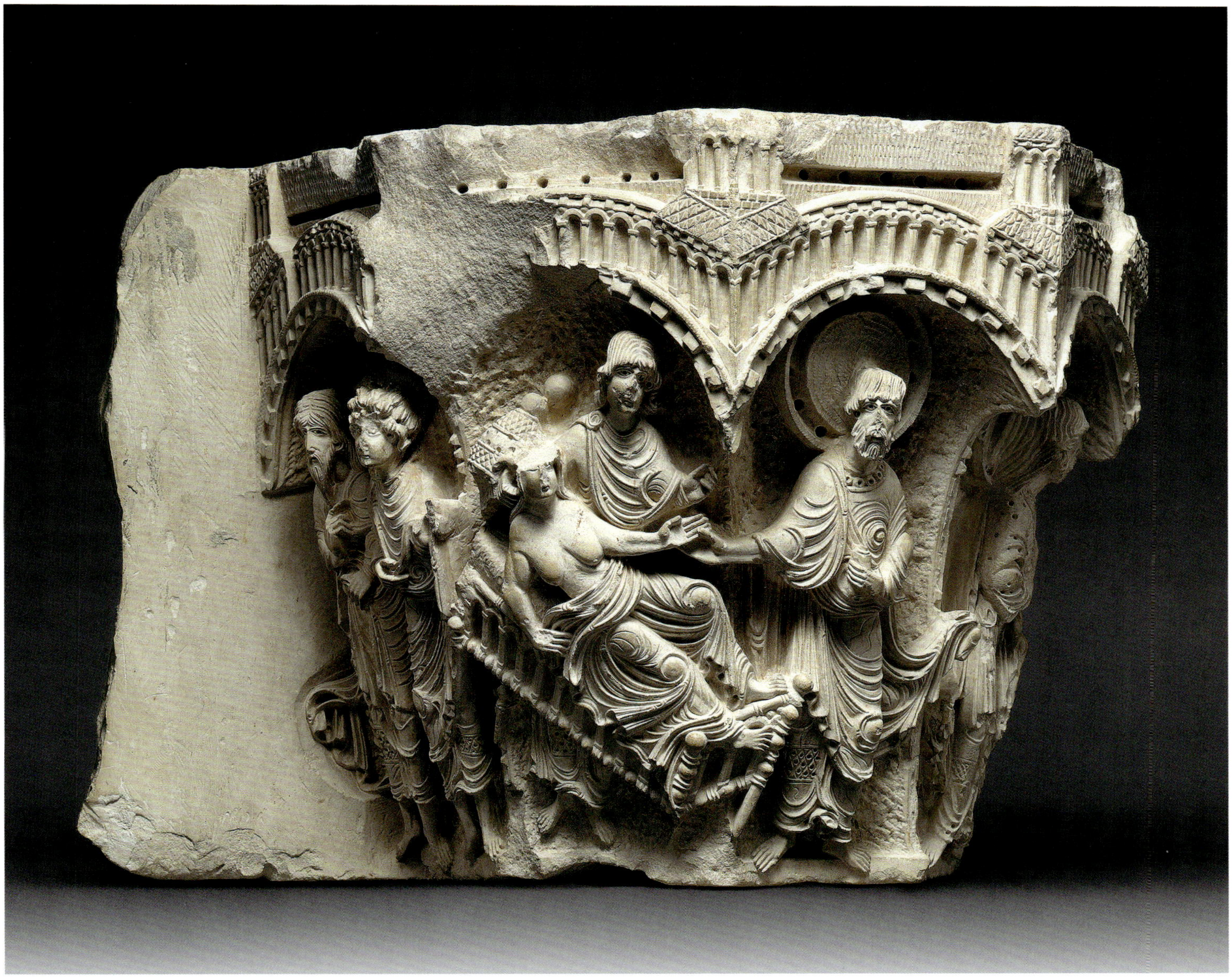

101b Peter heals Tabitha

Yet Islamic *muqarnas* do not include this roughened interior surface. There seems to be no doubt that the surface is intentional in these capitals. The plan may have been to cover them with gesso and paint at a later date, as sometimes seen in the West.[14] Yet here it seems more likely that the sculptor was trying to echo the cave-grotto setting inside the shrine in the north aisle of the church, an important visual aspect of the holy place (*loca sancta*) imagery so characteristic of religious sites in the Crusader Holy Land. By combining ideas from Romanesque architecture, Islamic *muqarnas*, and *loca sancta* imagery, the sculptor has created a uniquely Crusader program of capital sculpture for this distinctive holy site.

JF

Selected References: Viaud 1910, pp. 158–59; Enlart 1925–28, vol. 1, pp. 129–33, vol. 2, pp. 302, 306, atlas, pl. 132, figs. 416, 417; Folda 1986b, pp. 37–39, pls. 2–3, 16–17; Folda 1995, pp. 414–38; Stratford 2015, pp. 320–24.

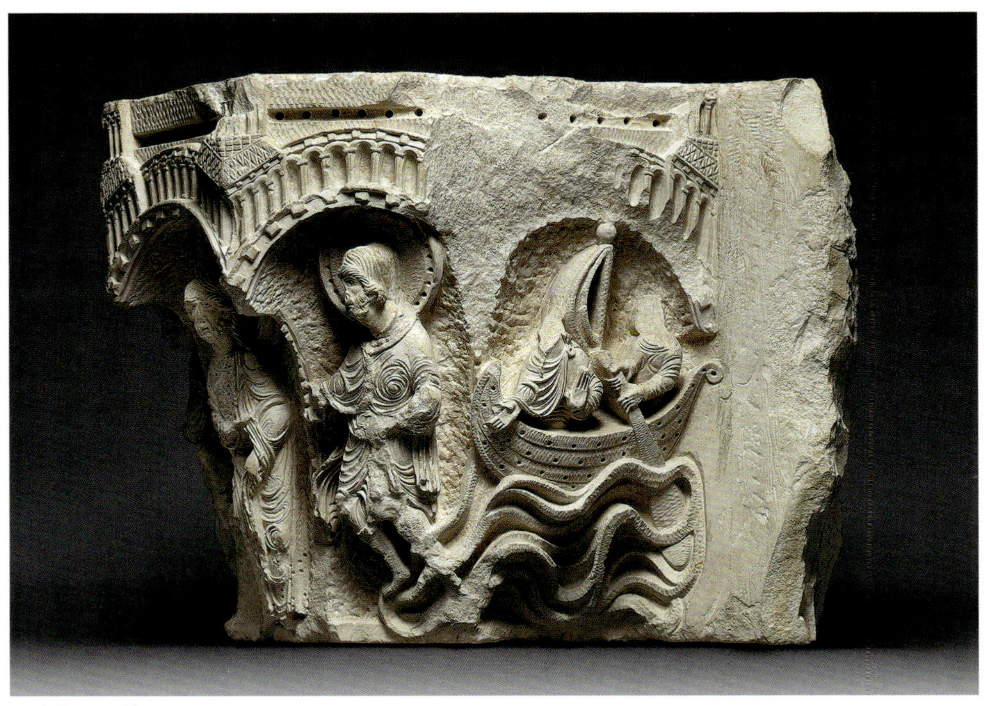

101b Peter walks on water

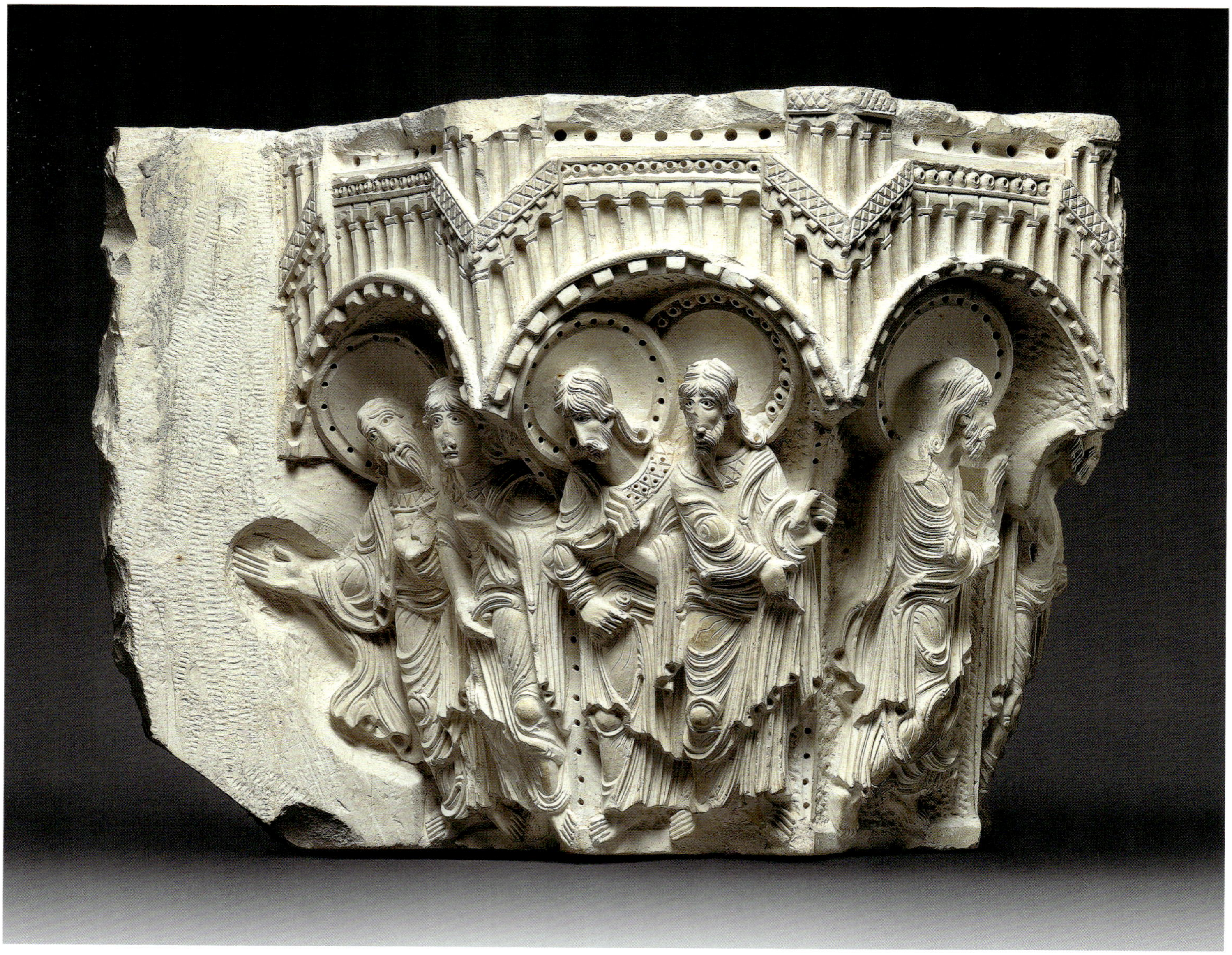

101c Apostles

101c

The Saint Thomas Capital

Nazareth, 1170s
Limestone
H. 16⅝ in. (42 cm), W. 21¼ in. (54 cm), D. 18½ in. (47 cm)
Terra Sancta Museum, Basilica of the Annunciation, Nazareth

Compared to other twelfth-century Crusader images, such as the colorful mosaic of Doubting Thomas in the Church of the Nativity in Bethlehem (cat. 96) or the compact composition in the miniature in the Psalter of Queen Melisende (cat. 121) where Christ is fully, even magnificently robed, this Nazareth capital features a seminude figure of Christ with a huge halo marked with a cross. Having pulled his tunic aside, Christ holds out his hand for Thomas to inspect. To each side, the apostles, standing in the upper room in Jerusalem, gesture as they witness the scene. The focus here is on the dramatic moment

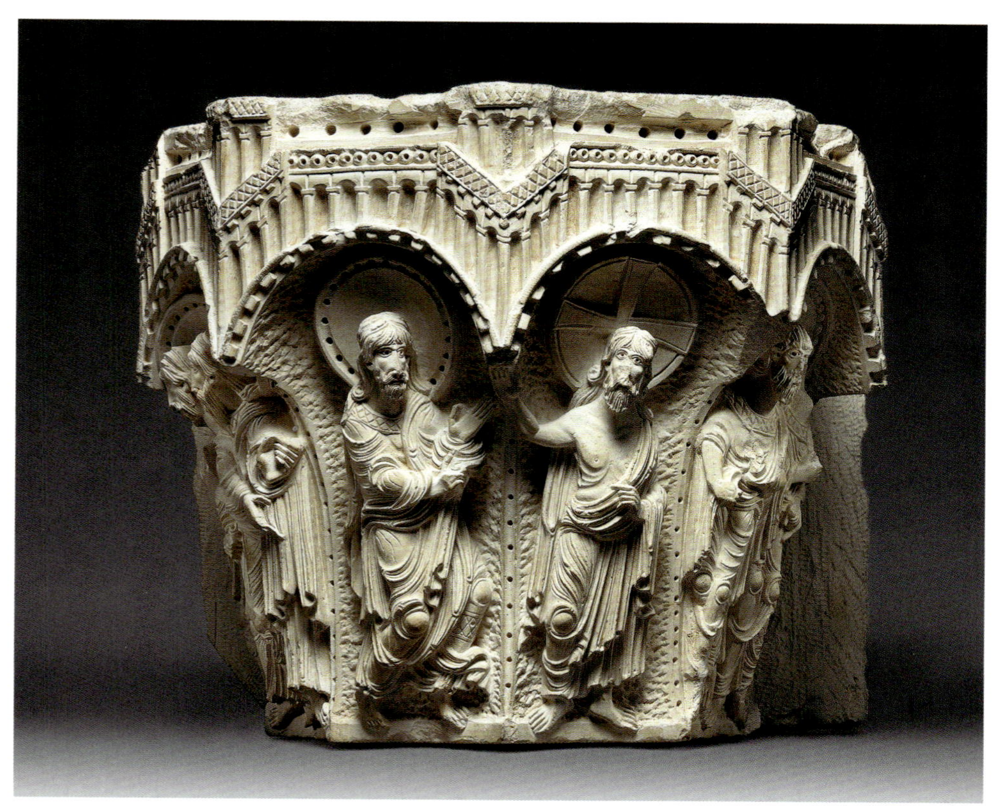

101c Thomas with the risen Christ

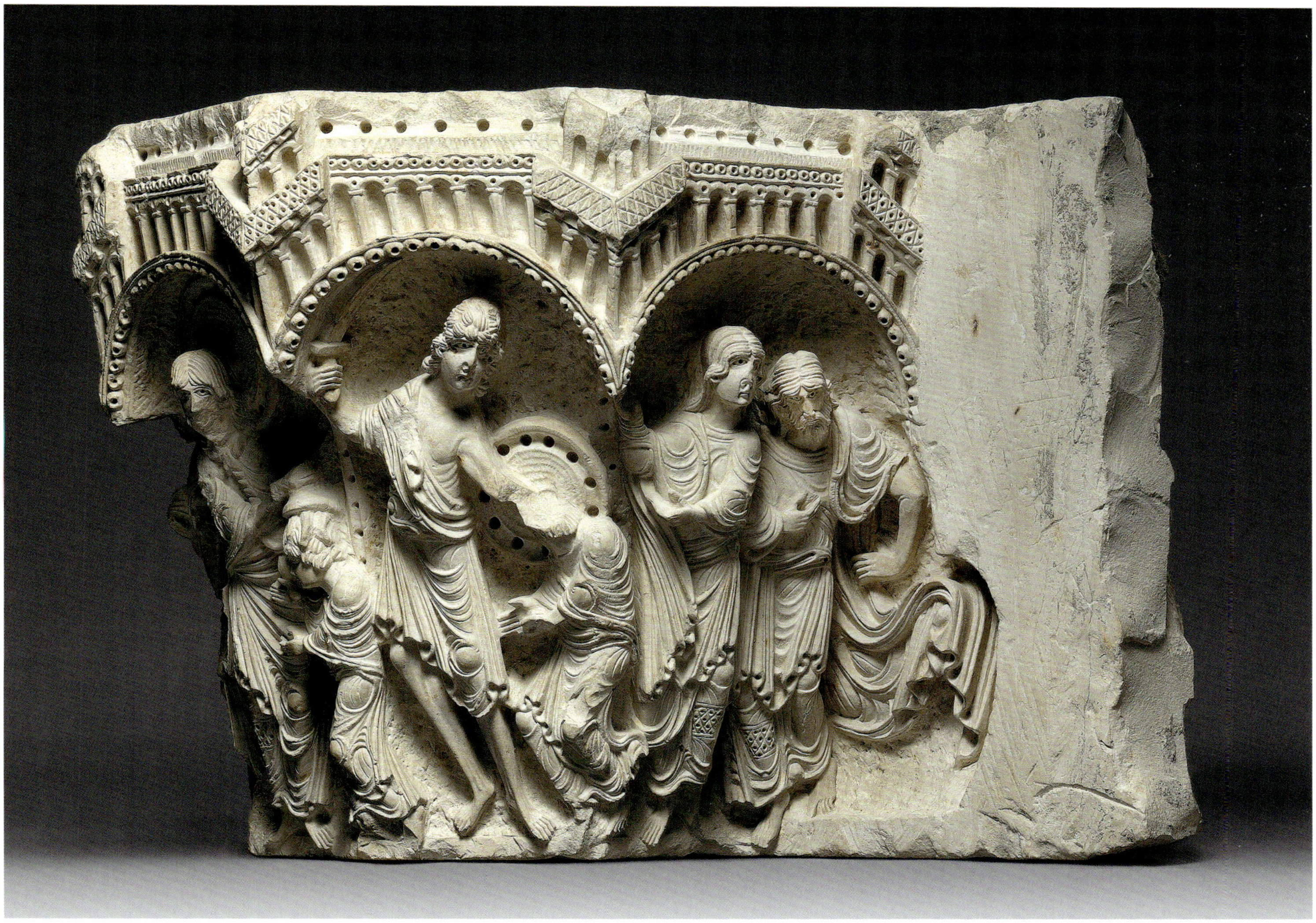

101d The beheading of James

rather than the narrative in the Gospel account (John 20:24–29). Since the composition features Jesus and Thomas aligned on the two central faces, it is likely that this capital was also placed in a prominent position on the arcaded canopy of the shrine for worshippers to view while standing in the nave.

By illustrating the Thomas scene that took place in Jerusalem, these sculptures create a link between Nazareth and the Holy City, similar to the Saint James capital, which also contains events that took place in Jerusalem. (The other two apostles — Peter and Matthew — are shown on their capitals pursuing their ministries out of town.) JF

Selected References: Viaud 1910, pp. 157–58; Enlart 1925–28, vol. 1, pp. 129–33, vol. 2, pp. 302, 305–6, atlas, pl. 131, figs. 414, 415; Folda 1986b, pp. 31–42, pls. 4, 7–10; Folda 1995, pp. 414–38; Stratford 2015, pp. 320–24.

101d

The Saint James the Greater Capital

Nazareth, 1170s
Limestone
H. 16⅝ in. (42 cm), W. 21¼ in. (54 cm), D. 18½ in. (47 cm)
Terra Sancta Museum, Basilica of the Annunciation, Nazareth

Saint James, son of Zebedee, a Galilean, was called by Jesus on the shores of the Sea of Galilee but died in Jerusalem. Indeed, James the Greater was the first apostle to be martyred, and the capital of Saint James is easily recognizable. On the first face, at the left side of the capital, James speaks with a sorcerer. The fifth face, on the right side, depicts his

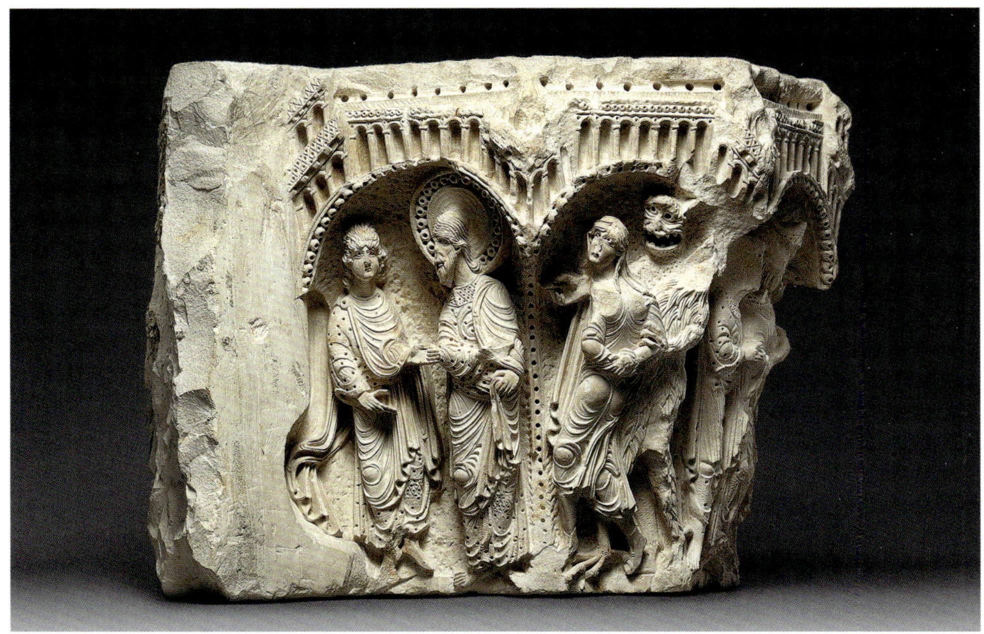

101d James speaks to a sorcerer

beheading (Acts 12:1–2). On the third face, the high priest, Abiathar, stands behind the prisoner James (on the fourth face, with a rope around his neck), speaking to an accomplice and pointing to the saint. In all three appearances, James has a large halo. In addition to the expected scenes from James's ministry, there are – as with the Saint Matthew capital (cat. 101e) – other scenes that are much more difficult to understand, but also seem to have been taken from the *Histories of the Apostles* (*Historiae apostolicae*) attributed to Saint Abdias.[15]

Saint James became the focus of a great pilgrimage at the site of Santiago de Compostela in Spain in the Middle Ages. It has been claimed that James preached in Spain before his martyrdom in Jerusalem, but there is no direct evidence for this. His relics are divided between Jerusalem, where his head reliquary is revered in the Armenian cathedral, and Santiago de Compostela, where his body relics, in a jeweled reliquary, continue to be reverenced by thousands of pilgrims every year. On this capital, the Nazareth artist focused on the strong link between James and Jerusalem and the Holy Land. JF

Selected References: Viaud 1910, pp. 159–61; Enlart 1925–28, vol. 1, pp. 129–33, vol. 2, pp. 302, 306, atlas, pl. 133, figs. 418, 419; Folda 1995, pp. 414–38; Pringle 1993–2009, vol. 2, pp. 123–39; Stratford 2015, pp. 320–24.

101e

The Saint Matthew Capital

Nazareth, early 1170s
Limestone
H. 16⅝ in. (42 cm), W. 21¼ in. (54 cm), D. 18½ in. (47 cm)
Terra Sancta Museum, Basilica of the Annunciation, Nazareth

The choice of Saint Matthew for this capital is unusual, as the story of his life and works is mostly obscure. He was a tax agent in the Galilee, in Capernaum not far from Nazareth, which is where Jesus called him to be an apostle. Thereafter, he wrote one of the four Gospels supposedly before being martyred. It is perhaps surprising that the artist chose to depict his ministry to the royal court in faraway Ethiopia. The source for the life of this saint comes not from the New Testament but from a text known as the *Histories of the Apostles* (*Historiae apostolicae*), attributed to Saint Abdias, first bishop of Babylon. These acts, initially written in Hebrew, were then translated into Latin by Julianus Africanus and eventually compiled in Gaul in the sixth century.[16] The content of this narrative about Matthew also made its way into the *Golden Legend* (*Aurea legenda*), the popular text by Jacobus de Voragine (1228/30–1298), bishop of Genoa, written about one hundred years after the Nazareth capitals were carved.

Matthew appears only once on this capital, on the fourth face, as the standing bearded apostle with a large halo who is blessing the tiny figure of Iphegenia, daughter of King Eglypus of Ethiopia. On the first face, King Eglypus himself is seated and joined by his young son, whom Matthew resurrected from the dead. Two sorcerers, Zaroes and Arphaxat, whom Matthew stripped of magical power, also appear on the second face. Years later, Hyrtacus, who succeeded Eglypus, lusted after the virgin Iphegenia, whom Matthew had dedicated to God. As seen on the capital, Hyrtacus attempted to win the hand of Iphegenia in marriage with the help of Zaroes and Arphaxat and a tiny demon, shown between the arches of the vault (between faces three and four), but he was rebuffed. Enraged at Matthew for thwarting his desire, Hyrtacus sent a soldier to kill him with a sword while he was praying at the altar (not depicted). Hyrtacus, stricken with leprosy for his evil deed, then took his own life, and as the final scene on the capital, on the sixth face, we see the devil seizing the soul of the loathsome king.

Understanding this arcane selection of episodes concerning Saint Matthew, unique in extant medieval imagery, requires careful observation of the figures on the capital and knowledge of the history of the apostles. Accordingly, the capital must have been placed on the superstructure of the Shrine of the Annunciation at a point where worshippers could read the scenes clearly. Making the link between Matthew and Nazareth in Galilee is not difficult, but the planner of this program of figural sculpture was quite imaginative in referencing Ethiopia, which is in fact linked to Jerusalem. Ethiopian monks have claimed a recorded historical presence in Jerusalem since the fourth century, and they are still found at the Holy Sepulchre today in their mud huts on the roof of the Chapel of Saint Helena. By choosing these particular stories of Saint Matthew, the Nazareth sculptor celebrated the diversity of Christianity found in Jerusalem.[17]

The dynamic style of this capital is exemplary among the Nazareth figural works. Although this sculpture has been linked with carvings from Plaimpied in the Berri and Vienne in the Rhone Valley,[18] the artist who made it was probably an experienced Crusader sculptor – meaning a resident of the Latin Kingdom with strong French ancestry, who may have worked in Jerusalem at the Holy Sepulchre before coming to Nazareth. Compared to French Romanesque antecedents, the features of his sculpture at Nazareth seem to be conditioned by the Late Antique, Byzantine, Syrian, and Islamic visual context of the Latin Kingdom.[19] JF

Selected References: Viaud 1910, pp. 161–62; Enlart 1925–28, vol. 1, pp. 129–33, vol. 2, pp. 302, 307, atlas, pl. 133, figs. 420, 421; Folda 1986b, pp. 41–42, pls. 6, 21–25; Pace 2005, pp. 219–25; Stratford 2015, pp. 320–24.

1. Folda 2005, pp. 204–29, 253–82.
2. Pringle 1993–2009, vol. 2, pp. 119–20.
3. Even so, during this period the Church of Our Lady and its shrine farther north in Tartus, Syria, had been built, inspired by the Nazareth ensemble; ibid., pp. 120–21.
4. This group consists of two life-size bearded heads carved in the distinctive Franco-Crusader Nazareth style; now glued together as part of one block. I am grateful to Melanie Holcomb for this observation. They were probably intended for column figures on a portal; ibid., p. 137.
5. According to my hypothetical reconstruction of the Shrine of the Annunciation, with its superstructure containing eight polygonal capitals, four more such capitals (in addition to those seen here) would have been intended, but if carved, they have not survived intact. It has been suggested that the other four capitals could have been devoted to John, Andrew, Bartholomew, and Philip, the other apostles from Galilee (Pringle 1993–2009, vol. 2, p. 136). Fragments of additional capitals were discovered during the most recent excavations, but so far reconstruction of other polygonal capitals has not been possible. The only other capital that survives in excellent condition is the larger one with a rectangular architectural canopy discussed above (cat. 101a).
6. Sculpture from the church of Saint Martin at Plaimpied, and the cathedral of Saint Maurice at Vienne, among other works in the Rhone Valley, are closely related. See the recent discussion of these related sculptures in Stratford 2015.
7. Folda 1995, p. 417, pl. 10.3d; Folda 1986b, pp. 4, 27, figs. 1, 5. See also Pringle 1993–2009, vol. 2, p. 136.
8. Folda 1986b, pp. 33–36.
9. Himmelfarb 1983, pp. 20–24, 178–79; Pernot 1900.
10. In Byzantine iconography the image of the Anastasis shows Christ trampling on the gates of hell and releasing Adam, Eve, and the other worthies of the Old Testament. Folda 1986b, pp. 43–48, with extended discussion.
11. Folda 1995, p. 142, pl. 6.8r.
12. Pringle has proposed that this capital and others of similar size whose fragments were found in the recent excavations "are in fact virtually identical in essential measurement to a surviving capital from one of the nave or aisle pilasters of the church itself." He suggests that this capital and another broken and damaged one of the same size would likely have been located on the nave arcade; Pringle 1993–2009, vol. 2, p. 137. See Folda 1986b, pls. 51, 52, for the damaged capital of similar size with an unidentified battle scene.
13. See, for example, Hoag 1977, pp. 146, 214, 216, figs. 181, 268, 271.
14. Folda 1986b, pp. 6–7, 69 nn. 15, 16.
15. Ibid., pp. 39–41.
16. See Folda 1986b, pp. 39–42, 78–79 n. 62, for the references to these arcane texts.
17. Wilkinson, Hill, and Ryan, eds. 1988, p. 273 (John of Würzburg); Hamilton, B., 1980, pp. 190, 209, 350–51.
18. Borg 1982; Krüger 2011, pp. 222–23. And see now Stratford 2015, pp. 307–24.
19. Pace 1984.

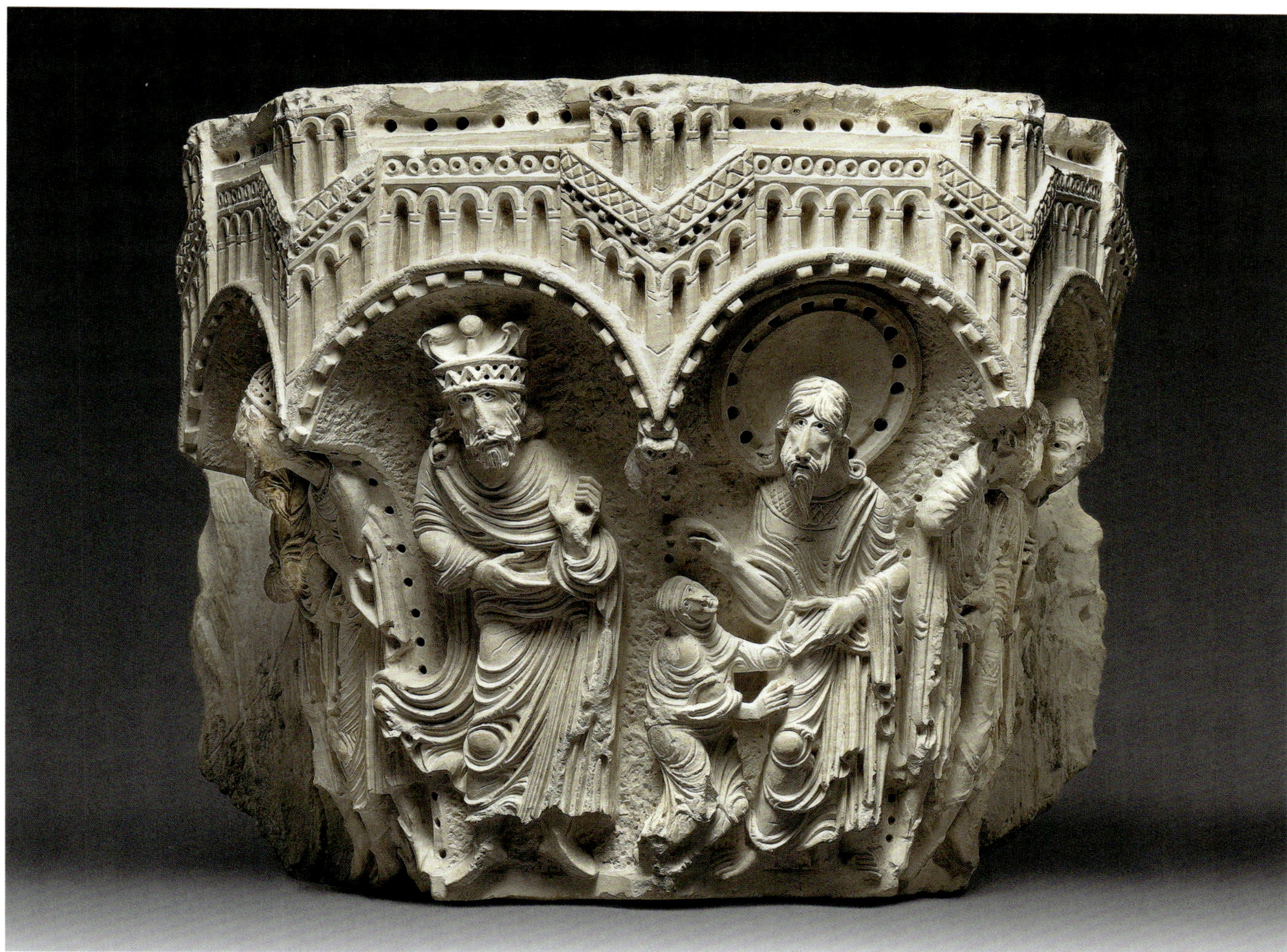
101e Matthew with Iphegenia and King Hyrtacus

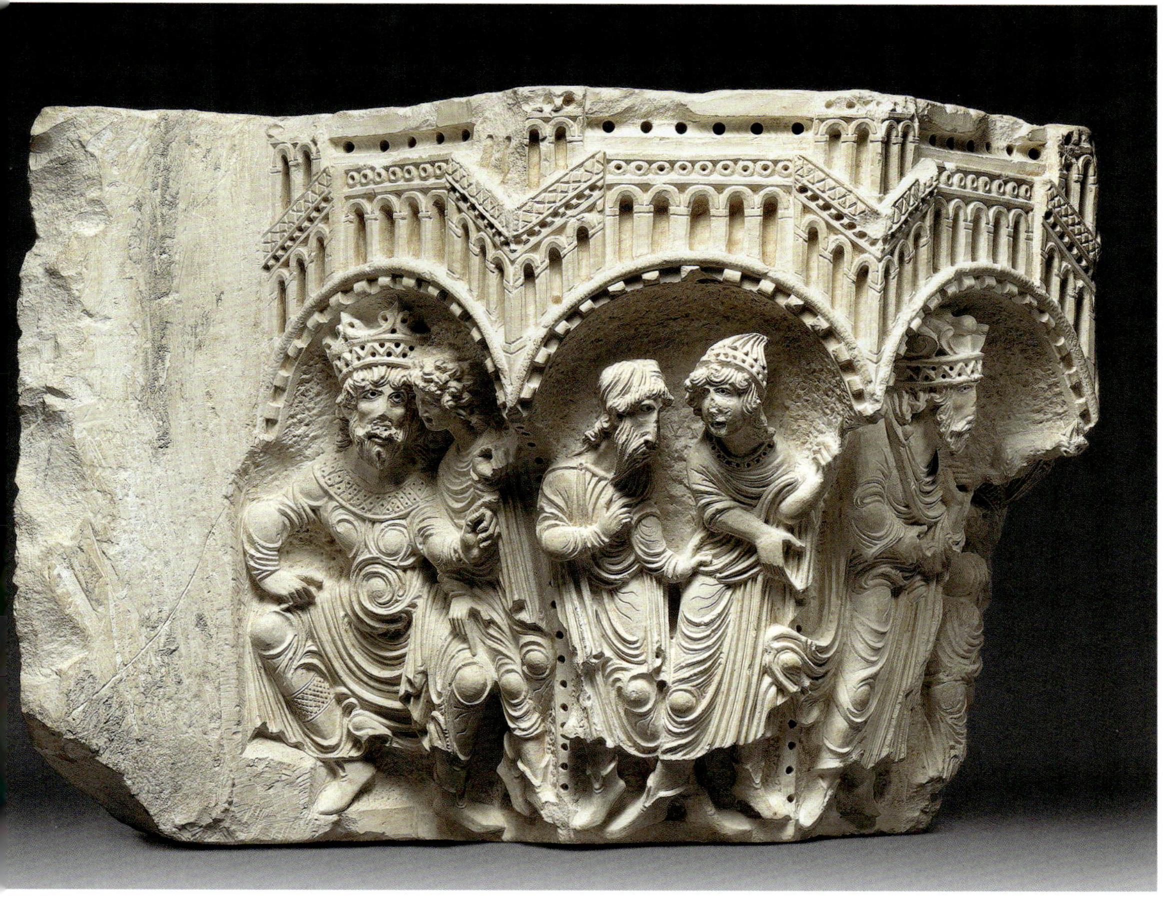
101e King Eglypus of Ethiopia with his son and two sorcerers

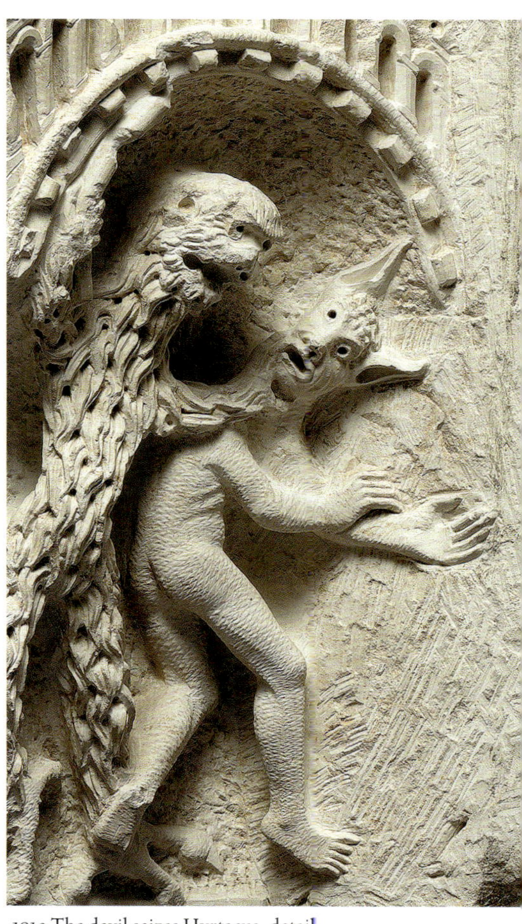
101e The devil seizes Hyrtacus, detail

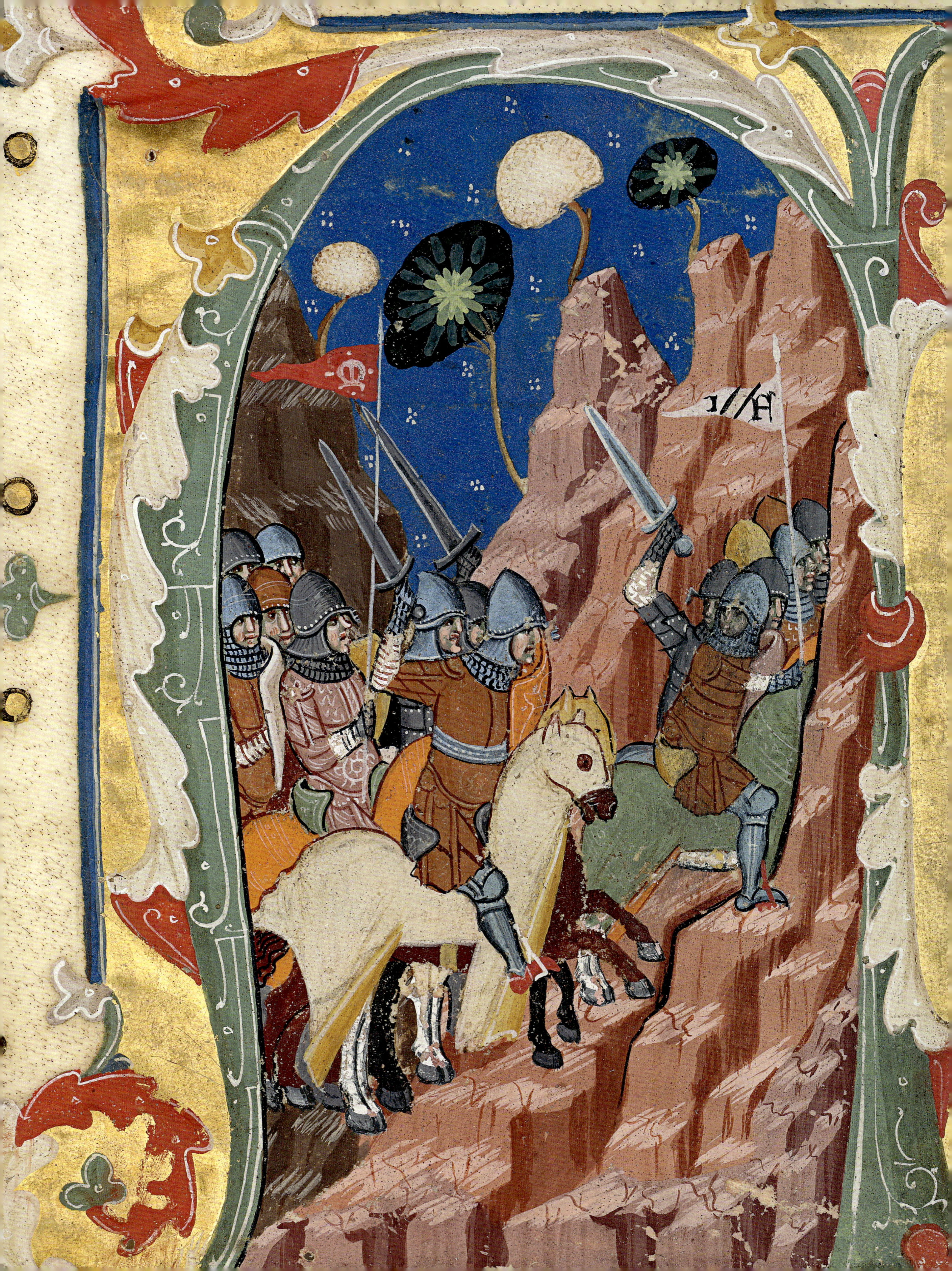

Holy War and the Power of Art

God has conferred remarkable glory in arms —Robert the Monk

BARBARA DRAKE BOEHM AND MELANIE HOLCOMB

IN A TREATISE written for Saladin in the second half of the twelfth century (cat. 104), designs for implements of war have become fine art, beautifully drawn and embellished in gold, with patterns suggesting enamel or niello.[1] A sword, shield, catapult, and even an elaborate crank for arming a bowstring (fig. 66) are presented as elegant specimens, graciously disposed on the page to show off their mesmerizing geometry. This is no mere user's manual but rather a testament to the technology that characterizes — and, in an artist's hands, dignifies — the machinery of war.

FACING PAGE
Fig. 65. Initial "A" with the Battle of the Maccabees. Italy, probably Bologna, ca. 1360–70. Tempera, gold, and ink on parchment. The Metropolitan Museum of Art, New York, Gift of Bashford Dean, 1923 (23.21.4)

Mardi ibn 'Ali of Tarsus (d. 1187), author of Saladin's treatise, was not a unique professional, having studied the arts of war with an arms specialist from Alexandria.[2] For their part, Europeans intent on crusade had their own such texts. One prepared for Philip VI of France in the fourteenth

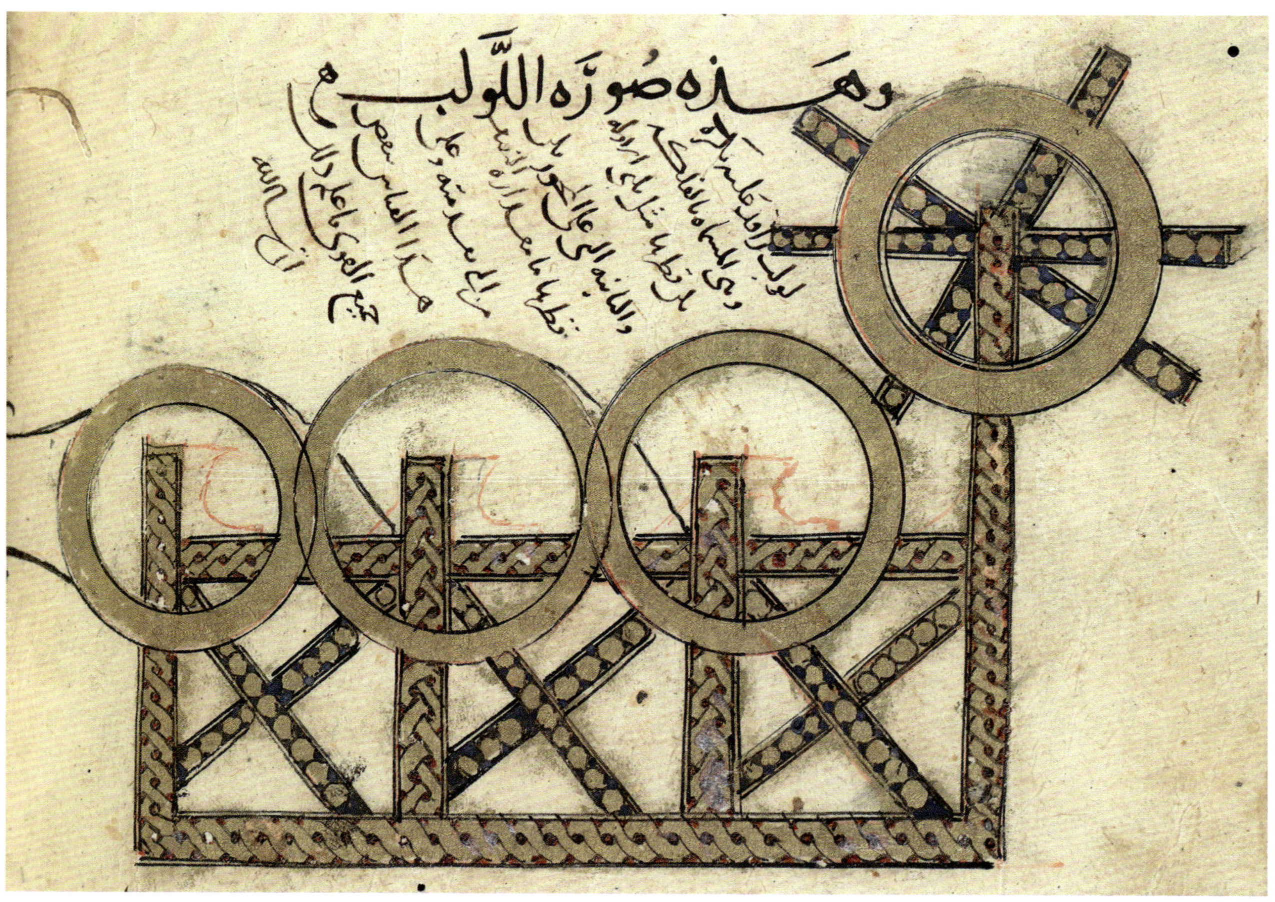

Fig. 66. Detail from Saladin's treatise on armor. Syria, ca. 1250–1300. Opaque watercolors, gold, and ink on paper. Bodleian Libraries, University of Oxford (MS Huntington 264, fol. 87v)

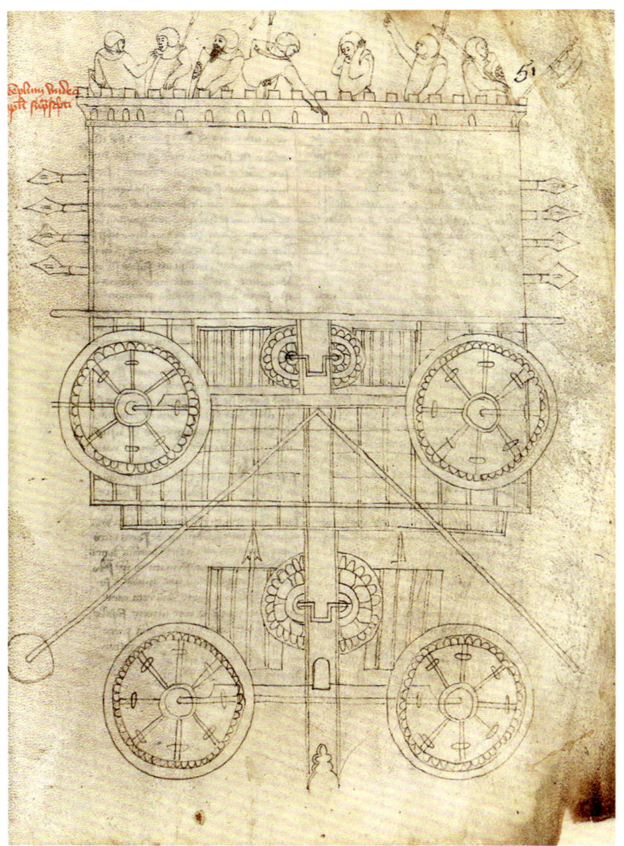

Fig. 67. Sketch of a crank wagon from a treatise for Philip VI of France by Guido da Vigevano. Italy, mid-14th century. Ink on paper. Bibliothèque Nationale de France, Département des Manuscrits, Paris (MS Latin 11015, fol. 51r)

century by the Italian inventor and physician Guido da Vigevano (ca. 1280–ca. 1349) contained delicately drawn sketches of technology for use in sieges, as well as for pontoon bridges and wind-powered devices for overland troop transport (fig. 67).[3] Before mocking the apparent absurdity of the last of these inventions, let us remember that Leonardo da Vinci's fanciful plans for flying machines and other military hardware are considered reflections of artistic genius. In all cases, the fact remains that such designs, however artistic, were proposals for deadly pursuits.

War is bent on destruction; art, on creation. Underpinning the unholy marriage that sometimes exists between these polar opposites is the concept of "holy war," fought in the name of God against those perceived as infidels. From the eleventh through fourteenth centuries the notion was widely and perversely promoted by admired and learned men across faiths in the context of the holy city of Jerusalem.

Pope Urban II (r. 1088–99) was one such man. An experienced and savvy leader, he convened an assembly of clerics and noblemen in 1095 that effectively launched the First Crusade. In his rousing speech on the penultimate day of the conference, he tempted potential soldiers with promises of "wars which contain the glorious reward of martyrdom, which will retain that title of praise now and forever."[4] Urban's ideas were echoed and elaborated in 1128 by the influential Cistercian abbot Bernard of Clairvaux (1090–1153) when he articulated the virtues of the Knights Templar, a Christian military order newly established in Jerusalem after the successful Crusader conquest.[5] Bernard, who would go on in 1144 to incite the Second Crusade, spoke admiringly of the "holy death" that awaited these honorable soldiers who wore the armaments of faith and steel. He asserted that to kill for Christ was no sin: "The Lord freely accepts the death of the foe who has offended him."[6]

Bernard grounded his arguments in Jerusalem and her monuments. The infidels to be struck down were those who "busy themselves to carry away the incalculable riches placed in Jerusalem by the Christian peoples, to profane the holy things and to possess the sanctuary of God as their heritage."[7] It was therefore fitting for these Christian defenders of the city to be quartered "in the very temple of Jerusalem"[8] – that is, in and around the Aqsa Mosque, which Christians understood as the Temple of Solomon. He described its stunning transformation from a house of God to a house of God's war. The facade was adorned "with weapons rather than jewels, and in place of the ancient golden crowns [within], its walls are hung round with shields. In place of candlesticks, censers and ewers, this house is well furnished with saddles, bits and lances."[9]

Such stirring rhetoric had a long life. Eudes of Châteauroux (ca. 1190–1273), an academic and a cardinal of the Church, wrote impassioned sermons urging Europeans to go on crusade.[10] This well-educated and highly placed churchman praised the sword as a sacred weapon: "This sword is holy, because everything that is blessed is blessed with the cross, and it blesses and purges those who take it."[11] In Germany, the blessing of swords is mentioned in 1101 as part of a special liturgy that included the singing of an antiphon linking the soldier's possession of the deadly weapon to the example of God himself: "Gird thy sword upon thy thigh, O thou most mighty."[12] More than a century later, after the reversal of Europe's fortunes in the eastern Mediterranean, William Durandus, bishop of Mende, France, created a liturgy for those bent on recapturing the Holy Land, during which each participant received a cross — likely of cloth or tin — that had been blessed (fig. 68). Turning Jesus's teaching of nonviolence and sacrifice on its head, Christians since the time of Constantine had converted the Cross into an emblem of battle, one that was widely recognized by their adversaries.[13] Qadi al-Fadil (1135–1199), a minister of Saladin, who ultimately defeated the Crusaders, declared that "they did not ever go forward into a danger without having it in their midst; they would fly around it like moths around the light."[14]

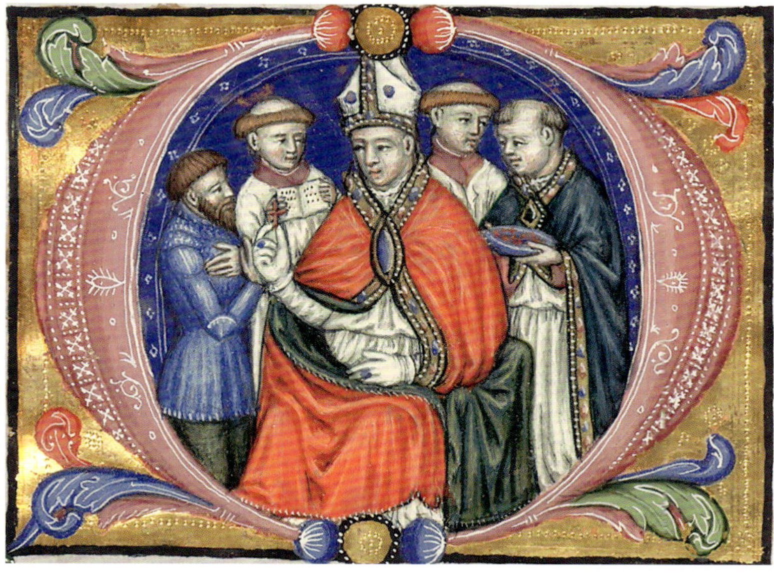

Fig. 68. Detail showing a bishop handing a blessed cross over to a crusader, from the *Calderini Pontifical*. Northern Italy, ca. 1380–ca. 1425. Tempera, gold, and ink on parchment. Houghton Library, Harvard University, Cambridge, Massachusetts (MS Typ 1, fol. 34v)

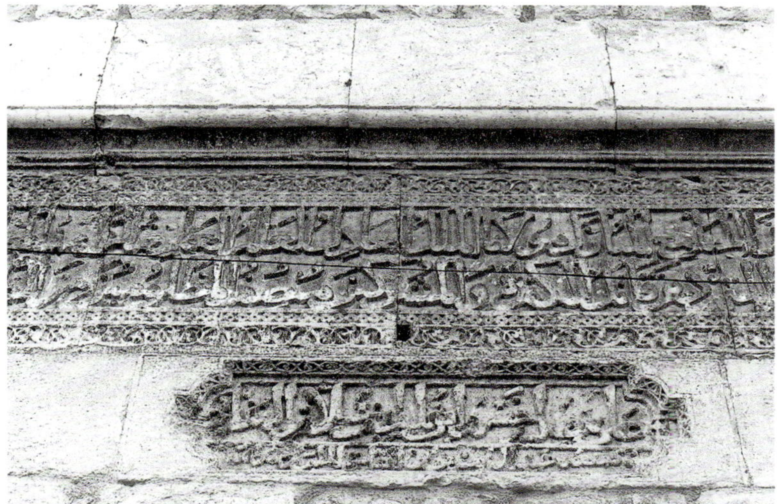

Fig. 69. Inscription on the outer north wall of the Nur al-Din Mosque. Hama, Syria, after 1157 (probably 1162–63 and later)

It is in this same period that Islamic scholars increasingly began to reinterpret Qur'anic discussions of jihad, or struggle, to embrace the concept of fighting as a religious duty, rather than an inner struggle or a defense of a community. This development is generally understood to have been fueled by Crusader incursions.[15] The concept was embraced by Nur al-Din (d. 1174), who sought to unite the region's varied Muslim communities in common cause against the Crusaders. As part of his strategy, he commissioned the religious scholar Ibn 'Asakir (d. 1176) to write a manual on jihad to be used for teaching and preaching.[16] Ibn 'Asakir was one of a group of scholars in Damascus — including several from Jerusalem displaced by the Crusader occupation — who articulated the virtues of military jihad as a religious obligation. He expressed his hope that his preparation of the manual would allow him to "receive the reward [from God]."[17] His text, studied with intensity in Damascus in the twelfth and thirteenth centuries, was meant "to stimulate the valiant jihad fighters . . . to uproot the unbelievers and tyrants who have terrorized the land."[18]

If Ibn 'Asakir's work constituted a "jihad of the pen,"[19] then the architectural patronage of Nur al-Din might be deemed a jihad of public space, for he used monuments and their inscriptions to wage an ideological battle within his own territories. The many madrasas, mosques, and minarets he sponsored trumpeted the orthodoxy of Sunni Islam and often explicitly encouraged jihad through their highly visible inscriptions. For instance, the colossal inscription on the Friday Mosque of Nur al-Din in Hama, Syria (fig. 69), which includes the *shahada*, the essential Muslim declaration of faith in God

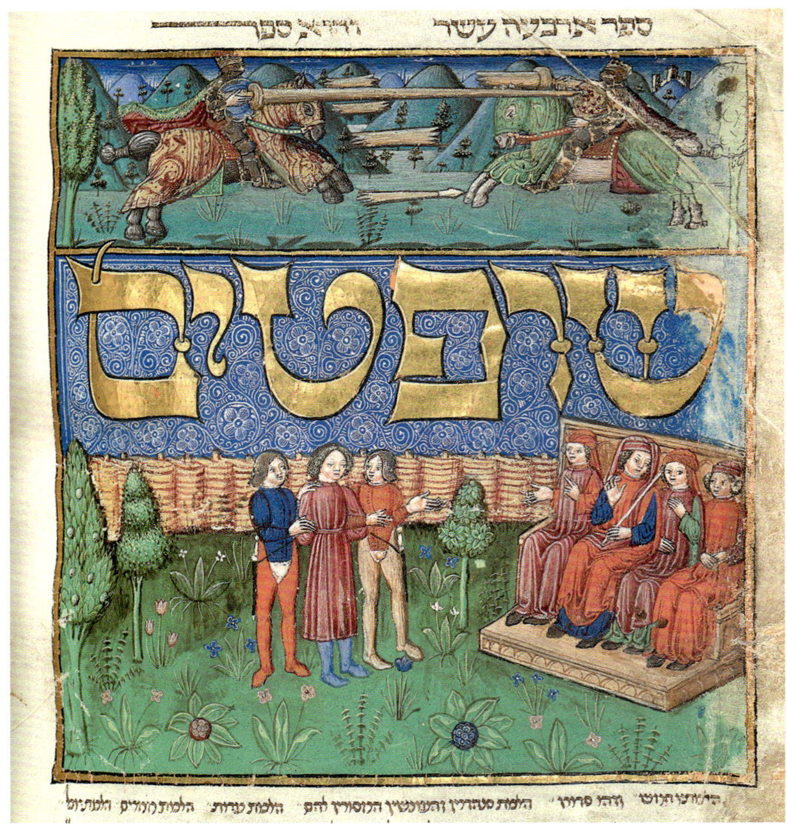

Fig. 70. "The Book of Judges," from the *Mishneh Torah* of Maimonides. Cat. 64, fol. 306v

and in the role of the Prophet, also acclaims Nur al-Din as a *mujahid* (fighter of jihad), a savior of the public, a vanquisher of rebels, and a slayer of infidels and polytheists.[20] By the later Mamluk period, inscriptions routinely heralded a sultan as a "holy warrior" alongside such universally lauded roles as being the "protector of the oppressed" and "one who establishes justice," both on monumental inscriptions, as seen as in the Cotton Market in Jerusalem, and on luxury brass vessels made for the sultan's use (cat. 129a–f).[21]

Nur al-Din possessed a searing obsession with Jerusalem.[22] The poet Ibn al-Qaysarani (d. 1154) expressed that desire on the sultan's behalf: "May it, the city of Jerusalem, be purified by the shedding of blood. The decision of Nur al-Din is as strong as ever, and the iron of his lance is directed at the Aqsa."[23] The lengthy inscriptions on the minbar (pulpit) that Nur al-Din commissioned for the Aqsa Mosque (cat. 93) — though he did not live to see it installed in the city he yearned for — included an invocation: "May he grant conquest to him [Nur al-Din] and at his own hands."[24] It is therefore not surprising that Nur al-Din's successor, Saladin, had the minbar brought to Jerusalem and installed at Aqsa once his victory over the city was complete. The scholar and jurist Ibn Shaddad (1145–1234) boasted that he had "collected for him [Saladin] a book on *jihad* in Damascus. . . . He liked it and used to study it constantly."[25]

Nor was the notion of divine sanction for war absent from Jewish scholarly and artistic tradition, even though medieval Jews controlled no armies. In the wake of the Romans' decisive quashing of the Bar Kokhba revolt in the second century, war figured rarely in rabbinic writings.[26] We find, however, in the twelfth and thirteenth centuries a willingness by two of the era's most prominent thinkers to reopen the issue of holy, or "commanded," war (*milhemet mitzvah*) as a theoretical discussion.

In compiling a systematic code of Jewish law, Maimonides explored the notion of righteous warfare. In his *Mishneh Torah* (cat. 64) he outlined the circumstances that permit a king to wage war.[27] "In all matters," he wrote, "[the king's] deeds shall be for the sake of heaven."[28] Influenced by contemporary Muslim theorists, Maimonides made a case for the destruction of idolatry in the world, citing in support commandments in the book of Deuteronomy (20:16 and 25:19) to destroy the Canaanite nations and the Amalekites, both timeless representatives of idolatrous people: "As it is said, 'You must not let a soul remain alive.'"[29] Given the absence of a Jewish polity, such a statement could hardly be understood as a call to arms. Rather, we might view it as a convincing demonstration of the applicability of Jewish law to the "hot topic" of the day, that is, holy war. The great rabbi Nachmanides (1194–1270), a critic of Maimonides, was no less severe in his interpretation of some of the same biblical passages, though his focus was on the Land of Israel (Eretz Yisrael): "We are commanded to engage in [its] conquest in every generation."[30] For Nachmanides, Jews, lacking the military means sanctioned by God, could fulfill the divine obligation of conquest by establishing Jewish communities in the Land of Israel.[31]

In contrast to some Jewish images that allude to the persecution Jews faced as minorities within often hostile cultures, the opening illustration of the book of Judges in a lavishly illustrated fifteenth-century copy of the *Mishneh Torah* imagines a different world.[32] To illustrate the "Laws Concerning Kings and War," the section of Maimonides's text that discusses *milhemet mitzvah*, the artist presents two kings jousting. Crowned and in full armor, the warriors charge toward each other astride colorfully appointed horses. The lance of one, presumably a defeated king of an idolatrous nation, has been shattered by the appointed king of Israel, whose own lance pierces his enemy's breastplate. An illustration of the miraculous crossing of the Red Sea from the Rylands Haggadah (fig. 71) presents an alternative view of military success within a Jewish context. In it, the fleeing Israelites appear not as downtrodden slaves but as able soldiers, outfitted with helmets, spears, swords, axes, shields, and body armor. Several men in their company clutch precious vessels looted from the Egyptian treasury, as described in the book of Exodus. Art allowed Jews to imagine themselves in the role of military victor.

Medieval accounts of battles in Jerusalem tell of precious goods lost to the enemy. Territory, slaves, cash, emblems of faith, and cultural heritage — all were prizes for the righteous warrior.[33] Indeed, throughout history, irreplaceable works of art have been among the uncounted fatalities of war; they, no less than the citizenry of an enemy state, were taken hostage. Yet art repeatedly champions the soldier and his physical prowess while minimizing his bloodstained work of destruction. It is a curious dance. In sculpture, Christian knights are represented for posterity as handsome, life-size heroes at peace (cat. 108), while "toy" knights graced the dinner table as aquamanilia for handwashing (cat. 116). In much the same way, the arts of Islam elevate the qualities and accoutrements of warriors, blurring the line between the bravado of a tournament and the actual peril of battle (fig. 72). The bands that encircle the *Baptistère de Saint Louis* present armor-clad warriors as part of a courtly entourage (fig. 73). Such images are a genteel step removed from battle.

Masterpieces of Western European Christian art celebrate the conflict over the Holy Land, echoing the voices heard in sermons and exhortations with images that offer a feast for the eyes, attempting to raise the grim realities of armed conflict to an elevated plane. Goldsmiths' work, manuscript illumination, and stained glass were all co-opted to proclaim the honor and rightness of war. The celebrated Morgan Picture Bible (cat. 109), for one, asserts that

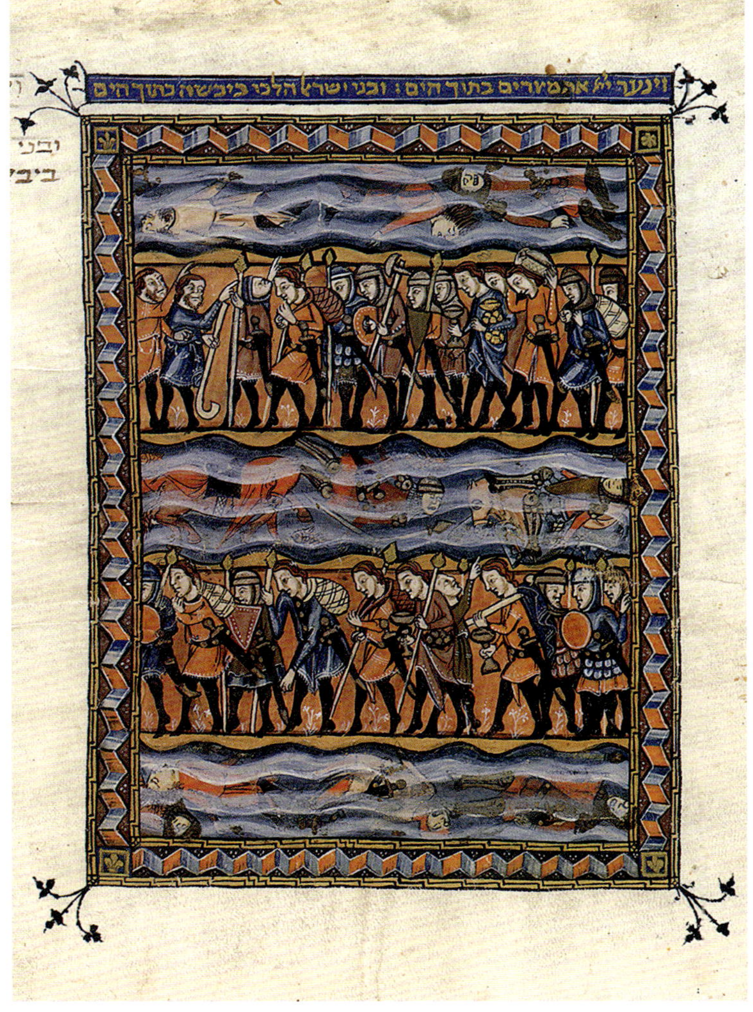

Fig. 71. "Crossing the Red Sea," from the Rylands Haggadah. Catalonia, mid-1300s. Tempera, gold, and ink on parchment. Courtesy of the Director and University Librarian, The John Rylands University Library, Manchester, England (Heb MS 6, fol. 19r)

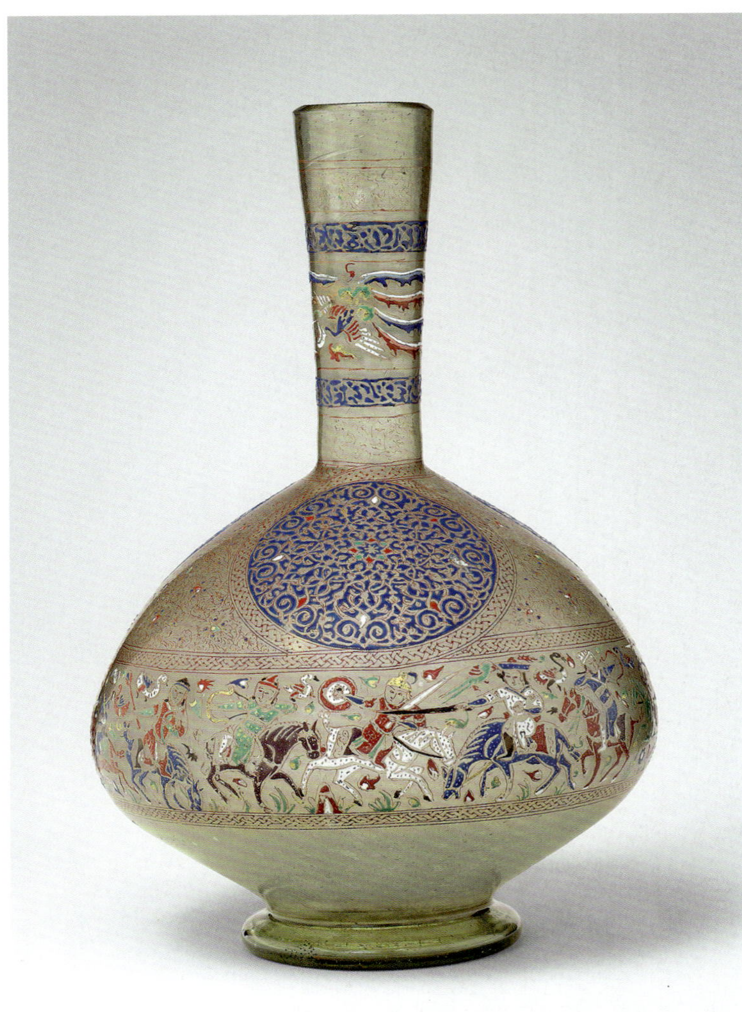

Fig. 72. Enameled and gilded bottle. Egypt, possibly Cairo, late 13th–early 14th century. Blown glass, enamel, and gold. The Metropolitan Museum of Art, New York, Rogers Fund, 1941 (41.150)

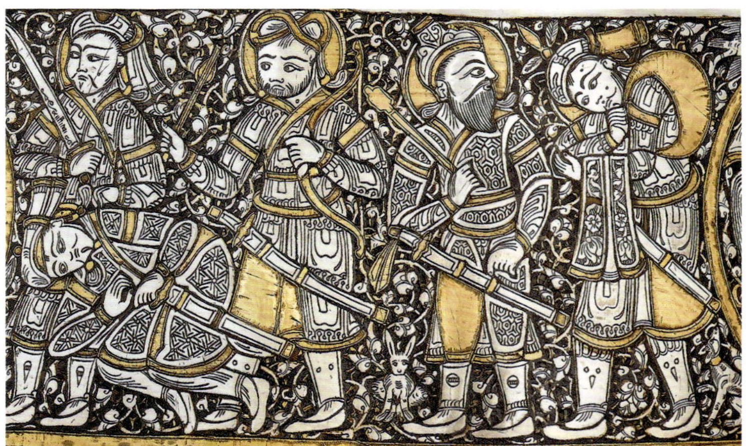

Fig. 73. Detail from the *Baptistère de Saint Louis*. Syria or Egypt, ca. 1330–40. Hammered brass, inlaid with gold, silver, and black paste. Musée du Louvre, Département des Arts de l'Islam, Paris (LP 16)

the Crusaders were following the righteous, yet militaristic, biblical tradition of Joshua and David.

On a single leaf from an Italian choir book, Crusaders claimed the historic mantle of the Maccabees (cat. 65). The name of the ancient Jewish tribe resonates with audiences today chiefly because of the Jewish festival of Hanukkah, which celebrates the miraculous rededication of the Temple of Jerusalem. The story, recounted in two books of the medieval Christian Bible, was well-known in Europe — not only for its miraculous happy ending in Jerusalem, but also for what preceded it: numerous battles and acts of violence against other Jews and pagans, all justified by the divinely ordained cause.[34] In the illumination, the Maccabees appear as a merry band of medieval knights, sporting impeccable armor and bright colors as they ride noble steeds through a rocky landscape. The resonance between images like this and medieval sermons extolling the Maccabees is abundantly clear. Pope Urban II had invoked them when he called for Westerners to "cleanse the Holy City": "If in olden times the Maccabees attained to the highest praise of piety because they fought for the ceremonies and the Temple, it is also justly granted you, Christian soldiers, to defend their liberty of your country by armed endeavor."[35]

Expressing a similarly clear agenda is the Stavelot Triptych (cat. 110), which proclaims the righteousness of fighting for Jerusalem. With shimmering images, it glorifies the example of the post-biblical history of Constantine (ca. 273–337), the first Christian emperor of Rome. At the triptych's very center are slivers of wood believed to be from the Cross of Jesus. The ensemble of enamels that surrounds it emphatically traces the relics of the Cross to Jerusalem's soil. The story unfolds on the wings. It begins at lower left with the sleeping emperor, to whom an angel appears, advising that he go into battle under the sign of the Cross (fig. 74). Heeding the angel's call, Constantine, in the second scene, at top, routs the enemy, his military victory affirming the righteousness of Christianity and vice versa. As a result of Constantine's newfound faith in the Cross and its powers, he is baptized as a Christian (the scene portrayed in the top left roundel of cat. 110). At upper right, compelled by the astonishing results her son had experienced in battle, the empress

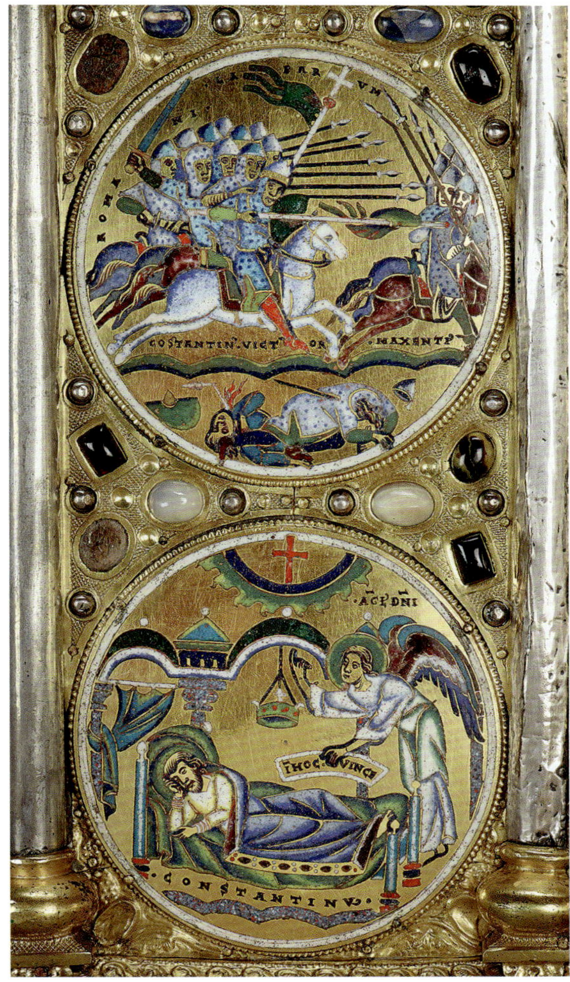

Fig. 74. At top, "Constantine's Victory at the Milvian Bridge"; below, "The Dream of Constantine." Detail of cat. 110

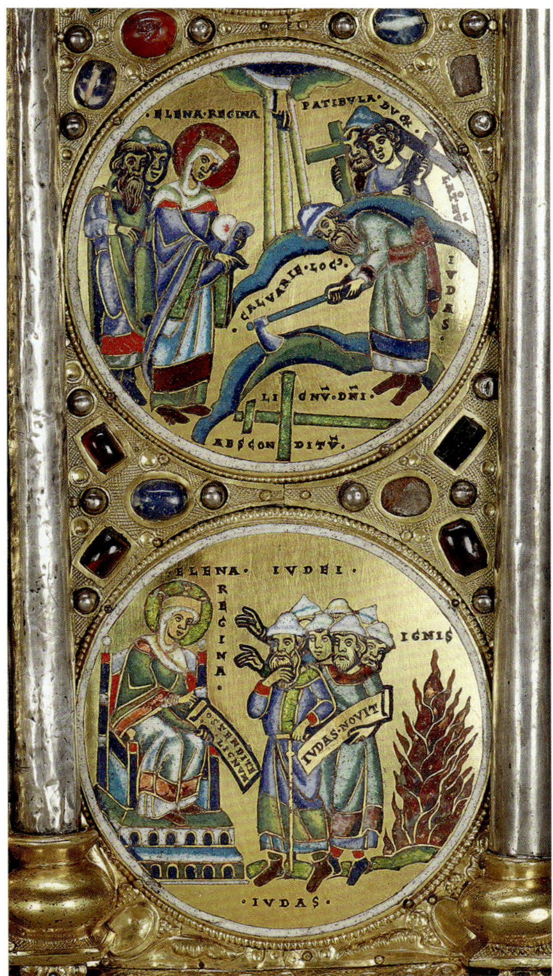

Fig. 75. At top, "Helena Oversees the Excavation of the Cross"; below, "Helena Questions Jewish Leaders as to Its Whereabouts." Detail of cat. 110

Helena undertakes an expedition to Jerusalem to find the Cross that ensured her son's triumph (fig. 75). The ensuing images demonstrate the authenticity of her find. Indeed, along with Helena the roundel presents perhaps the earliest instance of biblical archaeology, complete with pickax and a native worker who is exploited for his local knowledge (here, a Jew). In the roundel below, Jews have their feet put to the flames to pressure them into revealing the whereabouts of the Cross.

The triptych was created in a realm that felt keenly that it was on the verge of losing the hard-won prize of Jerusalem. The churchman generally considered to have been the patron of the triptych, Wibald (1098–1158), abbot of Stavelot, played an outsize role within a network of Crusader leaders. Wibald was a leading counselor to the German king Conrad III, an ardent disciple of Abbot Bernard of Clairvaux (1090–1153). Wibald, too, was a great admirer of Bernard, who traveled across Europe arguing for a "just war." The triptych conveys much the same message, combining a sense of historic entitlement, obligation, and mission into a visually compelling statement.

Subtly, the imagery of the Stavelot Triptych further embellishes the role of post-biblical heroes by adopting Byzantine saints who were considered "holy warriors." From left to right, top to bottom, enameled figures of saints George, Theodore, Procopius, and Demetrius stand, Cross in hand, to either side of the central Cross relic, protecting it along with Constantine, Helena, and the angels Gabriel and Michael. George, Demetrius, and, in one iteration of the story, Theodore were believed to have assisted the first Crusaders at the battle of Antioch in 1097–98 while on their way to Jerusalem.[36] As for

Procopius, his legend includes a miraculous vision of the Cross on the eve of battle and a voice urging, "in this sign, conquer," echoing the experience of the warring emperor Constantine. The juxtapositions are not accidental: these central "triptychs," though using Byzantine enamels, are assemblages made in the West when this work of art was created.

Like Constantine, the Holy Roman Emperor Charlemagne was also esteemed as a holy warrior and saint, with links to the Holy Land (cats. 111, 114). "Recruited" as holy warriors, the images of such post-biblical heroes sent an approving message to those who fought. Veterans of the First Crusade are honored in The Cloisters Apocalypse (cat. 140) as souls in white "under the altar, crying," as described by Saint John (fig. 76). He went on to ask, "How long before your blood be avenged on the earth?" The coats of arms that grace the altar confirm the figures' connection to the First Crusade: some are indecipherable, but most are of Norman families who went to the Holy Land to fight. Here, the connection to sacred violence has an even more troubling undertone, for it places the Crusaders' fight for Jerusalem squarely amid the horrors of the Final Days before the Last Judgment. This kind of link adheres to Jerusalem with unshakable, unfortunate tenacity and has taken its toll on works of art, most notably the minbar of Nur al-Din.[37] And indeed, by stoking sectarian violence, art was no less complicit than speech. It encouraged the hesitant and affirmed for the overeager the bloody necessity and valor of war.

NOTES FOR THIS ESSAY APPEAR ON PAGE 304
SEE CATS. 102–120

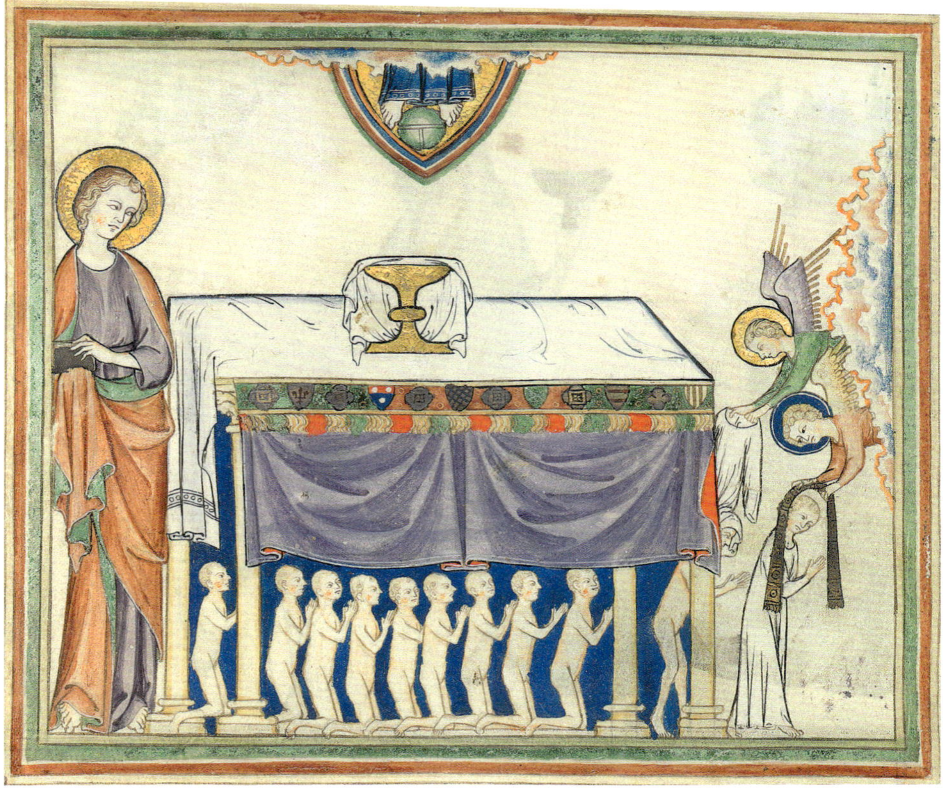

Fig. 76. "The Opening of the Fifth Seal: The Martyrs," from *The Cloisters Apocalypse*. Cat. 140, fol. 9v

JERUSALEM: THE CRUCIBLE OF HOLY WAR

James Carroll

DAYS AFTER the 9/11 attacks, British prime minister Tony Blair said that the terrorist violence of Mohamed Atta and the others was no more a reflection of true Islam than the Crusades were of the Gospel.[1] The Crusades remain a touchstone of an uneasy Western conscience precisely because grotesque acts of violence, centered on Jerusalem, were defined as holy. "God wills it!" was the Crusader battle cry, called out as thousands of Jews and Muslims were slaughtered. Europe came into being as the Europe we know during – and in part as a result of – the centuries-spanning sequence of assaults by Latin Christians against Muslims in the Levant and against Jews and Orthodox Christians encountered along the way. The Crusades epitomize Holy War, with Jerusalem as its crucible.

Today, defenders of religion, like Blair, want to separate violence from faith, arguing that "true" religion concerns love of neighbor and virtues like tolerance and compassion. Violent religion, the argument runs, is not actually religious. Thus, in such brutal civil wars as those that have in recent years wracked places as diverse as Northern Ireland, the former Yugoslavia, and Sri Lanka, nationalist and ethnic causes are emphasized by observers, even as participants themselves – Catholic, Protestant, Orthodox, Muslim, and Buddhist – define religion as key. The question of God-sanctioned killing remains salient as the murderous thugs of the so-called Islamic State, for example, advance their bloody cause with explicit appeals to the will of Allah. The global jihad is taken to be the Holy War of the twenty-first century. Yet because only a tiny minority of the world's billion-plus Muslims today adhere to any notion of killing in Allah's name, the aim to head off a rising Islamophobia by declaring the religion of Muhammad wholly innocent is understandable. But when it comes to violence rooted in zealotry, intolerance, and the apocalyptic, is any religion innocent? And what of so-called secular violence when it is ignited with religious reference, as happened when President George W. Bush blithely launched his war on terrorism as "this Crusade"?[2]

The Crusades marked a turning point in Christian history, a first unambiguous defining of bloodshed as willed by God. Because the campaigns' purpose was nothing less than rescuing God's own land – the Holy Land taken captive by Muslims – the end was taken to justify the means. Priests accompanied the cross-marked fighters not to forgive their savage deeds, as confessors had, say, during the conversion conquests of Charlemagne, but to send them into battle with a blessing, and, as repeatedly noted in Crusaders' own chronicles, under the sign of the Cross. Killing was the way to heaven.

The Holy War of the Crusades, far from being anomalous, showed what the Gospel had come to mean at the first millennium. Thus, the Crusades were underwritten by a violent theology of God that emphasized, for example in the schema described by Saint Anselm, that the redemption of the fallen world required the divinely willed crucifixion of God's own son. The Crusades were tied to the central authority of a justifying religious institution, with Crusader popes like Urban II summoning the fighters and saints like Bernard of Clairvaux offering expressly religious sanction for the killing. And the Crusades were animated by religiously justified contempt for the "perfidious," whether Jew or Muslim, and even by sacred texts of the New Testament, like the Apocalypse, which shows a warrior Christ leading God's army against the forces of evil at the end of history. The Crusades, that is, came right out of the sacred heart of Christendom.

Saint Bernard, the movement's leading preacher, summed up its ethos: "But the knights of Christ may safely do battle in the battles of their Lord, fearing neither the sin of smiting the enemy, nor the danger of their own downfall, inasmuch as death for Christ inflicted or endured, bears no taint of sin, but deserves

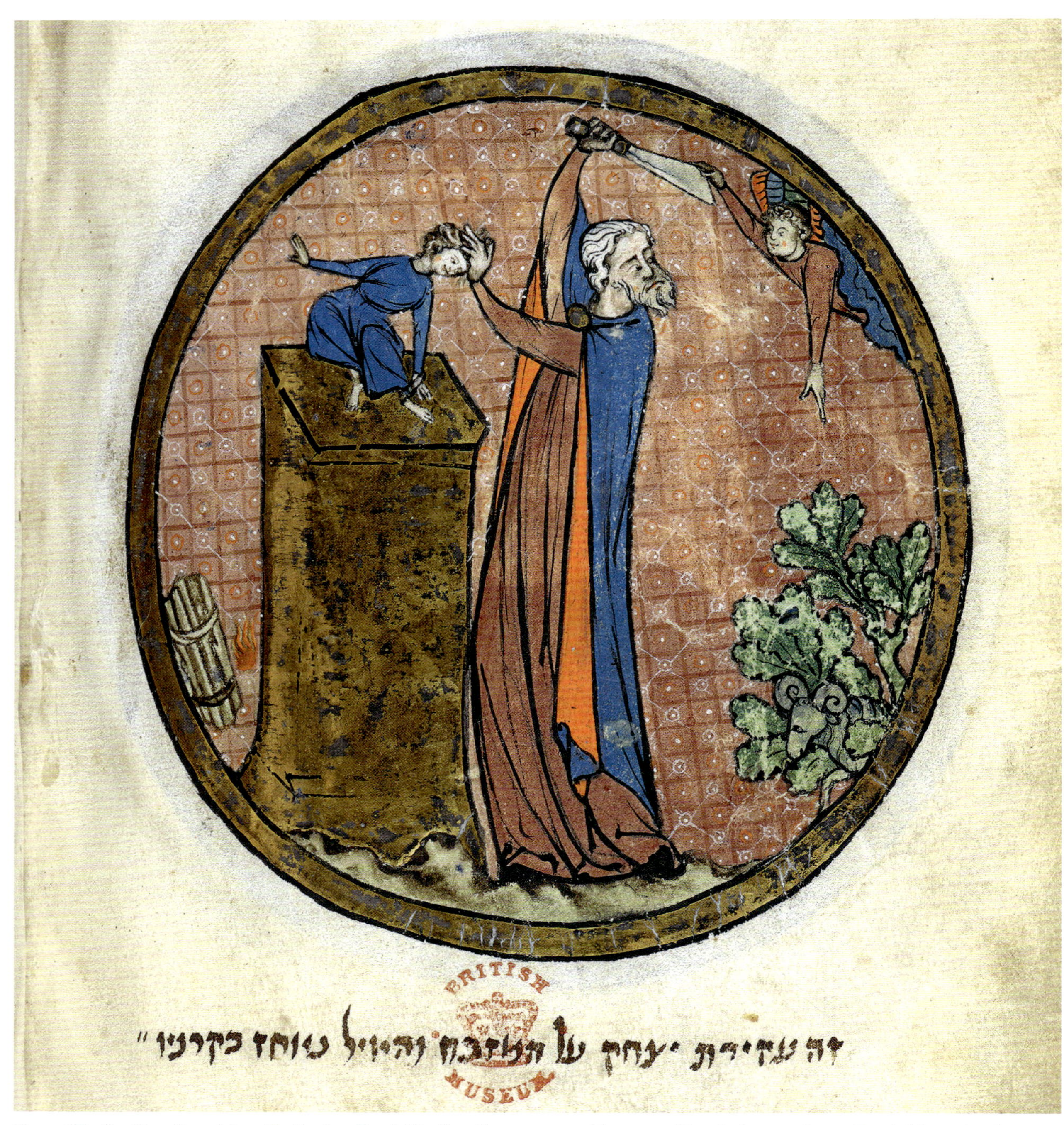

Fig. 77. "The Sacrifice of Isaac," from *The Northern French Miscellany*. France, 1277–86. Tempera, gold, and ink on parchment. British Library, London (Add. MS 11639, fol. 521v)

abundant glory."[3] The momentum of that paradigmatic Holy War would run on, eventually unleashing armies of Catholics and Protestants, all crying "God wills it!" as, across two centuries, they killed one another by the millions.[4]

Against those who target Islam, there is no crime of which Muslims can be accused that Christians do not stand accused of by history. Against religion's moralizing atheist critics, such history does not mean that faith itself is the prime source of violence or that the elimination of religion would lead the world to peace. After all, the most savage violence ever has unfolded in the modern era, during wars blithely regarded as "secular." But here again, Jerusalem is a clue. That the 1914 fevers of the Great War, despite its apparent secularity, drew on overheated religious currents running beneath the surface of power politics is suggested by the defining British war anthem, "Jerusalem." That early nineteenth-century lyric by William Blake was set to music only in 1916, as the epoch-shattering Battle of the Somme raged:

> And was Jerusalem builded here
> Among these dark Satanic Mills?
> Bring me my Bow of burning gold:
> Bring me my Arrows of desire:
> Bring me my Spear: O clouds unfold!
> Bring me my Chariot of fire![5]

As the Holy City had braced the imagination — and battle courage — of Crusaders, so it braced Englishmen, for whom it seemed only natural that the hated Hun had made his alliance with the Islamic Ottoman Empire. But now trenches became the altar of Abraham (fig. 77). There, old men, as Wilfred Owen put it, "slew half the seed of Europe, one by one."[6] Only a subliminal ideology of God-ordained sacrifice enabled such pointless carnage to occur between 1914 and 1918.

Rejecting the post-Reformation religious wars of Europe, the United States had erected its "wall of separation" between church and state. Nevertheless, an implicit ethos of Holy War formed a pillar of American attitudes, never more so than during the Cold War, when the apocalyptic fervor of a cosmic conflict between good and evil underwrote readiness to destroy the very planet as a way of saving it from "godless Communism." Indeed, the vision of America as the world-redeeming "City on a Hill," invoked by presidents from Kennedy to Reagan as they prepared for nuclear Armageddon, referred, in its ultimate source, yes, to Jerusalem — even if the politicians did not know it.[7] America's contest with the Soviet Union was as holy as any war ever was, and despite the Soviet demise, the American mind was set. At the dawn of the twenty-first century, world Communism was replaced by so-called fundamentalist Islam in that conflict offhandedly defined in Washington, as noted, in terms of the Crusades. By now, the drastic inappropriateness of cloaking the war on terror in God's will is clear.

Islam has its version of violence willed by God, but in the West, Holy War is taken to have its origins in biblical violence: the Old Testament with its hundreds of passages of bloody killing (fig. 77), stories that the Crusaders embraced as their own. But violence runs through the Bible because violence is the problem to which the Bible is responding. Jerusalem is its cockpit — a crossroads Hebrew city over which a succession of great empires fought, from Babylon and Egypt to Greece and Rome; from Latin Christians to Muslims; from the British Mandate to Zionists; and ultimately, from Israelis to Palestinians.

Although the Bible can be read as sponsoring violence, it can also be read as the story of violence told from the victim's point of view: therefore, anti-violence. So say the prophets of Israel, with, for example, Isaiah's plaintive cry about turning swords into ploughshares, spears into pruning hooks. And so says Jesus, who emphatically applied his commandment of love to the enemy (Isaiah 2:4; Luke 6:27). Interpretation is key, and so is learning from experience.

The Bible is the book of besieged Jerusalem, and as such it contains the hard lessons of sacred killing: that religion is never innocent; that appeals to God must always be subject to the test of what befalls the neighbor; and that self-criticism must be built into every claim to holiness. "Pray," the Psalmist pleads, "for the peace of Jerusalem" (Psalms 122:6).

NOTES FOR THIS ESSAY APPEAR ON PAGE 304

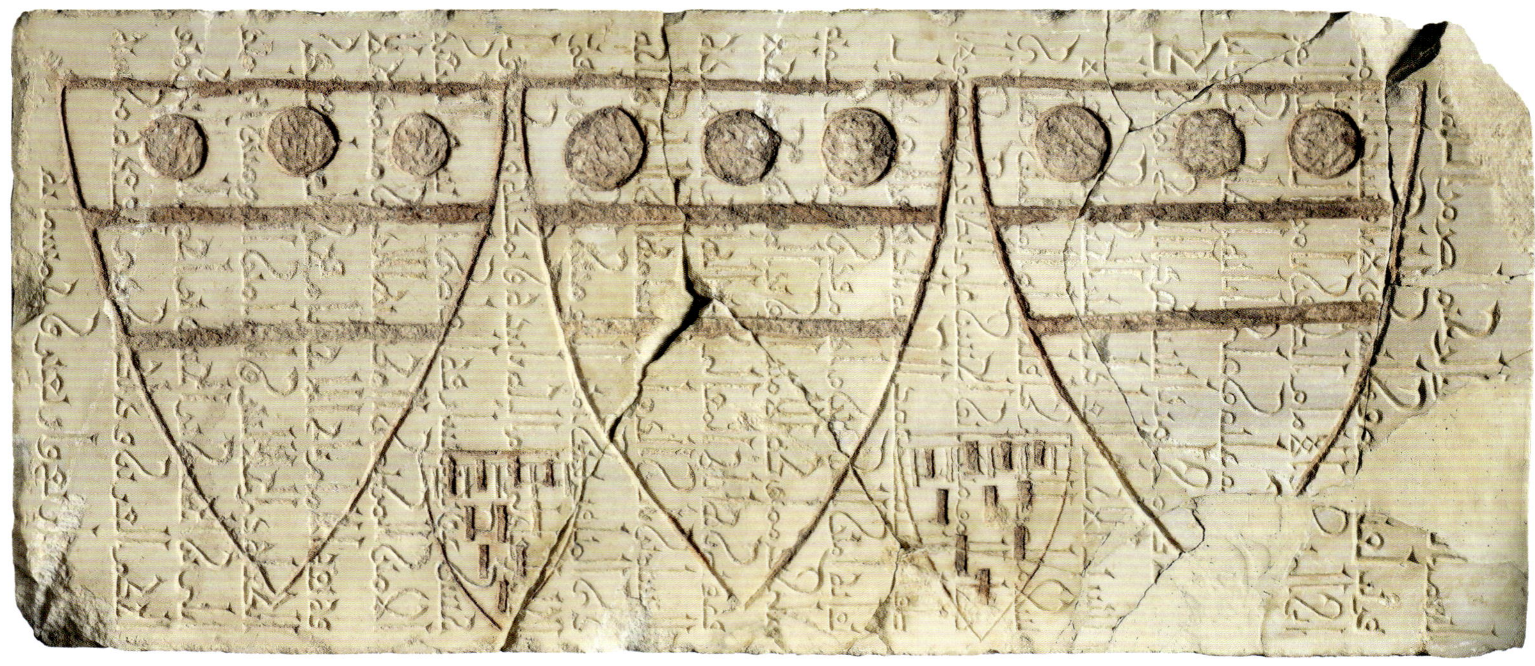

102

102

Three Coats of Arms of Sir Hugh Wake over a Royal Fatimid Inscription

Ascalon, 1150 and 1241
Marble, carved and painted
H. 24¾ in. (63 cm), W. 58⅝ in. (149 cm), D. 2⅞ in. (7.5 cm)
Courtesy of the Israel Antiquities Authority, exhibited at the Israel Museum, Jerusalem (IAA 1995-3731)

This plaque attests to the upheavals experienced in the city of Ascalon during a century of war. While the Arabic inscription commemorates the construction of the fortification tower, built in 1150 by the Fatimids against the Crusaders, the coats of arms of Sir Hugh Wake of County Lincoln in England were carved over it to attest to the 1241 Crusader restoration of the city's fortifications as protection against the Muslims.

The engraved Arabic inscription includes twenty-two lines of sophisticated late Fatimid Kufic royal script. The inscription relays that in the year A.H. 544 (1150), during the days of the Fatimid Sultan al-Zafir, a tower was built (in Ascalon) by the order of the Grand Vizier of Cairo. Construction was carried out by the governor and judge (qadi) of Ascalon. The inscription contains the titles and honorary titles of these officials, along with prayers and blessings.[1]

The inscription was discovered in the debris of the town's northern fortifications. Its large size and imperial nature suggest that the tower it commemorated guarded Ascalon's northern gate (known as the Jaffa Gate). In 1153, almost three and a half years after its construction, Ascalon, the last standing Muslim city on the Syrian-Palestinian coast, was captured by the Crusaders for the first of three times. During the third conquest, the Crusaders reused the stone, turning it widthwise and engraving over the inscription five heraldic red-painted shields. The three large shields are the arms of the principal knight, Sir Hugh Wake (d. 1241); they have two bars drawn across their widths and three roundels in the top of the shield. Two additional small shields, the arms of another, probably lesser, knight, consisting of ten billets arranged in four rows, fill the spaces between the lower portions of the three large ones.[2]

Wake, a baron of Norman origin, joined the crusade of Simon de Montfort, Earl of Leicester, along with nine other English and French knights. The group arrived in the Holy Land in 1240. Together with the knights of the expedition of Richard, Earl of Cornwall (brother of Henry III and brother-in-law of Simon de Montfort), Wake participated in the reconstruction of the Ascalon fortifications. By 1241 the work on the fortifications was completed.[3] Wake was buried in Ascalon, which fell to the Muslims in 1247 and was demolished by Sultan Baybars in 1270. NB

Selected Reference: Sharon 1995.

1. Sharon 1995, pp. 74–77; Sharon 1997, pp. 164–78.
2. As this is a very common pattern, it is difficult to determine who the owner of the smaller shields was. See Sharon 1995, pp. 63–64; Sharon 1997, pp. 178–83.
3. Sharon 1995, pp. 83–85; Lower 2005, p. 45; Tyerman 2006, pp. 757–63.

103

Map of Crusader Jerusalem

From a Picture Book
Saint-Bertin, France, late 12th century
Tempera, gold, and ink on parchment; 47 folios
10 × 6½ in. (25.5 × 16.5 cm)
Koninklijke Bibliotheek, The Hague (MS 76 F 5)

This early map is the most famous and the most beautiful of the circular maps of Jerusalem. It is linked to the First Crusade (1095–99) in several ways.[1] Its source is the *Deeds of the Franks Who Attacked Jerusalem* (*Gesta Francorum Hierusalem expugnantium*), an anonymous chronicle dealing with the history of the Crusades in the period from 1095 to 1106 and compiled before 1109 in Saint-Omer.[2] These *Gesta* were included almost verbatim by Lambertus of Saint-Omer in his *Book of Flowers* (*Liber floridus*). Unfortunately, the map is lost from the autograph manuscript of the *Liber floridus*, finished in 1121,[3] but it is preserved in two thirteenth-century copies, now in Leiden and Paris.[4] Moreover, the map is partly preserved in a manuscript closely connected and strictly contemporaneous to the autograph *Liber floridus*, of which the charred remnants are kept in London.[5]

Unique to the picture book in The Hague, a manuscript most likely initially intended to preface a psalter, is the scene below the city map. It represents Saint George and Saint Demetrius of Thessaloniki on horseback, charging a group of fleeing mounted Muslim warriors. The miniature is inspired by the legendary appearance of these Christian knights in the Crusaders' camp at the battle of Antioch. A leader in the capture of the city on June 28, 1098, was the Norman nobleman Bohemond I of Antioch (ca. 1058–1111). With good reason it is suggested that Bohemond was the key figure in the the origins of the *Gesta*.[6] His visit to Saint-Omer in the spring of 1106 is well documented.

The map was originally placed at the end of the book, after two Last Judgment scenes, showing that the Crusades and apocalyptic thought were closely connected.[7] EVDV

Selected References: Cologne 1985, vol. 3, pp. 76–77, no. H4; Simek 1992; Mainz 2004, pp. 337–40, no. 23; Meuwese 2005, p. 143; Van der Vlist et al. 2015, pp. 29–32, 206–7.

1. On this and other maps of Jerusalem, see Simek 1992; Rubenstein 2014.
2. An original manuscript of this chronicle is still partly preserved in Saint-Omer at the Bibliothèque Municipale, MS 776; it is the result of the collaboration between monks of the abbey of Saint-Bertin near Saint-Omer and Lambertus, canon of the collegiate church of Saint-Omer, the author of the *Liber floridus*. The map is on fol. 50v and accompanies a long description of Jerusalem; Derolez 2013.
3. Universiteitsbibliotheek, Ghent, MS 92. On this manuscript, see Derolez 2015.

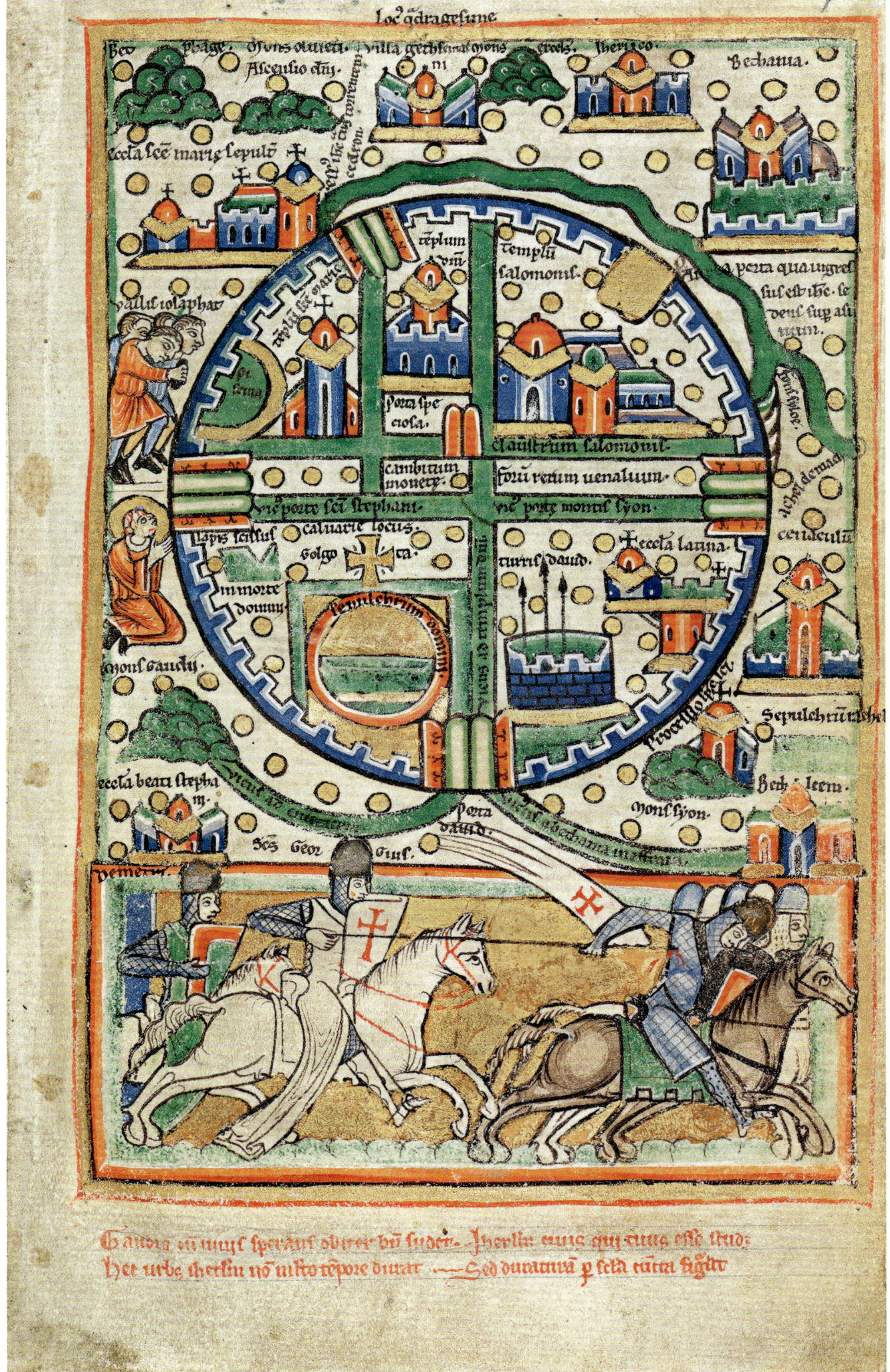

103, fol. 1r

4. Universiteitsbibliotheek, Leiden, MS VLF 31, fol. 85r; Bibliothèque Nationale de France, Paris, MS Lat. 8865, fol. 133r.
5. British Library, London, Cotton Fragments, vol. 1, no. 22. A copy in a fifteenth-century compilation is in the Grootseminarie, Bruges, MS 127/5, fol. 18r; Derolez 2005.
6. Derolez 2013.
7. On this connection, see Rubenstein 2011; Rubenstein 2012.

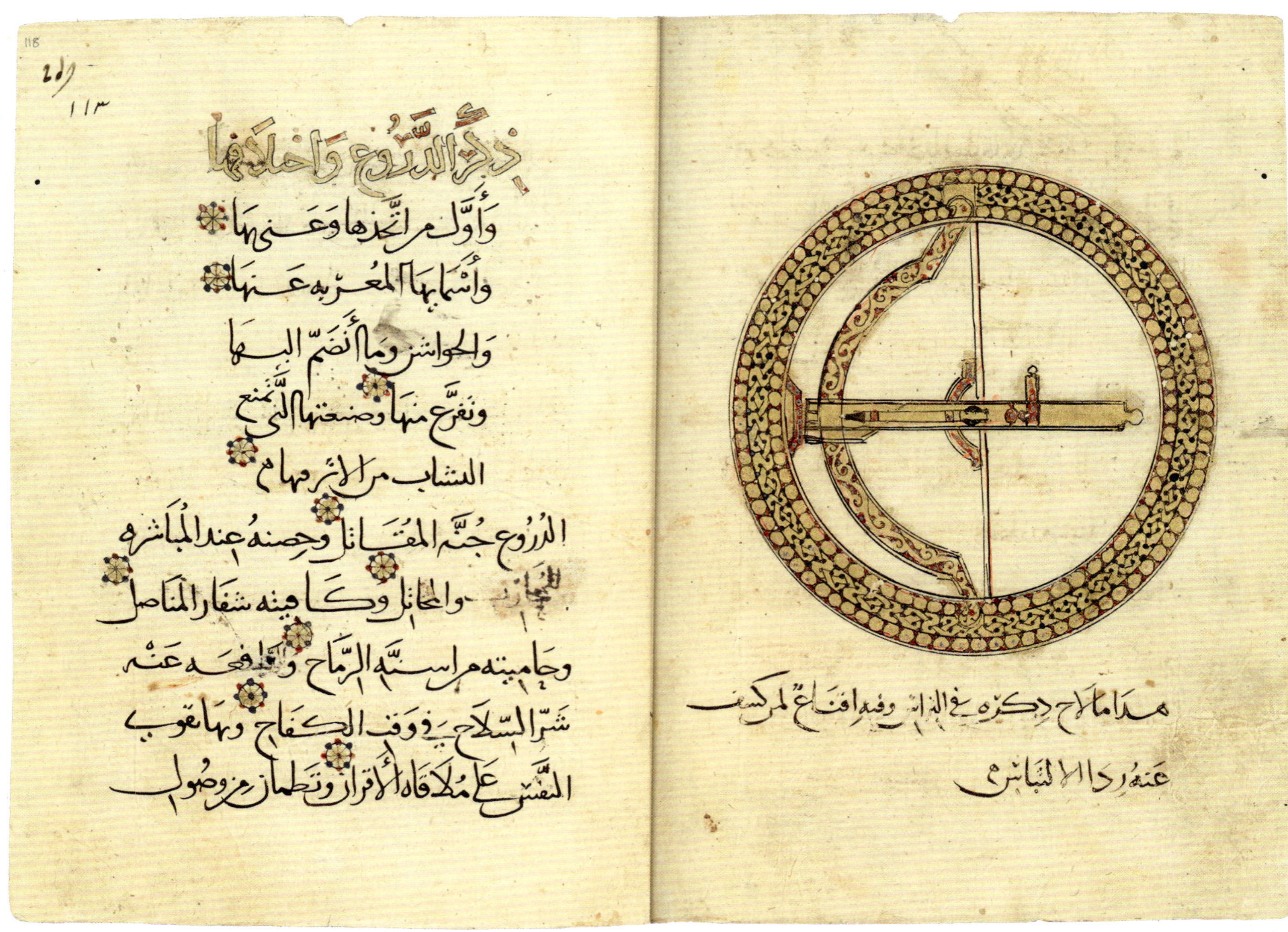

104 Combination shield and concealed crossbow, fols. 117b–118a

104

Saladin's Treatise on Armor

Syria, before 1187
Opaque watercolor, gold, and ink on paper; 217 folios
H. 9⅞ in. (25.2 cm), W. 7⅝ in. (19.5 cm), D. 2⅛ in. (5.5 cm)
Bodleian Libraries, University of Oxford
(MS Huntington 264)

On A.H. 20 Rajab 583 (September 25, 1187), a Friday, al-Malik al-Nasir Abu l-Muzaffar Yusuf ibn Ayyub, better known as Salah al-Din and westernized as Saladin, moved his armies from the west side of Jerusalem, where he had lain siege for five days, to the north side and pitched his tents. There he set up his mangonels — great siege engines for catapulting stones and other missiles toward the city walls. A contemporary chronicler described the mangonels as resembling "madmen competing with one another to hurl rocks."[1] Seven days later the walls were breached and the city taken, the siege engines having played a decisive role in the battle.

This copy of a treatise on the art of warfare was made for Saladin's own treasury by Mardi ibn 'Ali of Tarsus prior to the siege of Jerusalem. It describes swords — and their manufacture, including the technique known as damascening — spears, shields, siege engines such as catapults and great bows, and ends with a detailed and mathematical discussion of burning mirrors, whose use as a weapon goes back to ancient Greece. Not much is known about Mardi of Tarsus except that he died in 1193, the same year as Saladin, and that he studied with a master of the arts of war in Alexandria, Egypt. His treatise, however, shows the state of the art of medieval weaponry and may have contributed to the outcome of one of the most famous battles of the Middle Ages. AW

Selected References: al-Tarsusi 1948 ed.; Boudot-Lamotte 1968; al-Tarsusi 1998 ed.; al-Tarsusi 2004 ed.

1. Imad al-Din 1888 ed., p. 53.

105

Sword

Europe, before 1419
Steel and wood
Overall length: 43⅝ in. (110.9 cm); length of blade: 34⅛ in. (86.6 cm); width of cross guard: 12⅜ in. (31.4 cm)
The Metropolitan Museum of Art, New York, Bashford Dean Memorial Collection, Bequest of Bashford Dean, 1928 (29.150.143)

Swords were the premier weapons of the Crusading era and, beyond their lethal effectiveness, have remained the ultimate symbol of knighthood and the culture of chivalry. This sword represents the apogee of European cut-and-thrust weapons in the late Middle Ages. Its blade is extraordinarily wide at the top — 3½ inches (8.9 cm) — and narrows steeply to an acute point. Despite its massive silhouette, however, the blade is thin and flexible. Fitted with a wheel-shaped pommel as a counterweight and a long cross guard to protect the hands of the person wielding it, this sword is amazingly light, perfectly balanced, and easy to maneuver. Elegant in form and proportions, it represents a perfect combination of design and technology.

The Arabic inscription engraved at the top of the blade, "Donation of al-Malik al Mu'ayyad Abu al-Nasr Shaykh to the armory in the frontier city of Alexandria [in the] year [A.H.] 822 [1419],"[1] indicates that the sword was once part of the large group of European armor and weapons stored in the Mamluk arsenal in Alexandria, Egypt. Many of those pieces had been taken as booty in the battles between Muslim and Christian armies in the Middle East and Aegean regions; others were sent to the sultan as tribute, possibly by the king of Cyprus. DLR

Selected References: Von Kienbusch and Grancsay 1933, pp. 195–96, no. 138, pl. 52; Combe and de Cosson 1937, pp. 232–34, no. 4, fig. 4; Kalus 1982/1990, pp. 59–60, no. 59; Alexander 1985, p. 96 n. 35 and appendix I, p. 97; Thomas 2003, p. 40, no. 14, fig. 17.

1. Translation by David Alexander, as noted in the object file for 29.150.143, Department of Arms and Armor, The Metropolitan Museum of Art.

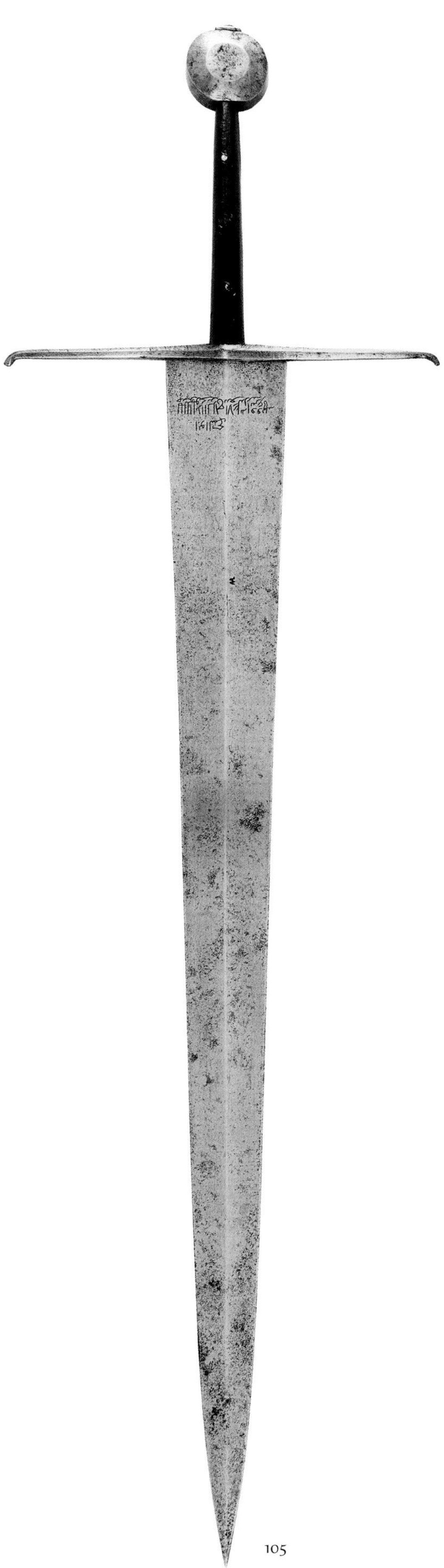

105

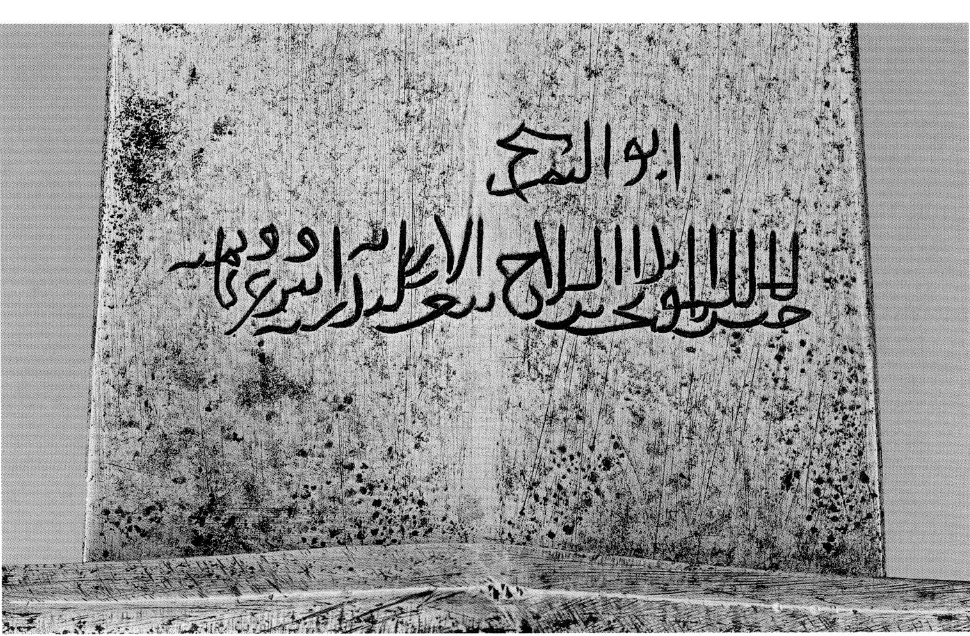

105 detail

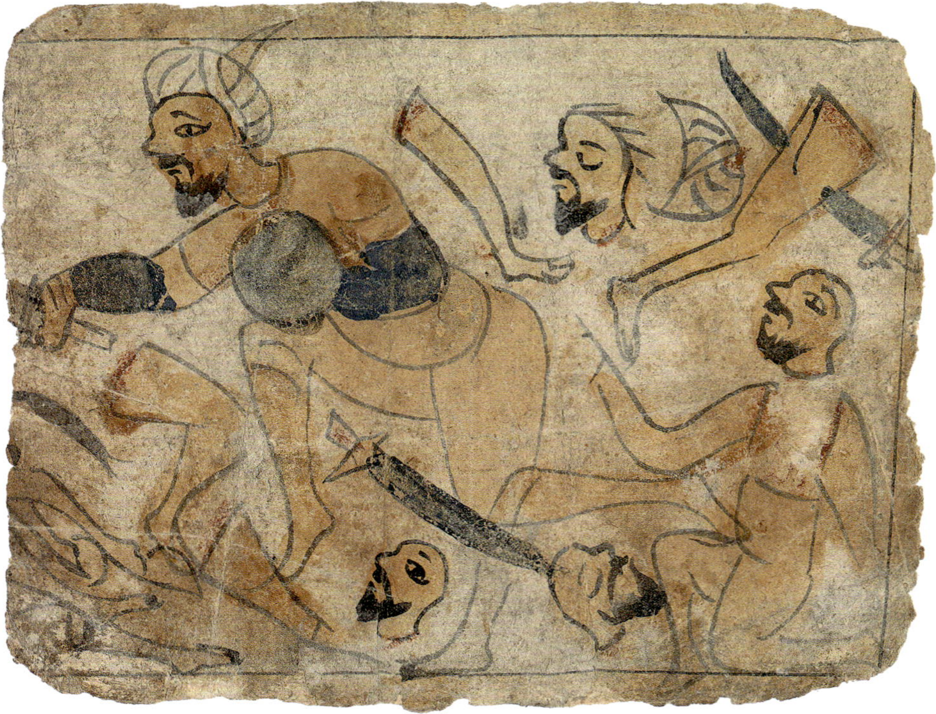

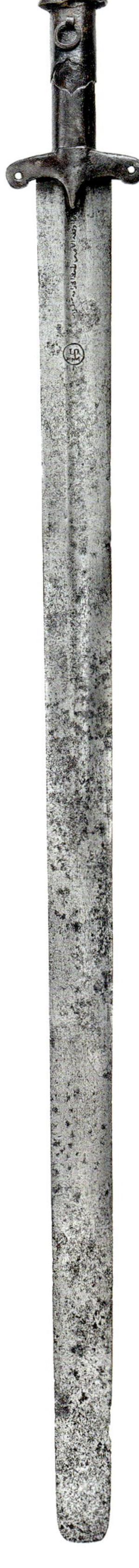

107

106

Scene of Carnage

Probably Egypt, 11th–13th century
Watercolor on paper
5½ × 7³⁄₁₆ in. (14 × 18.3 cm)
The Metropolitan Museum of Art, New York, Purchase, Mr. and Mrs. Jerome A. Straka Gift, Fletcher Fund and Margaret Mushekian Gift, 1975 (1975.360)

Using confident, simple lines, the artist responsible for this drawing captured the frenzied chaos of battle. The original context for this drawing is difficult to determine. The summary lines and thin wash used for the figures suggest that it may have been produced in Egypt. Informal excavations in Fustat in the early twentieth century yielded dozens of undated fragmentary drawings.[1]

There is no suggestion of glory or beauty in this war. The men appear naked; only one retains all his limbs. Severed heads, arms, and legs and a wounded man who has lost his hand are scattered across the paper. Headgear and swords provide few clues as to the date, and no specifics are given as to the site.[2] Indeed, such butchery could occur anywhere. The appearance of a fallen horse at the lower left poignantly mirrors the sad accounts of animal suffering during the wars for the Holy Land.[3]

BDB / MH

1. *Grove* 2009. For discussions of some of these drawings, see Unger 2002, pp. 90–94; Grube 1963; Grube 1976a.
2. One could compare this drawing to a watercolor sketch of a battle scene in the British Museum, London (1938,0312,0.1), which was found in Fustat. The artist of that work took a different tack, rendering the swords, shields, and setting with enough precision to date it with some confidence to the thirteenth century. See Paris 2001–2, p. 94, no. 62.
3. See, for example, Ibn al-Qalanisi 1932 ed, pp. 161, 287–88.

107

Sword

Cyprus or Anatolia, ca. 1366–ca. 1436
Steel, iron, and wood
L. 38¼ in. (97 cm)
Furusiyya Art Foundation (R-240)

The distinctive style of this sword, unique to a group of about a dozen known examples, results from the dynamic mix of Christian and Islamic martial culture in the Holy Land during the Middle Ages. The form and construction of its hilt show both late Byzantine and Mamluk influences. The straight double-edged blade, typical of Christian weapons, also echoes types used in the early centuries of Islam, before curved single-edge blades became favored in the Muslim world and straight blades were relegated mostly to ceremonial or symbolic uses. On this blade is a mark within a circle, which can be read as *IHS*, the sacred monogram for Jesus Christ, indicating it was made in Christian lands. It may be a maker's mark or simply talismanic.

Like other swords in this group, the blade is inscribed in Arabic: "This is a waqf [religious endowment] of the amir Yalbugha to the treasury of Alexandria."[1] The donor could be Amir Yalbugha (d. 1366), ruler of Cairo at the time of the invasion led by King Peter of Cyprus in 1365 as part of his ultimately unsuccessful plans to retake Jerusalem. Amirs of that name, however, also participated in the Mamluk conquest of Cyprus in 1436. Either event could have resulted in the sword being taken as booty and then given as a votive weapon in Alexandria, Egypt. The sword, along with the hundreds of other arms, was subsequently captured by the Ottomans from the Mamluks and transferred to the arsenal in the former Church of Hagia Irene in Istanbul.

DLR

Selected References: Kalus 1982/1990, p. 84, fig. 6, no. 90; Alexander 1985, pp. 87–89; Mohamed et al. 2008, p. 43, no. 12.

1. Mohamed et al. 2008, p. 43.

108

A Knight of the d'Aluye Family

Loire Valley, France, after 1248–by 1267
From his tomb in the Cistercian Abbey of La Clarté-Dieu, between Le Mans and Tours
Limestone
H. 83½ in. (212.1 cm), W. 34¼ in. (87 cm), D. 13 in. (33 cm)
The Metropolitan Museum of Art, New York, The Cloisters Collection, 1925 (25.120.201)

The person who ordered this image was very deliberate about presenting the deceased as an eternally youthful, and prayerful, warrior. There is no hint of the bloody battles in which he may have fought. His hair waves softly; the muscles of his arms and legs swell slightly in his mail. He lies at rest, his hood (known as a *coif*) about his shoulders, his mittens hanging from his wrists, his joined hands pointed heavenward.

For this warrior, fighting in the Holy Land was a family tradition, so much so that it is not entirely clear whether this knight is Jean II d'Aluye, as he was identified in 1865, or his son, Hugues VI, as identified in 1756. A history of the family written in 1665 is the earliest to mention that the abbey at La Clarté-Dieu housed a recumbent (*gisant*) figure of Jean d'Aluye, with a coat of mail, a sword, and a shield; however, it notes that "his son is shown the same way."

A document from 1241 reveals that Jean d'Aluye had traveled to the Holy Land and brought back a piece of the Cross, which the Abbey of La Boissière in Anjou purchased in 1244. He was following in the footsteps of his father, Hugues V, who had set out for the Holy Land about 1180 (apparently to make amends for aggressive acts against the priory of Braye); his own son, Hugues VI, would in turn set forth in 1248 with the Seventh Crusade, coincidentally the year his father died. What became of Hugues is unknown, but in 1267, the eldest of his four daughters, Marguerite, paid a fee owed to the Abbey of La Boissière for the execution of the will of her grandfather, Jean; her exercise of this authority suggests that her own father was already dead.

There is one anomaly in the carefully rendered armor of this knight of the d'Aluye family: his sword. Completely unlike any European sword, its form, with trefoil terminal, corresponds to Chinese swords of the time. Captured or abandoned weaponry was preserved as a treasured prize, as the European sword with added Arabic inscription (cat. 105) also demonstrates. Here it bears witness to a world beyond France, which this member of the d'Aluye family had seen and with which he wished to be linked in perpetuity. BDB

Selected References: Nickel 1991; Barnet and Wu 2012, pp. 88–89.

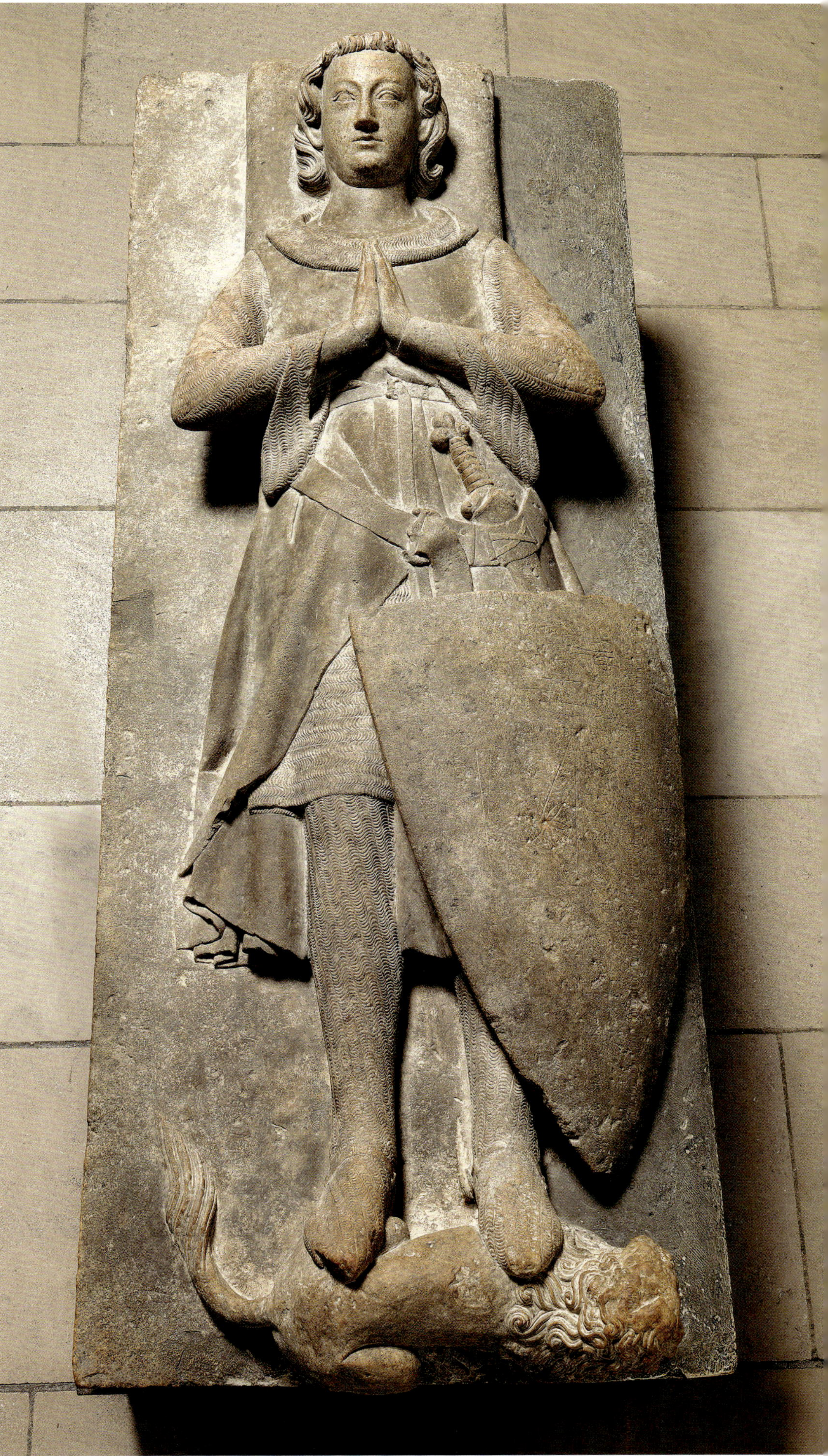

108

109

Slaughter of the Amalekites and Saul's Last Stand

From a Picture Bible
Paris, 1244–54
Tempera, gold, and ink on parchment
15⅜ × 11⅞ in. (39 × 30 cm)
Morgan Library and Museum, New York (MS M.638)

A dagger through the eyes, bodies pierced clean through by sword and arrow, bloody heads and limbs strewn about. The gruesomeness and pandemonium of battle are on full display in these images of the ancient Israelites at war, yet the jewel tones and glistening patches of gold give the whole an elegant sheen. War has never looked so good.

One of the most sumptuous manuscripts produced during the reign of the French crusading king Louis IX (r. 1226–70) — perhaps commissioned by Louis himself — the book presents some 340 separate scenes illustrating selected stories from the Hebrew Scriptures. A recurring theme is battle, with page after page showing the exploits of Joshua, David, Saul, and their armies. Seen here are two such episodes. At the top, David's army stages a devastating attack on the Amalekites as they feast, rescuing the women whom the Amalekites held captive. Below, Saul is fatally wounded in a pitched battle with the Philistines. Although the stories are ancient, the figures throughout the book are decidedly medieval. The soldiers wear the garb of French knights, their armor and weaponry presented in exacting detail. Scenes off the battlefield take place in a French courtly milieu and include specific allusions to the French king.[1] Given the French nobility's deep engagement in efforts to recapture Jerusalem at the time the book was made, the ideological message is clear: French Crusaders were the new "chosen people," following the righteous militaristic tradition of biblical heroes.[2]

Below and around each picture are identifying captions, in Latin, Persian, and Judeo-Persian, added by later owners. The original book contained no text, relying entirely on the power of mesmerizingly beautiful images to make a bold case for holy war.[3] MH

Selected References: Cockerell et al. 1927; Weiss 2002; Voelkle et al. 2014–15.

1. Weiss 2002.
2. Weiss 2004, pp. 3–4.
3. The Latin inscriptions were added in the early fourteenth century. The Persian inscriptions were added by Shah 'Abbas in the early seventeenth century, after it was presented to him by Pope Paul V. The Judeo-Persian texts date perhaps from the eighteenth century.

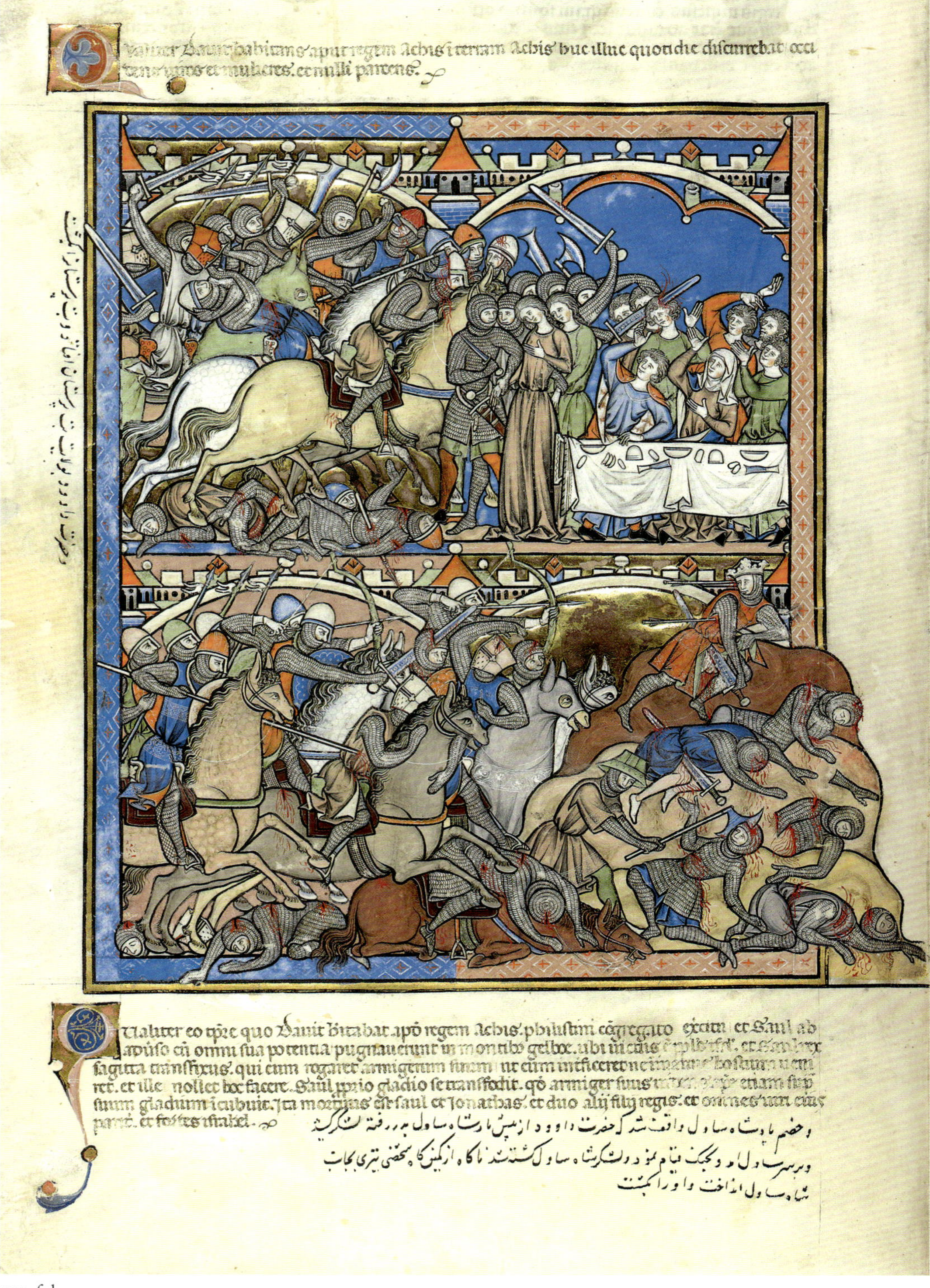

109, fol. 34v

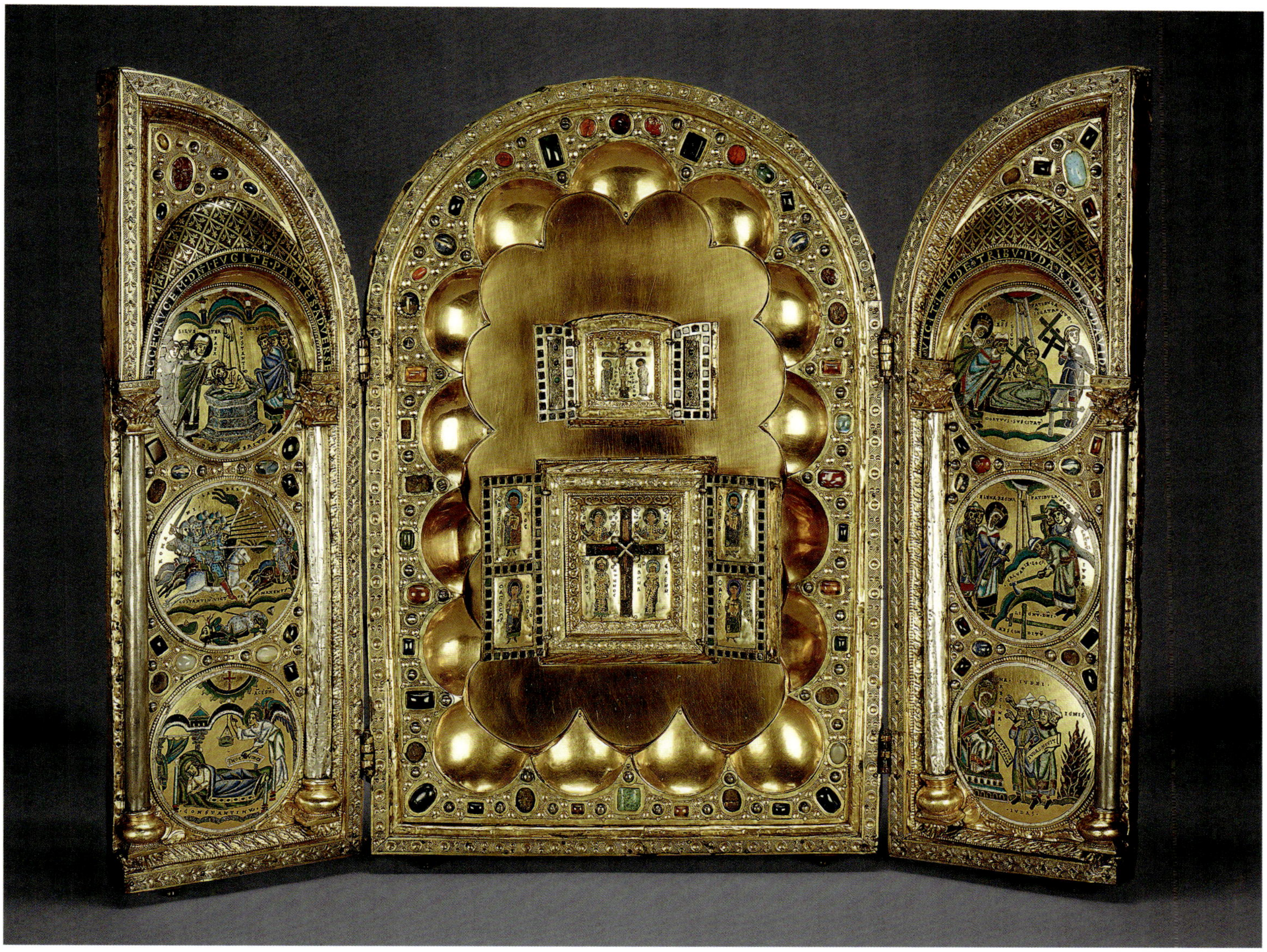

110

110

The Stavelot Triptych

Meuse Valley (present-day Belgium), ca. 1156–58
Gilded copper with champlevé and cloisonné enamel, silver, émail brun, and semiprecious stones
H. 19 in. (48.4 cm), W. 26 in. (66 cm), D. 3⅛ in. (8 cm)
Morgan Library and Museum, New York (AZ001)

In this opulent reliquary, probably made at the request of Wibald, abbot of Stavelot from 1130 to 1158, the importance of Jerusalem to the Latin Church is an overriding theme.[1] The larger of the two triptychs in the center section contains relics of the Cross, the dearest of relics from the Holy City, along with fragments from the Church of the Holy Sepulchre and the dress of the Virgin, all attested by an authenticating text in Latin.[2] The enameled scenes on the flanking wings, created in or near Stavelot, dramatically trace the relics' origins to Jerusalem's soil. They tell of Emperor Constantine's divinely orchestrated military victory leading to his conversion to Christianity, which in turn led to his

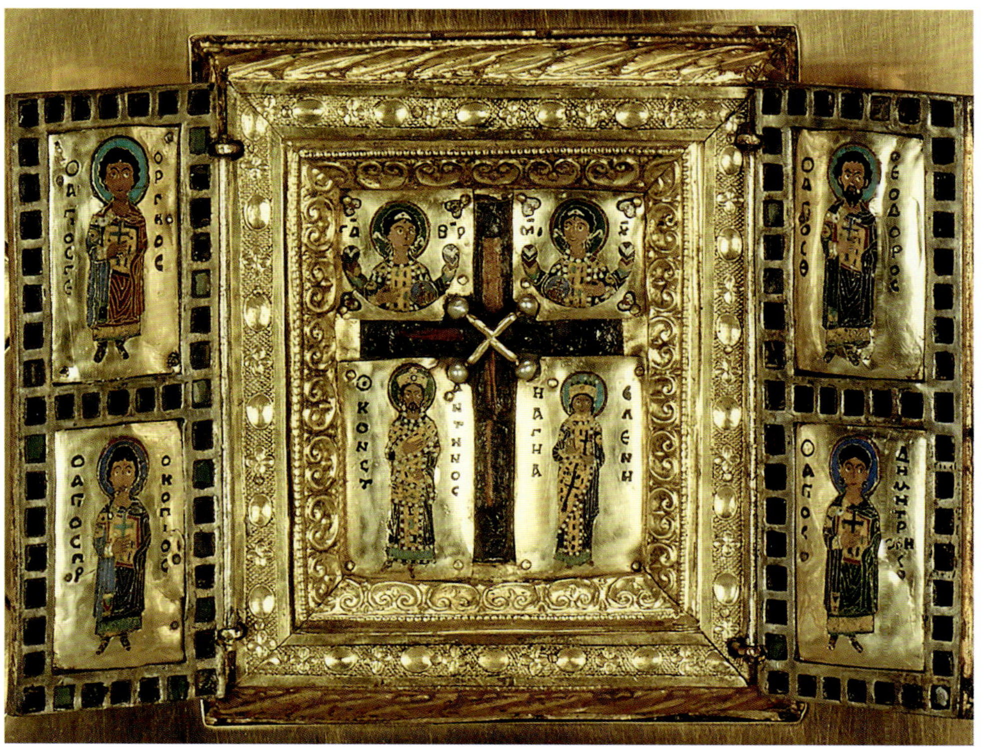

110 detail

mother Helena's obsession with excavating the original Cross on which Jesus was crucified on Golgotha. With a steady insistence, the roundels show the reasons why European Christians approached Jerusalem with such expectancy: like Helena, they were drawn to vestiges of the story of Jesus, the expectation of discovery that Jerusalem's bricks and soil offered, and the city's capacity for the miraculous.

This assemblage makes use of a rich and varied visual vocabulary to evoke the Christian East, creating a homogenous ensemble from disparate elements of refined goldsmiths' work. Unlike the roundels on the wings, created in or near Stavelot, the enamels set in the two triptychs at center are Byzantine in manufacture. Those on either side of the Cross relics feature Byzantine military saints of special importance to Latin Crusaders, who considered them local protectors of the Holy Land. In the smaller triptych above the one holding the relics, the role of the Cross in Christian history is made explicit by presenting Jesus crucified. The surrounding structure for the pair of triptychs takes the form of a lobed altar table from the first centuries of Christianity, examples of which could be found in the Holy Land and across the Mediterranean.[3]

The enameled components at center were created in Constantinople, but they were fashioned into triptychs in Western Europe.[4] As triptychs within a triptych, they heighten the drama of the relics' presentation. One set of doors opens into another, permitting a protracted reveal of the precious contents within. With architectural elements in silver and gold and dazzling jewels that fill the interstices, the reliquary as a whole calls to mind the splendor of the Heavenly Jerusalem, "adorned with all manner of precious stone" (Apocalypse 21:19).

BDB / MH

Selected References: New York 1980; Klein 2004, pp. 206–19; Hahn 2012.

1. For a detailed description of the reliquary, see William M. Voelkle in New York 1980.
2. Ibid., pp. 19–23; Hahn 2012, p. 214.
3. Voelkle in New York 1980, p. 23.
4. For example, the goldsmith's work immediately surrounding the central relic, with its characteristic thumbprint design, can be compared to that on a reliquary in a private collection in the United Kingdom (cat. 25a). See also Hahn 2012, p. 214.

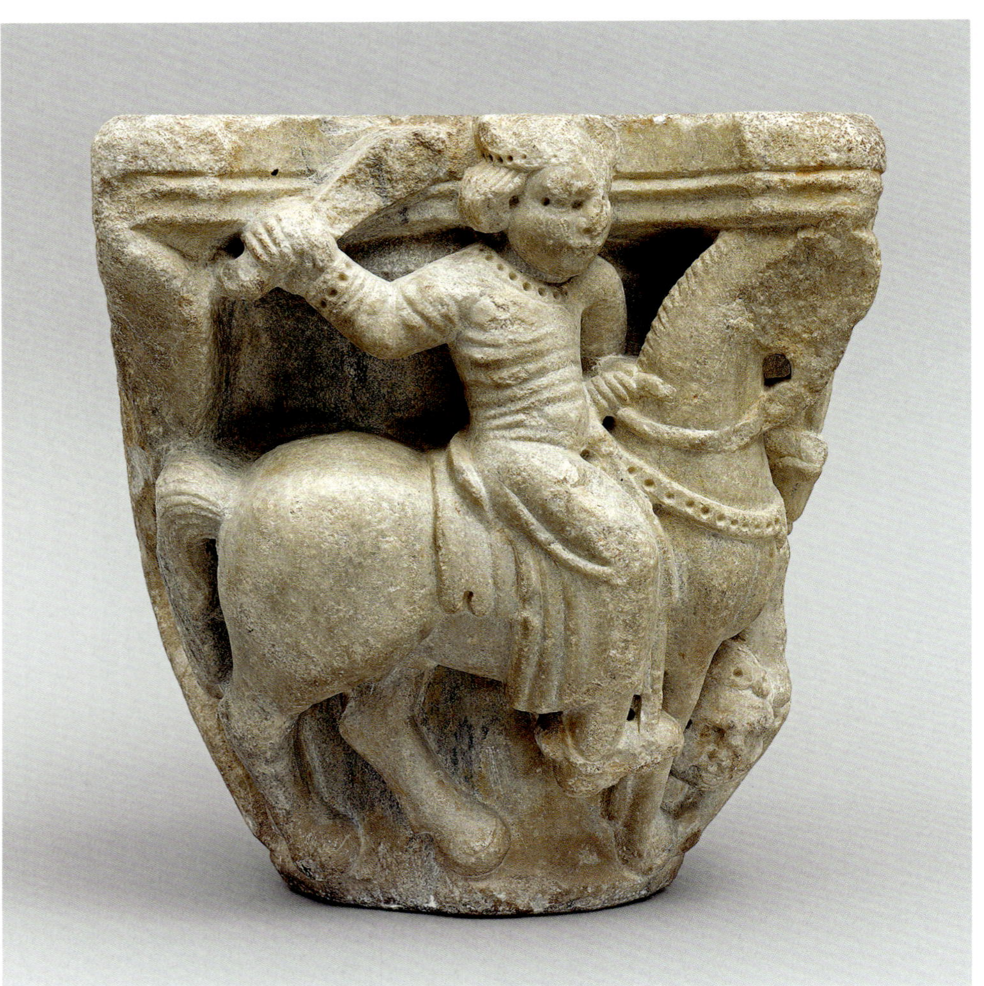

111

111

Capital with a Triumphant Prince Welcomed by a Woman at the Entrance to a City

Holy Land, second half of the 12th century (before 1186?)
Marble
H. 11⅞ in. (30 cm), W. 11½ in. (29 cm), D. 11⅞ in. (30 cm)
Musée du Louvre, Départment des Sculptures, Paris (RF 1994)

Many proposals have been put forward about the iconography of this capital, some not incompatible with one another. The most likely are that it shows Constantine trampling underfoot paganism and the Church or Charlemagne (or Roland) triumphant over King Marsile and Queen Bramimonde upon the reconquest of Saragossa from *The Song of Roland*. In any case, the scene must have been read through the prism of the local context, that is, as a model of the fight (and anticipated triumph) of the Crusaders against Islam, and more specifically, of the Crusaders' victorious entry into Jerusalem. The caricatured features of the figure trampled by the knight and the emphasis on his genitals thus have a derisive meaning. Although the work was acquired on the art market in Damascus in 1929, it must have come from a church in the Holy Land, not in Syria but from a territory farther south, like another, very similar capital (now probably lost) that was reused in the decoration of the early thirteenth-century Hanabila Mosque in Damascus.[1] The capital has been associated by turns with the sculpture in the cloister of Aosta in present-day Italy, with Provençal art, and, more recently, with sculpture from the Rhone Valley or Italy (cloister of Monreale). But, first, it is related to the capitals from the Cathedral of Saint John the Baptist in Sabastiya (now held in Istanbul) devoted to the history of that saint, especially the one of the dance of Salome, as others have argued.[2] The city of Sabastiya was lost by the Crusaders in 1186, a year before Jerusalem, and the Louvre capital must in any event predate that time.

PYLP

Selected References: Watzinger and Wulzinger 1921, pp. 110–12; Enlart 1925–28, vol. 1, pp. 127–28, vol. 2, pp. 101–2; Deschamps 1929; Folda 1995, p. 564 n. 110; Gaborit et al. 2005, pp. 105–6.

1. Herzfeld, E., 1948, p. 120; Boase 1967, p. 89; Boase 1977, p. 102 n. 29; Folda 1995, p. 564 n. 110.
2. Boase 1977, p. 102 n. 29; Folda 1995, p. 564 n. 110.

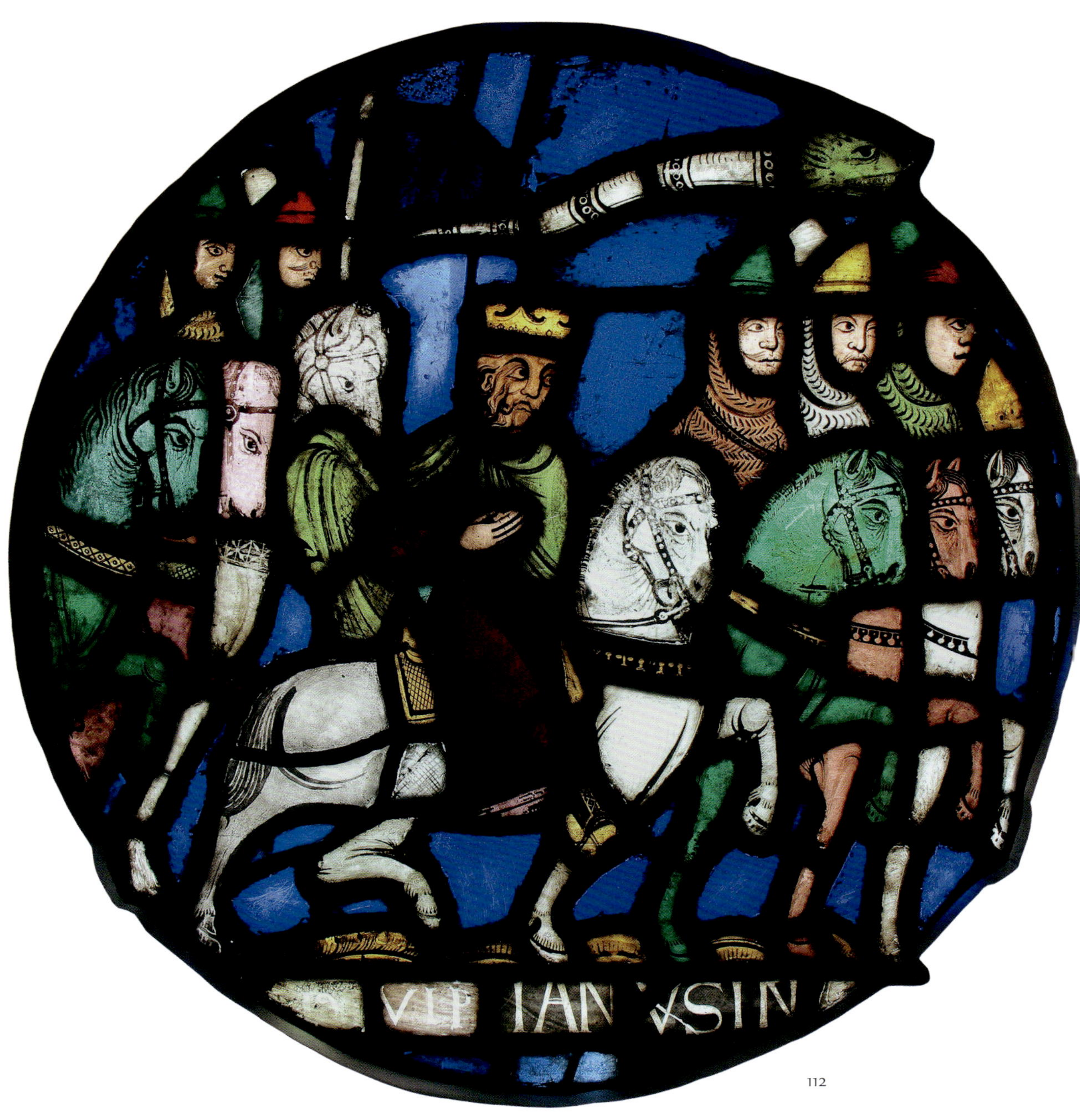

112

112

Crusaders Advance on Jerusalem

Abbey Church of Saint Denis, France, ca. 1158
Pot-metal glass
Diam. 19¾ in. (50.1 cm)
Glencairn Museum, Bryn Athyn, Pennsylvania (03.SG.156)

The two roundels from the Raymond Pitcairn Collection in the Glencairn Museum (cats. 112, 113) appear to be the sole surviving stained-glass components from the so-called Crusade Window, formerly located in one of the westernmost radiating chapels of the Abbey Church of Saint Denis. This edifice, made famous by Abbot Suger (1122–51), served as the burial church of the French monarchy and was the site of a number of important artistic innovations in the twelfth century. Suger's successor, Abbot Odo of Deuil (1151–62), apparently commissioned the unique Crusade Window about 1158.[1]

It has been proposed that the program of the Crusade Window with fourteen roundels combines the representation of specific historical events associated with the First Crusade with the symbolic pilgrimage of Charlemagne.[2] In this scheme the two Pitcairn pieces, paired at the bottom of the window, introduce this unique imagery by representing in the left roundel the Crusader army riding out toward their goal of the earthly Jerusalem and, at the right in the other extant roundel, the Crusaders crowned as martyrs for the faith surrounded on each side by others in the glory of Heavenly Jerusalem. JF

Selected References: Montfaucon 1729–33, vol. 1, pp. 277, 384–97, pls. 24, 25, 50–54; Grodecki 1976, pp. 115–21; New York 1981, pp. 94–95, no. 20; New York 1982, pp. 90–92; Brown and Cothren 1986.

1. As argued by Brown and Cothren 1986, pp. 21–39. The two Pitcairn roundels do not appear in the engraved reconstruction of the Crusade Window by Bernard de Montfaucon, published in 1729 from drawings done in 1721. They can be documented only from the 1830s, when they were installed in the axial chapel under the supervision of François Debret. They were not included in the 1840s church restoration supervised by Viollet-le-Duc and Baron de Guilhermy. Renewed scholarly attention after they entered Pitcairn's collection (1923 and 1937) included a reconstruction of the Crusade Window by Louis Grodecki (Grodecki 1976, pp. 115–21). Brown and Cothren (1986, pp. 33–37) located them as a pair at the base of the window, with all fourteen known roundels in a single window. The physical characteristics of the stained glass in these roundels link them with twelfth-century stained glass at Saint Denis, and the style of the painting has been loosely connected with three slightly earlier windows done at the time of Abbot Suger in the mid-1140s.
2. Brown and Cothren 1986, pp. 8–21.

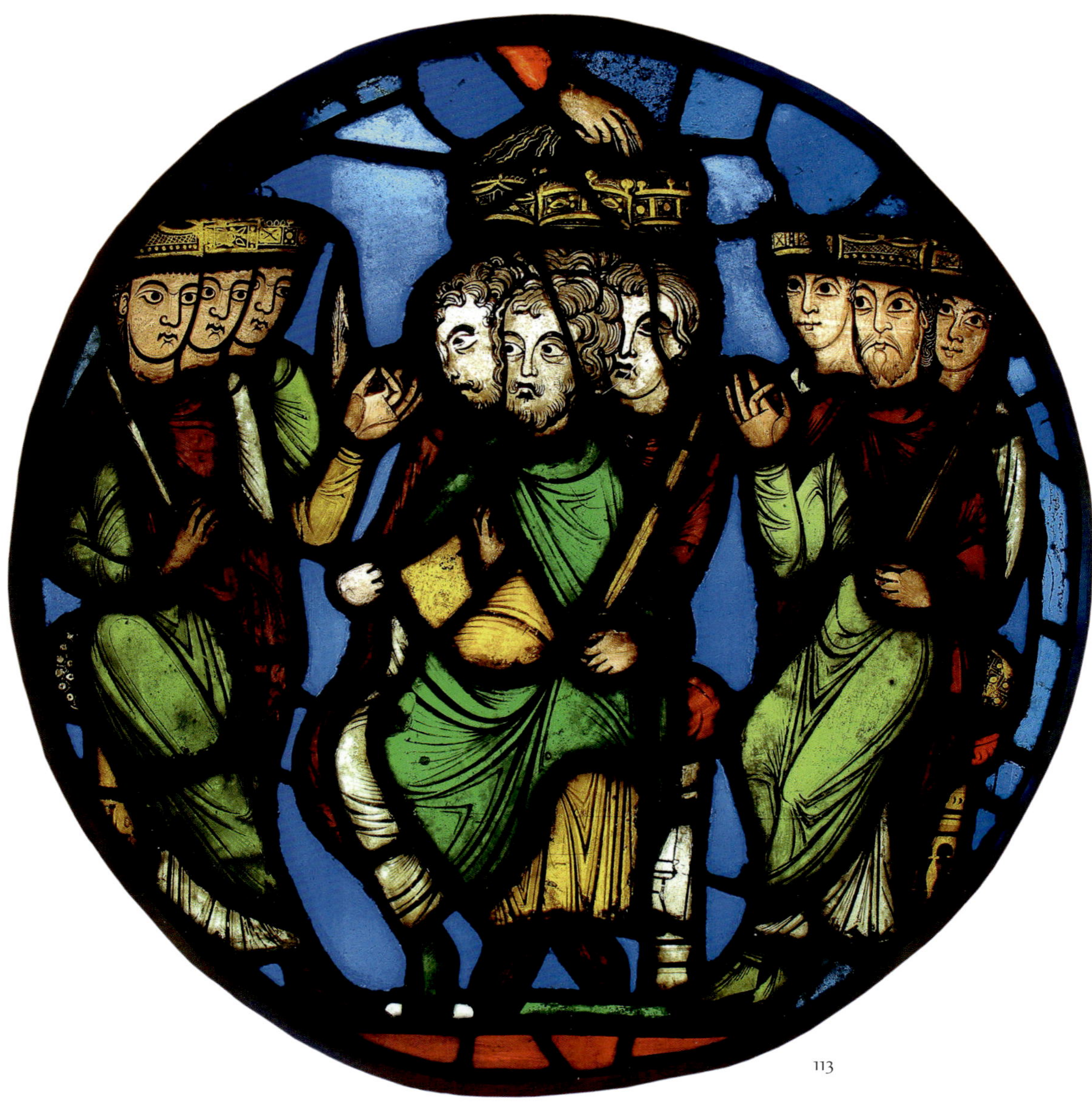

113

113

The Coronation of Three Men

Abbey Church of Saint Denis, France, ca. 1158
Pot-metal glass
Diam. 20⅝ in. (52.3 cm)
Glencairn Museum, Bryn Athyn, Pennsylvania (03.SG.111)

This roundel, sometimes called the Triple Coronation roundel, represents the hand of God conferring the crown of martyrdom on three men seated in the center, with two additional groups of three men, also crowned, at each side. It has been proposed that this image represents "all the martyred heroes who had died and who would die in holy battle" during the Crusades.[1] This interpretation is based on the imagery of these figures wearing or receiving crowns and holding palms. In a similar way, the interpretation of the Crusader Advance on Jerusalem (cat. 112), is based on the imagery of the mounted knights in mail and the mysterious "dragon" banner that floats above the heads of the crowned figure and the soldiers at the right. Unlike the representations of Crusader armies in the thirteenth-century manuscript illumination, in which the banners often were given cross insignias (see cat. 46), here the Crusader significance is inherent in the generic idea of an expedition against the infidel led by a royal figure.

Evidence points to two styles on this stained glass, possibly signifying two artists working in tandem on both roundels simultaneously.[2] The unity of the two roundels with regard to the use of color is notable, as seen in the green garments on the Coronation glass and the green horses on the Crusader army glass, both set against a deep blue ground. But perhaps the differences in the styles of the facial features pertain to more than the hands of two artists. Note the differences found, for example, in the faces of the three martyrs on the left side here, by the second artist: "The nostrils of the more substantial noses are terminated with an inward curl, and eyebrows are connected over the bridge of the nose with a thin, downward curving line. The upper lip is delineated by a tighter and bolder line, and the distinctive eyes are painted with one fluid stroke rather than with two stiff strokes of [the first artist]," who is identified as having done the three martyrs on the right side.[3] Could these differences not also reflect the intention of these artists to represent Western martyrs on the right, by one artist, and Eastern martyrs on the left, by the other? JF

Selected References: Montfaucon 1729–33, vol. 1, pp. 277, 384–97, pls. 24, 25, 50–54; Lasteyrie 1853–57, vol. 2, pl. 3; Labarte 1864–66, vol. 1, p. 318; Grodecki 1976, pp. 115–21; New York 1981, pp. 96–97, no. 21; New York 1982, pp. 93–95; Brown and Cothren 1986.

1. Brown and Cothren 1986, p. 11. The physical characteristics and style of the painting on the glass in this roundel link it to the Crusader Army roundel (cat. 112) and the other verifiable twelfth-century stained glass from Saint Denis, with the fourteen roundels included on the Crusade Window, as reconstructed by Elizabeth Brown and Michael Cothren; ibid., pp. 8–13, pls. 1, 5c, 7.
2. Ibid., pp. 33–34.
3. Ibid., and pls. 10a, 10d. Brown and Cothren are responsible for the artistic attributions.

114

Goblet of Charlemagne

Glass: Syria, second half of the 12th century; mount: France, 13th–14th century
Glass with gold and enamel; gilded silver
H. 9½ in. (24 cm)
Musée des Beaux-Arts, Chartres (5144)

First recorded in France in the seventeenth century, the so-called Goblet of Charlemagne comprises a Syrian enameled goblet set on a French gilded silver foot. It is a classic example of European artists' appreciation and adaptation of Islamic glass vessels for their own use. In this case, the goblet has assumed mythic status: according to tradition it represents Charlemagne's gift to the Abbey of the Magdalene at Châteaudun, to which it once belonged — an extraordinary feat given that Charlemagne lived some four hundred years before the work was made. Its inscription, likely not understood by its first European owner, is a formulaic expression of good wishes. BDB / MH

Selected Reference: Paris 2001–2, pp. 190–91, no. 203.

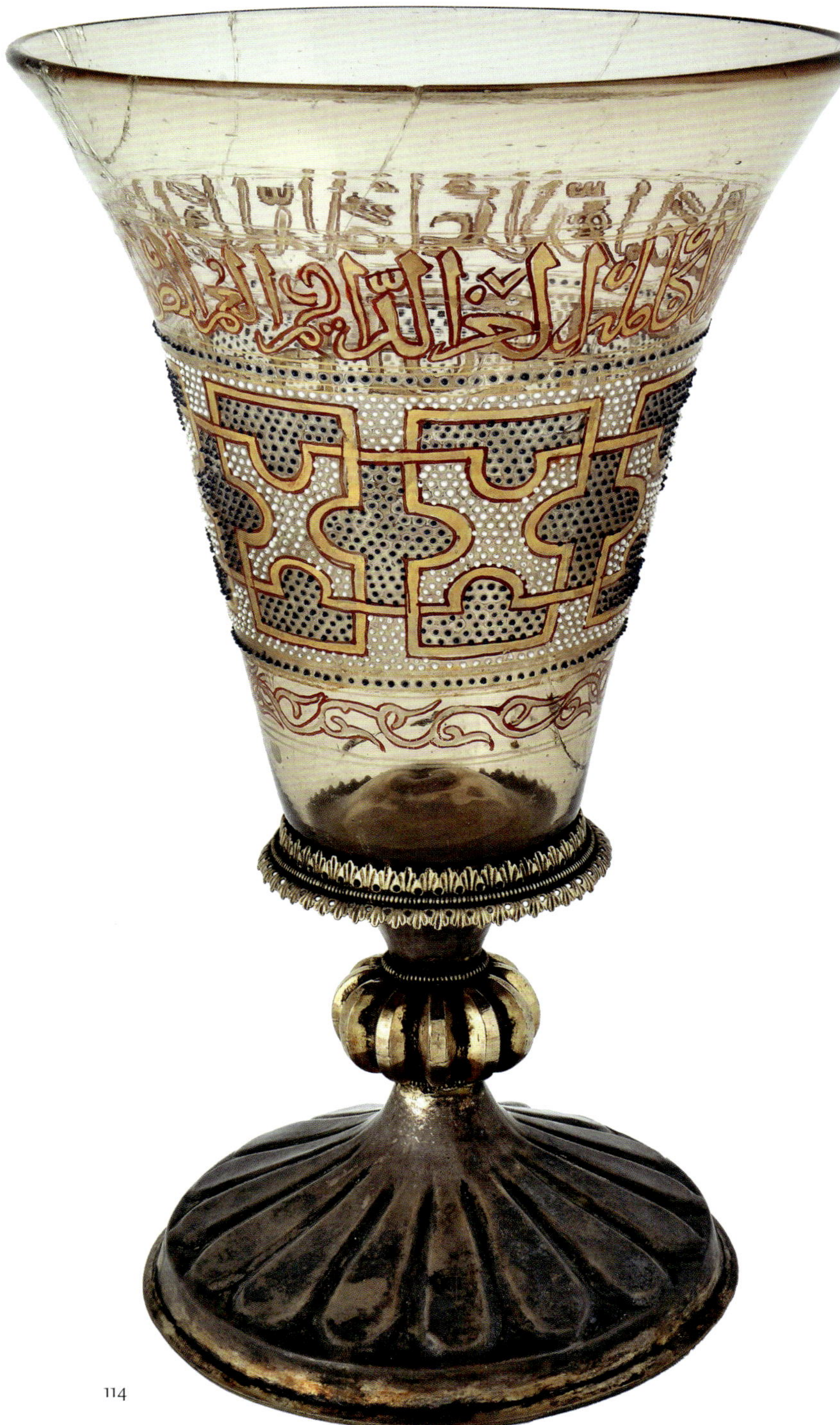

114

115

The Fall of Jerusalem

From the *History of Outremer* (*Livre d'eracles*) by William of Tyre (d. 1186)
Paris, ca. 1350
Tempera, gold, and ink on parchment; 175 folios
17⅛ × 12⅝ in. (43.5 × 32 cm)
Bibliothèque Nationale de France, Paris (MS Fr. 352)

Collapsing time and space to justify the concerns of its fourteenth-century French audience, this image exalts the actions of the eleventh-century Crusaders, commemorating their 1099 conquest of Jerusalem to inspire anew the desire to retake the city. Jerusalem appears as a Gothic building, part church, part castle, complete with portcullis. Within the church's lateral chapels we see episodes from the Passion of Christ. Biblical events unfold at the same moment as medieval soldiers, armed with trebuchets, crossbows, and swords, storm the city.

The most imposing of some twenty-eight illustrations in this condensed version of William's history of the Latin Kingdom of Jerusalem, the painting accompanies the author's description of the siege of the city in Book VIII, clearly marking that moment as the dramatic climax of his story. Though William's text takes pains to describe the "frightful havoc" of battle and the "unspeakable slaughter" that ensued with victory, the conquest of Jerusalem presented here is bloodless theater, with no enemies in sight.[1] Rather, we see a celebration of the encampments, the movable wooden towers, and the siege machines that made the victory possible.[2]

The Europeans' loss of Jerusalem to Saladin in 1187, followed by the fall of Acre in 1291, stimulated the production of French translations of William's story.[3] The popularity of the text seemed to both derive from and feed into French hopes for Jerusalem's recapture. The kings of France took the lead in preparations well into the next century, but ultimately no new large-scale Crusade was ever launched.[4] As the possibility for recovery grew ever more remote, the cycles of illumination in William's text grew ever more expansive, as if pretty pictures were consolation for the disappointment. MH

Selected References: Folda 1968, vol. 1, pp. 421–25; vol. 2, pp. 251–60, no. 39 (with complete list of illustrations).

1. See William's descriptions in bk. 8, chap. 19; William of Tyre 1943 ed., vol. 1, p. 370.
2. William clearly takes pleasure in discussing the machinery of war. See, for instance, bk. 8, chap. 8; ibid., p. 354: "They built engines, wove wickerwork frames, and spliced ladders together with the greatest care."
3. Folda 2012a.
4. Leopold 2000, pp. 37–45. See also Schein 1991.

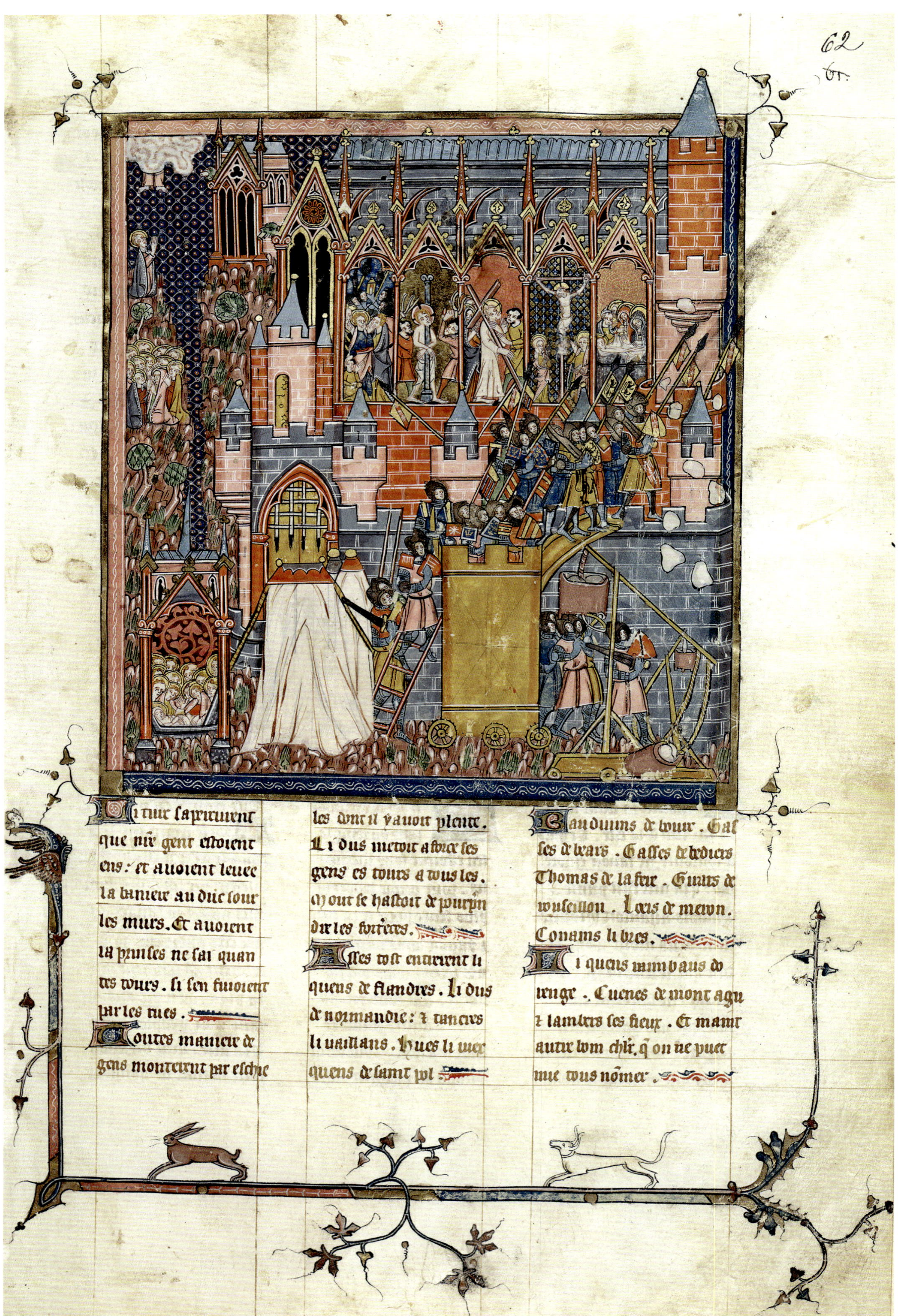
Ci tuit sapercurent
que nre gent estoient
ens: et auoient leuee
la baniere au duc sour
les murs. Et auoient
ia prinses ne sai quan
tes tours. si sen fuioient
par les rues.
Toutes maniere de
gens monterent par eschie
les dont il y auoit plente.
Li dus metoit a force ses
gens es tours a tous les.
Mout se hastoit de purp(re)n
dre les forteces.
Asses tost entrerent li
quens de flandres. Li dus
de normandie: et Tancres
li vaillans. Hues li mer
quens de saint pol
Bauduins de bour. Gas
ses de bears. Gasses de bediers
Thomas de la fere. Girars de
rousellon. Loeis de meion.
Conans li bres.
Li quens rembaus de
orenge. Cuenes de mont agu
et lambers ses fieux. Et maint
autre bon chlr. q on ne puet
mie tous nomer.

115, fol. 62r

116

Aquamanile in the Form of a Knight on Horseback

Germany, Lower Saxony, probably Hildesheim, mid-13th century
Copper alloy
H. 12⅞ in. (32.7 cm), W. 14¾ in. (37.3 cm), D. 5⅝ in. (14.3 cm)
The Metropolitan Museum of Art, New York, Gift of Irwin Untermyer, 1964 (64.101.1492)

Used to pour water for handwashing, aquamanilia take their name from the Latin words for water (*aqua*) and hand (*manus*). Hundreds of surviving European examples in animal and human form attest to their widespread use in religious and secular rituals. The production of hollow, three-dimensional sculptures was a significant technical challenge for medieval metalworkers, and European craftsmen were indebted to workshops in Islamic lands, which had preserved ancient techniques.

Gracing an object likely intended for domestic use, this horse and rider exemplify the courtly ideals of knighthood and the celebration of the warrior that pervaded Western medieval culture. The knight wears a helm surmounted by the remains of a crest, a mail shirt with long sleeves covering his hands, mail leggings (chausses) covered by padded leg protection (gamboised cuisses), and a surcoat decorated with chevrons. There are prick spurs on his feet, and the fittings for his shield, now lost, can be seen on the left side. He holds the reins of the horse in his raised left hand, and the extended right hand likely held a lance (or possibly a sword). The surface of the horse is enlivened by a pattern of crosshatched circles, probably meant to convey that the horse is a dappled gray war horse. First brought to Europe from Islamic lands, this breed is known to have been highly valued in this period. The aquamanile is filled through the hinged top of the helm, and the spout is cleverly formed by the horse's forelock.

The style of the knight's armor is consistent with the aquamanile's date of the middle of the thirteenth century. The relatively short helm with a flat top, for example, can be compared to the silver seal matrix of Robert FitzWalter (now in the British Museum, London) dated about 1213–19. The padded leg protection did not appear in European armor until about 1230–40, when it can be seen in the miniatures of the famous Morgan Picture Bible (cat. 109).

PB

Selected References: New York 2006, pp. 106–9, no. 11; Hildesheim 2008, pp. 332–34, no. 37; Scalini 2013.

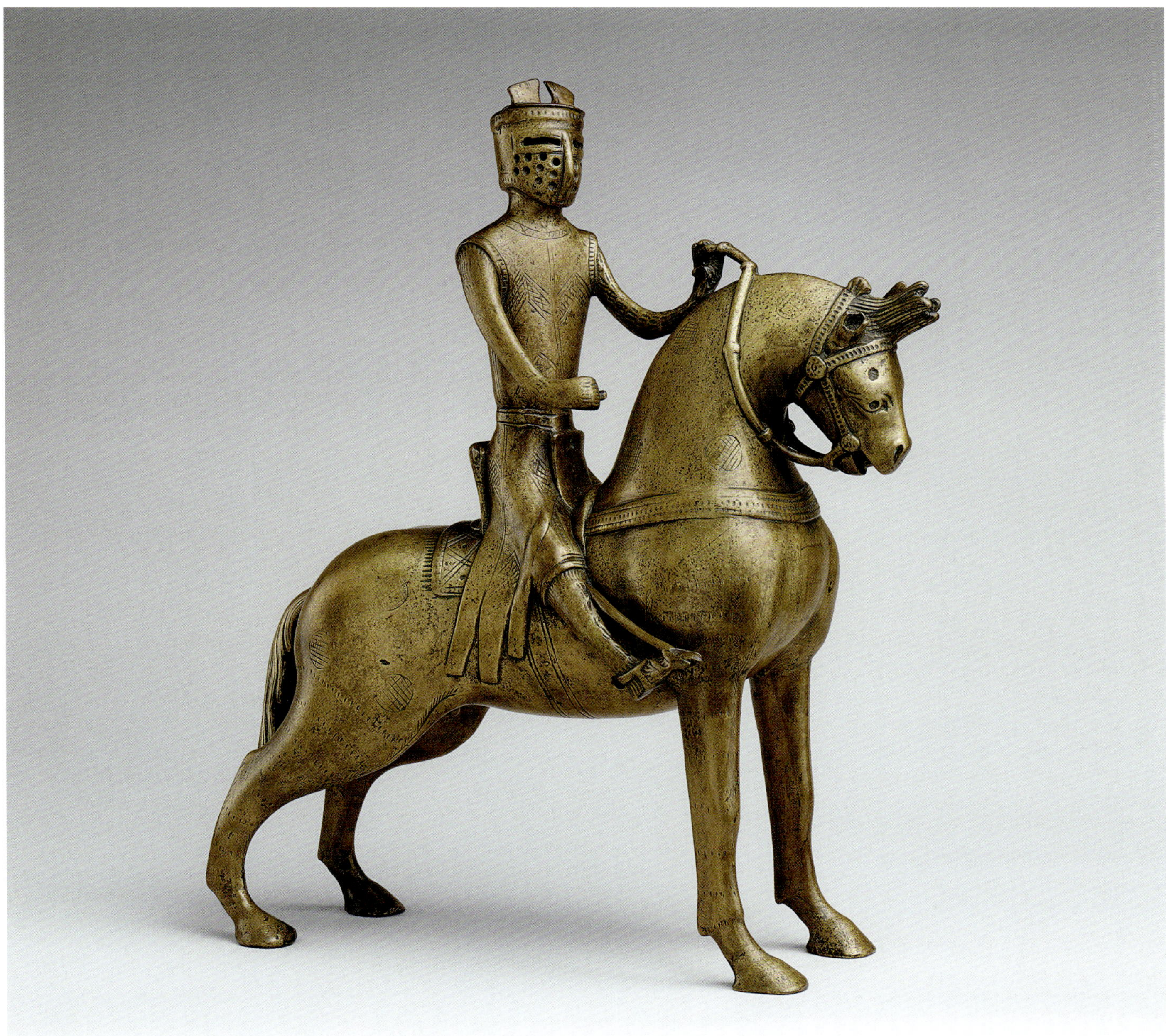

116

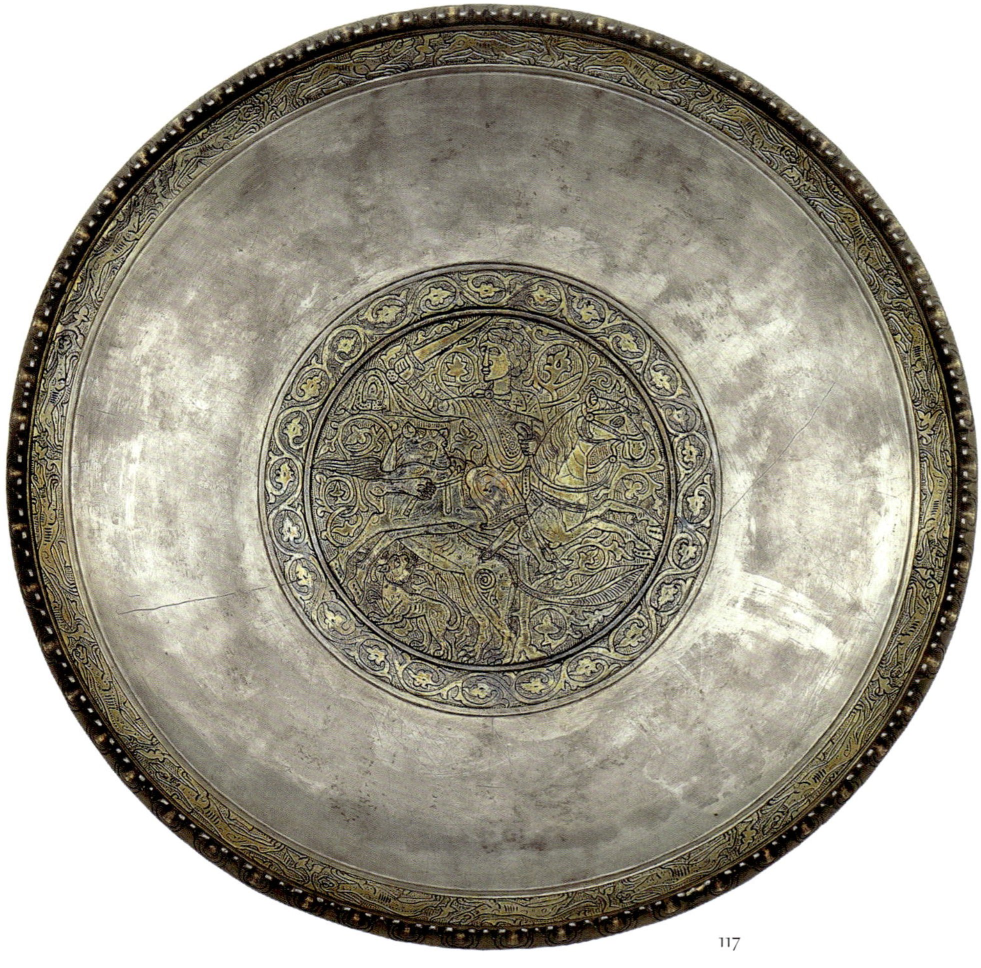

117

117

Bowl with Mounted Warrior

Byzantium (eastern Mediterranean), late 12th–early 13th century
Silver with gilding
Diam. 11⅛ in. (28.1 cm)
Private collection, United Kingdom

The image of the horse and rider at the center of this bowl can be related to a depiction of a haloed Saint George on a twelfth-century work from Beriozovo, Russia.[1] Yet this haloless rider and the hunting scene around the bowl's rim refer more to the pleasure of the aristocratic hunt than to religious protection. In many details, the work relates closely to a group of plates, including two with mounted riders, reported to have been discovered near the major Byzantine city of Philippopolis (in modern-day Bulgaria). They, with several others discovered earlier near the site, have been convincingly identified as Byzantine products developed in the cross-cultural milieu of the twelfth century, when the Byzantine court was closely interwoven with the Crusaders' world.[2] Another plate found in Siberia and displaying Alexander the Great, a hero to all rulers in the Middle East, has been attributed to early thirteenth-century Constantinople.[3] In contrast, this plate has been argued to be by a Frankish artist aware of Muslim motifs in the twelfth or thirteenth century.[4] As it is most closely related to the Philippopolis works, it should be understood as a Byzantine response to Crusader and Islamic motifs. No narrative source for the lioness has yet been identified.

HCE

Selected References: New York 1997, pp. 399–401, no. 267; Ballian and Drandaki 2003, pp. 47–68; Cutler 2004, pp. 263–68, 271; Christie's London 2006, pp. 382–91, lot 390.

1. Ballian and Drandaki 2003, pp. 51, 53, 58.
2. Ibid., pp. 47–68.
3. Boris Marshak in New York 1997, pp. 399–401, no. 267; Christie's London 2006, pp. 382–91, lot 390, uses the Ballian and Drandaki article and Marshak's attribution of the Alexander plate to attribute this plate to Constantinople in the late twelfth century.
4. Cutler 2004, pp. 268, 271.

118

Sketch of a Military Saint on Horseback

Abbey of Saint Mary in the Valley of Jehoshaphat, Jerusalem, 12th century (1150–80?)
Black charcoal on plaster
19¾ × 27½ in. (50 × 70 cm)
Courtesy of the Israel Antiquities Authority, Jerusalem, exhibited at the Israel Museum, Jerusalem (IAA 2009-1362/1)

This drawing of a charging knight on horseback was likely a preliminary sketch for a mural painting of a military saint, either now destroyed or never completed.[1] Such icons formed part of the painting program (ca. 1170)[2] of the Hospitallers' church in Abu Gosh near Jerusalem and were likewise depicted serially in late eleventh-to-thirteenth-century Syriac, Coptic, and Orthodox churches across Syria, Egypt, and the Levant. It is possible that this sketch from the Abbey of Saint Mary was also conceived as part of a series of images of military saints.

The rider wears a collared tunic with a mantle slung over his left shoulder. In his right arm he wields a thin lance with which he attacks something – possibly a dragon or a human adversary – that lay at the bottom right of the missing portion of the sketch. The galloping horse is remarkable for its expressiveness and realism, even though it oddly lacks a bridle. In contrast, the more static human rider is executed in hazy outline. The curvy feature on the rider's right might be a tree trunk, or a part of a dragon coiled from above, or a mountainous landscape. Visible behind the rider's left shoulder is an elongated shield. This type of "hidden shield" is characteristic of images of mounted military saints in twelfth- and thirteenth-century Syriac and Orthodox churches across the region[3] and recurs in thirteenth-century Crusader icons from Sinai that feature military saints in the guise of Crusader knights with banners.[4] A pair of red-painted lines extending downward from the lance's top end indicate an attached banner – a feature common in Romanesque, Crusader, and Syriac depictions of knights and military saints but atypical of Byzantine ones. Because of the state of the sketch, it is unclear whether the rider's bulging headwear was intended as a turban or simply denoted a full head of hair. If a turban, its Eastern source might reflect Crusader eclecticism and sublimation of Islamic costume and armor, also seen on a twelfth-to-thirteenth-century silver dagger from Syria-Levant inscribed with an Arabic blessing and an image of a military saint spearing a dragon, again with a hidden shield (cat. 120).[5]

The popularity of military-saint imagery in the eastern Mediterranean and Europe in

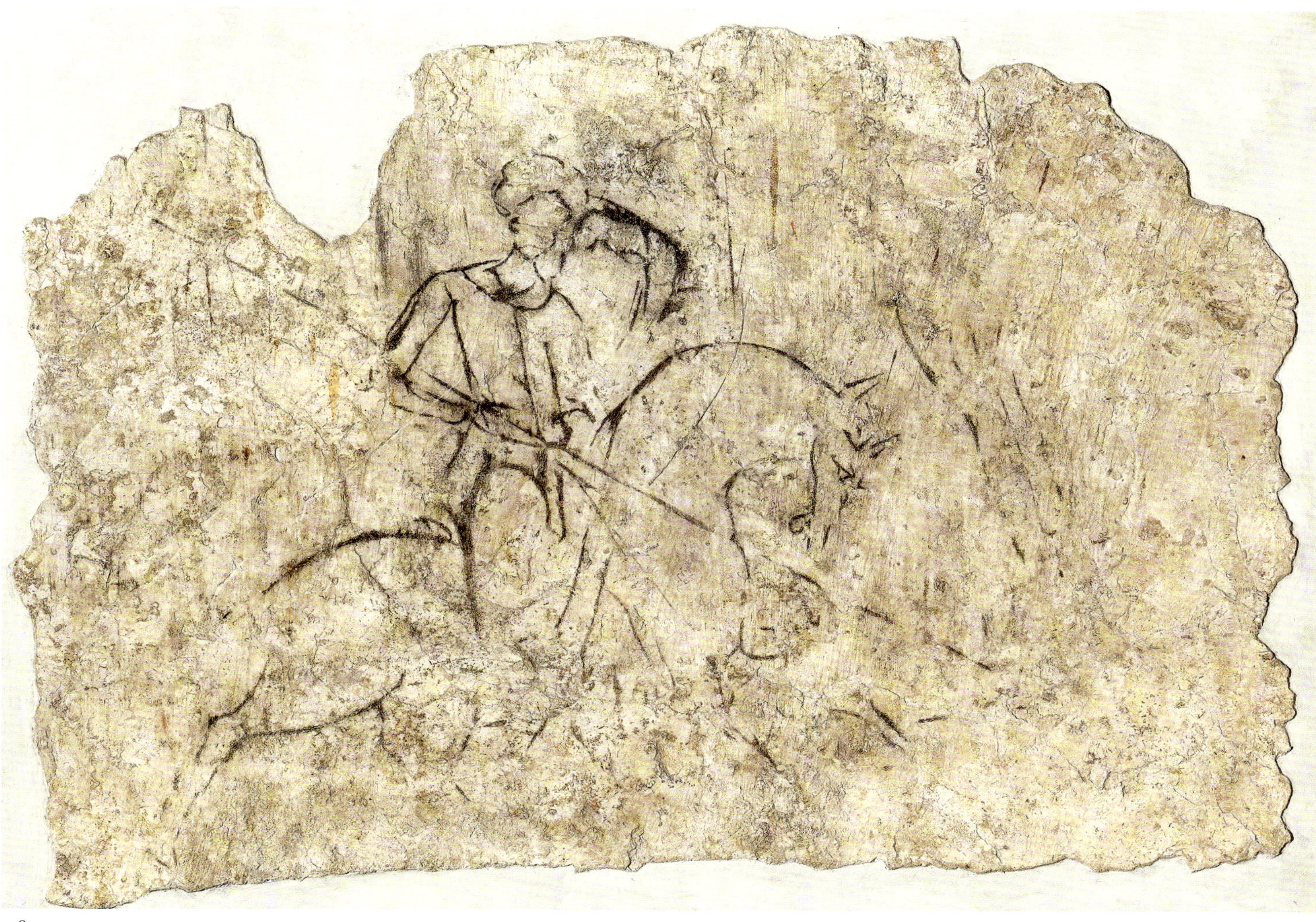

118

the twelfth to thirteenth century derived as much from the traditional veneration they had enjoyed in Byzantium and other Eastern Christian centers as from Crusader ideology that construed those saintly warriors — especially Saint George — as virtual embodiments of the Christian militant struggle against Islam. Hence, the sketch might reflect the political, ecclesiastical, and economical links that the Abbey of Saint Mary maintained with its dependencies and possessions in Sicily, southern Italy, Antioch, and northern Crusader principalities, including the spiritual center of Cluny in France.[6] Yet the sketch's dynamic and elegantly proportioned design brings to mind a similar drapery style in warring scenes from two churches near Venice: Santa Maria at Summaga (late twelfth–early thirteenth century)[7] and the crypt of Aquileia Cathedral (1161–82?).[8] The sketch from the Abbey of Saint Mary offers a unique testimony to the working methods of painters active in Crusader-era Jerusalem and the means of artistic and cultural transmission between Europe and the Levant. LK

Selected References: Seligman 2010, pp. 151–52, fig. 11; Seligman 2012, pp. 210–11, fig. 39.

1. Seligman 2012, pp. 197ff., figs. 15–39.
2. Kühnel, G., 1988, pp. 171–73, figs. 88, 106, 107.
3. Immerzeel 2004, pls. 1, 5, 14, 19–20, 29; Immerzeel 2009, pls. 35–36, 39, 40, 51, 65, 68, 70; Badamo 2011, figs. 3, 5, 29, 36–37, 39–41, 43, 45, 55, 57, 63, 68, 71, 74, 76, 80, 83.
4. Most recent scholarship ascribes this imagery to local Syrian, Palestinian, and Cypriot workshops. See Weitzmann 1982, pp. 343–57, figs. 49, 62–65; Jaroslav Folda in New York 1997, p. 395, no. 261: "His dark shield is visible to the right in the manner of a Crusader icon." For an overview of scholarship on these icons, see Folda 2005, pp. 329–42, figs. 183–85, 198–99.
5. Mohamed et al. 2008, pp. 155–57, no. 148; Kuehn 2011, fig. 111. The latter study extensively explores the interaction of Christian and Islamic dragon and dragon-slayer imagery.
6. Pringle 1993–2009, vol. 3, pp. 289–90, no. 337. On Sicilian connections, see White 1938, pp. 68–69, 207–14, 233.
7. Dale 1997, pp. 25–26, figs. 110–12.
8. Ibid., pp. 23–24, 26, 66–76, 115–18, figs. 97–101, pl. 6.

119

Icon with Saint George and the Young Boy of Mytilene

Holy Land, mid-13th century
Tempera and gold leaf on gesso and woven textile (linen?) over wood support
10½ × 7⅜ in. (26.8 × 18.8 cm)
British Museum, London (M and LA 1984, 6-1, 1)

Divine deliverance is the theme of this engaging icon, which represents Saint George on horseback, holding a protective arm around the boy who rides at his side. The jug and wineglass held by the youth connect the image to a popular miracle account in which a boy captured by Saracens is made to serve as cupbearer for an amir and pressured to convert to Islam. He prays for rescue, and Saint George responds.[1] Emphasizing his role as defender, Saint George appears in armor, equipped with a spear and shield. The background features a raised gesso pattern of scrolling vines, imitating icon revetments in precious metal to enhance the visual richness of the work.[2]

The icon highlights the dual role of the region as a center of exchange and site of military conflict. It belongs to a group of icons and murals characterized by an amalgamation of iconographic forms and styles that express affinities with both Eastern Christian and Crusader painting.[3] Appearing in local churches,[4] a Crusader castle,[5] and as icons,[6] these images often feature saints venerated across religious divides. Byzantines honored Saint George as a champion of the faith, wedding him to a conceptualization of warfare that regarded territorial expansion as concomitant with the defense of orthodoxy.[7] Devotion to Saint George reached new heights

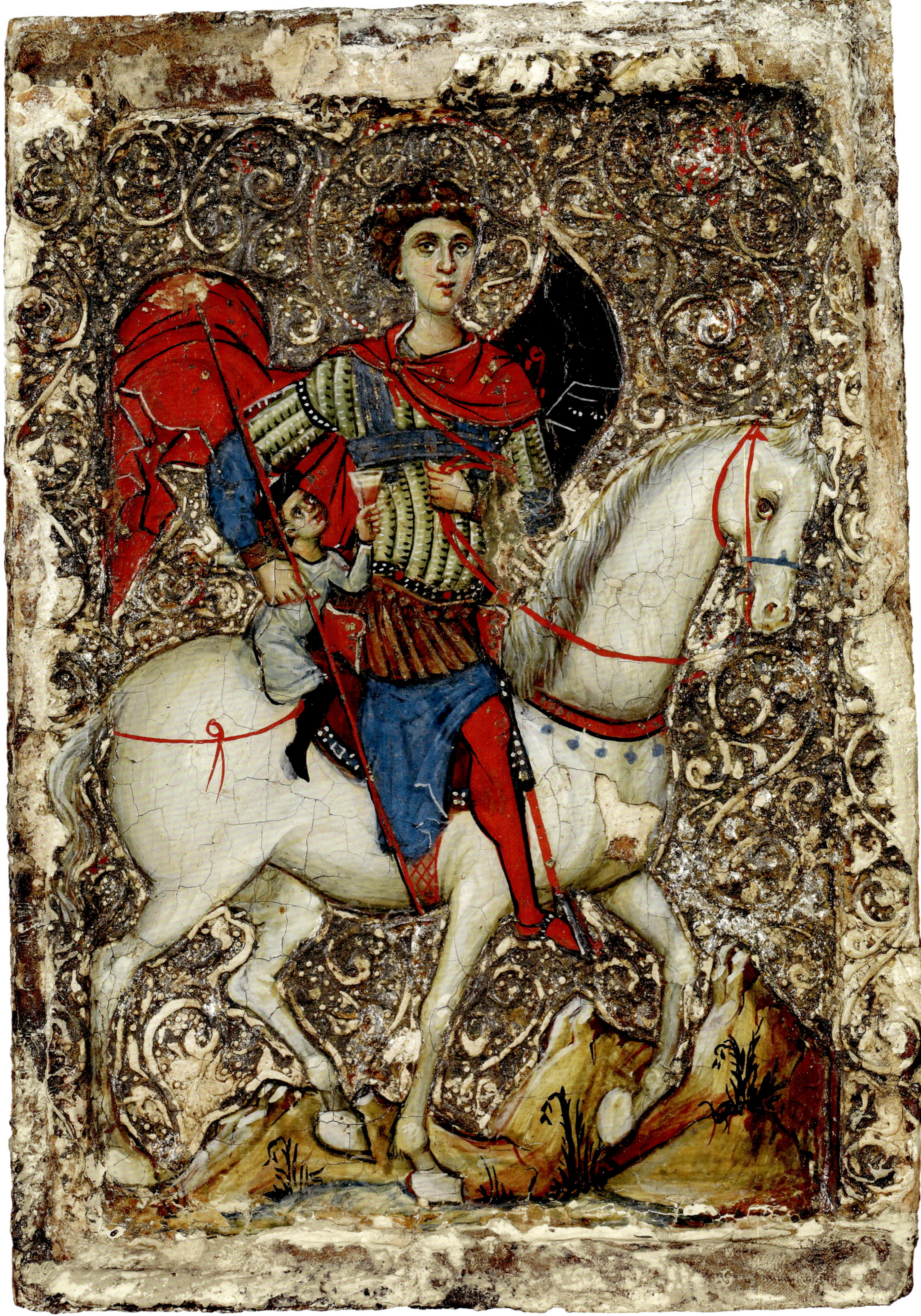

during the Middle Byzantine period, when he received imperial patronage for defending the frontiers of the empire.[8] The Crusaders, who adopted the Eastern martyr as their patron after he came to their aid in the conquest of the Holy Land, likely encountered images of Saint George as a cavalier and heard accounts of his miraculous interventions in battle while traveling in eastern Mediterranean lands.[9] After capturing Jerusalem, the Crusaders rebuilt his cathedral at Lydda, making it a site of shared devotion and perhaps facilitating the exchange of visual and religious ideas implicit in this work.[10]

The iconography here, which transforms the saint from combatant to protector, belongs to a period marked by constant skirmishes and memories of defeat at the hands of Saladin in the late twelfth century. At that time, the redemption of captives became regarded as a Christian duty.[11] With its theme of Christian deliverance from Islam, the icon presents the recovery of captives as a heroic deed and promises the faithful protection, spiritual as well as physical. HB

Selected References: Cormack and Mihalarias 1984; Folda 2005, pp. 329–31; Cormack 2007, pp. 69–83; Folda 2007, pp. 93–94.

1. The account belongs to his posthumous miracles; see *Miracula S. Georgii* 1913 ed. For a French translation, see Festugière, ed. 1971, pp. 313–15. Variations of the account have been gathered and analyzed in Grotowski 2003.
2. This was a common technique on Cypriot icons; see Ševčenko 1992, p. 67.
3. These icons, primarily representing warrior-saints, have been continuously reattributed to either Eastern Christian or Crusader painters. For a discussion of the arguments, see Carr 2007, pp. 93–95. The mechanisms through which this iconography moved are considered in Cutler 2004. Stylistically, this icon is best compared with manuscripts from the Acre school of painting; see Folda 2007, pp. 93–94.
4. Examples of this iconography appear in the Church of Mar Tadros in Lebanon and Deir Mar Musa in Syria; see Immerzeel 2004, pls. 11, 15–18; Dodd 2004, pp. 70–72, 150, pl. 85. There is a related painting in the Church of the Panagia in Moutoullas in Cyprus; see Carr 2009, p. 137, figs. 1, 5.
5. Folda 2005, pp. 98–99, fig. 56.
6. For icons with iconographical affinities, see Folda 2007, pp. 87–107, figs. 8.1–7; Cormack and Mihalarias 1984, pp. 136, 139, figs. 3–5, 7–8. For icons with stylistic comparisons, see Folda 2005, pp. 327–31, figs. 181–85.
7. Haldon 1999, pp. 17–22. This was distinct from crusading ideologies; see Kolbaba 1998, pp. 211–18.
8. Walter 2003, pp. 131–32; Nelson 2011–12, pp. 188–92.
9. He first appeared in the battle of Dorylaeum in Anatolia in 1097, then later at Antioch and Jerusalem; see Immerzeel 2004, p. 39. Such interventions had precedents in the Byzantine tradition; see Walter 2003, pp. 133–34.
10. The Byzantine church had been demolished by the Fatimid caliph al-Hakim (985–1021) as part of his efforts to reach rapprochement with Orthodox Sunnis; Pruitt 2013, p. 126. On the Crusader cathedral, see Pringle 1993–2009, vol. 1, pp. 19–27.
11. Eddé 2011, pp. 296–97; Richard 1999.

120

Dagger and Scabbard with Saint George (or Theodore) and Arabic Inscription

Syria, Palestine, or Anatolia, 13th century
Blade, steel; hilt and scabbard: silver, engraved and inlaid with niello
L. 15⅛ in. (38.5 cm)
Furusiyya Art Foundation (R-937)

Distinguished by its silver hilt and scabbard inlaid with niello, this dagger may be the only extant weapon of its type from the period. The scabbard features an inscription and motifs drawn from the artistic repertoire of the central Islamic lands. At the top of the scabbard, a laudatory epigram in Arabic wishes the owner "glory" and "good fortune." Below are running beasts set against a scrolling vine and a bird of prey attacking a gazelle.[1] The imagery, which evokes the hunt and courtly pastimes, is juxtaposed with a sacred iconography: a haloed rider impaling a serpent coiled beneath the hooves of his steed as the hand of God descends from the sky to bless him. The blessing-hand motif affiliates the image with Eastern Christian depictions of warrior-saints, particularly Theodore and George.[2]

Although the imagery derives from different contexts, it presents a unified theme of heroic pursuits. Eastern Christians revered saints George and Theodore as combatants against terrestrial adversaries, visualized here as demonic forces.[3] They received devotion not only from Christians but also from Muslims, who venerated them in the guise of al-Khidr, a sacred figure associated with a miraculous dragon slaying.[4] Both Christian and Muslim elites used images of dragon slayers to evoke valor in battle and the triumph of good over evil.[5] The inclusion of such imagery on this dagger points to an international courtly milieu governed by rules of display. Worn on the body, the iconography referred to the heroic stature of its wearer. In combat, it provided a powerful prophylactic for the owner and, perhaps, a warning for adversaries. HB

Selected References: Paris 2002–3, pp. 118–19, no. 57; New York 2004, p. 430, no. 257; Mohamed et al. 2008, pp. 155–57, no. 148; New York 2016, p. 146, no. 76.

1. Marilyn Jenkins-Medina noted close parallels in a variety of objects produced in the lands of the Ayyubids and Seljuq successor states; see New York 2004, p. 430.
2. The blessing-hand motif appears in wall paintings in Syria, Lebanon, Cyprus, and Egypt; see Carr 2009, p. 137, fig. 5; Immerzeel 2009, pp. 213, 232, 247, figs. 39, 65, 82; Bolman et al. 2002, pp. 42, 101, 120, figs. 4.8, 6.24, 7.31.
3. Walter 2003, p. 284.
4. Veneration to al-Khidr was especially strong in Syria, Palestine, and Anatolia; see Hasluck 1929, vol. 2, pp. 329–31; Wolper 2000, pp. 314–16.
5. For the Seljuq successor states, see Pancaroğlu 2004, pp. 157–60; for the Crusaders, see Metcalf 1983, p. 7; for Trebizond, see Eastmond 2004, p. 141; for the Byzantine Empire, see Walker 2012, pp. 125–27.

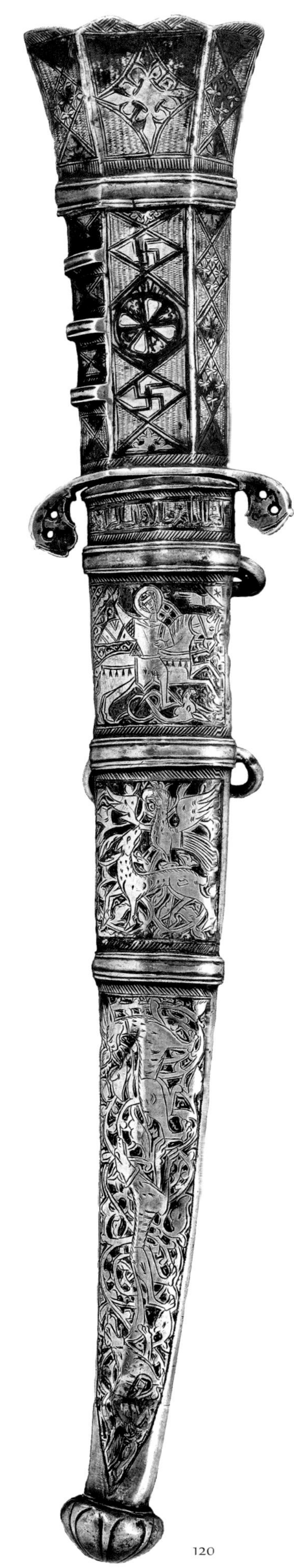
120

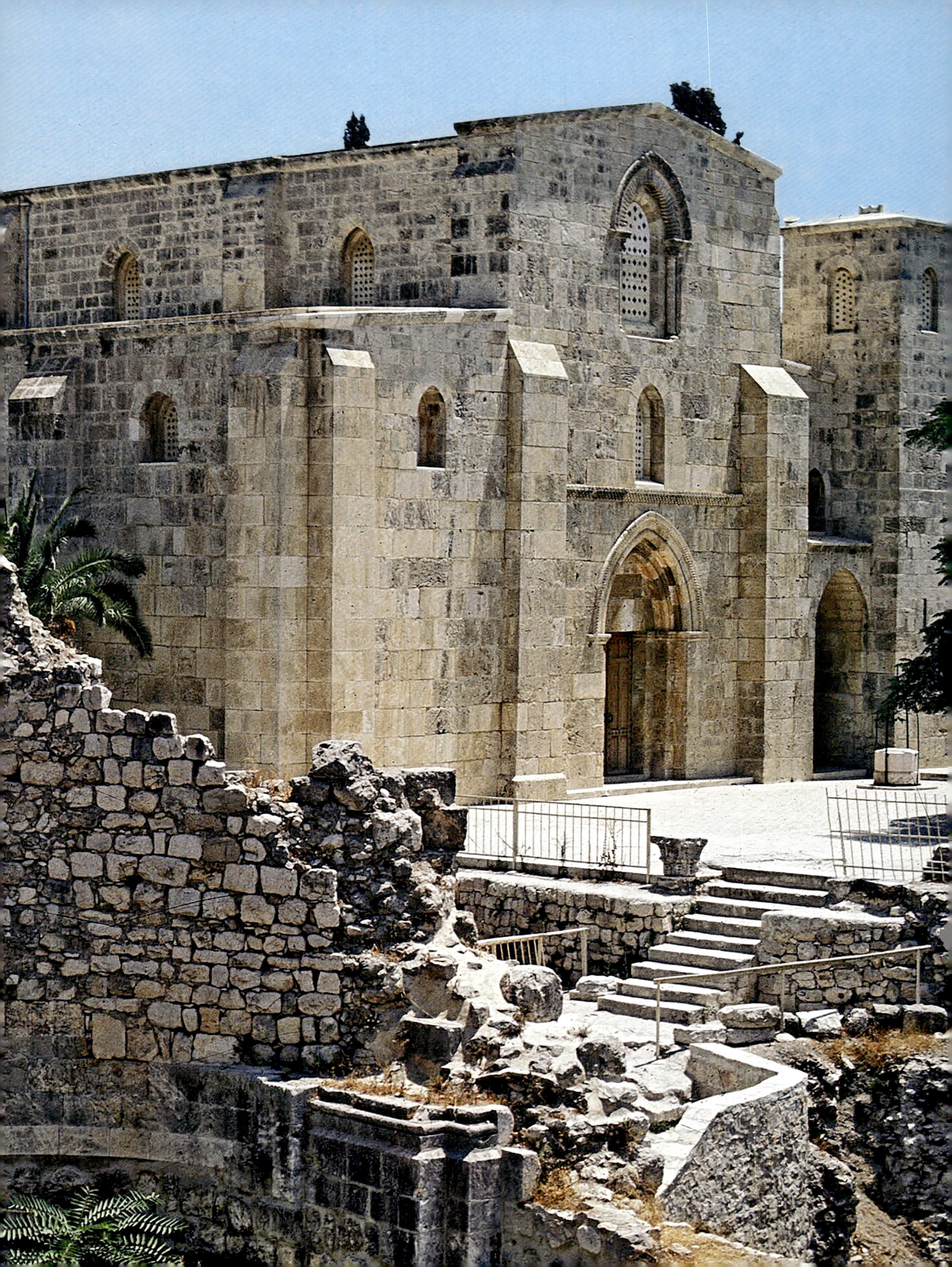

Patronage in Jerusalem

Constructing edifices of this world and the hereafter

— Ibn Shaddad 'Izz al-Din

MELANIE HOLCOMB AND BARBARA DRAKE BOEHM

FACING PAGE
Fig. 78. Church of Saint Anne, Jerusalem

IN 1149, MELISENDE, the Frankish queen of Jerusalem, displaying some anxiety lest her good works be forgotten, signed and sealed an official document attesting to her gift to the convent of Bethany, on the outskirts of Jerusalem.[1] History would prove her concerns well founded, for within a century the generously endowed and richly appointed convent was destroyed, leaving only her text and a field of ruined stones as witness.

The queen echoed the same thought when soon after she made a gift to the leper hospital of Saint Lazarus. This time, however, she recognized an obligation for charitable giving, continuing the work of her ancestors and setting an example for those who would follow: "It is the custom of wise men to record in writing their . . . works so that it is impossible to erase them from memory . . . and [thus] their successors may imitate what their ancestors have done."[2]

Little did she guess that her successors as patrons of the Holy City would be not her own descendants, but rather the Muslim rulers of Jerusalem. Nor could she have divined that one of them — Saladin — would impose his presence on a Christian foundation that her forebears, and she herself, had endowed: the Church, Shrine, and Convent of Saint Anne (fig. 78).[3] In 1192 Saladin transformed the complex into a madrasa bearing his name, proclaiming its new function on a stone slab set over the doorway (fig. 79).[4] There the inscription remains, although, through a later gift of the Ottoman rulers of Jerusalem to France, the building functions today as the Church of Saint Anne, where it quietly but unmistakably proclaims the importance of individual patrons who turned their attention to good works in the city.[5]

Good works, charity, and prayer are central tenets of all the religions that hold Jerusalem dear, and these fundaments possessed a special luster when done in or for that city. The twelfth-century poet Judah ha-Levi drew from long-held Jewish tradition when he stated that "the Land of Israel is especially distinguished by the Lord of Israel, and no action can be perfect except there."[6] Jewish teaching maintained that prayer should be directed toward Jerusalem and specifically the

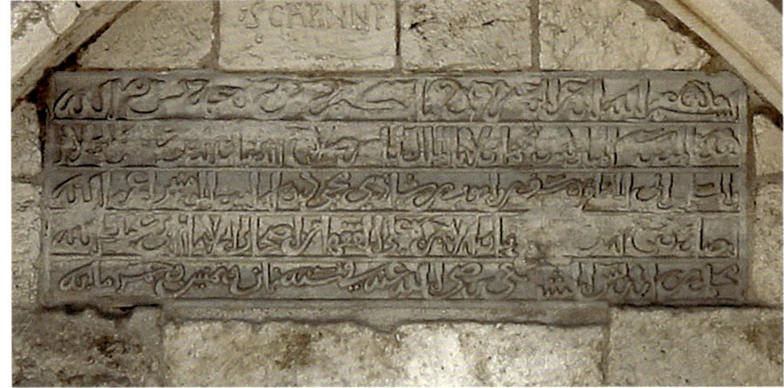

Fig. 79. Saladin's dedicatory inscription on the Madrasa al-Salahiyya, Jerusalem

site of the ancient Temple.[7] Medieval Muslim literature on the Merits of Jerusalem (Fada'il al-Quds)[8] asserted that by special reckoning a good deed done in the Holy City equals one thousand deeds performed elsewhere.[9] From an early period Muslim law protected endowments for places of worship in the city, including those of Christians and Jews.[10]

The city benefited materially from its privileged status. Patronage was manifested in various ways, from impressive architectural structures to charitable organizations, from endowments supporting activities in Jerusalem to precious works of art enriching its interior spaces. One did not need to live there to feel its pull. Its streets included many a building commissioned from afar; its churches, mosques, synagogues, schools, and libraries possessed works sent by devotees who never set foot inside its walls.

In fact, most patrons came from or lived far away: from Italy to India, England to Ethiopia, Gibraltar to Georgia.[11] Giving to Jerusalem continued even when the city's governors were from different lands or faith traditions, suggesting a degree of confidence in the abiding good will of those authorities. Charlemagne is reported to have founded a hospital and hospice for Latin pilgrims to Jerusalem, though local churches were under the sway of the Orthodox and the city ruled by Muslims.[12] The Byzantine emperor Manuel Comnenus (1118–1180) was instrumental in the physical reconstruction of Orthodox monasteries in the Latin Kingdom of Jerusalem, including, for example, Mar Elias, dedicated to the prophet Elijah and situated on the road from Jerusalem to Bethlehem.[13] Queen Tamar of Georgia (1184–1212), whose reign spanned that of the Franks and of Saladin, nevertheless invested funds for rebuilding monasteries and charities in the Holy Land.[14]

The most visible patrons were its rulers: emperors, kings, caliphs, sultans, queens, and princesses. Melisende was the matriarch of Frankish princesses, and her immediate female relatives followed her example (cat. 123). Saladin, the nemesis of the Frankish rulers, and his entourage were succeeded ultimately by the Mamluks, with Sultan al-Nasir Muhammad ibn Qala'un (1285–1341) evincing the greatest presence in Jerusalem. Still, the city's culture of philanthropy encouraged a wide spectrum of donors, with even the lowliest seeking opportunities to give. The city was enhanced not only by the largesse of resident ladies and merchants but also by scholars and pilgrims and the abiding presence of its many religious communities.

Then as now, impressive buildings were viewed as an enduring way for the powerful and the wealthy to leave their mark. From the eleventh to the fourteenth century, Jerusalem witnessed several periods of intense construction activity, as the ruling elite sought to remake portions of the city, asserting their political dominance through commanding architecture. That strategy proved effective, as the Jerusalem that billions of faithful hold in their minds today retains many features that visitors gazed upon centuries ago.

Though Western Christians controlled the city for less than a century, they wasted no time in translating their religious fervor into imposing edifices. To this day, the city bears material traces of sixty-one churches built or rebuilt when the Franks claimed Jerusalem as theirs.[15] Despite many subsequent renovations, the iconic Church of the Holy Sepulchre still has the striking architectural overlay that exuberant Crusaders imposed on it in the 1140s. Our sources are surprisingly quiet about its principal patrons, but the mid-twelfth-century Latin patriarchs William and his successor Fulcher undoubtedly played important roles, alongside King Fulk and Queen Melisende, who made it the state church for

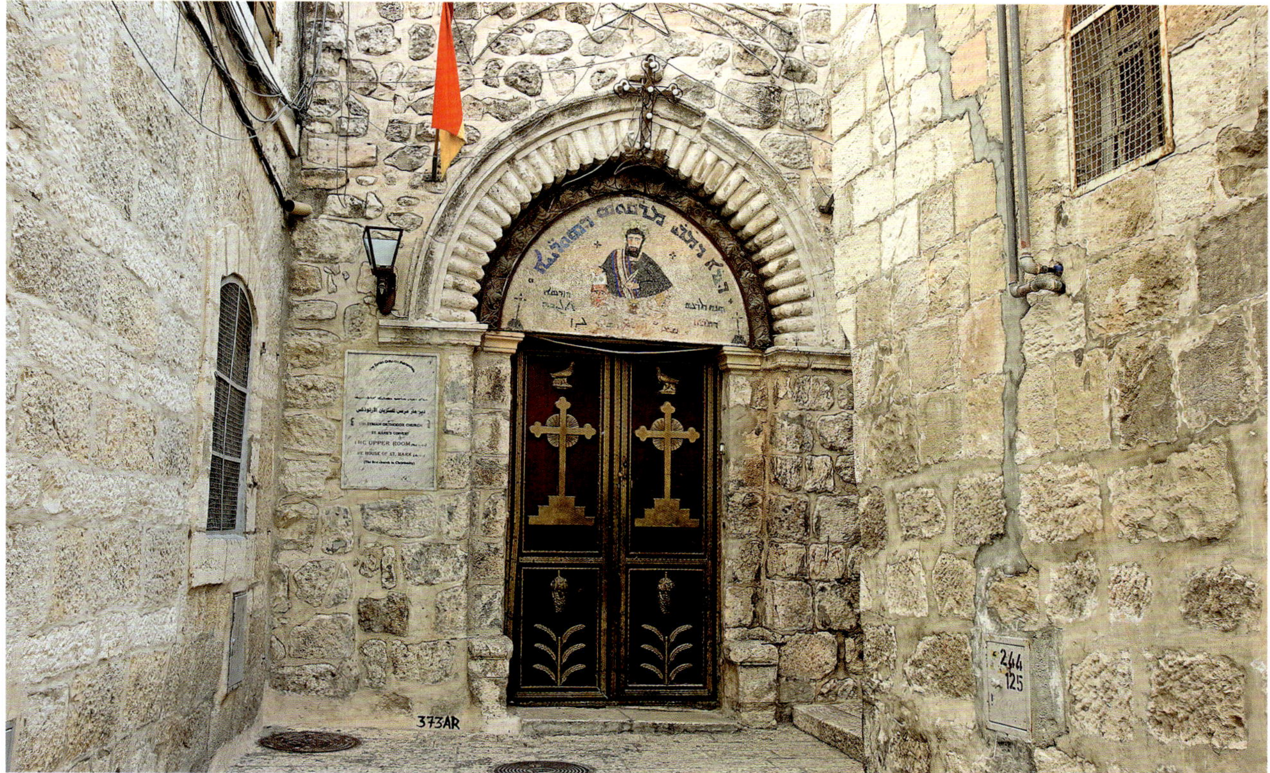

Fig. 80. The entrance to Saint Mark's Syrian Orthodox Monastery Church, Jerusalem

the Crusader kingdom.[16] Melisende's name is attached to many more surviving churches. Within the boundaries of the Old City, churches dedicated to saints Anne, James, and Mary (now Saint Mark; fig. 80) largely preserve their medieval contours, as do that of Saint Mary Jehoshaphat and the Chapel of the Ascension just outside the city walls. The prolific efforts of Melisende should not overshadow the contributions of her subjects. Tucked into today's Jewish Quarter overlooking the Western Wall, for instance, stand the substantial remains of the Church of Saint Mary of the Germans, built by an anonymous German merchant and his wife who had settled in Jerusalem (fig. 81).[17]

For their part, the Mamluks also dramatically changed the city, focusing their efforts on and around the Haram al-Sharif during the more than two hundred fifty years of their rule (1250–1517). The streets leading to that sacred esplanade are still graced by monuments from that period, including facades like that of the building now housing the Khalidi Library and gates like the Chain Gate (Bab al-Silsila), identifiable by their distinctive, dizzying honeycomb (*muqarnas*) decoration over the heads of visitors, their alternating colored marble slabs (*ablaq*), and deep porches. Though a relatively minor outpost within the Mamluk domain, the city nonetheless enjoyed the attention of sultans, who restored its shrines and constructed new buildings, creating a dazzling curtain of stone on the northern and western edges of the Haram. The magnificent complex erected by the amir Tankiz under the authority of al-Nasir Muhammad is one such structure. The exterior still bears his symbol (fig. 82) while the mosque within features an inscription that reads "Allah made his mosque the neighbor of the Aqsa Mosque and how goodly is a pure neighbor."[18] Many retired amirs who settled in the city built religious edifices on the streets approaching the Haram's gates, while private citizens had to content themselves with less valuable real estate.

As in many cities today, patrons of Jerusalem, whatever their affiliation, were eager to link their names to charitable institutions, notably hospitals and hostels, soup kitchens and schools. These

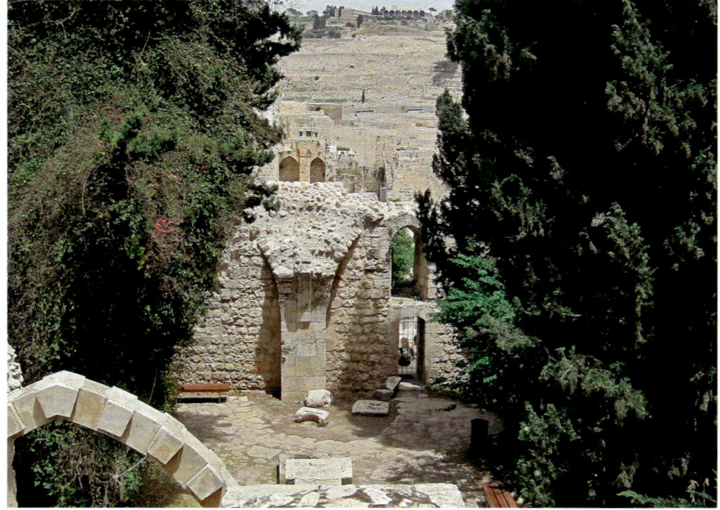

Fig. 81. The remains of the Church of Saint Mary of the Germans, Jerusalem

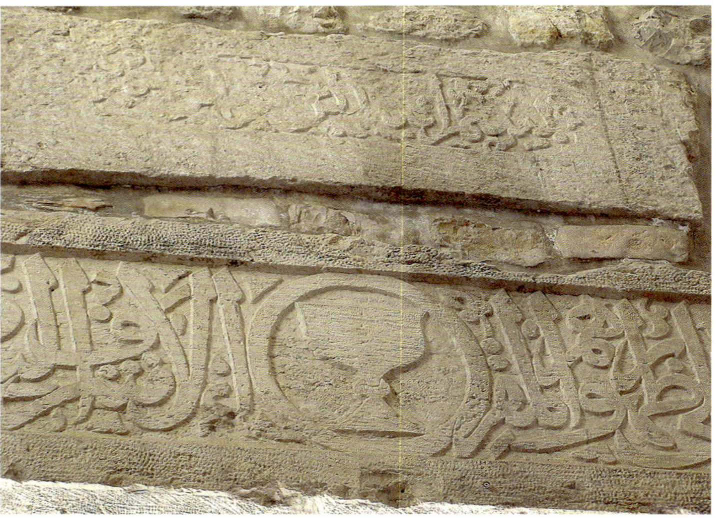

Fig. 82. The symbol of the amir Tankiz, a cup testifying to the trust placed in him as cupbearer to the sultan, on the exterior of the Tankiziyya Madrasa, Jerusalem

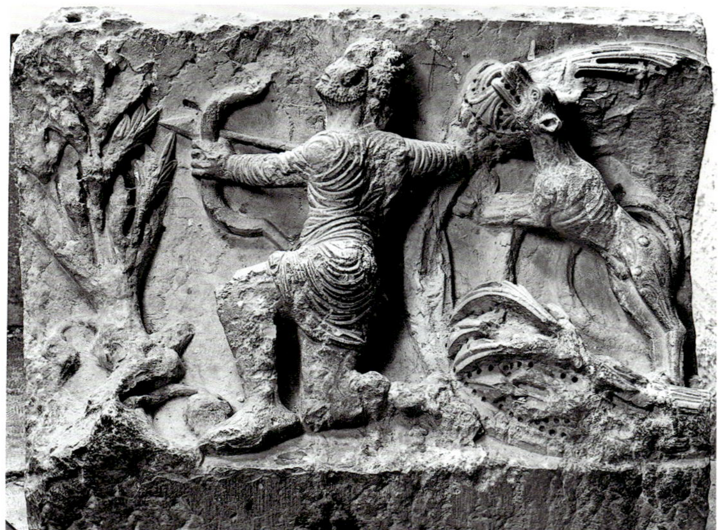

Fig. 83. Element from a 12th-century arch carved with a hunter. Limestone. Greek Orthodox Patriarchate, Jerusalem

practical institutions met the daily needs of Jerusalem's inhabitants and visitors, but their sculptural ornament and decorative furnishings, which often extended beyond the practical, reveal a greater ambition at play.

In 1047, before the arrival of the Franks, the Persian traveler Nasir-i Khusraw mentioned a "fine and heavily endowed" hospital whose doctors "draw their salaries from the endowment" without naming the patron.[19] Three hospitals were funded by merchants from Amalfi, in southern Italy, before the Crusader conquest of Jerusalem.[20] One, dedicated to Saint John the Baptist, came to be maintained by the Knights of Saint John (hence dubbed the Hospitallers). A monk from Iceland, visiting Jerusalem around 1140, called it "the most magnificent in the whole world."[21] There, four salaried doctors made rounds twice daily to ensure the well-being of nearly a thousand patients at the hospital. The twelfth-century pilgrim Theoderich also sang its praises, proclaiming that the hospital was richly appointed: "I would not trust anyone else to believe it if I had not seen with my own eyes how splendidly it is adorned with buildings with many rooms and bunks and other things poor people and the weak and sick can use. What a rich place this is and how excellently it spends the money for the relief of the poor."[22]

In his day, Saladin converted the convent church of Saint Mary Major (also known as Saint Mary Magdalene), one of the Amalfitan foundations, into a Muslim hospital in 1192, procuring "rare medicaments and drugs" for it.[23] Documents from the Mamluk era include the mention of a coppersmith with a house near the Damascus Gate that he established as an endowment to benefit the Hospital of Saladin.[24] While today many structures have been radically transformed or destroyed, the Muristan zone near the Holy Sepulchre, where these hospitals were clustered, retains a kind of neighborhood feeling, and the attentive visitor will find sculptural elements preserved there. Inside the nineteenth-century Lutheran Church of the Redeemer, one can find excavations of the Church of Saint Mary of the

Latins over which the modern church was built. Visible through the Plexiglas floor of a cloth merchant's shop in the Muristan are the fragments of Saint Mary Major.[25] Both churches were linked to the hospital (fig. 83). In addition, stonework from the complex bears masons' marks in the minaret and walls of the Mosque of 'Umar, opposite the Holy Sepulchre.

Jerusalem's patrons were aware that the city thrived on an international audience whose needs had to be accommodated, and throughout our period we find the steady construction of hospices for pilgrims. Within the Lyon Syriac Breviary of 1138 (cat. 73) is a testimonial to the intense building activity under the Syriac patriarch Ignatius (1125–1138).[26] He more than doubled the architectural footprint he inherited, adding vaulted rooms to serve as hostels for pilgrims. Similarly, from the surge in the construction of hospices (*ribats*) during the Mamluk period, the earliest is a pilgrim hospice sited near the edge of the Haram and endowed in 1267–68 "in favour of the poor who came on pilgrimage to Jerusalem."[27] Its patron, a certain 'Ala al-Din Aydughdi, though blind, served for many years as superintendent of the two sanctuaries of Jerusalem and Hebron.

Educational institutions drew many supporters. Saladin converted the complex at Saint Anne's into a madrasa, which was dedicated to Shafi'ite jurisprudence.[28] For his part, al-Mu'azzam Isa, one of Saladin's nephews, built a madrasa for Hanafites, a school of Sunni jurisprudence, in 1217–18.[29] His personal interest in scholarship represented more than a naming opportunity. In 1226 he convened a council outside the Dome of the Rock for the discussion of theological questions.[30] He rebuilt a *zawiya*, literally meaning "corners" and thus a gathering place, atop the Gate of Mercy on the eastern side of the Haram. Intended for the reciting of grammar and the Qur'an, it was endowed liberally with books.[31] Dramatically refashioning the urban landscape, the Mamluks established an astonishing sixty additional madrasas, along with *khanqa*s, hospices, a school for orphans, *zawiya*s, and mausoleums with living quarters.[32] Sufi students were paid salaries for participating in devotional prayer (*dhikr*); in addition, presaging today's work-study programs, they were given stipends for academic or menial jobs in the madrasa.[33] Moreover, the creation of madrasas for the Hanbali school of Sunni jurisprudence seems to have engendered a particular architectural form in Jerusalem, the double dome that became emblematic of its students' commitment to study.[34]

All these structures were conceived with posterity in mind. Their patrons were aware of the responsibility to provide for the future expenses and maintenance through a liberal endowment.[35] Funding was provided not only by cash gifts but also through properties and businesses that were obliged to channel income to the charitable institution on an ongoing basis. The Church of Saint Anne, for instance, rented space in "downtown" Jerusalem to Frankish merchants to offset the convent's expenses.[36] A number of shops in the triple market are marked to this day as church property. These shops may well have been a gift of Melisende, who is recorded as having completed a new street adjoining the money exchange.[37] The shops were later co-opted by Saladin to support a waqf, a charitable endowment or foundation, supporting the Madrasa al-Salahiyya. The waqf he established included income from shops as well as from land in Gethsemane and Silwan, a mill and an oven, a vegetable garden, baths, and springs.[38]

Income from such prudent patronage was not necessarily restricted to building maintenance. In 1263, for example, Sultan Baybars established an inn just outside Jerusalem, the income from which provided not only money but also bread for the sustenance of pilgrims, plus — fittingly — sandals for their weary feet.[39] The historian Mujir al-Din (1456–1522) related that all kinds of merchandise were sold in the caravanserai established at the end of the fourteenth century by Sultan Barquq as a waqf, netting four hundred dinars a year for the upkeep of the Haram al-Sharif.[40] Not only the ruling classes established endowments: Mujir al-Din noted that the widow of a Persian merchant from Abivard built a madrasa in Jerusalem near a tomb, presumably that of her late husband; endowed it with various carpets and utensils; and set up a waqf in 1367 to support it in perpetuity (cat. 136).[41]

Similar to the waqf was the Jewish institution of *heqdesh*, property set aside for charitable purposes, whether for the poor, synagogues, the ransom of captives, the burial of the dead, or the maintenance of hospitals, hospices, and schools.[42] Embedded in the notion was a link to Jerusalem. In biblical times, the *heqdesh* supported the upkeep of the Temple, and medieval fund-raising appeals equated gifts to the Jerusalem yeshiva with gifts to the Temple (cat. 65).[43] The city's Jewish community greatly benefited from — indeed depended on — donations from elsewhere. Documents recovered from the Geniza, the storeroom of a synagogue in Fustat (Cairo's Old City), reveal the poverty of many Jews living in the Holy City during the eleventh century. Local leaders regularly appealed for help for "the pained, the afflicted, the sad, the robbed, the deprived . . . the depressed and maimed . . . the poor and the impoverished."[44] The Diaspora responded through special vows, endowments, and bequests. Fustat was one of many cities that established foundations specifically to provide for the poor of Jerusalem.[45] In Ramle, income from certain shops was designated for the same purpose.[46] Most endowment money, however, went to education. The Palestinian Academy, a center for Talmudic study that had moved from Tiberias to Jerusalem in the tenth century before its relocation to Tyre in the late eleventh, profited from taxes assessed on Kosher butchering in Fustat.[47] A Maghrebi merchant set aside fifty-eight of the sixty dinars he earned from the sale of silk for the academy.[48]

A remarkable example of patronage across communities was set in 1092 — prior to the Franks' capture of Jerusalem — by an assistant to the Seljuq governor of the city, who built a church for the Copts.[49] Melisende, though the Crusader queen, took a special interest in the Eastern Christians of Jerusalem. As the eldest daughter of Baldwin II, the Frankish king of Jerusalem, and an Armenian mother whose father was Greek Orthodox, she had been reared in a multilingual, multicultural, and multidenominational environment. She provided an endowment to the Orthodox monastery of Saint Sabas outside Jerusalem (fig. 33) and to the Armenian Cathederal of Saint James (fig. 29).[50] In addition, she supported the Jacobite (Syrian Orthodox) Church of Saint Mary Magdalene near Herod's Gate, with which she was not affiliated. Melisende was apparently moved by the plight of Syrian refugees, for a colophon in a Syriac lectionary is inscribed with a prayer for King Baldwin and his mother Melisende for all they had done to aid the survivors of the loss of Edessa, which brought both Armenian and Syrian refugees to the city.[51] Later, in 1258, as if returning the favor, a Jacobite priest, Ignatius, willed half his possessions to his own church and the other half to the Frankish church.[52]

As noteworthy as Melisende's example of supporting projects across denominations may seem, there is a more exceptional circumstance at the Church of the Nativity in Bethlehem.[53] In an amazing joint sponsorship of the decoration of the church, two leaders from distinct communities and denominations formed an alliance to create an interior of dazzling splendor (fig. 84), bringing multiple artistic media to bear. In the church is an inscription from 1169, written in Latin and Greek, attesting to the completion of the work and naming the Byzantine emperor Manuel Comnenus and the Frankish king

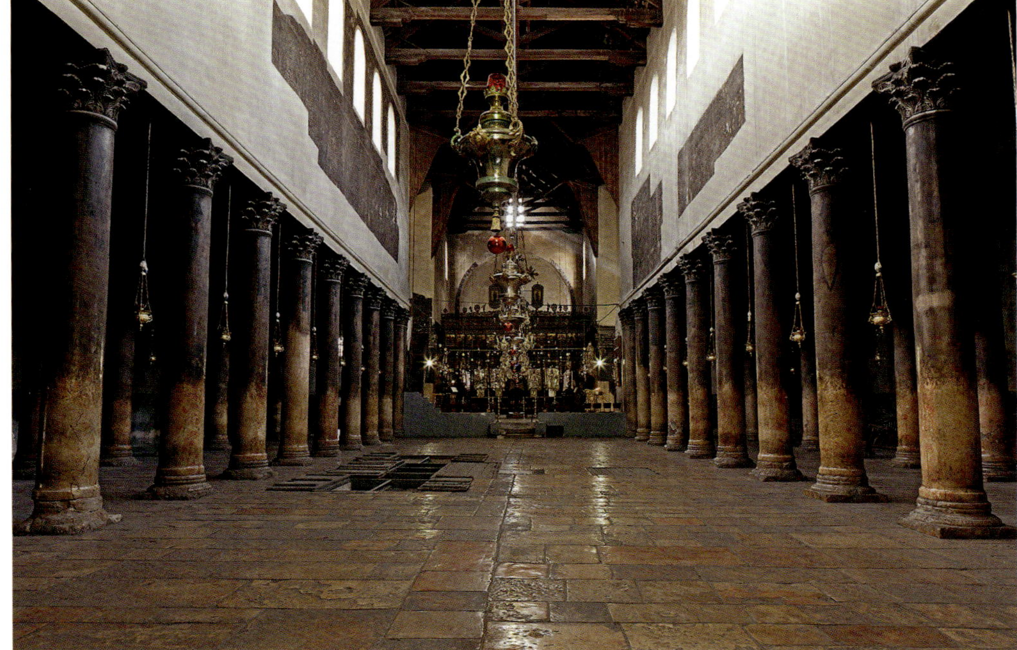

Fig. 84. Interior of the Church of the Nativity, Bethlehem

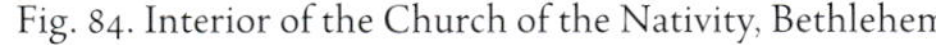

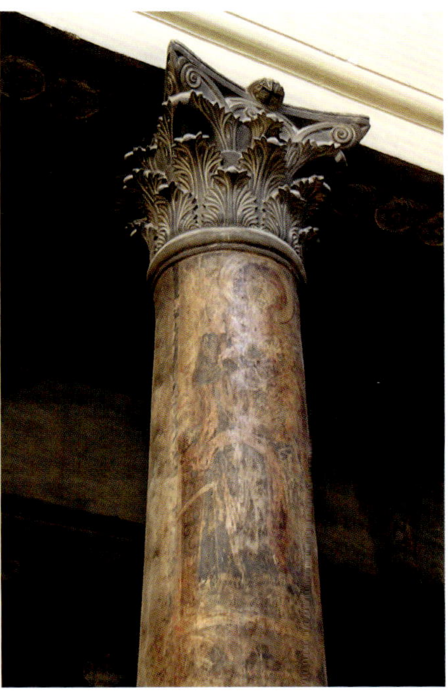

Fig. 85. Painted nave column of the Virgin, Church of the Nativity, Bethlehem

Amaury of Jerusalem, while not neglecting to mention the local Frankish church authority, Ralph, bishop of Bethlehem.[54] The workmanship, too, represents a surprising coalition, as the name of one artist, Ephraim, a Greek Orthodox monk, possibly from the region, is inscribed in Latin and Greek, along with the donors.[55] An additional inscription in Latin and another in Syriac – and possibly corresponding initials in Greek – highlight the work of a painter called Basilius, apparently a Syriac deacon.[56] It has been suggested that he is the same Basilius who painted some of the Melisende Psalter (cat. 121).[57]

In addition to images one might expect, such as the life of Jesus or processing angels, the mosaic decoration, extraordinarily, focuses on text, not standard prayers but esoteric proclamations of the historic Church councils convened to clarify points of doctrine. These dense and didactic texts are placed, virtually enshrined, on the wall above an altar, some set beneath a magnificent, domed church. Among them on the south wall are the texts of the seven ecumenical councils common to Orthodox and Western Christians (cat. 96).[58]

The paintings on the great columns of the nave (fig. 85) represent a mix of earlier and more recent decoration, as well as an unexpected assortment of saints: some common to East and West; some men, some women; some prominent, others obscure; some local like Sabas and Macarius, a fourth-century bishop of Jerusalem; and some foreign like Canute the Dane, Olaf of Norway, and Fusca, revered in Venice.[59] This panoply of holy figures could imply that international financial contributions were at play.

Why did the patrons support such an unusual decorative program? It cannot merely have been a question of sharing high costs. The varied saints were embraced as the common heritage of the worshippers who gathered there from across the known Christian world. The mosaic program celebrates the common history of the church, notwithstanding the fact that it was created at a time when the Eastern and Western churches had split and were no longer in communion. Perhaps they were massaging differences to present a united front against infidels.

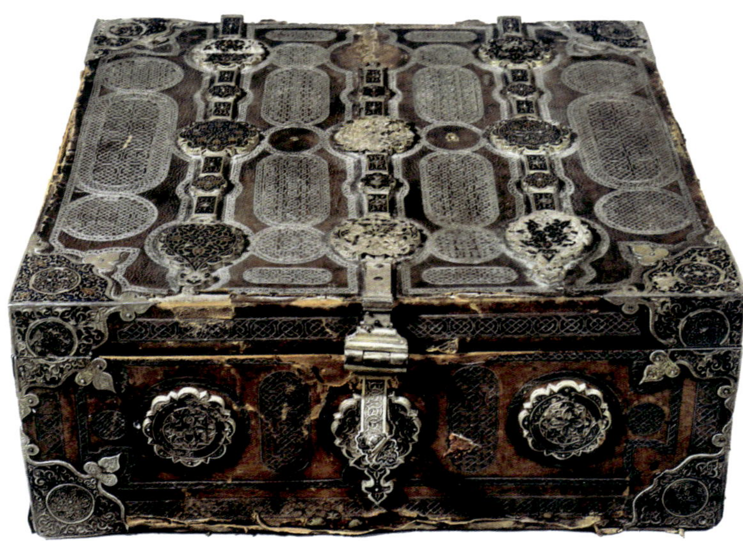

Fig. 86. Box for a thirty-volume Qur'an given by the Maghreb king Abu al-Hasan 'Abd Allah ibn 'Ali to Al-Aqsa Mosque, Jerusalem. Fez, A.H. 745 (1344/45). Wood, leather, silver, brass, and enamel. Islamic Museum and Al-Aqsa Library, Jerusalem

The embellishment of monumental structures with precious furnishings is seen throughout our period – in patrons' gifts and in visual and written memory. These began at the door, whether the richly carved wood door of the church in Bethlehem, bearing the name of the Armenian king Hetoum I (r. 1226–70), or the Cotton Gate rebuilt by the Mamluk sultan al-Nasir Muhammad (fig. 6).[60] The famous Arabic-language *Book of Treasures and Gifts* informs us that the Byzantine emperor Michael VII (ca. 1050–ca. 1090) sent gold, jewels, objects used in services, chandeliers to give light, vestments for priests to wear, "and other things of that sort that one finds in churches" to the Holy Sepulchre.[61] For his part, Henry the Lion, duke of Saxony (1129–1195), donated lamps to the Holy Sepulchre with a special endowment in perpetuity that complemented his commissioning of mosaics and silver doors at the entrance to the Chapel of the Cross.[62] William of Tyre notes that when Melisende founded the convent at Bethany, "she also presented to the convent a large number of sacred vessels of gold and silver adorned with gems. She likewise gave it silken stuffs for the adornment of the house of God and vestments of every description."[63] After her sister became abbess, "she made many additional gifts, such as chalices, books, and other ornaments pertaining to the service of the church."[64] While Melisende's precious gifts do not survive, the Cross of her stepdaughter Sibyl of Anjou, who resided at the convent of Bethany in later life, hints at the splendor of such works of art (cat. 123). So too does the precious lost Reliquary of the Cross of Byzantine manufacture, known through an eighteenth-century engraving that was given by another Sibyl – queen of Jerusalem – to the cathedral in Montferrat, Italy, after the death of her husband.[65]

Books were as prized as gold and silver and often embellished with them. The Missal of the Holy Sepulchre (cat. 77), created in Melisende's day, is indicative of the refined quality of manuscripts and other precious works of art created for the great churches of Jerusalem, as is the Psalter with ivory covers linked to her own name (cat. 121). After Saladin came to power in Egypt, the Armenian patriarch of Alexandria left Egypt in 1172 and settled in Jerusalem, bringing seventy-five codices, including a marvelous illuminated Gospel.[66] The future English king Henry IV (1367–1413) commissioned a lavish antiphonary for the Franciscans of the Holy Land (cats. 134a–c). Manuscripts made for Jerusalem's churches included not only service books but learned texts as well: a manuscript of John Chrysostom (347–407) now in the Greek Orthodox Patriarchate in Jerusalem has a note indicating that it was presented to the Monastery of Saint Euthymius in Jerusalem by Emperor Alexius II Comnenus of Trebizond (r. 1297–1330).[67]

Following his reconquest of Jerusalem, Saladin provided Qur'an manuscripts to the Haram. The historian Ibn al-Athir (1160–1233) specified that the ruler ordered entire Qur'ans as well as "sections" of the Holy Book and that they were "magnificent."[68] The finest examples from this period are often large and bound in multiple volumes (figs. 86, 87). Ibn al-Athir also related that the manuscripts and

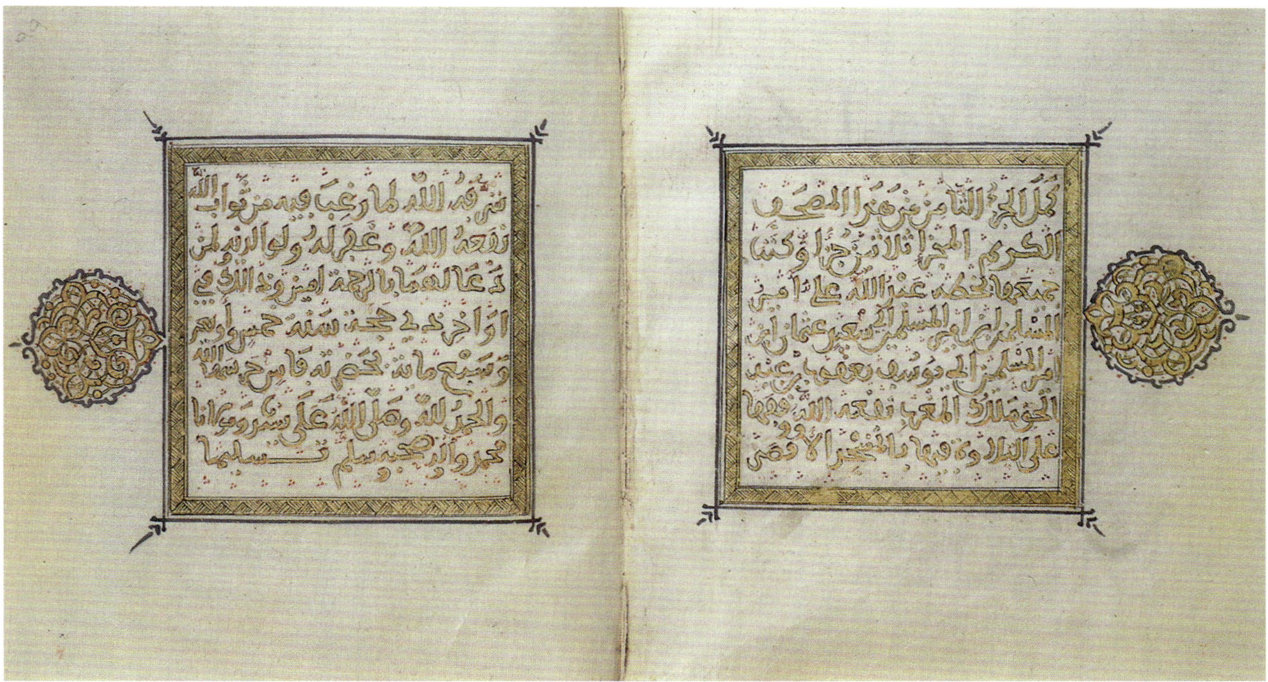

Fig. 87. Endowment text from the Qur'an given by the Maghreb king Abu al-Hasan 'Abd Allah ibn 'Ali to Al-Aqsa Mosque, Jerusalem. Fez, A.H. 745 (1344/45). Gold and ink on paper. Islamic Museum and Al-Aqsa Library, Jerusalem

their official reciters played a key role in restoring Islam "in full freshness and beauty."[69] Moreover, the volumes were "raised upon their lecterns and placed on their shelves in view of the visitors."[70] The preciousness and sacredness of the manuscripts are further evidenced by Saladin's appointing "custodians to keep [them] all in good condition," a responsibility that sounds like that of a museum professional.[71]

The need for light was both symbolic and practical. Byzantine, European, and Fatimid rulers alike chose to illuminate sacred buildings in Jerusalem. Nasir described a candle sent from Egypt: "I saw one enormous candle, seven cubits long and three spans thick; it was as white as camphor and mixed with ambergris. They said that every year the sultan of Egypt sends many candles, one of which was this one, for it had the sultan's name written in gold letters around the bottom."[72] In a land rich in olive oil, the gift of a wax candle that was double the height of a man, pure white in color, decorated with gold and infused with sweet-smelling, expensive ambergris, suggests a level of ostentation blended with a particular aesthetic sensibility. Nasir also recounted that hanging lamps at the Dome of the Rock advertised, by means of inscription, the weight of the silver they contained, again explicitly proclaiming the value of the gift.[73] The inscription on the silver candlesticks from Bethlehem provides neither the name of the donor nor the value of the gift; rather, it threatens eternal damnation to anyone who might have the audacity to remove them from the church (cat. 97). More humble offerings were important, too. Daniel the Abbot (1106–1178) spoke of his own gift of a large glass lamp to the Holy Sepulchre.[74] Al-Wasiti (d. after 1019), the main preacher at the Aqsa Mosque, observed that a pious Muslim could substitute an in-person visit to Jerusalem entirely with the donation of oil for lamps on the Haram.[75]

In another source we learn of the son of Rabbi Shemuel who gave money "for oil for the sanctuary at the western wall for the altar within." He refers to "the Cave," a synagogue under the western retaining wall of the Temple Mount.[76] Only a hint of its interior furnishings remains, but it appears that one Moses ben Jacob ordered "mats" from Alexandria especially for the synagogue in 1053.[77] Campaigns to raise funds for its upkeep and repair were particularly pressing following the earthquake of 1033. The

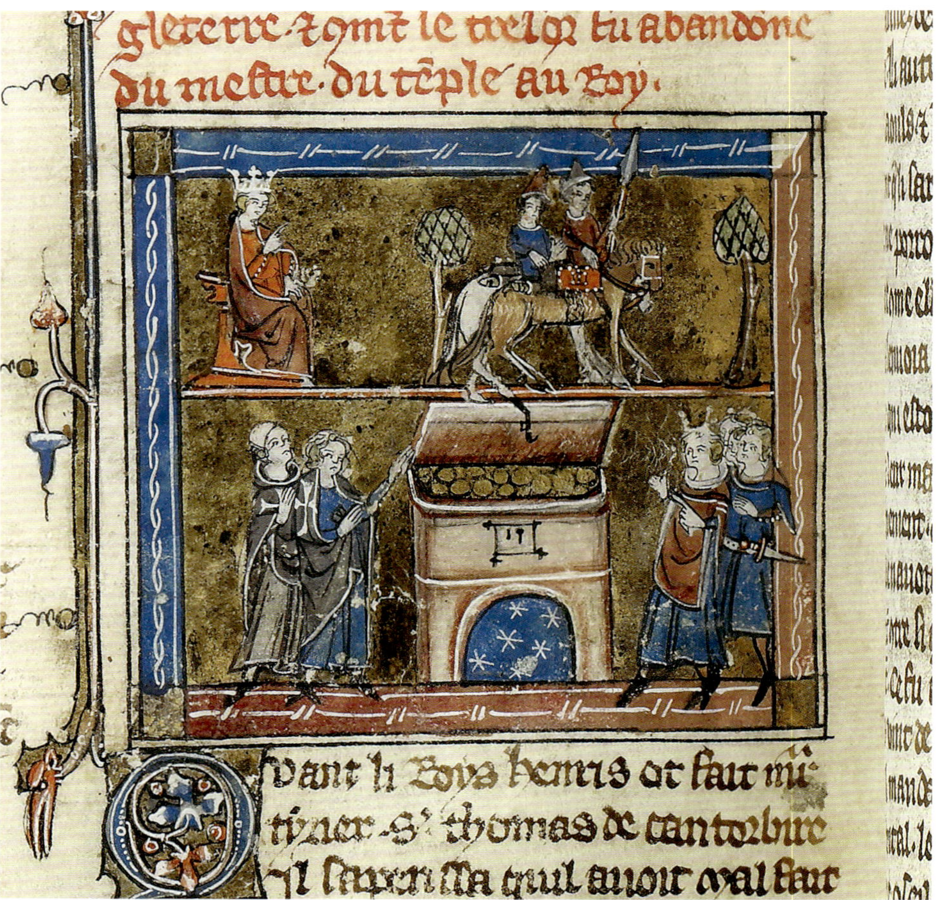

Fig. 88. At top, King Henry II of England sending his annual contribution for the aid of the Holy Land; below, the Master of the Temple distributing those funds, from the *Chronicle of Ernoul* (*Chronique d'Ernoul*). Paris, 14th century. Tempera, gold, and ink on parchment. Walters Art Museum, Baltimore (MS W.142, fol. 243v)

names of those who sponsored the rebuilding of the synagogue were read aloud on the last day of the Festival of Sukkoth, when Jews from near and far gathered on the Mount of Olives. Being so named was considered the highest of honors.[78]

Whatever their cultural, religious, or ethnic heritage, patrons of Jerusalem were bound by similar motivations. In any city, a yearning for both immediate recognition and an enduring legacy are among the forces that motivate philanthropy. From Melisende to Saladin, from a German merchant to a vendor of silk, what distinguishes their giving in Jerusalem is the city's inherent promise of eternity (fig. 88). Ibn Shaddad 'Izz al-Din's analysis of Sultan Baybars as a patron could apply to countless donors in the Holy Land across history: "When he . . . learned that the durability of buildings would fulfill for their builder the role of longevity and revive their name if forgotten, . . . he preoccupied himself with constructing [buildings, such as] earlier potentates had been unable [to build], and set up what [earlier] craftsmen had failed [to create]: chambers of edifices of this world and the hereafter, God would reward him who erected them."[79]

NOTES FOR THIS ESSAY APPEAR ON PAGES 304–5
SEE CATS. 121–136

JACQUES DE VITRY

Barbara Drake Boehm

As a patron, the churchman Jacques de Vitry (ca. 1160/70–1240) stands apart from the others celebrated in this volume and the exhibition it accompanies. He never commissioned a monument or a work of art for Jerusalem; in fact, he never set foot in the city. His deepest spiritual connection was to the Augustinian community at Oignies, in present-day France, near the Belgian border. Yet, Jacques de Vitry's legacy – his writings and precious objects – informs our understanding of the culture and art of the Holy Land in the early decades of the thirteenth century.

Jacques de Vitry's life journey led inexorably to the Holy Land. After studying at the University of Paris, he became the spiritual director for Marie of Oignies, a deeply religious ascetic to whom he was devoted, eventually becoming her biographer. By 1211 he was preaching in the diocese of Liège.[1] Renowned for his sermons exhorting men to take up the Cross, Jacques de Vitry attracted the attention of the pope and even Crusader chroniclers. And so it was, in 1214, that the canons of Acre – the port that had become the last outpost of European Christians in the Holy Land after the loss of Jerusalem to Saladin – elected him their bishop. Jacques de Vitry was at best ambivalent about this honor, and he tarried in Rome after his election. When no other post opened for him, he purchased a ship and stocked it with provisions, including thousands of books.[2] He arrived in Acre on November 4, 1216.[3]

While in the eastern Mediterranean, Jacques de Vitry wrote *History of the East and West* (*Historia orientalis et occidentalis*), weaving sacred history, Crusader adventure, natural history, and his own experience into a single narrative. Widely distributed in Europe,[4] the text conveyed with poetic cadence his longing for Jerusalem, which he called "the city of cities, the holy of holies, great among nations, princess among the provinces, by special prerogative called the city of the great king." He described the city in glowing terms as a woman: "She stands as if in the midst of the earth, in the centre of the world so all the nations shall flow into her. She is the possession of the patriarchs, the nursing mother of the prophets, the teacher of the apostles, the cradle of our salvation; the native country of the Lord, the mother of the faith, whereas Rome is the mother of the faithful; she had been chosen and sanctified by God, trodden by His feet, honoured by angels and frequented by every nation under heaven."[5]

By contrast, Acre's new bishop confessed that he was less impressed with the city where he was posted: "I found the town of Acre, like a monster or a beast, having nine heads, each fighting the other."[6] Still, in a flush of optimism, he recorded the efforts of resident Christians to secure their presence in the Holy Land: "Old churches were repaired, new ones built. Monasteries of regulars were constructed in suitable places. . . . Ministers of churches and other things required for divine worship and service were adequately and properly established everywhere. Holy men . . . sought out for themselves places appropriate to their way of life and greater devotion."[7]

Jacques de Vitry repeatedly emphasized appropriateness and propriety in religion, especially in his critique of Eastern Christians: "There were at that place [Acre] Jacobites with their archbishop, who in the manner of Jews, were circumcising their children and revealed their sins in confession to no one except to God . . . [and] when making the sign of cross signed themselves with one finger."[8] Concerning Syrian Christians, he observed, "Although their priests wore [clerical] headgear, they dressed their hair in the manner of lay people."[9] He further revealed that the abbots and priors under the direction of the patriarch of Jerusalem had the privilege of wearing insignia not usually accorded their rank: the crozier, miter, ring, and sandals.

Given his concerns about maintaining propriety, it is surprising that Jacques de Vitry gifted his own emblems of office to Oignies by 1221. It is also exceptionally fortunate, for few medieval church treasures of the Holy

Land have survived, or even are documented, from this period.[10] The crozier (cat. 124), ring (cat. 125), and, possibly, the Cross (cat. 126) shown here, together with his unusual parchment miter (fig. 89)[11] do not form a homogenous ensemble, and that is to be expected, for a number of chroniclers speak to the wealth and diversity of Acre's markets. The European chronicler Ludolph von Suchem, for one, claimed that in the city lived "the richest merchants under heaven, who were gathered together therein out of all nations . . . from sunrise to sunset all parts of the world brought merchandise thither."[12]

The bishop of Acre believed that most Muslims would convert to Christianity if given the option.[13] Thus, he equipped two ships at his own expense and on May 30, 1218, sailed to Damietta, in Egypt, with the Fifth Crusade.[14] The city fell in 1221, at which time Jacques de Vitry returned to Acre. Disheartened by the prospects for Christians in the Holy Land, he set his sights on home, traveling to Rome in 1223 and onward to Oignies in 1225. There, in 1227, he consecrated five new altars in the priory "for the adorning of which he had already sent gifts from the East"; relics in ivory boxes (cats. 127a–c) were likely among them.[15] Jacques de Vitry formally resigned as bishop of Acre and was named cardinal and bishop of Tusculum (modern Frascati, just south of Rome). As appropriate as it might have been, the claim that he was made titular Latin patriarch of Jerusalem at the end of his life stems from an early misreading of church documents.[16] He was buried in 1241 in Oignies, where his gift of silks, objects, relics, and treasured library of more than one thousand books was duly recorded.[17]

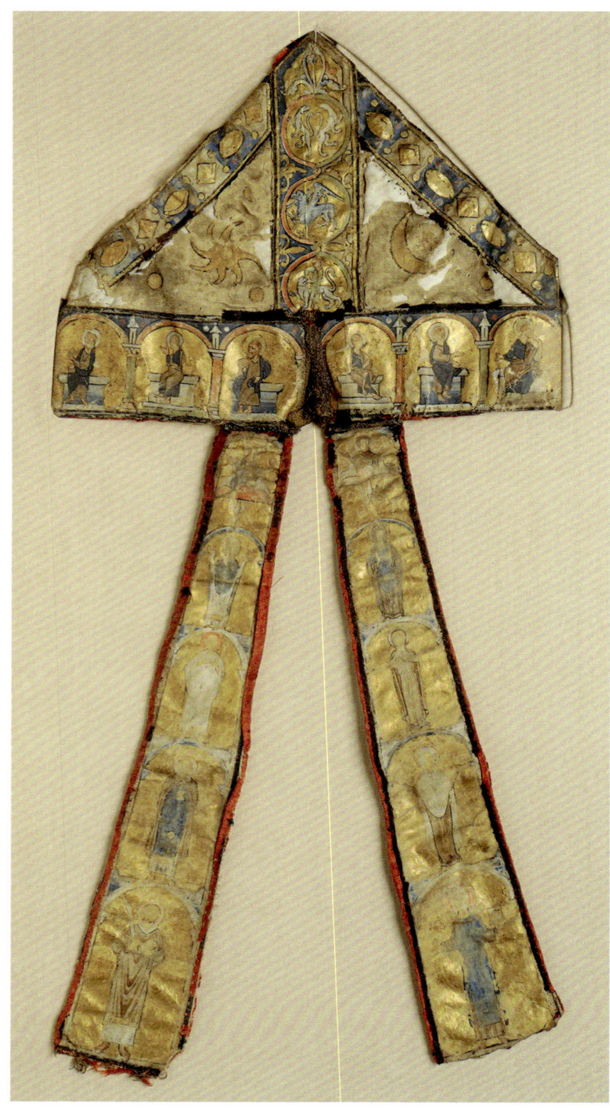

Fig. 89. Miter of Jacques de Vitry, Bishop of Acre. Latin Kingdom of Jerusalem (Acre), ca. 1216. Parchment and silk. Musée des Arts Anciens du Namurois, Namur

NOTES FOR THIS ESSAY APPEAR ON PAGE 305
SEE CATS. 124–127

THE ARMENIAN PRESENCE IN JERUSALEM

Helen C. Evans

FROM THE earliest days of the Christian faith, Armenians lived in and made pilgrimages to Jerusalem. According to tradition, the apostles Thaddeus and Bartholomew, seeking converts to Christianity, set out from the city along the northern trade routes to the Armenian homeland.[1] Cyril of Scythopolis (ca. 526–559), a monk in the Great Lavra of Saint Sabas, referred to Armenian pilgrims in Jerusalem in the late fifth century,[2] and floor mosaics in the city bearing Armenian inscriptions can be dated to the fifth to seventh century.[3] The largest and most handsome of these is a sixth-century memorial inscription on a floor just outside the Damascus Gate; it is decorated with an interlace pattern filled with birds, which in Armenian belief carry the souls of the dead to heaven (fig. 90).[4] Nearby, another inscription offers evidence of Armenian workers in the city about the same time: "Ewstat elder made this mosaic. Whoever enters this house, remember to Christ me and my brother Lukas."[5]

After Jerusalem fell to the Muslim Umayyad dynasty, in 638, Christian communities that were not aligned with the Orthodox Church of the Byzantine state, including the Armenians, grew in prominence.[6] In addition, the Armenian Church in Jerusalem

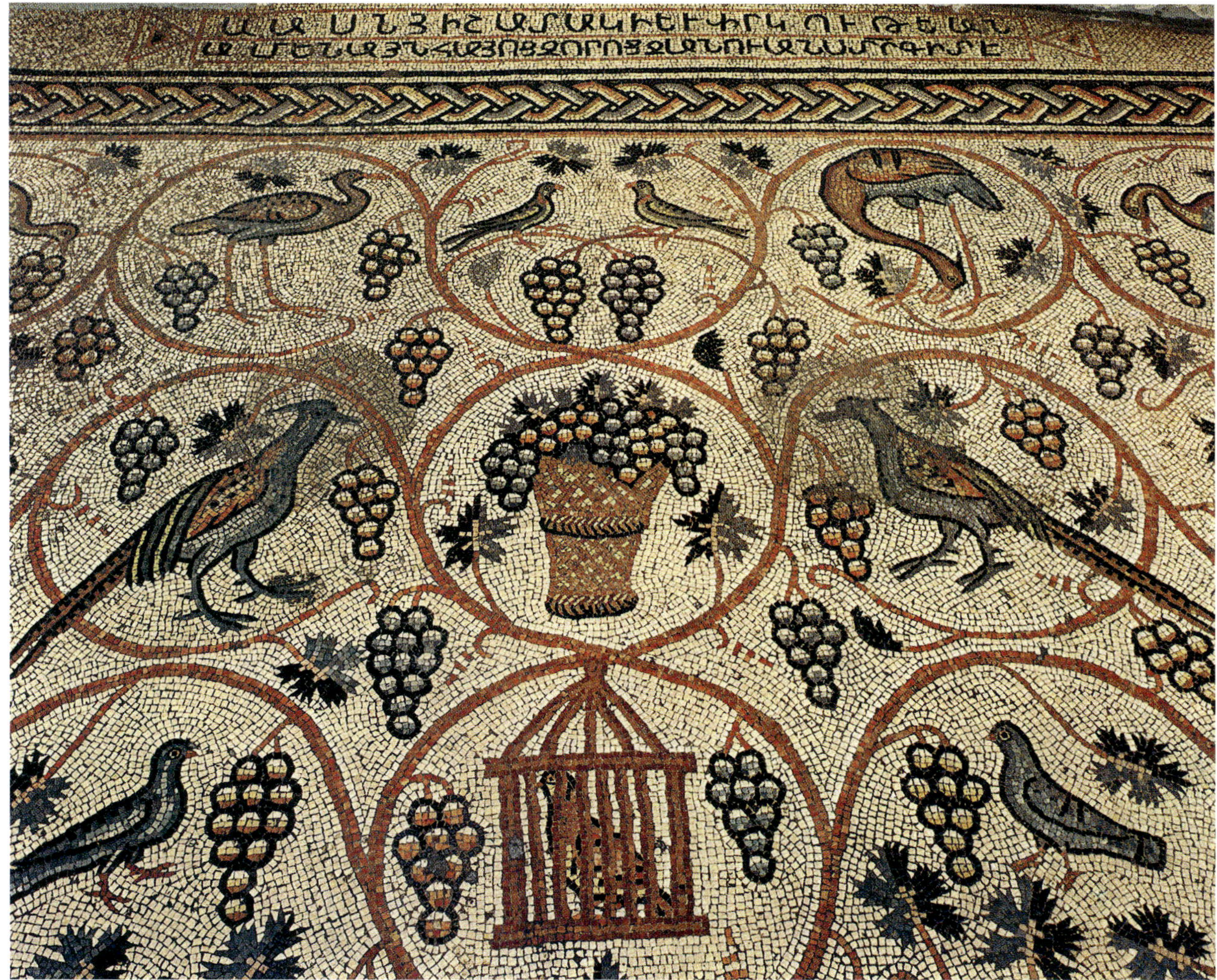

Fig. 90. Detail of an Armenian floor mosaic from a mortuary chapel near the Damascus Gate, Jerusalem. Jerusalem, 6th century

became increasingly independent of the patriarchate in the Armenian homeland amid the political turmoil resulting from the spread of Islam. By the fourteenth century the Armenian clergy in Jerusalem, called the Brotherhood of Saint James, enjoyed special status among the other major centers of the Armenian Church,[7] reflecting the traditional importance of the city's holy sites to the Christians of Greater Armenia. Indeed, at the beginning of the tenth century, Gagik Artsruni, the ruler of the Armenian kingdom of Vaspurakan in the Armenian homeland, had built a church on Mount Van evoking sacred spaces in Jerusalem, including the "upper room of the mystical celebration of the transmission of the new covenant" and "the crucifixion of the Lord at Golgotha."[8]

In the eleventh century, as Crusaders arrived from Europe, the Armenians, who had a similar social structure, became ready allies of their fellow Christians. Armenians connected to the kingdom of Edessa (which controlled the land in and around the city of Edessa, present-day Şanlıurfa, Turkey) were instrumental in aiding the Crusaders' approach to Jerusalem in the First Crusade.[9] The Armenian chronicler Matthew of Edessa (d. 1136/44) described the Crusaders' conquest of the city, in 1099, as "fulfilling the prophecy of the Armenian patriarch Nerses, who said 'The deliverance of Jerusalem will come from the Franks, but because of their sins the city once again will fall into the hands of the infidels.'"[10]

The emerging states of the Latin Kingdom profited from political alliances with and military assistance from the Armenians. In the mid-twelfth century Toros II (r. 1144/45–69), ruler of the Armenian kingdom of Cilicia, on the Mediterranean coast between Turkey and Syria, visited Jerusalem and offered Amalric of Jerusalem (r. 1163–74) thirty thousand Armenian settlers.[11] William, archbishop of Tyre (ca. 1130–1186), recorded the respect offered the Armenian Catholicos Krikor III Bahlavouni (1113–1166) when the latter came to Jerusalem in 1142 for a Latin church council.[12] As allies of the Crusaders, the Armenians, in turn, gained new authority within Jerusalem following the 1099 conquest. The power of Cilicia in the region is demonstrated by the fact that the early Crusader rulers of Jerusalem often had wives from prominent Armenian families: Baldwin of Edessa, the first king of Crusader Jerusalem (r. 1100–1118), was married to Arda, a niece of Constantin, who in the late eleventh century controlled the lands around the castle at Vahka in Cilicia (now in Feke, Turkey); Joscelin of Courtenay, ruler of Edessa (r. 1119–31), married Constantin's daughter; and Baldwin II, king of Jerusalem (r. 1118–31), spoke fluent Armenian and was married to Morfia, daughter of Gabriel, an Armenian of the Orthodox Greek faith who ruled Melitene.[13] Morfia's daughter, Queen Melisende of Jerusalem, was well aware that her mother was an Armenian, as evidenced by Melisende's relief efforts for Armenian and Syrian survivors of the fall of Edessa in 1144.[14]

Beginning in the medieval period (and continuing to this day), the Armenians occupied the southwestern quarter of the Old City and possessed a number of churches there.[15] In the twelfth century they erected the imposing Cathedral of Saint James (figs. 29, 91), believed to house the Armenian Church's most important relic, the head of Saint James the Greater. The German pilgrim John of Würzburg described the site about 1160 with an admiration echoed by later accounts, including those of Niccolo of Poggibonsi (ca. 1350) and John Poloner (1422).[16] The interior of the large structure joins a traditional Armenian domed, central-plan church to elements, such as surviving capitals, based on Crusader architecture.[17] Other medieval pilgrims recorded the presence of Armenians in the city and remarked on their role as guardians — along with the Byzantines and the Franciscans — of the Church of the Holy Sepulchre and the Church of the Nativity, in Bethlehem.[18] The intricately carved center door of the narthex in Bethlehem has an inscription identifying it as a gift in 1227 from Hetoum I, king of Cilicia.[19] (Today, the Armenians still control parts of the Church of the Nativity and the Holy Sepulchre, including the Chapel of Saint Helena (fig. 92), mother of Constantine the Great, which is also referred to as the Chapel of Saint Gregory the Illuminator, who is credited with converting the Armenian king Trdat and his people to Christianity at the beginning of the fourth century.)[20]

Jerusalem fell to Saladin, founder of the Ayyubid dynasty, in 1189. Two years later the Armenian Catholicos Grigor Tghay (1133–1193) wrote the long

"Poem of Lamentation over the Capture of Jerusalem." There decrying the loss of the city, he sought to place the Cilician ruling prince Leo II as the Eastern Christian leader who would aid in its reconquest by the newly declared Third Crusade. The poet's wish for the Rubenid prince to be king of an independent kingdom of Cilicia succeeded soon after the poem was written, as in 1198/99 Leo II received a king's crown through Pope Clement III (r. 1187–91) and the Holy Roman Emperor Frederick I (r. 1155–90).[21] By 1254 the kingdom was powerful enough that Louis IX of France, who led the Seventh Crusade against Ayyubid Egypt, left his young vassal, the heir to the Crusader kingdom of Antioch, as the Cilician king Hetoum I's ward.[22]

Following the defeat of Louis IX's forces and the collapse of the Ayyubid dynasty, power in the region shifted to the Mamluks. As a consequence, Armenians increasingly came to Jerusalem for safety, as they had in the past (the chronicler Abu Salih, probably writing in the thirteenth century, described the warm welcome the Armenian patriarch, fleeing Egypt with his church's treasure that included seventy-five books, had been given in 1172).[23] By the fourteenth century, however, the Mamluk sultanate extended its control to Jerusalem and was seen as a threat to the Armenians there, who feared reprisals for other conflicts in the region involving Armenians. In 1335, for example, the scribe Nerses Krakc'i wrote in a colophon that "we are told . . . they will assemble all Armenian Christians in one place and slaughter us" to avenge the deaths of Mamluks in Cilicia.[24] By the time another colophon was written, in 1373, Jerusalem was again stable enough that a monk from Greater Armenia could encourage pilgrimage to the city he believed to be "the centre from which all laws, grace and prophecy emanate."[25]

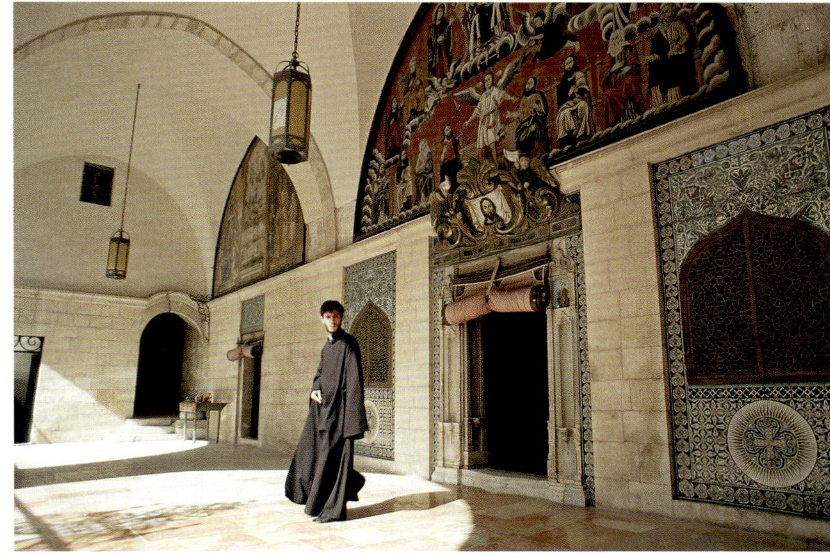

Fig. 91. Entrance to the Cathedral of Saint James, Jerusalem

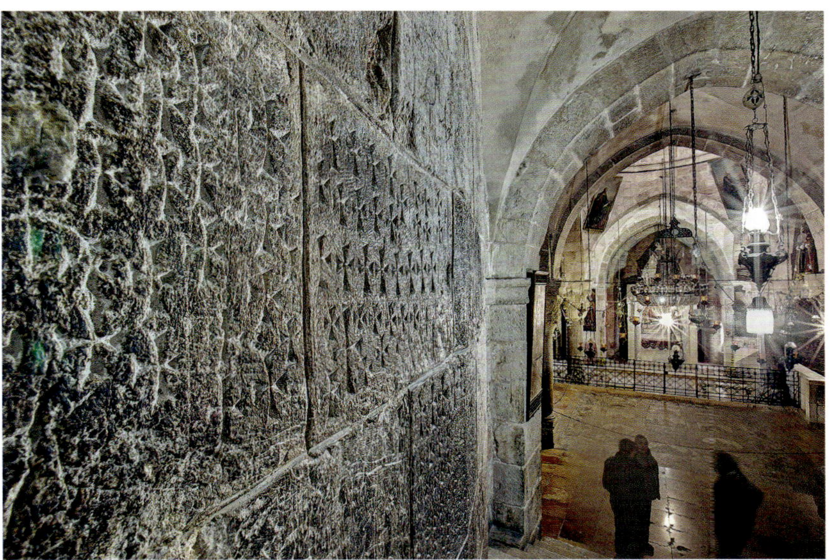

Fig. 92. Crosses carved by pilgrims into the walls of the Church of the Holy Sepulchre, Jerusalem, leading to the Armenian Chapel of Saint Helena

NOTES FOR THIS ESSAY APPEAR ON PAGE 305
SEE CATS. 49, 130, 131

FRANCISCANS IN JERUSALEM: THE EARLY HISTORY

Xavier John Seubert

THE FRANCISCAN order's association with the Holy Land began with Saint Francis of Assisi himself, who in 1219 accompanied the Fifth Crusade bound for Jerusalem. In his effort to preach to the Saracens (the European Christians' term for Muslims), he was captured and brought before Sultan Malik al-Kamil (r. 1218–38). Francis remained in the Saracen camp for what was likely about three weeks, during which time he and the sultan, known for his great learning, discussed their ideas on God. Their ensuing friendship tempered the friars' attitude toward Muslims and that of the sultans toward the Franciscans, both in Francis's time and for years to come.[1]

The Franciscans seek to emulate the life of their patron saint, who founded the order in the early thirteenth century in Italy. They live and preach the Gospel of Jesus Christ, taking vows of rigorous poverty and dedication to the poor. Unlike monks with a vow of stability, the original Franciscan brothers, although attached to a specific friary, were itinerant, preaching the Gospel wherever they moved around the world. That Jerusalem was a key destination was not unusual, since Francis encouraged travel to the Islamic lands: "Let those brothers who wish by divine inspiration to go among the Saracens or other non-believers ask permission to go from their provincial ministers."[2] The passage reflects what had occurred in Francis's exchange with al-Kamil and fostered Franciscan settlement in Morocco, Syria, and Palestine.[3]

By 1230 a group of Franciscans had secured a living space from the Latin Patriarchate in Jerusalem and use of a chapel in the Church of the Holy Sepulchre. The Monastery of the Holy Sepulchre was the second one established in Judea but the fifth in the province of Syria. The first and principal house was located on Mount Sion. From the letters of various sultans to the guardians, or superiors, of Mount Sion, it can be concluded that the friars obtained permission to live at the Holy Sepulchre from Salahad, son of al-Kamil, shortly after the capture of Jerusalem by the Khwarezmian Turks in 1244. Salahad further charged the friars with guarding the Tomb of Christ and, owing to his special regard for the order, engaged them as legates to Pope Innocent IV (r. 1243–54).[4]

At a major gathering of the Franciscans in Narbonne, in present-day France, in 1260, the Franciscan province of Syria (or of the Holy Land) was established and subdivided into two smaller units, or custodies. The provincial headquarters, housing sixty friars, was located at Acre, and after the fall of the city, in 1291, the plight of Christians living in Jerusalem became desperate.[5] The Franciscan presence was maintained only through extraordinary acts of diplomacy. Pope Nicholas IV (r. 1288–92), himself a Franciscan, requested from the sultan that Latin clergy be allowed to live in the Holy City. The sultan, assenting, asked the pope to send to Jerusalem clerics, monks, and peaceful men, further decreeing that daily alms be given to the hospital there.[6]

Taxation for the use of Christian shrines was a lucrative business for Muslims, and throughout their history in Jerusalem the Franciscans repeatedly needed to secure their presence through the political and financial intercession of powerful patrons. About a century after their first settlement at the Holy Sepulchre, James II, king of Aragon, "requested that the Friars Minor be able to enjoy a place of prayer in the Church of the Holy Sepulchre and another place close to this one where they ought to be able to serve God and welcome pilgrims. He requested further that they be able to circulate freely in the territories belonging to the sultan and that they be exempt from the payment of taxes, and other payments."[7]

In 1300 Robert of Anjou, king of Naples, voyaged as a pilgrim with safe-conduct from Sultan al-Nasir Muhammad ibn Qala'un to ascertain the state of affairs of Christians in Jerusalem. Nearly a decade later, in 1309, he journeyed to Egypt to beg the new sultan,

Baybars II, to turn over to the Franciscans jurisdiction of the church on Mount Sion, the Virgin's Chapel in the Church of the Holy Sepulchre, the Tomb of Saint Mary in the Valley of Jehoshaphat, and the Cave of the Nativity in Bethlehem, the right for which Robert paid 32,000 ducats.[8] That year, Baybars issued a document allowing the Franciscans to establish themselves on Mount Sion, at the Holy Sepulchre, and at the Church of the Nativity in Bethlehem (cat. 132).

Baybars's decree initiated a steady increase in the number of such documents, together with acts of purchase, juridical decisions, and friendly transactions, and by 1333 the Franciscan order had become the official representatives of Roman Catholicism in Jerusalem's holy places. They established their headquarters at the cenacle on Mount Sion, obtained from a "buyback" of sites from al-Nasir Muhammad, who had by then reassumed the Mamluk throne, for 20,000 ducats.[9] The Franciscan presence was confirmed canonically by Pope Clement VI in 1342 with the publication of his *We Give Thanks* (*Gratias agimus*) and *Some Time Ago* (*Nuper carissimae*), the bulls that established Franciscan Custody of the Holy Land (Custodia Terrae Sanctae).[10]

The order's influence in the Holy Land continued to grow; at its height in the fifteenth century, the brothers occupied four friaries in Jerusalem: at the Holy Sepulchre, Mount Sion, the Tomb of the Virgin, and the Garden of Gethsemane. Outside Jerusalem they had jurisdiction over the birthplace of Jesus at Bethlehem and a friary in Beirut.[11] A richly illuminated antiphonary (fig. 93; cat. 134a–c) bears beautiful witness to the daily devotions of the Franciscan community in the Holy Land in the late medieval period. It is this same devotion that marks the abiding Franciscan presence there to the present day.

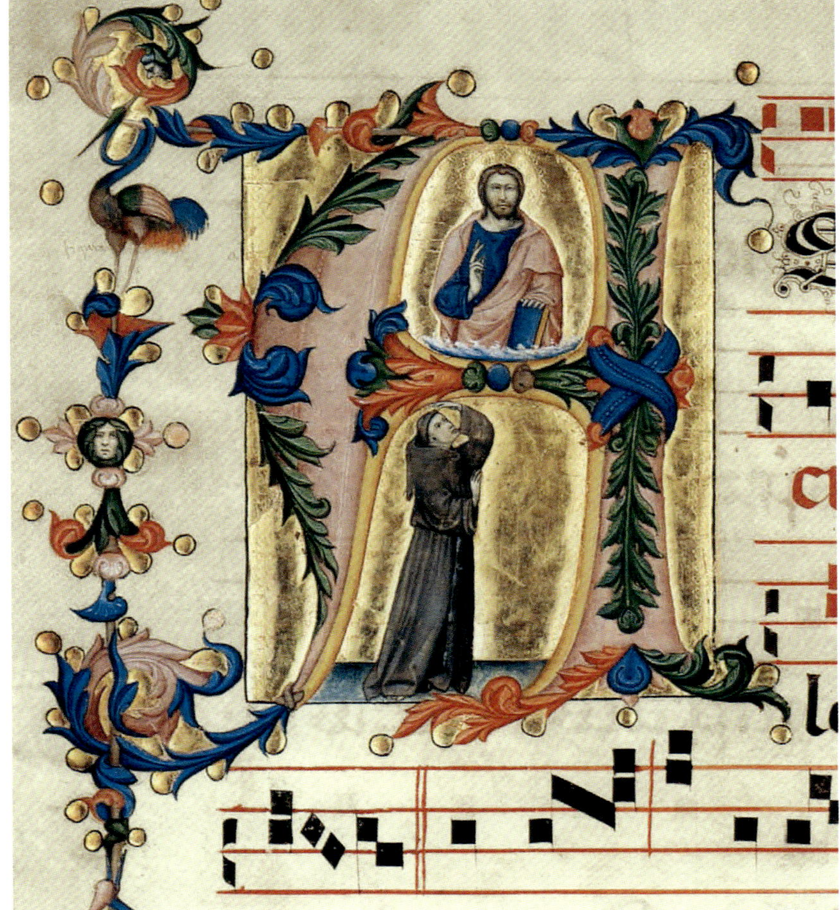

Fig. 93. Initial "A" with Christ blessing and a Franciscan friar, formerly bound with cat. 134a–c. Private collection, Europe

NOTES FOR THIS ESSAY APPEAR ON PAGE 305

SEE CATS. 101, 132–134

MUSLIM WOMEN PATRONS IN JERUSALEM

Yusuf Natsheh

WITHIN PATRIARCHAL societies of the time, Islam nevertheless established equality between men and women in religious duties and obligations and encouraged pious acts toward God and the search for knowledge by both.

The economic, cultural, and political status of some women in Jerusalem – among them princesses, wives of sultans, and mothers or wives of rulers and notables – led to their emergence in positions close to the governing power. These women played an extraordinary role in sponsoring charitable urban projects. Because of the lofty status of Jerusalem in Arab history and Islamic doctrine, the city attracted a number of devout wealthy women over the centuries, who embarked on the task of building beautiful monuments, which they secured for the future with generous endowments. The precursor for this directive can be attributed to the Abbasid period, when the mother of Caliph Muqtadir Billah (r. 903–32) took it upon herself to renovate the gates of the Dome of the Rock. During the Mamluk period, one of peace and stability, Jerusalem witnessed a variety of women's activities, ranging from caring for the poor and Sufi mystics to the endowment of larger copper cauldrons for local soup kitchens or providing Qur'an manuscripts for madrasas on the Haram al-Sharif, various theological schools, and Sufi foundations to undertaking monumental architectural projects.

Construction of the largest secular structure in Jerusalem, the Dar al-Sit Tinshuq (ca. 1388) – indeed the only palace in Jerusalem – is attributed to Lady Tunshuq al-Mazfariyya. Tunshuq, whose name in Turkish means "precious and wonderful," was a generous and compassionate woman, who fell in love with Jerusalem and gave the city a rare architectural jewel. Her wealth was evident from the massive size of her castle, its intricate ornamental details, and the amount of the endowment she created, reaching close to 100,000 dirhams, which was spent to purchase and endow a third of the village of Bayt Safafa in Jerusalem.

The largest and greatest social charitable institution from the Ottoman period, not only in Jerusalem but across Palestine and the Levant, is known as the Prosperous Building (1552–53). It was attributed to Roxelana, wife of the Ottoman sultan Süleyman the Magnificent (r. 1520–66). She was known by the name Khasqi Sultan, which indicates that she was the favorite and the beloved of the sultan, and in Turkish by the name Kharm, which holds many meanings, among them "the playful," "the cheerful," and "the joyful." It seems that her beauty, intelligence, and personality persuaded the sultan to free her from slavery and later to marry her. (It is well known that the sultan remained faithful to her from the time they met until her death.)[1] Khasqi Sultan was intent on administering the menu and the distribution of food for the building, stipulating that two kinds of soups be prepared daily. The building employed fifty people and was supported by the revenue of fifty towns and villages.

In addition, women established and endowed three schools, a tomb, and a shelter for the poor in Jerusalem. Turkan Khatoun, the daughter of an Uzbek prince who descended from Turkic sultans, decided to settle in the city and remained there until her death.[2] In 1352–53 she built for herself a tomb (*turba*), located on the northern side of the Bab al-Silsila road.[3] The building is a domed structure with a mihrab and a dedicatory inscription; red and cream-colored marble typical of Mamluk architecture and known as *ablaq* provides decoration at the windows.

The judge and historian Mujir al-Din recounted that two women from the city of Mardeen (Mardin, in present-day Turkey) embarked on building a shelter for the poor in Jerusalem about 1361.[4] Situated on the western side of Bab Hitta Street, the new building, known as the Mardeeni Hospice (Ribat al-Mardini), was linked to their city and designated for women visitors coming from the city of Mardeen. The influential Ottoman woman Asfahan Khatun, also known as Khanum, was involved in building and endowing what came to be known as the 'Uthmaniyya School in 1436–37.[5] This endowment covered the expenses of a caretaker, a teacher, a Qur'an reader, nine students, and a few Sufi

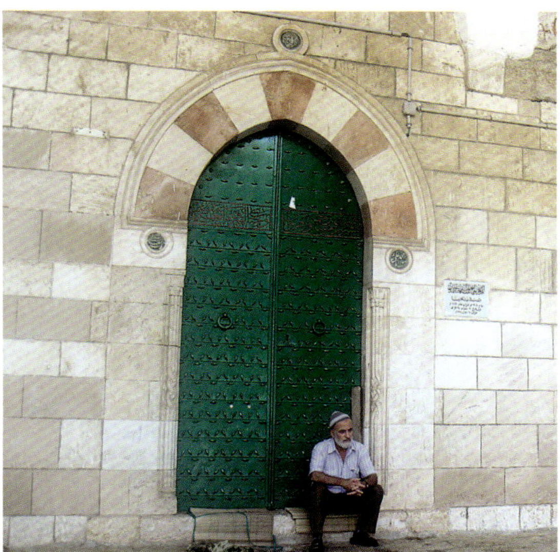

Fig. 94. Entrance to the Khatuni School, Jerusalem

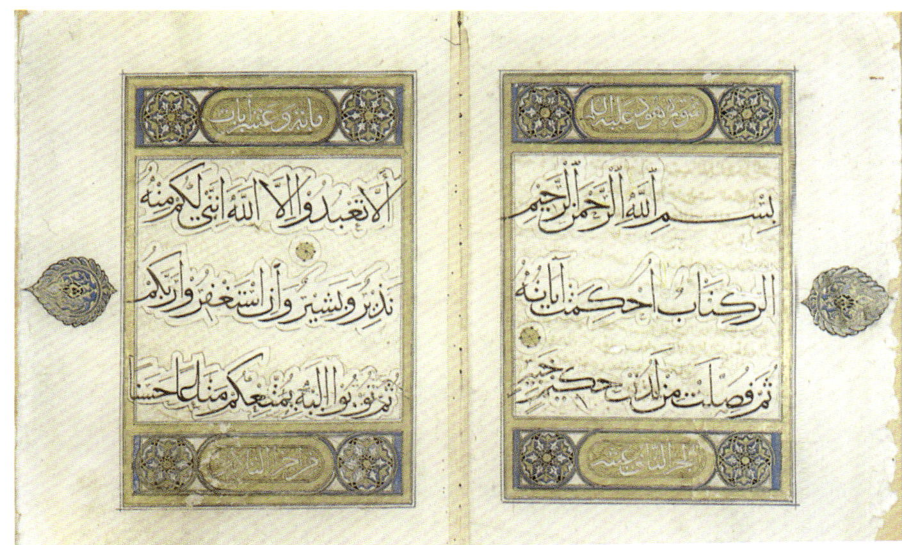

Fig. 95. Qur'an endowed by *Hajja* Ogul Khatun for the *zawiya* she had built in Jerusalem. 1358. Gold and ink on paper. Islamic Museum and Al-Aqsa Library, Jerusalem

mystics. The madrasa is located along the western wall of al-Aqsa Mosque.

The Qazani Baghdadi woman Ogul Khatun, daughter of Shams al-Din, built a *zawiya* (a type of school or lodging) in a prime location that came to be known as the Khatuni School (fig. 94). The school was part of the corridor found between the gate of the Cotton Market (Bab Suq al-Qattanin) and the Iron Gate (Bab al-Hadid). It contains an assembly hall with a mihrab and a tomb chamber (presumed to be that of the donor) marked by a dome.[6]

Construction of the Khatuni School was completed by 1380, which marked the date of a second endowment, by Isfahan Shah, daughter of the amir Qazan Shah. (Perhaps she was the daughter of Ogul Khatun, inspired to further her mother's charitable gift.)[7] The second endowment added land in Damascus and in Jerusalem, including a house in an area known as the Sion Quarter and a shop in the Cotton Market.

Although it has been suggested that both women were pilgrims, the commissioning of a Qur'an manuscript by Isfahan suggests that she was resident in Jerusalem for some time. The endowment (or waqf) describes Ogul Khatun as "the builder of charitable and pious [institutions], the special nurturer of princes and sultans, the *Hajja* Ogul Khatun, daughter of the emir Muhammad, son of the emir Thawr."[8] Inferring from the text of Mujir al-Din, it appears that the school was used in part as a residence for "emirs of some distinction sent to Jerusalem under a cloud."[9] Clearly it was in active use, because in 1574–75 the expenditures included repairs to the room for the Qur'an and the Qur'an stand, as well as new mats purchased for the madrasa.[10] The Qur'an manuscript would appear to correspond to the Rab'ah, all thirty volumes of which constitute a complete Qur'an, endowed in Ramadan 760 (July–August 1359), of which only one volume survives (fig. 95).[11]

Mujir al-Din attested that Misr Khatun, following in a similar tradition and acting on behalf of her husband, Nasir al-Din Muhammad bin Dilgar, the Turkman prince of Delgar, established the Ghadiriyya Madrasa in 1432 in the northern part of the Haram al-Sharif between the Lions' Gate (Bab al-Asbaat) and the Hitta Gate.[12] Originally a two-story structure, it was endowed with appropriate personnel, including fourteen Sufis. After his wife's death, the prince redoubled the endowment, augmenting its income with revenue from the Date Market in Aleppo. Moreover, he stipulated that the oversight of the waqf be placed in the hands of a daughter of the sultan, suggesting his awareness of and support for the key and abiding role played by women as patrons of the city of Jerusalem over the centuries.[13]

NOTES FOR THIS ESSAY APPEAR ON PAGE 305
SEE CAT. 136

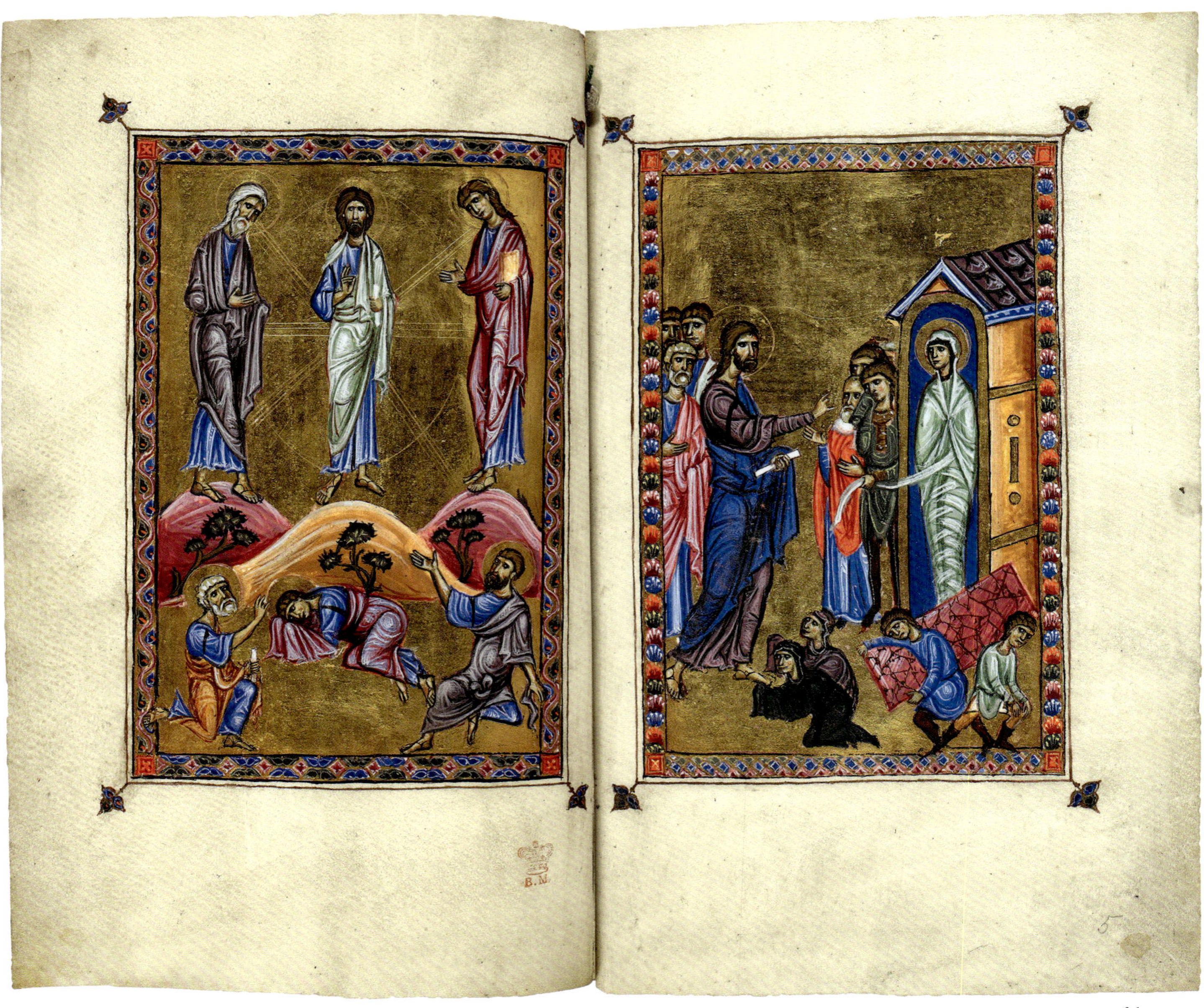

121, fols. 4v–5r

121

The Psalter of Melisende, Queen of Jerusalem

Jerusalem, Scriptorium of the Holy Sepulchre, ca. 1135
Tempera, gold, and ink on parchment; 218 folios
Binding: ivory covers with semiprecious stones and silk-embroidered spine
8½ × 5½ in. (21.6 × 14 cm)
British Library, London (Egerton MS 113; ivory covers held separately)

Basilius, a Byzantine-trained artist of European or Crusader origin, painted the twenty-four prefatory miniatures of the Melisende Psalter, to which the Transfiguration (folio 4 verso), the Raising of Lazarus (folio 5 recto), and the Entry into Jerusalem (folio 5 verso) belong. His signature appears on the Deesis miniature on folio 12 verso. Although a prefatory cycle of scenes from the Life of Christ for a psalter is a contemporary Western innovation, seen first in England, these miniatures are mainly Byzantine in inspiration. The Transfiguration demonstrates Basilius's command of the well-known imagery and figural style used to convey this important scene in eleventh- and twelfth-century manuscripts and icons, visible here in the handling of the mountaintops and the dynamic poses of the apostles Peter, John, and James below. On the other hand, the Entry into Jerusalem has been modified from its Byzantine sources, eliminating figures holding palm fronds in order to compress the scene into a vertical rectangular frame.

The Raising of Lazarus is of special interest, foremost for its unusual imagery: "the tomb is not carved out of the rock, as in most Byzantine representations of the scene, but forms the arched entrance of an ordinary building; and the tombstone is held in a slanting position in the right-hand corner, not . . . by one man only, but by two."[1] The composition recalls the Lazarus scene from about 1149 at the far left of the figural lintel of the Church of the Holy Sepulchre in Jerusalem, where Lazarus similarly emerges from beneath a prominent arch as two men handle the tombstone (fig. 45). Both cases represent the presence of the Western Romanesque in an otherwise strongly Byzantine-looking miniature. This latter point is particularly interesting in light of the fact that, in the late 1130s, Melisende helped commission a convent at Bethany dedicated to Saint Lazarus for her youngest sister, Iveta.[2] Melisende was also involved in the renovation and expansion of the Holy Sepulchre later in the 1140s, and the prominence of the Lazarus scene on the church's lintel might be linked to her patronage.

Basilius is only one of four painters who worked on this manuscript. A second Western artist painted medallions with signs of the zodiac in a handsome Romanesque style for the calendar. A third artist, fully the equal of

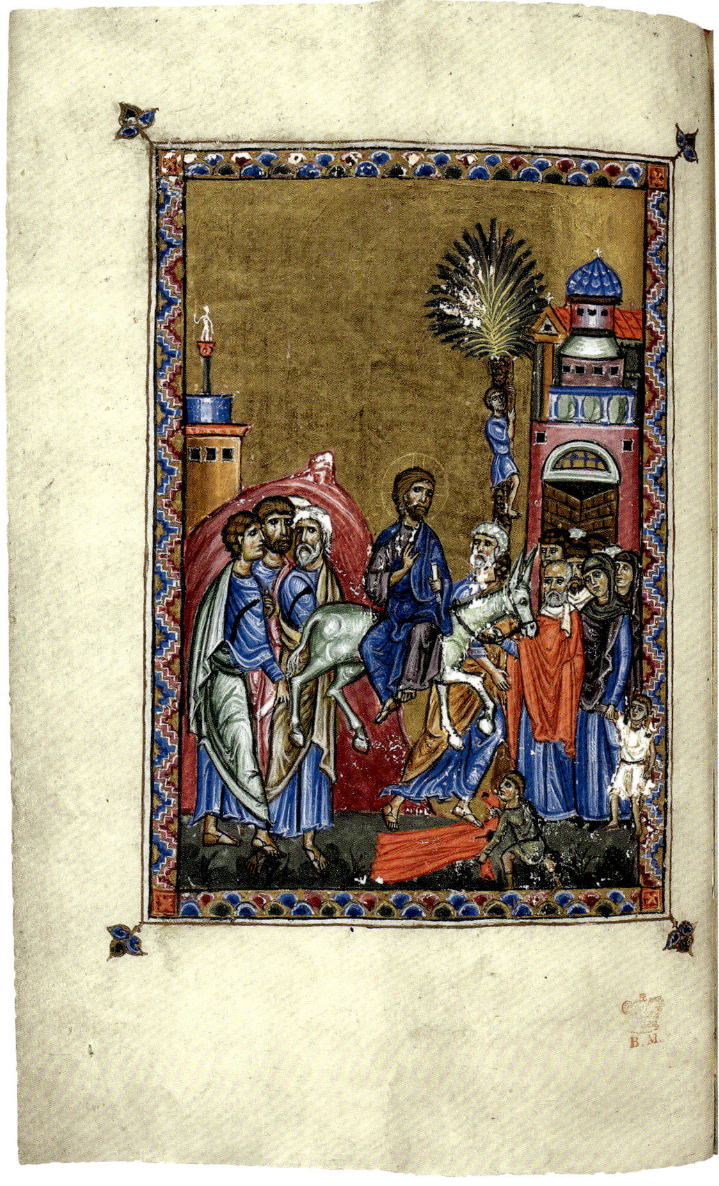

121, fol. 5v

Basilius in quality, combined Anglo-Italian figural decoration with geometric designs inspired by Islamic art for the eight divisions of the psalter text. A fourth illuminator painted a series of small icons, in effect, as headpieces for the prayers to nine saints following the psalter. This artist was trained in the Romanesque style but inspired by Byzantine art to produce figures that are flat, decorative, and abstract. This combination of Eastern and Western styles and iconography renders it both plausible and appropriate that these paintings by four diverse artists originated in a Crusader scriptorium in Jerusalem.

Other aspects of the text and decoration are relevant to Melisende. It is clear from the use of the noun *peccatrix* (the female form of "sinner") and from feminine adjective forms that the prayers following the litanies of the saints were tailored for a woman. That the intended reader was Iveta is unlikely, for the psalter lacks prayers to Lazarus — an expected inclusion for a manuscript made for a convent dedicated to the saint. Included instead are prayers to the Virgin and Mary Magdalene, which would have been of interest to Melisende owing to her likely membership in the confraternity founded about 1122 in connection with the abbey of Saint Mary in the Valley of Jehoshaphat in Jerusalem, at the site of the Tomb of the Virgin.[3] Indeed, Melisende ordered her own tomb placed at the entrance to the Virgin's sepulchre, where it survives to this day.

Other features linking the manuscript to Melisende concern her husband, King Fulk, to whom the inscription "Herodius" on the bottom cover has traditionally been thought to refer. The name appears above the large bird between the top two medallions, just below the outer border. This type of bird is known in bestiaries by the genus *Fulica*, hence the idea that Herodius is a rebus for Fulk. Melisende may have seen in these images of Crusader kings "the ideal of her husband, as the Christian ruler. This ruler is also a successor of David, the author of the Psalms, in a special way, as a king in Jerusalem. At the same time he is also the 'Blessed man' of the opening words of Psalm 1."[4]

One final, remarkable feature of this manuscript is the three-part program of decoration on the covers. Embellishing the top cover are six medallions with images from the life of David, the royal ancestor of Christ. The Virtues and Vices appear in the interstices in a representation of the *Contest of the Soul* (*Psychomachia*), the Classical allegory in which Virtue outnumbers and triumphs over Vice — in effect, a symbol of David's and the Crusaders' victory in the Holy Land.

The spine is decorated with silver-embroidered crosses, which find echoes in the red, green, and blue silk equal-armed crosses running along the vertical axis. The crosses may symbolize the Christian era in the Holy Land, for they provide a physical and symbolic link to the bottom cover and its six medallions with Christian royal figures performing the Corporal Works of Mercy (Matthew 25:35–36). The figures wear either Byzantine- or Western-style royal garments and exemplify Byzantine and Crusader rulers carrying out the charitable teachings of Jesus Christ.

The three elements of the binding are unified visually by their shared patterns of medallions and lozenges. In a much broader sense, however, they express the ideals of the royal presence in Jerusalem and the Holy Land as proclaimed in the Old and New Testaments. Compounding the symbolism is Christ's message referring to the Last Judgment and to the triumph of Christian ideals in the era of the New Covenant. Both are linked to the psalms and prayers contained within the psalter, to be read by its royal patron and its royal owner.

Were the patron and owner one and the same? In the absence of a colophon or other explicit indication by the book's French scribe, the book's ownership was assigned to Melisende by the nineteenth-century scholar Sir Frederic Madden, who, like others, observed that the calendar for this codex, which is remarkably English in its content, includes entries of particular relevance for her.[5] The entry for August 21, for instance, "Obiit Balduinus rex Ierusalem II," refers to the death of Melisende's French father, Baldwin II, which occurred in 1131. The entry for October 1, "Obiit Emorfia Ierusalem regina," refers to the death of her Armenian mother shortly after that of her father. Significantly, there is no entry for Fulk, who died in 1143, so he was presumably alive when this book was made. One other relevant entry is

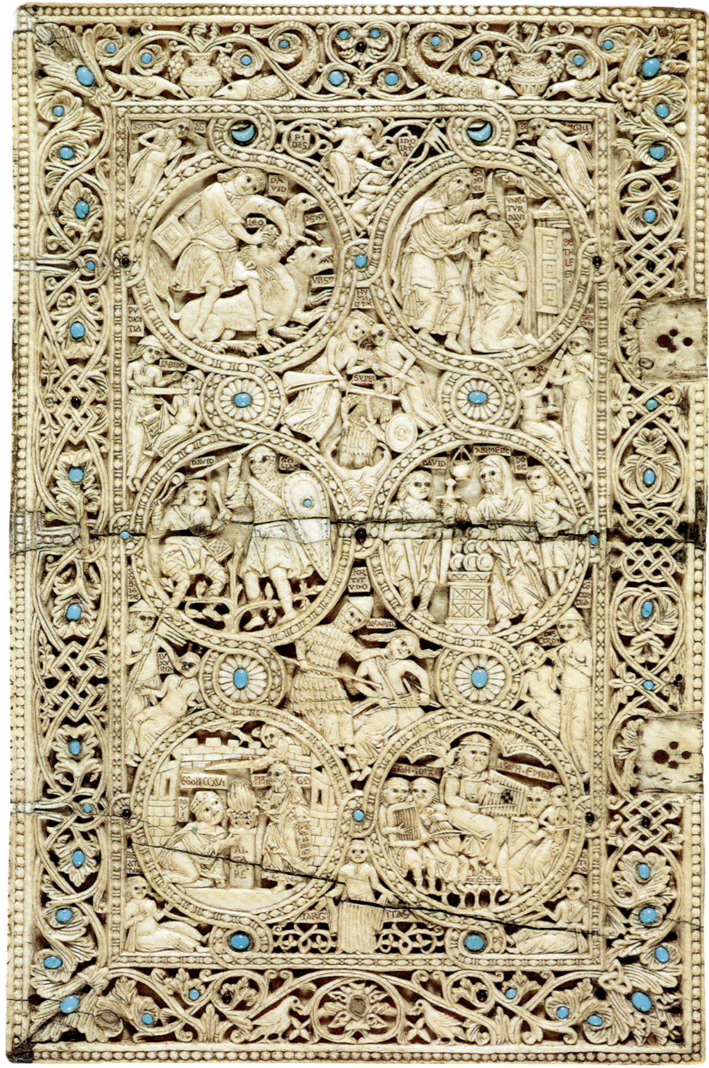

121 top cover

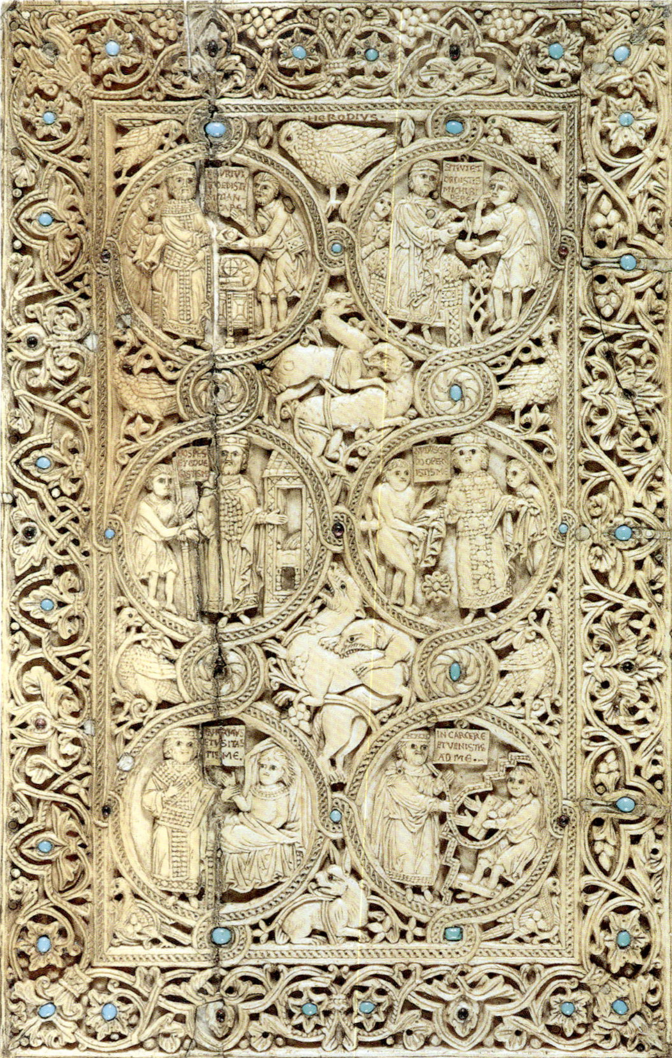

121 bottom cover

for July 15, "Eodem die capta est Ierusalem," which refers to the capture of Jerusalem during the First Crusade, in 1099. By contrast, there is no reference to the dedication of the Holy Sepulchre, on July 15, 1149, providing indications that this book was made between 1131 and 1143. But when exactly, and for whom?

The case has been made that King Fulk commissioned the psalter for his queen.[6] With no expense spared, so exquisite was its execution that this superb manuscript remains the best-known work of art associated with Melisende. Together with the four illuminators and one scribe mentioned above, at least two ivory carvers and one embroiderer were engaged to produce a book of the highest quality, one that reflected the rich heritage and stature of the queen of the multicultural city of Jerusalem.

The historical setting for this commission has been identified as the confrontation that began between king and queen in 1131, at the advent of their joint rule, and continued until their reconciliation in late 1134–early 1135. Fulk at first attempted to rule alone, despite the fact that, before he died, Baldwin II had conferred the *cura regni* and the *plena potestas* (full powers) on Fulk, Melisende, and their son, Baldwin III.[7] By 1134 Melisende had grown outraged at Fulk's attempt to deprive her of her proper role.[8] In response, in 1135 Fulk sought reconciliation with his wife and "did not attempt [thereafter] to take the initiative, even in trivial matters, without her knowledge and assistance."[9]

It is clear to the present author that Fulk ordered this magnificent psalter as a personal and important gift for his wife, one that reflected her royal stature, individual spirituality, refined tastes, and artistic sensibilities. He included references to himself to attest to his sincerity, hoping that this gift would repair the damage he had done to their relationship. He carried out this campaign of contrition as expeditiously as possible in 1135, with the goal of reestablishing peace with his "vigorous, proud, and ambitious" co-ruler of the Latin Kingdom of Jerusalem.[10] The fact that William of Tyre's detailed account of the confrontation makes no mention of this psalter suggests that it was an extremely private, personal gift from a king attempting to regain the confidence and high regard of his queen.

JF

Selected References: Manuscript illuminations: Buchthal and Wormald 1957, pp. 1–14, 122–28, 132–34, 139–40; Kühnel, B., 1994, pp. 53, 63, 64, 66, 95, 124, 166, 167; Folda 1995, pp. 137–59, pls. 8–10; Zeitler 2000; Folda 2012b, pp. 448–59. Covers and spine: Cahier 1874, pp. 1–14; Dalton 1909, pp. 22–26; Granger-Taylor 1994; Kühnel, B., 1994, pp. 67–125; Steenbock 2004, pp. 439–40; Backhouse 2006.

1. Hugo Buchthal in Buchthal and Wormald 1957, p. 5.
2. William of Tyre 1943 ed., vol. 2, bk. 15, chap. 26.
3. Francis Wormald in Buchthal and Wormald 1957, pp. 127, 132.
4. John Lowden in London 1994, pp. 165–66, no. 181.
5. Backhouse 2006, p. 459. Madden was Keeper of Manuscripts at the British Museum, London, from 1828 to 1866. On the English nature of the calendar, see Wormald in Buchthal and Wormald 1957, pp. 122–23, and Zeitler 2000, pp. 71–74. Zeitler places great stress on the English aspects of this manuscript as a whole.
6. Folda 1995, pp. 154–58; Folda 2012b, pp. 435, 437.
7. Mayer, H., 1972, p. 100. *Cura regni* is Latin for "care of the kingdom" and *plena potestas* "full power of government."
8. Ibid., pp. 100–104; Hamilton, B., 1978, pp. 149–51. There were other important problems as well that made Melisende so angry.
9. William of Tyre 1943 ed., vol. 2, and William of Tyre 1986 ed., bk. 14, chaps. 15–18.
10. Mayer, H., 1972, pp. 104–6; William of Tyre 1943 ed., vol. 2, and William of Tyre 1986 ed., bk. 15, chap. 26.

122

Initial "R" Showing the Death of King Baldwin II with Fulk and Melisende Looking On and the Coronation of Fulk

From *History of Outremer* (*Livre d'eracles*) by William of Tyre (d. 1186)
Books 1–22 (fols. 1–263 and 22 historical initials): Paris, ca. 1300; continuation (fols. 264ff. and 27 miniature panels): Paris, ca. 1340
Tempera, gold, and ink on parchment; 334 folios
13⅝ × 9½ in. (34.5 × 24 cm)
Walters Art Museum, Baltimore (MS 142)

This Old French text was one of the first secular histories to be illustrated in the Middle Ages in Paris, which became the main center for manuscript production in Europe during the thirteenth century.[1] The illustrations in such codices normally appeared, as here, as historiated initials, both in Paris and northern France as well as in the Latin Kingdom of Jerusalem. When the Old French continuation to 1261 was added about 1340, the scribe, fashion, and format, as well as the artist, had changed, and all the illustrations in the second half of this codex were executed as rectangular miniature panels. Despite the evident Western pictorialization of the scene, the artist used a Crusader manuscript illuminated in the Latin Kingdom as his model for all but two of the twenty-two historiated initials in the main text.

Shown here is the initial for book 14. It depicts, above, the mourning of King Baldwin II by his daughter Melisende and her husband, Fulk V of Anjou. William's text recounts how, prior to this moment, Fulk, Melisende, and their two-year-old son, the future King Baldwin III, had been called to Baldwin II's bedside in August 1131. In view of the patriarch, prelates, and nobles, the ailing king committed to them the care of and full power over the kingdom. Three and a half weeks later, on September 14, Fulk and Melisende were crowned co-rulers at the Church of the Holy Sepulchre. In this miniature, below, only Fulk is shown being crowned, with Melisende looking on.[2]

Although William of Tyre's text accords eminent status to Queen Melisende, revealing the significant role she played in the political affairs of the Latin Kingdom of Jerusalem, the artist treats her as a somewhat peripheral character. The upper register shows Baldwin II on his deathbed with Fulk and Melisende standing behind, hands joined, in mourning. In the lower register, Fulk appears at center flanked by two bishops, who place a crown on his head. Melisende, though co-regent, stands among the three witnesses, neither crowned nor wearing regal garments. It is a surprising diminution of her role, given both her prominence in the text and the number of other illustrated copies that show Melisende and Fulk as equals.[3] JF

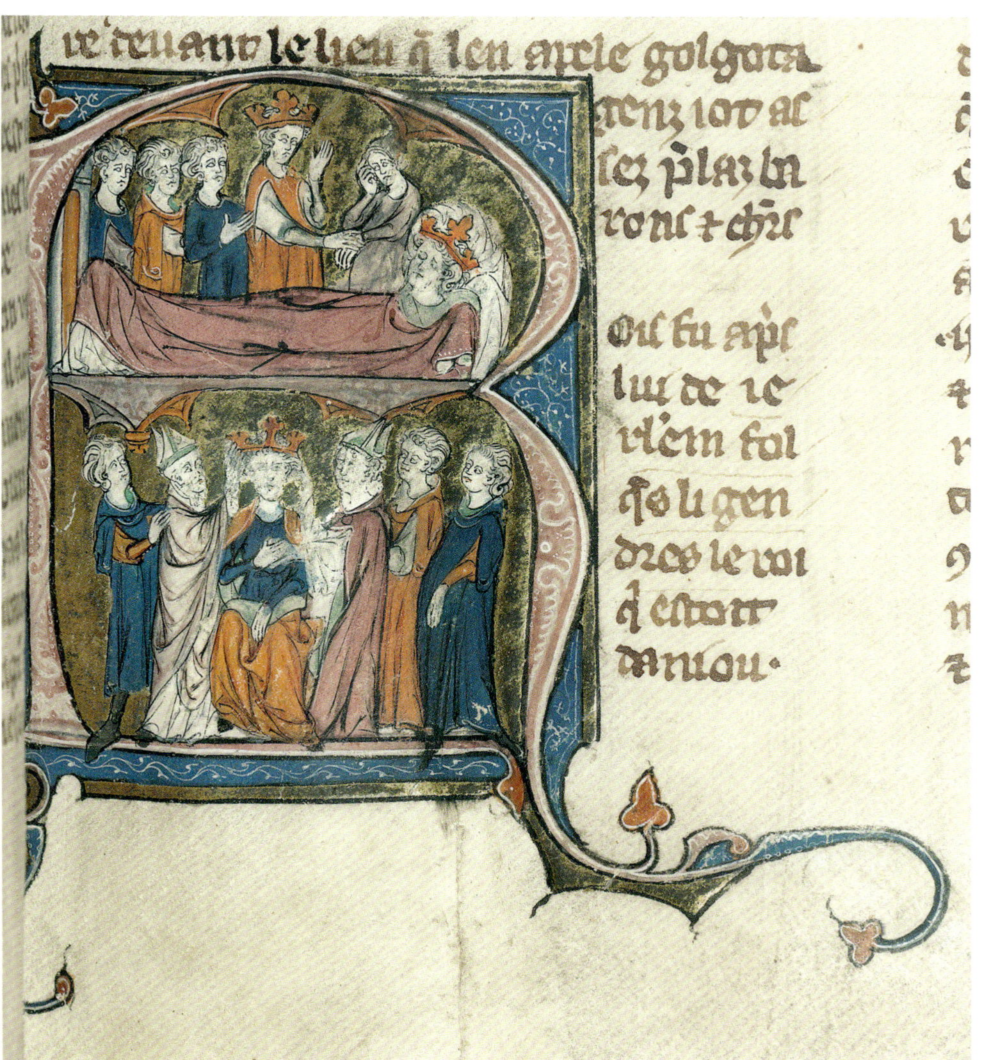

122 detail, fol. 122r

Selected References: Folda 1976, pp. 155–58, 212–13, no. 28; Randall 1989, pp. 133–38, no. 53; Folda 1993, pp. 102–5; Edbury 2007, pp. 77ff.; Handyside 2015, pt. 2, pp. 123ff.

1. Cat. 122 (Walters Art Museum, Baltimore, MS 142; MS Didot b) and Walters Art Museum, MS 137 (MS Didot a) are the only two manuscripts of the *History of Outremer* in the United States. They have a special historical importance with regard to scholarship on the Crusades, because they were owned at one time by Ambroise Firmin-Didot, the Parisian publisher, and as such were used by Paulin Paris as the basis for his 1879–80 Old French translation of the original Latin text. See William of Tyre 1879–80 ed., vol. 2, p. 469 n. 8. On Paris as a center of medieval manuscript production, see Morrison 2010–11; Rouse and Rouse 2000, vol. 1, pp. 17ff.
2. Folda 1993, pp. 102–5.
3. For example, Bibliothèque Nationale de France, Paris, MS Fr. 779, and British Library, London, Yates Thompson MS 12, both illustrated in Folda 1993, p. 104, figs. 11–12.

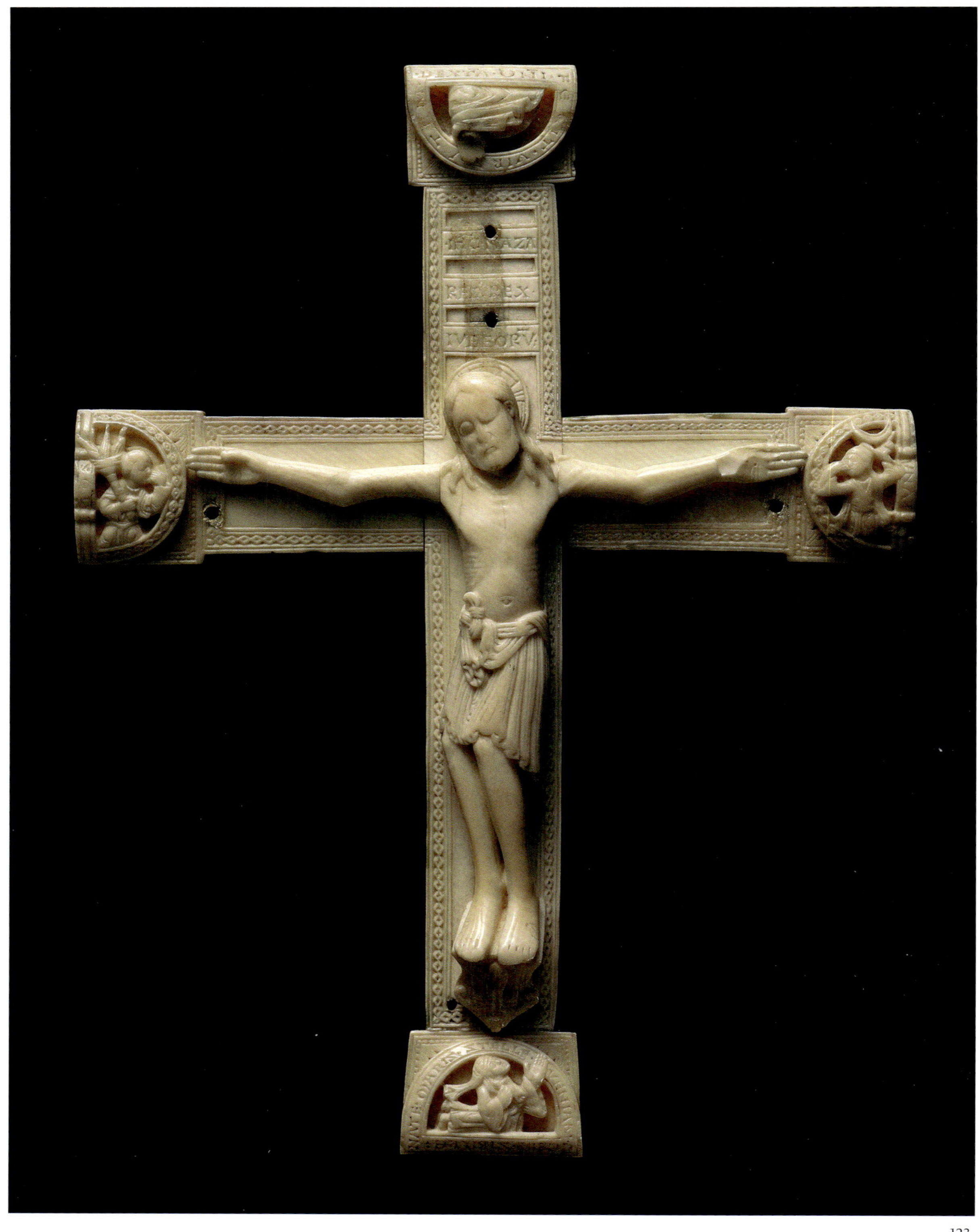

123

123

Cross of Sibyl of Anjou

Mosan, after 1134–before 1156
Walrus ivory
H. 7¼ in. (18.5 cm), W. 5½ (14 cm), D. ⅝ in. (1.6 cm)
Musée du Louvre, Départment des Objets d'Art, Paris (OA 2593)

This cross was once the centerpiece of a book cover created for Sibyl of Anjou (ca. 1112–1165). The daughter of Fulk V of Anjou and the stepdaughter of Melisende, queen of Jerusalem, Sibyl appears as a diminutive veiled figure at the foot of the cross. An inscription above her head asks for pardon from the crucified Christ, son of Mary.[1]

Sibyl of Anjou's life included more than a few adventures and several trips between Europe and the Holy Land. Considered together, they suggest the likely parameters for the creation of this cross. Sibyl first traveled to Jerusalem with her father on the occasion of his marriage to Melisende in the spring of 1129.[2] Five years later she married Count Thierry of Alsace of Flanders, who had come to the Holy Land on pilgrimage. They had five children together, the youngest of whom, Countess Margaret of Flanders, was born in Europe in 1145. Between 1147 and 1149, Sibyl served as regent in Flanders while her husband returned to the Holy Land with the Second Crusade.

Sibyl and Thierry met Bernard of Clairvaux during his tour of Flanders in 1157,[3] and that same year they traveled together to Jerusalem. She thereafter refused to return to Europe with her husband and entered the convent at Bethany, where her step-aunt Iveta, sister of Melisende, was abbess.

It can be reasonably suggested that the ivory, which conforms stylistically to work from the Mosan region (present-day Belgium), must have been made before Sibyl left Europe in 1156–57. Since she wears a veil, likely an indication that she is a married woman, the earliest possible date the work could have been commissioned is 1134, the year of her marriage. None of the "chalices, books, and other ornaments"[4] that Melisende presented to the lost convent at Bethany is known to have survived, but this ivory, owned by one of its nuns, hints at the community's wealth. BDB / MH

Selected Reference: Gaborit-Chopin et al. 2003, pp. 243–45, no. 80.

1. The inscription reads: "Nate. Maris. Stele. Veniam. C(on)cede. Sibille." ("You who are born of the star of the sea, grant pardon to Sibyl.") "Star of the sea" is a reference to the Virgin Mary that traces back to the time of Saint Jerome. The metaphor was used increasingly from the ninth century onward, with the Virgin as the North Star leading pilgrims through stormy waters to Christ.
2. According to Hans Eberhard Mayer, it was before June 2, 1129 (Mayer, H., 1972, p. 99: "shortly before Pentecost 1129").
3. Phillips, J., 2007, p. 104.
4. Described by William of Tyre. See Gaudette 2010, pp. 141–42.

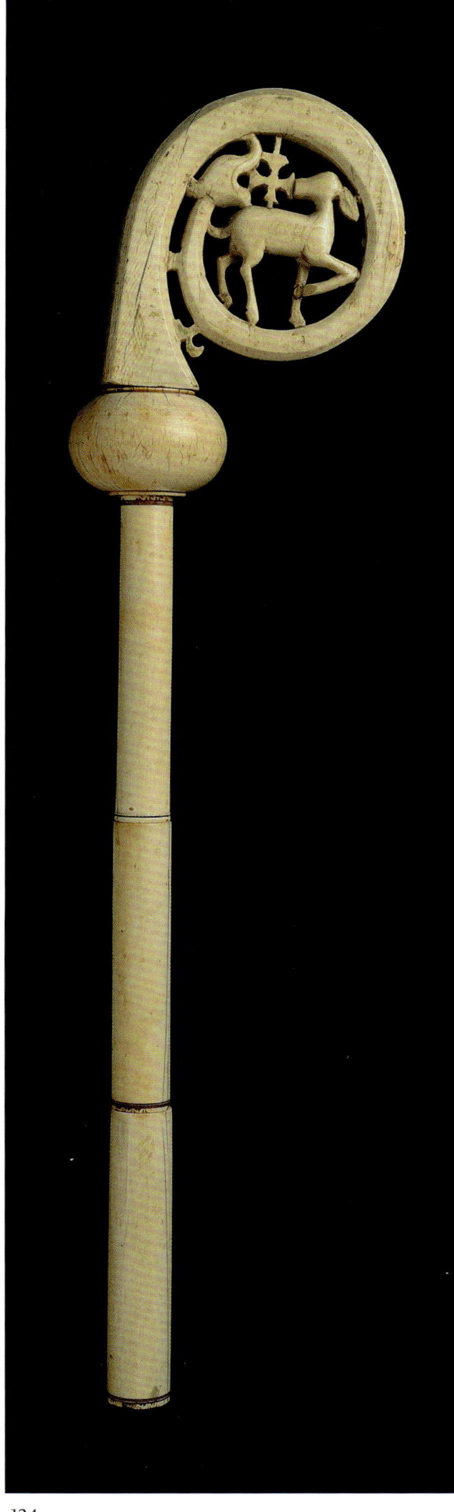

124

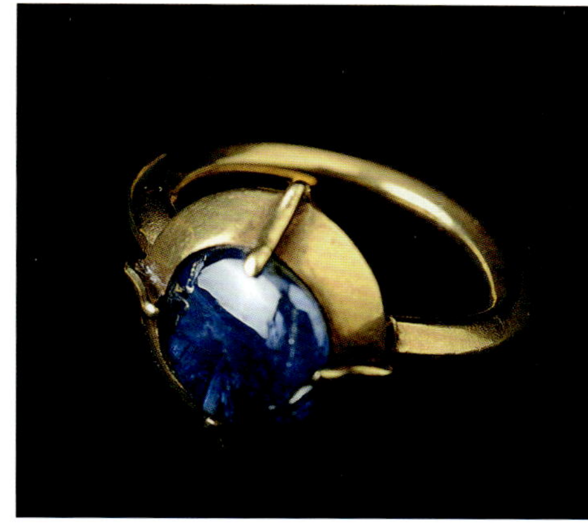

125

124

Crozier of Jacques de Vitry

Sicily (or Acre?), 1216–before 1240
Elephant ivory and bone
H. 22½ in. (57 cm), Diam. 4¾ in. (12 cm)
Musée des Arts Anciens du Namurois, Namur

Imitating the crooks used by shepherds to wrangle wayward sheep, croziers symbolize a bishop's role as herder of the faithful.[1] Here, the battle between good and evil that plays out in silhouette adds additional layers of symbolism. The head and neck of a serpent, emblematic of evil, form the top of the crook and encircle a ram, a representation of Christ, the Lamb of God. A cross at its back, however, protects him from the threat of the serpent's open maw.

First mentioned in 1628 in connection with Jacques de Vitry, bishop of Acre, this crozier reflects a standard type rather than a special commission; its association with Jacques de Vitry's tenure as bishop provides a time frame for its execution.[2] Likewise, his travels and career around the Mediterranean reinforce an attribution to that region, but whether Sicily, as is traditional for such works, or Acre, a center for the ivory trade, is not clear.[3] BDB / MH

Selected Reference: Namur 2003, pp. 278–79, no. 30.

1. The shaft originally would have been longer to accommodate its being carried in procession. According to Jacques Toussaint, the shaft is of bone.
2. As recognized by Danielle Gaborit-Chopin in her discussion of a similar example in the Musée du Louvre, Paris. See Gaborit-Chopin et al. 2003, pp. 225–26, no. 70.
3. Frescobaldi, Gucci, and Sigoli 1948 ed., p. 103.

125

Ring of Jacques de Vitry

Italy (or Latin Kingdom of Jerusalem), ca. 1216–40
Gold with sapphire
Diam. 1⅛ in. (2.9 cm)
Musée des Arts Anciens du Namurois, Namur

Emblematic of his episcopal office, this ring belonging to Jacques de Vitry, bishop of Acre, also appears to have been symbolic of the Holy Land. In his *History of the East* (*Historia orientalis*) he speaks poetically of sapphires, which he attributes to a land he calls "the property of patriarchs, the nourishing mother of the prophets and of the doctrine of the apostles, the mother of the faith." Moreover, the land itself is called "gold for those who are attached to it by love."[1]

The association of precious gems with the Holy Land is not unique to Jacques de Vitry, for reasons both spiritual and practical. The Apocalypse of Saint John (21:18–22) describes the precious stones adorning the walls and gates of the Heavenly City of Jerusalem (see cat. 141), while the twelfth-century Welsh chronicler Geoffrey of Monmouth's account of the First Crusade speaks of the large numbers of rare jewels "unknown in our part of the world" that were taken as booty.[2]

This ring is one of two from Oignies linked to Jacques de Vitry. Both are mentioned for the first time in 1628 and then listed in the 1648 inventory of the Oignies church treasury.[3]

BDB

Selected Reference: Namur 2003, p. 280, no. 31.

1. Jacques de Vitry 1825 ed., pp. 327–28.
2. *Gesta Regum Anglorum* 4.371; William of Malmesbury 1998–99 ed., vol. 1, p. 653.
3. Transcribed in Namur 2003, p. 401.

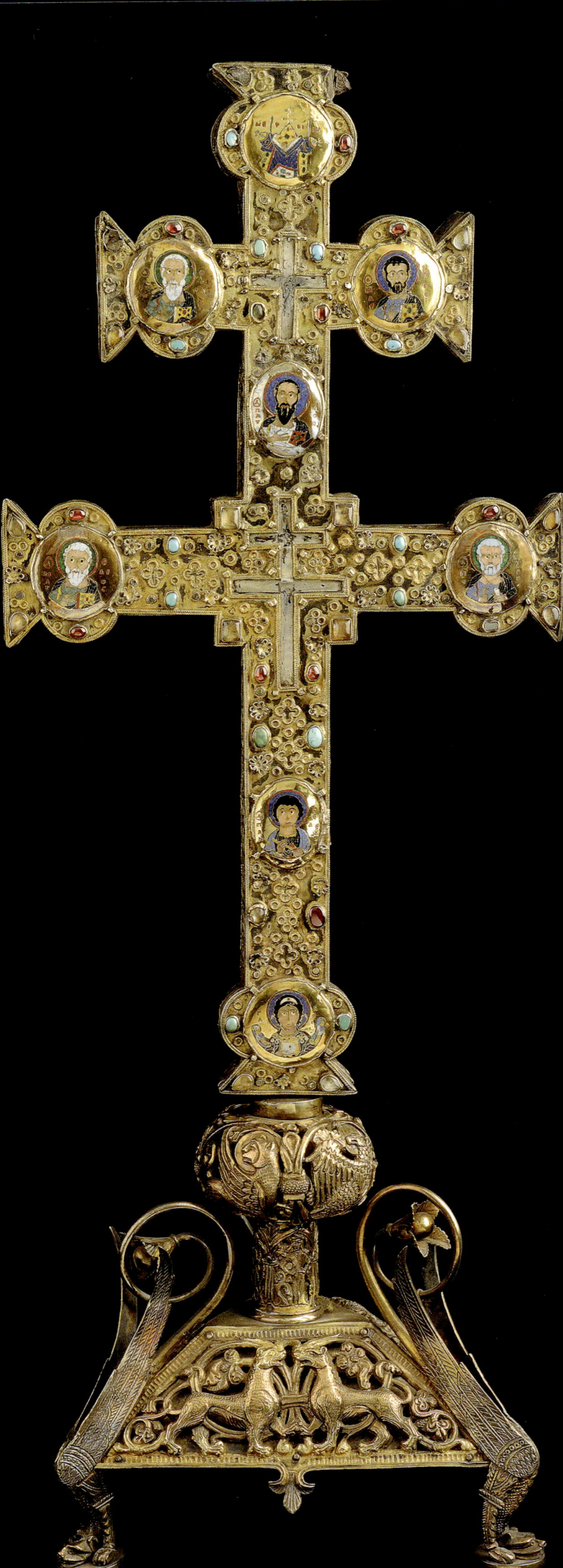

126

Reliquary Cross of Jacques de Vitry

Enamels: Byzantium, about 1160–80; cross: Acre, soon after 1216; base: Oignies, after 1228
Cross: gilded silver, cloisonné enamel on gold, semi-precious stones, and glass; base: gilded copper
H. 22⅛ in. (56.3 cm), W. 7⅛ in. (18 cm)
Musée des Arts Anciens du Namurois, Namur

The Byzantine enamels of saints embellishing this cross are clearly not original to the composition, as attested by two enamels that were trimmed from circles into ovals to fit the shaft better. Moreover, the saints make no sense as an ensemble as they compose an incomplete group of apostles with the addition of Saint Pantaleon, associated with healing and medicine, and the Archangel Gabriel. Their placement, meanwhile, defies hierarchy (Peter, for example, should logically appear opposite Paul, not Matthew). The goldsmith must not have read Greek, seemingly making juxtapositions partially on the basis of hair color, with dark-haired saints on the shaft of the cross and white-haired saints on the transverse. Only the image of the throne of God (*hetoimasia*), appears in its correct place, at the summit.

The embossed rosettes on the reverse resemble those on the somewhat earlier cross from Grandmont, in central France (cat. 25d). The only demonstrable link between Oignies and Grandmont is the European presence in the Holy Land, suggesting the common origin of these works of art there.[1]

The cross belonged to Jacques de Vitry, who from 1214 to 1227 was bishop of Acre, a city renowned for its international merchants. This cross offers key evidence that, among the myriad treasures and works of art available in Acre, European patrons and their goldsmiths had direct access to Byzantine material. BDB

Selected References: Frolow 1961, pp. 404–5, no. 489; Namur 2003, pp. 260–66; Folda 2005, pp. 141–42.

1. Folda 2005, pp. 141–42, proposes, and I concur, that the cross comes from Acre.

126 front view

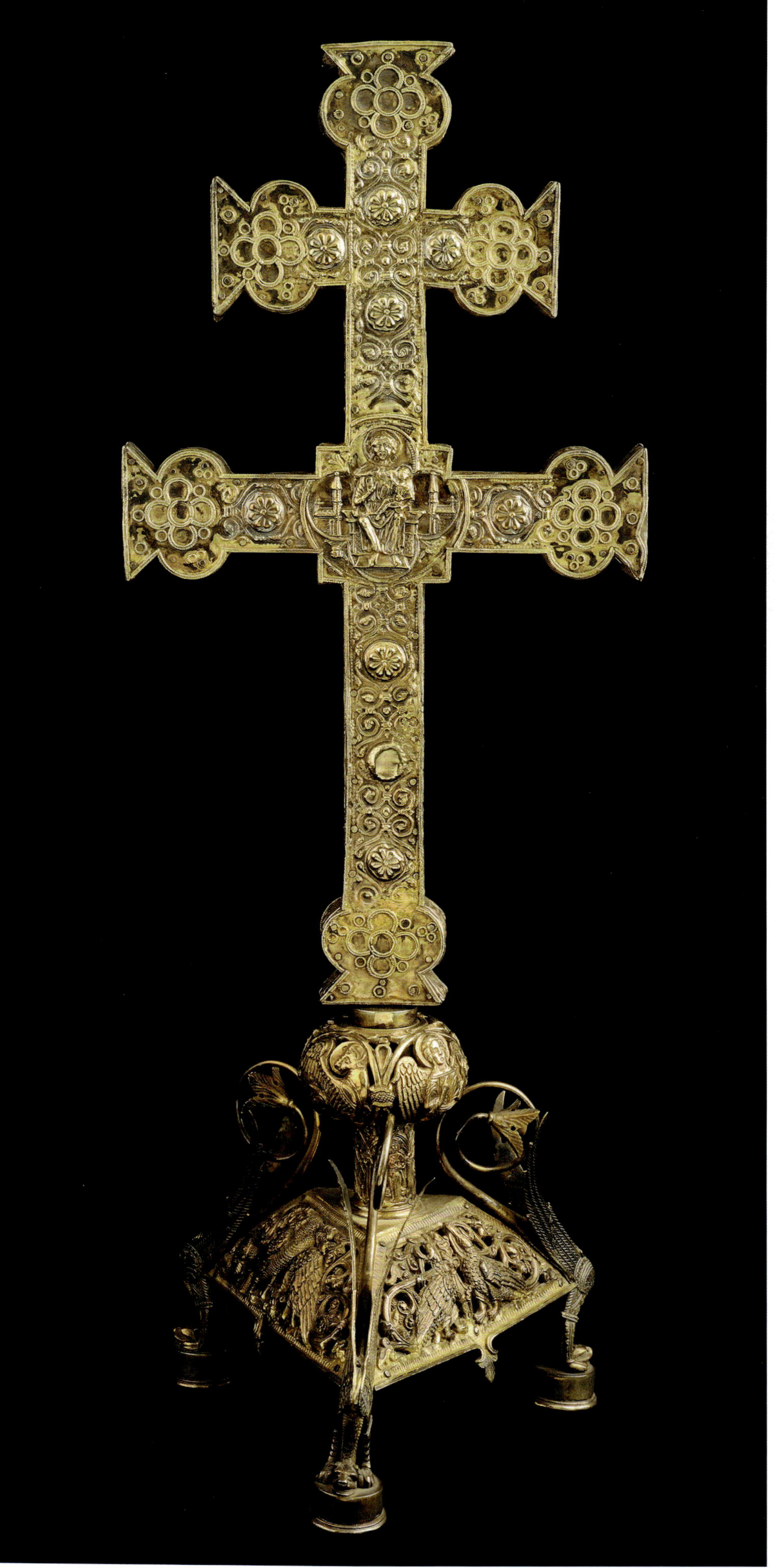

126 back view

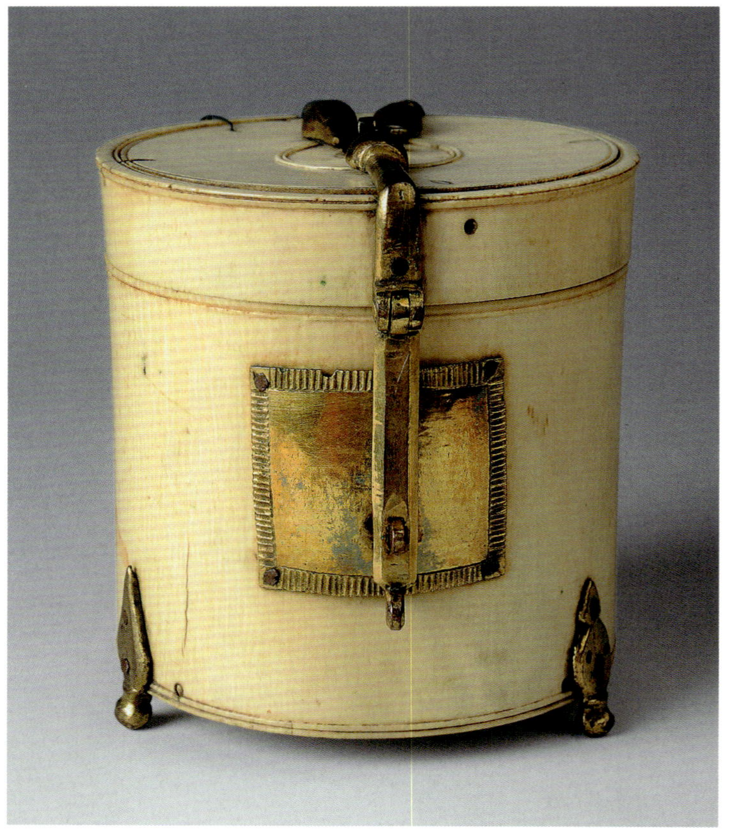

127a front view

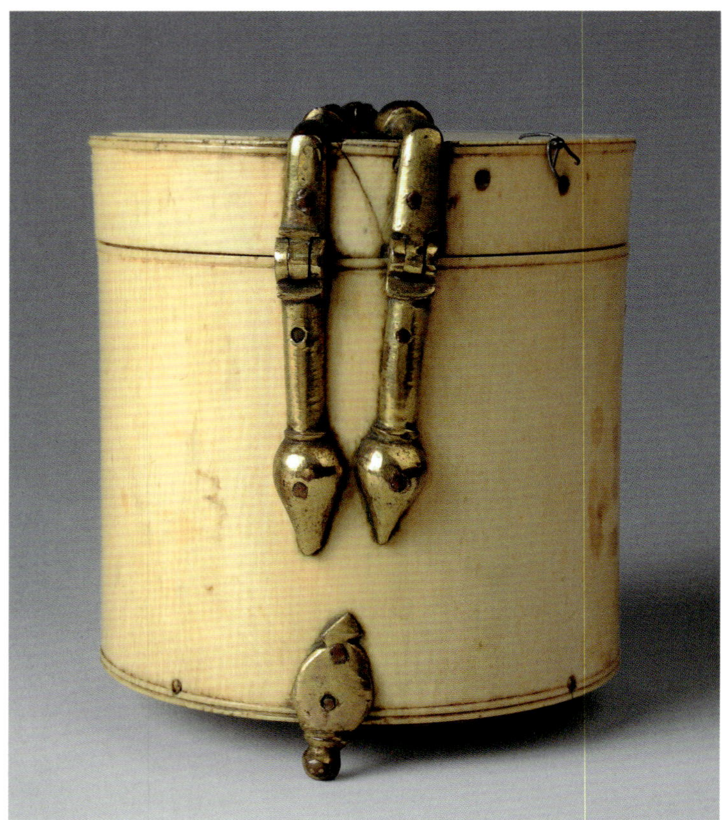

127b back view

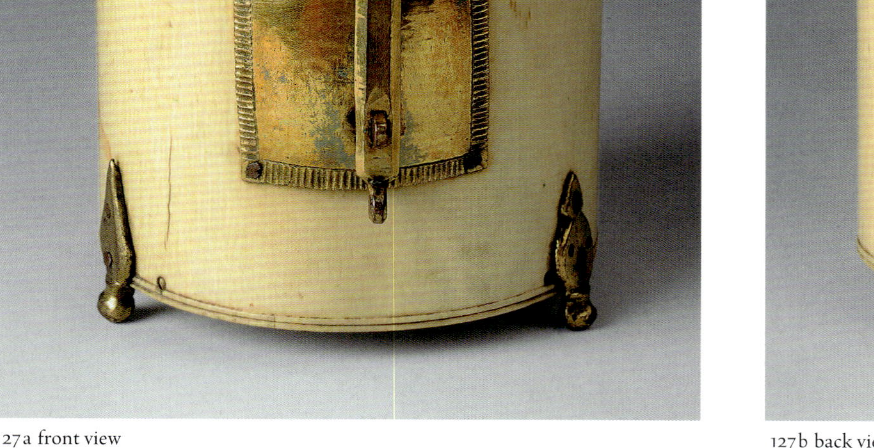

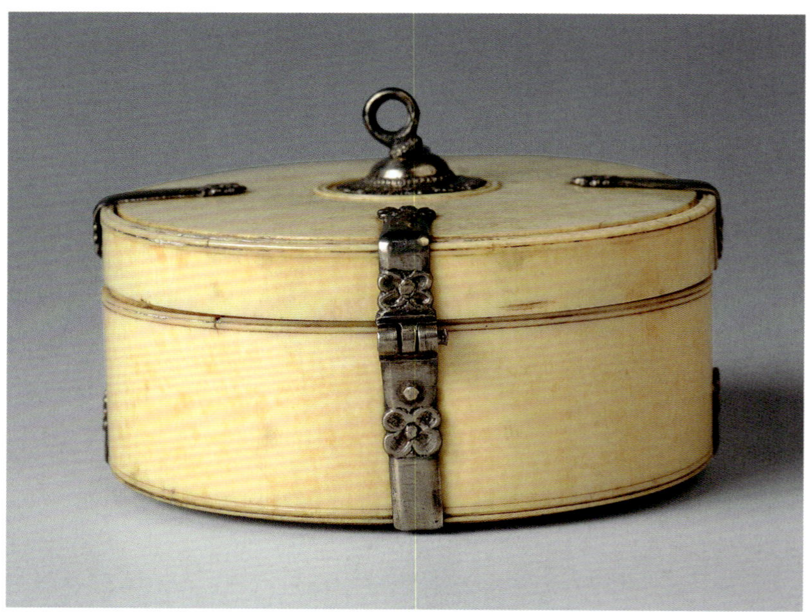

127b

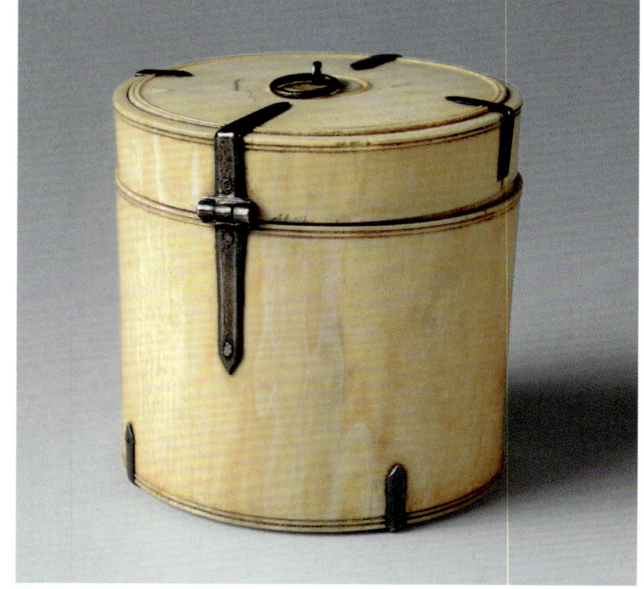

127c

127a–c

Reliquary Boxes of Jacques de Vitry

Sicily (or Acre?), 1216–before 1240
Elephant ivory and gilded-copper clasps
Dimensions variable
Musée des Arts du Anciens Namurois, Namur

The 1648 inventory of the priory of Oignies, of which Jacques de Vitry was the principal benefactor, lists ten ivory reliquaries of varying shapes and sizes. Relics were divided among the containers according to type, whether of "the Lord" and the Apostles, of martyrs, of confessor saints, of virgins, or unidentified. Listed separately is a small ivory box containing "oil of [the] Blessed Mary of Sardene [Saidnaya]."[1] It came from an icon of the Virgin that was carried from Jerusalem to a church in Syria, where it remains today a shrine for Christian and Muslim women.[2]

Notwithstanding their preciousness and apparent fragility, numerous similarly constructed boxes survive in churches across Europe, their widespread distribution facilitated by Mediterranean trade. Jacques de Vitry's biography suggests a timeline for their manufacture but not, given his travels, their localization. Such boxes are generally thought to have been made in Sicily. However, the oil from Saidnaya renders the Holy Land a possible place of origin as well. BDB / MH

Selected Reference: Namur 2003, pp. 258–59, no. 23a–f.

1. Number 32 in the inventory of 1648: "Item, une boite d'ivoir sucrite de oleo B. Marie Sardene, etc," cited in Namur 2003, p. 404.

2. On the Saidnaya icon, see "Trade and Tourism in Medieval Jerusalem," pp. 9–17, in this volume.

128
Single-Volume Qur'an

Cairo, A.H. 730 (1330)
Copied by Muhammad bin Bilik al-Muhsini al-Nasiri[1]
Opaque watercolor, gold, and ink on paper; 300 folios
14⅝ × 9⅞ in. (37 × 25 cm)
By kind permission of the Keir Collection, on long-term loan by Ranros Universal S.A. to the Dallas Museum of Art (VII 9)

This rich illumination marks the opening of a Qur'an manuscript produced in Cairo for the royal treasury of Sultan al-Nasir Muhammad ibn Qala'un, one of Jerusalem's most important patrons.[2] Despite its relatively small size, it follows the style of monumental Qur'an volumes of the Mamluk period, the geometric repertoire of which is distinct. The frontispiece carpet page is bordered by intricate arabesque vine scrolls, with a narrow gold strapwork border framing a geometric composition of stars and polygons. The gold and blue colors impart majesty, while the use of pale pink imbues the composition with warmth. The shimmering effect of light on the gold pigment is echoed by the raylike lines emanating from the carpet panel into the margin. Such extensive decoration declares reverence. Magnificent Qur'an manuscripts were often given as an endowment (waqf) to mosques and madrasas, including those in Jerusalem, as part of the sultan's declaration of piety and power across his dominion.

The ten-pointed star at the center of the pattern contains the words *hakim* and *hamid*, painted in reserve against a blue ground with gold arabesque. Al-Hakim (The All-Wise) and al-Hamid (The All-Praiseworthy) are two of the ninety-nine beautiful names of God. They appear here in reference to those verses that speak of the Qur'an itself as the Word of God.[3]

Relying on more than mathematical calculations, the illuminators drew with a precision guided by intuitive craftsmanship and honed through tradition, namely Qur'an manuscripts of the early Mamluk period.[4] Manuscripts in some ways served as pattern books, circulating designs and geometric motifs like the one seen here, with regard to not only the arts of the book but also media such as marble, metal, and wood.

Like calligraphy, geometry was considered a discipline of the soul in its aspiration to perfection. The potential of geometric patterns and arabesques to extend ad infinitum made them especially appropriate for expressing allusions to the Divine. Carpet pages such as this one spoke to a vision of cosmographic order wherein each piece is part of the whole.

SAK

Selected References: Robinson et al. 1976, p. 228; James 2007, pp. 7–8.

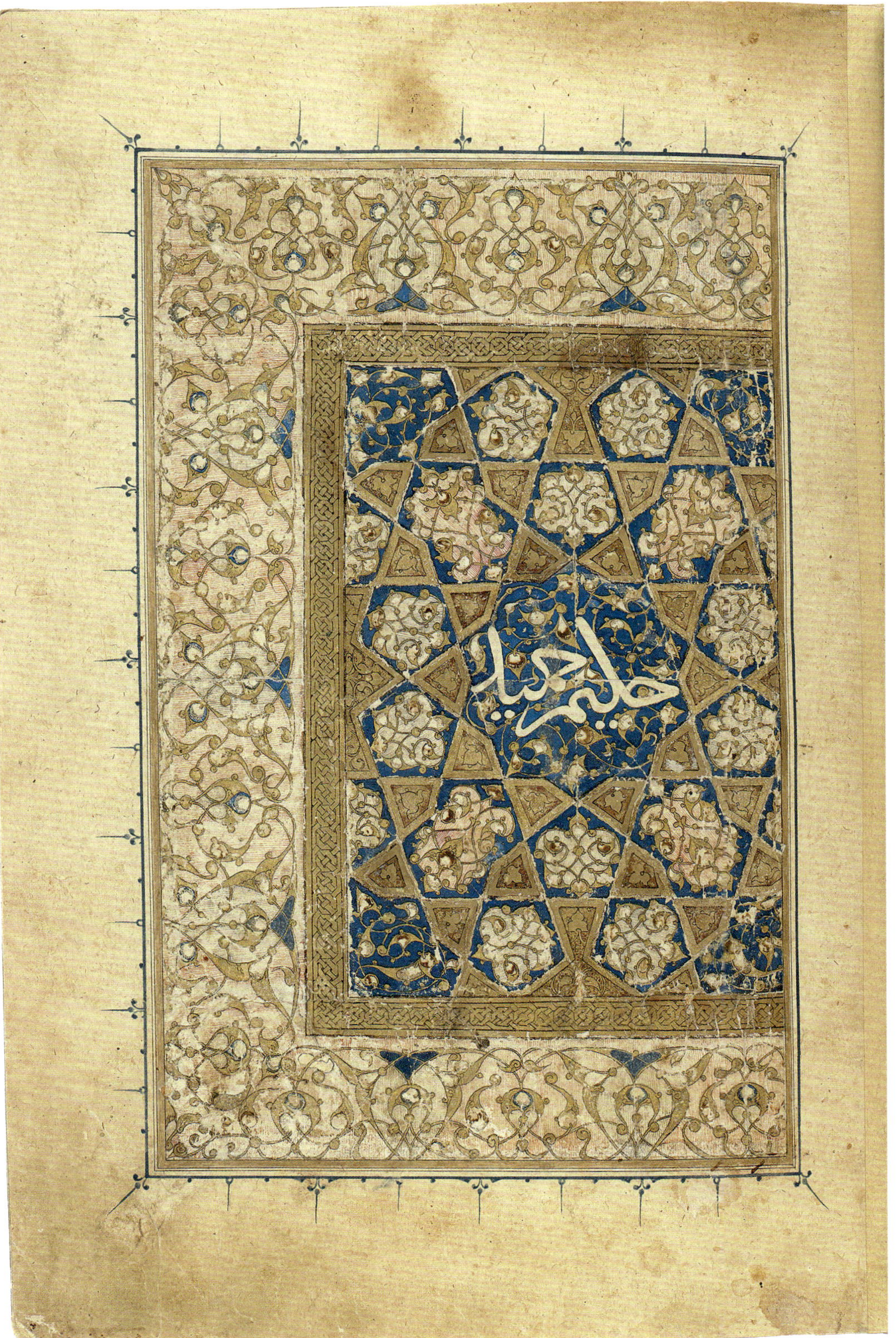

128, fol. 1

1. The name of the calligrapher was previously read, tentatively, as "Bilbek"; see Robinson et al. 1976, p. 228. However, close inspection of the colophon confirms the reading "Bilik," a name known during the Mamluk period. The supervisor (*mushrif*) who oversaw the building of the mosque and madrasa of Sultan Hasan, Muhammad bin Bilik al-Muhsini, could be the same person who copied this manuscript. See also James 2007.

2. Sultan al-Nasir Muhammad was known for his pious character, and some thirty mosques were built during his three periods of rule (1294–95, 1299–1309, 1310–41). He was an energetic patron of the arts, and his reign marked a peak in Mamluk power and culture.

3. "Those who reject the Qur'an when it comes to them — though it is an unassailable Scripture which falsehood cannot touch from any angle, a Revelation sent down from the Wise One, Worthy of All Praise" (Qur'an 2004 ed., 41:41–42).

4. See the Qur'an dated A.H. 705–14 (ca. 1306–15), illuminated by the renowned Sandal (Abu Bakr), in the Chester Beatty Library, Dublin (MS 1479), which has a very similar carpet page.

129 a–f

The Metalwork of Sultan al-Nasir Muhammad ibn Qala'un

a. Incense Box

Egypt or Syria, 14th century
Brass, gold, silver, and black compound
H. 2⅞ in. (7.5 cm), Diam. 4½ in. (11.5 cm)
Museum of Islamic Art, Doha (MW.468.2007)

b. Incense Burner

Egypt or Syria, 14th century
Brass, gold, silver, and black compound
14⅜ × 6½ in. (36.5 × 16.5 cm)
Museum of Islamic Art, Doha (MW.467.2007)

c. Basin

Egypt or Syria, 1310–14
Brass, silver, and gold
H. 8½ in. (21.6 cm), Diam. 19⅞ in. (50.5 cm)
Museo Nazionale di Capodimonte, Naples (112109/1145)

d. Water Vessel

Egypt or Syria, early 14th century
Brass and silver
H. 3⅞ in. (10 cm), Diam. 8⅝ in. (22 cm)
L. A. Mayer Museum for Islamic Art, Jerusalem (M 7–68)

e. Basin

Egypt or Syria, 1299–1340
Brass, silver, gold, and black compound
H. 29½ in. (75 cm), Diam. 45¼ in. (115 cm)
Museum of Islamic Art, Doha (MW.123.1999)

f. Tray

Egypt or Syria, 14th century
Brass, silver, and black compound
H. 4¼ in. (11 cm), Diam. 42¾ in. (108.6 cm)
Museum of Islamic Art, Doha (MW.35.1998)

Six of the more than forty surviving metalwork vessels that bear the name of the Mamluk sultan al-Nasir Muhammad ibn Qala'un are assembled here as both a brilliant testimony to his patronage of precious works of art and an evocation of the great architectural monuments he sponsored in Jerusalem.

The sultan chose his metalsmiths not by the locale for which the works were intended, nor even by the faith the artists practiced, but by the renown in which they were held. Some hailed from Baghdad or Damascus, while others, who used the suffix "al-Mawsili" (from Mosul) were active in the sultan's capital at Cairo.[1] Their creations were dispersed across and beyond the Mamluk world, including to the holy cities of Jerusalem and Hebron (al-Khalil). Mamluk buildings were also enriched by their patrons with appropriate works in metal, beginning at the doors, with their imposing brass fittings and knockers.[2]

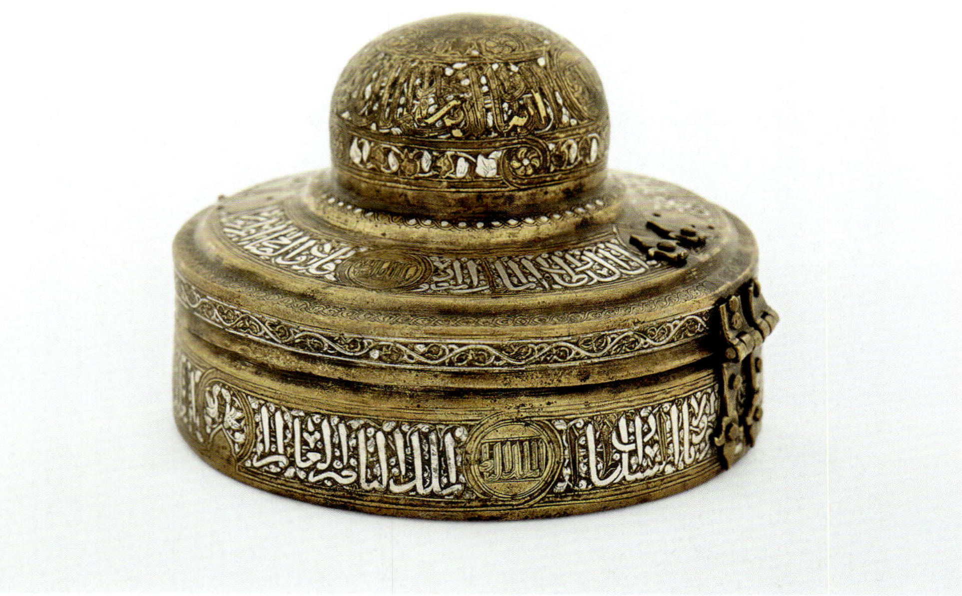

129a

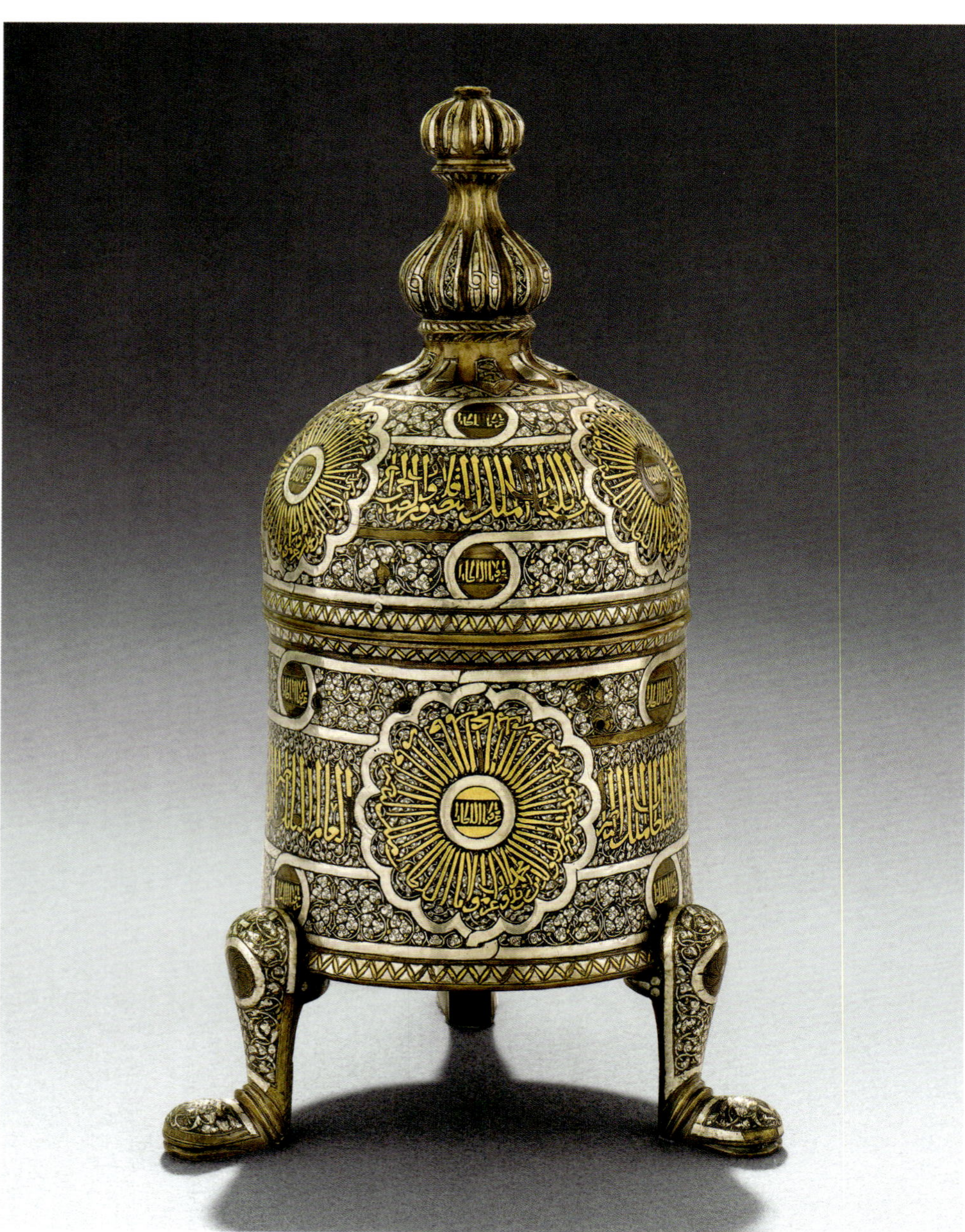

129b

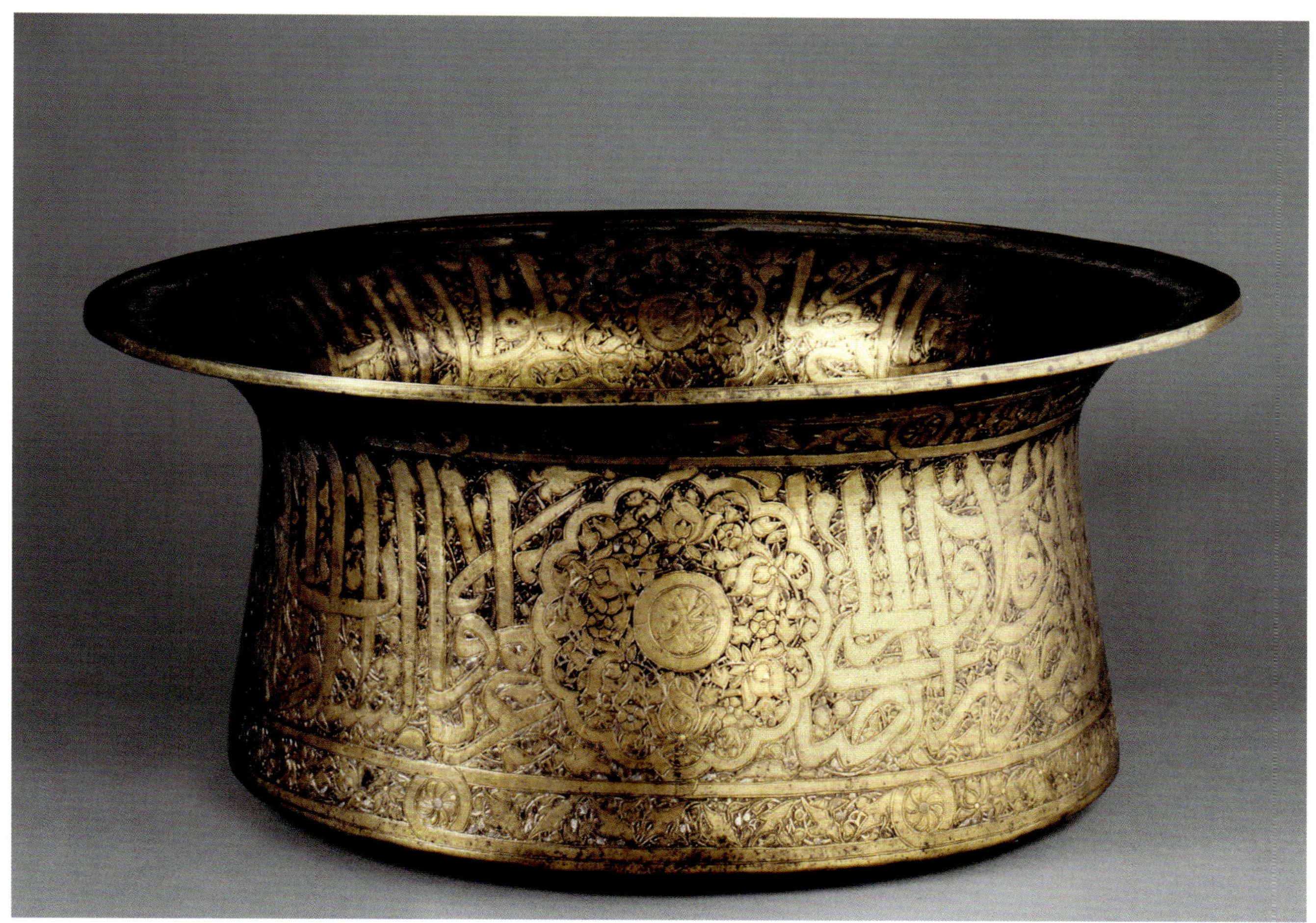

129c

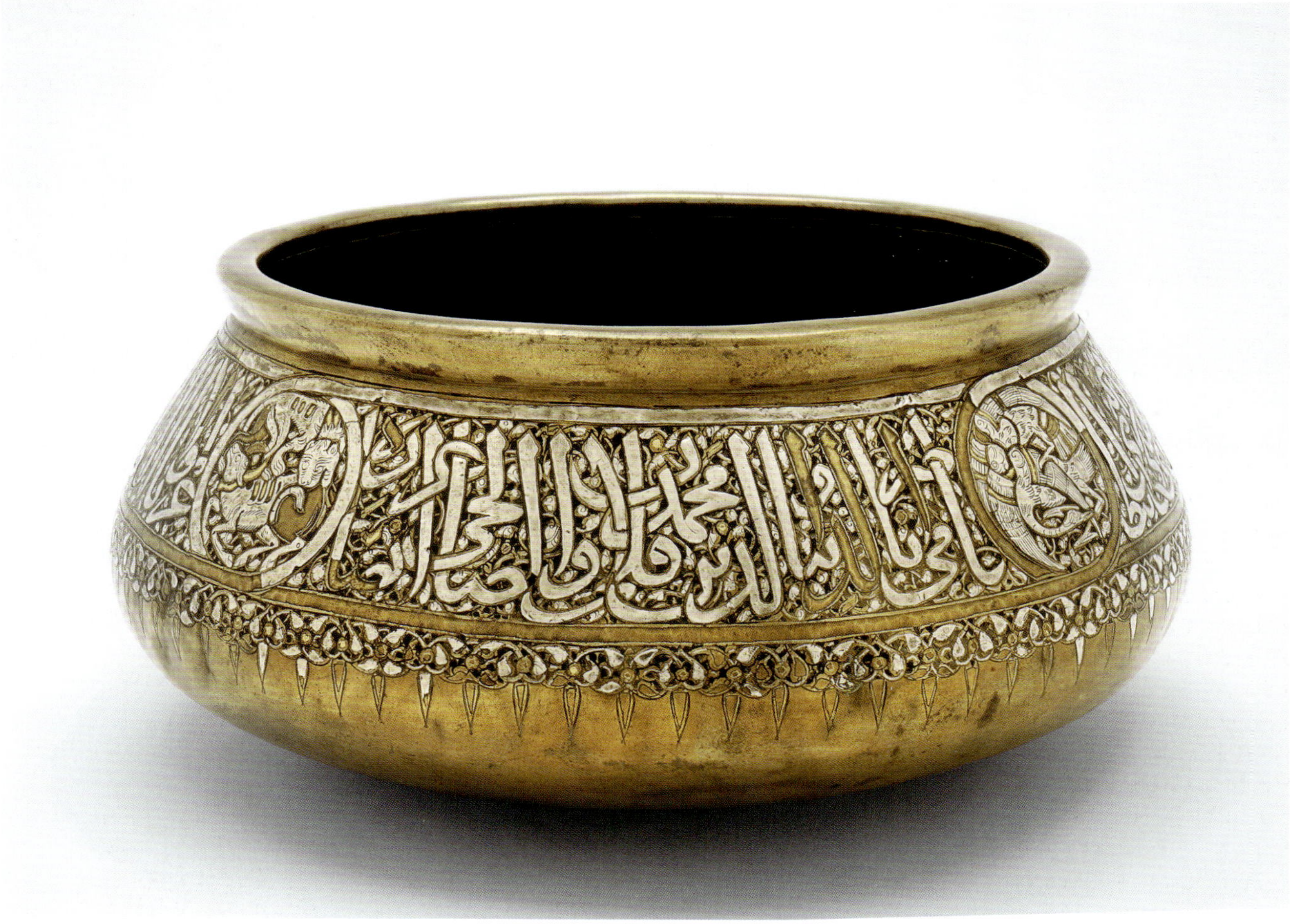

129d

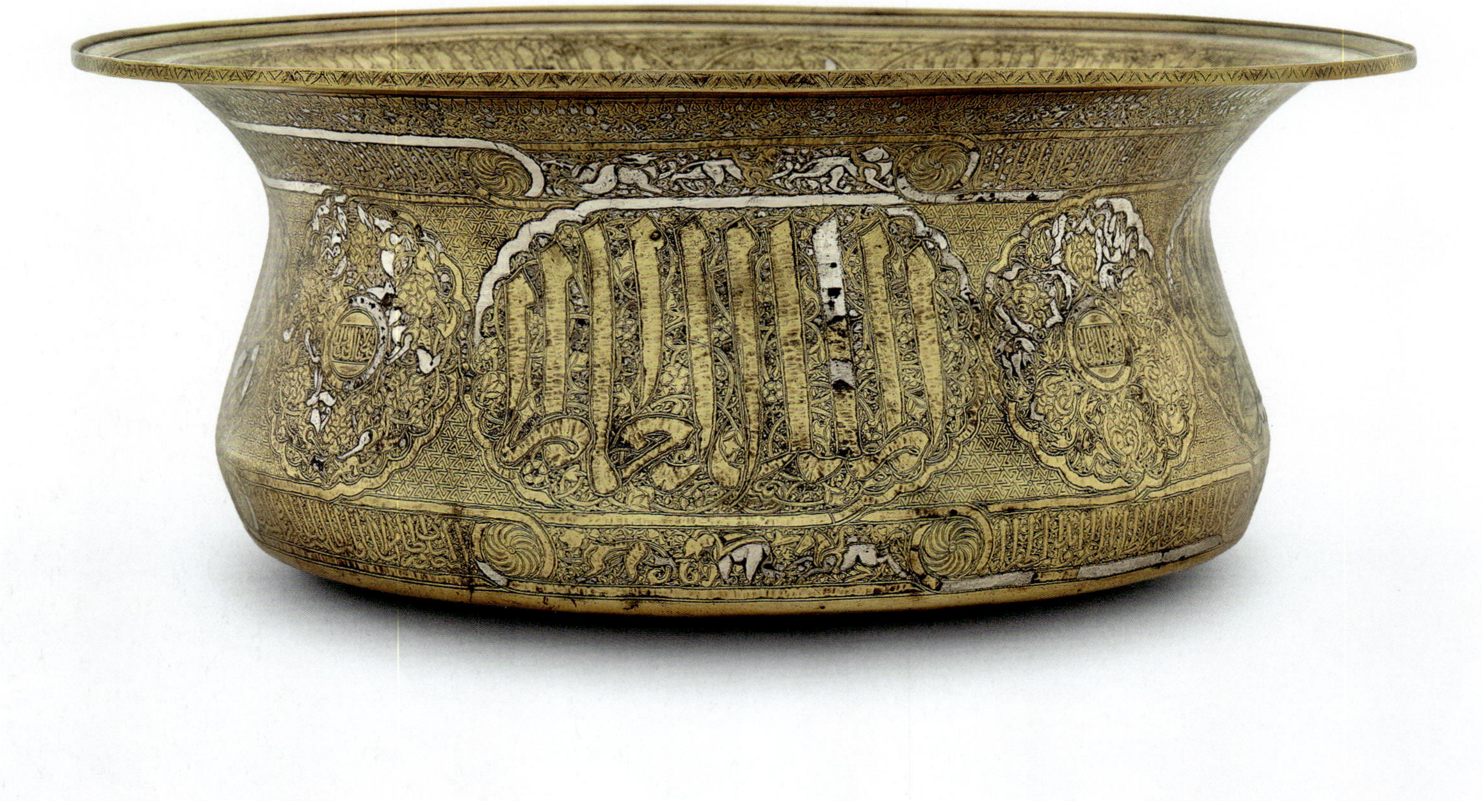

129e

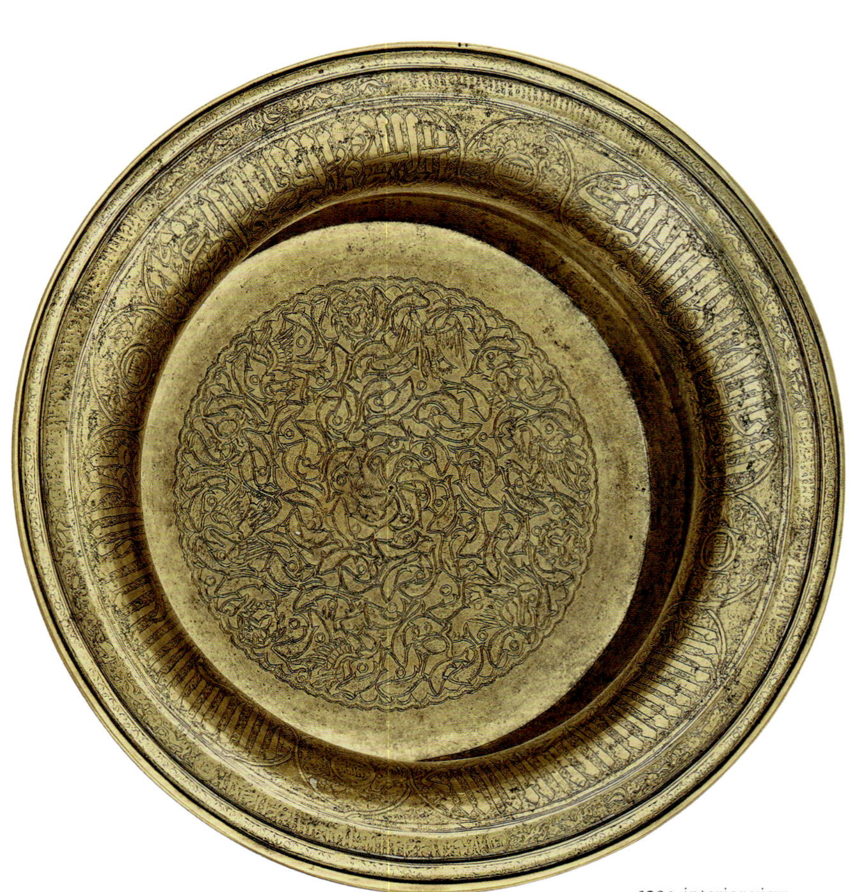

129e interior view

The very form of the incense box of al-Nasir Muhammad (cat. 129a) seems to acknowledge a symbiotic relationship between the arts of metalworking and architecture. Evocative of the domed structures of Jerusalem, the box suggests his role in restoring the domes of both the Aqsa Mosque and the Dome of the Rock, the latter project initiated a year after his 1317 visit to Jerusalem.[3] Nor is a linkage of this type of object with its patron accidental. From as early as the late twelfth century, the sultan was associated with "sweet, heady perfume."[4] The aromatics stored in the box and burned in the censer (cat. 129b) released a perfumed smoke that would emerge through the pierced metal, rising past the laudatory inscriptions to al-Nasir Muhammad on the lid, linking the sultan directly to the pleasurable scent.

In similar fashion, sultans were also compared to light, and a candlestick bearing the name of al-Nasir Muhammad was given to the Ibrahim Mosque in Hebron.[5] Paired candlesticks began to be placed in the mihrabs of mosques in Egypt and Syria in the thirteenth century, a practice that paralleled western European usage on Christian altars,

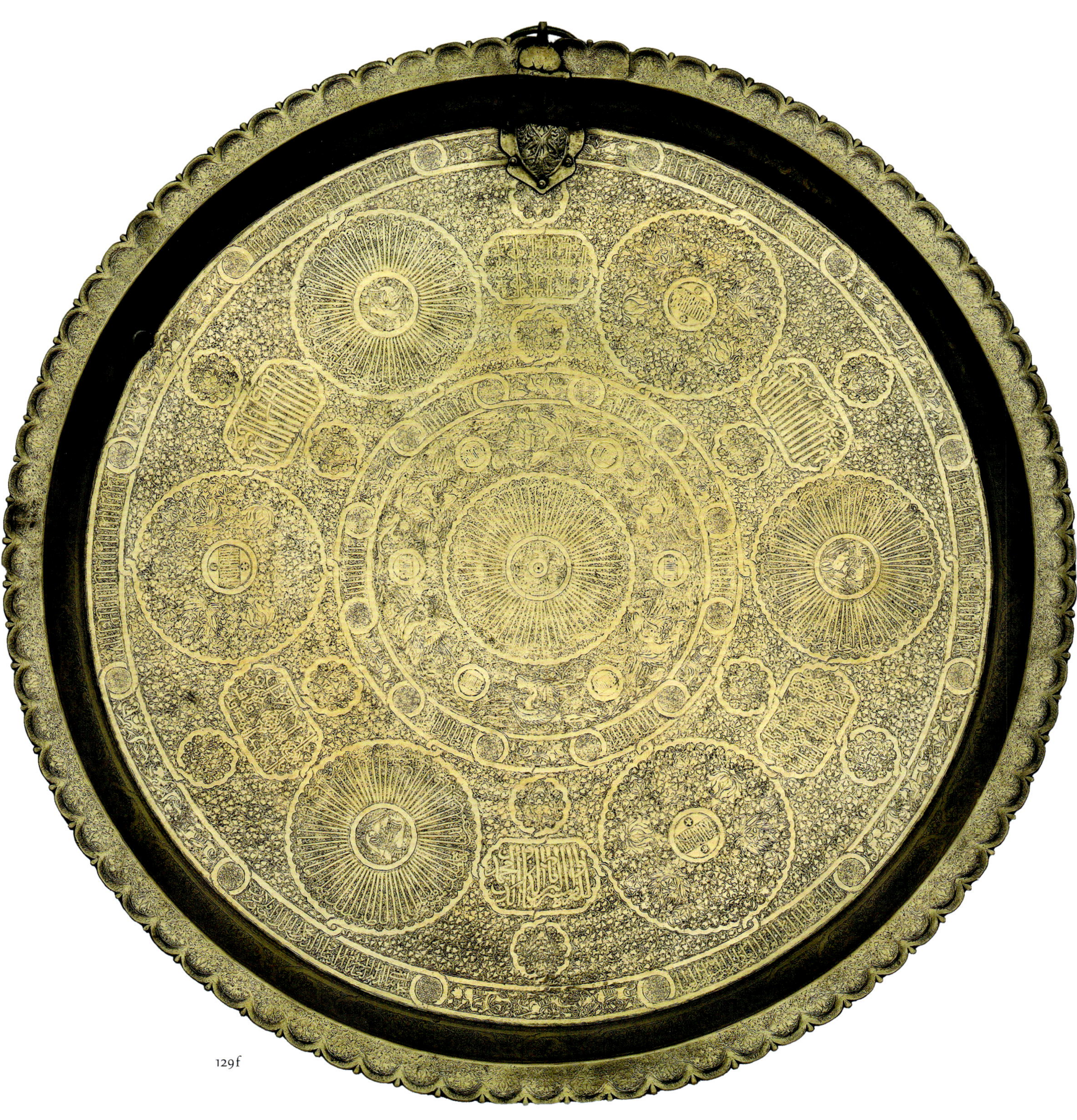

129f

and there are references to sending candles by caravan to Jerusalem even earlier, during the Fatimid period.[6] Moreover, the form of these candlesticks, crafted to accommodate tapers rather than oil, diverged from the more typical Islamic oil lamp, an example being the one dedicated to al-Nasir Muhammad recorded in the Dome of the Rock in 1932.[7]

Whether inlaid metal vessels had sacred or secular usages is almost impossible to determine with absolute certainty, for even common, utilitarian objects like ewers and basins (cats. 129c, e) had the potential for use in the daily practice of religious traditions, given the importance of both ritual washing and hospitality in Islam.[8] With regard to the latter, the tray (cat. 129f), by virtue of its size and the elaboration of its inscriptions, is one of the most luxurious objects linked to the name of the sultan, who was known for the lavish entertainment of his amirs and officers. The basins, the tray, and the bowl (cat. 129d) together exemplify the celebrated richness of the markets of Jerusalem, which, after all, surround the Aqsa Mosque and even today provide income to it in perpetuity through charitable endowment (waqf).

During al-Nasir Muhammad's reign, inscriptions giving his name and titles became the focus of the decorative programs on inlaid metal vessels in a new aesthetic, replacing the figures and animals seen on earlier metalwork.[9] The sultan's titles reflected his power and served as his official attribute. Not surprisingly, therefore, we see them on inscriptions embellishing the monuments in Jerusalem of which he was the patron, including the gate to the Cotton Market (fig. 6).

The sultan's list of titles may vary from object to object, and it is relevant to note that the metalwork repeatedly includes the title "the learned,"[10] a quality reflected in his patronage of madrasas (cat. 129b). On the tray now in Doha (cat. 129f), al-Nasir Muhammad is poetically referred to as the "light of the poor and the destitute" and politically as the "sultan of the Arabs and non-Arabs" and "the slayer of infidels and polytheists." It is most significant that the sultan is called both the "servant of the two noble holy places" on the tray and a "pilgrim" of the two holy places on a second basin (cat. 129e). In the Mamluk period, Jerusalem and Hebron were known as "the two noble sanctuaries," a title previously reserved for Mecca and Medina.[11] BDB

Selected References: 'Izzi 1972; al-Harithy 2000; Ward 2004.

1. Esin Atil in Washington, D.C., and other cities 2004–6, p. 51. James Allan in Doha 2002, p. 10, notes that not even use of the Arabic script indicates that the maker was Muslim, for a number of Egyptian and Syrian craftsmen were Christian.
2. See Mols 2006.
3. See Burgoyne et al. 1987, p. 77, for the date of the restoration and Kenney 2009, p. 84, for the trip to Jerusalem.
4. Quoted by Imad al-Din in Gabrieli, ed. 1969, p. 172. For further discussion of the sultan's connection to incense and evocation of that symbolism in cat. 129b, see Allan 1982, no. 15.
5. Imad al-Din also deemed the sultan, son of Saladin, to be "the cause of all shining light." Gabrieli, ed. 1969, p. 172.
6. Allan in Doha 2002, p. 9.
7. Wiet 1932, p. 27, no. 9; Ward 2004, p. 71.
8. Allan in Doha 2002, p. 9.
9. Ward 2004, p. 64.
10. 'Izzi 1972, p. 236.
11. Sharon 1997–2013, vol. 5, p. 8.

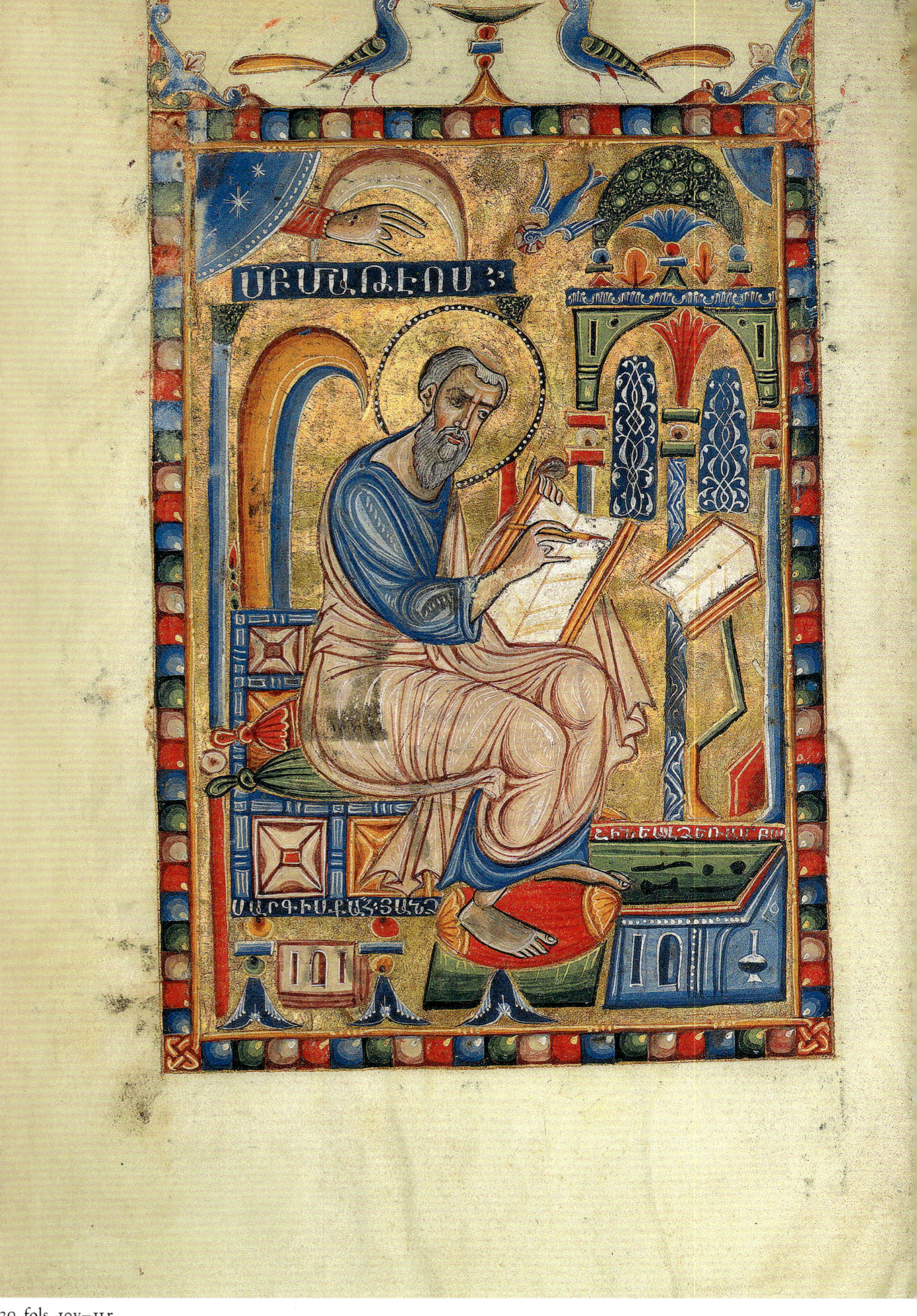

130, fols. 10v–11r

130

Gospel Book

Armenia, copied and decorated at the Monastery of Lazar, Taron; evangelist portraits: Sis, Cilicia (both, present-day Turkey), 1312
Written and decorated by Arak'el; evangelist portraits by Sargis Pidzak
Tempera, gold, and ink on paper; evangelist portraits: on parchment; 389 folios
10⅝ × 6¾ in. (27 × 17 cm)
Armenian Patriarchate, Jerusalem (MS 1949)

More than seventy years after its creation in 1312, this manuscript was brought by pilgrims to Jerusalem from Cilicia, the Armenian kingdom on the Mediterranean long allied with the Crusader states, as a donation. The text and decoration were produced by the scribe Arak'el at the famous Monastery of the Apostles (also known as the Monastery of Lazarus) in the province of Taron in the Armenian homeland; the evangelist portraits were painted in Sis by Sargis Pidzak, the most famous painter of his generation in Cilicia, and imported to be inserted into the manuscript on stubs of paper. The image of Saint Matthew, painted on expensive parchment, is one of the artist's earliest surviving works, which he signed "by the hand of the priest Sargis."[1] Here Saint Matthew is seated writing his Gospel before a table and stand in a format traditional throughout the Christian world. The vertical, blue foliate patterns in the building behind the table are suggestive of stained-glass windows that were known in the Frankish kingdom.[2] Divine inspiration appears above in the unusual combination of the hand of God extending from the arc of the heavens and the Holy Spirit, represented as a dove. The incipit, or opening on the first page, of the Gospel of Matthew (to the right of the portrait) and its text present figures that are less sophisticated

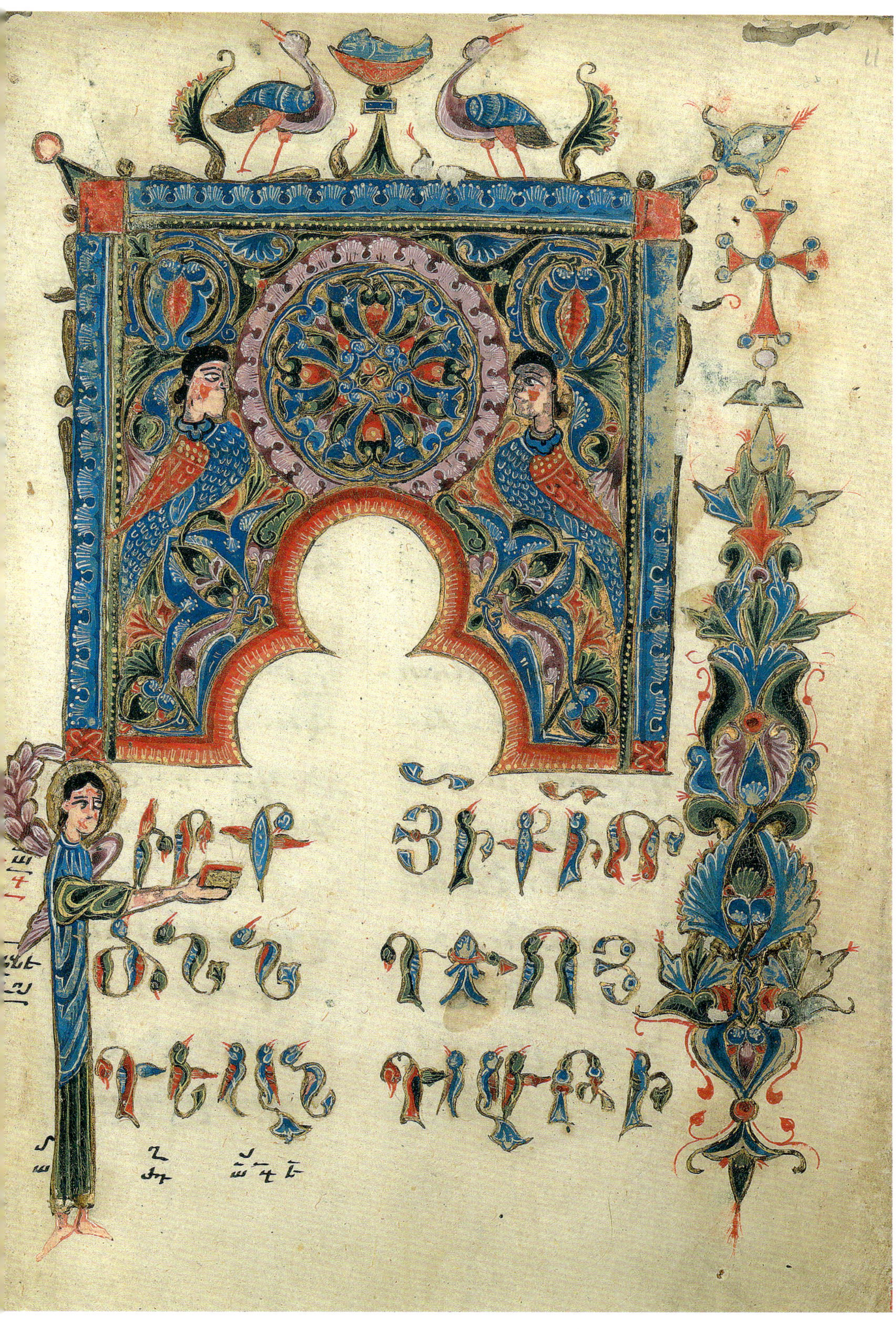

in their execution than the portraits but nonetheless lively and colorful within the Armenian tradition associated with Cilician art. The incipit letter shows Matthew's symbol, an angel holding the Gospel. The use of such symbols to decorate the opening of the evangelists' Gospels was introduced into Armenian art in Cilicia in the twelfth century, following long-established European practice.[3] HCE

Selected References: Narkiss, Stone, and Sanjian 1979, pp. 81–82, 151; Der Nersessian 1993, vol. 1, pp. 142–53.

1. Der Nersessian 1993, vol. 1, p. 143; Narkiss, Stone, and Sanjian 1979, pp. 81–82.
2. Dean 1927, pp. 5–46.
3. Evans 1990, pp. 51–68; New York and Baltimore 1994, pp. 46, 71, 73.

131

Gospel Book

Sis, Cilicia (present-day Turkey), 1346
Written by Nerses, a priest, and the scribe; illuminated by Sargis Pidzak
Text: tempera, gold, and ink on paper; illuminations tipped into the text: on parchment; 276 folios
6¾ × 4¾ in. (17 × 12 cm)
Armenian Patriarchate, Jerusalem (MS 1973)

In this Gospel, dedicated to the Armenian Queen Mariun and her daughter, Femi, the princess herself pours water from a ewer into the bath prepared for the child Jesus in the Nativity scene (folio 8 verso).[1] This is a busy moment, with angels, a shepherd, and magi in the company of the Virgin and Saint Joseph. The child appears twice: lying in his mother's arms, at center, and testing his own bathwater, at lower right.

Princess Femi appears again in the depiction of the Entry into Jerusalem (folio 114), where she assists by laying out a tunic on the same golden background inhabited by Christ on the donkey and his disciples Peter and Paul.[2] In the Descent from the Cross, her mother can be seen kneeling, with her name, "Mariun, Queen of the Armenians," inscribed in large Armenian script above her head (folio 258 verso). Dressed handsomely and wearing a large gold crown, the queen is nearly the same size as the Virgin standing and caressing Christ's hand on the other side of the cross.[3] Mariun, who was also mother of the future king, Kostandin, was queen of Cilicia at a time when the kingdom's rulers were increasingly closely allied with, and often married to, the Lusignans of Cyprus (cats. 19a, b) as the Mamluks of Egypt threatened both states.[4] After Cilician Armenia fell to the Mamluks, in 1374–75, Mariun became a nun at the Cathedral of Saint James in Jerusalem, where she was interred following her death, in 1377.[5] She most likely brought this manuscript with her to Jerusalem. HCE

Selected References: Der Nersessian 1973, pp. 161–62, figs. 118, 119; Narkiss, Stone, and Sanjian 1979, pp. 87, 152; Der Nersessian 1993, vol. 1, pp. 142–53.

1. Der Nersessian 1993, vol. 1, p. 146, vol. 2, fig. 598.
2. Ibid., p. 146; Der Nersessian 1978, p. 162; and Narkiss, Stone, and Sanjian 1979, p. 87, mistakenly identify the image as Queen Mariun.
3. Narkiss, Stone, and Sanjian 1979, p. 88, fig. 110; Der Nersessian 1978, p. 162; Der Nersessian 1993, vol. 1, pp. 146, 160, vol. 2, fig. 650.
4. Boase 1978, pp. 30–31; Der Nersessian 1993, vol. 1, p. 142.
5. Pringle 1993–2009, vol. 3, p. 170, citing Ervine 1999, p. 127.

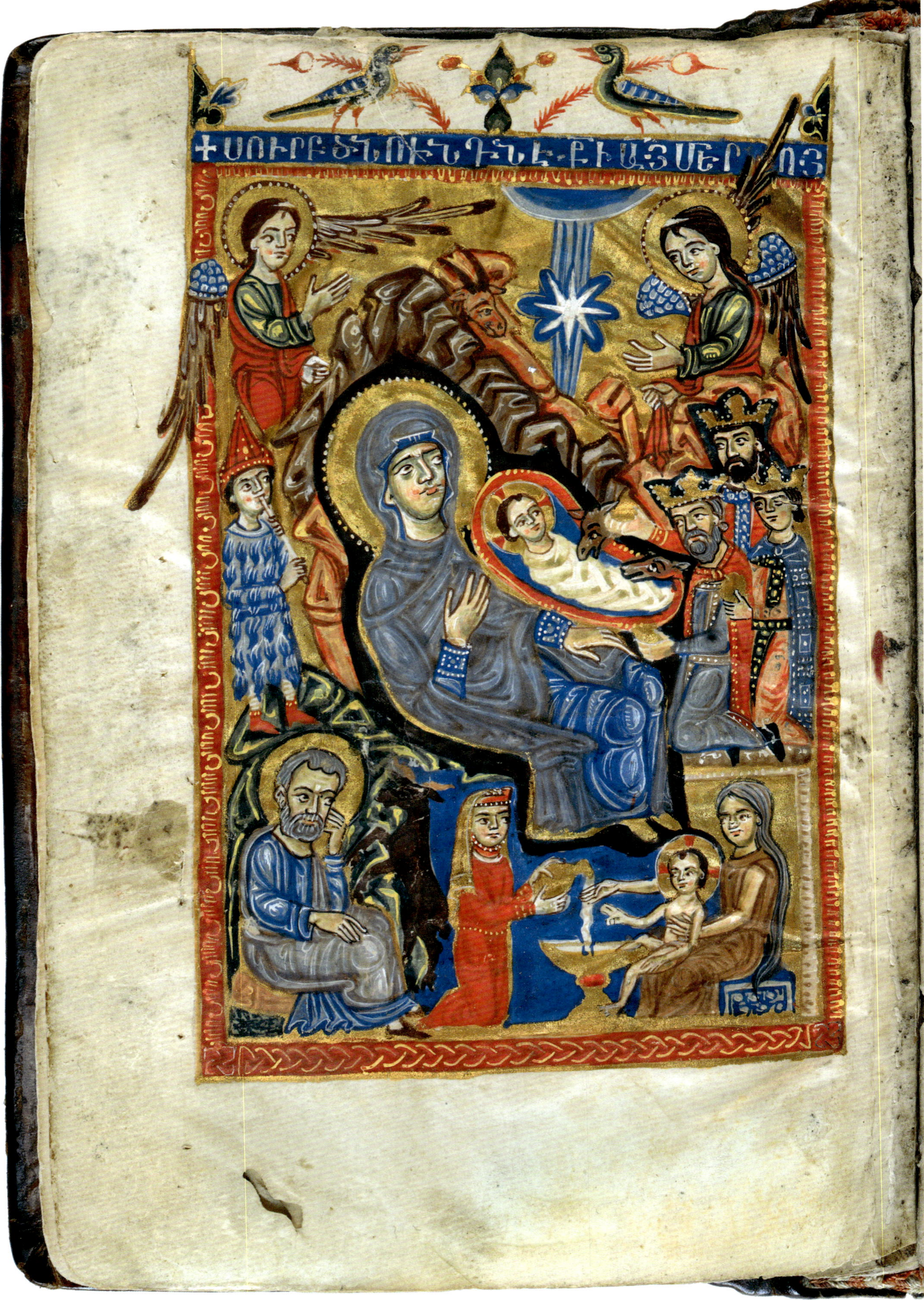

131, fol. 8v

132

Firman of Baybars II

Cairo, A.H. 1 Safar 709 (July 11, 1309)
Ink on paper
11⅞ × 8⅛ in. (30 × 20.5 cm)
Terra Sancta Museum, Historical Archive, Jerusalem

Despite the loss of Acre by the Crusaders in 1291, the Mamluk Egyptian sultan Baybars II[1] gave the "Brothers of the Cord," as Franciscan friars were called in the East, the right to establish themselves on Mount Sion, at the Church the Holy Sepulchre in Jerusalem, and at the Church of the Nativity in Bethlehem. They could occupy the sites but not own them. The firman of Baybars excluded from this grant all other religious orders of Franks, or Western Christians. It was the first Muslim document to favor the Franciscans and recognize them as guardians of the Christian sacred places. The decree also guaranteed the friars of Saint Francis protection against any who might oppose them.

In 1323, when James II of Aragon asked Sultan al-Nasir Muhammad ibn Qala'un to allow Christians to administer the Holy Sepulchre, a new era of Latin Christianity in the Holy Land began. The dream of military victory for the Crusaders had collapsed in the face of repeated defeat, and it took humility, patience, and faith on the part of the friars to remain in this hostile climate. This reality set the stage for Franciscan efforts toward peaceful dialogue with Muslims.[2]

The friars had visited the Holy Land many times in their attempt to secure access to the sacred places for Christian pilgrims. The establishment of the order in Jerusalem officially occurred in 1333 with its acquisition of Mount Sion, which was sold by al-Nasir Muhammad to Roger Guérin of Aquitane, an emissary for Robert of Anjou and Sancea of Majorca. The presence of the friars in the Holy Land was confirmed canonically by Pope Clement VI in 1342 with the publication of the papal bull *We Give Thanks* (*Gratias agimus*) and *Some Time Ago* (*Nuper carissimae*), which established the Franciscan Custody of the Holy Land (Custodia Terrae Sanctae).[3] HS

Selected References: Golubovich 1898, pp. 128–30; Florence 2015, pp. 320–22.

1. Golubovich 1898, pp. 128–30.
2. See De Sandoli 1990, p. 31.
3. Ciganotto, ed. 1909, pp. 13–15, 70–71.

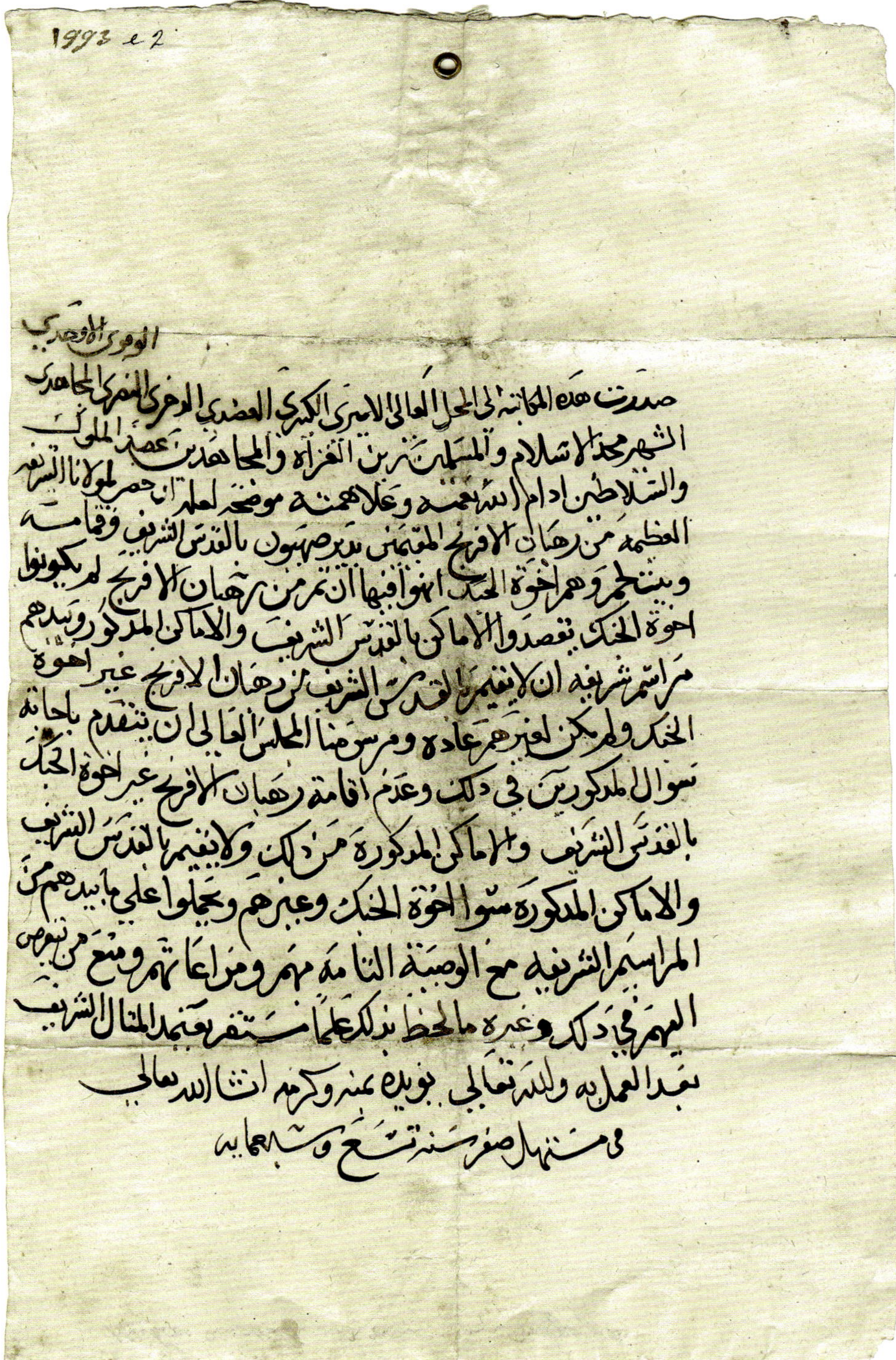

132

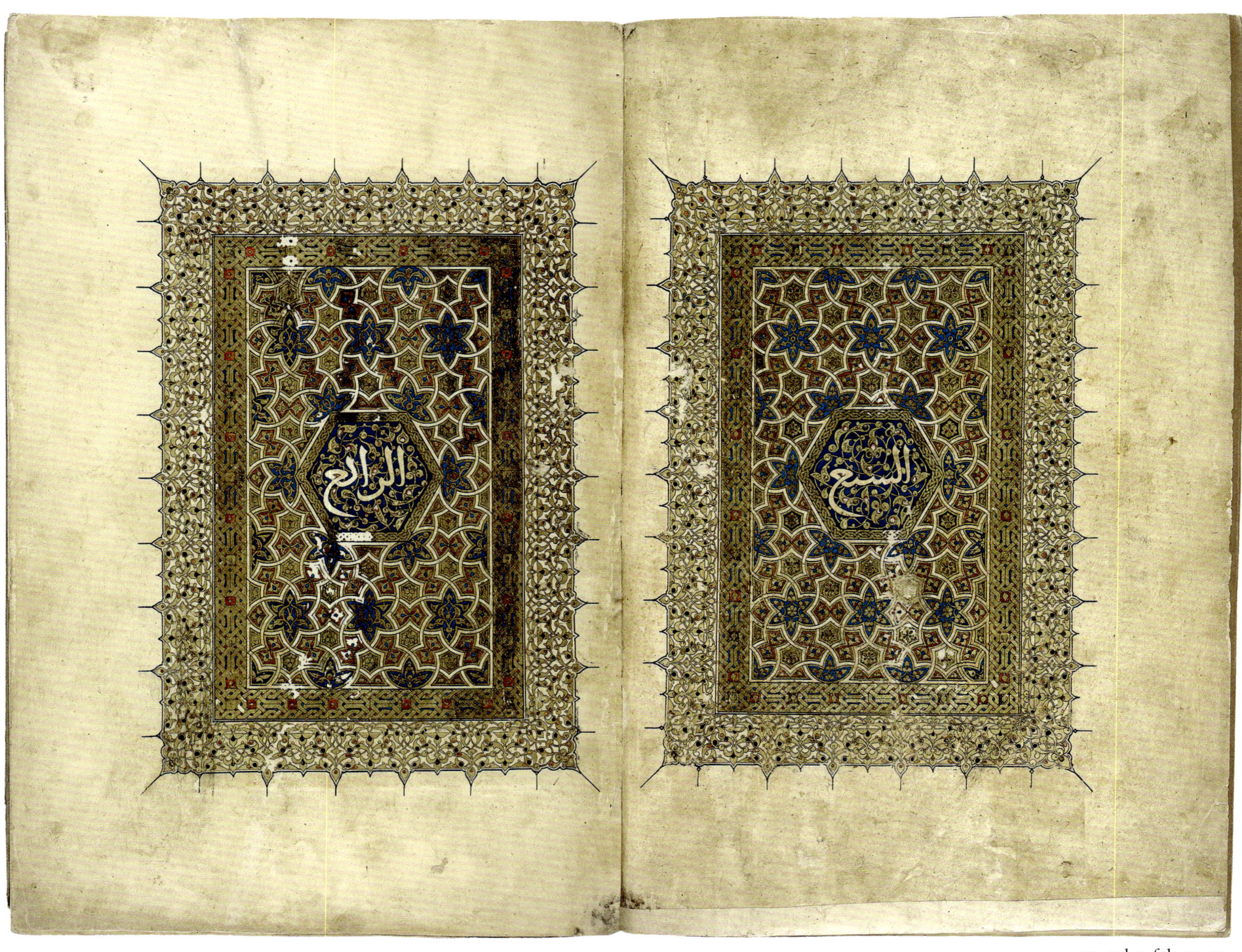

133, vol. 4, fols. 1v–2r

133

Volume Four of a Qur'an (Sura 14:23–52, 27)

Cairo, 1304–6
Calligraphy by ibn al-Wahid; illumination of this volume attributed to Muhammad ibn Mubadir
Opaque watercolor, gold, and ink on paper
19 × 12½ in. (48.5 × 32 cm)
British Library, London (Add. MS 22409)

This book is from a lavish seven-volume Qur'an produced for Baybars II, Mamluk sultan of Egypt from 1309 to 1310. In the preceding decade Baybars, as commander in chief at the court of the underage sultan al-Nasir Muhammad ibn Qala'un, had accumulated enough wealth to restore the minarets of the Mosque of al-Hakim (1302) and commission a dervish lodge (*khanqa*) in Cairo, completed in 1309. This Qur'an was made for and housed at the *khanqa*.[1]

In addition to being the earliest dated Mamluk Qur'an, the manuscript contains many exceptional features. Qur'ans often consist of multiple volumes, but the division here into seven parts (*sub'*) is unique, and the inclusion of six lines of text per page rather than the uneven number preferred by Mamluk calligraphers is highly unusual.[2] The copying of the text, in gold script outlined in black with silver diacriticals, probably took a year to complete. The illumination, meanwhile, carried out by three artists – Muhammad ibn Mubadir, responsible for this volume; Abu Bakr, known as Sandal; and Aydughdi ibn 'Abdallah – would have taken at least a year longer.

This volume contains several suras that have resonance with the Jewish and Christian traditions: "Ibrahim" (Sura 14) in part concerns the prophet Abraham, who brought his wife and his son Ishmael to the valley of Mecca; "The Night Journey" (*al-Isra'*, Sura 17) details the Prophet Muhammad's journey by night from Mecca to Jerusalem and onward to heaven and back; "The Cave" (*al-Kahf*, Sura 18) deals with the Seven Sleepers of Ephesus, who slept in a cave for 309 years; "Maryam" (Sura 19) notes the purity of Mary and the prophethood of Jesus (though denies that he is the son of God); and "The Prophets" (*al-Anbiya*, Sura 21) names Mary and sixteen prophets shared with the other Abrahamic faiths. In the Qur'an the prophets common to the three religions are harbingers of Islam and the "seal of the prophets," Muhammad. SRC

Selected References: London 1976, p. 52, nos. 66–69; James 1984; James 1988, pp. 34–73; Baker, ed. 2002.

1. James 1984, p. 148. James quotes Ibn Iyas's description of the manuscript and its placement in the *khanqa*.
2. Ibid.

134a–c

The Prophet Isaiah at the Walls of Jerusalem; The Maccabees' Battle for Jerusalem; The Emperor Heraclius Bringing the Cross to Jerusalem

From three volumes of an antiphonary made for the Franciscan community of Bethlehem
Venice, ca. 1401–4
Andrea di Bartolo (active in Siena and Venice, 1380–1429) and workshop
Tempera, gold, and ink on parchment
Isaiah volume (a): 22 × 15⅜ in. (56 × 39 cm)
Maccabees volume (b): 21⅝ × 13 in. (55 × 33 cm)
Emperor Heraclius volume (c): 22 × 15 in. (56 × 38 cm)
Terra Sancta Museum, Bibliotheca Custodialis, Jerusalem (MS 5, 6, 7)

Over the course of the fourteenth century, Italian painters established themselves as masters of the art of choir-book illumination. Known primarily on the Italian peninsula, the work of these artists reached distant new audiences with this commission. An inscription on the opening page of the first of the three books reveals that they formed part of an ensemble given to the Franciscans in the Holy Land by Henry IV of England, with the explicit intent that the friars pray for the soul of his father, John of Gaunt (1340–1399), duke of Lancaster.[1]

A remarkable collision of circumstances led to the creation of the ensemble, which originally comprised multiple volumes for daily use throughout the year. The chief mentor of Andrea di Bartolo, the artist responsible for the books' illumination, had sailed to the Holy Land on the same ship as the future Henry IV, forging a connection with Henry before he became king. The artist, in turn, was allied with the Contanini, a Venetian merchant family for whom support of the Franciscans in the Holy Land was among its active enterprises. Following a Contanini initiative in London in 1400, Henry contributed significantly to the work of the Franciscans at Bethlehem, likely commissioning this antiphonary at that time.

Among the wide-ranging subjects presented in the volumes, the dependence of Christian worship on the heritage of Judaism is evidenced in two of the images presented here. One scene, set within a letter *H*, shows the prophet Isaiah standing before the city of Jerusalem (cat. 134a). The accompanying chant is meant to be intoned during the season of Advent (coincident with the month of December), when the faithful prepare for the birth of Jesus, the Messiah. Thus, the words offer comfort: "Jerusalem, Thy salvation cometh quickly; why art thou wasted with sorrow? Is there no counselor in thee, that pangs have taken thee? Fear not, for I will save thee and deliver thee. / For I am the Lord, thy God, the Holy One of Israel, thy Saviour. / Fear not, for I will save thee, and deliver thee."[2]

A second such illumination portrays the battle of the Maccabees within a letter *A* (cat. 134b). Western European Christians fighting to regain the Holy Land considered the Maccabees, Jews living in the second century B.C., to be exemplars of the noble

134a, fols. 29v–30r

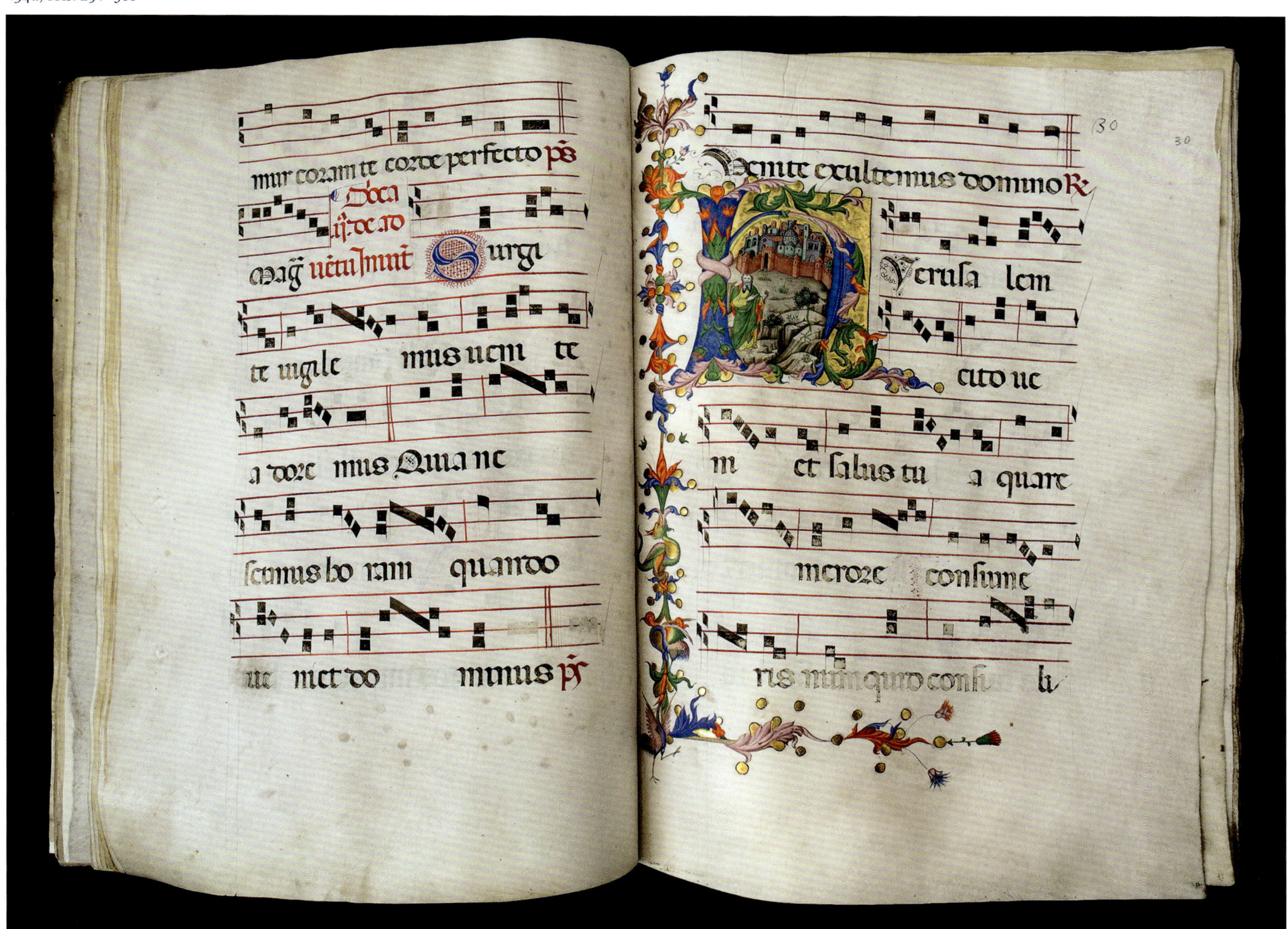

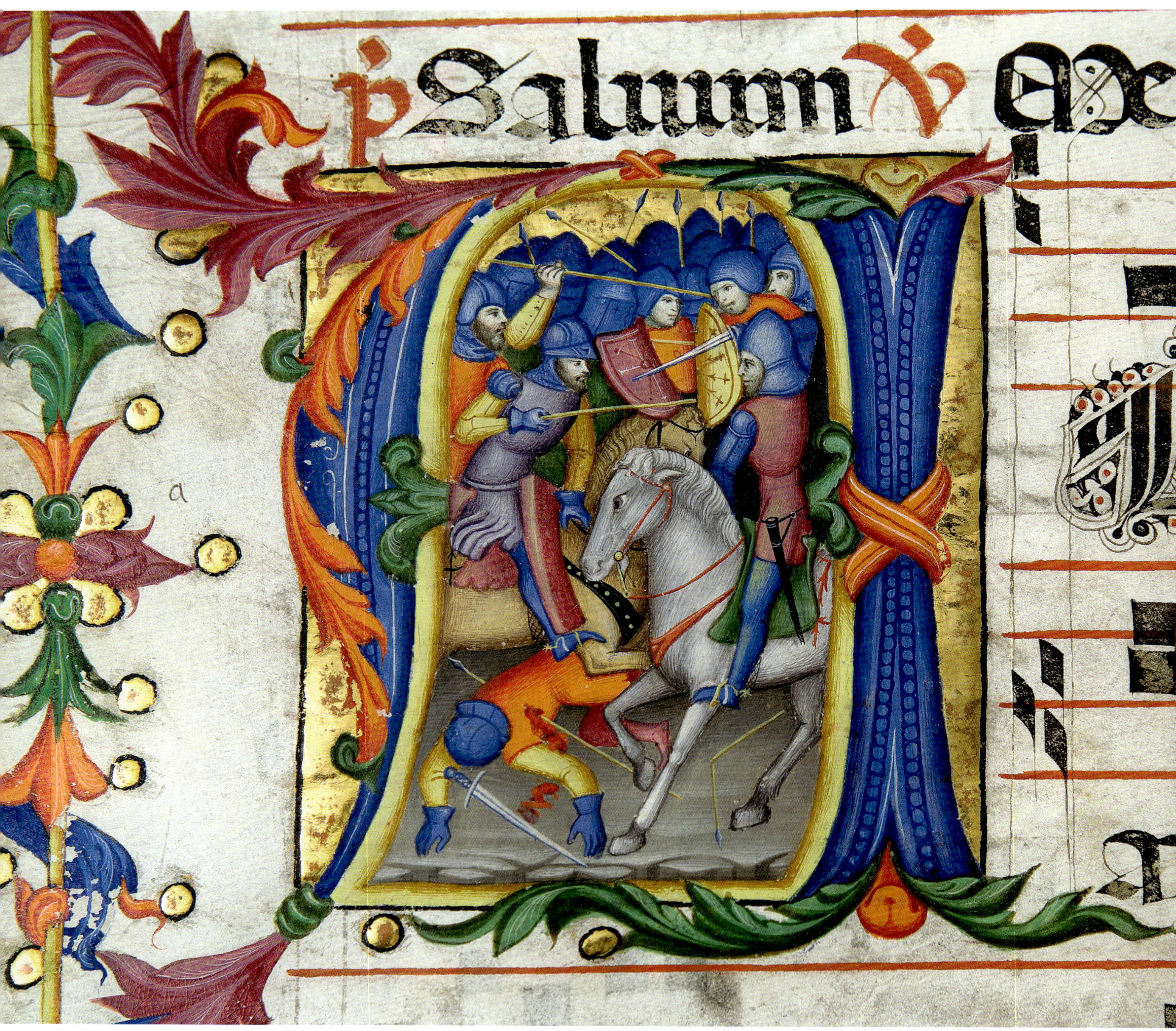

134b detail, fol. 254

struggle for Jerusalem, for against all odds they had wrested Jerusalem and the Temple back from the pagan king Antiochus IV Epiphanes. Centuries later, churchmen advocating crusade lauded the Maccabees' commitment to recapturing the Holy City, with Guibert, abbot of Nogent (1055–1124), drawing specifically on their story to justify combat: "If in olden times the Maccabees attained to the highest praise of piety because they fought for the ceremonies and the Temple, it is also justly granted you, Christian soldiers, to defend their liberty of your country by armed endeavor."[3] The image in the Franciscan choir book presents battle as a colorful event of almost balletic beauty, though a fallen soldier does lie trampled underfoot. The text to be sung is a plea for peace taken directly from the book of Maccabees: "The Lord open your hearts in His Law and commandments, and may the Lord our God send peace" (2 Macc. 1:4).[4]

An illumination from the third volume emphasizes the preservation of the Cross of Jesus, which had been taken forcibly from Jerusalem by Khusraw, king of Persia. Within a letter *D* the emperor Heraclius II, in perfect counterpoint to the illumination of Isaiah in the first volume, appears at the gates of Jerusalem (cat. 134c). It is the year 629, and the emperor, having recovered the Cross, returns it to the Holy City – not to his capital at Constantinople. The gate is open wide, and Jerusalem's sacred buildings are partly visible above the walls. Out of humility Heraclius has removed his elegant robe and crown; he enters barefoot. The hymn, written centuries earlier,

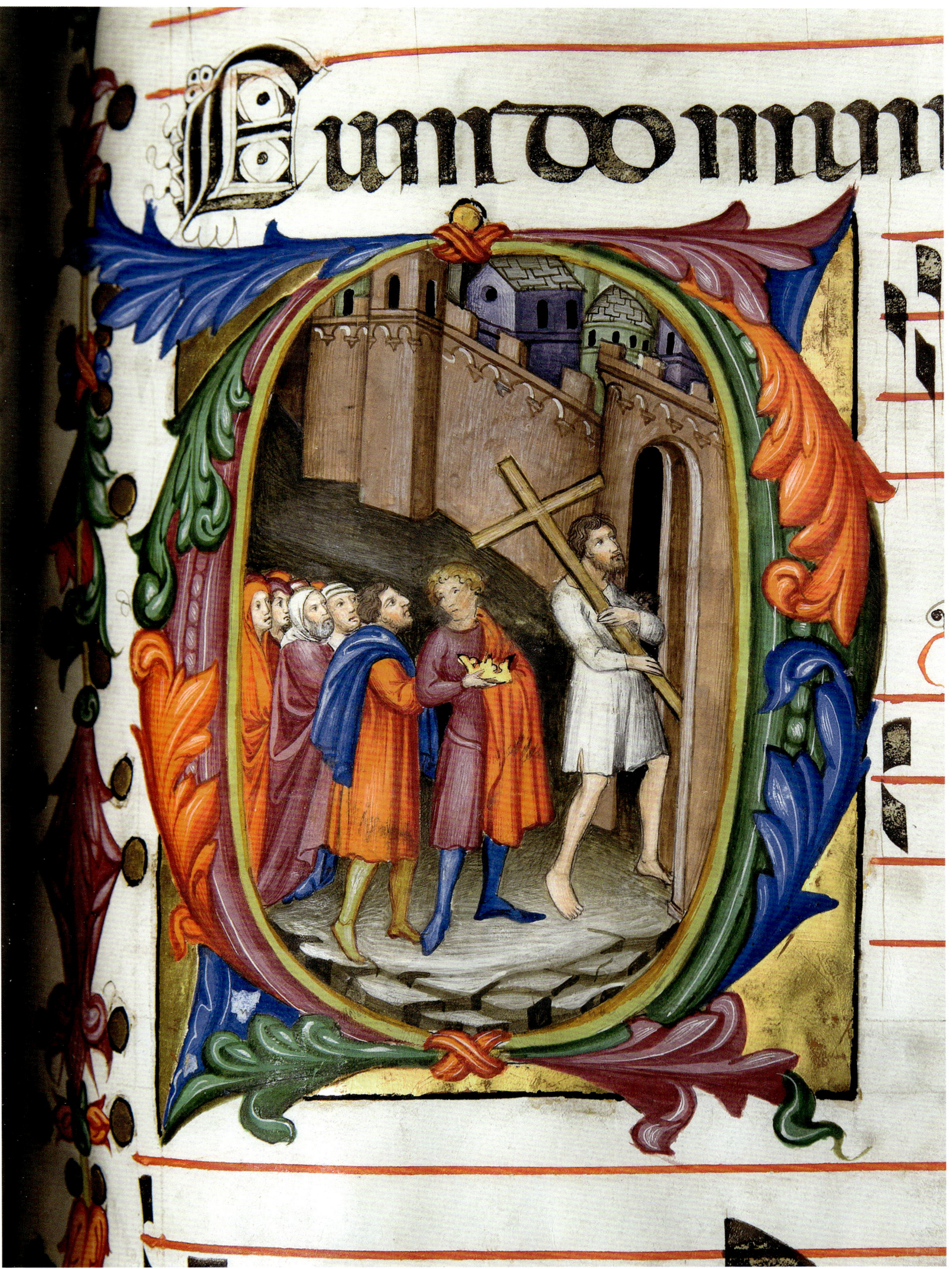

134c detail, fol. 48r

reflects devotion to the Cross for the feast of its veneration, celebrated on September 14: "O sweet wood, O sweet nails."[5] Whereas the text does not emphasize the city's importance as the place where the Cross is preserved, the illuminator focused on it as a matter of great importance to contemporary Christians and to the Franciscan community residing in the Holy Land, who served as guides to its visitors.

BDB

Selected References: Bux 1990, pp. 21, 52–78; De Benedictis et al. 2002, pp. 188–92, 340.

1. "Orate pro anima illustrissimi principis Domini Ioannis quondam ducis Lancastre filii regis. Anglorum Edwardi tertii, ac patris Henrici quarti de cuius elemosina scriptus est liber iste ac plenarie factus pro consolatione fratrum Sacri Montis Sion."
2. Chant for the second Sunday of Advent, first nocturn, first response: "Hyerusalem cito veniet salus tua quare moerore consumeris? namquid consiliarius non est tibi quia innovavit te dolor? Salvabo te, et liberabo te; noli timere. Ego enim sum Dominus Deus tuus, sanctus Israel, Redemptor tuus." Translation taken from Kiss, L., et al., eds. 2000– .
3. Cited in Guibert of Nogent 1997 ed., based on Krey 1921, pp. 36–40.
4. "Adaperiat dominus cor vestrum in lege sua et in preceptis suis, et faciat pacem Dominus Deus noster." The Maccabees' victory and the ensuing rededication of the Temple are celebrated by Jews during the feast of Hanukkah, beginning on the twenty-fifth day of Kislev. The Franciscans for whom this book was made feted the Maccabees on August 1.
5. "Dulce lignum, dulces clavos, dulce pondus sustinuit." The text is based on a sixth-century poem by Venantius Fortunatus, "Pange lingua, gloriosi." It was sung as the first nocturn of Matins.

135 a–e

Mosque Lamps of Sultan Barquq

Egypt or Syria, 1382–99
Glass with gold and enamel

a. 13 × 9⅞ in. (33 × 25 cm)
Nasser D. Khalili Collection of Islamic Art, London (GLS 572)

b. 13¾ × 10½ in. (34.7 × 26.8 cm)
Victoria and Albert Museum, London (321-1900)

c. 10 × 9¼ in. (25.4 × 23.5 cm)
Victoria and Albert Museum, London (325-1900)

d. 13⅝ × 10½ in. (34.7 × 26.8 cm)
Victoria and Albert Museum, London (326-1900)

e. 14⅝ in. × 9⅝ in. (37.1 × 24.4 cm)
The Metropolitan Museum of Art, New York, Gift of J. Pierpont Morgan, 1917 (17.190.989)

Sayf al-Din Abu Sa'id Barquq[1] was devoted to building, and his legacy includes a number of imposing monuments. Perhaps the most important is the madrasa that he built in Cairo in 1386, located between the Kamiliyya Madrasa and the Nasiriyya Madrasa, that was used by the four schools of Islamic law as well as for the Friday sermon and reading of the Qur'an. Additional building projects included the Sharia Bridge on the Jordan River and the Zawiyat Barzakh in Damietta, Egypt; a cistern, fountain, and library for orphans in the citadel, Cairo; and Qanat al-'Arub, a subterranean aqueduct, in Jerusalem.[2] Also in Jerusalem, he built the Khan al-Sultan, a travelers' inn and stables, in 1386[3] and renewed a rostrum in the Dome of the Rock in 1387.[4]

Lamps were an integral component of mosques and madrasas,[5] and approximately fifty-nine surviving examples can be attributed to the patronage of Sultan Barquq.[6] While the survival of such fragile material may seem surprising, their preservation over the centuries was assured by their continual use in their original context until the late nineteenth century. They are currently dispersed as follows: twenty-five are preserved in the Museum of Islamic Art, Cairo; twenty-two are in the Imam Husayn Mosque in Cairo; and twelve more are in various other museums and collections around the world.[7]

Research on these lamps has revealed a number of significant characteristics for this group. They all took a similar form, which

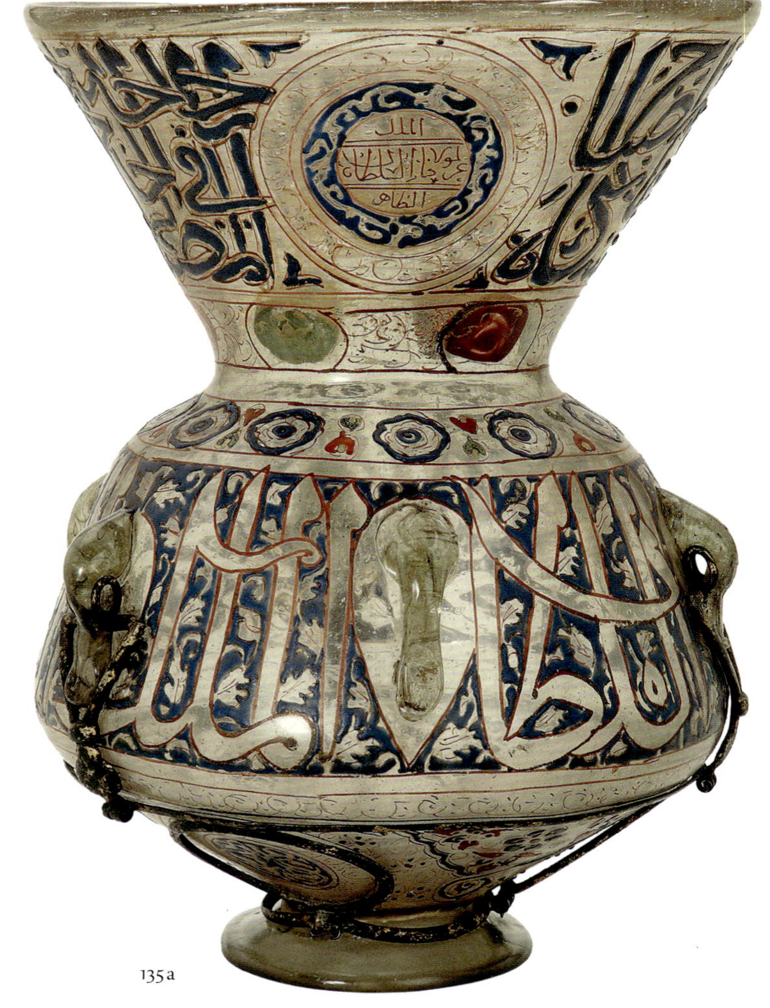

135a

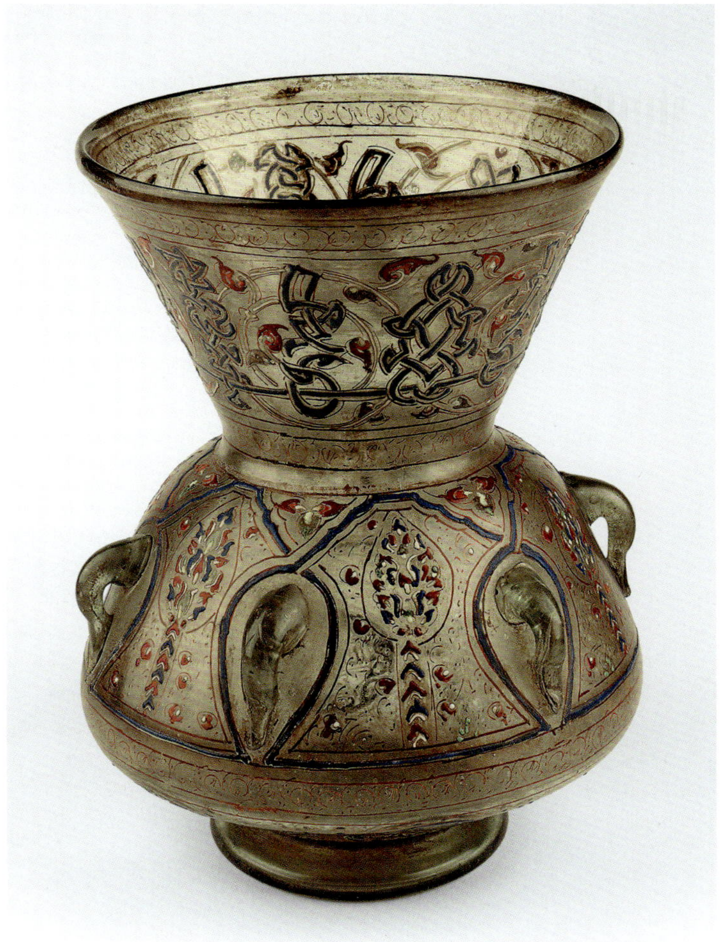

135b

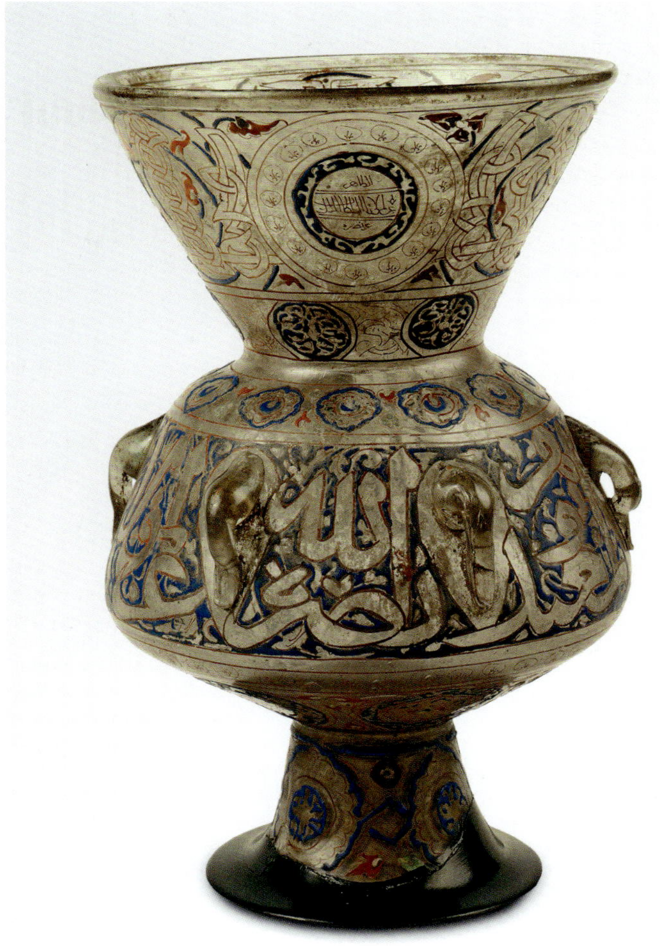

135c

consisted of a conical neck with a flaring mouth on top of a bulbous body, resting in turn on an attached foot, either splayed or short and ring-shaped.[8] The shape of the body may have been advantageous in terms of the lamp's ability to provide illumination.[9] It has also become evident that most mosque lamps of Barquq were made of glass so transparent that the decoration executed on the surface is visible from behind.[10]

Two styles of decoration are prevalent on the surfaces of the glass lamps: enamel and gilding. It is likely that during the fourteenth century, the period of Sultan Barquq, and thereafter, gilded decoration was unfired. This technique has less binding strength and is more susceptible to damage and loss due to the absence of a strong intermediary material binding the gilding to glass.[11]

Just as the decorative styles on the surfaces of the mosque lamps of Barquq are various, so too are the types of decorative elements. The first type of ornamentation is calligraphic, in which we find two forms of thuluth script. The first is characterized by the thickness of its letters[12] and was used to write such verses from the Qur'an as "God is the light of the heavens and the earth. His light is like a niche in which there is a lamp, the lamp made of glass" (24:35).[13] This distinguished verse is usually recorded on the neck of the lamp and appears on several examples preserved in the Museum of Islamic Art, Cairo. The script was less elegantly formed than that seen on the bodies of the vessels, a result of the smaller surface area of the neck.

The bulbous bodies of the vessels were considered the best place for invocatory expressions regarding Sultan Barquq, and these were written in a beautiful thuluth script. They read: "Glory to our lord the Sultan al-Malik al-Zahir Abu Sa'id, may God protect him!"[14] This expression is made up of four components: the first and last are invocations, appearing at the beginning and the end of such expressions, represented here by the phrases "Glory to our lord" and "May God protect him." The second component is the honorific title of Sultan Barquq, *al-Malik al-Zahir*, and the third element is the sultan's name, Abu Sa'id.

The second type of ornament found on the lamps is vegetal embellishment. Typical motifs include lotus blossoms with many petals,[15] composite flowers made up of six petals,[16] poplar-shaped trees, trefoils, vegetal branches and stems, and arabesques. Found on all parts of the lamp's body, although less commonly on the feet, these decorations were executed in polychrome enamels (various hues of blue, red, and white) as well as gilding.[17]

The third type of ornament that decorated the lamps is geometric, including roundels enclosing blossoms and mandorla-shaped fields enclosing the handles of the lamp. The mandorla-shaped fields are sometimes outlined with a single band of blue or red enamel but in other cases a double band is used. Lobed forms are also found and are usually executed in red enamel. Finally, there are semigeometric forms executed in red and interlace forms in blue. AEM

Selected References: Cat. 135a: Khalili 2008, p. 108. Cat. 135b: Wiet 1982, p. 176. Cat. 135c, d, e: Wiet 1982, p. 177.

I would like to thank both my colleague 'Abd al-Hamid 'Abd al-Salam and the Information Center, Museum of Islamic Art, Cairo.

1. This is how his name appears on the foundation inscription of the madrasa and *khanqa* located on Mu'izz li-Din Allah Street in Cairo, considered to be the first Circassian Mamluk construction. Built with funds from the waqf of the family of Sultan al-Nasir Muhammad, it was completed in 1386. See Mahir 2010, vol. 4, pp. 37–38.
2. See 'Umar Shukri, ed. 2002, pp. 90–91.
3. See Drory 1981, pp. 198–99; Burgoyne et al. 1987, p. 77.
4. See Sharon 1997–2013, vol. 5, p. 156, mentioned in relation to patronage in Hebron.
5. Glass was used for these mosque lamps so they could best serve their function of illumination. Some hanging lamps

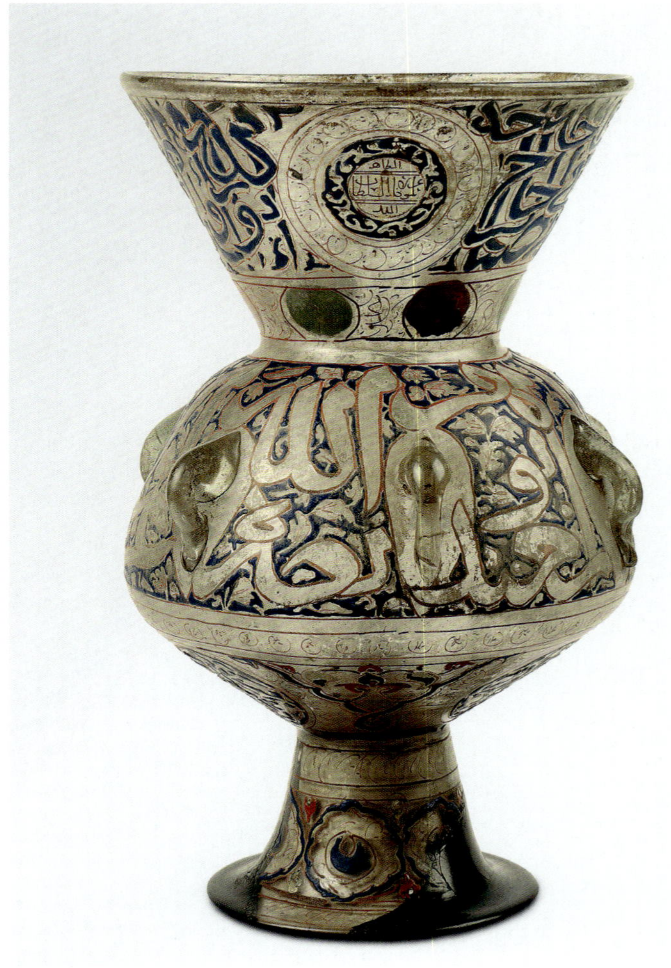

135d

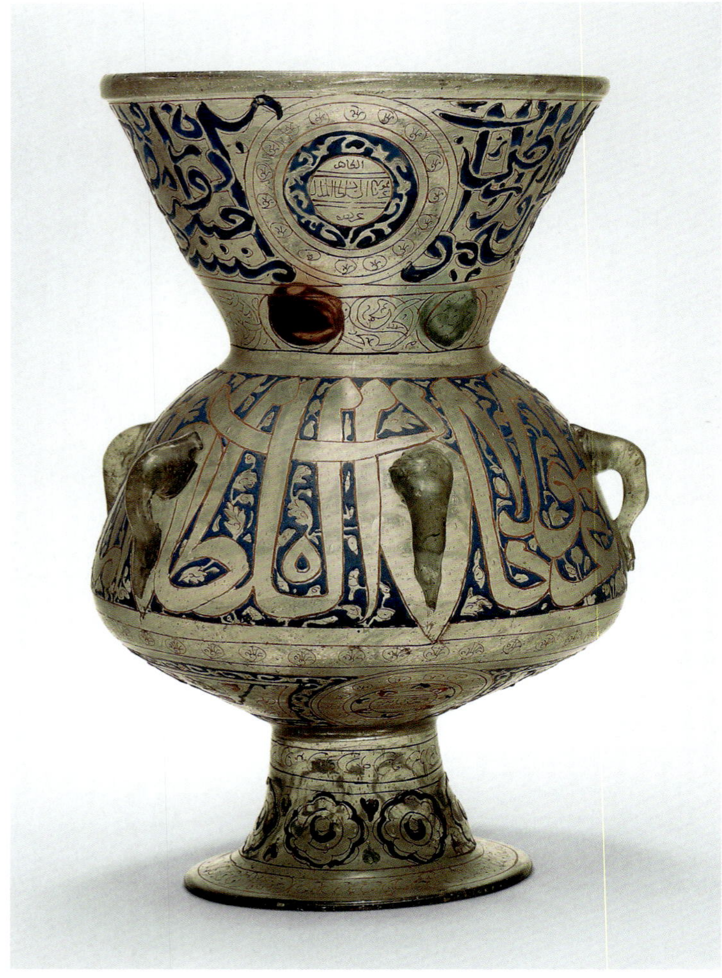

135e

were made of other materials, such as metal and ceramic. Although these took the same form as the glass mosque lamps, their function was not illumination. Rather, their function was decorative or to disperse pleasant scents, hence some of them were pierced. See cat. 91.

6. Dawud 1971, p. 468.

7. These include the Museum für Islamische Kunst in Berlin, the Victoria and Albert Museum in London, The Metropolitan Museum of Art, the Musée des Beaux-Arts in Lyon, and the Musée du Louvre in Paris (formerly the collection of Baron Edmond de Rothschild). For more information on these lamps, see Wiet 1982, pp. 175–79. I would like to thank Carine Juvin for notifying me that a lamp formerly housed in the collection of Edmond de Rothschild is now housed in the Louvre under inventory number OA 7568.

8. Numerous forms are known for lamps. Aside from the type under discussion here, there are cylindrical lamps, some examples of which were discovered in the Jazira Museum in Cairo and subsequently transferred to the Museum of Islamic Art in Cairo. A third type is shaped like a bowl equipped with a piece attached to the interior of the base used to fix the wick. A fourth type has a dented form without handles for hanging, as it would stand instead on a metal support. For more information, see Dawud 1971, p. 482.

9. Sa'id 1988, p. 5.

10. About twenty-two lamps preserved in the Mosque of Imam Husayn were made of glass tinged with red; see Dawud 1971, p. 467.

11. One study has shown that relative humidity and fluctuations in heat alongside air pollution are among the most serious factors leading to the damage of glass and loss of gilding from its surface. A hanging lamp of Sultan Barquq was used as an example in this study. See Dawi and 'Abd-Allah 1999, p. 583.

12. See Dhannun 1989, p. 108. On the characteristics of these types of scripts, see also Dawud 1991, p. 59.

13. Part of *Surat al-Nur*, "Light." All quotes from the Qur'an in this entry are from the al-Medina Qur'an.

14. An invocatory phrase that appears on many examples of applied art in the Ayyubid and Mamluk periods. For more information on this phrase, see Mahmud 2015, p. 255.

15. The lotus is a floral motif known since the Pharaonic age. See Fehérvári 1976, p. 151; Baer 1998, p. 20.

16. These decorations – the lotus and the composite flower – appear on either the neck or the body of most of the lamps of Barquq preserved in the Museum of Islamic Art.

17. Studies have confirmed that most of the feet of the lamps of Barquq were of the short, round type except in rare instances, such as an example in the collection of the Museum of Islamic Art, Cairo (no. 299), which has an elevated, cone-shaped foot.

136

Legal Document Concerning the Gift of Lady Sufra Khatun

Jerusalem, A.H. 26 Dhu al-Hijjah 770 (August 1, 1369)
Ink on paper
12⅝ × 16⅞ in. (32 × 43 cm)
Islamic Museum, Jerusalem (0168)

Lady Sufra Khatun was one of a number of wealthy women described by the historian Mujir al-Din who endowed madrasas and other religious structures in the vicinity of the Haram al-Sharif during the Mamluk period.[1] Descended from a family of merchants, Sufra also married a merchant—one Imad al-Din al-Bawardi, who traced his roots to the Mongol city of Sarai in southern Russia.[2] In 1367 she founded the Madrasa al-Bawardiyya as well as a mausoleum, undoubtedly for her husband, near the gate of the Aqsa Mosque.[3]

This document, dated two years after the establishment of the madrasa, acknowledges the endowment of furnishings for the complex, including brass trays and bowls, gilded lamps, and some fifteen carpets. The itemized list of carpets describes an Anatolian prayer rug in addition to carpets from the region of Hauran (present-day Syria and Jordan) and the city of Shoubak (in present-day Jordan). Once the site of the Crusader castle of Montreal, Shoubak seems to have become an important center for carpets by the end of the fourteenth century.[4] BDB / MH

Selected References: Little 1984a, pp. 194–95, no. 76 (with incorrect date); Little 1984b, p. 69; Müller 2008, pp. 177–79.

1. Mujir al-Din 1876 ed., pp. 158–59.
2. Little 1986, p. 85.
3. Burgoyne et al. 1987, p. 70.
4. Little 1986, pp. 85–87.

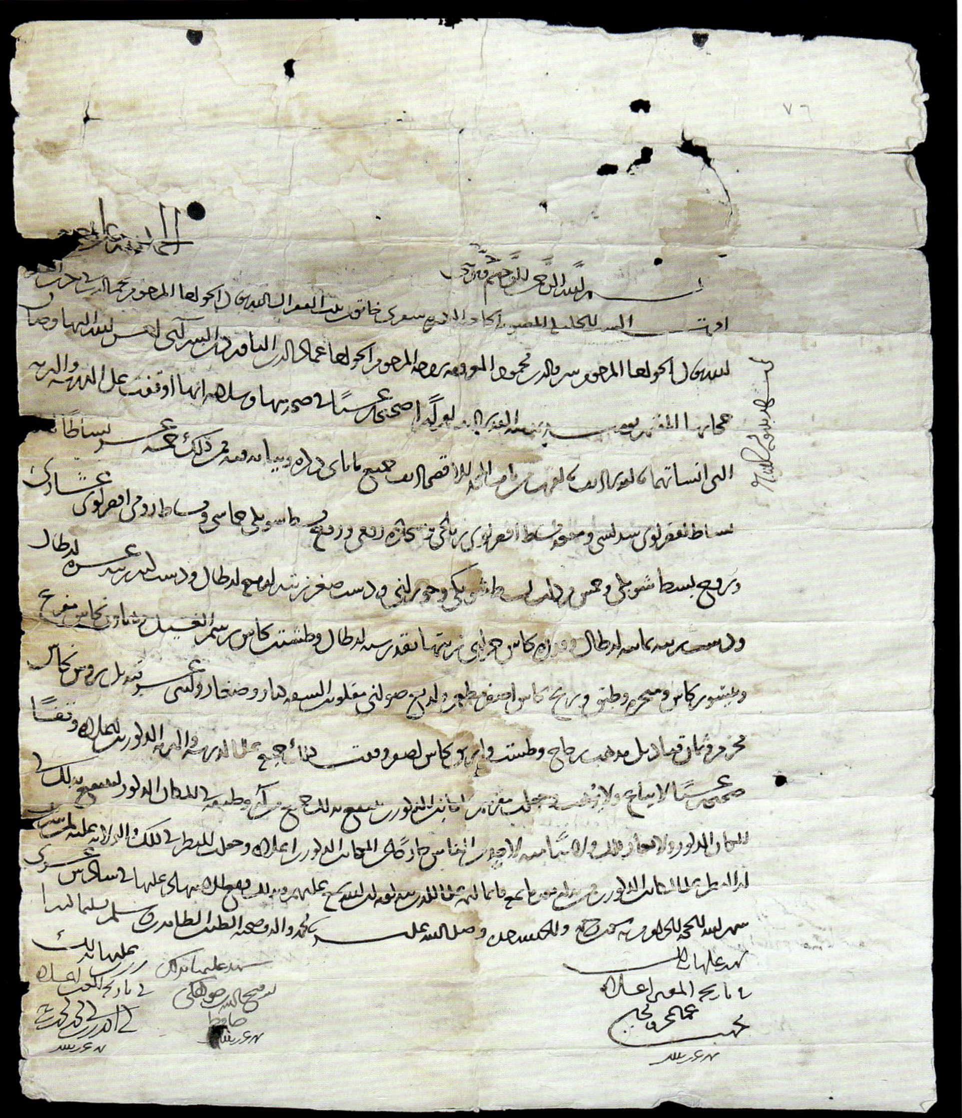

136

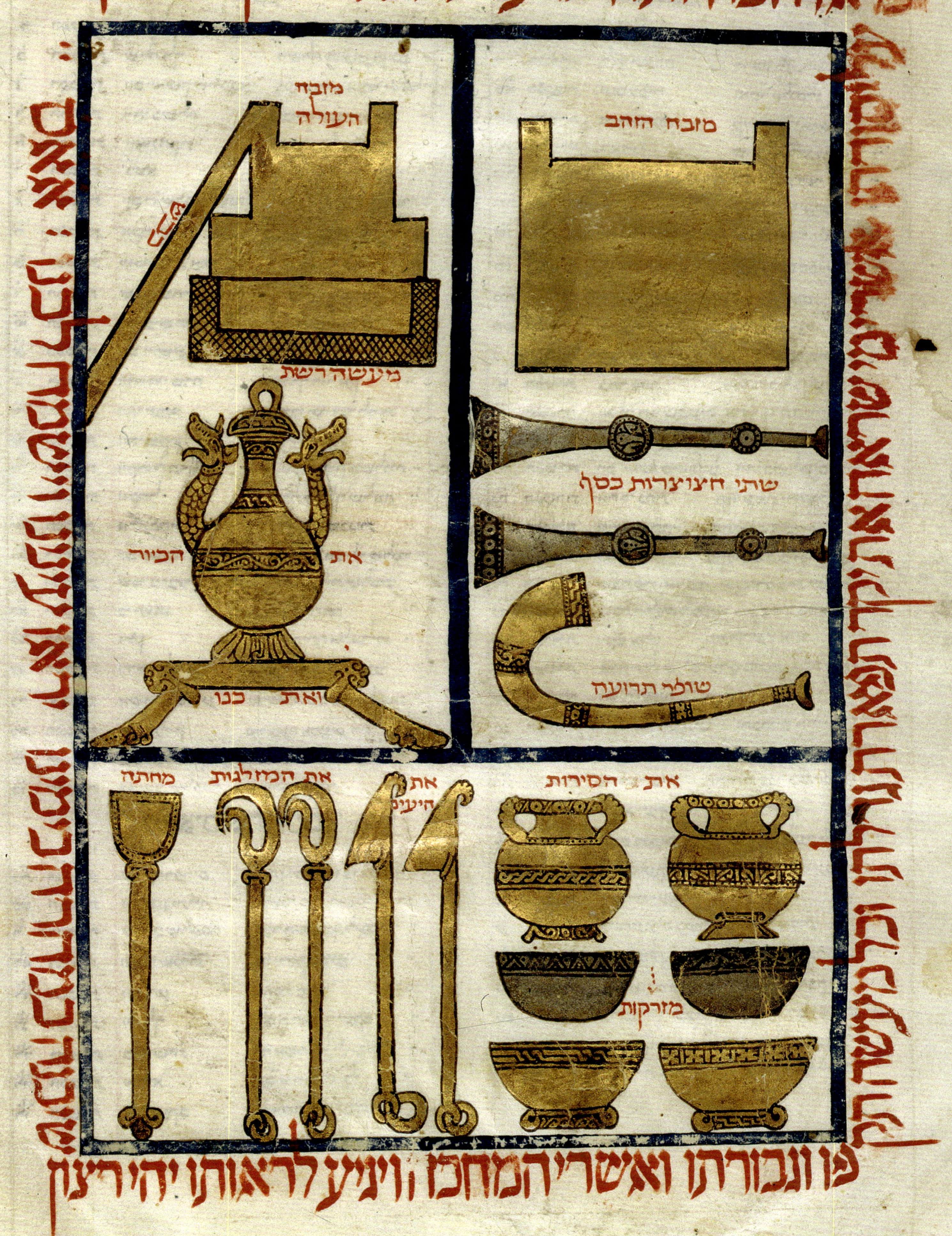

כל אלה כהיות היכל על מכונתו ומקדש הקדש
מזבח העולה
מזבח הזהב
מעשה רשת
את הכיור
ואת כנו
שתי חצוצרות כסף
שופר תרועה
מחתה
את המזלגות
את היעים
את הסירות
מזרקות
ואשרי המחכה ויגיע לראותו יהי רצון

Seeking the Eternal Jerusalem

Gates that face the open gates of heaven – Judah ha-Levi

ABBY KORNFELD

FACING PAGE
Fig. 96. Temple Implements, from the Perpignan Bible. Detail of cat. 137a, fol. 13r

THE SANCTITY OF Jerusalem depends as much on its biblical past as on its proximity to heaven. For Jerusalem was believed to be the closest point to the skies and the place on earth where the Messiah would appear, where humankind – living and dead, faithful and infidel – would be gathered and judged, where the final battles would be waged, and where the Heavenly City would emerge.[1] Although the city's significance and symbolism vary widely in Jewish, Christian, and Islamic traditions, there is a consensus that Jerusalem functions as the meeting place of God and man, the gateway to heaven, the terrestrial threshold of the eternal world. During the medieval period, cataclysmic events – natural disasters, bloody battles, political takeovers, and zealous destructions – shook the city repeatedly, sending reverberations across the known world. These upheavals were thought to signal the start of the End of Time, the arrival of the Kingdom of Heaven, the New Jerusalem.

The splendor of the Heavenly City of Jerusalem was described first by the prophet Ezekiel in the Hebrew Bible and later by John the Evangelist in the Apocalypse (book of Revelation). Both accounts combine vivid descriptions of the heavenly precinct with practical information: measurements, building materials, access points, and waterways. While both inspired expansive commentaries, homilies, sermons, and works of art, there are two key differences in their accounts. First, Ezekiel gives a detailed account of the space and contours of the future Temple – a structure so large that he initially mistakes it for a city (Ezekiel 40:2) – while John makes clear that there will be no Temple in the Heavenly City for "the Lord God Almighty is the temple thereof, and the Lamb" (Apocalypse 21:22). In addition, Ezekiel is led up to the top of a mountain, where he is shown the Heavenly City (Ezekiel 40:2), while John watches as it descends from heaven to a distant mountaintop (Apocalypse 21:2). Medieval artists relied on these two descriptive texts when depicting the New Jerusalem in illuminated manuscripts, precious objects, and monumental architecture.

"May it be your will that the Temple be speedily rebuilt in our days so that our eyes may see it and our hearts rejoice. Amen amen sela." This aspiration concludes the text inscribed around a depiction of ritual implements in the Hebrew Bible manuscript produced in Perpignan, France, in the year 1299 (cat. 137a; fig. 96).[2] Each object displayed is described in the Bible as a requisite element for God's dwelling place on earth, whether the portable sanctuary erected in the desert known as the Tabernacle or, later, the Temple in Jerusalem.[3] Beginning on the right, the towering seven-branched candelabrum (the menorah) stands aglow. Beneath it, the slender jar of manna is positioned between the barren rod and

Aaron's rod studded with stylized almond blossoms.[4] To the left, winged cherubs crown the Tablets of the Law, while twelve golden loaves are stacked on the shewbread table below. On the facing folio, at the top, the golden incense altar stands alongside the sacrificial altar with its ramp and grille. Finally, a collection of smaller ritual objects is displayed: two silver trumpets, the ram's horn (shofar), the copper laver on its stand (depicted here as a ewer), as well as various pots, basins, hooks, and shovels.[5]

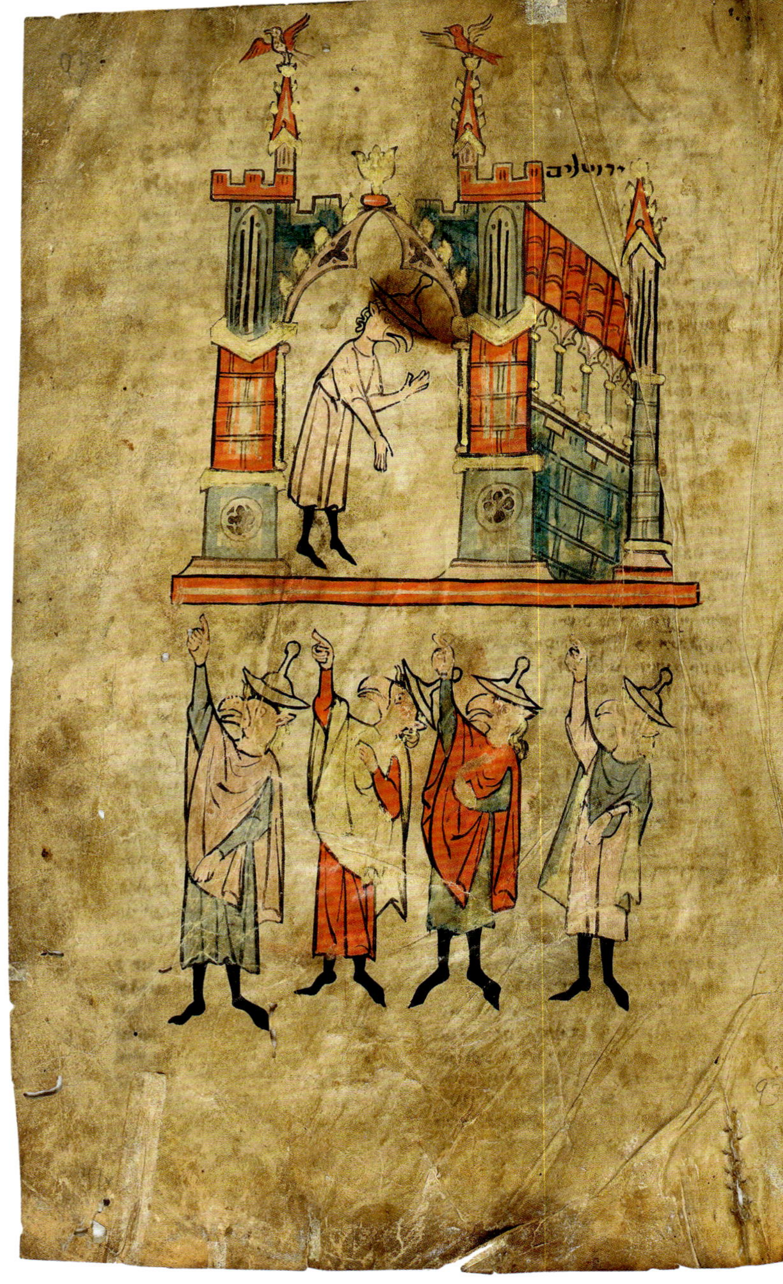

Fig. 97. "Next Year in Jerusalem," from the Birds' Head Haggadah. Upper Rhine (Mainz?), Germany, ca. 1310. Tempera and ink on parchment. The Israel Museum, Jerusalem (MS 180/57, fol. 47r)

Similar treasuries of shimmering ritual vessels appear in more than twenty large-scale illuminated Hebrew Bibles produced in Provence and Spain.[6] Differing only slightly from manuscript to manuscript, the arrangement of ritual objects remains remarkably stable throughout the fourteenth century.[7] The one significant addition is the Mount of Olives.[8] In a mid-fourteenth-century Hebrew Bible (cat. 137c), for example, the Mount of Olives is represented in the lower left corner as a diminutive mound topped by a slender, curved tree. A closer look reveals that the terrain has been cleaved in two, a division emphasized by curvilinear highlights. This detail refers to the prophet Zechariah's vision of the End of Days: the moment when all the nations are gathered in Jerusalem, God will set his feet on the Mount of Olives, and the "Mount of Olives shall cleft in the midst thereof toward the east and toward the west, so that there shall be a very great valley" (Zechariah 14:4).[9] By including the Mount of Olives, the collection of ritual implements is imbued with geographic and temporal specificity. As prophesied, these vessels will once again be necessary when the Messiah appears, the Temple is rebuilt, and the sacrificial service to God is restored.

There was great discussion among rabbinic exegetes about whether righteous individuals would need to rebuild the Temple or if it would descend from heaven fully formed.[10] According to the early seventh-century apocalyptic text *Book of Zerubbabel* (*Sefer Zerubbabel*), God "will bring down to earth the Temple that was built above, and the pillar of fire and the cloud of incense will ascend to heaven."[11] This idea was then repeated and expanded in various apocalyptic texts.[12] However, the philosopher

Sa'adia Gaon (882–942) famously rejected the idea that a heavenly precinct would descend to earth, finding neither biblical nor rabbinic support for such an interpretation.[13] The Talmudic scholar Hai Gaon (939–1038) conceded that some saw proof of the Heavenly City in the words of Psalms 122:3: "Jerusalem built up, a city knit together."[14] Later, Solomon ben Isaac of Troyes (1040–1105), better known as Rashi, would argue that the future Temple will descend from heaven already built and perfect. Maimonides (Moshe ben Maimon, 1135–1204), on the other hand, believed that the Jewish people would build the future Temple according to the specifications given in the Bible.[15]

On Passover, the annual Jewish festival commemorating the biblical Exodus from Egypt, the Messianic redemption was believed to be even more imminent, for the Talmud teaches that the past miracle anticipates the future one.[16] Therefore, by the late Middle Ages, the ritual banquet known as the Passover Seder would begin and end with the eschatological declaration "Next Year in Jerusalem."[17] In a Passover Haggadah produced in the early fourteenth century, this hope-filled affirmation faces an image of an architectural structure suspended above the outstretched arms of four animal-headed men (fig. 97).[18] This image is often said to represent the Heavenly City descending to earth and the Jewish exiles ascending to Jerusalem at the End of Days.[19] However, the pictorial layout (with a city seemingly suspended in air) is not unique in this manuscript: on folio 15 recto, for example, the store cities of Pithom and Raamses – Egyptian treasure cities believed to have been built by Jewish slaves at the direction of a tyrannical pharaoh – also appear to float in the middle of the folio. Certainly, no one would argue that Pithom and Raamses were heaven-sent. Perhaps the scene here imagines the moment when the Messiah (standing inside the lobed arch and making a gesture of speech) will stand up on the roof of the Temple and exclaim, "Humble ones, the time for your redemption has come."[20]

While Jewish commentators debated how the New Jerusalem would appear, Christian exegetes found their answer in John the Evangelist's account of the city's descent from heaven in the Apocalypse. He described it as "having the glory of God, and the light thereof was like to a precious stone, as to the jasper stone, even as crystal" (Apocalypse 21:10–11). This remarkable vision is imagined in works of art large and small.[21] In a mid-fourteenth-century Apocalypse manuscript (cat. 140), an angel takes John by the arm and gently guides him up to the top of a mountain, where they witness the luminous city descending to earth on a cloud.[22] The city, painted in silver, sparkles brightly, reflecting and refracting light. Neither sun nor moon is necessary, "for the glory of God hath enlightened it, and the Lamb is the lamp thereof" (Apocalypse 21:23). Here, the Heavenly Jerusalem is enclosed by a "wall great and high" with twelve gates – three on each of its cardinal sides – and its "foundations [are] . . . adorned with all manner of precious stones" (Apocalypse 21:12–13, 19). On the facing folio, the angel reveals "a river of water of life, clear as crystal, proceeding from the throne of God and of the Lamb" (Apocalypse 22:1). Not only do these images illuminate the biblical description verse by verse, they also provide the viewer with a vision of the heavenly precinct.[23]

John's description also inspired the form of the late twelfth-century Gozbert Censer (fig. 98).[24] Like the New Jerusalem, the Gozbert Censer was formed from gilded bronze and was built on a symmetrical (cruciform) plan. That it was intended to be seen in midair, swinging from side to side during liturgical processions and accompanied by plumes of sweet-smelling smoke, only further underscores John's vision of the city descending to earth on a cloud.[25] The iconography of the censer may well have been informed by the mid-twelfth-century treatise on the arts written by Theophilus, which plainly

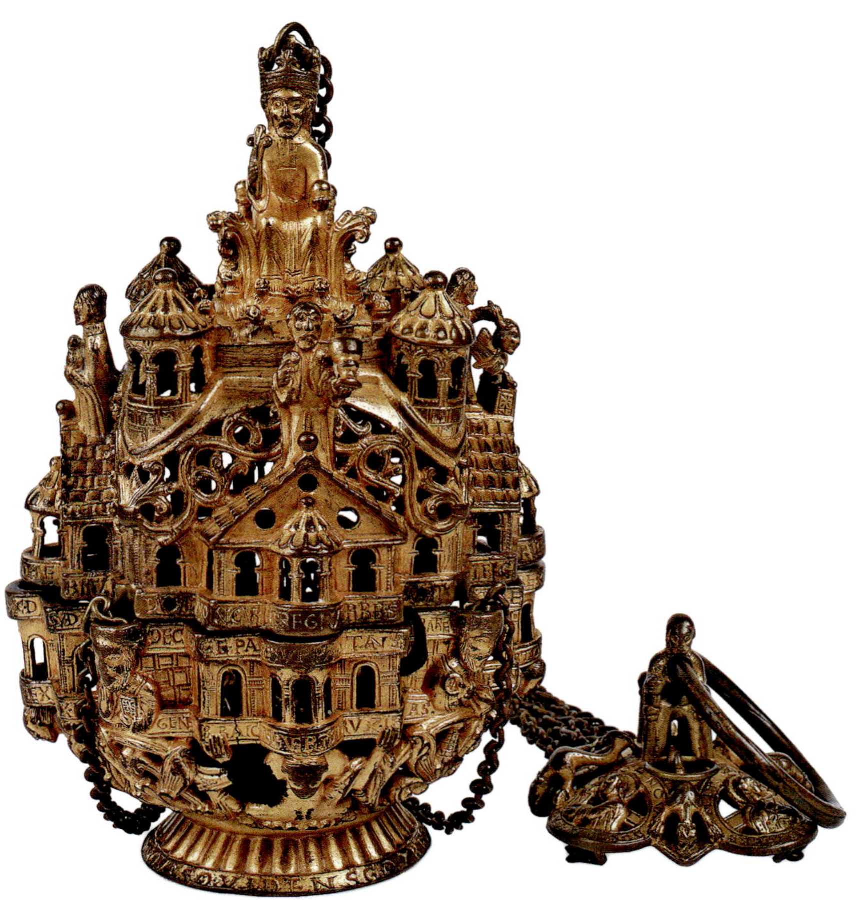

Fig. 98. The Gozbert Censer, representing the Heavenly Jerusalem. Meuse Valley (present-day Belgium), ca. 1100. Gilded bronze. Treasury of Trier Cathedral

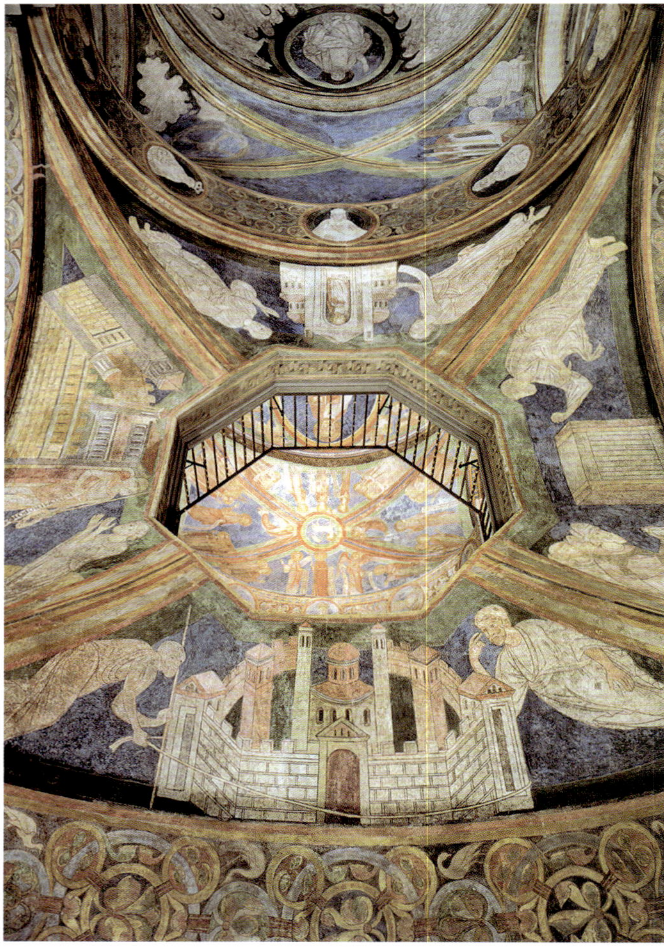

Fig. 99. Scene showing Ezekiel envisioning the Temple, from the nave of the lower church of Saint Clement, Schwarzrheindorf, Germany. Third quarter of the 12th century. Fresco. Doppelkirsch Schwarzheindorf, Germany

states that the preferred form for a cast-bronze censer is the Heavenly City itself.[26] The Gozbert Censer is ringed with figures and inscriptions that anticipate the coming of the Messiah and the New Jerusalem.[27] King Solomon, builder of the first Temple and noted administrator of the earthly city of Jerusalem, sits at the apex of the censer as a prefiguration of the End of Days, when all the souls on earth will be gathered up in Jerusalem and given eternal judgment.[28] A glimpse of this future vision is given by the appearance of Jesus enthroned at the top of the chain holder.

Although the Apocalypse makes it clear that there will be no Temple in the Heavenly City, images of the Temple occasionally appear in Christian art. The mid-twelfth-century fresco cycle of the lower church of Saint Clement in the Double Church in Schwarzrheindorf, Germany (fig. 99), features a detailed representation of Ezekiel's vision of the celestial city of Jerusalem and its Temple. [29] According to the prophet, the corrupt behavior of men – especially of those entrusted with the administration of the Temple and its sacrificial cult – will set the stage for the destruction of the terrestrial city. After its ruin, Ezekiel is led up to the top of a mountain, where God reveals the plan for the future city. Here, the frescoes depict the city being defiled as the wicked worship idols. The city is then decimated, and afterward its heavenly counterpart appears. Rising above the city's defensive walls is the restored Temple, which takes the form of a domed octagonal building, much like the Dome of the Rock, known to the Latin West as the Templum Domini or Temple of the Lord. These paintings were probably commissioned to provide comfort to the Crusaders, who had just returned home after being defeated in the Second Crusade and losing control of Jerusalem.[30] By drawing on Ezekiel's prophecy, this image cycle delivered a powerful message: Jerusalem's holy places were being polluted by the wicked;[31] these despicable actions will bring ruin to the earthly city and disgrace to the perpetrators; and the righteous will triumph in the Kingdom of Heaven at the End of Time.

While the Qur'an, believed by Muslims to be the final revelation from God as it was given to the Prophet Muhammad, does not elaborate on the city of Jerusalem or its heavenly counterpart, hadith literature reveals that late one night the angel Gabriel brought Muhammad from Mecca to Jerusalem and back again. In Jerusalem, Muhammad ascended to heaven, the "uppermost horizon," where he received further revelation.[32] A small domed structure – situated next to the much larger Dome of the Rock – is one site believed to commemorate the place from which Muhammad began his climb to heaven (fig. 100).[33] His journey is vibrantly depicted in a mid-fifteenth-century illuminated *Book of Ascension* produced in Herat (modern-day Iran).[34] On folio 5 verso, Muhammad arrives in Jerusalem at the Aqsa Mosque, where he is warmly welcomed by Abraham, Moses, Jesus, and other prophets who had gathered in anticipation of his arrival. The plume of golden fire that envelops Muhammad's body visually connotes his supremacy over his prophetic predecessors. Then, on folio 7, at Abraham's request, Muhammad kneels and leads the group in prayer (fig. 101). In this narrative, Jerusalem becomes more than the closest place to heaven; it is transformed into an extension of paradise, the gathering place for past and present prophets.[35] After praying, Muhammad ascends on a ladder of light to heaven, where he is welcomed and reintroduced to the very prophets with whom he had just prayed. In heaven, Muhammad witnesses the fertile gardens of paradise and the punishments of hell; he also receives the required number of daily prayers from God. This story of Muhammad's journey and ascension forms a fundamental part of Islamic sacred literature because it emphasizes his special relationship with God, his firsthand knowledge of heaven and hell, and his status as the first among the prophets and patriarchs of the Bible. In this narrative framework, the city of Jerusalem – not Mecca or Medina – functions as the gateway to heaven, the terrestrial threshold of the eternal world.[36]

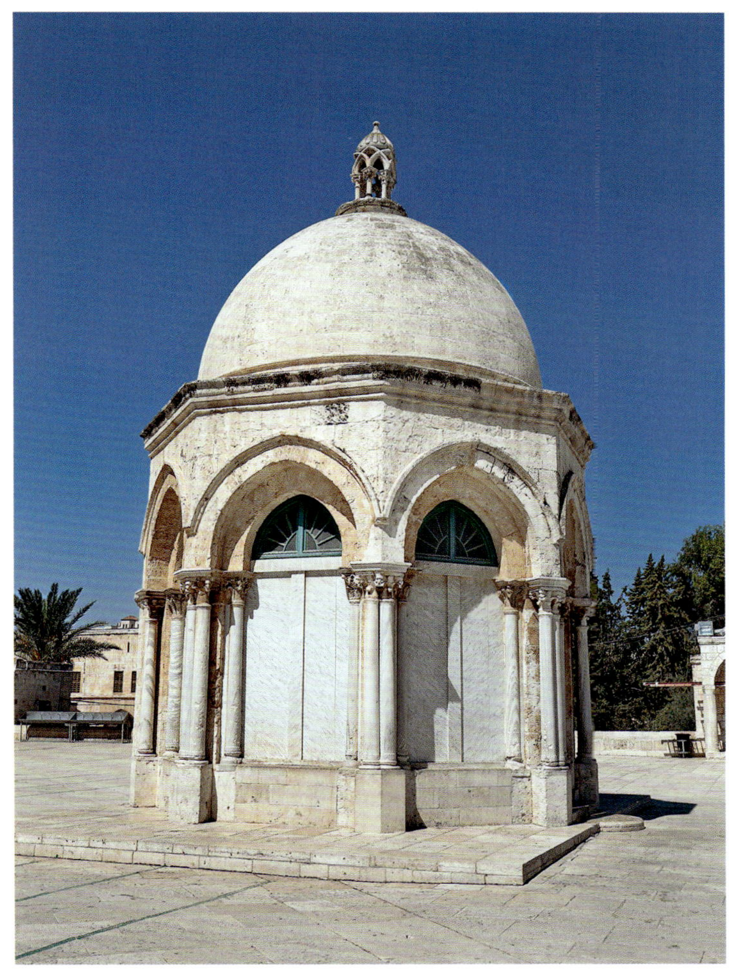

Fig. 100. Dome of the Ascension (Qubbat al-Mi'raj), Jerusalem

Medieval Muslim theologians sought to explain why God chose Jerusalem as the place where Muhammad would ascend to heaven. For the Sufi writer al-Qushayri (986–1073), Muhammad needed to go to Jerusalem for several interrelated reasons. First, in Jerusalem, Muhammad could see the traces of his prophetic predecessors. In addition, he explains that the city "faces the doorway to the heavens. Jerusalem is considered the closest location to the skies: it is only from there that the ascension can occur." And, finally, he writes that "God made Muhammad see Jerusalem in order to inform the

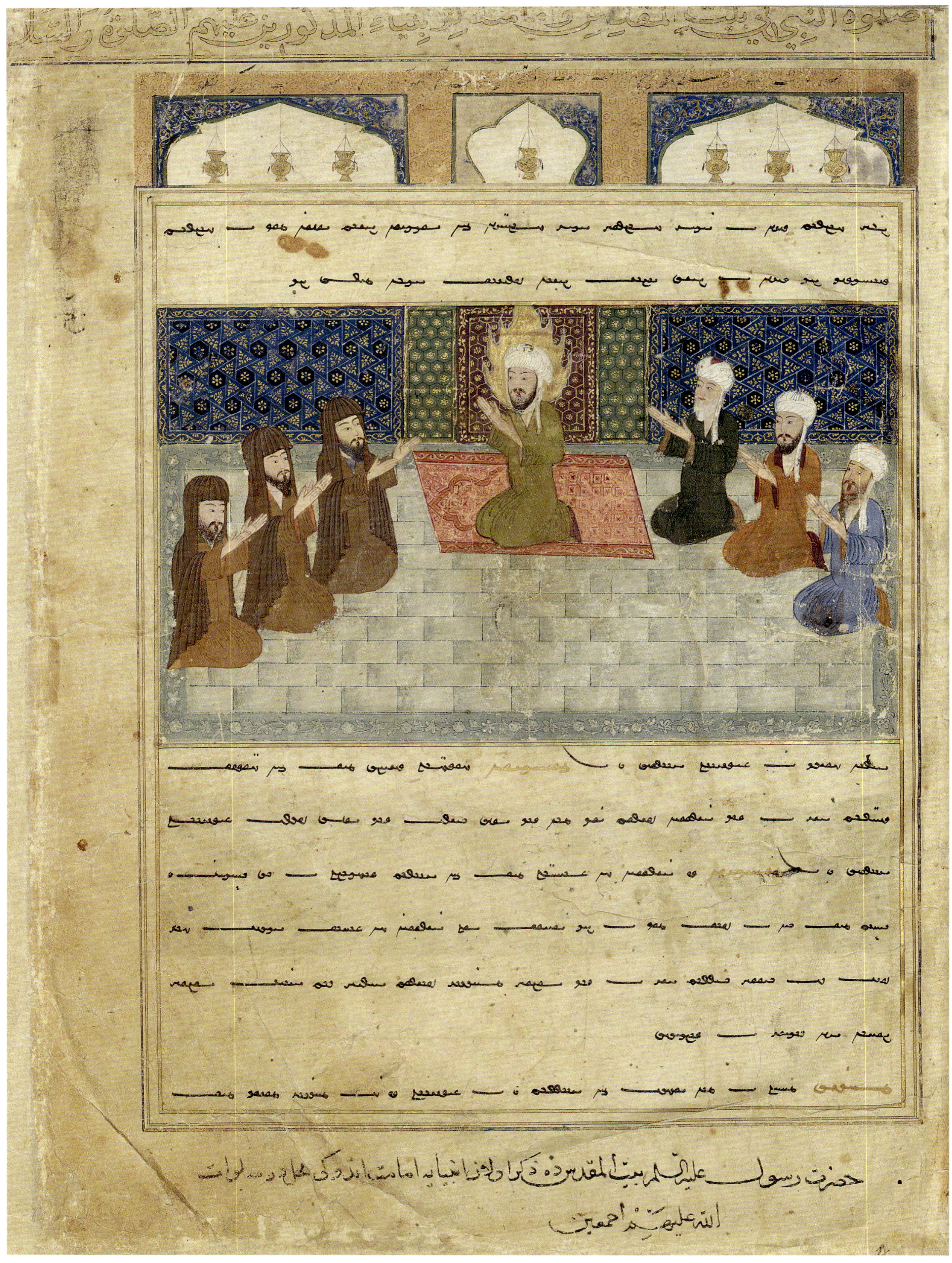

Fig. 101. "Muhammad Leading the Prophets in Prayer at Al-Aqsa Mosque," from a *Book of Ascension* (*Mi'rajnama*). Probably Herat (present-day Afghanistan), ca. 436. Opaque watercolor, gold, and ink on paper. Bibliothèque Nationale de France, Paris (suppl. turc 190, fol. 7r)

Quraysh [tribe] about it and thus prove his miracle . . . of the ascension to them."[37] This last rationale is brilliantly depicted in a mid-fourteenth-century *Book of Ascension* produced in Tabriz, Iran. Here, Muhammad sits on a rug facing two leaders of the powerful Quraysh tribe. As he speaks, a large angel swoops in, presenting him with a vision of the city. By providing a detailed account of the terrestrial city, complete with its architectural splendor and natural beauty, Muhammad is able to convince the dubious Qurayshes that he had been whisked away to Jerusalem and ascended to heaven.

Not only is Jerusalem the destination of Muhammad's Night Journey and the point of his entry into heaven; so too will it be the place of resurrection, gathering, and judgment at the End of Days.[38] When the angel Israfil sounds the trumpet, all of humankind will gather together in Jerusalem.[39] In a late fourteenth- or early fifteenth-century manuscript of the *Wonders of Creation* (*'Aja'ib al-Makhuqat*) by al-Qazwini (1202–1283) (cat. 148), the angel blows his slender trumpet, calling out to the dead and fulfilling the prophecy:[40]

> On the day they will certainly hear the sound of the trumpet and that will be the Day of Resurrection. We give life and cause things to die. To Us all things will return. On the day when the earth is rent asunder, they will quickly come out of their graves. This is how easy it is for Us to bring about the Day of Resurrection. (Qur'an 50:42–44)

Then God will descend to earth under a canopy of clouds in order to judge humankind: those who believe will find comfort in paradise, while nonbelievers will be sentenced to hell (Qur'an 2:210). At the End of Days, the Ka'ba and its Black Stone will be transported from Mecca, since the only pilgrimage will be to Jerusalem.[41] Jesus will return to Jerusalem to defeat the Antichrist.[42] Tremors of discord will portend the End of Time;[43] but it is the cry of Israfil's trumpet that will herald the beginning of the apocalypse.

From the eleventh to the fourteenth century, as the terrestrial city of Jerusalem suffered upheaval after upheaval – from natural disasters to the bloody clashes of empires and ideas – anticipation of its heavenly counterpart mounted.[44] According to Jewish, Christian, and Islamic traditions, these momentous and unsettling events signaled the End of Time, the arrival of the Kingdom of Heaven, the New Jerusalem. With these growing eschatological expectations came a flowering of works of art that imagined the splendors of the Heavenly City. By giving pictorial form to the prophetic visions of the Heavenly Jerusalem, these works brought the Messianic future to life. Jerusalem is the site of prophecy, the gateway to the heavens. And, once again, it will become the dwelling place of God on earth.

NOTES FOR THIS ESSAY APPEAR ON PAGES 305–6
SEE CATS. 137–149

137a–d

Temple Implements in Four Hebrew Manuscripts

a. The Perpignan Bible

Catalonia, Perpignan (present-day France), 1299
Tempera, gold, and ink on parchment; 517 folios
12⅝ × 9⅜ in. (32 × 23.7 cm)
Bibliothèque Nationale de France, Paris (MS Hebr. 7)

b. Hebrew Bible

Catalonia (present-day Spain), first quarter of the 14th century
Tempera, gold, and ink on parchment; 500 folios
15½ × 11½ in. (39.4 × 29.2 cm)
Jay and Jeannie Schottenstein, Columbus

c. The Duke of Sussex's Catalan Bible

Catalonia (present-day Spain), mid-14th century
Tempera, gold, and ink on parchment; 437 folios
14 × 11¼ in. (35.5 × 28.5 cm)
British Library, London (Add. MS 15250)

d. The Catalan Mahzor

Catalonia (present-day Spain), 1280
Tempera, gold, and ink on parchment; 154 folios
7⅝ × 6⅛ in. (19.5 × 15.5 cm)
The National Library of Israel, Jerusalem (MS Heb. 8°6527)

The glittering vessels of the Holy Temple beckon from the opening pages of thirteenth- and fourteenth-century Catalan Hebrew Bibles. After the destruction of the Temple, Bible study replaced sacrificial rite as the quintessence of religious practice. The tax once collected for communal offerings was instead allocated to poor Torah scholars for, as the sages stated, "a single day devoted to Torah outweighs one thousand sacrifices."[1] The Temple imagery gracing the opening pages of these Bibles functions not as an illustration of a specific passage but as a representation of the Bible as a whole — an embodiment of the holy book's then-popular epithet "Mikdashy'ah," or Temple of God.[2] A number of Bibles even explicitly introduce themselves as such in their dedicatory pages and colophons.[3] Correlation between the tripartite composition of each entity — the Bible's Pentateuch, Prophets, and Writings; the Temple's Holy of Holies, Holy Place, and Courtyard — further reinforces their parallels as spheres of religious worship.[4] The acceptance of Bible study as a surrogate form of Temple worship is visually established in the illumination of the Temple Implement folios.

The forms of the implements are artistically beautiful but also scholarly, adhering not only to the textual descriptions provided in the Bible[5] but also to the writings of Mishnaic sages and the foremost medieval exegetical scholars, Maimonides and Rashi. For example, the existence of the menorah's steps, the altar's ramp, and the frankincense dishes, as well as details such as the arrangement of the shewbread table, the configuration of the menorah, and the inward angling of the menorah's flames, are not enumerated in the Bible but are discussed in Maimonides's legal code, the *Mishneh Torah*, the eighth book of which focuses on the laws and measurements of the Temple (cat. 63).[6] Agreement with scholarly sources was of particular importance, for these illuminations not only stand in for the absent Temple but also manifest the concrete aspirations to rebuild the future one.

The Perpignan Bible (cat. 137a) contains what is likely the earliest illustration of this type, which served as the model on which subsequent ones were based. Graphically powerful images are surrounded by text frames that quote biblical passages describing the implements and then declare, "Happy was he who saw the grandeur of [the Temple's] glorious beauty and all its strength and power. Happy is he who awaits and will see it. May

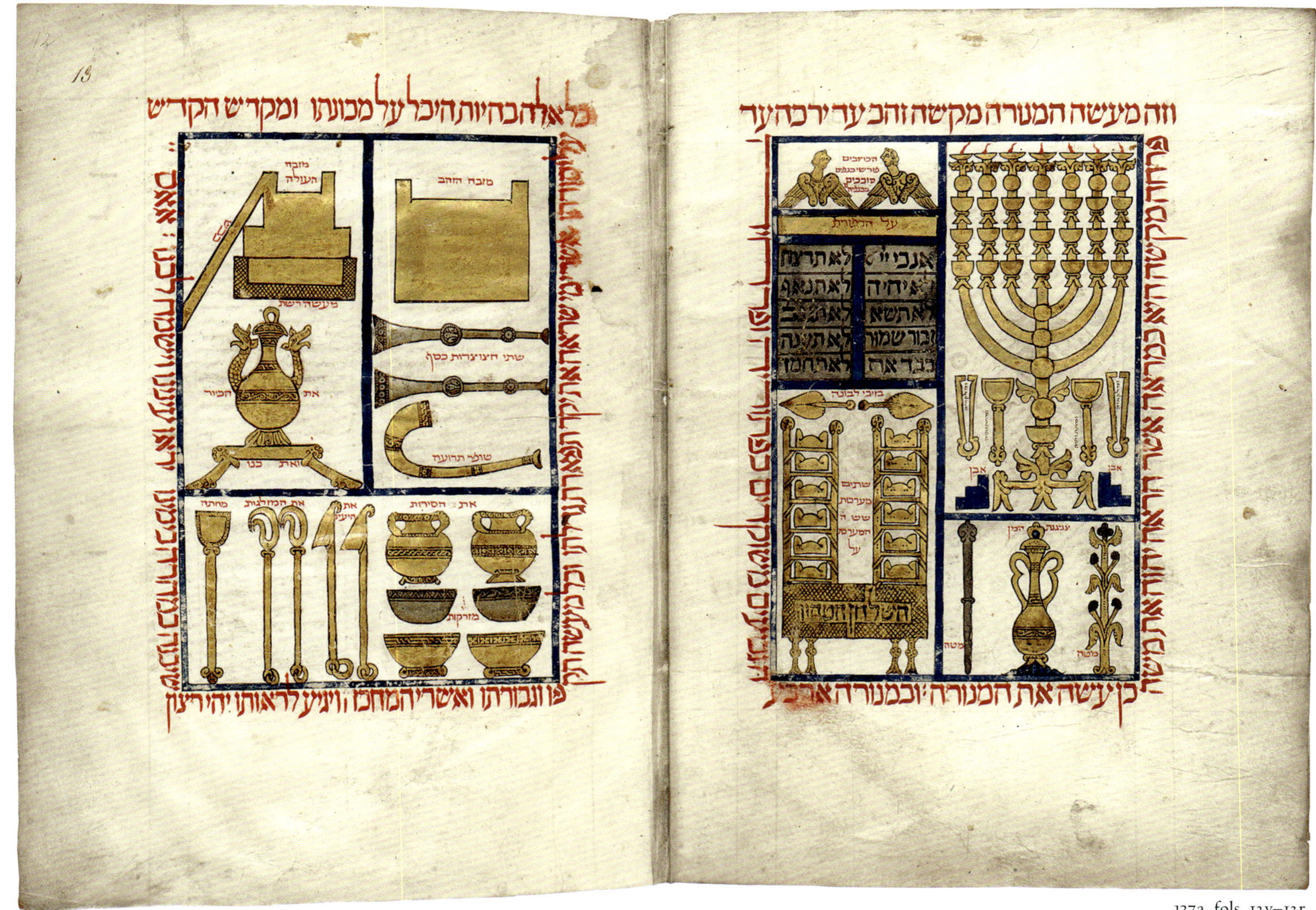

137a, fols. 12v–13r

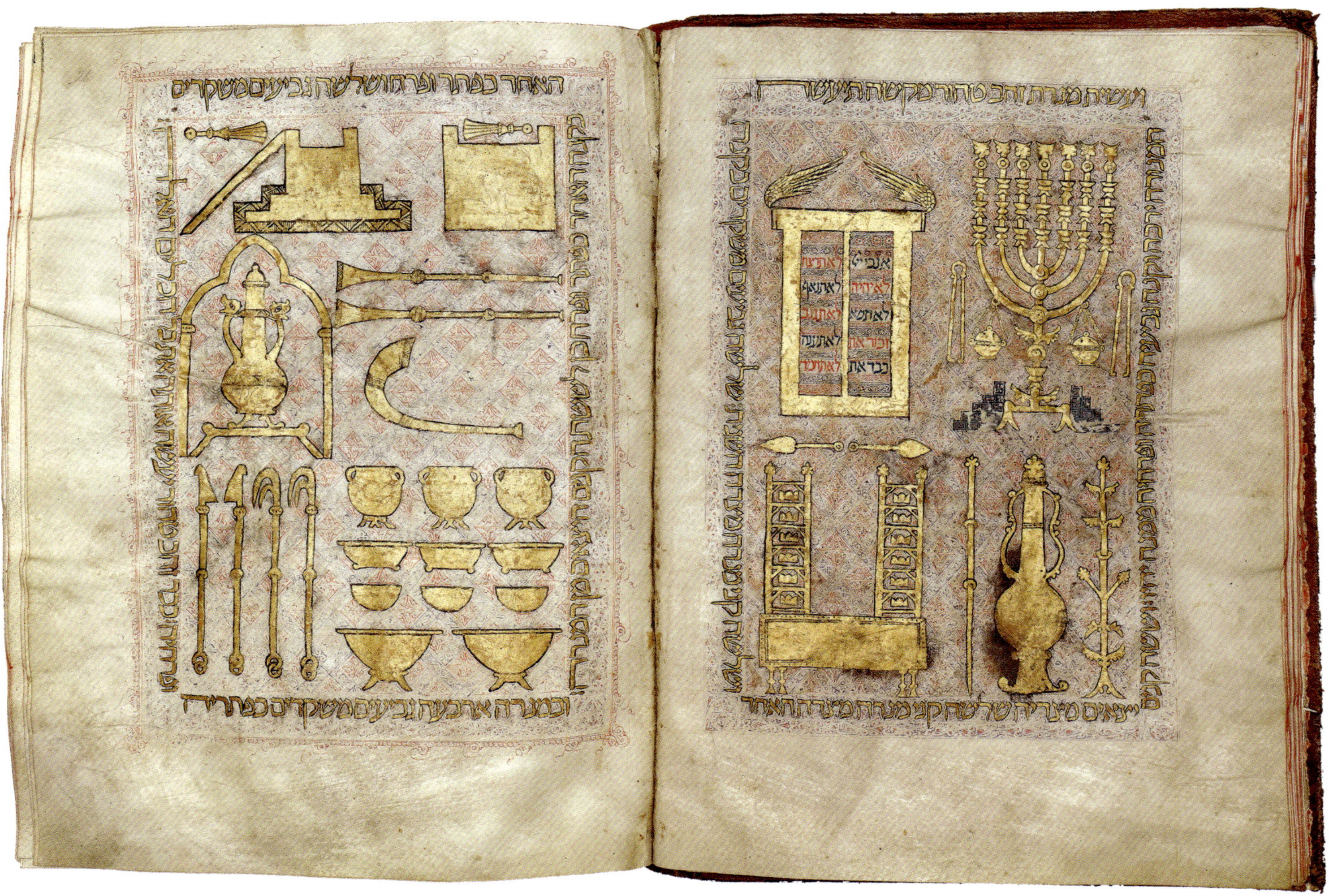

137b, fols. 25v–26r

it be God's will that He will rebuild it soon in our day. May our eyes see [it] and our hearts rejoice. Amen. Amen. Selah" (folios 12 verso–13 recto).[7]

Other Bibles frame the implements solely with the biblical passages that commanded their creation, visualizing the word of God in both its aural and material manifestations. Still other text frames reflect on the wisdom- and life-giving properties of Torah study, literally and figuratively reframing the vessels as the glittering keys to a life of fulfillment. A Hebrew Bible in the Schottenstein collection (cat. 137b) communicates both these themes by focusing specifically on the passages related to the creation of the menorah (folios 25 verso–26 recto), "for" — as stated in Proverbs and relayed in the text frames of similar Bibles — "the candle represents a Mitzvah, and the Torah represents light" (6:23).[8]

The implements are here preceded by an illustration of the High Priest's breastplate — a rare inclusion in Catalan Bibles[9] — and are followed by a folio bearing a compilation of passages that encapsulates the overriding message of the Temple Implement pages and of the time. They speak of the Temple's construction, of the awe elicited by the Divine Spirit's residence in this earthly home, of God Himself leading the nation to its homeland and of hope.[10]

Even in Bibles that forgo text frames entirely, the eschatological meaning of these images is made clear by the inclusion of an additional pictorial symbol — the Mount of Olives. The prophet Zechariah foretells the dawning of the Messianic era, when God will stand on the Mount of Olives, which shall cleave in two. A spring will flow from Jerusalem through the crevice to both the east and the west, and according to rabbinic literature, through this cleft God will open caverns in the earth whence the resurrected righteous will emerge.[11] This momentous episode is portrayed clearly in the Duke of Sussex's Catalan Bible (cat. 137c),[12] in which streams of water rush from the bifurcated Mount of Olives while caverns yawn below (folios 3 verso–4 recto).

It is from this peak that the High Priest will again look on the Temple while performing the ceremony of the red heifer, yet his view is not what the reader sees. The arrangement of the vessels and the Mount of Olives on the page does not conform to a map or plan but rather situates the entire composition in Messianic Jerusalem.[13] While Ashkenazi Messianic fervor at this time focused on the miraculous, such as the Feast of the Righteous (cat. 138), Sephardic expectations focused on a rationalist rebuilt Temple in Jerusalem.[14] The first step toward the fulfillment of this Messianic hope was the nation's habitation of the land, an idea addressed in the final manuscript of this group.[15]

The Catalan Mahzor (cat. 137d), a volume of liturgical poems for Rosh Hashana and Yom Kippur, is decorated through micrography, the art of using minute script to form beautiful patterns or figures. Originating in late ninth-century Hebrew manuscripts written in the Holy Land and Egypt, the art form is prevalent in Hebrew Bibles.[16] Here, amid hunt scenes and fantastical creatures, are two folios depicting the Temple Implements, intricately woven out of passages from Psalms (folios 11 verso–12 recto). The excerpts speak of hope in destitution, of God's protection of his people, of celebration of his glory, and, above all else, of Jerusalem.[17]

The vessels of the Temple spell out the Jewish nation's hope to renew their pilgrimage to the Holy City — to "encircle Sion and count its towers" (Psalms 48:13) and inhabit its walls and partake of its holiness. Through this return to Jerusalem the images on the page will be realized in the rebuilding of the Temple. In

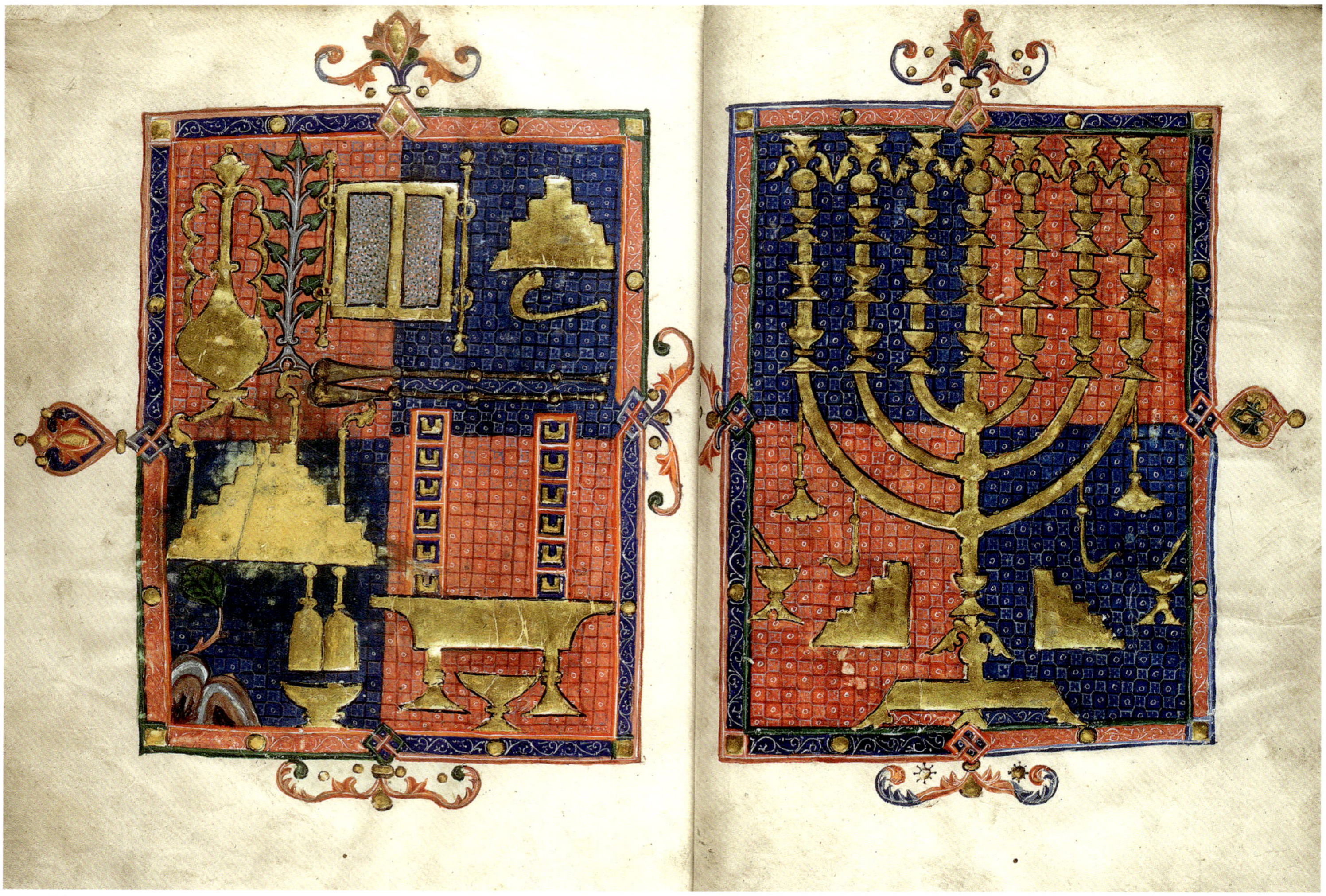

137c, fols. 3v–4r

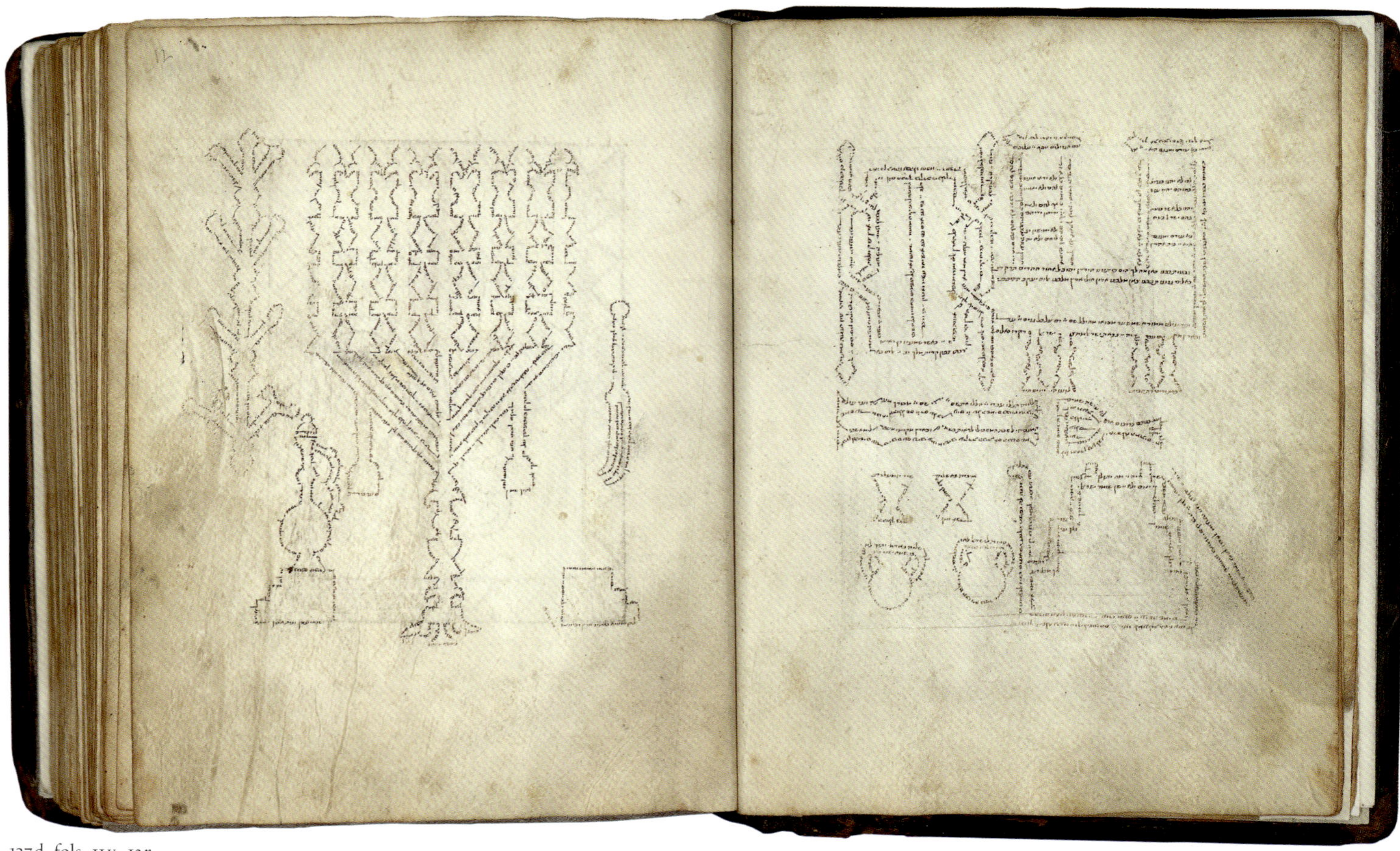

137d, fols. 11v–12r

a heart-wrenching prayer both to and for the city, the Temple Implements implore, "Pray for the peace of Jerusalem, may those who love you be at peace. May there be peace within your ramparts and tranquility in your citadels. For the sake of my family and friends, I pray for your well-being. For the sake of the House of the Lord our God, I shall plea for your prosperity" (Psalms 122:6–9). EE

Selected References: Cat. 137a: Nordström 1968, pp. 90–93; Metzger, T., 1969–70, pp. 419–20; Gutmann 1978, pp. 50–51, pls. 6, 7; Laderman 2003–4, pp. 111, 114–16; Kogman-Appel 2004, pp. 131–37, pls. 86, 87. Cat. 137b: Schilling and Swarzenski 1929, vol. 1, pp. 50–51, no. 48, vol. 2, pl. 29; Nordström 1968, p. 96, figs. 13–14; Metzger, T., 1969–70, pp. 426–30; Kogman-Appel 2004, pp. 138–40. Cat. 137c: Narkiss 1982, vol. 1, pp. 105–7, no. 19, vol. 2, figs. 310–23; Kogman-Appel 2004, pp. 145–47, pls. 106, 107; London 2007, p. 143; Tahan 2007, pp. 52–53. Cat. 137d: Kogman-Appel 2004, p. 143 n. 22; Halperin 2013.

1. Babylonian Talmud, Tractate Shabbat 30a; comp. Tractate Menachot 100a. See also Tractate Eruvin 63b: "Torah study is of more value than the offering of daily sacrifices." In English, Schottenstein Talmud 1990–2005, Tractate Shabbat (1996), p. 30a, and Schottenstein Talmud 1990–2005, Tractate Eruvin (1991), p. 63b.

2. Wieder 1957, p. 171.

3. Examples of Bibles that title themselves "Mikdashy'ah" are the King's Bible, British Library, London, King's MS I, fol. 2v; the National Library of Israel, Jerusalem, MS Heb. 4°780; and the Farhi Bible, formerly in the Sassoon Collection.

4. Scholars had already drawn the parallel between the tripartite compositions in the tenth century, but Profiat Duran, a fourteenth-century physician and scholar, went even further by declaring that "the very division of Scripture into three sections was *originally* made in imitation of the same division of the Temple" (Wieder 1957, p. 170).

5. Exodus 25 and Numbers 8.

6. For descriptions of the Temple implements, see Maimonides, *Mishneh Torah, Sefer Avodah*, Hilchot Beit ha-Bechira; for English, Maimonides 2007 ed., pp. 14–131. Bibles from the later fourteenth century even depict the Ark from above, emphasizing the carrying poles over the cherubim in accordance with Maimonides's own emphasis.

7. Translation by the author.

8. The King's Bible, British Library, London, King's MS I, and a Hebrew Bible, Communità Ebraica, Rome, MS 19a. See Frojmovic 2002, pp. 101–3, for transcriptions of these manuscripts' text frames and interpretations of the metaphor of light as knowledge, as well as Appendix I (pp. 125–27) for a list of twenty-three Bible manuscripts containing one or more double-page frontispieces featuring images of the Sanctuary vessels.

9. Also found in the Foa Bible (cat. 69) and the Farhi Bible.

10. 2 Chronicles 24:5; 1 Kings 8:27; Genesis 19:16 (partial); Numbers 32:42 (partial); Exodus 33:14; Psalms 27:14 (partial).

11. Zechariah 14:4, 8, with accompanying Rashi; Rashi 1993– ed. On the Mount of Olives as the site of the resurrection, see Gutmann 1976, p. 132 n. 30.

12. Indeed, it appeared as early as the third century in the Dura Europos Synagogue; see Gutmann 1967–68, p. 172 n. 30.

13. Revel-Neher 1998, p. 75.

14. Gutmann 1967–68, p. 171; Gutmann 1976, p. 129. According to Maimonides, the Temple "would be rebuilt in the Messianic period when a Jewish kingdom ruled by Jewish law would be established in the land of Israel under a king-messiah."

15. Yuval 1998, pp. 106–7.

16. Halperin 2013, p. 79.

17. Including Psalms 42–49, 113–15, 120–24. See Halperin 2013, pp. 250–69 for complete quotations.

138

The Feast of the Righteous

From the Ambrosian Bible
Germany (Ulm?), ca. mid-13th century
Tempera, gold, and ink on parchment; vol. 3, 136 folios
17½ × 13½ in. (44.5 × 34.3 cm)
Veneranda Biblioteca Ambrosiana, Milan
(MS B 32 inf.)

The last two folios of the third volume of the Ambrosian Bible contain two full-page miniatures. Unlike other illustrations in this Bible, these final images do not relate to the text. Depicted on the right (folio 135 verso) are the sun and moon, fifteen stars, and the heavenly spheres. The man, lion, ox, and eagle of the Divine Chariot described in Ezekiel (1:4–28) occupy the corners. In two registers on the facing page (folio 136 recto), eschatological imagery illustrates the Feast of the Righteous in the Messianic era. According to Jewish sources, the repast was to take place in the Garden of Eden.[1] It is likely that the creator of the unusual Messianic imagery in this Bible was influenced by contemporary Christian literary and artistic sources that associated the garden with Heavenly Jerusalem and therefore intended the scene to allude to both locales.

In keeping with a Jewish artistic tradition in southern Germany in the thirteenth and early fourteenth centuries, the artists who decorated this Bible avoided accurate depictions of human figures by replacing their heads with those of animals. The distortion of the man on the upper left in the depiction of the heavens was even more extreme, as he was rendered as a crowned rooster. The central figure in the banquet scene also has the head of a bird

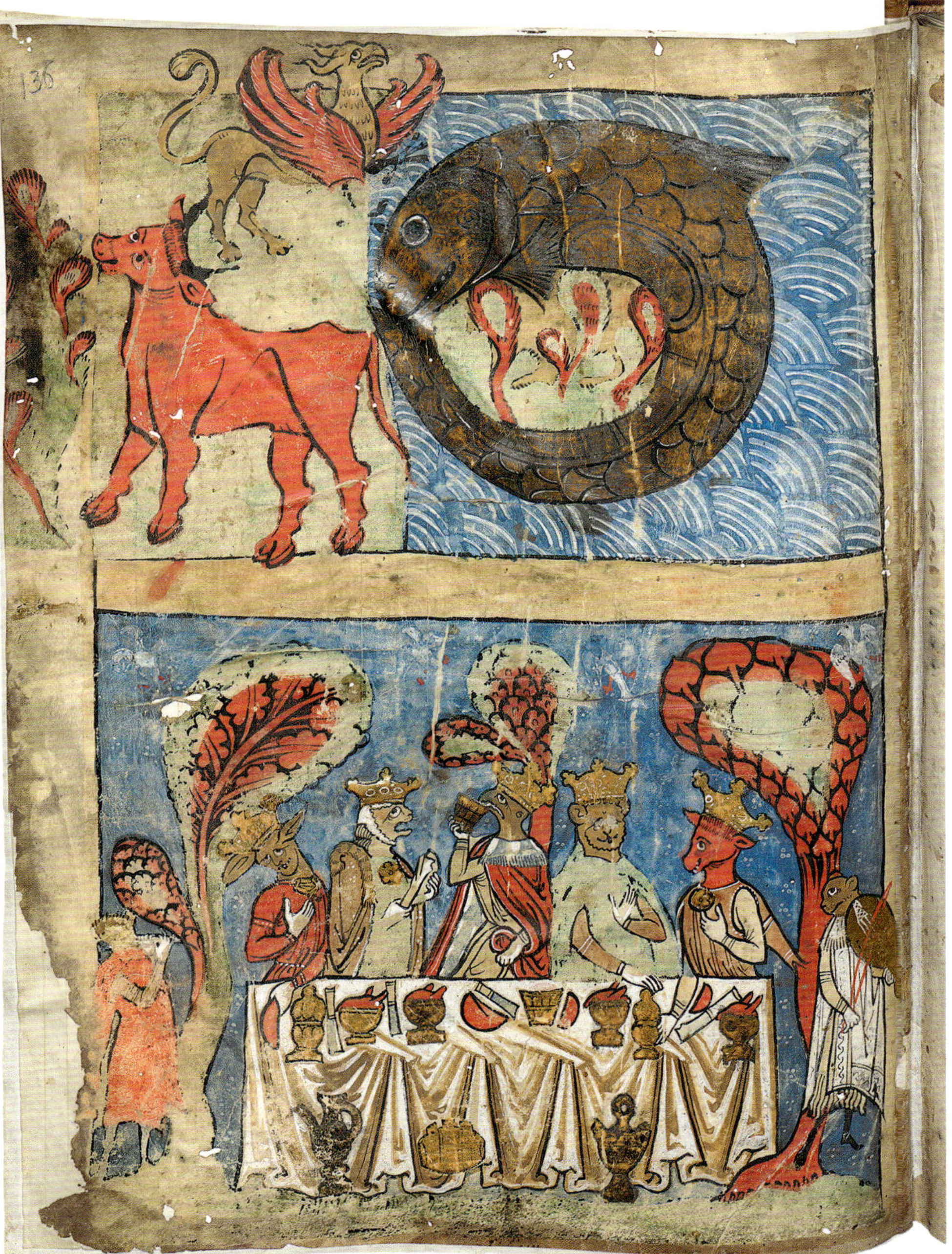

138, fol. 136r

while the others have heads of mammals; all wear crowns and luxurious garments. Standing under stylized trees behind a table laden with gold cups, bowls, and knives, the pious consume delicacies to the accompaniment of music played by the small figures standing to either side of the table.

Above are three mythological creatures, Ziz, Behemoth, and Leviathan. All are mentioned in the Bible, but none in conjunction with the Feast of the Righteous, a concept that developed in later Jewish legend. Ziz, usually thought of as a giant bird but portrayed here as a griffin, soars across the top of the page. Behemoth, the red ox, stands on the ground, inexplicably turning away from Leviathan, the curled fish afloat on stylized waves. It was believed that in Messianic times Behemoth and Leviathan would fight to the death, and their flesh would be consumed by the righteous. Remaining portions of Leviathan would be distributed in the markets of Jerusalem and its silver skin would be spread on the city's walls, making them shine.[2] In later writings, Ziz was included in eschatological imagery as well. Rather than conclude with a biblical scene, the artists of the Ambrosian Bible, therefore, created a unique image, one that indicates the desire of contemporary Jews to dwell among the righteous in the Messianic era. EMC

Selected References: Ameisenowa 1935; Gutmann 1967–68, pp. 168–75; Narkiss 1969, pp. 90–91, pl. 25; Mortara Ottolenghi 1972, pp. 119–25, pls. 11–28; Shalev-Eyni 2015.

1. See Shalev-Eyni 2015, pp. 463–67.
2. Schottenstein Talmud 1900–2005, Tractate Bava Batra (1994), p. 75a.

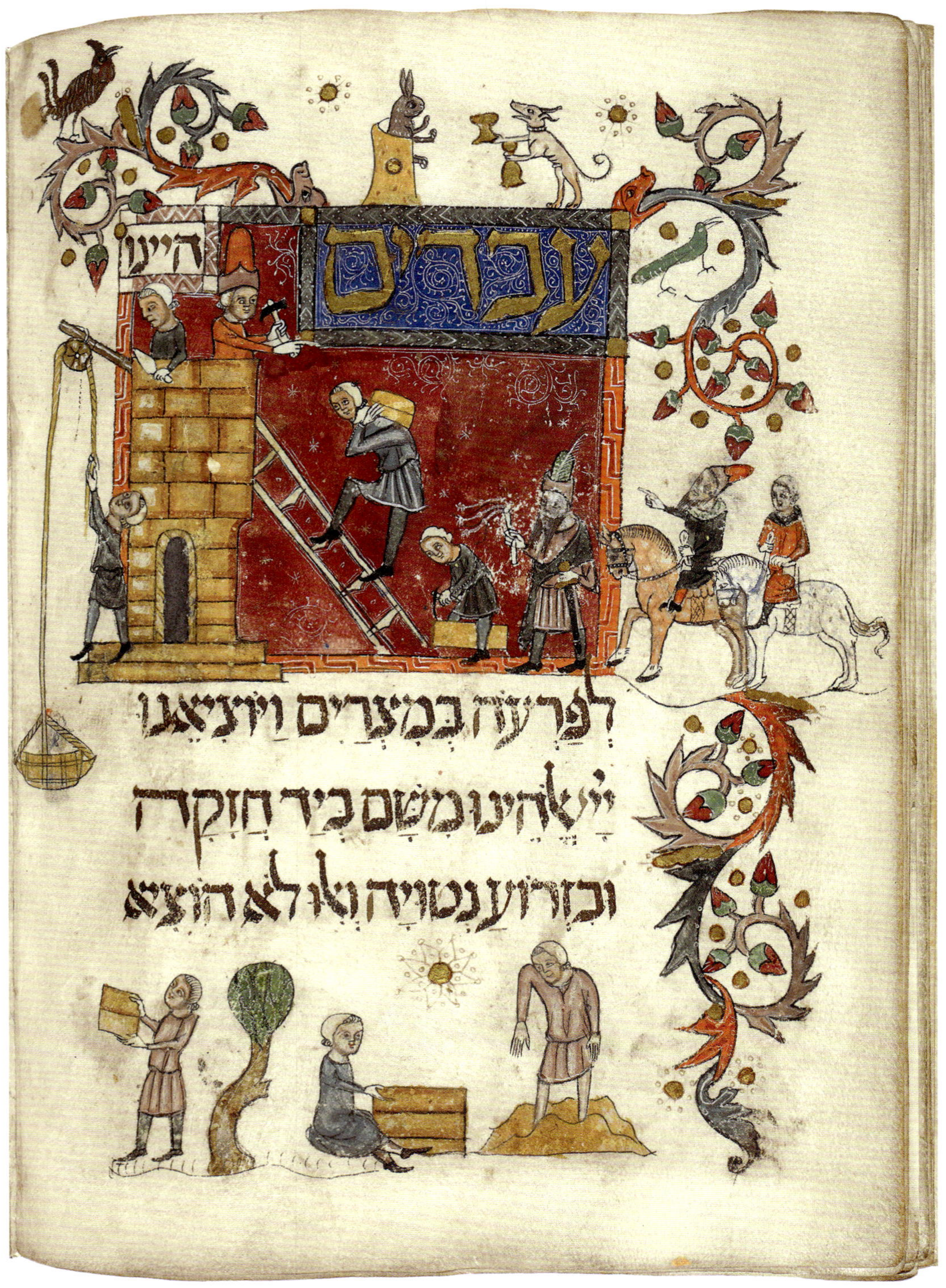

139, fol. 30v

139

Next Year in Jerusalem

From the Barcelona Haggadah
Catalonia (present-day Spain), ca. 1360–70
Tempera, gold, and ink on paper; 163 folios
10 × 7½ in. (25.5 × 19 cm)
British Library, London (Add. MS 14761)

Noteworthy for its iconographic richness and focus on ritual, the late fourteenth-century Barcelona Haggadah exemplifies the visual sophistication of the supposedly aniconic Jewish people. Contained within its folios is the liturgical text for Passover, the Jewish festival commemorating the Exodus from Egypt. Throughout the manuscript dogs scurry after rabbits, although at times this natural order is inverted. In folio 30 verso, for example, at top a rabbit sits on a throne, tended by a servile dog. This marginal vignette sharply contrasts with the text below, which reads, "We were slaves to Pharaoh in Egypt," and to the large depiction of Jewish laborers building a tower under the supervision of several taskmasters. The imagery suggests that, although the Jews were slaves, the oppressed would one day be liberated and the one-time servants would become rulers.

The web of hounds and hares forms an alternate path through the manuscript, one that culminates in the final proclamation of the Passover Seder: "Next Year in Jerusalem" (folio 88 recto). This eschatological declaration, which explicitly locates the future redemption in Jerusalem, shines against its decorative frame. Nestled between two smaller leaves in the center of the lower margin, a faintly drawn hare rests peacefully; in this vision of the world to come, there are no dogs at all. The Jewish people (shown here in the guise of a hare) will survive their earthly plight and be rewarded with redemption in the Heavenly Jerusalem. AK

Selected References: Schonfield et al. 1992; Epstein 1997, pp. 16–38, 128; Kornfeld 2013.

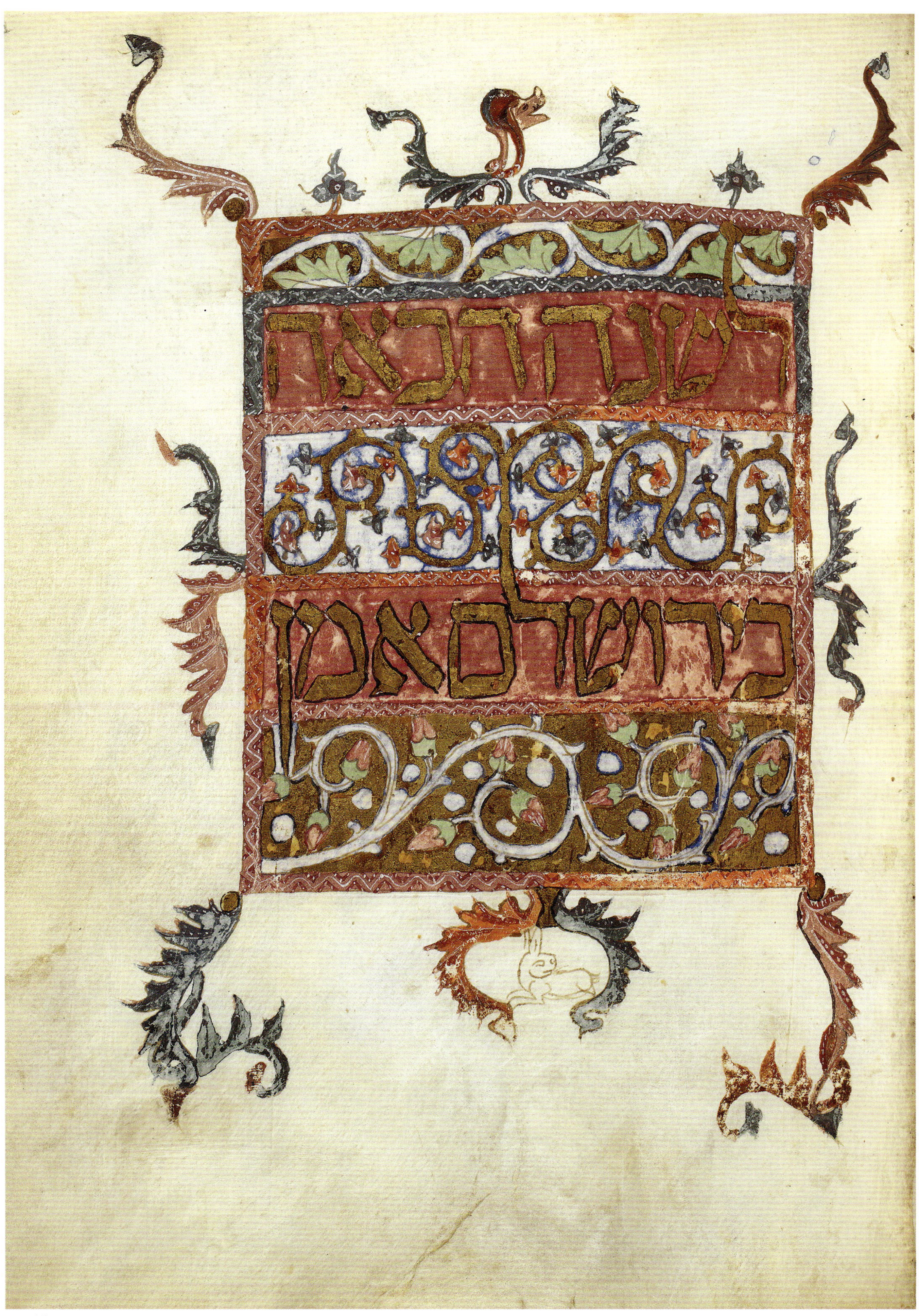

139, fol. 88r

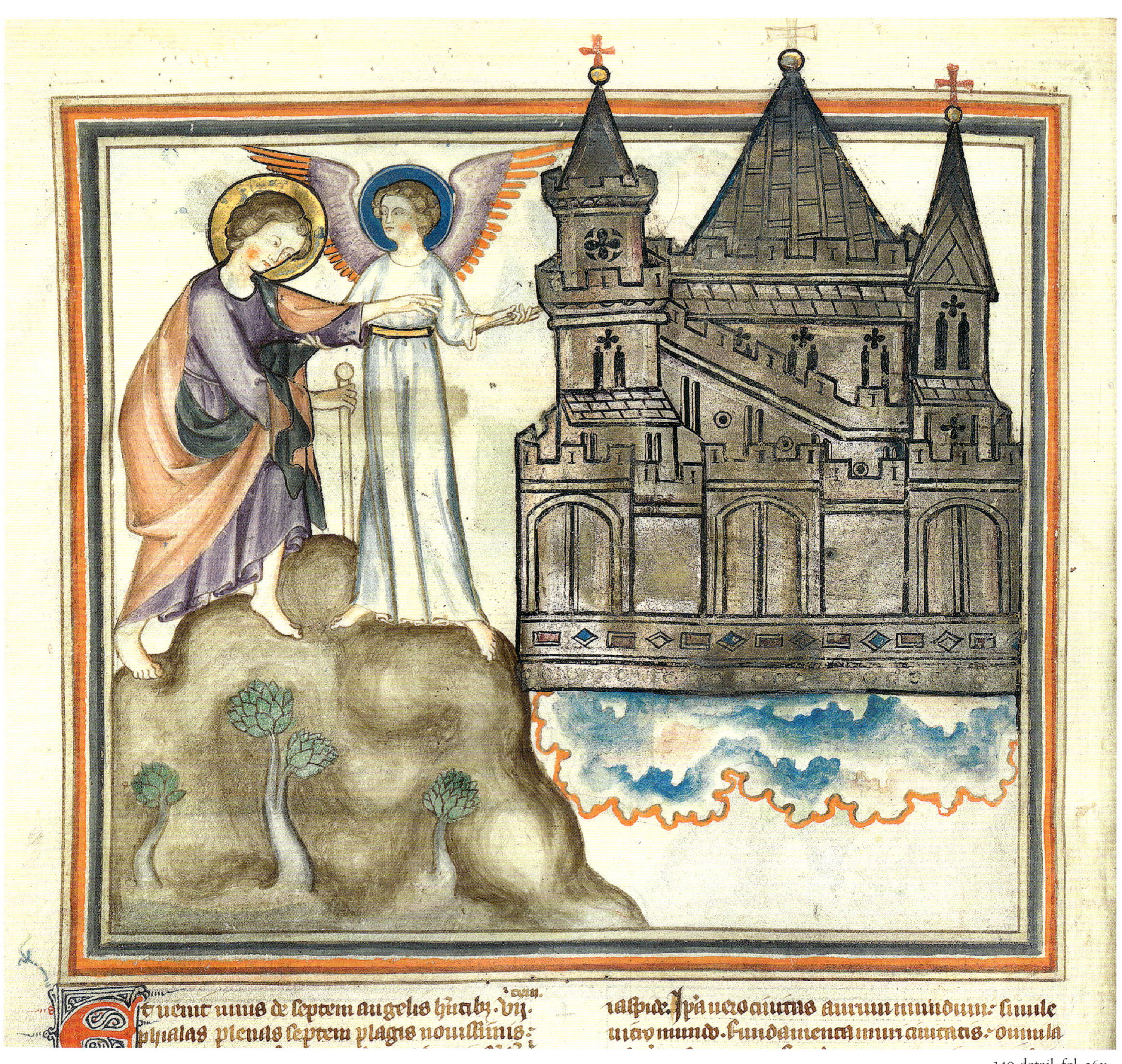

140 detail, fol. 36v

140

Saint John Sees the Heavenly Jerusalem

From The Cloisters Apocalypse
Normandy, France, ca. 1330
Tempera, gold, silver, and ink on parchment; 38 folios
12⅛ × 9 in. (30.8 × 22.9 cm)
The Metropolitan Museum of Art, New York, The Cloisters Collection, 1968 (68.174)

While exiled on the Greek island of Patmos, John the Evangelist bore witness to the tumultuous End of Days. His vision, recorded in the Apocalypse, was a frequent subject in medieval art. Here, an angel takes the Evangelist by the arm and guides him gently to a mountaintop, where he beholds the luminous City of Heaven descending to earth on a cloud (folio 36 verso). The text describes the city as "pure gold, like to clear glass" (Apocalypse 21:18), but the artist has chosen to render it using silver leaf. The opacity and sheen of the silver strikingly contrast with the painted scene around it, allowing Jerusalem to appear at once more solid and more ethereal than the mountain before it. Enclosing Jerusalem is a "wall great and high" with twelve gates — three on each of its cardinal sides — each with the name of one of the twelve tribes of the children of Israel. Its "foundations . . . [are] adorned with all manner of precious stones" (21:12–14, 19), each with the name of one of the twelve apostles. Neither their names nor those of the twelve tribes appear in the illumination.

On the facing folio (37 recto), the angel reveals "a river of water of life, clear as crystal, proceeding from the throne of God and of the Lamb. / In the midst of the street" (22:1–2). Not only would the pair of trees flanking the river bear fruit each month, but their leaves would also heal the nations. By depicting John the Evangelist's description in such detail, the illuminations allow the viewer to experience an analogous vision of the Heavenly Jerusalem.

AK

Selected References: Deuchler, Hoffeld, and Nickel 1971; Nickel 1972, pp. 60–62, 64, figs. 1–5, 7; Emmerson and Lewis 1984, p. 395, no. 86.

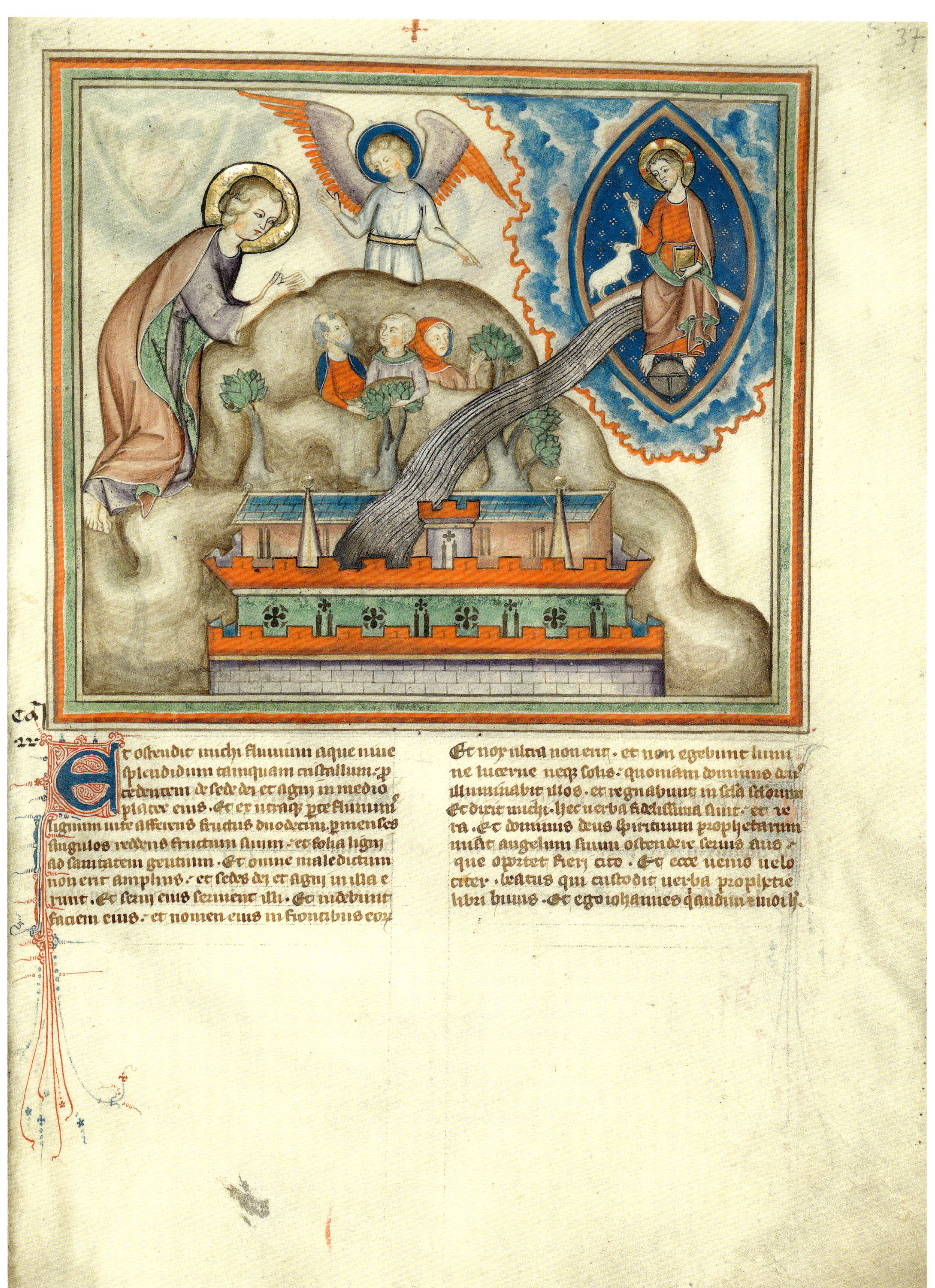

37

Cap. 22

Et ostendit michi fluuium aque uiue splendidum tamquam cristallum. procedentem de sede dei et agni in medio platee eius. Et ex utraque parte fluminis lignum uite afferens fructus duodecim. per menses singulos reddens fructum suum. et folia ligni ad sanitatem gentium. Et omne maledictum non erit amplius. et sedes dei et agni in illa erunt. Et serui eius seruient illi. Et uidebunt faciem eius. et nomen eius in frontibus eorum.

Et nox ultra non erit. et non egebunt lumine lucerne neque solis. quoniam dominus deus illuminabit illos. et regnabunt in secula seculorum. Et dixit michi. Hec uerba fidelissima sunt. et uera. Et dominus deus spirituum prophetarum misit angelum suum ostendere seruis suis que oportet fieri cito. Et ecce uenio uelociter. Beatus qui custodit uerba prophetie libri huius. Et ego iohannes qui audiui et uidi hec.

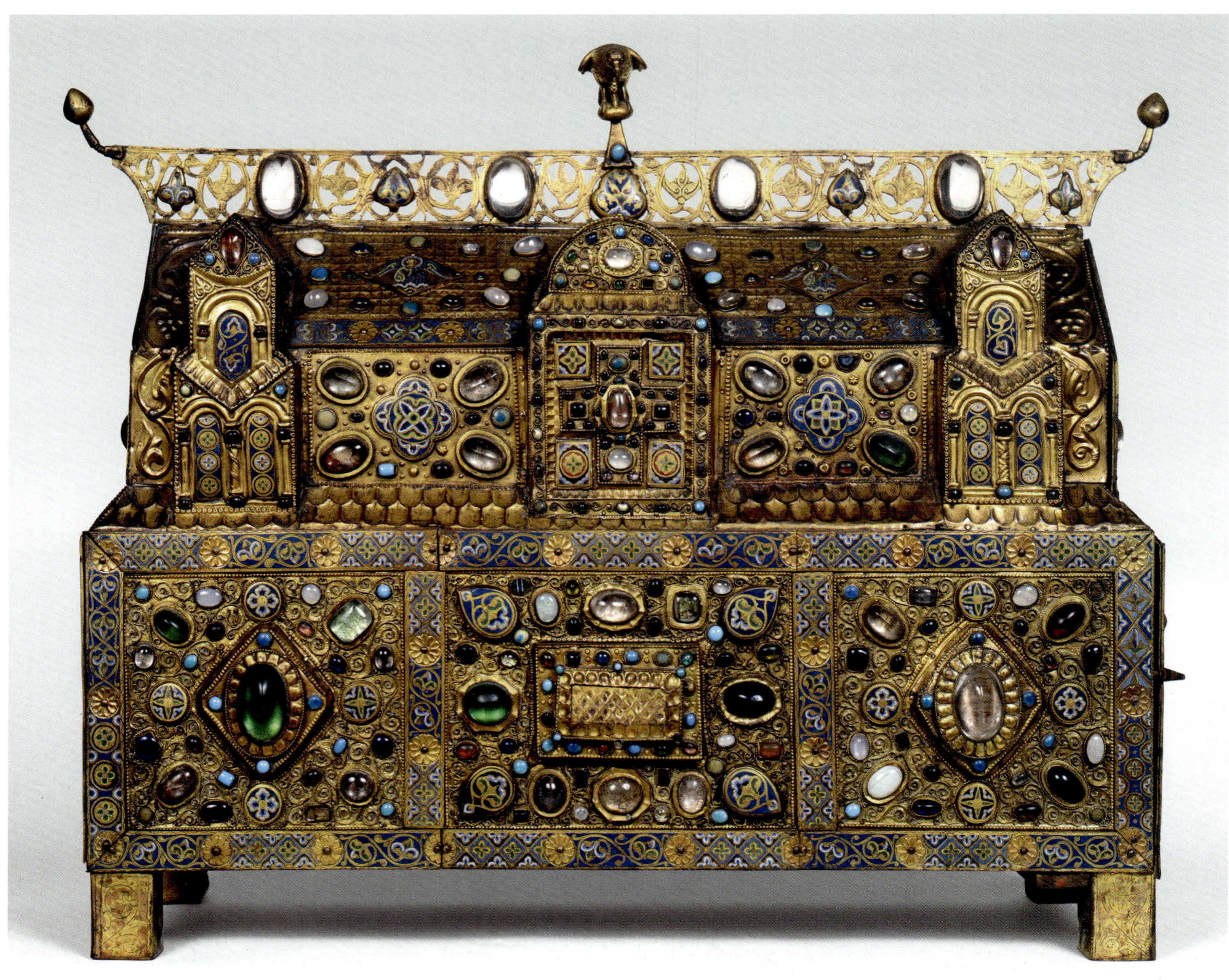

141 front view

141

Chasse of Ambazac

From the Treasury of Grandmont
Limoges, ca. 1180–90
Gilded copper, champlevé enamel, rock crystal, semiprecious stones, faience, and glass
H. 23⅛ in. (58.6 cm), W. 31⅛ in. (79 cm), D. 10¼ in. (26.2 cm)
Mairie d'Ambazac

This chasse is one of the most celebrated and technically accomplished reliquaries of the Middle Ages to survive. Exceptional among Limoges enamelwork, it has no figural imagery. Instead, it evokes the Heavenly Jerusalem, resplendent and bejeweled. Three domes appear on each side; angels hover between them on the front face. Enamels imitative of stained-glass windows fill the arcades of the domes on each side, while a cross figures prominently at center.

The goldsmith who created this reliquary did not attempt to accurately present each feature of the Heavenly City as described in the twenty-first chapter of the Apocalypse. Rather, like the illuminator of The Cloisters Apocalypse (cat. 140), he captured the overall effect of a city that "hath no need of the sun, nor of the moon, to shine in it. For the glory of God hath enlightened it" (Apocalypse 21:23). The New Jerusalem is "pure gold, like to clear glass," and "the foundations of the wall of the city were adorned with all manner of precious stones" (21:18–19).

A direct link with the eastern Mediterranean is evidenced by the decorative elements made of faience, a technology associated with Egypt but found across the region. One of the "gems" on The Cloisters Cross from Grandmont (cat. 25d) is also of faience.

At various points in its history, this reliquary housed the bones of different saints. Regardless of which holy relics were originally intended to be enshrined in it, the Heavenly City of Jerusalem would invariably have been the most appropriate home imaginable. BDB

Selected Reference: Paris and New York 1995–96, pp. 208–12, no. 55.

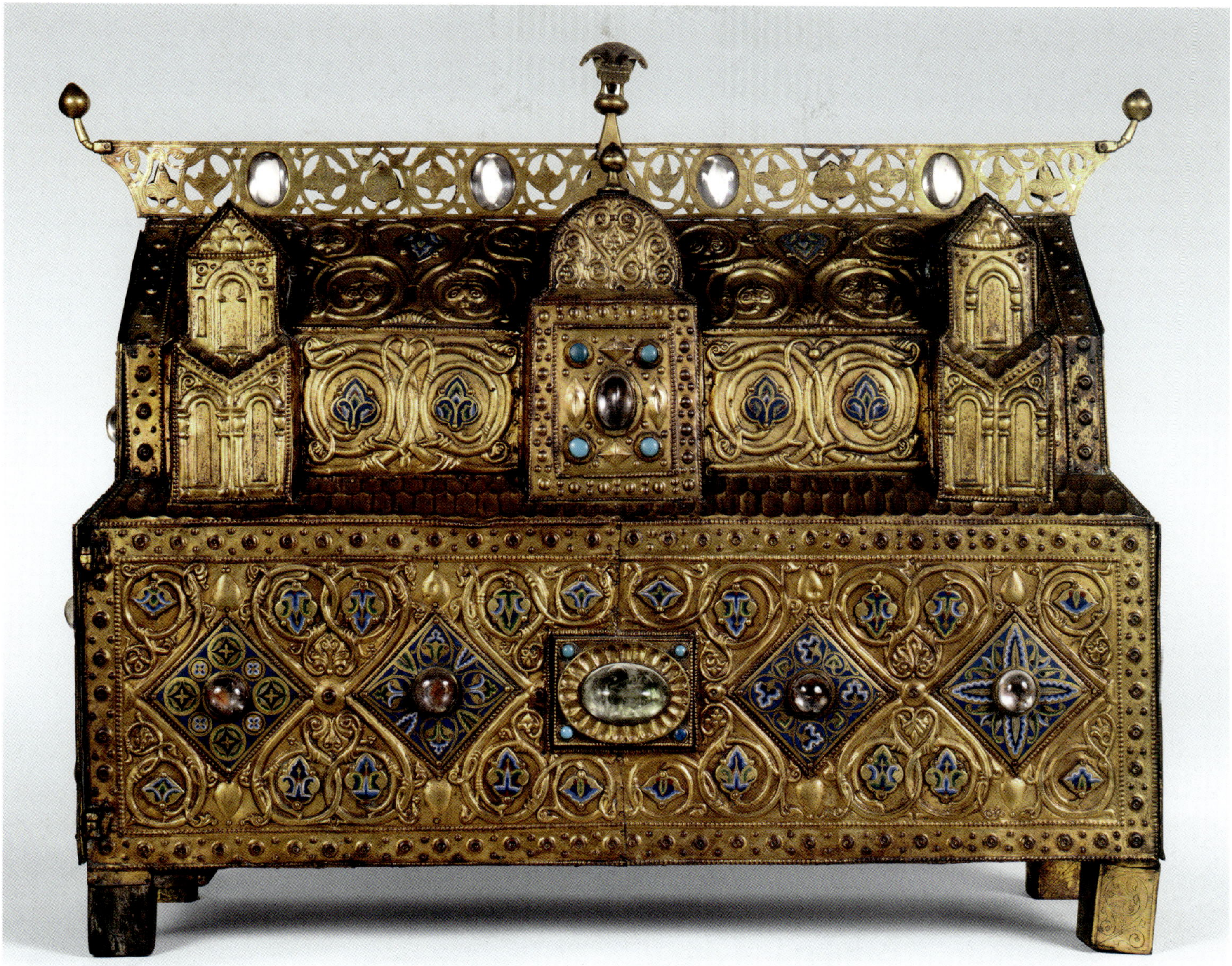

141 back view

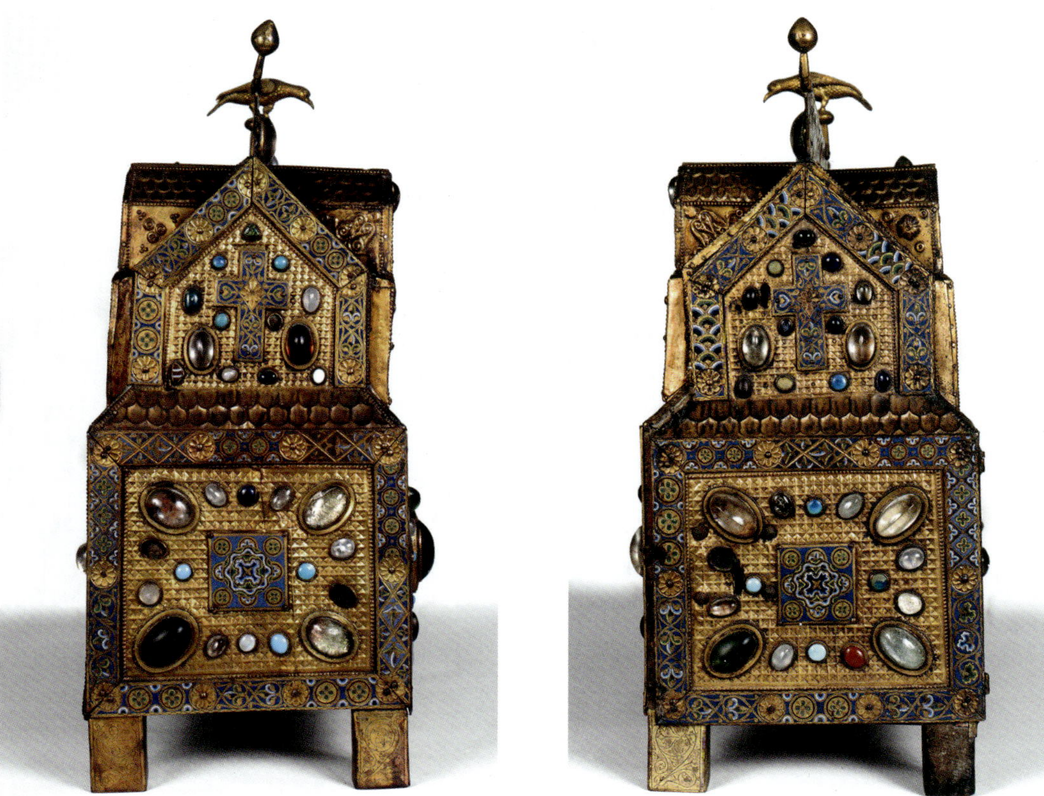

141 side views

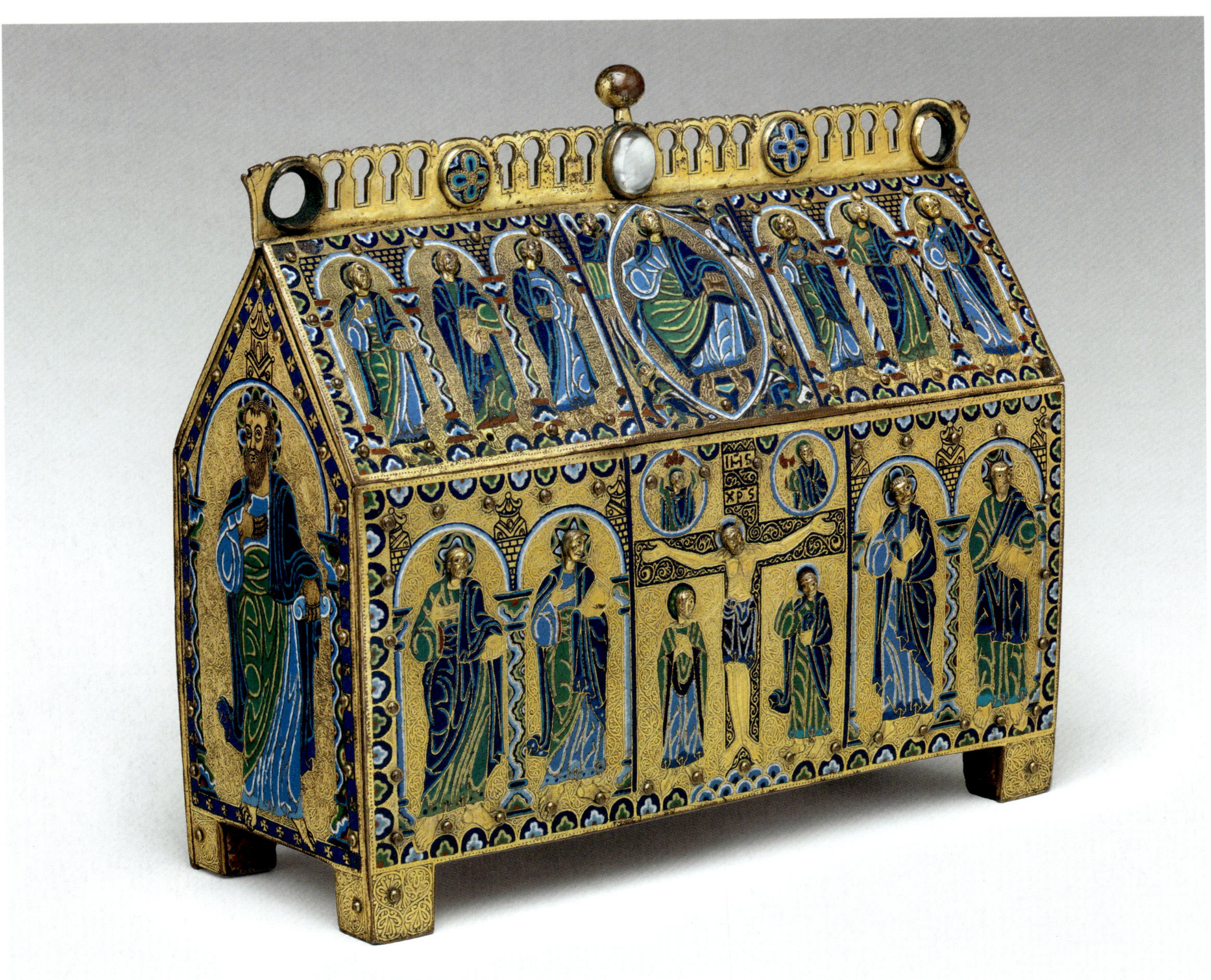

142

142

Chasse with the Crucifixion and Christ in Majesty

Limoges, ca. 1180–90
Gilded copper and champlevé enamel
H. 10⅜ in. (26.2 cm), W. 11⅞ in. (30.2 cm), D 4⅝ in. (11.6 cm)
The Metropolitan Museum of Art, New York, Gift of J. Pierpont Morgan, 1917 (17.190.514)

This reliquary depicts in the bottom register Christ's earthly death by crucifixion and in the top register the risen Christ in Majesty surrounded by symbols of the Four Evangelists. As such, it visually manifests Christ's Second Coming as described in the Apocalypse. To either side of the centermost panels, Christ's apostles stand within colorfully enameled arcades, which, together with the casket's gilded copper and predominantly blue, red, and green champlevé enamels, recall the gold and precious gems adorning the Heavenly Jerusalem as described in the Apocalypse (21:18–21).[1] Moreover, the vermicule decoration arguably evokes the Tree of Life.[2]

Because financial, logistic, and monastic limitations made pilgrimage to the earthly city of Jerusalem difficult for medieval Europeans, praying before such reliquaries may have served to facilitate a spiritual tour of the divine counterpart. Twelfth-century abbot Bernard of Clairvaux instructed that monks should "seek out not the earthly but the heavenly Jerusalem."[3] The imagery of Heavenly Jerusalem reliquaries would have made them useful visual props in a range of liturgical situations referencing the Apocalypse, such as the consecration or rededication of churches, Easter celebrations, Mass, and a saint's annual feast day when he or she was celebrated in the church.[4] With the increased building of new churches and the remodeling of old ones after 1000, the need for Heavenly Jerusalem reliquaries to adorn altars appears to have grown. Medieval Limoges workshops, famous for their champlevé enamelwork, produced numerous examples (cat. 143), which, facilitated by the French city's location on major trade, ecclesiastical, and pilgrimage routes, were disseminated throughout and beyond Western Europe.[5] MHA

Selected References: Marquet de Vasselot 1906, pp. 21–22, pl. 5; Pératé 1911, no. 49, figs. 24, 25; Gauthier 1987, pp. 181–82, no. 205, pl. N, ill. 21 (color), pl. CLXXXV, ills. 636–38; Paris and New York 1995–96, pp. 128–29, no. 24.

1. See also Garrison, El., 2010, pp. 24–26.
2. Apocalypse 22:2.
3. *PL* 1841–65, vol. 182, col. 612b, letter 399, and cited in Forsyth 1986, p. 79.
4. Hanan 2013, pp. 48–61, 87–98, 143–48.
5. Boehm 1996, p. 42.

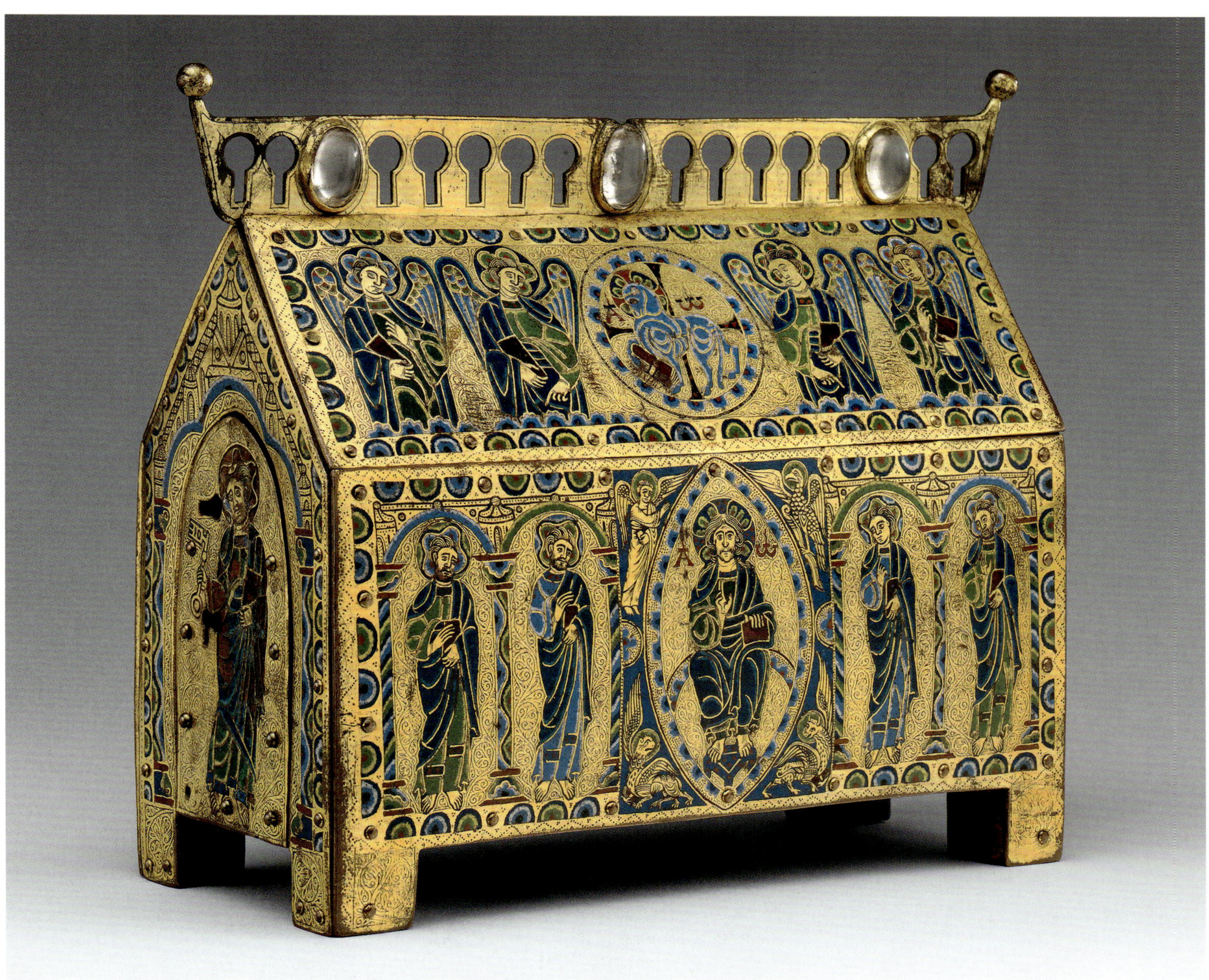

143

143

Chasse with Christ in Majesty and the Lamb of God

Limoges, ca. 1180–90
Gilded copper and champlevé enamel
H. 8⅝ in. (22 cm), W. 9¼ in. (23.5 cm), D. 4¼ in. (10.7 cm)
The Metropolitan Museum of Art, New York, Gift of J. Pierpont Morgan, 1917 (17.190.523)

With its pointed roof and enameled arcades, this small chasse resembles a medieval church, though its purpose hews more closely to that of a miniature sarcophagus made to contain relics, most likely the bones of a saint or pieces of cloth that came into contact with an object or place revered by medieval Christians.[1] The front of the reliquary displays Christ in Majesty enthroned between the inscribed Greek letters alpha and omega, as well as the symbols of the Four Evangelists. To either side stand saints under richly colored champlevé arches and columns. Above Christ, the Lamb of God, flanked by angels, appears between the alpha and omega, also inscribed. One of the chasse's sides features Saint Peter, who holds the key to the gates of heaven, a play on the fact that this pinion served as the lock plate for accessing the relics.

The depictions of Christ, the Lamb of God, the alpha and omega, the Evangelists, angels, Peter with his key, and other saints within an architectural framework indicate that the reliquary represents the Heavenly Jerusalem at the time of the Second Coming of Christ, as described in the Apocalypse.[2] Given the medieval requirement, drawn from Apocalypse 6:9, that altars be consecrated with relics, dedicatory liturgies described the church as a terrestrial version of the Heavenly City, as a medieval Mass antiphon makes clear: "City of blessed Jerusalem, called a vision of peace, built in heaven of living stones."[3] Worshippers could see these references reflected in the design of reliquaries such as this one during a church's consecration ceremony (see also cat. 142).[4] MHA

Selected References: Spitzer, ed. 1890–93, p. 103, no. Orfèvrerie religieuse 20, pl. 8; Marquet de Vasselot 1906, p. 24; Pératé 1911, no. 48, fig. 22; Gauthier 1987, p. 147, no. 150, pl. CXLI, ills. 514–16, pl. CXLIII, ill. 520; Paris and New York 1995–96, pp. 134–35, no. 27.

1. On this reliquary as a sarcophagus, see Gauthier 1987, p. 96.
2. Apocalypse 5:6–13, 21:6–22.
3. Hamilton, L., 2010, pp. 16–19 and n. 37 (translation by the author). On the development of church consecration requirements, see Crook 2000, pp. 13–14.
4. See Hanan 2013, pp. 56–61, 91–92.

144

Gospel Book

Ethiopia, Amhara region, late 14th–early 15th century
Tempera and ink on parchment; 178 folios
16½ × 11¼ in. (41.9 × 28.6 cm)
The Metropolitan Museum of Art, New York, Rogers Fund, 1998 (1998.66)

This large, handsomely decorated Gospel is based on models established in the first centuries of Ethiopian Christianity. In the fourth century the Ethiopian king of Aksum, in the northern Amhara region, along with his people converted to Christianity through the efforts of missionaries from Alexandria. Two centuries later the Gospels, including the Canon Tables, were translated from Greek into Geez, the classical, native language.[1] The manuscript follows the long-established Ethiopian tradition of concluding the Canon Tables, the concordance of the Gospels (cat. 71), with a circular structure known as a *tholos*.[2] The tenth table on the left has confronted birds flanking an elaborately mounted cross referring to the Heavenly Jerusalem on the top of its headpiece (cat. 76). In Ethiopia the multicolumned, conically domed *tholos* on the right represents the harmony of the four Gospels, as inscriptions on many of these images state.[3] The work is a product of the Solomonic dynasty (1270–1527), which proudly based its right to rule on the claim that it was directly descended from the ancient rulers of Aksum, said to be descendants of Menilek. In Ethiopian belief Menilek was born to the Queen of Sheba after her visit to King Solomon in Jerusalem.[4] This manuscript was probably made for a member of the court at the Dabra Hayg Estifanos Monastery, known for its support of the dynasty and its production of exceptional manuscripts.[5] HCE

Selected References: LaGamma et al. 1998, p. 69; Evans, Holcomb, and Hallman 2001, p. 63; New York 2004, p. 441, no. 267.

1. Alisa LaGamma in New York 2004, p. 441, no. 267.
2. Paris and Girona 2000–2001, p. 54.
3. Marilyn Heldman in Baltimore and other cities 1993–96, p. 131.
4. The biblical book of Kings attests to the rich train that accompanied Sheba, with "camels that carried spices, and an immense quantity of gold, and precious stones" (3 Kings 10:2).
5. Heldman in Baltimore and other cities 1993–96, p. 141.

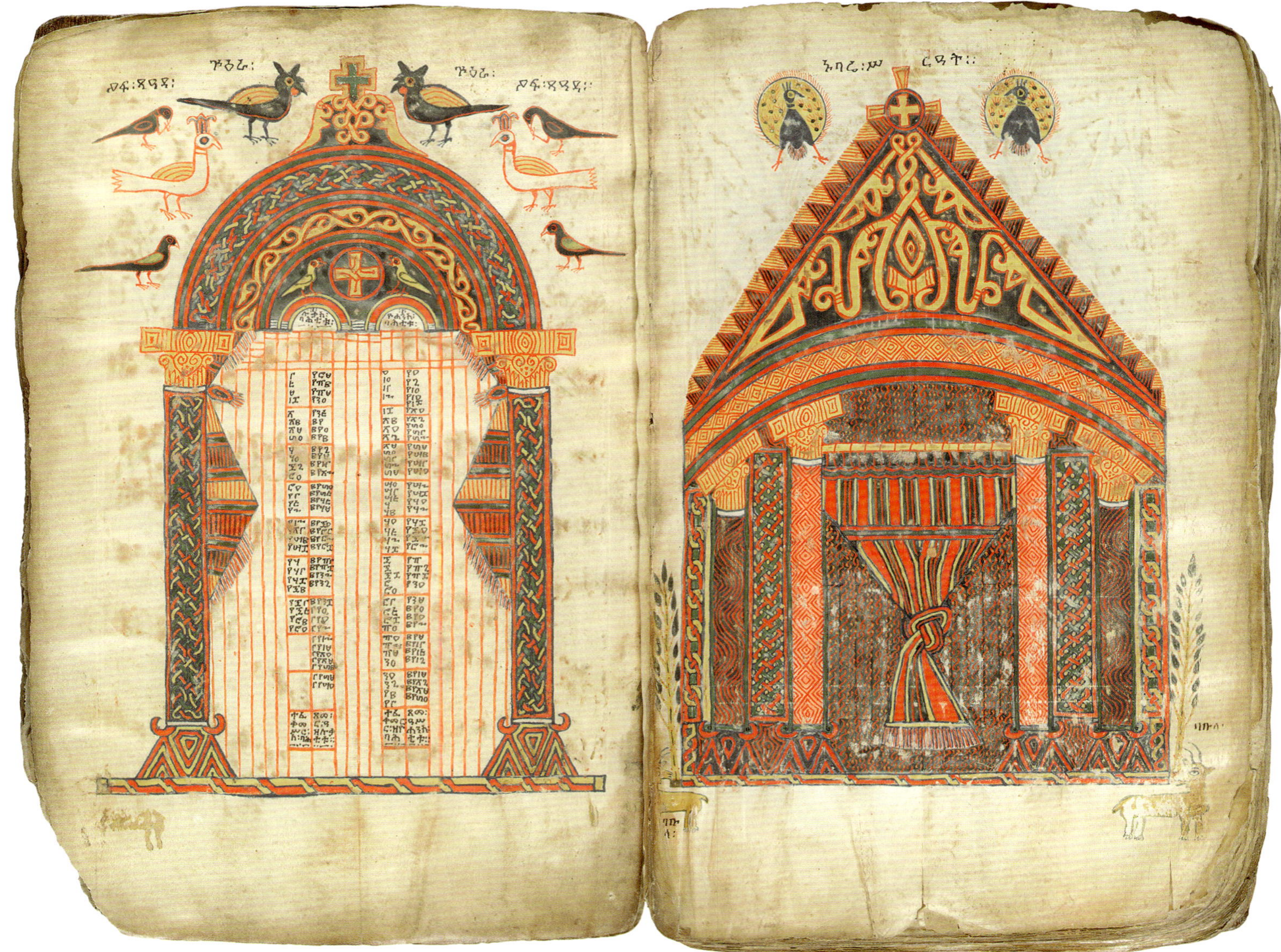

144, fols. 15v–15r

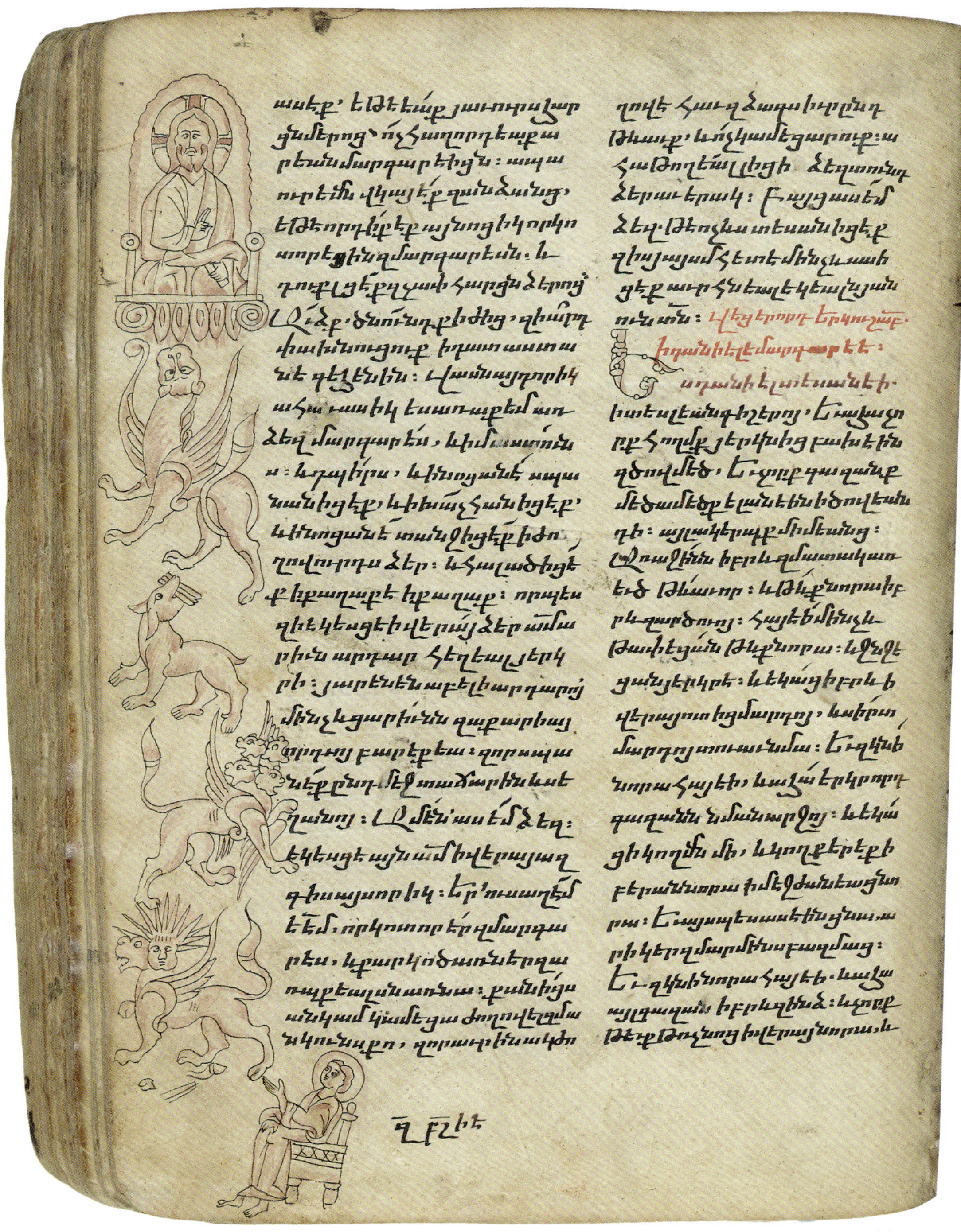

145, fol. 102v

145

The Vision of Daniel

From a lectionary
Vahnashen (present-day Turkey), 1334
Illustrated by Mkrtich'; written by Varden and sons
Ink and colored washes on paper; 477 folios
9¼ × 12⅞ in. (23.5 × 32.5 cm)
Morgan Library and Museum, New York (MS M. 803)

This image of the Vision of Daniel accompanies the reading on the sixth Monday of Lent (folio 102 verso).[1] The text maintains the early Jerusalem lectionary format that provides instructions for the ceremonies performed on important feast days at the holy places in and around the city, while its handsome medieval Armenian *bolorgir*-style script confirms its later date.[2] Small temples appear in the margins of the text when the Temple of Jerusalem is mentioned in the opening sentence of a reading, a motif often found in Armenian lectionaries and Gospels.[3] On this page, Daniel is shown as seated in a chair at the bottom of the page viewing his vision as it rises in the left margin. At the top, the Ancient of Days appears with Christ seated on a throne supported by wheels of fire (Daniel 7:9), although the flames are not represented. Below are several strange animals mentioned in Daniel 7:3–8: a lion with eagle's wings; a bear with three ribs in its mouth; a leopard with four wings of a fowl and four heads; and at the bottom the dreadful beast with iron teeth and eleven horns (and an extra head).[4] The style of the illustration, which relates the work more closely to those from the southern and eastern provinces of Greater Armenia than to those from Cilicia, demonstrates the lasting influence of Jerusalem on the Armenian Church in its homeland.[5] HCE

Selected References: Der Nersessian 1954; New York and Baltimore 1994, no. 67, fig. 148.

1. Morgan Library and Museum, New York, museum website catalogue record, MS M. 803, fol. 102v.
2. Der Nersessian 1954, p. 231.
3. Ibid.
4. Ibid., pp. 235–36.
5. Ibid., p. 237.

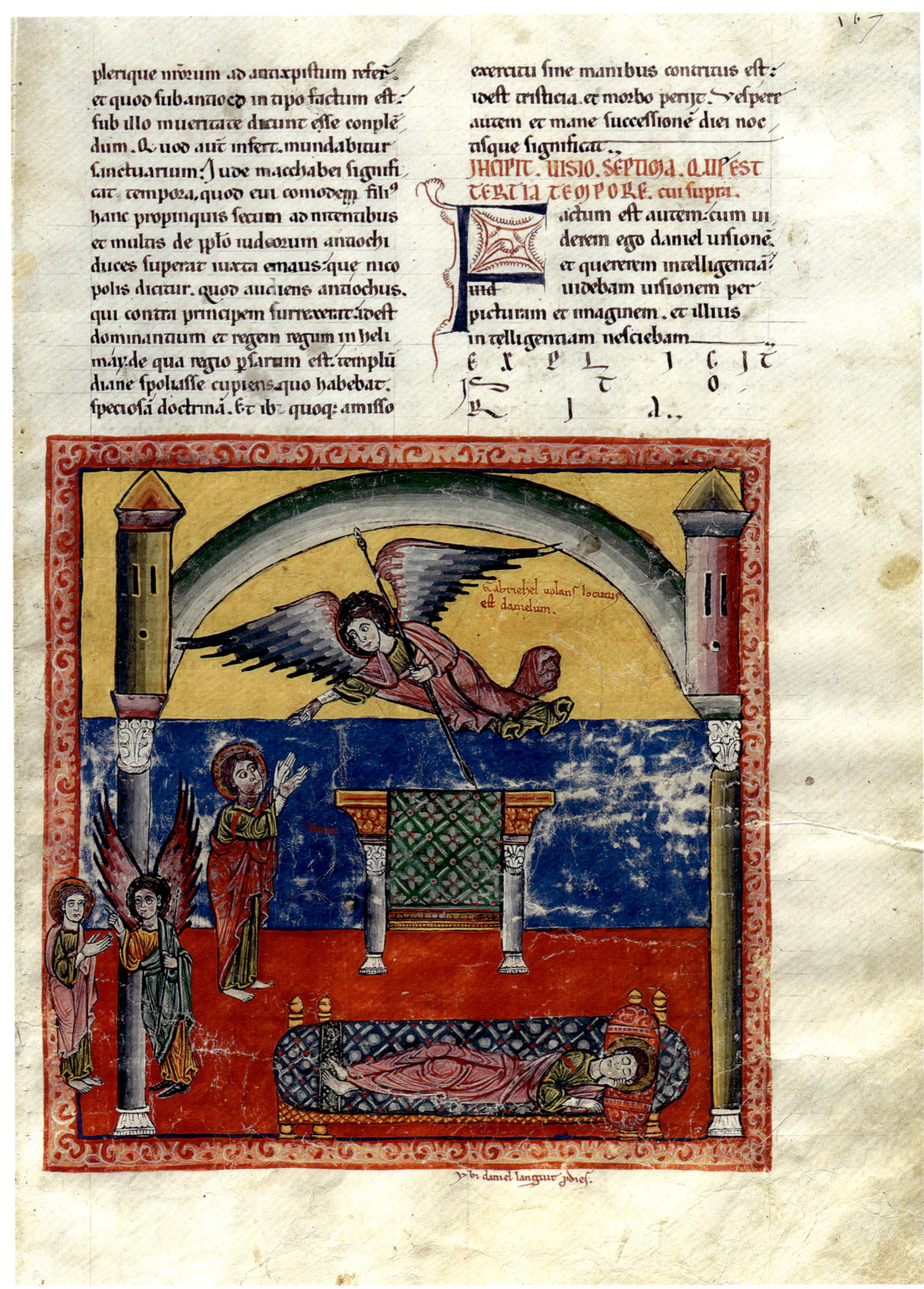

146, fol. 167

146

Gabriel Appears to Daniel

From the Las Huelgas Apocalypse
Spain, possibly Toledo, 1220
Tempera, gold, and ink on parchment; 184 folios
20⅞ × 13⅜ in. (53 × 34 cm)
Morgan Library and Museum, New York (MS M. 429)

The Apocalypse was not the only book of the Christian Bible to offer an account of the end of the present age. The Old Testament book of Daniel includes an apocalyptic vision with many of the hallmarks of the genre: monstrous beasts, celestial agents, numerology, and the destruction and restoration of Jerusalem.

This image illustrating the commentary on Daniel by the church father Saint Jerome (d. 420) combines two moments described in the biblical text. At bottom left, the angel Gabriel explicates for Daniel a series of symbols that foretells a battle between the Persians and the Greeks. So distressed is Daniel that he languishes ill in bed for several days. In the second image, Gabriel swoops down as Daniel performs the evening sacrifice to tell him of Jerusalem's seventy years of desolation.

The vivid palette and banded background are typical of the twenty-six Spanish manuscripts (dating from the ninth to the thirteenth centuries) that illustrate Beatus of Liébana's commentary on the Apocalypse, which the Spanish monk compiled in the late eighth century. The Las Huelgas Apocalypse is a particularly fine example from the group of Beatus manuscripts that also includes Jerome's commentary on Daniel's vision. MH

Selected References: Williams, J., 1994–2003, vol. 2, pp. 38–42; Voelkle et al. 2007.

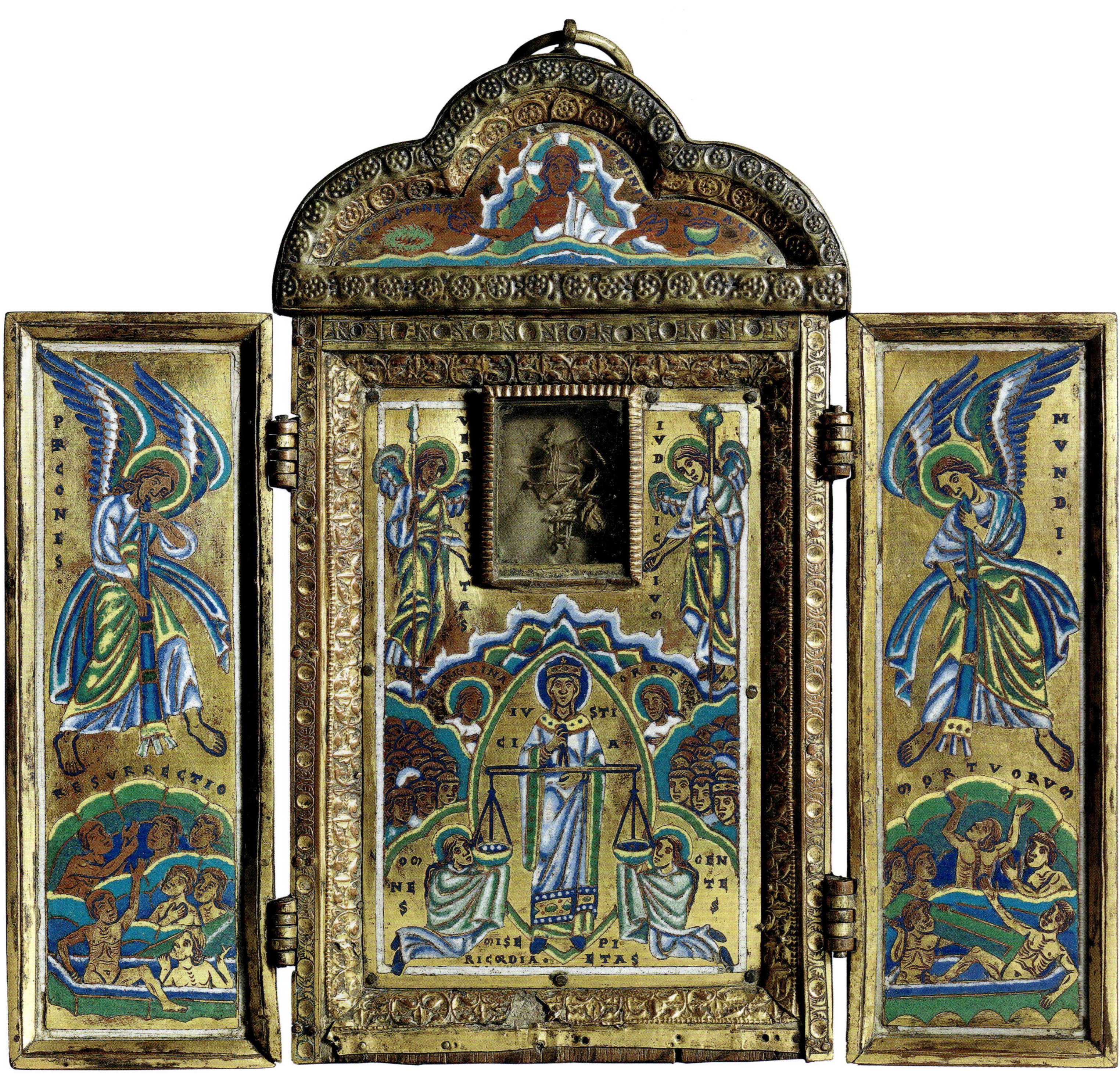

147

147

Triptych Reliquary of the Cross

Meuse Valley, probably Liège, ca. 1160–70
Gilded copper, champlevé enamel, émail brun, and rock crystal
Open: H. 10⅝ in. (26.9 cm), W. 11½ in. (29.2 cm)
Private collection, United Kingdom

Christ, identified by the cross of his halo and the inscription labeling him "the Son of Man," appears amid clouds of heaven at the top of this reliquary. Only when the object is open do we perceive that he presides over the End of Days.

Angels are the principal agents orchestrating the event. Those representing Truth and Judgment stand to either side of now-lost relics, certainly of the Cross and perhaps also of the Crown of Thorns pictured at Christ's side. Larger angels, identified as "heralds of the world," appear on the wings of the triptych. At the sounding of their trumpets, the dead rise from their graves; Justice stands ready to weigh souls.

The work has a hopeful, even joyful quality that draws on the meaning of the Cross. There are no devils, no fires of hell, no gnashing of teeth. Instead, the dead rise energetically, lifting their arms heavenward, while Mercy and Piety keep the scales evenly balanced. Significantly, and as the inscription indicates, they do so on behalf of "all people" (*omnes gentes*). BDB

Selected References: Frolow 1961, p. 356, no. 394; Fro ow 1965, pp. 33, 58, 233, 250; Cleveland, Baltimore, and London 2010–11, pp. 180–81, no. 89.

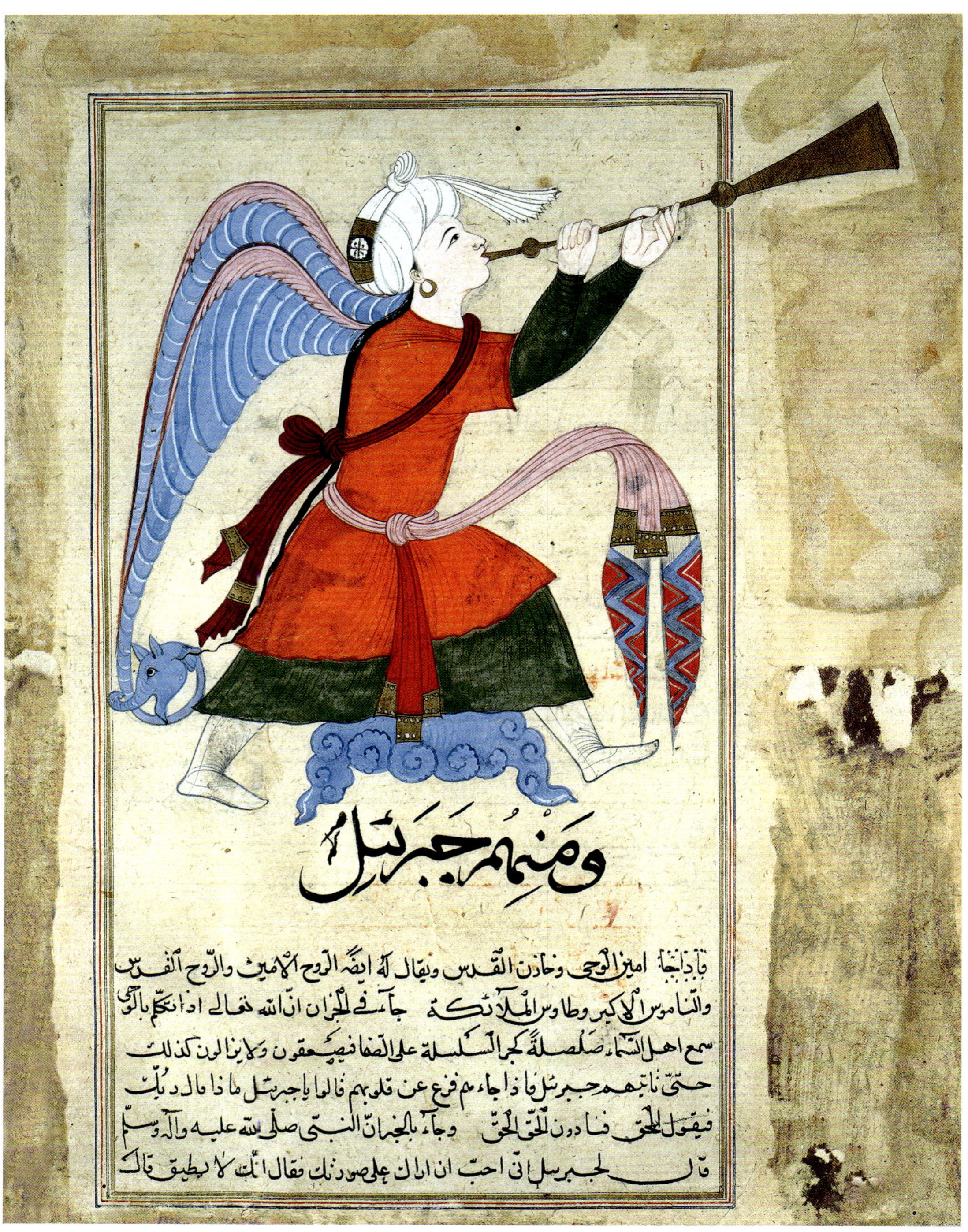

148

148

The Archangel Israfil

From *The Wonders of Creation and Oddities of Existence* (*'Aja'ib al-Makhluqat*) by al-Qazwini (1202–1283)
Egypt or Syria, late 14th–early 15th century
Opaque watercolor and ink on paper
15⅜ × 9⅝ in. (38.9 × 24.6 cm)
British Museum, London (1963,0420,0.1)

In Islamic belief, as in Christianity, archangels will play a key role in the Last Judgment. One, unnamed in the Qur'an (50:41–42), blows a trumpet. From very early on, especially in the Merits of Jerusalem (Fada'il al-Quds) literature, that angel came to be identified with Israfil, and the place with the Rock in Jerusalem. Moreover, Muqatil, an eighth-century commentator on the Qur'an, specified that Israfil would be "standing on the rock of Jerusalem, which is the nearest place on earth to heaven, at a distance of eighteen miles." He noted further that "all the creatures will hear [the trumpet and his terrifying call] and they will assemble in Jerusalem, and it is the middle of the Earth."[1]

This illustration comes from a text by al-Qazwini, a widely trained and prominent scholar, who studied in Mosul and was a contemporary of the historian Ibn al-Athir, who famously chronicled the life of Saladin.[2] In his systematic attempt to present the wonders of God's creation, al-Qazwini discussed all things celestial, including archangels.

The text on the reverse of this single leaf describes Israfil. The text immediately under the image names Gabriel in large letters, which at first appears to be a caption for the image, and then describes Gabriel's role as "keeper of the holy" and as a translator of what God says to his people. It seems, therefore, that the text beneath the figure represents the subsequent chapter devoted to Gabriel, rather than the identification of the figure in this image.

BDB / MH

1. See Livne-Kafri 2006, pp. 388–89.
2. See Carboni 2015, p. 14.

149a–f

Folios from the *Paths of Paradise* (*Nahj al-faradis*) of al-Sara'i

Herat (present-day Iran), ca. 1466
Commissioned by the Timurid ruler Abu Sa'id
Opaque watercolor, gold, and ink on paper
16⅛ × 11⅝ in. (41 × 29.6 cm)

a. "The Prophet Muhammad Arriving at the Fourth Heaven" (recto) and "The Prophet Muhammad Encountering Jesus in the Bayt al-Ma'mur" (verso)

Private collection, London

b. "The Prophet Muhammad Encountering the Angel 'Azra'il" (recto) and "The Prophet Muhammad Arriving at the White Sea" (verso)

Sarikhani Collection, Oxfordshire

c. "The Prophet Muhammad before the Angel with Seventy Heads" (recto) and "The Prophet Muhammad Encounters the Angel with Ten Thousand Wings and the Four-Headed Angel" (verso)

David Collection, Copenhagen (14/2012)

d. "The Prophet Muhammad in the Place of Seventy Thousand Veils" and "The Prophet Muhammad in the Place of Seven Hundred Thousand Tents"

Sarikhani Collection, Oxfordshire

e. "The Prophet Muhammad at the Gates of Paradise" (verso)

David Collection, Copenhagen (15/2012)

f. "The Prophet Muhammad Visiting the Heavenly Pavilion of Abraham" (recto) and "The Prophet Muhammad Visiting the Pavilions Made from Rubies in Paradise" (verso)

Private collection, London

After Mecca and Medina, Jerusalem is considered the third holiest city in Islam. This "holy abode" (*bayt al-maqdis*) served as the original direction of prayer (qibla) for members of the early Muslim community before it was revealed to Muhammad to change the qibla to Mecca. Jerusalem's sacredness did not, however, diminish as a result. On the contrary, it was enhanced by the many narratives of the Prophet's Night Journey (*isra'*) to and ascension (*mi'raj*) from the Holy City. In Islamic tradition Muhammad's visit to Jerusalem, where he leaped into the heavens, is widely believed to have left an imprint of his foot on the rocky outcrop. This mark comprises the Prophet's major contact relic, as sheltered and displayed in the Dome of the Rock.[1]

Tales of Muhammad's *mi'raj* have proved highly popular in Islamic storytelling and literature, because they provide a dramatic glimpse into the Prophet's greatest miracle along with awe-inspiring descriptions of the angels (cat. 149c), prophets, God, heaven (cat. 149f), and hell.[2] Just as significantly, these bio-apocalyptic narratives confirm Muhammad's supreme standing among the Abrahamic prophets while concurrently placing the city of Jerusalem within a larger Islamic prophetic and eschatological landscape.

Many ascension texts were penned in Arabic during the first few centuries of Islam and spread to eastern Islamic lands by the medieval period. After 1300 Muslim dynasties in Persia and Central Asia began to commission illustrated manuscripts to commemorate this momentous event, itself a major holiday in the Islamic calendar.[3] At least three so-called

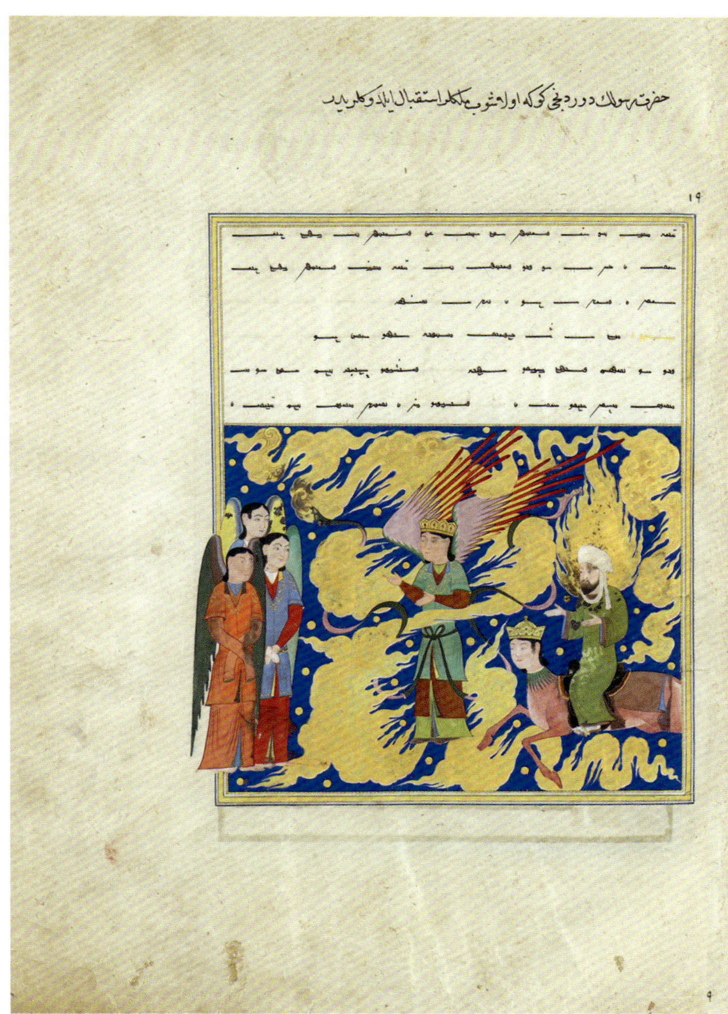

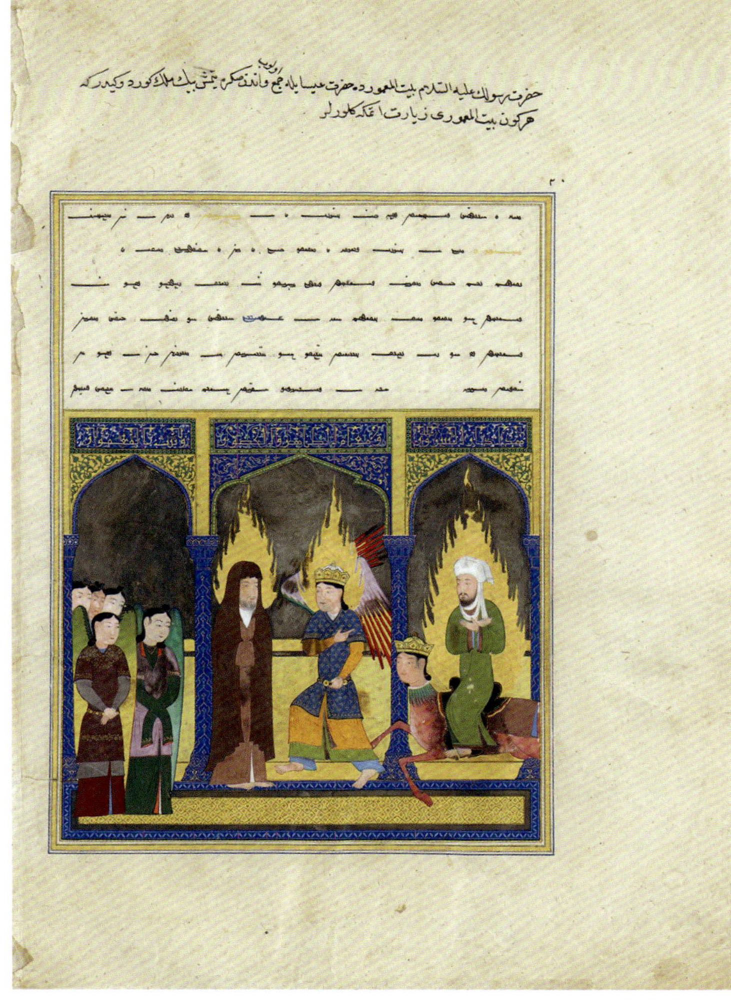

149a "The Prophet Muhammad Arriving at the Fourth Heaven" and "The Prophet Muhammad Encountering Jesus in the Bayt al-Ma'mur"

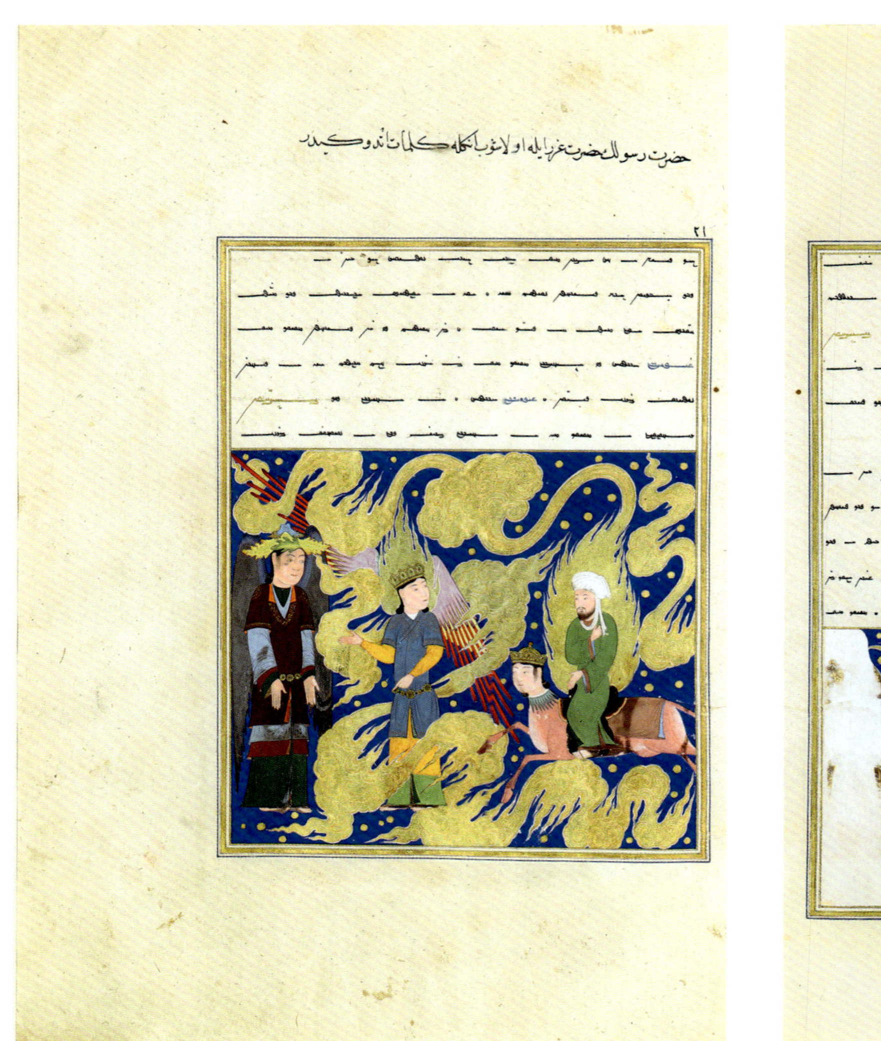

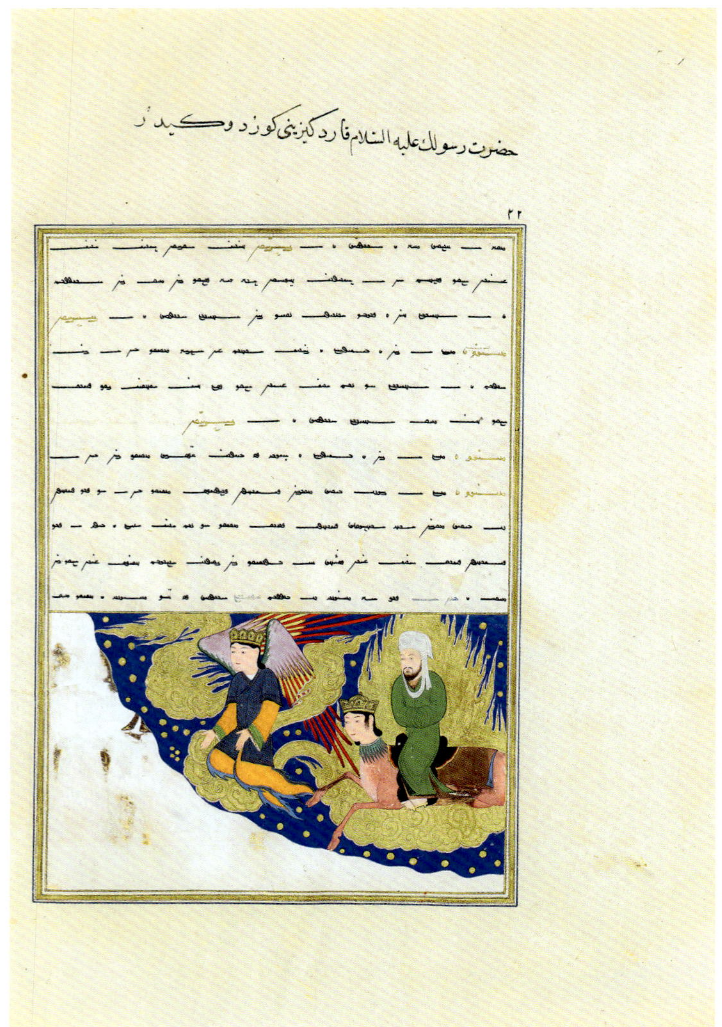

149b "The Prophet Muhammad Encountering the Angel 'Azra'il" and "The Prophet Muhammad Arriving at the White Sea"

Books of Ascension (*Mi'rajnamas*) written in Persian and Turkic languages and made between 1300 and 1470 are extant today.[4] Each manuscript contains an elaborate cycle of paintings that is important for various reasons, among them its contribution to the ways in which Muhammad was depicted in Islamic artistic traditions.[5]

One of these lavishly illustrated manuscripts, made about 1466 for the Timurid monarch Abu Sa'id (r. 1451–69), is identified as a "book of images of the Prophet on the night of the ascension (as described) in the hadith."[6] The hadith, or saying of the Prophet, that launches this text and its subsequent elaboration composes al-Sara'i's *Paths of Paradise* (*Nahj al-faradis*), a Turkic-language narrative written in the mid-fourteenth century. Thus, the illustrated *Paths of Paradise* from which catalogues 149a–f derive is essentially a hadith — that is, a religious text second only to the Qur'an in its theological status — elaborated into a longer tale and put to picture.

The *Paths of Paradise* is like other *Mi'rajnamas* in that it describes and illustrates Muhammad's arrival in Jerusalem, at which time he enters the so-called faraway mosque (*al-masjid al-aqsa*), frequently identified as the Dome of the Rock.[7] While there, he meets the Judeo-Christian prophets, including Adam, Noah, Abraham, Moses, and Jesus. They welcome him and ask him to serve as their prayer leader or imam, an act of selection confirming Muhammad's supreme rank as the "seal of prophets."[8] In Islamic *mi'raj* narratives Jerusalem thus serves as the locus of prophetic congregation where Muhammad is recognized as an apostle. This collective act of confirmation precedes his journey through the heavens, where he encounters further prophets and angels — including 'Azra'il, the angel of death (cat. 149b) — and traverses many tents and veils guarded by angels (cat. 149d) before finally arriving in God's presence.

In a number of Islamic ascension tales, Jerusalem also plays a key role at the very end — rather than at the beginning — of Muhammad's *mi'raj*. Upon his return to Mecca, Muhammad is dared by his adversary Abu Jahl to describe the city of Jerusalem, which he had never visited during his lifetime, in order to prove the veracity of his celestial ascent. Numerous texts describe this climactic conclusion, and at least one painting, from a *Book of Ascension* made about 1317–35, depicts Gabriel offering a vision of the Holy City to Muhammad.[9] Upon the Prophet's accurate elucidation of Jerusalem's architectural and natural sites, members of the Quraysh tribe who doubted or disbelieved his ascension convert to Islam on the spot. Jerusalem thus provides the ultimate proof of Muhammad's miraculous ascent as well as the final argument in favor of conversion to the Islamic faith.

The medieval mystical writer al-Qushayri (d. 1073) perhaps captures best the many virtues (*lata'if*) of Jerusalem in his *Book of Ascension* (*Kitab al-mi'raj*), in which he offers the following laudatory remarks: "Jerusalem allows the Prophet Muhammad to witness the traces (*athar*) of the prophets and their tombs. Also, the rock (*sakhra*) faces the doorway to the heavens. Jerusalem is considered the closest location to the skies: it is only from it that the ascension can occur. It is also where the angels descend and where all the souls of the prophets and messengers are gathered. Finally, God made Muhammad see Jerusalem to inform the

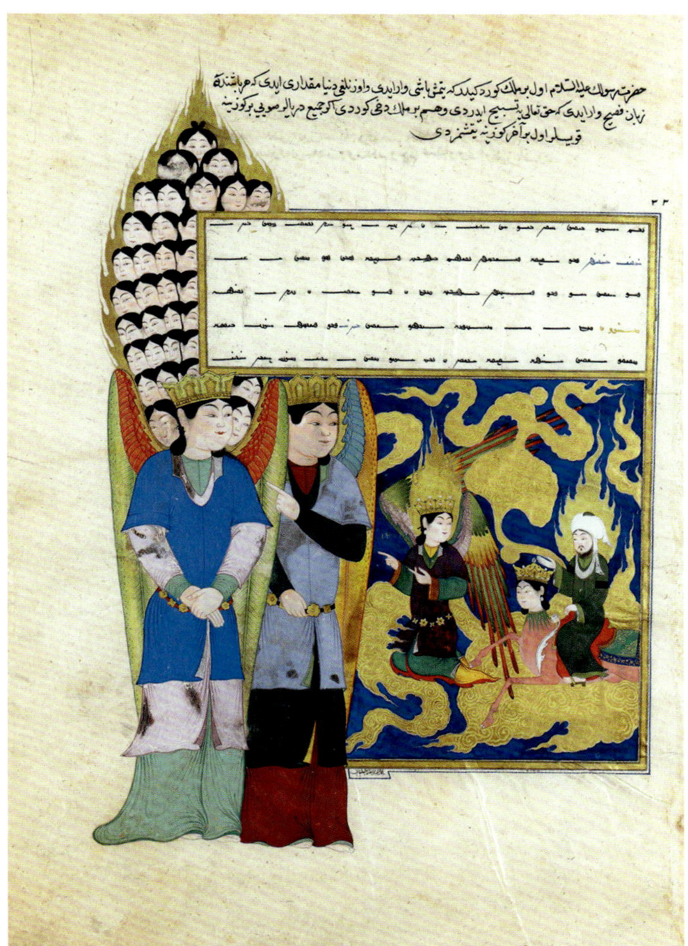

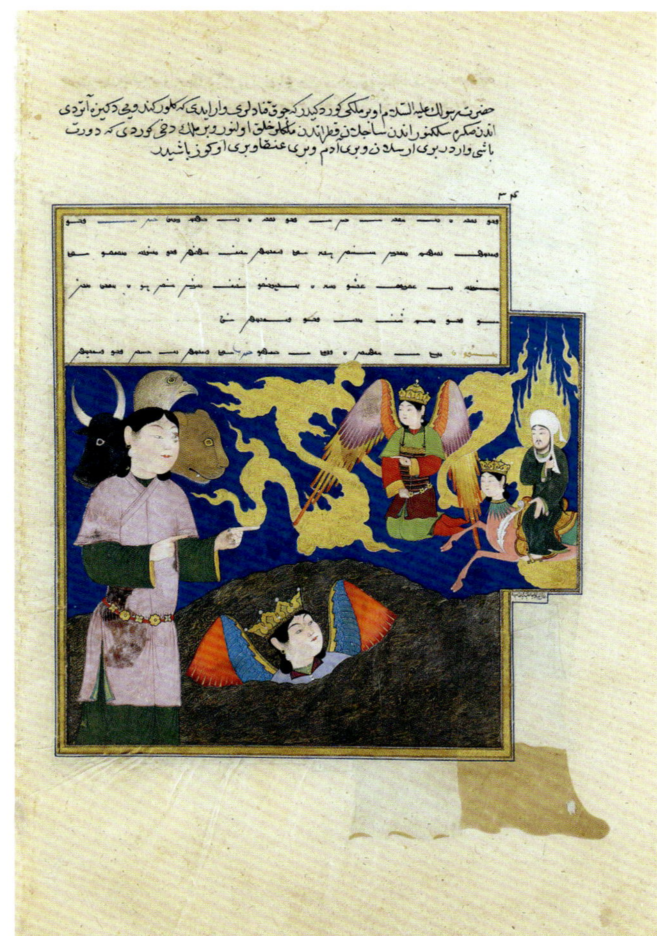

149c "The Prophet Muhammad before the Angel with Seventy Heads" and "The Prophet Muhammad Encounters the Angel with Ten Thousand Wings and the Four-Headed Angel"

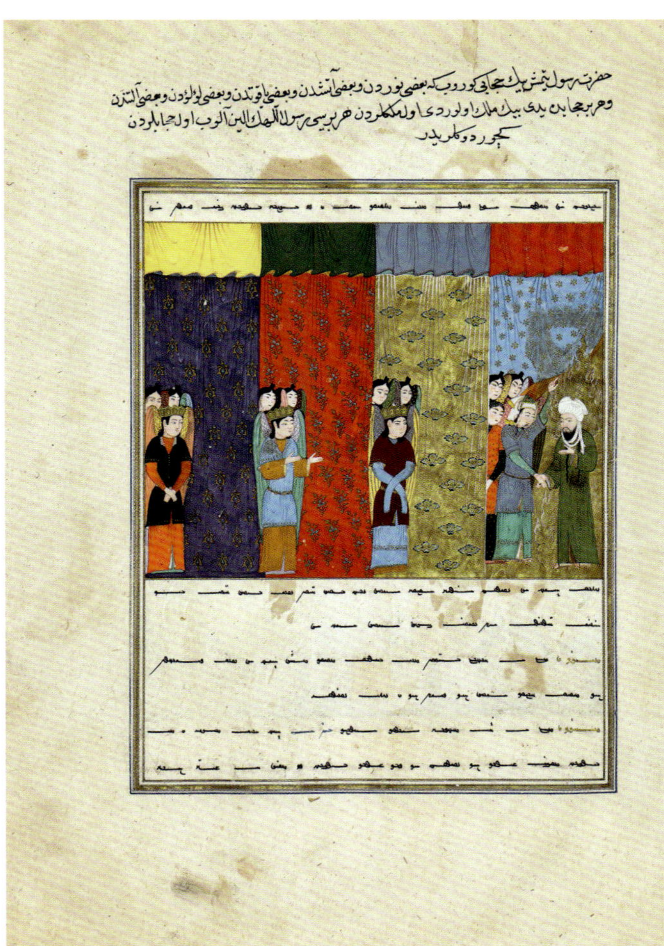

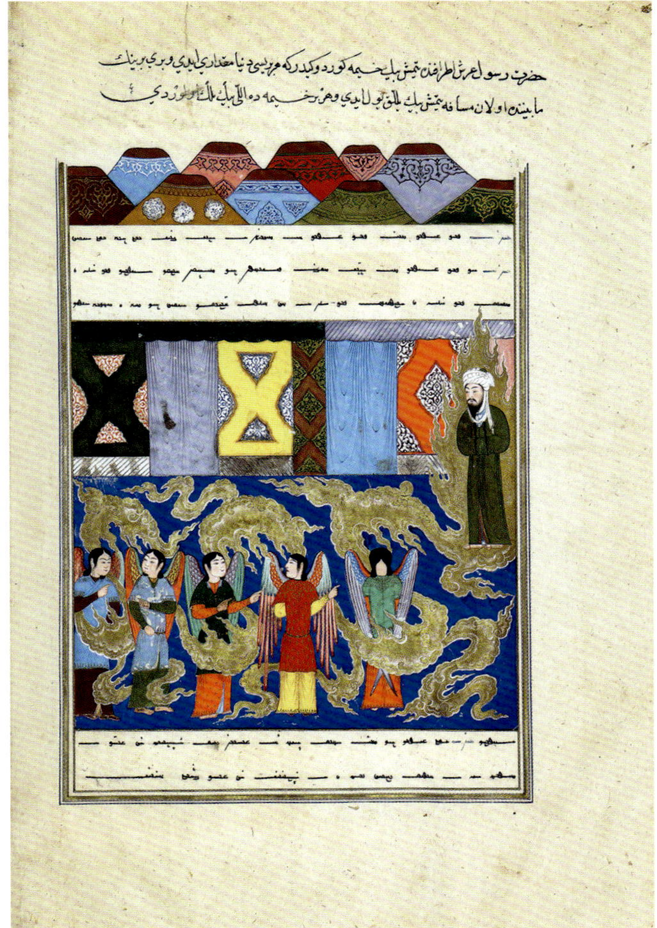

149d "The Prophet Muhammad in the Place of Seventy Thousand Veils" and "The Prophet Muhammad in the Place of Seven Hundred Thousand Tents"

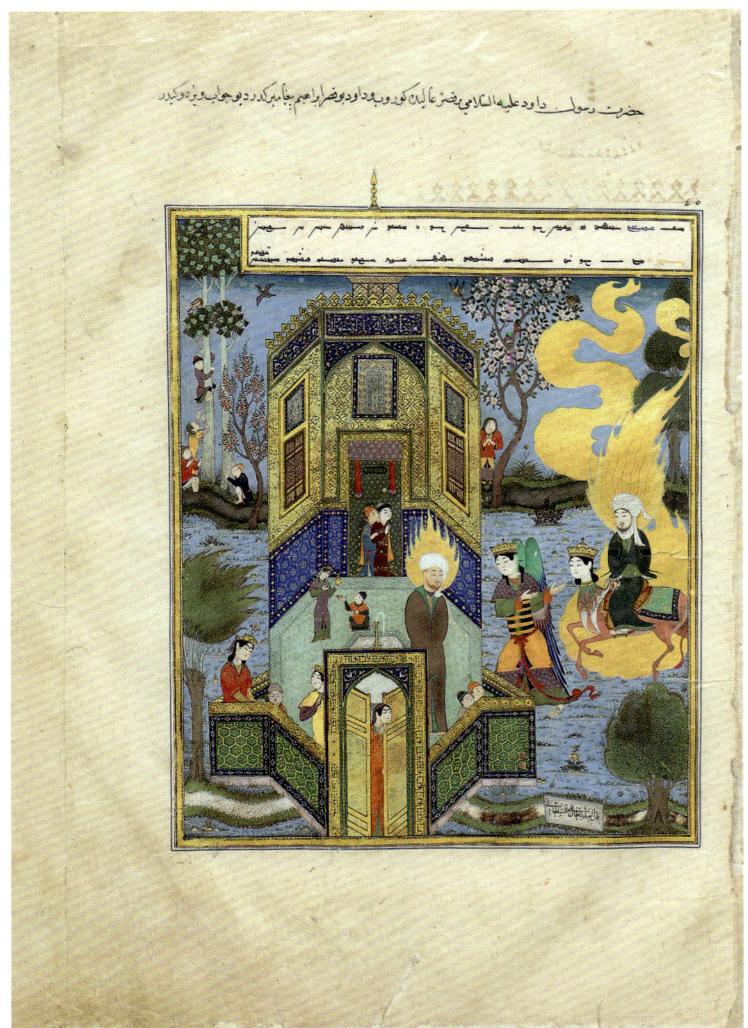
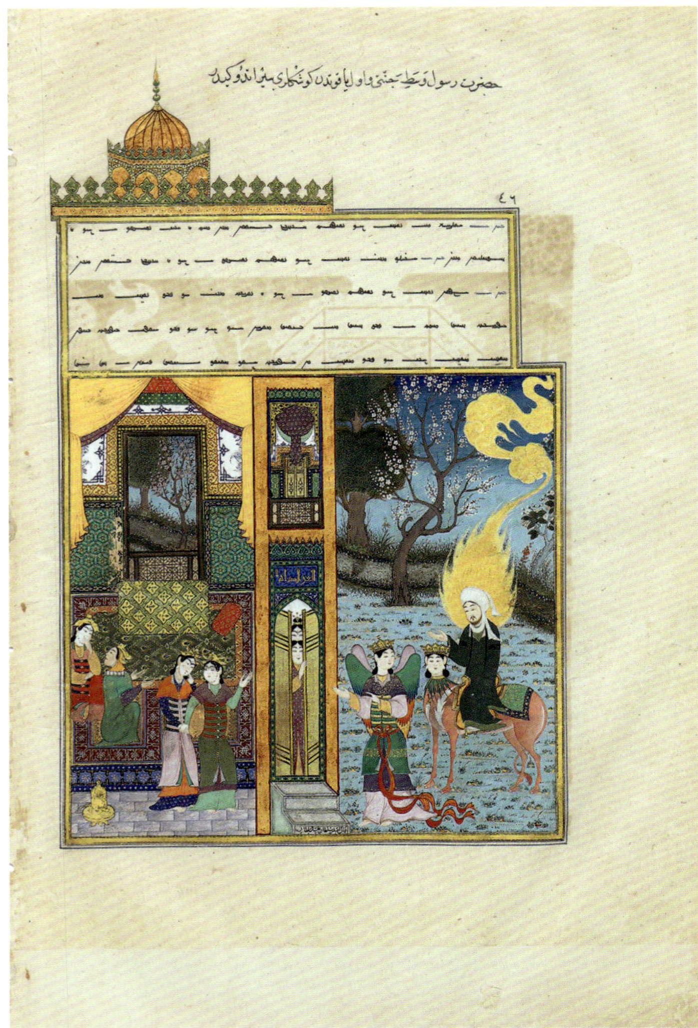

149f "The Prophet Muhammad Visiting the Heavenly Pavilion of Abraham" and "The Prophet Muhammad Visiting the Pavilions Made from Rubies in Paradise"

Quraysh about it and thus prove his miracle (*mu'jizat*) of the ascension to them."[10] Within Islamic ascension texts and images, the Holy City therefore functions as a place of prophetic initiation, a way station to the celestial spheres, and irrefutable proof of Muhammad's chief miracle. CG

Selected References: Gruber 2008, pp. 330–36; Sims 2014.

1. On the Dome of the Rock, see especially Grabar, O., et al. 1996 and Rabbat 1989.

2. For an overview of Islamic ascension tales, see Amir-Moezzi 1996; Colby 2008; Gruber and Colby, eds. 2010.

3. Muhammad's ascension is typically celebrated on 27 Rajab. In the Muslim world, the feast day is known as the "night of ascension" (Arabic, *laylat al-mi'raj*), and it is often accompanied by evening prayers, musical ceremonies, and/or the distribution of food.

4. On the Ilkhanid *Book of Ascension* of about 1317–35, see Gruber 2010 and Ettinghausen 1957. On the two Timurid ascension manuscripts of about 1436–69, see Gruber 2008; Sims 2014; and Séguy 1977.

5. For a general discussion of representations of the Prophet in Islamic figural arts, see Gruber 2009.

6. "Kitab ashkal al-nabi, 'alayhi al-salam, fi laylat al-mi'raj fi'l-hadith"; see Gruber 2008, p. 331; and Sims 2014, p. 88, fig. 1.

7. On the many interpretations of the term *al-masjid al-aqsa*, see Busse 1998, Bevan 1914, Hasson 1996, and Plessner 1957.

8. For Muhammad's meeting with the prophets in Jerusalem as described in the Ilkhanid and Timurid illustrated *Books of Ascension*, see Gruber 2010, pp. 43–44; Eckmann, ed. 1995–98, vol. 1, p. 39; Thackston 1994, p. 267; and Pavet de Courteille 1975 ed., pp. 3–4. For the two Timurid *Mi'rajnama* paintings illustrating Muhammad's arrival and prayer in Jerusalem, see Séguy 1977, pls. 4–5.

9. For a discussion of this painting and its related text, see Gruber 2010, pp. 29, 74, and pl. 12.

10. Al-Qushayri 1964 ed., p. 103.

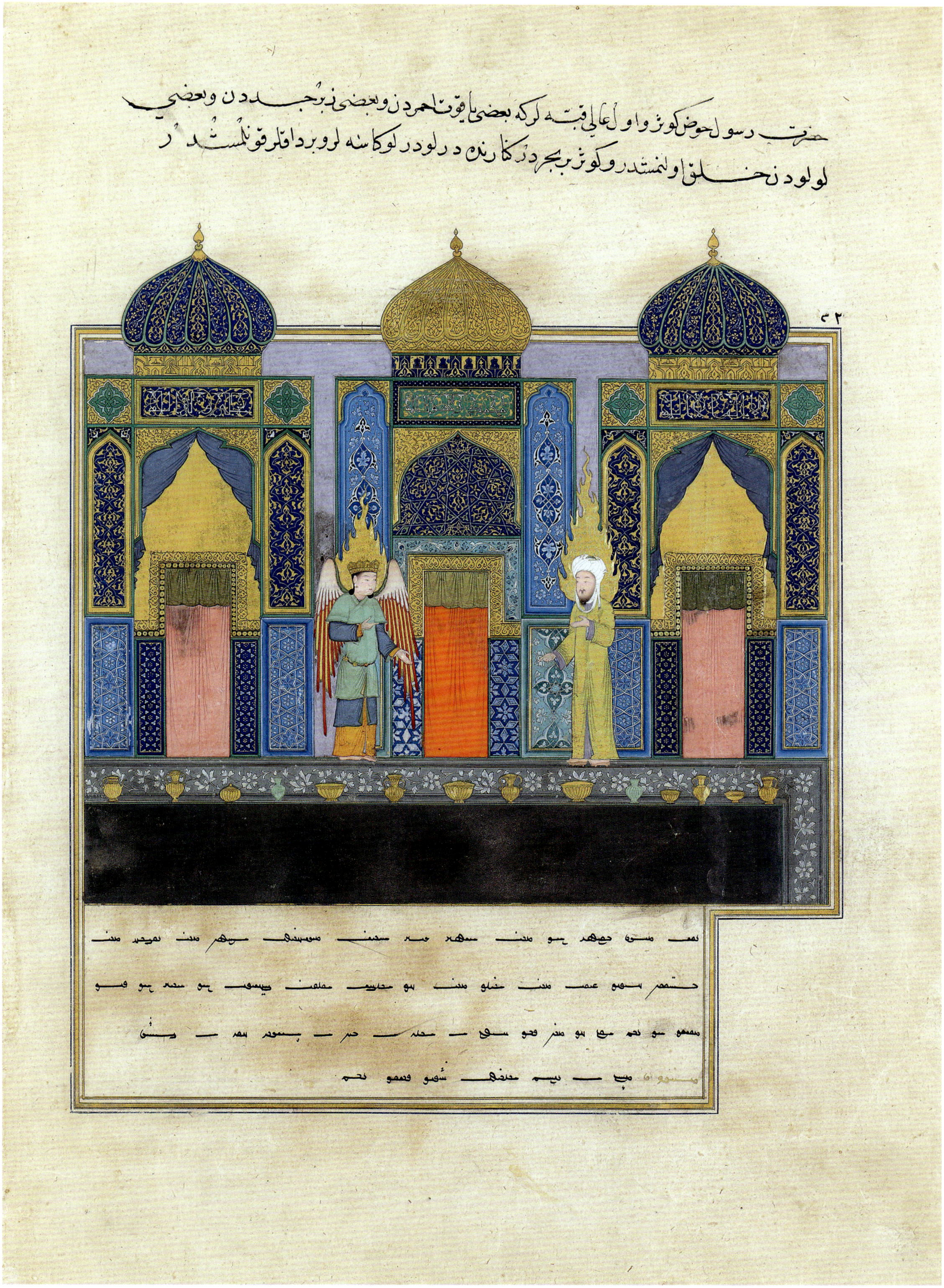

149e “The Prophet Muhammad at the Gates of Paradise”

NOTES

Art and Medieval Jerusalem

1. Bar-El et al. 2000, pp. 86–87.

2. Ibid., p. 88.

3. Berlin 1995–96.

4. Rome 1997; Jerusalem 1999; Oldenburg 2005–6; Schallaburg 2007.

5. Vienna 1998–99; Paris 2001–2; Washington, D.C., and other cities 1981–83.

6. *The Meeting of Two Worlds: The Crusades and the Mediterranean Context*, the publication accompanying the exhibition of the same name held at the University of Michigan Museum of Art (Ann Arbor 1981), was in the vanguard of efforts to take a cross-cultural approach to the art of the Mediterranean, though without a specific focus on Jerusalem.

7. Auld and Hillenbrand 2000, vol. 2, pp. 689–92.

8. A carved inscription in Arabic indicates that it was built by Sultan Süleyman the Magnificent in 1537.

9. Bahat 1996, p. 45.

10. Gil 1992, pp. 635–53.

11. Boas 2001, p. 88.

12. On this point, see the nuanced remarks in Grabar, O., et al. 1996, p. 145.

13. Boas 2001, pp. 83–93.

14. Peters 1985, pp. 357–59.

15. Schaefer 1985, pp. 305–29; Mujir al-Din 1876 ed., pp. 174–75.

16. Inspired by the Acts of the Apostles (2:5), the thirteenth-century bishop Jacques de Vitry described Jerusalem as "honored by angels and frequented by every people under heaven" (*ab Angelis honorata & ab ab omni natione, quae sub caelo est frequentata*). Jacques de Vitry in Bongars 1611, p. 1077.

Trade and Tourism in Medieval Jerusalem

1. Jacques de Vitry 1960 ed., pp. 79–97, no. 2; Jacques de Vitry arrived in Acre on November 7, 1216. The epigraph is from Ibn Jubayr (1952 ed., p. 300).

2. On Saewulf's voyage, see Wilkinson, Hill, and Ryan, eds. 1988, pp. 94–95. For Judah ha-Levi's poetic description of the dangers he faced, see Scheindlin 2008, pp. 214–47, poems 23–30.

3. Bird, Peters, and Powell, eds. 2013, p. 438.

4. A Marseillaise statute of 1253 reveals that ships transporting one thousand pilgrims were not exceptional. See Jacoby, D., 2001, p. 106.

5. Spufford 2002, p. 401.

6. Fabri 1893 ed., vol. 1, pt. 1, p. 13.

7. Jacques de Vitry 1896 ed., pp. 90–91.

8. Al-Muqaddasi 1994 ed., p. 151.

9. Nasir-i Khusraw 1986 ed., p. 22.

10. Pietro Casola 1907 ed., p. 251.

11. Frescobaldi, Gucci, and Sigoli 1948 ed., p. 180. See similar remarks by the Italian rabbi Obadiah of Bertinoro in Adler, ed. 1930, p. 236.

12. The Cotton Market was built by Tankiz, governor of Damascus and viceroy of Syria from 1312 to 1340, during the reign of Mamluk Sultan al-Nasir Muhammad ibn Qala'un. See pp. 227–28, fig. 82, in this volume.

13. Mujir al-Din on Cotton Market merchants and the three suqs, as cited in Peters 1985, pp. 400–401.

14. Al-Umari, 1347, as cited in ibid., p. 402.

15. On the various commercial districts of Jerusalem, see the remarks of the anonymous early thirteenth-century writer of *The Condition of the City of Jerusalem* (*City of Jerusalem* 1896 ed., pp. 6–7), and later, the fifteenth-century descriptions of the markets by both Mujir al-Din, cited in Peters 1985, pp. 400–401, and Obadiah of Bertinoro in Adler, ed. 1930, pp. 236–37.

16. "On the right hand of this Market [where cheese, chickens, eggs and birds were sold] are the shops of the Syrian gold-workers. . . . On the left hand of the Market are the shops of the Latin gold-workers." *City of Jerusalem* 1896 ed., p. 7.

17. Al-Muqaddasi 1994 ed., p. 166.

18. Gil 1996, pp. 188–90.

19. In the thirteenth century Jews paid for the right to practice dyeing in the Latin Kingdom of Jerusalem and were involved in glassmaking north of the city; Prawer 1988, p. 124.

20. "Many of them [Jews] carry on the work of goldsmiths or shoemakers; some deal in silks, the men doing the buying and selling, the women the actual work." Elijah of Ferrara in Adler, ed. 1930, pp. 152–53. "The soil is excellent, but it is not possible to gain a living by any branch of industry, unless it be that of a shoemaker, weaver, or goldsmith; even such artisans as these gain their livelihood with great difficulty." Obadiah of Bertinoro in Adler, ed. 1930, p. 238.

21. See the remarks of the twelfth-century historian Imad al-Din in Gabrieli, ed. 1969, pp. 161–62: "The Franks began selling their possessions and taking their precious things out of safe-keeping to sell them for nothing in the market of abjection. People made bargains with them and bought the goods at very low prices. They sold things worth more than ten *dinar* for less than one and were forced to put together all that they could find of their scattered possessions. So they scavenged in their own churches, stripped them of their ornaments and carried off candelabra and vases of gold and silver, gold and silken curtains and draperies. They broke open and emptied the boxes in the churches and took from the storage chests the treasures they contained. The Grand Patriarch gathered up all that stood above the Sepulchre, the gold plating and gold and silver artifacts, and collected together the contents of the Church of the Resurrection, precious things of both metals and of the two sorts of fabric."

22. Haarmann 1984, p. 329.

23. For an English translation of the document, see the appendix in Janin, H., 2002, pp. 221–22.

24. Pietro Casola 1907 ed., p. 251; Frescobaldi, Gucci, and Sigoli 1948 ed., p. 180.

25. Fabri 1893 ed., vol. 2, pt. 1, p. 111.

26. Gayraud 2012, p. 78.

27. Al-Muqaddasi 1994 ed., p. 152.

28. Burchard of Mount Sion 1896 ed., pp. 99–102.

29. Gil 1996, p. 186.

30. Mujir al-Din, as noted in Goitein 1968, p. 142. See, too, the remarks of Obadiah of Bertinoro, who also marveled at the novel banana and oversize grape. "Here, in Jerusalem, I have seen several kinds of fruits which are not to be found in our country. There is one tree with long leaves, which grows higher than a man's stature and bears fruit only once; it then withers, and from its roots there rises another similar one, which again bears fruit the next year. And the same thing is continually repeated. The grapes are larger than in our country, but neither cherries, hazelnuts, nor chestnuts are to be found. All the necessaries of life, such as meat, wine, olives, and sesame oil can be had very cheap." Adler, ed. 1930, pp. 237–38.

31. Nasir-i Khusraw 1986 ed., p. 36.

32. Al-Muqaddasi 1994 ed., p. 156.

33. The inscription is dated Jumada I, 720 (June–July 1320). See Sharon 1997–2013, vol. 5, pp. 109–10, fig. P13.

34. Cited in Jacobs, M., 2014, p. 106.

35. Cited in ibid.

36. Cited in ibid. Meshullam supplemented his letters to Lorenzo de Medici with game from his hunting expeditions in the Volterran countryside. Ibid., p. 39.

37. Behrens-Abouseif 2014, p. 63.

38. Nasir-i Khusraw 1986 ed., p. 21.

39. *City of Jerusalem* 1896 ed., pp. 6–7. This anonymous text was written shortly after 1187.

40. Nasir-i Khusraw 1986 ed., p. 21.

41. Fabri 1893 ed., vol. 2, pt. 1, p. 84.

42. Ludolph von Suchem 1895 ed., p. 106.

43. Fabri 1893 ed., vol. 2, pt. 1, p. 90.

44. Ibid., pp. 86–88.

45. Frescobaldi, Gucci, and Sigoli 1948 ed., pp. 68, 69, 71, 80.

46. Kempe 2015 ed., p. 107.

47. Kohler, ed. 1899, pp. 2–9; see also Pringle 1993–2009, vol. 3, p. 284.

48. See, for example, Los Angeles 2006–7, pp. 144–45, no. 9.

49. Kedar 2001; Hamilton, B., 2000.

50. See Jacoby, D., 2004, p. 101.

51. As cited in n. 23 above. Janin, H., 2002, pp. 221–22. Nompar mentioned "roses d'outremer," but the meaning is unclear. He could be referring to hollyhocks (*Alcea rosea*), "desert roses," crystal clusters of gypsum, or rose of Sharon (*Hibiscus syriacus*).

52. Ibn Jubayr 1952 ed., p. 300.

53. Eddé 2011, p. 451, cited in Christie 2014, p. 75.

54. For European views on lodging in Muslim mercantile centers, see Christie 2014, p. 75.

55. Ibid.

56. Jacques de Vitry 1825 ed., p. 129.

57. Elijah of Ferrara in Adler, ed. 1930, p. 153.

58. Many pilgrims' accounts mention guides. Abbot Daniel, for instance, who traveled to the Holy Land in 1106, describes how "the chief of the Saracens, armed, escorted us as far as Bethlehem and conducted us all round those places; otherwise we should not have reached those holy places because of the pagans . . . [who] carry on brigandage in those mountains." Wilkinson, Hill, and Ryan, eds. 1988, p. 150.

59. Ibn Jubayr 1952 ed., pp. 300–301.

Domestic Goods from the Suq to the Home

1. Maps in Ben-Dov 2002, pp. 198, 200.

2. Ghabin 2009.

3. Ibid., pp. 216–45.

4. Nasir-i Khusraw 2001 ed., p. 28.

5. Ciggaar 2005.

6. As Judaism forbids the discarding of writings related to the name of God, worn-out holy books — or even letters invoking God in their benedictory salutations — were collected in repositories (*genizot*) until they could be given a solemn burial. Among the extensive scholarly literature on this topic are the recent Goldberg 2012 and a popular account of the discovery of the Geniza in Hoffman, A., and Cole 2011.

7. Goitein 1977, pp. 107–10, doc. I; Goitein 1967–93, vol. 4, pp. 314–17, appendix D, doc. I.

8. Goitein 1977, pp. 93–98, doc. III; Goitein 1967–93, vol. 4, pp. 322–25, appendix D, doc. III.

9. Chazaud 1871.

10. The text specifies, for example, "la toile qui fu achetée à Troies," "la toile la duchoise de Borgoingne," and "xxxvi granz napes nueuves que Afetiez livra," to name only a few examples. Ibid., p. 484.

11. A summary and partial translation is in Little 1984b. See also Little 1985.

12. Little 1998.

13. Goitein 1973, p. 107.

14. Shamir and Baginski 2002.

Jewish-Muslim Encounters in the Holy Land

1. Jacobs, M., 2014.

2. Scheindlin 2008.

3. Meri 1999; Meri 2002.

4. Quoted in Jacobs, M., 2014, p. 112.

5. On the pilgrimage as a "liminal" or "liminoid" experience that transcends social boundaries, see Turner 1973; Turner and Turner 1978, pp. 1–20. On tomb veneration as a shared experience among women of different faiths, see Cuffel 2005.

Terra Miracula: Blessed Souvenirs from the Holy Land

1. Herzfeld, M., 2014, p. 127. See also Yalouri 2001, p. 133.

2. On tourism and mass-produced souvenirs, see mainly Hume 2014, esp. chaps. 3 and 4, pp. 21–83; see also Phillips, R., and Steiner 1999; Stewart 1984; MacCannell 1976; Dorfles et al. 1968; Kjellman-Chapin et al. 2013.

3. For the continuity of production during the early Muslim period (seventh–ninth centuries), see Raby 1999. The production of souvenirs during the Crusades is well demonstrated by the luxurious Ayyubid metalwork with Christian imagery. See Schneider 1973; Katzenstein and Lowry 1983; Baer 1989; Hoffman, E., 2004; and recently Ecker and Fitzherbert 2012, with extensive literature, esp. p. 190 n. 2; Fitzherbert 2012.

4. See Wharton 2006, esp. p. 20.

5. For example, the anonymous writer who accompanied Antoninus of Piacenza on his pilgrimage noted: "In the place where the Lord's body was laid, at the head, has been placed a bronze lamp. It burns there day and night, and we took a blessing from it. Earth is brought to the tomb and put inside, and those who go in take some as a blessing." Wilkinson 1977, pp. 79–89. For the different substances collected in the Holy Land such as sanctified oil, earth, stones, dust, balsam, water, and even milk and manna, see Shalem 1996, pp. 17–31. See also Bagatti 1949.

6. For the earliest account of biting the Cross, see Egeria, who visited the Levant between 381 and 384, in Wilkinson 2002a, p. 155. As for the chipping of sacred stones during the Crusade era, see the accounts of the Russian Abbot Daniel, who visited the Holy Land between 1106 and 1107, cited in Lidov 2014, p. 243, and of Imad al-Din (1125–1201), Saladin's biographer, cited in Gabrieli, ed. 1969, pp. 170–71. See also Klein 2010–11.

7. Lidov 2014.

8. See Fricke 2014, and for further bibliography esp. pp. 246–47 n. 2; Kessler 2014. For phials and ampoules, see Grabar, A., 1958; Barag and Wilkinson 1974; Kötzsche-Breitenbruch 1984; Elsner 1997; Raby 1999. For the clay flat-bottle containers, see mainly Kauffmann 1910; Metzger, C., 1981; Kiss, Z., 1989; Martin, A., 2006. For expensive, fragile materials, see mainly Shalem 1999. On enameled glass souvenirs, see cat. 24, in this volume.

9. See the account of Father Simon Fitzsimonis cited in Hoade 1952, p. 44.

10. Wilkinson 2002b, p. 139.

11. Cited in ibid., p. 87.

12. Niccolo of Poggibonsi 1945 ed., p. 47.

13. Ibid., p. 107. Frescobaldi, who visited the Holy Land in 1384, claims that manna issued from Saint Catherine's ears and was collected as a sanctified substance by pilgrims. See Frescobaldi, Gucci, and Sigoli 1948 ed., p. 58.

14. Hoade 1952, p. 31; see also Milwright 2003.

15. See mainly Skarlakidis 2011; Auxentios 1999 ed. The earliest accounts are in the writings of the Abbasid historian al-Jahiz (d. 869) and in 865 that of the Latin pilgrim Bernard; see Lidov 2014, p. 241.

16. Hahn 1990, esp. p. 91.

17. On the idea of time collapsing in the pilgrim experience, see Vikan 1990. For the vision of the holy and its modifications, see Ousterhout 2009.

18. See Boertjes 2014. Souvenirs with these particular depictions are discussed in cat. 24, in this volume.

19. Boertjes 2014; Rahmani 2003. Levi Yitzhak Rahmani has proposed medicinal purposes for this type of object, a very plausible idea that suggests another function of these blessings.

20. See Shalem 2016; see also Shalem 2007.

21. See, for example, the case of the bread stamp from Jerusalem in Galavaris 1970; see also Wharton 2006.

Pluralism in the Holy City

1. The epigraph is from Benjamin of Tudela (1983 ed., p. 82).

2. Ezekiel 5:5.

3. That this heterogeneity is deliberate is evidenced by comparison with the sister manuscript in the Vatican (Biblioteca Apostolica Vaticana, MS Syriaco 559). Although the composition is identical, the population is shown as homogenous rather than diverse.

4. As quoted in Noble 2014, pp. 163–64.

5. See, for example, discussions by Kedar 1990; MacEvitt 2008; Peri 2001, pp. 38–43; or Cohen, M., 1994, esp. pp. 52–74, though the latter is not specific to Jerusalem.

6. William of Tyre 1943 ed., vol. 1, p. 507 (bk. XI.27). On the not always easy relations between Western and Eastern Christians during the century of Crusader rule, see MacEvitt 2008 and Murray 2013. On the little-remarked presence of Jews in the Frankish Kingdom of Jerusalem, see Prawer 1988, pp. 93–127.

7. On the relationship between Jerusalem and Mecca, see Peters 1986.

8. Jacques de Vitry 1896 ed., p. 68.

9. Jean of Tournai 2012 ed., p. 189.

10. See Kohlberg and Kedar 1988, p. 119 n. 26.

11. Ibid., p. 118. See also the remarks on Muslim dress regulations in Prawer 1988, pp. 104–5.

12. Radulfus Niger 1977 ed., pp. 193–94 (bk. III.83).

13. See Classen 2013, pp. 98–100, 107.

14. Fabri 1893 ed., vol. 1, pt. 1, p. 209.

15. Armstrong, K., 1996, p. 255 n. 15.

16. Pataridze 2013, p. 49.

17. Pahlitzsch 2008, p. 375.

18. Arnold von Harff 1946 ed., pp. 129–32, for the Arabic lexicon and pp. 217–20 for the Hebrew. Through his extensive travels, Arnold von Harff, who is also known in the literature as Arnulf of Harff, was inspired to develop a list of phrases for several languages, including Greek, Turkish, and Slavonic (a dialect of Serbo-Croatian). His is a multicultural approach; from Arnold we learn how to proposition a woman in Slavonic and Greek as well as Arabic and Hebrew.

19. Maspero 1911, pp. 175–212. On this manuscript, see also Kedar 1998b, pp. 215–16; and Tuley 2013, p. 323 n. 44.

20. Maspero 1911, p. 196.

21. Fulcher of Chartres 1969 ed., p. 272 (bk. III.XXXVII .2–7). On Arabic-French patois, see Tuley 2013, p. 323.

22. Jacoby, D., 1986, pp. 161–63.

23. Galadza 2013, p. 74.

24. From the *Typikon of the Anastasis*, cited in Galadza 2013, p. 75.

25. Tuley 2013, pp. 320–21.

26. Al-Muqaddasi 1994 ed., p. 166.

27. Ibn Jubayr 1952 ed., p. 317.

28. Maspero 1911, p. 178.

29. Discussed in Kedar 1990, pp. 157–58.

30. Raimond d'Aguilers, *Historia Francorum*, chap. XIII.108, as cited in Tuley 2013, p. 319.

31. Rubin 1998, p. 153, citing Jacques de Vitry.

32. Tuley 2013, p. 333, from Richard the Lion-Hearted's chronicle of the Third Crusade; Imad al-Din informs us that Saladin himself relied on interpreters. See ibid., p. 335.

33. Goitein 1967–93, vol. 1, pp. 14–15. Not surprisingly, given the role of Italy in Mediterranean commerce, Italian — in a variety of dialects — was also a required language for shipping and commerce. See Jacoby, D., 2004, p. 115 and n. 137.

34. Cuffel 1999, pp. 73–75.

35. Though the largest community of Samaritans was (and is still) in Nablus, according to contemporary accounts, they lived throughout Palestine. This included Jerusalem, at least until the Crusader conquest of that city. See Prawer 1988, p. 18; see also Kedar 1989. The twelfth-century traveler Benjamin of Tudela wrote of the Samaritans and their form of Hebrew: "Their alphabet lacks three letters *He*, *Cheth*, and *Ain*. . . . In place of these letters, they make use of the *Aleph*, by which we can tell that that they are not of the seed of Israel, although they know the law of Moses with the exception of these three letters." Benjamin of Tudela 1983 ed., p. 81.

36. For the Fatimids, see Grabar, O., et al. 1996, pp. 135–69; Bloom 2007, pp. 81–83. John of Würzburg, writing in the twelfth century, made an effort to enumerate the "people of every race and tongue" that he encountered at the Christian holy sites of Jerusalem: "For there are Greeks, Latins, Germans, Hungarians, Scots, people of Navarre, Britons, Angles, Ruthenians, Bohemians, Georgians, Armenians, Syrians, Jacobites, Nestorians, Indians, Egyptians, Copts, Capheturici, Maronites and many others which it would be a long task to list." Wilkinson, Hill, and Ryan, eds. 1988, p. 273. On doctrinal differences among Christian sects in Jerusalem, see the useful summary in MacEvitt 2008, pp. 7–10.

37. Quoted in Armstrong, K., 2014, p. 217, citing Nicholson 1963, p. 105.

38. Kedar 1997, p. 194.

39. Golb 1965, p. 155.

40. Kedar 1997, p. 191.

41. Quoted in ibid.

42. Burgoyne 2009b, p. 198; on Copts converting to Islam, see Little 1990.

43. Brentjes 2011, p. 340.

44. Usama ibn Munqidh 2000 ed., p. 164. For a discussion of Usama, see Irwin 1998.

45. Usama ibn Munqidh 2000 ed., p. 160.

46. Fulcher of Chartres, in a famous passage asserting that "Occidentals" had become "Orientals," noted that "some have taken wives not merely of their own people, but Syrians, or Armenians, or even Saracens who have received the grace of baptism." Fulcher of Chartres 1969 ed., p. 272 (bk. III. XXXVII.3–4).

47. Fabri 1893 ed., vol. 1, pt. 1, p. 199.

48. Per Loenertz 1948, as cited in Jotischky 1995, p. 90 n. 70.

49. From Fustat, Israel ben Nathan received paper, a ruler for marking the margins, and a second ruler to fix the width. Gil 1996, p. 190.

50. We find a similar instance of cooperation among different Christian sects in the Church of the Nativity in Bethlehem, where the mosaics are graced with statements of faith (texts of the creeds) in both Latin and Greek.

51. Margoliouth 1897, p. 439. See "The Karaites," pp. 79–81, in this volume.

52. Ibid.

53. Ben-Shammai 1996, pp. 211–14.

54. Mujir al-Din 1876 ed., pp. 139–67. Mujir al-Din organized the list by location relative to the Aqsa Mosque, reinforcing the link between scholarship and religious pursuits.

55. Little 2000, p. 192.

56. Burgoyne et al. 1987, p. 71.

57. Mujir al-Din 1876 ed., pp. 61–66. For Fada'il literature, see Sivan 1971; Hasson 1981; Asali 1981; and "The Merits of Jerusalem (Fada'il al-Quds)," pp. 84–85, in this volume. Islamic scholars were among the casualties of the Crusader conquest of Jerusalem, including Makki al-Rumayli, a jurist who lectured on the "merits of Jerusalem." See Dajani-Shakeel 1990, p. 164.

58. Zaimeche 2005; Badawy 1972; Burgoyne et al. 1987, pp. 70–74.

59. Haarmann 1984, p. 331.

60. Ibn al-'Arabi, to his father, ca. 1093–96, cited in Drory 2004, p. 114. See also the discussion in Jarrar 1998, pp. 75–78.

61. Hillenbrand, C., 1999, p. 49. On Ibn al-'Arabi's assessment of Jerusalem vis-à-vis Cairo, see Jarrar 1998, p. 76.

62. See Burgoyne et al. 1987, p. 71.

63. Cuffel 1999; Kanarfogel 1986.

64. Cited in Prawer 1988, p. 78.

65. On his character and interests as well as a review of the literature, see Edbury and Rowe 1988.

66. On the impact of William of Tyre's early education at Jerusalem on his writings about his former teacher Jean, archdeacon of Tyre and later a cardinal, see Mayer, H., 1988.

67. We are grateful to David P. Bardeen for his synthesis of William of Tyre's contribution, reflected here.

68. Prologue in William of Tyre 1943 ed., vol. 1, pp. 56–57.

69. Ibid., vol. 2, pp. 358–59 (bk. XX.11). On William of Tyre's attitude toward Islam, see Schwinges 2001, pp. 124–32.

70. William of Tyre 1943 ed., vol. 2, p. 394 (bk. XX.31).

71. Ibid., pp. 292–93 (bk. XVIII.34).

72. Usama ibn Munqidh 2000 ed., pp. 162–63.

73. Brentjes 2011, p. 339.

74. Kohlberg and Kedar 1988, p. 114.

75. Kedar 1998b, p. 221.

76. Kedar 1998a.

77. Gil'adi 1979. More recently, for English, see Stroumsa, S., 2009, pp. 25–26.

78. Jarrar 1998, pp. 76, 77.

79. Miller, R., 2005, p. 201.

80. Gabrieli, ed. 1969, p. 270.

81. Niccolo of Poggibonsi 1945 ed., p. 25.

Saint Sabas and the Monks of the Holy Land

1. The epigraph may be found in Griffith 2002, p. 28.

2. The facts of Saint Sabas's life are known from his *Vita*, written by Cyril of Scythopolis (Cyril of Scythopolis 1939 ed. and 1991 ed.; for French, Cyril of Scythopolis 1961 ed.).

3. Patrich 1995, pp. 203–5, 255–58.

4. There were many variations of lavriote living throughout the Christian world, including, for example, having novitiates live communally while only more experienced monks lived as solitaries. Even at Mar Sabas there have been variations over time, such as after the Persians invaded, when all monks lived communally for safety reasons.

5. Patrich 1995, p. 41.

6. Pringle 1993–2009, vol. 2, p. 259. On Saint Sabas's feast today, candles are illuminated in each cave, creating this effect.

7. Hirschfeld 1992, pp. 20–25.

8. Ibid., p. 27.

9. According to a Greek pilgrim of 1187; Pringle 1993–2009, vol. 2, p. 261.

10. Ibid., p. 260.

11. *St. Sabbas the Sanctified Orthodox Monastery* 1999– .

12. Hirschfeld 1992, p. 247.

13. Krueger 2014, pp. 5–6.

14. The monks at Stoudios were called "sleepless" for these vigils, which were eventually stopped by Theodore of Stoudios. Miller, T., 2000, p. 67.

15. Ševčenko 2004, p. 274.

16. Noble and Treiger, eds. 2014, p. 19.

17. Flusin 2011.

18. Galadza 2013, p. 64.

19. Jotischky 2001, p. 90. The place of the "Archimedes Palimpsest" in the history of Mar Saba is still debated. See Netz 2001.

20. Jotischky 2001, pp. 86–87.

21. MacEvitt 2008, pp. 132–33.

22. Ibid., p. 92.

23. Laboa 2003, p. 94.

The Karaites

1. For detailed essays on the medieval origins of Karaism as well as its history and literature, see Polliack, ed. 2003.

2. For detailed historical studies, see Gil 1992; Goitein 1967–93, vol. 5, pp. 358–91 (schism and counter-reformation); Erder 2003; Mann, J., 1970; Prawer and Ben-Shammai, eds. 1996.

3. For more on each genre, see Polliack, ed. 2003.

4. See Walfish and Kizilov 2011.

Maimonides and Jerusalem

1. See the discussion in Kraemer 2008, pp. 116–24.

2. Although the letter is quoted in a commentary erroneously attributed to him, it is accepted as genuine by scholars. See Prawer 1988, p. 142 n. 37.

3. Ibid., p. 142.

4. All of these teachings may be found in his *Mishneh Torah*, Laws of Kings, chap. 5.

5. *Mishneh Torah*, Laws of Marriage, chap. 13, end.

6. *Mishneh Torah*, Laws of the Chosen House 6:16.

7. This is Maimonides's opinion expressed in Laws of the Chosen House 7:7.

Merits of Jerusalem (Fada'il al-Quds)

1. For further discussion of the Merits of Jerusalem (Fada'il al-Quds) literature, see Hillenbrand, C., 1999, pp. 162–65, 175–79; Sivan 1971.

2. Al-Wasiti 1979 ed.; Ibn al-Murajja' al-Magdisi 1995 ed.

3. Muqatil 1979–89 ed.

4. Nasir-i Khusraw 1881 ed.

5. Ibn al-Jawzi, *Fada'il al-Quds al-sharif*, Princeton University Library, MS Garrett, Arabic 586.

Experiencing Sacred Art in Jerusalem

1. The epigraph is from Saladin as cited by Imad al-Din in Gabrieli, ed. 1969, p. 152. In addition to Ibn Jubayr (see note 2 below), the historians Ibn al-Athir (1160–1233) and Imad al-Din (1125–1201) each discussed the commissioning of the minbar by Nur al-Din. See Hillenbrand, C., 1999, pp. 152–56. See also "The Minbar of Nur al-Din," pp. 136–37, in this volume.

2. Ibn Jubayr, as cited in Tabbaa 1986, p. 232.

3. Based on Gabrieli, ed. 1969, pp. 271–72.

4. Fabri 1893 ed., vol. 1, pt. 2, p. 280.

5. Kempe 2000 ed., p. 161.

6. Burchard of Mount Sion 1896 ed., pp. 2–3.

7. Mann, J., 1935, pp. 464–65; Fleisher 1998, pp. 298–327.

8. Adler, ed. 1930, p. 103.

9. On the significance of domes in Jerusalem, see Kenaan-Kedar 1986; Jarrar 1998. See also Grabar, O., 1963, pp. 191–98; and Grabar, O., 1990, pp. 15–21.

10. Al-Muqaddasi 1994 ed., p. 146. It was said in the ninth century that Thomas Tamriq, Patriarch of Jerusalem, was instructed when rebuilding the Dome of the Holy Sepulchre not to make it higher than that of the Dome of the Rock, lest he be flogged. See Kaplony 2004, p. 43.

11. Prawer 1988, pp. 106, 173–74.

12. Al-Wasiti cited in Cornell 2008, p. 277.

13. Al-Muqaddasi 1994 ed., p. 153.

14. Found in the French translation, Fulcher of Chartres 1825 ed., pp. 109–10.

15. Lindner 1992, pp. 87–92.

16. On the Byzantine restoration of the church, see Ousterhout 1989. On the changes to the church over its long history, see Corbo 1981–82.

17. Folda 1995, pp. 177–229. See also the useful outline and critique of the medieval changes to the church in Ousterhout 2003.

18. Wilkinson, Hill, and Ryan, eds. 1988, p. 281.

19. Ibid., p. 224.

20. It was mentioned by Arculfus in the eighth century (Arculfus 1889 ed., p. 7), by Daniel the Abbot (Wilkinson, Hill, and Ryan, eds. 1988, p. 170) in the twelfth century, and by Arnold von Harff in the fifteenth century (Arnold von Harff 1946 ed., p. 196); it also figures in the inventory of Nompar de Caumont of 1420 (Janin, H., 2002, pp. 221–22).

21. Theoderich in Wilkinson, Hill, and Ryan, eds. 1988, p. 279.

22. Al-Idrisi in ibid., p. 224. The open dome is mentioned by others including Daniel the Abbot in ibid., p. 127; and Burchard of Mount Sion 1896 ed., pp. 75–76.

23. John of Würzburg in Wilkinson, Hill, and Ryan, eds. 1988, p. 261. Daniel the Abbot describes a baldachin covered with silver plates. John of Würzburg a few decades later seemed to have encountered a larger aedicule built by the Crusaders; Folda 1995, pp. 79–82. On the aedicule, see Wilkinson 1972, pp. 83–97; and Biddle 1999.

24. Theoderich in Wilkinson, Hill, and Ryan, eds. 1988, p. 279. The marble Theoderich described was part of the Crusaders' refurbishment.

25. See, for instance, Burchard of Mount Sion 1896 ed., pp. 75–76: "The cave . . . is entirely cased with marble on the outside, but within it is bare rock, even as it was at the time of his burial."

26. Daniel the Abbot in Wilkinson, Hill, and Ryan, eds. 1988, p. 128.

27. Theoderich in ibid., p. 279.

28. John Phocas in ibid., p. 324.

29. Daniel the Abbot in ibid., p. 129.

30. Theoderich in ibid., p. 285.

31. Ibid., p. 284.

32. Nasir-i Khusraw 1893 ed., p. 60. Concerning the mosaics, he observed, "Inside the church is everywhere adorned with Byzantine brocade [i.e., mosaics] worked in gold with pictures."

33. Cited in Gabrieli, ed. 1969, p. 148.

34. It also bears mentioning that the occasional Jew visited the Church of the Holy Sepulchre, although these accounts tell us little. Jacob ha-Cohen, for instance, traveled to the Holy Land from Europe sometime in the twelfth century and remarked, "I stood by the grave of Jesus four cubits from the place where he was stoned." Adler, ed. 1930, p. 99.

35. Noted in Hillenbrand, C., 1999, p. 319. This refers to the Qur'an verse *Surat Al 'Imran* (3:46): "He shall speak to people while still in the cradle, and in manhood, and he shall be from the righteous." The reference to the Magi's robes comes from *Surat Ta-ha* (20:63–73).

36. Of vestments, altar furnishings, and manuscripts used at the time, precious little survives. Compare cats. 72, 77.

37. Theoderich in Wilkinson, Hill, and Ryan, eds. 1988, p. 282.

38. Among medieval visitors who describe the ceremony of the Holy Fire are Ibn al-Qalanisi, Mujir al-Din, al-Biruni, and Bernard the Wise; Peters 1985, pp. 259–63.

39. Daniel the Abbot in Wilkinson, Hill, and Ryan, eds. 1988, p. 167.

40. Nasir-i Khusraw 1986 ed., p. 24.

41. Ibid., p. 24. On Fatimid changes to the Haram al-Sharif, see Grabar, O., et al. 1996, pp. 135–70, which also sensitively discusses Nasir-i Khusraw's reactions. See also Kaplony 2002, pp. 83–114, 559–789. On Nasir-i himself, see Hunsberger 2000.

42. Al-Muqaddasi 1994 ed., p. 155.

43. Al-Idrisi in Wilkinson, Hill, and Ryan, eds. 1988, p. 225.

44. Theoderich, who visited when Latin Christians controlled Jerusalem and hence the Haram al-Sharif, suggested that the Knights Templar made the most of the Haram's singular environment when they established their "remarkable complex" there. He described an area that "is full of houses, dwellings and outbuildings for every kind of purpose, and it is full of walking-places, lawns, council-chambers, porches, consistories and supplies of water." Wilkinson, Hill, and Ryan, eds. 1988, p. 294.

45. Nasir-i Khusraw 1986 ed., p. 28.

46. Ibid.

47. Ibid., p. 30.

48. This feature was not lost on Daniel the Abbot when he visited. "The whole house was supplied with water," he reported. Wilkinson, Hill, and Ryan, eds. 1988, pp. 132–33.

49. Nasir-i Khusraw 1986 ed., p. 27.

50. Al-Idrisi in Wilkinson, Hill, and Ryan, eds. 1988, p. 225.

51. Nasir-i Khusraw 1986 ed., p. 30.

52. Ibid.

53. Ibid.

54. "Men say that on the face of the world there is no more wonderful structure to look upon, none loftier or more marvelously built, than this dome [in Damascus], save what is reported of the Dome (of the Rock) in Jerusalem, which is said to be still higher in the skies than this." Ibn Jubayr 1952 ed., p. 308.

55. Al-Muqaddasi 1994 ed., pp 154–55.

56. In 1545 Süleyman the Magnificent removed the mosaics on the exterior and replaced them with tiles, beginning a tradition that continues to this day.

57. Cited in Little 2009, p. 178 n. 4, citing Ibn Battuta 1958 ed., pp. 78–79.

58. John of Würzburg in Wilkinson, Hill, and Ryan, eds. 1988, p. 247.

59. Nasir-i Khusraw 1986 ed., pp. 30–34.

60. Gucci in Frescobaldi, Gucci, and Sigoli 1948 ed., p. 128.

61. Cited in Little 2009, p. 180 n. 6.

62. Pietro Casola 1907 ed., p. 251.

63. Al-Idrisi: "The Masjid al Aksa is the Great Mosque, and in the whole earth there is no mosque of greater dimensions than this." Wilkinson, Hill, and Ryan, eds. 1988, p. 224.

64. Nasir-i Khusraw 1986 ed., p. 26.

65. Ibid., p. 27.

66. Mujir al-Din 1876 ed., p. 138.

67. "Many ampullae burn there continually." Arnold von Harff 1946 ed., p. 208.

68. The Christian names had widespread currency, even in surprising places. Al-Idrisi referred to the Aqsa Mosque as the Temple of Solomon: "You come to the holy house built by Solomon, the son of David. This in the time of the Jews, was a mosque to which pilgrimage was made . . . but when the days of Islam came . . . the spot came once more to be venerated, as the Masjid al Aksa" (Wilkinson, Hill, and Ryan, eds. 1988, p. 224). Benjamin of Tudela, a Jewish traveler from Spain, referred to "our ancient Temple, now called Templum Domini" and to the Aqsa Mosque, which then housed the Knights Templar, as "the palace built by Solomon." Benjamin of Tudela 1983 ed., p. 83.

69. Mentioned by numerous visitors, including Theoderich, al-Hawari, Imad al-Din, and others, but described in greatest detail by John of Würzburg. Wilkinson, Hill, and Ryan, eds. 1988, pp. 246–48.

70. On the balustrade, see Nasir-i Khusraw 1986 ed., p. 47. Fulcher of Chartres said the rock was covered over and paved in marble; Fulcher of Chartres 1969 ed., p. 16. Ibn al-Athir reported that the rock was covered because fragments were broken off to sell to pilgrims; Gabrieli, ed. 1969, p. 145.

71. Gabrieli, ed. 1969, p. 169.

72. John of Würzburg: "The sign of the Holy Cross has been fixed to the top by Christians, which is annoying to the Saracens." Wilkinson, Hill, and Ryan, eds. 1988, p. 248.

73. See Jacoby, Z., 1982; Folda 1995, pp. 441–56.

74. Gabrieli, ed. 1969, pp. 168–71.

75. Ibid., pp. 144–45.

76. Burgoyne 2009a, pp. 155–56.

77. Ibid., p. 170; see also Hillenbrand, R., 2009, p. 43.

78. Korn 2004, pp. 83–85.

79. Gabrieli, ed. 1969, p. 165.

80. An important point noted in Prawer 1988, pp. 173–74.

81. Cited in Jacobs, M., 2014, p. 88. A number of writers have discussed this phenomenon, Jacobs most compellingly. See especially his remarks on pp. 83–97.

82. Al-Harizi 1965–73 ed., vol. 2, pp. 419–21.

83. Adler, ed. 1930, p. 204.

84. Ibid., p. 194.

85. Nachmanides 2009 ed., p. 791.

86. Al-Harizi 1965–73 ed., vol. 2, p. 419.

87. Prawer 1988, p. 174.

88. On the medieval Hebrew graffiti in the Gates of Mercy, see Gera 1991. On the archaeological evidence of ancient Temple gates below the current gates, see Fleming 1983 and Ritmeyer 1992, p. 40.

89. Holtz, ed. 1971, pp. 122–23.

90. Nachmanides 2009 ed., p. 795.

91. Adler, ed. 1930, p. 117.

92. Throughout the medieval period, Jewish access to the Temple Mount itself was limited; it was most restricted during the Crusader occupation of Jerusalem, when Jews were banned from living in the city; see Prawer 1988, pp. 47–49. Before and after the Crusader ban, however, Jews gathered at certain structures within the city. One building was regularly mentioned, particularly before 1099: a synagogue under the western retaining wall of the Temple Mount, known as the Cave. This underground structure was an important place of assemblage for both local and visiting Jews. Geniza documents mention it as a place where the Torah was read, the community gathered on holidays, and communal proclamations were declared. Al-Muqaddasi, who described it as a "cave under a rock," said it had room for 69 people; another text, however, indicated 960. See Gil 1992, pp. 244, 607–9. See also "Patronage in Jerusalem," pp. 233–34, in this volume.

93. See, for instance, the remark of Jacob the Emissary in Adler, ed. 1930, p. 117.

94. Gil 1992, p. 627.

95. "Lift up your heads, O Gates, so that the King of Glory may enter" (Psalms 24:7). Fleisher 1998, p. 316.

96. Gil 1992, pp. 626–30.

97. Adler, ed. 1930, p. 190.

98. Ibid., pp. 118–19.

99. Ibid., pp. 88–89.

100. Follower of Obadiah of Bertinoro cited in Wilhelm 1948, p. 25.

The Closed Gate

1. Wightman 1993, pp. 231–32. On early traditions related to the gate, see Kaplony 2002, pp. 188–90, 277–80, 459–60, 638–44. See also Schick 2012, pp. 373–77.

2. Nasir-i Khusraw 1986 ed., pp. 25–26.

3. *City of Jerusalem* 1896 ed., p. 14.

4. Jacob the Emissary in Adler, ed. 1930, p. 117.

5. Niccolo of Poggibonsi 1945 ed., pp. 45–46; Obadiah of Bertinoro in Adler, ed. 1930, p. 240.

6. Fabri 1893 ed., vol. 1, pt. 2, pp. 458–61.

7. Babylonian Talmud, Tractate Shabbat 30a; for English, Schottenstein Talmud 1990–2005, Tractate Shabbat (1996), p. 30a.

8. Saewulf in Wilkinson, Hill, and Ryan, eds. 1988, p. 105; Theoderich in ibid., p. 276.

9. Petachya of Regensburg, cited in Adler, ed. 1930, p. 90; Niccolo of Poggibonsi 1945 ed., pp. 45–46. Mujir al-Din 1876 ed., pp. 127–28.

10. Saladin, as cited by Imad al-Din in Gabrieli, ed. 1969, p. 152.

11. John of Würzburg in Wilkinson, Hill, and Ryan, eds. 1988, pp. 250–51; Theoderich in ibid., p. 296.

12. On the route of the coronation ceremony, see Kenaan-Kedar 1986, p. 114, and Mayer, H., 1967, p. 170.

Sharing the Church of the Holy Sepulchre during the Crusader Period

1. Sebag Montefiore 2011, p. xxi.

2. These remarks follow the admirable characterization in Elie 2003, p. x.

3. Hamilton, B., 1980, p. 159.

4. Biddle 2000, pp. 84–91. See MacEvitt 2008, p. 120, and Hunt 1995.

5. John of Würzburg in Wilkinson, Hill, and Ryan, eds. 1988, p. 273. The identity of the "Capheturici" remains a mystery.

6. For Scandinavian pilgrims, the original research was carried out by Paul Edouard Didier, Le Comte Riant (Riant 1865–69). Abbot Daniel, a major Russian pilgrim, wrote a detailed account of his visit, which appears as "The Life and Journey of Daniel, Abbot of the Russian Land," in Wilkinson, Hill, and Ryan, eds. 1988, pp. 120–71.

7. Prawer 1988, passim; Prawer 1985, pp. 94–101; and Prawer 1972, pp. 233–51.

8. Prawer 1972, pp. 241, 244–45. See also the analysis of the text by David Simha Segal in al-Harizi 2001 ed., pp. 241, 555–57. For the original Hebrew, see al-Harizi 1952 ed., p. 248, ll. 14–16.

9. Bashear 1991, p. 273.

10. Albera 2012, p. 11. For Mary's appearance in the Qur'an, see Gregg 2015, pp. 547–62.

11. Albera 2012, pp. 11–13. The Tomb of the Virgin even contained a mihrab for prayer.

12. Jotischky 2013, esp. pp. 247–49.

13. Gabrieli, ed. 1969, p. 175.

14. Cited in Gabrieli, ed. 1956, pp. 146–75.

15. Gabrieli, ed. 1969, pp. 174–75.

16. On shared sacred space, see Limor 2007, p. 220; Kedar 2001.

17. Folda 1998. See also the discussions in Pringle 1993–2009, vol. 3, pp. 54–58, and Krüger 2011, pp. 218–21.

18. Ousterhout 2003, pp. 18–21. Ousterhout believes the cornices are both Roman imperial spolia; see his other discussion of the sculpture on the south transept facade in this important article.

19. See, e.g., Georgopolou 2004, p. 123.

20. Folda 1998, p. 252.

21. Biddle 2000, p. 118.

22. Zander 1971, pp. 199–201.

23. This version of Psalms 122:6–9 is from the New American Bible, Saint Joseph edition.

The Minbar of Nur al-Din

1. John 1:1: "In the beginning was the Word, and the Word was with God, and the Word was God."

2. *Surat al-'Alaq* (Clots of Blood, 96:3–5): "Recite! Your Lord is the Most bountiful One who by the pen taught man what he did not know." All quotes from the Qur'an in this essay are from Qur'an 1990 ed.

3. See the chapters on geometry in Islam in Singer, ed. 2008, pp. 67–82, 106–24. An unpublished doctoral thesis suggests that the shapes are an indication of the gateway to the holy; Jakeman 1993.

4. The names are Salman ibn Ma'ali (twice), Humaid ibn Tafir (four times), Abu'l-Hasan ibn Yahya (twice), and his brother Fada'il. See Auld 2009b, p. 72.

5. Van Berchem 1927, pp. 393–97, nos. 277 and 278, with a discussion on the meaning of "finished" (*tammamahu*), p. 398 n. 1. The "appropriation," or claiming ownership of something that added blessings or kudos, was not unusual; see ibid., p. 231.

6. Photographs of both the fragments and the minbar before its destruction can be seen in Auld 2005, pls. 1–9, and Auld 2009b, pls. 4.1–4.18.

7. Ibn al-Athir in Gabrieli, ed. 1969, p. 145; Ibn Jubayr 1952 ed., pp. 262–63; on contemporary wood, see Bloom 2009.

8. The minbar and its designs are drawn and more fully analyzed with regard to contemporary works in Auld 2009b. The concept of the inlay's "dressing" the underlying construction recalls the practice of draping significant religious monuments, for example, the annual covering of the Ka'ba with a newly woven honorific *kiswa*.

9. Van Berchem 1927, pp. 50ff., inscription no. 277.

10. In translation, the inscription reads, "Its construction has been ordered by the slave, the one needful of His Mercy, the one thankful for His grace, the fighter of *jihad* in His path, the one who defends [the frontiers] against the enemies of His religion, the just king, Nur al-Din, the pillar of Islam and the Muslims, the dispenser of justice to those who are oppressed in the face of the oppressors, Abu 'l-Qasim Mahmud ibn Zengi Aqsunqur, the helper of the Commander of the Faithful."

11. Van Berchem 1927, p. 401 n. 2; see also Elisséeff 1952–54; Elisséeff 1967.

12. Van Berchem 1927, pp. 398–401; Nur al-Din's obsession with the conquest of Jerusalem and letter to the caliph 'Adid dated A.H. 565 (1169–70), both quoted in ibid., p. 401 n. 2. On Saladin's transport of the minbar to Jerusalem some twenty years after the conquest, see ibid., pp. 398 n. 6, 399 n. 1, 400. Ibid., p. 402 n. 2, quotes Imad al-Din on Saladin's fulfillment of Nur al-Din's vow: "Salah al-Din thought of that which al-Malik 'Adil Nur al-Din Mahmud had made for Jerusalem some twenty years before. He ordered that they write to Aleppo to reclaim it; once it had been transported to Jerusalem, it was there put to the use for which it had been intended."

13. See cat. 23, in this volume, and a fragment of a pilgrim scroll from 1544–45 (Topkapı Sarayı Museum, Istanbul,

H. 1812), with the Aqsa identified by the pulpit labeled *minbar al-nabi* (pulpit of the Prophet); a similar depiction, of the Haram al-Sharif again identified as *minbar al-nabi*, in a Book of Pilgrimage, dated 1643–44 (Jewish National and University Library, Jerusalem, Yah. MS 117, fol. 40v). Both are illustrated in Baer 1997–98, pp. 389, 391, figs. 6, 8.

14. Singer, ed. 2008.

The Cradle of Jesus and the Oratory of Mary on Jerusalem's Haram al-Sharif

1. See el-Khatib 2001, pp. 43–44.

2. Grabar, O., 2006, p. 50. Sabri Jarrar has a brief discussion of the cradle and the oratory (Jarrar 1998, pp. 85–87). See also Andreas Kaplony's magisterial *The Haram of Jerusalem, 324–1099* (2002, pp. 599–606 and 664–75).

3. Stephan 1939, p. 101 n. 2.

4. See St. Laurent and Awwad 2013.

5. Muqatil 1979–89 ed., vol. 2, p. 514. Ibn al-Firkah (1262–1329) cites Muqatil's observation in "Ba'ith al-nufus ila ziyarat al-Quds al-Sharif al-mahrus" (Ibn al-Firkah 2000 ed., p. 102).

6. Al-Muqaddasi 1896 ed., p. 166.

7. Antrim 2012.

8. Quoted in Mujir al-Din 1973 ed., vol. 1, p. 296.

9. Al-Muqaddasi 1896 ed., p. 36.

10. See a graphic description in Ibn al-Murajja' al-Maqdisi 2002 ed., pp. 300–301.

11. Matthews 1936.

12. Al-Nabulusi 1991 ed., p. 146.

13. Matthews 1935, p. 75.

Holy War and the Power of Art

1. The epigraph is from Robert the Monk, recounting Pope Urban II's call to crusade, found in Munro, ed. 1895, p. 6.

2. Cahen 1947–48, p. 103.

3. *Texaurus Regis Francie*, Bibliothèque Nationale de France, Paris, MS Lat. 11015, fols. 32r–54v. Vigevano 1993 ed. See also Tyerman 1985, p. 35.

4. Pope Urban II, as cited by Guibert, abbot of Nogent (ca. 1055–1124); Guibert of Nogent 1997 ed., based on Krey 1921, pp. 36–40.

5. Bernard of Clairvaux 1977 ed.

6. Ibid., p. 39.

7. Ibid., pp. 40–41.

8. Ibid., p. 48.

9. Ibid.

10. See the summary of his career in Maier 2000, p. 9, with earlier literature in French. On the notion of crusade into the modern era, see Phillips, J., 2009.

11. Ibid., pp. 149–51.

12. See Gaposchkin 2013b, p. 8; and Gaposchkin 2013a, pp. 48, 51, 52, with earlier literature on the liturgy of the sword. The antiphon is based on Psalms 44:34.

13. See Buc 2015, pp. 23–25.

14. Cited in Hillenbrand, C., 1999, p. 307.

15. See ibid., pp. 89–255, which includes Qur'anic texts, especially Sura 9, that came to underpin this notion. For a thorough and nuanced view of the interpretation of these verses by Muslim exegetes over the centuries, see Afsaruddin 2013, especially the conclusion, pp. 269–98, and p. 275 on the link to the Crusades. Additional discussion can be found in a number of sources, including Waterson 2010; Hillenbrand, C., 1994; Afsaruddin 2013; Armstrong, K., 1988; and Lyons and Jackson 1982.

16. Mourad and Lindsay 2012.

17. Ibid., p. 134.

18. Ibid.

19. On the role of poetry, see Dajani-Shakeel 1976. We thank Samuel England for this reference.

20. Tabbaa 1986.

21. Kenney 2009, p. 130: "This blessed gate was renewed in the days of our Lord the Sultan, the King, the Assisted, the Wise, the Ruler, the Fighter in the Holy War, the Champion of the Faith, the Frontier Defender, the Helper, the Victorious, the Sultan of Islam and of the Muslims, the Slayer of unbelievers and polytheists, the One who re-establishes justice in the worlds, the Protector of the oppressed from the oppressor, the Helper of the Muslim community, Nasi al-Dunya wa'l-Din Muhammad, son of the Sultan."

22. Hillenbrand, C., 1999, p. 123.

23. Cited in ibid., p. 151.

24. Cited in ibid., p. 152, acknowledging the research of Yasser Tabbaa, ibid., p. 155.

25. Cited in ibid., p. 182.

26. Firestone 2012, pp. 3–5.

27. Maimonides, *Mishneh Torah, Sefer Shoftim*, Hilchot Melachim u'Milchamot, Laws of Kings and Wars, chaps. 5–6; for English, Maimonides 2001 ed., pp. 78–127. See also Maimonides's discussion in the *Book of Divine Commandments* (originally published in Arabic, *Kitab al-Farai'd* or *Sefer Hamitzvot*), positive commandments 187–88; for English, Maimonides 1940 ed., p. 200.

28. Maimonides, Laws of Kings and Wars 4:10; Maimonides 2001 ed., pp. 532–33.

29. Maimonides, Laws of Kings and Wars 5:4; Maimonides 2001 ed., pp. 536–37. On parallels between Maimonides's and Islamic theories of holy war, see Blidstein 1991. On the development of Maimonides's ideas on this topic, see Wilkes 2012. See also Firestone 2012, pp. 114–26.

30. Nachmanides, *Hassagot*, positive commandment 4. Cited in Firestone 2012, p. 130.

31. Firestone 2012, pp. 131–32.

32. Hunt imagery, for instance, appears with relative frequency in medieval Hebrew manuscripts and is generally understood to signify persecution. See Offenberg 2011, p. 9 n. 9, with earlier literature.

33. For example, Fulcher of Chartres, in his account of a battle in 1113 by the Sea of Galilee, reported: "The king fled, losing his flag and his fine tent with many furnishings and silver vessels. Likewise the patriarch who was present also fled." Fulcher of Chartes 1969 ed., p. 173. Imad al-Din praised Saladin for his restraint in not confiscating the church and monastic treasure of the Patriarch of Jerusalem, saying, "Let them go. They will talk about our benevolence." Cited in el-Moctar 2012, p. 209.

34. On the often contradictory evocations of the Maccabees in Crusader-era writings, see Lapina 2015, pp. 97–121.

35. An intriguing counterpoint can be found in volume 1 of the Leipzig Mahzor (Universitätsbibliothek, Leipzig, MS V 1102). Extending across the bottom of folios 72v–73r are the Israelites pursued by the Egyptians as Moses divides the Red Sea. Extraordinarily, the artist has portrayed the enemy Egyptians as medieval knights.

36. See Lapina 2015, pp. 10, 54–74.

37. See "The Minbar of Nur al-Din," pp. 136–37, in this volume.

Jerusalem: The Crucible of Holy War

1. *Independent* 2001.

2. The president used the phrase at a press conference a week after 9/11. Ford 2001.

3. Bernard of Clairvaux 1977 ed.

4. The post-Reformation religious wars included the German Peasants' War in the early sixteenth century, the French wars of religion in the late sixteenth century, the continent-spanning Thirty Years' War in the first half of the seventeenth century, and the English Civil War in the middle of the seventeenth century. Obviously, these conflicts had economic and political aspects, but they drew their ferocity from their centrally religious character.

5. Blake 1907 ed., p. 2.

6. Wilfred Owen's 1918 poem, "The Parable of the Old Man and the Young," in Owen 1983 ed., vol. 1, p. 166.

7. Jesus invoked the image in the Sermon on the Mount (Matthew 5:14). John Winthrop used it to define the Puritan enterprise in the New World. Before taking office, Kennedy picked up the image, and Reagan cited it in first accepting the Republican nomination. The City on a Hill is the emblem of American exceptionalism.

Patronage in Jerusalem

1. The epigraph is from Taragan 2006, p. 56.

2. From a letter written in 1149, translated and transcribed on the Columbia University website *Epistolae: Medieval Women's Latin Letters*. See Melisende 2014 ed., with slight revisions to the translation made by Melanie Holcomb.

3. The wife of the previous king of Jerusalem, Baldwin I, was a nun there, and Melisende's sister Iveta was at the convent prior to the founding of the abbey at Bethany, of which she became the abbess. See Pringle 1993–2009, vol. 3, pp. 142–43.

4. Saladin may in fact have been restoring the site to its pre-Crusader function; see ibid., p. 143. Curiously, the exterior retained its painted representations of Anna and Joachim, the parents of the Virgin Mary, which were creatively reinterpreted as images of the Prophet Muhammad by a "Saracen" woman who served as a self-appointed docent for Christian visitors, as described in a fourteenth-century pilgrimage account, Ludolph von Suchem 1895 ed., p. 101. Other images were covered with plaster.

5. A mihrab was removed during nineteenth-century restorations of the church. See Pringle 1993–2009, vol. 3, p. 145.

6. Ha-Levi 1964 ed., p. 293.

7. Babylonian Talmud, Tractate Berachot 30a; in English, Schottenstein Talmud 1990–2005, Tractate Berachot (1997), p. 30a.

8. See "Merits of Jerusalem (Fada'il al-Quds)," pp. 84–85, in this volume.

9. See Mourad 2008, p. 93, citing the tradition of al-Wasiti and Abu al-Ma'ali, both from the eleventh-century, reiterated by al-Ramli in the seventeenth century. The claim also appears in the writing of Ibn al-Jawzi. See Patel 2006, p. 76.

10. Gil 1984, pp. 156–57.

11. Still active today, a hospice for Sufi pilgrims from India was established by Hazrat Farid ud-Din Ganj Shakar (Baba Farid) about 1200 and was recently featured in Sarna 2014. From northern Africa, the Marinid king of the Maghreb Abu al-Hasan 'Abd Allah ibn 'Ali gave a thirty-part Qur'an and storage box decorated with enamels to the Aqsa Mosque in 1344/45. See Salameh 1999, pp. 66–83, and fig. 86, p. 232, in this volume.

12. On Latin foundations before the first Crusade, see Jotischky 1995, pp. 50–51, drawing on evidence from *Commemoratorium de casis Dei vel monasteriis* (ca. 808). The chronicler Bernard, a Frankish monk from about 870, noted the presence of a hospital for Latin pilgrims that had been founded by Charlemagne.

13. See Jotischky 1995, p. 83.

14. Rose 1992, p. 240.

15. Pringle 1982.

16. Folda 2012b, pp. 460–65. On Melisende, see also Gaudette 2010.

17. Pringle 1993–2009, vol. 3, pp. 228–36, no. 333.

18. Armstrong, K., 1996, pp. 310–11.

19. Nasir-i Khusraw 1986 ed., p. 23. For more on the hospital, see Murphy-O'Connor 2012, p. 283.

20. Pringle 1993–2009, vol. 3, p. 236.

21. Murphy-O'Connor 2012, p. 261.

22. Cited by Rosen-Ayalon 1999, p. 345; also Murphy-O'Connor 2012, p. 263. Notwithstanding the hospital's wealth, between 1139 and 1143 Pope Innocent II initiated a "capital campaign" to benefit the hospital. See Murphy-O'Connor 2012, p. 273.

23. Pringle 1993–2009, vol. 3, pp. 198, 254.

24. See Burgoyne et al. 1987, p. 66. See also Bahat 2002.

25. Folda 1995, pp. 274–82. The merchant is Bilal Abu Khalaf.

26. See Kenaan 1973, p. 175.

27. Burgoyne 2009b, p. 194.

28. The expertise of the professors was more wide-ranging than one might infer. The mathematician Ahmad ibn Muhammad ibn al-Ha'im taught there in the fourteenth century. See Ismail et al., eds. 1995, p. 19.

29. Jarrar 1998, p. 73.

30. Ibid., pp. 73–74.

31. Ibid., p. 74.

32. The full range of Mamluk patronage in Jerusalem can best be appreciated in Burgoyne's magisterial survey; see Burgoyne et al. 1987.

33. Haarmann 1984, p. 331.

34. Jarrar 1998, esp. pp. 94–95.

35. For an introduction to the institution of the endowment (waqf), see Bakhoum 2011. On its historic basis, see Hennigan 2004.

36. Folda 2012b, pp. 467–68.

37. Pringle 1993–2009, vol. 3, p. 143.

38. See Frenkel 1999, p. 8. For a translation of the endowment terms, see Pahlitzsch 2004, pp. 63–68.

39. Constable 2003, p. 253.

40. Burgoyne et al. 1987, pp. 479, 484.

41. Ibid., p. 70.

42. Cohen, M., 2005a, pp. 200–204; Gil 1976.

43. Gil 1992, p. 603.

44. Ibid., p. 601.

45. Ibid.

46. Gil 1984, pp. 169 (Fustat), 171 (Ramle).

47. Gil 1992, p. 603.

48. Ibid., p. 606.

49. Pringle 1993–2009, vol. 3, p. 323.

50. Folda 2012b, pp. 468–69.

51. Kenaan-Kedar 1998, p. 80.

52. Cited in Kedar 1998b, p. 211.

53. Bacci et al. 2012.

54. On the mosaics, see Folda 1995, pp. 347–64; Hunt 1991, p. 87.

55. On Ephraim, see Cutler 1986–87, pp. 179–83.

56. Folda 1995, pp. 91–97, 351–53; Kühnel, G., 1984, p. 512.

57. See Hunt 1991, pp. 69–85.

58. These seemingly unlikely choices are, with one exception, in Greek; the council of Nicaea combines Latin and Greek characters.

59. On the column paintings, see Folda 1995, pp. 364–71.

60. For the door naming King Hetoum I, see Sharon 1997–2013, vol. 5, pp. 184–87. For the Cotton Gate, see Burgoyne et al. 1987, p. 277.

61. See Ousterhout 1989, p. 77 n. 40, citing an Arabic source, Ibn al-Zubayr 1959 ed., pp. 74–76.

62. Folda 1995, p. 392.

63. Folda 2012b, p. 442, citing William of Tyre 1943 ed., vol. 2, bk. 15, chap. 26, p. 133.

64. Gaudette 2010, pp. 141–42.

65. See Irico, ed. 1748, vol. 1, illustrated on two engravings just after p. LVI.

66. Prawer 1985, p. 86.

67. Jotischky 1995, p. 83.

68. Ibn al-Athir, cited in Gabrieli, ed. 1969, p. 145.

69. Ibid.

70. Imad al-Din in Gabrieli, ed. 1969, p. 170.

71. Ibid.

72. Nasir-i Khusraw 1986 ed., p. 32.

73. Ibid.

74. See "Experiencing Sacred Art in Jerusalem," p. 121, in this volume.

75. Kaplony 2004, p. 38.

76. Bonfil, Ro., 2009, pp. 334–36.

77. See Gil 1992, pp. 244, 607–9.

78. Ibid., p. 608.

79. Taragan 2006, p. 56.

Jacques de Vitry

1. Namur 2003, p. 38.

2. On his voyage, see Crane 1890, pp. xxviii–xxix.

3. For Jacques de Vitry's early biography, see Crane 1890, p. xxvii. For his arrival in Acre, see Eduardo Formigoni in Namur 2003, p. 44 n. 24.

4. On the distribution of his text, see Bird 2003.

5. Jacques de Vitry 1896 ed., p. 32. Jacques was struck by the multilingual character of the Holy Land. In another passage (ibid, p. 26), he again emphasized the presence of "every nation under heaven," drawn by "the odour of the saints and of the Holy Places." Jacques also saw the practical necessity of the diverse population to the economy of the Holy Land. See "Trade and Tourism in Medieval Jerusalem," pp. 16–17, in this volume.

6. Jacques de Vitry 2001 ed., n.p.

7. Quoted in Pringle 2003, p. 165.

8. Jacques de Vitry 2001 ed., n.p.

9. Ibid. It should be noted that Jacques is equally critical of the Italians and other Europeans born in the Holy Land for their lax morals and inadequate practice of their faith. Elsewhere, he mentions Georgians, who process freely in Jerusalem, carrying banners. Janin, R., 1913, citing Jacques de Vitry 1896 ed., p. 84.

10. See Folda 2005, pp. 86–87, for the 1209 inventory of the treasury of Antioch, and pp. 87–92, for the Resafa silver treasure of liturgical objects preserved in Damascus.

11. An example of an emblem of ecclesiastical office in ivory coming from the Holy Land is the tau given to Angers by King Fulk of Jerusalem, a gift to him from the "sultan of Babylon." See Riley-Smith 1997, pp. 55–56. Though the reference postdates Jacques de Vitry by more than a century, it is worth noting that, in 1384, Giorgio Gucci noted seeing elephant tusks during his travels to holy places in Egypt, Sinai, Palestine, and Syria. He indicated that the ones in Cairo were mediocre, better ones could be found in Venice, and the principal fourteenth-century Mediterranean trade centers "via which ivory reached Europe were Alexandria, Acre, and Famagusta." See Frescobaldi, Gucci, and Sigoli 1948 ed., p. 103. On Jacques de Vitry and his miter, see Folda 2005, pp. 108–10, 142–44.

12. Ludolph von Suchem 1895 ed., p. 53.

13. Jacques de Vitry betrayed a strong anti-Islamic position, claiming Muhammad was "disguised as an angel of light." See Jacques de Vitry 1825 ed., p. 14. On his and others' attitude toward Muslims, see Kedar 1984.

14. Crane 1890, p. xxx. In Egypt, he busied himself ransoming and baptizing children, though not failing to remark on the quantity of gold, silver, and silks seen there, and writing his history; ibid., p. xxxii.

15. Quoted in ibid., p. xxxiii. After the loss of Jerusalem, relics salvaged from the city together with new acquisitions were taken to Acre, lending new sanctity to that city. See Jacoby, D., 2004, p. 100. His gift of a relic of Mary, "matris apostolorum Joannis et Jacobi" (mother of the apostles John and James), is mentioned in a document of about 1224; Namur 2003, p. 40.

16. The claim still appears in the *Catholic Encyclopedia* website, which reprints Bréhier 1910. See, however, Funk 1909, pp. 63–64.

17. As cited in a document of 1245; see Saint-Genois 1847, p. 9. It also mentions the gift of money to purchase land for viticulture.

The Armenian Presence in Jerusalem

1. Thomson 1988–89/1994, p. 29.

2. Thomson 1985/1994, p. 78.

3. Hintlian 1976, pp. 13–15; Greenwood 2004, pp. 89–91; Thomson 1985/1994, p. 78; Stone et al. 2011, p. 232.

4. Evans 1982, p. 219; Greenwood 2004, p. 89.

5. Greenwood 2004, p. 91.

6. Thomson 1988–89/1994, pp. 31–45; Narkiss, Stone, and Sanjian 1979, p. 12.

7. Narkiss, Stone, and Sanjian 1979, pp. 17–18; Vrej Nersessian in London 2001, pp. 57–59.

8. Jones 2007, pp. 101–5; Thomson 1985/1994, pp. 84–85.

9. Boase 1978, pp. 4–7; Evans 1990, pp. 18–20.

10. Dostourian 1993, pp. 172–73; Evans 1990, p. 41 and n. 113, where Nerses is identified as a fourth-century patriarch.

11. Boase 1978, pp. 4–8, 13. The plan foundered over issues related to the taxation of non-Latins.

12. Hintlian 1976, p. 21; Narkiss, Stone, and Sanjian 1979, p. 12.

13. Boase 1978, pp. 6–7, 9, 11; Hintlian 1976, p. 18.

14. Boase 1978, p. 10; Hintlian 1976, pp. 25–28; Evans 1990, p. 58.

15. Boas 1999, p. 25.

16. Narkiss, Stone, and Sanjian 1979, pp. 121–23; Hintlian 1976, pp. 54–55; Boas 2001, pp. 126–27.

17. Narkiss, Stone, and Sanjian 1979, pp. 121–22; Georgopolou 2004, pp. 122–23.

18. Hintlian 1976, pp. 38–45; Narkiss, Stone, and Sanjian 1979, p. 11.

19. Boas 1999, pp. 166–68; Hintlian 1976, pp. 42–43.

20. Hintlian 1976, pp. 40–44.

21. Boyadjian forthcoming.

22. Evans 1990, p. 37.

23. Abu Salih, the Armenian 1895 ed., pp. 5–6; Boas 2001, p. 39.

24. Sanjian 1969, pp. 74–75; La Porta 2007, p. 113.

25. La Porta 2007, p. 105 and n. 30.

Franciscans in Jerusalem: The Early History

1. Rout 2011. See also Warren 2003; Cusato 2008; Gallant 2006. On the friendship of Francis Piacenza, guardian of the Mount Sion Friary, and Sultan Qa'it Bay, see Suriano 1949 ed., pp. 126–27.

2. Armstrong, R., Hellman, and Short, eds. 1999, p. 106.

3. Flood 1992, p. 69.

4. Ibid., p. 82.

5. Fabri 1893 ed., vol. 2, pt. 2, pp. 378–79.

6. Peters 1985, p. 421.

7. Barriuso 2000, col. 1106.

8. It should be noted that Robert's uncle, Saint Louis of France, was a member of the Third Order of Saint Francis, a lay confraternity based on a rule of the saint for those who wished to live in the world while cultivating a deeper religious sensibility. It is not unlikely that Robert was, too, particularly in light of his donations of great artworks to Franciscan churches in Italy. Robert's wife, Queen Sancea, was also intimately involved in the support of the Franciscans in the Holy Land.

9. Collin 1982, p. 126.

10. Barriuso 2000, cols. 1106–7. Felix Fabri describes the continued support from the monarchs of Europe to the Franciscans in the Holy Land. See Fabri 1893 ed., vol. 2, pt. 2, p. 382. See also Benvenuti 2014 for the involvement, among others, of the Medici.

11. Barriuso 2000, col. 1107.

Muslim Women Patrons in Jerusalem

1. Natsheh 2000, p. 794.

2. *Khatoun* in medieval Turkish means "princess."

3. See Burgoyne et al. 1987, pp. 321–24, no. 28, and pp. 89, 92.

4. On this hospice, see ibid., pp. 412–14, no. 37.

5. Ibid., p. 544.

6. Ibid., p. 348. The original dome was replaced after it collapsed in 1919–20.

7. Suggested by ibid., p. 343.

8. Little 1984a, pp. 194–95, no. 76.

9. Burgoyne et al. 1987, p. 344.

10. Ibid., p. 345.

11. Salameh 1999, pp. 84–85, no. 18.

12. Burgoyne et al. 1987, pp. 526–33, no. 54.

13. Ibid., p. 527.

Seeking the Eternal Jerusalem

1. The epigraph is from Scheindlin 2008, p. 193, poem 18, p. 193. For an overview of the role of Jerusalem at the End of Time in Jewish, Christian, and Islamic contexts, see Grossman 1996, pp. 295–310; Stroumsa, G., 2009; Livne-Kafri 2006.

2. For this manuscript, see Frojmovic 2015.

3. Thérèse Metzger divided these depictions into two groups: those objects associated with the desert Tabernacle and those associated with Solomon's Temple. Eva Frojmovic, on the other hand, discusses them together as "sanctuary vessels." See Metzger, T., 1969–70 and Metzger, T., 1970–71; Frojmovic 2002, esp. pp. 92–93.

4. When the first Temple was destroyed, the Ark of the Covenant and its contents were lost or, according to rabbinic tradition, hidden. Those contents included the Tablets of the Law, the jar of manna, and the flowering rod

of Aaron. See Babylonian Talmud, Tractate Yoma 52b. For Christian discourse about the whereabouts of these objects, see Oftestad 2014.

5. Most of these implements are described in detail in Exodus 25–30. For the rest, see Exodus 16:33–34 (jar of manna), Numbers 10:2–10 (trumpets), Numbers 17:18–25 (flowering staff of Aaron).

6. Kogman-Appel 2004. For a partial list of manuscripts, see Gutmann 1976, esp. pp. 134–38 and n. 6; and Frojmovic 2002, pp. 126–27. For the often neglected fifteenth-century manuscripts, see Contessa 2012.

7. At times, the menorah is given its own folio. Some of the details derive from the commentary of Solomon ben Isaac (known as Rashi), while others draw upon the descriptions given by Moshe ben Maimon (known as Maimonides). Some include the pillars Jachin and Boaz (3 Kings 7:15–22); others add the lyre, harp, and cymbals, which were used as part of the Temple service. Nordström 1968.

8. Katrin Kogman-Appel cites the Bible produced in 1336 and currently housed in the Karaite Synagogue, Istanbul, as the first to include the Mount of Olives as part of the sanctuary implements. Kogman-Appel 2004, pp. 143–44. The importance of the Mount of Olives during the early Middle Ages is evident from the numerous attempts by Jews to buy it. See Gil 1978, esp. pp. 131–32.

9. This verse from Zechariah is the single appearance of the name "Mount of Olives" in the Hebrew Bible and further solidifies the connection between the image and its textual source. In an illuminated Bible written by Vidal Satorre in 1404 in Saragossa, Spain, the image of the Mount of Olives is given a full page and is surrounded by the verses of Zechariah's prophecy (Bibliothèque Nationale de France, Paris, MS Hebr. 31, fol. 4r). The Bible produced in 1384 in Solsona, Spain, has labeled the grassy hill topped by a single tree as "Mount of Olives" (British Library, London, King's MS 1, fol. 3v).

10. Aptowitzer 1931; Grossman 1996.

11. Himmelfarb, trans. 1990, p. 79.

12. See *Book of Elijah*, *Mysteries of Rabbi Simeon ben Yohai*, *The Story of Daniel*, *Vision of Daniel*, and *Prayer of Rabbi Simeon b. Yohai* in Even-Shemuel, ed. 1954; Schwartz 1997; Bonfil, Re., 1979. For a selection of these apocalyptic texts in English, see Patai 1979.

13. While the belief in a heavenly Temple appears in numerous early rabbinic texts, none makes explicit mention of its miraculous descent to earth. See, for example, Mishnah Taanit 4:1, Berachot 4:5; Babylonian Talmud, Taanit 5a and 25b, Haggigah 12b; Jerusalem Talmud, Berachot 4:1 (31a), 4:5 (35b); Midrash Tehilim 122:3. Avigdor Aptowitzer believes that this idea was redacted from Jewish sources after it was described in the Apocalypse and embraced by Christian exegetes. See Aptowitzer 1931, pp. 271–72; Gaon, S., 1948 ed., pp. 290–332, esp. 309–10.

14. Gaon, H., 1934 ed., pp. 72–75, esp. 74.

15. Rashi, Babylonian Talmud, Sukkot 41a, using Exodus 15:17 as a proof text. For Maimonides, see *Mishneh Torah*, Hilchot Melachim u'Milchamoteihem 11:1, 4.

16. "In [the month of] Nissan we were redeemed and in Nissan we will be redeemed." Babylonian Talmud, Rosh Hashanah 11a. Rashi discusses the idea that the future Temple will be built on the first day of Passover (Babylonian Talmud, Sukkot 41a, and Rosh Hashana 30a).

17. For varying opinions on the genesis of reciting the passage beginning "This is the bread of Affliction" at the start of the Passover Seder and the call "Next Year in Jerusalem," see Kulp 2005, esp. pp. 111–16; Safrai and Safrai 1998, pp. 109–12, 189, 246; Tabory 2008, pp. 60–61; Glatzer, N., ed. 1989, pp. 24–25.

18. For this manuscript, see Epstein 2011, pp. 19–128.

19. Shalev-Eyni 2004, esp. pp. 176–81; Epstein 2011, pp. 125–26.

20. Yalkut Shimoni, sec. 499, on Isaiah 60:1.

21. Gousset 1974; Gousset 1982; Milan 1983; Kühnel, B., 1987; Emmerson and McGinn, eds. 1992; Losito 2011.

22. Deuchler, Hoffeld, and Nickel 1971. See also Trinity College, Cambridge, R.16.2, fol. 25v; British Library, London, Yates Thompson MS 10, fol. 19r; British Library, London, Add. MS 42555, fol. 79v; Angers Apocalypse Tapestry.

23. Lewis, S., 1995; Lewis, S., 1991; Carruthers 1998.

24. Many thanks to Joseph Ackley for his thoughtful suggestions concerning this censer and the concept of microarchitecture as a symbol of the Heavenly Jerusalem. Bayer 1991; Gousset 1982; Grabar, A., 1957; Westermann-Angerhausen 2014, esp. pp. 85–108 and 214–23; Westermann-Angerhausen 2011;Westermann-Angerhausen 1988; Anton von Euw in Cologne 1985, vol. 1, p. 478; Bayer 1991.

25. While a case can certainly be made for an iconography of the Heavenly Jerusalem, it is important to note that the form of the object deviates from the biblical cityscape described by John in several significant ways. For instance, the censer is not ringed with twelve gates or with the twelve apostles. Neither does it show the walls of the city. Instead, it features a range of figures from the Hebrew Bible that foreshadow the coming of the Messiah and the Heavenly Kingdom. See Westermann-Angerhausen 2014, p. 104.

26. For an overview of Theophilus's *De diversis artibus*, see Gearhart 2010. For a translation of this text, see Theophilus 1961 ed., pp. 110–20.

27. Beginning on the bottom, there are half-length busts of Moses, Isaiah, Jeremiah, and Aaron, each of whom presaged the arrival of the Messiah. Above them, Melchizedek holds bread and wine; Abraham is about to sacrifice his son Isaac on an altar; a blind Isaac unknowingly blesses his younger son, Jacob; and finally Abel brings a lamb offering to God. All these moments from the Hebrew Bible were believed by Christians to foreshadow God's sacrifice of his son, Jesus, and to confirm the path to salvation given through the sacrament of the Eucharist. Westermann-Angerhausen 2011.

28. The correlation between Solomon and the Second Coming of Christ is made explicit in the inscription: "Solomon, while caring for the terrestrial realm, prefigures the true king of peace through all times, he surrounds the order of prophets prophesying Christ coming to take upon Himself the death of the flesh." As translated in Westermann-Angerhausen 2011, p. 236.

29. Neuss 1912, pp. 265–97. Other examples include the Roda Bible (Bibliothèque Nationale de France, Paris, MS Lat. 6), the Farfa Bible (Vatican Library, MS Lat. 5729), the commentary on Ezekiel by Haymo of Auxerre (Bibliothèque Nationale de France, Paris, MS Lat. 12302), a copy of the Moralized Bible (Bibliothèque Nationale de France, Paris, MS Lat. 11560), and a window of the Sainte-Chapelle (see Grodecki 1976, pls. 408–27).

30. Derbes 1992. For a mystical reading of these frescoes, see Odell 2011.

31. As Derbes has shown, the calls to crusade used the language of Ezekiel – specifically his description of the desecration of holy sites (Ezekiel 22:26, 23:8, 23:38) – as a means of rallying support. Derbes 1992, pp. 143–44.

32. The earliest account of these events appears in the Qur'an (17:1 and 53:6–18). However, the Qur'an does not explicitly link the trip to Jerusalem with the Prophet's ascension. Understood as Jerusalem, the destination of Muhammad's Night Journey is described as the "furthest place of worship [*al-masjid al-aqsa*] whose precincts We have blessed" (17:1). By the tenth century, the two narratives had been soldered together and the contours of the narrative had been more or less codified. For the development of this tradition, see Busse 1998; Colby 2008; el-Khatib 2001; Gruber 2010, esp. pp. 1–31. For a historiographic critique, see Nor 2011.

33. The exact date for the construction of the Dome of the Ascension (Qubbat al-Mi'raj) remains unknown. It may well have been built during the Umayyad period, perhaps as early as the second reign of al-Walid (705–15). However, the lack of documentary and archaeological evidence makes this dating difficult to prove. Furthermore, there is a fair amount of controversy surrounding the precise location for this crucial event. Several important sources place the Prophet's ascension not in the Dome of the Ascension but in the Dome of the Rock. Others imply that he climbed to heaven from the spot now commemorated as the Dome of the Prophet. For more on these contradictory traditions, see Elad 1999, pp. 48–50; Grabar, O., 1987, pp. 48–49.

34. For this manuscript, see Gruber 2008; Gray et al. 1979, pp. 161–76; Subtelny 2010. For earlier examples, see Ettinghausen 1957.

35. This version of the narrative is not unique to the manuscript. Earlier accounts include Ibn Sa'd's ninth-century *Tabaqat*, Muslim's ninth-century *Sahih*, and Ibn Ishaq's *Sira*, among others. For an overview of the many variations of this text and their importance, see Vuckovic 2005.

36. This is not to say that Jerusalem was considered to be more important than either Mecca or Medina. According to hadith, Jerusalem is considered to be the third holiest city for Muslims. For the comparative status of Jerusalem, see Hillenbrand, C., 1999, pp. 141–61; Kister 1969; Livne-Kafri 1993; Livne-Kafri 1998; Abu-Sway 2009.

37. Al-Qushayri 1964 ed., p. 103, as translated in Gruber 2010, p. 6.

38. The Qur'an describes the End of Days as the imminent "Hour" when earthly life ends in resurrection and judgment, but it provides very little other information on the subject. As a body of literature on the Merits of Jerusalem (Fada'il al-Quds) took shape in the eighth century and continued to expand in subsequent centuries, more elaborate layers of importance were added to the city of Jerusalem. See Necipoğlu 2008, esp. pp. 23–45; Bashear 1993; Livne-Kafri 1998.

39. Qur'an 17:52, 50:41. Shihab al-Din bin Ahmad al-Muqaddasi (d. 1364) wrote, "The Rock originated in paradise;/Jerusalem is the 'chief' among places just as the Rock in Jerusalem is the 'chief' among rocks;/Allah said to the Rock: In you is my Garden of Eden and my Gehenna . . . happy is he who visited thee;/The Rock is on a date tree;/Upon thee will I place my throne of glory . . . ;/You are my earthly throne of glory." Al-Muqaddasi as quoted and translated in Hasson 1996, p. 375.

40. The enlarged text immediately below the angel's feet refers to the angel Gabriel. However, the text on the verso describes the role of the angel Israfil blowing his horn to signify the arrival of the Day of Judgment. Thank you to Michael Chagnon for his help in translating this text.

41. Shoemaker 2012, esp. pp. 192–265.

42. The Qur'an does not specifically mention a messianic figure (*mahdi*) that will appear at the End of Days. By the early ninth century, the prevalent belief was that Jesus would appear on Mount Afiq and slay the Antichrist, but this did not necessarily mean that he was the Messiah. Instead, there was much speculation about a Messiah born from Muhammad's family. And there were many competing claims to this title. See Bashir 2003, esp. pp. 3–13; Madelung 1981; Campbell 1995; Yücesoy 2009, pp. 38–58; Ahmed 2011.

43. The Qur'an never names civil disorder as a harbinger of the End of Days. Nevertheless, as Hayrettin Yücesoy has argued, civil discord became linked to the End of Days during the bloody and tumultuous fighting immediately following the death of Muhammad. See Yücesoy 2009, pp. 38–40. See also Arjomand 2002; Stowasser 2004; Bashear 1993.

44. Sylvia Schein has gone so far as to suggest that when Christians were ruling Jerusalem, the apocalyptic importance of the city waned, but when they lost control of the city, there was a dramatic surge in eschatological expectation. Schein 2005, esp. pp. 141–57.

BIBLIOGRAPHY

Aachen 1972
Der Aachener Domschatz. Exh. cat., Museumsverein Aachen, 1972. Catalogue by Ernst Günther Grimme and Erich Stephany. *Aachener Kunstblätter* 42. Düsseldorf, 1972.

Abu Salih, the Armenian 1895 ed.
Abu Salih, the Armenian. *The Churches and Monasteries of Egypt and Some Neighbouring Countries.* Translated by B[asil] T[homas] A[lfred] Evetts; annotated by Alfred J[oshua] Butler. Anecdota Oxoniensia, Semitic Series, 7. Oxford, 1895.

Abu-Sway 1996
Abu-Sway, Mustafa. *Al-Ghazzaliyy: A Study in Islamic Epistemology.* Kuala Lumpur, 1996.

Abu-Sway 2009
Abu-Sway, Mustafa. "The Holy Land, Jerusalem and the Aqsa Mosque in the Islamic Sources." In Grabar, O., and Kedar, eds. 2009, pp. 334–43.

Abweini et al. 2013
Abweini, Walid H., et al. "Reconstructing Salah al-Din Minbar of al-Aqsa Mosque: Challenges and Results." *International Journal of Conservation Science* 4, no. 3 (July–September 2013), pp. 307–16.

Adler, ed. 1930
Adler, Elkan Nathan, ed. *Jewish Travellers.* London, 1930. Reprinted with variant titles.

Afsaruddin 2013
Afsaruddin, Asma. *Striving in the Path of God: Jihad and Martyrdom in Islamic Thought.* Oxford and New York, 2013.

Ahmed 2011
Ahmed, Asad Q. *The Religious Elite of the Early Islamic Hijaz: Five Prosopographical Case Studies.* Oxford, 2011.

Albera 2012
Albera, Dionigi. "Combining Practices and Beliefs: Muslim Pilgrims at Marian Shrines." In *Sharing the Sacra: The Politics and Pragmatics of Inter-communal Relations around Holy Places,* edited by Glenn Bowman, pp. 10–24. New York and Oxford, 2012.

Aldsworth et al. 2002
Aldsworth, Fred, et al. "Medieval Glassmaking at Tyre, Lebanon." *Journal of Glass Studies* 44 (2002), pp. 49–66.

Alexander 1985
Alexander, David Geoffrey. "European Swords in the Collections of Istanbul: Part 1, Swords from the Arsenal of Alexandria." *Waffen- und Kostümkunde: Zeitschrift der Gesellschaft für historische Waffen- und Kostümkunde* 27 (1985), pp. 81–118.

Allan 1982
Allan, James W. *Islamic Metalwork: The Nuhad Es-Said Collection.* London, 1982.

d'Allemagne 1899
d'Allemagne, Henry-René. "Notice sur un bassin en cuivre éxécuté pour Hugues IV de Lusignan, Roi de Chypre (1324–1361)." In *L'art Gothique et la Renaissance en Chypre,* edited by C[amille] Enlart, vol. 2, pp. 743–56. 2 vols. Paris, 1899.

d'Allemagne and Janneau 1948
d'Allemagne, Henry-René, and Guillaume Janneau. *La maison d'un vieux collectionneur.* 2 vols. Paris, 1948.

Ameisenowa 1935
Ameisenowa, Zofja. "Das messianische Gastmahl der Gerechten in einer hebräischen Bibel aus dem XIII. Jahrhundert: Ein Beitrag zur eschatologischen Ikonographie bei den Juden." *Monatschrift für Geschichte und Wissenschaft des Judentums* 79, no. 6, n.s. 43 (November–December 1935), pp. 409–22.

Amir-Moezzi 1996
Amir-Moezzi, Mohammad Ali. *Le voyage initiatique en terre d'Islam: Ascensions célestes et itinéraires spirituels.* Paris, 1996.

Amitai-Preiss 1992
Amitai-Preiss, Nitzan. "A Fatimid Gold Bead from Caesarea." *'Atiqot* 21 (1992), pp. 171–72, n.p. pl.

Angar 2016
Angar, Mabi. *The Reliquary of St. Anastasios the Persian in Aachen: Middle Byzantine Head Reliquaries and the Role of the 1204 Conquest of Constantinople in Their Reception and Perception in the West.* Wiesbaden, 2016.

Ann Arbor 1981
The Meeting of Two Worlds: The Crusades and the Mediterranean Context. Exh. cat., University of Michigan Museum of Art, Ann Arbor, 1981. Catalogue by Christine Verzár Bornstein and Priscilla Parsons Soucek. Ann Arbor, Mich., 1981.

Antiochus Strategos 1909 ed.
Antiochus Strategos. *The Persian Conquest of Jerusalem in 614* (in Russian). Translated by N. la. Marr. St. Petersburg, 1909.

Antrim 2012
Antrim, Zayde. *Routes and Realms: The Power of Place in the Early Islamic World.* Oxford and New York, 2012.

Aptowitzer 1931
Aptowitzer, Avigdor. "The Celestial Temple as Viewed in the Agada" (in Hebrew). *Tarbiz* 2 (1931), pp. 137–53, 257–87.

Aptowitzer 1989
Aptowitzer, Victor [Avigdor]. "The Celestial Temple as Viewed in the Aggadah." In *Studies in Jewish Thought,* edited by Joseph Dan, pp. 1–29. Binah: Studies in Jewish History, Thought, and Culture, 2. New York, 1989. Abridged English translation of Aptowitzer 1931.

Arberry 1955
Arberry, Arthur J. *The Koran Interpreted.* 2 vols. in one. London and New York, 1955.

Arculfus 1889 ed.
The Pilgrimage of Arculfus in the Holy Land (about the Year A.D. 670). Translated and annotated by James Rose MacPherson. Palestine Pilgrims' Text Society, 3, no. 1. London, 1889.

Arjomand 2002
Arjomand, Said Amir. "Messianism, Millennialism and Revolution in Early Islamic History." In *Imagining the End: Visions of the Apocalypse from the Ancient Middle East to Modern America,* edited by Abbas Amanat and Magnus Bernhardsson, pp. 106–25. London and New York, 2002.

Armstrong, K., 1988
Armstong, Karen. *Holy War: The Crusades and Their Impact on Today's World.* London and New York, 1988.

Armstrong, K., 1996
Armstrong, Karen. *Jerusalem: One City, Three Faiths.* New York, 1996.

Armstrong, K., 2014
Armstrong, Karen. *Fields of Blood: Religion and the History of Violence.* New York and Toronto, 2014.

Armstrong, R., Hellman, and Short, eds. 1999
Armstrong, Regis J., J. A. Wayne Hellman, and William J. Short, eds. *Francis of Assisi.* Vol. 1, *The Saint: Early Documents.* Hyde Park, N.Y., 1999.

Arnold von Harff 1946 ed.
Arnold von Harff. *The Pilgrimage of Arnold von Harff, Knight, from Cologne through Italy, Syria, Egypt, Arabia, Ethiopia, Nubia, Palestine, Turkey, France, and Spain, Which He Accomplished in the Years 1496 to 1499.* Edited by Malcolm Letts. Works Issued by the Hakluyt Society, Second series, 94. London, 1946.

Asali 1981
Asali, Kamil Jamil. *Fada'il bayt al-Maqdis Manuscripts: A Study and Bibliography* (in Arabic). Amman, 1981.

Ashtor 1969
Ashtor, Eliyahu. *Histoire des prix et des salaires dans l'Orient médiéval.* Monnaie, prix, conjoncture, 8. Paris, 1969.

Auld 2005
Auld, Sylvia. "The Minbar of al-Aqsa: Form and Function." In *Image and Meaning in Islamic Art,* edited by Robert Hillenbrand, pp. 42–60. London, 2005.

Auld 2009a
Auld, Sylvia. "Cross-Currents and Coincidences: A Perspective on Ayyubid Metalwork." In Hillenbrand, R., and Auld, eds. 2009, pp. 45–71.

Auld 2009b
Auld, Sylvia. "The Minbar of Nur al-Din in Context." In Hillenbrand, R., and Auld, eds. 2009, pp. 72–93.

Auld and Hillenbrand 2000
Auld, Sylvia, and Robert Hillenbrand, with Yusuf Natsheh. *Ottoman Jerusalem: The Living City, 1517–1917.* 2 vols. London, 2000.

Auxentios 1999 ed.
Auxentios, Bishop, of Photiki. *The Paschal Fire in Jerusalem: A Study of the Rite of the Holy Fire in the Church of the Holy Sepulchre.* Berkeley, 1999.

Avigad 2007
Avigad, Nahman. "Seal, Seals." In *Encyclopaedia Judaica* 2007, vol. 18, pp. 225–28.

Avissar 2003
Avissar, Miriam. "Early Islamic through Mamluk Pottery" In *Jewish Quarter Excavations in the Old City of Jerusalem Conducted by Nahman Avigad, 1969–1982,* vol. 2, *The Finds from Areas A, W and X–2,* edited by Hillel Geva, pp. 433–41. Jerusalem, 2003.

Avissar and Stern 2005
Avissar, Miriam, and Edna J. Stern. *Pottery of the Crusader, Ayyubid, and Mamluk Periods in Israel.* IAA Reports, 26. Jerusalem, 2005.

el-Awaisi 2008
el-Awaisi, Khalid A. *Geographical Dimensions of Islamic Jerusalem.* Newcastle upon Tyne, 2008.

Azkari 1981 ed.
Azkari, Elazar ben Mordecai. *Sefer Charedim* (in Hebrew) Jerusalem, 1981.

Bacci et al. 2012
Bacci, Michele, et al. "Historical and Archaeological Analysis of the Church of the Nativity." *Journal of Cultural Heritage* 13, no. 4 (2012), pp. e5–e26.

Backhouse 2006
Backhouse, Janet. "The Case of Queen Melisende's Psalter: An Historical Investigation." In *Tributes to Jonathan J. G. Alexander: The Making and Meaning of Illuminated Medieval and Renaissance Manuscripts, Art and Architecture,* edited by Susan L'Engle and Gerald Guest, pp. 457–70. London and Turnhout, 2006.

Badamo 2011
Badamo, Heather A. "Image and Community: Representations of Military Saints in the Medieval Eastern Mediterranean." Ph.D. diss., University of Michigan, Ann Arbor, 2011.

Badawy 1972
Badawy, Ahmad Ahmad. *Intellectual Life in Egypt and Syria in the Age of Crusades* (in Arabic). Cairo, [1972].

Baer 1983
Baer, Eva. *Metalwork in Medieval Islamic Art.* Albany, 1983.

Baer 1989
Baer, Eva. *Ayyubid Metalwork with Christian Images.* Studies and Sources in Islamic Art and Architecture, 4. Leiden, 1989.

Baer 1997–98
Baer, Eva. "Visual Representation of Jerusalem's Holy Islamic Sites." *Jewish Art* 23–24 [*The Real and Ideal Jerusalem in Jewish, Christian, and Islamic Art: Studies in Honor of Bezalel Narkiss on the Occasion of His Seventieth Birthday,* edited by Bianca Kühnel] (1997–98), pp. 384–92.

Baer 1998
Baer, Eva. *Islamic Ornament.* Edinburgh, 1998.

Bagatti 1930
Bagatti, B[ellarmino]. *Il Museo della Flagellazione in Gerusalemme.* Jerusalem, 1930.

Bagatti 1949
Bagatti, Bellarmino. "Eulogie Palestini." *Orientalia Cristiana Periodica* 15 (1949), pp. 126–66.

Bagatti 1952
Bagatti, Bellarmino. *Gli antichi edifici sacri di Betlemmein seguito agli scavi e restauri praticati dalla Custodia di Terra Santa (1948–51).* Publications of the Studium Biblicum Franciscanum, 9. Jerusalem, 1952.

Bagatti and Alliata 1984
Bagatti, Bellarmino, and Eugenio Alliata. *Gli scavi di Nazaret.* Vol. 2, *Dal secolo XII ad oggi.* Publications of the Studium Biblicum Franciscanum, Collectio maior, 17. Jerusalem, 1984.

Bahat 1996
Bahat, Dan. "The Physical Infrastructure." In Prawer and Ben-Shammai, eds. 1996, pp. 38–100.

Bahat 2002
Bahat, Dan. "Hospices and Hospitals in Mamluk Jerusalem." In *Towns and Material Culture in the Medieval Middle East,* edited by Yaacov Lev, pp. 73–88. The Medieval Mediterranean: Peoples, Economies and Cultures, 400–1453, 39. Leiden, Boston, and Cologne, 2002.

Baker, ed. 2002
[Baker, Colin F., ed. and annot.]. *Sultan Baybar's Qur'an.* In *Turning the Pages.* British Library. London, [2002]; http://www.bl.uk/turning-the-pages/?id0354fafo-a67a-11db-87d3-0050c2490048&typebook (accessed February 9, 2016).

Bakhoum 2011
Bakhoum, Dina Ishak. "The Waqf System: Maintenance, Repair, and Upkeep." In *Held in Trust: Waqf in the Islamic World,* edited by Pascale Ghazaleh, pp. 179–96. Cairo and New York, 2011.

al-Bakri 1913 ed.
al-Bakri, Abu 'Ubayd. *Description de l'Afrique septentrionale.* Translated by William MacGuckin Slane. Algiers, 1913.

Ball 2005
Ball, Jennifer. *Byzantine Dress: Representations of Secular Dress in Eighth- to Twelfth-Century Painting.* New York, 2005.

Ballian 2009
Ballian, Anna. "Three Medieval Islamic Brasses and the Mosul Tradition of Inlaid Metalwork." *Mouseio Benake* 9 (2009), pp. 113–41.

Ballian and Drandaki 2003
Ballian, Anna, and Anastasia Drandaki. "A Middle Byzantine Silver Treasure." *Mouseio Benake* 3 (2003), pp. 47–80.

Baltimore 2001
Ethiopian Art: The Art Museum. Exh. cat., Walters Art Museum, Baltimore, 2001. Catalogue by Kelly M. Holbert and others. Baltimore, 2001.

Baltimore and other cities 1990
Islamic Art and Patronage: Treasures from Kuwait [The al-Sabah Collection]. Exh. cat., Walters Art Gallery, Baltimore, and other venues, 1990. Catalogue by Esin Atil and others. New York, 1990.

Baltimore and other cities 1993–96
African Zion: The Sacred Art of Ethiopia. Exh. cat., Walters Art Gallery, Baltimore; The Schomburg Center for Research in Black Culture, New York; The Menil Collection, Houston; and five other venues, 1993–96. Catalogue by Marilyn Heldman and others. New Haven, 1993.

Baltimore and Princeton 2012–13
Revealing the African Presence in Renaissance Europe. Exh. cat., Walters Art Museum, Baltimore; Princeton University Art Museum, 2012–13. Catalogue by Joaneath Spicer and others. Baltimore, 2012.

Barag and Wilkinson 1974
Barag, Dan, and John Wilkinson. "The Monza – Bobbio Flasks and the Holy Sepulchre." *Levant: The Journal of the Council for British Research in the Levant* 6, no. 1 (1974), pp. 179–87.

Bar-El et al. 2000
Bar-El, Yair, et al. "Jerusalem Syndrome." *The British Journal of Psychiatry* 176, no. 1 (January 2000), pp. 86–90.

Barnes 1997
Barnes, Ruth. *Indian Block-Printed Textiles in Egypt: The Newberry Collection in the Ashmolean Museum, Oxford.* Oxford and New York, 1997.

Barnet and Wu 2012
Barnet, Peter, and Nancy Wu. *The Cloisters: Medieval Art and Architecture.* New York, 2012.

Baron et al. 1996
Baron, Françoise, et al. *Sculpture française.* Vol. 1, *Moyen Âge.* [Catalogue], Musée du Louvre. Paris, 1996.

Barriuso 2000
Barriuso, P. García. "Jérusalem. IV: La custodie franciscaine." In *Dictionnaire d'histoire et de géographie ecclésiastiques,* edited by Alfred Aubert, vol. 27 (2000), cols. 1106–10. 31 vols. Paris, 1912– .

Bashear 1991
Bashear, Suliman. "Qibla Musharriqa and Early Muslim Prayer in Churches." *The Muslim World* 81, nos. 3–4 (October 1991), pp. 267–82.

Bashear 1993
Bashear, Suliman. "Muslim Apocalypses and the Hour: A Case-Study in Traditional Reinterpretation." *Israel Oriental Studies* 13 (1993), pp. 75–99.

Bashir 2003
Bashir, Shahzad. *Messianic Hopes and Mystical Visions: The Nurbakhshiya between Medieval and Modern Islam.* Columbia, S.C., 2003.

Basset 1960
Basset, René. "Burda." In *EI2* 1960–2009, vol. 1 (1960), pp. 1314–15.

Van Bastelaer 1880
Van Bastelaer, D. A. *Étude sur le précieux reliquaire phylactère du XIIe siècle provenant du prieuré de Sart-les-Moines, à Gosselies, et probablement originaire de l'abbaye de Lobbes: Émail et dorure sur cuivre bronzé.* Antwerp, 1880.

Bayer 1991
Bayer, Clemens M. M. "Zum Gozbertus-Rauchfass in der Trierer Domschatzkammer." In *Schatzkunst Trier: Forschungen und Ergebnisse,* edited by Franz J. Ronig, pp. 45–88. Treveris Sacra, 4. Trier, 1991.

Behrens-Abouseif 2007
Behrens-Abouseif, Doris. *Cairo of the Mamluks: A History of the Architecture and Its Culture.* London and New York, 2007.

Behrens-Abouseif 2014
Behrens-Abouseif, Doris. *Practising Diplomacy in the Mamluk Sultanate: Gifts and Material Culture in the Medieval Islamic World.* London and New York, 2014.

Beit-Arié 1985
Beit-Arié, Malachi. "The Worms Mahzor: Its History and Its Paleographic and Codicological Characteristics." In *Worms Mahzor: MS. Jewish National and University Library Heb. 4°781/1,* edited by Malachi Beit-Arié, vol. [2], pp. 13–35. 2 vols. Jerusalem and Vaduz, 1985.

Beit-Arié et al. 1994
Beit-Arié, Malachi, et al. *Catalogue of the Hebrew Manuscripts in the Bodleian Library: Supplement of Addenda and Corrigenda to Vol. I (A. Neubauer's Catalogue).* Oxford, 1994.

Ben-Dov 1985
Ben-Dov, Meir. *In the Shadow of the Temple: The Discovery of Ancient Jerusalem.* Jerusalem and New York, 1985.

Ben-Dov 2002
Ben-Dov, Meir. *Historical Atlas of Jerusalem.* New York, 2002.

Benjamin of Tudela 1983 ed.
Benjamin of Tudela. *The Itinerary of Benjamin of Tudela: Travels in the Middle Ages.* Malibu, 1983.

Ben-Shammai n.d.
Ben-Shammai, Haggai. "The Seal of Tsemach son of Asah, the Prince: Historical and Literal Context." In "The Seal of Tsemach Son of Asah, the Prince." Unpublished manuscript, n.d.

Ben-Shammai 1996
Ben-Shammai, Haggai. "The Karaites." In Prawer and Ben-Shammai, eds. 1996, pp. 201–24.

Ben-Shammai 2007
Ben-Shammai, Haggai. "Japheth ben Eli Ha-Levi." In *Encyclopaedia Judaica* 2007, vol. 11, pp. 86–87.

Benvenuti 2014
Benvenuti, Anna. "Gerusalemme: Gli osservanti e la 'sindrome da abbandono.'" In *I Francescani e la crociata: Atti dell'XI Convegno di Greccio; Greccio, 3–4 maggio 2013,* edited by Alvaro Cacciotti and Maria Melli, pp. 245–61. Biblioteca di Frate Francesco, 15. Milan, 2014.

Van Berchem 1927
Van Berchem, Max. *Matériaux pour un Corpus inscriptionum Arabicum.* Pt. 2, *Syrie du Sud.* Vol. 2, *Jérusalem "Haram."* Mémoires publiés par les membres de l'Institut Français d'Archéologie Orientale du Caire, 44. Cairo, 1927.

Berger 2012
Berger, Pamela. *The Crescent on the Temple: The Dome of the Rock as Image of the Ancient Jewish Sanctuary.* Boston, 2012.

Berlin 1989
Europa und der Orient, 800–1900. Exh. cat., Martin-Gropius-Bau, Berlin, 1989. Catalogue by Gereon Sievernich, Hendrik Budde, and others. Berlin, 1989.

Berlin 1995–96
Die Reise nach Jerusalem: Eine kulturhistorische Exkursion in die Stadt der Städte; 3000 Jahre Davidsstadt. Exh. cat., Grossen Orangerie Schloss Charlottenburg Berlin, 1995–96. Catalogue by Hendrik Budde, Andreas Nachama, and others. Berlin, 1995.

Bernard of Clairvaux 1977 ed.
Bernard of Clairvaux. *Treatises III: On Grace and Free Choice; In Praise of the New Knighthood.* Translated by Conrad Greenia. Cistercian Fathers Series, 19. Kalamazoo, 1977.

Bernsted 2003
Bernsted, Anne-Marie Keblow. *Early Islamic Pottery: Materials and Techniques.* London, 2003.

Bevan 1914
Bevan, A[nthony] A[shley]. "Mohammed's Ascension to Heaven." In *Studien zur semitischen Philologie und Religionsgeschichte: Julius Wellhausen zum siebzigsten Geburtstag am 17. Mai 1914 gewidmet von Freunden und Schülern und in ihrem Auftrag herausgegeben,* edited by Karl Marti, pp. 49–61. Beihefte zur Zeitschrift für die alttestamentliche Wissenschaft, 27. Giessen, 1914.

Biddle 1999
Biddle, Martin. *The Tomb of Christ.* Gloucestershire, 1999.

Biddle 2000
Biddle, Martin. *The Church of the Holy Sepulchre.* New York, 2000.

Bijovsky and Berman 2008
Bijovsky, Gabriela, and Ariel Berman. "The Coins." In Hirschfeld et al. 2008, pp. 63–103.

Bird 2003
Bird, Jessalynn. "The *Historial Orientalis* of Jacques de Vitry: Visual and Written Commentaries as Evidence of a Text's Audience, Reception, and Utilization." *Essays in Medieval Studies: Proceedings of the Illinois Medieval Association* 20 (2003), pp. 56–74.

Bird, Peters, and Powell, eds. 2013
Bird, Jessalynn, Edward Peters, and James M. Powell, eds. *Crusade and Christendom: Annotated Documents in Translation from Innocent III to the Fall of Acre, 1187–1291.* The Middle Ages Series. Philadelphia, 2013.

Bitton-Ashkelony 2010
Bitton-Ashkelony, Brouria. "From Sacred Travel to Monastic Career: The Evidence of Late Antique Syriac Hagiography." *Adamantius* 16 (2010), pp. 353–70.

Blackman and Redford 2005
Blackman, M. James, and Scott Redford. "Neutron Activation Analysis of Medieval Ceramics from Kinet, Turkey, Especially Port Saint Symeon Ware." *Ancient Near Eastern Studies* 42 (2005), pp. 83–186.

Blackmore 2009
Blackmore, Josiah. *Moorings: Portuguese Expansion and the Writing of Africa.* Minneapolis, 2009.

Blair 2014
Blair, Sheila. *Text and Image in Medieval Persian Art.* Edinburgh, 2014.

Blake 1907 ed.
Blake, William. *The Prophetic Books of William Blake: Milton.* Edited by E. R. D. Maclagan and A. G. B. Russell. London, 1907.

Blidstein 1991
Blidstein, Gerald J. "Holy War in Maimonidean Law." In *Perspectives on Maimonides: Philosophical and Historical Studies* [Proceedings of a colloquium held at Tel Aviv University in June 1982], edited by Joel L. Kraemer, pp. 209–20. Littman Library of Jewish Civilization. Oxford, 1991.

Bloom 2007
Bloom, Jonathan M. *Arts of the City Victorious: Islamic Art and Architecture in Fatimid North Africa and Egypt.* New Haven and London, 2007.

Bloom 2009
Bloom, Jonathan M. "Woodwork in Syria, Palestine, and Egypt during the 12th and 13th Centuries." In Hillenbrand, R., and Auld, eds. 2009, pp. 129–46.

Boas 1999
Boas, Adrian J. *Crusader Archaeology: The Material Culture of the Latin East.* London and New York, 1999.

Boas 2001
Boas, Adrian J. *Jerusalem in the Time of the Crusades: Society, Landscape and Art in the Holy City under Frankish Rule.* London and New York, 2001.

Boase 1967
Boase, Thomas S. R. *Castles and Churches of the Crusading Kingdom.* London and New York, 1967.

Boase 1977
Boase, Thomas S. R. "Ecclesiastical Art in the Crusader States in Palestine and Syria: B. Mosaic, Painting, and Minor Arts." In *A History of the Crusades,* vol. 4, *The Art and Architecture of the Crusader States,* edited by Harry W. Hazard, pp. 117–39, pls. 30–49. 2nd ed. Madison, Wisc., and London, 1977.

Boase 1978
Boase, T[homas] S. R. *The Cilician Kingdom of Armenia.* Edinburgh, 1978.

Boehm 1996
Boehm, Barbara Drake. "*Opus Lemovicense*: The Taste for and Diffusion of Limousin Enamels." In Paris and New York 1996, pp. 40–47.

Boehm 2006
Boehm, Barbara Drake. "Une croix reliquaire limousine au Musée du Berry." *La revue des musées de France: Revue du Louvre* 56, no. 4 (2006), pp. 28–37.

Boehm 2014
Boehm, Barbara Drake. "Un chapiteau des croisés de la mosquée Ali al-Bakka d'Hebron." *Bulletin de la Société Nationale des Antiquaires de France,* 2014, forthcoming.

Boehm and Holcomb 2014
Boehm, Barbara Drake, and Melanie Holcomb. "Mishneh Torah." *The Metropolitan Museum of Art Bulletin,* n.s., 72, no. 2 [*Recent Acquisitions: A Selection, 2012–2014*] (Fall 2014), p. 23.

Boertjes 2014
Boertjes, Katja. "The Reconquered Jerusalem Represented: Tradition and Renewal on Pilgrimage Ampullae from the Crusader Period." In *The Imagined and Real Jerusalem in Art and Architecture,* edited by Jeroen Goudeau, Mariëtte Verhoeven, and Wouter Weijers, pp. 169–89. Radboud Studies in Humanities, 2. Leiden and Boston, 2014.

Bolman et al. 2002
Bolman, Elizabeth S., et al. *Monastic Visions: Wall Paintings in the Monastery of St. Antony at the Red Sea.* New Haven, 2002.

Bonfil, Re., 1979
Bonfil, R[euven]. "The Vision of Daniel as an Historical and Literary Document" (in Hebrew). *Zion* 44 (1979), pp. 111–47.

Bonfil, Ro., 2009
Bonfil, Robert. *History and Folklore in a Medieval Jewish Chronicle: The Family Chronicle of Ahima'az ben Paltiel.* Studies in Jewish History and Culture, 22. Leiden and Boston, 2009.

Bongars 1611
Bongars, Jacques. *Gesta Dei per francos, sive orientalium expeditionum et regni francorum hierosolimitani historia.* Hanover, 1611.

Borg 1982
Borg, Alan. "Romanesque Sculpture from the Rhone Valley to the Jordan Valley." In *Crusader Art in the Twelfth Century,* edited by Jaroslav Folda, pp. 97–119. BAR International Series, 152. Oxford, 1982.

Van den Bossche et al. 2007
Van den Bossche, Benoît, et al. *L'art mosan: Liège et son pays à l'époque romane du XIe au XIIIe siècle.* Alleur, Liège, Belgium, 2007.

Boudot-Lamotte 1968
Boudot-Lamotte, Antoine. *Contribution à l'étude de l'archerie musulmane, principalement d'après le manuscrit d'Oxford Bodléienne Huntington N[r] 264.* Damascus, 1968.

Boyadjian forthcoming
Boyadjian, Tamar M. "Crusader Antioch: The Sister-City in the Armenian Laments of Grigor Tłay and Nersēs Šnorhali." In *East and West in the Medieval Eastern Mediterranean,* vol. 3, *Antioch from the Byzantine Reconquest until the End of the Crusader Principality.* Orientalia Lovaniensia analecta. Leiden, forthcoming.

Bréhier 1910
Bréhier, Louis. "Jacques de Vitry." In *The Catholic Encyclopedia,* edited by Charles G. Herbermann et al., vol. 8, p. 266. New York, 1910.

Brenk et al. 2010
Brenk, Beat, et al. *La Cappella Palatina a Palermo / The Cappella Palatina in Palermo.* Mirabilia Italiae, 17. Modena, 2010.

Brentjes 2011
Brentjes, Sonja. "Ayyubid Princes and Their Scholarly Clients from the Ancient Sources." In *Court Cultures in the Muslim World, Seventh–Nineteenth Centuries,* edited by Albrecht Fuess and Jan-Peter Hartung, pp. 326–56. SOAS/Routledge Studies on the Middle East, 13. London and New York, 2011.

Bresc-Bautier 1971
[Bresc-]Bautier, Geneviève. "L'envoi de la relique de la Vraie Croix à Notre-Dame de Paris en 1120." *Bibliothèque de l'École des chartes* 129, no. 2 (July–December 1971), pp. 387–97.

Briquel-Chatonnet 1997
Briquel-Chatonnet, Françoise. *Manuscrits syriaques de la Bibliothèque Nationale de France (nos. 356–435 entrés depuis 1911), de la Bibliothèque Méjanes d'Aix-en-Provence, de la Bibliothèque Municipale de Lyon et de la Bibliothèque Nationale et Universitaire de Strasbourg: Catalogue.* Paris, 1997.

Brodt 2011a
Brodt, Eliezer. "The Death and Burial of Rabbi Yehudah Halevi in the Land of Israel and the Cairo Genizah" (in Hebrew). *Yeshurun: Me'asaf Torani* 21 (2011), pp. 754–75.

Brodt 2011b
Brodt, Eliezer. "The Legend of R. Yehuda Halevi's Death: Truth or Fiction and the Cairo Genizah." In *The Seforim Blog.* [Ramat Gan, Israel], August 10, 2011; http://seforim.blogspot.com/2011/08/legend-of-r-yehuda-halevis-death-truth.html (accessed April 23, 2016).

Brosh 1986
Brosh, N[a'ama]. "Ceramic Remains. A: Pottery of the 8th–13th Centuries C.E. (Strata 1–3)." In *Excavations at Caesarea Maritima: 1975, 1976, 1979 – Final Report,* edited by Lee I. Levine and Ehud Netzer, pp. 66–89. Qedem: Monographs of the Institute of Archaeology, 21. Jerusalem, 1986.

Brosh 1987
Brosh, Na'ama. *Islamic Jewelry.* Katalog, Muze'on Yisra'el, 281. Jerusalem, 1987.

Brown and Cothren 1986
Brown, Elizabeth A. R., and Michael W. Cothren. "The Twelfth-Century Crusading Window of the Abbey of Saint-Denis: *Praeteritorum Enim Recordatio Futurorum est Exhibitio.*" *Journal of the Warburg and Courtauld Institutes* 49 (1986), pp. 1–40, pls. 1–12.

Browne 1975
Browne, Roland A. *The Holy Jerusalem Voyage of Ogier VIII, Seigneur d'Anglure.* Gainesville, Fla., 1975.

Buber, ed. 1899
Buber, Salomon, ed. *Midrash Ekhah rabah* [Lamentations] (in Hebrew). Vilna, 1899.

Buc 2015
Buc, Philippe. *Holy War, Martyrdom, and Terror: Christianity, Violence, and the West, ca. 70 C.E. to the Iraq War.* Philadelphia, 2015.

Buchthal and Wormald 1957
Buchthal, Hugo, and Francis Wormald. *Miniature Painting in the Latin Kingdom of Jerusalem.* Oxford, 1957.

al-Bukhari 2011– ed.
al-Bukhari, Muhammad. "Kitab al-Libas/Book of Dress." In *Sahih al-Bukhari,* translated by M. Muhsin Khan, in *The Hadith of the Prophet Mohammad at Your Fingertips.* 2011– ; http://sunnah.com/bukhari/77 (accessed February 18, 2016).

Burchard of Mount Sion 1896 ed.
Burchard of Mount Sion, A.D. 1280. Translated by Aubrey Stewart; annotated by C[harles R.] Conder. Palestine Pilgrims' Text Society, 12, no. 1. London, 1896.

Burgoyne 2009a
Burgoyne, Michael Hamilton. "1187–1260: The Furthest Mosque (Al-Masjid al-Aqsa) under Ayyubid Rule." In Grabar, O., and Kedar, eds. 2009, pp. 150–75.

Burgoyne 2009b
Burgoyne, Michael Hamilton. "1260–1516: The Noble Sanctuary (al-Haram al-Sharif) under Mamluk Rule – Architecture." In Grabar, O., and Kedar, eds. 2009, pp. 188–209.

Burgoyne et al. 1987
Burgoyne, Michael Hamilton, et al. *Mamluk Jerusalem: An Architectural Study.* British School of Archaeology in Jerusalem. [London], 1987.

Buschhausen 1978
Buschhausen, Helmut. *Die Süditalienische Bauplastik im Königreich Jerusalem von König Wilhelm II. bis Kaiser Friedrich II.* Vienna, 1978.

Busse 1998
Busse, Heribert. "Jerusalem in the Story of Muhammad's Night Journey and Ascension." In *The Life of Muhammad,* edited by Uri Rubin, pp. 279–318. The Formation of the Classical Islamic World, 4. Aldershot, Hampshire, 1998.

Bux 1990
Bux, Nicola. *Codici liturgici latini di Terra Santa/Liturgic Latin Codices of the Holy Land.* Studium Biblicum Franciscanum Museum, 8. Fasano, Brindisi, 1990.

Cahen 1947–48
Cahen, Claude. "Une traité d'armuerie composé pour Saladin." *Bulletin d'études orientales* 12 (1947–48), pp. 103–63.

Cahier 1874
Cahier, Charles. *Nouveaux mélanges d'archéologie, d'histoire et de littérature sur le Moyen Âge.* Vol. 2, *Ivoires, miniatures, émaux.* Paris, 1874.

Campbell 1995
Campbell, Sondra. "Millennial Messiah or Religious Restorer? Reflections on the Early Islamic Understanding of the Term *Mahdi.*" *Jusur* 11 (1995), pp. 1–11.

Canby 2012
Canby, Sheila R. "The Scented World: Incense Burners and Perfume Containers from Spain to Central Asia." *Arts of Asia* 42, no. 5 (September–October 2012), pp. 119–27.

Carboni 2001–2
Carboni, Stefano. "Painted Glass." In Corning, New York, and Athens 2001–2, pp. 198–207.

Carboni 2015
Carboni, Stefano. *The Wonders of Creation and the Singularities of Painting: A Study of the Ilkhanid London Qazvini.* Edinburgh Studies in Islamic Art. Edinburgh, 2015.

Carboni, Lacerenza, and Whitehouse 2003
Carboni, Stefano, Giancarlo Lacerenza, and David Whitehouse. "Glassmaking in Medieval Tyre: The Written Evidence." *Journal of Glass Studies* 45 (2003), pp. 139–49.

Carr 1987
Carr, Annemarie Weyl. *Byzantine Illumination, 1150–1250: The Study of a Provincial Tradition.* Text vol. and microfiche facsimile. Studies in Medieval Manuscript Illumination; Chicago Visual Library Text-Fiche, 47. Chicago, 1987.

Carr 2007
Carr, Annemarie Weyl. "Perspectives on Visual Culture in Early Lusignan Cyprus: Balancing Art and Archaeology." In *Archaeology and the Crusades: Proceedings of the Round Table, Nicosia, 1st February 2005,* edited by Peter Edbury and Sophia Kalopissi-Verti, pp. 83–110. Athens, 2007.

Carr 2009
Carr, Annemarie Weyl. "Iconography and Identity: Syrian Elements in the Art of Crusader Cyprus." *Church History and Religious Culture* 89 (2009), pp. 127–51.

Carruthers 1998
Carruthers, Mary. *The Craft of Thought: Meditation, Rhetoric, and the Making of Images, 400–1200.* Cambridge Studies in Medieval Literature, 34. New York, 1998.

Carswell 1998
Carswell, John. "The Baltimore Beakers." In Ward, ed. 1998, pp. 61–63, 182–83, color pl. L.

Casey 1951
Casey, Robert Pierce. "New Testament Manuscripts in the Pierpont Morgan Library." *The Journal of Theological Studies,* n.s., 2, no. 1 (1951), pp. 64–68.

Cerulli 1943–47
Cerulli, Enrico. *Etiopi in Palestina: Storia della comunità etiopica di Gerusalemme.* 2 vols. Rome, 1943–47.

Chazaud 1871
Chazaud, M[artial Alphonse]. "Inventaire et comptes de la Succession d'Eudes, Comte de Nevers (Acre 1266)." *Mémoires de la Société Nationale des Antiquaires de France*, ser. 4, 2 (1871), pp. 164–206.

Christie 2014
Christie, Niall. *Muslims and Crusaders: Christianity's Wars in the Middle East, 1095–1382, from the Islamic Sources.* Seminar Studies in History. London and New York, 2014.

Christie's London 1999
Islamic Art, Manuscripts and Printed Books of Iranian Interest. Sale cat., Christie's London, April 19–20, 1999, sale 6098. London, 1999.

Christie's London 2006
Important Early European Furniture, Sculpture and Tapestries, including Three Private European Collections. Sale cat., Christie's London, November 9, 2006. London, 2006.

Ciampini 1693
Ciampini, [Giovanni Giusto]. *De sacris aedificiis a Constantino Magno constructis: Synopsis historica.* Rome, 1693.

Ciganotto, ed. 1909
Ciganotto, Ludovico, ed. "Bullarium franciscanum Terrae Sanctae." *Diarium Terrae Sanctae* 2 (1909), pp. 1–140.

Ciggaar 2005
Ciggaar, Krijnie. "Painters, Paintings and Pilgrims in Medieval Jerusalem: Some Witnesses from East and West." *Eastern Christian Art* 2 (2005), pp. 127–38.

***City of Jerusalem* 1896 ed.**
The City of Jerusalem. Translated by C[harles] R. Conder. Palestine Pilgrims' Text Society, 6, no. 2. London, 1896.

Classen 2013
Classen, Albrecht. "Encounters between East and West in the Middle Ages and Early Modern Age: Many Untold Stories about Connections and Contacts, Understanding and Misunderstanding." In Classen, ed. 2013, pp. 1–222.

Classen, ed. 2013
Classen, Albrecht, ed. *East Meets West in the Middle Ages and Early Modern Times: Transcultural Experiences in the Premodern World.* Fundamentals of Medieval and Early Modern Culture, 14. Berlin and Boston, 2013.

Clermont-Ganneau 1885
Clermont-Ganneau, Ch[arles]. "Rapports sur une mission en Palestine et en Phénicie entreprise en 1881 par M. Ch. Clermont-Ganneau." In *Archives des missions scientifiques et littéraires: Choix de rapports et instructions,* ser. 3, 11 (1885), pp. 157–251.

Clermont-Ganneau 1896
Clermont-Ganneau, Charles. *Archaeological Researches in Palestine during the Years 1873–1874, with Numerous Illustrations from Drawings Made on the Spot by A. Lecomte du Noüy.* Vol. 2. Palestine Exploration Fund. London, 1896.

Cleveland, Baltimore, and London 2010–11
Treasures of Heaven: Saints, Relics, and Devotion in Medieval Europe. Exh. cat., Cleveland Museum of Art; Walters Art Museum, Baltimore; British Museum, London, 2010–11. Catalogue by Martina Bagnoli and others. Baltimore, 2010.

Cockerell et al. 1927
Cockerell, Sydney Carlyle, et al. *A Book of Old Testament Illustrations of the Middle of the Thirteenth Century Sent by Cardinal Bernard Maciejowski to Shah Abbas the Great, King of Persia, Now in the Pierpont Morgan Library at New York.* Cambridge, 1927.

Cohen, A., ed. 1965
Cohen, A., ed. *The Minor Tractates of the Talmud: Massektoth Ketannoth.* 2 vols. London, 1965.

Cohen, M., 1994
Cohen, Mark R. *Under Crescent and Cross: The Jews in the Middle Ages.* Princeton, N.J., 1994.

Cohen, M., 2005a
Cohen, Mark R. *Poverty and Charity in the Jewish Community of Medieval Egypt.* Jews, Christians, and Muslims from the Ancient to the Modern World. Princeton, N.J., 2005.

Cohen, M., 2005b
Cohen, Mark R. *The Voice of the Poor in the Middle Ages: An Anthology of Documents from the Cairo Geniza.* Princeton, N.J., 2005.

Cohen-Mushlin 1985
Cohen-Mushlin, Aliza. "Later Additions to the Worms Mahzor." In *Worms Mahzor: MS. Jewish National and University Library Heb. 4°781/1,* edited by Malachi Beit-Arié, vol. [2], pp. 94–96, and vol. [1], facsimile. 2 vols. Jerusalem and Vaduz, 1985.

Colby 2008
Colby, Frederick S[tephen]. *Narrating Muhammad's Night Journey: Tracing the Development of the Ibn 'Abbas Ascension Discourse.* Albany, N.Y., 2008.

Collin 1982
Collin, Bernadin. *Recueil de documents concernant Jerusalem et les lieux saints.* Jerusalem, 1982.

Cologne 1963–64
Monumenta Judaica: 2000 Jahre Geschichte und Kultur der Juden am Rhein. Exh. cat., Kölnischen Stadtmuseum, Cologne, 1963–64. Catalogue by Konrad Schilling and others. Cologne, 1963.

Cologne 1985
Ornamenta Ecclesiae: Kunst und Künstler der Romanik. Vol. 1, *Ordo et artes, fabrica, liturgica.* Vol. 2, *Coloniensia, ornamenta ecclesiarum.* Vol. 3, *Antike und Byzanz, sacrae reliquiae.* Exh. cat., Schnütgen-Museum, Josef-Haubrich-Kunsthalle, Cologne, 1985. Catalogue by Anton Legner and others. 3 vols. Cologne, 1985.

Combe and de Cosson 1937
Combe, Etienne, and A[nthony] F[rancis] C[harles] de Cosson. "European Swords with Arabic Inscriptions from the Armoury of Alexandria." *Bulletin de la Société Royale d'Archéologie d'Alexandrie,* n.s., 31 (1937), pp. 225–46.

Connolly 2009
Connolly, Daniel K. *The Maps of Matthew Paris: Medieval Journeys through Space, Time, and Liturgy.* Woodbridge, Suffolk, 2009.

Constable 2003
Constable, Olivia Remie. *Housing the Stranger in the Mediterranean World: Lodging, Trade, and Travel in Late Antiquity and the Middle Ages.* Cambridge and New York, 2003.

Contessa 2012
Contessa, Andreina. "Sephardic Illuminated Bibles: Jewish Patrons and Fifteenth-Century Christian Ateliers." In *The Hebrew Bible in Fifteenth-Century Spain: Exegesis, Literature, Philosophy, and the Arts,* edited by Jonathan Decter and Arturo Prats, pp. 61–72, 282–94. Études sur le judaïsme médiéval, 54. Leiden and Boston, 2012.

Corbo 1981–82
Corbo, Virgilio C. *Il Santo Sepolcro di Gerusalemme: Aspetti archeologici dalle origine al periodo crociato.* 3 vols. Collectio maior, 29. Jerusalem, 1981–82.

Cormack 2000
Cormack, Robin. "The Mother of God in Apse Mosaics." In *Mother of God: Representations of the Virgin in Byzantine Art,* edited by Maria Vassilaki, pp. 91–105. Milan, 2000.

Cormack 2007
Cormack, Robin. *Icons.* Cambridge, Mass., 2007.

Cormack and Mihalarias 1984
Cormack, Robin, and Stavros Mihalarias. "A Crusader Painting of St. George: 'Maniera greca' or 'lingua franca'?" *The Burlington Magazine* 126, no. 972 (March 1984), pp. 132–39, 141.

Cornell 2008
Cornell, Vincent J. "Theologies of Difference and Ideologies of Intolerance in Islam." In *Religious Tolerance in World Religions,* edited by Jacob Neusner and Bruce Chilton, pp. 274–96. West Conshohocken, Pa., 2008.

Corning Museum of Glass 2002–
Corning Museum of Glass. *Glass Dictionary.* Corning, N.Y., 2002– ; http://www.cmog.org/research/glass-dictionary.

Corning, New York, and Athens 2001–2
Glass of the Sultans. Exh. cat., Corning Museum of Glass; The Metropolitan Museum of Art, New York; The Benaki Museum, Athens, 2001–2. Catalogue by Stefano Carboni, David Whitehouse, and others. New York, 2001.

Cotsonis 1994
Cotsonis, John A. *Byzantine Figural Processional Crosses.* Dumbarton Oaks Byzantine Collection Publications, 10. Washington, D.C., 1994.

Crane 1890
Crane, Thomas Frederick. *The Exemplar or Illustrative Stories from the Sermones Vulgares of Jacques de Vitry.* Publications of the Folklore Society, 26. London, 1890.

Croker et al. 1853
Croker, Thomas C., et al. *Catalogue of a Collection of Ancient and Mediaeval Rings and Personal Ornaments Formed for Lady Londesborough.* London, 1853.

Crook 2000
Crook, John. *The Architectural Setting of the Cult of Saints in the Early Christian West, c. 300–1200.* Oxford Historical Monographs. Oxford and New York, 2000.

Cuffel 1999
Cuffel, Alexandra. "Call and Response: European Jewish Emigration to Egypt and Palestine in the Middle Ages." *The Jewish Quarterly Review* 90, nos. 1–2 (July–October 1999), pp. 61–101.

Cuffel 2005
Cuffel, Alexandra. "From Practice to Polemic: Shared Saints and Festivals as 'Women's Religion' in the Medieval Mediterranean." *Bulletin of the School of Oriental and African Studies, University of London* 68, no. 3 (2005), pp. 401–19.

Cusato 2008
Cusato, Michael F. "Healing the Violence of the Contemporary World: A Franciscan Paradigm for Dialogue with Islam." *Spirit and Life: A Journal of Contemporary Franciscanism* 12 [*Daring to Embrace the Other: Franciscans and Muslims in Dialogue,* edited by Daria Mitchell] (2008), pp. 1–37.

Cutler 1986–87
Cutler, Anthony. "Ephraim, Mosaicist of Bethlehem: The Evidence from Jerusalem." *Jewish Art* 12–13 (1986–87), pp. 179–83.

Cutler 2004
Cutler, Anthony. "Everywhere and Nowhere: The Invisible Muslim and Christian Self-Fashioning in the Culture of Outremer." In Weiss and Mahoney, eds. 2004, pp. 253–81.

Cyril of Scythopolis 1939 ed.
Cyril of Scythopolis. "Vita Sancti Sabae." In *Kyrillos von Skythopolis,* edited by Eduard Schwartz. Texte und Untersuchungen zur Geschichte der altchristlichen Literatur, ser. 4, 4/49, pt. 2. Leipzig, 1939.

Cyril of Scythopolis 1961 ed.
Cyril of Scythopolis. *Les moines de Palestine.* Vol. 3, *Vie des saints Jean l'Hésychaste, Kyriakos, Théodose, Théognios, Abraamios; Vie de saint Théodosios.* Translated by A[ndré] J[ean] Festugière. Les moines d'Orient, 3. Paris, 1961.

Cyril of Scythopolis 1991 ed.
Cyril of Scythopolis. *Lives of the Monks of Palestine.* Translated by R. M. Price. Cistercian Studies Series, 114. Kalamazoo, Mich., 1991.

Dajani-Shakeel 1976
Dajani-Shakeel, Hadia. "Jihad in Twelfth-Century Arabic Poetry: A Moral and Religious Force to Counter the Crusades." *The Muslim World* 66, no. 2 (April 1976), pp. 96–113.

Dajani-Shakeel 1990
Dajani-Shakeel, Hadia. "Natives and Franks in Palestine: Perceptions and Interaction." In *Conversion and Continuity: Indigenous Christian Communities in Islamic Lands, Eighth to Eighteenth Centuries,* edited by Michael Gervers and Ramzi Jibran Bikhazi, pp. 161–84. Papers in Mediaeval Studies, 9. Toronto, 1990.

Dale 1997
Dale, Thomas E. A. *Relics, Prayer, and Politics in Medieval Venetia: Romanesque Painting in the Crypt of Aquileia Cathedral.* Princeton, N.J., 1997.

Dalton 1909
Dalton, O[rmonde] M[addock]. *Catalogue of the Ivory Carvings of the Christian Era with Examples of Mohammedan Art and Carvings in Bone in the Department of British and Mediaeval Antiquities and Ethnography of the British Museum.* London, 1909.

Davidson 2004
Davidson, Herbert A. *Moses Maimonides: The Man and His Works.* New York, 2004.

Dawi and 'Abd-Allah 1999
Dawi, Salwa Jad al-Karim, and Ramadan 'Awad 'Abd-Allah. "Gold-Enameled Monumental Glass, Arts, Factors and Aspects of Damage, Maintenance, and Restoration in the Light of the Islamic Art Museum Collection" (in Arabic). *Majallat Kulliyyat al-Adab, Jami'at Hulwan* 5 (January 1999), pp. 575–606.

Dawud 1971
Dawud, Mayisa Mahmud. "Glass Lamps in the Mamluk Era" (in Arabic). Master's thesis, Cairo University, 1971.

Dawud 1991
Dawud, Mayisa Mahmud. *Arabic Inscriptions on Islamic Archaeology from First Century to Late 12th Century A.H. (7–18 A.D.)* (in Arabic). Cairo, 1991.

Dayagi-Mendeles and Rozenberg 2010
Dayagi-Mendeles, Mikhal, and Silvia Rozenberg. *Chronicles of the Land: Archaeology in the Israel Museum, Jerusalem.* Jerusalem, 2010.

Dean 1927
Dean, Bashford. "A Crusaders' Fortress in Palestine: A Report of Explorations Made by the Museum, 1926." *The Metropolitan Museum of Art Bulletin* 22, no. 9, pt. 2 (September 1927), pp. 1–47.

De Benedictis et al. 2002
De Benedictis, Cristina, et al. *La miniatura senese, 1270–1420.* Milan, 2002.

Degenhard and Schmitt 1973
Degenhard, Bernhard, and Annegrit Schmitt. "Marino Sanudo und Paolino Veneto: Zwei Literaten des 14. Jahrhunderts in ihrer Wirkung auf Buchillustrierung und Kartographie in Venedig, Avignon, and Neapal." *Römisches Jahrbuch für Kunstgeschichte* 14 (1973), pp. 1–137.

De Hond and Mols 2011
De Hond, Jan, and Luitgard Mols. "A Mamluk Basin for a Sicilian Queen." *The Rijksmuseum Bulletin* 59, no. 1 (2011), pp. 6–33.

Dekker 2013
Dekker, Elly. *Illustrating the Phaenomena: Celestial Cartography in Antiquity and the Middle Ages.* Oxford, 2013.

Derbes 1992
Derbes, Anne. "The Frescoes of Schwarzrheindorf, Arnold of Wied and the Second Crusade." In *The Second Crusade and the Cistercians,* edited by Michael Gervers, pp. 141–54. New York, 1992.

Der Nersessian 1954
Der Nersessian, Sirarpie. "An Armenian Lectionary of the Fourteenth Century." In *Studies in Art and Literature for Belle da Costa Greene,* edited by Dorothy Miner, pp. 231–37, figs. 179–85. Princeton, N.J., 1954.

Der Nersessian 1973
Der Nersessian, Sirarpie. *Armenian Manuscripts in the Walters Art Gallery.* Baltimore, 1973.

Der Nersessian 1978
Der Nersessian, Sirarpie. *Armenian Art.* 1977. Basel, 1978.

Der Nersessian 1993
Der Nersessian, Sirarpie. *Miniature Painting in the Armenian Kingdom of Cilicia from the Twelfth to the Fourteenth Century.* 2 vols. Dumbarton Oaks Studies, 31. Washington, D.C., 1993.

Der Nersessian et al. 2013
Der Nersessian, Sirarpie, et al. *A Digital Facsimile of Selections from Ms. W.538, Gospels.* Baltimore, 2013; https://issuu.com/the-walters-art-museum/docs/w538_82e4a172fe84e9 (accessed April 5, 2016).

Derolez 2005
Derolez, Albert. "*Codex Aldenburgensis,* Cotton Fragments Vol. 1, and the Origins of the *Liber Floridus.*" *Manuscripta: A Journal for Manuscript Research* 49, no. 2 (2005), pp. 139–63.

Derolez 2013
Derolez, Albert. "The Abbey of Saint-Bertin, the *Liber Floridus,* and the Origin of the *Gesta Francorum Hierusalem expugnantium.*" *Manuscripta: A Journal for Manuscript Research* 57, no. 1 (2013), pp. 1–28.

Derolez 2015
Derolez, Albert. *The Making and Meaning of the* Liber Floridus: *A Study of the Original Manuscript, Ghent, University Library, MS 92.* Turnhout, 2015.

De Sandoli 1990
De Sandoli, Sabino. *La liberazione pacifica dei Luoghi Santi nel sec. XIV: Ossia il terzo ritorno del clero franco o latino nella custodia e servizio dei Luoghi Santi mediante ufficiali trattative (1333).* Jerusalem, 1990.

Deschamps 1929
Deschamps, Paul. "Un chapiteau roman provenant de Terre-Sainte." *Bulletin des musées de France* 1, no. 11 (November 1929), pp. 243–45.

Deuchler, Hoffeld, and Nickel 1971
Deuchler, Florens, Jeffrey M. Hoffeld, and Helmut Nickel. *The Cloisters Apocalypse: An Early Fourteenth-Century Manuscript in Facsimile.* 2 vols. The Metropolitan Museum of Art. New York, 1971.

Dhannun 1989
Dhannun, Yusuf. "Thuluth Script in Sources on Islamic Art" (in Arabic). In *Islamic Art: Common Principles, Forms and Themes; Proceedings of the International Symposium Held in Istanbul in April 1983,* edited by Ahmed Mohammed Issa and Tahsin Ömer Tahaoğlu, pp. 107–27. Damascus, 1989.

Dimand 1942
Dimand, M[aurice] S. "Two Abbasid Straw Mats Made in Palestine." *The Metropolitan Museum of Art Bulletin,* n.s., 1, no. 1 (Summer 1942), pp. 76–79.

Dimand 1944
Dimand, M[aurice] S. *A Handbook of Muhammadan Art.* 2nd ed. 1930. New York, 1944.

Di Salvo 2006
Di Salvo, Mario. *Crosses of Ethiopia: The Sign of Faith; Evolution and Form.* Milan, 2006.

Dodd 2004
Dodd, Erica Cruikshank. *Medieval Paintings in the Lebanon.* Sprachen und Kulturen des christlichen Orients, 8. Wiesbaden, 2004.

Doha 2002
Metalwork Treasures from the Islamic Courts. Exh. cat., Marriott Gulf Hotel, Doha, Qatar, 2002. Catalogue by James [W.] Allan and Francis Maddison. Doha, 2002.

Dorfles et al. 1968
Dorfles, Gillo, et al. *Kitsch: The World of Bad Taste.* New York, 1968.

Dostourian 1993
Dostourian, Ara E., trans. and annot. *Armenia and the Crusades, Tenth to Twelfth Centuries: The Chronicle of Matthew of Edessa.* Lanham, 1993.

Drory 1981
Drory, Joseph. "Jerusalem during the Mamluk Period (1250–1517)." In *The Jerusalem Cathedra,* edited by Lee I. Levine, pp. 190–213. Studies in the History, Archaeology, Geography and Ethnography of the Land of Israel, 1. Jerusalem and Detroit, 1981.

Drory 2004
Drory, Joseph. "Jerusalemites in Egyptian Society during the Mamluk Period." In Pahlitzsch and Korn, eds. 2004, pp. 109–16.

Eastmond 2004
Eastmond, Antony. *Art and Identity in Thirteenth-Century Byzantium: Hagia Sophia and the Empire of Trebizond.* Birmingham Byzantine and Ottoman Monographs, 10. Aldershot, Hampshire, and Burlington, Vt., 2004.

Ecker and Fitzherbert 2012
Ecker, Heather, and Teresa Fitzherbert. "The Freer Canteen, Reconsidered." *Ars Orientalis* 42 (2012), pp. 176–93.

Eckmann, ed. 1995–98
Eckmann, János, ed. and trans. *Nehcu'l-Feradis.* 3 vols. in 2. Ankara, 1995–98.

***E-Corpus* 2011–12**
"Bréviaire syrien orthodoxe (Fenqito)." In *E-Corpus.* Arles, 2011–12; http://www.e-corpus.org/eng/notices/113801-Bréviaire-syrien-orthodoxe-Fenqito-.html (accessed April 28, 2016).

Edbury 1997
Edbury, Peter W. "The Lyon Eracles and the Old French Continuations of William of Tyre." In *Montjoie: Studies in Crusader History in Honour of Hans Eberhard Mayer,* edited by Benjamin Z. Kedar, Jonathan Riley-Smith, and Rudolph Hiestand, pp. 139–53. Aldershot, Hampshire, and Brookfield, Vt., 1997.

Edbury 2007
Edbury, Peter [W.]. "The French Translation of William of Tyre's *Historia:* The Manuscript Tradition." *Crusades* 6 (2007), pp. 69–105.

Edbury and Rowe 1988
Edbury, Peter W., and John Gordon Rowe. *William of Tyre: Historian of the Latin East.* Cambridge Studies in Medieval Life and Thought, ser. 4, 8. Cambridge, 1988.

Eddé 2011
Eddé, Anne-Marie. *Saladin.* 2008. Cambridge, Mass., 2011.

Edson 2004
Edson, Evelyn. "Reviving the Crusade: Sanudo's Schemes and Vesconte's Maps." In *Eastward Bound: Travels and Travelers, 1050–1550,* edited by Rosamund Allen, pp. 131–55. Manchester and New York, 2004.

Ehrhard 1892
Ehrhard, A. "Das Kloster zum hl. Kreuz bei Jerusalem und seine Bibliothek." *Historisches Jahrbuch* 13 (1892), pp. 158–72.

***EI2* 1960–2009**
The Encyclopaedia of Islam. Edited by H[amilton] A. R. Gibb et al. New ed. 11 vols.; supplements 1–6; glossaries; index. 1913–36. Leiden, London, and Boston, 1960–2009. Entries also available online at http://www.brill.com/publications/encyclopaedia-islam.

Elad 1999
Elad, Amikam. *Medieval Jerusalem and Islamic Worship: Holy Places, Ceremonies, Pilgrimage.* 2nd ed. Islamic History and Civilization, 8. 1995. Leiden and Boston, 1999.

Elie 2003
Elie, Paul. *The Life You Save May Be Your Own: An American Pilgrimage.* New York, 2003.

Elisséeff 1952–54
Elisséeff, Nikita. "La titulature de Nur al-Din d'après ses inscriptions." *Bulletin des études orientales* 14 (1952–54), pp. 155–96.

Elisséeff 1967
Elisséeff, Nikita. *Nur ad-Din: Un grand prince musulman de Syrie au temps des Croisades (511–569 h./1118–1174).* Damascus, 1967.

Elsner 1997
Elsner, John. "Replicating Palestine and Reversing the Reformation: Pilgrimage and Collecting at Bobbio Monza and Walsingham." *Journal of the History of Collections* 9, no. 1 (1997), pp. 117–30.

Emmerson and Lewis 1984
Emmerson, Richard K., and Suzanne Lewis. *Census and Bibliography of Medieval Manuscripts Containing Apocalypse Illustrations, ca. 800–1500.* New York, 1984.

Emmerson and McGinn, eds. 1992
Emmerson, Richard K., and Bernard McGinn, eds. *The Apocalypse in the Middle Ages.* Ithaca, 1992.

***Encyclopaedia Judaica* 2007**
Berenbaum, Michael, and Fred Skolnik, eds. *Encyclopaedia Judaica.* 2nd ed. 22 vols. 1971–72. Detroit, 2007.

Enlart 1925–28
Enlart, Camille. *Les monuments des Croisés dans le royaume de Jérusalem: Architecture religieuse et civile.* 2 vols. and atlases. Haut-commissariat de la République française en Syrie et au Liban: Service des antiquités et des beaux arts. Bibliothèque archéologique et historique, 7–8. Paris, 1925–28.

Epstein 1997
Epstein, Marc Michael. *Dreams of Subversion in Medieval Jewish Art and Literature.* University Park, Pa., 1997.

Epstein 2011
Epstein, Marc Michael. *The Medieval Haggadah. Art, Narrative, and Religious Imagination.* New Haven and London, 2011.

Erder 2003
Erder, Yorum. "The Mourners of Zion: The Karaites in Jerusalem in the Tenth and Eleventh Centuries." In Polliack, ed. 2003, pp. 213–35.

Ermete, Gleba, and Endlich 2006
Ermete, Karen, Gudrun Gleba, and Corinna Endlich. *Syrien in der Zeit Saladins: Begleitschrift zur Sonderausstellung "Saladin und die Kreuzfahrer" im Landesmuseum für Natur und Mensch vom 05.03–02.07.2006.* Oldenburg, 2006.

Ervine 1999
Ervine, Roberta. "Women Who Left the World: The Armenian Nuns of Jerusalem." In *Patterns of the Past, Prospects for the Future: The Christian Heritage in the Holy Land,* edited by Thomas Hummel, Kevork Hintlian, and Ulf Carmesund, pp. 124–34. London, 1999.

Ettinghausen 1957
Ettinghausen, Richard. "Persian Ascension Miniatures of the Fourteenth Century." In *Accademia Nazionale dei Lincei, Fondazione Alessandro Volta, Istituto dalla Società Edison di Milano: XII Convegno Volta promosso dalla classe di scienze morali, storiche e filologiche,* pp. 360–83. Rome, 1957.

Ettinghausen, Grabar, and Jenkins-Madina 2001
Ettinghausen, Richard, Oleg Grabar, and Marilyn Jenkins-Madina. *Islamic Art and Architecture, 650–1250.* 2nd ed. Pelican History of Art. 1987. New Haven and London, 2001.

Eusebius 1993– ed.
"Eusebius Pamphilius: Church History, Life of Constantine, Oration in Praise of Constantine." In *Christian Classics Ethereal Library,* edited by Harry Plantinga. Grand Rapids, Mich., 1993– ; http://www.ccel.org/ccel/schaff/npnf201.iii.vi.vii.html (accessed February 16, 2016).

Evans 1982
Evans, Helen C. "Nonclassical Sources for the Armenian Mosaic near the Damascus Gate in Jerusalem." In *East of Byzantium: Syria and Armenia in the Formative Period,* edited by Nina G. Garsoïan, Thomas F. Mathews, and Robert W. Thomson, pp. 217–22. Washington, D.C., 1982.

Evans 1990
Evans, Helen C. "Manuscript Illumination at the Armenian Patriarchate in Hromkla and the West." Ph.D. diss., Institute of Fine Arts, New York University, 1990.

Evans, Holcomb, and Hallman 2001
Evans, Helen C., Melanie Holcomb, and Robert Hallman. "The Arts of Byzantium." *The Metropolitan Museum of Art Bulletin,* n.s., 58, no. 4 (Spring 2001), pp. 1–68.

Evelyn-White, 1926–33
Evelyn-White, Hugh G. *The Monasteries of the Wadi 'n Natrûn.* 3 pts. Egyptian Expedition. Publications of the Metropolitan Museum of Art Egyptian Expedition, 2, 7, 8. New York, 1926–33.

Even-Shmuel, ed. 1954
Even-Shmuel, Yehudah, ed. *Midrashim of Redemption: An Anthology of Jewish Apocalyptic Literature from the Conclusion of the Talmud to the Thirteenth Century* (in Hebrew). Jerusalem, 1954.

Fabri 1893 ed.
The Wanderings of Felix Fabri. Translated by Aubrey Stewart. 2 vols. Palestine Pilgrims' Text Society, 7–10. London, 1893.

Farcy 1898
Farcy, L[ouis] de. "Le cor d'ivoire de la cathédrale, au Musée Archéologique d'Angers." *Revue de l'art chrétien* 47 [48] (November 1898), pp. 468–70.

Fedorov-Davydov, ed. 2001
Fedorov-Davydov, G[erman] A., ed. *The Silk Road and the Cities of the Golden Horde.* Berkeley, 2001.

Fehérvári 1976
Fehérvári, Géza. *Islamic Metalwork of the Eighth to the Fifteenth Century in the Keir Collection.* The Keir Collection. London, 1976.

Festugière, ed. 1971
Festugière, A[ndré] J[ean], ed. and trans. *Sainte Thècle, Saints Côme et Damien, saints Cyr et Jean (extraits), saint Georges.* Collection grecques de miracles. Paris, 1971.

Fiey 1966
Fiey, Jean-Maurice. "Saint 'Azziza et son village de Zérini." *Le muséon: Revue d'études orientales* 79 (1966), pp. 429–33.

Firestone 2012
Firestone, Reuven. *Holy War in Judaism: The Fall and Rise of a Controversial Idea.* New York, 2012.

Fitzherbert 2012
Fitzherbert, Teresa. "The Freer Canteen: Jerusalem or Jazira?" In *Islamic Art, Architecture and Material Culture: New Perspectives,* edited by Margaret S. Graves, pp. 1–6. BAR International Series, 2436. Oxford, 2012.

Fleisher 1998
Fleisher, Ezra. "On the Issue of Pilgrims' Prayer at the Gates of Jerusalem" (in Hebrew with English summary). In *Mas'at Moshe: Studies in Jewish and Islamic Culture Presented to Moshe Gil* (in Hebrew), edited by Ezra Fleisher, Mordechai A. Friedman, and Joel A. Kraemer, pp. 298–327. Jerusalem, 1998.

Fleming 1983
Fleming, James. "The Undiscovered Gate Beneath Jerusalem's Golden Gate." *Biblical Archaeology Review* 9, no. 1 (January–February 1983), pp. 24–37.

Flemming 1977
Flemming, B[arbara]. "Literary Activities in Mamluk Halls and Barracks." In *Studies in Memory of Gaston Wiet,* edited by Myriam Rosen-Ayalon, pp. 248–60. Jerusalem, 1977.

Flood 1992
Flood, David. "Assisi's Rules and People's Needs." *Franciscan Digest* 2, no. 2 (1992), pp. 69–89.

Florence 2015
L'arte di Francesco: Capolavori d'arte italiana e terre d'Asia dal XIII al XV secolo. Exh. cat., Galleria dell'Accademia, Florence, 2015. Catalogue by Angelo Tartuferi, Francesco D'Arelli, and others. Florence, 2015.

Flusin 2011
Flusin, Bernard. "Palestinian Hagiography (Fourth–Eighth Centuries)." In *The Ashgate Research Companion to Byzantine Hagiography,* vol. 1, *Periods and Places,* edited by Stephanos Efthymiadis, pp. 199–226. Farnham, Surrey, and Burlington, Vt., 2011.

Folda 1968
Folda, Jaroslav. "The Illustrations in Manuscripts of the *History of Outremer* by William of Tyre." 3 vols. Ph.D. diss., Johns Hopkins University, Baltimore, 1968.

Folda 1976
Folda, Jaroslav. *Crusader Manuscript Illumination at Saint-Jean d'Acre, 1275–1291.* Princeton, N.J., 1976.

Folda 1986a
Folda, Jaroslav. "Problems of the Crusader Sculptures at the Church of the Annunciation in Nazareth." In *The Meeting of Two Worlds: Cultural Exchange between East and West during the Period of the Crusades,* edited by Vladimir P. Goss and Christine Verzár Bornstein, pp. 132–44, figs. 3–7. Studies in Medieval Culture, 21. Kalamazoo, Mich., 1986.

Folda 1986b
Folda, Jaroslav. *The Nazareth Capitals and the Crusader Shrine of the Annunciation.* University Park, Pa., and London, 1986.

Folda 1993
Folda, Jaroslav. "Images of Queen Melisende in Manuscripts of William of Tyre's *History of Outremer,* 1250–1300." *Gesta* 32, no. 2 (1993), pp. 97–112.

Folda 1995
Folda, Jaroslav. *The Art of the Crusaders in the Holy Land, 1098–1187.* Cambridge, 1995.

Folda 1998
Folda, Jaroslav. "The South Transept Façade of the Church of the Holy Sepulchre in Jerusalem: An Aspect of 'Rebuilding Zion'" In France and Zajac, eds. 1998, pp. 239–57.

Folda 2005
Folda, Jaroslav. *Crusader Art in the Holy Land, from the Third Crusade to the Fall of Acre, 1187–1291.* Cambridge, 2005.

Folda 2007
Folda, Jaroslav. "Mounted Warrior Saints in Crusader Icons: Images of the Knighthoods of Christ." In *Knighthoods of Christ. Essays on the History of the Crusades and the Knights Templar, Presented to Malcolm Barber,* edited by Norman Housley, pp. 87–108. Aldershot, Hampshire, and Burlington, Vt., 2007.

Folda 2012a
Folda, Jaroslav. "Commemorating the Fall of Jerusalem: Remembering the First Crusade in Text, Liturgy, and Image." In Paul and Yeager, eds. 2012, pp. 125–45.

Folda 2012b
Folda, Jaroslav. "Melisende of Jerusalem: Queen and Patron of Art and Architecture in the Crusader Kingdom." In *Reassessing the Roles of Women as 'Makers' of Medieval Art and Architecture,* edited by Therese Martin, vol. 1, pp. 429–77, color pl. 17. 2 vols. Visualising the Middle Ages, 7. Leiden, 2012.

Folda 2015
Folda, Jaroslav, with Lucy Wrapson and Adele Wright. *Byzantine Art and Italian Panel Painting: The Virgin and Child Hodegetria and the Art of Chrysography.* Cambridge, 2015.

Ford 2001
Ford, Peter. "Europe Cringes at Bush 'Crusade' against Terrorists." *The Christian Science Monitor,* September 19, 2001; http://www.csmonitor.com/2001/0919/p12s2-woeu.html (accessed March 13, 2016).

Forsyth 1986
Forsyth, Ilene H. "The *Vita Apostolica* and Romanesque Sculpture: Some Preliminary Observations." *Gesta* 25, no. 1 (1986), pp. 75–82.

France and Zajac, eds. 1998
France, John, and William G. Zajac, eds. *The Crusades and Their Sources: Essays Presented to Bernard Hamilton.* Aldershot, Hampshire, and Brookfield, Vt., 1998.

Frank 2004
Frank, Daniel. *Search Scripture Well: Karaite Exegetes and the Origins of the Jewish Bible Commentary in the Islamic East.* Études sur le judaïsme médiéval, 29. Leiden and Boston, 2004.

Frenkel 1999
Frenkel, Yehoshu'a. "Political and Social Aspects of Islamic Religious Endowments (*awqaf*): Saladin in Cairo (1169–73) and Jerusalem (1187–93)." *Bulletin of the School of Oriental and African Studies, University of London* 62, no. 1 (1999), pp. 1–20.

Frescobaldi, Gucci, and Sigoli 1948 ed.
Frescobaldi, Leonardo, Giorgio Gucci, and Simone Sigoli. *Visit to the Holy Places of Egypt, Sinai, Palestine and Syria in 1384 by Frescobaldi, Gucci and Sigoli.* Translated by Theophilus Bellorini, Eugene Hoade, and Bellarmino Bagatti. Publications of the Studium Biblicum Franciscanum, 6. Jerusalem, 1948.

Fricke 2014
Fricke, Beate. "Tales from Stones, Travels Through Times: Narrative and Vision in the Casket from the Vatican." *West 86th: A Journal of Decorative Arts, Design History, and Material Culture* 21, no. 2 (Fall–Winter 2014), pp. 230–50.

Friedlander, ed. 1916
Friedlander, Gerald, ed. *Pirkê de Rabbi Eliezer: The Chapters of Rabbi Eliezer the Great According to the Text of the Manuscript Belonging to Abraham Epstein of Vienna.* London and New York, 1916.

Friedman 1981
Friedman, Mordechai Akiva. *Jewish Marriage in Palestine: A Cairo Geniza Study.* Vol. 2, *The Ketubba Texts.* Tel Aviv and New York, 1981.

Fritz 1982
Fritz, Johann Michael. *Goldschmiedekunst der Gotik in Mitteleuropa.* Munich, 1982.

Frojmovic 2002
Frojmovic, Eva. "Messianic Politics in Re-Christianized Spain: Images of the Sanctuary in Hebrew Bible Manuscripts." In *Imagining the Self, Imagining the Other: Visual Representation and Jewish-Christian Dynamics in the Middle Ages and Early Modern Period,* edited by Eva Frojmovic, pp. 91–128, fig. 1. Cultures, Beliefs and Traditions, 15. Leiden, Boston, and Cologne, 2002.

Frojmovic 2007
Frojmovic, Eva. "Framing: The Resisting Viewer in a Medieval Jewish Image of the Circumcision Ritual." In *Conceptual Odysseys: Passages to Cultural Analysis,* edited by Griselda Pollock, pp. 10–22. New York, 2007.

Frojmovic 2009
Frojmovic, Eva. "Early Ashkenazic Prayer Books and Their Christian Illuminators." In *Crossing Borders: Hebrew Manuscripts as a Meeting-Place of Cultures,* edited by Piet van Boxel and Sabine Arndt, pp. 45–56. Oxford, 2009.

Frojmovic 2012
Frojmovic, Eva. "Translating Jerusalem: Jewish Authenticators of the Cross." In *Jerusalem as Narrative Space/Erzählraum Jerusalem,* edited by Annette Hoffman and Gerhard Wolf, pp. 155–86. Visualising the Middle Ages, 6. Leiden and Boston, 2012.

Frojmovic 2015
Frojmovic, Eva. "Inscribing Piety in Late-Thirteenth-Century Perpignan." In *The Late Medieval Hebrew Book in the Western Mediterranean: Hebrew Manuscripts and Incunabula in Context,* edited by Javier del Barco, pp. 107–47. Études sur le judaïsme médiéval, 65. Leiden and Boston, 2015.

Frolow 1961
Frolow, A[natole]. *La relique de la Vraie Croix: Recherches sur le développement d'un culte.* Archives de l'Orient chrétien, 7. Paris, 1961.

Frolow 1965
Frolow, A[natole]. *Les reliquaires de la Vraie Croix.* Archives de l'Orient chrétien, 8. Paris, 1965.

Fulcher of Chartres 1825 ed.
Fulcher of Chartres. *Histoire des croisades.* In *Histoire des croisades par Foulcher de Chartres/Histoire de la croisade de Louis VII par Odon de Deuil.* Translated and annotated by François [Pierre Guillaume] Guizot. Collection des mémoires relatifs à l'histoire de France, [24]. Paris, 1825.

Fulcher of Chartres 1969 ed.
Fulcher of Chartres. *A History of the Expedition to Jerusalem, 1095–1127.* Translated by Frances Rita Ryan; edited by Harold S. Fink. Knoxville, Tenn., 1969.

Funk 1909
Funk, Philipp. *Jakob von Vitry: Leben und Werke.* Leipzig and Berlin, 1909.

Gaborit-Chopin 1992
Gaborit-Chopin, Danielle. "La Croix de la Roche-Foulques." *Bulletin de la Société Nationale des Antiquaires de France,* 1992, pp. 408–25.

Gaborit-Chopin et al. 2003
Gaborit-Chopin, Danielle, et al. *Ivoires médiévaux, Ve–XVe siècle.* Catalogue, Musée du Louvre, Département des Objets d'Art. Paris, 2003.

Gaborit et al. 2005
Gaborit, Jean-René, et al. *L'art roman au Louvre.* Trésors du Louvre. Paris, 2005.

Gabrieli 1962
Gabrieli, Francesco. "The Arabic Historiography of the Crusades." In *Historians of the Middle East,* edited by Bernard Lewis and P. M. Holt, pp. 98–107. Historical Writing on the Peoples of Asia. London, 1962.

Gabrieli, ed. 1956
Gabrieli, Francesco, ed. and trans. *Arab Historians of the Crusades.* Translated by E. J. Costello. London, 1956.

Gabrieli, ed. 1969
Gabrieli, Francesco, ed. and trans. *Arab Historians of the Crusades.* Translated by E. J. Costello. [2nd ed.]. 1956. London, 1969.

Gagoshidze 2001
Gagoshidze, George. "Georgian Churches Dedicated to St. Sabas the Purified." In Patrich, ed. 2001, pp. 363–84.

Galadza 2013
Galadza, Daniel. "Worship of the Holy City in Captivity: The Liturgical Byzantinization of the Orthodox Patriarchate of Jerusalem after the Arab Conquest (8th–13th c.)." Ph.D. diss., Pontifical Oriental Institute, Rome, 2013.

Galavaris 1970
Galavaris, George. *Bread and the Liturgy: The Symbolism of Early Christian and Byzantine Bread Stamps.* Madison, Wisc., 1970.

Gallant 2006
Gallant, Laurent. "Francis of Assisi: Forerunner of Inter-religious Dialogue; Chapter 16 of the Earlier Rule Revisited." *Franciscan Studies* 64 (2006), pp. 53–82.

Gaon, H., 1934 ed.
Gaon, Hai. *Otzar ha-Gaonim.* Vol. 6, *Tractate Yoma and Sukkah.* Edited by Benjamin Manasseh Lewin. Haifa, 1934.

Gaon, S., 1948 ed.
Rosenblatt, Samuel, ed. and trans. *Saadia Gaon, The Book of Beliefs and Opinions.* Yale Judaica Series, 1. New Haven, 1948.

Gaposchkin 2013a
Gaposchkin, M. Cecilia. "From Pilgrimage to Crusade: The Liturgy of Departure, 1095–1300." *Speculum* 88, no. 1 (January 2013), pp. 44–91.

Gaposchkin 2013b
Gaposchkin, M. Cecilia. "The Place of Jerusalem in Western Crusading Rites of Departure (1095–1300)." *The Catholic Historical Review* 99, no. 1 (January 2013), pp. 1–28.

Garel 1979
Garel, Michel. "The Foa Bible." *Journal of Jewish Art* 6 (1979), pp. 78–85.

Garrison, Ed., 1949
Garrison, Edward B. *Italian Romanesque Panel Painting: An Illustrated Index.* Florence, 1949.

Garrison, El., 2010
Garrison, Eliza. "A Curious Commission: The Reliquary of St. Servatius in Quedlinburg." *Gesta* 49, no. 1 (2010), pp. 17–29, pls. 1–5.

Gaudette 2010
Gaudette, Helen A. "The Spending Power of a Crusader Queen: Melisende of Jerusalem." In *Women and Wealth in Late Medieval Europe,* edited by Theresa Earenfight, pp. 135–48. New Middle Ages. New York, 2010.

Gauthier 1983
Gauthier, Marie-Madeleine. *Les routes de la foi: Reliques et reliquaires de Jérusalem à Compostelle.* Fribourg, 1983.

Gauthier 1987
Gauthier, Marie-Madeleine, with Geneviève François. *Émaux méridionaux: Catalogue international de l'oeuvre de Limoges.* Vol. 1, *L'époque romane.* Corpus des émaux méridionaux, 1. Paris, 1987.

Gayraud 2012
Gayraud, Roland-Pierre. "Ceramics in the Mamluk Empire: An Overview." In *The Arts of the Mamluks in Egypt and Syria — Evolution and Impact,* edited by Doris Behrens-Abouseif, pp. 77–94. Mamluk Studies, 1. Göttingen, 2012.

Gearhart 2010
Gearhart, Heidi C. "Theophilus' *On Diverse Arts*: The Persona of the Artist and the Production of Art in the Twelfth Century." Ph.D. diss., The University of Michigan, Ann Arbor, 2010.

Geneva 1985
Treasures of Islam. Exh. cat., Musée Rath, Geneva, 1985. Catalogue by Toby Falk and others. London, 1985.

Geneva and Paris 1993–94
Tissus d'Egypte, témoins du monde arabe, VIIIe–XVe siècles: Collection Bouvier. Exh. cat., Musée d'Art et d'Histoire, Geneva; L'Institut du Monde Arabe, Paris, 1993–94. Catalogue by Georgette Cornu. Thonon-les-Bains, 1993.

George 2012
George, Alain. "Orality, Writing and the Image in the *Maqamat*: Arabic Illustrated Books in Context." *Art History* 35, no. 1 (February 2012), pp. 10–37.

Georgopolou 2004
Georgopoulou, Maria. "The Artistic World of the Crusaders and Oriental Christians in the Twelfth and Thirteenth Centuries." *Gesta* 43, no. 2 (2004), pp. 115–28.

Gera 1991
Gera, Shulamit. "The Hebrew Inscriptions in the Golden Gate" (in Hebrew). *Cathedra: For the History of Eretz Israel and Its Yishuv* 61 (1991), pp. 176–81.

Getatchew 2008–14
Getatchew, Haile. "Ms. W.836, Ethiopian Gospels," in "Digitized Manuscripts," in *The Digital Walters.* Baltimore, 2008–14; http://www.thedigital.org/Data/Manuscripts/html/W836/description.html (accessed April 30, 2016).

Ghabin 2009
Ghabin, Ahmad. *Hisba: Arts and Craft in Islam.* Arabisch-Islamische Welt in Tradition und Moderne, 7. Wiesbaden, 2009.

al-Ghazali 2010 ed.
al-Ghazali. *Kitab sharh aja'ib al-qalb/The Marvels of the Heart: Book 21 of the Ihya ulum al-din/The Revival of the Religious Sciences.* Translated by Walter James Skellie; foreword by T. J. Winter. Louisville, Ky., 2010.

Gibson 2005
Gibson, Melanie. "Admirably Ornamented Glass." In *Glass: From Sassanian Antecedents to European Imitations,* by Sidney M. Goldstein, pp. 262–91. The Nasser D. Khalili Collection of Islamic Art, edited by Julian Raby, vol. 15. London, 2005.

Gil 1976
Gil, Moshe. *Documents of the Jewish Pious Foundations from the Cairo Geniza.* Publications of the Diaspora Research Institute, 12. Leiden, 1976.

Gil 1978
Gil, Moshe. "Immigration and Pilgrimage in the Early Arab Period (634–1099)" (in Hebrew). *Cathedra: For the History of Eretz Israel and Its Yishuv* 8 (1978), pp. 124–33.

Gil 1983
Gil, Moshe. *Palestine during the First Muslim Period (634–1099)* (in Hebrew). 3 vols. Publications of the Diaspora Research Institute, 41, 57–58. Tel Aviv, 1983.

Gil 1984
Gil, Moshe. "Dhimmi Donations and Foundations for Jerusalem (638–1099)." *Journal of the Economic and Social History of the Orient* 27, no. 2 (1984), pp. 156–74.

Gil 1992
Gil, Moshe. *A History of Palestine, 634–1099.* Cambridge and New York, 1992.

Gil 1996
Gil, Moshe. "The Jewish Community." In Prawer and Ben-Shammai, eds. 1996, pp. 163–200.

Gil'adi 1979
Gil'adi, Avner. "A Short Note on the Possible Origin of the Title Moreh Ha-Nevukhim" (in Hebrew). *Tarbiz* 48 (1979), pp. 346–47.

Giuzalian 1968
Giuzalian, L. T. "The Bronze Qalamdan (Pen-Case) 542/1148 from the Hermitage Collection (1936–1965)." *Ars Orientalis* 7 (1968), pp. 95–119.

Glatzer, M., n.d.
Glatzer, Mordechai. "Description of the Seal, the Script Style and the Spelling." In "The Seal of Tsemach Son of Asah, the Prince." Unpublished manuscript, n.d.

Glatzer, N., ed. 1989
Glatzer, Nahum N., ed. *The Passover Haggadah: Introduction and Commentary Based on the Studies of E. D. Goldschmidt.* New York, 1989.

Goitein 1967–93
Goitein, S[helomoh] D[ov]. *A Mediterranean Society: The Jewish Communities of the Arab World as Portrayed in the Documents of the Cairo Geniza.* 6 vols. Berkeley and Los Angeles, 1967–93.

Goitein 1968
Goitein, S[helomoh] D[ov]. "The Sanctity of Jerusalem and Palestine in Early Islam." In *Studies in Islamic History and Institutions,* by S[helomoh] D[ov] Goitein, pp. 135–48. 2nd ed. Leiden, 1968.

Goitein 1973
Goitein, S[helomoh] D[ov]. *Letters of Medieval Jewish Traders.* Princeton, N.J., 1973.

Goitein 1977
Goitein, Shelomo[h] Dov. "Three Trousseaux of Jewish Brides from the Fatimid Period." *Association for Jewish Studies Review* 2 (1977), pp. 77–110.

Goitein 1980
Goitein, Shelomoh Dov. "Moses Maimonides, 'A Man of Action': A Revision of the Master's Biography in Light of the Geniza Documents." In *Hommage à Georges Vajda: Études d'histoire et de pensée juives,* edited by Gérard Nahon and Charles Touati, pp. 155–67. Louvain, 1980.

Goitein and Friedman 2007
Goitein, Shelomo[h] Dov, and Mordechai Akiva Friedman. *India Traders of the Middle Ages: Documents from the Cairo Geniza.* India Book, 1. Leiden, 2007.

Golb 1965
Golb, Norman. "Obadiah the Proselyte: Scribe of a Unique Twelfth-Century Hebrew Manuscript Containing Lombardic Neumes." *The Journal of Religion* 45, no. 2 (April 1965), pp. 153–56.

Golb 2004
Golb, Norman. *The Autograph Memoirs of Obadiah the Proselyte of Oppido Lucano and the Epistle of Barukh b. Isaac of Aleppo, together with an Appendix Containing the Music of Obadiah the Proselyte.* Chicago, 2004; http://oi.uchicago.edu/sites/oi.uchicago.edu/files/uploads/shared/docs/autograph_memoirs_obadiah.pdf.

Goldberg 2012
Goldberg, Jessica L. *Trade and Institutions in the Medieval Mediterranean: The Geniza Merchants and Their Business World.* Cambridge Studies in Economic History. Cambridge, 2012.

Goldhill 2008
Goldhill, Simon. *Jerusalem: City of Longing.* Cambridge, Mass., 2008.

Goldman 2005
Goldman, Esther. "Maimonides' Illustration of the Temple in Jerusalem as a Model for Later Copies." In *Manuscripts in Transition: Recycling Manuscripts, Texts and Images; Proceedings of the International Congress Held in Brussels (5–9 November 2002),* edited by Brigitte Dekeyzer and Jan van der Stock, pp. 93–98. Corpus of Illuminated Manuscripts, 15; Corpus of Illuminated Manuscripts, Low Countries Series, 10. Paris, 2005.

Golubovich 1898
Golubovich, Girolamo. *Serie cronologica dei Reverendissimi Superiori di Terra Santa.* Jerusalem, 1898.

Gorin-Rosen 2004
Gorin-Rosen, Yael. "Glass Vessels from a Salvage Excavation at Sarafand el-Kharab, Nes Ziyyona" (in Hebrew with English summary). *'Atiqot* 46 (2004), pp. 59–64, 131*–32*.

Gousset 1974
Gousset, Marie-Thérèse. "La représentation de la Jérusalem céleste à l'époque carolingienne." *Cahiers archéologiques* 23 (1974), pp. 47–60.

Gousset 1982
Gousset, Marie-Thérèse. "Un aspect du symbolisme des encensoirs romans: La Jérusalem céleste." *Cahiers archéologiques* 30 (1982), pp. 81–106.

Grabar, A., 1957
Grabar, Andre. "Le reliquaire byzantin de la cathédrale d'Aix-la-Chapelle." In *Karolingische und ottonische Kunst: Werden, Wesen, Wirkung,* pp. 282–97. Forschungen zur Kunstgeschichte und christlichen Archäologie, 3. Wiesbaden, 1957. Reprinted in *L'art de la fin de l'Antiquité et du Moyen Âge,* edited by Andre Grabar, vol. 1, pp. 427–33. 3 vols. Paris, 1968.

Grabar, A., 1958
Grabar, André. *Ampoules de terre sainte (Monza–Bobbio).* Paris, 1958.

Grabar, O., 1963
Grabar, Oleg. "The Islamic Dome, Some Considerations." *Journal of the Society of Architectural Historians* 22, no. 4 (December 1963), pp. 191–98.

Grabar, O., 1970
Grabar, Oleg. "The Illustrated *Maqamat* of the Thirteenth Century: The Bourgeoisie and the Arts." In *The Islamic City: A Colloquium,* edited by A[lbert] H. Hourani and S[amuel] M[iklos] Stern, pp. 207–22. Oxford, 1970.

Grabar, O., 1984
Grabar, Oleg. *The Illustrations of the Maqamat.* Text vol. and microfiche facsimile. Studies in Medieval Manuscript Illumination; Chicago Visual Library Text–Fiche, 45. Chicago, 1984.

Grabar, O., 1987
Grabar, Oleg. *The Formation of Islamic Art.* Rev. ed. 1973. New Haven and London, 1987.

Grabar, O., 1990
Grabar, Oleg. "From Dome of Heaven to Pleasure Dome." *Journal of the Society of Architectural Historians* 49, no. 1 (March 1990), pp. 15–21.

Grabar, O., 2006
Grabar, Oleg. *The Dome of the Rock.* Cambridge, Mass., 2006.

Grabar, O., and Kedar, eds. 2009
Grabar, Oleg, and Benjamin Z. Kedar, eds. *Where Heaven and Earth Meet: Jerusalem's Sacred Esplanade.* Jerusalem and Austin, 2009.

Grabar, O., et al. 1996
Grabar, Oleg, et al. *The Shape of the Holy: Early Islamic Jerusalem.* Princeton, N.J., 1996.

Graf 1944–53
Graf, Georg. *Geschichte der christlichen arabischen Literatur.* 5 vols. Vatican City, 1944–53.

Granger-Taylor 1994
Granger-Taylor, Hero. *Report on the Embroidered Silk Spine of the Melisende Psalter.* British Library, Manuscripts Departmental Pamphlet 3338. London, 1994.

Gray et al. 1979
Gray, Basil, et al. *The Arts of the Book in Central Asia: 14th–16th Centuries.* Boulder, Colo., 1979.

Greenwood 2004
Greenwood, Timothy. "A Corpus of Early Medieval Armenian Inscriptions." *Dumbarton Oaks Papers* 58 (2004), pp. 27–91.

Gregg 2015
Gregg, Robert C. *Shared Stories, Rival Tellings, Early Encounters of Jews, Christians, and Muslims.* Oxford and New York, 2015.

Griffith 1992
Griffith, Sidney H[arrison]. *Arabic Christianity in the Monasteries of Ninth-Century Palestine.* Aldershot, Hampshire, and Brookfield, Vt., 1992.

Griffith 1998
Griffith, Sidney H[arrison]. "Christians, Mulsims, and Neo-Martyrs: Saints' Lives and Holy Land History." In Kofsky and Stroumsa, eds. 1998, pp. 163–207.

Griffith 2002
Griffith, Sidney H[arrison]. *The Beginnings of Christian Theology in Arabic: Muslim-Christian Encounters in the Early Islamic Period.* Aldershot, Hampshire, 2002.

Griffith 2012
Griffith, Sidney H[arrison]. "Arab Christians." In New York 2012, p. 60.

Grodecki 1976
Grodecki, Louis. *Les vitraux de Saint-Denis: Étude sur le vitrail au XIIe siècle.* Vol. 1, *Histoire et restitution.* Corpus vitrearum Medii Aevi, France, Série "Études" 1. Paris, 1976.

Grossman 1996
Grossman, Avraham. "Jerusalem in Jewish Apocalyptic Literature." In Prawer and Ben-Shammai, eds. 1996, pp. 295–310.

Grotowski 2003
Grotowski, Piotr L. "The Legend of St. George Saving a Youth from Captivity and Its Depiction in Art." *Series Byzantina* 1 (2003), pp. 27–77.

***Grove* 2009**
"Drawing." In *The Grove Encyclopedia of Islamic Art and Architecture,* edited by Jonathan M. Bloom and Sheila S. Blair, vol. 2, pp. 20–21. 3 vols. Oxford and New York, 2009.

Grube 1963
Grube, Ernst J. "Three Miniatures from Fustat in the Metropolitan Museum of Art in New York." *Ars Orientalis* 5 (1963), pp. 89–95, pls. 1–6.

Grube 1965
Grube, Ernst J. "A Bronze Bowl from Egypt." *Journal of the American Research Center in Egypt* 4 (1965), pp. 141–43, pl. 33.

Grube 1976a
Grube, Ernst J. "Fostat Fragments." In Robinson et al. 1976, pp. 23–66.

Grube 1976b
Grube, Ernst J. *Islamic Pottery of the Eighth to the Fifteenth Century in the Keir Collection.* The Keir Collection. London, 1976.

Gruber 2008
Gruber, Christiane J. *El "libro De La Ascensión" (mi'rajnama) Timúrida: Estudio de Textos e Imágenes en un Contexto Panasiático/The Timurid "Book of Ascension" (mi'rajnama): A Study of Text and Image in a Pan-Asian Context.* Valencia, 2008.

Gruber 2009
Gruber, Christiane [J.]. "Between Logos (*Kalima*) and Light (*Nur*): Representations of the Prophet Muhammad in Islamic Painting." *Muqarnas* 26 (2009), pp. 229–62.

Gruber 2010
Gruber, Christiane J. *The Ilkhanid Book of Ascension: A Persian-Sunni Devotional Tale.* London, 2010.

Gruber and Colby, eds. 2010
Gruber, Christiane [J.], and Frederick Colby, eds. *The Prophet's Ascension: Cross-Cultural Encounters with the Islamic Mi'raj Tales.* Bloomington and Indianapolis, 2010.

Guibert of Nogent 1997 ed.
Guibert of Nogent. "4. Version of Guibert de Nogent." In "Urban II (1088–1099): Speech at Council of Clermont, 1095, Five Versions of the Speech," in *Internet Medieval Sourcebook,* edited by Paul Halsall, in *Fordham University Center for Medieval Studies.* Bronx, N.Y., 1997; http://www.fordham.edu/halsall/source/urban2-5vers.html (accessed March 31, 2016).

Guidi 1888
Guidi, Ignazio. *Le traduzioni degli evangeli in arabo e in etiopico.* Atti della R. Accademia dei Lincei, Classe di scienze, morali, storiche e filologiche, memorie, ser. 4, no. 4. Rome, 1888.

Guthrie 1994
Guthrie, Shirley. *Arab Social Life in the Middle Ages: An Illustrated Study.* London, 1994.

Gutmann 1967–68
Gutmann, Joseph. "When the Kingdom Comes: Messianic Themes in Medieval Jewish Art." *Art Journal* 27, no. 2 (Winter 1967–68), pp. 168–75.

Gutmann 1976
Gutmann, Joseph. "The Messianic Temple in Spanish Medieval Hebrew Manuscripts." In *The Temple of Solomon: Archaeological Fact and Medieval Tradition in Christian, Islamic, and Jewish Art,* edited by Joseph Gutmann, pp. 125–45. Religion and the Arts, 3. Missoula, Mont., 1976.

Gutmann 1978
Gutmann, Joseph. *Hebrew Manuscript Painting.* New York, 1978.

Haarmann 1984
Haarmann, Ulrich. "The Library of a Fourteenth Century Jerusalem Scholar." *Der Islam: Zeitschrift für Geschichte und Kultur des islamischen Orients* 61 (1984), pp. 327–33.

Haddon 2012
Haddon, Rosalind A. Wade. "Mongol Influences on Mamluk Ceramics in the Fourteenth Century." In *The Arts of the Mamluks in Egypt and Syria — Evolution and Impact,* edited by Doris Behrens-Abouseif, pp. 95–113. Mamluk Studies, 1. Göttingen, 2012.

Hahn 1990
Hahn, Cynthia. "Loca Sancta Souvenirs: Sealing the Pilgrim's Experience." In *The Blessings of Pilgrimage,* edited by Robert Ousterhout, pp. 85–96. Illinois Byzantine Studies, 1. Urbana, Ill., 1990.

Hahn 2012
Hahn, Cynthia. "A Case Study: Wibald of Stavelot as Patron." In *Strange Beauty: Issues in the Making and Meaning of Reliquaries, 400–circa 1204,* by Cynthia Hahn, pp. 209–21. University Park, Pa., 2012.

Haifa 1999
The Richness of Islamic Caesarea (in English, Hebrew, and Arabic). Exh. cat., Reuben and Edith Hecht Museum, University of Haifa, 1999. Catalogue by Avner Raban and others. Haifa, 1999.

Haldon 1999
Haldon, John. *Warfare, State and Society in the Byzantine World, 565–1204.* London, 1999.

ha-Levi 1964 ed.
ha-Levi, Judah. *The Kuzari/Kitab al Khazari: An Argument for the Faith of Israel.* Introduction by Henry Slonimsky; translated by Hartwig Hirschfeld. New York, 1964.

Halperin 2013
Halperin, Dalia-Ruth. *Illuminating in Micrography: The Catalan Micrography Mahzor — MS Heb 8°6527 in the National Library of Israel.* Leiden and Boston, 2013.

Hamilton, B., 1978
Hamilton, Bernard. "Women in the Crusader States: The Queens of Jerusalem, 1100–1190." In *Medieval Women,* edited by Derek Baker, pp. 143–74. Oxford, 1978.

Hamilton, B., 1980
Hamilton, Bernard. *The Latin Church in the Crusader States: The Secular Church.* London, 1980.

Hamilton, B., 2000
Hamilton, Bernard. "Our Lady of Saidnaiya: An Orthodox Shrine Revered by Muslims and Knights Templar at the Time of the Crusades." In *The Holy Land, Holy Lands, and Christian History: Papers Read at the 1998 Summer Meeting and the 1999 Winter Meeting of the Ecclesiastical History Society,* edited by R. N. Swanson, pp. 207–15. Studies in Church History, 36. Woodbridge, England, 2000.

Hamilton, L., 2010
Hamilton, Louis I. *A Sacred City: Consecrating Churches and Reforming Society in Eleventh-Century Italy.* Manchester and New York, 2010.

Hamilton, R., 1947
Hamilton, R. W. *The Church of the Nativity, Bethlehem: A Guide.* 2nd ed. Palestine Department of Antiquities. 1939. Jerusalem, 1947.

Hanan 2013
Hanan, Melanie. "Romanesque Casket Reliquaries: Forms, Meanings, and Development." Ph.D. diss., Institute of Fine Arts, New York University, 2013.

Handyside 2015
Handyside, Philip. *The Old French William of Tyre.* Leiden, 2015.

Hansmann and Hohmann 2002
Hansmann, Wilfried, and Jürgen Hohmann. *Die Gewölbe und Wandmalereien in der Kirche zu Schwarzrheindorf: Konservierung – Restaurierung – Neue Erkenntnisse.* Arbeitsheft der Rheinischen Denkmalpflege, 55; Veröffentlichung des Landschaftsverbandes Rheinland. Worms, 2002.

al-Harithy 2000
al-Harithy, Howayda. "The Patronage of al-Nasir Muhammad ibn Qalawun, 1310–1341." *Mamluk Studies Review* 4 (2000), pp. 219–44.

al-Harizi 1952 ed.
al-Harizi, Judah. *Sefer Tahkemoni* (in Hebrew). Edited by Y. Toporovski and Israel Zmora. Tel Aviv, 1952.

al-Harizi 1965–73 ed.
al-Harizi, Judah. *The Tahkemoni of Judah al-Harizi.* Translated by Victor Emanuel Reichert. 2 vols. Jerusalem, 1965–73.

al-Harizi 2001 ed.
al-Harizi, Judah. *The Book of Tahkemoni: Jewish Tales from Medieval Spain.* Translated and annotated by David Simha Segal. Littman Library of Jewish Civilization. Portland, 2001.

Harvey, P., 2012
Harvey, P[aul] D. A. *Medieval Maps of the Holy Land.* British Library. London, 2012.

Harvey, W., 1922
Harvey, William. "Colour in Architecture." *Royal Institute of British Architects Journal* 29, no. 16 (June 1922), pp. 485–501.

Hasluck 1929
Hasluck, F[rederick] W[illiam]. *Christianity and Islam under the Sultans.* 2 vols. Oxford, 1929.

Hasson 1981
Hasson, Isaac. "Muslim Literature in Praise of Jerusalem: Fada'il bayt al-Maqdis." In *The Jerusalem Cathedra,* edited by Lee I. Levine, pp. 168–84. Studies in the History, Archaeology, Geography and Ethnography of the Land of Israel, 1. Jerusalem and Detroit, 1981.

Hasson 1996
Hasson, I[saac]. "The Muslim View of Jerusalem: The Qur'an and Hadith." In Prawer and Ben-Shammai, eds. 1996, pp. 349–85.

Helmecke 2009
Helmecke, Gisela. "Textiles for the Interiors: Some Remarks on Curtains in the Written Sources." In *Clothing the House: Furnishing Textiles of the 1st Millennium A.D. from Egypt and Neighbouring Countries; Proceedings of the 5th Conference of the Research Group "Textiles from the Nile Valley," Antwerp, 6–7 October 2007,* edited by Antoine de Moor, Cäcilia Fluck, and Susanne Martinssen-von Falck, pp. 48–53. Tielt, 2009.

Henderson 2002
Henderson, Julian. "Tradition and Experiment in First Millennium A.D. Glass Production: The Emergence of Early Islamic Glass Technology in Late Antiquity." *Accounts of Chemical Research* 35, no. 8 (August 2002), pp. 594–602.

Hennigan 2004
Hennigan, Peter C. *The Birth of a Legal Institution: The Formation of the Waqf in Third-Century A.H. Hanafi Legal Discourse.* Studies in Islamic Law and Society, 18. Leiden and Boston, 2004.

Henschel-Simon 1946
Henschel-Simon, E. "Note on a Romanesque Relief from Jerusalem." *The Quarterly of the Department of Antiquities in Palestine* 12 (1946), pp. 75–76, pl. 24.

Herzfeld, E., 1948
Herzfeld, Ernst. "Damascus: Studies in Architecture – IV." *Ars islamica* 13–14 (1948), pp. 118–38, figs. 15–38.

Herzfeld, M., 2014
Herzfeld, Michael. "Po-Mo-Med." In *A Companion to Mediterranean History,* edited by Peregrine Horden and Sharon Kinoshita, pp. 122–35. Chichester, West Sussex, 2014.

Hildesheim 2008
Bild und Bestie: Hildesheimer Bronzen der Stauferzeit. Exh. cat., Dom-Museums Hildesheim, 2008. Catalogue by Michael Brandt. Regensburg, 2008.

Hillenbrand, C., 1994
Hillenbrand, Carole. "Jihad Propaganda in Syria from the Time of the First Crusade Until the Death of Zengi: The Evidence of Monumental Inscriptions." In *The Frankish Wars and Their Influence on Palestine: Selected Papers Presented at Birzeit University's International Academic Conference Held in Jerusalem, March 13–15, 1992,* edited by Khalil Athaminah and Roger Heacock, pp. 60–69. Birzeit, 1994.

Hillenbrand, C., 1999
Hillenbrand, Carole. *The Crusades: Islamic Perspectives.* New York, 1999.

Hillenbrand, R., 2009
Hillenbrand, Robert. "The Art of the Ayyubids: An Overview." In Hillenbrand, R., and Auld, eds. 2009, pp. 22–44.

Hillenbrand, R., and Auld, eds. 2009
Hillenbrand, Robert, and Sylvia Auld, eds. *Ayyubid Jerusalem: The Holy City in Context, 1187–1250.* London, 2009.

Himmelfarb 1983
Himmelfarb, Martha. *Tours of Hell: An Apocalyptic Form in Jewish and Christian Literature.* 1981. Philadelphia, 1983.

Himmelfarb, trans. 1990
Himmelfarb, Martha, trans. "Sefer Zerubbabel." In *Rabbinic Fantasies: Imaginative Narratives from Classical Hebrew Literature,* edited by David Stern and Mark Jay Mirsky, pp. 67–90. Philadelphia and New York, 1990.

Hintlian 1976
Hintlian, Kevork. *History of the Armenians in the Holy Land.* Jerusalem, 1976.

Hirschfeld 1992
Hirschfeld, Yizhar. *The Judean Desert Monasteries in the Byzantine Period.* New Haven and London, 1992.

Hirschfeld et al. 2008
Hirschfeld, Yizhar, et al. *Tiberias: Excavations in the House of the Bronzes; Final Report.* Vol. 1, *Architecture, Stratigraphy and Small Finds.* Qedem: Monographs of the Institute of Archaeology, 48. Jerusalem, 2008.

Hoade 1952
Hoade, Eugene. *Western Pilgrims: The Itineraries of Fr. Simon Fitzsimons O.F.M. (1322–23), a Certain Englishman (1344–45), Thomas Brygg (1392), and Notes on Other Authors and Pilgrims.* Jerusalem, 1952.

Hoag 1977
Hoag, John D. *Islamic Architecture.* New York, 1977.

Hoffman, A., and Cole 2011
Hoffman, Adina, and Peter Cole. *Sacred Trash: The Lost and Found World of the Cairo Geniza.* New York, 2011.

Hoffman, E., 1982
Hoffman, Eva R. "The Emergence of Illustration in Arabic Manuscripts: Classical Legacy and Islamic Transformation." Ph.D. diss., Harvard University, Cambridge, Mass., 1982.

Hoffman, E., 1999
Hoffman, Eva R. "A Fatimid Book Cover: Framing and Re-framing Cultural Identity in the Medieval Mediterranean World." In *L'Égypte Fatimide son art et son histoire: Actes du colloque organisé à Paris les 28, 29 et 30 mai 1998,* edited by Marianne Barrucand, pp. 403–19. Paris, 1999.

Hoffman, E., 2000
Hoffman, Eva R. "The Beginnings of the Illustrated Arabic Book: An Intersection between Art and Scholarship." *Muqarnas* 17 (2000), pp. 37–52.

Hoffman, E., 2004
Hoffman, Eva R. "Christian-Islamic Encounters on Thirteenth-Century Ayyubid Metalwork: Local Culture, Authenticity, and Memory." *Gesta* 43, no. 2 (2004), pp. 129–42.

Holtz, ed. 1971
Holtz, Avraham, ed. *The Holy City: Jews on Jerusalem.* New York, 1971.

Horn 1962 ed.
Horn, Elzear. *Ichnographiae monumentorum Terrae Sanctae, 1724–1744.* Translation by Eugene Hoade, annotated by Bellarmino Bagatti. 2nd ed. Publications of the Studium Biblicum Franciscanum, 15. Jerusalem, 1962.

Houston 2015–17
Arts of Islamic Lands: Selections from The al-Sabah Collection, Kuwait. Exh. cat., Museum of Fine Arts, Houston, 2015–17. Catalogue by Giovanni Curatola and Salam Kaoukji, with Aimée Froom. Houston, 2015.

Hume 2014
Hume, David L. *Tourism Art and Souvenirs: The Material Culture of Tourism.* Routledge Advances in Tourism, 32. New York, 2014.

Hunsberger 2000
Hunsberger, Alice C. *Nasir Khusraw, the Ruby of Badakhshan: A Portrait of the Persian Poet, Traveller and Philosopher.* Ismaili Heritage Series, 4. London and New York, 2000.

Hunt 1985
Hunt, Lucy-Anne. "Christian-Muslim Relations in Painting in Egypt of the Twelfth to Mid-Thirteenth Centuries: Sources of Wallpainting at Deir es-Suriani and the Illustration of the New Testament MS Paris, Copt-Arabe 1/Cairo, Bibl. 94." *Cahiers archéologique* 33 (1985), pp. 111–55.

Hunt 1991
Hunt, Lucy-Anne. "Art and Colonialism: The Mosaics of the Church of the Nativity in Bethlehem (1169) and the Problem of 'Crusader' Art." *Dumbarton Oaks Papers* 45 (1991), pp. 69–85.

Hunt 1995
Hunt, Lucy-Anne. "Artistic and Cultural Inter-Relations between the Christian Communities at the Holy Sepulchre in the 12th Century." In *The Christian Heritage in the Holy Land,* edited by Anthony O'Mahoney with Göran Gunner and Kevork Hintlian, pp. 57–96. London, 1995.

Hunt 2005–6
Hunt, Lucy-Anne. "Orientalische Christen: Kunst und Kultur zur Zeit der Kreuzfahrer." In Oldenburg 2005–6, pp. 191–203.

Husband 2009
Husband, Timothy. "The Asseburg-Hedwig Glass Re-emerges." In *The Four Modes of Seeing: Approaches to Medieval Imagery in Honor of Madeline Harrison Caviness,* edited by Evelyn Staudinger Lane, Elizabeth Carson Pastan, and Ellen M. Shortell, pp. 44–62. Burlington, Vt., 2009.

Ibn al-Firkah 2000 ed.
Ibn al-Firkah. "The Book of Arousing Souls to Visit the Divinely Guarded Jerusalem" (in Arabic). In *Arba' rasa'il f fada'il al-Masjid al-Aqsa,* edited by Muhammad Zaynahum, pp. 99–103. Cairo, 2000.

Ibn al-Murajja' al-Maqdisi 1995 ed.
Ibn al-Murajja' al-Maqdisi, Abu al-Ma'ali al-Musharraf. *Fada'il bayt al-Maqdis* [The Merits of Jerusalem]: *Edited Text of Tübingen MS Ma VI 27* (in Arabic with introduction in English). Edited and introduced by Ofer Livne-Kafri. Shfaram, 1995.

Ibn al-Murajja' al-Maqdisi 2002 ed.
Ibn al-Murajja' al-Maqdisi, Abu al-Ma'ali al-Musharraf. *Fada'il bayt al-Maqdis* [The Merits of Jerusalem] (in Arabic). Edited by Aiman Nasr-ad-Din al-Azhari. Beirut, 2002.

Ibn al-Qalanisi 1932 ed.
Ibn al-Qalanisi. *The Damascus Chronicle of the Crusades, Extracted and Translated from the Chronicle of Ibn al-Qalanisi.* Edited and translated by H[amilton] A. R. Gibb. University of London Historical Series, 5. London, 1932.

Ibn al-Zubayr 1959 ed.
Ibn al-Zubayr, Ahmad ibn al-Rashid. *Kitab al-Dhakha'ir Wa al-Tuhaf* (Book of Treasures and Gifts). Edited by Muhammad Hamid Allah. Turath al-'Arabi, 1. Kuwait, 1959.

Ibn Battuta 1958 ed.
Ibn Battuta. *The Travels of Ibn Battuta, A.D. 1325–1354.* Vol. 1. Translated and edited by H[amilton] A. R. Gibb. Works Issued by the Hakluyt Society, Second series, 110. London, 1958.

Ibn Jubayr 1952 ed.
Ibn Jubayr, Muhammad ibn Ahmad. *The Travels of Ibn Jubayr, Being the Chronicle of a Mediaeval Spanish Moor Concerning His Journey to the Egypt of Saladin, the Holy Cities of Arabia, Baghdad the City of the Caliphs, the Latin Kingdom of Jerusalem, and the Norman Kingdom of Sicily.* Translated by R. J. C. Broadhurst. London, [1952].

Ibn Majah 2011– ed.
Ibn Majah al-Qazvini, Muhammad bin Yazid. "Establishing the Prayer and the Sunnah Regarding Them." In *Sunan Ibn Majah,* in *The Hadith of the Prophet Mohammad at Your Fingertips;* http://sunnah.com/urn/1282900 (accessed June 21, 2016).

Idal 1991
Idal, Moshe. "Jerusalem in Thirteenth Century Jewish Thought" (in Hebrew). In *The History of Jerusalem: Crusaders and Ayyubids, 1099–1250* (in Hebrew), edited by Joshua Prawer and Haggai Ben-Shammai, pp. 264–86. Jerusalem, 1991.

Imad al-Din 1888 ed.
Imad al-Din. *Kitab al-Fath al-qussi fi 'l-fath al-Qudsi/Conquête de la Syrie et de la Palestine par Salah ed-din* (in Arabic). Edited by Carlo Landberg. Leiden, 1888.

Immerzeel 2004
Immerzeel, Mat. "Holy Horsemen and Crusader Banners: Equestrian Saints in Wall Paintings in Lebanon and Syria." *Eastern Christian Art* 1 (2004), pp. 29–60.

Immerzeel 2009
Immerzeel, Mat. *Identity Puzzles: Medieval Christian Art in Syria and Lebanon.* Orientalia Lovaniensia analecta, 184. Leuven and Walpole, Mass., 2009.

***Independent* 2001**
"Blair Warns Taliban of Military Strikes." *Independent,* October 2, 2001.

Innemée 1992
Innemée, Karel C. *Ecclesiastical Dress in the Medieval Near East.* Studies in Textile and Costume History, 1. Leiden and New York, 1992.

Irico, ed. 1748
Irico, Joannis Andreae, ed. *Sacrosanctus Evangeliorum Codex S. Eusebii Magni . . . Basilicae Vercellensis . . .* 2 vols. Mediolani, 1748.

Irwin 1998
Irwin, Robert. "Usamah ibn Munqidh: An Arab-Syrian Gentleman at the Time of the Crusades Reconsidered." In France and Zajac, eds. 1998, pp. 71–87.

Irwin 2003
Irwin, Robert. "Mamluk Literature." *Mamluk Studies Review* 7, no. 1 (2003), pp. 1–29.

Isaac 1984–86
Isaac, Ephraim. "Shelf List of Ethiopian Manuscripts in the Monasteries of the Ethiopian Patriarchate of Jerusalem." *Rassegna di studi etiopici* 30 (1984–86), pp. 53–80.

Ismaīl et al., eds. 1995
Ismail, Mourad, et al., eds. *Mathematical Analysis, Wavelets, and Signal Processing: An International Conference on Mathematical Analysis and Signal Processing, January 3–9, 1994, Cairo University, Cairo, Egypt.* Contemporary Mathematics, 190. Providence, R.I., 1995.

'Izzi 1972
'Izzi, Wafiyya. "Objects Bearing the Name of An-Nasir Muhammad and His Successors." In *Colloque international sur l'histoire du Caire, 27 mars–5 avril 1969,* pp. 234–41. Cairo, 1972.

Jacobs, J., and Wolf 1906
Jacobs, Joseph, and Albert Wolf. "Seal." In *The Jewish Encyclopedia,* edited by Joseph Jacobs, vol. 11, pp. 134–40. 12 vols. New York and London, 1906.

Jacobs, M., 2014
Jacobs, Martin. *Reorienting the East: Jewish Travelers to the Medieval Muslim World.* Philadelphia, 2014.

Jacoby, D., 1986
Jacoby, David. "Knightly Values and Class Consciousness in the Crusader States of the Eastern Mediterranean." *Mediterranean Historical Review* 1, no. 2 (1986), pp. 158–86.

Jacoby, D., 2001
Jacoby, David. "Pilgrimage in Crusader Acre: The *Pardouns dAcre.*" In *De Sion exibit lex et verbum domini de Hierusalem: Essays on Medieval Law, Liturgy and Literature in Honour of Amnon Linder,* edited by Yitzhak Hen, pp. 105–17. Cultural Encounters in Late Antiquity and the Middle Ages, 1. Turnhout, 2001.

Jacoby, D., 2004
Jacoby, David. "Society, Culture and the Arts in Crusader Acre." In Weiss and Mahoney, eds. 2004, pp. 97–137.

Jacoby, Z., 1979
Jacoby, Zehava. "The Tomb of Baldwin V, King of Jerusalem (1185–1186) and the Workshop of the Temple Area." *Gesta* 18, no. 2 (1979), pp. 3–14.

Jacoby, Z., 1982
Jacoby, Zehava. "The Workshop of the Temple Area in Jerusalem in the Twelfth Century: Its Origin, Evolution and Impact." *Zeitschrift für Kunstgeschichte* 45, no. 4 (1982), pp. 325–94.

Jacques de Vitry 1825 ed.
Jacques de Vitry. *Histoire des croisades.* Translated and annotated by F[rançois Pierre Guillaume] Guizot. Collection des mémoires relatifs à l'histoire de France, [22]. Paris, 1825.

Jacques de Vitry 1896 ed.
The History of Jerusalem, A.D. 1180, by Jacques de Vitry. Translated by Aubrey Stewart. Palestine Pilgrims' Text Society, 11, no. 2. London, 1896.

Jacques de Vitry 1960 ed.
Jacques de Vitry. *Lettres de Jacques de Vitry, 1160/1170–1240, évêque de Saint-Jean d'Acre.* Edited by R. B. C. Huygens; translated by Iris Rau. Leiden, 1960.

Jacques de Vitry 2001 ed.
Jacques de Vitry. "A Letter of Jacques de Vitry." Translated by G. A. Loud and Iris Rau. In *Leeds Medieval History Texts in Translation.* Leeds, 2001; http://www.leeds.ac.uk/arts/download/1147/a_letter_of_jacques_de-vitry_1121617.

Jakeman 1993
Jakeman, Jane. "Abstract Art and Communication in 'Mamluk' Architecture." Ph.D. diss., Oxford University, 1993.

James 1984
James, David [Lewis]. "Some Observations on the Calligrapher and Illuminators of the Koran of Rukn al-Din Baybars al-Jashnagir." *Muqarnas* 2 [*The Art of the Mamluks,* edited by Oleg Grabar] (1984), pp. 147–57.

James 1988
James, David Lewis. *Qur'ans of the Mamluks.* London, 1988.

James 1992
James, David [Lewis]. *The Master Scribes: Qur'ans of the 10th to 14th Centuries A.D.* The Nasser D. Khalili Collection of Islamic Art, edited by Julian Raby, vol. 2. London, 1992.

James 1999
James, David [Lewis]. *Manuscripts of the Holy Qur'an from the Mamluk Era.* 1988. [Riyadh], 1999.

James 2007
James, D[avid] L[ewis]. "More Qur'ans of the Mamluks." *Manuscripta Orientalia: International Journal for Oriental Manuscript Research* 13, no. 2 (June 2007), pp. 3–16.

Janin, H., 2002
Janin, Hunt. *Four Paths to Jerusalem: Jewish, Christian, Muslim, and Secular Pilgrimages, 1000 B.C.E. to 2001 C.E.* Jefferson, N.C., 2002.

Janin, R., 1913
Janin, R[ené]. "Les Géorgiens à Jérusalem." *Echos d'Orient* 16, no. 98 (1913), pp. 32–38.

Jarrar 1998
Jarrar, Sabri. "Suq al-Ma'rifa: An Ayyubid Hanbalite Shrine in al-Haram al-Sharif." *Muqarnas* 15 (1998), pp. 71–100.

Jaspert 2014
Jaspert, Nikolas. "The True Cross of Jerusalem in the Latin West: Mediterranean Connections and Institutional Agency." In Kühnel, B., Noga-Banai, and Vorholt, eds. 2014, pp. 207–21.

Jean of Tournai 2012 ed.
Jean of Tournai. *Le voyage de Jean de Tournai.* Edited, translated, and annotated by Fanny Blanchet-Broekaert and Denise Péricard-Méa. Cahors, 2012.

Jenkins 1986
Jenkins, Marilyn. "Islamic Glass: A Brief History." *The Metropolitan Museum of Art Bulletin,* n.s., 44, no. 2 (Fall 1986), pp. 1–56.

Jenkins 1988a
Jenkins, Marilyn. "Mamluk Jewelry: Influences and Echoes." *Muqarnas* 5 (1988), pp. 29–42.

Jenkins 1988b
Jenkins, Marilyn. "*Sa'd*: Content and Context." In *Content and Context of Visual Arts in the Islamic World: Papers from a Colloquium in Memory of Richard Ettinghausen, Institute of Fine Arts, New York University, 2–4 April 1980,* [edited] by Carol Manson Bier, pp. 67–89. New York, 1988.

Jenkins et al. 1983
Jenkins, Marilyn, et al. *Islamic Art in the Kuwait National Museum: The al-Sabah Collection.* London, 1983.

Jenkins-Madina 2006
Jenkins-Madina, Marilyn. *Raqqa Revisited: Ceramics of Ayyubid Syria.* New York, 2006.

Jerusalem 1985
Selected Manuscripts and Prints: An Exhibition from the Treasures of the Jewish National and University Library. Exh. cat., The Jewish National and University Library, Jerusalem, 1985. Catalogue by Mordekhai Nadav, Rafael Weiser, and others. Jerusalem, 1985.

Jerusalem 1987
Early Islamic Jewellery. Exh. cat., L. A. Mayer Museum for Islamic Art, Jerusalem. Catalogue by Rachel Hasson. Jerusalem, 1987.

Jerusalem 1995
The Art of Islamic Calligraphy (in Hebrew with English pamphlet). Exh. cat., L. A. Mayer Museum for Islamic Art, Jerusalem. Catalogue by Rachel Hasson. Jerusalem, 1995.

Jerusalem 1999
Knights of the Holy Land: The Crusader Kingdom of Jerusalem. Exh. cat., Weisbord Exhibition Pavilion, The Israel Museum, Jerusalem, 1999. Catalogue by Silvia Rozenberg and others. Jerusalem, 1999.

Jerusalem 2000
Treasures Revealed from the Collections of the Jewish National and University Library in Honor of the 75th Anniversary of the Hebrew University of Jerusalem, 1925–2000. Exh. cat., The Jewish National and University Library, Jerusalem, 2000. Catalogue by Rafael Weiser and Rivka Plesser. Jerusalem, 2000.

Jerusalem 2000–2001
Daughter of Zion: Orthodox Christian Art from Ethiopia. Exh. cat., The Israel Museum, Jerusalem, 2000–2001. Catalogue by Miloš Simović. Jerusalem, 2000.

Jerusalem Talmud 2000 ed.
Guggenheimer, Heinrich W., ed. and trans. *The Jerusalem Talmud: First Order; Zeraïm and Tractate Berakhot* (in Hebrew and English). Berlin and New York, 2000.

Jones 2007
Jones, Lynn. *Between Islam and Byzantium: Aght'amar and the Visual Construction of Medieval Armenian Rulership.* Aldershot, Hampshire, and Burlington, Vt., 2007.

Jotischky 1995
Jotischky, Andrew. *The Perfection of Solitude: Hermits and Monks in the Crusader States.* University Park, Pa., 1995.

Jotischky 2001
Jotischky, Andrew. "Greek Orthodox and Latin Monasticism around Mar Saba under Crusader Rule." In Patrich, ed. 2001, pp. 85–96.

Jotischky 2013
Jotischky, Andrew. "Pilgrimage, Procession and Ritual Encounters between Christians and Muslims in the Crusader States." In *Cultural Encounters during the Crusades,* edited by Kurt Villads Jensen, Kirsi Salonen, and Helle Vogt, pp. 245–62. University of Southern Denmark Studies in History and Social Sciences, 445. Odense, 2013.

al-Jubeh 1991
al-Jubeh, Nazmi. "Hebron (al-Halil): Kontinuität und Integrationskraft einer islamisch-arabischen Stadt." Ph.D. diss., Eberhard-Karls-Universität, Tübingen, 1991.

al-Jubeh 2015
al-Jubeh, Nazmi. "Column Capital." In *Discover Islamic Art, Museum with No Frontiers.* Vienna, 2015; http://www.discoverislamicart.org/database_item.php?idobject;ISL;pa;Mus01;15;en (accessed April 30, 2016).

al-Jubeh 2016
al-Jubeh, Nazmi. "Pieces from the Nur al-Din Zangi *Minbar.*" In *Discover Islamic Art, Museum with No Frontiers.* Vienna, 2016; http://www.discoverislamicart.org/database_item.php?idobject;ISL;pa;Mus01;16;en (accessed April 30, 2016).

Kaentzeler 1858
Kaentzeler, P. St. "Ein griechischer Reliquienbehälter im Aachener Münster." *Zeitschrift für christliche Archäologie und Kunst* 2 (1858), pp. 130–33.

Kalus 1982/1990
Kalus, Ludvik. "Donations pieuses d'epées médiévales à l'arsenal d'Alexandrie." *Revue des études Islamiques* 50 (1982 [published 1990]), pp. 1–174.

Kalus and Naffah 1983
Kalus, Ludvik, and Christiane Naffah. "Deux écritoires mameloukes des collections nationales françaises." *Revue des études Islamiques* 51 (1983), pp. 89–124.

Kanarfogel 1986
Kanarfogel, Ephraim. "The *'Aliyah* of 'Three Hundred Rabbis' in 1211: Tosafist Attitudes toward Settling in the Land of Israel." *The Jewish Quarterly Review* 76, no. 3 (January 1986), pp. 191–215.

Kaplony 2002
Kaplony, Andreas. *The Haram of Jerusalem, 324–1099: Temple, Friday Mosque, Area of Spiritual Power.* Freiburger Islamstudien, 17. Stuttgart, 2002.

Kaplony 2004
Kaplony, Andreas. "Manifestations of Private Piety: Muslims, Christians and Jews in Fatimid Jerusalem." In Pahlitzsch and Korn, eds. 2004, pp. 33–45.

Kashouh 2011
Kashouh, Hikmat. *The Arabic Versions of the Gospels: The Manuscripts and Their Families.* Arbeiten zur neutestamentlichen Textforschung, 42. Berlin, 2011.

Katzenstein and Lowry 1983
Katzenstein, Ranee A., and Glenn D. Lowry. "Christian Themes in Thirteenth-Century Islamic Metalwork." *Muqarnas* 1 (1983), pp. 53–68.

Kauffmann 1910
Kauffmann, Carl Maria. *Menas, Saint of Mareotis.* Cairo, 1910.

Kedar 1984
Kedar, Benjamin Z. *Crusade and Mission: European Approaches toward the Muslims.* Princeton Legacy Library. Princeton, N.J., 1984.

Kedar 1989
Kedar, Benjamin Z. "The Frankish Period." In *The Samaritans,* edited by Alan D[avid] Crown, pp. 82–94. Tübingen, 1989.

Kedar 1990
Kedar, Benjamin Z. "The Subjected Muslims of the Frankish Levant." In *Muslims under Latin Rule, 1100–1300,* edited by James M. Powell, pp. 134–74. Princeton, N.J., 1990.

Kedar 1997
Kedar, Benjamin Z. "Multidirectional Conversion in the Frankish Levant." In *Varieties of Religious Conversion in the Middle Ages,* edited by James Muldoon, pp. 190–99. Gainesville, Fla., 1997.

Kedar 1998a
Kedar, Benjamin Z. "A Twelfth-Century Description of the Jerusalem Hospital." In *The Military Orders.* Vol. 2, *Welfare and Warfare,* edited by Helen Nicholson, pp. 3–26. Aldershot, Hampshire, 1998.

Kedar 1998b
Kedar, Benjamin Z. "Latins and Oriental Christians in the Frankish Levant, 1099–1291." In Kofsky and Stroumsa, eds. 1998, pp. 209–22.

Kedar 2001
Kedar, Benjamin Z. "Convergences of Oriental, Christian, Muslim, and Frankish Worshippers: The Case of Saydnaya and the Knights Templar." In *The Crusades and the Military Orders: Expanding the Frontiers of Medieval Latin Christianity,* edited by Zsolt Hunyadi and József Laszlovszky, pp. 89–100. CEU Medievalia. Budapest, 2001.

Kedar, ed. 1992
Kedar, Benjamin Z., ed. *The Horns of Hattin: Proceedings of the Second Conference of the Society for the Study of the Crusades and the Latin East, Jerusalem and Haïfa, 2–6 July 1987.* Jerusalem, 1992.

Kempe 2000 ed.
Kempe, Margery. *The Book of Margery Kempe.* Edited by Barry [A.] Windeatt. Longman Annotated Texts. Harlow, 2000.

Kempe 2015 ed.
Kempe, Margery. *The Book of Margery Kempe.* Translated by Anthony Bale. Oxford World's Classics. Oxford, 2015.

Kenaan 1973
Kenaan, Nurith. "Local Christian Art in Twelfth Century Jerusalem." *Israel Exploration Journal* 23, no. 3 (1973), pp. 167–75.

Kenaan-Kedar 1986
Kenaan-Kedar, Nurith. "Symbolic Meaning in Crusader Architecture: The Twelfth-Century Dome of the Holy Sepulcher Church in Jerusalem." *Cahiers archéologiques* 34 (1986), pp. 109–17.

Kenaan-Kedar 1998
Kenaan-Kedar, Nurith. "Armenian Architecture in Twelfth-Century Crusader Jerusalem." *Assaph, Section B: Studies in Art History* 3 [*East Meets West: Art in the Land of Israel,* edited by Aser Ovadya and Nurith Kenaan-Kedar] (1998), pp. 77–92.

Kenesson 1998
Kenesson, Summer S. "Islamic Enamelled Beakers: A New Chronology." In Ward, ed. 1998, pp. 45–49, 176–77, color pl. I.

Kenney 2009
Kenney, Ellen V. *Power and Patronage in Medieval Syria: The Architecture and Urban Works of Tankiz al-Nasiri.* Chicago Studies on the Middle East. 2004. Chicago, 2009.

Kermer 1967
Kermer, Wolfgang. "Studien zum Diptychon in der sakralen Malerei von den Anfängen bis zur Mitte des sechzehnten Jahrhunderts, mit einem Katalog." Ph.D. diss., Eberhard-Karls-Universität, Tübingen, 1967.

Keshman 2013
Keshman, Anastasia. "Crusader Wall Mosaics in the Holy Land: Gustav Kühnel's Work in the Church of the Nativity in Bethlehem." *Arte Medievale,* ser. 4, 3 (2013), pp. 257–70.

Kessler 2014
Kessler, Herbert L[eon]. "Arca arcarum: Nested Boxes and the Dynamics of Sacred Experience." *Codex Aquilarensis: Cuadernos de investigación del Monasterio de Santa María la Real* 30 (2014), pp. 83–108.

Khalili 2008
Khalili, Nasser D. *Islamic Art and Culture: Timeline and History.* Cairo, 2008.

Khamis 2013
Khamis, Elias. *Tiberias: Excavations in the House of the Bronzes; Final Report.* Vol. 2, *The Fatimid Metalwork Hoard from Tiberias.* Qedem: Monographs of the Institute of Archaeology, 55. Jerusalem, 2013.

Khan 1992
Khan, Geoffrey. "The Medieval Karaite Transcriptions of Hebrew into Arabic Script." *Israel Oriental Studies* 12 (1992), pp. 157–76.

el-Khatib 2001
el-Khatib, Abdallah. "Jerusalem in the Qur'an." *British Journal of Middle Eastern Studies* 28, no. 1 (2001), pp. 25–53.

von Kienbusch and Grancsay 1933
von Kienbusch, Carl Otto, and Stephen V. Grancsay. *The Bashford Dean Collection of Arms and Armor in The Metropolitan Museum of Art.* Portland, Me., 1933.

King 1999
King, David A. "Bringing Astronomical Instruments Back to Earth: The Geographical Data on Medieval Astrolabes (to ca. 1100)." In *Between Demonstration and Imagination: Essays in the History of Science and Philosophy Presented to John D. North,* edited by Lodi Nauta and Arjo Vanderjagt, pp. 3–53. Brill's Studies in Intellectual History, 96. Leiden, 1999.

King and Maier 1996
King, David A., and Kurt Maier. "The Medieval Catalan Astrolabe of the Society of Antiquaries, London." In *From Baghdad to Barcelona: Studies in the Islamic Exact Sciences in Honour of Prof. Juan Vernet,* edited by Josep Casulleras and Julio Samsó, vol. 2, pp. 673–718. 2 vols. Anuari de Filologia [Universitat de Barcelona], 19 (1996) B–2. Barcelona, 1996.

Kiss, Laszlo, et al., eds. 2000–
Kiss, Laszlo, et al., eds. "S. Damasi Papae et Confessoris – Duplex." In *The Divinum Officium Project.* [Forrest Lake, Ill., 2000–]; http://divinumofficium.com/cgi-bin/horas/Pofficium.pl?date112-11-2014&commandprayMatutinum&versionReduced%201955&testmodeseasonal&lang2English&votive chant for the 2nd Sunday of Advent, first nocturn, first response (accessed February 9, 2016).

Kiss, Z., 1989
Kiss, Zsolt. *Les ampoules de Saint Ménas découvertes à Kôm el-Dikka (1961–1981).* Alexandrie, 5. Warsaw, 1989.

Kister 1969
Kister, M. J. "'You Shall Only Set out for Three Mosques': A Study of an Early Tradition." *Le muséon: Revue d'études orientales* 82 (1969), pp. 173–96.

Kjellman-Chapin et al. 2013
Kjellman-Chapin, Monica, et al. *Kitsch: History, Theory, Practice.* Newcastle upon Tyne, 2013.

Klein 2004
Klein, Holger A. *Byzanz, der Westen und das "wahre" Kreuz: Die Geschichte einer Reliquie und ihrer künstlerischen Fassung in Byzanz und im Abendland.* Spätantike, frühes Christentum, Byzanz, ser. B, Studien und Perspektiven, 17. Wiesbaden, 2004.

Klein 2010–11
Klein, Holger A. "Sacred Things and Holy Bodies: Collecting Relics from Late Antiquity to Early Renaissance." In Cleveland, Baltimore, and London 2010–11, pp. 54–67.

Kofsky and Stroumsa, eds. 1998
Kofsky, Arieh, and Guy G. Stroumsa, eds. *Sharing the Sacred: Religious Contacts and Conflicts in the Holy Land, First–Fifteenth Centuries C.E.* Jerusalem, 1998.

Kogman-Appel 2004
Kogman-Appel, Katrin. *Jewish Book Art between Islam and Christianity: The Decoration of Hebrew Bibles in Medieval Spain.* Medieval and Early Modern Iberian World, 19. Leiden and Boston, 2004.

Kogman-Appel 2009
Kogman-Appel, Katrin. "Sephardic Ideas in Ashkenaz: Visualizing the Temple in Medieval Regensburg." *Simon Dubnow Institute Yearbook,* 2009, pp. 246–77.

Kohlberg and Kedar 1988
Kohlberg, Etan, and Benjamin Z. Kedar. "A Melkite Physician in Frankish Jerusalem and Ayyubid Damascus: Muwaffaq al-Din Ya'qub b. Siqlab." *Asian and African Studies* 22 (1988), pp. 113–26.

Kohler, ed. 1899
Kohler, C., ed. "Documents inédits concernant l'Orient latin et les croisades (XIIe–XIVe siècles)." *Revue de l'Orient latin* 7 (1899), pp. 1–37.

Kolbaba 1998
Kolbaba, Tia M. "Fighting for Christianity: Holy War in the Byzantine Empire." *Byzantion: Revue internationale des études byzantines* 68 (1998), pp. 194–221.

Korn 2004
Korn, Lorenz. "The Structure of Architectural Patronage in Ayyubid Jerusalem." In Pahlitzsch and Korn, eds. 2004 pp. 70–89.

Kornfeld 2013
Kornfeld, Abby. "Meanings in the Margins: Between Text and Image in the Barcelona Haggadah." Ph.D. diss., Institute of Fine Arts, New York University, 2013.

Kotzabassi, Ševčenko, and Skemer 2010
Kotzabassi, Sofia, and Nancy Patterson Ševčenko, with Don C. Skemer. *Greek Manuscripts at Princeton, Sixth to Nineteenth Century: A Descriptive Catalogue.* Department of Art and Archaeology and Program in Hellenic Studies, Princeton University. Princeton, N.J., 2010.

Kötzsche-Breitenbruch 1984
Kötzsche-Breitenbruch, Lieselotte. "Pilgerandenken aus dem Heiligen Land: Drei Neuerwerbungen des Württembergischen Landesmuseums in Stuttgart." In *Vivarium: Festschrift Theodor Klauser zum 90. Geburtstag,* edited by Ernst Dassmann and Klaus Thraede, pp. 229–46. Jahrbuch für Antike und Christentum, Supplement 11. Muenster, 1984.

Kraemer 2008
Kraemer, Joel L. *Maimonides: The Life and World of One of Civilization's Greatest Minds.* New York, 2008.

Krey 1921
Krey, August C. *The First Crusade: The Accounts of Eye-Witnesses and Participants.* Princeton, N.J., 1921.

Krueger 2014
Krueger, Derek. *Liturgical Subjects: Christian Ritual, Biblical Narrative, and the Formation of the Self in Byzantium.* Divinations. Philadelphia, 2014.

Krüger 2011
Krüger, Jürgen. "Architecture of the Crusaders in the Holy Land: The First European Colonial Architecture?" In *The Crusades and the Near East: Cultural Histories,* edited by Conor Kostick, pp. 216–28. London and New York, 2011.

Kuehn 2011
Kuehn, Sara. *The Dragon in Medieval East Christian and Islamic Art.* Islamic History and Civilization, 86. Leiden and Boston, 2011.

Kühnel, B., 1977
Kühnel, Bianca. "Crusader Sculpture at the Ascension Church on the Mount of Olives in Jerusalem." *Gesta* 16, no. 2 (1977), pp. 41–50.

Kühnel, B., 1987
Kühnel, Bianca. *From the Earthly to the Heavenly Jerusalem: Representations of the Holy City in Christian Art of the First Millennium.* Römische Quartalschrift für christliche Altertumskunde und Kirchengeschichte, Supplementheft 42. Rome, 1987.

Kühnel, B., 1994
Kühnel, Bianca. *Crusader Art of the Twelfth Century: A Geographical, an Historical, or an Art Historical Notion?* Berlin, 1994.

Kühnel, B., Noga-Banai, and Vorholt, eds. 2014
Kühnel, Bianca, Galit Noga-Banai, and Hanna Vorholt, eds. *Visual Constructs of Jerusalem.* Cultural Encounters in Late Antiquity and the Middle Ages, 18. Turnhout, 2014.

Kühnel, G., 1984
Kühnel, Gustav. "Neue Feldarbeiten zur musivischen und malerischen Ausstattung der Geburts-Basilika in Bethlehem." *Kunstchronik* 37 (1984), pp. 507–13.

Kühnel, G., 1988
Kühnel, Gustav. *Wall Painting of the Latin Kingdom of Jerusalem.* Frankfurter Forschungen zur Kunst, 14. Berlin, 1988.

Kühnel, G., 1993–94
Kühnel, Gustav. "Die Konzilsdarstellungen in der Geburtskirche in Bethlehem: Ihre kunsthistorische Tradition und ihr kirchenpolitisch-historischer Hintergrund." *Byzantinische Zeitschrift* 86–87, no. 1 (1993–94), pp. 86–107, pls. 6–11.

Kühnel, G., 1999
Kühnel, Gustav. "Crusader Monumental Painting and Mosaic." In Jerusalem 1999, pp. 202–15.

Kulp 2005
Kulp, Joshua. "The Origins of the Seder and Haggadah." *Currents in Biblical Research* 4, no. 1 (2005), pp. 109–34.

Labarte 1864–66
Labarte, Jules. *Histoire des arts industriels au Moyen Âge et à l'époque de la Renaissance.* 4 vols. Paris, 1864–66.

Laboa 2003
Laboa, Juan María. *The Historical Atlas of Eastern and Western Christian Monasticism.* Collegeville, Minn., 2003.

Lachter 2015
Lachter, Hartley, with Marc Michael Epstein. "Other Worlds: Fantastic Horizons and Unseen Universes." In *Skies of Parchment, Seas of Ink: Jewish Illuminated Manuscripts,* by Marc Michael Epstein et al., pp. 193–203. Princeton, N.J., 2015.

Laderman 2003–4
Laderman, Shulamit. "Images of the Temple in Jewish Art and Their Parallels in Literary Sources." In *Envisioning the Temple: Scrolls, Stones and Symbols,* pp. 97–126. Exh. cat., The Israel Museum, Jerusalem, 2003–4. Catalogue by Adolfo [Daniel] Roitman and others. Katalog 483. Jerusalem, 2003.

LaGamma et al. 1998
LaGamma, Alisa, et al. "Africa, Oceania, and the Americas." *The Metropolitan Museum of Art Bulletin,* n.s., 56, no. 2 [*Recent Acquisitions: A Selection, 1997–1998*] (Autumn 1998), pp. 69–71.

Lamm 1929–30
Lamm, Carl Johan. *Mittelalterliche Gläser und Steinschnitt-arbeiten aus dem Nahen Osten.* 2 vols. Forschungen zur islamischen Kunst, 5. Berlin, 1929–30.

Lämmerhirt 2010
Lämmerhirt, Maike. "Zur Geschichte der Juden im Mittelalterlichen Erfurt." In Ostritz, ed. 2010a, pp. 334–75.

Landsberger 1961
Landsberger, Franz. "The Illumination of Hebrew Manuscripts in the Middle Ages and Renaissance." In *Jewish Art: An Illustrated History,* edited by Cecil Roth, pp. 377–422. London, 1961.

Lapina 2015
Lapina, Elizabeth. *Warfare and the Miraculous in the Chronicles of the First Crusade.* University Park, Pa., 2015.

La Porta 2007
La Porta, Sergio. "The Armenian Episcopacy in Mamluk Jerusalem in the Aftermath of the Council of Sis (1307)." *Journal of the Royal Asiatic Society,* ser. 3, 17, no. 2 (April 2007), pp. 99–114.

Lasteyrie 1853–57
Lasteyrie, Ferdinand de. *Histoire de la peinture sur verre d'après ses monuments en France.* 2 vols. Paris, 1853–57.

Le Bon 1884
Le Bon, Gustave. *La civilisation des Arabes.* Paris, 1884.

Leopold 2000
Leopold, Antony. *How to Recover the Holy Land: The Crusade Proposals of the Late Thirteenth and Early Fourteenth Centuries.* Aldershot, Hampshire, and Burlington, Vt., 2000.

Leroy 1964
Leroy, Jules. *Les manuscrits syriaques à peintures conservés dans les bibliothèques d'Europe et d'Orient: Contribution à l'étude de l'iconographie des églises de langue syriaque.* 2 vols. Bibliothèque archéologique et historique, 77. Paris, 1964.

Lester 1991
Lester, Ayala. "A Fatimid Hoard from Tiberias." In *Jewellery and Goldsmithing in the Islamic World: International Symposium, The Israel Museum, Jerusalem, 1987,* edited by Na'ama Brosh, pp. 21–29. Jerusalem, 1991.

Lester 2004
Lester, Ayala. "Glass and Metal Objects." In *Excavations at Tiberias, 1989–1994,* edited by Yizhar Hirschfeld and Roni Amir, pp. 59–68. Jerusalem, 2004.

Lester 2011
Lester, Ayala. "Typological and Stylistic Aspects of Metalware of the Fatimid Period." Ph.D. diss., Haifa University, 2011.

Lester 2013
Lester, Ayala. "Metal Hoards from the Fatimid Period and the Geniza Documents from the Ibn-Ezra Synagogue at Fustat" (in Hebrew). In *Hoards and Genizot as Chapters in History,* edited by Ofra Guri-Rimon, pp. 71–81. Haifa, 2008.

Lester 2014
Lester, Ayala. "Reconsidering Fatimid Metalware." In *Proceedings of the 8th International Congress on the Archaeology of the Ancient Near East, 10 April–4 May 2012, University of Warsaw,* vol. 3, *Archaeology of Fire, Conservation, Preservation and Site Management . . . ,* edited by Piotr Bieliński, pp. 437–54. Wiesbaden, 2014.

Lev 2007
Lev, Yaacov. "Saladin's Economic Policies and the Economy of Ayyubid Egypt." In *Egypt and Syria in the Fatimid, Ayyubid and Mamluk Eras,* vol. 5, *Proceedings of the 11th, 12th and 13th International Colloquium Organized at the Katholieke Universiteit Leuven in May 2002, 2003 and 2004,* edited by Urbain Vermeulen and K. D' Hulster, pp. 307–48. Orientalia Lovaniensia analecta, 169. Leuven, 2007.

Lewis, B., 1955
Lewis, Bernard. "The Isma'ilites and the Assassins." In *A History of the Crusades,* vol. 1, *The First Hundred Years,* edited by Marshall W. Baldwin, pp. 99–132. Philadelphia, 1955.

Lewis, S., 1987
Lewis, Suzanne. *The Art of Matthew Paris in the Chronica Majora.* California Studies in the History of Art, 21. Berkeley, Los Angeles, and London, 1987.

Lewis, S., 1991
Lewis, Suzanne. "The English Gothic Illustrated Apocalypse, *Lectio divina,* and the Art of Memory." *Word and Image* 7, no. 1 (1991), pp. 1–32.

Lewis, S., 1995
Lewis, Suzanne. *Reading Images: Narrative Discourse and Reception in the Thirteenth-Century Illuminated Apocalypse.* Cambridge and New York, 1995.

Lidov 2014
Lidov, Alexei. "The Holy Fire and Visual Constructs of Jerusalem, East and West." In Kühnel, B., Noga-Banai, and Vorholt, eds. 2014, pp. 241–49.

Limor 2007
Limor, Ora. "Sharing Sacred Space: Holy Places in Jerusalem between Christianity, Judaism, and Islam." In *In Laudem Hierosolymitani: Studies in Crusades and Medieval Culture in Honour of Benjamin Z. Kedar,* edited by Iris Shagrir, Ronnie Ellenblum, and Jonathan Riley-Smith, pp. 219–31. Aldershot, Hampshire, and Burlington, Vt., 2007.

Lindner 1992
Lindner, Molly. "Topography and Iconography in Twelfth-Century Jerusalem." In Kedar, ed. 1992, pp. 81–98, pls. 38–68.

Lisbon 1997–98
Arte Islâmica e mecenato: Tesouros do Kuwait; Exposição cedida pela Colecção al-Sabah, Dar al-Athar al-Islamiyyah, Museu de Arte Islâmica do Kuwait. Exh. cat., Museu Calouste Gulbenkian, Lisbon, 1997–98. Catalogue by Esin Atil. Lisbon, 1997.

Little 1984a
Little, Donald P. *A Catalogue of the Islamic Documents from al-Haram as-Sarif in Jerusalem.* Beiruter Texte und Studien, 29. Beirut, 1984.

Little 1984b
Little, Donald P. "The Haram Documents as Sources for the Arts and Architecture of the Mamluk Period." *Muqarnas* 2 [*The Art of the Mamluks,* edited by Oleg Grabar] (1984), pp. 61–72.

Little 1985
Little, Donald P. "Haram Documents Related to the Jews of Late Fourteenth Century Jerusalem." *Journal of Semitic Studies* 30, no. 2 (1985), pp. 227–64.

Little 1986
Little, Donald P. "Data from the Haram Documents on Rugs in Late 14th Century Jerusalem." In *Carpets of the Mediterranean Countries, 1400–1600: Based upon the Special Sessions of the 4th International Conference on Oriental Carpets, London, 1983,* edited by Robert Pinner and Walter B. Denny, pp. 83–93. Oriental and Carpet Textile Studies, 2. London, 1986.

Little 1990
Little, Donald P. "Coptic Converts to Islam during the Bahri Mamluk Period." In *Conversion and Continuity: Indigenous Christian Communities in Islamic Lands, Eighth to Eighteenth Centuries,* edited by Michael Gervers and Ramzi Jibran Bikhazi, pp. 262–88. Papers in Mediaeval Studies, 9. Toronto, 1990.

Little 1998
Little, Donald P. "Documents Related to the Estates of a Merchant and His Wife in Late Fourteenth Century Jerusalem." *Mamluk Studies Review* 2 (1998), pp. 93–192.

Little 2000
Little, Donald P. "Jerusalem under the Ayyubids and Mamluks, 1187–1516 A.D." In *Jerusalem in History: 3,000 B.C. to the Present Day,* edited by Kamil J. Asali, pp. 177–99. London and New York, 2000.

Little 2009
Little, Donald P. "1260–1516: The Noble Sanctuary (al-Haram al-Sharif) under Mamluk Rule — History." In Grabar, O., and Kedar, eds. 2009, pp. 176–87.

Littmann 1902
Littmann, Enno. "Aus den abessinischen Klöstern in Jerusalem." *Zeitschrift für Assyriologie und verwandte Gebiete* 16, no. 1 (1902), pp. 102–24.

Livne-Kafri 1993
Livne-Kafri, Ofer. "Jerusalem: 'The Navel of the World' in Muslim Tradition." *Cathedra: For the History of Eretz Israel and Its Yishuv* 69 (1993), pp. 79–105.

Livne-Kafri 1998
Livne-Kafri, Ofer. "The Muslim Traditions 'in Praise of Jerusalem' (*Fada'il al-Quds*): Diversity and Complexity." *Annali (Istituto Universitario Orientale)* 58, nos. 1–2 (1998), pp. 165–92.

Livne-Kafri 2006
Livne-Kafri, Ofer. "Jerusalem in Early Islam: The Eschatological Aspect." *Arabica* 53, no. 3 (July 2006), pp. 382–403.

Loenertz 1948
Loenertz, R. J. "L'épître de Théorien le Philosophe aux prêtres d'Oreine." In *Mémorial Louis Petit: Mélanges d'histoire et d'archéologie byzantines,* pp. 317–35. Archives de l'Orient chrétien, 1. Bucharest, 1948.

London 1976
The Qur'an: Catalogue of an Exhibition of Qur'an Manuscripts at the British Library, 3 April–15 August 1976. Exh. cat., British Library, London, 1976. Catalogue by Martin Lings and Yasin Hamid Safadi. London, 1976.

London 1978
The Christian Orient. Exh. cat., British Library, London, 1978. Catalogue by John Mitchell. London, 1978.

London 1994
Byzantium: Treasures of Byzantine Art and Culture from British Collections. Exh. cat., British Museum, London, 1994. Catalogue by David Buckton. London, 1994.

London 2001
Treasures from the Ark: 1700 Years of Armenian Christian Art. Exh. cat., British Library, London, 2001. Catalogue by Vrej Nersessian. London, 2001.

London 2003–4
Saved!: 100 Years of the National Art Collections Fund. Exh. cat., Hayward Gallery, London, 2003–4. Catalogue by Richard Verdi and others. London, 2003.

London 2007
Sacred Books of the Three Faiths: Judaism, Christianity, Islam. Exh. cat., British Library, London, 2007. Catalogue by John Reeve and others. London, 2007.

London and other cities 2001
Treasury of the World: Jewelled Arts of India in the Age of the Mughals. Exh. cat., British Museum, London, and other venues, 2001. Catalogue by Manuel Keene with Salam Kaoukji. London, 2001.

Los Angeles 2006–7
Holy Image, Hallowed Ground: Icons from Sinai. Exh. cat., J. Paul Getty Museum, Los Angeles, 2006–7. Catalogue by Robert S. Nelson and Kristen M. Collins. Los Angeles, 2006.

Los Angeles and Houston 2011–12
Gifts of the Sultan: The Arts of Giving at the Islamic Courts. Exh. cat., Los Angeles County Museum of Art; Museum of Fine Arts, Houston, 2011–12. Catalogue by Linda Komaroff and others. New Haven and London, 2011.

Losito 2011
Losito, Maria. *Il Santo Sepolcro e la Gerusalemme celeste: Da architettura costantiniana a modello universale.* Acta e monumenta. Bari, [2011].

Lower 2005
Lower, Michael. *The Barons' Crusade: A Call to Arms and Its Consequences.* Philadelphia, 2005.

Löwy, ed. 1872–77
Löwy, A[lbert], ed. *Miscellany of Hebrew Literature.* 2 vols. Publications of the Society of Hebrew Literature. London, 1872–77.

Ludolph von Suchem 1895 ed.
Ludolph von Suchem's Description of the Holy Land, and of the Way Thither, Written in the Year A.D. 1350. Translated by Aubrey Stewart. Palestine Pilgrims' Text Society, 12, no. 3. London, 1895.

Lupis 2012
Lupis, Vinicije B. "*Staurotheca di Gerusalemme* u Dubrovniku." *Starohrvatska prosvjeta* 3, no. 39 (2012), pp. 183–92.

Lyons and Jackson 1982
Lyons, Malcolm Cameron, and D. E. P. Jackson. *Saladin: The Politics of the Holy War.* University of Cambridge Oriental Publications, 30. Cambridge and New York, 1982.

MacCannell 1976
MacCannell, Dean. *The Tourist: A New Theory of the Leisure Class.* New York, 1976.

MacEvitt 2008
MacEvitt, Christopher. *The Crusades and the Christian World of the East: Rough Tolerance.* The Middle Ages Series. Philadelphia, 2008.

Machado 2009
Machado, Pedro. "Awash in a Sea of Cloth: Gujarat, Africa, and the Western Indian Ocean, 1300–1800." In *The Spinning World: A Global History of Cotton Textiles, 1200–1850,* edited by Giorgio Riello and Prasannan Parthasarathi, pp. 161–79. Oxford and New York, 2009.

Maddison and Savage-Smith 1997
Maddison, Francis, and Emilie Savage-Smith. *Science, Tools and Magic.* Pt. 1, *Body and Spirit, Mapping the Universe.* The Nasser D. Khalili Collection of Islamic Art, edited by Julian Raby, vol. 12, pt. 1. London and Oxford, 1997.

Madelung 1981
Madelung, Wilferd. "'Abd Allah b. al-Zubayr and the Mahdi." *Journal of Near Eastern Studies* 40, no. 4 [*Arabic and Islamic Studies in Honor of Nabia Abbott, Part Two*] (October 1981), pp. 291–305.

Mahir 2010
Mahir, Su'ad. *Egypt's Mosques and Their Saints* (in Arabic). 4 vols. Cairo, [2010].

Mahmud 2015
Mahmud, 'Ala al-Din. "Artistic and Archaeological Study for a New Collection of Ayyubid and Mamluk Glass" (in Arabic). Ph.D. diss., University of Cairo, 2015.

Maier 2000
Maier, Christoph T. *Crusade Propaganda and Ideology: Model Sermons for the Preaching of the Cross.* Cambridge and New York, 2000.

Maimonides 1910 ed.
Maimonides [Moshe ben Maimon]. *Responsa of Maimonides.* Edited by Alfred Freimann. Jerusalem, 1910.

Maimonides 1940 ed.
Maimonides [Moshe ben Maimon]. *The Book of Divine Commandments: The Sefer ha-Mitzvoth of Moses Maimonides.* Vol. 1, *The Positive Commandments.* Translated and annotated by Charles B[er] Chavel. London, 1940.

Maimonides 1987 ed.
Maimonides [Moshe ben Maimon]. *Igrot ha-Rambam* [Letters and Essays of Moses Maimonides] (in Hebrew). Edited and translated by Isaac Shailat. 2 vols. Jerusalem, 1987.

Maimonides 1989a ed.
Maimonides [Moshe ben Maimon]. *Mishneh Torah, Hilchot Kri'at Shema/The Laws of Kri'at Shema, and Hilchot Tefilah [I]/The Laws of Prayer.* Translated by Boruch Kaplan. New York and Jerusalem, 1989.

Maimonides 1989b ed.
Maimonides [Moshe ben Maimon]. *Mishneh Torah, Hilchot Yesodei HaTorah/The Laws [Which Are] the Foundations of the Torah.* Translated by Eliyahu Touger. New York and Jerusalem, 1989.

Maimonides 2001 ed.
Maimonides [Moshe ben Maimon]. *Mishneh Torah: A New Translation with Commentaries and Notes.* Vol. 14, *Sefer Shoftim/The Book of Judges.* Translated by Eliyahu Touger. New York and Jerusalem, 2001.

Maimonides 2005 ed.
Maimonides [Moshe ben Maimon]. *Mishneh Torah, Sefer Zeraim/The Book of Agricultural Ordinances.* Translated by Eliyahu Touger. New York and Jerusalem, 2005.

Maimonides 2007 ed.
Maimonides [Moshe ben Maimon]. *Mishneh Torah, Sefer ha-'Avodah/The Book of [Temple] Service.* Translated by Eliyahu Touger. New York and Jerusalem, 2007.

Mainz 2004
Die Kreuzzüge: Kein Krieg ist heilig. Exh. cat., Bischöfliches Dom- und Diözesanmuseum, Mainz, 2004. Catalogue by Hans-Jürgen Kotzur and others. Mainz, 2004.

Makariou et al. 2002
Makariou, Sophie, et al. *Nouvelles acquisitions, Arts de l'Islam, 1988–2001: Catalogue.* Musée du Louvre, Département des Antiquités Orientales. Paris, 2002.

Makariou et al. 2012
Makariou, Sophie, et al. *Islamic Art at the Musée du Louvre.* Paris, 2012.

Mann, J., 1935
Mann, Jacob. *Texts and Studies in Jewish History and Literature.* Vol. 2. *Karaitica.* Philadelphia, 1935.

Mann, J., 1970
Mann, Jacob. *The Jews in Egypt and in Palestine under the Fatimid Caliphs: A Contribution to Their Political and Communal History, Based Chiefly on Genizah Material Hitherto Unpublished, and a Second Supplement to "The Jews in Egypt and in Palestine under the Fatimid Caliphs."* 2 vols. in 1. New York, 1970.

Mann, V., 1988
Mann, Vivian B. "'New' Examples of Jewish Ceremonial Art from Medieval Ashkenaz." *Artibus et Historiae* 9, no. 17 (1988), pp. 13–24.

al-Maqrizi 1980 ed.
al-Maqrizi, Amad ibn 'Ali. *A History of the Ayyubid Sultans of Egypt.* Translated by R. J. C. Broadhurst. Library of Classical Arabic Literature, 5. Boston, 1980.

Marçais and Poinssot 1948–52
Marçais, Georges, and Louis Poinssot, with Lucien Gaillard. *Objets kairouanais IXe au XIIIe siècle: Reliures, verreries, cuivres et bronzes, bijoux.* Tunisia — Direction des antiquités et arts: Notes et documents, 11. Tunis, 1948–52.

Margoliouth 1897
Margoliouth, G. "Ibn al-Hiti's Arabic Chronicle of Karaite Doctors." *The Jewish Quarterly Review* 9, no. 3 (April 1897), pp. 429–43.

Marmorstein 1916
Marmorstein, A. "Fragments du commentaire de Daniel al-Kumisi sur les Psaumes." *Journal asiatique,* ser. 11, 7 (1916), pp. 177–237.

Marquet de Vasselot 1906
Marquet de Vasselot, J[ean]-J[oseph]. *Les émaux limousins à fond vermiculé (XIIe et XIIIe siècles).* Paris, 1906.

Martin, A., 2006
Martin, Alain. "Dix ampoules de saint Ménas aux Musée Royaux d'Art et d'Histoire." *Chronique d'Égypte* 161–62 (2006), pp. 383–93.

Martin, J., 1888–89
Martin, Jean-Pierre Hippolyte. "Les premiers princes croisés et les Syriens Jacobites de Jérusalem." *Journal asiatique,* 8th ser., 12 (1888), pp. 471–90; ser. 8, 13 (1889), pp. 33–79.

Mason 2004
Mason, Robert B. J. *Shine Like the Sun: Lustre-Painted and Associated Pottery from the Medieval Middle East.* Bibliotheca Iranica, Islamic Art and Architecture Series, 12. Costa Mesa, Calif., 2004.

Maspero 1911
Maspero, G. *Bibliothèque égyptologique contenant les oeuvres des égyptologues français . . .* Vol. 27. Études de mythologie et d'archéologie égyptiennes, 5. Paris, 1911.

Mathews 1982
Mathews, Thomas F. "The Early Armenian Iconographic Program of the Ējmiacin Gospel (Erevan, Matenadaran MS 2374, *olim* 229)." In *East of Byzantium: Syria and Armenia in the Formative Period,* edited by Nina G. Garsoïan, Thomas F. Mathews, and Robert W. Thomson, pp. 199–215. Washington, D.C., 1982.

Mathews et al. 1991
Mathews, Thomas F., et al. *Armenian Gospel Iconography: The Tradition of the Glajor Gospel.* Dumbarton Oaks Studies, 29. Washington, D.C., 1991.

Matthews 1935
Matthews, C[harles] D. "The *'kitab ba'itu–n-nufus'* of Ibnu-i-Firkah." *The Journal of the Palestine Oriental Society* 15 (1935), pp. 51–87.

Matthews 1936
Matthews, Charles D. "A Muslim Iconoclast (Ibn Taymiyyeh) on the 'Merits' of Jerusalem and Palestine." *Journal of the American Oriental Society* 56, no. 1 (March 1936), pp. 1–21.

May 1957
May, Florence Lewis. *Silk Textiles of Spain: Eighth to Fifteenth Century.* Hispanic [Society of America] Notes and Monographs, Peninsular Series. New York, 1957.

Mayer, H., 1967
Mayer, Hans Eberhard. "Das Pontifikale von Tyrus und die Krönung der Lateinischen Könige von Jerusalem. Zugleich ein Beitrag zur Forschung über Herrschaftszeichen und Staatssymbolik." *Dumbarton Oaks Papers* 21 (1967), pp. 141–232, figs. 1–7.

Mayer, H., 1972
Mayer, Hans Eberhard. "Studies in the History of Queen Melisende of Jerusalem." *Dumbarton Oaks Papers* 26 (1972), pp. 93–182.

Mayer, H., 1988
Mayer, Hans Eberhard. "Guillaume de Tyr à l'école." *Mémoires de l'Académie des Sciences, Arts et Belles-Lettres de Dijon* 127 (1988), pp. 257–65.

Mayer, L., 1956
Mayer, L[eo] A[ry]. *Islamic Astrolabists and Their Works.* Geneva, 1956.

Meinecke 1972
Meinecke, Michael. "Zur mamlukischen Heraldik." *Mitteilungen des deutschen Archäologischen Instituts, Abteilung Kairo* 28, no. 2 (1972), pp. 213–87.

Melikian-Chirvani 1986
Melikian-Chirvani, A[ssadullah] S[ouren]. "State Inkwells in Islamic Iran." *The Journal of the Art Gallery* 44 (1986), pp. 70–94.

Melisende 2014 ed.
"A Letter from Melisende." In *Epistolae: Medieval Women's Latin Letters.* New York, 2014; https://epistolae.ccnmtl.columbia.edu/letter/25215.html (accessed April 2[illegible], 2016).

Meri 1999
Meri, Josef W. "Aspects of Baraka (Blessings) and Ritual Devotion among Medieval Muslims and Jews." *Medieval Encounters* 5, no. 1 (1999), pp. 46–69.

Meri 2002
Meri, Josef W. *The Cult of Saints among Muslims and Jews in Medieval Syria.* Oxford Oriental Monographs. Oxford and New York, 2002.

Metcalf 1983
Metcalf, D[avid] M[ichael]. *Coinage of the Crusades and the Latin East in the Ashmolean Museum, Oxford.* Royal Numismatic Society, Special Publication 15. London, 1983.

Metzger, C., 1981
Metzger, Catherine. *Les ampoules à eulogie du Musée du Louvre.* Notes et documents des musées de France, 3. Paris, 1981.

Metzger, T., 1969–70
Metzger, Thérèse. "Les objets du culte, le sanctuaire du désert et le temple de Jérusalem, dans les Bibles hébraïques médiévales enluminées, en Orient et en Espagne: Part 1." *Bulletin of the John Rylands Library* 52 (1969–70), pp. 397–436.

Metzger, T., 1970–71
Metzger, Thérèse. "Les objets du culte, le sanctuaire du désert et le temple de Jérusalem, dans les Bibles hébraïques médiévales enluminées, en Orient et en Espagne: Part 2." *Bulletin of the John Rylands Library* 53 (1970–71), pp. 169–209.

Metzger, T., and Metzger 1982
Metzger, Thérèse, and Mendel Metzger. *Jewish Life in the Middle Ages: Illuminated Hebrew Manuscripts of the Thirteenth to the Sixteenth Centuries.* New York, 1982.

Meurer 1985
Meurer, Heribert. "Zu den Staurotheken der Kreuzfahrer." *Zeitschrift für Kunstgeschichte* 48 (1985), pp. 65–76.

Meuwese 2005
Meuwese, Martine. "Representations of Jerusalem on Medieval Maps and Miniatures." *Eastern Christian Art in Its Late Antique and Islamic Contexts* 2 (2005), pp. 139–48.

Milan 1983
La Gerusalemme celeste. Exh. cat., Università Cattolica del S. Cuore, Milan, 1983. Catalogue by Maria Luisa Gatti Perer and others. Milan, 1983.

Milan 2000
In Terrasanta: Dalla Crociata alla Custodia dei Luoghi Santi. Exh. cat., Palazzo Reale, Milan, 2000. Catalogue by Michele Piccirillo. Florence, 2000.

Miller, R., 2005
Miller, Roland E. *Muslims and the Gospel: Bridging the Gap; A Reflection on Christian Sharing.* Minneapolis, 2005.

Miller, T., 2000
Miller, Timothy, trans. "Theodore Studites: Testament of Theodore the Studite for the Monastery of St. John Stoudios in Constantinople." In *Byzantine Monastic Foundation Documents: A Complete Translation of the Surviving Founders'* Typika *and Testaments,* edited by John Thomas and Angela Constantinides Hero with Giles Constable, vol. 1, pp. 67–83. 5 vols. Dumbarton Oaks Studies, 37. Washington, D.C., 2000.

Milwright 2003
Milwright, Marcus. "The Balsam of Matariyya: An Exploration of a Medieval Panacea." *Bulletin of the School of Oriental and African Studies, University of London* 66, no. 2 (2003), pp. 193–209.

Milwright 2009
Milwright, Marcus. "The Pottery of Ayyubid Jerusalem." In Hillenbrand, R., and Auld, eds. 2009, pp. 408–17.

***Miracula S. Georgii* 1913 ed.**
Aufhauser, Joannes B., ed. *Miracula S. Georgii.* Bibliotheca scriptorum graecorum et romanorum Teubneriana, Auctores graeci, 1540. Lipsiae, 1913.

Mirsky 1985
Mirsky, Aaron. *The Origins of Forms of Early Hebrew Poetry* (in Hebrew). Studies of the Research Institute for Hebrew Poetry in Jerusalem, 7. Jerusalem, 1985.

***Mishnah* 1933 ed.**
The Mishnah. Translated by Herbert Danby. Oxford, 1933.

Mitchell 2004
Mitchell, Piers D. *Medicine in the Crusades: Warfare, Wounds, and the Medieval Surgeon.* New York, 2004.

el-Moctar 2012
el-Moctar, Mohamed. "Saladin in Sunni and Shi'a Memories." In Paul and Yeager, eds. 2012, pp. 197–214.

Moelin 1960 ed.
Moelin, Jacob ben Moshe ha-Levi. *Sefer ha-Maharil* (in Hebrew). Brooklyn, 1960.

Mohamed et al. 2008
Mohamed, Bashir, et al. *The Arts of the Muslim Knight: The Furusiyya Art Foundation Collection.* Milan, 2008.

Mols 2006
Mols, Luitgard. *Mamluk Metalwork Fittings in Their Artistic and Architectural Context.* Delft, 2006.

Mols 2012
Mols, Luitgard. "Arabic Titles, Well-Wishes and a Female Saint: A Mamluk Basin in the Rijksmuseum, Amsterdam." In *Metalwork and Material Culture in the Islamic World: Art, Craft and Text; Essays Presented to James W. Allan,* edited by Venetia Porter and Mariam Rosser-Owen, pp. 201–13. London and New York, 2012.

Montfaucon 1729–33
Bernard de Montfaucon. *Les monumens de la monarchie françoise, qui comprennent l'histoire de France, avec les figures de chaque règne que l'injure des tems à éparnées.* 5 vols. Paris, 1729–33.

Moore 2010
Moore, Kathryn Blair. "Textual Transmission and Pictorial Transformations: The Post-Crusade Image of the Dome of the Rock in Italy." *Muqarnas* 27 (2010), pp. 51–78.

Morgan 1973
Morgan, Margaret Ruth. *The Chronicle of Ernoul and the Continuations of William of Tyre.* Oxford Historical Monographs. [London], 1973.

Morgan 1982
Morgan, M[argaret] R[uth]. "The Rothelin Continuation of William of Tyre." In *Outremer: Studies in the History of the Crusading Kingdom of Jerusalem Presented to Joshua Prawer,* edited by Benjamin Z. Kedar, H[ans] E[berhard] Mayer, R. C. Smail, pp. 244–57. Jerusalem, 1982.

Morrison 2010–11
Morrison, Elizabeth. "From Sacred to Secular: The Origins of History Illumination in France." In *Imagining the Past in France: History in Manuscript Painting, 1250–1500,* pp. 9–25. Exh. cat., The J. Paul Getty Museum, Los Angeles, 2010–11. Catalogue by Elizabeth Morrison, Anne D. Hedeman, and others. Los Angeles, 2010.

Mortara Ottolenghi 1972
Mortara Ottolenghi, Luisa. *Hebraica Ambrosiana.* Vol. 2, *Description of Decorated and Illuminated Hebrew Manuscripts in the Ambrosian Library.* Milan, 1972.

Mortara Ottolenghi 1993–94
Mortara Ottolenghi, Luisa. "Scribes, Patrons and Artists of Italian Illuminated Manuscripts in Hebrew." *Jewish Art* 19–20 (1993–94), pp. 86–97.

Mourad 2008
Mourad, Suleiman Ali. "The Symbolism of Jerusalem in Early Islam." In *Jerusalem: Idea and Reality,* edited by Tamar Mayer and Suleiman A. Mourad, pp. 86–102. London and New York, 2008.

Mourad and Lindsay 2012
Mourad, Suleiman Ali, and James E. Lindsay. *The Intensification and Reorientation of Sunni Jihad Ideology in the Crusader Period: Ibn 'Asakir of Damascus (1105–1176) and His Age, with an Edition and Translation of Ibn 'Asakir's "The Forty Hadiths for Inciting Jihad."* Islamic History and Civilization, 99. Leiden and Boston, 2012.

Mujir al-Din 1876 ed.
Mujir al-Din. *Histoire de Jérusalem et d'Hébron depuis Abraham jusqu'à la fin du XVe siècle de J.-C.: Fragments de la Chronique de Moudjir-ed-Dyn traduits sur le texte arabe.* Edited and translated by Henry Sauvaire. Paris, 1876.

Mujir al-Din 1973 ed.
Mujir al-Din. *The Glorious History of Jerusalem and Hebron* (in Arabic). 2 vols. in 1. 1968. Amman, 1973.

Müller 2008
Müller, Christian. "A Legal Instrument in the Service of People and Institutions: Endowments in Mamluk Jerusalem as Mirrored in the Haram Documents." *Mamluk Studies Review* 12, no. 1 (2008), pp. 173–91.

Müller-Wiener 2009
Müller-Wiener, Martina. "Science as the Handmaiden of Power: Science, Art and Technology in Ayyubid Syria." In Hillenbrand, R., and Auld, eds. 2009, pp. 418–22.

Munich 1910
Meisterwerke muhammedanischer Kunst auf der Ausstellung München, 1910: Teppiche, Waffen, Miniaturen, Buchkunst, Keramik, Glas und Kristall, Stein-, Holz- und Elfenbeinarbeiten, Stoffe, Metall, Verschiedenes. Exh. cat., Munich, 1910. Munich, 1912.

Munro, ed. 1895
Munro, Dana C., [ed.]. *Urban and the Crusaders.* Translations and Reprints from the Original Sources of European History 1, no. 2. Philadelphia and London, 1895.

al-Muqaddasi 1896 ed.
*Description of Syria, including Palestine by Mukaddasi (Circ. 985 A.D.).*Translated and annotated by Guy Le Strange. Palestine Pilgrims' Text Society, 3, no. 3. London, 1896.

al-Muqaddasi 1994 ed.
al-Muqaddasi. *The Best Divisions for Knowledge of the Regions: A Translation of Ahsan al-taqasim fi Ma'rifat al-aqalim.* Translated by Basil Anthony Collins. Reading, U.K., 1994.

Muqatil 1979–89 ed.
Muqatil ibn Sulëyman. *Tafsir Muqatil b. Sulëyman* (in Arabic). Edited by Abd Allah Mahmud Shihatah. 5 vols. Cairo, 1979–89.

Murphy-O'Connor 2012
Murphy-O'Connor, Jerome. "The Hospital of Saint John of Jerusalem." In *Keys to Jerusalem: Collected Essays,* by Jerome Murphy-O'Connor, pp. 261–85. Oxford, 2012.

Murray 1998
Murray, Alan V. "Mighty Against the Enemies of Christ: The Relic of the True Cross in the Armies of the Kingdom of Jerusalem." In France and Zajac, eds. 1998, pp. 217–38.

Murray 2013
Murray, Alan V. "Franks and Indigenous Communities in Palestine and Syria (1099–1187): A Hierarchical Model of Social Interaction in the Principalities of Outremer." In Classen, ed. 2013, pp. 291–309.

al-Nabulusi 1991 ed.
al-Nabulusi, Abd al-Ghani. *Al-Hadra al-Unsiyya fi al-Rih la al-Qudsiyya: Min 17 Jumada al-Akhirah hatta ghurrat Sha'ban sanat 1101 H.* Edited by Akram Hasan al-'Ulabi. Beirut, 1991.

Nachmanides 2009 ed.
Nachmanides [Moshe ben Nachman]."Prayer at the Ruins of Jerusalem." In *Writings of the Ramban,* translated and annotated by Charles Ber Chavel, vol. 2, pp. 771–806. 2 vols. Brooklyn, 2009.

Namur 2003
Autour de Hugo d'Oignies. Exh. cat., Musée des Arts Anciens du Namurois, Namur, Belgium, 2003. Catalogue by Robert Didier and Jacques Toussaint. Monographies (Musée des Arts Anciens du Namurois), 25. Namur, 2003.

Narkiss 1969
Narkiss, Bezalel. *Hebrew Illuminated Manuscripts.* Jerusalem, 1969.

Narkiss 1982
Narkiss, Bezalel. *Hebrew Illuminated Manuscripts in the British Isles: A Catalogue Raisonné.* Vol. 1, *The Spanish and Portuguese Manuscripts.* 2 vols. Oxford, 1982.

Narkiss 1998
Narkiss, Bezalel. "The Menorah in Illuminated Hebrew Manuscripts of the Middle Ages." In *In the Light of the Menorah: Story of a Symbol,* pp. 81–86. Exh. cat., The Israel Museum, Jerusalem, 1998. Catalogue by Yael Israeli and others. Israel Museum Catalogue, 406. Jerusalem, 1999.

Narkiss, Stone, and Sanjian 1979
Narkiss, Bezalel, Michael E. Stone, and Avedis K. Sanjian. *Armenian Art Treasures of Jerusalem.* Jerusalem, 1979.

Nasir-i Khusraw 1881 ed.
Nasir-i Khusraw. *Sefer nameh: Relation du voyage de Nassiri Khosrau en Syrie, en Palestine, en Égypte, en Arabie et en Perse pendant les années de l'Hégire 437–444 (1035–1042).* Translated by Charles Schefer. Publications de l'École des Langues Orientales Vivantes, 2, no. 1. Paris, 1881.

Nasir-i Khusraw 1893 ed.
Diary of a Journey through Syria and Palestine by Nasir-i-Khusrau, in 1047 A.D. Translated and annotated by Guy Le Strange. Palestine Pilgrims' Text Society, 4, no. 1. London, 1893.

Nasir-i Khusraw 1986 ed.
Nasir-i Khusraw. *Naser-e Khosraw's Book of Travels/Safarnama.* Translated by W[heeler] M. Thackston, Jr. Persian Heritage Series, 36. Albany, N.Y., 1986.

Nasir-i Khusraw 2001 ed.
Nasir-i Khusraw. *Nasir-i Khusraw's Book of Travels/ Safarnamah.* Edited and translated by W[heeler] M. Thackston, Jr. Bibliotheca Iranica, Intellectual Traditions Series, 6. Costa Mesa, Calif., 2001.

Natsheh 2000
Natsheh, Yusuf. "The Architecture of Ottoman Jerusalem: Catalogue of Buildings." In Auld and Hillenbrand 2000, vol. 2, pp. 657–1085.

Necipoğlu 2008
Necipoğlu, Gülru. "The Dome of the Rock as Palimpsest: 'Abd al-Malik's Grand Narrative and Sultan Süleyman's Glosses." *Muqarnas* 25 [*Frontiers of Islamic Art and Architecture: Essays in Celebration of Oleg Grabar's Eightieth Birthday,* edited by Gülru Necipoğlu and Julia Bailey] (2008), pp. 17–105.

Nelson 2011–12
Nelson, Robert S. "'And So, With the Help of God': The Byzantine Art of War in the Tenth Century." *Dumbarton Oaks Papers* 65–66 (2011–12), pp. 169–92.

Netz 2001
Netz, Reviel. "Archimedes in Mar Saba: A Preliminary Notice." In Patrich, ed. 2001, pp. 195–99.

Neusner and Bashan 2007
Neusner, Jacob, and Eliezer Bashan. "Exilarch." In *Encyclopaedia Judaica* 2007, vol. 6, pp. 600–607.

Neuss 1912
Neuss, Wilhelm. *Das Buch Ezechiel in Theologie und Kunst bis zum Ende des 12. Jahrhunderts, mit besonderer Berücksichtigung der Gemälde in der Kirche zu Schwarzrheindorf: Ein Beitrag zur Entwicklungsgeschichte der Typologie der Christlichen Kunst, Vornehmlich in den Benediktinerklöstern.* Beiträge zur Geschichte des alten Mönchtums und des Benediktinerordens, pts. 1–2. Münster in Westf., 1912.

Newman 2008
Newman, Andrew J. "Burda." In *Encyclopedia of Islamic Civilisation and Religion,* edited by Ian Richard Netton, pp. 110–11. Curzon Encyclopedias of Religion. London and New York, 2008.

New York 1970
The Year 1200: A Centennial Exhibition at The Metropolitan Museum of Art. Exh. cat., The Metropolitan Museum of Art, New York, 1970. Catalogue by Konrad Hoffmann and others. Cloisters Studies in Medieval Art, 1–2. New York, 1970.

New York 1980
The Stavelot Triptych: Mosan Art and the Legend of the True Cross. Exh. cat., Pierpont Morgan Library, New York, 1980. Catalogue by William M. Voelkle. New York, 1980.

New York 1981
The Royal Abbey of Saint-Denis in the Time of Abbot Suger (1122–1151). Exh. cat., The Cloisters, The Metropolitan Museum of Art, New York, 1981. Catalogue by Sumner McKnight Crosby and others. New York, 1981.

New York 1982
Radiance and Reflection: Medieval Art from the Raymond Pitcairn Collection. Exh. cat., The Metropolitan Museum of Art, New York, 1982. Catalogue by Jane Hayward, Walter Cahn, and others. New York, 1982.

New York 1988–89
A Sign and a Witness: 2,000 Years of Hebrew Books and Illuminated Manuscripts. Exh. cat., New York Public Library, 1988–89. Catalogue by Leonard Singer Gold. Studies in Jewish History. New York, 1988.

New York 1997
The Glory of Byzantium: Art and Culture of the Middle Byzantine Era, A.D. 843–1261. Exh. cat., The Metropolitan Museum of Art, New York, 1997. Catalogue by Helen C. Evans, William D. Wixom, and others. New York, 1997.

New York 1999
Mirror of the Medieval World. Exh. cat., The Metropolitan Museum of Art, New York, 1999. Catalogue by William D. Wixom and others. New York, 1999.

New York 2000–2001
Scripture and Schism: Samaritan and Karaite Treasures from The Library of The Jewish Theological Seminary. Exh. cat., The Library of The Jewish Theological Seminary, New York, 2000–2001. Catalogue by Marina Rustow, Sharon Liberman Mintz, and Elka Deitsch. New York, 2000.

New York 2001
Precious Possessions: Treasures from The Library of The Jewish Theological Seminary. Exh. cat., The Library of The Jewish Theological Seminary, New York, 2001. Catalogue by Sharon Liberman Mintz, Elka Deitsch, and Havva Charm. New York, 2001.

New York 2004
Byzantium: Faith and Power (1261–1557). Exh. cat., The Metropolitan Museum of Art, New York, 2004. Catalogue by Helen C. Evans, Sarah T. Brooks, and others. New York, 2004.

New York 2006
Lions, Dragons, and Other Beasts: Aquamanilia of the Middle Ages, Vessels for Church and Table. Exh. cat., The Bard Graduate Center for Studies in the Decorative Arts, Design, and Culture, New York, 2006. Catalogue by Peter Barnet, Pete Dandridge, and others. New York, 2006.

New York 2010–11
Three Faiths: Judaism, Christianity, Islam. Online exh. cat., New York Public Library, 2010–11. Catalogue by George Fletcher and others. New York, 2010; http://www.nypl.org /events/exhibitions/three-faiths-judaism-christianity-islam.

New York 2011
Masterpieces from the Department of Islamic Art in The Metropolitan Museum of Art. Exh. cat., The Metropolitan Museum of Art, New York, 2011. Catalogue by Maryam D. Ekhtiar, Priscilla P. Soucek, and others. New York, 2011.

New York 2012
Byzantium and Islam: Age of Transition, 7th–9th Century. Exh. cat., The Metropolitan Museum of Art, New York, 2012. Catalogue by Helen C. Evans, Brandie Ratliff, and others. New York, 2012.

New York 2016
Court and Cosmos: The Great Age of the Seljuqs. Exh. cat., The Metropolitan Museum of Art, New York, 2016. Catalogue by Deniz Beyazit, Martina Rugiadi, and others. New York, 2016.

New York and Baltimore 1994
Treasures in Heaven: Armenian Illuminated Manuscripts. Exh. cat., Pierpont Morgan Library, New York; Walters Art Gallery, Baltimore, 1994. Catalogue by Thomas F. Mathews, Roger S. Wieck, and others. New York, 1994.

Niccolo of Poggibonsi 1945 ed.
Niccolo of Poggibonsi. *A Voyage Beyond the Seas (1346–1350).* Translated and edited by T[heophilus] Bellorini and E[ugene] Hoade. Publications of the Studium Biblicum Franciscanum, 2, pt. 2. Jerusalem, 1945.

Nicholson 1963
Nicholson, Reynold A[lleyne]. *The Mystics of Islam.* London, 1963.

Nickel 1972
Nickel, Helmut. "A Theory about the Early History of the Cloisters Apocalypse." *Metropolitan Museum Journal* 6 (1972), pp. 59–72.

Nickel 1991
Nickel, Helmut. "A Crusader's Sword: Concerning the Effigy of Jean d'Alluye." *Metropolitan Museum Journal* 26 (1991), pp. 123–28.

Noble 2014
Noble, Samuel. "Sulayman al-Ghazzi." In Noble and Treiger, eds. 2014, pp. 160–70.

Noble and Treiger, eds. 2014
Noble, Samuel, and Alexander Treiger, eds. *The Orthodox Church in the Arab World, 700–1700: An Anthology of Sources.* Orthodox Christian Series. DeKalb, Ill., 2014.

Nor 2011
Nor, Mohd Roslan Mohd. "Orientalists' View on the Night Journey: An Analysis." *Journal of Islamic Jerusalem Studies* 11 (Summer 2011), pp. 59–74.

Nordström 1968
Nordström, Carl-Otto. "Some Miniatures in Hebrew Bibles." In *Synthronon: Art et archéologie de la fin de l'Antiquité et du Moyen Âge; Recueil d'études,* edited by André Grabar, pp. 89–105. Bibliothèque des cahiers archéologique, 2. Paris, 1968.

Odell 2011
Odell, Margaret S. "Reading Ezekiel, Seeing Christ: The Ezekiel Cycle in the Church of St. Maria and St. Clemens, Schwarzrheindorf." In *After Ezekiel: Essays on the Reception of a Difficult Prophet,* edited by Paul M. Joyce and Andrew Mein, pp. 115–36. New York, 2011.

Offenberg 2011
Offenberg, Sara. "Illuminations of *Kol Nidrei* in Two Ashkenazi Mahzorim." *Ars Judaica* 7 (2011), pp. 7–16.

Offenberg 2014
Offenberg, Sara. "A Jewish Knight in Shining Armour: Messianic Narrative and Imagination in Ashkenazic Illuminated Manuscripts." *The University of Toronto Journal of Jewish Thought* 4 (2014), pp. 1–14.

Oftestad 2014
Oftestad, Eivor Andersen. "Beyond the Veil: Roman Constructs of the New Temple in the Twelfth Century." In Kühnel, B., Noga-Banai, and Vorholt, eds. 2014, pp. 171–78.

O'Kane 2012
O'Kane, Bernard. "Text and Paintings in the Al-Wasiti *Maqamat.*" *Ars Orientalis* 42 (2012), pp. 41–55.

O'Kane et al. 2012
O'Kane, Bernard, et al. *The Illustrated Guide to the Museum of Islamic Art in Cairo.* Cairo and New York, 2012.

Oldenburg 2005–6
Saladin und die Kreuzfahrer. Exh. cat., Landesmuseum für Vorgeschichte Halle (Saale) and Landesmuseum für Natur und Mensch, Oldenburg, 2005–6. Catalogue by Alfried Wieczorek, Mamoun Fansa, and others. Mainz, 2005.

Olszowy-Schlanger 1998
Olszowy-Schlanger, Judith. "The Karaite Nesiim." In *Karaite Marriage Documents from the Cairo Geniza: Legal Tradition and Community Life in Mediaeval Egypt and Palestine,* edited by Judith Olszowy-Schlanger, pp. 143–55. Études sur le judaïsme médiéval, 20. Leiden, New York, and Cologne, 1998.

O'Mahony 1996
O'Mahony, Anthony. "Between Islam and Christendom: The Ethiopian Community in Jerusalem before 1517." *Medieval Encounters* 2, no. 2 (1996), pp. 140–54.

Ostritz, ed. 2010a
Ostritz, Sven, ed. *Die Mittelalterliche jüdische Kultur in Erfurt* Vol. 1, *Der Schatzfund: Archäologie — Kunstgeschichte — Siedlungsgeschichte.* Thüringisches Landesamt für Denkmalpflege und Archäologie. Weimar, 2010.

Ostritz, ed. 2010b
Ostritz, Sven, ed. *Die Mittelalterliche jüdische Kultur in Erfurt.* Vol. 2, *Der Schatzfund: Analysen — Herstellungstechniken — Rekonstruktionen.* Weimar, 2010.

Otavsky and Salim 1995
Otavsky, Karel, and Muhammad 'Abbas Muhammad Salim. *Mittelalterliche Textilien.* Vol. 1, Ägypten, Persien und Mesopotamien, Spanien und Nordafrika. Abegg-Stiftung, Textilsammlung der Abegg-Stiftung. Riggisberg, 1995.

Ousterhout 1989
Ousterhout, Robert. "Rebuilding the Temple: Constantine Monomachus and the Holy Sepulchre." *Journal of the Society of Architectural Historians* 48, no. 1 (March 1989), pp. 66–78.

Ousterhout 2003
Ousterhout, Robert. "Architecture as Relic and the Construction of Sanctity: The Stones of the Holy Sepulchre." *Journal of the Society of Architectural Historians* 62, no. 1 (March 2003), pp. 4–23.

Ousterhout 2009
Ousterhout, Robert. "'Sweetly Refreshed in Imagination': Remembering Jerusalem in Words and Images." *Gesta* 48, no. 2 (2009), pp. 153–68, pls. 9–16.

Owen 1983 ed.
Owen, Wilfred. *The Complete Poems and Fragments.* Edited by Jon Stallworthy. 2 vols. London, 1983.

Pace 1984
Pace, Valentino. "I capitelli di Nazaret e la scultura 'franca' del XII secolo a Gerusalemme." In *Scritti di storia dell'arte in onore di Roberto Salvini,* edited by Cristina De Benedictis, pp. 87–95, pls. 29–31. Florence, 1984.

Pace 2005
Pace, Valentino. "Bildprogramme in der Figuralplastik des Heiligen Landes zur Zeit der Kreuzzüge." In Oldenburg 2005–6, pp. 216–25.

Pahlitzsch 2004
Pahlitzsch, Johannes. "The Transformation of Latin Religious Institutions into Islamic Endowments by Saladin in Jerusalem." In Pahlitzsch and Korn, eds. 2004, pp. 46–69.

Pahlitzsch 2008
Pahlitzsch, Johannes. "Documents on Intercultural Communication in Mamluk Jerusalem: The Georgians under Sultan an-Nasir Hasan in 759 (1358)." In *Diplomatics in the Eastern Mediterranean 1000–1500: Aspects of Cross-Cultural Communication,* edited by Alexander D. Beihammer, Maria G. Parani, and Christopher D. Schabel, pp. 373–94. The Medieval Mediterranean: Peoples, Economics and Cultures, 400–1500, 74. Leiden and Boston, 2008.

Pahlitzsch and Korn, eds. 2004
Pahlitzsch, Johannes, and Lorenz Korn, eds. *Governing the Holy City: The Interaction of Social Groups in Jerusalem between the Fatimid and Ottoman Period.* Wiesbaden, 2004.

Pancaroğlu 2004
Pancaroğlu, Oya. "The Itinerant Dragon-Slayer: Forging Paths of Image and Identity in Medieval Anatolia." *Gesta* 43, no. 2 (2004), pp. 151–64, pl. 2.

Paris 1998
Trésors fatimides du Caire. Exh. cat., L'Institut du Monde Arabe, Paris, 1998. Catalogue by Marianne Barrucand. Paris, 1998.

Paris 2001–2
L'Orient de Saladin: L'art des Ayyoubides. Exh. cat., L'Institut du Monde Arabe, Paris, 2001–2. Catalogue by Sophie Makariou and others. Paris, 2001.

Paris 2002–3
Chevaux et cavaliers arabes dans les arts d'Orient et d'Occident. Exh. cat., L'Institut du Monde Arabe, Paris, 2002–3. Catalogue by Jean-Pierre Digard and others. Paris, 2002.

Paris and Girona 2000–2001
L'arche éthiopienne: Art chrétien d'Éthiopie. Exh. cat., Pavillon des Arts, Paris; Fundació Caixa de Girona, Spain, 2000–2001. Catalogue by Béatrice Riottot El-Habib, Jacques Mercier, and others. Paris, 2000.

Paris and New York 1995–96
Enamels of Limoges, 1100–1350. Exh. cat., Musée du Louvre, Paris; The Metropolitan Museum of Art, New York, 1995–96. Catalogue by Barbara Drake Boehm, Marie-Madeleine Gauthier, and others. New York, 1996.

Paris, Brooklyn, and Doha 2006–7
From Cordoba To Samarqand: Masterpieces from the Museum of Islamic Art in Doha. Exh. cat., Musée du Louvre, Paris; Brooklyn Museum; Fahd bin Ali Palace, Doha, Qatar, 2006–7. Catalogue by Sabiha al-Khemir and others. Milan, 2006.

Patai 1979
Patai, Raphael. *The Messiah Texts.* Detroit, 1979.

Pataridze 2013
Pataridze, Tamar. "Christian Literature Translated from Arabic into Georgian: A Review." *Annual of Medieval Studies at CEU* 19 (2013), pp. 47–65.

Patel 2006
Patel, Ismail Adam. *Virtues of Jerusalem: An Islamic Perspective/ Fada'il al-Quds.* Leicester, 2006.

Patitucci-Uggeri 1979
Patitucci-Uggeri, Stella. "Protomaiolica brin-disina: Gruppo I." *Faenza* 65, no. 6 (1979), pp. 241–55.

Patrich 1995
Patrich, Joseph. *Sabas, Leader of Palestinian Monasticism: A Comparative Study in Eastern Monasticism, Fourth to Seventh Centuries.* Dumbarton Oaks Studies, 32. Washington, D.C., 1995.

Patrich, ed. 2001
Patrich, Joseph, ed. *The Sabaite Heritage in the Orthodox Church from the Fifth Century to the Present.* Orientalia Lovaniensia analecta, 98. Leuven, 2001.

Paul and Yeager, eds. 2012
Paul, Nicholas, and Suzanne Yeager, eds. *Remembering the Crusades: Myth, Image, and Identity.* Rethinking Theory. Baltimore, 2012.

Pauty 1930
Pauty, Edmond. *Bois sculptés d'églises coptes (époque fatimide)/ Matbu'at Mathaf al-Fann al-Islami.* Cairo, 1930.

Pavet de Courteille 1975 ed.
Pavet de Courteille, Abel, trans. *Miradj-Nameh: Récit de l'ascension de Mahomet au ciel, composé A.H. 840 (1436/1437).* Publications de l'École des Langues Orientales Vivantes, ser. 2, 6. Amsterdam, 1975.

Peeters 1912
Peeters, Paul. "De codice Hiberico Bibliothecae Bodleianae Oxoniensis." *Analecta Bollandiana* 31 (1912), pp. 301–18.

Peled 1999
Peled, Anat. "The Local Sugar Industry under the Latin Kingdom." In Jerusalem 1999, pp. 250–57.

Peradze 1935
Peradze, G[rigol]. "Georgian Manuscripts in England." *Georgica* 1 (1935), pp. 80–88.

Pératé 1911
Pératé, André. *Collections Georges Hoentschel.* Vol. 1, *Émaux du XIIe au XVe siècle.* Paris, 1911.

Peri 2001
Peri, Oded. *Christianity under Islam in Jerusalem: The Question of the Holy Sites in Early Ottoman Times.* Ottoman Empire and Its Heritage, 23. Leiden, Boston, and Cologne, 2001.

Pernot 1900
Pernot, H. "Descente de la Vierge au Enfers d'après les manuscrits grecs de Paris." *Revue des études grecques* 13 (1900), pp. 233–57.

Peters 1985
Peters, F[rank] E. *Jerusalem: The Holy City in the Eyes of Chroniclers, Visitors, Pilgrims, and Prophets from the Days of Abraham to the Beginnings of Modern Times.* Princeton, N.J., 1985.

Peters 1986
Peters, F[rank] E. *Jerusalem and Mecca: The Typology of the Holy City in the Near East.* New York University Studies in Near Eastern Civilization, 11. New York, 1986.

Petersen 2005
Petersen, Andrew. *The Towns of Palestine under Muslim Rule A.D. 600–1600.* BAR International Series, 1381. Oxford, 2005.

Phillips, J., 2007
Phillips, Jonathan. *The Second Crusade: Extending the Frontiers of Christendom.* New Haven and London, 2007.

Phillips, J., 2009
Phillips, Jonathan. "The Call of the Crusades." *History Today* 59 (November 11, 2009); http://www.historytoday.com /jonathan-phillips/call-crusades.

Phillips, R., and Steiner 1999
Phillips, Ruth B., and Christopher B. Steiner. "Art, Authenticity, and the Baggage of Cultural Encounter." In *Unpacking Culture: Art and Commodity in Colonial and Postcolonial Worlds,* edited by Ruth B. Phillips and Christopher B. Steiner, pp. 3–19. Berkeley and Los Angeles, 1999.

Pietro Casola 1907 ed.
Pietro Casola. *Canon Pietro Casola's Pilgrimage to Jerusalem in the Year 1494.* Edited by Margaret M. Newett. Publications of the University of Manchester, Historical Series, 5. Manchester, 1907.

***PL* 1841–65**
Migne, J[acques]-P[aul], et al. *Patrologiae cursus completus . . . : Series . . . latinae.* 221 vols. Paris, 1841–65.

Plessner 1957
Plessner, Martin. "Muhammed's Clandestine 'Umra in the Du 'l-Qa'da 8 H. and Sura 17,1." *Rivista degli Studi Orientali* 32 [*Scritti in onore di Guiseppe Furlani, Part II*] (1957), pp. 525–30.

Pletteau 1876
Pletteau, T. "Annales ecclésiastiques d'Anjou: Guillaume de Beaumont, Évêque d'Angers, 1202–1240." *Revue historique, littéraire et archéologique de l'Anjou* 17 (1876), pp. 144–80.

Polliack, ed. 2003
Polliack, Meira, ed. *Karaite Judaism: A Guide to Its History and Literary Sources.* Handbuch der Orientalistik, 1; Der Nahe und der Mittlere Osten, 73. Leiden and Boston, 2003.

Prawer 1972
Prawer, Joshua. *The Latin Kingdom of Jerusalem: European Colonialism in the Middle Ages.* London, 1972.

Prawer 1985
Prawer, Joshua. "Social Classes in the Crusader States: The 'Minorities.'" In *A History of the Crusades,* vol. 5, *The Impact of the Crusades on the Near East,* edited by Norman P. Zacour and Harry W. Hazard, pp. 59–115. Madison, Wisc., and London, 1985.

Prawer 1988
Prawer, Joshua. *The History of the Jews in the Latin Kingdom of Jerusalem.* Oxford, 1988.

Prawer and Ben-Shammai, eds. 1996
Prawer, Joshua, and Haggai Ben-Shammai, eds. *The History of Jerusalem: The Early Muslim Period, 638–1099.* Jerusalem and New York, 1996.

Princeton 1973
Illuminated Greek Manuscripts from American Collections: An Exhibition in Honor of Kurt Weitzmann. Exh. cat., Princeton University Art Museum, 1973. Catalogue by Gary Vikan and others. Princeton, N.J., 1973.

Princeton 1986
Byzantium at Princeton: Byzantine Art and Archaeology at Princeton University. Exh. cat., Firestone Library, Princeton University, 1986. Catalogue by Slobodan Ćurčić and Archer St. Clair. Princeton, N.J., 1986.

Pringle 1982
Pringle, Denys. "Les édifices ecclésiastiques du royaume latin de Jérusalem: Une liste provisoire." *Revue biblique* 89, no. 1 (1982), pp. 92–98.

Pringle 1993–2009
Pringle, Denys. *The Churches of the Crusader Kingdom of Jerusalem: A Corpus.* 4 vols. Cambridge, 1993–2009.

Pringle 2003
Pringle, Denys. "Churches and Settlement in Crusader Palestine." In *The Experience of Crusading,* vol. 2, *Defining the Crusader Kingdom* [The Second of 2 Volumes Presented to Jonathan Riley-Smith on His Sixty-fifth Birthday], edited by Peter Edbury and Jonathan Phillips, pp. 161–78. Cambridge, 2003.

Provo 2012
Beauty and Belief: Crossing Bridges with the Arts of Islamic Culture. Exh. cat., Brigham Young University Museum of Art, Provo, 2012. Catalogue by Sabiha al-Khemir. Provo, 2012.

Pruitt 2013
Pruitt, Jennifer. "Method in Madness: Reconsidering Church Destructions in the Fatimid Era." *Muqarnas* 30 (2013), pp. 119–39.

Quaresmius 1639
Quaresmi[us], Francisc[us]. *Historica, Theologica et Moralis Terrae Sanctae Elucidatio* . . . 2 vols. Antwerp, 1639.

Qur'an 1990 ed.
The Koran with a Parallel Arabic Text. Translated and annotated by N. J. Dawood. London, 1990.

Qur'an 1992–93 ed.
The Holy Qur'an: English Translation of the Meanings and Commentary. Edited by the Presidency of Islamic Researches, IFTA, Call and Guidance. Medina, [1992–93].

Qur'an 2004 ed.
The Qur'an. Translated by M. A. S. Abdel Haleem. Oxford, 2004.

al-Qushayri 1964 ed.
al-Qushayri, Abu'l-Qasim. *Kitab al-Mi'raj* (in Arabic). Edited by 'Ali Hasan 'Abd al-Qadir. Maktabat al-adab al-Sufiyah, 2. Cairo, [1964].

Rabbat 1989
Rabbat, Nasser. "The Meaning of the Umayyad Dome of the Rock." *Muqarnas* 6 (1989), pp. 12–21.

Rabinowitz 1985
Rabinowitz, Zvi Meir. *Mahzor piyute Rabi Yanai la-Torah vela mo'adim . . . The Liturgical Poems of Rabbi Yannai* (in Hebrew). Jerusalem, 1985.

Raby 1999
Raby, Julian. "In Vitro Veritas: Glass Pilgrim Vessels from 7th-Century Jerusalem." In *Bayt al-Maqdis,* pt. 2, *Jerusalem and Early Islam,* edited by Jeremy Johns, pp. 113–90. Oxford Studies in Islamic Art, 9. Oxford, 1999.

Raby 2012
Raby, Julian. "The Principle of Parsimony and the Problem of the 'Mosul School of Metalwork.'" In *Metalwork and Material Culture in the Islamic World: Art, Craft and Text; Essays Presented to James W. Allan,* edited by Venetia Porter and Mariam Rosser-Owen, pp. 11–85. London and New York, 2012.

Raby 2014
Raby, Julian. "Mosul Metalworkers after the Mongols." In *Court and Craft: A Masterpiece from Northern Iraq,* pp. 56–67. Exh. cat., Courtauld Gallery, London, 2014. Catalogue by Rachel Ward and others. London, 2014.

Radulfus Niger 1977 ed.
Radulfus Niger. *De re militari et triplici via peregrinationis ierosolimitane (1187–88).* Edited by Ludwig Schmugge. Beiträge zur Geschichte und Quellenkunde des Mittelalters, 6. Berlin and New York, 1977.

Rahmani 2003
Rahmani, Levi Yitzhak. "On Some Roman to Early Medieval Lead Miniature Amphorae." *Israel Museum Studies in Archaeology* 2 (2003), pp. 33–62.

Randall 1989
Randall, Lilian M. C. *Medieval and Renaissance Manuscripts in the Walters Art Gallery.* Vol. 1, *France, 875–1420.* Baltimore and London, 1989.

Rashi 1993– ed.
Rashi [Solomon ben Isaac of Troyes]. *The Complete Jewish Bible with Rashi Commentary.* [Brooklyn], 1993– ; http://www.chabad.org/library/bible_cdo/aid/16218/jewish/Chapter-14.htm#showrashitrue.

Rashi 1995–2008 ed.
Rashi [Solomon ben Isaac of Troyes]. *Rashi: The Torah with Rashi's Commentary.* Edited by Yisrael Isser Zvi Herczeg et al. 5 vols. Artscroll Series, Sapirstein Edition. Brooklyn, 1995–2008.

Rashid al-Din 2015 ed.
"Rashid al-Din's 'World History,' 1314 – A Masterpiece of Islamic Painting" [with link to facsimile of Edinburgh University Library, MS Arab 20]. In *The University of Edinburgh, School of Literatures, Languages and Cultures, Islamic and Middle Eastern Studies.* Edinburgh, 2015; http://www.ed.ac.uk/literatures-languages-cultures/islamic-middle-eastern/news-events/visual-world-persian-culture/rashad-al-din (accessed April 23, 2016).

Redford 2004
Redford, S. "On Saquis and Ceramics: Systems of Representations in the Northeast Mediterranean." In Weiss and Mahoney, eds. 2004, pp. 282–312.

Reiner 1999
Reiner, Elchanan. "A Jewish Response to the Crusades: The Dispute over Sacred Places in the Holy Land." In *Juden und Christen zur Zeit der Kreuzzüge,* edited by Alfred Haverkamp, pp. 209–31. Vorträge und Forschungen, 47. Sigmaringen, 1999.

Reiner 2002
Reiner, Elchanan. "Traditions of Holy Places in Medieval Palestine – Oral versus Written." In *Offerings from Jerusalem: Portrayals of Holy Places by Jewish Artists,* edited by Rachel Sarfati, pp. 9–19. Catalogue [Muzeon Yisrael], 463. Jerusalem, 2002.

Reiner 2004
Reiner, Elchanan. *"All Rivers Run to the Sea, All of Israel Converge in Jerusalem, May It be Rebuilt Speedily": The Pilgrimage to Jerusalem after the Destruction* (in Hebrew; provisional unpublished edition, Accademia.edu.). Jerusalem, 2004; https://www.academia.edu/11208366 (accessed August 6, 2015).

Revel-Neher 1998
Revel-Neher, Elisabeth. *Le témoignage de l'absence: Les objets du sanctuaire à Byzance et dans l'art juif du XIe au XVe siècle.* Paris, 1998.

Riant 1865–69
Riant, Paul Edouard Didier, comte. *Expéditions et pèlerinages des Scandinaves en Terre Sainte au temps des Croisades.* 2 vols. Paris, 1865–69.

***RIBA* 1962**
Obituary of William Harvey. *Royal Institute of British Architects Journal* 69 (1962), p. 224.

Rice, D. S., 1950
Rice, D. S. "The Brasses of Badr al-Din Lu'lu'." *Bulletin of the School of Oriental and African Studies, University of London* 13, no. 3 (1950), pp. 627–34, pls. 13–16.

Rice, D. T., 1976
Rice, David Talbot. *The Illustrations to the World History of Rashid al-Din* [Edinburgh University Library, MS Arab 20]. Edited by Basil Gray. Text vol. and microfiche facsimile. Edinburgh, 1976.

Richard 1999
Richard, Jean. "Les prisonniers et leur rachat au cours des croisades." In *Fondations et oeuvres charitables au Moyen Âge,* edited by Jean Dufour and Henri Platelle, pp. 63–74. Paris, 1999.

Riley-Smith 1997
Riley-Smith, J[onathan]. "King Fulk of Jerualem and 'The Sultan of Babylon.'" In *Montjoie: Studies in Crusader History in Honour of Hans Eberhard Mayer,* edited by Benjamin Z. Kedar, Jonathan Riley-Smith, and Rudolph Hiestand, pp. 55–66. Aldershot, Hampshire, and Brookfield, Vt., 1997.

Ritmeyer 1992
Ritmeyer, Leen. "Locating the Original Temple Mount." *Biblical Archaeology Review* 18, no. 2 (March–April 1992), pp. 24–45, 64–65.

Riyadh 1985
The Unity of Islamic Art: An Exhibition to Inaugurate the Islamic Art Gallery of the King Faisal Center for Research and Islamic Studies, Riyadh, Saudi Arabia, 1405 A.H./1985 A.D. Exh. cat., Islamic Art Gallery of the King Faisal Center for Research and Islamic Studies, Riyadh, Saudi Arabia, 1985. Catalogue by Oliver Hoare and others. Riyadh, 1985.

Robinson et al. 1976
Robinson, B[asil] W[illiam], et al. *Islamic Painting and the Arts of the Book.* The Keir Collection. London, 1976.

Rodríguez Arribas 2014
Rodríguez Arribas, Josefina. "Medieval Jews and Medieval Astrolabes: Where, Why, How, and What For?" In *Time, Astronomy, and Calendars in the Jewish Tradition,* edited by Sacha Stern and Charles Burnett, pp. 221–72. Time, Astronomy, and Calendars, 3. Leiden and Boston, 2014.

Rogers 1973
Rogers, J. Michael. "Evidence for Mamluk-Mongol Relations, 1260–1360." In *Colloque international sur l'histoire du Caire,* [edited by André Raymond, J. Michael Rogers, and Magdi Wahba], pp. 384–403. Berlin and Cairo, 1973.

Rogers 1998
Rogers, J. M[ichael]. "European Inventories as a Source for the Distribution of Mamluk Enamelled Glass." In Ward, ed. 1998, pp. 69–73, 187–88, color pl. D.

Rome 1997
Le Crociate: L'Oriente e l'Occidente da Urbano II a San Luigi, 1096–1270. Exh. cat., Palazzo Venezia, Rome, 1997. Milan, 1997.

Rose 1992
Rose, Richard B. "The Native Christians of Jerusalem, 1187–1260." In Kedar, ed. 1992, pp. 239–49.

Rosen-Ayalon 1977
Rosen-Ayalon, Myriam. "A Silver Ring from Medieval Islamic Times." In *Studies in Memory of Gaston Wiet,* edited by Myriam Rosen-Ayalon, pp. 194–201. Jerusalem, 1977.

Rosen-Ayalon 1991
Rosen-Ayalon, Myriam. "The Islamic Jewellery from Ashkelon." In *Jewellery and Goldsmithing in the Islamic World: International Symposium, The Israel Museum, Jerusalem, 1987,* edited by Na'ama Brosh, pp. 9–19. Jerusalem, 1991.

Rosen-Ayalon 1999
Rosen-Ayalon, Myriam. "Three Perspectives on Jerusalem: Jewish, Christian, and Muslim Pilgrims in the Twelfth Century." In *Jerusalem: Its Sanctity and Centrality to Judaism, Christianity, and Islam,* edited by Lee I. Levine, pp. 326–46. New York, 1999.

Rosen-Ayalon 2008
Rosen-Ayalon, Myriam. "Gold Jewellery of the Fatimid Period." In *Ashkelon 1: Introduction and Overview (1985–2006),* edited by Lawrence E. Stager, J. David Schloen, and Daniel M. Master, pp. 639–44. Final Reports of the Leon Levy Expedition to Ashkelon. Winona Lake, Ind., 2008.

Rosenberg, trans. 2000
Rosenberg, A. J., trans. *Ezekiel: A New English Translation.* Vol. 2. Judaica Books of the Prophets. New York, 2000.

Ross 2014
Ross, Elizabeth. *Picturing Experience in the Early Printed Book: Breydenbach's Peregrinatio from Venice to Jerusalem.* University Park, Pa., 2014.

Roupp 1902
Roupp, N. "Die älteste äthiopische Handschrift der vier Bücher der Könige." *Zeitschrift für Assyriologie und verwandte Gebiete* 16, no. 2 (1902), pp. 296–343.

Rouse and Rouse 2000
Rouse, Richard H., and Mary A. Rouse. *Manuscripts and Their Makers: Commercial Book Producers in Medieval Paris, 1200–1500.* 2 vols. Turnhout, 2000.

Rout 2011
Rout, Paul. "St. Francis of Assisi and Islam: A Theological Perspective on a Christian-Muslim Encounter." *Al-Masaq: Journal of the Medieval Mediterranean* 23, no. 3 (2011), pp. 205–15.

Roxburgh 2008
Roxburgh, David J. "Pilgrimage City." In *The City in the Islamic World,* edited by Salma K. Jayyusi et al., vol. 2, pp. 753–74. 2 vols. Handbook of Oriental Studies, 94. Leiden and Boston, 2008.

Roxburgh 2013
Roxburgh, David J. "In Pursuit of Shadows: Al-Hariri's *Maqamat.*" *Muqarnas* 30 (2013), pp. 171–212.

Rubenstein 2011
Rubenstein, Jay. *Armies of Heaven: The First Crusade and the Quest for Apocalypse.* New York, 2011.

Rubenstein 2012
Rubenstein, Jay. "Lambert of Saint-Omer and the Apocalyptic First Crusade." In Paul and Yeager, eds. 2012, pp. 69–95.

Rubenstein 2014
Rubenstein, Jay. "Heavenly and Earthly Jerusalem: The View from Twelfth-Century Flanders." In Kühnel, B., Noga-Banai, and Vorholt, eds. 2014, pp. 265–76.

Rubin 1998
Rubin, Milka. "Arabization versus Islamization in the Palestinian Melkite Community during the Early Muslim Period." In Kofsky and Stroumsa, eds. 1998, pp. 149–62.

Rüdt de Collenberg 1977
Rüdt de Collenberg, W[eyprecht]-H[ugo]. "L'héraldique de Chypre." *Cahiers d'héraldique* 3 (1977), pp. 85–158 and plates.

Ruíz 2012
Ruíz, Rafael Azuar. *Los bronces islámicos de Denia.* Museo Arqueológico Provincial [Alicante], Serie mayor, 10. Alicante, 2012.

Rutschowscaya 2000
Marie-Hélène Rutschowscaya. "The Mother of God in Coptic Textiles." In *Mother of God: Representations of the Virgin in Byzantine Art,* edited by Maria Vassilaki, pp. 219–25. Milan, 2000.

Safadi 1978
Safadi, Yasin Hamid. *Islamic Calligraphy.* London, 1978.

Safrai and Safrai 1998
Safrai, Shmuel, and Zev Safrai. *Haggadah of the Sages: Haggadah of Passover* (in Hebrew). Jerusalem, 1998.

Safran 2014
Safran, Linda. *The Medieval Salento: Art and Identity in Southern Italy.* The Middle Ages Series. Philadelphia, 2014.

Sa'id 1988
Sa'id, Mustafa 'Abd al-Rahim Muhammad. "Islamic Glass Lamps as Light Energy-Saving Vessels: An Analytical Study" (in Arabic). Unpublished conference paper, "The Greatest Products Designed and Produced in Egypt," Helwan University, Faculty of Applied Arts, Industrial Designs Department, Glass Section; Cairo, 1988.

Saint-Genois 1847
Saint-Genois, Jules Ludger Dominique Ghislain de. *Sur des lettres inédites de Jacques de Vitry, évêque de Saint-Jean-d'Acre, Cardinal et légat du pape, écrites en 1216.* Mémoires de l'Académie Royale des Sciences, des Lettres et des Beaux-Arts de Belgique, 23, no. 5. Brussels, 1847.

Salameh 1999
Salameh, Khader. *The Qur'an Manuscripts in the Al-Haram al-Sharif Islamic Museum, Jerusalem.* Reading, U.K., 1999.

Sanjian 1969
Sanjian, Avedis K. *Colophons of Armenian Manuscripts, 1301–1480.* Harvard Armenian Texts and Studies, 2. Cambridge, 1969.

Sanjian 1976
Sanjian, Avedis K. *A Catalogue of Medieval Armenian Manuscripts in the United States.* University of California Publications; Near Eastern Studies, 16. Berkeley, 1976.

Sanudo 2011 ed.
Sanudo Torsello, Marino. *The Book of the Secrets of the Faithful of the Cross/Liber Secretorum Fidelium Crucis.* Translated by Peter Lock. Crusade Texts in Translation, 21. Farnham, Surrey, and Burlington, Vt., 2011.

Sarfati 2002
Sarfati, Rachel. "The Illustrations of Yihus ha-Avot: Folk Art from the Holy Land." In *Offerings from Jerusalem: Portrayals of Holy Places by Jewish Artists,* edited by Rachel Sarfati, pp. 21–29. Catalogue [Muzeon Yisrael], 463. Jerusalem, 2002.

Sarna 2014
Sarna, Navtej. *An Indian Corner in Jerusalem.* New Delhi, 2014.

Saunders 1982
Saunders, W. B. R. "The Aachen Reliquary of Eustathius Maleinus, 969–970." *Dumbarton Oaks Papers* 36 (1982), pp. 211–19.

Savage-Smith 1985
Savage-Smith, Emilie. *Islamicate Celestial Globes: Their History, Construction, and Use.* Smithsonian Studies in History and Technology, 46. Washington, D.C., 1985.

Savage-Smith 1992
Savage-Smith, Emilie. "Celestial Mapping." In *The History of Cartography,* vol. 2, bk. 1, *Cartography in the Traditional Islamic and South Asian Societies,* edited by J. B. Harley and David Woodward, pp. 12–70. Chicago and London, 1992.

Savage-Smith 2003
Savage-Smith, Emilie. "Memory and Maps." In *Culture and Memory in Medieval Islam: Essays in Honour of Wilferd Madelung,* edited by Farhad Daftary and Josef W. Meri, pp. 109–27. London, 2003.

Scalini 2013
Scalini, Mario. "Il Maestro dell'acquamanile Palagi di Bologna." In *L'acquamanile del Museo Civico Medievale di Bolgna,* edited by Mark Gregory D'Apuzzo and Massimo Medica, pp. 33–51. Milan, 2013.

Schaefer 1985
Schaefer, Karl R. "Jerusalem in the Ayyubid and Mamluk Eras." Ph.D. diss., New York University, 1985.

Schallaburg 2007
Kreuzritter: Pilger, Krieger, Abenteurer. Exh. cat., Schallaburg Kulturbetriebsges, 2007. Catalogue by Barbara Sternthal and others. Schallaburg, Austria, 2007.

Schaus, ed. 2006
Schaus, Margaret, ed. *Women and Gender in Medieval Europe: An Encyclopedia.* Routledge Encyclopedias of the Middle Ages, 14. New York, 2006.

Schechner 2008
Schechner, Sara. "Astrolabes and Medieval Travel." In *The Art, Science, and Technology of Medieval Travel,* edited by Robert Bork and Andrea Kann, pp. 181–210. AVISTA Studies in the History of Medieval Technology, Science and Art, 6. Aldershot, Hampshire, and Burlington, Vt., 2008.

Scheiber 1983
Scheiber, Sándor. *Jewish Inscriptions in Hungary from the 3rd Century to 1686/Corpus inscriptionum Hungariae Judaicarum, a temporibus saeculi III., quae exstant, usque ad annum 1686.* Budapest and Leiden, 1983.

Schein 1991
Schein, Sylvia. *Fidelis Crucis: The Papacy, the West, and the Recovery of the Holy Land, 1274–1314.* Oxford, 1991.

Schein 2005
Schein, Sylvia. *Gateway to the Heavenly City: Crusader Jerusalem and the Catholic West (1099–1187).* Church, Faith, and Culture in the Medieval West. Aldershot, Hampshire, and Burlington, Vt., 2005.

Scheindlin 2008
Scheindlin, Raymond P. *The Song of the Distant Dove: Judah Halevi's Pilgrimage.* Oxford, 2008.

Schick 2012
Schick, Robert. "Christian Identifications of Muslim Buildings in Medieval Jerusalem." In *Jerusalem as Narrative Space/Erzählraum Jerusalem,* edited by Annette Hoffman and Gerhard Wolf, pp. 367–89. Visualising the Middle Ages, 6. Leiden and Boston, 2012.

Schilling and Swarzenski 1929
Schilling, Rosy, and Georg Swarzenski. *Die illuminierten Handschriften und Einzelminiaturen des Mittelalters und der Renaissance in Frankfurter Besitz.* 2 vols. Frankfurt, 1929.

Schimmel 1992
Schimmel, Annemarie. "Islamic Calligraphy." *The Metropolitan Museum of Art Bulletin,* n.s., 50, no. 1 (Summer 1992), pp. 1–56.

Schneider 1973
Schneider, Laura T. "The Freer Canteen." *Ars Orientalis* 9 [*Freer Gallery of Art Fiftieth Anniversary Volume*] (1973), pp. 137–56, pls. 1–13.

Schonfield et al. 1992
Schonfield, Jeremy, et al. *The Barcelona Haggadah: An Illuminated Passover Compendium from 14th-Century Catalonia in Facsimile (MS British Library Additional 14761).* 2 vols. London, 1992.

Schottenstein Talmud 1990–2005
Goldwurm, Hersh, et al., eds. *Talmud Bavli/The Gemara; The Classic Vilna Edition, with an Annotated, Interpretive Elucidation as an Aid to Talmud Study.* Schottenstein Edition. 73 vols. Artscroll Series. Brooklyn, N.Y., 1990–2005.

Schultz, ed. 1910
Schultz, R[obert] Weir, ed. *The Church of the Nativity at Bethlehem.* Byzantine Research Fund. London, 1910.

Schwarb 2010
Schwarb, Gregor. "Yusuf al-Basir." In *Encyclopedia of Jews in the Islamic World,* edited by Norman A. Stillman. 5 vols. Leiden, 2010.

Schwartz 1997
Schwartz, Dov. *Messianism in Medieval Jewish Thought* (in Hebrew). Ramat-Gan, [1997].

Schwinges 2001
Schwinges, Rainer Christoph. "William of Tyre, the Muslim Enemy, and the Problem of Tolerance." In *Tolerance and Intolerance: Social Conflict in the Age of the Crusades,* edited by Michael Gervers and James M. Powell, pp. 124–32. Syracuse, N.Y., 2001.

Seawulf 1892 ed.
Seawulf (1102, 1103 A.D.). Translated by William Robert Bernard Brownlow. Palestine Pilgrims' Text Society, 4, no. 2. London, 1892.

Sebag Montefiore 2011
Sebag Montefiore, Simon. *Jerusalem: The Biography.* New York, 2011.

Sed-Rajna 1975
Sed-Rajna, Gabrielle. *Ancient Jewish Art: East and West.* Paris, 1975.

Sed-Rajna 1983
Sed-Rajna, Gabrielle. *Le Mahzor enluminé: Les voies de formation d'un programme iconographique.* Leiden, 1983.

Sed-Rajna 1986–87
Sed-Rajna, Gabrielle. "Filligree Ornaments in Fourteenth-Century Hebrew Manuscripts: Methodology and Practice." *Jewish Art* 12–13 (1986–87), pp. 45–54.

Sed-Rajna 1994
Sed-Rajna, Gabrielle. *Les manuscrits hébreux enluminés des bibliothèques de France.* Leuven, 1994.

Séguy 1977
Séguy, Marie-Rose. *The Miraculous Journey of Mahomet: Miraj Nameh, Bibliothèque Nationale, Paris (Manuscrit supplément turc 190).* Translated by Richard Pevear. New York, 1977.

Seligman 2010
Seligman, Jon. "A Crusader Wall Painting from the Abbey of the Virgin Mary in the Valley of Jehoshaphat, Jerusalem" (in Hebrew). In *New Studies in the Archaeology of Jerusalem and Its Region: Collected Papers* (in Hebrew), vol. 4, edited by David Amit, Orit Peleg-Barkat, and Guy D. Stiebel, pp. 141–57. Jerusalem, 2010.

Seligman 2012
Seligman, Jon. "A Wall Painting, a Crusader Flood Diversion Facility and Other Archaeological Gleanings from the Abbey of the Virgin Mary in the Valley of Jehoshaphat, Jerusalem." In *Christ is Here!: Studies in Biblical and Christian Archaeology in Memory of Michele Piccirillo O.F.M.,* edited by L[eslaw] Daniel Chrupcała, pp. 185–220. Collectio maior, 52. Milan, 2012.

Ševčenko 1991
Ševčenko, Nancy Patterson. "Menologion." In *The Oxford Dictionary of Byzantium,* edited by Alexander P. Kazhdan et al., vol. 2, p. 1341. 3 vols. New York and Oxford, 1991.

Ševčenko 1992
Ševčenko, Nancy Patterson. "Vita Icons and 'Decorated' Icons of the Komnenian Period." In *Four Icons in the Menil Collection,* edited by Bertrand Davezac, pp. 56–69, pl. 3. The Menil Collection Monographs, 1. Houston, 1992.

Ševčenko 2004
Ševčenko, Nancy P[atterson]. "The Liturgical *Typikon* of Symeon of Sinai." In *Metaphrastes, or, Gained in Translation: Essays in Honour of Robert H. Jordan,* edited by Margaret Mullet, pp. 274–86. Belfast Byzantine Texts and Translations, 9. Belfast, 2004.

Seville and Dallas 2013–14
Nur/Light: Light in Art and Science from the Islamic World. Exh. cat., Focus-Abengoa Foundation, Seville; Dallas Museum of Art, 2013–14. Catalogue by Sabiha Al Khemir and others. Seville, 2013.

Sezgin, Ehrig-Eggert, and Neubauer 2007
Sezgin, Fuat, Carl Ehrig-Eggert, and E. Neubauer. *Al-haram Ash-Sharif in Jerusalem: Texts and Studies.* 4 vols. Frankfurt am Main, 2007.

Shalem 1996
Shalem, Avinoam. *Islam Christianized: Islamic Portable Objects in the Medieval Church Treasuries of the Latin West.* Ars faciendi, 7. Frankfurt am Main, 1996.

Shalem 1998
Shalem, Avinoam. "Some Speculations on the Original Cases Made to Contain Enamelled Glass Beakers for Export." In Ward, ed. 1998, pp. 64–68, 184–86.

Shalem 1999
Shalem, Avinoam. "Islamic Rock Crystal Vessels – Scent or Ampullae?" In *Bamberger Symposium: Rezeption in der islamischen Kunst; Vom 26.6.–28.6.1992,* edited by Barbara Finster et al., pp. 289–99. Beiruter Texte und Studien, 61. Stuttgart, 1999.

Shalem 2007
Shalem, Avinoam. "From Individual Manufacturing to Mass-Production: Notes on the Aesthetic of the Islamic Traded Ivories of the Crusader Era." In *Facts and Artefacts: Art in the Islamic World; Festschrift for Jens Kröger on his 65th Birthday,* edited by Annette Hagedorn and Avinoam Shalem, pp. 231–49. Islamic History and Civilization, 68. Leiden and Boston, 2007.

Shalem 2014
Shalem, Avinoam. *Die Mittelalterlichen Olifante: Elfenbeinobjekte in einem Zeitalter des ästhetischen Wandels.* 2 vols. Die Elfenbeinskulpturen, 8. Berlin, 2014.

Shalem 2016
Shalem, Avinoam. "The Poetics of Portability." In *Histories of Ornament from Global to Local,* edited by Gülru Necipoğlu and Alina Payne, pp. 250–61. Princeton, N.J., 2016.

Shalev-Eyni 2004
Shalev-Eyni, Sarit. "Jerusalem and the Temple in Hebrew Illuminated Manuscripts: Jewish Thought and Christian Influence." In *L'interculturalità dell'ebraismo,* edited by Mauro Perani, pp. 173–91. Tessere, 8. Ravenna, 2004.

Shalev-Eyni 2015
Shalev-Eyni, Sarit. "Between Carnality and Spirituality: A Cosmological Vision of the End at the Turn of the Fifth Jewish Millennium." *Speculum* 90, no. 2 (April 2015), pp. 458–82.

Shamir and Baginski 2002
Shamir, Orit, and Alisa Baginski. "Medieval Mediterranean Textiles, Basketry, and Cordage Newly Excavated in Israel." In *Towns and Material Culture in the Medieval Middle East,* edited by Yaacov Lev, pp. 135–57. The Medieval Mediterranean: Peoples, Economies and Cultures, 400–1453, 39. Leiden, Boston, and Cologne, 2002.

Sharon 1995
Sharon, Moshe. "A New Fâtimid Inscription from Ascalon and Its Historical Setting." *'Atiqot* 26 [*Early Islamic and Medieval Studies*] (1995), pp. 61–86.

Sharon 1997
Sharon, Moshe. "Ashkelon." In Sharon 1997–2013, vol. 1, pp. 130–84.

Sharon 1997–2013
Sharon, Moshe. *Corpus inscriptionum Arabicarum Palaestinae.* 5 vols. in 6. Handbuch der Orientalistik, 1; Der Nahe und der Mittlere Osten, 30. Leiden, 1997–2013.

Sheffer and Druks 2000
Sheffer, Avigail, and Adam Druks. "A Bowl from Acre Depicting a Woman Spinning" (in Hebrew). *Qadmoniot: A Journal for the Antiquities of Eretz-Israel and Bible Lands* 119 (2000), pp. 63–65.

Shoemaker 2012
Shoemaker, Stephen J. *The Death of a Prophet: The End of Muhammad's Life and the Beginnings of Islam.* Divinations: Rereading Late Ancient Religion. Philadelphia, 2012.

Simek 1992
Simek, Rudolf. "'Hierusalem civitas famosissima': Die erhaltenen Fassungen des hochmittelalterlichen *Situs Jerusalem* (mit Abbildungen zur gesamten handschriftlichen Überlieferung)." *Codices manuscripti* 16 (1992), pp. 121–53.

Sims 2014
Sims, Eleanor. "The *Nahj al-Faradis* of Sultan Abu Sa'id ibn Sultan Muhammad ibn Miranshah: An Illustrated Timurid Ascension Text of the 'Interim' Period." *Journal of the David Collection* 4 (2014), pp. 88–147.

Singer, ed. 2008
Singer, Lynette, ed. *The Minbar of Saladin: Reconstructing a Jewel of Islamic Art.* London, 2008.

Sivan 1971
Sivan, Emanuel. "The Beginnings of the 'Fada'il al-Quds' Literature." *Israel Oriental Studies* 1 (1971), pp. 263–72.

Skarlakidis 2011
Skarlakidis, Haris. *Holy Fire – The Miracle of Holy Saturday at the Tomb of Christ: Forty-Five Historical Accounts (9th–16th C.).* Athens, 2011.

Sklare 1995
Sklare, David E. "Yusuf al-Basir: Theological Aspects of His Halakhic Works." In *The Jews of Medieval Islam: Community, Society, and Identity; Proceedings of an International Conference Held by the Institute of Jewish Studies, University College London, 1992,* edited by Daniel Frank, pp. 248–70. Études sur le judaïsme médiéval, 16. New York, 1995.

Snelders 2010
Snelders, Bas. *Identity and Christian-Muslim Interaction: Medieval Art of the Syrian Orthodox from the Mosul Area.* Orientalia Lovaniensia analecta, 198. Leuven and Walpole, Mass., 2010.

Spallanzani 2012
Spallanzani, Marco. *Vetri islamici a Firenze nel primo Rinascimento.* Florence, 2012.

Spatharakis 1981
Spatharakis, Io[h]annis. *Corpus of Dated Illuminated Greek Manuscripts to the Year 1453.* 2 vols. Byzantina Neerlandica, 8. Leiden, 1981.

Sperber 1989
Sperber, Daniel. *The Customs of Israel* (in Hebrew). Jerusalem, 1989.

Sperling n.d.
Sperling, Abraham Isaac. *The Book of the Reasons for the Customs and Sources for the Laws* (in Hebrew). Jerusalem, n.d.

Spitzer, ed. 1890–93
Spitzer, Frédéric, ed. *La collection Spitzer: Antiquité – Moyen-Âge – Renaissance.* Vol. 1. Paris, 1890–93.

Spufford 2002
Spufford, Peter. *Power and Profit: The Merchant in Medieval Europe.* London, 2002.

Stantchev 2014
Stantchev, Stefan K. *Spiritual Rationality: Papal Embargo as Cultural Practice.* Oxford, 2014.

Stautz 1999
Stautz, Burkhard. *Die Astrolabiensammlungen des Deutschen Museums und des Bayerischen Nationalmuseums.* Abhandlungen und Berichte [Deutsches Museum], 12. Munich, 1999.

Steenbock 2004
Steenbock, Frauke. "Psalters with Pictorial Bindings/ Psalterien mit kostbaren Einbänden." In *The Illuminated Psalter: Studies in the Content, Purpose and Placement of Its Images,* edited by F. O. Büttner, pp. 435–40, pls. 441–55. Turnhout, 2004.

Steensgaard et al. 1971
Steensgaard, N., et al. "Harir." In *EI2* 1960–2009, vol. 3 (1971), pp. 209–21, pls. 1–8.

Stephan 1939
Stephan, St[ephan] H[anna]. "Evliya Tshelebi's Travels in Palestine, VI." *The Quarterly of the Department of Antiquities in Palestine* 9 (1939), pp. 81–104.

Stern, D., 2012
Stern, David. "The Hebrew Bible in Europe in the Middle Ages: A Preliminary Typology." *Jewish Studies, an Internet Journal* 11 (2012), pp. 1–88.

Stern, E., 1999
Stern, Edna J. "Ceramic Ware from the Crusader Period in the Holy Land." In Jerusalem 1999, pp. 258–65.

Stern, E., 2012
Stern Edna J., with Anastasia Shapiro and Sylvie Yona Waksman. *Akko I: The 1991–1998 Excavations; The Crusader-Period Pottery.* 2 vols. IAA Reports, 51. Jerusalem, 2012.

Stern, H., 1936
Stern, Henri. "Les représentations des conciles dans l'Église de la Nativité à Bethléem." *Byzantion: Revue internationale des études byzantines* 11 (1936), pp. 101–52.

Stern, H., 1938
Stern, H[enri]. "Les représentations des conciles dans l'Église de la Nativité à Bethléem. Deuxieme partie: Les inscriptions." *Byzantion: Revue internationale des études byzantines* 13 (1938), pp. 415–59.

Stern, H., 1948
Stern, Henri. "Nouvelles recherches sur les images des conciles dans l'Église de la Nativité à Bethléem." *Cahiers archéologiques* 3 (1948), pp. 82–105.

Stern, H., 1957
Stern, Henri. "Encore les mosaïques de l'Église de la Nativité à Bethléem." *Cahiers archéologiques* 9 (1957), pp. 141–45.

Stern, S., 1955
Stern, S[amuel] M[iklos]. "Autographs of Maimonides in the Bodleian Library." *The Bodleian Library Record* 5, no. 4 (October 1955), pp. 180–202.

Stetkevych 2006
Stetkevych, Suzanne Pinckney. "From Text to Talisman: Al-Busiri's *Qasidat al-Burdah* (*Mantle Ode*) and the Supplicatory Ode." *Journal of Arabic Literature* 37, no. 2 (2006), pp. 145–89.

Stetkevych 2010
Stetkevych, Suzanne Pinckney. *The Mantle Odes: Arabic Praise Poems to the Prophet Muhammad.* Bloomington and Indianapolis, 2010.

Stewart 1984
Stewart, Susan. *On Longing: Narratives of the Miniature, the Gigantic, the Souvenir, the Collection.* Baltimore, 1984.

Stillman 2000
Stillman, Yedida Kalfon. *Arab Dress from the Dawn of Islam to Modern Times: A Short History.* Themes in Islamic Studies, 2. Leiden and Boston, 2000.

Stillman 2003
Stillman, Yedida Kalfon. *Arab Dress from the Dawn of Islam to Modern Times: A Short History.* 2nd ed. Themes in Islamic Studies, 2. Leiden, 2003.

St. Laurent and Awwad 2013
St. Laurent, Beatrice, and Isam Awwad. "The Marwani Musalla in Jerusalem: New Findings." *Jerusalem Quarterly* 54 (Summer 2013), pp. 7–30.

Stone et al. 2011
Stone, Michael E., David Amit, Jon Seligman, and Irina Zilberbod. "A New Armenian Inscription from a Byzantine Monastery on Mt. Scopus, Jerusalem." *Israel Exploration Journal* 61, no. 2 (2011), pp. 230–35.

Stowasser 2004
Stowasser, Barbara Freyer. "The End Is Near: Minor and Major Signs of the Hour in Islamic Texts and Contexts." In *Apocalypse and Violence,* edited by Abbas Amanat and John J. Collins, pp. 45–67. YCIAS Working Paper Series. New Haven, 2004.

Stratford 2015
Stratford, Neil. "Le chapiteau de la tentation du Christ à Plaimpied revisité." *Bulletin Monumental* 173–74 (2015), pp. 307–31.

Strong and Brown 1976
Strong, Donald, and David Brown. *Roman Crafts.* New York, 1976.

Stroumsa, G., 2009
Stroumsa, Guy G. "Christian Memories and Visions of Jerusalem in Jewish and Islamic Context." In Grabar, O., and Kedar, eds. 2009, pp. 320–33.

Stroumsa, S., 2009
Stroumsa, Sarah. *Maimonides in His World: Portrait of a Mediterranean Thinker.* Jews, Christians, and Muslims from the Ancient to the Modern World. Princeton, N.J., 2009.

***St. Sabbas the Sanctified Orthodox Monastery* 1999–**
"St. Sabbas the Sanctified Monastery – Jerusalem." In *St. Sabbas the Sanctified Orthodox Monastery.* Harper Woods, Mich., 1999– ; http://stsabbas.org/jerusalem.html (accessed June 1, 2016).

Stürzebecher 2010
Stürzebecher, Maria. "Der Schatzfund aus der Michaelisstrasse in Erfurt." In Ostritz, ed. 2010a, pp. 60–323.

Subtelny 2010
Subtelny, Maria E. "The Jews at the Edge of the World in a Timurid-Era Mi'rajnama: The Islamic Ascension Narrative as Missionary Text." In Gruber and Colby, eds. 2010, pp. 50–77.

Suriano 1949 ed.
Suriano, Francesco. *Treatise on the Holy Land.* Translated by Theophilus Bellorini and Eugene Hoade. Publications of the Studium Biblicum Franciscanum, 8. Jerusalem, 1949.

Tabbaa 1986
Tabbaa, Yasser. "Monuments with a Message: Propagation of Jihad under Nur A-Din (1146–1174)." In *The Meeting of Two Worlds: Cultural Exchange between East and West during the Period of the Crusades,* edited by Vladimir P. Goss and Christine Verzár Bornstein, pp. 222–40, figs. 22–28. Studies in Medieval Culture, 21. Kalamazoo, Mich., 1986.

Tabbaa 1991
Tabbaa, Yasser. "The Transformation of Arabic Writing: Part I, Qur'anic Calligraphy." *Ars Orientalis* 21 (1991), pp. 119–47.

Tabbaa 2001
Tabbaa, Yasser. *The Transformation of Islamic Art during the Sunni Revival.* Publications on the Near East. Seattle, 2001.

Tabory 2008
Tabory, Joseph. *JPS Commentary on the Haggadah: Historical Introduction, Translation, and Commentary.* Philadelphia, 2008.

Tahan 2007
Tahan, Ilana. *Hebrew Manuscripts: The Power of Script and Image.* London, 2007.

Tait, ed. 1986
Tait, Hugh, ed. *Jewelry, 7,000 Years: An International History and Illustrated Survey from the Collections of the British Museum.* New York, 1986.

Tait et al. 1991
Tait, Hugh, et al. *Five Thousand Years of Glass.* London, 1991.

Tal, Kool, and Baidoun 2013
Tal, Oren, Robert Kool, and Issa Baidoun. "A Hoard Twice Buried?: Fatimid Gold from Thirteenth Century Crusader Arsur (Apollonia-Arsuf)." *Numismatic Chronicle* 173 (2013), pp. 261–92, pls. 43–48.

Tamrat 1972
Tamrat, Taddesse. *Church and State in Ethiopia, 1270–1527.* Oxford Studies in African Affairs. Oxford, 1972.

Taragan 2000
Taragan, Hana. "Politics and Aesthetics: Sultan Baybars and the Abu Hurayra/Rabbi Gamliel Building in Yavne." In *Milestones in the Art and Culture of Egypt,* edited by Asher Ovadiah, pp. 117–43. Assaph Book Series. Tel Aviv, 2000.

Taragan 2005
Taragan, Hana. "The 'Speaking' Inkwell from Khurasan: Object as 'World' in Iranian Medieval Metalwork." *Muqarnas* 22 (2005), pp. 29–44.

Taragan 2006
Taragan, Hana. "Sign of the Times: Reusing the Past in Baybar's Architecture in Palestine." In *Mamluks and Ottomans: Studies in Honour of Michael Winter,* edited by David J. Wasserstein and Ami Ayalon, pp. 54–66. Routledge Studies in Middle Eastern History, 5. London and New York, 2006.

al-Tarsusi 1948 ed.
al-Tarsusi, Mardi ibn 'Ali. *Instruction of the Valiant on Prevailing in War* (in Arabic). Edited and introduced by Claude Cahen. Beirut, 1948.

al-Tarsusi 1998 ed.
al-Tarsusi, Mardi ibn 'Ali. *Dictionary of Ancient Weapons* (in Arabic). Edited by Karin Sadir. Beirut, 1998.

al-Tarsusi 2004 ed.
al-Tarsusi, Mardi ibn 'Ali. *Instruction of the Valiant on Prevailing in War* (in Arabic). Edited and introduced by Fuat Sezgin. Frankfurt, 2004.

Thackston 1994
Thackston, W[heeler] M. "The Paris *Mi'rajnama.*" *Journal of Turkish Studies/Türklük Bilgisi Araştirmalari* 18 (1994), pp. 263–99.

Theophilus 1961 ed.
Theophilus. *De Diversis Artibus/The Various Arts.* Translated and annotated by C[harles] R[eginald] Dodwell. London, 1961.

Thomas 2003
Thomas, Clive. "A Distinctive Group of Swords from the Arsenal of Alexandria." In *The 20th Anniversary London Park Lane Arms Fair* [February 16, 2003, The Marriott Hotel, Grosvenor Square, London], edited by Nigel McKinley, pp. 29–44. London, 2003.

Thomson 1985/1994
Thomson, Robert W. "Jerusalem and Armenia." *Studia Patristica* 18 [*Historica – Theologica – Gnostica – Biblica: Papers of the Ninth International Conference on Patristic Studies, Oxford 1983,* edited by Elizabeth A. Livingstone] (1985), pp. 77–91. Reprinted in *Studies in Armenian Literature and Christianity,* by Robert W. Thomson. Aldershot, Hampshire, and Brookfield, Vt., 1994.

Thomson 1988–89/1994
Thomson, Robert W. "Mission, Conversion, and Christianization: The Armenian Example." *Harvard Ukrainian Studies* 12–13 [*Proceedings of the International Congress Commemorating the Millennium of Christianity in Rus'-Ukraine*] (1988–89), pp. 28–45. Reprinted in *Studies in Armenian Literature and Christianity,* by Robert W. Thomson. Aldershot, Hampshire, and Brookfield, Vt., 1994.

Thurston 1908
Thurston, Herbert. "Chalice." In *The Catholic Encyclopedia,* edited by Charles G. Herbermann et al., vol. 3, pp. 561–64. New York, 1908.

Tibbetts 1992
Tibbetts, Gerald R. "The Balkhi School of Geographers." In *The History of Cartography,* vol. 2, bk. 1, *Cartography in the Traditional Islamic and South Asian Societies,* edited by J. B. Harley and David Woodward, pp. 108–36, pls. 6, 7. Chicago and London, 1992.

Timm 2006
Timm, Frederike. *Der Palästina-Pilgerbericht des Bernhard von Breidenbach und die Holzschnitte Erhard Reuwichs: Die* Peregrinatio in terram sanctam *(1486) als Propagandainstrument im Mantel der gelehrten Pilgerschrift.* Stuttgart, 2006.

Toaff 1993
Toaff, Ariel. *The Jews in Umbria.* Vol. 1, *1245–1435.* Studia Post Biblica, 43. New York, 1993.

Tuley 2013
Tuley, K. A. "A Century of Communication and Acclimatization: Interpreters and Intermediaries in the Kingdom of Jerusalem." In Classen, ed. 2013, pp. 311–39.

Turner 1973
Turner, Victor. "The Center Out There: Pilgrim's Goal." *History of Religions: An International Journal for Comparative Historical Studies* 12, no. 3 (February 1973), pp. 191–230.

Turner and Turner 1978
Turner, Victor, and Edith L. B. Turner. *Image and Pilgrimage in Christian Culture: Anthropological Perspectives.* New York, 1978.

Tushingham et al. 1985
Tushingham, A[rlotte] D[ouglas], et al. *Excavations in Jerusalem, 1961–1967: Report of the Joint Expedition, the British School of Archaeology in Jerusalem, the Royal Ontario Museum, L'École Biblique et Archéologique Française, Jérusalem.* Vol. 1. Toronto, 1985.

Twersky, ed. 1972
Twersky, Isadore, ed. *A Maimonides Reader.* Library of Jewish Studies. Springfield, N.J., 1972.

Tyerman 1982
Tyerman, C[hristopher] J. "Marino Sanudo Torsello and the Lost Crusade: Lobbying in the Fourteenth Century." *Transactions of the Royal Historical Society,* ser. 5, 32 (1982), pp. 57–73.

Tyerman 1985
Tyerman, Christopher J. "Philip VI and the Recovery of the Holy Land." *The English Historical Review* 100, no. 394 (January 1985), pp. 25–52.

Tyerman 2006
Tyerman, Christopher [J.]. *God's War: A New History of the Crusades.* London, 2006.

Tzaferis 1981
Tzaferis, Vassilios. "The Wall Mosaics in the Church of the Nativity, Bethlehem."In *Actes du XVe Congrès International d'Études Byzantines, Athènes – Septembre 1976,* vol. 2, pt. B, *Art et archéologie: Communications,* pp. 891–900. Athens, 1981.

'Umar Shukri, ed. 2002
'Umar Shukri, Iman, ed. *Al-Sultan Barquq, Founder of the Jarakasian al-Mamalik State, through the Manuscript of Iqd al-juman fi tarikh ahl al-zaman li-Badr al-Din al-'Ayni* (in Arabic). Cairo, 2002.

Unger 2002
Unger, Edmund de. "Fragments of Drawings and Paintings from Fustat." In *Cairo to Kabul: Afghan and Islamic Studies Presented to Ralph Pinder-Wilson,* edited by Warwick Ball and Leonard Harrow, pp. 90–94. London, 2002.

Usama ibn Munqidh 2000 ed.
Usama ibn Munqidh. *An Arab-Syrian Gentleman and Warrior in the Period of the Crusades: Memoirs of Usamah ibn-Munqidh (Kitab al-I'Tibar).* Translated by Philip K[huri] Hitti. New ed. Records of Western Civilization. 1929. New York, 2000.

Viaud 1910
Viaud, Prosper. *Nazareth et ses deux églises de l'Annonciation et de Saint-Joseph d'après les fouilles récentes.* Paris, 1910.

Vienna 1998–99
Schätze der Kalifen: Islamiche Kunst zur Fatimidenzeit. Exh. cat., Kunsthistorischen Museums Wien, Künstlerhaus, Vienna, 1998–99. Catalogue by Wilfried Seipel and others. Vienna, 1998.

Vigevano 1993 ed.
Vigevano, Guido da. *Le macchine del re: Il Texaurus Regis Francie di Guido da Vigevano . . . codice lat. 11015 della Bibliothèque nationale di Parigi.* Edited, translated (into Italian), and annotated by Giustina Ostuni. Vigevano, 1993.

Vikan 1990
Vikan, Gary. "Pilgrims in Magi's Clothing: The Impact of Mimesis on Early Byzantine Pilgrimage Art." In *The Blessings of Pilgrimage,* edited by Robert Ousterhout, pp. 97–107. Illinois Byzantine Studies, 1. Urbana, Ill., 1990.

Vincent and Abel 1914
Vincent, [Louis-]H[ugues], and F[élix-]M[arie] Abel. *Bethléem: Le Sanctuaire de la Nativité.* Paris, 1914.

Vincent and Abel 1912–26
Vincent, [Louis-]Hugues, and F[élix-]M[arie] Abel. *Jérusalem: Recherches de topographie, d'archéologie et d'histoire.* 2 vols. Paris, 1912–26.

Van der Vlist et al. 2015
Van der Vlist, Ed, et al. *Biblia ilustrada de La Haya (KB 76 F 5): Libro de estudios.* [Madrid, 2015].

Voelkle et al. 2007
[Voelkle, William M., et al.]. "Apocalypse Then: Medieval Illuminations from the Morgan." In *The Morgan Library and Museum.* Online exh. cat., The Morgan Library and Museum, New York, 2007. New York, [2007]; http://www.themorgan.org/collection/Apocalypse-Then-Medieval-Illuminations-from-the-Morgan (accessed March 28, 2016).

Voelkle et al. 2014–15
Voelkle, William M., et al. "The Crusader Bible." In *The Morgan Library and Museum.* Online exh. cat., The Morgan Library and Museum, New York, 2014–15. New York, [2014]; http://www.themorgan.org/collection/Crusader-Bible (accessed April 1, 2016).

Vuckovic 2005
Vuckovic, Brooke Olson. *Heavenly Journeys, Earthly Concerns: The Legacy of the Mi'raj in the Formation of Islam.* Religion in History, Society, and Culture, 5. New York, 2005.

Walfish and Kizilov 2011
Walfish, Barry Dov, and Mikhail Kizilov. *Bibliographia Karaitica: An Annotated Bibliography of Karaites and Karaism.* Karaite Texts and Studies, 2; Études sur le judaïsme médiéval, 43. Leiden and Boston, 2011.

Walker 2012
Walker, Alicia. *The Emperor and the World: Exotic Elements and the Imagining of Middle Byzantine Imperial Power, Ninth to Thirteenth Centuries C.E.* Cambridge, 2012.

Walter 2003
Walter, Christopher. *The Warrior Saints in Byzantine Art and Tradition.* Burlington, Vt., 2003.

Ward 1989
Ward, Rachel [M.]. "Metallarbeiten der Mamluken-Zeit, Hergestellt für den Export nach Europa." In Berlin 1989, pp. 202–9.

Ward 1993
Ward, Rachel [M.]. *Islamic Metalwork.* London, 1993.

Ward 1998
Ward, Rachel [M.]. "Glass and Brass: Parallels and Puzzles." In Ward, ed. 1998, pp. 30–34, 161–65, color pls. B, I.

Ward 2004
Ward, Rachel M. "Brass, Gold and Silver from Mamluk Egypt: Metal Vessels Made for Sultan Al-Nasir Muhammad: A Memorial Lecture for Mark Zebrowski, Given at the Royal Asiatic Society on 9 May 2002." *Journal of the Royal Asiatic Society,* ser. 3, 14, no. 1 (April 2004), pp. 59–73.

Ward 2005
Ward, Rachel [M.]. "Style versus Substance: The Christian Iconography on Two Vessels Made for the Ayyubid Sultan al-Salih Ayyub." In *The Iconography of Islamic Art: Studies in Honour of Robert Hillenbrand,* edited by Bernard O'Kane, pp. 309–24. Edinburgh, 2005.

Ward 2007
Ward, Rachel [M.]. "Plugging the Gap: Mamluk Export Metalwork 1375–1475." In *Facts and Artefacts: Art in the Islamic World; Festschrift for Jens Kröger on his 65th Birthday,* edited by Annette Hagedorn and Avinoam Shalem, pp. 263–84. Islamic History and Civilization, 68. Leiden and Boston, 2007.

Ward, ed. 1998
Ward, Rachel [M.], ed. *Gilded and Enamelled Glass from the Middle East.* British Museum. London, 1998.

Wardrop et al. 2003
Wardrop, David, et al. *Arabic Treasures of the British Library from Alexandria to Baghdad and Beyond.* London, 2003.

Warren 2003
Warren, Kathleen. *Daring to Cross the Threshold: Francis of Assisi Encounters Sultan Malek al-Kamil.* Rochester, Minn., 2003.

Washington, D.C. 1985–86
Islamic Metalwork in the Freer Gallery of Art. Exh. cat., Freer Gallery of Art, Smithsonian Institution, Washington, D.C., 1985–86. Catalogue by Esin Atil and others. Washington, D.C., 1985.

Washington, D.C. 2012
To Know Wisdom and Instruction: A Visual Survey of the Armenian Literary Tradition from the Library of Congress. Exh. cat., Library of Congress, Washington, D.C., 2012. Catalogue by Levon Avdoyan. Washington, D.C., 2012.

Washington, D.C., and other cities 1981–83
Renaissance of Islam: Art of the Mamluks. Exh. cat., National Museum of Natural History, Washington, D.C., and other venues. Catalogue by Esin Atil. Washington, D.C., 1981.

Washington, D.C., and other cities 2004–6
Palace and Mosque: Islamic Art from the Victoria and Albert Museum. Exh. cat., National Gallery of Art, Washington, D.C.; Kimbell Art Museum, Fort Worth; Setagaya Art Museum, Tokyo; Millennium Galleries, Sheffield, 2004–6. Catalogue by Tim Stanley, Mariam Rosser-Owen, and Stephen Vernoit. London, 2004.

al-Wasiti 1979 ed.
al-Wasiti, Abu-Bakr Muhammad Ibn-Ahmad. *Fada'il al-bayt al-Muqaddas.* Edited by Isaac Hasson. The Max Schloessinger Memorial Series, 3. Jerusalem, 1979.

Waterson 2010
Waterson, James. *Sacred Swords: Jihad in the Holy Land, 1097–1291.* London, 2010.

Watin-Grandchamp, Cabau, and Cazes 2007
Watin-Grandchamp, Dominique, Patrice Cabau, and Daniel and Quitterie Cazes. "Le coffret reliquaire de la Vraie Croix de Saint-Sernin de Toulouse." *Les cahiers de Saint-Michel de Cuxa* 38 (2007), pp. 37–46.

Watson 1998
Watson, Oliver. "Pottery and Glass: Lustre and Enamel." In Ward, ed. 1998, pp. 15–19, 156.

Watt 2002–3
Watt, James C. Y. "A Note on Artistic Exchanges in the Mongol Empire." In *The Legacy of Genghis Khan: Courtly Art and Culture in Western Asia, 1256–1353,* pp. 62–73. Exh. cat., The Metropolitan Museum of Art, New York; Los Angeles County Mueum of Art, 2002–3. Catalogue by Linda Komaroff, Stefano Carboni, and others. New York, 2003.

Watzinger and Wulzinger 1921
Watzinger, Carl, and Karl Wulzinger. *Damaskus, die antike Stadt.* Wissenschaftliche Veröffentlichungen des Deutsch-Tükischen Denkmalschutz-Kommandos, 4. Berlin and Leipzig, 1921.

Wedepohl 2005
Wedepohl, Karl Hans. *Die Gruppe der Hedwigsbecher.* Nachrichten der Akademie der Wissenschaften in Göttingen, 2, Mathematisch-Physikalische Klasse, 1. Göttingen, [2005].

Weiss 1997–98
Weiss, Daniel H. "*Hec est Domus Domini firmiter edificata*: The Image of the Temple in Crusader Art." *Jewish Art* 23–24 [*The Real and Ideal Jerusalem in Jewish, Christian, and Islamic Art: Studies in Honor of Bezalel Narkiss on the Occasion of His Seventieth Birthday,* edited by Bianca Kühnel] (1997–98), pp. 210–17.

Weiss 2002
Weiss, Daniel [H.]. "Portraying the Past, Illuminating the Present: The Art of the Morgan Library Picture Bible." In *The Book of Kings: Art, War and the Morgan Library's Medieval Picture Bible,* pp. 10–35. Exh. cat., Walters Art Museum, Baltimore, 2002. Catalogue by William Noel, Daniel Weiss, and others. Baltimore, 2002.

Weiss 2004
Weiss, Daniel H. "The Old Testament Image and the Rise of Crusader Culture in France." In Weiss and Mahoney, eds. 2004, pp. 3–21.

Weiss and Mahoney, eds. 2004
Weiss, Daniel H., and Lisa Mahoney, eds. *France and the Holy Land: Frankish Culture at the End of the Crusade.* Parallax. Baltimore and London, 2004.

Weitzmann 1982
Weitzmann, Kurt. *Studies in the Arts at Sinai: Essays.* Princeton Series of Collected Essays. Princeton, N.J., 1982.

Welch 1976
Welch, Stuart Cary. *Royal Persian Manuscripts.* London, 1976.

Welch et al. 1987
Welch, Stuart Cary, et al. *The Islamic World.* The Metropolitan Museum of Art Series, 11. New York, 1987.

Wellesz 1959
Wellesz, Emmy. "An Early al-Sufi Manuscript in the Bodleian Library in Oxford: A Study in Islamic Constellation Images." *Ars Orientalis* 3 (1959), pp. 1–26, pls. 1–27.

Westermann-Angerhausen 1988
Westermann-Angerhausen, Hiltrud. "Zwei romanische Thuribula im Trierer Domschatz – und Überlegungen zu Theophilus und dem Gozbert-Rauchfass." *Zeitschrift des Deutschen Vereins für Kunstwissenschaft* 42, no. 2 (1988), pp. 45–60.

Westermann-Angerhausen 2011
Westermann-Angerhausen, Hiltrud. "Incense in the Space between Heaven and Earth – The Inscriptions and Images on the Gozbert Censer in the Cathedral Treasury of Trier." In *Inscriptions in Liturgical Spaces,* edited by Kristin B. Aavitsland and Thomas K. Seim, pp. 227–42. Acta ad archaeologiam et artium historiam pertinentia, 24. Rome, 2011.

Westermann-Angerhausen 2014
Westermann-Angerhausen, Hiltrud. *Mittelalterliche Weihrauchfässer von 800 bis 1500.* Denkmäler deutscher Kunst; Bronzegeräte des Mittelalters, 7. Petersberg, 2014.

Whalen 2001
Whalen, Brett E. "The Discovery of the Holy Patriarchs: Relics, Ecclesiastical Politics and Sacred History in Twelfth-Century Crusader Palestine." *Historical Reflections/Reflexions historiques* 27, no. 1 (Spring 2001), pp. 139–76.

Wharton 2006
Wharton, Annabel Jane. *Selling Jerusalem: Relics, Replicas, Theme Parks.* Chicago and London, 2006.

Whatley 2014
Whatley, Laura J. "Experiencing the Holy Land and Crusade in Matthew Paris's Maps of Palestine." In Kühnel, B., Noga-Banai, and Vorholt, eds. 2014, pp. 295–305.

White 1938
White, Lynn Townsend, Jr. *Latin Monasticism in Norman Sicily.* The Medieval Academy of America, 31. Cambridge, Mass., 1938.

Whitehouse 2010
Whitehouse, David. *Islamic Glass in the Corning Museum of Glass.* Vol. 1. Corning, N.Y., 2010.

Wiedemann and Plessner 1960
Wiedemann, E., and M. Plessner. "al-Anbik." In *EI2* 1960–2009, vol. 1 (1960), p. 486.

Wieder 1957
Wieder, Naftali. "'Sanctuary' as a Metaphor for Scripture." *The Journal of Jewish Studies* 8 (1957), pp. 165–75.

Wiet 1932
Wiet, Gaston. *Catalogue général du Musée Arabe du Caire: Objets en cuivre.* Cairo, 1932.

Wiet 1982
Wiet, Gaston. *Catalogue général du Musée Arabe du Caire: Lampes et bouteilles en verre émaillé.* [Cairo], 1982.

Wightman 1993
Wightman, G. J. *The Walls of Jerusalem from the Canaanites to the Mamluks.* Mediterranean Archaeology, suppl. 4. Sydney, 1993.

Wild and Wild 2005
Wild, John Peter, and Felicity Wild. "Rome and India: Early Indian Cotton Textiles from Berenike, Red Sea Coast of Egypt." In *Textiles in Indian Ocean Societies,* edited by Ruth Barnes, pp. 11–16. Indian Ocean Series. London, 2005.

Wilhelm 1948
Wilhelm, Kurt, ed. *Roads to Zion: Four Centuries of Travelers' Reports.* New York, 1948.

Wilkes 2012
Wilkes, George R. "Religious War in the Works of Maimonides: An Idea and Its Transit across the Mediterreanean." In *Just Wars, Holy Wars, and Jihads: Christian, Jewish, and Muslim Encounters and Exchanges,* edited by Sohail H. Hashmi, pp. 146–64. New York and Oxford, 2012.

Wilkinson 1972
Wilkinson, John. "The Tomb of Christ: An Outline of Its Structural History." *Levant: The Journal of the Council for British Research in the Levant* 4, no. 1 (1972), pp. 83–97.

Wilkinson 1977
Wilkinson, John. *Jerusalem Pilgrims before the Crusades.* Warminster, 1977.

Wilkinson 1987
Wilkinson, John. *Column Capitals in Haram al Sharif from 138 A.D. to 1118 A.D.* Jerusalem, 1987.

Wilkinson 2002a
Wilkinson, John. *Egeria's Travels.* 3rd ed. 1971. Warminster, 2002.

Wilkinson 2002b
Wilkinson, John. *Jerusalem Pilgrims before the Crusades.* 2nd ed. 1977. Warminster, 2002.

Wilkinson, Hill, and Ryan, eds. 1988
Wilkinson, John, with Joyce Hill and W. F. Ryan, eds. *Jerusalem Pilgrimage 1099–1185.* Works Issued by the Hakluyt Society, Second series, 167. London, 1988.

William of Malmesbury 1998–99 ed.
William of Malmesbury. *Gesta Regum Anglorum/The History of the English Kings.* Edited and translated by R. A. B. Mynors; completed by R[odney] M. Thomson and M[ichael] Winterbottom. 2 vols. Oxford Medieval Texts. Oxford, 1998–99.

William of Tyre 1879–80 ed.
William of Tyre. *Guillaume de Tyr et ses continuateurs.* Translated by Paulin Paris. 2 vols. Paris, 1879–80.

William of Tyre 1943 ed.
William of Tyre. *A History of Deeds Done beyond the Sea.* Translated and annotated by Emily Atwater Babcock and A. C. Krey. 2 vols. Records of Civilization, Sources and Studies, 35. New York, 1943.

William of Tyre 1986 ed.
William of Tyre. *Guillaume de Tyr Chronique.* Edited by R. B. C. Huygens with H[ans] E[berhard] Mayer and G[erhard] Rösch. 2 vols. Corpus Christianorum Continuatio Medievalis, 63–63A. Turnhout, 1986.

Williams, G., 2013
Williams, Gregory. "'Fayyumi Ware': Variations, Imitations, and Importation of an Early Islamic Glazed Ceramic Type." Master's thesis, American University in Cairo, 2013.

Williams, J., 1994–2003
Williams, John. *The Illustrated Beatus: A Corpus of the Illustrations of the Commentary on the Apocalypse in Five Volumes.* London, 1974.

Wischnitzer 1935
Wischnitzer, Rachel. "Les manuscrits à miniatures de Maimonide." *Gazette des Beaux-Arts,* ser. 6, 14 (1935), pp. 47–52.

Wischnitzer 1960
Wischnitzer, Rachel. "The Money Changer with the Balance: A Topic of Jewish Iconography." *Eretz-Israel* 6 (1960), pp. 23–25.

Wischnitzer 1974
Wischnitzer, Rachel. "Maimonides' Drawings of the Temple." *Journal of Jewish Art* 1 (1974), pp. 16–27.

Wolper 2000
Wolper, Ethel Sara. "Khidr, Elwan Çelebi and the Conversion of Sacred Sanctuaries in Anatolia." *The Muslim World* 90 (2000), pp. 309–22.

***World Heritage Encyclopedia* n.d.**
World Heritage Encyclopedia. "Jilu." In *World Public Library.* N.p., n.d.; http://www.worldlibrary.org/articles/jilu (accessed May 12, 2016).

Yalouri 2001
Yalouri, Eleana. *The Acropolis: Global Fame, Local Claim.* Materializing Culture. Oxford, 2001.

Yota 2001
Yota, Elisabeth. "Le tétraévangile Harley 1810 de la British Library: Contribution à l'étude de l'illustration des tétraévangiles du Xe au XIIIe siècle." Ph.D. diss., Université de Fribourg, Switzerland, 2001.

Yücesoy 2009
Yücesoy, Hayrettin. *Messianic Beliefs and Imperial Politics in Medieval Islam: The 'Abbasid Caliphate in the Early Ninth Century.* Charleston, S.C., 2009.

Yuval 1998
Yuval, Israel Jacob. "Jewish Messianic Expectations towards 1240 and Christian Reactions." In *Toward the Millenium: Messianic Expectations from the Bible to Waco,* edited by Peter Schäfer and Mark [R.] Cohen, pp. 105–21. Studies in the History of Religions (*Numen* Book Series), 77. Leiden, Boston, and Cologne, 1998.

Zaimeche 2005
Zaimeche, Salah. "Jerusalem: Its Sites, Scholars and Scholarship before the Crusades." In *Muslim Heritage.* Manchester, [2005]; http://www.muslimheritage.com/article/jerusalem-its-sites-scholars-and-scholarship-crusades.

Zander 1971
Zander, Walter. *Israel and the Holy Places of Christendom.* New York, 1971.

Zeitler 2000
Zeitler, Barbara. "The Distorting Mirror: Reflections on the Queen Melisende Psalter (London, B.L., Egerton 1139)." In *Through the Looking Glass: Byzantium through British Eyes: Papers from the Twenty-ninth Spring Symposium of Byzantine Studies, London, March 1995,* edited by Robin Cormack and Elizabeth Jeffreys, pp. 69–83. Aldershot, Hampshire, and Burlington, Vt., 2000.

INDEX

Page numbers in **bold** refer to catalogue entries. Page numbers in *italics* refer to figures.

D

E

PHOTOGRAPHY CREDITS

Figs. 1, 9 and cats. 71, 80a, 101a–e, 134a–c: © Marie-Armelle Beaulieu / Custodia Terræ Sanctæ; figs. 3, 63 and cats. 13a, 13d, 33, 55–56, 82, 88, 135b–d: © Victoria and Albert Museum, London; fig. 5: photograph by Diego Delso; fig. 6: © Boaz Rottem / Alamy Stock Photo; fig. 7: Paris 2001–2, p. 106; fig. 10: Scala / Art Resource, NY; fig. 11: © Patrimonio Nacional; fig. 12: Courtesy Rabbi Mark Glickman (photograph by Jacob Glickman); fig. 16 and cats. 25c, 25f, 30: © The Cleveland Museum of Art; fig. 17: © The Israel Museum, Jerusalem (photograph by Avraham Hay); figs. 20, 25, 41, 51, 77 and cats. 27, 31, 45, 54, 66, 100, 121, 133, 137c, 139: © The British Library Board; fig. 21: Courtesy Rijksmuseum, Amsterdam; fig. 22: © Musée du Louvre, Dist. RMN-Grand Palais / photograph by Hervé Lewandowski / Art Resource, NY; fig. 23: © Dommuseum Wien; fig. 24: © Rheinisches Bildarchiv Köln; fig. 29: © robertharding / Alamy Stock Photo; fig. 30: Narkiss, Stone, and Sanjian 1979, p. 77; fig. 31: Courtesy of the Ben-Zvi Institute, Jerusalem (photograph by Ardon Bar-Hama); fig. 32: © 2016 Museum Associates / LACMA, licensed by Art Resource, NY; fig. 33: © Eddie Gerald / Alamy Stock Photo; fig. 42: Le Bon 1884, pp. 154–55; figs. 43 *left*, 50: Courtesy Corbis Images; fig. 43 *right*: © dov makabaw / Alamy Stock Photo; fig. 45: Courtesy of the Israel Antiquities Authority; fig. 47: Biddle 2000, p. 83; fig. 48: Reuters / Nir Elias; fig. 49: DEA / Archivio J. Lange; fig. 53: DEA / S. Vannini; fig. 55: © Creswell Archive, Ashmolean Museum; fig. 56: Auld and Hillenbrand 2000, p. 536; fig. 58: Klaus E Göltz, Halle (Saale); fig. 59: Thüringisches Landesamt für Denkmalpflege und Archäologie (photograph by B. Stefan); fig. 60: Buschhausen 1978, pl. 87; fig. 61: Horn 1962 ed., pp. 50–56; fig. 62: Courtesy of Merav Mack; fig. 64: Image reproduced by permission of Chatsworth Settlement Trustees; fig. 69: Geneva and Paris 1993–94, pl. 3.13; fig. 73: © RMN-Grand Palais / Art Resource, NY (photograph by Franck Raux); figs. 74–75 and cats. 34, 109–10, 145–46: Morgan Library and Museum, New York; fig. 78: © www.BibleLandPictures.com / Alamy Stock Photo; fig. 79: © Museum With No Frontiers (Discover Islamic Art); fig. 80: © dbimages / Alamy Stock Photo; fig. 83: Courtesy the University of Haifa Library; fig. 84: © stefano baldini / Alamy Stock Photo; fig. 85: © Hanan Isachar / Alamy Stock Photo; figs. 86–87, 95: Salameh 1999, pp. 69, 74, 85; fig. 89 and cats. 124–27: photographs by Guy Focant, Vedrin; fig. 90: Der Nersessian 1978, fig. 45; fig. 91: photograph by Hanan Isachar; fig. 92: photograph by Gavin Hellier; fig. 99: Hansmann and Hohmann 2002, p. 12; fig. 100: © Daniel Greenhouse / Alamy Stock Photo; cat. 2a: © Bayerisches Nationalmuseum München (photograph by Walter Haberland); cat. 3: Hillenbrand, C., 1999, p. 270; cat. 4: Courtesy of the Israel Antiquities Authority (photograph by Clara Amit); cats. 5–6, 10–11, 91–92, 102, 118: © The Israel Museum, Jerusalem (photographs by Elie Posner); cats. 7–8, 57: © The al-Sabah Collection, Dar al-Athar al-Islamiyyah, Kuwait; cat. 14: © The Israel Museum (photograph by Meidad Suchowolski); cats. 17, 52: © 2016 Biblioteca Apostolica Vaticana; cat. 19a: © RMN-Grand Palais / Art Resource, NY (photograph by René-Gabriel Ojeda); cats. 19b, 83, 129d: Avshalom Avital; cats. 23, 43, 129a–b, 129e–f: The Museum of Islamic Art, Doha; cat. 24c: © IMA (photograph by Philippe Maillard); cats. 25b, 98: © Musées d'Angers (photographs by P. David); cat. 25e: © DRAC Midi-Pyrénées (photograph by Jean-François Peiré); cat. 62b: © RMN-Grand Palais / Art Resource, NY; cat. 62c: Thüringisches Landesamt für Denkmalpflege und Archäologie (photograph by B. Stefan); cats. 63, 119: © The Israel Museum, Jerusalem (photographs by Ardon Bar-Hama); cat. 70: © Domkapitel Aachen (photograph by Ann Münchow); cats. 78, 111: © RMN-Grand Palais / Art Resource, NY (photographs by Stéphane Maréchalle); cat. 97: © Silvano Migani / Custodia Terræ Sanctæ; cats. 107, 120: Courtesy Furusiyya Art Foundation (photographs by Noël Adams); cat. 114: Cliché Musée des Beaux-Arts de Chartres; cat. 123: © RMN-Grand Palais / Art Resource, NY (photograph by Jean-Gilles Berizzi); cat. 132: © Custodia Terræ Sanctæ; cat. 137b: photograph by Ardon Bar-Hama; cat. 141: © Region Aquitaine-Limousin-Poitou-Charentes, Service de l'Inventaire et du Patrimoine Culturel (photograph by Philippe Rivière, 1993); cat. 148: © The Trustees of the British Museum; cats. 149a, 149d, 149f: Courtesy of Francesca Galloway, London; cat. 149b: John Bodkin / Dawkins Colour; cats. 149c, 149e: photographs by Pernille Klemp.

This catalogue is published in conjunction with "Jerusalem, 1000–1400: Every People Under Heaven," on view at The Metropolitan Museum of Art, New York, from September 26, 2016, through January 8, 2017.

The exhibition is made possible by The David Berg Foundation; The al-Sabah Collection, Kuwait; the Sherman Fairchild Foundation; the William S. Lieberman Fund; The Polonsky Foundation; Diane Carol Brandt; The Andrew W. Mellon Foundation; the Ruddock Foundation for the Arts; and Mary and Michael Jaharis.

Additional support is provided by the National Endowment for the Arts.

The catalogue is made possible by The Andrew W. Mellon Foundation; the Michel David-Weill Fund; Tauck Ritzau Innovative Philanthropy; the Ruddock Foundation for the Arts; Christopher C. Grisanti and Suzanne P. Fawbush; and Helen E. Lindsay.

Published by The Metropolitan Museum of Art, New York
Mark Polizzotti, Publisher and Editor in Chief
Gwen Roginsky, Associate Publisher and General Manager of Publications
Peter Antony, Chief Production Manager
Michael Sittenfeld, Senior Managing Editor

Edited by Cynthia Clark and Kamiah Foreman
Designed by Christopher Kuntze
Production by Chris Zichello
Bibliography and notes edited by Penny Jones and Ellen Hurst
Image acquisitions and permissions by Crystal Dombrow

Photographs of works in the Metropolitan Museum's collection are by the Imaging Department, The Metropolitan Museum of Art, unless otherwise noted; new photography is by Anna-Marie Kellen, Peter Zeray, and Hyla Skopitz. Additional photography credits appear on p. 335.

Typeset in Agmena and Sava Pro
Printed on 150 gsm Perigord
Separations by Professional Graphics, Inc., Rockford, Illinois
Printed and bound by Conti Tipocolor S.p.A., Florence, Italy

Jacket illustrations: (front) *Syriac Lectionary*, detail of cat. 27, fol. 115; (back) *Map of Crusader Jerusalem*, detail of cat. 103, fol. 1r

Endpapers: *View of Jerusalem*, detail of cat. 20

Frontispieces: p. ii: *The Archangel Israfil*, detail of cat. 148; p. vi: *Menorah*, cat. 66, fol. 136r

First Printing

The Metropolitan Museum of Art
1000 Fifth Avenue
New York, New York 10028
metmuseum.org

Distributed by
Yale University Press, New Haven
yalebooks.com/art
yalebooks.co.uk

Cataloging-in-Publication Data is available from the Library of Congress.
ISBN 978-1-58839-598-6

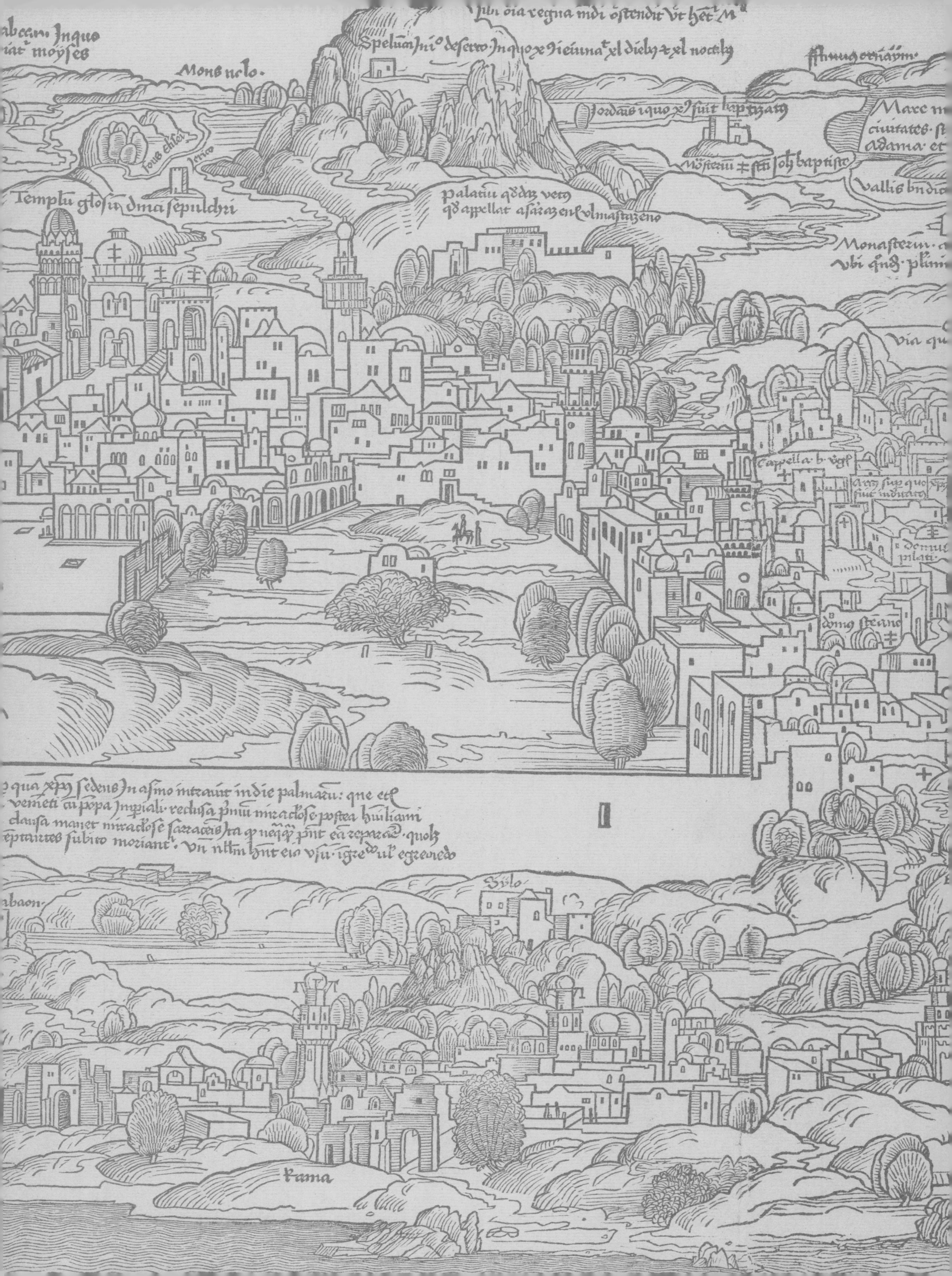

Mons uelo
Jordanis in quo xps fuit baptizatus
Maxe
ciuitates
Adama et
Vallis
Monasterium
Via qu
Capella
Rama